A History of the British Steam Tram

by David Gladwin

Volume 7 Part 2

It had been intended to contain this volume within one book; however it became clear that this would be too unwieldy and put undue strain on the binding, leading to distortion. It has therefore been split into two parts.

Published by Adam Gordon

ISBN: 978-1-874422-80-8

A catalogue entry for this book is available from the British Library.

Publication no. 84.

Print run limited to 400.

Published 2010 by Adam Gordon, Kintradwell Farmhouse, Brora, Sutherland KW9 6LU.
Tel: 01408 622660. E-mail: adam@ahg-books.com

Printed by 4edge Limited, 7a Eldon Way, Eldon Way Industrial Estate, Hockley, Essex SS5 4AD

Production and design by Trevor Preece: trevor@epic-gb.com

Contents

Part 1

Part 2

LOCOMOTIVE AND ROLLING STOCK FITTINGS

NEW AND REVISED

ILLUSTRATED CATALOGUE OF

BRASS

TRAM CAR FITTINGS, &c.

MANUFACTURED BY

GABRIEL & CO.,

4 & 5 A. B. ROW,

BIRMINGHAM.

ENTERED AT STATIONERS' HALL.

MOLE & NICHOLS, BIRMINGHAM.

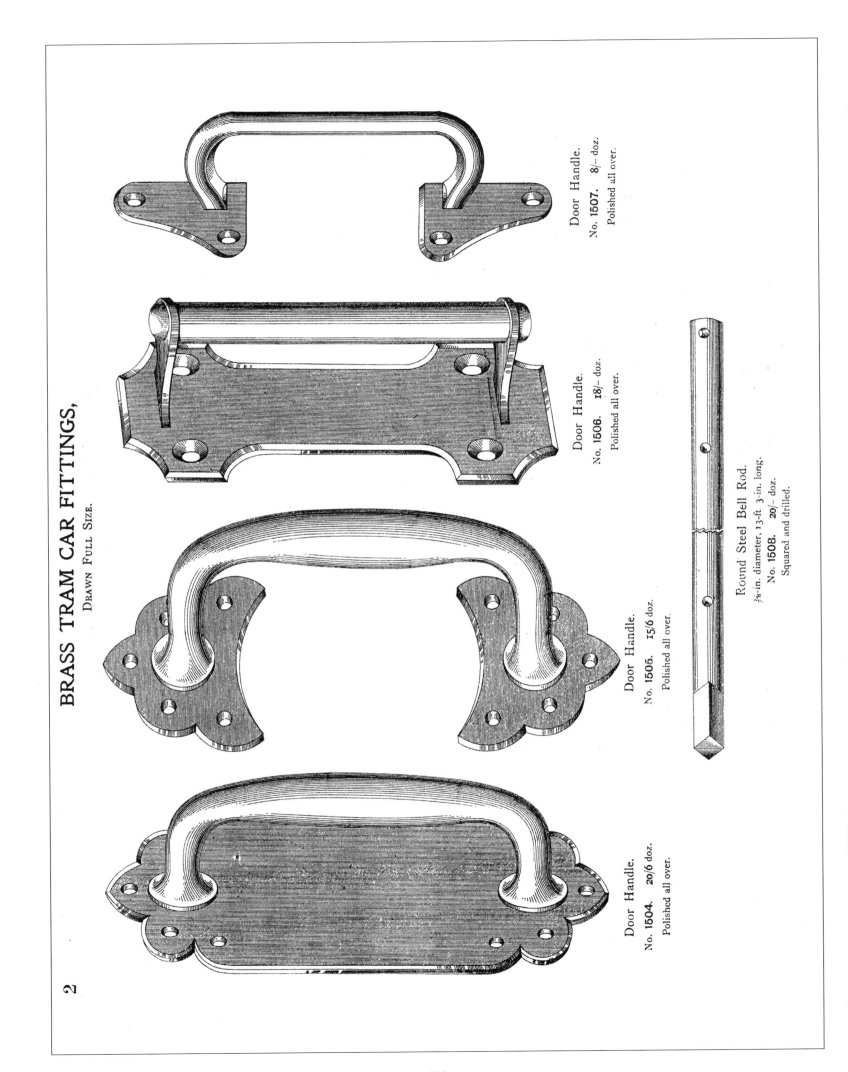

BRASS TRAM CAR FITTINGS,

DRAWN FULL SIZE.

Door Handle.
No. 1507. 8/- doz.
Polished all over.

Door Handle.
No. 1506. 18/- doz.
Polished all over.

Door Handle.
No. 1505. 15/6 doz.
Polished all over.

Door Handle.
No. 1504. 20/6 doz.
Polished all over.

Round Steel Bell Rod.
$\frac{3}{8}$-in. diameter, 13-ft 3-in. long.
No. 1508. 20/- doz.
Squared and drilled.

2

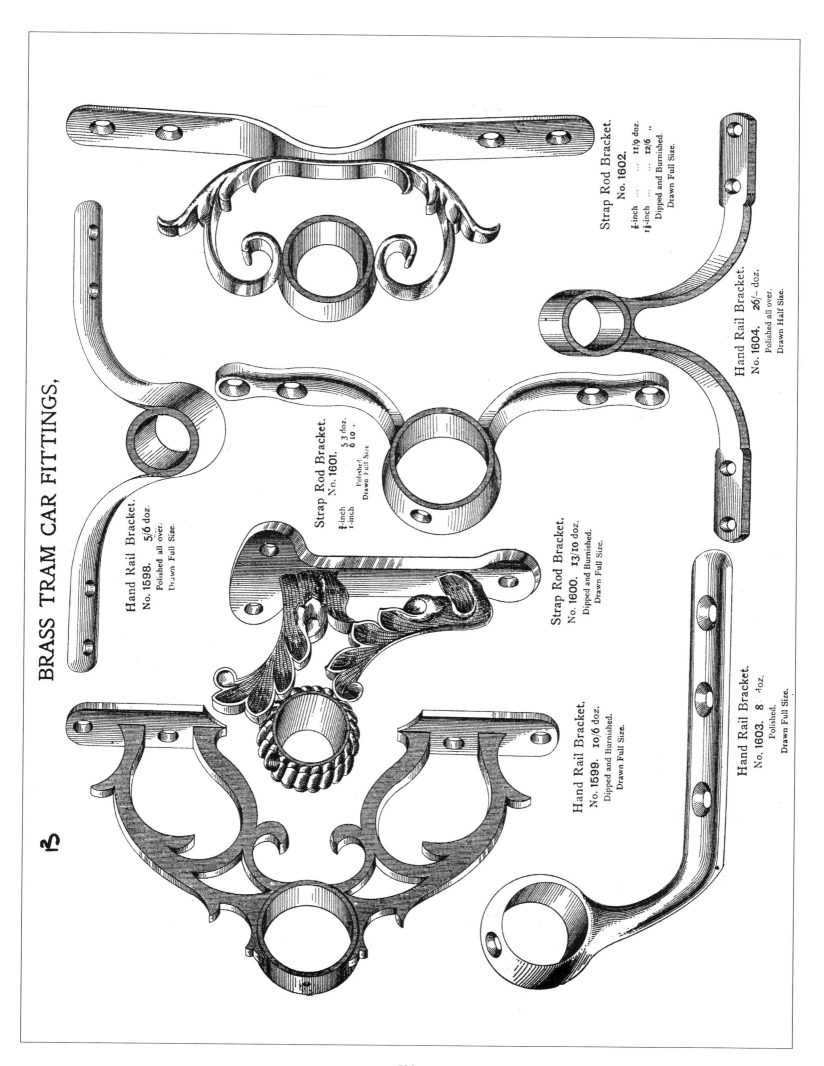

BRASS TRAM CAR FITTINGS,

Strap Rod Bracket.
No. 1602.

⅞-inch ... ... 11/9 doz.
1⅛-inch ... ... 12/6 "
Dipped and Burnished.
Drawn Full Size.

Hand Rail Bracket.
No. 1604. 26/- doz.
Polished all over.
Drawn Half Size.

Hand Rail Bracket.
No. 1598. 5/6 doz.
Polished all over.
Drawn Full Size.

Strap Rod Bracket.
No. 1601. 5 3 doz.
6 10 "
Polished.
Drawn Full Size.

⅞-inch
1-inch

Strap Rod Bracket.
No. 1600. 13/10 doz.
Dipped and Burnished.
Drawn Full Size.

Hand Rail Bracket.
No. 1599. 10/6 doz.
Dipped and Burnished.
Drawn Full Size.

Hand Rail Bracket.
No. 1603. 8 4 oz.
Polished.
Drawn Full Size.

BRASS TRAM CAR FITTINGS,

DRAWN FULL SIZE.

Cast Brass Sunk Flush Lift with Half-Round Stamped Back.
No. **1647.** **4/9 doz.**
Polished.

Window Lift.
No. **1652.** **1/3 doz.**
Cast, Dipped and Burnished.

Window Strap Plate.
No. **1655.** **3/4 doz.**
Cast and Polished.

Cupboard Catch.
No. **1658.** **4/- doz.**
Polished

Window Lift.
No. **1651.** **3/4 doz.**
Cast and Polished.

Cast Brass Finger Plate.
No. **1646.** **2/7 doz.**
Polished.

Stamped Brass Sunk Flush Lift.
No. **1650.** **2/- doz.**
Polished.

Window Lift with Leather Tab and Stud.
No. **1654.** **10/7 doz.**
Cast and Polished.

Cast Brass Sunk Lift with Square Stamped Back.
No. **1645.** **5/9 doz.**
Polished.

Window Lift.
No. **1649.** **1/9 doz.**
Cast and Dipped.

Window Lift.
No. **1648.** **4/8 doz**
Cast and Polished.

Cast Brass Finger Plate.
No. **1653.** **3/7 doz.**
Polished.

Door Catch and Plate.
No. **1656.** **3/1 doz.**
Polished.

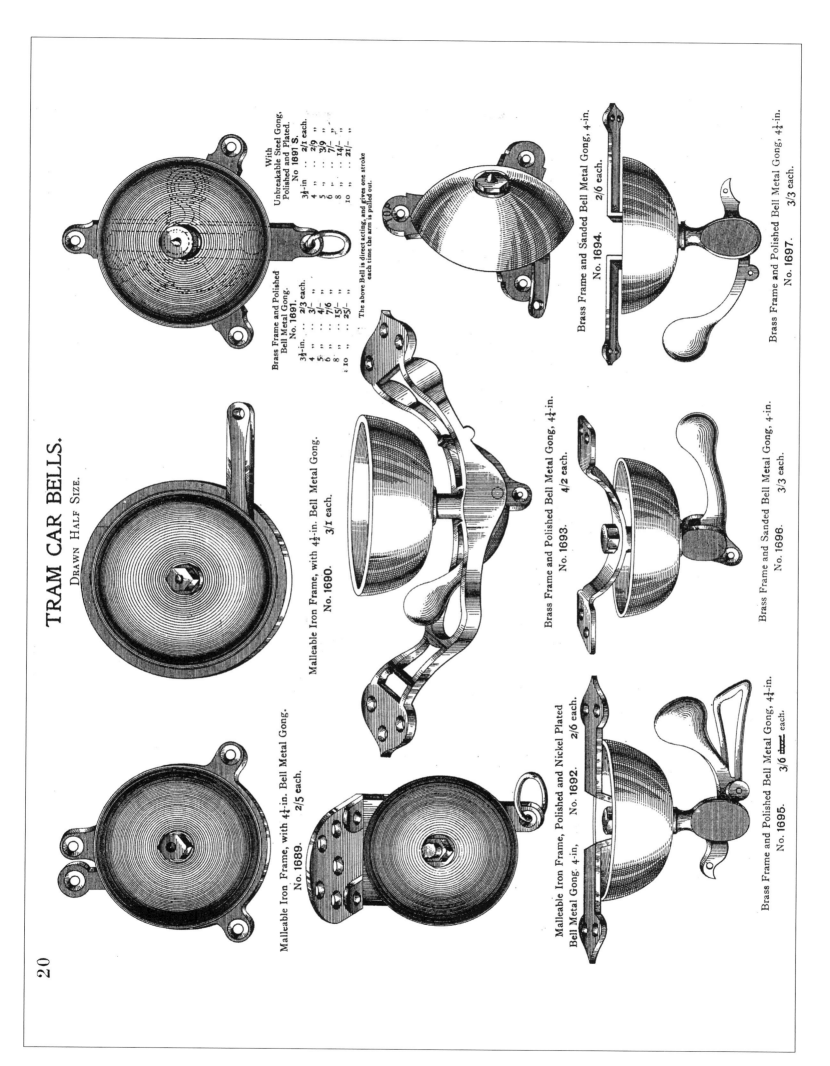

TRAM CAR BELLS.

DRAWN HALF SIZE.

Malleable Iron Frame, with 4¼-in. Bell Metal Gong.
No. 1689. 2/5 each.

Malleable Iron Frame, Polished and Nickel Plated
Bell Metal Gong. 4-in, No. 1692. 2/6 each.

Malleable Iron Frame, with 4¼-in. Bell Metal Gong.
No. 1690. 3/1 each.

Brass Frame and Polished Bell Metal Gong, 4¼-in.
No. 1693. 4/2 each.

Brass Frame and Polished Bell Metal Gong, 4¼-in.
No. 1695. 3/6 ——— each.

Brass Frame and Polished
Bell Metal Gong.
No. 1691.

3½-in.	...	...	2/3 each.
4 "	...	...	3/— "
5 "	...	...	4/— "
6 "	...	...	7/6 "
8 "	...	...	15/— "
10 "	...	...	25/— "

With
Unbreakable Steel Gong,
Polished and Plated.
No. 1691 S.

3½-in	...	2/1 each.
4 "	...	2/9 "
5 "	...	3/9 "
6 "	...	7/— "
8 "	...	14/— "
10 "	...	21/— "

The above Bell is direct acting, and gives one stroke
each time the arm is pulled out.

Brass Frame and Sanded Bell Metal Gong, 4-in.
No. 1694. 2/6 each.

Brass Frame and Sanded Bell Metal Gong, 4-in.
No. 1696. 3/3 each.

Brass Frame and Polished Bell Metal Gong, 4¼-in.
No. 1697. 3/3 each.

20

TRAM CAR FITTINGS.

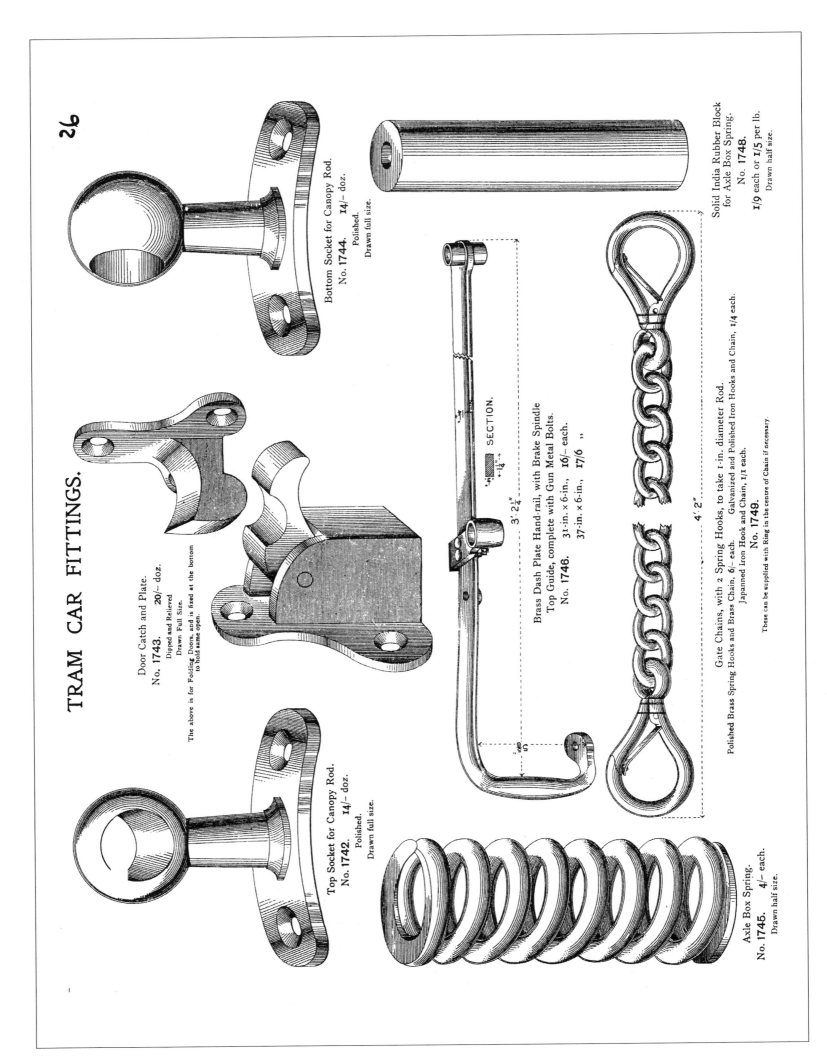

Bottom Socket for Canopy Rod.
No. 1744.　14/- doz.
Polished.
Drawn full size.

Door Catch and Plate.
No. 1743.　20/- doz.
Dipped and Relieved
Drawn Full Size.

The above is for Folding Doors, and is fixed at the bottom
to hold same open.

Top Socket for Canopy Rod.
No. 1742.　14/- doz.
Polished.
Drawn full size.

**Brass Dash Plate Hand-rail, with Brake Spindle
Top Guide, complete with Gun Metal Bolts.**
No. 1746.　31-in. × 6-in.,　16/- each.
　　　　　37-in. × 6-in.,　17/6　,,

SECTION.

3′ 2¼″

**Solid India Rubber Block
for Axle Box Spring.**
No. 1748.
1/9 each or 1/5 per lb.
Drawn half size.

Gate Chains, with 2 Spring Hooks, to take 1-in. diameter Rod.
Polished Brass Spring Hooks and Brass Chain, 6/- each.　Galvanized and Polished Iron Hooks and Chain, 1/4 each.
Japanned Iron Hook and Chain, 1/1 each.
No. 1749.
These can be supplied with Ring in the centre of Chain if necessary.

4′ 2″

Axle Box Spring.
No. 1745.　4/- each.
Drawn half size.

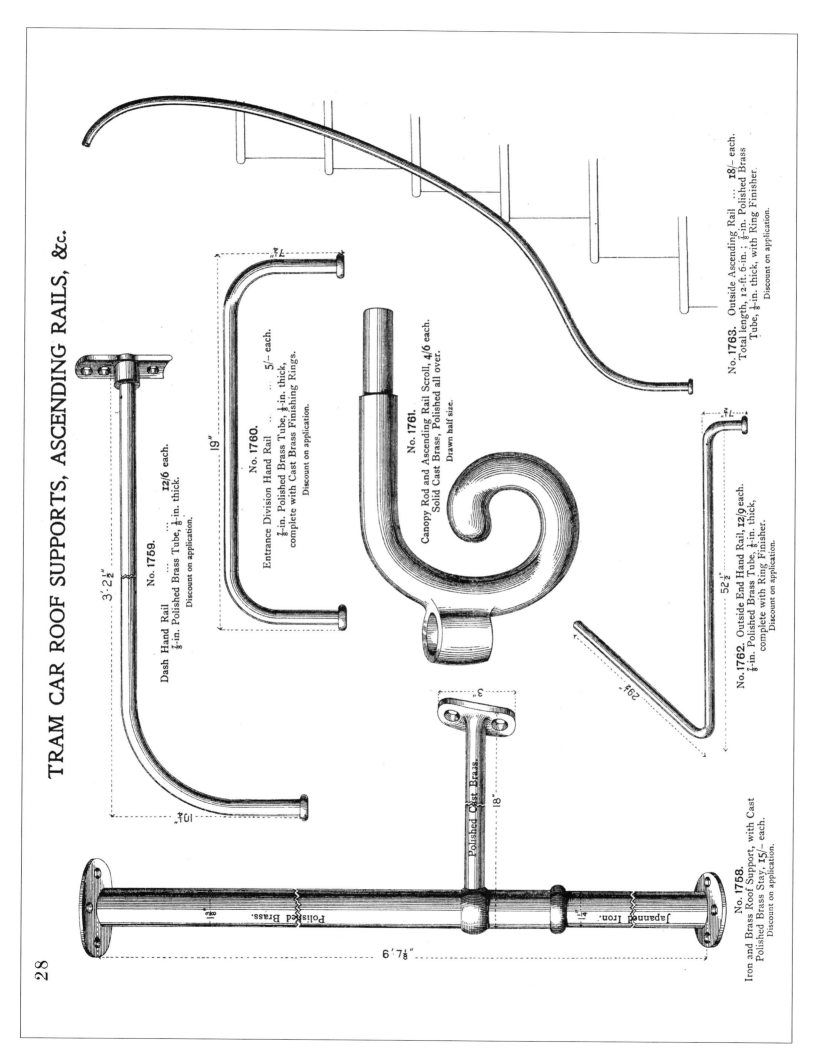

TRAM CAR ROOF SUPPORTS, ASCENDING RAILS, &c.

28

No. 1759.
Dash Hand Rail ... ... 12/6 each.
⅞-in. Polished Brass Tube, ⅛-in. thick.
Discount on application.

3' 2½"

10¾"

No. 1760.
Entrance Division Hand Rail ... ... 5/- each.
⅞-in. Polished Brass Tube, ⅛-in. thick,
complete with Cast Brass Finishing Rings.
Discount on application.

7½"

19"

No. 1761.
Canopy Rod and Ascending Rail Scroll, 4/6 each.
Solid Cast Brass, Polished all over.
Drawn half size.

No. 1762. Outside End Hand Rail, 12/9 each.
⅞-in. Polished Brass Tube, ⅛-in. thick,
complete with Ring Finisher.
Discount on application.

7½"

52½"

29¾"

No. 1763. Outside Ascending Rail ... 18/- each.
Total length, 12-ft. 6-in.; ⅞-in. Polished Brass
Tube, ⅛-in. thick, with Ring Finisher.
Discount on application.

No. 1758.
Iron and Brass Roof Support, with Cast
Polished Brass Stay, 15/- each.
Discount on application.

Polished Cast Brass.

3"

18"

Polished Brass.

Japanned Iron.

1¼"

6' 7⅛"

527

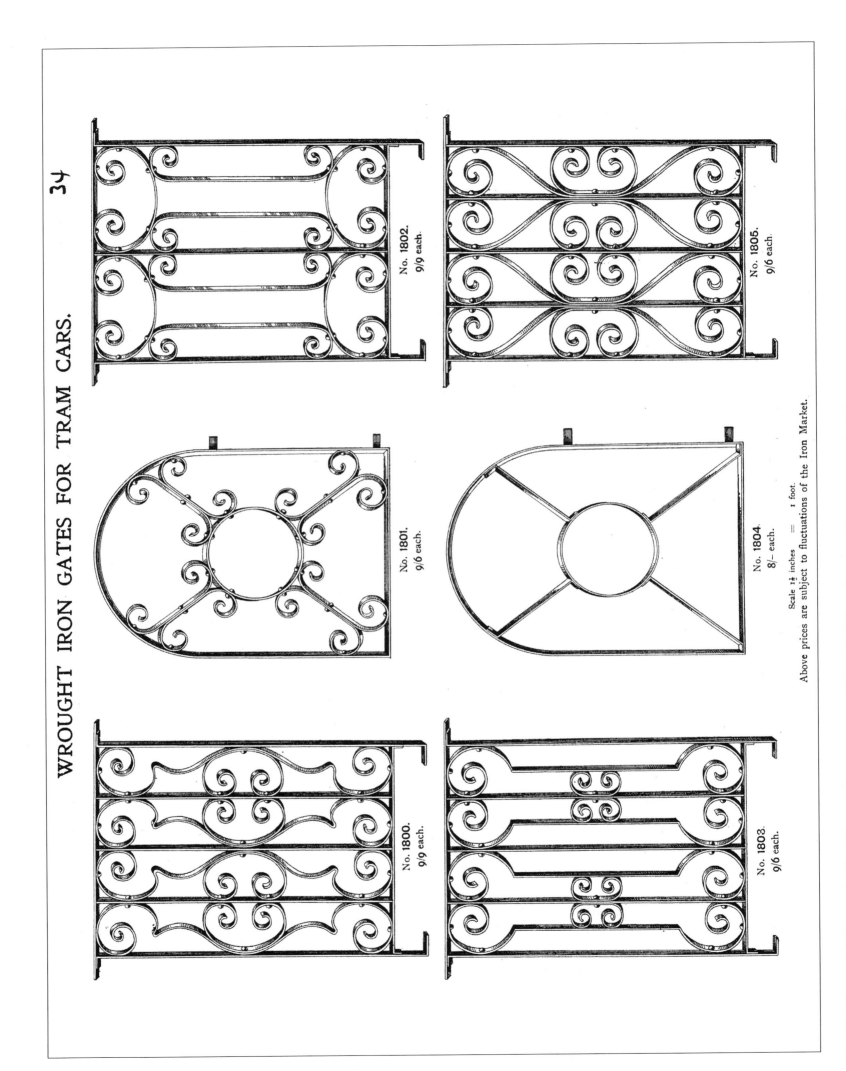

WROUGHT IRON GATES FOR TRAM CARS.

34

No. 1802.
9/9 each.

No. 1805.
9/6 each.

No. 1801.
9/6 each.

No. 1804.
8/- each.

No. 1800.
9/9 each.

No. 1803.
9/6 each.

Scale 1½ inches = 1 foot.

Above prices are subject to fluctuations of the Iron Market.

TRAM CAR LAMP BURNERS, LENSES AND LAMP GLASSES.

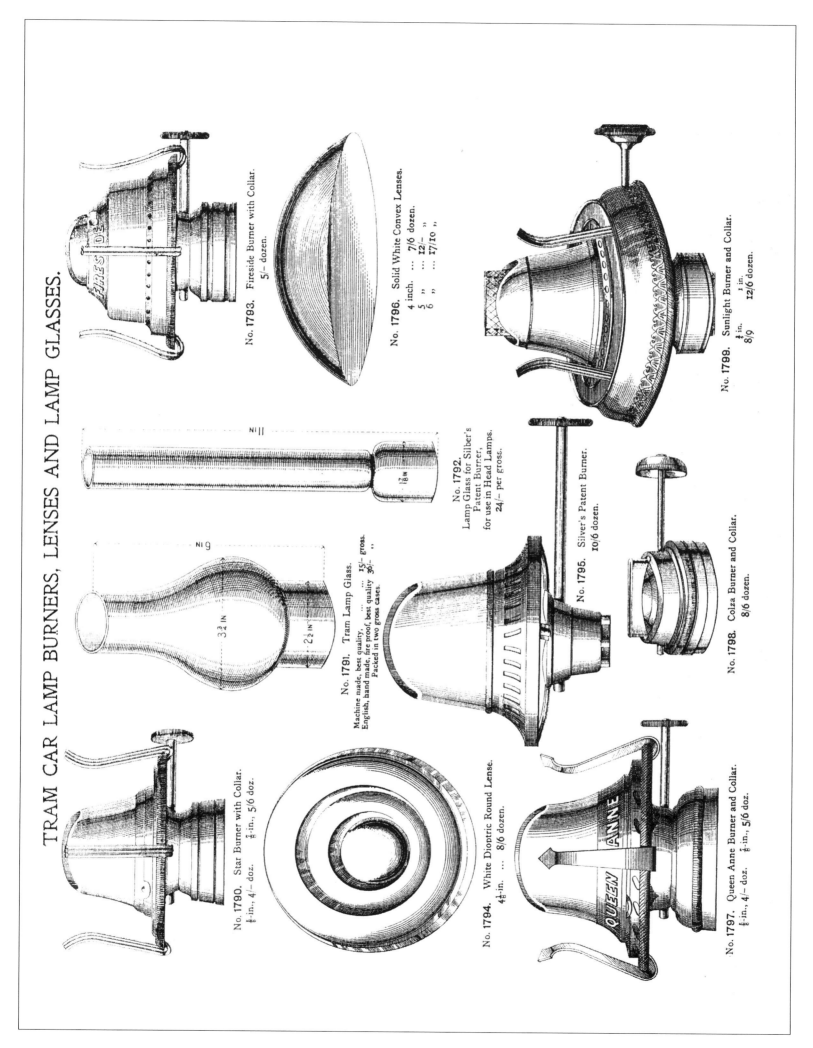

No. 1793. Fireside Burner with Collar.
5/- dozen.

No. 1796. Solid White Convex Lenses.
4 inch. ... 7/6 dozen.
5 " ... 12/- "
6 " ... 17/10 "

No. 1799. Sunlight Burner and Collar.
1 in.
8/9   12/6 dozen.

No. 1792.
Lamp Glass for Silber's Patent Burner, for use in Head Lamps.
24/- per gross.

No. 1791. Tram Lamp Glass.
Machine made, best quality, ... 15/- gross.
English, hand made, fire proof, best quality 30/- "
Packed in two gross cases.

No. 1795. Silver's Patent Burner.
10/6 dozen.

No. 1798. Colza Burner and Collar.
8/6 dozen.

No. 1790. Star Burner with Collar.
⅞-in., 4/- doz. ⅞-in., 5/6 doz.

No. 1794. White Dioptric Round Lense.
4½-in. ... 8/6 dozen.

No. 1797. Queen Anne Burner and Collar.
⅞-in., 4/- doz. ⅞-in., 5/6 doz.

Section 13

PATENTS

A few years ago I tried to add up the number of patents issued from 1860 to 1900 having some relevance to tramways in all their manifold forms. My guess is in excess of 2,500 in the UK alone. Many were incredibly ingenious and well meaning attempts to assist the horse or horses to start laden cars or assist them uphill and took the form of springs or some form of clockwork. Trouble is all of these gadgets would rely upon someone to maintain the mechanical unit; it would add weight and although the clockwork would probably work well enough the animal had to wind up the springs on the level road, an extra load it could not cope with.

Lifeguards there were a-plenty and some of these could work well enough on a model – I've found Gauge 1 to be about adequate for testing – but could not make much allowance for the pitching of a steam tram engine on a rough road hauling a laden trailer, but gradually they changed from the 'snowplough' style to the underslung 'catcher' net.

Tracklaying and maintenance led to another plethora of designs but few offered more than a small increment in efficiency and as an example if we are honest there was little point in bringing out a (steam or oil driven) motor to cut rails when cheap labour was so easily available, and the sheer weight of gizmos for bending and aligning rails ensured our old friend the 'Jim Crow' remained in use.

Improvements in the engines were often acceptable, and were mostly designed to keep as many of the working parts of the motion clear of the foul grunge the wheels lived in as could be attained. It says much for the Beyer Peacock/Wilkinson geared drive that it was so successful and relatively maintenance-free. The tramcars themselves were the subject of a number of patents mainly relating to either the drawbar gear or the brakes. Our predecessors had a justified fear of the trailer breaking away and running amok. I suspect this happened more often than I have seen recorded – even main line handbrakes were far from ideal – and until recently it did not take much to knock a hand-braked motor-car down a hill; my old Alfa Romeo had a separate set of drums and shoes just to ensure this did not happen to it. Later in electrical days, when passengers found they were bereft of even the skeletal protection given upstairs on a steam car trailer, many were the fiendish plans (worthy of Dr No) for ever-dry seats upstairs.

I have included a number of foreign patents. Our Antipodean predecessors were very fond of re-designing things – in general their improvements were of a robust nature, although Continental engineers grappled with, and more-or-less overcame, the same problems we had.

It will be understood these patents are merely a sample intended to wet the appetite, and most are presented chronologically, to record the flow and ebb of steam trams, with the exception of Alfred Dickinson's output which are grouped together, many of which being the product of a working engineer's mind were accepted for use not only on 'his' tramway, then South Staffs., but others. In order we have the date, the unique number of the patent within that date-year, and a key to the originator/content. Have fun with these products of fertile minds; their dreams may not have been realised but they are worthy of our attention and, dare I say, admiration.

1860-02895 George Francis Train Patent

A surprisingly little known Patent was granted to George Francis Train on 26 November 1860 – I repeat eighteen sixty A.D. This is reproduced in its entirety partly because of the age of the Patent, to a degree so that modellers may seize upon it with alacrity, leading (I hope) to a plethora of strange model steam trams turning up and also because the drawings alone show a great degree of misguided Yankee ingenuity.

The oldest steam tram car we can reasonably recognise is one which pre-dated G.F. Train's by a year and was built by a man named A.B. Latter, but after that, as is the way of steam trams, facts become cloudy. Our 'vade mecum', Kinnear Clark's *Tramways – Their Construction and Working* states that "The second application was made by Messrs Grice and Long, of Philadelphia, who constructed a long car on two four-wheel trucks or bogies – one under each end of the car. To one of the trucks steam power was applied by means of toothed gear. In 1860, five or six steam-cars were in use in the United States, in which the engine and boiler were placed within the car, the whole being carried on two bogie trucks. Mr G.F. Train, in 1860, patented a steam-car, on a Bissell-truck at one end and a pair of wheels at the other end, driven by a double-cylinder steam-engine with a vertical boiler, with intervening spur-gearing ..."

It was not entirely coincidental that at Birkenhead on 30 August 1860 there was a magnificent banquet given by our George Francis to "inaugurate the opening of the First Street Railway in Europe."

Compliments flowed like the wine and one by one Mr Pliny Miles makes sad reading today when the importance of Train's work is almost forgotten and never taught in schools.

"Alluding to the class of gentlemen, or noblemen, or whoever they were – old fogies was a more correct term – who resisted all improvements – he advised them to lose no time in opposing the first introduction of this Street Railway system in England, for he assured them that, as soon as one railway was fairly established it would lead to the general adoption of the plan. He would, therefore, say, with due regard to Mr Train's character, and without any reflection upon the ladies of England that one 'Train' would beget a very large number, and that the 'Trains' would shortly become so very thick upon the ground that he feared they would almost forget their friend George, the founder. (Laughter and cheers). The only reason why Mr Train was not the inventor of steam was, that steam had been invented before his birth. (Laughter and loud cheers)".

However, here we are – another 'what might have been'.

A.D. 1860, *26th November.* N° 2895.

Steam Carriages, &c.

LETTERS PATENT to George Francis Train, of Liverpool, in the County of Lancaster, Merchant, for the Invention of "IMPROVEMENTS IN STEAM CARRIAGES, AND THE RUNNING GEAR FOR STREET AND OTHER RAILWAYS."—A communication from abroad by Messrs. Grice and Long, residing in the City of Philadelphia, in the United States of America.

Sealed the 22nd May 1861, and dated the 26th November 1860.

PROVISIONAL SPECIFICATION left by the said George Francis Train at the Office of the Commissioners of Patents, with his Petition, on the 26th November 1860.

I, GEORGE FRANCIS TRAIN, of Liverpool, in the County of Lancaster,
5 Merchant, do hereby declare the nature of the said Invention for "IMPROVEMENTS IN STEAM CARRIAGES, AND THE RUNNING GEAR FOR STREET AND OTHER RAILWAYS," to be as follows (that is to say):—

This Invention is peculiarly adapted to railways in the streets of towns, or other railways having sharp curves, and where an ordinary locomotive, from
10 its size and weight, would be objectionable, and where a lighter and less costly engine would be a sufficient substitute, high velocity not being essential.

To construct according to this Invention a steam carriage for, say, the conveyance of passengers on street or other railways, the body of the carriage it is preferred to construct of an enclosed oblong form, having a stage or
15 platform at each end, one of which serves to enter the vehicle by, and the other to carry the engine and boiler, and which is constructed so as to allow

---

the frame of the engine to be brought down almost in contact with the driving wheels. The boiler is placed on one side of the platform and the engine on the other, the space between being for the engineer. It is preferred to place the engine and boiler on the forward platform, that the engineer may be in a better position to keep a look-out on the road, but the engine can be worked 5 with equal facility in opposite directions. The water tank is placed across the forward end of the body of the carriage in rear of the boiler and engine. In some cases the tank may, with advantage, be extended lengthwise beneath the seats in the body of the car. The boiler preferred to be used is a vertical tubular boiler with internal furnace. 10

The engine consists of two cylinders placed at angles of, say, about 30°, with their piston rods working through the lower ends thereof between guide frames, the connecting rods being coupled to a pair of crank arms on the ends of a transverse toothed or friction pinion shaft, which has its bearings on the lower side of the engine frame. The toothed pinion or small friction wheel on 15 the transverse shaft gears into a large toothed or friction grooved wheel staked on to the axle of the driving wheels. In some cases it is preferred to use an endless chain band in place of the cog or friction gear described.

The hinder part of the carriage body, in place of being supported upon an axletree and pair of wheels in the ordinary way, is mounted upon a truck 20 having either one or two pairs of wheels with their transverse axles. This truck is attached to the carriage body by a vertical pin which projects through the bottom of the carriage some distance in front of the truck wheels, and through a hole in the fore part of the truck, which is elongated for the purpose, or a rigidly fixed horizontal projecting arm, with a vertical hole through the 25 outer end thereof, may be used in place of extending the truck from beyond the running wheels. The waggon frame has a number of vertical antifriction rollers placed in one or more curved lines forming a part of a circle, the radius of which is taken from the vertical pin. The bottom of the body of the carriage, which is provided with suitable curved metal plates, rests upon the 30 antifriction rollers, which arrangement admits of the carriage readily passing round sharp curves.

The system of mounting upon trucks as herein-before described may be readily adapted to all kinds of railway carriages. When applied to railway waggons it is preferred to mount the body upon two trucks, which may be 35 constructed with either one or two pairs of wheels each, or one of the trucks may be provided with one pair, and the other two pairs of wheels. The object in using two trucks is that the vehicle can be driven either end first. When drawn by an engine the front truck would require to be locked, but when

---

drawn by a horse or other draught animal, by connecting the shafts or poll to the leading truck, it would be better to allow it to turn under the body of the vehicle.

To prevent undue vibration at the rear end of the car body when upon a
5 straight track, and to keep it in a line parallel with it, employ a spiral spring resting in a cylinder of nearly the same diameter internally, and about the same length, within this spring, and hanging upon the top of it by its larger head or a shoulder, is a bolt projecting some distance above it, and having at its outer and upper end an antifriction roll, the cylinder containing the spring
10 and bolts, being secured to the curved end of the truck at its centre by suitable lugs and bolts, causes the aforesaid spring to act through the said bolt and its antifriction roller upon an inverted double inclined plane secured to the bottom of the car body, the apex of the inclined plane being placed in the centre of the car body, transversely in a line perpendicular to the bolt, when the truck
15 to which it is attached is square with the body of the carriage upon a straight track.

SPECIFICATION in pursuance of the conditions of the Letters Patent, filed by the said George Francis Train in the Great Seal Patent Office on the 25th May 1861.

20 **TO ALL TO WHOM THESE PRESENTS SHALL COME,** I, GEORGE FRANCIS TRAIN, of Liverpool, in the County of Lancaster, Merchant, send greeting.

WHEREAS Her most Excellent Majesty Queen Victoria, by Her Letters Patent, bearing date the Twenty-sixth day of November, in the year of our
25 Lord One thousand eight hundred and sixty, in the twenty-third year of Her reign, did, for Herself, Her heirs and successors, give and grant unto me, the said George Francis Train, Her special licence that I, the said George Francis Train, my executors, administrators, and assigns, or such others as I, the said George Francis Train, my executors, administrators,
30 and assigns, should at any time agree with, and no others, from time to time and at all times thereafter during the term therein expressed, should and lawfully might make, use, exercise, and vend, within the United Kingdom of Great Britain and Ireland, the Channel Islands, and Isle of Man, an Invention for "IMPROVEMENTS IN STEAM CARRIAGES, AND THE RUNNING GEAR FOR
35 STREET AND OTHER RAILWAYS," as communicated to me from abroad by Messrs. Grice and Long, residing in the City of Philadelphia, in the United States of America, upon the condition (amongst others) that I, the said George Francis

---

Train, my executors or administrators, by an instrument in writing under my, or their, or one of their hands and seals, should particularly describe and ascertain the nature of the said Invention, and in what manner the same was to be performed, and cause the same to be filed in the Great Seal Patent Office within six calendar months next and immediately after the date of the 5 said Letters Patent.

NOW KNOW YE, that I, the said George Francis Train, do hereby declare the nature of my said Invention, and in what manner the same is to be performed, to be particularly described and ascertained in and by the following statement (that is to say):— 10

This my said Invention is peculiarly adapted to railways in the streets of towns, or other railways having sharp curves, and where an ordinary locomotive, from its size and weight, would be objectionable, and where a lighter and less costly engine would be a sufficient substitute, high velocity not being essential. 15

To construct, according to this my said Invention, a steam carriage suitable for, say, the conveyance of passengers on street or other railways :—The body of the carriage I prefer to construct of an enclosed oblong form, having a stage or platform at each end, one of which serves to enter the vehicle by, and the other to carry the engine and boiler, and which I construct so as to 20 allow the frame of the engine to be brought down almost in contact with the driving wheels. The boiler I place on one side of the platform, and the engine on the other, the space between being for the engineer. I prefer to place the engine and boiler on the forward platform, that the engineer may be in a better position to keep a look-out on the road, but the engine can be 25 worked with equal facility in opposite directions. The water tank I place across the forward end of the body of the carriage in rear of the boiler and engine, but in some cases the tank may with advantage be extended lengthwise beneath the seats in the body of the car. The boiler I prefer to use is a vertical tubular boiler with internal furnace. 30

The engine consists of two cylinders placed at an angle of, say, about 30°, with their piston rods working through the lower ends thereof between guide frames, the connecting rods being coupled to a pair of crank arms on the ends of a transverse toothed or friction pinion shaft, which has its bearings on the lower side of the engine frame. The toothed pinion or small friction wheel on 35 the transverse shaft gears into a large toothed or friction-grooved wheel staked on to the axle of the driving wheels. In some cases I prefer to use an endless chain band in place of the cog or friction gear described.

The hinder part of the carriage body, in place of being supported upon an

---

Train's Improvements in Steam Carriages, &c. for Street and other Railways.

axletree and pair of wheels in the ordinary way, is mounted upon a truck having either one or two pairs of wheels, with their transverse axles. This truck I attach to the carriage body by a vertical pin, which projects through the bottom of the carriage some distance in front of the truck wheels, and

5 through a hole in the fore part of the truck which is elongated for the purpose, or a rigidly fixed horizontal projecting arm with a vertical hole through the outer end thereof may be used in place of extending the truck frame beyond the running wheels. The waggon frame has a number of vertical antifriction rollers placed in one or more curved lines, forming a part of a circle, the

10 radius of which is taken from the vertical pin. The bottom of the body of the carriage, which is provided with suitable curved metal plates, rests upon the antifriction rollers, which arrangement admits of the carriage readily passing round sharp curves.

This system of mounting upon trucks, as herein-before described, may be

15 readily adapted to all kinds of railway carriages. When applied to railway waggons, I prefer to mount the body upon two trucks, which may be constructed with either one or two pairs of wheels each, or one of the trucks may be provided with one pair, and the other two pairs of wheels. The object in using two trucks is that the vehicle can be driven either end first.

20 When drawn by an engine, the front truck would require to be locked, but when drawn by a horse or other draught animal, by connecting the shafts or poll to the leading truck, it would be better to allow it to turn under the body of the vehicle.

To prevent undue vibration at the rear end of the car body when upon a

25 straight track, and to keep it in a line parallel therewith, I employ a spiral spring resting in a cylinder of nearly the same diameter internally, and about the same length. Within this spring, and hanging upon the top of it by its larger head or a shoulder, is a bolt projecting some distance above it, and having at its outer and upper end an antifriction roller. The cylinder con-

30 taining the spring and bolt is secured to the curved end of the truck at its centre by suitable lugs and bolts. The spring acts through the bolt and its antifriction roller upon an inverted double-inclined plane secured to the bottom of the car body. The apex of the inclined plane is placed transversely in the centre of the car body in a line perpendicular to the bolt when the truck

35 to which it is attached is square with the body of the carriage upon a straight track.

That this my said Invention may be the more readily seen and understood, I have hereunto annexed Drawings showing the practical application thereof; like letters and figures marked thereon have reference to similar parts.

Train's Improvements in Steam Carriages, &c. for Street and other Railways.

Figure 1 is a side elevation of one of the improved steam cars, shown with part of the external casing and the fore wheel removed for the purpose of exposing to view the engine and boiler, and the mode of connecting the running wheels therewith; Figure 2 is a partial front view of the same, showing

5 the position of the boiler, steam cylinders, cranks, spur gearing, and the eccentric on the revolving axle of the driving wheels for working the force pump for supplying the steam boiler.

Figure 3 is a side elevation of a truck constructed with double-swivelling axles, each fitted with a pair of wheels, and Figure 4 is a top view of the

10 same, the flooring or stage boards being removed to show the plan and mode of action of the working parts.

Figure 5 is a vertical sectional elevation of a truck fitted with swivelling axle frames, one of which is carried on an axle and one pair of running wheels, and the other upon a pair of axles and two pairs of running wheels;

15 and Figure 6 is a plan of the under side of the same carriage, showing the position of the hinder swivelling axle frame on a curved line of rail.

Figure 7 is a top view or plan of a swivelling axle frame, shown detached, fitted with two pairs of running wheels, and Figure 8 is a vertical transverse section of a truck, showing the self-adjusting arrangements used for cen-

20 tralising the running wheels when on a straight line of railway.

A, the body of the steam passenger car; B, the steam boiler; C, the steam cylinders; D, piston rods, which by E, connecting rods, are coupled to F, cranks on shaft of G, a pinion wheel working into H, a cog wheel staked on to the fixed axle of I, the driving wheels; K, engine frame; L, platform of

25 the steam carriage; M, frame of truck platform; N, swivelling axle frames; O, swivel pins of axle frames; p, lock pins to secure the swivelling axle frames; P, revolving axles of Q, the running wheels; q, antifriction wheels fitted to swivelling axle frames; R, a double inclined plane, against which presses S, an antifriction roller on the head of T, a vertical spindle, sur-

30 rounded by a helix spring, which works up and down in U, a vertical cylinder.

Having now fully described and ascertained the nature of this my said Invention, and how I believe the same may be best carried into effect, I wish it to be understood that I do not confine myself to the precise details or relative dimensions, as it will be readily seen that they may be

35 considerably varied without departing from the Invention; but what I claim as new is,—

First, a steam engine, boiler, and water tank constructed and arranged on the platforms or floors of railway cars, substantially and in the manner herein-before set forth and described, or any mere modification of the same.

Train's Improvements in Steam Carriages, &c. for Street and other Railways.

Secondly, mounting the driving pinion (G) on the frame of the engine.

Thirdly, swivelling axle frames pivoted at a point not over the axle or axles in combination with the antifriction rollers mounted in the axle frame, which work upon suitable bearing surfaces on the bottom of the carriage body,

5 substantially and in the manner herein-before described.

Fourthly, the application to swivelling axle carriages of an antifriction roller mounted on the head of a vertical spindle, surrounded with and acted upon by a helix spring in combination with a double inverted inclined plane beneath the bottom of the carriage body, substantially and in the manner

10 herein-before described and set forth.

And, lastly, the peculiar arrangement and combination of the various parts herein-before described, or any mere modification of the same, when applied to the construction of railway carriages with swivelling axletrees.

In witness whereof, I, the said George Francis Train, have hereunto

15   set my hand and affixed my seal, this Twenty-fifth day of May, in the year of our Lord One thousand eight hundred and sixty-one.

GEO. FRANCIS (L.S.) TRAIN.

Witness,

    J. I. Isaacson,

20   of 16, Norfolk Street,

        Strand, London, W.C.

Redhill: Printed for His Majesty's Stationery Office, by Love & Malcomson, Ltd.
[G 7308—25—6/1903.]

With Mr. Train's Compliments.]

FIRST

STREET RAILWAY BANQUET

IN THE OLD WORLD

BIRKENHEAD
1860

K & WOODSIDE-FERRY

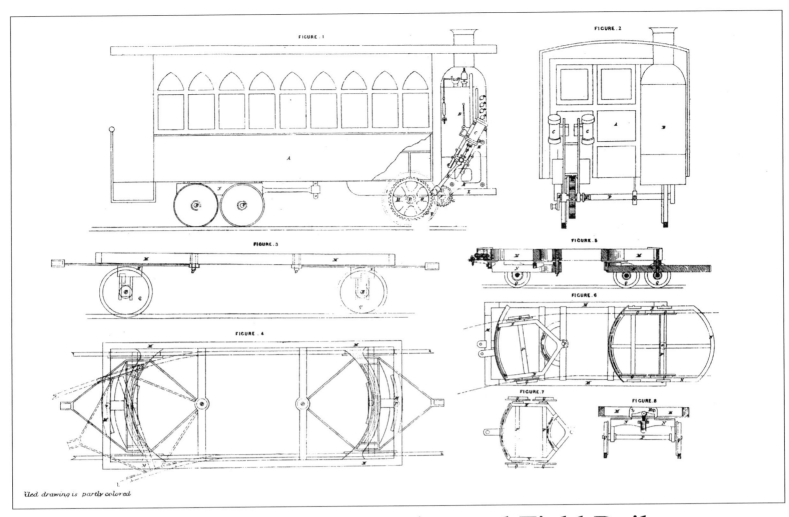

FIGURE.1   FIGURE.2   FIGURE.3   FIGURE.4   FIGURE.5   FIGURE.6   FIGURE.7   FIGURE.8

iled drawing is partly colored.

1862-02956 Merryweather and Field Boilers

[Third Edition.]

A.D. 1862, 1st *November*. N° 2956.

Steam Fire Engines, &c.

LETTERS PATENT to Moses Merryweather, Richard Moses Merryweather, both of Long Acre, London, Fire-engine Manufacturers, and Edward Field, of Buckingham Street, Adelphi, London, Consulting Engineer, for the Invention of "**Improvements in Steam Fire-engines, Parts of which Improvements are applicable also to other Purposes.**"

Sealed the 13th January 1863, and dated the 1st November 1862.

PROVISIONAL SPECIFICATION left by the said Moses Merryweather, Richard Moses Merryweather, and Edward Field at the Office of the Commissioners of Patents, with their Petition, on the 1st November 1862.

5   We, Moses Merryweather, Richard Moses Merryweather, both of Long Acre, London, Fire-engine Manufacturers, and Edward Field, of Buckingham Street, Adelphi, London, Consulting Engineer, do hereby declare the nature of the said Invention for "**Improvements in Steam Fire-engines, Parts of which Improvements are applicable also to other Purposes,**" to be as

10   follows:—

A steam fire-engine constructed according to this Invention consists of a framed carriage mounted, when for land service, on travelling wheels; at the hinder end of the frame is the boiler, in front of which is placed the steam cylinder and pump. The boiler consists of a vertical fire-box with a water

15   and steam chamber above, from the plate of which descend a number of tubes, arranged around the entrance to the smoke flue, the lower ends of some of them converging inwards to bring them into more immediate contact with the

M. & R. M. Merryweather & Field's Improvements in Steam Fire Engines, &c.

main body of the fire. Within these tubes are smaller ones open at top and bottom, their upper ends being wide mouthed or trumpet-shaped to facilitate the entrance and downward passage of currents of solid water unaffected by

5 the steam which rises externally around them. The exhaust pipe from the steam cylinder on entering the chimney passes downward to a chamber (the lower surface of which forms a baffle plate) from whence the steam is projected upwards to increase the draught in the fire-box. Provision is made for cushioning the piston in the steam cylinder by causing it to pass beyond

10 and close the main ports, the steam and exhaust being then led through a smaller channel capable of nice adjustment. Steam is admitted to the working cylinder of the engine by a slide valve acted upon by a smaller steam valve which receives its motion from connecting rods attached to the piston rod of the engine.

The foregoing improvements in the construction of the boiler, and in the arrangement and method of working the slide valves of steam fire-engines may also be advantageously applied to steam boilers and engines for other purposes.

SPECIFICATION in pursuance of the conditions of the Letter Patent, filed by the said Moses Merryweather, Richard Moses Merryweather, and Edward Field in the Great Seal Patent Office on the 30th April 1863.

20

TO ALL TO WHOM THESE PRESENTS SHALL COME, we, MOSES MERRYWEATHER, RICHARD MOSES MERRYWEATHER, both of Long Acre, London, Fire-engine Manufacturers, and EDWARD FIELD, of Buckingham Street, Adelphi, London, Consulting Engineer, send greeting.

25 **WHEREAS** Her most Excellent Majesty Queen Victoria, by Her Letters Patent, bearing date the First day of November, in the year of our Lord One thousand eight hundred and sixty-two, in the twenty-sixth year of Her reign, did, for Herself, Her heirs and successors, give and grant unto us, the said Moses Merryweather, Richard Moses Merryweather, and Edward Field,

30 Her special licence that we, the said Moses Merryweather, Richard Moses Merryweather, and Edward Field, our executors, administrators, and assigns, or such others as we, the said Moses Merryweather, Richard Moses Merryweather, and Edward Field, our executors, administrators, and assigns, should at any time agree with, and no others, from time to time and at all

35 times thereafter during the term therein expressed, should and lawfully

M. & R. M. Merryweather & Field's Improvements in Steam Fire Engines, &c.

might make, use, exercise, and vend, within the United Kingdom of Great Britain and Ireland, the Channel Islands, and Isle of Man, an Invention for "IMPROVEMENTS IN STEAM FIRE-ENGINES, PARTS OF WHICH IMPROVEMENTS ARE APPLICABLE ALSO TO OTHER PURPOSES," upon the condition (amongst others) that

5 we, the said Moses Merryweather, Richard Moses Merryweather, and Edward Field, our executors or administrators, by an instrument in writing under our or their hands and seals, or under the hand and seal of one of us or them, should particularly describe and ascertain the nature of the said Invention, and in what manner the same was to be performed, and cause the same

10 to be filed in the Great Seal Patent Office within six calendar months next and immediately after the date of the said Letters Patent.

NOW KNOW YE, that I, the said Moses Merryweather, on behalf of myself and the said Richard Moses Merryweather, and Edward Field, do hereby declare the nature of the said Invention, and in what manner the

15 same is to be performed, to be particularly described and ascertained in and by the following statement thereof, that is to say :—

This improved steam fire-engine consists of a framed carriage, mounted when intended for land service, on travelling wheels ; at the hinder end of the frame is the boiler, in front of which is placed the steam cylinder and pump. The boiler

20 consists of a vertical fire-box with water and steam chamber above, from the lower plate of which descend a number of tubes arranged around the entrance to the smoke flue, the lower ends of some of them converging inwards to bring them into more immediate contact with the main body of the fire. Within these tubes are smaller ones open at top and bottom, their upper ends being

25 wide mouthed or trumpet-shaped to facilitate the entrance and downward passage of currents of solid water, unaffected by the steam which rises externally around them. The exhaust pipe from the steam cylinder on entering the chimney passes downward to a chamber (the lower surface of which forms a baffle plate) from whence the steam is projected upwards to increase the

30 draught in the fire-box. Provision is made for cushioning the piston in the steam cylinder by causing it to pass beyond and close the main ports, the steam and exhaust being then led through a smaller channel capable of nice adjustment. Steam is admitted to the working cylinder of the engine by a slide valve, acted upon by a smaller steam valve which receives its

35 motion from connecting rods attached to the piston rod of the engine.

The foregoing improvements in the construction of the boiler, and in the arrangement and method of working the slide valves of steam fire-engines, may also be advantageously applied to steam boilers and engines for other purposes.

M. & R. M. Merryweather & Field's Improvements in Steam Fire Engines, &c.

And in order that the manner of performing this our Invention may be more fully understood, reference is had to the Drawings hereunto annexed, and to the following description thereof, that is to say :—

Figures 1 and 2, on Sheet 1, are respectively an elevation and plan view of a single cylinder steam fire-engine for land service, constructed agreeably to our 5 said Invention ; and Figure 3 is a vertical longitudinal section of the steam cylinder and valves appertaining thereto. The framing of the machine *a*, *a*, is formed principally of angle iron, supported on springs, and carried by the travelling wheels *b*. The boiler *c* (shewn in detail, and herein-after explained with reference to Sheet 2,) is attached to and carried by the framing at a 10 level below the steam and water spaces, so that the bolts employed for fixing do not pass into either of them, thus avoiding liability to leakage. It communicates by the steam pipe *d* with the valve chest *e*, as also by a small pipe *d*¹ with the valve chest *e*¹, made use of for regulating the motion of the piston valve, whereby the ingress and egress of steam to and from the main cylinder 15 are regulated. The construction of the cylinder and valves is clearly shewn at Figure 3, in which the same letters are employed to indicate the same parts as in the other Figures. The two pistons *f*, *f*¹, of a piston valve work in a suitable cylindrical valve chamber or chest *e*, into which steam is led from the steam pipe *d*. The rod *f*² of the piston valve is continued forward, and fitted 20 with a small piston *i* working in a cylinder *i*¹, to which steam is admitted alternately on each side of the piston as required by means of a small slide valve *i*² of ordinary construction. The valve chamber *e* communicates with the main cylinder *j* by means of four passages *k*, *k*¹, and *l*, *l*¹, which open into the thoroughfares *m*, *m*¹, communicating respectively with the forward and back- 25 ward ends of the cylinder. Small passages *n*, *n*¹, lead into the main thoroughfares *m*, *m*¹, and are formed with cocks for the purpose of regulating the escape of steam after cushioning. The action of the valve piston is regulated by means of levers *o*, *o*¹, connected by links *p*, *p*¹, with the piston rod, common to both the steam cylinder *j* and pump *q*. The levers *o*, *o*¹, communicate 30 motion to a rocking shaft *r*, upon which is keyed a disc *s*, fitted with adjustable stops, which act alternately upon each side of a tongue lever *t*, taking into the rod of the slide *i*². In the position of the parts as shewn, the piston *j*¹ propelled by steam (admitted through the opening *k* to its forward side), has just completed its backward stroke, and by closing the backward main port has 35 caused the steam behind the piston to form a cushion, whereby the momentum of the piston has been checked sufficiently to avoid injury to the end of cover of the cylinder ; while the steam forming the cushion has, at the same time, been gradually escaping through the opening *n* into the exhaust passage *l*¹.

M. & R. M. Merryweather & Field's Improvements in Steam Fire Engines, &c.

The piston rod during its backward action has given motion in that direction to the levers *o*, *o*¹, the shaft *r*, and disc *s* ; the latter moving through a great portion of its arc without moving the tongue lever *t*. When, however, the corresponding adjustable stop has come into contact with the forward side of the tongue lever, the slide *i*² is immediately moved into the position shewn, and 5 steam is thereby admitted to the forward side of the small piston *i*, thus driving it backward, and carrying the pistons *f*, *f*, into the position shewn by the dotted lines, and causing the piston *j* to be moved in the contrary or forward direction, firstly, by the passage of steam through the small passage *n* to the back of the piston, which upon passing, and thus laying 10 open the back port, is continued in its forward motion by the full volume of steam entering thereby, until upon the piston *j*¹ arriving near to the end of its forward stroke, the piston *i* is again moved, and the contrary action takes place. It is obvious that the frame boiler, and general arrangement herein represented and described with reference to this engine may also be 15 applied to engines having two or more cylinders and pumps.

The boiler *c* is shewn in detail in Sheet 2, Figure 4 being a vertical section ; Figure 5, a plan view (partly in section) of the same ; and Figure 6 an enlarged section of one pair of the tubes detached. The fire-grate *u* fed with fuel through the opening *u*¹ is of the ordinary or any other suitable construc- 20 tion, and is enclosed in a casing *v* depending from the water and steam space *u*, *u*¹. From the tube plate *x* depend and descend into the furnace a series of tubes *x*¹, curved or otherwise as found most convenient for the economical employment of the heat generated in the furnace. These tubes *x*¹ contain other tubes *x*², which are notched or otherwise made so as to be freely 25 open at bottom, and are formed with enlarged trumpet mouths at their upper ends, or are otherwise equivalently shaped to deflect the steam and water ascending from the annular spaces contained between the inner and outer tubes, in such manner as to facilitate and not to interfere with the downward current of colder and solid water descending by the inner tube to replenish 3 that which has passed upward by evaporation or otherwise between the inner and outer tubes. This deflection of the upward current may be effected by various arrangements, differing more or less from the trumpet mouth herein-before described and shewn ; as, for example, by the use of a dish or cup-shaped top to the inner tube, as shewn at Figure 7 ; or by an annular disc or 35 washer as at Figure 8 ; both of which are substantially equivalent to although in our opinion less suitable than the trumpet mouth. We do not in respect of this boiler lay any claim to novelty in respect of the employment of one tube within another for the purpose of separating the downward and upward

M. & R. M. Merryweather & Field's Improvements in Steam Fire Engines, &c.

currents from each other, as such an arrangement had been employed prior to the date of these our Letters Patent; but we believe that in no case had any arrangement for diverting the upward current of steam and heated water by a trumpet-mouthed inner tube, or by any equivalent thereto, been used.

By this employment of an enlarged or trumpet-shaped top, or equivalent, to the inner tube, a smooth and rapid circulation is induced, not otherwise obtainable. This arrangement of double tubes, formed as described, is obviously applicable to boilers and heating apparatus for various other purposes, as well as to the generation of steam, and owing to the rapidity and perfection of the circulation it induces, will be found highly economical in fuel. Thus, for example, it may be advantageously employed in apparatus for heating by hot water, for heating brewers' coppers, in distilling apparatus, and in numerous other cases in which it is required to heat a liquid in a rapid and economical manner. The steam after passing through the engine, as described, is carried off by an exhaust pipe y, which terminates in a box or chest y, having an opening opposite to the bottom of the chimney; from which opening the steam rushes upward, and increases the draught of air through the fire-grate; the lower side or surface of the box or chest acting at the same time as a baffle plate, deflecting the flame and heated gases; and preventing their too rapid escape up the chimney. The circumference of the tube plate x is bent downward so as to form an annular pocket x^3 for the collection of mud or sediment thrown up and ejected from the tubes, and which after settling in the pocket may be got rid of when required by openings provided for that purpose.

Figure 9, Sheet 2, is a vertical section of a boiler constructed on the same principle as the foregoing: and intended for stationary purposes; and Figure 10 a plan (partly in section) of the same. In this case the boiler c is set in brickwork, and is formed with a mud pocket as before described. The gases from the furnace in this case instead of being carried off by a central chimney or flue passing upward through the boiler pass outward through the annular mud pocket or water space by a series of flue tubes c^1 into the main flue c^2 communicating with the chimney. The steam generated passes by pipes as shewn into and through the segmental chamber c^3, wherein it becomes more or less superheated, and passes off to its work by the pipe c^4 as shewn. The grate and other parts corresponding with those of the boiler herein-before previously described, are marked with similar letters and figures, and require no description. The same system of double tubes, the inner tubes having trumpet mouths, or being otherwise equivalently formed for the purpose of facilitating the downward and deflecting the upward currents of water and

---

M. & R. M. Merryweather & Field's Improvements in Steam Fire Engines, &c.

steam, and ensuring a steady and sufficient downward current, may obviously be employed in boilers of various other forms and for various other purposes not herein particularly specified, wherein it is required to impart heat to fluid or liquid bodies in a rapid and economical manner. We do not therefore limit or confine our use or application of tubes as herein-before described to steam boilers, or hot water apparatus alone, neither do we limit ourselves to the precise forms of tubes as delineated; but we claim,—

Firstly, the use or employment in apparatus for heating fluids by double tubes of a trumpet mouth or other suitably formed guide or deflector for the purpose of preventing the interference of the ascending with the descending currents of fluid, and of ensuring a sufficient and steady circulation, substantially as herein-before described.

Secondly, the use of a hollow baffle plate or chamber into which steam is admitted, and from which it issues up the chimney for the purpose of increasing the draft and preventing the baffle plate becoming overheated.

Thirdly, the general construction and arrangement of parts constituting a steam fire-engine, substantially as herein-before described.

In witness whereof, I, the said Moses Merryweather, have hereunto set my hand and seal, this Thirtieth day of April, in the year of our Lord One thousand eight hundred and sixty-three.

MOSES MERRYWEATHER. (L.S.)

Witness,
Wᴹ. BADDELEY,
   Patent Agent,
      Islington.

Redhill: Printed for His Majesty's Stationery Office, by Love & Malcomson, Ltd.   [G. 8211—25—9/1904]

A.D. 1862. Nov. 1. N°. 2956.

M. MERRYWEATHER & FIELD'S SPECIFICATION.

3rd Edition

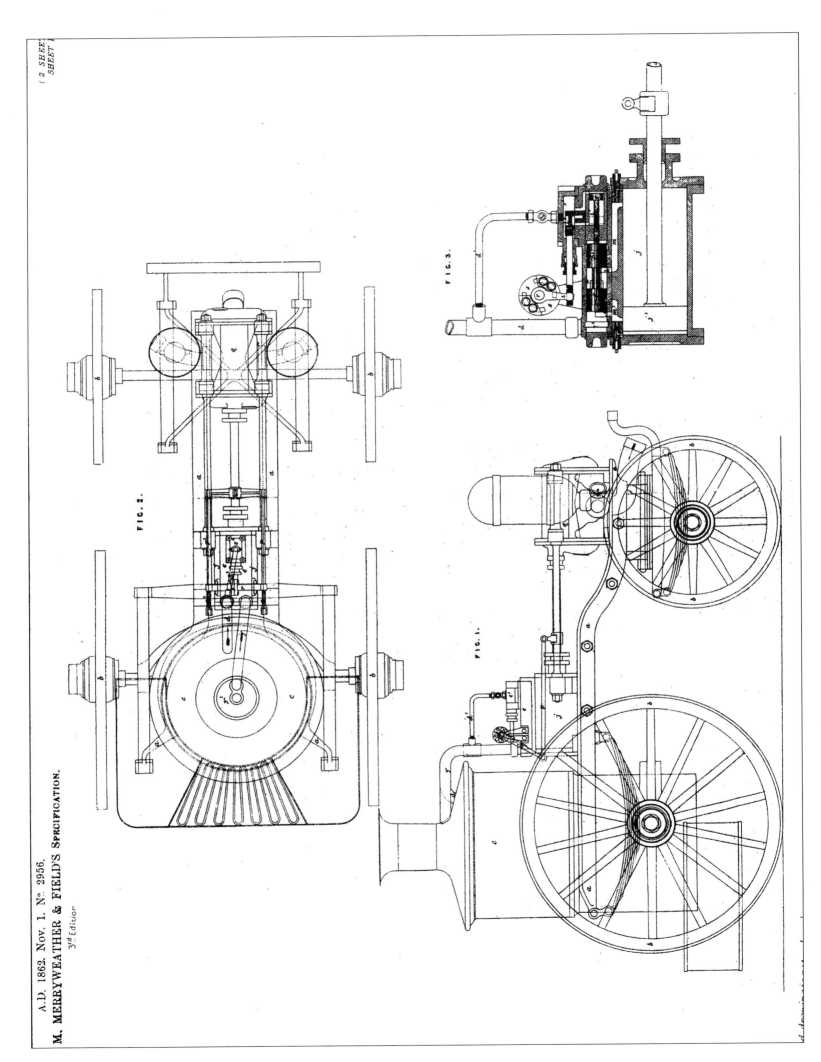

FIG. 2.

FIG. 3.

FIG. 1.

A.D. 1862. Nov. 1. Nº. 2956.

M. & R. M. MERRYWEATHER & FIELD'S SPECIFICATION.

3rd Edition)

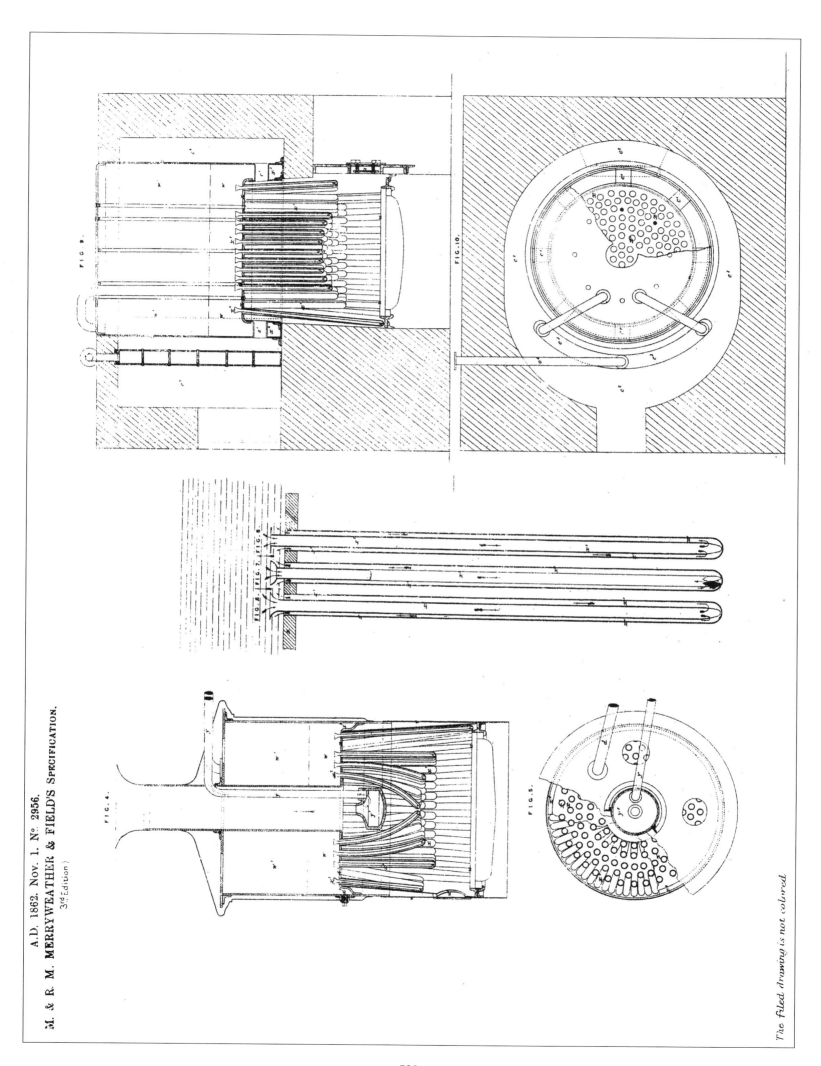

FIG. 9.

FIG. 10.

FIG. 8. FIG. 7. FIG. 6.

FIG. 4.

FIG. 5.

The filed drawing is not colored

1869-01519 A.M. Clark (agent for Jean Larmanjat) on Tramway and other Loco Engines

A.D. 1869, *18th* MAY. N° 1519.

Tramway and other Locomotive Engines, &c.

LETTERS PATENT to Alexander Melville Clark, of 53, Chancery Lane, in the County of Middlesex, Patent Agent, for the Invention of "IMPROVEMENTS IN TRAMWAY AND OTHER LOCOMOTIVE ENGINES AND CARRIAGES, AND IN THE PERMANENT WAY FOR THE SAME."—A communication from abroad by Jean Larmanjat, of 13, Boulevart St. Martin, Paris, Mechanical Engineer.

Sealed the 16th November 1869, and dated the 18th May 1869.

PROVISIONAL SPECIFICATION left by the said Alexander Melville Clark at the Office of the Commissioners of Patents, with his Petition, on the 18th May 1869.

I, ALEXANDER MELVILLE CLARK, of 53, Chancery Lane, in the County
5 of Middlesex, Patent Agent, do hereby declare the nature of the said Invention for "IMPROVEMENTS IN TRAMWAY AND OTHER LOCOMOTIVE ENGINES AND CARRIAGES, AND IN THE PERMANENT WAY FOR THE SAME," to be as follows :—

This Invention relates to improvements in tramway and other
10 locomotives and carriages, and also in the arrangement of the permanent way.

Clark's Improvements in Tramway and other Locomotive Engines, &c.

5 NOW KNOW YE, that I, the said Alexander Melville Clark, do hereby declare the nature of the said Invention, and in what manner the same is to be performed, to be particularly described and ascertained in and by the following statement, reference being had to the Sheet of Drawings hereunto annexed, and to the letters and figures marked thereon (that is 10 to say) :—

This Invention relates to improvements in tramway and other locomotives and carriages, and also in the arrangement of the permanent way. I will first describe the improvements in loco-
15 motives.

Ordinary railway locomotives are incapable of ascending inclines above a certain degree of steepness, 1st, in consequence of their weight ; 2ndly, from a want of sufficient adhesion, notwithstanding their weight. They further usually possess but one system of driving wheels
20 which serves alike for working inclines and levels.

According to the improvements of this Invention I make locomotives as small and as light as possible, the parts being made of steel, and hollow where practicable. These locomotives are relatively of great power, but at same time save much wear and tear of the road. I
25 provide two arrangements of driving wheels, one consisting of large wheels for running on levels and slight inclines, and a system of smaller wheels for ascending steep inclines. One or other of these two systems of wheels is used at a time according to the nature of the road, and each receives motion from the same driving power. Thus the small wheels
30 would be used for steep gradients, the engine travelling at a slower rate by which means greater power is obtained, permitting of the ascent of steeper gradients than has hitherto been possible. With the same object (namely, of ascending steep inclines) in order to obtain increased adhesion at any moment, I cause the driving wheels of the locomotive (supporting
35 a minimum weight) to run on the ground, while the remaining portion of the weight of the locomotive and load would be carried either on two rails, or it may be on a single rail, as will be herein-after described.

Clark's Improvements in Tramway and other Locomotive Engines, &c.

The driving wheels of the locomotive which run on the ground when two rails are employed may either be placed inside or outside said rails.

In order to enable the engine to turn curves of very small radius each
5 end of the driving axle is placed in connection with the driving wheels by means of coiled springs, so that the one wheel when on a curve may make a greater number of revolutions than the other by the coiling of the spring. The engine before starting stores the power in the two springs, which are sufficiently coiled by the time the engine and train is
10 in motion. In order to ensure the horizontal position of the boiler when ascending steep inclines I make the fore carriage of the engine to rise and fall in guides when travelling. For example, in ascending an incline the fore end is lowered, so as to bring the boiler to a horizontal line and keep the tubes well covered with water. This arrangement
15 of the generator, combined with the arrangement of wheels, herein-after referred to, further allows of adjusting the minimum of weight on the driving wheels for procuring only just the exact amount of adhesion desired. I may also reduce or increase the weight on the driving wheels and ensure the horizontal position of the boiler by making
20 the axis of the fore guide wheel to move horizontally in inclined guides formed on the framing, which is thereby raised or lowered as required.

These improvements may be adapted to locomotives running on one, two, or more rails, or to those used on common roads. Where two rails are employed the leading wheels and frame would be pivotted
25 as well as the trailing wheels.

I will now describe the improvements in the permanent way for use with the locomotives of this Invention designed with a view to economy. I use a single central rail placed on small wood sleepers, on blocks of stone or brickwork, with or without chairs. This single rail may be
30 made of any suitable section, and I thus economize the cost of one rail and its sleepers. The locomotives of this Invention travelling on the single rail have one carrying and guiding wheel at the front part, the axis of which is movable at all times, so as to be capable of being raised or lowered for the purpose of adjusting the boiler in a horizontal
35 position on inclines. The driving wheels, which may be in two sets, large and small, to be used alternately as before mentioned run on each side of the central rail, either on the ordinary road or on narrow wood,

---

macadamized, paved, or otherwise prepared surfaces placed parallel therewith. These wheels serve to maintain the equilibrium of the vehicle with the ground for their point of support. At the rear end of the locomotive, there is also a carrying wheel running on the central rail. In this manner only just the amount of weight required to 5 produce the necessary adhesion is brought to bear on the driving wheels. As before mentioned, to mount inclines I increase the adhesion by lowering the axis of the fore wheel, thus throwing more weight on the driving wheels, which at same time re-establishes the horizontal position of the boiler and increases the adhesion of the 10 driving wheels. I reverse the above action when descending inclines. In single rail lines the carriages composing the train attached to the locomotive are also provided with two kinds of wheels, 1st, two central bearing wheels mounted on independent axles, one at either end of the carriage; 2ndly, two supporting or balancing wheels mounted on the 15 same axle and running on the ground or other prepared surface, one at either side of the carriage. The weight in each carriage is brought to bear as equally as possible on the wheels running on the central rail by a combination of levers, the weight might also be brought to bear on the balancing wheels. 20

The improvements above described may be applied either separately or in combination both to road and rail locomotives with double or single rails.

The improvements of this Invention are illustrated in the accompanying Drawings, Figure 4 of which shows a plan, and Figure 5 an 25 elevation of a railway engine with boiler removed designed for running on a single rail. The leading guiding wheel is mounted in the manner previously described, but not shown in these Figures, and only one of the driving wheels is shown in Figure 4; these parts are however shown clearly in Figures 7 and 8. *a*, framing of the combined tender and 30 locomotive carrying the boiler and driving gear, which latter acts either directly on wheels *b*, as in ordinary, or by means of connecting rods, endless chains, or otherwise, suitable reversing gear being also provided. On axle *d* of wheels *b* are mounted levers *e*, which may be raised on turning a screw *f* by the aid of crank handle *g* for lifting the small 35 wheels *h*, in which case the large wheels *b*, *b*, alone would rest on the ground, a greater speed being thereby attainable. On the contrary, by

lowering the levers *e, e*, the small wheels *h, h*, are caused to rest on the ground, and the larger wheels *b, b*, would be raised. In this case the large wheels *b, b*, communicate motion to wheels *h, h*, by means of endless chain or other gearing not shown connecting axles *d* and *h*¹. Thus disposed greater power is attainable in consequence of the di- 5 minished speed. *l* steering wheel, which is moved to the right or left by the aid of a hand wheel.

Figure 6 shows the mode of transmitting the power from the engine to the wheels by means of coiled springs. One end of the spring is fixed to the driving axle *a*, the other end being connected to the box *e* 10 of wheel *b*. The axle *a* in turning coils the spring *c*, and so stores power, and when the power equals the resistance a start is effected. Further this arrangement enables one driving wheel when on a curve to make more revolutions than the other, thereby causing a variation in the coiling of the springs; and when the train returns to a straight 15 line an equilibrium is established between the two springs by the slipping of the wheel whose spring is most coiled.

Figures 1 and 2 of the Drawings show a plan and sectional elevation of the under frame of a carriage arranged to run on a single central rail. Figure 3 is a transverse section of same. The same letters apply to the 20 three Figures. *a*, framing; *b*, carrying wheels running on a central rail *c*, here shown as supported by a chair *d* on a base *e*. The wheels *b* are mounted on inclined pivots *f*, carried on framing *a* for facilitating the passing of curves; *g*, balance wheels mounted on the same axle *h*. These wheels run either on the macadamized or paved road or on tram- 25 ways on either side, for example on longitudinal wood sleepers. These wheels carry only a portion of the load, and serve to balance the carriage. *i*, lever provided with a screw *j*, and jointed to the spring of the balance wheels with the object of bringing the weight on the carrying wheels; *k*, macadamized trams on which run the driving wheels of the 30 locomotive and also the carrying wheels of the carriages. I have before mentioned that the driving wheels of the locomotive may run either on an ordinary road or on wood, macadamized, paved, or otherwise prepared surfaces laid parallel with the rail. Instead of having two such prepared surfaces disposed one on either side of the central rail I may 35 have but one such surface which would be laid on the side the most conveniently adapted for it, viz., that least occupied by ordinary vehicles.

This single tram would be protected from the wheels of ordinary vehicles by the rail which forms a guard therefor. The improved system of vehicle and single railway of this Invention may also be used with animal power or stationary traction engines.

I have before mentioned that the locomotives may be either adapted 5 for running on common roads, or on two, or it may be a single rail. I may also as before mentioned adapt a fourth wheel to the locomotive, which would take more or less of the weight on inclines, so that only just the necessary weight for obtaining adhesion and drawing the load will be applied on those wheels which run on the ground. This fourth 10 wheel may be placed in rear of the driving wheels, the whole series being arranged as follows, viz.:—1st, the fore guide wheel running on the rail; 2ndly, the driving wheels running on the road; 3rdly, the rear guide wheel running on the rail.

Figures 7 and 8 of the Drawings show a side elevation and plan of the 15 locomotive of this Invention.

It will be seen by the Drawing that the weight on the fore wheel A is regulated by a screw B and hand wheel C. The spiral spring connecting the driving axle D to driving wheels E is also shown in these Figures; F, rear guide wheel. The fourth wheel A running on the 20 single rail, as before mentioned, is capable of being moved longitudinally with the object of regulating the weight on the driving wheels. This arrangement of weight regulating wheels is also applicable on lines with two or more rails. In this case two of these wheels would be mounted on the same carriage. 25

In the course of experiments I have made on the improved mode of transport on a single rail I have found that in certain cases it is preferable to employ lateral supporting surfaces for the locomotive driving wheels and also for the carriage wheels, and that the friction between the iron rims of the wheels and the wood trams will ensure 30 sufficient adhesion for ascending all practical inclines. Hence in order to reduce the expense of laying, and the wear and tear of said trams, I propose to construct them of wood and iron combined. For this purpose I use wood sleepers of a comparatively small size, on which I place an iron sole piece of the same breadth as the rims of the 35 locomotive wheels, which latter I make of wood with the grain disposed so that the fibres may resist the wear. The friction between the wood

wheels of the locomotive on the iron sole of the tram is above mentioned, sufficient to produce the required adhesion for ascending any incline. These iron soles may also be roughened or grooved for increasing the adhesion, if desired. The iron soles are attached to the sleepers in any suitable manner. These combined wood and iron trams 5 are shown in transverse section in Figure 9 of the accompanying Drawings. *a*, iron sole of sufficient width to support the wood wheels of the locomotive at all points; *b*, wood sleeper to be made as light as possible. The parts *a*, *b*, are connected together by a screw *c* or otherwise, the sole *a* projecting beyond the sleeper on either side. 10 Figures 10 and 11 show a side view and transverse section of a wheel composed of wood in the manner above described. *d*, axle; *e, e*, discs uniting by means of bolts the several segments *f* of wood, each having the grain disposed endwise to the wear. I may also adopt the following arrangement for the locomotives:—Instead of having two driving wheels 15 there may be but one disposed centrally and running on the ground or tramway for obtaining the required adhesion, while I dispose the carrying wheels to run on rails as well as those of the carriages the same as in ordinary. In this case I also employ mechanism for regulating the weight on the driving wheel so as to obtain only just 20 the required amount of adhesion. The boilers of these locomotives with a single driving wheel may be formed in two parts with a fire-box between them.

Having described the nature of this Invention, and the manner of performing the same, I declare that what I claim as the Invention to 25 be protected by the herein-before in part recited Letters Patent is,—

1st. I claim the application to locomotives of two systems of driving wheels to be used alternately and receiving motion from the same driving power. The large wheels to be used when running on a horizontal surface or on inclines, and the small wheels for steep inclines 30 so as to obtain greater tractive power when required, both systems being applicable for use on common roads or on lines having one, two, or more rails, all as herein-before described.

2ndly. I claim the herein described method of supporting either a whole or a portion of the locomotive on the ground while the load is 35 carried on one, two, or more rails or trams for the purpose of increasing the adhesion of the motor, and of diminishing that of the carriages to be drawn.

3rdly. I claim transmitting motive power to the wheels by means of coiled springs which store power to aid in starting and also permit of the one wheel turning faster than the other to facilitate turning curves of small radius, said improvements being applicable to road locomotives or to locomotives running on one, two, or more rails.   5

4thly. I claim the application of carrying wheels disposed as described for adjusting or regulating the weight on the driving wheels in combination with the adjustable axis of the guide wheel, the whole designed with a view to bring only the minimum weight required on the driving wheels which run on the ground, and also to permit of maintaining the 10 horizontal position of the boiler when on inclines, the above improvements being applicable to road locomotives or to locomotives running on one, two, or more rails, all as herein-before described.

5thly. I claim constructing a single line railway of any form and fixed in a roadway in any known manner with or without the addition 15 of paved, macadamized, wood, or other tramway or ways disposed parallel to the central line and on which trams the driving wheels run, as also the balancing wheels of the carriages to be drawn, the central rail serving to support the weight regulating and guide wheels of the motor as well as the carrying wheels of the carriages, substantially 20 as herein-before described and shown in the Drawings.

6thly. I claim constructing rail or tramway carriages, as herein-before described, with two carrying wheels mounted on independent pivoted axes and running on the rail, and with two balancing wheels to run on the ground mounted loose on the same axle, said carriages being 25 also provided if desired with an arrangement of levers for bringing the weight on to the carrying wheels running on the rail, all as herein-before described.

7thly. I claim the application of this single line railway and carriages with carrying or balancing wheels where animal motors or stationary 30 engines are employed.

8thly. I claim the improved combined iron and wood tram in connection with the wood wheels in the manner shown and for the purpose specified.

9thly. I claim the application in these improved locomotives of a 35 single central driving wheel in lieu of two, as before described.

10thly. I claim the herein-before described improvements applied either separately or in combination, as and for the purposes specified.

In witness whereof, I, the said Alexander Melville Clark, have hereunto set my hand and seal, this Seventeenth day of November, in the year of our Lord One thousand eight hundred and sixty-nine.   5

A. M. CLARK.   (L.S.)

Witness,
    JAMES DAISH,
        53, Chancery Lane,   10
        London.

LONDON:
Printed by GEORGE EDWARD EYRE and WILLIAM SPOTTISWOODE,
Printers to the Queen's most Excellent Majesty.   1869.

A.D. 1872, 26th APRIL. N° 1246.

Locomotive Engines and Carriages, &c.

LETTERS PATENT to Alexander Melville Clark, of 53, Chancery Lane, in the County of Middlesex, Patent Agent, for the Invention of "IMPROVEMENTS IN LOCOMOTIVE ENGINES AND CARRIAGES AND PERMANENT WAY FOR THE SAME."—A communication from abroad by Jean Larmanjat, of Paris, Engineer.

Sealed the 10th October 1872, and dated the 26th April 1872.

PROVISIONAL SPECIFICATION left by the said Alexander Melville Clark at the Office of the Commissioners of Patents, with his Petition, on the 26th April 1872.

I, ALEXANDER MELVILLE CLARK, of 53, Chancery Lane, in the County of Middlesex, Patent Agent, do hereby declare the nature of the said Invention for "IMPROVEMENTS IN LOCOMOTIVE ENGINES AND CARRIAGES AND PERMANENT WAY FOR THE SAME," to be as follows:—

In the construction of a locomotive engine the chief aim is to obtain such an amount of adhesion that the weight of the train shall never

---

overcome the adhesion of the driving wheels and cause them to slip or revolve without advancing. Thus a locomotive of the ordinary construction and weight has a maximum of tractive power which cannot be exceeded on an ordinary railway except some practical means be provided to prevent slipping in conjunction with a means of multiplying 5 the power without increasing the weight.

The method of increasing the tractive power beyond that obtained by the adhesion of the wheels on the ordinary smooth rails proposed by the present Inventor consists in the employment of a single toothed rail or rack placed alongside the ordinary rail and secured in a similar 10 manner. A ring of teeth carried by one of the driving wheels of the locomotive is caused to gear with the toothed rail, which is laid at points where increased tractive power is required, the speed of the locomotive being also reduced by a system of gearing provided for the purpose when ascending steep gradients. Since the toothed rack serves merely 15 as an auxiliary to the rail it will form no impediment to the passage of the train in the contrary direction, as the gearing is placed on one side only of the engine which is turned round for returning. The rack rail would be placed now on one and now on the other side of the line according as the ground rises or falls, but when descending the train 20 can travel at any speed desired, as the rack at those places is always on the opposite side to the gearing on the engine.

By these improvements railways in which two rails are employed may be laid in localities having steep gradients, but where it is not desired to communicate with an ordinary line of railway it is preferable 25 to employ the single rail system herein-after referred to, in which the same method of obtaining adhesion at the expense of speed is applied although in a different manner. The single rail system allows of curves of very small radius, whereby the expense of the road is greatly reduced, and even on curves of a fourth of a chain radius the tractive 30 effort required is not increased, and the use of turntables is dispensed with.

Vehicles are employed for use on such lines having four wheels, one at each end, placed centrally or in the longitudinal axis of the vehicle, and one at either side at mid length. The two first mentioned wheels 35 are grooved to run on the rail, and are mounted on pivots. They serve to guide the vehicle and they also sustain a greater portion of the load. The other two wheels serve merely to maintain the equipoise of the

Clark's Improvements in Locomotive Engines and Carriages.

vehicle by bringing the weight on the central rail. The vehicle is entered at either end and has longitudinal central seats. A single central buffer is placed at each end of the framing, which is curved to an arc of a circle, and beneath it is placed the coupling link, which
5 connects to a radiating bar pivoted to a transverse lever placed at a certain distance from the end of the carriage, on which the bar moves as a centre. The fulcrum of this lever may be movable and connected to a spring. The other extremity of the lever is connected with the corresponding end of the lever at the opposite end of the carriage by
10 a screw coupling adjusted by a worm shaft, operated by a ball lever at either side of the carriage. By this means the strain is sustained by the draw bars and does not effect the carriage framing. The springs on which the carriage is supported are located in the hollow central back of the passengers' seats and connected by suitable yokes with the
15 bearings of the central guide wheels. The vehicle is constructed for use on ordinary roads by making the fore and rear grooved guide wheels removable and attaching shafts. This system of traction is also applicable for towing barges or vessels on canals by laying the rail along the towing path. The locomotive applicable for single rail lines is also
20 provided with four wheels, one at front and one at rear running on the rail, forming guide wheels, while the other two are driving wheels running on the ground or on trams for obtaining adhesion and are furnished with india-rubber tires.

A further means of preserving both the rubber surface and the roadway
25 is obtained by making the driving wheels bear more or less thereon according to the tractive power required by the aid of an adjusting screw which causes the engine to preponderate either on the side wheels or on the central rail. The engine is arranged to work at two different speeds and so as to double the tractive power when working on inclines
30 or drawing heavy loads.

The chief feature of novelty in the construction of the locomotive consists in the method of varying the speed. In order to adapt the locomotive to turn curves of small radius one of the driving wheels is loose on its axle (which is not the cranked axle), and each is provided
35 with a toothed wheel or circle on the boss of the wheel for high speeds, while for low speeds a larger toothed circle concentric with the other is placed within a ring fixed on the driving wheel, both toothed circles being capable of turning loosely. A pinion is keyed at either end of

Clark's Improvements in Locomotive Engines and Carriages.

the crank axle and placed between the inner and outer toothed circle to gear with both at once. It will be evident that by fixing one or other of the toothed circles to the driving wheels the engine may be driven at a high or low speed as desired. The toothed circles may
5 be fixed by means of locking wedges or keys, and by fixing those of the one driving wheel to which only the power would be applied the engine may be turned on the other driving wheel as on a pivot.

The bearings of the wheel axle and cranked driving shaft are made in one piece, so that the two will always preserve their relative positions
10 and keep in gear notwithstanding the vertical movements of the engine caused by the yielding of the springs.

For double rail lines I employ a locomotive with two pairs of wheels which may be coupled. One pair is provided with the system of gearing above described and is driven by a separate cranked shaft. One wheel
15 of this pair is also provided with an outer ring of teeth fixed inside the tire of the wheel to gear with the rack laid alongside the rail as before described.

SPECIFICATION in pursuance of the conditions of the Letters Patent, filed by the said Alexander Melville Clark in the Great Seal Patent Office on the 25th October 1872.
20

TO ALL TO WHOM THESE PRESENTS SHALL COME, I, ALEXANDER MELVILLE CLARK, of 53, Chancery Lane, in the County of Middlesex, Patent Agent, send greeting.

WHEREAS Her most Excellent Majesty Queen Victoria, by Her Letters Patent, bearing date the Twenty-sixth day of April, in the year of
25 our Lord One thousand eight hundred and seventy-two, in the thirty-fifth year of Her reign, did, for Herself, Her heirs and successors, give and grant unto me, the said Alexander Melville Clark, Her special licence that I, the said Alexander Melville Clark, my executors, administrators, and assigns, or such others as I, the said Alexander Melville
30 Clark, my executors, administrators, and assigns, should at any time agree with, and no others, from time to time and at all times thereafter during the term therein expressed, should and lawfully might make, use, exercise, and vend, within the United Kingdom of Great

Clark's Improvements in Locomotive Engines and Carriages.

Britain and Ireland, the Channel Islands, and Isle of Man, an Invention for "IMPROVEMENTS IN LOCOMOTIVE ENGINES AND CARRIAGES AND PERMANENT WAY FOR THE SAME," a communication to me from abroad by Jean Larmanjat, of Paris, Engineer, upon the condition (amongst others)
5 that I, the said Alexander Melville Clark, my executors or adminis-trators, by an instrument in writing under my, or their, or one of their hands and seals, should particularly describe and ascertain the nature of the said Invention, and in what manner the same was to be performed, and cause the same to be filed in the Great Seal Patent Office within
10 six calendar months next and immediately after the date of the said Letters Patent.

NOW KNOW YE, that I, the said Alexander Melville Clark, do hereby declare the nature of the said Invention, and in what manner the same is to be performed, to be particularly described and ascer-
15 tained in and by the following statement, reference being had to the Sheet of Drawings hereunto annexed, and to the letters and figures marked thereon (that is to say) :—

In order to work local or branch railways having steep gradients the locomotive if of the ordinary type would have to be of such power and
20 weight and the permanent way of such an expensive character that in most cases the expenses would exceed any possible returns.

This Invention relates to the construction of locomotive engines capable of working at two different speeds according to the requirements of the traffic, and therefore peculiarly adapted for service on such lines.
25 An engine so constructed weighing between 13 and 14 tons and capable of hauling a dead weight of 118 tons on inclines of about 1 in 80 (when arranged to run on rails in the ordinary manner and the weight of the engine being sufficient to obtain the necessary adhesion) may by simply changing the speed be used for hauling a train of the same weight up
30 inclines of about 1 in 40. The tractive power which is equal in the first case to about 2 tons becomes doubled in the second case owing to the change in the speed of the locomotive, thus power is gained at the expense of speed.

In the construction of a locomotive engine the chief aim is to obtain
35 such an amount of adhesion that the weight of the train shall never overcome the adhesion of the driving wheels and cause them to slip or revolve without advancing. A locomotive of the ordinary construction

Clark's Improvements in Locomotive Engines and Carriages.

and of a certain weight has a maximum tractive power which cannot be exceeded (as it would however require to be in order to ascend a steep incline) unless some means be provided to prevent slipping, in conjunction with a means of multiplying the power and diminishing the speed
5 without increasing the weight.

The method of increasing the adhesion beyond that of the wheels on the smooth rails of an ordinary railway proposed by the present Inventor consists in the employment of a single toothed rail or rack placed along-side the ordinary rail and secured in a similar manner. A ring of teeth
10 carried by one of the driving wheels of the locomotive is caused to gear with the toothed rail, which is laid at points where increased tractive power is required, the speed of the locomotive being reduced to 6 or 7 miles an hour by a system of gearing provided for the purpose when ascending steep gradients. Since the toothed rack serves merely as an
15 auxiliary to the rail it will form no impediment to the passage of the train in the contrary direction, as the gearing is placed on one side only of the engine which is turned round at the end of the line. The rack rails would therefore be placed now on one and now on the other side of the line according as the ground rises or falls, but when descending
20 the train can travel at any speed desired, as the gearing on the engine is always at the opposite side to the rack provided at those places for engines travelling in the contrary direction.

By these improvements railways in which two rails are employed as usual may be laid in localities having steep gradients, but where it is
25 not desired to form a junction with an ordinary line of railway it is preferable to employ the single rail system herein-after referred to, in which increased adhesion is obtained by partly running on the ordinary roadway, and the same method of obtaining greater tractive power at the expense of speed is applied although in a different manner.

30 The single rail system which facilitates the laying of lines alongside of roads allows of curves of very small radius, whereby the expense of the line is greatly reduced, and even on curves of a fourth of a chain radius the tractive effort required is not increased and the use of turn-tables is dispensed with.

35 The vehicles, both locomotives and carriages, employed on such lines have four wheels, one at each end, placed centrally or in the longitudinal axis of the vehicle, and one at either side. The two first mentioned wheels are grooved to run on the rail and are mounted in pivoted frames.

Clark's Improvements in Locomotive Engines and Carriages.

They serve to guide the vehicle and also sustain the greater portion of the load, while the other two wheels serve to maintain the equipoise of the vehicle by throwing the weight on the central rail.

I have taken as an example an engine of the comparatively light
5 weight of 14 tons, although it will be found that in the majority of cases engines weighing from 5 to 8 tons only and capable of hauling a train of four or five trucks carrying from 15 to 20 tons of goods up inclines of 1 in 25 will suffice for local purposes. With light engines heavy rails and sleepers are not required and but little ballast, while by
10 the adoption of these gradients the heavy expenses inseparable from the construction of ordinary lines are not incurred.

This system of traction is also applicable for towing barges or vessels on canals by laying the rail along the towing path. The locomotive applicable for single rail lines is illustrated in the accompanying
15 Drawings, Figure 1 of which shows a longitudinal vertical section thereof; Figure 2 is a transverse section taken through the fire-box and tender; Figure 3 is a longitudinal section below the boiler; Figure 4 shows a face view on a larger scale of the driving wheel with gear for changing the speed; Figure 5 is a section of same, while
20 Figures 6 and 7 show a part sectional elevation and plan of the crank shaft and driving axle detached. The same reference letters serve for all these Figures.

The locomotive is provided with four wheels, of which one *a* is placed at front and one *b* at rear, running on the rail, forming guide wheels,
25 while the other two *c, c,* are driving wheels running on the ground or on trams for obtaining adhesion and are furnished with india-rubber tires to prevent damage to the trams or road, and which serve to reduce the weight on the square inch to less than 26 lbs. The driving wheels are made capable of adjustment so as to bear more or less on the track
30 according to the tractive power required by the aid of an adjusting screw *d* by which the engine may be caused to preponderate either on the side wheels or on the central rail *e,* Figure 2.

The engine is arranged to work at two different speeds so as to double the tractive power when working on inclines or drawing heavy loads.
35 The locomotive shown in the Drawing is so geared that for the higher speed the crank makes three revolutions for one of the driving wheel, and for the lower speed five revolutions to one of the driving wheel.

Clark's Improvements in Locomotive Engines and Carriages.

The chief feature of novelty in the construction of the locomotive consists in the method of changing the speed. In order to adapt the locomotive to turn curves of small radius one of the driving wheels *c*
5 is loose on its axle *f* (which is not the cranked axle), and each is provided with a toothed wheel *g* or circle on the boss *h* of the wheel for high speed, while for low speed and increased tractive power a larger toothed circle *i* concentric with the other is placed within a ring *j,* fixed on the driving wheel, both toothed circles being capable of turning loosely
10 when not fixed or keyed. A pinion *l* is keyed at either end of the crank axle *k* and placed between the inner and outer toothed circles *g, i,* to gear with both at once. It will be evident that by fixing one or other of the toothed circles to the driving wheels the engine may be driven at a high or low speed as desired. Sufficient space is left between the
15 two toothed rings *g, i,* for the insertion of a hooked or locking bolt *m,* which passes through the body or web of the wheel, and is provided with a handle *n* and nut *o.* If it is desired to run at a low speed the larger toothed ring *i* is locked against the wheel *c* by the bolt *m* and nut *o,* while on the contrary for running at a high speed the key *m* is unlocked
20 and reversed by its handle *n,* so as to lock the smaller toothed ring *g* against the wheel. Turntables are not required with an engine of this construction, and in order to turn it within a circle of 5 or 6 yards radius the toothed rings of the inside wheel are unlocked by releasing the bolt *m,* so that the wheel which runs on the outside curve only will be
25 driven (one of the wheels being loose on the axle), and the engine may therefore be turned sharp round, as at the corner of a road for example. The bearings *p* of the wheel axle *f* and cranked driving shaft are made in one piece, so that the two will always preserve their relative positions and keep in gear notwithstanding the vertical movements of the engine
30 caused by the yielding of the springs.

In double rail lines having gradients higher than 1 in 80, I employ a locomotive with two pairs of wheels coupled and capable of working at either of two speeds. The arrangement of gearing is the same as that for the single rail locomotive before described and the same
35 reference letters serve to indicate the same parts.

Figure 8 shows a longitudinal vertical elevation of the mechanism; Figure 8^a the continuation of the incline shown at Figure 8, while Figures 9 and 9^a show plans of Figures 8 and 8^a respectively. The general arrangement of the engine is shown at A; *r, r, c, c,* two pairs

Clark's Improvements in Locomotive Engines and Carriages.

of driving wheels coupled together, the latter pair being provided with the system of gearing before described for changing the speed; f, wheel axle; g, small ring of teeth for high speed; h, nave of driving wheels; j, circular rib or flange within which is carried the large toothed ring
5 for low speed; l, pinion fixed on each end of the crank axle k; m, bolt, and o nut for locking one or other of the toothed rings; n, handle of same; s, s, pair of rails with a rack t placed at one side, on inclines only. With this rack gears a ring of teeth u on one of the driving wheels c.

10 Figure 10 shows a longitudinal vertical section of a passenger carriage adapted for the single line railway before referred to, Figure 11 an end view, and Figure 12 a transverse section of same, while Figure 13 shows a plan of the under framing, the flooring being removed. The same reference letters apply to all these Figures.

15 The following are the features of novelty in this vehicle :—The vehicle if for passenger service is entered at either end from platforms a^1, a^1, and has longitudinal central seats b^1; a single central buffer c^1 is placed at each end of the framing. The face of the buffer is curved in a horizontal but not in a vertical direction, and the ends of the framing are also
20 curved to an arc of a circle. Beneath the framing is placed the coupling link which connects to a radiating bar pivoted at d^1 to a transverse lever placed at a certain distance from the end of the carriage on which the bar moves as a centre. The fulcrum of this lever is at e^1, which may be movable within fixed limits and connected to a spring. The other
25 extremity f^1 of the lever is connected by rods g^1 with the corresponding end of a similar lever at the opposite end of the carriage, a screw coupling $-h^1$ being provided in said rods g^1 for tightening up when required. The coupling is adjusted by a worm shaft i^1 operated by a ball lever j^1 at either side of the carriage. By this means the strain
30 is sustained by the draw bars alone and does not affect the carriage framing. The springs on which the carriage is supported are located in the hollow central back of the passengers' seats and connected by suitable yokes with the bearings of the central guide wheels. The vehicle is constructed for use on ordinary roads by making the fore
35 and rear grooved guide wheels removable and attaching shafts.

Having described the nature of the Invention, and in what manner the same is to be performed, I declare that what I claim as the Invention to be protected by the herein-before in part recited Letters Patent

---

Clark's Improvements in Locomotive Engines and Carriages.

is, the system of locomotive constructed as set forth to work either at a high speed or at a low speed when increased tractive power is required whether for a single rail line or for an ordinary line, the latter being provided with a rack rail at steep gradients, also the improved
5 construction of passenger carriage for single rail lines, the whole constituting improvements in railways based on the novel means of traction above specified, and illustrated in the Drawings.

In witness whereof, I, the said Alexander Melville Clark, have hereunto set my hand and seal, this Twenty-fifth day of October,
10 in the year of our Lord One thousand eight hundred and seventy-two.

A. M. CLARK. (L.S.)

LONDON:
Printed by GEORGE EDWARD EYRE and WILLIAM SPOTTISWOODE, Printers to the Queen's most Excellent Majesty. 1872.

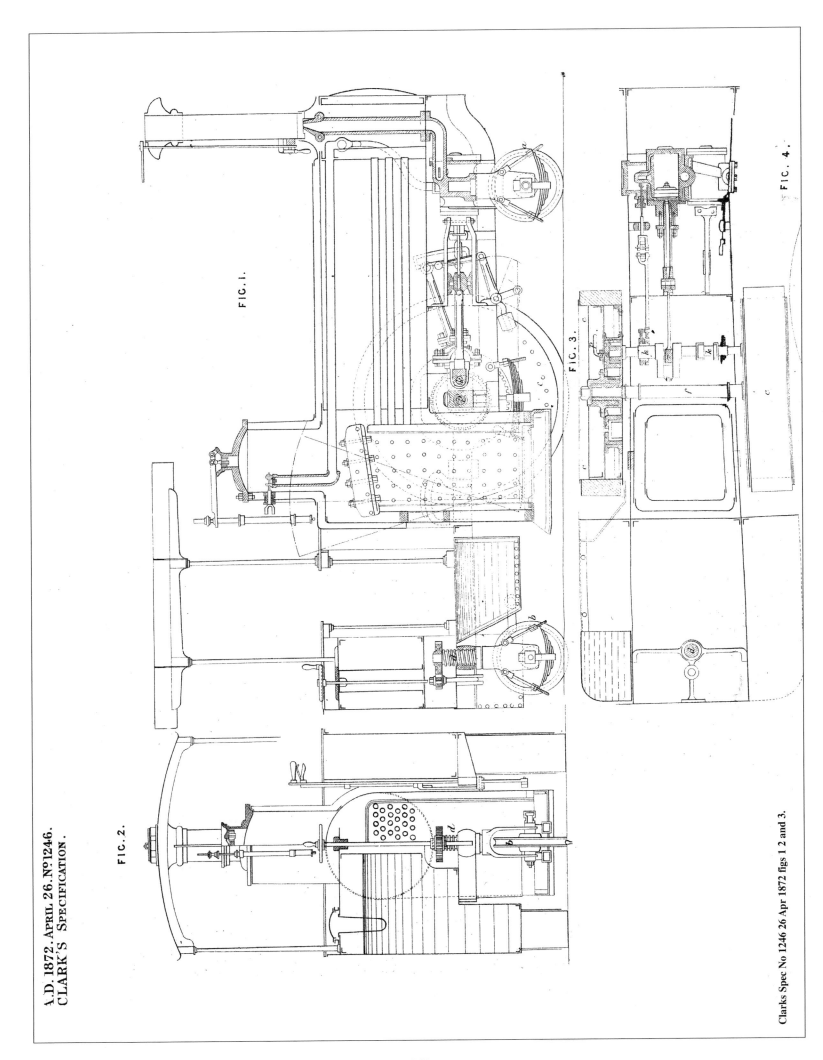

FIG. 1.

FIG. 2.

FIG. 3.

FIG. 4.

Clarks Spec No 1246 26 Apr 1872 figs 1 2 and 3.

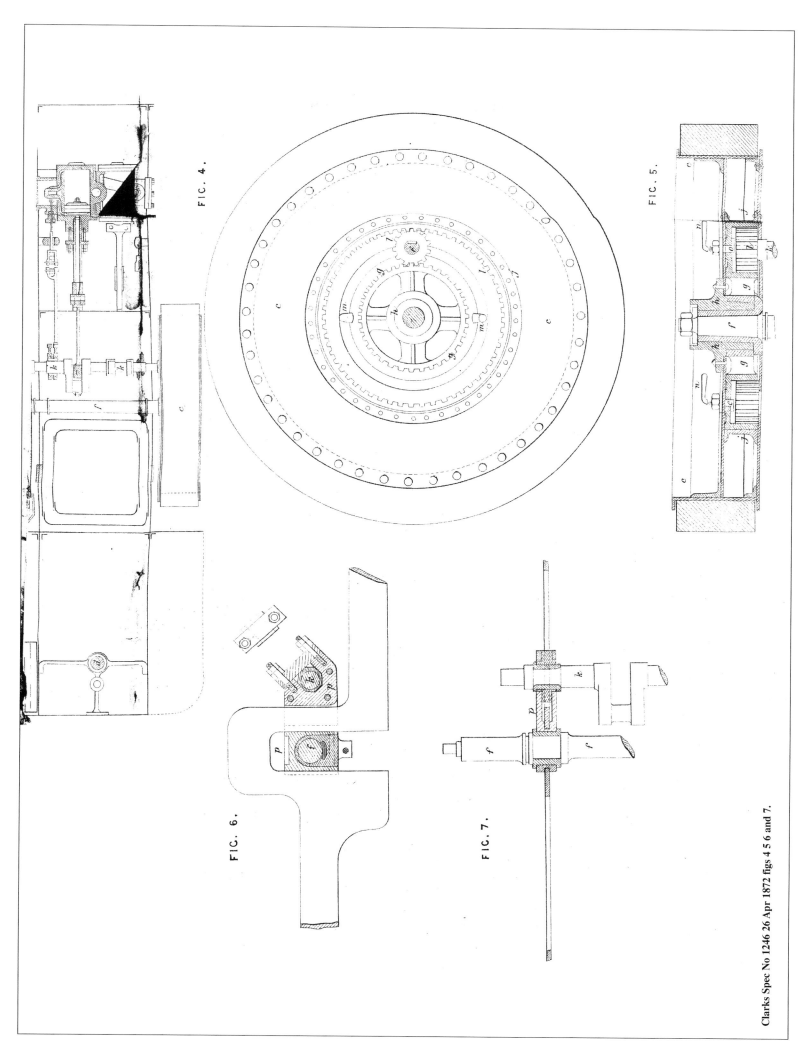

FIC. 4.

FIC. 5.

FIC. 6.

FIC. 7.

Clarks Spec No 1246 26 Apr 1872 figs 4 5 6 and 7.

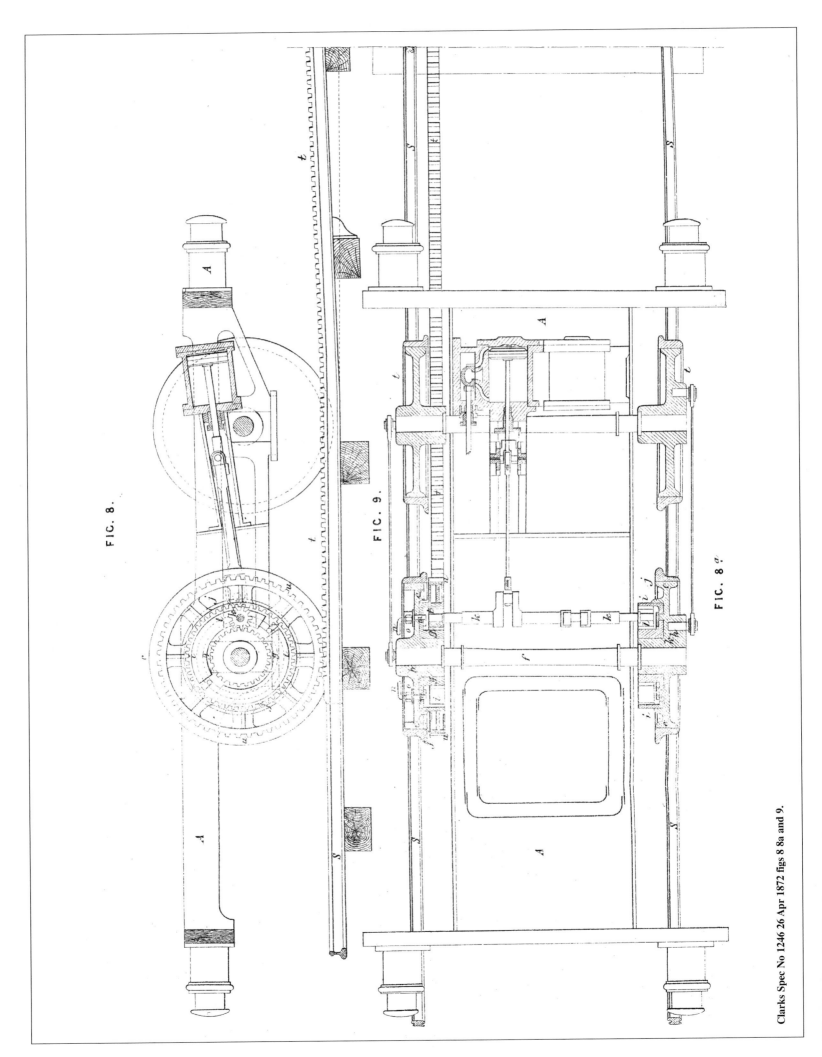

FIC. 8.

FIC. 9.

FIC. 8ª.

Clarks Spec No 1246 26 Apr 1872 figs 8 8a and 9.

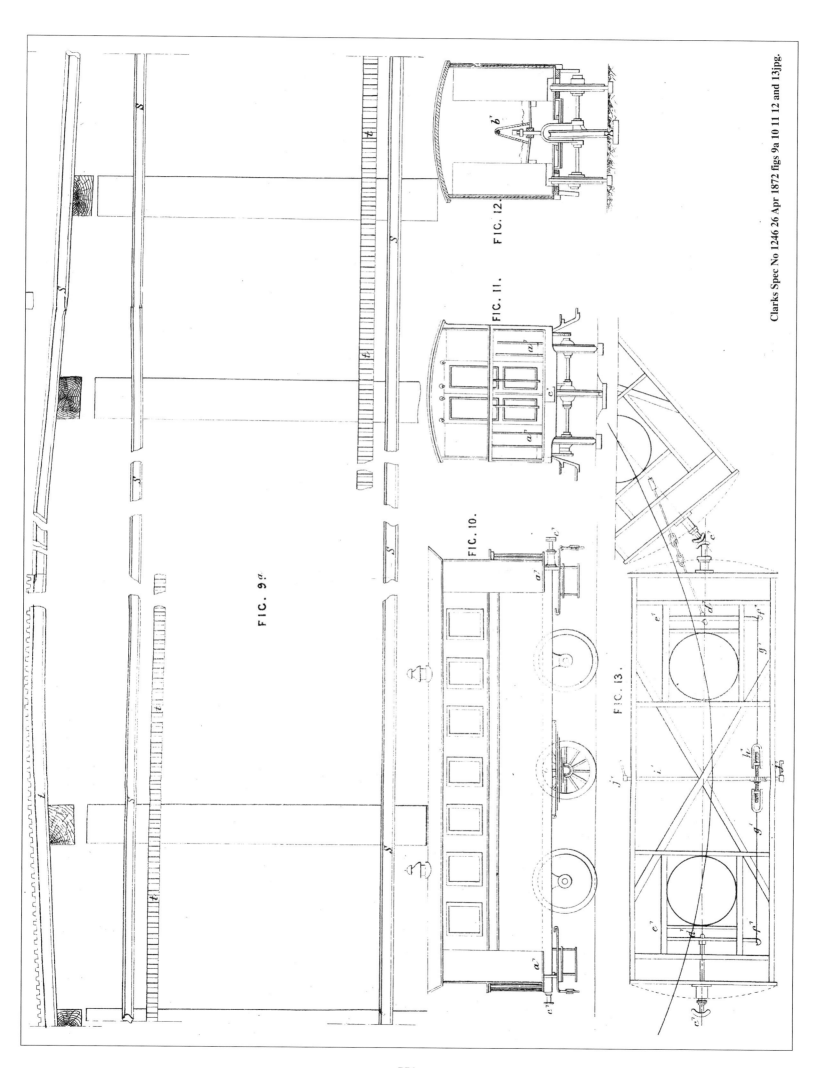

FIC. 9ª.

FIC. 10.

FIC. II.

FIC. 12.

FIC. 13.

Clarks Spec No 1246 26 Apr 1872 figs 9a 10 11 12 and 13jpg.

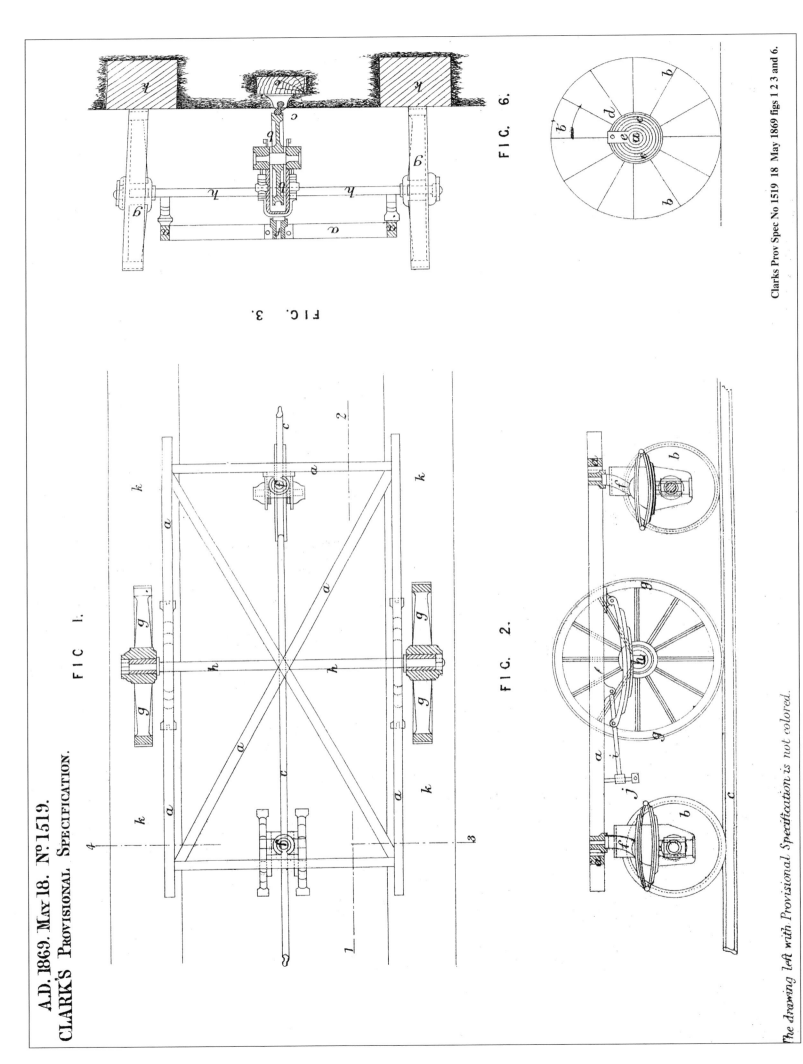

FIG. 1.

FIG. 2.

FIG. 3.

FIG. 6.

Clarks Prov Spec No 1519 18 May 1869 figs 1 2 3 and 6.

The drawing left with Provisional Specification is not colored.

552

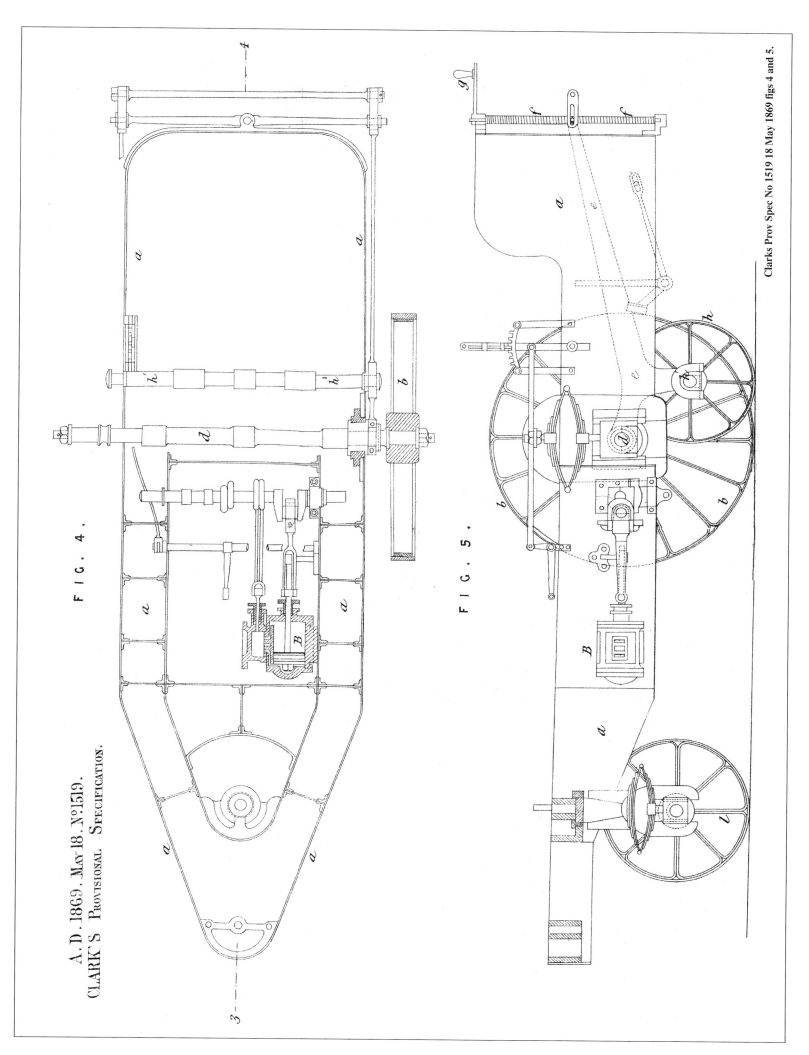

A.D. 1869. May 18. №1519.

CLARK'S PROVISIONAL SPECIFICATION.

FIG. 4.

FIG. 5.

Clarks Prov Spec No 1519 18 May 1869 figs 4 and 5.

553

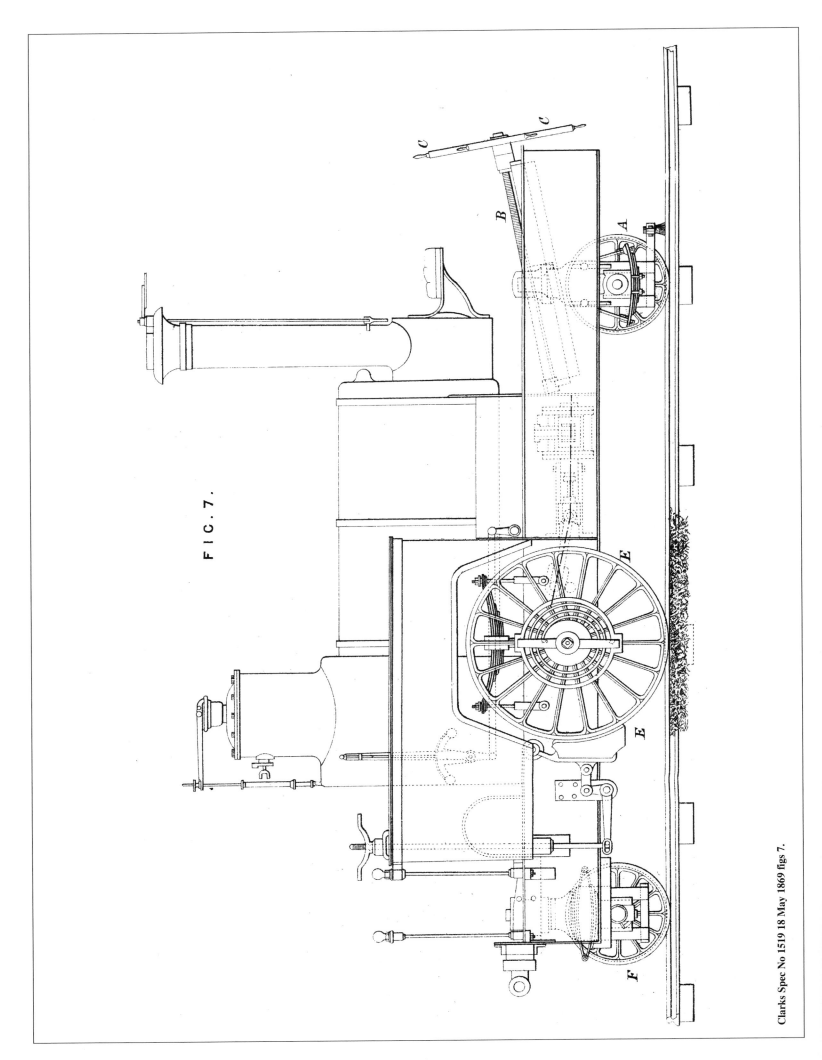

F I C . 7 .

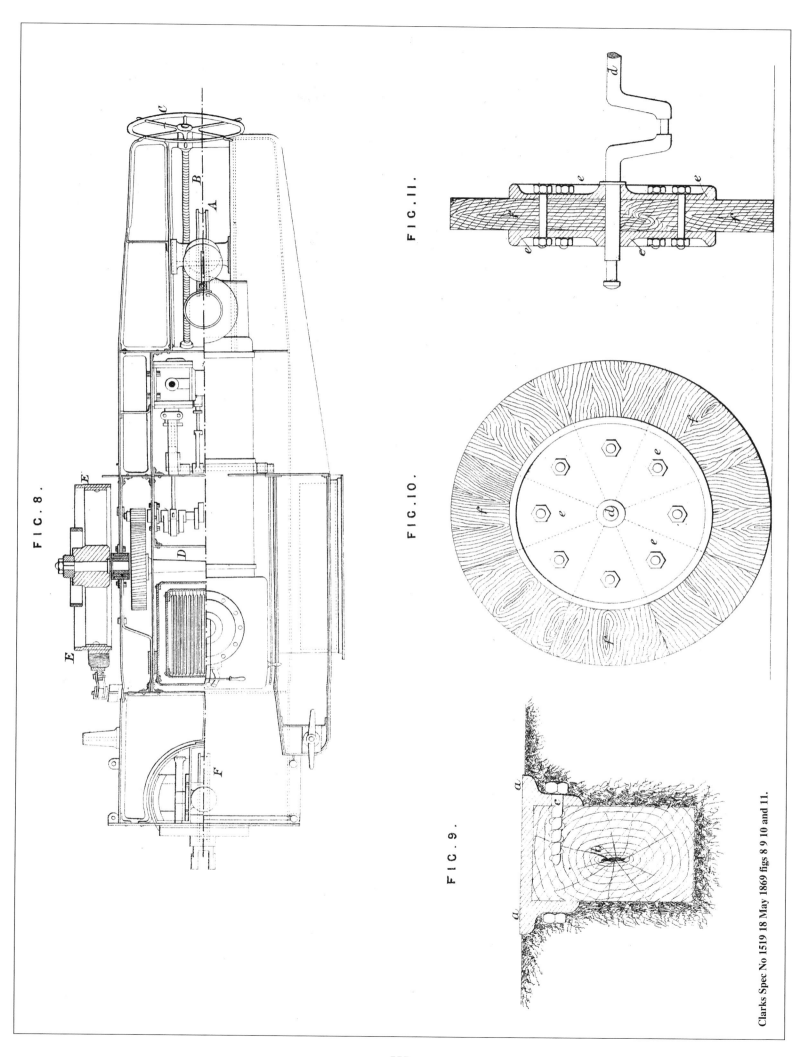

FIG. 8.

FIG. 9.

FIG. 10.

FIG. 11.

Clarks Spec No 1519 18 May 1869 figs 8 9 10 and 11.

1875-03373 Palmer Harding
Hughes Exhaust System

An interesting twist on the story of Hughes' locomotives in Bristol lies in that strange exhaust system used. The photograph which previously appeared in volume 2 page 205 is reproduced below to show the device.

During patent research on our behalf at the Science Library, Birmingham, Ted Hunt found No. 3373 of 1875 issued to Gustavus Palmer Harding which he thought might be of interest. In fact this basically covers "Locomotive Tramway Carriages" but a part includes the Hughes' chimney pattern. Clearly, given the number of engines the works made for Palmer Harding for use on his continental franchises there was a very close relationship between the two men.

Part of the provisional specification dated 27 September 1875 reads:

"I, GUSTAVUS PALMER HARDING, of 8, Old Jewry, London, E.C., do hereby declare the nature of the said Invention for "IMPROVEMENTS IN LOCOMOTIVE TRAMWAY CARRIAGES, AND IN THE LOCOMOTIVES IN CONNECTION WITH TRAMWAY CARRIAGES' to be as follows:

This Invention of improvements in locomotive tramway carriages, and in the locomotives in connection with tramway carriages consists –

Firstly. In improvements in disposing of the products of combustion, waste steam, and vapour passing off from the furnace and engine whether such furnace and engine forms part of the carriage conveying the passengers, or is arranged in a separate carriage from the passenger carriages. With this object the chimney is led off at a certain height horizontally, either below the seats of the carriage or along the roof, and where the chimney starts from the centre of the carriage it leads into a horizontal chimney in the direction of the length of the carriages, either at the middle or towards one end. I prefer to have one end of this tube open, facing the direction in which the carriage is travelling; and when the passenger carriage is attached to the engine carriage I extend the horizontal chimney along such passenger carriage or carriages. I also in some cases fit to the end of such chimney facing the direction the carriage is travelling the well-known blow pipe cowl for the purpose of creating a draft. It is obvious that all these arrangements can be adopted to comply with the necessary change of direction in the engine or cars in any suitable manner. In place of the blow pipe I may also use at the reverse end a rotating fan for drawing away the products of combustion, &c., and dispersing them in the wake of the car, the object of these several arrangements being to prevent annoyance to the passengers ... Having thus explained the nature of my improvements, as well as the best means that I am acquainted with for carrying the same into practical operation, I claim as my Invention –

Firstly. The means or their mechanical equivalents above described and illustrated in Figures 1 to 7 inclusively of the products of combustion.

Secondly. The means or their mechanical equivalents above described and illustrated in the same Figures for cultivating the draft by means of the sliding funnel-shaped sleeve. Thirdly. The means above described and illustrated in the same Figures or their mechanical equivalents for activating the draft by means of a fan."

Part of the relevant drawings and the letter key follow:

"First improvement, Figures 1 to 7 inclusively. In order to dispose of the products of combustion, waste steam and vapour passing off from the furnace and engine, whether such furnace and engine forms part of the carriage conveying the passengers, or are arranged in a separate carriage from the passengers' carriages, I adapt (in the case of an independent locomotive) on the boiler 1, Figures 1 and 2, a vertical chimney 2 rising to a height corresponding approximately to that of the roof of the passenger carriages; at that height by means of an elbow I give it a horizontal direction through the axis of the carriages, and on the roof of the latter I place a horizontal tube 4, Figures 3 and 4, running the entire length with its open ends or extremities on the same level as the elbow 3 on the locomotive, but on the vehicles being connected these pipes do not come in contact, and I then unite their extremities by means of a sleeve fitted to one or the other extremity, and by sliding which I advance it forward so as to cover the extremity opposite. In this matter the products of combustion or the steam are directed entirely to the rear of the passenger carriages, for this system of connection can be readily and speedily adapted to a train of carriages, and also disconnected as regards the said pipe by simply sliding back the sleeve. I also adapt this system of piping on the sides of the carriages underneath the overhanging edge of

the roof, as shown in dotted lines, Figures 1 and 3, or under the platforms or frames, preferably in the axis of the same, as shown in dotted lines, Figures 2 and 4. As in most cases locomotives have to run in both directions I arrange the elbow 3 on the boiler 1 so that it can be readily and rapidly turned round in both directions.

In order to augment automatically the draft in this system of piping, I make use of preferably at the place where two pipes join of a funnel sleeve 5, one end of which is cylindrical and slides freely on one of the pipes, whilst the other is conical and receives the extremity of the second pipe with however a considerable amount of play in which the air is driven by the progression of the vehicles, and thus stimulates considerably and automatically the draft. With the same end in view augmenting the draft I also adapt if desired to this system of piping a fan 7 shewn in elevation at Figure 2, and in plan Figure 6, to which I impart the required rotary motion by means of a cord 8 driven by a pulley mounted on the driving shaft. This apparatus may work conjointly with the conical sleeves, although I have shewn it adapted to the elbow 3; on account of the reversing of the engine it is preferable to adapt it on the chimney 2, so that when the direction of the locomotive is changed it is merely necessary to open the driving belt instead of crossing it; on the other hand the connection with the pipe on the carriage next to the engine is made by reversing the elbow 3 as it has been explained above; Figures 6 and 7 are intended to indicate specially the application of my above-mentioned first improvement to composite vehicles, that is to say, vehicles provided with an engine and also carrying passengers."

I think, and hope you will agree, this was all rather fabulous for 1875.

Seven engines were supposed to have been tried in Bristol. This one is a product of Henry Hughes' works, Loughborough. That curious chimney must have caused enormous back pressure.

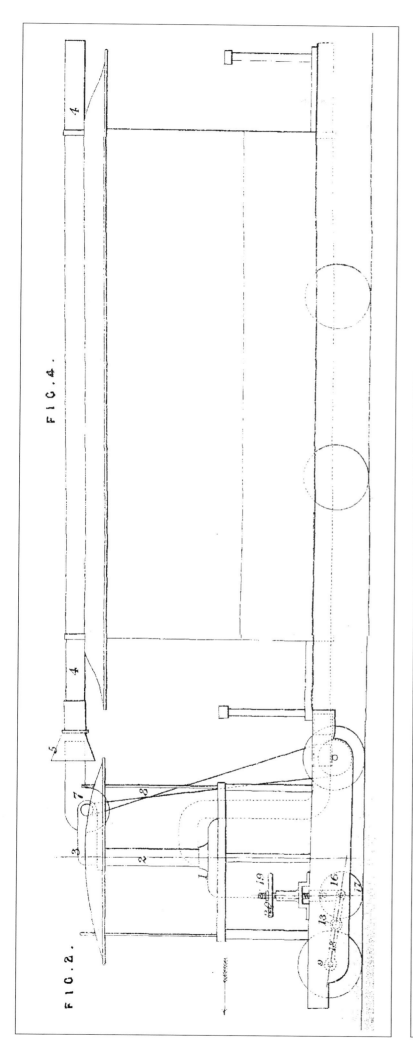

FIG.2.

FIG.4.

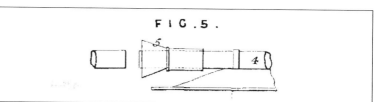

FIG.5.

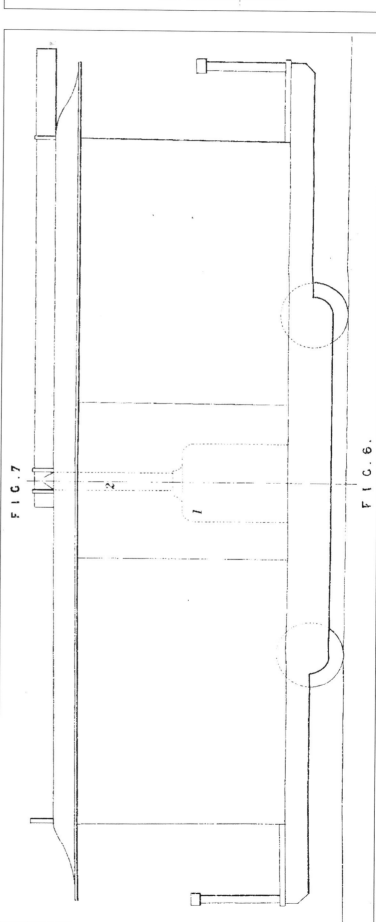

FIG.7.

FIG.6.

A.D. 1879, 5th NOVEMBER. N° 4512.

Motive Power Engines.

LETTERS PATENT to John Hawthorn Kitson, of Leeds, in the County of York, Engineer, for the Invention of "IMPROVEMENTS IN THE MEANS FOR WORKING THE VALVES AND CONTROLLING THE SPEED OF MOTIVE POWER ENGINES."

Sealed the 27th January 1880, and dated the 5th November 1879.

PROVISIONAL SPECIFICATION left by the said John Hawthorn Kitson at the Office of the Commissioners of Patents on the 5th November 1879.

JOHN HAWTHORN KITSON, of Leeds, in the County of York, Engineer. "IMPROVEMENTS IN THE MEANS FOR WORKING THE VALVES AND CONTROLLING THE SPEED OF MOTIVE POWER ENGINES."

The first part of my Invention relates to the valve gear of motive power engines, and consists of an arrangement of parts, the object of which is to give the required movement to the valve by a combination of a motion derived from the cross head with a motion at right angles thereto derived from some other convenient part of the machinery without the intervention of an excentric sheave or its equivalent.

One arrangement consists of a lever, one end of which is coupled by a link or other suitable arrangement to the cross head and the other to the valve spindle. To an intermediate point on this lever one end of a radius rod is coupled, the other end being coupled to a die working in the curved slot of a link pivotted to a fixed point at about the middle of its length. Opposite this point of attachment the link is provided with a tail piece, the end of which is connected by a link rod with a point on the connecting or coupling rod of the engine as may be most convenient. The slotted link is furnished with pivots at or near to the centre line of the curved slot, and a bracket or other suitable means is provided for carrying these pivots in a certain fixed position, thus forming a fulcrum on which the curved slotted link oscillates.

By means of an ordinary weigh bar shaft and lifting links the die can be placed in such a position in the slotted link as will give any desired amount of expansion or a reversed motion.

In some cases, instead of coupling the connecting or coupling rod direct to the tail piece of the link, I attach one end of a link rod to the coupling or connecting rod, whilst to the other end of this rod I joint a second link rod which I connect to the tail piece.

[Price 8d.]

Kitson's Improvements in Motive Power Engines.

The second part of this Invention relates to an arrangement of apparatus for controlling the speed of engines, more particularly tramcar and locomotive engines. On an axle of such an engine I fit two discs, one of which is keyed fast while the other is free to slide on a feather. Between these discs I place a loose pulley, to which is attached a chain leading to a brake apparatus and also connected with the throttle valve.

I also fix on the opposite sides of the axle two pivots which form centres for two rock levers. Between the extremities of these levers two weights are fastened, and I also attach a pin or fulcrum near the middle of their length, which I couple by means of links with corresponding pins in the sliding disc before mentioned. Opposite to one of the weights and on the other side of the axle I fix a **T** shaped piece carrying springs in tension, which are connected at their other ends with the opposite weight.

The tension on these springs is such that until the required limited speed is exceeded no action takes place, but when it is exceeded the centrifugal force of the weights overcoming the resistance of the springs will cause the disc to slide forward on the axle and grip the loose pulley between it and the fixed disc, thereby causing the pulley to wind up the chain. The tension thus put on the chain, which is attached both to the brake and the steam valve, will simultaneously put on the brakes and shut off the steam, and thus prevent any required speed being exceeded.

Kitson's Improvements in Motive Power Engines.

SPECIFICATION in pursuance of the conditions of the Letters Patent filed by the said John Hawthorn Kitson in the Great Seal Patent Office on the 5th May 1880.

JOHN HAWTHORN KITSON, of Leeds, in the County of York, Engineer. "IMPROVE-
MENTS IN THE MEANS FOR WORKING THE VALVES AND CONTROLLING THE SPEED
OF MOTIVE POWER ENGINES."

This Invention relates, firstly, to a novel arrangement of valve gear for motive power engines, the object being to give the required "supply," "cut off," and "reverse" motions to the valves by a combination of a motion derived from the cross head with a motion at right angles thereto derived from some other convenient part of the engine, without the intervention of an excentric or its equivalent specially provided for the purpose; secondly, to apparatus for controlling the speed of tramcar and other locomotive engines, by bringing into action a friction brake and cutting off the steam automatically so soon as a given speed is exceeded. In Sheet I. of the accompanying Drawings the first part of my Invention is shewn as applied to a locomotive engine, and in Sheet II. as applied to a marine-engine, a slight modification in the apparatus being made for this purpose. In both arrangements the same letters of reference are employed to indicate like parts. A is the steam-cylinder; B, the cross-head; and C, the rod by which the cross-head is connected to the crank D of the driving wheel (Sheet I.) or crank-shaft (Sheet II.); E is a lever which is pivoted at its upper end at its upper end and by a rod G to the rod F of the slide valve, and is connected at its lower end by a rod G to the cross-head B. This lever is also connected near its upper end by means of a rod H with the ordinary slotted link I, which is mounted on a suitable standard or support so that it may pivot on a central trunnion I*. The rod H is pivoted to a sliding block which fits in the segment shaped slot of the link I, and is free to be set in any desired position in the slot by means of the rock bar, levers, and links K, K, in the manner common to link motions. Projecting from the slotted link I and forming one piece therewith is a tail piece I*, which is connected by a rod L with the head of the connecting rod C.

From the foregoing description of the parts it will be understood that when the engine is set in action the connecting rod C will impart, through the rod L, an oscillating motion to the slotted link I, and at the same time the cross head B will, by reason of its connection through the rod C with the lever E, impart a rocking motion to that lever. The Drawing shews the sliding-block of the link I at its dead point, but when shifted to either side thereof the link in its oscillations will cause the rod H to actuate the lever E and move the slide valve with which it is connected, thereby admitting steam to and cutting it off from the cylinder as required.

The action of the link motion as respects the movements of the slide-valve will be similar to that of the link motions in common use, but the mechanism employed for imparting motion to the slotted link will by this Invention be greatly simplified.

In the arrangement shewn in Sheet II. instead of connecting the tail I* of the link I with the crank rod C by means of the rod L, an intermediate rock lever M and rod N are employed, the lever M having its fulcrum on an independent standard. This modification is introduced as a convenient means for communicating the motion from the crank rod to the slotted link.

The second part of my Invention is illustrated in Sheet III., Fig. 1 being a side view of the apparatus by which the motion for putting on the brakes and for cutting off the steam is obtained, and Fig. 2 being a cross section of the same taken in the line 1, 2, of Fig. 1.

Kitson's Improvements in Motive Power Engines.

Upon the axle A of one pair of travelling wheels of a locomotive or tramcar engine a friction disc B is keyed. This axle is provided with a feather for receiving a similar friction disc C, which is capable of sliding freely towards and from the fixed disc. Between the two discs is mounted loosely upon the axle A a pulley D, to which a chain E is attached in such manner as to allow of its being wound up upon the pulley when rotary motion is imparted thereto. By connecting this chain E with a brake and with a lever in connection with the steam-supply valve any tension put upon the chain by the pulley will throw the brake into action and cut off the steam, thereby instantly checking the progress of the engine. The rotation of the pulley D to effect the winding up of the chain E is produced by the gripping of the pulley between the discs B and C while the axle A is in rapid rotation. This gripping of the pulley is effected automatically by the following means:—Pivotted to the axle A is a rocking frame F which is weighted at its extremities to give the frame a tendency, as the speed of rotation of the axle A increases, to move to a position at right angles to the axle. This tendency is counteracted by means of coiled springs G, which tie one end of the frame elastically to a fixed T-piece H projecting from the axle A. The strength of these springs will be such as to retain the frame in its normal position, as shewn in the Drawings, so long only as the axle A rotates at its proper minimum speed. When this speed is exceeded the springs will yield to the centrifugal action of the loaded frame, and the frame will then move on its pivots in the direction of the arrow in Fig. 1. I, I, are rods which serve to connect the disc C with the oscillating frame F. When therefore this frame is caused to take the dotted position Fig. 1 the disc C will by means of the connecting rods I be thrust forward against the loose pulley D, which will be gripped firmly between the two friction discs and caused to rotate therewith. This rotation of the pulley D will put such a tension on the chain E as to bring the brake in connection therewith into action, and to shut the steam supply valve. I have not thought it necessary to trace the connection of the chain E with either the brake or the steam supply valve, as that will vary according to the arrange-ment of the engine and the brake apparatus employed. The manner however of effecting this connection will be obvious to any competent mechanic whatever may be the controlling circumstances of the case.

Having now set forth the nature of my Invention of "Improvements in the Means for Working the Valves and Controlling the Speed of Motive Power Engines," and explained the manner of carrying the same into effect, I wish it to be under-stood that under the above in part recited Letters Patent I claim,—

First. The means above described for obtaining the motion for working the slide-valves of motive power engines from the cross heads and cranks of such engines.

Second. The means above described for obtaining automatically the motion for controlling the speed of tram-car and other locomotive engines.

In witness whereof, I, the said John Hawthorn Kitson, have hereunto set my hand and seal, the Seventeenth day of April, in the year of our Lord One thousand eight hundred and eighty.

J. HAWTHORN KITSON. (L.S.)

LONDON: Printed by GEORGE EDWARD EYRE and WILLIAM SPOTTISWOODE,
Printers to the Queen's most Excellent Majesty.
For Her Majesty's Stationery Office.

1880.

A.D.1879. Nov.5. N° 4512.
KITSON'S SPECIFICATION.

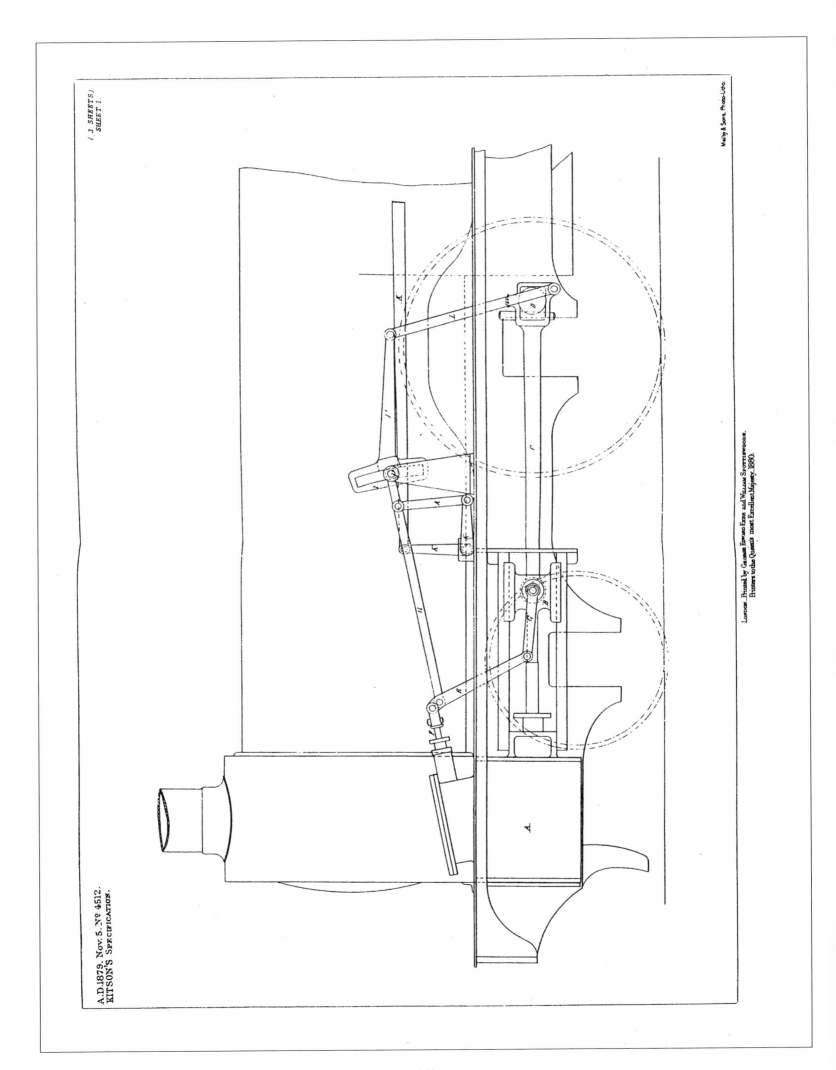

London. Printed by GEORGE EDWARD EYRE and WILLIAM SPOTTISWOODE,
Printers to the Queen's most Excellent Majesty. 1880.

Malby & Sons, Photo-Litho.

(3 SHEETS)
SHEET 3.

FIG. 2.

FIG. 1.

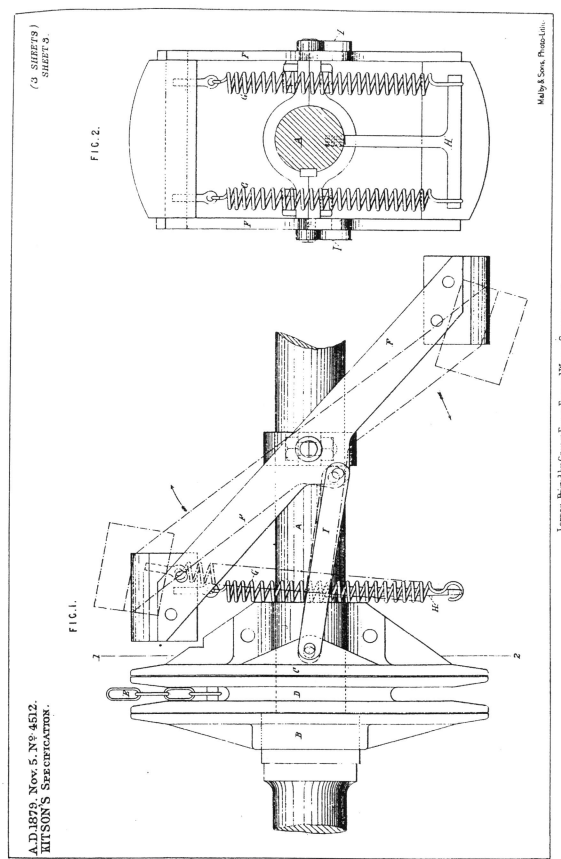

London. Printed by George Edward Eyre and William Spottiswoode.
Printers to the Queen's most Excellent Majesty. 1880.

Malby & Sons, Photo-Litho.

561

2   A.D. 1883.—N° 4526.

Peacock & Lange's Improvements in Tramway or other Road Engines.

This valve is placed between the cylinders and the steam regulator, and shuts off steam automatically and beyond the control of the driver, when the engine exceeds a certain rate of speed, which rate of speed can be determined by a Governor or any other suitable mechanical contrivance. It opens again auto- 5 matically and without action on the part of the driver as soon as the speed of the Engine is reduced below the fixed limit

This valve is further arranged to admit steam automatically into the steam brake cylinders of the Engine and cars (if any) and thus apply the brakes automatically without the control of the driver.

This valve is also arranged to come into action through an independent drivers 10 brake valve when it will shut off steam and apply the brakes

This valve is also arranged to open automatically and thus again admit the steam into the cylinders and release the brakes after the speed of the engine is reduced or after the driver has shut his brake valve.

A.D. 1883, 21*st* SEPTEMBER. N° 4526.

Tramway or other Road Engines.

LETTERS PATENT to Ralph Peacock and Hermann Ludwig Lange of Gorton Foundry Gorton in the County of Lancaster Engineers for an Invention of "IMPROVEMENTS IN TRAMWAY OR OTHER ROAD ENGINES"

PROVISIONAL SPECIFICATION left by the said Ralph Peacock and Hermann Ludwig Lange at the Office of the Commissioners of Patents on the 21st September 1883.

RALPH PEACOCK and HERMANN LUDWIG LANGE of Gorton Foundry Gorton 5 in the County of Lancaster; Engineers—IMPROVEMENTS IN TRAMWAY OR OTHER ROAD ENGINES.

Our invention relates to Tramway or other Road engines and the objects of our invention are first to dispose of the exhaust and waste steam and at the same time to deaden the beat of the engine, and, secondly to provide an automatic speed 10 regulator stop and brake valve.

In performing the first part of our invention we place a metal pot on the top of the vertical boiler over the vertical flue. This pot has an annular chamber and into this chamber we conduct the exhaust steam from the cylinders, the waste steam from the safety valves, the exhaust steam from the Brake cylinders and 15 other waste steam—In this annular chambers, which is heated by the hot gases from the vertical flue, and from being in close contact with the hot Boiler top on which it rests, the exhaust and waste steam is dried and heated before it escapes either into another superheater placed inside the firebox or into the chimney. We cover the metal pot on the outside with papier maché or some other nonconducting 20 material to prevent radiation.

We form recesses or corrugations on one of the inner sides of the annular chamber and projections or ribs on the other inner side of the annular chamber so as to bring the exhaust steam in contact with a large amount of heated surface whilst passing from the inlet to the outlet, and also to break up the exhaust and 25 thereby soften or deaden the beat of the engine as much as possible.

In performing the second part of our invention we construct an automatic speed regulator stop and brake valve to fulfil the functions described below.

[*Price 6d.*]

SPECIFICATION in pursuance of the conditions of the Letters Patent filed by the said Ralph Peacock and Hermann Ludwig Lange in the Patent Office on the 21st March 1884.

RALPH PEACOCK and HERMANN LUDWIG LANGE, of Gorton Foundry, Gorton, in the County of Lancaster, Engineers, "IMPROVEMENTS IN TRAMWAY OR OTHER ROAD ENGINES"

Our invention relates to tramway or other engines, and the objects of our Invention are first, to dispose of the exhaust and waste steam and at the same time to deaden the beat of the engine and secondly to provide an automatic speed regulator stop and brake valve.

And in order that our Invention may be fully understood and readily carried into effect we will proceed to describe the accompanying two Sheets of drawings, reference being had to the figures and letters marked thereon.

On Sheet 1.—Fig. 1 is a sectional elevation. Fig. 2 a plan and Fig. 3 an elevation, partly in section of part of the boiler of an engine to which our Improvements are applied and on Sheet 2. Figs. 4, 5 and 6 are enlarged views of our automatic speed regulator stop and brake valve.

We place a metal pot a on the top of the vertical boiler over the vertical flue: this pot has an annular chamber a^1 and into this chamber we conduct the exhaust steam from the cylinders d (through the pipe d^1) the waste steam from the safety valves c, the exhaust steam from the brake cylinders (through the pipe d^2) and other waste steam. In this annular chamber a^1 which is heated by the hot gases from the vertical flue, and from being in close contact with the hot boiler top on which it rests, the exhaust and waste steam is dried and heated before it escapes into another super-heater,—(placed inside the fire-box,)—on its way to the chimney. We cover the metal pot on the outside with papier maché or some other non-conducting material to prevent radiation. We form recesses or corrugations (see Fig. 2) on the inner ring of the annular chamber a^1 and projections or ribs on the inner side of the outer ring of this chamber so as to bring the exhaust steam in contact with a larger amount of heated surface whilst passing from the inlet to the outlet, and also to break up the exhaust and thereby soften or deaden the beat of the engine as much as possible.

In performing the second part of our Invention we construct an automatic speed regulator, stop and brake valve b to fulfill the functions described below.

This valve is placed between the cylinders and the steam regulator and shuts off steam automatically and beyond the control of the driver, when the engine exceeds a certain rate of speed, which rate of speed can be determined by a governor or any other suitable mechanical contrivance. It opens again automatically and without action on the part of the driver, as soon as the speed of the engine is reduced below the fixed limit. This valve is farther arranged to admit steam automatically into the steam brake cylinders of the engine and cars (if any) and thus apply the brakes automatically without the control of the driver. This valve is also arranged to come into action through an independent driver's brake valve f when it will shut off steam and apply the brakes. This valve is also arranged to open automatically and thus again admit the steam into the cylinders d and release the brakes after the speed of the engine is reduced, or after the driver has shut his brake valve f.

Our improved valve is shown on Sheet 2. Figs. 4 and 5 being sectional elevations of the valve with the passage to the brake cylinder closed, and the passage to admit steam to the power cylinder open and Fig. 6 being a sectional elevation of the valve with the passage to the brake cylinder open, and the passage to the power cylinder closed.

This valve is placed in the steam pipe between the steam regulator on the boiler, and the cylinders, and steam, to reach the cylinders, passes through the valve chamber i, lifting the valve j from its seating.

When the engine reaches its maximum speed, a separate valve actuated by the governor or any other means admits steam through the pipe k and the hole l, to the piston m, which is fixed on the same spindle as the valve j, and having a larger area than the valve j, is enabled to overcome its resistance, and being forced down by the steam from the pipe k, closes the valve j and shuts off steam from the cylinders. This downward movement of the piston m, brings a groove n, turned in the piston spindle opposite the orifice of the steam pipe k, and opens a way for steam to pass into the pipe leading to the brake cylinder and so set the brake. The speed of the engine then being checked both by the application of the brake and the non-admission of steam to the cylinders, the governor valve closes and prevents farther admission of steam through the pipe k, to the piston m, and the pressure against the piston becomes reduced by leakage through the small hole o, until it is overcome by the pressure acting against the valve j, which re-opens, re-admits steam to the cylinders, and foreing up the piston spindle closes the steam passage to the brake cylinder and brings a second groove p on the spindle opposite the openings q which permits the escape of steam from the brake cylinder into the hot-pot a on the boiler, or the ash pan or any other convenient place and releases the brake

Having stated the nature of our Invention and described the manner of performing the same

We declare that we claim

1.—The pot a, substantially as and for the purposes herein shown and described.

2.—The improved automatic speed regulator stop and brake valve, substantially as and for the purposes herein specified and as shown on Sheet 2 of the annexed drawings.

In witness whereof I the said Hermann Ludwig Lange for myself and on behalf of the said Ralph Peacock have hereunto set my hand and seal this nineteenth day of March in the year of Our Lord One thousand eight hundred and eighty four.

HERMANN L. LANGE.   (L.S.)

LONDON: Printed by EYRE AND SPOTTISWOODE, Printers to the Queen's most Excellent Majesty. For Her Majesty's Stationery Office.

1884.

A.D. 1883. SEP. 21. Nº 4526.
PEACOCK & LANGE'S SPECIFICATION.

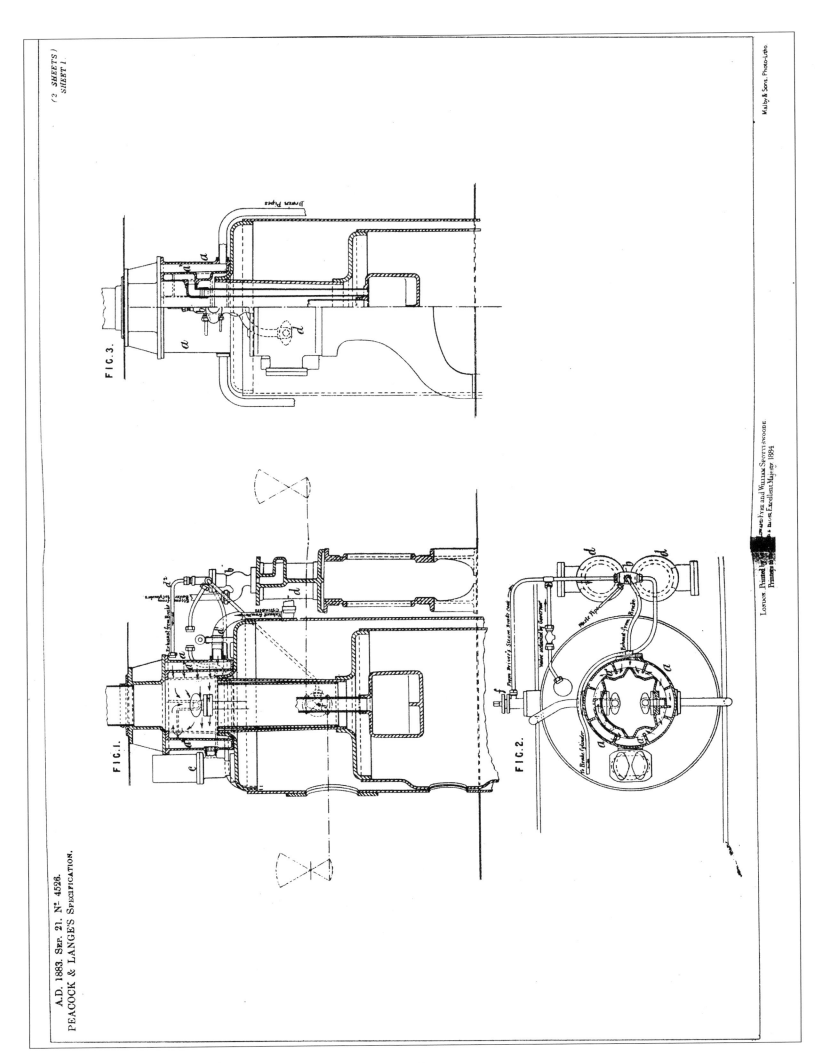

FIG. 3.

FIG. 1.

FIG. 2.

Maltby & Sons. Photo-Litho.

LONDON. Printed by ... worthe and William Spottiswoode
Printers to ... os. Excellent Majesty 1884

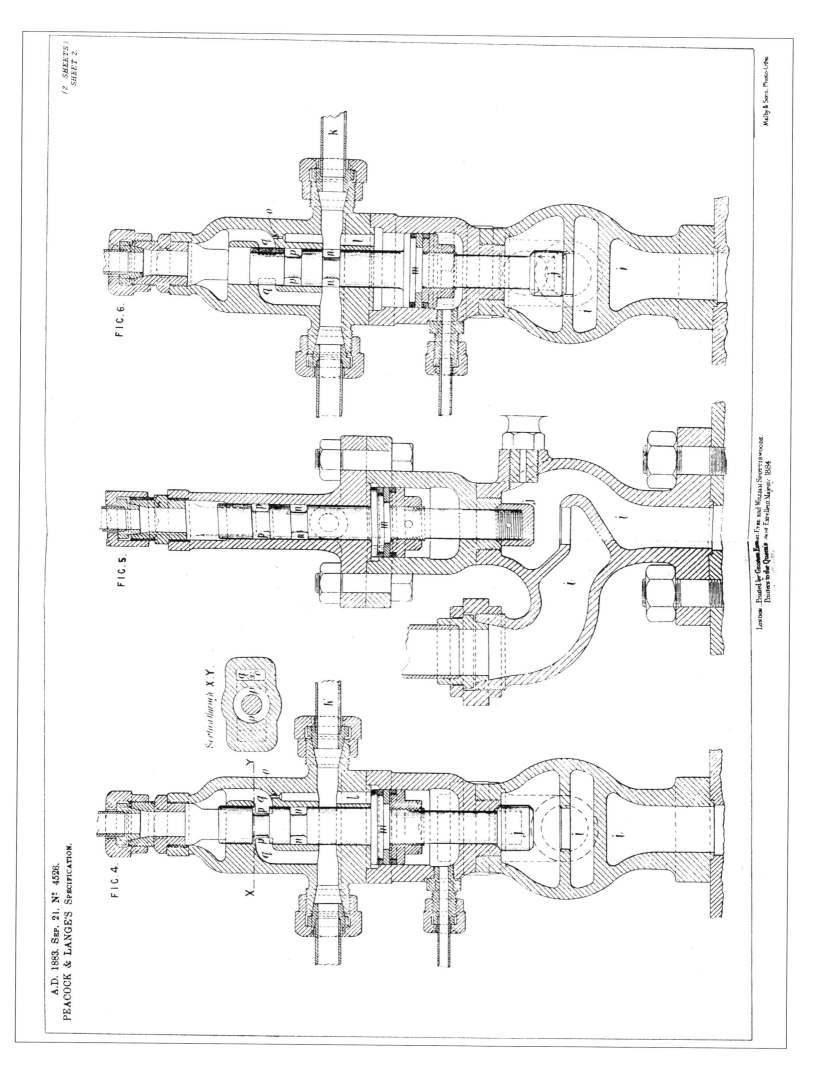

FIG. 4.

FIG. 5.

FIG. 6.

Section through X.Y.

London Printed by George Edward Eyre and William Spottiswoode,
Printers to the Queen's most Excellent Majesty. 1884.

Malby & Sons, Photo-Litho.

COMPLETE SPECIFICATION.

Improvements in Means for Condensing the Exhaust Steam of Tramway Engines.

I NORMAN SCOTT RUSSELL of the Falcon Engine Works 41 Coleman Street in the City of London Engineer do hereby declare the nature of this invention and in what manner the same is to be performed, to be particularly described and ascertained in and by the following statement:—

The object of my Invention is to perfect the condensation of the exhaust Steam of tramway Engines so that at all times whilst the vehicle is running whether with or without the consumption of Steam the cooling effect of the air is utilized for the purpose of such condensation—According to my Invention I employ a nest of tubes or their equivalents constituting a water cooler and situated on the roof of the vehicle or at other convenient part thereof where the said cooler will be exposed to the air and through the cooler I pass or circulate water to be cooled therein by the cooling effect of the air and I employ the water so cooled for condensing the exhaust steam by passing the said water into a condenser situated at any convenient part of the engine. This condenser may be of any suitable kind such as an ordinary jet condenser or a surface condenser like those used in marine engines. In this condenser the water cooled in the before mentioned cooler is utilized for the condensation of the exhaust steam from the engine. I use a pump or pumps for circulating the water through the said cooler and condenser. This pump may be of any suitable kind and either direct acting or centrifugal. I may use separate pumps to circulate the water and to create a vacuum in the condenser or I may use one pump for both these purposes. These pumps may be operated from any suitable part of the engine.

And in order that this Invention may be fully understood I shall now proceed more particularly to describe the same and for that purpose shall refer to the several figures on the annexed sheets of drawings the same letters of reference indicating corresponding parts in all the figures.

Figures 1 and 2 are sections at right angles to each other of apparatus arranged according to my Invention.

The exhaust steam leaving the cylinder or cylinders or the last of the cylinders (A) in case the engine is compound (which I prefer) passes by the pipe B and its branches into the surface condensers C and C¹ which are preferably formed of copper tubes fixed in brass boxes the outer surface of the tubes of the said condensers C and C¹ being entirely covered by cold water contained in the tank I. In this tank I a double acting pump D is situated its plunger being worked by means of an eccentric off the axle E this pump D acts on the one side H as an air pump and draws the air vapour and water from the condensers C C¹ through the pipes $h\,h$ and forces them into the tank G and from this tank the water is pumped into the boiler in the usual way. The opposite side of the pump at F acts as a circulating pump to circulate, and in the circulation to cool, the water for the tank I This circulation is effected by the pump taking the water by the pipes $i\,i$ from the highest part of the tank I and forcing it up through the pipe L into the cooler K on the roof of the vehicle the said water thence passing by the pipe L¹

A.D. 1885, 6th *JANUARY*. Nº 195.

PROVISIONAL SPECIFICATION.

Improvements in Means for Condensing the Exhaust Steam of Tramway Engines.

I, NORMAN SCOTT RUSSELL of The Falcon Engine Works 41 Coleman Street in the City of London Engineer do hereby declare the nature of said Invention for "IMPROVEMENTS IN MEANS FOR CONDENSING THE EXHAUST STEAM OF TRAMWAY ENGINES" to be as follows:—

The object of my Invention is to perfect the condensation of the exhaust Steam of Tramway Engines so that under all conditions and whether the Engines be working or not the cooling effect of the air is utilized for the purposes of such condensation. According to my Invention I employ a nest of tubes or their equivalents situated on the roof of the Engine or other convenient part thereof where the said tubes or passages will be exposed to the air and through these tubes or passages I pass or circulate water to be cooled therein by the cooling effect of the air and I employ the water so cooled for condensing the exhaust Steam by passing it into another condenser situated at any convenient part of the Engine This condenser may be of any suitable kind such as an ordinary jet condenser or a surface condenser like those used in marine Engines. In this condenser the water cooled in the first mentioned tubes or passages is utilized for the condensation of the exhaust steam from the Engine. I may use separate pumps to circulate the water and to create a vacuum in the condenser or I may use one pump for both these purposes. These pumps may be operated from any suitable part of the Engine,

Dated the 6th day of December 1885.

J. HENRY JOHNSON,
47, Lincoln's Inn Fields, W.C.,
Agent for the said Norman Scott Russell.

[Price 6d.]

Russell's Means for Condensing the Exhaust Steam of Tramway Engines.

into the tank M and therefrom by the pipe L² back into the tank I. The tanks, pipes, and tubes, of the circulating system, are all filled with water nearly to the top of the boxes N which are open at top and admit of the escape of air. By the foregoing means a constant circulation of the condensing water is maintained and

5 the cooling effect of the atmosphere is utilized very effectually and the water is received back into the tank I in a cold condition to rapidly effect the condensation of the exhaust steam entering the tubes of the condensers C, C¹ and I gain the advantage of cooling the condensing water continuously and of storing cold water whilst the engine is going down hill, to use it for condensing the exhaust steam

10 when the engine is going up hill.

In the tank G there may be provided a pipe P leading therefrom into the chimney This pipe P is connected with the pipe B there being a weighted valve at R between the pipes B and P, acting as a safety valve to the condenser as if the pressure of exhaust steam should exceed the limit for which the valve at R is

15 weighted the excess of steam will blow off through the said valve and pipe P into the chimney.

Figures 3 and 4 are sections at right angles to each other of a modified arrangement. In this arrangement the exhaust steam from the cylinder or cylinders or from the last of compounded cylinders passes by the pipe B into the tank I

20 meeting the cooled condensing water entering the tank I by the pipe L². The pump D worked from the axle E draws the water from the tank I by the inlets *i i* into the valve chamber F and thence forces it by the pipe L into the tank M and thence by the pipe L¹ into the cooler K through which it passes (being therein subjected as in the former example to the cooling effect of the atmosphere playing

25 around the said tubes) and returns by the pipe L² into the tank L P is a pipe which may if required be provided to admit of excess steam and air passing from the tank I into the smoke box, but if this be used there will of course be no vacuum in the condenser I. Water from the tank I is taken by the pipe *s* to feed the boiler in the usual way.

30 Having now particularly described and ascertained the nature of my said Invention and in what manner the same is to be performed I declare that what I claim is

First. In Tramway engines the combination of a condenser and cooler the latter continuously cooling water for use in the former a pump or pumps being used for

35 maintaining circulation through both cooler and condenser substantially as hereinbefore described.

Second. In Tramway engines the system of circulating tanks pipes and tubes arranged and combined together and with a pump to cause circulation of condensing water or of condensing water and water of condensation therein substan-

40 tially as hereinbefore described and illustrated by the Drawings.

Third. For condensing exhaust steam of tramway engines an arrangement and combination of parts substantially as hereinbefore described and illustrated in Figures 1 and 2 of the accompanying drawings.

Fourth. For condensing exhaust steam of tramway engines the arrangement and

45 combination of parts substantially as hereinbefore described and illustrated in Figures 3 and 4 of the accompanying drawings.

Dated this sixth day of October 1885.

N. SCOTT RUSSELL.

LONDON : Printed by EYRE AND SPOTTISWOODE,
Printers to the Queen's most Excellent Majesty.
For Her Majesty's Stationery Office.

1885.

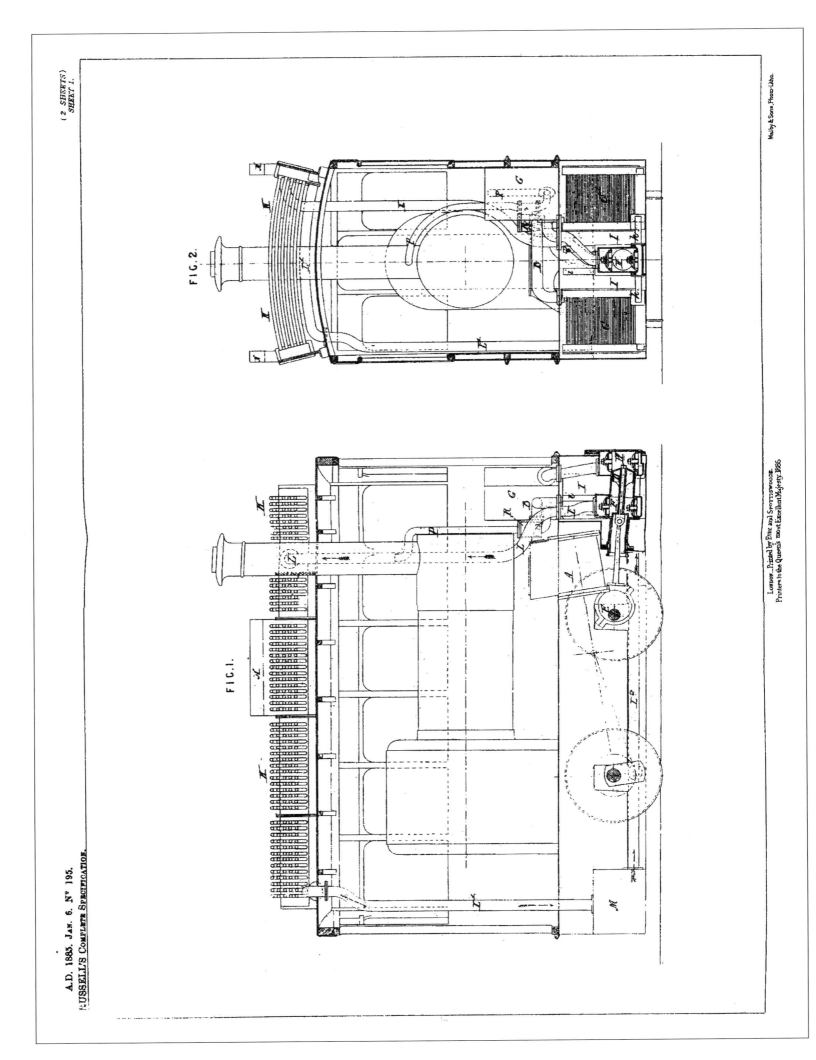

FIG. 1.

FIG. 2.

London _ Printed by Eyre and Spottiswoode.
Printers to the Queen's most Excellent Majesty. 1885.

Malby & Sons. Photo-Litho.

(2 SHEETS)
SHEET 2.

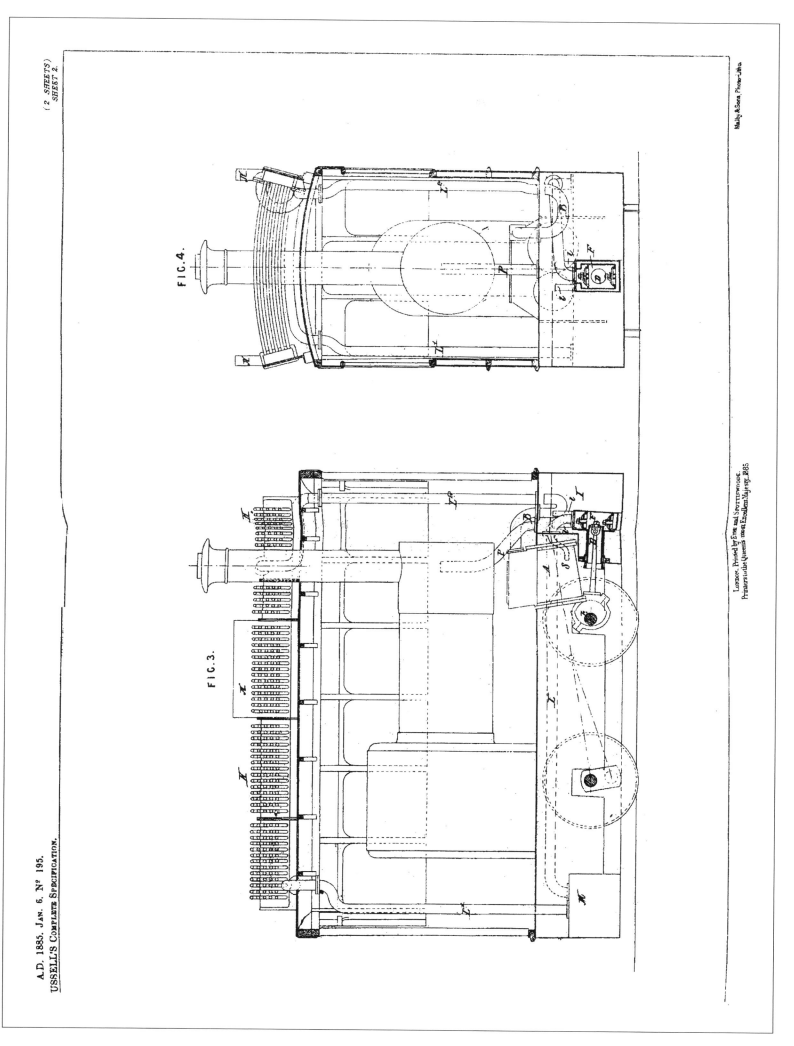

FIG. 3.

FIG. 4.

London. Printed by Eyre and Spottiswoode.
Printers to the Queen's most Excellent Majesty. 1885.

Malby & Sons. Photo-Litho.

1885-00785 Kirk Specification on Chairs and Sleepers

COMPLETE SPECIFICATION.

Improvements in Combined Metallic Chairs and Sleepers for Railways.

I PETER KIRK of Bankfield Workington in the County of Cumberland Iron and Steel Manufacturer do hereby declare the nature of the said Invention for "IMPROVEMENTS IN COMBINED METALLIC CHAIRS AND SLEEPERS FOR RAILWAYS" and in what manner the same is to be performed to be particularly described and ascertained in and by the following statement and accompanying drawings:— 5

My Invention relates partly to a former Invention for which on the twenty second day of November in the year 1884 I made application for the grant of Letters Patent. In the specification of my said former Invention I proposed to roll steel or iron sleepers with recessed rolls so as to produce the sleepers with parts of increased thickness at the places which would come below the rail and in these 10 thicker parts I punched slots and riveted or welded jaws or chairs to the said thicker parts. In my present Invention I employ suitable means and methods of operating to obtain sleepers having parts or places of increased thickness at the desired points but in place of welding or securing chairs or jaws to the sleeper, I form the holding jaws or clips out of the substance of the sleeper at the thicker 15 places by cutting, slitting or punching the metal and by pressing out parts of the same which are only partly detached from the body of the sleeper so as to form clips or jaws which are made of forms suitable to the section of the rail which is to be held.

In the accompanying drawings examples are given of the forms in which these 20 holding jaws or clips may be made. In the said drawings Fig. 1 represents a longitudinal section of part of a cross sleeper with a rail in position as when secured to the sleeper and Fig. 2 is a plan of the same parts. In the said Figs. a is the sleeper and a^1 are the parts which are made to be of increased thickness. In practice I prefer to obtain the increased thickness by rolling in the manner 25 and by means forming the subject matter of an application for Letters Patent made by me on the twenty-ninth day of August last but any suitable method of rolling, welding or pressing may be used. The holding jaws are represented by b, c. These jaws are produced by a punching operation the punch being so formed as to sever the metal on three sides of a rectangle without cutting the 30 fourth side. The punch and die are so formed as to press this partly severed part outward from the face of the sleeper and to curve and shape it into the required form as represented in the drawing or into any other form suitable to the requirements. It may be necessary or desirable to complete the shaping of the jaws or clips by a subsequent pressing or shaping operation especially in 35 the example illustrated by Figs. 1 and 2 wherein the parts to form the jaws have to be turned over and bent inward toward each other. In Figs. 3 and 4 the formation of the jaws or clips is simplified. It will be seen that in this case the parts to form the jaws are only pressed outward and at the same time shaped into form. This method is the one I prefer to adopt for the indicated section of rail as 40 the shaping of the jaws is more readily effected. To secure the rail of the indicated

---

A.D. 1885, 20th JANUARY. N° 785.

PROVISIONAL SPECIFICATION.

Improvements in Combined Metallic Chairs and Sleepers for Railways.

I PETER KIRK of Bankfield Workington in the County of Cumberland Iron and Steel Manufacturer do hereby declare the nature of the said Invention for "IMPROVEMENTS IN COMBINED METALLIC CHAIRS AND SLEEPERS FOR RAILWAYS" to be as follows:—

5 My Invention relates partly to a former Invention for which on the twenty second day of November in the year 1884 I made application for the grant of Letters Patent. In the specification of my said former Invention I proposed to roll steel or iron sleepers with recessed rolls so as to produce the sleepers with parts of increased thickness at the places which would come below the rail and in 10 these thicker parts I punched slots and riveted or welded jaws or chairs to the said thicker parts. In my present Invention I pursue the same method of operating so far as the rolling of the sleeper is concerned and I thereby obtain sleepers having parts or places of increased thickness at the desired points but in place of welding or securing chairs or jaws to the sleeper, I form the holding jaws or clips out of the 15 substance of the sleeper at the thicker places by cutting slitting or punching the metal and by pressing out parts of the same which are only partly detached from the body of the sleeper so as to form clips or jaws which are made of forms suitable to the section of the rail which is to be held. In some cases the parts to form the jaws or clips are turned up and over and toward each other and 20 pressed or moulded into form. In other cases the said parts are simply raised above the top of the sleeper and shaped into form either by the punching operation or by a subsequent operation. I may obtain the increased thickness by welding or pressing on pieces at the required places.

Dated this 19th day of January 1885.

EDWARD K. DUTTON,
Agent,
41, John Dalton Street, Manchester.

25

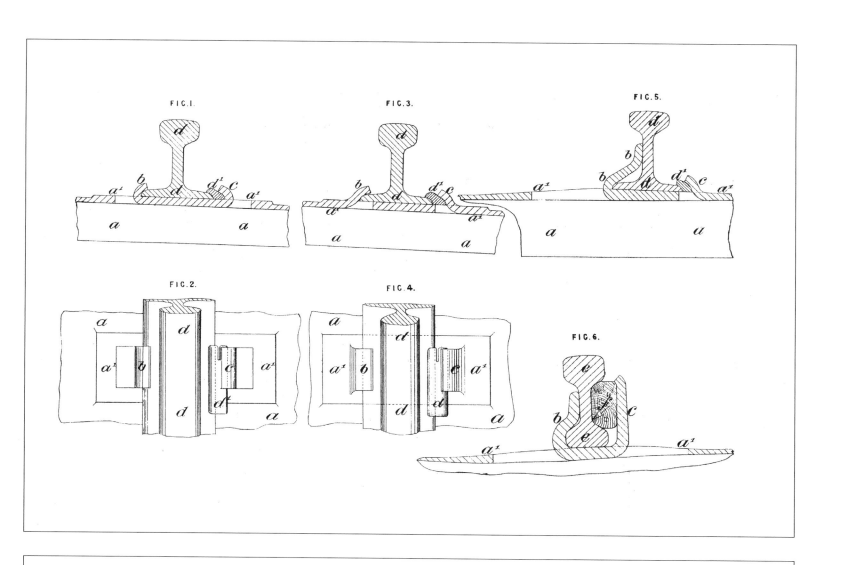

FIG.1.

FIG.3.

FIG.5.

FIG.2.

FIG.4.

FIG.6.

Kirk's Improvements in Combined Metallic Chairs and Sleepers for Railways.

form to the improved sleeper it is only necessary to drive a key d between the foot of the rail and the jaw c. In the example this key is split at one end so that it can be expanded to prevent accidental loosening of the fastening. I do not confine myself to the exact forms of the jaws b, and c, nor to the rectangular form of the

5 thickened parts of the sleeper. I may make the thicker parts extend entirely across the width of the sleeper and be either of uniform thickness or be tapered down to the thickness of the main body of the sleeper. In the examples illustrated by Figs. 5 and 6 the thicker parts of the sleepers are in each case made in the form of a swelling which dies out gradually at each end to the general thickness

10 of the sleeper top and which may or may not also die out toward the sides of the sleeper in the same manner. The same Figs. illustrate variations in the form of the jaws which hold the rails the said jaws being made comparatively thicker and longer or larger so as to give support to the vertical web of the rail. In Fig. 6 the jaws are shaped into forms suitable to the retention of an ordinary double headed

15 rail which is indicated in section by e. The rail is secured by means of an ordinary wooden key f, as in the cases of ordinary chairs but any other suitable means for securing the rail may be adopted. I do not claim as novel the method of forming the holding jaws or clips excepting when the sleeper is made thicker at the required places so as to obtain jaws of a suitable strength as jaws so formed

20 in a sleeper made of the usual thickness throughout would be much too weak for their intended purpose.

Having now particularly described and ascertained the nature of my said Invention and in what manner the same is to be performed I declare that what I claim is

25   1. The sleeper with holding jaws or clips b, c, for holding a rail formed out of the metal of the sleeper the sleeper being made thicker at the places where the jaws or clips are to be formed substantially as and for the purpose set forth and indicated.

    2. A steel or iron sleeper for permanent way made thicker in two places in its

30 length and having parts of these thicker portions punched or cut so as to be partly separated and raised or pressed out so as to form jaws or clips to answer as chairs to hold rails or a rail substantially as set forth and indicated.

Dated this 19th day of October 1885.

DUTTON & FULTON,
Agents,
1, St. James' Square, Manchester.

35

LONDON : Printed by EYRE AND SPOTTISWOODE,
Printers to the Queen's most Excellent Majesty.
For Her Majesty's Stationery Office.

1885.

Date of Application, 10th June, 1887
Complete Left, 12th Mar., 1888
Complete Accepted, 27th Apr., 1888

A.D. 1887, 10th June. N° 8380.

PROVISIONAL SPECIFICATION.

Improvements in Means for Operating Tram Cars by Electricity.

We ALEXANDER LOGIN LINEFF and WILLIAM JONES both of 12, Buckingham Street, Adelphi, in the City of Westminster, Consulting Engineers and Electricians do hereby declare the nature of this invention to be as follows :—

The objects of this invention are to render the motor unaffected by the vertical movements of the car, whereby the use of flexible joints is rendered unnecessary, and the friction, and consequent loss of power in transmitting the pull of the motor to the axle of the car, is reduced, and also to provide means by which, when the car meets any obstruction, the current is automatically cut off, and is thrown into an electro-magnet actuating the car brake, the brushes being at the same time reversed, and ultimately, when the speed of the motor is sufficiently reduced, the current is put on automatically again, while the brushes are in the reversed position, and the car can thus be moved backwards until the obstacle in the road is cleared.

In carrying out our invention, we mount the motor in a suitable frame, one end of which is carried by the car axle, and the other end is supported by a link, or springs, from the underside of the car floor.

The end of this frame, which is carried by the car axle, is so constructed as to form a chamber in which is enclosed a worm wheel keyed upon the axle, and is provided with bearings for a prolongation of the motor spindle, on which is mounted a worm to gear with the worm wheel.

By these means, the gearing is not in any way disturbed or affected, if the outer end of the motor frame is raised or lowered.

The link or other means for supporting the outer end of the frame is preferably attached to the frame at the centre of gravity of the motor.

The worm and worm wheel chamber is intended to contain a quantity of oil or other lubricant in which the worm and the lower part of the worm wheel are immersed, thus reducing the friction to a minimum.

As the worm on the motor shaft is geared into the lower side of the worm wheel, the motor shaft is inclined, and on emerging from the chamber, passes through a gland with which the chamber is provided, and which prevents any leakage of the lubricant.

[Price 1s. 8d.]

---

2   A.D. 1887.—N° 8380.

Lineff & Jones' Improvements in Means for Operating Tram Cars by Electricity.

To further obviate any strain on the motor gearing, through the unavoidable jolting of the car, the hinged frame or links may support the trunnions of the motor by means of springs.

The electric motor arranged in the above described manner may be provided with the usual reversing gear under the control of the driver. But in order to lessen the chances of accident on the road, through neglect or carelessness on the part of attendants, we hinge or otherwise movably secure, at each end of the car, a fender or board, which is kept in its normal position by means of a spring.—When pressed against by any obstacle on the road, the fenders swing inwards through a certain portion of an arc.—This movement of either fender is utilized to actuate a circular three-way switch at each end of the car, with which the fender is connected by means of a chain or rope passing round a pulley on the axle of the switch.

The middle (second) way contact piece occupies the greater part of the circumference of the switch, the two remaining ways (first and third) consisting of narrow contact pieces.

When the fender is in its normal position, the current on its way to the motor passes through the above mentioned switches, entering through the centre of the first switch to the first contact piece, thence through the centre of the second switch and its first contact piece to the motor ; thus both the switches are electrically in series.

The second (wide) contact piece of each switch is in connection with the Brake magnet, and the third in direct connection with the motor. When the switch arm of either of the switches leaves the first contact piece, the motor is cut out ; when it begins to travel over the second (wide) piece, the current is thrown into the brake magnet, and both car and motor slacken speed. As it is important to do this effectually before reversing the current in the motor, the other end of the chain or rope attached to the fender, and which actuates the switch, is connected with the piston of a pneumatic or hydraulic cylinder, the contents of which can be regulated in their escape (under the pressure of a spring at the back of the piston, or in any other convenient manner) by means of a cock or valve.—Thus the time occupied by the switch arm in passing over the second contact piece can be regulated at will.—In some cases we prefer to make the third way of the automatic switch of two or more separate pieces electrically connected to each other by suitable resistances. Thus, when the switch arm leaves the second way and slowly passes over the several contact pieces of the third, the current, before it reaches the motor, has to pass through a series of resistances, which are gradually cut out until the last contact piece of the series is reached, when the full power of the current is thrown into the motor.

The fender, while swinging on the hinge and actuating the switch, also reverses the brushes of the motor.—This is effected by means of a sleeve sliding on a rod flexibly connected to the lever actuating the brushes, and fitted with a suitable gripping mechanism which is connected by a strut to the fender.—When the fender moves inward, the strut presses the gripping mechanism against the rod, and thus jams it against the sleeve, whereby the rod is pushed forward and actuates the brushes.

When the switch arm comes to touch the third contact piece, the reversing of the brushes is already accomplished, and the current passes through the motor in an opposite direction to that in which it was passing when the car was moving forward.

When the obstruction has been removed, the switch and the other parts will be returned automatically to their normal position by the fender spring, and the backward motion of the car will be stopped by the driver reversing the brushes. A bridge piece may also be provided to keep the current from the brake magnet while the hand of the automatic switch above described is travelling backwards over the second (wide) contact piece, or the current may be split between the brake magnet and the motor ; while the brake magnet actuates the brake blocks only feebly.—In some cases we may insert between the third contact piece and the motor a suitable resistance,

Lineff & Jones' Improvements in Means for Operating Tram Cars by Electricity.

and thus regulate the current while the automatic backward motion of the motor is going on.

Reversing as well as brake mechanism capable of being operated by hand may also be provided, such mechanism being of the usual construction. Of course, both actions (automatic and by hand) of brake, and reversing of the motor, are quite independent of each other.

Dated this 10th day of June 1887.

NEWTON & SON,
Agents for the Applicants.

COMPLETE SPECIFICATION.

Improvements in Means for Operating Tramcars by Electricity.

We ALEXANDER LOGIN LINEFF and WILLIAM JONES, both of 12 Buckingham Street, Adelphi in the City of Westminster, Consulting Engineers and Electricians, do hereby declare the nature of this invention and in what manner the same is to be performed, to be particularly described and ascertained in and by the following statement:—

The objects of this invention are to render the motor unaffected by the vertical movements of the car, whereby the use of flexible joints is rendered unnecessary, and the friction, and consequent loss of power, in transmitting the pull of the motor to the axle of the car, is reduced; and also to provide means by which, when the car meets any obstruction, the current is automatically cut off, and is thrown into an electro magnet actuating the car brake, the brushes being at the same time reversed, and ultimately, when the speed of the motor is sufficiently reduced, the current is put on automatically again while the brushes are in the reversed position, and the car can thus be moved backwards until the obstacle in the road is cleared.

In the accompanying drawings:—

Fig. 1, Sheet I, shows in side elevation, and on an enlarged scale, the arrangement of the worm gearing which we use in carrying out our invention.

Fig. 2 is a plan view of the same.

Fig. 3 is a longitudinal section showing a mode of mounting the worm spindle, and

Figs. 4 show a slight modification of the same.

In Sheets II, III, and IV, we have shown the means we employ for arresting the motion of the car in case of meeting with an obstruction on the line, Fig. 5, Sheet II, being a side elevation, partly in section, of a portion of a car, with the apparatus in position; Fig. 6 a partial front view; Fig. 7 a partial plan view of the same.—

Lineff & Jones' Improvements in Means for Operating Tramcars by Electricity.

Fig. 8, Sheet III, is a side elevation of the pneumatic apparatus and switch detached, and Fig. 9 is a plan view, partly in section, of the same.—Fig. 10, Sheet IV, is a diagram showing a mode of changing the brushes of a motor of any suitable construction, and mounted transversely of the car.—Figs. 11 and Figs. 12, Sheet IV, show modifications in the arrangements of gripping mechanism, and Fig. 13, Sheet V, shows an arrangement of brake magnet in side elevation, partly in section. This part of the invention can be applied to the cars of any other system of electrical driving.

Referring now to Sheet I, A is the frame of the car, and B the wheel axle, the periphery of the wheel being shown by the dotted line. C is a metal framework, one end of which is supported at C^1 from the frame A.—The other end of the frame C is pendent from the axle B, and is constructed so as to form a chamber or casing C^2 within which works a worm wheel D and worm D^1, the worm wheel D being keyed on the axle B. Mounted in bearings in the frame, is a spindle or axle E, upon which are mounted a commutator or commutators E^1, and an armature of an electro-motor, of which E^2 are the field magnets.—The lower end of this spindle projects into the casing C^3, and carries the worm D^1 (see Figs. 3 and 4). A thrust block or device D^2 is provided to take up the thrust arising from the working of the worm, and this device may consist of a series of annular grooves in the casing, and a series of half rings placed round the spindle between collars, as shown at Fig. 3; or in place of the half rings, we may use rings of the shape shown at Figs. 4, which will be placed in pairs on opposite sides of the spindle, so that they will cross one another, and thus form a complete ring, which will have more even bearing surface than two half rings. These rings can readily be removed when worn, and replaced with new rings, by removing the lower part of the casing C^2.—The casing C^2 is kept full of oil or other suitable lubricant, and thus the worm and wheel will rotate in the lubricant, and the friction will be reduced to a minimum.

The gearing in the above described arrangement will not in any way be disturbed or affected, as the outer end of the motor frame C is raised or lowered, by the movement or jolting of the car.

The electric motor will be provided with the usual starting, stopping, and reversing gear under the control of the driver. But in order to lessen the chances of accident on the road through neglect or carelessness on the part of the attendants, we hinge or otherwise moveably secure, at each end of the car, a fender or board, which is kept in its normal position by means of a spring, and when pressed against by an obstacle on the road, the fenders swing inwards through a certain portion of an arc. This movement of either fender is utilized to actuate a switch at each end of the car, by means of a chain or rope passing from the fender round a pulley on the axle of the switch to a pneumatic apparatus, to cut off the current, throw it into a brake magnet, and then gradually to put on the current again, the brushes of the motor having meantime been reversed also by the movement of the fender.

In Sheets II and III, we have shown our arrangement of automatic apparatus which comes into operation when the tramcars meet any obstruction on the road.

R is a fender or board, which is hinged or otherwise moveably secured at each end to, and transversely of the frame of the car, so as to be near the ground. This fender or board, as shown in the figures, is secured to arms which are pivotted to the car frame, and it is kept in its normal position by means of springs R^1 secured at one end to the frame of the car, and at the other to projections of the arms above the pivot or hinge, either direct or through an arrangement of rods and levers, as shown at Figs. 6 and 7.

A chain, band, or rope R^2, which passes round a chain wheel or pulley R^3 (Fig. 9) on the axle of a switch S, is connected at one end to the fender R, and at its other end to the piston rod of a pneumatic apparatus R^4, suitably carried by the car frame. This apparatus consists of a cylinder R^4 (see the detail views Figs. 8 and 9) containing a piston, on the rod of which, inside the cylinder, is mounted a coiled spring R^5, the tendency of which is to drive the piston forward as soon as the tension of the spring R^1 is overcome by an obstacle in the road forcing back the fender and slackening the

Lineff & Jones' Improvements in Means for Operating Tramcars by Electricity.

chain R^2.—The opposite ends of the cylinder are connected by the pipe R^5, which is provided with a throttle valve to regulate the flow of air from one end to the other of the cylinder, according to the speed at which it is desired the piston should move. Other means may of course be provided for regulating the escape of the air from the cylinder.—The outer end of the cylinder may be provided with a valve opening inwards, so that as the piston returns to its normal position, air may be drawn in to fill up any vacuum that may be formed, and the inner end of the cylinder may be more or less open for the exit of air, so that there shall be no unnecessary pressure on the back of the piston during its return movement.

The switch S may be said to be an ordinary switch, though certain modifications are made therein to adapt it for our purposes. Round a disc or plate of insulating material, are secured insulated contact pieces 1, 2, 3, 4, 5, 6.—A fixed arm S^1, mounted on the axle S^3 of the switch, extends beyond the periphery of the disc, and forms the road by which the current enters the switch. The axle S^3 works in a metal sleeve S^2 (see Fig. 9), and on its rear end, and insulated therefrom, the chain wheel R^3 before referred to is mounted. On the front end of this axle S^3 is mounted an arm S^4, provided at its outer end with a sleeve S^5, in which a rubber S^6 slides, pressure being applied to the rubber by a spring S^7. If desired, the rubber may press against an arm of copper S^8, also mounted on the axle S^3, and which serves to somewhat shorten the circuit.—S^9 and S^{10} are stops to arrest the movement of the switch arm S^4 on one or other of the contacts 1 or 6, as required.

The electric current will always enter the switch by the arm S^1, and under normal conditions will pass out at contact 1 to the motor. Should an obstruction take place, the switch arm S^4 will be moved off contact 1 by the pneumatic apparatus R^4 (which will cut off the current from the motor), and onto contact 2. This contact is in connection with the brake magnet, so that the current will then pass to that mechanism, and put on the brake.—As the current to the brake magnet must be maintained for some time, to allow for stopping the car, we make the contact piece 2 of considerable length, nearly half the circumference of the disc, so that as the arm S^4 is moving over the face of the switch, ample time will be allowed for the action of the brake.

The switch arm S^4 will next pass successively over contacts 3, 4, 5, and 6, between each of which a resistance is or may be placed, so that the current will pass through varying resistances to the motor on the car, and will gradually, owing to the changed position of the brushes, drive the motor and the car in the reverse direction, so as to clear the obstruction, which can then be removed. The action of the pneumatic apparatus will be somewhat slow towards the end of the stroke of the piston, and this will give ample time for the motor to be driven in the reverse direction, without unduly heating the wires.

The diagram on Sheet II shows how the several operations which take place when the tramcar meets an obstruction are effected. The entry and exit of the current is indicated by the arrows. S^1 S^2 are the automatic switches at opposite ends of the car, connected in series. R represents resistances, H S a hand switch, B M brake magnet, M motor, and D dynamo.—Under normal conditions, the current enters the car, and passes through S^1, wire 2, S^2, wire 3 to H S, thence by wire 4 and M to earth. In this case, the contact arm of the H S would be over contact r^4.

If an obstruction occurs, the current passes from either S^1 or S^2 according to the direct in which the car is moving, by wire 5, to B M, and then, as the arm of switch S^1 or S^2 passes over the contacts successively through the wires 6, 7, and 8, the gradually decreasing R, and wire 4, to M. When the full power is attained, the current will pass direct from either S^1 or S^2, by lines 9, to M, and thence to earth.

The hand switch is used for starting and stopping the car under ordinary circumstances. When the handle is in the position shown in the diagram, the car is standing still, and no current passes to M. By moving the handle successively over the contacts r, r^1, r^2, r^3, r^4, the current passes through R with gradually increasing force until contact r^4 is reached, when the current passes direct to M by line 4. To stop the car, the handle is moved to r^4, and the current then passes by lines 5* and 5 to B M.

Lineff & Jones' Improvements in Means for Operating Tramcars by Electricity.

We may here mention that the hand switch forms no part of the present invention.

The reversing of the brushes of the motor by the movement of the fender R is effected by means of the rod R^7 attached at one end to the fender, and carrying at the other end a lever gripping device, through which passes a cord or rod R^6 connected with the brushes of the motor, which cord or rod R^8 is gripped as the rod R^7 advances, and is drawn or pushed forwards to change the position of the brushes. This lever gripping device is indicated at Figs. 11.

In place of a lever gripping device, I may use a ring gripping device, as shown at Figs. 12.—R^9 is the ring, which is placed on the rod R^8 and inside a recess in the sleeve R^{10}, with a slight spring behind it.—This spring is formed with a lug at its lower part, to which the rod R^7 is attached. As this rod is pushed forward by the fender R, it causes the ring to cant and grip the rod R^8.

We have shown, at Fig. 10, a well known arrangement for changing the brushes for the purpose of illustrating our invention; thus the brushes T of the motor are carried at opposite ends of two bell cranks T^1 pivoted at a plate T^2 secured to the motor frame. At their lower ends, the two bell cranks are connected by the rod T^3, to which is secured the notched plate T^4. This plate is held in position by the spring T^5, and it is also connected to the rod, cord, or chain R^8. As the rod R^8 is pulled in either direction, the plate T^4 is pulled with it, which rocks the bell cranks on their pivots, and brings, say, the top right hand, and the bottom left hand brushes, into contact with the commutator.

To change the direction of the current, the rod R^8 is pulled in the opposite direction, which draws the brushes above named out of contact, and throws the other two in. The notches on the plate T^4 catch against the shoulders of the plate T^2, and are thus held in position against the jolting of the car.—When the current is to be cut off entirely, the plate T^4 is brought to a central position, in which case none of the brushes touch.

In some cases, we may dispense with the automatic reversing of the motor, the action of the fender being limited to simply put the brake on, and when the car is thus arrested, the obstacle is removed, which brings the fender to its normal position. In such case, the gripping arrangement and the pneumatic device become unnecessary, the fender actuating a modified two-way switch by means of a lever or levers and connecting rods.

In Sheet V, we have shown the form of brake magnet which we propose to use.

It consists of two sucking bobbins U U, which are conveniently secured to the frame or bracket U^1, and a horse shoe magnet or armature U^2, the two arms of which enter the bobbins. The ends of these arms are rounded off so as to make the magnetic action equal through the whole length of the stroke. They are each provided with a non-magnetic guide a to keep the cores of the armature central of the bobbins, and a similar washer b to prevent the opposite poles touching one another.

The frame or bracket U^1 carries two pieces of metal V, which project into the bobbins about one third of their length.—These pieces are cup shaped at their upper ends, to correspond to the cores of the armature, and they are drilled centrally right through to receive the guides a.

The armature is connected with a lever, which is arranged to actuate the brake blocks. The electric current passes the bobbins in such a manner as to produce the polarity as marked on the figure.

In Sheets VI and VII, we have shown a general view of a tramcar, with the mechanism for stopping the car when meeting an obstruction in position, Sheet VI showing a side elevation, partly in section, and Sheet VII and underside plan view.

Having now particularly described and ascertained the nature of our said invention and in what manner the same is to be performed, we declare that what we claim is:—

1st. The arrangement of worm driving gear for electrical tramcars substantially as herein shown and described.

[This Drawing is a reproduction of the Original on a reduced scale.]

(7 SHEETS)
SHEET 1

A.D. 1887. JUNE 10. Nº 8380.

LINEFF & JONES' COMPLETE SPECIFICATION.

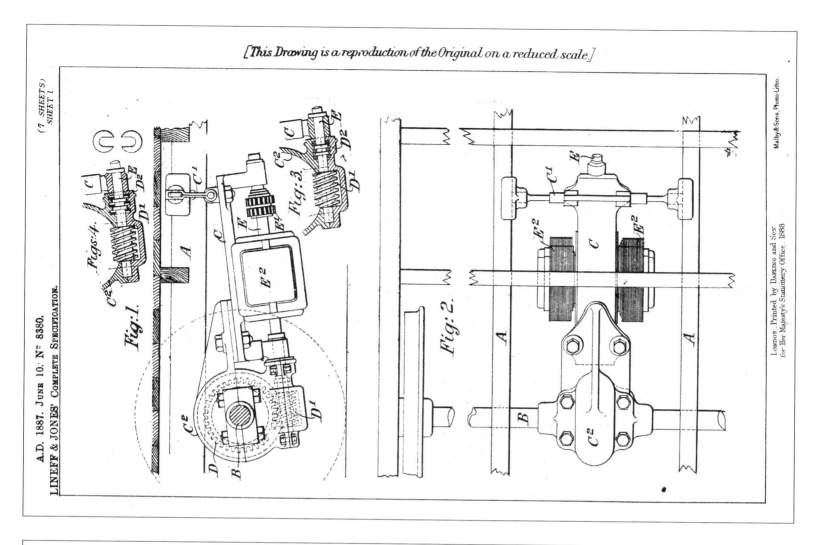

Fig: 4.

Fig: 1.

Fig: 3.

Fig: 2.

LONDON. Printed by DARLING and SON
for Her Majesty's Stationery Office. 1888.

Malby & Sons, Photo-Litho.

Lineff & Jones' Improvements in Means for Operating Tramcars by Electricity.

2nd. The means substantially as herein shown and described for arresting the motion of, and backing the car, in case of meeting with an obstruction on the track, as set forth.

3rd. In means for arresting the motion of the car, the application and use of a
5 fender, or equivalent apparatus, in combination with a switch for diverting the electric current from the motor to a brake magnet, as described.

4th. In means for arresting the motion of the car, the combination of a fender or equivalent apparatus, a switch, and a pneumatic apparatus, substantially as described.

10 5th. The modified construction of switch herein described.

6th. The combination of a fender, a gripping device connected with the fender, and a rod, chain, or rope in connection with the brush, ring or carrier, as and for the purpose set forth.

7th. The construction of brake magnet substantially as described.

15   Dated this 12th day of March 1888.

NEWTON & SON,
Agents for the Applicants.

LONDON: Printed for Her Majesty's Stationery Office,
By DARLING AND SON, LTD.

1888.

575

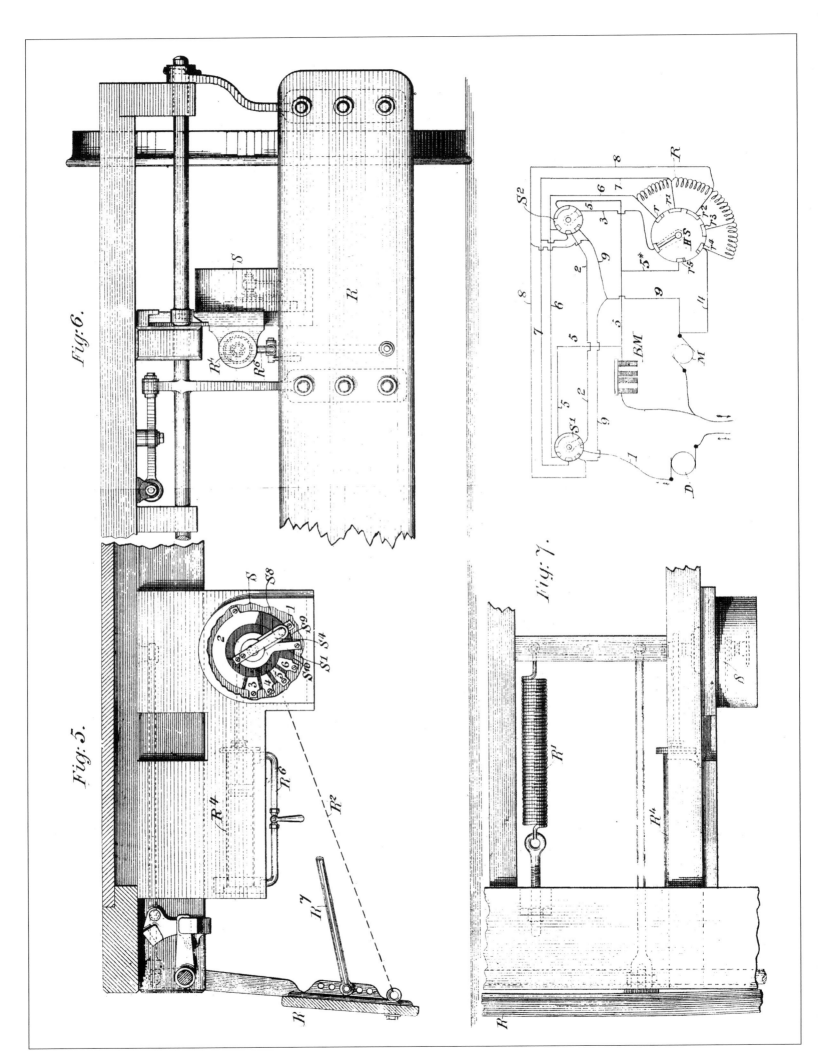

Fig. 6.

Fig. 5.

Fig. 7.

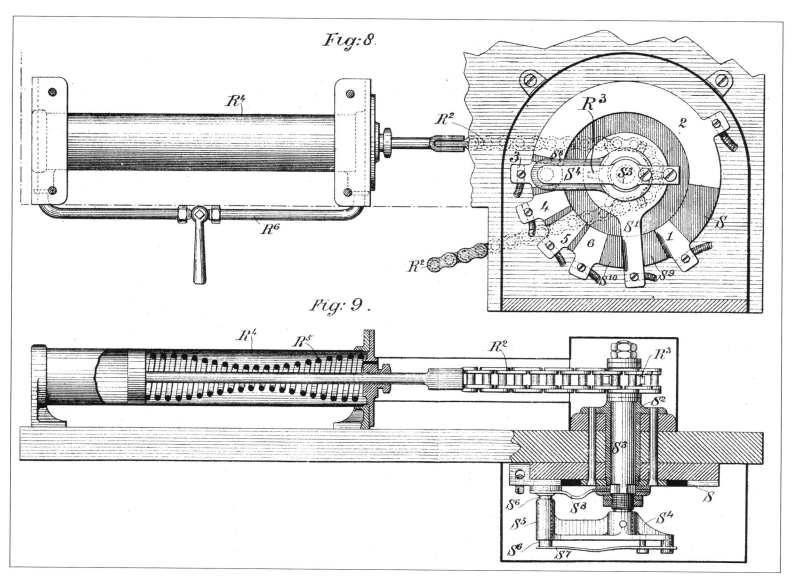

Fig: 8.

Fig: 9.

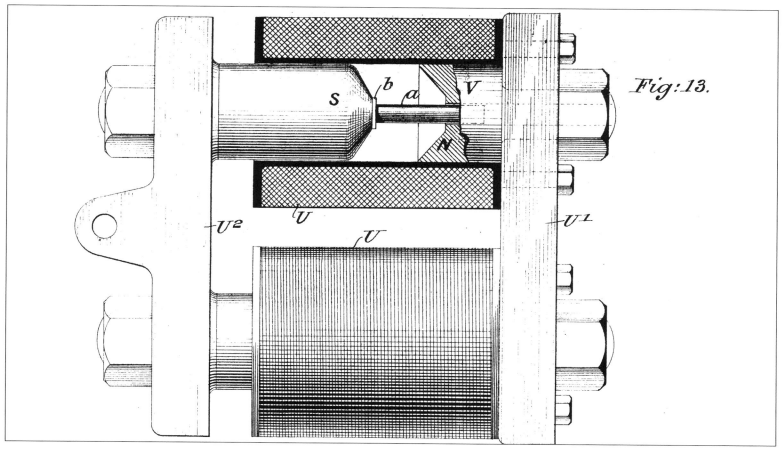

Fig: 13.

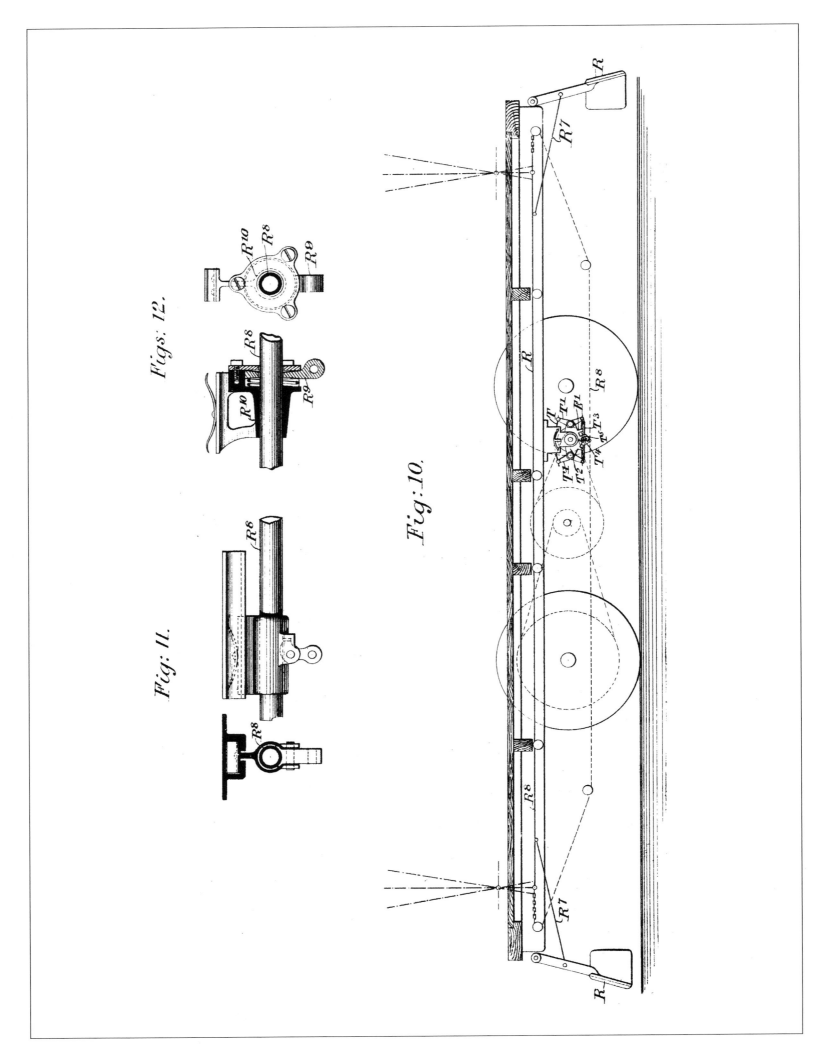

Figs: 12.

Fig: 11.

Fig: 10.

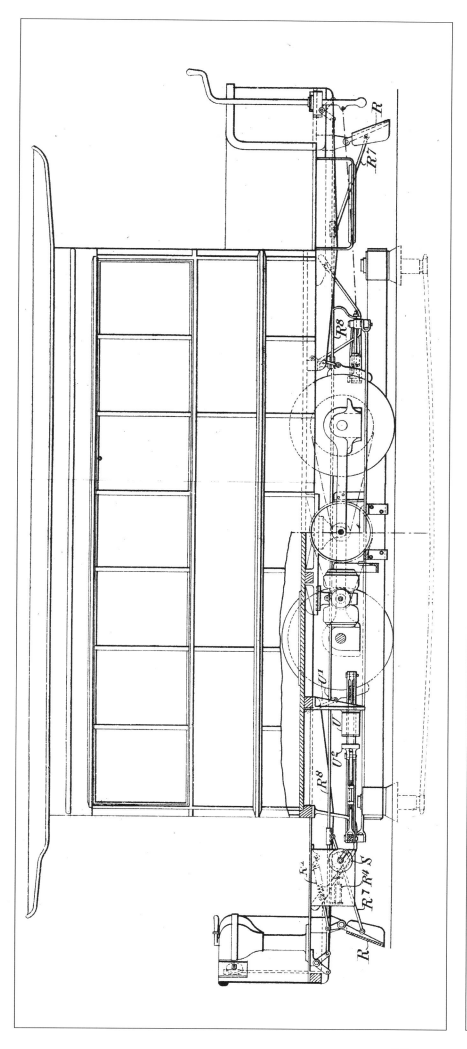

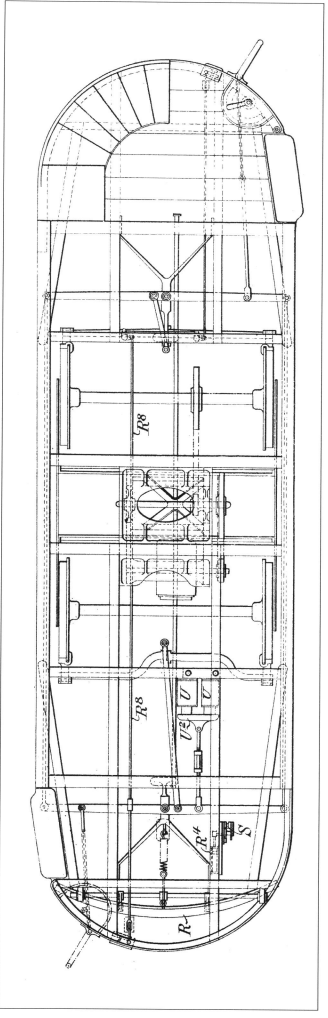

1887-10227 Cock Specification on Track Cleaner

2

A.D. 1887.—N° 10,227.

Cock's Improved Means and Apparatus for Removing Debris from Tram Rails.

COMPLETE SPECIFICATION.

Improved Means and Apparatus for Removing Debris from Tram Rails.

I WILLIAM JOSEPH COCK of 225 St. Johns Street, Clerkenwell, Middlesex, Engineer, do hereby declare the nature of my said invention and in what manner the same is to be performed to be particularly described and ascertained in and by the following statement :—

The object of this invention is to remove dirt from tram rails by the onward motion of a trolley or vehicle carrying an endless chain of blades which travel up an incline or spout the corner part of which is provided with a spike or scoop point to run in the groove of the tram rail and lift the dirt by said onward movement, the dirt pushing itself into the lower part of the incline from which the blades take it into a side or other shoot for falling into the trolly. [5]

The chain of blades is driven by any suitable gear from the travelling wheels and the incline is pivoted or suspended that the driver by means of a foot plate and levers can raise or lower the bottom end of the scoop to suit the depth of groove or to raise the appliance clear of the rails when not required for work. [10]

The upper part of the scoop has a hanging plate the edge of which rides successively on the chain blades to remove any dirt that may adhere to them. [15]

My invention will be understood by reference to the annexed drawings in which at Figures 1 and 2 I show elevation and plan of a trolly with the parts in position for cleaning the grooves of tram rails by the onward motion of the trolly.

Figure 3 is a side elevation of the same trolly with the cleaning apparatus lifted out of gear such as when travelling on rails without the cleaner being at work. [20]

Figure 4 is a detached view of one of the detachable scoops by which the dirt is first lifted.

Figure 5 is a detached view of the appliance for removing any dirt that may adhere to the lifter blades to ensure the dirt falling from the scoop into the [25] vehicle.

Figure 6 is an elevation of the body part of the trolly turned at right angles to the direction of travel so that when the doors are opened the contents can be shovelled out to the side of the line.

The portion of the body at Figure 2 shows, when the doors are opened that the [30] rubbish may be shovelled out on to the track or into a vehicle backed against the trolly to receive the dirt, the body of the trolly having an all round motion when a bolt is released for the dirt to be discharged at any point.

A is the body of the trolly of rectangular shape, mounted upon a lower frame B by means of a centre pin or perch C as seen more clearly at Figure 2. This centre pin [35] is socketed in the lower frame and the two ends of said frame are provided with a slot D for the reception of bolt E to lock the trolly body in the required position to suit the travel for lifting the dirt.

The body A and lower frame B are mounted upon travelling wheels F, F, two of which, at opposite corners, are provided with toothed gear for engaging into a first [40] motioned wheel G which through the intermediate gear wheels H and I drive the pinions J which are mounted upon a transverse shaft K so that the two sets of chains L, M

Date of Application, 21st July, 1887
Complete Left, 18th Apr., 1888
Complete Accepted, 18th May, 1888

A.D. 1887, 21st JULY.   N° 10,227.

PROVISIONAL SPECIFICATION.

Improved Means and Apparatus for Removing Debris from Tram Rails.

I, WILLIAM JOSEPH COCK of 225 St. Johns Street, Clerkenwell, Middlesex, Engineer, do hereby declare the nature of this invention to be as follows :—

The object of this invention is to remove dirt from tram rails by the onward motion of a trolley or vehicle carrying an endless chain of blades which travel up an incline or spout, the lower part of which is provided with a spike or scoop [5] point to run in the groove of the tram rail and lift the dirt by said onward movement, the dirt pushing itself into the lower part of the incline from which the blades take it into a slide or other shoot for falling into the trolley.

The chain of blades is driven by any suitable gear from the travelling wheels and the incline is so pivoted or suspended that the driver by means of a foot [10] plate and levers can raise or lower the bottom end of the scoop to suit the depth of groove or to raise the appliance clear of the rails when not required for work. The upper part of the scoop has a hanging plate the edge of which rides successively on the chain blades to remove any dirt that may adhere to them.

Dated this 21st day of July 1887. [15]

H. GARDNER,
166, Fleet Street, London,
Agent for the said William Joseph Cock.

[*Price 8d.*]

Cock's Improved Means and Apparatus for Removing Debris from Tram Rails.

are operated at the same time, the chains being on either side of the trolly for cleaning the grooves of the two rails simultaneously.

The chains L, M, are carried by sprocket wheels which give motion to them from the gear wheels.

5　The transverse shaft K is supported in bearings forming part of the two shoots or inclines N, N, these being pivotted at P so that they, with the chains can have a tilting or rising motion from the bottom by means of the hand lever Q and short arm R both of which are pivotted to the bracket S.

The intermediate wheel H is mounted on a centre or pivot pin which carries a

10　strap T on one side of the trolly, said trap T carrying the first motioned wheel G and the intermediate wheel I so that when the wheels have to be put out of gear such as when the scoops are not required to work it is only necessary to lift the handle U Figure 1 or depress the foot plate U Figure 3 to do so. In which Figure the chains and scoops are lifted above the rails by the throw over of the

15　lever Q in which position it can be locked by any appliance.

If the lever U is arranged as at Figure 3 only the wheel G is removed from gear but if arranged as at Fig. 1 the wheels G and I are simultaneously thrown out.

The lower part of each shoot or incline is shaped to receive a bottom scoop V with

20　a nose piece W shown separately at Figure 4 this having a tang X to be forced into a slot between the incline N and the bracket or lower strap Y.

This scoop may bear upon the surface of the rail for lifting any dirt that may be thereon.

Z, Z, are doors at one end of the trolley, see Figure 6, which can after

25　removing the latch fastener a be thrown open to enable the contents of the trolly to be shovelled out.

As the dirt lifted by the nose piece and scoop accumulates in the pocket of the scoop it is lifted up the incline by the blades b. b of the chain and as each blade in succession approaches the top of the incline a clearing blade c, shown

30　separately in Figure 5, rides against the inner end of the blade next the chain and as the chain continues its motion the scraping blade c which is suspended from the pivot d rides outwards on the chain blade and so scrapes the dirt off so that it falls into a side box e and from thence into the body of the trolly.

As soon as the chain blade has passed the edge of the scraping blade c the scraping

35　blade by its weight f resumes its normal position to act upon the next succeeding chain blade and so on each blade of the chain being operated on in a similar manner.

The object of making the scoop separately from the incline is to facilitate easy renewal when worn.

Having now particularly described and ascertained the nature of my said inven-

40　tion and in what manner the same is to be performed I declare that what I claim is:—

1. The apparatus constituting a trolly with dirt lifting appliances for clearing tram rails and their grooves of dirt the construction being substantially as shown in the annexed drawings Figures 1. 2. 3 and 6.

45　2. The detachable and affixable scoop V constructed as set forth and substantially as shown at Figure 4 of the annexed drawings.

3. The scraping blade c, see Figure 5, having a free motion for scraping the chain blades as and for the purpose described.

The 18th day of April 1888.

H. GARDNER,
166, Fleet Street, London,
Agent for the said W. J. Cock.

LONDON : Printed for Her Majesty's Stationery Office,
By DARLING AND SON, LTD.
1888.

50

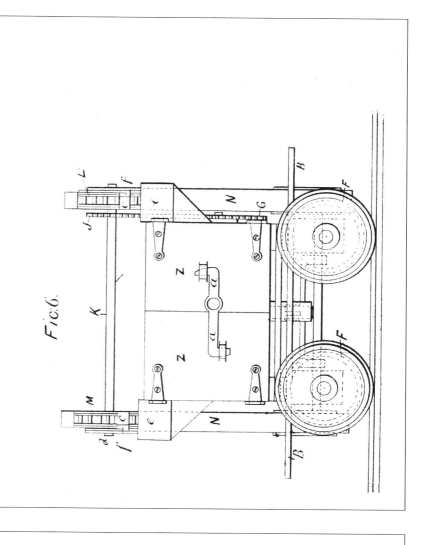

FIG. 3

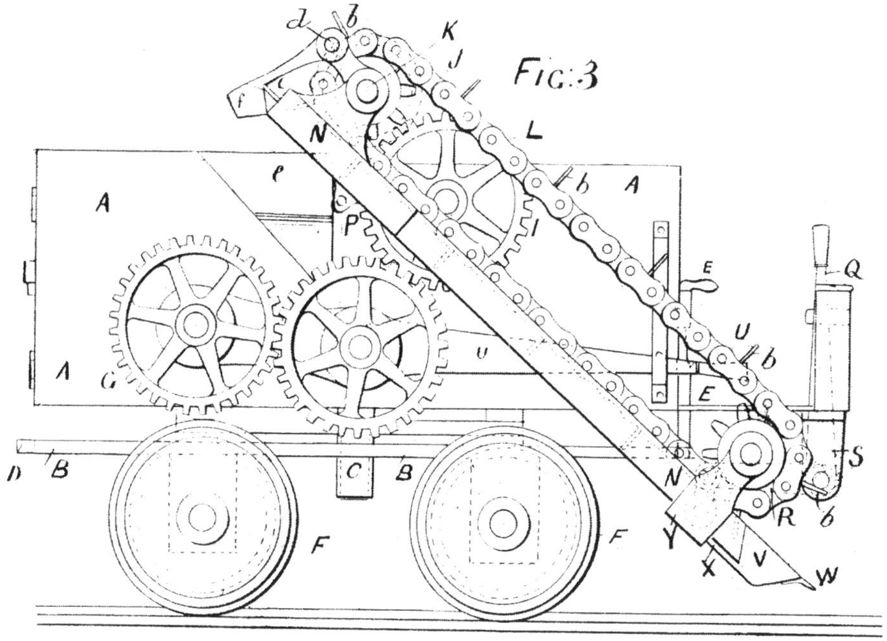

FIG. 6.

A.D. 1887.—N° 13,498.

Pauwels' Improved Apparatus for Cleaning Tramway Lines.

COMPLETE SPECIFICATION.

An Improved Apparatus for Cleaning Tramway Lines.

I JOHANNES CORNELIS WILHELMUS PAUWELS, of Tasman Straat No. 78, The Hague, Netherlands Civil Engineer do hereby declare the nature of this invention and in what manner the same is to be performed, to be particularly described and ascertained in and by the following statement:—

My invention relates an improved apparatus for cleaning the rails or lines of 5 tramways, which consists chiefly of two circular brushes provided with steel wires in lieu of bristles, and mounted upon a steel shaft.

Over and in front of the axles of the wheels of tramway cars, I fix two transverse bars of iron or other suitable metal whose extremities are bent at right angles and provided with a perforation through which passes the steel shaft above mentioned. 10

And in order that my invention may be more fully understood I have shewn the same in the accompanying drawing in which Fig. 1 is a view of the underside of a tramway car shewing only the wheels, the rails whereon they stand and the mechanism for rotating the brushes.

Fig. 2 is an end elevation of the under frame of a tram car shewing the mode of 15 attachment of the bar carrying the brushes, to the said under frame.

B is a bar riveted or otherwise fixed to the under frame of the car C and whose bent extremities $d\ d^1$ carry the shaft s which rotates in circular perforations formed therein. Upon the shaft S are mounted the two circular brushes $b\ b^1$ formed with steel wires and bearing upon the rails $r\ r^1$ or tramway line as shewn in fig. 2. 20

These brushes are shewn in Fig. 1, two in front and two behind the wheels $w,\ w,$ $w^1\ w^1$ of the tram car respectively thus cleaning the line in front and at the rear thereof. They may however if required be placed both in front or both at the rear of the said wheels, or the two front brushes may be found sufficient to effect the cleaning, and the hind brushes may be dispensed with. 25

Upon the axles A A of the wheels $w,\ w,\ w^1\ w^1$ are mounted two chain wheels $c\ c^1$ gearing by means of two chains $h\ h^1$ with two other chain wheels $a\ a^1$ mounted upon the shaft s of the brushes $b\ b^1$. When the car is in motion the rotation of its wheels imparts a rotary motion to the chain wheels $c\ c^1$ and through the chains $h\ h^1$ to the chain wheels $a\ a^1$ thus causing the brushes to revolve and to clean the rails or line as 30 shewn.

In wintry weather when the grooves of the rails are likely to be filled with ice, I arrange two strong bent springs $o\ o^1$ in front of the car as shewn in Fig. 1 (not

---

Date of Application, 5th Oct., 1887
Complete Specification Left, 4th Aug., 1888
Complete Specification Accepted, 5th Oct., 1888

A.D. 1887, *5th* OCTOBER. N° 13,498.

PROVISIONAL SPECIFICATION.

An Improved Apparatus for Cleaning Tramway Lines.

I JOHANNES CORNELIS WILHELMUS PAUWELS, of Tasman Straat No. 78 The Hague Netherlands Civil Engineer, do hereby declare the nature of this invention to be as follows:—

My invention relates to an improved apparatus for cleaning tramway lines, which consists chiefly of two circular brushes provided with steel wires in lieu of bristles 5 and mounted upon a steel axis. Upon the axles of the wheels of the tramway cars, I fix two long bars of iron or other suitable metal whose extremities are bent at right angles and provided with a perforation through which passes the steel axis above mentioned.

Upon the axles of the tramcar are mounted two chain wheels gearing by means 10 of an endless chain with two other chain wheels mounted upon the axis of the brushes so that the rotary motion of the axles when the tramcar is being propelled will cause the brushes to revolve upon the line and hence to clean the rails.

In wintry weather when the grooves of the rail are likely to be filled with ice, 15 I arrange a strong spring in front of the car provided with teeth or serrations which break such ice.

Dated 5th October 1887.

EDE WILDE,
Rathbone Place, Oxford Street, W.,
For the Applicant.

20

[*Price 8d.*]

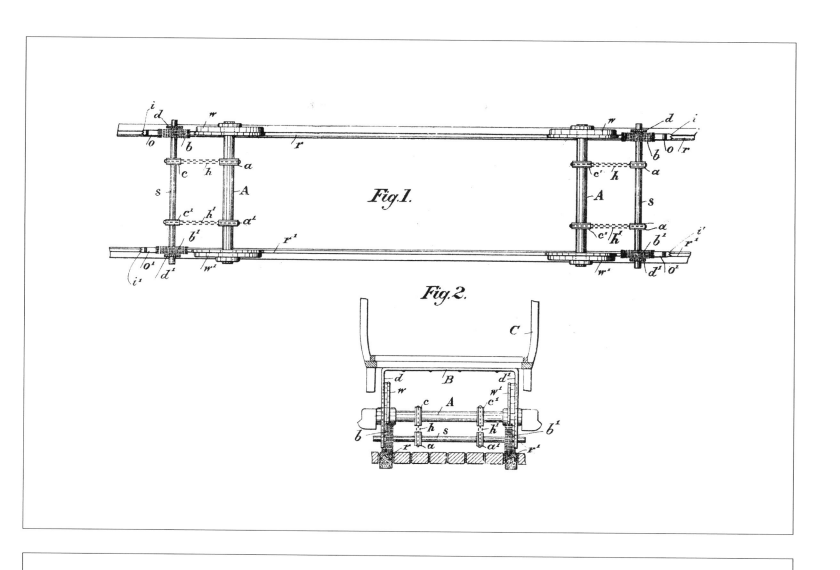

Fig.1.

Fig.2.

Pauwels' Improved Apparatus for Cleaning Tramway Lines.

shewn in Fig. 2) provided with teeth or serrations i, i, i^1 i^1 for the purpose of breaking such ice.

Having now particularly described and ascertained the nature of my said 5 Invention and in what manner the same is to be performed, I declare that what I claim is :—

The improved apparatus for cleaning tramway rails or lines, arranged, constructed and operating substantially as hereinbefore described and for the purpose set forth.

Dated this 4th day of August 1888.

10

EDE WILDE,
Rathbone Place, W., and Green Lanes, N.,
Agent for the Applicant.

LONDON : Printed for Her Majesty's Stationery Office,
By DARLING AND SON, LTD.

1888.

2   **N° 20,834.—A.D. 1889.**

Bullough's Improvements in Brakes for Tramcars or other Vehicles and Machinery.

and other machinery from running away as well as insuring a permanent brake in the absence of the attendant or operator, or in the event of any accident by the breaking of any portion of the brake gear or otherwise.

According to this my said invention behind the ordinary brake blocks I place spiral or flat springs fixed to brackets attached to the bottom of the car or other vehicle, or in a suitable position in connection with other machinery.

These springs bear against the brake blocks in such a manner, as to cause a permanent brake to such car, other vehicle or machinery until removed by the attendant.

The brake may be released when desired by means of a fulcrum lever, fixed at or near the centre of the tram car or other vehicle, this fulcrum lever being operated by means of connecting rods attached to the spindles of the brake wheels. Fulcrum levers may be placed at one side and near or attached to each brake block and operated by connecting rods for the purpose of taking off the brake.

The brake wheel or handle operates the connecting rod which in turn operates the fulcrum lever so pushing or pulling the brake blocks out of contact with the wheels of the car, other vehicle or other machinery, and as soon as the driver or operator leaves the brake wheel or lever the brake automatically applies itself by means of the springs bearing against the brake blocks, as before described.

For the purpose of controlling the brake I fix upon the spindle of the brake wheel one or two pulleys or wheels, around which and running in a groove are fixed belts connected with fulcrum levers to act as brakes upon the brake wheels, and which may be operated by hand or foot as required.

Such being the nature, and object of my said invention the following is a complete description of same reference being made to the accompanying drawings in which :—

Fig. 1 is a plan view (looking from underneath) of my improved brake and appliances connected therewith, as used in connection with a tram car or similar vehicle.

Fig. 2 is a longitudinal sectional elevation of Fig. 1.

Fig. 3 is a side elevation of the apparatus for controlling the brake.

Fig. 4 is a plan view of Fig. 3.

Figs. 5 and 6 is a detail drawn on an enlarged scale.

According to this my said invention the brake blocks 1. 1 are fixed to and carried by the ordinary cross bars 2. 2 and these cross bars are connected, and drawn towards each other by the spiral springs 3. 3 and links 4. 4, and to or near the centre of each one the cross bars 2. 2 is fixed a connecting rod, or bar 5. 5, the opposite end of each of the rods or bars 5. 5 being held by the studs 6. 6 one on each side of the centre or fulcrum 7 of the fulcrum lever 8 which is carried in suitable bearings 9 at or near and underneath the body 10 of the tram car or other vehicle. Connected to each end of the fulcrum lever 8 is a connecting rod 11. 11 one passing to each end of the tram car or other vehicle and being connected by a short chain 12 to the spindle 13 of the brake wheel or lever 14 (see Figs. 3 and 4).

The brake wheel is constructed in the ordinary manner and the lever consists of the lever 14 working on a fulcrum stud 15 on which is also fixed one end of a band of steel 16 which passes nearly all round the periphery of the pulley or wheel 17 on the spindle 13, and the other end of the band 16 is fixed to the end 17ᴬ of the lever 14.

The action is as follows :—If the brake is "on", or applied to the wheels 18. 18 and it is desired to remove same, then the spindle 13 is turned round by the ordinary brake wheel, and the chain 12 is wound around the spindle 13 shortening its length, and consequently drawing the connecting rod 11 with it, and so turning the fulcrum lever 8 on its centre or fulcrum 7 and pushing back the rods or bars 5. 5 and moving away from each other the cross bars 2. 2 which carry the brake blocks 1. 1 so that the latter are removed from contact with the peripheries of the wheels 18. 18. When in this position the attendant will, by hand or foot press the lever 14 moving the same on its fulcrum stud 15 and tightening the steel band 16 around the pulley 17 thereby holding the latter, and also the spindle 13 and preventing any turning of the latter in either direction, and the brake is "off" or removed from the wheels. When the

---

N° 20,834   **A.D. 1889**

Date of Application, 28th Dec, 1889
Complete Specification Left, 18th Oct, 1890—Accepted, 29th Nov., 1890

PROVISIONAL SPECIFICATION.

Improvements in Brakes for Tramcars or other Vehicles and Machinery.

I EDWIN JAMES BULLOUGH of 1 Richmond Terrace, Blackburn in the County of Lancaster, Incorporated Accountant, do hereby declare the nature of this invention to be as follows :—

The object of this invention is to construct a brake calculated to minimise accidents by preventing tramcars, vehicles, and other machinery from running away, as well as insuring a permanent brake.

I construct my brake as follows :—Behind the ordinary brake blocks I place spiral or flat springs fixed in brackets attached to the bottom of the car, or other vehicle, or in a suitable position in connection with other machinery.

These springs bear against the brake blocks in such a manner as to cause a permanent brake to such car or other vehicle, or machinery. The brake may be released as desired by means of a fulcrum lever fixed to the centre of the cross bar upon the ends of which are fixed the brake blocks.

This fulcrum lever is operated by means of a connecting rod attached to the spindle of the brake wheel ; fulcrum levers may be placed at one side and near or attached to each brake block operated by connecting rods for the purpose of taking off the brake.

The brake wheel or handle operates the connecting rod which in turn operates the fulcrum lever, so pushing or pulling the brake blocks out of contact with the wheels of the car, vehicle, or machinery.

As soon as the driver or operator leaves the brake wheel or lever, the brake automatically applies by means of the springs bearing against the brake blocks, as before described.

For the purpose of controlling the brake I fix upon the spindle of the brake wheel two pulleys or wheels, around which and running in a groove are fixed belts connected with fulcrum levers to act as brakes upon the brake wheels, and which may be operated by hand or foot as required.

As a further safeguard, I apply as an emergency, brake shoes or slippers composed of any suitable material suspended from the bottom or side of the car, or other vehicle, and made to fit the wheel and rail, operated by means of levers, connecting rods and springs by which means the shoes or slippers are lowered on to the rail or raised as required.

Dated this Twenty-seventh day of December 1889.

E. J. BULLOUGH,
Applicant.

COMPLETE SPECIFICATION.

Improvements in Brakes for Tramcars or other Vehicles and Machinery.

I, EDWIN JAMES BULLOUGH of No. 1 Richmond Terrace, Blackburn in the County of Lancaster, Incorporated Accountant, do hereby declare the nature of this invention and in what manner the same is to be performed, to be particularly described and ascertained in and by the following statement :—

This invention relates to improvements in the construction of and method employed for operating brakes of tramcars and other vehicles and machinery and the object is to construct a brake calculated to minimise accidents by preventing tramcars, vehicles,

[*Price 11d.*]

FIG. 6

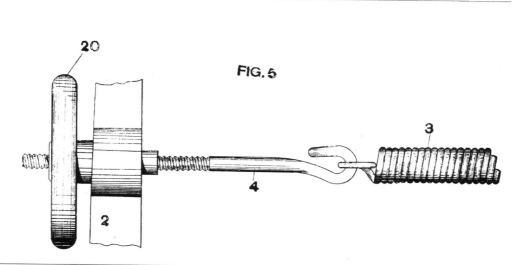

FIG. 5

Bullough's Improvements in Brakes for Tramcars or other Vehicles and Machinery.

attendant removes his foot or hand from the lever 14 the tension of the springs 3. 3 at once draw the cross bars 2. 2 carrying the brake blocks 1. 1 towards each other, and the brake is thus automatically applied.

In order to allow of the tension of the springs 3. 3 being readily varied on the end of one of the connecting links 4. 4 which pass through the cross bars 2. 2 (see Fig. 5) I place a small hand wheel 20 by turning which in one direction or the other the tension of the spring 3 is made greater or less as desired.

The link 4 may be attached to the spring 3 either by hook as shewn in Fig. 5 or the link 4 may be threaded and screw into a block 21 fixed to the end of of the springs 3.

By the use of the above described appliances great saving in time, in applying the brake is obtained, which in case of emergency may prevent an accident caused by the vehicle "running away," and the improved brake is less liable to fail in its action, as if one of the springs, connecting rods or links should break or give way the remaining three are not rendered useless, but would act equally as well as before breakage the stays 9. 9 acting as reserve links or connections, which has not been the case in brakes as heretofore constructed.

Although I have described the improved brake as applied to tram cars it will be understood that the improved brake is equally applicable to waggonettes and other vehicles of like class.

Having now particularly described and ascertained the nature and object of my said invention, and in what manner same is to be performed, I declare that what I claim is :—

The general construction, combination and arrangement of parts substantially as and for the purpose, and acting in the manner herein described and as illustrated by the drawings annexed.

Dated the 27th day of October 1890.

EDWIN JAMES BULLOUGH.

By his Agent, Walter Brierley,
Central Chambers, Halifax.

London Printed for Her Majesty's Stationery Office. by Darling & Son. Ltd —1890

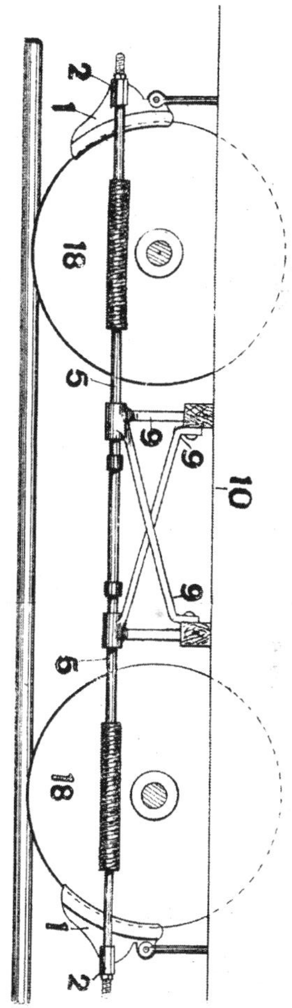

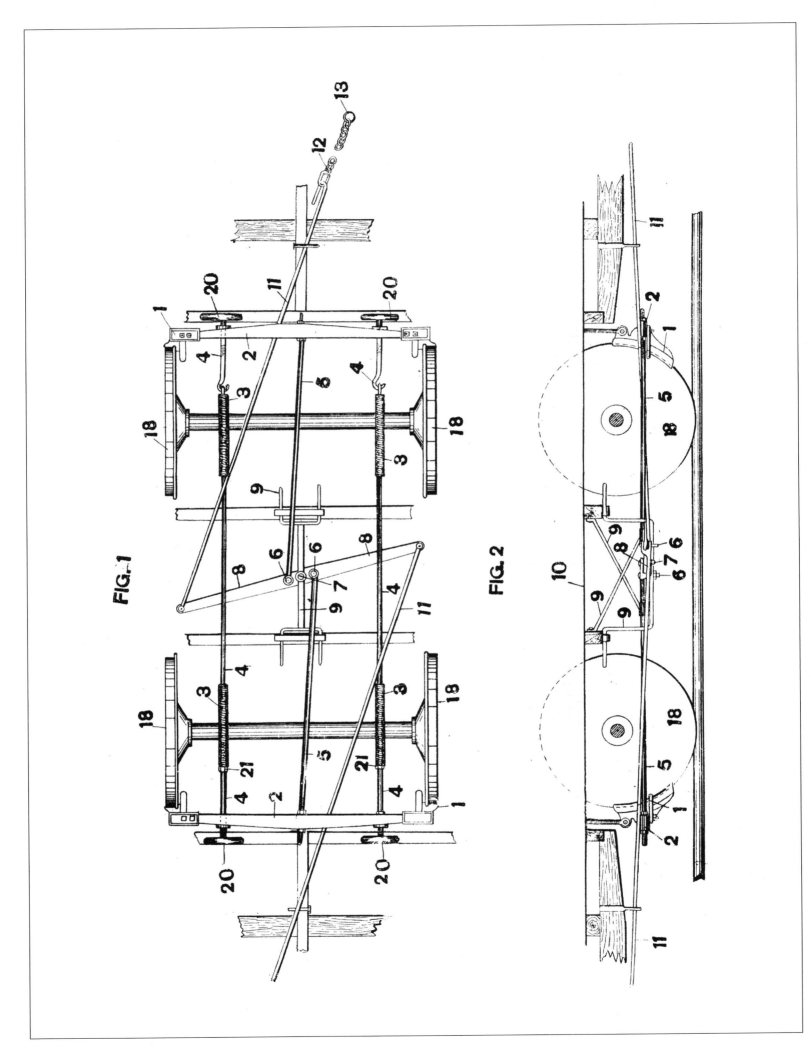

FIG. 1

FIG. 2

586

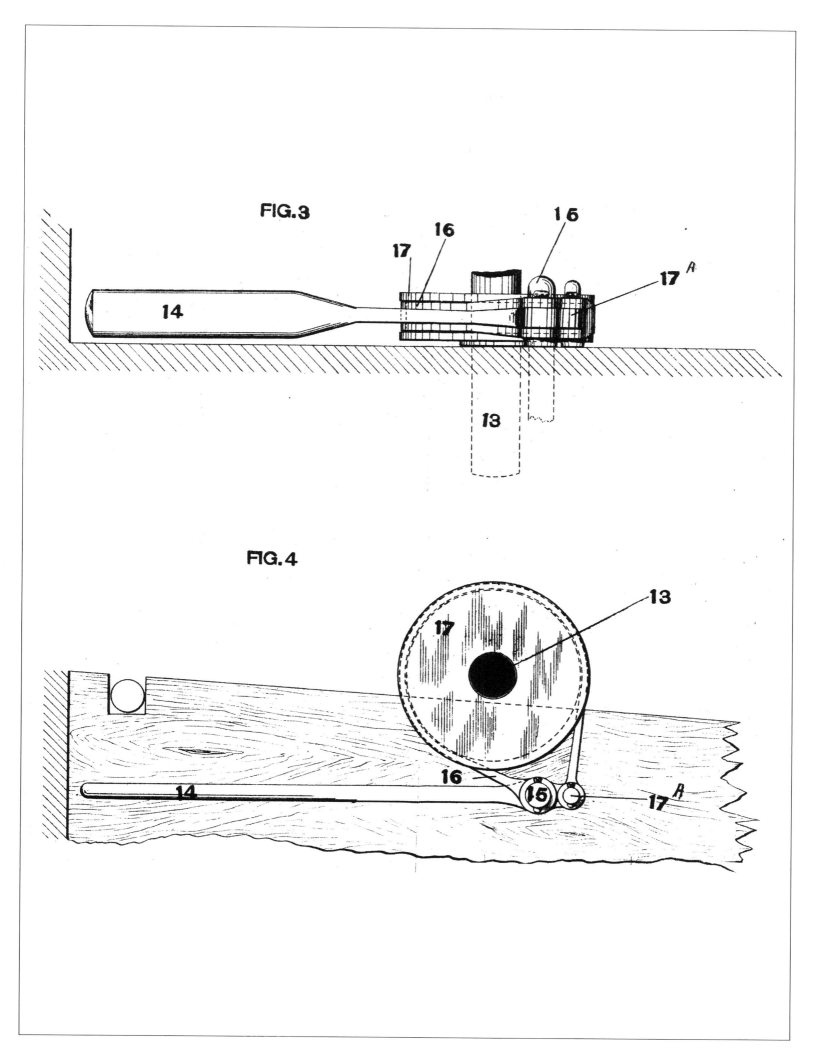

FIG.3

FIG.4

N° 250  A.D. 1890

Date of Application, 7th Jan., 1890
Complete Specification Left, 19th Feb., 1890—Accepted, 12th Apr., 1890

PROVISIONAL SPECIFICATION.

Improved Means for Cleaning Tramway Rails and for Removing Snow and Sand therefrom.

WILLIAM ROCHE Tailor 145 Weston Street Long Lane Borough, S.E. ALBERT ROCHE Tailor 145 Weston Street Long Lane Borough S.E. do hereby declare the nature of this invention to be as follows :—

5   A travelling machine to be screwed to bottom of car in front of the wheels near as can with revolving brush the shaft holding machine is telescoped with india rubber spring inside telescope shaft to work with the springing of the car.

   The travelling wheel brush and cog wheels are covered in with a case that can be unscrewed the shaft or telescope is screwed to the top of case. It can be used with or without the plough. The plough has two shafts with two sockets to hook on

10 the fronts axles outside the case with pins and chains attached.

   The guiding pin is fixed in telescope and a screw in front working in two slots.

   Dated this 6th day of January 1890.

WILLIAM ROCHE.
ALBERT ROCHE.

15   COMPLETE SPECIFICATION.

Improved Means for Cleaning Tramway Rails and for Removing Snow and Sand therefrom.

WILLIAM ROCHE and ALBERT ROCHE 145 Weston Street Long Lane Borough S.E. Tailors do hereby declare the nature of this invention and in what manner the same

20 is to be performed, to be particularly described and ascertained in and by the following statement :—

   Tramway brush machine for cleaning the metals to be fitted to the bottom of car with screw and 2 bolts it has one travelling wheel 2 cog wheels and 1 circular brush covered within a case or box with a small steel comb inside case over brush.

25   Telescope attached to bar for the india rubber spring with small giding bar at back and screw in front that works in 2 slots in telescope case steel bar on a disk going ⅔ of height of spring through center thereof attachment a plough to hook on with pins and chains attached.

   Sheet No. 1 Fig. 1st & 2nd section shewing A. revolving brush to run in grove of

30 metal and cog wheels with reversing action by cog wheels at C—B india rubber spring fitted in gun metal tube E screwed and bolted to wrought iron casing for wheels F.

   D shewing revolving nut for screw with fixed wheel for turning screw G.

   H plates fixed on car and on braces of machine to hold revolving nut in position.

35   I screw to adjust machine and cylinders to hold spring B and E.

   J pivot in slot of cylinder attached to screw to prevent machine from dropping, K wheel to run on surface of metals.

   L tramway metals.

   Sheet No. 2 Fig. 3 showing snow plough for fixing in front of machine and to form

40 guard at front of wheels and machine.

   A shewing cutters in steel: fixed in slot at B with spring & loose plate at C the cutter so fixed will rise or fall to any unequality of the roadway D are screwed pivots to hold cutters in position E is guard plate at front of machine the plough can be easily removed from machine by removing screw plate at E Fig. 4.

45   Sheet 3 Fig. 4.

   Shewing method of fixing machine to car at A.

   [*Price 6d.*]

---

2   N° 250.—A.D. 1890.

W. & A. Roche's Improved Means for Cleaning Tramway Rails, &c.

   B shewing braces to hold machine in proper position over the tram metals C showing snow plough fixed and front guard D showing tram metals E showing method of fixing plough to machine.

   Having now particularly described and ascertained the nature of our said invention and in what manner the same is to be performed we declare that what we 5 claim is

   1st. The revolving brush.
   2nd. Telescope with india rubber spring.
   3rd. The elevator.
   4th. Plough.   10

   Dated this 7th day of January 1890.

WILLIAM ROCHE.
ALBERT ROCHE.

A.D. 1890. JAN. 7. Nº 250.

ROCHE & another's COMPLETE SPECIFICATION.

(3 SHEETS)
SHEET 3.

SHEET 2.

SHEET 1.

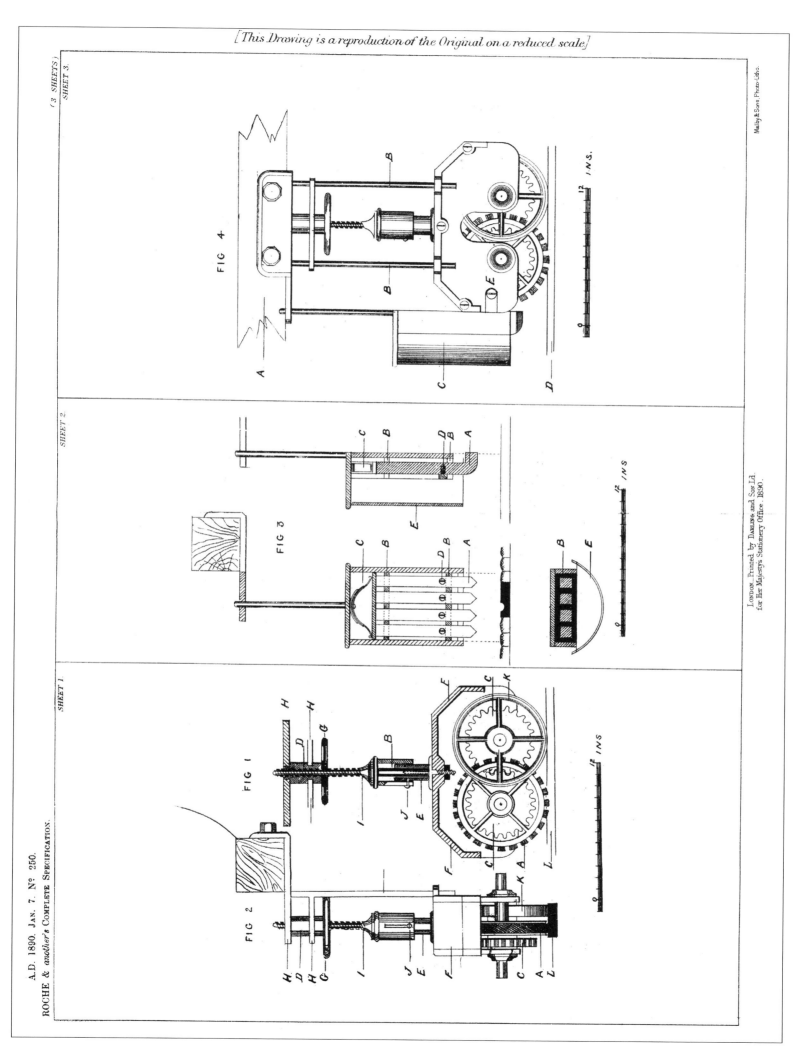

FIG 4

FIG 3

FIG 1

FIG 2

N° 549

A.D. 1890

Date of Application, 11th Jan., 1890

Complete Specification Left, 8th Nov., 1890—Accepted, 13th Dec., 1890

PROVISIONAL SPECIFICATION.

Improvements in Machinery for Stopping and Starting Tramway Cars.

We, JOSEPH HEWINS of Eleanor Street, Great Grimsby, Builder, and CHARLES HARDY, of 53 Willingham Street, Great Grimsby, Contractor's Foreman, both in the County of Lincolnshire, do hereby declare the nature of our invention to be as follows:—

5 This invention consists in improved machinery for stopping and starting tramway cars, to be used instead of tyre or other brakes.

In the improved machinery on each of the two car axles is a friction wheel adapted to be brought into respective engagement with one of two corresponding friction wheels on shafts journalled in the respective ends of a swinging or oscillating frame.

10 On each of said shafts are also four pulleys two geared by two crossed chains with the respective pulleys on the other shaft, and two having connected to them chains adapted to be wound thereon by action of the friction wheels when the latter are in engagement respectively with one or other axle friction wheel, and so bring into tension springs attached to the other ends of said chains.

15 Lever gear is provided to be operated by the driver to move the frame aforesaid so as to bring the friction wheels into respective engagement. The springs tensioned by the action of the friction wheels of one axle may be thus made to operate for assistance in starting the car by engagement of the friction wheel on the other axle.

Dated this 11th day of January 1890.

20 HERBERT & Co.,
Agents to Applicants.

COMPLETE SPECIFICATION.

Improvements in Machinery for Stopping and Starting Tramway Cars.

25 We, JOSEPH HEWINS Builder of Eleanor Street and CHARLES HARDY, Contractor's Foreman of 53 Willingham Street, both in Great Grimsby in the County of Lincolnshire do hereby declare the nature of this invention and in what manner the same is to be performed to be particularly described and ascertained in and by the following statement:—

30 This invention consists in improved machinery for stopping and starting tramway cars to be used instead of tyre or other brakes.

The object of this invention is to collect the force usually lost when stopping the vehicle when in motion to store the collected force and apply the same when required to

35 relieve the horse, engine or other motive power from the extra strain required to put the vehicle again into motion.

In the accompanying drawing Fig. 1 is a vertical longitudinal section and Fig. 2 a sectional plan of the under carriage of a tram car fitted with the improved machinery.

In applying this invention we fix at convenient positions two powerful springs A B,

40 the one end being fixed, the other carrying loose plates C C which are connected to the pulleys D and E by rods and chains. The pulleys D and E are respectively fixed on oscillating shafts F and G working upon centres H H at one end respectively thereof. At or near this end is fixed on each shaft a chain wheel I, the two chain wheels being geared by a cross chain to transmit the motion of the shaft F in a contrary direction

45 to the shaft G or *vice-versâ*. At the free or outer ends of the shafts F and G we fix pinion wheels J and K which can be put in and out of gear with the spur wheels L and M on the main axles by the connecting links N and O between shafts F and G

Hewins & Hardy's Impts in Machinery for Stopping and Starting Tramway Cars.

2 **N° 549.   A.D. 1890.**

and levers P Q. The levers P Q work on a common fulcrum, and are, as illustrated, so arranged that the apparatus can be put into work from either end.

In place of toothed gear L J, K M, frictional surface gear may be used; but the toothed gear is preferred for the reason of being more certain of engagement, more

5 especially during the period of inactivity of the mechanism with force stored in the tensioned springs thereof after the stopping and previous to the restarting of the vehicle.

The levers P, Q, pass through slots in each of the connecting links N O, the slots being larger than the levers so that their free movement of the links upon the levers is permitted within the limits of the slots. These limits are such that when the levers

10 are held in their intermediate or central position each connecting link may move to sufficiently only to allow the respective pinion thereon to move into engagement or out of engagement with the respective spur wheel as the tension of the springs bearing on the links or the respective oscillating shafts may determine.

When the lever P is drawn back by rod R through turning the handle V which

15 operates chain wheel V¹ on which gears an endless chain R² connected to the lever R¹, the other end of which is connected to the rod R, if the vehicle is travelling in such a direction that the handle V is at the fore end of it the connecting link N moved by the lever P puts the pinion J into gear with the revolving spur wheel L which, if the direction is as above stated is on the rear axle which instantly causes both shafts G and

20 F to revolve they being connected by the chain on wheels I I until the revolving drums D, E have drawn the two springs A and B until the pressure of these stops the vehicle. The man in charge then turns the handle V so that the lever P is put on the centre again which liberates both connections N & O enabling the springs A and B to draw the pinions J and K respectively into gear, which at once locks the whole.

25 When it is required to use the force in the two springs A and B for starting the vehicle the lever P is moved so that N draws pinion J out of gear with the spur wheel L which allows the whole of the force in the two springs A and B to start the vehicle by turning the spur wheel M on the leading axle. When the force in the springs A and B is spent the lever P is again put back on its centre when the connections N &

30 O are free from the pull of the springs A and B, the springs X and Y acting on the links N and O draw and hold the two pinions J and K out of gear with the spur wheels L and M respectively, liberating all so that the vehicle can proceed freely. When the vehicle proceeds in the opposite direction the handle W is used with the same result, only that it acts on and by the lever Q. Should the man in charge turn

35 either handle W or V the wrong way, the only difference it would make would be that he would brake on the front wheel and start on the rear which is the opposite to that above described.

The stored up force may be utilized to propel the vehicle backwards by moving the handle V or W respectively so the pinion and spur wheel which were beforehand

40 brought in contact for storing the force may be alone left in contact for utilizing the force so stored which will react then in the contrary direction.

Having now particularly described and ascertained the nature of our said invention and in what manner the same is to be performed we declare that what we claim is

45 The combination of the spur wheels L M in connection with the wheels of the vehicle or the revolving axles thereof, the oscillating or movable shafts F G connected by a crossed chain or equivalent to each other, the pinions J and K on said shafts the links N and O the lever or levers P Q movable through suitable mechanism, the springs X Y, the pulleys D E on said shafts respectively the springs A and B and

50 chains or equivalents connecting said springs A and B to said pulleys D and E respectively all substantially as and for the purpose described.

Dated this 8th day of November 1890.

HERBERT & Co.,

18, Buckingham Street, Strand, London, W.C., Agents to Applicants.

London : Printed for Her Majesty's Stationery Office, by Darling & Son, Ltd.—1891

A.D. 1890. Jan. 11. N° 549.

HEWINS & another's Complete Specification.

(1 SHEET)

Malby & Sons, Photo-Litho.

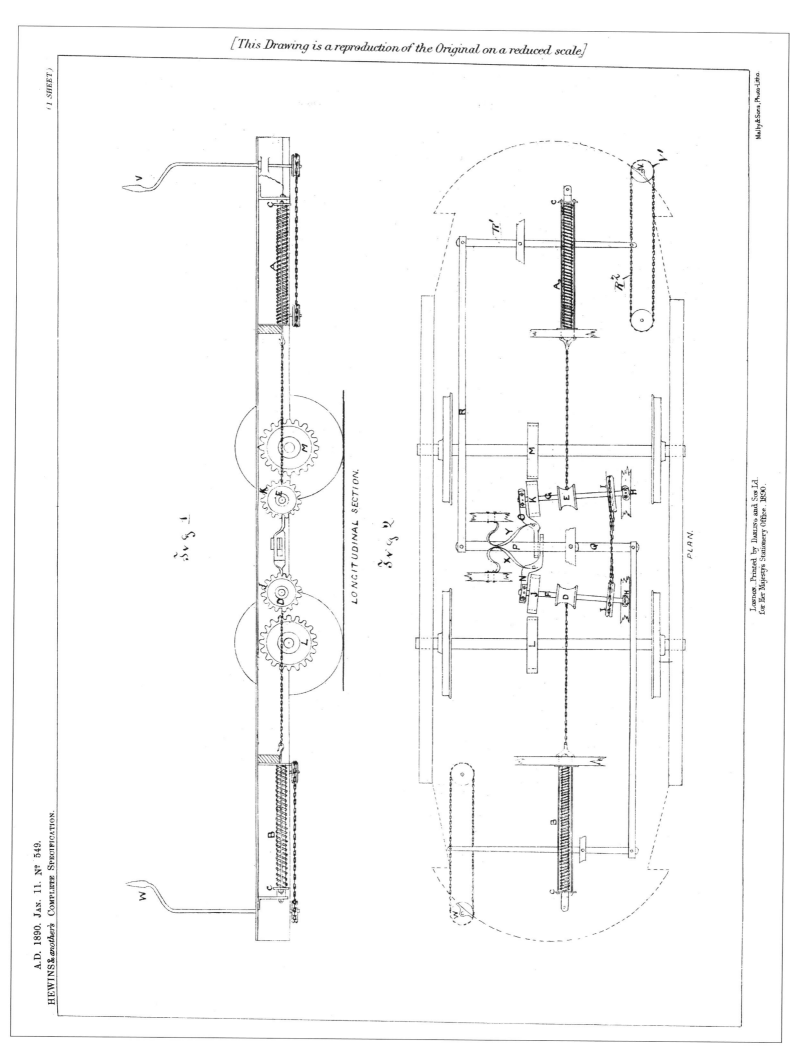

LONGITUDINAL SECTION.

Fig. 1

Fig. 2

PLAN.

London. Printed by Darling and Son Ld.
for Her Majesty's Stationery Office. 1890.

N° 8502   A.D. 1893

Date of Application, 27th Apr., 1893—Accepted, 1st July, 1893

COMPLETE SPECIFICATION.

Improvements in Electrical Railways and Tramways.

A communication from abroad by ALFRED DIATTO, of 12, Piazza Gran Madre di Dio, Turin, Italy, Engineer.

I, WILLIAM LLOYD WISE of 46 Lincoln's Inn Fields in the County of London, Consulting Engineer and Chartered Patent Agent, do hereby declare the nature of this invention and in what manner the same is to be performed to be particularly described and ascertained in and by the following statement:—

5 Owing to the increased use of electricity for various purposes within recent years, attention has been drawn to the inconveniences of aerial conductors used for conveying powerful currents, and particularly for currents of variable intensity, by reason of their inductive action on telegraph and telephone wires.

In large towns moreover, the appearance of these conductors is objectionable,
10 especially where they have to be supported on posts arranged at relatively short distances apart, or upon supports attached to houses, the general appearance and arrangement of the conductors and supports being both unpleasant and inconvenient. As is well known there are other disadvantages inherent to this system, especially if the conductors are not insulated.

15 For the reasons above mentioned, the construction of electrical tramways with underground conductors in preference to aerial conductors has been regarded with favor; and the great advantages likely to result therefrom have caused many electricians to undertake this problem with the view of arriving at a satisfactory solution. Several systems have heretofore been proposed and tried but so far as I
20 know they are all more or less objectionable for one at least of the following reasons:—too complicated construction; or too high cost of installation; or too high cost of maintenance.

Of the systems that have heretofore been proposed, one of the most satisfactory is Siemen's system, as employed and at the present time still worked in the town of
25 Buda-Pesth. It has however the drawback of requiring a net work of underground conduits that is not practicable in all towns, or which if possible, is too expensive.

In the system forming the subject of this invention I have endeavoured to reconcile as far as possible technical advantages with financial requirements. It
30 may be applied to any line of tramway or railway which is already being worked. The negative pole of the dynamo is placed in communication with the rails, and the underground conductor starts from the positive pole of the dynamo and is buried at a suitable depth say of about 30 centimetres along the various branches of the line. From this conductor, which constitutes the main conductor of the
35 whole system, branches are led to contact boxes located between the two rails at distances apart that are about equal to the length of a car, as in arrangements heretofore proposed.

My invention relates to improvements in the construction and operation of the contact boxes; in the manner in which these are arranged; in the means employed
40 for supplying electric current directly from the boxes without opening them; and in a very simple manner of solving the important question of insulation.

In the accompanying drawings,

Figs. 1 and 2 are respectively a longitudinal section, and a transverse section showing the arrangement of a car and the adjacent part of the track according to
45 my invention.

Fig. 3 is a part section to a larger scale showing the arrangement of one of the contact boxes one of the holding down bolts having been omitted, and part of the contact piece broken away.

[*Price 8d.*]

---

2   N° 8502.—A.D. 1893.

Wise's Improvements in Electrical Railways and Tramways.

Fig. 4 is a diagrammatic plan of a part of the same.
Fig. 4A is a vertical cross section to a smaller scale, showing a cylindrical contact box made of cast iron.
Figs. 5, 6 7 and 8 are detail views hereinafter referred to.

As shown in Fig. 1 the contact box A^1 is not in operation, so that it is not
5 transmitting current to the car, whereas the contact box A^2 is in operation. The boxes remain always closed, and the enclosed devices operate to place the underground cable in communication with a metal piece b^1 which is suitably insulated and fitted in the cover of the box, as shown in Figs. 3 and 6 in longitudinal and transverse section respectively. From this piece b^1 the current
10 passes to the electro-motor on the car by means of the plate b^2 (Figs. 1, 3 and 6) of metal and of suitable dimensions, which connects with an arrangement of springs c^1, c^2, and d^1, d^2 (Fig. 1) that have for object to impart to it suitable tension and elasticity. From the motor the current passes to the rails to return to the negative pole of the dynamo.

15 In order to obtain the above stated tension and elasticity in the plate b^2, the springs $c^1 d^1$ and $c^2 d^2$ (Fig. 1) are mounted on slides capable of being moved by means of a screw and hand wheel, in such a manner that they can be moved in a longitudinal direction to produce the necessary tension which it is desired to give to the plate, and in a vertical direction in order to establish a suitable contact of
20 the latter with the pieces b^1 of the boxes. As the construction of these slides and screws here referred to, is obvious, they are not shown in the drawings.

The springs $d^1 d^2$ are suitably insulated at their point of attachment to the slides, and they are connected to the springs $c^1 c^2$ in such a manner that the thin part of the former has attached to it the thick part of the latter. The bolt which holds
25 them together is preferably square, so as not to allow the springs $c^1 c^2$ to rotate thereon.

The current might be taken from the boxes ($A^1 A^2$) by means of a series of brushes; it is however obvious that the means I have described are less costly, are
30 stronger, and require less expense of maintenance.

The manner in which at the desired instant, communication is established or is interrupted between the underground cable and the contact piece b^1 is shown more clearly in Figs. 3 and 4. The insulated wire, which enters the contact box at the point B starting from the main conductor, is attached to the safety fuse v. From
35 the latter another wire leads to a small mercury vessel r^1 being secured by means of the screw s which also serves to fix the said mercury vessel upon the insulating piece e. Another wire attached in the same manner to a mercury vessel r^2 (Fig. 4) is connected to a stirrup b^6 by means of the fastening pin f of the stirrup and a screw s^1 (Figs. 3 and 5) so that it communicates with the contact piece b^1 by a
40 holding down bolt b^3 which is arranged in the same manner and serves the same purpose as the other holding down bolt b^3 which might be connected to a second stirrup b^5. As will be obvious the mercury cup r^2 might be electrically connected with the stirrup b^5 and bolt b^3 or with each of the stirrups and bolts and thus with the contact piece b^1.

45 It is required when the car is to pass the contact box, that connection shall be made between r^1 and r^2, thus placing the underground conductor in communication with the contact piece b^1, and after the car has passed that the connection shall be broken. This is effected in the following manner:—

m^1 and m^2 are two permanent magnets connected together at their centre and
50 capable of rocking in the supports l^1 and l^2. They are arranged in such a manner as to each have the south pole on one and the same side of a vertical plane passing through the axes about which the magnets turn, the north pole being consequently at the opposite side of such plane. Now assuming that the south poles of these two magnets are on the left hand side, and that a vertical electro-magnet (M^1 or M^2
55 Fig. 1) having its north pole pointing to the ground, passes over to the cover of the box, the system of magnets $m^1 m^2$ will partly turn upon its axis in the direction indicated by arrows in Fig. 3 and the contacts at the end of the wires o will be

Wise's Improvements in Electrical Railways and Tramways.

raised out of the mercury in the cups r^1 r^2. Thus the communication between b^1 and the underground cable previously established by the wire O, which starting from the vessel r^1 suitably winds around the magnets m^1 m^2 (Figs. 3 and 4) and passes into r^2, will be broken.

By the use of the insulated wire O it is unnecessary to insulate the system of magnets m^1 m^2, while the latter are from time to time replenished with magnetism which without the arrangement described, they would have a tendency to lose in the course of time.

The electro-magnets M^1 M^2 (Fig. 1) each having only a single pole directed towards the contact box might be replaced by electro magnets of horse shoe or U-form arranged to attract and move a piece of iron in the interior of the box against the action of a spring or gravity, the movements of the piece of iron being utilised in various ways to make and break the electric circuit, but this arrangement besides necessitating a larger quantity of electro magnetic force, could scarcely offer all the advantages of the one just referred to.

For example with my system it is not necessary that the electro magnets should be kept in circuit during stoppages, and assuming that the current should fail from any cause, even for an instant, the car will be able to continue its progress at once. For this purpose it will be sufficient to push the car backwards as far as the last contact box which will have remained included, and which will not be very far because the driver will have taken care to stop the car immediately he perceived that there was no longer any current. This difficulty in other known systems is sometimes met with the aid of accumulators which are very expensive, very heavy to draw, and very troublesome to maintain.

In other systems in which the current is taken up from insulated bars, it is also usual to employ accumulators in order to start the car at the stopping stations, because it is necessary to interrupt communication between the under ground cable and the bar in order that a person crossing the rails quite close to the car shall not be liable to receive a strong electric discharge.

It should also be noted (which is of great importance) that the cut out which I have adopted makes and breaks communication at a time when no current is passing, thereby obviating the possibility of producing sparks which would have amongst other drawbacks that of consuming gradually the mercury contained in the vessels r^1 r^2. I have not the intention of dilating here upon all the advantages of the cut out which I have described nor upon a great number of advantages relative to the general arrangement of my system of electric railways.

The description which follows will render more clear that which I have just set forth.

Referring to the car shown in Fig. 1 and assuming it to be travelling in the direction indicated by the arrow, the electro magnets M^1 M^2 are excited in series in such a manner that if one has its south pole pointing to the ground, the other will present its north pole to the ground, and *vice versa* if the current which circulates round them be reversed. Let us now assume that the magnets m^1 m^2 of the contact boxes present their south poles to the left hand of the person viewing Figure 3, then the electro magnet M^1 should be so arranged as to have its south pole pointing towards the ground, whilst M^2 will have its north pole pointing to the ground, so as in the first case to depress the contacts on the pivoted magnets, and in the second case to raise them.

In the position in which the car is shown in Fig. 1 communication in the contact box A^1, is shortly about to be established between r^1 r^2, whilst in A^2 this communication is about to be interrupted immediately after the car shall have passed; and it will be seen that for this reason the boxes will not be at all dangerous when they are not quite underneath the car, so that traffic can take place freely around said boxes at the stopping stations.

As long as a contact box is underneath the car it will be in circuit, which will allow the car to resume its travel.

In order to ensure that the magnets m^1 m^2 shall positively remain in the required

Wise's Improvements in Electrical Railways and Tramways.

position after being operated, a light spring pressure may be applied, or the said magnets may be made hollow and be each provided internally with a round weight such for instance as a small ball of lead which when the magnets are operated will fall to the lower part and thus aid the magnets to remain in the desired position.

If it be desired to cause the car to travel backwards, it will be sufficient to reverse the current in the electro magnets M^1 M^2 whilst operating in the usual manner as to the rest.

In order to prolong the action of the electro-magnets M^1 M^2 upon the magnets m^1 m^2 of the contact boxes it will be necessary (especially if the carriages are run at a high speed) to keep the said magnets M^1 M^2 at some distance above the ground, and to provide their lower end, lengthwise of the carriage, with an iron plate, as shown in Fig. 1, forming a $\perp$ cross section.

The sides top and bottom of the contact box which play a very important part with respect to insulation, are of wood, but they may be formed of any other suitable material so long as the arrangement satisfies the essential condition of insulation.

When the four sides and the bottom of the box have been put together, they are immersed in a bath of thin tar or of suitable varnish at a temperature sufficiently high to allow them to become thoroughly impregnated for the purpose of protecting them from moisture and of imparting to them a better insulating property. After this there is applied to the bottom and to the sides, up to about the point P (Fig. 3) a covering of suitable metal such as zinc, which should also be coated with varnish, for better preservation.

From the point P upwards and to the cover which will have been treated in a similar manner as just described there will be applied a plentiful coating of tar, which should be subsequently renewed from time to time, as regards the cover and which will constitute one of the slight expenses of maintenance that will have to be incurred.

By the construction described leakage of current, is very effectually prevented and the necessary insulation of the piece b^1 from the ground (Figs. 3 & 6) is ensured.

The piece b^1 is bedded upon a sheet or strip g^1 of suitable insulating material such as india rubber, and the cover of the box of which only one, viz. b^3 is shown, placed between its edges and the sides of the box as seen in Fig. 3. These rubber strips also serve to effect a hermetic closure of the contact box.

It will thus be seen that the current cannot leak to the rails after leaving the contact piece b^1, save through the insulating material at g^1 and g^2, and also in addition the resistance of the suitably prepared or treated wooden cover itself.

Fig. 4^A represents one form of cast iron contact box.

The openings through the contact piece b^1 in the cover of each box are hermetically closed by the holding down bolts of which only one, viz. b^3 is shown, and which have countersunk heads and are screwed at their lower ends on to the stirrups b^5 and b^6 (Fig. 3) a section of one of which is shown in Fig. 5. Either or both of these bolts may be used to communicate the current to the contact piece although usually, one as described is ample.

At the points where the stirrups above mentioned are connected to the cross piece t, the latter is covered with a strip g^3 of india rubber (Figs. 3 and 5), the mode of attachment of the stirrups being clearly shown in the drawings.

When the contact box is once closed, arrangements may be made to prevent the bolts of the stirrups being improperly removed as it is only for repairs that removal is required.

The contact box may rest on a foundation of concrete and should be so strong that heavy loads which may pass over it will not damage it. The cover as shown in Fig. 3, forms with the cross piece t by means of the bolts and the stirrups of attachment, a compound beam. Moreover it can easily be arranged by notices or otherwise that heavy carts are not to pass over the boxes and this can be more

Wise's Improvements in Electrical Railways and Tramways.

easily avoided as the boxes are located about 6 metres distant from one another. However the said boxes are made sufficiently strong to prevent injury in case of a heavy waggon going over them.

The contact boxes have a height of about 25 centimetres so that the soil need be excavated only to a very small depth in order to lay the contact boxes and the insulated main conductor and thus avoiding the drawback of meeting with gas, water or sewer pipes. The said boxes will not cause inconvenience to foot passengers, or to vehicular traffic, because the centre of the cover will be only about 4 cm. at the highest point, above the ground the said 4 cm. forming the rise of an arc of a circle having a chord of about 40 cm. that is to say the curve of the cover will be scarcely felt.

For tramways or railways where the roadway is private or where the rails project above the surface of the track, the boxes may also project from the ground to a height of several centimetres which projecting portion is suitably coated with tar, and then the track between the two rails has no longer need of any special treatment.

It will in all cases where the contact boxes are almost flush with the roadway, be well to make use of a special stone clearer to protect the current collecting plate b^3 from pebbles or other obstructions which might be in line therewith and apt to come in contact with it. This stone-clearer may be of very simple construction.

One form is shown in Figs. 7 and 8 which are views at right angles to one another. It comprises a wheel of a width slightly greater than the plate journalled in a fork F of a steel spring arm L secured to the underframe of the car by a flexible joint I. This wheel is normally situated slightly above the ground (at a height of about 2 cm.) and is capable of rotating in F on the axle D. In order to enable it to pass over the contact boxes, the aforesaid stirrup is made capable of yielding below the point of attachment I. The wheel R has at its periphery a rubber tyre.

In winter, if necessary, there may be employed a snow clearer N (Fig. 1) and a suitable brush which will precede the electro-magnets and will clean the contact pieces.

By employing two plates b^2 on the cars and two contact pieces on the contact boxes, a return cable for the electric current may be used instead of utilizing the rails and the earth for this purpose although this would detract from the simplicity of the various apparatus and the working, besides increasing the cost of installation of the apparatus.

It is obvious that in adopting the system forming the subject of the present application, the details of construction may be modified without departing from the nature of the invention, and I therefore do not intend to restrict my invention to the constructional details described and illustrated in the accompanying drawings.

Having now particularly described and ascertained the nature of the said invention and in what manner the same is to be performed I declare that what I claim is :—

1. In the underground distribution of an electric current for electrical railways and tramways by means of contact pieces arranged along the track and of a collecting plate secured to the vehicle to be propelled, and sliding upon the said contact pieces, the arrangement by means of which the contact pieces b^1 are connected to the underground conductor comprising mercury vessels r^1, r^2, and a conductor o surrounding a permanent magnet $m^1 m^2$ operated by the vehicle itself through the electro-magnets $M^1 M^2$, which cause the said permanent magnet to assume a position for making or breaking the electric connection between the main conductor and the motor on the vehicle substantially as described and shown for the purpose specified.

2. In the arrangement referred to in the preceding claim, for the purpose of

Wise's Improvements in Electrical Railways and Tramways.

avoiding sparkling in the mercury vessels r^1, r^2, the arrangement of the electro-magnets M^1, M^2, at a suitable distance from the collecting plate b^3, so as to complete the electric connection when the said plate comes into sliding contact with the contact piece b^1 and not to interrupt such connection until the plate has left the said contact piece, substantially as described and shown for the purpose specified.

3. In the arrangement described in Claim 1, a device for collecting the current, consisting of a plate b^3 secured to two sets of springs c^1, d^1, c^2, d^2, capable of a longitudinal and transverse movement, substantially as described and shown for the purpose specified.

4. In electrical railways and tramways, the arrangement of the device for making and breaking the connection between the underground cable and the contact pieces in permanently closed boxes A^1 A^2, in the covers of which and projecting more or less from the ground, are arranged the insulated contact pieces b^1 for the purpose of effecting a direct distribution of the current, without opening the boxes, substantially as described and shown for the purpose specified.

Dated this 27th day of April 1893.

W. LLOYD WISE,
Per F. J. Brougham,
46, Lincoln's Inn Fields, London, W.C.

London : Printed for Her Majesty's Stationery Office, by Darling & Son, Ltd.—1898.

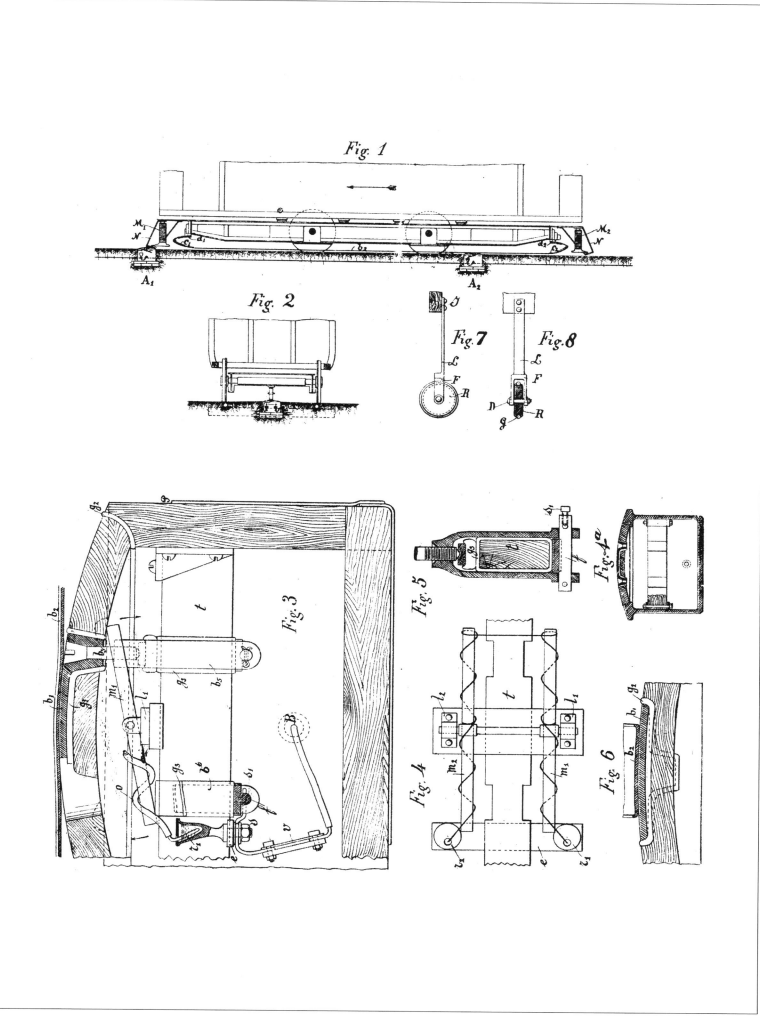

Fig. 1

Fig. 2

Fig. 7

Fig. 8

Fig. 3

Fig. 4

Fig. 5

Fig. 4ª

Fig. 6

N° 8516

A.D. 1893

Date of Application, 27th Apr., 1893—Accepted, 21st Oct., 1893

COMPLETE SPECIFICATION.

Apparatus for Sanding Street Railway Car Tracks.

We, DAVID ALBERT GHENT, and OCTAVIUS SYDNEY COLBRAN, both of Burlington, in the County of Halton, in the Province of Ontario, Dominion of Canada, Gentlemen, do hereby declare that we are in possession of an invention for AN APPARATUS FOR SANDING STREET RAILWAY CAR TRACKS, and in what manner the same is to be performed, to be particularly described and ascertained in and by the following statement:—

The invention relates to a very simple, but handy and useful device for sanding street railway car tracks, when the conditions are such as to cause the wheels to slide on the track when the car cannot be stopped short with the brakes, and which can be operated instantly by the driver pressing his foot on a projecting knob on the platform floor of a car.

The device consists, first, in a reservoir of any shape, preferably of sheet metal, filled with fine sand and bolted to or otherwise secured on the floor of a car in any convenient place, such as at both ends under the seat, resting on the floor. It is provided with a valve seat and valve, with a rubber tube attached to conduct the sand to the track.

Second. An eccentric wheel is secured to the valve spindle, said wheel having a connecting rod leading to and connected with a second eccentric attached to a block affixed to the floor beams of a car, and on the opposite side of the eccentric is attached an operating rod made to pass up through the floor of the car a very short distance, convenient to be pressed down by the foot of the driver to open the valve to allow sand to escape when necessary.

Third. A counter balance weight is attached to the large eccentric which by its gravity always keeps the valve closed automatically until it is wished to open it for sanding the track to prevent the wheels from sliding when the track is wet or greasy from any cause.

Reference being made to the accompanying drawing in which Fig. 1 is a side section of a street car.

Fig. 2 is an end view of valve-seat and valve closed with eccentric.

Fig. 3, shows the eccentrics and balance weight when the valve is open and the sand running out.

Fig. 4, is a side view of valve-spindle in the position it is when open.

In the drawing A represents any ordinary street car, B the wheels, one only thought necessary to represent. C, is the platform for the driver. D, is a reservoir of sheet metal preferably secured in front of the wheels at each end of a car under the seat, and with an opening through the bottom of it immediately over the rails. M, is a valve seat attached to the reservoir D, having a vertical opening a through it, and a horizontal opening b at right angles to and crossing the vertical one a, to contain a valve spindle d, having a valve opening e cut through it as shown at Fig. 2 for the admission of sand from the reservoir to the rubber tube D¹ attached to the under side of the valve-seat M, when the said opening e is in a vertical position in the valve as in Fig. 4. E, is an eccentric wheel secured to the valve spindle d, to which a connecting screw rod F is attached to another eccentric G, secured on a short shaft or stud e^1 attached to a block H bolted to the floor beams of a car. I, is a vertical operating rod pivoted to a stud f on the eccentric G on the opposite side from where the connecting rod F is secured; the said rod projects through an opening in the floor of a car but not far enough to be operated by a driver's foot without a movable hollow cap g being placed over it, when the device is easily operated by the driver, pressure of his foot downwards on it opens the valve d, through the medium of the eccentric G, connecting rod F and eccentric E,

[*Price 8d.*]

---

2   N° 8516.—A.D. 1893.

Ghent & Colbran's Apparatus for Sanding Street Railway Car Tracks.

and the sand runs out of the spout D¹ by its gravity as long as the driver's foot is kept on the cap g. When he releases his foot from the cap g, the valve d closes immediately by means of the counterbalance weight h attached by a rod to the large eccentric G; when the valve is closed the balance-weight is in the position shown at Fig. 1; when the valve is open the weight is in the position shown at Fig. 3.

It will be seen that when the atmospheric or other conditions are such that car wheels will not revolve when the brakes are applied, but slide on the track, as they usually do in wet weather, the driver has at his control a simple device to sand the track by pressure of his foot, when in any case of emergency he wishes to instantly stop his car, to prevent accident, which can now easily be done by turning off the power and applying the brakes and opening the sand valve. Many collisions occur at railway crossings in a city when an electric street car crashes into a passing railway train, on account of the difficulty of stopping a car in a short distance, or on down grade, when the tracks are in such a condition (as often happens) when the car wheels slide on them after the brakes are applied.

Having now particularly described the nature of our said invention and in what manner the same is to be performed, we declare that what we claim is,—

1st. In combination with a street railway car, a sand reservoir attached thereto having a valve adjusted to the same and an eccentric secured to it, and a connecting rod from it to a second eccentric to which is fastened a vertical operating foot lever to open the valve to admit sand to the track rails, and a counter-balance weight attached on one of the eccentrics to automatically close the valve and shut off the sand when pressure is removed from the operating lever-rod, substantially as specified.

2nd. In combination with a street railway car, the reservoir D, valve seat M, valve d, eccentric E, connecting rod F, eccentric G on the stud e^1, operating rod I, substantially as and for the purpose specified.

3rd. In combination with a street railway car, the reservoir D, valve seat M, valve spindle d, eccentric E on valve spindle d, adjustable connecting-rod F, attaching eccentric E to eccentric G, operating rod I, counter-balance weight h, and pipe D¹, all constructed substantially as and for the purpose specified.

Dated, at Hamilton, Ontario, this 7th day of April 1893.

DAVID ALBERT GHENT.
OCTAVIUS SYDNEY COLBRAN.

Signed in the presence of
R. J. FITZGERALD.
W. BRUCE.

London : Printed for Her Majesty's Stationery Office, by Darling & Son, Ltd.—1893.

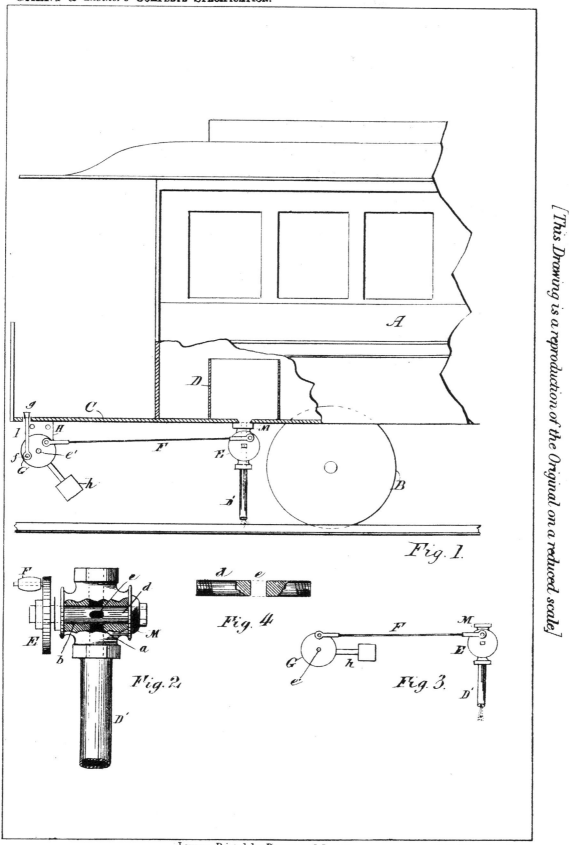

Fig. 1.

Fig. 2.

Fig. 3.

Fig. 4.

[This Drawing is a reproduction of the Original on a reduced scale]

London.—Printed by Darling and Son Ld.
for Her Majesty's Stationery Office. 1893.

Malby & Sons, Photo-Litho.

2   Nº 15,560.—A.D. 1894.

ImpꝮts. in connection with Motive Power Engines for Driving Tramway Cars, &c.

supported and the engine for working the pump is mounted in the body of the vehicle. The supply pipe or passage for water from the pump to the hydraulic engine or engines passes through the axis or axes of the bogie or bogies and through an outer pipe through which the water after acting in the hydraulic engine or engines returns to the tank from which the pump draws the water. These pipes are provided with stuffing boxes which permit of the required movements of the bogie or bogies and between the pump and the hydraulic engine or engines a valve is or valves are provided by means of which the driver can as desired or when required cause the water to pass from the pump direct to the tank from which the said pump is supplied and thereby prevent the water from entering the hydraulic engines to drive the vehicle. In order that my invention may be well understood I will further describe the same with reference to the accompanying drawings which illustrate the application of the said invention to a tramcar having a driving bogie at one end only of the car it being obvious however that a driving bogie may be provided at each end of the car if desired.

Figure 1 is a sectional elevation of so much of the tramcar as is necessary to illustrate the invention.

Figures 2 and 3 are respectively a sectional elevation and a plan of the driving bogie and

Figure 4 is a vertical section (drawn to a larger scale) of the pipes or passages through the axis of the bogie for water to and from the hydraulic engines.

A is the frame or bottom of the main body of the car beneath one end of which is a water tank B from which water is pumped into the hydraulic engines C carried ou a bogie D on which the opposite end of the body of the car is supported. E are pumps the suction pipes e of which enter the tank B and the delivery pipes f communicate by a pipe g with a chamber h in proximity to the hydraulic engines C. The pumps E are worked by a gas, oil, or other suitable motor F situated in the body of the car the piston of the said motor imparting rotation by a rod k to a pinion l in gear with a wheel m on a shaft or spindle n carrying an eccentric p in connection with the piston rod of the pumps the said eccentric being provided with a link or lever motion or other suitable means by which the stroke of the pump pistons may be varied as required. The chamber h communicates with the cylinder of the hydraulic engine C, by pipes or passages G and H arranged concentrically one within the other as shewn in Figure 4 the said concentric pipes passing through the axis of the bogie D the said pipes being free to turn in stuffing boxes or cup leathers q in the chamber h to admit of the turning of the bogie when passing round curves. The chamber h is divided by a partition r into two compartments s s^2 the pipe or passage G which is the inlet passage to the hydraulic engine opening into the upper compartment s and the pipe or passage H which is the exhaust passage from the hydraulic engine communicating with the lower compartment S^2 from which compartment the exhaust fluid is conducted by a pipe i into the tank B. The piston or plunger of the hydraulic engine is connected by a rod t with a crank u on one of the axles of the bogie so that by the reciprocation of the said piston or plunger rotation is given to the wheels of the bogie to propel the car. In the delivery pipe g in connection with the pumps E is a valve v and a branch pipe w leading to the tank B the said valve v being capable of being operated by the driver by means of a lever x so as to conduct the water from the pumps either through the pipe g into the hydraulic engines or through the branch pipe w back into the tank from which it was pumped. By this means the necessity for stopping the motor F when the car is required to be stopped is obviated as by turning the valve v so as to conduct the water back to the tank the pumps may continue to work as the water will simply circulate through the pump and the tank, whilst the car can be readily started by simply turning the valve v so as to conduct the water through the pipe g into the hydraulic engine. By varying the stroke of the pumps by means of a link or lever the motion as shown or equivalent means the speed of the car can be regulated as required.

Nº 15,560   A.D. 1894

Date of Application, 15th Aug, 1894

Complete Specification Left, 15th May, 1895—Accepted, 6th July, 1895

PROVISIONAL SPECIFICATION.

Improvements in connection with Motive Power Engines for Driving Tramway Cars and other Vehicles.

I, Sir EUSTACE FITZMAURICE PIERS, Bart. of 41 Finsbury Pavement in the City of London Mechanical Engineer do hereby declare the nature of this invention to be as follows:—

This invention relates to certain improvements upon apparatus for driving tramway cars and other vehicles for which Letters Patent were granted to me bearing date as of the 6th day of February 1889 No, 2144 my present invention consisting of an improved arrangement of the hydraulic engine or engines and the engine for working the pumps by which water is forced into the hydraulic engine or engines is or are carried on a bogie or on bogies upon which the body of the vehicle is supported and the engine for working the pump is mounted in the body of the vehicle. The supply pipe or passage for water for working the pump to the hydraulic engine or engines passes through the axis or axes of the bogie or bogies and the engine or engines passes through an outer pipe through which the water after acting in the hydraulic engine or engines returns to the tank from which the pump draws the water. These pipes are provided with stuffing boxes which permit of the required movements of the bogie or bogies and between the pump and the hydraulic engine or engines a valve is or valves are provided by means of which the driver can as desired or when required cause the water to pass from the pump direct to the tank from which the said pump is supplied and thereby prevent the water from entering the hydraulic engines to drive the vehicle.

Dated this 16th day of August 1894.

JOHNSONS & WILLCOX,
Agents.

COMPLETE SPECIFICATION.

Improvements in connection with Motive Power Engines for Driving Tramway Cars and other Vehicles.

I, Sir EUSTACE FITZMAURICE PIERS, Bart., of 41 Finsbury Pavement, in the City of London, Mechanical Engineer, do hereby declare the nature of this invention and in what manner the same is to be performed to be particularly described and ascertained in and by the following statement:—

This invention relates to certain improvements upon apparatus for driving tramway cars and other vehicles for which Letters Patent were granted to me bearing date as of the 6th day of February 1889 No. 2144 my present invention consisting of an improved arrangement of the hydraulic engine or engines and the engine for working the pumps by which water is forced into the hydraulic engine or engines is or are carried on a bogie or on bogies upon which the body of the vehicle is

[*Price 8d.*]

Impts. in connection with Motive Power Engines for Driving Tramway Cars, &c.

Having now particularly described and ascertained the nature of my said invention and in what manner the same is to be performed I declare that what I claim is :—

1. In connection with motive power engines for driving tram cars or other vehicles the combination of a primary motor situated in the body of the vehicle and a secondary motor or motors carried on a bogie or on bogies on which the main body of the vehicle is carried the primary motor operating a pump or pumps for supplying fluid under pressure to the secondary motor the said fluid passing through passages in the axis or axes of the bogie or bogies to and from the secondary motor or motors substantially as hereinbefore described.

2. The combination and arrangement of parts constituting means for driving tram cars and other vehicles substantially as hereinbefore described and illustrated by the accompanying drawing.

Dated this 15th day of May 1895.

JOHNSONS & WILLCOX,
Agents.

London : Printed for Her Majesty's Stationery Office, by Darling & Son, Ltd.—1895

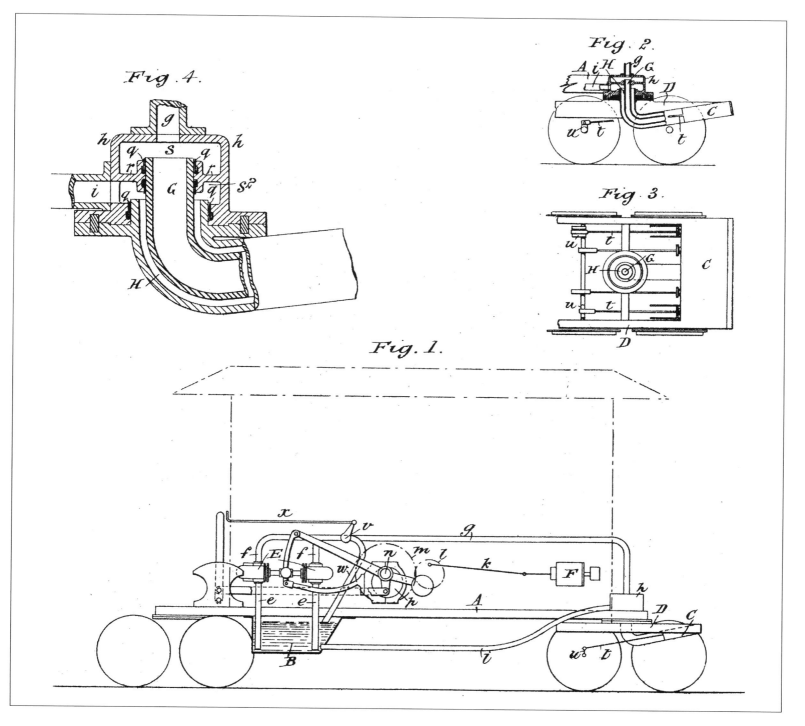

Fig. 4.

Fig. 2.

Fig. 3.

Fig. 1.

N° 24,573

A.D. 1894

Date of Application, 18th Dec., 1894—Accepted, 2nd Feb., 1895

COMPLETE SPECIFICATION.

Improvements in or connected with the Working of the Points or Switches of Tramway and Railway Lines.

I, JAMES WALKER LITTLEJOHN, of The Anchorage, by Kilmalcolm, in the County of Renfrew, North Britain, Wine Merchant, do hereby declare the nature of this invention and in what manner the same is to be performed, to be particularly described and ascertained in and by the following statement :—

5 This invention relates to improvements in or connected with the working of the points or switches of tramway and railway lines, and consists as follows :—

In carrying out my said invention I provide the free end of the pivoted point or switch with projecting arms and inclined plane portions ; either of which may be actuated when desired by the driver, through the medium of suitable arrangements
10 of levers and wheels which may be actuated by foot or otherwise ; one of said arrangements being mounted at each end of the car or other vehicle.

But in order that my said invention may be more readily understood, and easily carried into effect, I will proceed to describe the same with reference to the accompanying drawings.

15 Figure 1 is a plan and Figure 2 a sectional elevation of a tramway line having my improvements attached.

Figure 3 is a part end elevation, Figure 4 a part side elevation and Figure 5 an under plan of a tramway car having my improvements attached.

Referring to Figures 1 and 2 of the said drawings, I attach to both sides of the
20 free end a, of the pivoted point or switch A, projecting arms B, B¹, having inclined plane portions C, C¹ attached to their outer ends as shown. The said arms B, B¹, and inclined plane portions C, C¹ being mounted in a suitable casing or box, which is embedded in the road or street so that its top side will be level with the surface of the road or street ; this box is formed with two tracks or grooves E
25 for enabling the the inclined plane portions C, C¹ to be acted upon.

Referring to Figures 3, 4 and 5, I provide each end of the tramway car or other vehicle with an arrangement of actuating levers and wheels, that is to say, I pivot, screw or otherwise mount, below the foot plate F, a pair of levers G, H, the outer ends of which are provided with loosely mounted revolving rollers or wheels G¹, H¹,
30 one for each of the inclined plane portions C, C¹ of the point or switch A. The said levers G and H are provided with depressing rods g and h, the upper ends of which pass through the foot plate F and are provided with small foot plates g¹ and h¹, so as to enable the driver by means of his foot to press down one or other of the wheels G¹, H¹ into the tracks E of the bore D ; said wheels G¹, H¹ being
35 returned to their normal positions (as shown) on the downward pressure being removed or withdrawn, by means of the spring portions g² and h², of the levers G and H ; also if desired one or both of the said levers may be provided with guide brackets G³.

The whole arrangement is such, that supposing a car is upon the main line of
40 rails J (Figures 1 and 2) and driving in the direction of the arrow, with the point or switch A lying in any position ; now if the driver wishes to continue on the same straight line of rails J, all he requires to do is to depress the foot plate g¹ and so cause the wheel G¹ to enter into the track E of the box and so place the point or switch A into the position shown by means of the wheel G¹ pressing past the
45 plane portion C, and thus enabling the car to go straight on ; but on the other hand should the driver wish to go along the other line of rails J¹ he would depress

[*Price 8d.*]

2

N° 24,573.—A.D. 1894.

Impts. in the Working of the Points or Switches of Tramway and Railway Lines.

the foot plate h¹ and wheel H¹ and so cause the point A to be pushed into the opposite position than that shown and so enable the car to pass on to the branch or other line J¹.

A similar arrangement to the foregoing may be employed on railway lines, the
5 actuating lever arrangements being mounted on the locomotive.

Having now particularly described and ascertained the nature of my said invention and in what manner the same is to be performed, I declare that what I claim is :—

1st. The general arrangement, construction and combination of the various parts,
10 constituting the improvements in working the points or switches of tramway and railway lines, substantially as hereinbefore described and shown in the accompanying drawings.

2nd. In working the points or switches, of tramway and railway lines, providing the free end of the point or switch with two projections or arms and inclined plane
15 portions, capable of moving sideways in an embedded box or case, substantially as hereinbefore and shown in Figures 1 and 2 of the accompanying drawings.

3rd. In working the points or switches of tramway or railway lines, providing each end of the car with an arrangement of levers G and H, having wheels or rollers G¹ and H¹, and their connections whereby the driver is enabled to actuate
20 the point or switch in the direction required, substantially as hereinbefore described and shown in Figures 3, 4 and of the accompanying drawings.

Dated this 17th day of December 1894.

JOHNSONS,
115, St. Vincent Street, Glasgow, Applicant's Agents.

London : Printed for Her Majesty's Stationery Office, by Darling & Son, Ltd.—1895

(2 SHEETS)
SHEET 1.

A.D. 1894. Dec. 18. Nº. 24,573.
LITTLEJOHN'S COMPLETE SPECIFICATION.

Malby & Sons, Photo-Litho.

London: Printed by Darling and Son Ld.
for Her Majesty's Stationery Office. 1895.

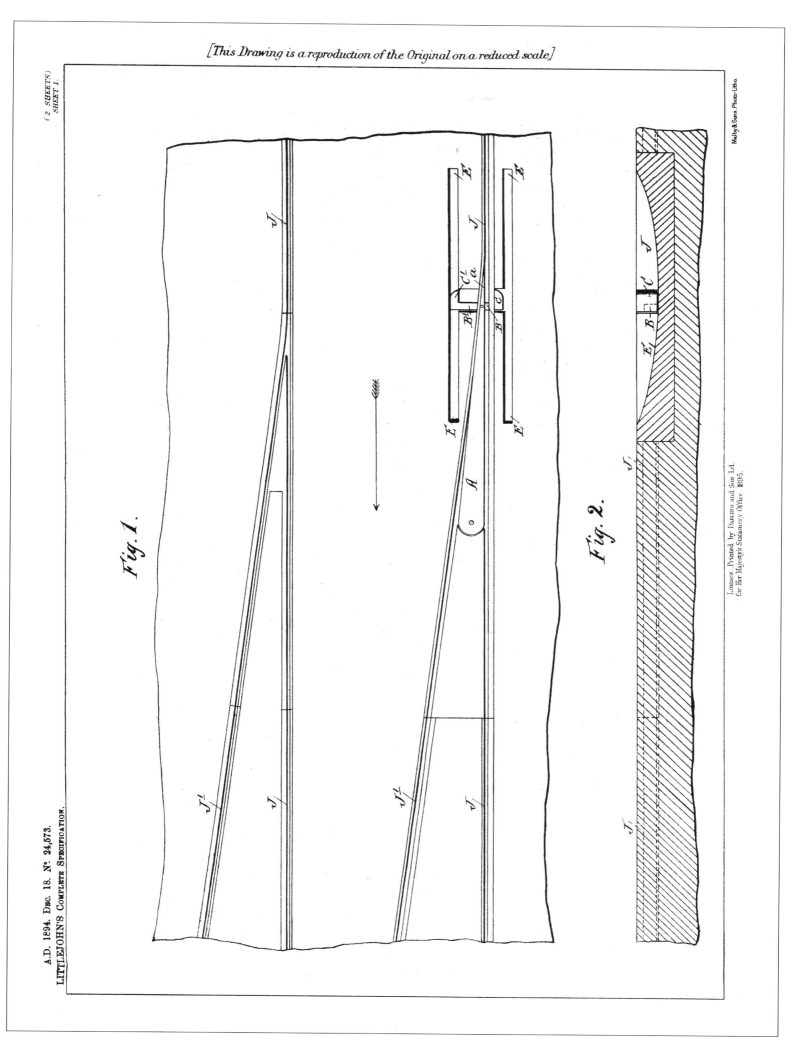

Fig. 1.

Fig. 2.

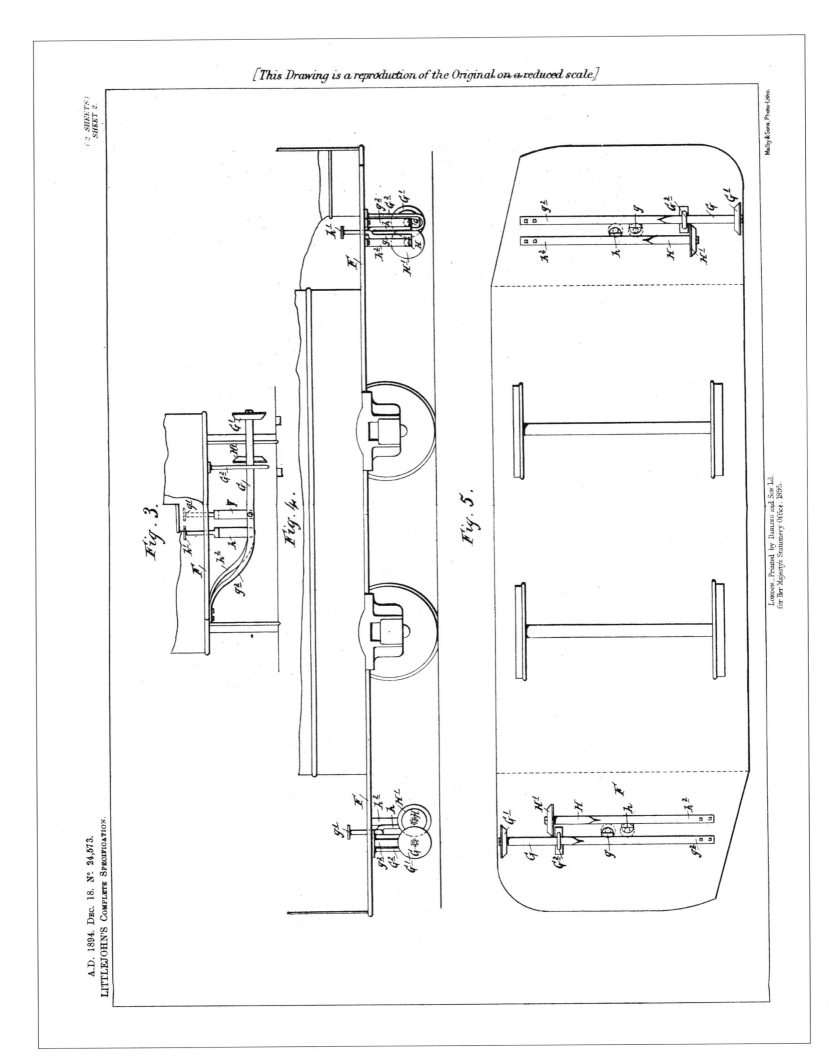

A.D. 1894. Dec. 18. Nº 24,573.

LITTLEJOHN'S Complete Specification.

(2 SHEETS)
SHEET 2.

Malby & Sons, Photo-Litho.

London. Printed by Darling and Son Ld.
for Her Majesty's Stationery Office. 1895.

Fig. 3.

Fig. 4.

Fig. 5.

N° 2123   **A.D. 1895**

Date of Application, 30th Jan., 1895

Complete Specification Left, 16th Oct., 1895—Accepted, 16th Nov., 1895

PROVISIONAL SPECIFICATION.

Improvements in Rail-clearing and Safety Appliances for Tramcars.

I, HANS HINRICH STÖLTING, of 36 Lornsenstrasse, Altona, Germany, Gentleman, do hereby declare the nature of this invention to be as follows:—

In consequence of the ever increasing extension of mechanical and electrical power propulsion for tramways, and of the accidents resulting therefrom, there is felt more and more the want of a suitable and reliable safety appliance. The rail-clearers provided in front of railway locomotives have to be situated at a considerable height above the rails, in order that they shall not come in contact with the track and be destroyed by it when commencing to climb a rising gradient.

In consequence of the sharp curves on tramways, the wheel base is usually very short and therefore necessitates a much longer understructure for the front and hind portions of the car, so that a rail-clearer of the kind referred to would have to be situated considerably higher than is the case in railway locomotives, and would thus do more damage than it would be of use.

Now this invention relates to a rail-clearing device, with catching apparatus, that is arranged underneath the car as near as possible to and in front of the wheels, and which can therefore be situated and fixed within a very short distance of the rails, or can be made movable, as illustrated in the accompanying drawings.

The apparatus is illustrated in Figs. 1 & 2, in side elevation, and in Fig. 3 in plan, and consists of two hook-shaped hangers or drag-links a and b, which are connected together by means of a cross-piece c. These hangers oscillate in eye-bolts a^1 and b^1 which are elastically guided in casings d by means of springs, rubber buffers or the like. The hook-shaped ends of the hangers slide along on the rails. A net or catching cloth f attached to the car is connected to the hangers in such a manner as to slide over the track and catch up any article lying thereon. A net composed of strong ropes and made with wide meshes can advantageously be used, because a person who might happen to be lying on the track is able to hold on with his hands in the meshes, whilst small articles such as stones or the like, will fall through the same.

A suitable raising and lowering device g, h enables the rail-clearer to be raised during the journey as shewn in Fig. 1, and to be immediately dropped into the position shewn in Fig. 2 in case of need, even though a person should fall down directly in front of the car, or actually be knocked down by it. To prevent the hanging net from becoming entangled with any fixed obstacles, such as projecting stones on the track, and to diminish the sudden jerk exerted thereby upon the eye-bolts a^1 b^1 the latter are mounted in an elastic manner.

In the case of narrow gauges the hooked ends of the hangers or drag-links are bent inwards, or guard plates are fixed on the sides of the same in order to prevent any articles that have been pushed aside by the rail-clearers, from getting under the hind wheels.

Dated this 30th day of January 1895.

F. WISE HOWORTH,
46, Lincoln's Inn Fields, London, W.C., Agent for the Applicant.

[*Price 8d.*]

Stölting's Improvements in Rail-clearing and Safety Appliances for Tramcars.

COMPLETE SPECIFICATION.

Improvements in Rail-clearing and Safety Appliances for Tramcars.

I, HANS HINRICH STÖLTING, of 36, Lornsenstrasse, Altona, Germany, Gentleman, do hereby declare the nature of this invention and in what manner the same is to be performed to be particularly described and ascertained in and by the following statement:—

In consequence of the ever increasing extension of mechanical and electrical power propulsion for tramways, and of the numerous accidents resulting therefrom, there is felt more and more, the want of a suitable and reliable safety-appliance. The rail-clearers heretofore provided in front of railway locomotives have to be situated at a considerable height above the rails, in order that they shall not come into contact with the track and be thereby destroyed when commencing to climb a rising gradient. In consequence of the sharp curves on tramways, the wheel-base is usually very short and therefore necessitates that the front and hind portions of the car project much further, so that a rail-clearer of the kind referred to would have to be situated considerably higher than is the case in railway locomotives, and would thus be more harmful than useful.

Now this invention relates to a rail-clearing device, with catching apparatus, that is arranged underneath the car as near as possible to, and in front of, the wheels, and which can be situated and fixed so as to be within a very short distance of the rails, or can be raised above the rails, as I will now proceed to explain by aid of the illustrative drawings filed with my Provisional Specification, wherein

Figs. 1 & 2 are side elevations and Fig. 3 a plan, showing the apparatus applied to a tramcar, Fig. 1 showing it in its inoperative position and Fig. 2 in its operative position.

It comprises two hook-shaped hangers or drag-links a and b, connected together by means of a crosspiece c. These hangers oscillate in eye-bolts a^1 and b^1 which are elastically guided in casings d by means of springs, india-rubber buffers, or the like. The hook-shaped ends of the hangers are adapted to slide along on the rails. A net or catching-cloth f attached to the car is connected to the hangers in such a manner as to slide over the track and catch up any article lying loose thereon. A net composed of strong ropes and made with wide meshes can advantageously be used because a person who might happen to be lying on the track would, after being caught in the net, be able to hold on with his hands in the meshes thereof, whilst small articles, such as stones, would fall through the same.

A suitable raising and lowering device g, h is provided to enable the rail-clearer to be raised during the journey into the position shown in Fig. 1, and to be immediately dropped into that shown in Fig. 2 in case of need—even if a person should fall down directly in front of the car, or actually be knocked down by it.

To prevent the hanging net from becoming entangled with or damaged by any fixed obstacles, such as projecting stones on the track, by diminishing the sudden jerk exerted thereby upon the eye-bolts a^1 b^1, these bolts are mounted in an elastic manner as hereinbefore described and shewn in the drawings.

In the case of narrow gauge tracks, the hooked ends of the hangers a b are bent inwards in a lateral direction, or guard-plates are fixed on the sides of the same, in order to prevent any articles that may have been pushed aside by the rail-clearers, from getting under the travelling wheels of the tramcar.

Stirling's Improvements in Rail-clearing and Safety Appliances for Tramcars.

Having now particularly described and ascertained the nature of this invention and in what manner the same is to be performed I declare that what I claim is :—

1. A rail-clearing device with catching apparatus, comprising two hangers or
5 drag-links *a b*, adapted to be attached to a tram car so as to be held over the track or the rails or to be lowered so as to slide along the said track or rails, and a drag-net or catching cloth *f* connected with the said hangers, substantially as hereinbefore described.

2. In a rail-clearing device of the kind specified in the preceding claim,
10 mounting the hangers or drag-links in an elastic or yielding manner, substantially as hereinbefore described for the purpose set forth.

3. My improved tramcar-rail-clearing and safety appliance constructed arranged and operating as hereinbefore described with reference to and shown in the drawings referred to.

15   Dated this 16th day of October 1895.

F. WISE HOWORTH,
46, Lincoln's Inn Fields, London, W.C., Agent for the Applicant.

London : Printed for Her Majesty's Stationery Office, by Darling & Son, Ltd.—1895

A.D. 1895 Jan 30. Nº 2123.

STOLTING'S PROVISIONAL SPECIFICATION.

(1 SHEET)

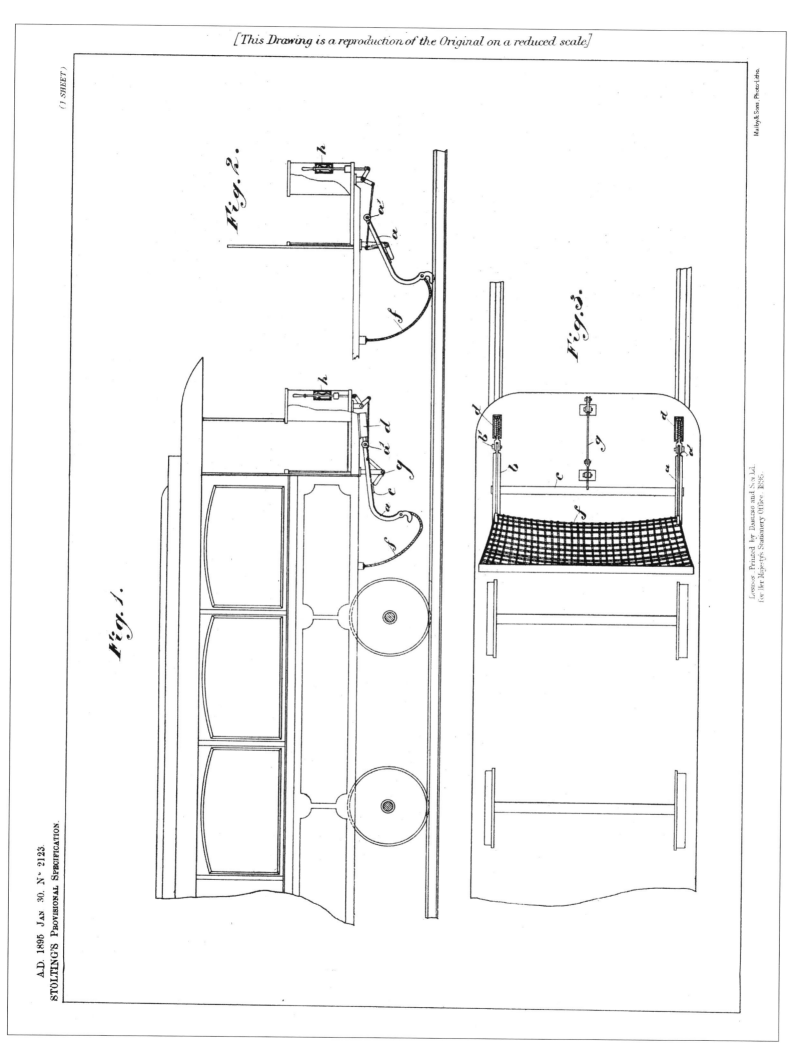

Fig. 1.

Fig. 2.

Fig. 3.

Malby & Sons. Photo-Litho.

London: Printed by Darling and Son Ld.
for Her Majesty's Stationery Office. 1895.

McEwen's Improvements in Apparatus for Stopping and Starting Tram-cars, &c.

COMPLETE SPECIFICATION.

Improvements in Apparatus for Stopping and Starting Tram-cars and other Vehicles.

I, MATTHEW McEWEN, of East Street and Quay, Ramsey, Isle of Man, Ironmonger, do hereby declare the nature of this invention and in what manner the same is to be performed, to be particularly described and ascertained in and by the following statement :—

This invention relates to improved apparatus for stopping and starting tram-cars and other vehicles and has for object to enable the power stored up when the car is stopped to be utilized not only for restarting the car or other vehicle in the same direction but to move it in the reverse direction if desired.

In carrying out my invention I mount two bevel wheels loosely on a shaft fixed to a frame attached to the car or other vehicle, a third bevel wheel mounted loosely on a second spindle, fixed to the said frame at right angles to the first named shaft, gearing with the said two bevel wheels.

The two bevel wheels are provided on their inner faces with clutch teeth, with either set of which a double clutch mounted loosely on the fixed shaft between the two bevel wheels is adapted to engage. In connection with this double clutch a chain wheel is mounted through the medium of which the motion of one or both of the car axles is imparted to the double clutch. In practice the two ends of the clutch are formed separately and connected by rods which slide through the chain wheel so as to permit of the double clutch moving laterally without moving the said chain wheel. To the boss of each of the two bevel wheels is connected one end of a spiral spring, the other end of the spring being connected to the framing attached to the car. These two springs are coiled in opposite directions and adapted to be wound and unwound simultaneously.

To the back of the third bevel wheel is fixed a ratchet provided with a pawl to prevent the springs from unwinding unless it is so desired.

The pawl and the clutches are controlled by the driver of the car or other vehicle by any suitable means.

To enable my invention to be fully understood I will describe the same by reference to the accompanying drawings, in which :—

Figure 1 is a sectional elevation of the lower part of a tram-car having my improved apparatus applied thereto :

Figure 2 is a plan of the framing of the car provided with my improved apparatus, and,

Figures 3, 4 and 5 are views of details.

a is the frame of the car and *b*, *b* the axles of the same, *c* is a shaft supported in bearings *d*, *d* and *e*, *f* are the two bevel wheels mounted loosely on the same. *g* is the third bevel wheel mounted loosely on the spindle *h* secured in a framing *i* attached to the frame *a* of the car.

j, *k* are the clutch teeth on the inner face of the bevel wheels *e f* respectively and *l*, *l*¹ are the two ends of the double clutch mounted loosely on the shaft *c* and connected together by rods *m*, *m*, *n* is a chain wheel mounted loosely on the shaft *c* between the two ends *l* and *l*¹ of the double clutch. The rods *m*, *m* connecting the two clutch-ends pass through the said chain-wheel *n* so that the double clutch can be caused to slide on the shaft *c* to enable either the clutch end *l* to engage with the clutch teeth *j* on the bevel wheel *e* or the clutch end *l*¹ to engage with the clutch teeth *k* on the bevel wheel *f* without the chain wheel moving on the said shaft. *o* is a chain transmitting motion to the chain wheel *n* from a chain wheel *p* on one of the car axles *b*.

q, *q*¹ Figures 3 and 4 are the spiral springs one end of each being attached to the boss of one of the bevel wheels on the shaft *c*, that is to say, one end of the spring *q*

N° 6496 A.D. 1895

Date of Application, 29th Mar., 1895

Complete Specification Left, 30th Dec., 1895—Accepted, 1st Feb., 1896

PROVISIONAL SPECIFICATION.

Improvements in Apparatus for Stopping and Starting Tram-cars and other Vehicles.

I, MATTHEW McEWEN, of East Street and Quay, Ramsey, Isle of Man, Ironmonger, do hereby declare the nature of this invention to be as follows :—

This invention relates to improved apparatus for stopping and starting tram-cars and other vehicles and has for object to enable the power stored up when the car is stopped to be utilized not only for restarting the car or other vehicle in the same direction but to move it in the reverse direction if desired.

In carrying out my invention I mount two bevel wheels loosely on a shaft fixed to a frame attached to the car or other vehicle, a third bevel wheel mounted loosely on a second spindle, fixed to the said frame at right angles to the first named shaft, gearing with the said two bevel wheels.

The two bevel wheels are provided on their inner faces with clutch teeth, with either set of which a double clutch mounted loosely on the fixed shaft between the two bevel wheels is adapted to engage. In connection with this double clutch a chain wheel is mounted through the medium of which the motion of one or both of the car axles is imparted to the double clutch. In practice the two ends of the clutch are formed separately and connected by rods which slide through the chain wheel so as to permit of the double clutch moving laterally without moving the said chain wheel. To the boss of each of the two bevel wheels is connected one end of a spiral spring, the other end of the spring being connected to the framing attached to the car. These two springs are coiled in opposite directions and adapted to be wound and unwound simultaneously.

To the back of the third bevel wheel is fixed a ratchet provided with a pawl to prevent the springs from unwinding unless it is so desired.

The pawl and the clutches are controlled by the driver of the car or other vehicle by any suitable means.

When the car or other vehicle is in motion the double clutch is not in gear with either of the bevel wheels but when it is desired to stop the car one end of the clutch is put into gear with the corresponding teeth on the face of one of the bevel wheels and both the springs are thereby wound up by the clutch which revolves with the chain wheel.

If it be desired to restart the car, the double clutch is moved to gear with the teeth on the face of the other bevel wheel and the pawl released. If, however, it be desired to restart the car in the opposite direction the pawl only is released, the position of the clutch remaining unaltered.

Dated the 29th day of March 1895.

G. F. REDFERN & Co.,
4, South Street, Finsbury, London, Agents for the Applicant.

McEwen's Improvements in Apparatus for Stopping and Starting Tram-cars, &c.

being attached to the boss r of the bevel wheel e and one end of the spring q^1 being attached to the boss r^1 of the bevel wheel f. The other ends of these two springs are connected to the frame i on the car by means of screws s, s^1 respectively.

These spiral springs are enclosed in casings t, t^1 as shewn in Figures 3 and 4 and 5 are right and left hand whereby they are adapted to be coiled at the same time by the bevel wheels e and f which rotate simultaneously in opposite directions.

u is the ratchet on the back of the bevel wheel g and v is the pawl by means of which the springs are prevented from unwinding, the said pawl, as shewn in Figures 2 and 5, being part of a lever w pivoted at w^1 and actuated by the 10 conductor of the car through the medium of the foot levers x, x and of the chains y, y attached to the lever w as shewn clearly in Figure 2. z is a spring connected to one end of the lever w and to the framing i on the car so as to hold the pawl v in engagement with the ratchet u. Instead of the foot levers x x and chains y y I may employ hand levers and rods respectively.

15 To operate the double clutch I may employ any suitable arrangement such for instance as that shewn in Figures 1 and 2 of the drawings in which one end l^1 of the double clutch is actuated by a forked lever a^1 keyed to a rocking shaft b^1 mounted in bearings c^1 attached to the frame of the car and provided at each end with a crank d^1 adapted to be oscillated by the hand levers e^1 through the medium 20 of the arrangement of rods and bell-crank levers f^1.

The operation of the apparatus is as follows :—When the car is in motion the double clutch l, l^1 is not in gear with either of the bevel wheels e or f, that is to say, it occupies the position represented in Figure 2. When, however, it is desired to stop the car one end of the double clutch l or l^1, according to the direction in 25 which the car is running, is put into engagement with the clutch teeth j or k thereby causing both the wheels e and f to rotate in opposite directions through the medium of the chain wheels p and n, which transmit the motion of the car axle b to the double clutch, whereby the springs q and q^1 are both coiled up.

If it be desired to restart the car in the same direction the double clutch is 30 moved to gear with the teeth on the face of the other bevel wheel and the pawl v is released by means of one of the foot levers x, x.

If, however, it be desired to restart the car in the opposite direction it is only necessary to release the pawl v in the manner described leaving the position of the clutch unaltered.

35 It will be obvious that if desired one of the springs q or q^1 can be dispensed with.

Having now particularly described and ascertained the nature of my said invention and in what manner the same is to be performed, I declare that what I claim is :—

40 1. In apparatus for stopping and starting tram-cars and other vehicles the combination with the spring or springs for storing up the energy of momentum of the car, of a train of three bevel wheels mounted loosely on two shafts at right angles and adapted to be engaged by a double clutch placed between the two opposite bevel wheels, of ratchet mechanism for preventing the uncoiling of the 45 spring or springs and of means for releasing the spring or springs from the ratchet mechanism, substantially as described.

2. The improved apparatus for stopping and starting tram-cars and other vehicles consisting of the parts constructed and combined, substantially as hereinbefore described and illustrated in the accompanying drawings, and operating as 50 and for the purposes set forth.

Dated the 30th day of December 1895.

G. F. REDFERN & CO.,
4, South Street, Finsbury, London, Agents for the Applicant.

London: Printed for Her Majesty's Stationery Office, by Darling & Son, Ltd.—1896

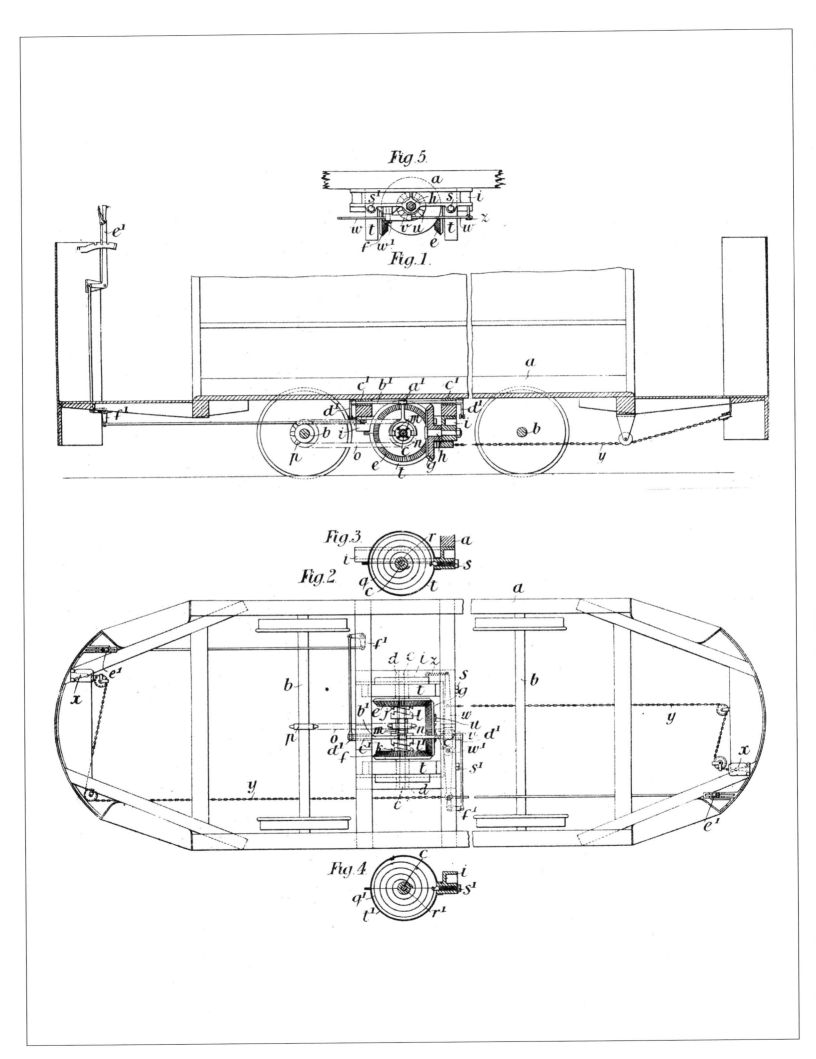

Fig.5.

Fig.1.

Fig.3.

Fig.2.

Fig.4.

N° 10,109   A.D. 1895

Date of Application, 22nd May, 1895—Accepted, 29th June, 1895

COMPLETE SPECIFICATION.

Improvements in Apparatus for Stopping and Starting Tramcars, Omnibuses, and such like Vehicles.

I, ARTHUR DANIEL HOPKINS, of 19, Lower Grove, St. Anne's Hill, Wandsworth, Engineer, do hereby declare the nature of this invention and in what manner the same is to be performed, to be particularly described and ascertained in and by the following statement :—

This invention relates to improvements in apparatus for stopping and starting vehicles such as tramcars, omnibuses etc., whereby the force or energy used for stopping the car or other vehicle is stored up and utilized again for restarting it.

For this purpose I provide the car or vehicle with an air pump actuated by means of eccentrics from one of the wheel axles and this air-pump is connected to a reservoir or chamber wherein the air from the pump is stored up.

This reservoir is connected by a pipe to a cylinder provided with a piston and rod the outer end of which is attached to a horizontal rack which gears with a toothed pinion loosely mounted upon a transverse shaft carried in bearings fixed underneath the floor of the car. This pinion is carried on a squared portion of the said shaft along which it is slid in or out of gear with the rack by means of a lever which operates this rod or bar being likewise connected to another bell crank engaging with a coupling sleeve carried upon a squared portion of the axle which operates the pump eccentrics, which latter are connected together by a sleeve loosely mounted upon the said axle. Thus as the said pinion is brought into gear with the rack, the coupling sleeve is likewise moved into engagement with the eccentrics sleeve causing the latter to be turned by the revolving axle and so to operate the pump. This action of the parts also closes a valve placed in the pipe connecting the aforesaid air reservoir and cylinder thus causing the air to accumulate in the said reservoir as it is pumped therein. The shaft carrying the pinion is geared to the pump actuating axle by means of a series of four toothed wheels, one of which is mounted on the said shaft and another on the axle whilst the intermediate ones are carried by a triangular plate loosely mounted on the axle. This constitutes a reversing motion, one or other of the intermediate wheels being brought into gear with the others according to which direction the car is moving, by raising or lowering the said triangular plate.

When required to start the car the aforesaid action is reversed thus opening the valve between the reservoir and power cylinder whereby the air from the former passes into the latter pressing its piston and rack forwards and operating the pinion so as to cause the axle to turn in the direction in which the car is proceeding. The bell-crank connected to the pinion is provided with a slot so as not to be operated by this movement of the mechanism, thus the pinion is kept in gear with the rack until the latter arrives at the end of its forward stroke when an inclined projection, formed on the rear end of the rack, bears against one side of the pinion and forces it out of gear with the rack, thus permitting the latter making its return stroke without operating the pinion.

The power cylinder is provided with a slide valve whose rod is formed with a projection which comes against one or other of two stops formed on a bar connected to the sliding rack so as to open the said valve when the rack is at the end of its forward stroke and close it at the end of its backward stroke. The said

[Price 8d.]

---

valve is thus opened when the starting gear has finished its work thus permitting the escape of the air from the cylinder and allowing the piston and rack to be drawn back by means of a spring into their normal position.

In the accompanying sheet of drawings illustrating my invention

Fig. 1 is a plan of the mechanism applied to a tram-car, two only of the wheels and the axles being shown without any of the framing of the car.

Fig. 2 is a side elevation of the said mechanism, and Figs. 3, 4 and 5 are details.

a, a^1, are the axles of the car upon the latter of which are mounted the eccentrics b b, connected together by the loose sleeve b^1 and operating the double acting air-pump c. This pump is connected to the air reservoir d by the branch pipes d^1 fitted with non-return valves d^2 d^2. The storage reservoir d is connected with the power cylinder e by the pipe e^1 provided with a valve e^2. The piston rod e^3 of this cylinder is connected to the horizontal rack f which gears with the pinion g loosely mounted upon a squared portion h^1 of the transverse shaft h carried in bearings h^2 fixed underneath the car flooring. The pinion g is connected to a sleeve g^1 also mounted loosely on the part h^1 along which it is slid by the bell-crank g^2, i is the rod or bar operating the bell-crank g^2, the latter being formed with a slot g^3 for preventing its operation during the reverse movement of the rod i. The rod i is connected at one end to a lever j for operating the valve e^2, and at the other end to a lever k operated by toothed wheels k^1 and a hand-wheel k^2 fitted to the end platform of the car, it being understood that similar operating gear is to be fitted to the other end platform. The lever k is likewise connected to a bell-crank l for operating a coupling sleeve or clutch l^1 mounted so as to slide on a squared portion of the axle a^1.

The operation of my improved apparatus is as follows :—

In Fig. 1 the parts are shown in their normal position, and in order to stop the car the driver turns the hand-wheel k^2 so as to move the lever k in the direction of the arrow ; this pulls the rod i forward and closes the valve e^2, and also causes the bell-crank l to couple the clutch l^1 with the loose sleeve b^1, thus transferring the motion of the axle a^1 to the eccentrics b and operating the air-pump c which fills the reservoir d with air to a pressure sufficient to stop the car. This movement of the bar i also causes the bell-crank g^2 to slide the pinion g underneath and in line with the rack f as shown in Fig. 3.

For re-starting the car the hand-wheel k^2 is reversed thus forcing the rod i back and opening the valve e^2 to permit of the escape of the air, stored up in the reservoir d, into the cylinder e, such air forcing the piston and rod e^3 and the rack f forward, thus causing the latter to gear with and turn the pinion g and with it the shaft h and gear wheels m, m^1, m^2, m^2, so as to cause the axle a^1 to turn in the direction in which the car is proceeding. The said movement of the lever k also causes the bell-crank l to uncouple the clutch l^1 from the sleeve b^1 thereby preventing the eccentrics b actuating the pump c. The rack f travels forward until the inclined projection f^1 on its end bears against the pinion g as shown in Fig. 3, which projection pushes the pinion along the shaft h out of gear with the rack f. As soon as this is accomplished a projection n^1 on the bar n (connected at f^2 to the rack f) bears against a projection o^1 on the rod o^2 of the sliding valve o causing the valve o to open so as to permit of the escape of the air behind the piston in the cylinder e, whereupon a coiled spring p is free to draw the piston and rack f back into their normal positions. This spring bears at one end against the bracket q fixed to the underpart of the floor r (Fig. 2) of the car, whilst its other end bears against the projection s^1 of the bar s which is guided by the rod t supported by the brackets q, q^1. When the rack f and bar n are brought back into their normal positions the projection n^2 on the said bar bears against the projection o^1 and pushes the valve o into its closed position.

Fig. 4 is a separate view of the reversing gear one or other of the wheels m^1 or m^3 being raised or lowered so as to gear with the wheels m and m^2 by means of the triangular plate m^4 operated by the bell-crank lever m^5 (see Fig. 2) from the

3

Hopkins' Improvements in Apparatus for Stopping and Starting Tramcars, &c.

car platform, thus permitting the axle a^1 to be turned in one or the other direction.

The rack f is provided with a guide or support u shown in cross section in Fig. 5, to keep it firm and steady in its forward and backward motions.

In applying my invention to other vehicles in which the axles are fixed I may attach a toothed wheel to the hub of one of the wheels which would gear with and actuate a separate shaft, similar to the axle a^1, shown in the drawings, for operating similar mechanism, and when applied to such vehicles the reversing gear shown in Fig. 4 would of course not be required.

Having now particularly described and ascertained the nature of my said invention and in what manner the same is to be performed, I declare that what I claim is :—

1. The improved apparatus for stopping and starting tram-cars and other vehicles consisting of an air-pump or air-pumps actuated from one of the axles and connected to a reservoir for storing up the pressure caused thereby, and a power cylinder, rack and pinion operated by the said air pressure on its release from the storage reservoir substantially as described and shown in the accompanying drawings.

2. In apparatus as above claimed the means for stopping a car or other vehicle consisting of the eccentrics $b, b,$ actuating the air-pump c and mounted upon the loose sleeve b^1, the sliding clutch l^1 for coupling the loose sleeve to the axle a^1, the bell-crank l, lever k, gear wheels k^1, hand wheel k^2, and storage reservoir d substantially as described and for the purposes specified.

3. In apparatus for starting tram-cars or other vehicles the combination of the air-pump c reservoir d, power-cylinder e, pipe e^1, valve e^2, rack f, pinion g, shaft h, operating rod i, lever j, and gearing $m, m^1. m^2, m^3,$ substantially as described and for the purposes specified.

4. In apparatus such as specified in Claim 3 the combination with the cylinder e and rack f of the inclined projection f^1, clutch g^1, bell-crank g^2, bar n, provided with projections $n^1, n^2,$ valve o, valve rod o^2 having a projection o^1, spring p brackets q, q^1 bar s, projection s^1, guide rod t, and guide or support u substantially as and for the purposes specified.

5. The improved apparatus for stopping and starting tram-cars and other vehicles substantially as described and shown in the accompanying sheet of drawings.

Dated this 19th day of April 1895.

F. G. CASSELL,

Of Cassell & Co.,

22, Glasshouse Street, Regent Street, London, W.,

Agent for the Applicant.

London : Printed for Her Majesty's Stationery Office, by Darling & Son, Ltd.—1895

A.D. 1895. May 22. No. 10,109.

HOPKINS' Complete Specification.

(1 SHEET.)

Malby & Sons Photo-Lith.

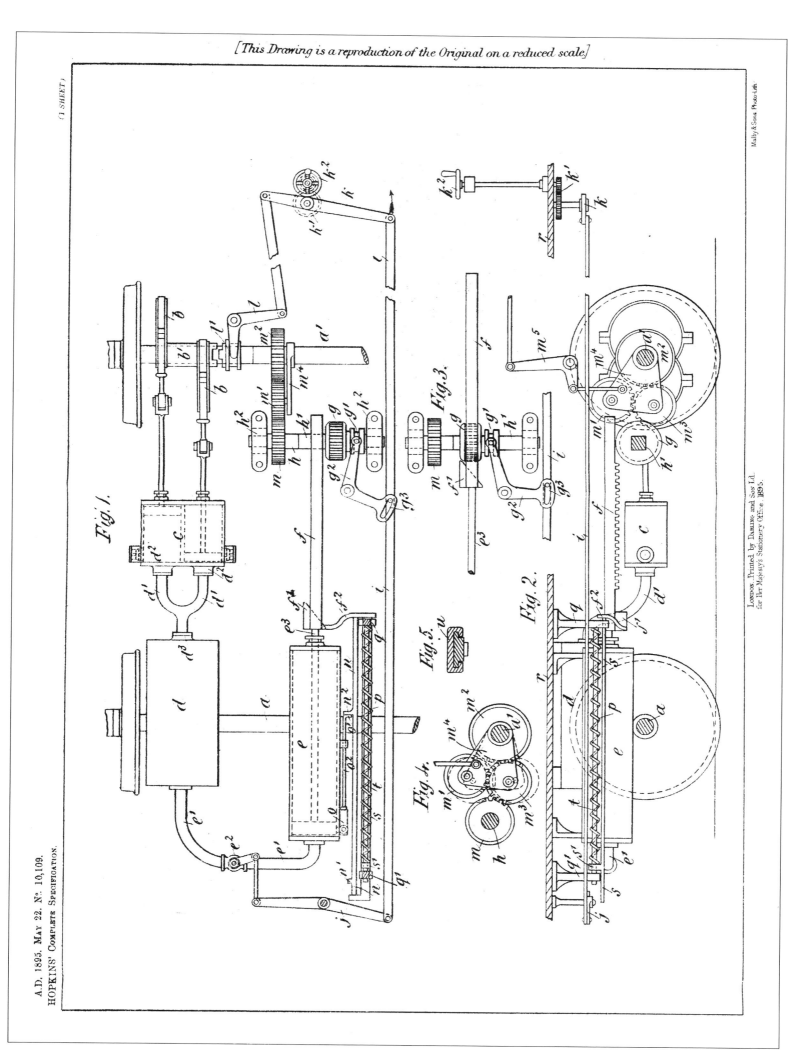

Fig. 1.

Fig. 2.

Fig. 3.

Fig. 4.

Fig. 5.

London. Printed by Darling and Son Ld.
for Her Majesty's Stationery Office. 1895.

N° 13,412   A.D. 1895

Date of Application, 12th July, 1895
Complete Specification Left, 13th Apr., 1896—Accepted, 12th Oct., 1896

PROVISIONAL SPECIFICATION.

Improvements in Apparatus for Lessening the Load at Starting of Tramcars by Horse Propulsion.

I, JOHN BARAGWANATH KING of 13 St. George's Terrace in the Parish of Stonehouse County of Devon Engineer and FREDERICK ROUSE POOL of 16 Durnford Street Parish of Stonehouse in the County of Devon Engineer do hereby declare the nature of this invention to be as follows:—

Our invention relates to improvements in apparatus for lessening the load at starting of tramcars by horse propulsion and is as follows. A bell crank or elbow lever is supported to the tramcar front by a suitable bracket or brackets, the said lever being free to move preferably in an horizontal plane, one end of the said lever is connected by pin and cheek joint to the ordinary pole or chain attachment of the horses the other end of the said lever is connected in a similar manner by pin and cheek joint to a connecting rod or link the opposite end of which is provided with serrated teeth which is free to engage in one direction with a circular ratchet wheel which is secured and revolves with the axle of the said tramcar. A spring is connected to one end of the said connecting rod or link, a stop is also provided for throwing out of gear the teeth engagement with the said ratchet wheel, this stop is preferably arranged so as to be operated at will by the driver of the said tramcar.

The positions of the pins of the said bell crank lever are approximately at right angles to each other, giving a differential motion and leverage to the connecting rod or link on being operated at starting by the horses. In case of tramcars being operated from either end two complete sets of said apparatus are to be employed. In case of tramcars being reversed while the axles remain stationary two sets of ratchet wheels are provided one on each axle with the teeth set to pull in the direction of motion.

Dated this 10th day of July 1895.

JOHN BARAGWANATH KING.
FREDERICK ROUSE POOL.

COMPLETE SPECIFICATION.

Improvements in Apparatus for Lessening the Load at Starting of Tramcars by Horse Propulsion.

We, JOHN BARAGWANATH KING, of 13 St. George's Terrace, in the Parish of Stonehouse in the County of Devon, Engineer, and FREDERICK ROUSE POOL, of 16 Durnford Street, in the Parish of Stonehouse in the County of Devon, Engineer, do hereby declare the nature of this invention and in what manner the same is to be performed to be particularly described and ascertained in and by the following statement:—

Our invention relates to apparatus for lessening the load at starting of tramcars by horse propulsion, as we shall describe referring to the accompanying drawings.

Fig. 1 is an elevation and Fig. 2 is a plan of apparatus according to our invention;

Fig. 3 is an elevation and Fig. 4 a plan of the apparatus somewhat modified,

[Price 8d.]

---

2   N° 13,412.—A.D. 1895.

Apparatus for Lessening the Load at Starting of Tramcars by Horse Propulsion.

Figs. 5, 6 and 7 are respectively a side and end view and a plan of the elbow lever to which the swingle tree or other organ of traction is attached.

Referring first to Figs. 1 and 2, we fix on an axle of the car a ratchet wheel A and mount by the side of it free on the axle a lever carrying a pawl B, which is usually disengaged from the teeth of the wheel A but can be engaged when desired by depressing a treadle C, which is connected to an arm D that bears against the tail of the pawl B. A rod E jointed to the pawl lever has its one end attached to a tensile spring F, and its other end connected to the one arm G of an elbow lever, which is mounted on a vertical pin J at the front of the car and which has its other arm H attached to the swingle tree.

When the car is stopped, and there is no pull of the arm H, the spring F draws the elbow lever to the position shewn, its arm G being in line with the rod E. When the car is to be started, the treadle C is depressed so as to engage the pawl B with the teeth of the ratchet wheel A, thereupon the horses in pulling the arm H towards the position indicated by the dotted lines H¹ (Fig. 2) cause the arm G to move, at first through a very small versed sine, and therefore transmit through the rod E very great tension, so that the pawl B turns with great force the ratchet wheel A and the axle on which it is fixed, thus starting the car.

In the modified arrangement shewn in Figs. 3 and 4, the rod E has part of it e formed as a ratchet rack which is usually held out of gear with the ratchet wheel A by a tensile spring L acting on two levers K, each having a pair of rollers between which the rod E passes. On depressing the treadle C, the levers K K are moved so as to engage the rack teeth e with the teeth of the wheel A, and then the pull of the rod E effects the starting of the car with great force, as above described with reference to Figs. 1 and 2.

We are aware that, in the Specification No. 14309 of 1888, it is proposed to start a vehicle by pulling the long arm of an elbow lever, the short arm of which is connected to a pawl engaging a ratchet wheel on an axle of the vehicle; but, in this case, the engagement of the pawl is not effected by a treadle, and advantage is not taken of the great tractive force obtained by starting the arm of the elbow lever from a position in which it is in line with the rod connecting it to the pawl. We therefore make no claim to apparatus such as is described in the Specification No. 14309 of 1888 above referred to, but

Having now particularly described and ascertained the nature of this invention, and in what manner the same is to be performed, we declare that what we claim is:—

1. The herein described method of lessening the load at starting a tramcar by transmitting the pulling strain of the horses, through an elbow lever and rod, to a ratchet wheel on an axle of the car, the rod and the arm of the elbow lever to which it is connected being in line at starting.

2. Apparatus for facilitating the starting of a tramcar in the manner above referred to by means of a treadle to throw the pawl into gear with the ratchet wheel and an elbow lever having an arm in a line with the connecting rod at the moment of starting, constructed and operating substantially as described with reference to the accompanying drawings.

Dated this 10th day of April 1896.

HARRIS & MILLS,
23 Southampton Buildings, London, W.C., Agents.

London: Printed for Her Majesty's Stationery Office, by Darling & Son, Ltd.—1896

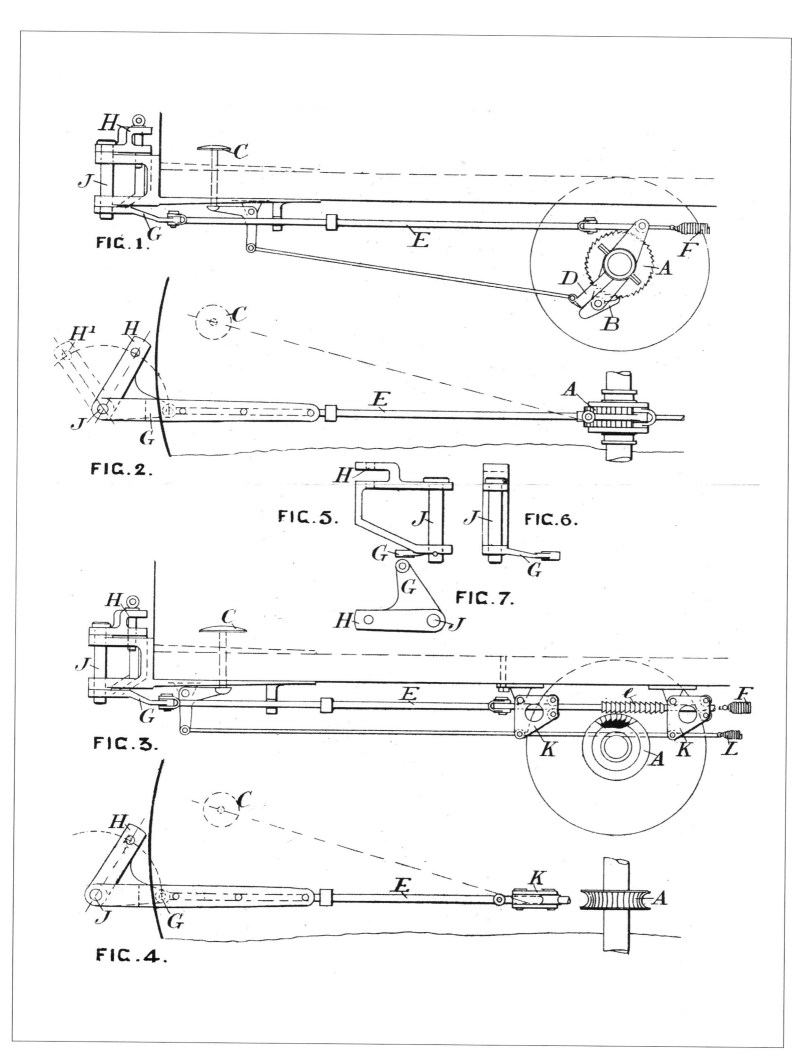

FIG.1.

FIG.2.

FIG.5.

FIG.6.

FIG.7.

FIG.3.

FIG.4.

613

N° 18,819   **A.D. 1895**

Date of Application, 8th Oct., 1895

Complete Specification Left, 8th July, 1896—Accepted, 8th Aug., 1896

PROVISIONAL SPECIFICATION.

Improvements in and relating to Tramcars.

I, WILLIAM GOODING, of North Road, Holloway, in the County of Middlesex, Manufacturer, do hereby declare the nature of this invention to be as follows:—

This invention relates to tramcars, and it consists in using plain wheels instead of flanged wheels and in the use of auxiliary small flanged wheels adapted to run in the grooves of the rails and guide the car so that its plain wheels run on the rails, the object being to provide a ready and simple means of allowing tramcars to be run off the rails in case of accident or obstruction.

In carrying my invention into effect I mount at each end of the tramcar a suitable frame in which is mounted a pair of small flanged wheels the flanges of which are adapted to run in the grooves of the tram rails, the said wheels being controlled by suitable springs and fitted with any suitable lifting gear whereby the flanges of the wheels may be raised clear of the rails when it is desired to run the car off the rails. As an alternative construction only one flanged wheel may be used at each end of the car.

Dated this 8th day of October 1895.

ROBERT E. PHILLIPS, Assoc. M Inst. C.E., M.I. Mech. E,
Consulting Engineer and Patent Agent,
70, Chancery Lane, London, W.C., Agent for the Applicant.

COMPLETE SPECIFICATION.

Improvements in and relating to Tramcars.

I, WILLIAM GOODING of North Road, Holloway, in the County of Middlesex, Manufacturer, do hereby declare the nature of this invention and in what manner the same is to be performed to be particularly described and ascertained in and by the following statement:—

This invention relates to tramcars, and it consists in using plain wheels instead of flanged wheels and in the use of auxiliary small wheels adapted to run in the grooves of the rails and guide the car so that its plain wheels run on the rails, the object being to provide a ready and simple means of allowing tramcars to be run off the rails in case of accident or obstruction.

In carrying my invention into effect I mount at each end of the tramcar a suitable frame in which is mounted a pair of small wheels adapted to run in the grooves of the tram rails, the said wheels being controlled by suitable springs and fitted with any suitable lifting gear whereby the said wheels may be raised clear of the rails when it is desired to run the car off the rails,

I will now more particularly describe my invention making reference to the accompanying drawings in which:—

Figure 1 is a broken view in side elevation of one form my invention may assume as applied to a tramcar.

Figure 2 is a broken view in plan thereof.

[*Price 8d.*]

Figure 3 is a broken view in side elevation of a modification a.. tramcar.

Figure 4 is a broken view in plan thereof.

Figure 5 is a detail end view, and

Figure 6 is a similar view of a modification.

Throughout the views similar parts are marked with ..e letters of reference. X designates the tramcar fitted with whee..ch have plain or unflanged peripheries and are adapted to run o.. the usua.. .s Y. On each or either end of the tramcar X is mounted a pair of small wheels B, B. These wheels B, B are mounted on a framing C in such a manner as to allow the said wheels to be easily raised or lowered from or on to the rails, so that when it is desired to run the car off the rails for any purpose it is only necessary to raise the said wheels B, B clear of the rails as shown in Figure 1. The framing carrying the wheels is pivotted at c and the end c^1 of the framing is adapted to be raised or lowered, thus lowering or raising its opposite end (as shown by dotted lines in Figure 1), by means of a screw adapted to be operated by a handle or other arrangement. A spring c^2 may or may not be used for returning the wheels to their lower position, or the wheels B, B may be operated in any other way either directly or indirectly.

When it is desired to use my invention in connection with existing tramcars I prefer the form illustrated by Figures 1 and 2, wherein the small wheels B, B are mounted slightly in advance of the ordinary wheels A, A, the said ordinary wheels having their flanges turned down so as to convert them into wheels having plain or unflanged peripheries.

When the tramcar is built specially for use with my invention I prefer the construction shown by Figures 3 and 4 of the accompanying drawings in which it will be seen the wheels A, A have a narrower tread and therefore allow the small wheels B, B to be mounted in the same axial line as the wheels A, A, in this position it will be seen they are practically unnoticeable. The small wheels B, B may either be plain, narrow treaded wheels adapted to enter the groove in the rail as illustrated by Figures 1, 2, 3, 4 and 5 of the accompanying drawings, or they may be flanged wheels as shown by Figure 6 of the accompanying drawing.

As an alternative construction only one of the small wheels B, B may be used at each end of the car.

Having now particularly described and ascertained the nature of my said invention and in what manner the same is to be performed, I declare that what I claim is:—

(1.) The improvements in and relating to tramcars, substantially as hereinbefore described and illustrated by the accompanying drawings.

(2.) In tramcars capable of being used on tram lines, rails or ways and having plain or unflanged wheels, the use of two or more auxiliary wheels either flanged or not, adapted to be mounted so as to be raised or lowered into the groove of the rails, as and for the purpose set forth.

Dated this 8th day of July 1896.

ROBERT E. PHILLIPS, Assoc. M. Inst. C.E., M.I. Mech. E.,
Consulting Engineer and Patent Agent,
70, Chancery Lane, London, W.C., Agent for the Applicant.

London · Printed for Her Majesty's Stationery Office, by Darling & Son. Ltd.—1896

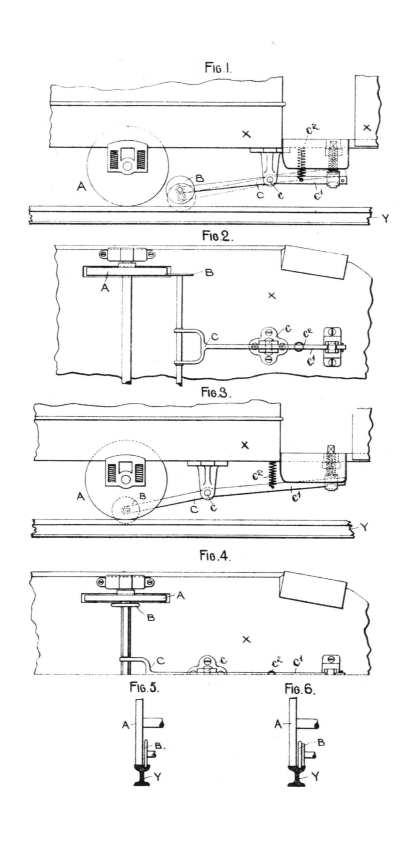

FIG.1.

FIG.2.

FIG.3.

FIG.4.

FIG.5.

FIG.6.

N° 25,168   **A.D. 1897**

Date of Application, 30th Oct., 1897

Complete Specification Left, 30th July, 1898—Accepted, 29th Oct., 1898

PROVISIONAL SPECIFICATION.

Improved Safety-guard for Steam Tramcars and other Carriages Propelled by Mechanical Power.

I, GUSTAVUS ADOLPHUS JOHN SCHOTT, of No. 48, Richmond Road, Bradford, in the County of York, Manufacturer, do hereby declare the nature of this invention to be as follows:—

My invention refers more particularly to safety-guards applied to tramcars or motor cars propelled by electricity or other mechanical power and to the steam engines used for drawing tramcars and to other road engines of that nature.

The contrivances most in favour at present for this purpose consist of a flat table or platform fixed in front of the engine or car at a height of from 2 to 4 inches from the ground, that is to say as near to the ground as has been found practically feasible; the intention being that any person caught thereby in front of the car shall be scooped off the ground, so to speak, and deposited upon the said platform. This plan, though effecting its object in many cases, has also been found to fail frequently, more particularly in the case of children, owing to the clothing or a limb getting into the space between the guard and the ground and the body being thus drawn under the guard and the car. Many accidents of this nature have occurred and resulted in serious bodily injury or death.

The main object of my present invention is to bring the guard into such close contact with the ground that the danger of a body getting under the guard is greatly reduced, if not absolutely eliminated.

To this end I use by preference a guard in the form of a flat or slightly basin-shaped table, similar to the platforms at present in use, but other forms may be adopted. A strong stiff broom four or five inches thick, formed of any suitable material and standing upright or inclined with the bottom end forward, is fixed along the whole breadth of the guard at its front edge in such manner that the broom extends a few inches, say about three, below the guard and its top may stand about the same distance above the guard, so as to prevent a body deposited upon the guard from rolling off it. In place of the broom I may use mechanical equivalents, such for example as a thick band of indiarubber. The back edge of the guard I may form of an iron rod, capable of turning in eyes fixed to the front of the car or engine. On the said back rod of the guard I fix a lever extending upwards, the upper end of which is connected with a suitable catch mechanism, which ordinarily keeps the lever in such a position that the front portion of the platform or guard is suspended above the ground to such an extent that the bottom of the broom beforementioned is a few inches above the ground, same as the ordinary guard at present in use is carried now. A short distance say 18 inches or so in front of the broom and across the whole length of it are stretched one above the other a number of horizontal cords parallel to each other and an inch or two apart from each other. The lowest cord may be ordinarily about two inches from the ground and the highest about a foot or fifteen inches. These cords are carried by two iron rods, one of which is fixed to the car on each side

[*Price 8d.*]

---

2   **N° 25,168.—A.D. 1897.**

Improved Safety-guard for Steam Tramcars, &c., Propelled by Mechanical Power.

of the guard, and each cord is tied to one of the said rods and passed through an eye or hole provided for it in the other bearer. After passing through the said eyes of the one bearer the cords unite into a single one, which proceeds to a slide or trigger in connection with the before mentioned catch mechanism, which I will now describe more particularly. In connection with any convenient revolving part of the mechanism of the engine or car I mount a catch or clutch wheel to which a continual turning motion is imparted as long as the car is in motion. Corresponding to this catch wheel and moving with it, when in gear therewith for the necessary distance, is a catch, which however is ordinarily held out of gear with the revolving catch wheel by the before mentioned slide or trigger, but when the latter is pulled or withdrawn, the said catch engages with the revolving catch wheel and a lever or rod to which the catch is attached is moved thereby. This lever or rod is so connected and arranged that its motion liberates the catch which holds the guard suspended above the ground, and allows the front part of the guard to drop upon the ground.

The action of the combination of mechanism so far described is as follows:
Suppose a person falling in front of or being otherwise overtaken by a moving tram-car, the body will evidently first come in contact with one or more of the cords stretched across the front of the guard, whereby the said cords are pulled or bent inwards towards the car and the trigger to which the cords are attached is also pulled, allowing the catch to engage with the revolving catch-wheel, whereby the guard is released and the broom drops upon the ground and is pushed along it by the advancing car, whilst one or more catches fixed to the car, which act upon corresponding catch wheels fixed upon the back rod of the guard prevent the guard from rising and thus keep the broom in close contact with the ground, so that the object in front cannot get under the guard, but is pushed forward by the broom and in many cases scooped off the ground and thrown upon the guard. I may construct the front part of the guard and the broom curved, that is to say rounding off from the middle to both sides, which would have a tendency to brush the obstacle in front aside out of the track of the car, if it is not scooped off the ground and deposited upon the platform. The motion of the rod or lever which liberates the guard and allows the broom to drop upon the ground I may also utilise for working at the same time a steam whistle or alarm bell for the purpose of signalling the engine driver and guard of the car to stop the car. I may further utilise it for applying an automatic brake, with which the car may be fitted.

After the apparatus has been in action in the manner above described, its various parts would of course have to be readjusted and, so far as they may have been damaged, repaired, and reset or brought into their normal position of readiness for action on the next occasion.

It will be obvious that though primarily intended to save life and injury to persons overtaken by the moving car, the apparatus may also act usefully in brushing aside or removing other obstacles which may have got upon the track of the car.

Dated this 29th day of October 1897.

GUSTAVUS ADOLPHUS JOHN SCHOTT.

COMPLETE SPECIFICATION.

Improved Safety-guard for Steam Tramcars and other Carriages Propelled by Mechanical Power.

I, GUSTAVUS ADOLPHUS JOHN SCHOTT, of No. 48, Richmond Road, Bradford, in the County of York, Manufacturer, do hereby declare the nature of this inven-

Improved Safety-guard for Steam Tramcars, &c., Propelled by Mechanical Power.

tion and in what manner the same is to be performed, to be particularly described and ascertained in and by the following statement:—

My invention refers more particularly to safety-guards applied to tramcars or motor cars propelled by electricity or other mechanical power and to the steam engines used for drawing tramcars and to other road engines of that nature.

The contrivances most in favour at present for this purpose consist of a flat table or platform fixed in front of the engine or car at a height of from 2 to 4 inches from the ground, that is to say as near to the ground as has been found practically feasible; the intention being that any person caught thereby in front of the car shall be scooped off the ground, so to speak, and deposited upon the said platform. This plan, though effecting its object in many cases, has also been found to fail frequently, more particularly in the case of children, owing to the clothing or a limb getting into the space between the guard and the ground and the body being thus drawn under the guard and the car. Many accidents of this nature have occurred and resulted in serious bodily injury or death.

The main object of my present invention is to construct the guard in such a manner that the danger of a body getting under the guard is greatly reduced, if not absolutely eliminated.

To this end I use by preference a guard in the form of a flat or slightly basin-shaped table, similar to the platform at present in use, but other forms may be adopted.

My improved guard is ordinarily carried a few inches above the ground but when any object in front comes against it it falls and parts of it come into close contact with the ground. The guard is forcibly held in this position until released, so that the object in front cannot pass under it but is swept aside out of the track of the car, if the front of the guard is suitably curved, or deposited upon the platform of the guard. The motion of parts of the guard, which takes place as a consequence of contact with the obstructing object, I utilise also for releasing the catch of an alarm bell, whereby a signal is given to the driver of the tramcar to stop, or if the car is fitted with an automatic brake the said motion may by suitable connections be made to apply the brake. These are the general or leading features of my improved safety guard, which may be attained by various combinations of detail mechanism. One of these I have already shortly described in words in the Provisional Specification and will now describe more fully with the assistance of the annexed drawings, of which

Fig. 1 shows the safety-apparatus attached to the front of a steam tram engine, ready for action. The broom "B" is elevated above the ground.

Fig. 2, the same after action, with the broom "B" held in close contact with the ground.

Fig. 3, shows the guard "A," with its fittings, seen from above.

Fig. 4, shows the arrangement of the bearers "F," with the cords, "E" and net "S" attached.

I use the same letters of reference for corresponding parts in the four drawings. "A" is a platform, similar to those at present often used. A strong, stiff broom "B," 5 or 6 inches thick, made of birch or broom twigs, or any suitable material, and standing inclined with the bottom end forward, is fixed along the whole breadth of the guard at its front edge in such manner that the broom extends a few inches, say about three, below the guard, and its top may stand about the same distance above the guard, so as to prevent a body deposited upon the guard from rolling off it. At the back of the guard is fixed a lever "C," extending upwards, the upper end of which is connected with a catch "D," which ordinarily keeps the lever "C" in such a position that the bottom of the broom "B." is a few inches above the ground, as shown in Fig. 1, and same as the ordinary guard at present in use is carried now. A short distance, say 18 inches or so, above the broom and across the whole length of it are stretched, one above the

Improved Safety-guard for Steam Tramcars, &c., Propelled by Mechanical Power.

other, a number of horizontal wires or cords "E," parallel to each other and an inch or two apart from each other. The lowest cord may be ordinarily about 2 inches from the ground, and the highest say 15 inches.

These cords are carried by a framework fixed to the car and consisting in the main of two bearers "F," one of which is situated on each side of the guard, and each cord is tied to one of the said bearers and passed through an eye or hole provided for it in the other bearer. These bearers don't touch the ground and are so constructed that if a body in front should come against them, they turn up and allow the body to pass under them. In that event by pressing against the slide "O," the top of the bearers "F" will move the trigger "G," which is attached to the slide "O." After passing through the eyes of the one bearer some or all of the cords "E," may unite into a single one, which is also connected to the trigger "G" by way of the double-armed lever "PO1," which pivots on a stud fixed to the bearer "V."

In connection with any convenient revolving part of the mechanism of the engine or car is mounted a catch-wheel, "H," to which a continual turning motion is thus imparted as long as the car is in motion. Corresponding to this catch-wheel and moving with it, when in gear therewith for the necessary distance, is a catch "I" which however is ordinarily held out of gear with the revolving catch-wheel by the before-mentioned trigger "G," but when the latter is moved the catch "I" falls and engages with the revolving catch-wheel "H," and the lever "L," to which the catch is attached, is partially turned thereby and causes the rod, "T," upon which the lever "L," is fixed to turn also. This motion of the rod "T," liberates the catch "D," which held the guard suspended above the ground, and allows the broom "B" to drop upon the ground, as shown in Fig. 2.

The action of this combination of mechanism is as follows:—Suppose a person falling in front of or being otherwise overtaken by a moving tramcar, the body will evidently first come in contact with one or more of the cords "E," or one of their bearers "F," whereby the cords are bent inwards towards the car, and the trigger "G," is moved, allowing the catch "I" to engage with the revolving catch-wheel "H," whereby the guard is released and the broom "B" drops upon the ground and is pushed along it by the advancing car, whilst the catches "M," fixed to the car, engage with corresponding toothed racks "N," fixed upon the back-rod of the guard, prevent the guard from rising and thus keep the broom "B." in close contact with the ground, so that the object in front cannot get under the guard, but is pushed forward by the broom and in many cases scooped off the ground and thrown upon the guard. The front part of the guard and the broom are curved, which has a tendency to brush the obstacle in front aside out of the track of the car if it is not deposited upon the platform. The motion of the rod "T," which liberates the guard and allows the broom to drop upon the ground as already described, or of any other convenient part of the mechanism, is at the same time utilised for working a steam-whistle or alarm bell "R" for the purpose of signalling the engine-driver and conductor to stop the car. The same motion might also be utilised for applying an automatic brake, if the car is fitted with one.

It is advisable to attach to the bearers "F" behind the cords "E" a bag or net "S", as shown in the drawings, as in many cases persons, when falling, would be caught therein, and thus be preserved from the more serious consequences if falling to the ground and coming in contact with the guard "A," or broom "B."

After the apparatus has been in action in the manner above described, its various parts must be put right so far as they have been deranged by the collision, and brought into their normal position of readiness for action on the next occasion.

It will be obvious that though primarily intended to save life and injury to persons overtaken by the moving car, the apparatus may also act usefully in brushing aside or removing other obstacles which may have got upon the track of the car.

The mechanism described in the foregoing serves to illustrate the general

[This Drawing is a reproduction of the Original on a reduced scale.]

(1 SHEET)

A.D. 1897. Oct. 30. Nº. 25,168.
SCHOTT'S COMPLETE SPECIFICATION.

Malby & Sons, Photo-Litho.

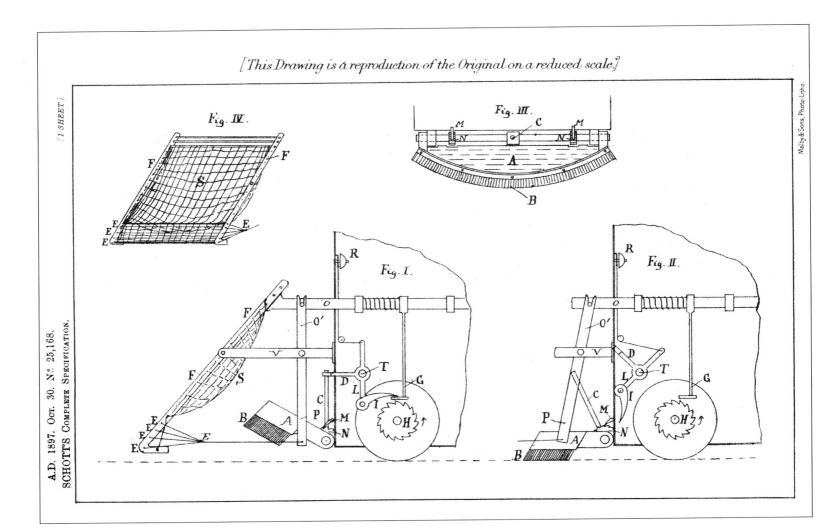

Fig. IV.

Fig. III.

Fig. I.

Fig. II.

Improved Safety-guard for Steam Tramcars, &c., Propelled by Mechanical Power.

principles of the apparatus and of its action. It will be obvious that the details of the said mechanism will have to be varied and adapted in accordance with the particular construction of the car to which it is applied, and the accommodation which is available for it in the said car, and I therefore dont bind myself to the
5 precise details given.

Having now particularly described and ascertained the nature of my said invention and in what manner the same is to be performed, I declare that what I claim is:—

1. A safety-guard for tramcars and similar vehicles, which is ordinarily sus-
10 pended above the ground, but on touching a person or similar obstruction in front, drops to the ground and thus prevents the passage of the said object under it and the car, whilst at the same time signalling the car attendants to stop or putting in action an automatic brake, substantially as described in the foregoing and shewn in Figs. 1 to 4.

15 2. In a safety-guard for tramcars or similar vehicles the combination of a movable platform "A," broom "B," lever "C," catch "D," wires or cords "E," bearers "F," trigger "G," catch wheel "H," catch "I," lever "L," catches "M," toothed racks "N," slide "O" lever "PO¹," bell "R," net "S," rod "T," and bearer "V," substantially for the purposes set forth, and as described and illus-
20 trated in Figs. 1 to 4.

3. Utilising the motion imparted to a safety-guard for tramcars and other vehicles by collision with an object in front for transmitting a signal to the car attendants to stop, as set forth.

Dated this Twenty-ninth day of July 1898.

GUSTAVUS ADOLPHUS JOHN SCHOTT.

Redhill: Printed for Her Majesty's Stationery Office, by Malcomson & Co., Ltd.—1898

N° 5997   A.D. 1898

Date of Application, 11th Mar., 1898

Complete Specification Left, 12th Dec., 1898—Accepted, 4th Feb., 1899

PROVISIONAL SPECIFICATION.

Improvements in Awnings or like Coverings for Tramway Cars, Lorries and other Road Vehicles.

I, CARRINGTON WILLIAM AYLES, of the Firm of Barrett and Company, Aerated Water Manufacturers, 37, Clarendon Street, in the City of Glasgow, do hereby declare the nature of this invention to be as follows:—

This invention, which relates to awnings or like coverings for tramway cars, lorries and other road vehicles, has for its object to provide a covering which may be readily wholly or in part withdrawn to uncover the vehicle or to give access to goods carried by it, and which may not require special stowing when not in use.

The improved awning or covering is composed of a narrow ridge or roof part which is permanently or removably maintained by end supports or uprights at any desired height longitudinally over the body of the car or vehicle and under which are secured in suitable housings or bearings the ends of rollers carrying blinds of canvas or other material. A single blind or two or more blinds may be provided in the length of the car upon each side of the ridge piece, and each blind may be kept normally rolled upon its carrying roller by springs or pulleys and cords or other means. The outer or lower end of each blind is preferably fitted with a bar extending through it and attached at its ends to lever arms jointed to the end supports or uprights in such wise that by drawing down these arms the blind or blinds is or are drawn more or less off the rollers and stretched out in an inclined plane in roof-like form over the top of the car or vehicle so as to protect passengers or goods situated below whilst also serving to deflect rain over the sides. The blinds or any of them may be secured in the covering position by catches engaging the lever arms above mentioned and on releasing these catches the blinds may be drawn up by means of the springs in the rollers or by other devices provided for the purpose.

Dated this 10th day of March 1898.

WALLACE FAIRWEATHER,
Of the Firm of Cruikshank & Fairweather,
Chartered Patent Agents, 62, Saint Vincent Street, Glasgow,
Agent for the Applicant.

COMPLETE SPECIFICATION.

Improvements in Awnings or like Coverings for Tramway Cars, Lorries and other Road Vehicles.

I, CARRINGTON WILLIAM AYLES, of the Firm of Barrett and Company, Aerated Water Manufacturers, 37, Clarendon Street, in the City of Glasgow, do hereby,

[Price 8d.]

---

2   *Ayles's Improvements in Awnings or like Coverings for Tramway Cars, &c.*

N° 5997.—A.D. 1898.

declare the nature of this invention and in what manner the same is to be performed, to be particularly described and ascertained in and by the following statement:—

This invention, which relates to awnings or like coverings for tramway cars, lorries and other road vehicles, has for its object to provide a covering which may be readily wholly or in part withdrawn to uncover the vehicle or to give access to goods carried by it, and which may not require special stowing when not in use.

The invention is illustrated by the accompanying drawings, Figure 1 being a transverse vertical section on the line x—x Figure 2, Figure 2 a longitudinal vertical section on the line y—y Figure 1, of the improved awning or covering shewn as applied to a lorry, and Fig. 3 a part view similar to Fig. 1 of a modified method of carrying the awning.

The improved awning or covering is composed of a narrow ridge or roof part A which is permanently or removably maintained by end supports or uprights B at any desired height longitudinally over the body of the car or vehicle C and under which are secured in suitable housings or bearings D the ends of rollers E carrying blinds F of canvas or other material. A single blind, or two, as shewn, or more blinds may be provided in the length of the lorry, car, or other vehicle upon each side of and beneath the ridge piece A, and each blind F may be kept normally, almost completely, rolled upon its carrying roller E, as shewn at Z, Figure 1, by springs or pulleys and cords or other means. The outer or lower end of each blind F is preferably fitted with a bar F^1 extending through it and attached at its ends to lever arms H jointed to the end supports or uprights B at H^1 as shewn at Fig. 3 about midway between the topmost and lowermost position of the blind in such wise that by drawing down these arms the blind F or blinds is or are drawn more or less off the rollers and stretched out in an inclined plane in roof-like form over the top of the car or vehicle C so as to protect passengers or goods situated below whilst also serving to deflect rain over the sides. The blinds F or any of them may be secured in the covering position by catches F^2 upon them engaging the lever arms above mentioned, and on releasing these catches the blinds may be drawn up by means of the springs in the rollers or by other devices provided for the purpose. Or instead of lever arms guide rods B^1 may be secured upon the upper surface of the uprights or end supports B along the top of which the edges of the blinds F rest when in the covering position, hooks B^2 on the lower ends of these rods B^1 engaging eyes F^2 on the lower ends of the blinds.

Having now particularly described and ascertained the nature of my said invention, and in what manner the same is to be performed, I declare that what I claim is:—

The improved awning or like covering for tramway cars, lorries and other road vehicles constructed and arranged substantially as described.

Dated this 10th day of December 1898.

WALLACE FAIRWEATHER,
Of the Firm of Cruikshank & Fairweather,
Chartered Patent Agents, 62, Saint Vincent Street, Glasgow,
Agent for the Applicant.

Redhill: Printed for Her Majesty's Stationery Office, by Malcomson & Co., Ltd.—1819

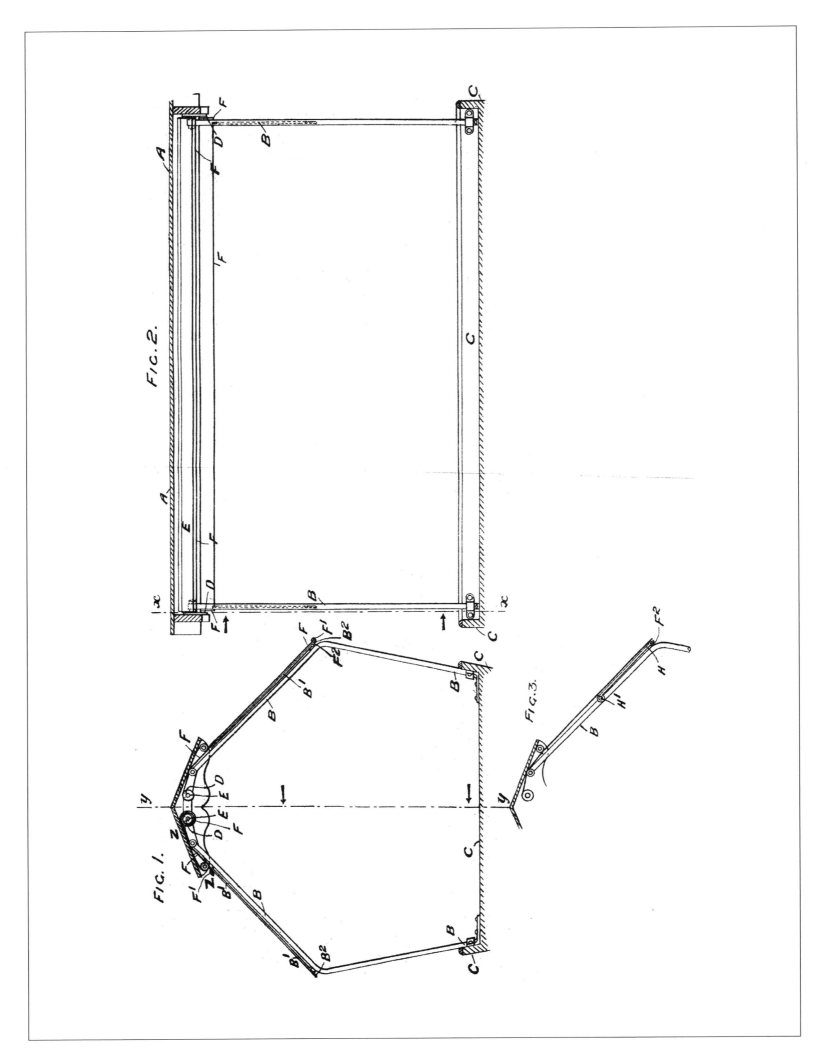

FIG. 2.

FIG. 1.

FIG. 3.

N° 20,109   A.D. 1899

Date of Application, 6th Oct., 1899—Accepted, 11th Nov., 1899

COMPLETE SPECIFICATION.

Improvements in Fenders for Tramway and like Vehicles.

I, JOHANN VON HOLT, of 1, Jacobstrasse, 11, Hamburg, in the Empire of Germany, Labourer, do hereby declare the nature of this invention and in what manner the same is to be performed, to be particularly described and ascertained in and by the following statement:—

5   This invention relates to a fender for street tram or railway-vehicles for preventing persons being run over.

The arrangement consists broadly of an elastic frame arranged in front of the wheels and fitted with a number of vertical rollers. The frame is arranged at an incline with the longitudinal axis of the vehicle in such a manner that

10   normally a person caught by the fender is pushed towards that side where there is no danger from vehicles coming in an opposite direction.

My invention will be readily understood by reference to the accompanying drawings, in which:—

Figure 1 is a perspective view of a portion of a tram-car showing the im-

15   proved fender applied thereto.

Figure 2 is a reversed plan of Figure 1.

Figure 3 is a front elevation of the fender.

Figure 4 shows the rollers and their mountings drawn to a larger scale.

Figure 5 is a side-elevation of the sliding supports for the fender-frame.

Figure 6 is a reversed plan of Figure 5.

Figure 7 shows the top-bar of the fender.

Figure 8 is a sectional view on the line A—B Figure 5.

Below the ordinary platform of the tram-vehicle upon which the driver

25   stands, a bar a is arranged at right angles to the longitudinal axis of the car and such bar is adapted to move forward and rearward owing to the action of slotted bearings b having movable sliding blocks c which by means of bracket pieces d supports the bar a.

The blocks c are constantly urged forward by means of strong helical springs e

30   which normally hold them in such forward position.

To the bar a is connected a vertically arranged frame adapted to reach down to the ground as far as is practical.

The said frame comprises the bars i, i^1 and $j j^1$ the portions of which are respectively secured together by hinge-joints $f f^1$, the purpose of which will

35   be hereinafter explained. The articulation divides the frame into the parts $g—f$ and $f—h$. The upper bar $i i^1$ of the frame is bent at parts so as to adapt itself to the car and various apparatus carried below the floor such as the brake, the steps and so on, while the lower bar $j j^1$ is straight. The rollers k mounted between the bars $i i^1$ and $j j^1$ are made of soft rubber and of a reduced diameter

40   at the middle somewhat as shown.

The frame furnished with the rollers is mounted at a sharp angle with its supporting bar a to which it is connected by means of arms $l l^1 l^2$. The arm l^1 carries the joint f and the arm l^2 forms a guide in which the frame-portion $f—h$ can slide, this latter being normally held in its forward position by the pull

45   of a helical spring m.

If now a person owing to an accident is caught by the fender it is in most cases in the middle of the apparatus that such is caught. The form of the

[Price 8d.]

---

2   N° 20,109.—A.D. 1899.

Holt's Improvements in Fenders for Tramway and like Vehicles.

rollers is such as to adapt themselves somewhat to the rounded form of the body and therefore obviously as the car has a certain momentum, the tendency of the rollers is to push the person onward and at the same time sidewise outside the rails towards the receding portion g by reason of the inclined position of

5   the frame. This action is facilitated by the adoption of rotary rollers whereby friction is obviated between the person and the protecting fender.

If the person however falls in front of the portion $f h$ the force of the spring is overcome and the said portion assumes a position as is indicated by the dotted line in Figure 2 and the person is then pushed towards this side as this is the

10   nearest side.

The wheels are advantageously cased in by a side plate or board n so as to prevent the person ejected by the fender from coming within reach of the wheels of the tram.

The forward movable end of the fender is connected with the side-boards by

15   an intermediary part n^1 which is guided in the side-board n and which can move rearward sufficiently to admit of the motion of the fender-portion $f—h$ and thus all danger from the wheels is obviated.

In a trailing-car the fender may be constructed without the hinge-joint as accidents can here only occur on entering or descending the car and access to

20   the car takes place from one side only.

In order to reduce the shock by contact more than already effected by the soft rubber rollers k I make the entire structure elastic i.e. to yield by enabling the blocks carrying the bar a to slide in the slotted bearings b and compress the springs e.

25   Thus the shock is transmitted to the springs e and in this manner is lessened upon the person.

In Figures 2, 5 and 6 of the drawing it is shown how the projection c^1 of the sliding-block c can be used to form an electric-contact with a spring controlled stud o which latter then switches off the current and at the same time starts

30   an electric-brake.

Having now particularly described and ascertained the nature of my said invention and in what manner the same is to be performed, I declare that what I claim is:—

1. A protecting fender for tramway and like vehicles characterized by a ver-

35   tical frame, with elastic rollers k, arranged at an incline with the longitudinal axis of the vehicle and adapted to remove obstructions during the journey from the front of the vehicle towards the furthest removed portion of the frame and finally outside the permanent-way which is facilitated by the action of the rollers k, substantially as hereinbefore described with reference to the accom-

40   panying drawings.

2. A protecting fender for tramway and like vehicles as claimed in Claim 1, in which the frame carrying the rollers k consists of a rigid portion $g—f$ and a movable or hinged portion $f—h$ so as to enable an obstruction, if laying in a certain position, to be removed after pushing rearward the portion $f—h$ to

45   one side of the car, while ordinarily obstructions are removed to that side of the car where it is free from danger through the traffic coming in an opposite direction, substantially as hereinbefore described with reference to the drawing.

3. In a protecting fender for tramway and like vehicles as claimed in Claims 1 and 2 the method of securing the frame of the fender to a sliding-bar a so as

50   to reduce shock by contact with the obstruction by means of springs, while the sliding motion of the fender may serve in bringing a brake into operation, sub-stantially as hereinbefore described.

Dated this 6th day of October 1899.

HASELTINE, LAKE & Co.,
45, Southampton Buildings, London, W.C., Agents for the Applicant.

Redhill: Printed for Her Majesty's Stationery Office, by Malcomson & Co., Ltd.—1899.

[This Drawing is a reproduction of the Original on a reduced scale.]

A.D. 1899. Oct. 6. No. 20,109.
VON HOLT'S COMPLETE SPECIFICATION.

(2 SHEETS)
SHEET 2.

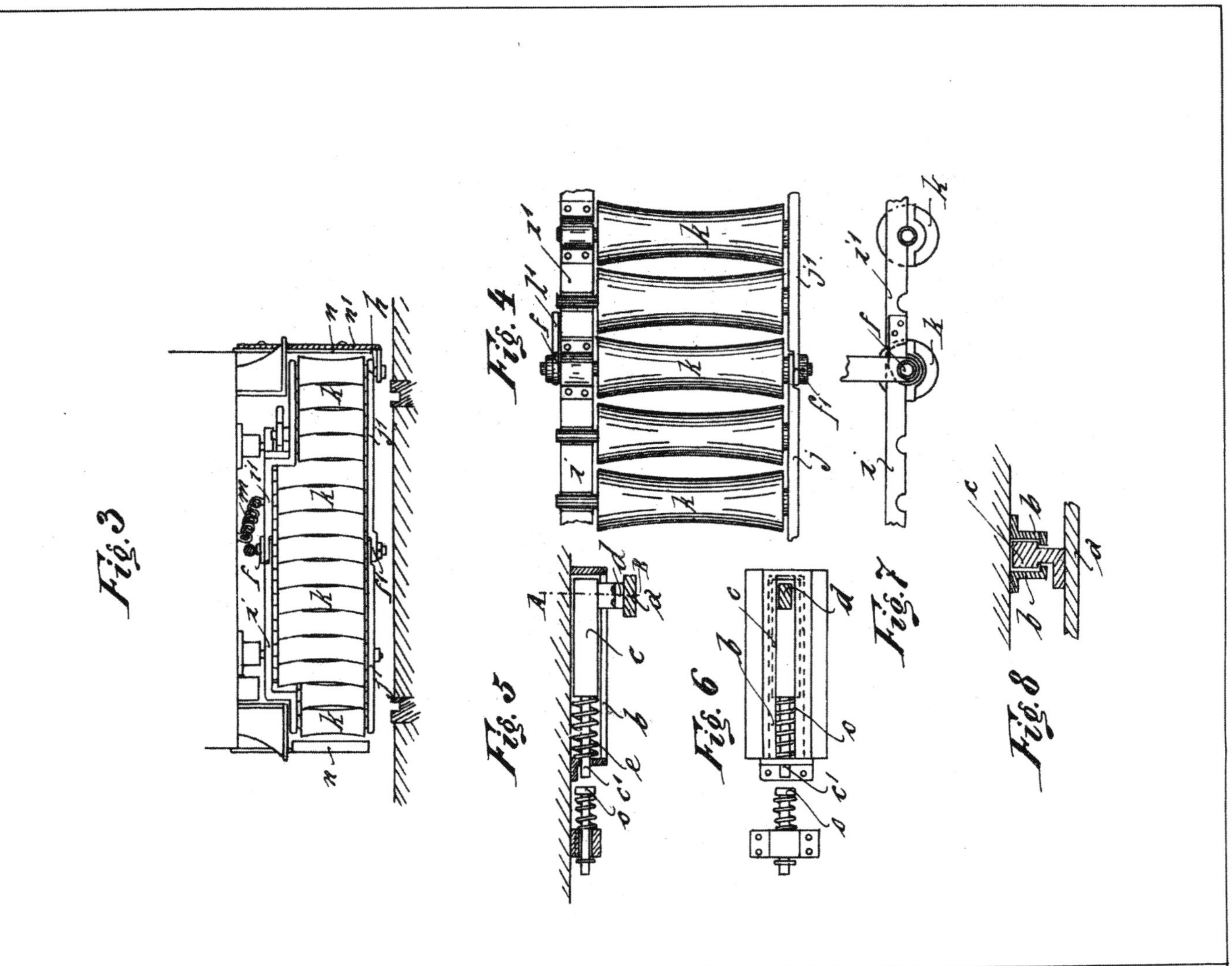

SHEET 1.

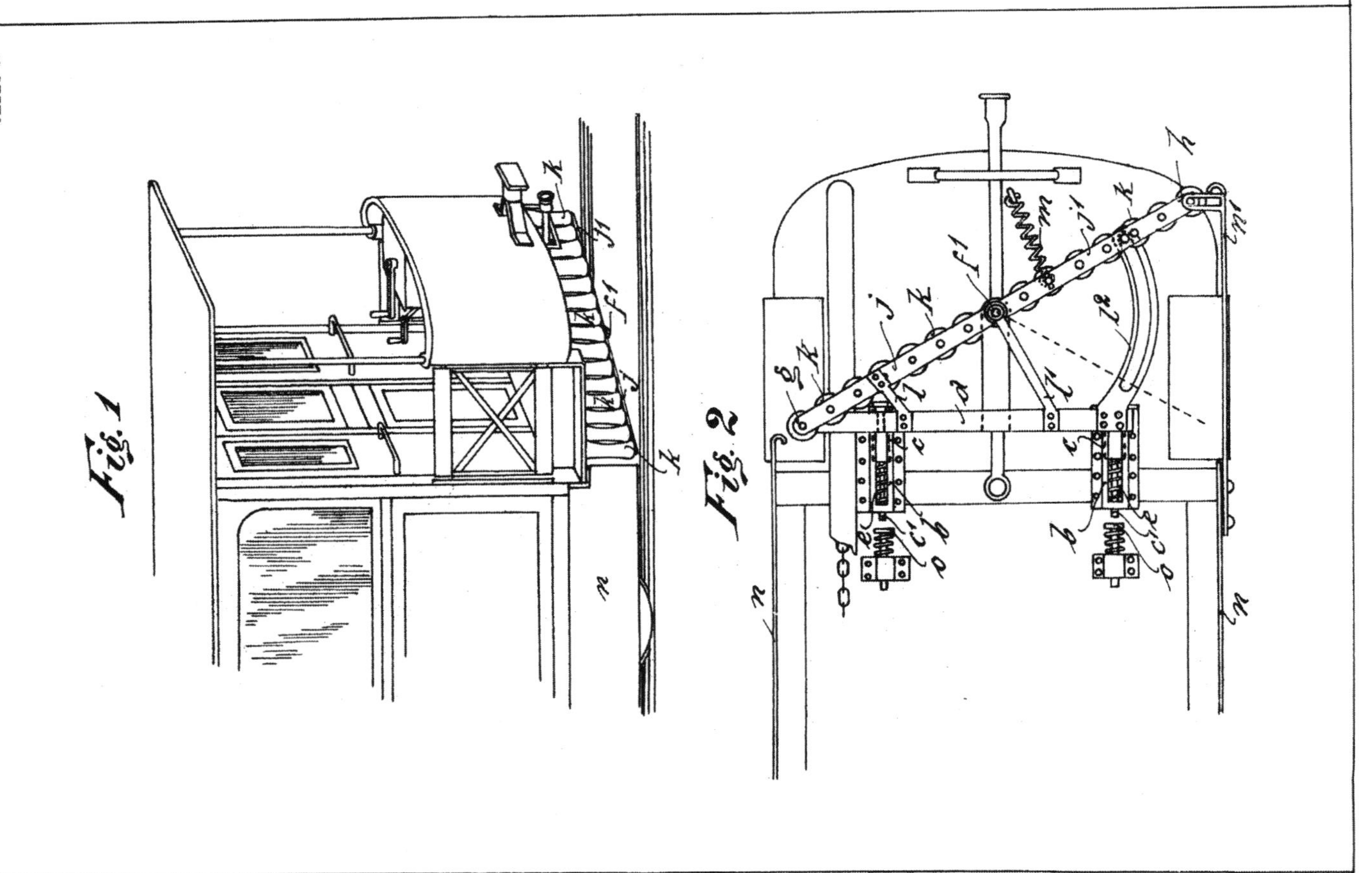

Malby & Sons, Photo-Litho

N° 25,225   A.D. 1901

Under International Convention.

Date claimed for Patent under Sect. 103 of Act, being date of first Foreign Application (in Switzerland), 11th May, 1901

Date of Application (in United Kingdom), 10th Dec., 1901

Complete Specification Left, 10th Dec., 1901—Accepted, 23rd Jan., 1902.

COMPLETE SPECIFICATION.

"Improved Means for Replacing Derailed Tramcars."

I, JEAN DUCIMETIÈRE, Gentleman, of Rue de Hesse, Geneva, Switzerland, do hereby declare the nature of this invention and in what manner the same is to be performed, to be particularly described and ascertained in and by the following statement:—

The present invention relates to a tram car provided with a device, which, in case of derailment, allows the car to be held up by one of its ends and to be replaced in position by rolling it on to the rails.

The accompanying drawings illustrate different methods of carrying the invention into effect, in which,

Figure 1 is a partial elevation of a car fitted with the apparatus,
Figure 2 is a front view of the same car,
Figure 3 illustrates a modification, and
Figure 4 a view of a detail.

In carrying out the invention as illustrated in Figures 1 and 2 of the drawings which show the apparatus for raising the car by one of its ends and for holding it in the raised position, a support a is employed fitted at its lower end with a movable part b—such as a ball or roller—which allows the raised car to be rolled laterally on to the rails.

The said support a forms the rack of a lifting jack attached in a removable manner to the car, so that it may be moved from one platform to the other. For this purpose each platform is fitted with clamps or similar devices necessary for receiving and securely holding the body of the jack c.

To raise the car at one end, it is sufficient to lower the support a by means of the crank handle of the jack, and to facilitate the displacement of the car thus raised, the support a rests upon a beam or wedge of hard wood d, with which the car is provided and which will ordinarily be carried with the lifting jack, under a seat or in any other suitable place on the car.

The face of the wedge upon which the support a is placed may be concave as shown in Figure 1 to prevent the support from sliding off. The wedge d is placed on the ground with its point lying on the side of the track so that the car may be rolled into place almost without effort.

In the modification represented in Figure 3 the car is fitted with two fixed supports a, one under each platform. In this case it is necessary to raise the car by means of an ordinary lifting jack or in some other manner, and to pack up the support a underneath with wood,

---

Ducimetière's Improved Means for Replacing Derailed Tramcars.

In another modification the support a may be of the form represented in Figure 4 consisting of a screwed bar which enters into the body e as illustrated. This form of support may be readily removed from the car it being sufficient for this purpose to unscrew it from its socket e fixed on the frame or under part of the car.

The invention is not limited to the exact details hereinbefore described and illustrated as obviously such modifications may be made as are necessary for adapting the device for use upon cars of different forms or to meet any other requirements.

Having now particularly described and ascertained the nature of my said invention and in what manner the same is to be performed, I declare that what I claim is:—

1.—A tramcar provided with an apparatus for use when a derailment of the car occurs which allows the car to be held up by one of its ends and to be replaced, by rolling, on to the rails, consisting of a support having a movable part such as a ball or roller at its lower end, substantially as described.

2.—A tramcar provided with an apparatus for use when a derailment of the car occurs as claimed in the first claim, arranging the support so as to serve as a means of leverage, substantially as described.

3.—A tramcar provided with an apparatus for use when a derailment of the car occurs as claimed in the first claim arranging the support in a removable manner so that it may be transported from one end of the car to the other substantially as described.

4.—A tramcar provided with an apparatus for use when a derailment of the car occurs, as claimed in the first claim, the provision of a wedge serving as a base and a guide for the support substantially as described.

5.—A tram-car provided with apparatus for use when a derailment of the car occurs, arranged and operating substantially as hereinbefore described and as illustrated in the accompanying drawings.

Dated this 10th day of December 1901.

MARKS & CLERK
18, Southampton Buildings, London, W.C.
13, Temple Street, Birmingham, and
25, Cross Street, Manchester,
Agents.

Redhill: Printed for His Majesty's Stationery Office, by Malcomson & Co., Ltd.—1902.

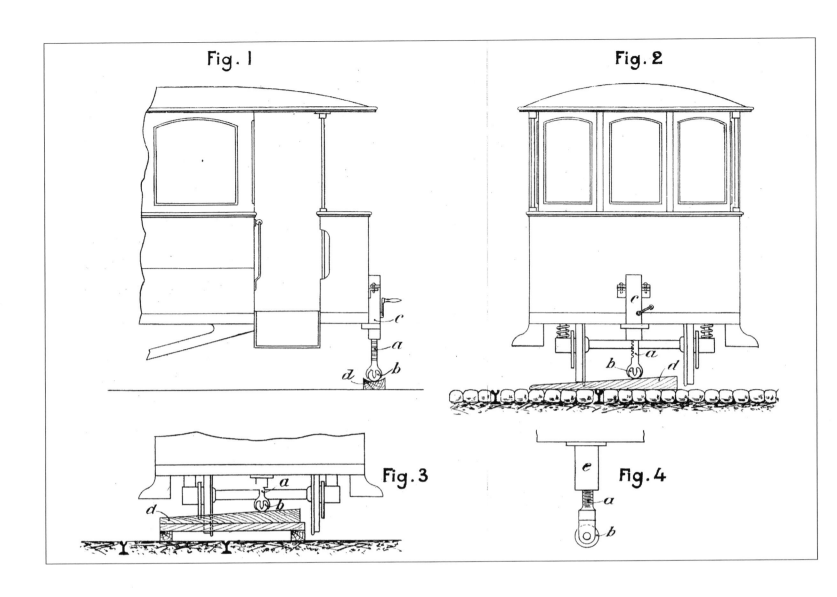

Fig. 1

Fig. 2

Fig. 3

Fig. 4

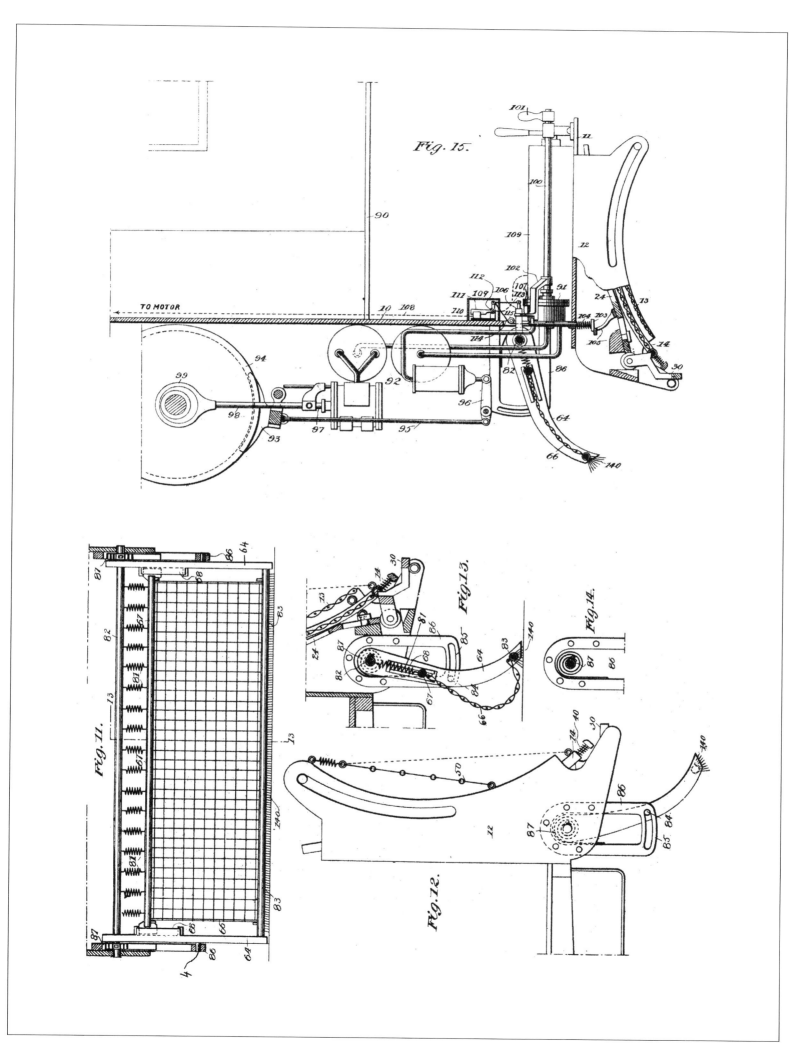

Fig. 15.

TO MOTOR

Fig. 11.

Fig. 13.

Fig. 14.

Fig. 12.

N° 26,239   A.D. 1902

Date of Application, 28th Nov., 1902

Complete Specification Left, 28th Aug., 1903—Accepted, 8th Oct., 1903

PROVISIONAL SPECIFICATION.

Improvements in Brake Blocks for Tramway or Railway Vehicles.

We, FREDERICK KENNINGTON, of 26 Sholebroke Avenue, Leeds, in the County of York, Commercial Traveller, and HENRY LEWIS WHITE, of Willow House, Cleethorpes, in the County of Lincoln, Tramway Manager do hereby declare the nature of this invention to be as follows:—

This invention relates to a novel construction of brake block applicable to tramway or railway vehicles whereby advantages are obtained in a more effective grip with less pressure than in the case of metal blocks and greater endurance than in the case of wooden blocks and less irregular wear upon the tyres than in the case of metal blocks respectively when made wholly of those materials.

To carry this invention into effect we employ a metal body for the block it being preferably in form a segment of a circle thus following the contour of the wheel to which it is to be applied.

In the tread of such block we insert by dove-tailing or in other convenient manner a segment of wood or composition slightly projecting, when new, beyond the surrounding metal tread.

When worn down flush either material supports the other and as the friction grip of the wood or composition sandwich gives a quicker retardation to the wheel with less pressure than when the block is entirely metal, the manipulation is easier for the brakesman and the irregularity of the wear and tear upon the tyres is less for our compound block than for a metal block.

The powdered detritus produced by use from the sandwiched wood or composition, being also spread over the adjoining metal faces of the block aids the latter in a prompt and effective grip upon the wheel with a minimum of pressure.

Dated this 28th day of November, 1902.

FELL & JAMES,
1 Queen Victoria Street, London, E.C.
Agents for the Applicants.

COMPLETE SPECIFICATION.

"Improvements in Brake Blocks for Tramway or Railway Vehicles."

We, FREDERICK KENNINGTON, late of 26 Sholebroke Avenue, but now of 10 Avenue Hill, Leeds, in the County of York, Commercial Traveller, and HENRY LEWIS WHITE, of Willow House, Cleethorpes, in the County of Lincoln, Tramway Manager, do hereby declare the nature of this invention and in what manner the same is to be performed to be particularly described and ascertained in and by the following statement:—

This invention relates to a novel construction of a brake-block, applicable to

[Price 8d.]

N° 26,239.—A.D. 1902.

Improvements in Brake Blocks for Tramway or Railway Vehicles.

tramway or railway vehicles whereby advantages are obtained in a more effective grip with less pressure than in the case of metal blocks, and greater endurance than in the case of wooden blocks, and less irregular wear upon the tyres than in the case of metal blocks, when the blocks respectively are made wholly of those materials.

To carry this invention into effect, we employ a metal body for the block, it being preferably in form, a segment of a circle, thus following the contour of the wheel to which it is to be applied.

In the tread of such block we insert, by dove-tailing, a segment or segments of wood slightly projecting, when new, beyond the surrounding metal tread.

When worn down flush, either material supports the other, and as the frictional grip of the wood insertion gives a quicker retardation to the wheel with less pressure, than when the block is entirely metal, the manipulation is easier for the brakesman, and the irregularity of the wear upon the tyres is less for our compound block than for a metal block.

The powdered detritus produced by use from the inserted wood, being also spread over the adjoining metal faces of the block aids the latter in a prompt and effective grip upon the wheel with a minimum of pressure.

And in order that our invention may be the better understood, we will now proceed to describe the same with reference to the drawings hereto annexed and to the figures and letters marked thereon.

Like letters refer to similar parts in the various figures.

Figure 1 is an elevation.

Figure 2 is an under plan and

Figure 3 is a transverse section of one form of our compound brake block, taken on the line $x\,y$ of Figure 1.

Figure 4 is an elevation,

Figure 5 is an under plan and

Figure 6 is a transverse section of a modified form of our compound brake block, taken on the line $v\,w$ of Figure 4.

a is the metal body of the block which may be conveniently of cast iron and which may be of any convenient form or metal.

b, b^1 are the tenoned insertions of wood let into the tread of the block.

In Figures 1 to 3, we show a continuous strip b of wood extending through the length of the tread of the shoe or block, the said strip being tenoned into a dove-tailed groove.

In Figures 4 to 6, we show transverse strips b^1 of wood or composition, extending across the tread of the shoe or block which also are tenoned in transverse dove-tailed grooves.

It is to be understood that we may vary the angle of these transverse strips and place them obliquely across the tread should we so desire.

Having now particularly described and ascertained the nature of our said invention and in what manner the same is to be performed, we declare that what we claim is:—

1st. A compound brake-block for tramway and railway vehicles, consisting of a metal body or shoe, in the tread of which is inserted a strip or strips of wood, secured in place by tenon ends in dove-tailed grooves.

2nd. The construction and arrangement of compound brake-blocks in metal and wood for tramway and railway vehicles, substantially as herein described and as illustrated herewith.

Dated this 28th day of August, 1903.

FELL & JAMES,
1 Queen Victoria Street, London, E.C.
Agents for the Applicants.

Redhill: Printed for His Majesty's Stationery Office, by Love & Malcomson, Ltd.—1903.

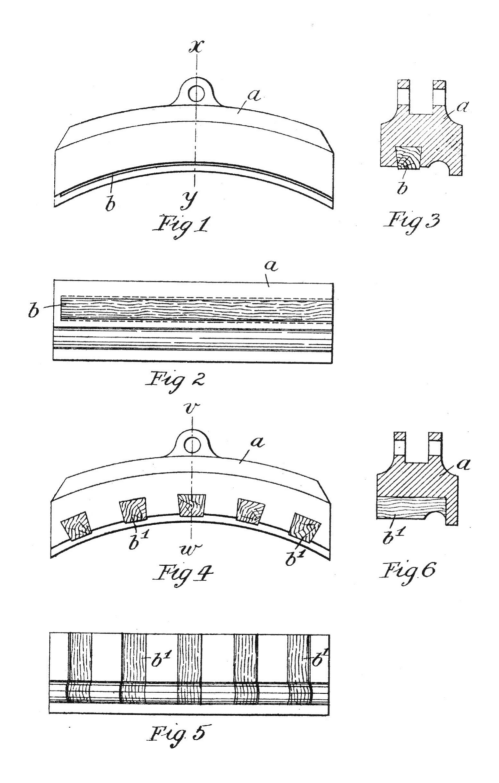

Fig 1

Fig 3

Fig 2

Fig 4

Fig 6

Fig 5

N° 23,999.—A.D. 1904.

A New Drilling Cramp for Tramway and Railway Rails.

Having now particularly described and ascertained the nature of my said invention, and in what manner the same is to be performed, I declare that what I claim is:—

First.—The new drilling cramp for tramway and railway rails consists of the tube A, the clips B and B¹, the rod D, and other devices, as shewn, all constructed and combined substantially as described with reference to the accompanying drawings and operating as and for the purpose above specified.

Second.—A new drilling cramp, being light and portable, arranged substantially, as shewn, for the purpose of obtaining rigidity as hereinbefore specified.

Third.—A rigid drilling cramp suitable for drilling in any position that may be required when laying down or repairing rails in the manner hereinbefore specified.

Dated this Third day of November 1904.

WILLIAM KEMMISH, Junior.
157, Osborne Road Portswood Southampton

Redhill: Printed for His Majesty's Stationery Office, by Love & Malcomson, Ltd.—1904.

N° 23,999   A.D. 1904

Date of Application, 7th Nov., 1904—Accepted, 8th Dec., 1904

COMPLETE SPECIFICATION.

A New Drilling Cramp for Tramway and Railway Rails.

I, WILLIAM KEMMISH, Junior of 157, Osborne Road Portswood, Southampton, in the County of Hants, Blacksmith, do hereby declare the nature of this invention and in what manner the same is to be performed, to be particularly described and ascertained in and by the following statement:—

My invention relates to a new drilling cramp for tramway and railway rails, to obtain rigidity in drilling holes with ratchet or other braces.

The main object of my said invention is to provide a simple and effective apparatus for the aforesaid purpose.

In the accompanying drawings I have shewn what I consider to be the best means of carrying out my said invention, in which—

Figure 1 shews an elevation of my apparatus

Figure 2, a plan of same.

Figures 3, 4, 5 and 6 are sectional views taken on the lines aa, bb, cc and dd. respectively. Like letters indicate corresponding parts throughout the drawings.

In carrying out my said invention I provide the tube A with clips B and B¹ for gripping the bullhead of the rails C—the rod D and moveable arm E, for the purpose hereinafter described.

Upon one end of the rod D, which runs through the tube A projecting beyond ends of same I place the clip B which is arranged to slide upon the rod D, and with the tube A to a limited extent regulated by means of the key nut F.

The rod D has a screw thread cut at both ends, one being considerably longer than the other.

B¹ is a collar rest and clip combined, slid on the tube A, and fixed by means of a grip tightened by the screw G, provided with a handle and can be placed in any position on the tube A, according to the guage or spacing of rails.

H. is a collar rest shrunk on the tube A. or fixed by any other suitable means.

The disc J is fixed by the rivets K, or any other means found most suitable.

Through the disc J the rod D projects, upon which I place the nut F¹, for fixing the rod D, to obtain pressure on the clip B, by means of the key-nut F, when desirous of gripping the rails C for drilling as shewn in the drawings.

The moveable arm E is fitted on the tube, A in the same manner as the clip B¹, and has two steel plates L L fitted in dovetailed groves or recesses, see Figure 5, against which the ratchet or other braces rest, to obtain pressure for drilling.

The plates L L are kept in position by the rivet M, which is punched out for removing and renewing of the plates when worn by the centres of ratchet or other braces.

In the accompanying drawings I have shown only one moveable arm E, but it is obvious I may, if required, fit two moveable arms on the aforesaid device, thus I am able to drill both rails at one time.

When drilling in the neighbourhood of points I may require to place the clips B, and B¹ close together, and the arm E outside to obtain the necessary space between same and the rail C. to be drilled for the working of the ratchet or other braces

[*Price 8d.*]

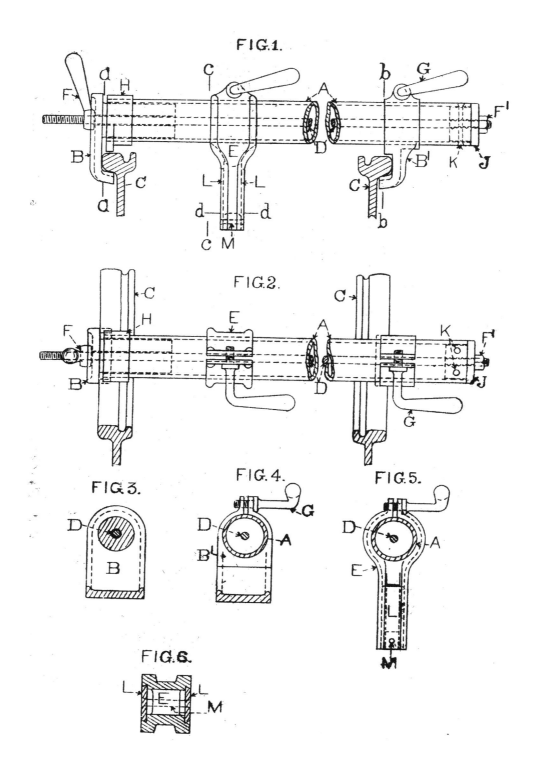

FIG.1.

FIG.2.

FIG.3.

FIG.4.

FIG.5.

FIG.6.

629

Alfred Dickinson's Patents

It does appear that Alfred Dickinson is one of those tramway pioneers to whom history has not done justice. It may be that in the eyes of late Victorians and Edwardians he was tarnished by his association with Joseph Ebbsmith and Carruthers Wain, both of whom we now know were crooks of the first water. Details are given in our volume 4 pp224 to 227 but of vital importance as evidence at their trial were the Patents of Alfred Dickinson, taken out when he was the Engineer and General Manager, based at Darlaston, of the South Staffordshire & Birmingham District Tramway Company. His patents seem in the main to have been purchased by Ebbsmith for quite nominal sums and resold to The Dickinson Appliance Company, a 'creature' virtually wholly owned by Ebbsmith. Many were then licensed (at a profit) for use by the South Staffs., notwithstanding that the research work was carried out by the South Staffs labour force in the company's time. Whatever the truth of the matter it does seem as though Dickinson made precious little money from the products of his fecund brain.

Space/time constraints preclude us including all of his patents with any degree of detail but the patent numbers and dates are listed at the end of this item thanks to assistance given by Rachel Ford then of Business Insight (Patents Office) at the Birmingham Central Library.

The most important of these patents related to ro-rail vehicles. The first, 6164 of 1885, was joint with Louis Clavering Clovis, who had been appointed manager of the South Staffs the year before, but by the time of the second, 11,353 of 1887, Alfred Dickinson had moved from being the Locomotive Superintendent at the Tramway Depot, Kings Hill, Wednesbury, to the General Manager's house at this yard, now known as the Darlaston Depot, where he was to remain at least until 1894.

6164 depicted a normal cart or wagon which, said Dickinson, "has proved very successful especially where a number of these vehicles may be connected one behind the other when drawn on rails by steam power so as to more fully economise the power of the engine", whereas 11,353 was a quite ingenious form of container transporter where "one, two or three or more ... special bodies [can be] placed one above the other on the centre of the rail vehicle", each box carrying one or two tons of goods; not dissimilar to today's air-freight methods for part loads.

Not only was fare-dodging rife on steam tramways but it was always understood by the men (if not the management) right through to the 1960s at least that the conductor (or rather the company) bought breakfast for himself and the driver.

Alfred Dickinson was aware of the manner in which waybills could be 'adapted' and patented (9157 of 1887) an improved "way bill frame which prevents the persons using them from tampering therewith and thus greater security is obtained against fraud". Not that this prevented fraud for the *Tramway & Railway World* in March 1892 stated "The sentence by the stipendiary [in Birmingham] of a tramguard to three weeks imprisonment with hard labour for embezzlement of fares will prove a salutary lesson to dishonest guards. The prisoner was charged with issuing a 'dead' ticket on a recent night to a passenger on the Small Heath route, and although the amount involved was only a penny the magistrate stated that the thieving must be stopped, and he therefore imposed the severe sentence."

The South Staffs engines were, in March 1886, so bad Handsworth Council made a bitter protest to the Board of Trade: "... they make a great noise and clatter, [and] emit smoke and steam". The drivers, who were fined with regularity "say the engines are badly constructed and in bad repair and they cannot stop them emitting smoke for these reasons" and were leaving (after being fined too often) with Dickinson having to send out 17-year-old lads. Typically the Handsworth Local Board in January 1886 "recommended that proceedings should be taken against four of the drivers employed on the Central Tramways, and four drivers employed on the South Staffordshire Tramways, for allowing steam to be emitted from their engines." The Board of Trade Inspector, Major-General Hutchinson, made various suggestions and in 1887 another patent, 5469, emerged headed "Improvements in Condensers", part of the text and the drawings are reproduced as they show clearly the working of a condenser; although most of the South Staffs engines were built to Wilkinson vertical boiler design with only a superheater and no external condensers, but one seems to have been retro-fitted, presumably with Dickinson's own design; even if possible, I would imagine, it would not be an easy conversion.

It is, of course, possible that these experiments lay behind the purchase of engine no.38, the Falcon bought secondhand from Hartlepools in 1885 and sold on shortly afterwards to Coventry as their no.7.

Another of Dickinson's clever moves was his development of the flexible wheel which reduced both the impact of the engine on the rails and the vibration inherent in bad trackwork. 9782 of 1886 stated in its preamble that this device would "minimise the noise produced by the running of such wheels [on the locomotive] which is now felt to be so objectionable." Between the tyres and the wheel proper were interspersed fillets of "india-rubber, lead, asbestos or other material."

1442 of 1887 was for a modified type of point blade or "moveable tongue", single of course as urban tramways did not normally have the railway type of two blades operated together by a lever and tie-bar but instead a double grooved rail is fitted on one (normally right) side and on the left a moveable tongue which would be sprung to guide the wheels on to either road. As they wore (being only chilled iron) the tongue could lay over and throw the tram 'wrong road' and even fifty years later a point or pry bar could be of great use. Dickinson's plan seems to have been the forerunner of the 20th century 'tadpole' pattern of point tongue.

However his 151 of 1887 seems to have been an oddity. The design was intended "to avoid any undue lifting of the vehicle passing [through a crossing] thus minimising the shake or jar caused thereby". Very reasonable when one thinks of an eight-ton engine munching its way over worn trackwork. But his patent required "a rubber or other flexible ring for the purpose of keeping the joint around the top part quite tight". This is shown between 'M' and "K" in the drawing. Underneath the tongue 'K' and resting on the base 'R' is a "coiled or other spring which permits the loose piece to sink as the Car, Engine or other Tramway Vehicle passes along in the direction requiring it and the top is formed with a natural groove a little way along the groove ... then rising sufficiently to form the necessary obstacle against vehicles entering in the other direction". This, he hoped, would prove a steady loose point which could act vertically without fear of injury from water. Perhaps ... I wonder if he ever assembled one of these? Permanent way

---

Date of Application, 29th July, 1886.
Complete Left, 12th Mar., 1887.
Complete Accepted, 15th Apr., 1887.

A.D. 1886, 29th July. N° 9782.

PROVISIONAL SPECIFICATION.

Improvements in Wheels.

I, ALFRED DICKINSON of Tramway Depot Darlaston in the County of Stafford Tramway Manager do hereby declare the nature of the said invention to be as follows :—

My invention has for its object improvements in wheels which are more especially 5 intended for use upon Tramways and Railways where the wear and tear would be considerable such for instance as where brakes are constantly applied to the wheels and where the tyre would often require to be renewed which can be done by my invention very effectively and so as to minimize the noise produced by the running of such wheels which is now felt to be so objectionable.

10 My tyres are made of steel or other hard tough wearing metal and are formed with an internal flange at the plain side and the flange is bored out slightly taper. The internal part or arms are turned to fit the taper in the tyre but slightly larger and a recess is formed around the circumference of the rim of the internal part connecting the arms or forming the centre of the wheel in which I place a ring of india rubber, 15 lead, asbestos or other material having a deadening effect upon the sound produced by concussion with the rails.

I also introduce a facing between the flange face and tyre face and I further form the point of the arms or centre block of a hexagonal or other equivalent shape so as to relieve the bolts which pass through the flanges to secure the two together from any 20 undue strain so that the tendency of the tyre to turn is entirely prevented. Or the points of the arms may be let into the flange of the tyre which answers the same purpose. When the two are forced together the packings are compressed and no jar can occur and the noise is considerably reduced.

Dated this 28th day of July 1886.

25   JOHN KENDRICK,
                            77, Colmore Row, Birmingham,
                            Agent for Applicant.

[*Price 8d.*]

Provisional Specification No. 9782 dated 29 July 1886.

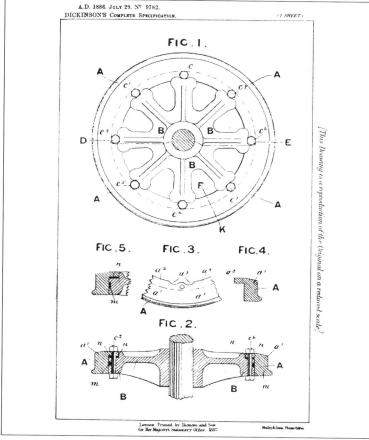

FIC. 1.

FIC. 5.   FIC. 3.   FIC. 4.

FIC. 2.

[This Drawing is a reproduction of the Original on a reduced scale.]

London: Printed by Eyre and Son
for Her Majesty's Stationery Office. 1887.

Malby & Sons. Photo-Litho.

Drawing from Specification No. 9782 dated 29 July 1886.

men have always had an implacable (and sensible) hatred of complicated 'gizmos' that could and would go wrong. Dickinson did however add that if any water got inside the gadget it would pass away through the bottom ...

If the drawing for his 6370 of 1890 is accurate his combined fishplate and soleplate looks quite sensible but I suspect very expensive to cast compared with the norm. The nuts and bolts should be reasonably accessible in use; like all of their kind they would need 'nobbling-up' in due course. Unfortunately he does not state the

proposed length of the fittings – presumably Alfred Dickinson intended these to fit standard drilled rail ends; one problem suggested is that there is no allowance whatsoever for expansion or contraction.

Probably the best, and certainly the one most used of Alfred Dickinson's patents was 6846 of 1890 – his "Improved Auxiliary Brake for Tramway Cars". Simply he wanted it to be possible to stop the trailers either by the action of the conductor/guard who could apply the brake either by a sort of ship's wheel or by a lever, not dissimilar to those used on early cars (Bentleys and the like), or if the engine broke away it would automatically wind a chain on to the wooden drum set on the middle axle, thus pulling up the brake blocks, they then being locked by a ratchet. This would have some chance of working – whether or not it is 'newspaper speak' or an excuse for the conductor/guard (or even if it is true) we do not know, but the bulk of accident reports imply the guard was 'on top', or in the middle of the saloon, at the time of the accident and thus unable to wind on his handbrake. That said and done I sympathise with these men (some were boys of 15, alas) who had probably never gone faster than the 8 or 10mph of the tram and were suddenly faced with an incredibly noisy trailer running away, swaying from side to side and accelerating; at some points the bogie wheels would leave the track and crash down again until they did not and the inevitable happened. It is frightening enough to be on an electric 4-wheel tram doing 'wheelies' let alone one of those behemoths. Even if the guard got to the brake, he would need many turns to take up the slack in the chain while he was jostled and shouted or shrieked at by frightened passengers.

The same year, 1890, another patent, No. 18516, covered a rather unusual "metal

box fitted under and to the web of the tramway rail, having holes for connecting to drains, the upper portion of the box forming the frame for the lid or cover, and the cover forming the check of the tramway rail, the check and bottom of groove of rail being cut away to form a slot to admit the water into the box." I use the word unusual as he introduces a weakness by milling a slot in the groove of the rail right at the point where strength is most needed. If Fig.4 is correct the whole structure is dreadfully weak and after a year or two given the tishy bearing surface F and that slot the whole rail might well twist and in an extreme case fall into the conduit.

Alfred Dickinson was clearly a most amazing man, inventive and yet practical. I do not know what happened to him after Ebbsmith and Wain left the Board of the South Staffs in 1894 – clearly as their protégée he had to resign. Although no patents in his name can be traced after 1894 I cannot believe he sunk into total obscurity; to encourage further research a list of his patents between 1885 and 1894 follows, although one query relates to patent 13211 of 1886 shown as originating from R.H. Dickinson for a "life protector and snow plough" but by the entry are the "void, never published". Was this "life protector" one of those credited to Smith/Ebbsmith?

DICKINSON PATENTS 1885-1894

1885	No. 5368 Tramway points
	No. 6164 Carriages for railways & roadways
1886	No.3630 Dummy points for tramways
	No.4903 Cleaning rails of tramways
	No.7672 Cleaning rails for tramways
	No.9782 Wheels
	No. 14178 Axle Boxes
	No. 16251 Cleaning rails of tramways
	No.16316 Wheels
	No.16805 Wheel journals
	No.16876 Tramway rail cleaners
1887	No.151 Points or crossings of tramways
	No.1442 Movable points of crossings
	No.5469 Condensors
	No.9157 Waybill frame & box
	No.11353 Transmitting material from road to rail
	No.12233 Tramway etc engines
1888	No.16931 Gearing for tramway engines & cars
1889	No.15155 Storing secondary batteries of tramcars
	No.16808 Welding links, hoops etc.
	No.18638 Driving electrical vehicles
1890	No.6370 Fishing & supporting joints of tramways
	No.6846 Brake for tramway cars
	No.18516 Surface, etc. drains for tramways
1891	No.5461 Masts & trolleys for electric traction
	No.8359 Cable tramways
1892	No.9486 Switches & crossings for trolley wires for overhead traction
1893	No patents
1894	No.4244 Overhead electric tramways
	No.9399 Electric railways & tramways
	No.13728 Pole & lamp post for supporting overhead wires for tramways

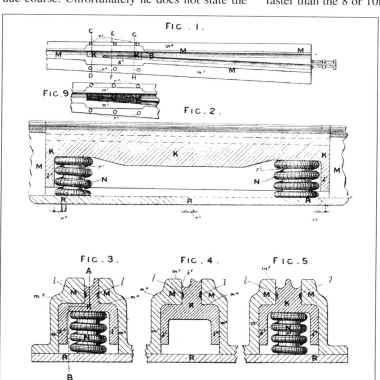

Drawing from Specification No.151 dated 5 January 1887.

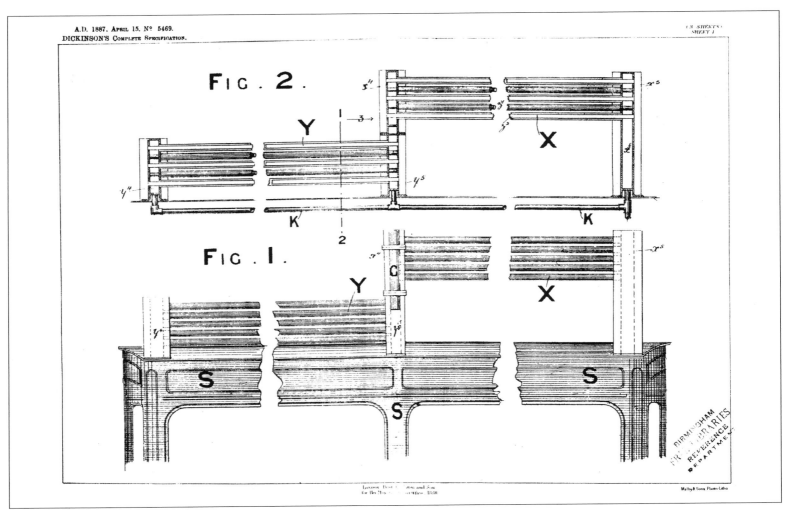

Drawings from Specification No. 5469 dated 15 April 1887.

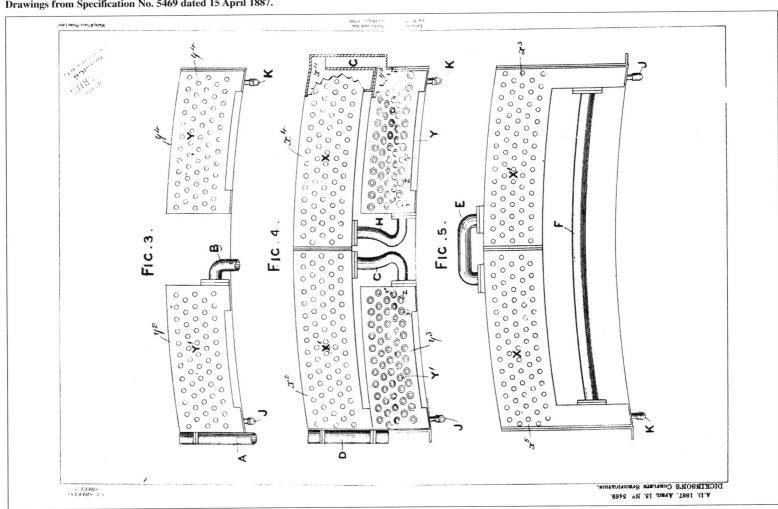

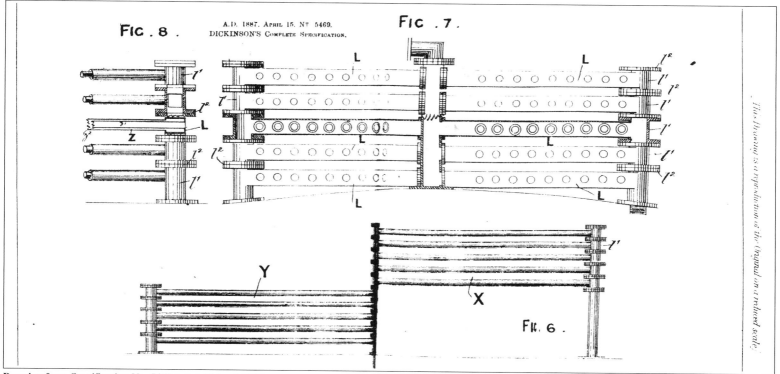

A.D. 1887. April 15. N° 5469.
DICKINSON'S COMPLETE SPECIFICATION.

FIC . 8 .   FIC . 7 .

FIc. 6 .

Drawing from Specification No. 5469 dated 15 April 1887.

A.D. 1887. — N° 5469.

Dickinson's Improvements in Condensers.

Figure 7 is an end view of the same to an enlarged scale a portion being shewn in section.

Figure 8 is a part of the side elevation also enlarged and shewing portions of the pipe L and chamber l^1 in section.

5 My condensers consist of two or more steps or groups of pipes but upon these drawings there are two shewn, namely :—X and Y Figure 1 which are each again divided into two distinct sections thereby forming two other groups which we will distinguish as X^1 and Y^1.

Each of these steps groups or sections are composed of a series of outer pipes Z
10 Figure 4 with inner pipes z^1 of smaller diameter so as to leave the annular space z^2 between the inner diameter of the outer pipe Z and the outer diameter of the inner pipe z^1 in which the steam circulates. Though I lay no exclusive claim to the annular space itself and the circulation of a cooling medium such as air or water inside and outside simultaneously. For the purpose of distributing the steam equally through
15 each pipe each group of pipes are provided with a collecting or distributing chamber at each end, group Y^1 having the chambers y^2 and y^3 group X^1 the chambers x^2 and x^2, group X the chambers x^4 and x^5, and group Y the chambers y^4 and y^5.

The steam from the exhaust pipe is either split up into two parts or the steam from
20 of the group Y^1 at opposite corners by means of the connecting pipes A and B and the steam is thereby forced to distribute itself equally into each annular space in its passage through group Y^1 into the collecting chamber y^3 out of which it again passes by means of the pipes C and D at opposite corners into the upper chamber x^2 and along the pipes X^1 into chamber x^3 from which it is transferred by the connecting
25 pipes E and F into the adjoining chamber x^5 and along pipes X into x^4 and by pipes G and H into the lower chamber y^5 and by group Y into the last chamber y^4. As the steam is condensed it is drained by the pipes J K into the collecting tank ready for pumping back to the boiler. Figures 6 7 and 8 upon sheet 3 shew more clearly the practical method of constructing the distributing and collecting chamber which are
30 formed of a number of square pipes L each having a circular end l^1 and flanges l^2 for bolting to each other to enable any defective pipe to be readily renewed and at the same time allows ample circulation around the outside of the pipes. In this arrangement the course of the steam, the connections from one chamber to another and pipes, are exactly similar to the last.

35 It will be readily seen that by raising one portion of the groups of pipes above another as shewn I am enabled to get a fresh supply of cold air for the latter portion of the pipes which under ordinary circumstances would have been heated by passing through or over the first portion.

Having now particularly described and ascertained the nature of my said
40 invention and in what manner the same is to be performed I declare that what I claim is

First :—In condensers the arrangement of a series of groups and sections of pipes at two or more levels each group having a collecting or distributing chamber at each
45 end into which the steam is supplied from the exhaust and circulated by separate inlets arranged at opposite corners of the chambers substantially as and for the purpose herein set forth.

Second :—The improvements in condensers herein described and as illustrated upon the drawings.

Dated this 13th day of January 1888.

50
GEORGE BARKER,
77, Colmore Row, Birmingham,
Agent for Applicant.

LONDON : Printed for Her Majesty's Stationery Office,
By DARLING AND SON, LTD.

1888.

Specification No. 5469 dated 15 April 1887.

N° 6370   A.D. 1890

Date of Application, 26th Apr., 1890—Accepted, 31st May, 1890
COMPLETE SPECIFICATION.

Improvements in the Methods of Fishing and Supporting the Joints of Tramway and other Rails.

I ALFRED DICKINSON of Tramway Depot Darlaston in the County of Stafford Tramway Manager and Engineer do hereby declare the nature of this invention and in what manner the same is to be performed, to be particularly described and ascertained in and by the following statement :—

5 The Invention has for its object the improvement in the method of fishing and supporting the joints of tramway and other rails and of preventing the springing and other defects that exist with the previous methods of jointing.

In order that my invention may be properly understood and carried into practical effect without difficulty I have appended hereunto one sheet of drawings upon which
10 five figures of various parts of the chair upon a rail are given.

Figure 1 is a plan shewing the casting with the rails fixed in position and secured to the sole of the casting D by means of the bolts E which may be fixed after the chair is in position by being passed through the holes F and held in position by the fillet plate G which also forms an even bearing with the flange of the rail for
15 the washers H which together with the nuts J hold the flange of the rail in position the top portion of the casting has a chequered surface forming the paving block K.

Figure 2 is a section through the casting and rail on the line C. C. Figure 1 shewing the web of the rail secured to the back of the casting L which is provided with fillet M by means of the bolts N and the ordinary fish plate O.

20 Figure 3 is an end elevation of the casting and section through the rail shewing an end view of the stiffening wings P and the chequered surface or paving block K.

Figure 4 is an elevation on the line A. A Figure 1 giving a view of the back L the stiffening wings P the chequered surface or paving block K and also the heads of the bolts E & N.

25 Figure 5 is an elevation on the line B. B Figure 1 shewing the ordinary fish plate O. the fillet plate G the bolts E and N the holes F and the washers H.

The combination of the figures tending to shew the method in its completed form the rails being secured and held in position as hereinbefore described.

Having now particularly described and ascertained the nature of my said Inven-
30 tion and in what manner the same is to be performed I declare that what I claim is :—

1st. The improvements in the method of fishing and jointing tramway and other rails by which means an even bearing is obtained for the flange and head of the rails and greater steadiness is obtained substantially as and for the purpose set forth and
35 shewn upon the accompanying drawing.

2nd. A casting of iron steel or other approved metal forming a combined fish chair and sole plate in conjunction with the ordinary fish plate and bolts substantially as herein set forth and shewn upon the drawing.

3rd. The method of inserting the bolts after the casting is in position by means of
40 the holes F and securing the same in position by means of the fillet plate G substantially as herein set forth and shewn upon the drawing.

Dated this Twenty-third day of April 1890.

ALFRED DICKINSON.

London : Printed for Her Majesty's Stationery Office, by Darling & Son, Ltd.—1890.

[*Price 6d.*]

Specification No. 6370 dated 26 April 1890.

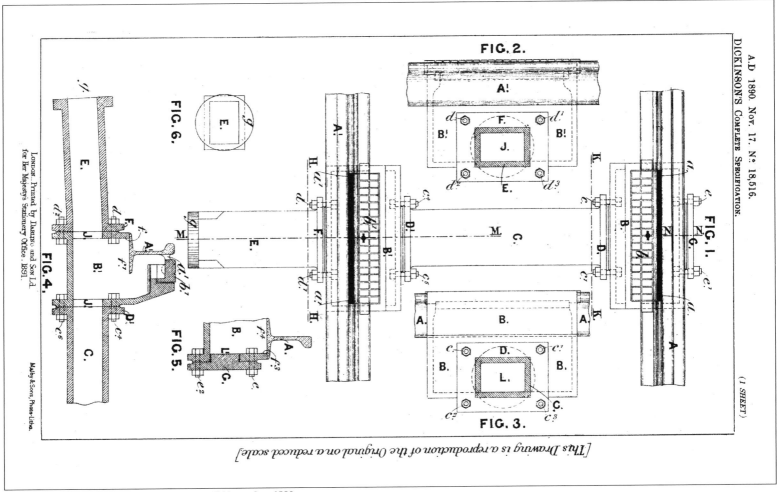

Drawing from Specification No. 18516 dated 17 November 1890.

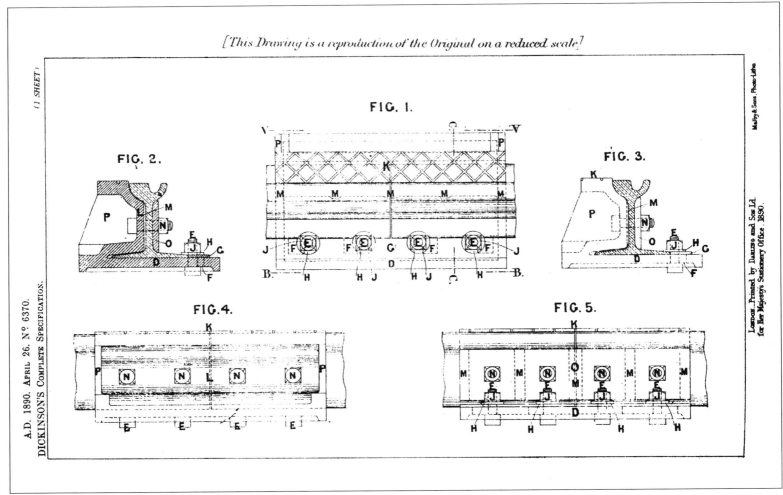

Drawing from Specification No. 6370 dated 26 April 1890.

Section 14

LIFU

Liquid Fuel Engineering Co., Cowes, Isle of Wight

This firm built an extensive range of advanced road vehicles in the late Victorian period. Henry Alonzo House, M.I.M.E., the American M.D. and Engineer had a fertile mind, and it was fortunate that the profits from his steam launch and yacht engines helped to subsidise his other work.*

In 1891, Henry Alonzo started a shipyard by the Thames at Teddington, to build fast launches fired by kerosene. Being American, he considered that the laws of the Conservators of the River Thames did not apply to him and was duly summonsed to appear in court for speeding on the water, and was fined £10 plus costs. It was this over-reaching arrogance that ensured in due course he was to leave Cowes, Isle of Wight, where he next moved his works to. In all his new factory on the IoW was to employ 200 men, many of whom commuted from Southampton.

The first lorry or van utilising House's newly designed boiler and twin compound engines

*One time and another this long lived man (1840-1930) invented an automatic buttonhole machine (1862), a steam horseless carriage (1866) and fascinatingly he was, with his son Henry A. House Jr., heavily involved in the design and building of Sir Hiram Maxim's 300 horsepower steam powered flying machine (1889).

appeared in 1896 or 1897, more or less simultaneously with our steam tram, the latter being put to work on the Portsmouth Town Hall to North End route of the Provincial Tramways Company during peak periods, where the capacity of 60 plus the ability to tow two trailers made it invaluable. Fired by refined petroleum oil or kerosene the boiler, manufactured by Noakes and Company of East London, could be up to a working pressure of 250psi in 20 minutes, consuming one gallon of fuel for this but thereafter requiring, in ideal conditions, 4.54 gallons of water per mile run, as well as 0.655 gallons of fuel.

The regular driver, a Mr D. Bundy, found (as with LIFU's lorries and buses) that once fired up little further attention was required for the boiler, engine or gear, which given the centre location of the equipment quite remote from the driver, was just as well. Following municipalisation of LIFU's tram route in 1901, the car was put aside. In March 1902 it reappeared on the Portsdown and Horndean Light Railway (really a tramway, LRO on 2 September 1899) where this by now rather tired tram operated rather erratically on passenger work certainly until 1917, and probably later, ending up as the works shunter at Cowplain recovering failed electric cars and moving them within the depot. LIFU is known to

still have been in existence 1936-7 as a store, her glory days gone.

One problem found by House at Cowes was that the locals took umbrage at his charging around the lanes test driving his lorries, buses and cars (these latter suffered from temperamental burners and were described as "clumsy things of heavy construction"; odd really for a firm that specialised in fast light launches) and in due course he was again fined for speeding. Ultimately, though, it may well have been the fact that all materials had extra ferry costs to the Island, and completed vehicles carried the same cost penalty that forced a move in 1900 for his works to Southampton. Delays and damage to parts was given as another reason.

As a final note on Henry Alonzo House it was he that developed a new system for baking, handling and packing shredded wheat biscuits for the eponymous company, which could produce 456,000 biscuits every 24 hours. It was derivatives of his machines that first produced 'Welgar Shredded Wheat' in the new ideal Welwyn Garden City factory (opened 1926, closed 2008).

[NOTE: It does now seem probable from the researches of Alan Brotchie that a second LIFU-derived tram operated in Glasgow. We do know that Messrs Robertson, Morton and Co of Wishaw made a number of LIFU pattern steam wagons under licence from the main company and all the components given by Alan in our Volume 5, pp168/9 reek of 'our' paraffin burner.]

There is some doubt exactly what happened to the LIFU/Collis combination. Southampton City Archives carried out some research on this for me and I quote from an email from the Collections Access Officer, to whom I must express my sincere thanks.

"Although I cannot find the Liquid Fuel Engineering Co. anywhere I have found A.B. Collis. In the 1900 directory he is listed as Arthur Bentall Collis, engineer & steam launch builder, West Quay. He is not listed in the 1904 directory but by our next one, the 1909/10, he is at Quayside, Bitterne Park. He is not in the 1911/12 directory".

Was the booklet a last fling or is there more to the story?

The following notes are drawn from a 1910 LIFU catalogue which has been reproduced

A very well known photograph of LIFU probably taken, heavily retouched, on delivery. One of the odd, rather quaint, trailers is shown, together with the spring centre coupling. The skirt of the trailer is lifted, and whether the BoT ever saw the power-car, bereft as it is of any lifeguards, has to be a matter of debate. (Courtesy Geoff Lumb)

100-I.H.P. LIFU Boiler with case on.

100-I.H.P. LIFU Boiler with case off.

under the aegis of the Steam Boat Association in 2005 and we are grateful to this enthusiastic society for facilitating its use.

On the face of it, operating a paraffin fired boiler and its engine should be more or less like working with a Primus stove or Tilley lamp, but the reality is that a really good and intelligent

ship's engineer was well worth his corn, and I have no doubt there was a knack in handling LIFU products which enabled short-cuts to be taken, commensurate with meeting safety requirements. The following guidelines tell us how it should be done, be it working a lorry, car, steam boat or tram!

LIQUID FUEL

"Before describing in detail the system in use by this Company, it may be mentioned that the object aimed at has been the application of ordinary mineral oil, of the very commonest and cheapest quality, as fuel in the furnaces of Steam Boilers.

ITS ADVANTAGES

The advantages of using such a fuel are daily becoming better known and appreciated, but it may be well to mention that petroleum contains – bulk for bulk – twice as many heat units as coal, thereby needing only half the storage space to give the same calorie effect; whilst its cleanliness, its freedom from waste, the facility with which it may be handled, together with the entire absence of obnoxious fumes, all lead one to the opinion that dictates of economy, no less than comfort, must cause mineral oil to take its place in the front rank of fuels within a very short time, and eventually to replace altogether such wasteful fuels as coal and wood.

WHERE TO BE OBTAINED

The recent discoveries of fresh petroleum fields on the European as well as on the American Continent, the prompt measures taken to lay pipe lines to the sea coast where necessary, and the construction of tank steamers on the newest and most improved principles, have combined

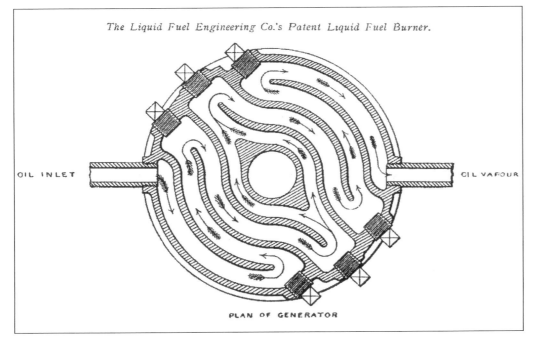

The Liquid Fuel Engineering Co.'s Patent Liquid Fuel Burner.

OIL INLET

OIL VAPOUR

PLAN OF GENERATOR

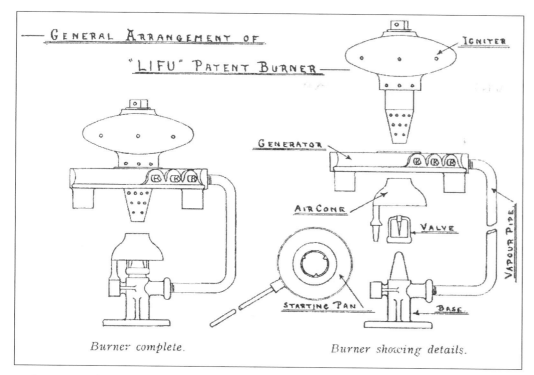

GENERAL ARRANGEMENT OF "LIFU" PATENT BURNER

Burner complete.   *Burner showing details.*

to place mineral oil in almost every port of the world, where it can be bought at prices ranging between 2d. and 6d. per gallon.

SYSTEM ADOPTED BY THIS COMPANY

In order to remedy the various defects already mentioned, a series of elaborate and exhaustive experiments were carried out at great cost, and extending over a period of more than six years, with the result that the Company has been enabled to offer to the public a burner of simple construction and automatic action by means of which

a) Steam at 100lb. Pressure can be raised in 12 to 15 minutes from everything cold.
b) The oil is not sprayed but burned as a vapour.
c) In the event of the fire being put out from a sudden jar or gust of wind, it will re-light even after 10 minutes or more have elapsed.

MACHINERY

"LIFU" BURNER

The burner now used by the Company is of very simple construction, consisting of only four or six parts, according to size and power. An integral part of the apparatus consists of a flat, hollow plate called the "generator". Through this the oil is made to flow under a slight atmospheric pressure by a circuitous route, entering cold and liquid, and issuing from it in the form of hot gas or vapour. This vapour is conducted by a pipe to the burner proper, being compelled on its way to lift a weighted valve forming the "air cone". This automatically regulates the quantity, not only of vapour consumed during a given period of time, but, what is of equal importance, of the atmospheric air to be consumed with it in order to obtain perfect combustion. On the top of the generator (with a nozzle passing through it) is placed an iron receptacle, called the "igniter".

IGNITER

This is filled with small pieces of fire-brick or other material capable of retaining heat for a

considerable period, and in the event of the fire being accidentally extinguished by the presence of water in the oil or a sudden gust of wind it will immediately re-light.

STARTER

The fire is started by means of a flat, shallow pan called a Starter, filled with Asbestos Wool. On the latter a quantity of Methylated Spirit or Oil is poured, and lighted, and the Starter is then placed under the generator on top of the burner. Sufficient heat is thereby generated to volatise a small quantity of oil, and the vapour thus formed is itself ignited on issuing from the burner.

REGULATOR

The furnace will then remain alight as long as any oil is allowed to pass to the generator, the amount being easily regulated by mans of a cone valve to which is attached a dial showing approximately the number of pounds of oil consumed per hour. As before stated, the oil used is the cheapest quality of lamp oil, ordinary paraffin, or even brown oil, and the consumption per I.H.P. per hour is about 1½ to 3lb.

BOILERS

It has been found in practice that in order to obtain perfect combustion of the Liquid Fuel, a correct admixture of atmospheric air is absolutely essential, and to secure this we have introduced a water tubular boiler

having a furnace specially arranged to obtain this result. The base of the furnace is formed into a well, in which the burner is placed, the air being carried round the base of the burner and mixed with the vapour before the latter is ignited. In some cases where it is not practical to use oil fuel, we also make Lifu Boilers to burn coal or wood, and being provided with large heating surfaces and grate area, ample steam can be maintained without the use of artificial draught.

WATER TUBES

The water tubes are seamless (drawn on a central mandril), bent in a double curve to allow for expansion and contraction, and fixed at top and bottom by means of our Patent Detachable Joint, by means of which any single tube can be readily taken out for inspection or renewal, and replaced with an ordinary spanner, a perfect joint being obtained without packing or expanding of the ends.

PATENT JOINT

It must be evident that the danger of explosion in such a boiler is reduced to a minimum, for even if in consequence of carelessness the feed water should be cut off and the furnace still be left alight, the only result would be that a tube (the weakest part) would open, and the small amount of steam in the boiler would escape up the funnel.

TESTING

Every boiler before being fitted is tested to 500 lb hydraulic pressure per square inch, the safety valve being set at 250 lbs.

CASING

All valves and fittings are of the very latest design, and all cocks are asbestos packed."

The following directions will be of interest, and show a greater degree of skill, more akin to that of a 'mecanicien' than a shunt engine driver, was required to get the best from a LIFU machine.

Class.	I.H.P. of Boiler.	Length.	Width.	Height.	Approximate Weights.
B	7	2 ft. 3 in.	1 ft. 8 in.	2 ft. 6 in.	2 cwts.
C	10	2 ft. 9 in.	2 ft. 2 in.	2 ft. 9 in.	3 ,,
D	15	3 ft. 0 in.	2 ft. 6 in.	3 ft. 0 in.	5 ,,
F	25	3 ft. 5½ in.	2 ft. 10 in.	3 ft. 3 in.	7½ ,,
H	35	3 ft. 8 in.	3 ft. 6 in.	4 ft. 2 in.	10 ,,
J	50	4 ft. 8 in.	3 ft. 6 in.	4 ft. 2 in.	12½ ,,
K	65	5 ft. 2 in.	3 ft. 9 in.	4 ft. 8 in.	15 ,,
L	80	6 ft. 0 in.	4 ft. 1 in.	5 ft. 3 in.	20 ,,
N	125	7 ft. 0 in.	4 ft. 1 in.	5 ft. 3 in.	30 ,,

This table gives the reletive sizes and weights of our standard types of boilers.

Class.	I.H.P. of Engine	Length.	Breadth.	Height.	Weight in lbs.	Steam Pressure lbs.	Rev. per Minute.
B	7	2 ft. 3 in.	1 ft. 6 in.	0 ft. 10 in.	200	225	600
C	10	2 ft. 6 in.	1 ft. 10 in.	1 ft. 0 in.	300	250	600
D	15	2 ft. 6 in.	1 ft. 10 in.	1 ft. 0 in.	300	250	600
F	25	2 ft. 10 in.	2 ft. 2 in.	1 ft. 3 in.	400	250	550
H	35	3 ft. 0 in.	2 ft. 6 in.	1 ft. 6 in.	500	250	450
J	50	3 ft. 6 in.	1 ft. 8 in.	1 ft. 6 in.	600	250	400
K	65	4 ft. 6 in.	2 ft. 2 in.	4 ft. 0 in.	1250	250	350
L	80	5 ft. 2 in.	2 ft. 7 in.	4 ft. 4 in.	2100	250	300
N	125	5 ft. 7 in.	3 ft. 0 in.	4 ft. 6 in.	2800	250	300

This table shows the comparative weights and dimensions of our various sizes of engine and pumps complete. Engines of 7 to 50 I.H.P. are horizontal, closed in, with all working parts running in oil.

"DIRECTIONS FOR RAISING STEAM IN WATER TUBULAR BOILERS FITTED WITH PATENT LIQUID FUEL BURNERS, AND FOR WORKING COMPOUND ENGINES MANUFACTURED BY THE LIQUID FUEL ENGINEERING COMPANY

FIRST

See that the water in the boiler is two-thirds up the glass gauge. If not, fill the desired height by opening the "auxiliary feed valve" which connects the reserve water tank, using the hand feed pump to force the water into the boiler, and taking care to shut the "auxiliary feed valve" when the boiler is filled to the desired level. See that the cover is on the funnel.

SECOND

Take the "Starter" (a flat pan filled with asbestos wool) and pour in methylated spirit until the wool is thoroughly saturated; light the spirit and place the "Starter" on top of the burner cone, allowing it to remain there from ten to fifteen minutes. This heats the generator, and thereby vaporises the liquid fuel.

Lubricate the engine as follows: Fill the brass reservoir box on the frame of the engine; fill the four oil boxes on the sides of the eccentric rods, and the one on the top of the pump plunger, and also put a few drops of oil on all the moving parts of the links and connections.

With our improved type enclosed engine, it is only necessary to fill the engine case level with the top of guides and fill oil box on pump plunger.

THIRD

Raise the pressure on the air gauge to 9 or 10 pounds by the use of the hand air-pressure pump. See that the "oil cock" (with square spindle) is opened, the hand-regulating oil valve being closed. When the "Starter" has been on as long as necessary, open the oil valve to figure 4 on the dial. Watch the burner, and when oil comes out and lights, close the valve for a moment to allow the condensed vapour to burn, then open the valve again to about number 4, when the burner will start with a slight splutter. The cover on the funnel should then be taken off and the oil valve opened to about number 6. Should the air pressure drop, give a few strokes with the hand pump to raise it again to the required pressure. The "Starter" can then be taken off the burner. When the steam pressure has reached about 40 pounds, open the drain cock on the receiver; then open the main steam valve a little, and also the low pressure starting valve, letting steam into the second cylinder to warm up; then work the reversing lever forwards and backwards. When the engine has made a few revolutions ahead and astern, close the low

pressure starting valve, and if there is no clicking in the cylinders caused by the presence of water, the drain cock may be closed.

During the summer months in 1898 and 1899 this LIFU parcels van and passenger trailer plied the eight miles between Fairford and Cirencester. Operated by the Midland and South Western Junction Railway the objective was to establish if there was sufficient demand to justify laying in a rail link. Although the parcels side was successful (the van could carry 3 tons) the passenger demand was so little that the LIFU ensemble was replaced with a horse bus.

GENERAL

Should there be any smoke coming from the funnel, open the blast valve very slightly. By this means a forced draught is obtained, which at ordinary speeds will not be required. To maintain the desired steam pressure open the oil valve to number 12, or as near that number as may be found necessary.

In making a landing, close the oil valve to about number 3 or 5, and then slow down by closing the main steam valve.

If the engine should not start instantly, either ahead or astern, open the low pressure starting valve, letting steam into the second cylinder, and close again immediately the engine starts.

In case of a long stop, it is better to open the drain cock to let the condensed steam out of the receiver.

Should the fire go out by a jar or puff of wind when the burner is turned too low, turn off the oil-regulating valve, open the blast valve for a few seconds, put a little methylated spirit on the "Starter"; light and place by the side of the burner; turn on the liquid fuel, and it will immediately re-light.

When the engines are stopped for the day, turn off the main and regulating oil valves, open the drain cock, and put the cover on the funnel.

The safety valve is set at 250 lb, and will not allow the pressure to get above that point.

Should the feed pump on the engine fail to work satisfactorily, open the small air cock and partially close a few times; this releases the air which sometimes gets under the valves.

It is advisable to take out the pump valves occasionally in order to clean them. This can be done by unscrewing the cap on the valve box. Be sure to replace the valves and springs in their right positions, the stiffest spring always on the top valve.

Never have a strong fire when the water is low. When the water is not in sight *turn the fire out*, and use the hand-feed pump or donkey pump. Never completely fill the oil tank; an air space of three inches at the least must always be left.

Use only the best engine oil for bearings.

Should the boiler prime in consequence of the water being greasy, put in a handful of common soda dissolved in water, raise the steam to 150 lb, and allow it to remain overnight. In the morning raise steam to 50 lb or 100 lb and blow out boiler, then re-fill with fresh water."

25-I.H.P. LIFU Burner in Blast.

TANGLED WEBS

Manchester, Bury, Rochdale & Oldham Rules & Regulations 1885

The MBRO Rules and Regulations, for not only their Servants but also their Officers, are redolant of those made apparent to the staff of any traffic grade who joined the old 'Big Four', and later British Railways. We have shown elsewhere in this series that these Rules were often not sustainable in Court, and it is difficult to believe that the Company's directors really thought their men could read, let alone understand some of the nuances apparent. Personally I like the

Honesty!
Punctuality!
Obedience!
Sobriety!
Civility!

that was asked of the men (and the occasional clerkess) and only regret the loss recently of so many public transport employees who tried to follow this creed, only to find out how venal managements could be. I do not think as a generality the MBRO directors were a bad crew, and no matter how hard these Rules may appear to be some humanity was shown in the 'Glee Parties', outings and Jamborees arranged for the employees.

Our set of these Rules was incomplete and we are grateful to the Local Studies staff at Touchstones, Rochdale, for copies of the missing pages.

𝔯𝔲𝔩𝔢𝔰 𝔞𝔫𝔡 𝔯𝔢𝔤𝔲𝔩𝔞𝔱𝔦𝔬𝔫𝔰

FOR THE

OFFICERS AND SERVANTS

OF THE

MANCHESTER, BURY, ROCHDALE, AND

OLDHAM STEAM TRAMWAYS COMPANY.

BURY:
PRINTED BY JOHN H. SHAW, 4, COOPER STREET.
1885.

THE MANCHESTER, BURY, ROCHDALE, & OLDHAM STEAM TRAMWAYS COMPANY.

Notice is Hereby Given, that a breach of the Company's Rules and Regulations for the time being in force will render any Servant of the Company committing the same liable to a fine.

By order of the Directors.

1st January, 1885.

GENERAL REGULATIONS.

1. All the *officers and servants* of the company shall, at the time of their engagement, be furnished with a copy of the Rules and Regulations of the Company in force for the time being, in which will be inserted the employee's name, and it shall be held as forming an express condition of their engagement, that the same is made and accepted of, subject to the said Rules and Regulations, and under an obligation on their part, (1) To abide by, observe, fulfil, and comply with the same, and with the Bye-Laws and Regulations made by the Manchester, Bury, Rochdale, and Oldham Steam Tramways Company, under the powers conferred on them by the Tramways Act, 1870, and all orders made in pursuance thereof (all of which are declared to form a part of these Rules and Regulations) in all respects, in so far as applicable to their several and respective classes or departments,

The word " Car " in these Rules and Regulations shall include " Omnibus."

2 Every servant is required when on duty to have in his possession a copy of these Rules, Regulations, and Bye-laws, in which will be inscribed his name, and he must produce the same when required. If lost, a fresh copy will be supplied, and a charge of sixpence made for same.

3 Every servant is expected to be neat in appearance polite to all, and to abstain from improper language and misconduct.

4 Every servant in the company's service found under the influence of drink will be forthwith discharged.

5 It is as much the driver's duty as the conductor's to look out for passengers, and when the conductors are collecting fares they must use extra diligence.

6 Any servant using improper language, entering into altercation with the public or his fellow servants when on duty, absenting himself without permission, disobeying orders, smoking on the company's premises or on duty, being intoxicated, or feeing any other servant of the company, will be liable to be discharged.

7 It is the duty of all subordinates to report to their respective Inspector any occurrences coming under their notice affecting the proper working of the traffic, or which may effect the company in any way, or the convenience and accommodation of the public.

8 *No servant of the company must give or receive from any other servant of the company any fee or gratuity of any nature, and any servant from whom any such gratuity is demanded must immediately report the same to the head of his department.*

THE LOCOMOTIVE FOREMAN

Is responsible as follows :—

1. For the efficient performance of duty by all men working under his supervision, the proper working order of engines and cars, in accordance with the authorised time tables, the cleanliness and efficient lighting of the cars.

2. For a strict observance of the Bye-Laws and Regulations, of which copies are annexed, and of the rules laid down by the company for the drivers.

3. For the punctual starting of cars from the depot when commencing for the day.

4. For each car running its booked number of journeys, and to report in writing, and to obtain the drivers' reports, and hand them to the locomotive superintendent, explaining any trips lost,

of the cars in use. The cars shall be examined every morning and unless they are thoroughly cleaned, without injury to the advertisements therein or thereon, report the matter in full.

2. For a strict observance of the Bye-Laws and Regulations made by the Company, and all orders made in pursuance thereof, and of the Rules laid down by the company for Time-keepers, Conductors, Drivers, &c.

3. For the timely starting of the Cars from the Depot, so as to give them time to reach and leave the terminus at the time stated in the time-table.

4. For cars being supplied before leaving the yard with time-tables and fare bills, route and destination boards, and with keys for ticket drawers, and all articles required to be kept in the Cars.

Inspectors are required

5. To regulate their watches daily and to see that the clocks at the Cash Offices are kept to time.

6. To report every morning if the Cars running in their district on the previous day have made all their stated journeys and if not to explain the reason.

7. In the event of a fire occurring in their district while they are on duty, to arrange with the proper authorities that the traffic may not be suspended in consequence.

8. When an accident, **no matter how trivial**, to person or property occurs, or when a car or other vehicle breaks down, to make a full investigation at once, obtaining names and addresses of all witnesses and reporting the facts to the Traffic Manager or Superintendent of accidents in writing, at the same time forwarding the Conductor's official report.

5. To examine reports of engine-drivers and conductors as to defects in engines or cars, and sign the same as a voucher that such report has been read, and have the defects (if any) remedied before starting-time in the morning.

6. When an accident, *no matter how trivial*, involving injury to person or property occurs, or when a car breaks down, to proceed to the spot with all necessary appliances, and spare neither time nor trouble to arrange for the speedy resumption of the traffic, to make a full investigation at once, and report the facts to the locomotive superintendent in writing, and to obtain the driver's report.

7. To report immediately any driver who quits his post without permission, or until he has been relieved.

8. To be prepared to go on duty at any time when required.

9. When a car is more than five minutes late to obtain the driver's (if necessary) explanation of the cause, and hand the same to the locomotive superintendent.

10. To keep private all information he may possess with regard to the receipts or other matters he may be cognisant of.

11. Study to treat all men under him with consideration and kindness, but firmness.

INSPECTORS.

Inspectors shall be responsible

1. For the proper and efficient working of all employees in their respective districts, the good conduct of their subordinates, and the cleanliness

9. When misconduct is observed in another district, to report the same at once to the Traffic Manager, and also to the Inspector in whose district the misconduct has taken place.

10. To report immediately any Time-keeper, Driver, or Conductor leaving his work before or until he has been relieved.

11. To be courteous to and co-operate with their colleagues, and avoid all jealous or unfriendly feeling.

12. To keep every man to his time and proper duty, and report every breach of these Rules which may come under his notice.

13. To see that the gas is not burnt extravagantly or the water wasted.

14. To examine and collect from time to time as they may be instructed, the tickets of passengers by the company's cars, for the purpose of ascertaining if the proper fares have been paid, and the proper tickets issued and punched.

15. Before entering any car they must count the passengers both in and out, and see that the proper number are marked on the way bill, and before leaving the car they must require the production of a ticket or the payment of a fare from every passenger unprovided with a pass.

16. In the event of any passenger (not having a pass) being found without a ticket, either on Engine or Car, they must compel payment of the proper fare and report the circumstance.

17. They must see that all tickets are properly punched.

18 Should any passenger refuse to produce his ticket or to pay the fare legally demandable, his name and address must be taken and a report made of the circumstance in writing giving full particulars.

19. Inspectors must in like manner report every case of a passenger who has paid a fare being without a ticket, or with an unpunched ticket, or with a ticket the number of which does not correspond with the way-bill as being in use for that journey, who may state that the conductor has failed to deliver to him a ticket, or to punch it, with the name and address of such passenger, and if possible the name and address of any other passenger who may have witnessed the fact of the conductor receiving a fare without giving a ticket, or punching it.

20. They must record on the forms supplied to them for the purpose full particulars of their work, specifying under the respective headings the information required, and at the close of each day's work, or oftener if necessary, will fill up their daily report forms, with full particulars of all cases of irregularities which they may have met with, as well as all cases of fast driving, bad timekeeping, or other breaches of these rules and regulations, and forward the same to the Traffic Manager.

21. Inspectors must not enter into conversation with conductors, except as business may require. They must keep an independent position, and any Inspector failing to do this will be immediately discharged.

22. Inspectors are required to see that conductors keep their cars clean and well ventilated, that the lighting is perfect, and the flame not too high to smoke the glasses and lamp boxes.

23. Each Inspector must see that the Water Boy keeps the road cleanly swept in his respective district, and also that the Points Boy keeps the points clean. They must also report to the Traffic Manager any defect in the permanent way which comes under their notice.

24. They must rigidly enforce a strict obedience to the rules laid down for timekeepers, drivers, conductors, and road cleaners, and all others under their supervision.

25. They must thoroughly examine every day the cars running on their route, reporting in writing to the Traffic Manager any defects they may observe, and must, under no circumstances, allow a car or horses to run when not in proper order or condition.

TIME-KEEPERS.

Time-keepers are required

1. To be on duty at the appointed time, and never to leave their post unless relieved or until the last car for the day has left the station.

2. To provide themselves with a suitable watch and whistle.

3. To do all in their power to insure that the drivers and conductors keep time to a minute, and to report to the Traffic Manager any man who fails to do so.

4. To initial the conductor's way bills and inspect his tickets each run, and to mark thereon the time when each car arrives at a terminus, or at the point at which they may be stationed.

5. To see that drivers and conductors obey the rules laid down for their guidance.

6. To enter, if required, the arrival and departure of each car, the number of passengers carried, and check-tickets sold.

7. To attend promptly to any breakdown, or collision, or accident to person or property, happening on the company's lines in their im-

mediate district, and to leave a full written report of same at once, giving the names and addresses of all witnesses, to the Traffic Manager or Superintendent of Accidents.

ENGINE-DRIVERS.

Engine-drivers are required—

1. To be on duty at least twenty minutes before their engines are booked to leave the shed, for the purpose of ascertaining if the engine is all right and properly supplied with the requisite tools, sand boxes filled, to oil all round, &c.; also, should they find any defects reported the previous night not attended to, they must report the same to the foreman, and they must see that an entry is made on their Report Sheet.

2. Each engine is supplied with a set of tools, a list of which are entered up in a book and signed for by each engine-driver on taking charge of an engine, and each engine-driver will be held responsible for the full number and good usage—wear and tear excepted—upon whatever engine he may be engaged.

3. Engine-drivers must not, upon any pretence whatever, leave their engines when in the streets.

4. Engine-drivers must light the engine headlight immediately after sunset.

5. The speed at which the engine and car must travel upon the straight in ordinary weather is eight miles per hour, but when passing over crossings the speed must not exceed two miles per hour. On passing streets which cross a speed of four miles per hour must not be exceeded, and at these points the engine-driver must keep a very sharp look out and ring his bell. Any breach of this Rule will be severely punished.

6. At all times must an engine-driver keep a sharp look out. When approaching restless horses he must at once bring the engine to a stand until the horses have passed.

7. The alarm must be frequently sounded when passing through the busy portion of the route, care being taken not to pull up opposite cross streets, but just clear in order not to interfere with the ordinary traffic of the streets.

8. In view of cross streets (see also 5), and traffic and pedestrians, engine-drivers must at all times have their engines and cars well under control, and be prepared to pull up at once.

9. The passing places are noted on the sheets for the purpose, and may vary from time to time. Engine-drivers must satisfy themselves that no engine or car is approaching them from the next crossing place in advance.

10. When a man in charge of any cart, vehicle, or lurry makes no attempt to get out of the way, the engine-driver must stop the engine and car and ask the man civilly to get out of the way. If he does not do so in a reasonable time obtain his name and address.

11. Engine-drivers are strictly forbidden to erect any temporary sheeting or weather board which shall in any way interrupt a full view of the road immediately before them.

12. Engine-drivers must keep a sharp look out for persons, particularly children, crossing the streets.

13. Engine-drivers are required to keep a sharp look out for persons down cross streets and on the road side who may indicate a wish to ride. They must not wait for the signal to stop from the conductor, but pull up at once when it is seen that there are intending passengers.

14. Engine-drivers are held responsible for damages to property caused by their negligence, and they will be required to pay the amount claimed. The money will be deducted from their wages.

15. Engine-drivers are required to observe the following signals between the conductor and themselvse.

Rings of the Bell:

Once, STOP.
Once, GO ON.
Three times, FULL.

In case of accident, or to prevent one, the conductor will ring the bell repeatedly, when the driver must stop and ascertain what is the matter. In the event of the driver finding he cannot, through a failure of a brake on the engine, safely take an engine and car down an incline, he must ring his bell violently until the conductor's attention is gained, who will immediately apply the brake of the car. Should the driver require the assistance of the conductor for any purpose, he must ring the conductor's bell three times slowly and repeatedly.

16. Engine-drivers are strictly forbidden to start the car by any other signal than the bell (except in case the bell is out of order, when a whistle will be used), and drivers must not look back into the car for the purpose of ascertaining if a passenger has got into the car or alighted.

17. When passing a car, the car which first reaches the crossing must come to a stand until the car running in the opposite direction has got quite clear. After dark the engine-driver who first reaches the crossing must signal to the approaching car by waving a green light that the crossing is clear for the car to proceed. **Any disregard of this Rule will be severely punished.** In foggy weather the greatest possible care must be exercised in running. Under no circumstances must the proper crossing place be passed until ten minutes have elapsed without hearing or seeing anything of the car running opposite. After that time the car must proceed at four miles an hour, the driver continuously ringing the alarm bell until the next crossing is reached, and the approaching car has passed. Drivers must **sound the alarm bell almost continuously during foggy weather, particularly when passing through busy streets.**

18. When two cars meet on the single lines, the one nearest the crossing places, after obtaining the requisite signal from the conductor to do so must put back at the speed of four miles an hour. The signal to put back is by waving of the arm by day and a green light by night. Drivers are required to avoid overrunning the crossing places as much as possible, and when it becomes necessary to put back, every care must be exercised to prevent accidents. Any damage done will have to be paid by the men in fault if it is proved the damage was the result of carelessness.

19. No driver must leave his engine unless relieved by another man, before seeing that his hand brakes are screwed hard on, and the engine put in middle geer. Any breach of this rule will result in instant dismissal.

20. It is as much the driver's duty as the conductor's to look out for passengers; and when the conductor is collecting fares the driver must use extra diligence.

21. Drivers' wages will accrue from day to day but be paid once a week only, and will only accrue and be paid for such days or parts of days as the driver may be actually at work it not being the intention of the company to ensure constant daily employment to the driver. The rate of wages will be fixed at the time of the driver entering the company's service, but may be varied at any time on giving twenty-four hours' notice to the driver.

22. Drivers will be held responsible for all injury and damage caused by their neglect or carelessness.

23. They must not annoy or harass any conductor by unduly increasing or diminishing the speed of his car, or by not promptly stopping for passengers upon the usual signal being given.

Each Driver is specially required

24. Not to turn curves especially in narrow streets, until there is space enough for the rear end of the car as it swings round, to pass without colliding with other vehicles which may be in the street, and **to use great caution in passing cross streets.**

25. When two engines are meeting near a facing-point (whether such facing-point leads to a junction, siding, or cross-over) both drivers will apply the brakes and bring their engines to almost a standstill until each engine has passed the point safely. **The engine about to take a point shall have the precedence of the other.**

26. To give wide space to winged wagons and heavily loaded carts, and to keep a good look-out for children improperly or incautiously straying or walking in the streets.

27. To come to a full stop for all persons wishing to enter the car, unless the conductor strikes the bell to go on.

28. To have the brake always under control, and to use his utmost endeavours to avoid collisions with vehicles **whether those in charge of such vehicles are in the wrong or not.**

29. To obey the Inspectors and Time-keepers

HORSE CAR DRIVERS.

1. Drivers' wages will accrue from day to day, but be paid once a week only, and will only accrue and be paid for such days or parts of days as the driver may be actually at work, it not being the intention of the company to ensure constant daily employment to the driver. The rate of wages will be fixed at the time of the driver entering the company's service, but may be varied at any time on giving twenty-four hours' notice to the driver.

2. Drivers will be held responsible for all injury and damage caused by their neglect or carelessness.

A Driver is expressly forbidden

3. To leave his car for the purpose of changing switches, or to yoke or unyoke trace-horses, it being the duty of the conductor to do so in the absence of an appointed person.

4. To annoy or harass any conductor by unduly increasing or diminishing the speed of his car, or by not promptly stopping for passengers upon the usual signal being given.

5. To ill-treat his horses or to leave them unattended.

6. To accept any fee or gratuity for carrying parcel, box, package, basket, or barrel, whether full or empty.

Each Driver is specially required

7. To be at the yard 10 minutes before the appointed time of his starting, to take out his car, also to see that it is properly put up at nights.

8. To provide himself with a proper whip and whistle.

9. To be careful and considerate in the treatment of his horses, holding the reins firmly, so that should a horse slip, he will be enabled to prevent a fall. **All falls must be reported to the Traffic Manager in writing and to the Horse-keeper when the horses are returned to the stables.**

10. To report to the Traffic Manager any horses unfit for work—either from sore shoulders loose shoes, or any other cause, **and to report any horse-keeper missing a shift or not bringing the horses out at the proper time.**

11. To start the horses by the bell.

12. To see that his horses are properly harnessed and the draw bars fixed before leaving a terminus,

13. To stand erect when passing through busy thoroughfares.

14. To keep a sharp look out for persons in side streets, who may indicate a wish to ride.

15. **To allow no one to enter or leave the Car by the front platform.**

16. To speak pleasantly to drivers in charge of other conveyances when requesting them to remove out of the way.

17. To apply the brake when approaching a machine upon the track, so as to give sufficient room to get out of the way if the wheels should slide.

18. To give the conductor the signal by the bell when a parcel is put on the front platform, so that the fare for it can be collected.

19. To look back and see that passengers are safely received and landed before starting.

20. As a general rule not to start without the signal from the conductor.

21. Never to drop the bar when changing the horses from one end of the car to the other, and to obtain the conductor's assistance when changing if necessary.

22. Not to stop when going up a steep incline for the purpose of taking up or setting down passengers, **and not to drive his horses faster than an ordinary trot going down an incline.**

23. When approaching facing-points on an incline, the driver of a down car is to **stop** until the up car has undoubtedly passed the point.

24. To tap the bell three times quickly, in emergencies, when the rear brake requires to be applied.

25. To ring the bell once when the assistance of the conductor is absolutely necessary.

26. When the street is blocked so that the cars cannot proceed, to stop his car before arriving at the place where the block occurred, so as to keep an open space of 100 yards be-

tween each car. In case the car is stopped by any block so long as to bring more than two cars together, the foremost car must, after the way is clear, be driven along so that the time lost by the delay may be gradually made up as soon as possible, but it must not be driven faster than six miles an hour. This rule applies to two or more cars following each other on the same route only.

27. Not to turn curves, especially in narrow streets, until there is space enough for the rear end of the car as it swings round, to pass without colliding with other vehicles which may be in the street. and **to use great caution in passing cross streets.**

28. When two cars are meeting near a facing point (whether such facing-point leads to a junction, siding, or cross-over) both drivers will apply the brakes and bring their horses to a walk until each car has passed the point safely. **The Car about to take a point shall have the precedence of the other.**

29. To give wide space to winged wagons and heavily loaded carts, and to keep a good look-out for children improperly or incautiously straying or walking in the streets.

30. When following vehicles, to allow ample space so that in the event of the former pulling up suddenly no collision may result therefrom.

31. When passing another car, to slacken the speed of his horses and gently put on the brake, to guard against running over persons who may be unguardedly crossing the street, in the rear of or alighting from the other car. **Cars are never to be stopped abreast of each other.**

32. To exercise great caution on inclines, curves, switches, connections with other roads, and in streets where the track runs so near the footpath as not to allow a carriage to pass without a collision.

33. To drive the horses no faster than a trot when driving down inclines, and over all curves, switches, turnouts, and crossings, and at other times to drive at a regular and steady pace, and in no instance to exceed six miles an hour.

34. In case of fire, to give all the accommodation possible to fire engines, and stop his car, if necessary, for them to pass.

35. To prevent any one except the authorised officials of the company from standing on the platform with him.

36. To remain at the yard when the car is not running, seeing he may be required at any time.

37. To allow **no one** to drive for him without first obtaining permission from the Traffic Manager or Inspector.

38. To come to a full stop for all persons wishing to enter the car, unless the conductor strikes the bell to go on.

39. To have the brake always under control and to use his utmost endeavours to avoid collisions with vehicles **whether those in charge of such vehicles are in the wrong or not.**

40. To **stop** the car in cases where the conductor may have more passengers on than the authorised number, until the latter has got them off.

41. To leave the brakes off the wheels when the car is run into the yard, and never to link up the brake-chains so as to impede the perfect working of the wheels.

43 To report himself to the Inspector before leaving the depot at the end of the day's work.

CONDUCTORS.

1. Parties wishing to become conductors, must in the first instance prove themselves competent to manage a car before they will be allowed to take charge of one. They will be put on a car to practice with a selected conductor who will be held responsible for the learner's competency when passed.

2. Conductor's wages will accrue from day to day, but be paid once a week only, and will only accrue and be paid for such days or parts of days as the conductor may be actually at work by order of the company or their Traffic Manager; it not being the intention of the company to ensure constant daily employment to the conductor. The rate of wages will be fixed at the time of the conductor entering the company's service, but may be varied at any time by the Traffic Manager on giving twenty-four hours' notice to the conductor.

A conductor shall be responsible for

3. The cleanliness and ventilation of his car, the proper state of the seats, aprons, lamps, and other fittings; also to see that the proper lighting is perfect, and that the flame is not kept too high to smoke the glasses and lamp-boxes.

4. The fare of every passenger riding in a car, in terms of the Table of Fares.

5. The comfort and safety of the passengers.

6. All accidents and casualties (however trivial) not duly reported by him.

7. The careful changing of the switches in the absence of the point-boys.

A conductor is expressly forbidden

8. To start a car from a terminus until he has taken his position on the rear platform, and marked off on his Way Bill the number of passengers on his car, which (when not collecting fares or providing seats for passengers) shall form his standing-place, from which to look out in the opposite direction from that in which the car is going.

9. To allow any person to travel without paying the proper fare, except in the case of a person producing a ticket, or a " Complimentary " or " Employee " Pass.

10. To allow an intoxicated person to be received on, or any person to smoke while inside the car, or on the platforms, or to allow any person to remain upon either platform, excepting an officer of the company.

11. To sit down inside or on the outside of the car when on duty; or to allow any passenger to sit on the guard rail, or to stand on the roof or on either platform, except when in the act of entering or leaving the car.

12. To allow the distribution of Advertisements or Tracts of any kind or nature in or on the cars, or the sale of Newspapers or any article without permission from the Head Office in writing.

13. To collect or receive money for any employee, to be applied in paying fines or penalties.

14. To allow anyone to change a switch where there is no pointsboy, it being the conductor's duty to attend to matters such as these.

15. To stop the car on street-crossings, or while going up heavy inclines.

Each conductor is required

16. To be at the yard 10 minutes before the appointed time of his starting, to see that the car is in order when taken from the yard, and that it is properly put up at night.

17. To provide himself with a proper whistle.

18. To go to the front when he gets the signal from the driver, and assist the driver in every possible way.

19. To report on the proper form all injury done to the car, or accidents caused by it, either to person or property, **no matter how trivial.** In all cases of injury to person, to show sympathy and render every assistance, and to send a report of same to the head office at once, so that inquiries can be immediately instituted.

20. To ascertain, and report in writing on the proper form, the names and addresses of the party or parties causing any damage, as well as of any person or persons who may have been injured, and also the names and addresses of witnesses.

21. To call the attention of the night inspector or watchman to any damage which may have been done to the car, horses, or harness during the day, as well as making out the formal report to be sent to the head office.

22. **Any neglect to report an accident, however slight, will be deemed sufficient cause for dismissal. All Reports must be written in ink, and signed by driver and conductor.**

23. To direct the driver entirely by the bell when on the platform or inside, as regards, starting and stopping, viz., one tap; when on the top of the car, collecting fares, the whistle

is to be blown once to stop the car; the driver will start when he sees the passenger or passengers safely on or off the car.

24. To make a written report of all deviations from the Time Table by his car.

25. To report any driver who does not stop his car when the signal is given, or who unduly increases the speed of the car or in any way harasses the conductor, or is guilty of any misconduct, or negligence in the discharge of his duties.

26. In the morning to count his Tickets and see that they agree with the total Way-bill, and to examine **every part** of his car and report to the Inspector anything out of order or place. Should the Inspector not attend to the matter at once, to report his neglect to the Traffic Manager.

27. To keep a vigilant look out for passengers on both sides of the car, particularly at cross streets, and to announce the principal streets immediately before the car arrives at them, especially in the evening.

28. To allow no boxes, barrels, trunks, baskets, or merchandise of any description in the car to the annoyance of any passenger; all such articles are to be placed upon the front platform. **All Parcels carried on the front platform will be charged for according to the rates fixed from time to time by the Traffic Manager. Conductors must collect for and punch and deliver a ticket for all such parcels, as soon as placed on the car, and will take the name and address of any passenger refusing to pay. Personal Luggage to the amount of 28lbs. may be carried inside the Car free, when accompanied by the owner.**

29. To allow no offensive article to be placed on the cars.

30. To act as extras when appointed, until a vacancy occurs.

31. To obey the Inspectors and Time-keepers.

32. To remain at the yard when their car is not running, seeing they may be required at any time.

33. **To request all Passengers to alight on the side of the car nearest the foot-path, and to be particular not to start the car until all passengers are safely received or landed.**

34. The fares for the various distances on each route being marked on a Table of Fares in the cars the same must either be paid in money to the conductor, or the prepayment of them to the company, must be vouched to the conductor by the production of Tickets called "Scholars' Tickets," which have been previously sold by the company. Children under three years of age may travel free if not occupying a seat.

35. A conductor must collect the fares from passengers **before, or as soon as the car leaves a terminus, and afterwards as each passenger enters,** and he must immediately punch and deliver a ticket as provided for in next rule. This rule also applies for the collection of fares for parcels.

36. Whenever a passenger who has paid a fare travels beyond the distance for which he has paid, the Conductor must collect from him the additional fare due for the extra distance, and punch and deliver to him a check-ticket as above provided.

37. Way-bills are not to be made up until all fares are collected and the car is within 300 yards of its terminus.

38. When the drawings of a conductor are less than the average takings of the car on the line on which he works, and a satisfactory reason cannot be given for it he will be considered unfit for the position. It is necessary that each conductor should see that the car preceding his own does not loiter; that the one he is running does not go ahead of time, that his driver keeps a vigilant look out for passengers, and that the fare is collected from every passenger for the full distance travelled.

39. Conductors are forbidden to enter the Ticket Offices, Engine Workshops. Lamp-rooms, or Stables.

40. Conductors will be careful to enter the correct number of passengers, inside and outside, in the first column of their Way Bill, BEFORE starting their car from either Terminus.

41. Whilst proceeding on their journey they must be careful from time to time to enter in the columns of their Way Bill each passenger or passengers immediately they are received upon the car.

42. Passengers entering the car during the conductor's unavoidable absence from the rear platform must be entered on the Way Bill immediately upon their return. They must therefore upon all such occasions use great care to accurately check their passengers and see that they correspond with the number entered on the Way Bill, as any omission may be construed into an intention to neglect making a correct return.

43. It frequently occurs that an inside passenger pays for one or more outside, or vice-versa.

It must be distinctly understood that the party who pays must in every such case receive the tickets he or she pays for.

44. Conductors are cautioned against taking the nails out of the tickets they are using, as they are liable to get mixed. They must tear each ticket off the nail as required. and always in the passenger's presence.

45. Any Conductor shown to have, (under any circumstances) taken a ticket from a passenger after this date, will be discharged forthwith.

Conductors may examine tickets, but are bound to return them *immediately* to the passenger or passengers.

46. All persons riding upon their car must be accounted for and appear on the Way Bill. Those having authority to ride free must be marked in the usual way, and their names, or the number of their pass, shown below.

47. Passengers changing their seats from inside to outside, or *vice versa*, must be re-entered on the Way Bill, and the circumstance duly noted on the Way Bill.

48. *On approaching the Terminus, Conductors will enter their totals. This must be done in full view of the passengers, and under no circumstances are they to remove the Way Bill from the case until their arrival at the Termini, when they will reverse the Way Bill for the return journey.*

49. Upon the completion of each journey conductors will promptly deposit money and Way Bill in the Receiving Office.

50. Treat every passenger with attention and courtesy, and wait until all elderly ladies and gentlemen are seated; by observing this they will be less liable to accidents, and give better satisfaction to passengers and the company.

51. Any neglect to report an accident, however slight, will be severely dealt with.

52. Conductors will be held responsible for any misconduct or carelessness on the part of their driver, unless they report the same to the Traffic Manager at the first opportunity. Drivers missing points or continually getting off the line, must be reported.

53. Should any driver attempt to diminish the receipts of his conductor by increasing or decreasing the speed of the car, or by not promptly stopping the car for passengers upon being signalled by the conductor, or directly or indirectly harass the conductor, or be guilty of any misconduct, it is the duty of the conductor to make a report in writing, forwarding it to the Traffic Manager.

ENGINE CLEANERS.

Engine Cleaners are required

1. To clean the engines thoroughly by means of a scraper and moderate use of waste and grease.

2. To coil the hose pipes and hang them up in a dry place when not in use.

3. To exercise economy in the consumption of water.

4. To assist in other departments when wanted.

COKEMEN.

Cokemen are required

1. To exercise the greatest care in breaking the coke, and to see that as little as possible is powdered.

2. To be careful with the coke bags, not trailing them on the ground, but lifting them clear when moving them about or carrying them to the engines at any time.

3. To keep a correct account of the number of bags delivered to each engine.

4. To fill the bags evenly; 56lbs. is the nett weight each bag must contain.

5. To assist in other departments when wanted.

ROAD CLEANERS, POINTS-MEN, AND WATER BOYS.

Road Cleaners, Pointsmen, and Water Boys are under the direction of the Inspector of their respective districts, to whom they are responsible for the proper performance of the duties required of them.

STABLEMEN.

1. Attendance at the stables will be required each morning at 6-0.

2. Smoking on any part of the premises is strictly forbidden.

3. No stableman is permitted to absent himself from the depot during working hours without leave.

4. No stableman must leave duty at night until the last change has been put to their respective cars, their harness cleaned, and stables put ready for inspection.

5. Each stableman must be accountable for the tools with which he works; and in case of loss the value to be deducted from his wages.

6. Each stableman will be on night duty at the depot every week in his turn to assist to unhorse last cars.

7. In going to or from changing horses, stopping to drink at public-houses on the road, or taking their horses above a walking pace, will not be allowed.

8. Stablemen in liquor, incapable of attending to their duties, or acting contrary to their orders, will render themselves liable to instant dismissal.

9. No stableman will be allowed to introduce strangers or discharged servants into the stables.

10. Discharged servants will not be allowed in the stables, and if found loitering there will be treated as trespassers.

11. Turning out horses when suffering from the effects of sudden illness, lameness, or sore shoulders, must be carefully guarded against.

12. Illusing the horses will not be tolerated under any circumstances.

13. Obscene language and noisy behaviour or smuggling liquor into the stables is strictly prohibited.

Board of Trade Regulations and Bye-Laws.

(COPY.)

R. 4505.

The Board of Trade, under and by virtue of the powers conferred upon them in this behalf, do hereby order that the following Regulations for securing to the public reasonable protection against danger in the exercise by the Manchester, Bury, Rochdale, and Oldham Steam Tramways Company (hereinafter called "The Company") of the powers conferred by Parliament upon the Company with respect to the use of Steam power on all or any of the Tramways of the Company, on which the use of such power has been authorised (hereinafter called "The Tramways") be substituted for all other Regulations in this behalf, contained in any Tramway Act or Tramway Order confirmed by Act of Parliament, or in any Order of the Board of Trade heretofore made thereunder. And the Board of Trade do also hereby rescind and annul all Bye-Laws heretofore made by them with regard to all or any of the Tramways aforesaid, and do hereby make the following Bye-Laws with regard to all or any of such Tramways:—

REGULATIONS.

1.—The engine or engines to be used on the Tramways shall comply with the following requirements, that is to say:

(a) Each coupled-wheel shall be fitted with a brake block, which can be applied by a screw or treadle, or by other means, and also by steam.

(b) A governor, which cannot be tampered with by the driver shall be attached to each engine, and shall be so arranged that at any time when the engine exceeds a speed of ten miles an hour, it shall cause the steam to be shut off, and the brake applied.

(c) Each engine shall be numbered, and the number shall be shown in a conspicuous part thereof.

(d) Each engine shall be fitted with an indicator by means of which the speed is shown; with a suitable fender to push aside obstructions; and with a special bell to be sounded as a warning, when necessary.

(e) Arrangement shall be made enabling the driver to command the fullest possible view of the road before him.

(f) Each engine shall be free from noise produced by blast and from the clatter of machinery such as to constitute any reasonable ground of complaint either to the passengers or to the public; the machinery shall be concealed from view at all points above four inches from the level of the rails, and all fire used on such engines shall be concealed from view.

II.—Every carriage used on the tramways shall be so constructed as to provide for the safety of passengers, and for their safe entrance to, exit from, and accommodation in, such carriages, and for their protection from the machinery of any engine used for drawing or propelling such carriages.

III.—The Board of Trade and their officers may, from time to time, and shall, on the application of the Local Authority of any of the districts through which the said Tramways pass, inspect such engines or carriages used on the Tramways and the machinery therein, and may, whenever they think fit, prohibit the use on the Tramways of any of them which in their opinion are not safe for use.

IV.—The speed at which such engines and carriages shall be driven or propelled along the Tramways shall not exceed the rate of eight miles an hour, and the speed at which such engines shall pass through facing points, whether fixed or moveable, shall not exceed the rate of four miles an hour.

V. The engines and carriages shall be connected by double couplings.

VI.—The speed of the engines and carriages shall not exceed four miles an hour at the following places:

In the Borough of Rochdale,

(a) In descending the incline in Drake Street, between Water Street and Fleece Street.

(b) In passing over the junction line opposite the Wellington Hotel.

(c) In descending the incline from the commencement of the double line, north of Moor Street.

(d) At the crossing of Church Stile and Milkstone Road.

(e) In Yorkshire Street, between Whitehall Street and West Street.

In the Borough of Bury,

(f) In descending the inclines commencing at the intersection of Castlecroft with Bolton Street, and at the intersection of Irwell Street with Bolton Street.

(g) In rounding the corner by the Bridge Inn.

In the Township of Whitworth,

(h) In Market Street, between Union Street and New Inn.

In the Borough of Heywood,

(i) In Manchester Street, between Rochdale Road and Rochdale Lane.

(j) In Manchester Street, between Rock Street and Hall Street.

VII.—The speed of the engines and carriages on the Tramway, over the present Heap Bridge, over the River Roach, and its approaches, shall not exceed the rate of four miles an hour, and no engine or carriage on the Tramway shall cross such Bridge while any other vehicle is upon it.

VIII.—The speed of the engines and carriages shall not exceed the rate of four miles an hour in descending the inclines at the following places:

In the Borough of Heywood,

(a) From the Passing Loop, Prettywood, for a distance of 220 yards nearing Bury. And from the Passing Loop next on the Bury side of Boo Hole Farm, for a distance of 200 yards.

(b) In Bury Street, between Lord Street and Peel Street.

(c) Between the Britannia Inn and the Commercial Inn in Bridge Street.

(d) In the narrow part of Market Street, between Ashton Street and Pitt Street.

PENALTY.

NOTE.—The Company or any person using steam power on the Tramways contrary to any of the above Regulations, is for every such offence subject to a penalty not exceeding ten pounds, and also in the case of a continuing offence to a further penalty not exceeding five pounds for every day after the first during which such offence continues.

BYE-LAWS.

I.—The special bell shall be sounded by the driver of the engine from time to time, when it is necessary, as a warning.

II.—No smoke or steam shall be emitted from the engines so as to constitute any reasonable ground of complaint to passengers or to the public.

III.—Whenever it is necessary, to avoid impending danger, the engine shall be brought to a standstill.

IV.—The entrance to, and exit from, the carriages shall be by the hindermost or conductor's platform.

V.—The engine shall be brought to a standstill at the following places :

(a) Immediately before entering any passing loop situated on a falling gradient of 1 in 25 or steeper.

In the Borough of Rochdale,

(b) At the junction of John Street with Smith Street, at the junction of Ramsey Street with Entwistle Road, and at the junction of Entwistle Road with Yorkshire Street.

(c) At the junction of Oldham Road with Milnrow Road.

(d) At the corner of South Parade and Drake Street.

(e) At the entrance of the passing loop, south of Moor Street, on the descending journey.

(f) At the junction of Manchester Road, on the outward journey.

(g) At the corner of Yorkshire Street and Whitworth Road.

(h) At the intersection of Princess Street with Whitworth Road.

(i) At the passing place in Whitworth Road, opposite the Post Office at Healey.

In the Borough of Bury,

(j) At the intersection of Castlecroft with Bolton Street.

(k) At the Intersection of Irwell Street with Bolton Street.

In the Borough of Heywood,

(l) At the intersection of Rock Street with Manchester Street, (Hopwood Line.)

(m) Immediately before commencing to descend the inclines at each of the places mentioned in Regulation No. VIII. above mentioned.

VI.—The Company shall place, and keep placed, in a conspicuous position inside of each carriage in use on the Tramways, a printed copy of these Regulations and Bye-laws.

PENALTY.

NOTE.—Any person or corporation offending against or committing a breach of any of these Bye-Laws is liable to a penalty not exceeding forty shillings.

The provisions of "The Tramways Act, 1870," with respect to the recovery of penalties is applicable to the penalties for the breach of these Regulations or Bye-laws.

Signed, by order of the Board of Trade, this Fourth day of July, 1884,

(*Signed*)

HENRY G. CALCRAFT,

An Assistant Secretary to the Board of Trade.

BYE-LAWS AND REGULATIONS

OF THE

MANCHESTER, BURY, ROCHDALE, AND OLDHAM STEAM TRAMWAYS COMPANY.

Under the powers conferred on the Company by the Tramways Act, 1879.

1. The Bye-Laws and Regulations hereinafter set forth shall extend and apply to all carriages of the Company, and to all places with respect to which the Company have power to make Bye-Laws or Regulations.

2. Every passenger shall enter or depart from a carriage by the hindermost or conductor's platform, and not otherwise.

3. No passenger shall smoke inside any carriage.

4. No passenger or other person shall, while travelling in or upon any carriage, play or perform upon any musical instrument.

5. A person in a state of intoxication shall not be allowed to enter or mount upon any carriage, and if found in or upon any carriage, shall be immediately removed by or under the direction of the conductor.

6. No person shall swear or use obscene or offensive language whilst in or upon any carriage, or commit any nuisance in or upon or against any carriage, or wilfully interfere with the comfort of any passenger.

7. No person shall wilfully cut, tear, soil, or damage the cushions or linings, or remove or deface any number plate, printed or other notice, in or on the carriage, or break or scratch any window of, or otherwise wilfully damage any carriage. Any person acting in contravention of this Regulation shall be liable to the penalty prescribed by these Bye-Laws and Regulations, in addition to the liability to pay the amount of any damage done.

8. A person whose dress or clothing might, in the opinion of the conductor of a carriage, soil or injure the linings or cushions of the carriage, or the dress or clothing of any passenger, or a person who, in the opinion of the conductor, might for any other reason be offensive to passengers, shall not be entitled to enter or remain in the interior of any carriage, and may be prevented from entering the interior of any carriage, and shall not enter the interior of any carriage after having been requested not to do so by the conductor, and, if found in the interior of any carriage, shall, on request of the conductor, leave the interior of the carriage upon his fare, if previously paid, being returned.

9. Each passenger shall, upon demand, pay to the conductor or other duly authorised officer of the Company, the fare legally demandable for the journey.

10. Each passenger shall show his ticket (if any) when required so to do to the conductor or any duly authorised servant of the Company, and shall also, when required so to do, either deliver up his ticket or pay the fare legally demandable for the distance travelled over by such passenger.

11. A passenger not being an artisan, mechanic, or daily labourer, within the true intent and meaning of the Acts of Parliament relating to the Company, shall not use or attempt to use any ticket intended only for such artisans, mechanics, or daily labourers.

12. Personal or other luggage (including the tools of artisans, mechanics, and daily labourers) shall, unless otherwise permitted by the conductor, be placed on the front or driver's platform, and not in the interior or on the roof of any carriage.

13. No passenger or other person, not being a servant of the company, shall be permitted to travel on the steps or platforms of any carriage, or stand either on the roof or in the interior, or sit on the outside rail on the roof of any carriage, and shall cease to do so immediately on request by the conductor.

14. No person, except a passenger or intending passenger, shall enter or mount any carriage, and no person shall hold or hang on by or to any part of any carriage, or travel therein otherwise than on a seat provided for passengers.

15. When any carriage contains the full number of passengers which it is licensed to contain, no additional person shall enter, mount, or remain in or on any such carriage when warned by the conductor not to do so.

16. When a carriage contains the full licensed number of passengers, a notice to that effect shall be placed in conspicuous letters, and in a conspicuous position on the carriage.

17. The conductor shall not permit any passenger beyond the licensed number to enter or mount or remain in or upon any part of a carriage.

18. No person shall enter, mount, or leave, or attempt to enter, mount, or leave any carriage whilst in motion.

19. No dog or other animal shall be allowed in or on any carriage, except by permission of the conductor, nor in any case in which the conveyance of such dog or other animal might be offensive or an annoyance to passengers. No person shall take a dog or other animal into any carriage after having been requested not to do so by the conductor. Any dog or other animal taken into or on any carriage in breach of this Regulation shall be removed by the person in charge of such dog or other animal from the carriage immediately upon request by the conductor, and in default of compliance with such request may be removed by, or under the direction of the conductor.

20. No person shall travel in or on any carriage of the Company with loaded fire-arms.

21. No passenger shall wilfully obstruct or impede any officer or servant of the Company in the execution of his duty, upon or in connection with any carriage or tramway of the Company.

22. The conductor of each carriage shall enforce or prevent the breach of these Bye-Laws and Regulations to the best of his ability.

23. Any person offending against or committing a breach of any of these Bye-Laws or Regulations shall be liable to a penalty not exceeding forty shillings.

24. The expression "conductor" shall include any officer or servant in the employment of the Company and having charge of a carriage.

25. There shall be placed and kept placed in a conspicuous position inside of each carriage in use a printed copy of these Bye-Laws and Regulations.

26. These Bye-Laws shall come into force on the 25th day of October, 1883.

The above is a true copy of the Bye-laws and Regulations made by the above-named Company.
THOMAS JERVIS, *Secretary*,

22nd August, 1883.

The Common Seal of the above-named Company was affixed hereto.

I hereby certify that a true copy of the foregoing Bye-laws and Regulations has, in accordance with the provisions of Section 46 of the Tramways Act, 1870, been laid before the Board of Trade not less than two calendar months before such Bye-Laws and Regulations came into operation, and that such Bye-Laws and Regulations have not been disallowed by the Board of Trade within the said two calendar months.

(Signed) HENRY G. CALCRAFT,
An Assistant Secretary to the Board of Trade.

24th October, 1883.

All Servants of the Company (not provided with a Pass) must pay their fares when travelling on the cars off duty.

Conductors are cautioned to mark off a number on their Way Bill, for every person travelling on their Car, whether a passenger holding a pass or otherwise.

The Manchester, Bury, Rochdale, and Oldham Steam Tramways Company, require of all Employees,

Honesty!
Punctuality!
Obedience!
Sobriety!
Civility!

In every case where a person is injured, or an accident of any kind affecting the Company occurs, no matter how small it may be, the full Names and Addresses of all witnesses must be sent to the Head Office.

By Order.

Mr O'Hagan

Rochdale Observer, Saturday, 5 June 1886

"THE TRAMWAY COMPANY v. THE CITY OF LONDON CONTRACT CORPORATION.
(From Our Own Reporter)
LONDON, Thursday.

To-day Mr Graham Tinge, Q.C. (Mr Swinfer Eady with him) moved in the action instituted by the Manchester, Bury, Rochdale, and Oldham team Tramways Company against the City of London Contract Corporation – before Mr Justice Kay, sitting in the Chancery Division of the High Court of Justice – in the following terms: – That the defendant corporation, their solicitor and agents be restrained from proceeding under an arbitration named in a deed of agreement of the 15th February, 1886, made between the plaintiff company and the defendant corporation, until the trial of the action or further order. The learned counsel said that the object of the action was to have it declared that the agreement entered into was ultra vires on the part of the plaintiff company or, in the alternative, that the deed mentioned should be given up by the defendant corporation to the plaintiff company to be cancelled. The questions involved were questions of law and of fact; the first – the question of law – being whether the plaintiff company had authority under their statutory powers, or under the general acts of Parliament, to enter into a deed of submission to arbitrate, and refer to arbitration and agreement something which was ultra vires. Before dealing with the question of law he would first of all put his lordship in possession of the material facts of the case, presenting them, of course, from his own point of view, there being some dispute between him and the other side as to what the precise facts were. It appeared that there was a firm known as that of Charles Phillips and Company, who carried on the business of contractors with Mr Phillips. Mr H. Osborne O'Hagan was associated, and he was in fact the principal in the firm. In the year 1881 an Order, known as the Bury and District Tramways Order, was obtained by Mr Charles Phillips, and this act authorised the construction of tramways between Bury and various places in the district, duly specified. In the same year another tramways order was obtained on the motion of Mr Charles Phillips, and that order was known as the Rochdale Tramways Order, 1881, for Rochdale and District. Having obtained these two orders the plaintiff company was registered (probably sanctioned before the month of November). The company was of that kind which was commonly known as a contractor's company – that was a company promoted by contractors – and it was registered under the Company's Act, 1862, as a limited company, and the orders were taken over by Charles Phillips and Company, who promoted and obtained them in Parliament. On the 26th of November, the company then having been registered, two agreements were entered into between Chas. Phillips on the one part and the limited company on the other part. By the first agreement it was agreed that the contractors

should sell to the plaintiff company the undertaking authorised by the Bury and District Tramways Order, 1881, By this deed the contractors (Phillips and Company) were to execute all the necessary works, and the company were to pay to the contractors the sum of £91,000 in addition to £7,741 paid by way of Parliamentary deposit. Clause 13 of the agreement provided that the two engineers were to be the sole judges of all matters relating to the works, their decision in all cases to be binding and conclusive on both parties and there was also a provision for the making of alterations in plans, and for modifying their certificates. By clause 34 Mr Newton and another gentleman were to be the two engineers. By the 16th clause it was provided that the contractors were to pay to the holders of the first 10,000 shares in the company any interest until the works were completed, at the rate of 6 per cent per annum. The other agreement, bearing the same date (26th March, 1881), relating to the Rochdale and District Tramways Order was substantially in the same terms. Messrs Phillips and Co. were by that deed to execute, all necessary works, and to sell the tramway to the plaintiffs for the sum of £85,000 in addition to a further sum of £7,741.2s.8d. paid under the statute as a Parliamentary deposit. This agreement contained clauses similar to those already referred to as contained in the agreements relating to the Bury and District Tramways Company. This having been done, then the plaintiff Company, in the same year, as promoters, obtained a further order which was known as the Manchester and Bury Extension Order, 1882; and the company which had been a company under the statute became a limited company established for the purpose of constructing certain tramways in the borough of Bury, Rochdale, Oldham, and other districts in the county of Lancashire. In the same year the Corporation of Oldham obtained an order known as the Oldham Borough Tramway Extension Order, 1882, by which they were authorised to construct and maintain certain tramways in their borough. In this state of things a dead was executed dated March 14th, 1883, and that deed purported to be entered into between the defendant Corporation, which was called the City of London Contract Corporation, Limited, – a Company which, as its name implied, was established for the purpose of carrying on the work which had been contracted for by private firms –and the limited company on the other part. That deed recited that by an agreement entered into by the Corporation of Oldham and Mr Charles Phillips, it was agreed that the Corporation should construct the tramways and that Charles Phillips and Co. should enter into to an agreement to lease the tramways – and there was a further agreement as to the price at which the work was to be executed. On the 25th July, 1884, an Act of Parliament was passed, entitled "The Manchester, Bury, Rochdale and Oldham Steam Tramways Act, 1884." By that act the limited company was dissolved, and the plaintiff company incorporated for the purpose of constructing, completing and maintaining the tramways authorised by the Bury and District Order of 1881, the Rochdale District

order of 1881, and the Manchester, &c, Order of 1882; and they were also incorporated for the purpose of taking on lease the tramways comprised in the Oldham Tramways as comprised in No. 4 agreement already referred to. The act contained the usual clauses, and incorporated certain portions of the Tramways Act and General Act. The company having thus been incorporated, the business went on – the tramways were completed, and the Oldham Corporation granted the lease above-mentioned. The five gentlemen named as the defendants of the City of London Contract Corporation were Mr Waine, Mr Handyside, Mr Busby, Mr Luke Bishop and Mr Fishwick, and these five gentlemen were the directors of the plaintiff company down to the 27th February, 1886 – Mr Luke Bishop being the chairman of the plaintiff company in addition to being the vice-chairman of the defendant Corporation. The allegation on the part of the plaintiff company was that these gentlemen were in point of fact in the habit of acting as directors of the company with which Mr O'Hagan was connected and therefore that they were not disposed to look unfavourably on anything put before them by Mr O'Hagan. At the end of 1885, and the beginning of 1886, considerable dissatisfaction was expressed amongst the shareholders of the plaintiff company at the manner in which the affairs of the company had been conducted; and apparently this discontent was not without reason, because it appeared that under the rule of these gentlemen it had been customary to pay the defendant corporation considerable sums of money in excess of the certificates given by the engineers, and consequently proceedings were taken by the shareholder, which resulted in a charge in the personnel of the board of directors. Before this was done, however, and with the object of concluding the matter and binding the plaintiff company a question was raised which resulted in this submission to arbitration it was now sought to set aside, viz., this deed of the 15th February, 1886. That agreement was come to before any change took place in the personnel of the board of directors and one of the questions of fact in controversy now was who it was who first proposed this submission to arbitration? That, however, in the opinion of the learned counsel, Was not a question of importance, although according to the view which they took of it the negotiations for submitting the questions in dispute to arbitration were entered into by the directors of the plaintiff company after a special committee of investigation had expressed dissatisfaction with the conduct of the directors, and a change of directors was being carried out. On the 3rd February last to Mr O'Hagan wrote to Mr Luke Bishop urging him to attend a meeting of the defendant corporation to be held in London, but without intimating that the question of arbitration would be submitted. Mr Bishop attended the meeting, which was held at the office of the defendant corporation, and at that meeting a deed of submission to arbitration was submitted, and Mr Digby Seymour, W.C., was appointed referee. On the 11th February, at a board meeting of the defendant company, it was resolved that the deed of submission should be

sealed. On the 17th February, at a special meeting of the defendant board, Mr O'Hagan (the manager of the defendant company) produced a statement of accounts, and £2,000 was paid him on account of work done. On the 27th February a meeting of the plaintiff company was held, when a committee of investigation was appointed, and they at once commenced to work. The first meeting of the arbitrator was held on the 11th March. The committee of investigation showed that the deed of submission which had been sealed so hurriedly was of such a character as to tie the hands of the plaintiff company in such a way that no one interested in it could have consented to. On the 18th March the board met, and amongst their other work they discharged their solicitors and appointed fresh ones, and the writ in this action was issued. The claim of the defendant Corporation was originally £52,000, but that had been reduced to £51,000.

His Lordship: And you seek to have the deed of submission set aside?

Mr Graham Hastings: Or in alternative to have it given up to be cancelled. It is suggested that the interests of the plaintiff company were not properly looked after by the board of directors.

His Lordship: Your main ground is that which was done was in ultra vires.

Mr Graham Hastings: Yes, that is my first point. I say that they had no power to go to arbitration with such an agreement. The learned counsel then proceeded to support his contention by references to the company's Acts, 1862, and to the Lands Clauses Acts, and at this stage the Court adjourned.

The arguments will be resumed on Saturday.

Mr Rigby, Q.C., and Mr Bradford appeared for the defendant Corporation.

Extracts from *"Leaves from my life"* by H. Osborne O'Hagan, volumes 1 & 2, published by John Lane The Bodley Head Ltd., in 1929.

Volume 1, page 3 [O'Hagan had an accident on a swing-boat at school and was carried home apparently lifeless. He lay unconscious for 4 days with concussion of the brain, and was then kept in a dark room for another 10 days.] "When I recovered, my father, a severe man, but who ... had sat by my bedside during the whole of the first two nights of my illness, said that in my accident I had lost the whole of my brains and the empty space had been filled in with mashed turnips ... I made this an excuse for not attempting to work. Why should I, if I had no brains..."

Page 21: "I have always collected amusing stories, until I have now over eighteen thousand of them, and even they have helped to keep my memory bright and at times they have been useful. I have rarely conducted any negotiation without a smiling face and one or two anecdotes. There were many other methods I pursued to improve the memory until I could claim to have an almost perfect one. I think I may say that I have only met one or two men who appeared to me to have better ones. At the age of 76, and having left my business and dropped out of active work for the last five years, I am writing these reminiscences without a diary, a book, or a paper, relying entirely upon my memory, which is as clear today for events which occurred forty or fifty years ago as for matters which happened last week...."

Page 22: "I soon came to the conclusion that in business success did not come to the man who was merely clever and learned; many other

qualities were essential. What was more material than anything else was "good address, good manners, industry, determination, persistence, and good judgment, good temper and tact – above everything, tact – a certain amount of assertiveness with the avoidance of offensiveness, unselfishness, and a willingness at all times to go out of your way to help others."

Page 57: [Reminiscing on his taking over the Hanley and Burslem tramway] ("a wretched old concern in a dilapidated state"): "Living on the road upon which we proposed to construct tramways was a dentist, and opposite the house in which he resided our proposed tramways could come within 9 feet 6 inches of the kerb or pavement. Under the General Tramways Act, where this occurred the frontager thus affected could dissent from the scheme, and if opposition came from two-thirds of such frontagers and they could not be induced to withdraw their dissent, the scheme was killed.

I had ascertained that this dentist, who was on the Hanley Town Council, had sent in a dissent, and that he was agitating amongst the frontagers in the hope of throwing out the scheme. I sought an interview with him. There were patients in his waiting-room, but when my card was taken in he saw me at once and expressed himself as pleased at my calling. I spent some time in trying to persuade him of the great advantages the tramways would be to all the people living in the district, that they would greatly develop the four towns and add to their prosperity, afford the required facilities for getting about in these straggling towns, benefit the shopkeepers, keep the roads in proper repair, relieve the rate, and generally prove a boon to all concerned, and as I had learned that he was a Hanley town councillor he would no doubt feel it his duty to give his townspeople the benefit of his support to the introduction of the tramways. He replied that he was not so sure about that. He would like to know what he was to get out of it?

I said that he certainly would derive great personal benefit if the tramways were constructed, for they would bring to his door patients from all the four towns. Who could doubt that his practice would increase when anyone could get into a tramcar in any of the towns and be brought straight to his door?

"Yes" he replied; "but what is my vote worth to you? Surely it is worth £100."

I appeared astonished, and said "What would your townsmen say if they heard that I had paid you £100 for your vote?"

"Oh, but we can get over that," said he. "I will extract one of your teeth, and out of gratitude for the relief from pain you can pay me £100." I said that I could be no party to purchasing a councilman's vote. I would prefer to keep both my molar and my money, and if I had his continued opposition I should know how to deal with it. As I left, he came with me to the door and said, "You'll be sorry, my young friend, that you have not secured my support."

That evening came the battle before the Hanley Town Council, a meeting having been called to hear me in support of the scheme, and to determine whether the consent should be given or withheld. Mr Bradford was very sanguine about the result of the voting. He said that I had a great point in my favour that I had obtained the support of Mr Minton Campbell, the Mayor of Stoke-on-Trent, and he had taken care to spread it about that Mr. Minton Campbell had obtained for me the consent of the Council. He went on to say that the name of Minton Campbell was one to conjure with throughout the Potteries.

I attended the meeting and made my usual address on the great advantages of tramways, particularly in such a district as the Potteries, where greater prosperity might well be looked for with all their straggling towns coupled up. I soon found I had an appreciative audience, and I thought I could introduce with advantage a little humour, so I said it was a pity there were no steam tramways anywhere near, as could they see them running they would no doubt feel as I did about them. There was naturally much that they would like to know about such tramways. Would they frighten the horses and other things in the streets? They knew that Parliament was prepared to sanction the introduction of steam tramways into the public streets under certain restrictions. But Parliament had taken great care to investigate the matter very fully before they were willing to give such sanction. They had empowered a Committee of the House of Lords to inquire into the subject. I had given evidence before that Committee, having first visited Paris, Strasburg, and Milan, where steam tramways were in use. I gave their lordships one or two instances of what I had seen in connection with this class of traffic. When I was in Paris in the Avenue de la Grande Armeé, as a steam-car was going along at a good pace, a child, running out of a side-street, went right in front of it. Had it been a horse-car the child would in all probability have been killed. The driver, who was in front, brought his engine to a dead stop in an instant, and picked up the child into the cab of his engine.

After giving a good deal of evidence, one of the Committee asked me how the horses took to the innovation; he supposed I would say they appeared to like it.

"No," I replied; "I could not go so far as that, because they appeared very distressed and no doubt resented their introduction."

"Can you tell me why?" asked the noble lord.

"Yes," I replied; "they looked as though they were afraid the engines were going to take the bread out of their mouths." I then said there was no fear for the horses, they soon got used to the new traffic.

When I sat down after a long speech I thought I had the meeting with me, when a member of the Council arose. I at once recognised him as my dentist friend, who began a tirade against strangers coming into the town to force tramways upon them. He had proceeded thus far when up jumped Mr. Alderman Bradford, who thundered out: "Strangers indeed! Had the gentleman paid you a hundred pounds to have a tooth out this afternoon he would have been your friend, and no stranger," and amidst roars of laughter Mr. Bradford proceeded to say that one of his daughters with a friend was in the dentist's waiting-room that afternoon, and overheard a conversation between Mr. O'Hagan and the dentist, when the latter asked for £100 for his vote and suggested that to cover the matter he should take out one of Mr. O'Hagan's molars.

The dentist sat down in confusion, and the Council at once proceeded to vote, gave me the required consent, and within a couple of days the other local authorities followed suit."

Pages 68-75 contain some most amusing accounts of how O'Hagan brought Council members to his side by wining and dining them with champagne and oyster luncheons and other alcoholic and gastronomic ministrations.

Pages 76-77 contain a novel way of avoiding an overdraft: "In these old tramway days I remember one occasion only when I was short of money to pay my monthly accounts, and that happened on a day when an unusually large amount had to be paid in cash. I had been engaged in the country on business, and had been unable to be present at two directors' meetings, where I could have drawn substantial amounts, and then the day before our pay-day, which was on the tenth of each month, I attended a meeting of a company where a very large amount, £40,000, was due to me, but I did not get a cheque owing to the engineer being ill and failing to certify the amount due. Unfortunately this occured just at a time when my bank accounts were low, owing to the fact that acceptances for nearly £60,000 had just fallen due.

What was to be done? A sum of nearly £50,000 was required. I have no doubt my bankers would have lent the money on the case being put before them, but I had always avoided an overdraft, and attributed my high standing in "Seyds' Book" to that fact. I resorted to a very innocent little trick which never came to light. I had cheques drawn to the various firms for the amounts of their accounts. Then before signing the cheques I had all the letters and envelopes in which the cheques were to go brought into my room, and as I signed the cheques I put them in the wrong envelopes; that is to say, Beyer Peacock, of Manchester, to whom £9,000 odd was due, would receive a cheque for £6,500 payable to the Stockton Forge Company. It took three or four days to correct this mistake, as each firm returned the cheque received to have the mistake rectified, and during those three days I obtained my certificates and cheques, placing my bank in ample funds..."

Volume 2, pages 454-459 is devoted to The City of London Contract Corporation Ltd., which was mentioned in volumes 1 and 4 of this series.

Note from the publisher: O'Hagan's Leaves are most readable and remind me of those of George Francis Train, but I suspect the former's veracity is much more credible than that of the latter!

HARRIET OSBORNE O'HAGAN was the sister of Henry and lived from 1830 to 1921. Born in Dublin she rapidly showed her promise as an artist, first exhibiting at the Royal Hibernian Academy at the age of 19. Her tutor, George Sharp, encouraged her to go to Paris with its less stultified air and, more particularly, greater freedom for lady artists, which move took place around 1866. She is said to have established the first properly structured academy for women artists in Paris, but seeking a harder clearer air moved to Normandy in 1880, where she became domiciled. A good collection of her drawings and two of her oil on canvas paintings are held in the National Gallery of Ireland, although one delightful oil 35x46cm (14"x18") showing an adjacent farmhouse in Normandy sold in 2005 for €3,800. Other works have included an 'alive' interior oil on panel, one of Eugénie O'Hagan, rather winsome for today, but in charcoal, and similar treatment was given to her sister, Marguerite, although this is an almost photographic study. I like to think of her, painting equipment to hand, boarding the French steam tram as it trundled across the countryside!

John Fell

John Fell proved a rather strange adage that no matter how good you were, to be a contractor for steam tramways was to write your own debt.

Born in 1848, this Leamington-bred man began life as a particularly gifted builder, proved when at the relatively young age of 33 his tender for the building of the prestigious Town Hall in the town was accepted by the council. Shortly after this his contract to build the Leamington and Warwick horse tramway was accepted, this opening on 21 November 1881. Thereafter he undertook work for the Barrow-in-Furness Tramways Co. (opened July 1885), the Coventry & District (September 1884), Birmingham & Midland (July 1885), Birmingham Central (various contracts 1884 to 1887), Dudley and Stourbridge (May 1884) and, from his angle the most ill-fated of all, the Magdeburg Tramways. At the time of his death in December 1925, at the ripe old age of 77, it was stated he also lost £18,000 for work on Potteries tramways, £20,000 at Malaga, and £6,000 plus on a singularly ill-fated involvement in the Cairo-Pyramids scheme.

On the social side he was a Gladstonian Liberal*, initially standing as the candidate in Bewdley, Worcs., later being elected to the Leamington Town Council and then Mayor in November 1885 – not bad for a 37 year-old builder. Around 1888 he was appointed as a J.P., although the previous year John Fell found himself inadvertently involved in the affairs of a crooked bank – Greenways of Warwick and Leamington, detailed in our volume 6, and the forced sale of their holdings in Magdeburg tramways (valued at £11,921. 10s. 2d.) led to the Financial World in March 1888 stating "The market in shares in this company [Magdeburg] having been artificially worked up ... it has given way and there are now no dealings again ... the public will not be hoodwinked into relieving the Greenways' creditors of the shares they hold..."

We find a note in *The Times*, 22 December "Mr John Fell (Mayor of Leamington), the contractor to the [Magdeburg] company, stated at the time the bank failed the dividend warrants were out, and he had made himself responsible for their payment. After going through matters with the bank, he had made an arrangement with the company to take their claim for £11,700 and to deal with it as best he could, on account of the sum due to him under his contract". A resolution was passed by the shareholders thanking him for ensuring they were paid their dividends. The contract price had been about £108,000 (about £8,000 per mile) but it is interesting to note that as he was responsible for the provision of loco-motive and rolling stock, the engines were ex Berlin, second hand Schwartzkopf products. His own share-holding taken in lieu of cash would be severely depreciated.

---

*Harold Perkin in The Origins of Modern English Society (R&KP 1969) "Gladstone, having inherited Peel's mantle and carried it with him into the Liberal Party, found it, to his own surprise, to be the aegis of the symbolic representative not so much of the middle class, as of the middle-class civilisation of mid-Victorian England."

Although the amount John Fell had to pay out was painful, it does show the profits a competent contractor could make as he was still busy around the Leamington and Warwick areas. However there was a flip side to all his myriad activities (he had been re-elected Mayor in 1889) when the stresses and strains forced him to withdraw his candidature as M.P. for Stratford on Avon in November 1889, on the grounds of ill-health. Worse was to follow as the debenture holders in John Fell Ltd (which I assume was his holding company, although there were four John Fells extant at this time) forced a meeting on 17 June 1892 to elect trustees, one of whom turned out to be ... John Fell!! Another of his companies came unglued in July 1892.

Another new company emerged from the ashes of the old when *"The Money Market"* reported on 9 January, 1893 that a new firm had been formed, Gordon and Fell, Ltd., with a capital of £100,000, 'the whole of which it is stated has been taken by the vendors in respect of their purchase-money. There are besides that Five per cent. First Mortgage Profit debentures for £100,000 ... the company has been formed for the purposes of taking over, and carrying on, as from 1 January 1893, the electrical business of J.E.H. Gordon Ltd., ... of 11 Pall Mall, and the general contracting business of John Fell of Leamington.'

In the meantime he had not lost all his political aspirations although when the Gladstonian Liberals asked him to contest the seat in Leamington Spa during early March 1895, he agreed only if no one else would stand, finally declining on the 19th, although they kept trying until 1 April. In those far-off days it cost the Member money to hold his position – no nice fat trough then. A very 'posh'

THE LEAMINGTON CYCLE COMPANY (LIMITED).

A winding-up order having been made against this company on the 9th ult. the statutory meetings of creditors and contributories were held yesterday at the Board of Trade offices, Carey-street, Lincoln's-inn. Mr. G. S. Barnes, Senior Official Receiver, presided.

Messrs. Field, Roscoe, and Co. and Messrs. Ward, Perks, and M'Key appeared as solicitors on behalf of creditors.

The CHAIRMAN stated that the accounts had been submitted in draft, and they showed liabilities £17,629, of which £7,417 were expected to rank, with assets £11,630, subject to loans on debenture bonds, £10,196, thus leaving net assets to meet the unsecured claims amounting to £1,434. As regards contributories the deficiency was returned at £25,758. The company was registered on June 27, 1896, with a nominal capital of £60,000 in shares of £1 each. It was formed to acquire as a going concern three cycle businesses in the neighbourhood of London ; and also to take over the freehold works at Bedford-street, Leamington, the property of Messrs. John Fell (Limited). An agreement was entered into between the company and Mr. F. H. Brady (the vendor to and promoter of the company) under which the former were to acquire the properties for £65,000, payable as to £13,100 in cash, £39,400 in cash or shares, and £12,500 in debentures. The vendor was to fit up the Leamington works with machinery sufficient to turn out 250 cycles per week. A prospectus was issued under date June 25, 1896, and it contained the following statement :— " Subscriptions for debentures and shares have already been guaranteed for sums more than sufficient to pay so much of the purchase money as is payable in cash and provide the working capital. The directors will therefore proceed to allotment on July 2 next." The first directors appointed by the signatories were Mr. John Fell, J.P., Mr. R. G. Webster, M.P., Mr. W. Heron Maxwell, Mr. Russell Dowse, and Mr. H. Lincoln Tangye. Mr. Dowse never attended board meetings and his post became vacant under the articles. Mr. Tangye retired in January of this year, and in June last Mr. Cohen was elected a director. In all 5,981 shares had been subscribed for, and 14,000 shares were issued as fully paid to the vendor. The Official Receiver was informed that guarantees to subscribe for shares and debentures as mentioned in the prospectus had been produced to the directors, but, so far as had been yet ascertained, no applications had been received by the persons who signed them, and no steps had been taken to enforce the guarantees. In consequence of the inability of Mr. Brady to carry out the original arrangement a modified agreement was executed in October, 1896, which was concurred in by the shareholders, under which only the Leamington works were acquired, the purchase price being £25,000, payable as to £4,000 in cash, £14,000 in fully-paid shares, and £7,000 in first mortgage debentures. Mr. Brady undertook, if called upon, to purchase or find subscribers for 2,000 six per cent. debentures at £90. Owing to the delay in carrying out the necessary alterations and fitting up the machinery the company was unable to commence operations until Christmas last, and in the following June Mr. Brady's account was settled at £24,400. The company received an offer from Mr. Bagshawe to take 2,000 cycles, and the company made special arrangements to supply them, but owing to the bankruptcy of Mr. Bagshaw, the contract was never completed. The failure of the company was ascribed to inability to realize stock as payments for goods became due, and also to delay in commencing business. An execution was levied in July last, and the debenture-holders appointed a receiver, who was now carrying on the business.

Mr. John Fell addressed the meeting and stated that both his wife and himself had invested large sums in the company. The works at Leamington were all that could be desired, and it was a great pity that the undertaking had been brought into its present position. He understood that several large firms would be prepared to make an offer to purchase the property for a sum which would be sufficient to pay the claims of the debenture-holders and creditors, and perhaps leave a balance for the shareholders. The assets were valued in the accounts at less than half the amount they actually cost.

The proceedings at both meetings resulted in resolutions being passed in favour of the appointment of Mr. G. G. Poppleton, chartered accountant, as liquidator, a committee of inspection being also nominated consisting of Messrs. John Fell, J.P., D. Russell, E. O. French, and Arthur Cohen.

The Times, 8 September 1897.

do around this time was the First Annual Ladies' House Dinner held at the National Liberal Club. The three hundred guests included Mr and Mrs Fell, and his Jewish banker partner in a couple of tramway ventures, Emile Oppert, and his wife.

In 1896, during the arbitration proceedings between the London County Council and the London Tramways Company Ltd., he, described as "a contractor of great experience in the construction of tramways", was called as an Expert Witness … to give a valuation of the company's horses! ... which he put at an average of £23. By contrast, on 8 September 1897 another of his companies went bottoms up.

His life becomes rather vague hereafter, although he continued his contracting business – we must assume Gordon and Fell as a company either never took off or failed as on 12 April 1898 he was the co-signatory on a raft of contracts relating to the Potteries Electric Tramways Company, in company with S.P.W. Sellon, Francis Ashby, and Emile Garcke including one between British Electric Traction (Pioneer) with Brush Electrical Company, and a final signature on an agreement directly between B.E.T. and John Fell was signed on 15 November 1898, showing that his reputation must have still been high.

Sadly if this is 'our' John Fell (and I suspect it is) things were going wrong for him as three years later (11 July 1906 a Receiving Order under the Bankruptcy Acts was issued against John Fell, who had left Leamington in 1899 for London and who was described as an 'Engineer and Contractor of Victoria Street, SW., Arundel Gardens, Ladbroke Grove [his home].

A later report in the Leamington Spa Courier 27 August 1906 would seem to indicate he was getting back on to an even keel, although whether the Nova Scotia railways were ever built I do not know.

HIGH COURT OF JUSTICE.
KING'S BENCH DIVISION.
(*Before* MR. JUSTICE DARLING.)
GARLAND V. LAWSON AND ANOTHER.

This was an action on a promissory note for £1,100, dated December 18, 1903, made by the defendant Mr. H. J. Lawson and endorsed by the other defendant Mr. John Fell.

Mr. Chester Jones appeared for the plaintiff ; neither of the defendants appeared or was represented.

Mr. CHESTER JONES stated that the note was to be paid in instalments of £220 each, and in default of payment of any instalment the whole of the balance was to become due. Default was made in the payment of the first instalment, and the plaintiff as holder of the note now sought to recover the balance.

MR. JUSTICE DARLING asked if Mr. Fell was present in Court.

Mr. CHESTER JONES.—He has not appeared to the writ, but is coming as a witness if necessary.

MR. JUSTICE DARLING.—Mr. Lawson is not here, is he ?

Mr. CHESTER JONES.—No, my Lord.

MR. JUSTICE DARLING.—There must be judgment for the plaintiff for £1,100 and costs.

The Times, 6 June 1904.

10 August 1906:

"The Affairs of Mr John Fell His losses on Abortive Schemes The Press Association.

On Thursday a sitting was held before Mr Registrar Hope, at the London Bankruptcy Court, for the public examination of John Fell, late builder and contractor, Denby Buildings, Regent Grove, Leamington, now described as of 25 Victoria Street, Westminster, engineer for the construction of tramways, etc. The debtor, who was twice Mayor of Leamington and candidate for the S-W division of Warwickshire, has placed before the creditors a scheme for the payment of a composition of 7s.6d. in the £ extending over a period guaranteed, and which is to be considered by creditors on Friday. He applied to pass upon accounts showing gross liabilities £7,299.16s.8d, of which £3,932.13s.2d is returned as fully secured, with assets valued at £2,914.12s.6d, consisting mainly of household furniture £1,500, surplus from securities, £767, book debts £499, various shares £32226, and bank balance £2.

From the observations of the official Receiver it appears that the books of account appeared to record the bulk of his building transactions, but did not describe his financial position. Of the unsecured liabilities, £1,112 represented moneys borrowed and interest; £478 claims under guarantees; £307 goods supplied and medical and other services rendered; £129 calls on shares; £61 solicitors' charges; and £38 office rent not recoverable by distress. He attributed his failure mainly to pressure by creditors, to loss on a contract for the construction of a tramway in the Potteries district, to losses in connection with the projected construction of a bridge across the Tyne at South Shields, on a contract for the construction of a tramway between Derby and Nottingham and other abortive schemes, over which he lost some thousands of pounds. In examination by the Official Receiver (Mr E. Leadam Hough), the debtor stated that he started in business at Leamington as a builder and contractor in 1870, and about 1891 he transferred it to a limited company, "John Fell & Co. Ltd." of which he acted as managing director till 1896, when the company went into liquidation. The creditors were all paid in full. Mr Hough: Under that liquidation? – The debtor: They were all paid in full. – It was a one man company, was it not? – Yes. It never went public. All the creditors were paid in full.

Today, Friday, the creditors met before Mr E. Leadam Hough, Official Receiver, to consider the scheme of arrangement of the affairs of John Fell. It appeared from the report of the Official Receiver, that the debtor had lodged a proposal for a scheme providing first of all for the payment of all costs, charges and expenses, and priority debts. It then provided for the vesting of the estate in a trustee to realise and pay dividend to the creditors, pro rata. It was further agreed that the debtor should pay to the trustee one half of his net earnings, or income, for a period of three years from the date of the approval by the Court of the scheme, after deducting therefrom an allowance for maintenance of £500 per annum. Guarantees were to be provided for the sum of not less than £1,250, approved by the Official Receiver, and a committee of inspection to be appointed by the creditors. The guarantors should only become

operative in the event of the assets not having, within six months of the approval of the scheme, realised sufficient to pay the creditors a dividend of 7s.6d. in the £. The maximum liability of the guarantee was not to exceed the sum of £1,250, and should such a sum not be required to make up a dividend of 7s.6d in the £, the payments by the guarantors to be reduced.

The amount of the guarantees were to be payable within six months of the approval of the scheme by the Court. The remuneration of the trustee was to be fixed by the Committee of Inspection. The Official Receiver further reported that he was not satisfied that the unsecured liabilities returned by the debtor at £3,932 were correct, inasmuch as proofs to the amount of a further £1,500 had been tendered in addition to that a proof for £200 had been put in for income tax for 1905. The claim had not been scheduled and was disputed by the debtor. He was further of opinion that the realisable value of the assets returned at £3,173 had been over-estimated. In the event of claims for £1,500 and the income tax, standing security to the amount of £2,420 would have to be provided to satisfy the provisions of the Bankruptcy Act, requiring reasonable security for not less than 7s.6d in the £ on all probable debts. He was of the opinion that the scheme was calculated to benefit the creditors but doubts whether it provides the security required by the Act. Upon the voting being taken, the Chairman stated that proofs to the amount of £5,305 had been put in, and had been admitted for £3,325, of that amount the creditors for £3,131 had voted in favour of the scheme and £190 against, it was therefore accepted practically unanimously. –Mr Thomas Ford, CA, 1 Guildhall Chambers, London, was appointed trustee of the estate, with a Committee of Inspection. –The Chairman said that upon the public examination being concluded a day would be applied for to obtain the Court's confirmation of the scheme. The proceedings terminated."

Unusually for a contractor, despite research by Allan C. Baker and Russell Wear of the Industrial Locomotive Society, only one engine can definitely be traced as working for John Fell. This is W.B. Bagnall-built W/no.840 3' 0" gauge 0-4-0ST with 8" x 12" (203 x 305mm) outside cylinders, new as their JUBILEE to H. Fotherby in March 1887 for use on the Burnley Corporation Cant Clough Reservoir. From this owner it passed c.1889 to John Sagar of Clough Quarries, Salterforth, near Skipton, finally surfacing in John Fell's hands during 1896, when he was working on the contract to clean the lake at Blenheim Palace. The last mention of this hard worked little engine seems have been with John Shelbourne, a contractor working in Rainham Essex around 1903.

Leamington Spa Courier, 24 August 1906:

"THE AFFAIRS OF MR. JOHN FELL
The case of Mr. John Fell, engineer and contractor, of Victoria Street, Westminster came before Mr Registrar Linklater, at the London Bankruptcy Court, on Tuesday, upon adjourned public examination. The debtor originally started business as a builder and contractor at Leamington, in which town he laboured for many years and attained highest civic honours. His business after a few years developed into that of a contractor for and constructor of public works, largely concerned in the tramway system of various provincial towns. He, however, had unfortunately made considerable losses over those contracts, and had now come to the Court owing £3,932.13s.2d, unsecured and assets £2,914.12s.6d.

He had laid a scheme before his creditors providing for the payment to them of a composition of 7s.6d. in the £, he agreeing to vest his estate in a trustee and to set aside one-half of his net earnings or income for a period of three years, after deducting £500 a year for his maintenance. The prospects of his earning money were very good because he was interested in the construction of a railway in Nova Scotia, for which a charter had been granted. He had, already made the necessary surveys, and substantial progress would be made next spring. He would be entitled as the works proceeded to a remuneration of £5 per cent on the cost.

Upon the case being called on, Mr Haigh senior Official Receiver, said that on the last occasion, after the debtor had been examined at very considerable length, the examination was adjourned to enable a deficiency account to be filed, and to enable the creditors to consider the scheme which had been laid before them. The day after the examination the creditors had met, and had accepted the proposal, which would come before the Court for confirmation in due course. Under those circumstances he had no further questions to put.

The Registrar ordered the public examination to be concluded."

Gordon and Fell (Limited) is a new company which has been formed with a share capital of £100,000, the whole of which has been taken, it is stated, by the vendors in respect of their purchase-money. There are besides Five per Cent. First Mortgage Profit debentures for £100,000, divided into 2,000 bonds of £50 each. The present is an issue of £100,000 Five per Cent. First Mortgage Profit debentures, repayable at the expiration of 21 years from the date of issue, but redeemable at the option of the company after five years at 5 per cent. premium. These debentures will receive interest at the rate of 5 per cent. per annum, and will, in addition thereto, be entitled to one-fourth of the net profits of the company in each year after 5 per cent. dividend has been paid upon the shares. The company has been formed for the purpose of taking over and carrying on, as from January 1, 1886, the electrical business of J. E. H. Gordon and Co. (Limited), electrical engineers and contractors, of 11, Pall-mall, London, and the general contracting business of John Fell, of Leamington.

The Times, 9 January 1886.

Fell, Mr. A. L. C., M.I.E.E., is *electrical engineer* of the Sheffield Corporation.

Fell, Mr. J., Leamington, is a *director* of the—
Barrow-in-Furness Tramways, Limited.
Dudley and Wolverhampton Tramways, Limited (*chairman*).
Worcester Tramways, Limited.

The Subscription List will be Closed on or before Thursday, May 27th.

THE WESTON-SUPER-MARE, CLEVEDON, and PORTISHEAD (STEAM) TRAMWAYS COMPANY (with Junctions with the Great Western Railway). Incorporated by special Act of Parliament 48 and 49 Vict., cap. 182, whereby the liability of each shareholder is absolutely limited to the amount unpaid on his subscription. Capital £60,000 in 6,000 shares of £10 each. Payable £1 on application, £1 on allotment, and the balance in calls not exceeding £2, at intervals of not less than two months.

DIRECTORS.

Until the first meeting of the Company.

SIR EDMUND HARRY ELTON, Bart., Chairman, Clevedon-court, Somerset.

Samuel Edward Baker, Esq., Weston-super-Mare.

Henry Daniel, Esq., Tyndall's-park, Clifton.

John Griffin, Esq., Kenn, Somerset.

Henry Wansbrough, Esq., Weston-super-Mare.

Engineer—F. O. Stileman, Esq., C.E., Great George-street, Westminster.

Solicitors—Messrs. Osborne, Ward, Vassall, and Co., Bristol.

Bankers—The National Provincial Bank of England, London, Bristol, and Portishead; Stuckey's Banking Company, Weston-super-Mare and Clevedon.

Brokers—Messrs. Godwin and Walter, 8, Finch-lane, London, E.C.

Secretary—J. F. R. Daniel, Esq. (late Secretary and General Manager Bristol and Portishead Railway and Docks).

Offices (temporary)—70, Queen's-square, Bristol, and 21, Threadneedle-street, London, E.C.

Agent—Mr. Samuel Dawes, Birklands, Clevedon, and High-street, Weston-super-Mare.

PROSPECTUS.

The title of the Company, as incorporated by special Act of Parliament obtained in 1885, is the Weston-super-Mare, Clevedon, and Portishead Tramways Company.

The object of the Company is to construct and work, by locomotive power, a tramway 14 miles in length, for carriage of passengers and goods, on lands to be purchased by the Company, adjacent to and easily accessible from existing highways, between the important and increasing towns of Weston-super-Mare, Clevedon, and Portishead, the intermediate villages and the large import docks and warehouses at Portishead; also to construct certain sections of tramway upon public roads; and to build and maintain a bridge over the river Yeo, with road approaches.

The advantages of this undertaking are very great, there being at present no direct railway or tramway communication between Portishead, Clevedon, and Weston, the only route from Portishead to Weston being viâ Bristol, and though only 13 miles apart, a to and fro journey takes a longer time than between either place and London, more than ten times the distance.

With the facilities that will be given by this Tramway, it is estimated that the large population, consisting of residents and visitors and inhabitants generally, of the rising watering-places of Weston, Clevedon, and Portishead will give a constant passenger traffic, increasing with the development at various points of the route of the numerous beautiful building sites now unavailable for want of access, while the picturesque nature of the country through which the line passes will insure a large tourist traffic.

Portishead, with its fine docks and warehouses, is so naturally the port of this part of the West of England, that cheap and easy transit of goods by this Tramway, together with the collection of agricultural produce for the town markets, the carriage of building materials, and the development of the valuable mines and quarries of the district, will provide a steady paying and increasing goods traffic.

For these kinds of traffic a steam tramway near but not running on the roads is the best that can be provided, having regard to cheapness of construction, working, time, and convenience.

The cost of construction, £3,000 per mile, exclusive of land, is less than one-tenth of the average cost of English railways, and less than one-third that of street tramways, while even upon that cost most of the latter are yielding good dividends. The average receipts per mile are very nearly as much for tramways as for railways.

Taking the capital expenditure of this undertaking at £60,000, and the gross receipts at one-third only of those averaged by the tramways of the United Kingdom, and making a liberal reduction for working expenses, it is calculated that the dividend earned should be at the rate of at least 7¼ per cent., which it is fair to presume will be increased upon the natural development of the traffic.

The Bristol and Portishead Railway (now taken over by the Great Western Railway Company), ten miles in length, and having cost about £30,000 per mile, earned over £550 per month from the time the first train was run; similar receipts per mile on this tramway line, with its small cost of construction and working, would give enough to pay ten per cent. dividends. Previous to the construction of the Bristol and Portishead Railway, the only public conveyance to Bristol was an omnibus, which at present is the means of transit between Portishead and Clevedon.

There are no cuttings or embankments, and the gradients are practically level throughout, the line running through most picturesque valleys. There are also no stations, and only one bridge (this being over the river Yeo, which in itself will be a great boon to the district, providing much required means of transit over that portion of the river, and it is estimated that the tolls (as allowed by Act of Parliament) will of themselves produce a revenue sufficient to pay interest on the capital expended on the bridge), which will be approached by a new road to be constructed by the Company. The cost of traction is very small, as compared either with railway, road omnibus, or horse tramways, and the terminal and staff expenses will be trifling. In practice the tramcar stops whenever and only when passengers have to be taken up or set down.

Junctions with the Great Western Railway have been agreed upon, and the tramway line is in other respects constructed to take ordinary railway rolling stock, so that the traffic between railway and tramway will be easily interchanged.

This economical class of steam tramway running on its own land, and combining, at the low cost above-mentioned the most valuable advantages of a railway and tramway, is a new departure in locomotion, and certain to have a great future.

A contract has been entered into with Mr. John Fell, of Leamington, the well-known tramway contractor, who agrees to complete the line for the cost above stated, within six months from the date of commencement, when the Company will be in a position to begin earning dividends.

The preliminary expenses of the Company are limited to the actual outlay, incurred in obtaining the Act of Parliament, &c.

The special Act of Parliament, &c., can be inspected at the offices of the Company's Solicitors and Brokers.

A settlement and quotation on the Stock Exchange will be applied for in due course.

If no allotment is made the deposit will be returned in full.

Prospectus and forms of application may be had at the Bankers and Brokers.

Dated May 20th, 1886.

20 May 1886.

Opinions of the Financial Press.

The Money Market Review.

A seven per cent. investment: the Magdeburg Tramways Company (Limited).—Seven per cent. is a fine rate of interest, and an investment offering a secured 7 per cent. is likely to be a good deal sought after. Under these circumstances a more than usually cordial reception is likely to be given to the Magdeburg Tramways Company (Limited), whose prospectus was issued yesterday. Firstly, let us see what prospect there is that the promised 7 per cent. will be a reality and not a myth. The directors, in whose number are included the chairmen of some of the most successful tramways in this kingdom, give it as their distinct opinion, after close personal inspection on the spot, that when the lines at Magdeburg are in full operation the shareholders may depend upon dividends of at least 7 per cent.; but, as a precautionary measure, and in order to allow time for necessary development, the have obtained a guarantee from the contractor of that rate of dividend for three years from the 1st of July last. This is, therefore, an immediate 7 per cent. investment, for the shares so allotted rank for dividend on the full £10 as from the first day of the current half-year—namely, the 1st of July last. It furthermore appears that, in support of his guarantee, the contractor "deposits security approved by the directors."

Magdeburg is one of the most important commercial centres and rapidly-growing cities in Germany, being excellently situated at the junction of six railways, and upon the navigable river Elbe. The lines in question are already a "going concern," being nearly 12 miles in length, and only one and a half mile remain to be constructed. It is mentioned that "the results of the working of the lines opened have been highly satisfactory." The cost, which includes price paid for the concession (one arranged on specially favourable terms), the construction of 13½ miles of line, and an ample equipment of engines, horses, and cars, as well as substantial depots, is at the rate of £8,000 per mile, a price which compares very favourably with that of any of our English lines.

German tramways have invariably proved successful. For example, the Tramways Company of Germany, owning lines in Hanover and Dresden, which are not far distant from Magdeburg, is a conspicuous success, and has always paid steady dividends of about 7 per cent., and its shares stand at 50 per cent. premium. As a matter of fact, tramways abroad when under English control and management are to be preferred to tramways at home, as there is a much more general movement of the population and much more out-of-door life, especially in the evenings.

The Railway News.

The Magdeburg Tramway.—It is proposed to raise a capital of £120,000, of which £8,500 is now offered for subscription, to complete a system of tramways in the city of Magdeburg. The cost, including the concession, the construction of 13½ miles of tramway, with ample equipment of engines, horses, and cars, is at the rate of £8,000 per mile, a sum which compares favourably with that of most of the tramways of this country. Only about 1½ miles of the tramway remain to be completed. Considering that the success with which the Tramways Company of Germany have worked tramways in that country, the favourable estimates formed by the directors of the Magdeburg appear reasonable and well founded. The contractor guarantees a dividend of 7 per cent. on the shares for three years from the 1st July last.

The Bullionist.

The Magdeburg Tramways Company.—It is strange how social and national habits find their counterpart in economic and commercial operations. The particular fact that illustrates this generalization is the Continental habit of outdoor enjoyment as opposed to the attractions of English homes. In Germany, when business is done, there is in the evenings a general movement towards places of amusement, and this habit of the people has a distinct effect on the earnings of the tramway companies in the cities and towns of the empire. This broad and general observation leads us up to the consideration of the affairs of the Magdeburg Tramways Company, the capital of which is £120,000 in shares of £10. The directors are:—

Thos. J. Moore, Chairman of the Birmingham Central Tramway Company (Limited).

Edward Pritchard, Chairman of the Birmingham and Aston Tramways Company (Limited).

George Cattell Greenway, Chairman of the Dudley and Stockbridge Tramways Company (Limited).

Herr Edward Nehse, Dresden.

These directors, and especially the English ones, are connected with some of the most successful tramways in the United Kingdom, and they have committed themselves to this undertaking with the full conviction that it has in it all the elements of success. They have, after a close personal inquiry, announced their deliberate opinion that, as soon as the lines shall be in full operation, the shareholders may depend upon a dividend at least of 7 per cent. from the beginning, with a good prospect of larger dividends in the immediate future; in fact the contractor has guaranteed a 7 per cent. rate for three years from the 1st July last, and he has already deposited security such as is approved by the directors for the due payment of this dividend. This Company has hitherto been a private one, and was incorporated in 1884, but it has been found necessary to raise additional capital in order to complete the system of lines, and to pay off the contractor, Mr. John Fell, of Leamington. The shares allotted in this issue will rank for dividend in the full £10 shares from 1st July, 1886.

The concern is handed over to the Company as a going concern, and with 1½ mile only remaining to be completed, and when this has been finished there will be a total length of 13½ miles. The results of the working hitherto have been highly satisfactory. The one-horse cars are yielding a return of £2 per day, and the steam line to Herrenkrug has given on special days as much as £20 per engine, drawing two cars. The sphere of this enterprise has been well chosen, for Magdeburg is certainly one of the most improving cities on the Continent of Europe. It is the headquarters of the sugar industry, and possesses numerous iron, spirit, tobacco, and other manufactures. It is situated at the junction of six railways and upon the navigable river of the Elbe, and the railway and river traffic makes it the centre for 6,000,000 of inhabitants. The price at which the Company acquires the whole property is £108,000, and is at the rate of £8,000 per mile. The contractor will receive in part payment of this amount £25,000 of five per cent. debentures. The purchase includes the concession, which is for 39 years, as compared with the 21 years of English tramways, and a complete equipment of cars, horses, engines, and freehold property for stables, depots, &c. The lines have been laid down with steel girder rails, and are decidedly superior in their construction and stability to German tramways generally. An older tramway in the same city, and running through similar thoroughfares, now pays a dividend of nine to 10 per cent., and its shares are quoted at 90 per cent. premium. But tramways in Germany are almost invariably successful, and especially when they are under English administration, for English promoters have been quick to perceive that the general habits of the people in German cities demand exactly the facilities for locomotion which tramways provide. As another illustration of successful enterprise in this direction, we may allude to the Tramways Company of Germany, which is also under English administration. It possesses tramways in Hanover and Dresden, which are in the vicinity of Magdeburg. This company steadily divides 10 per cent., and the £10 fully-paid shares are quoted at 14½ to 15. The most conservative and cautious of investors can have no hesitation in taking a moderate stake in this enterprise. It seems to possess every recognized element of success.

A Seven per Cent. German Tramway Investment.
THE MAGDEBURG TRAMWAYS COMPANY

(Limited).—Incorporated under the Companies Acts, 1862 to 1883.—Nominal capital £120,000, in 12,000 shares of £10 each.—FIRST ISSUE £85,000, in 8,500 SHARES, of which about half have already been allotted and are fully paid. The balance (together with shares held by the contractor) are offered to the public at par. Payable—£1 per share on application, £4 per share on allotment, and £5 per share on 15th December, 1886. Upon these shares a minimum dividend of 7 per cent. is secured for three years.

DIRECTORS.

THOMAS J. MOORE, Esq. (Chairman Birmingham Central Tramways Company, Limited), Chairman.
Edward Pritchard, Esq., Chairman Birmingham and Aston Tramways Company (Limited).
George Cattell Greenway, Esq., Chairman Dudley and Stourbridge Tramways Company (Limited).
Herr Edward Nehse, Dresden, Germany, Manufacturer.
Local Representative—Herr Paul Stahlknecht, Magdeburg.
Bankers—Messrs. Greenway, Smith, and Greenways, Warwick and Leamington ; and their London Agents, Messrs. Glyn, Mills, Currie, and Co., Lombard-street, London.
Engineer—E. Pritchard, Esq., M.Inst.C.E., 2, Storey's-gate, Westminster.
Solicitors—Messrs. Hawkes, Weekes, and Howlett.
Auditors—Messrs. Carter and Carter.
Secretary (pro tem.).—Mr. Robert Green.
Offices (pro tem.).—2, Storey's-gate, Westminster, London.

PROSPECTUS.

This Company, which has hitherto been a private one, was incorporated in 1884, and has nearly completed its routes of tramways, some of which have been worked for 18 months and others for a short period. It being now necessary to raise more capital to pay off the contractor (Mr. John Fell, of Leamington), who is also desirous of disposing of some of the shares allotted to him, in lieu of cash, this prospectus is issued, and applications for shares are invited from the public on the following terms :—

1. Payment to be made £1 per share on application, £4 per share on allotment, £5 per share on 15th December, 1886.
2. The shares allotted to rank for dividend on the full £10 per share from 1st July last.
3. The provisions of the Companies Acts as to the setting out of all agreements in a prospectus are to be considered as waived, so far as any such contracts or agreements may have been entered into in the formation and management of the Company up to the date of the contract hereinafter referred to, bearing date the 20th day of October, 1886, and made between the Company of the one part and John Fell of the other part.
4. The contractor deposits security approved by the Directors to ensure a dividend at a rate not less than 7 per cent. per annum for three years from 1st July last.

The Directors have made a personal inspection of the tramway, and, having also made a careful investigation into its position and prospects, are of opinion that a 7 per cent. dividend may fairly be expected when the lines are fully developed, but to provide for any possible delay in such development they have arranged for the guarantee aforesaid.

The tramways already constructed are between 11 and 12 miles in length, the greater portion traversing the city of Magdeburg, and the

remainder (about 3½ miles) is a steam line running to the Herrenkrug, which is the great park and fête ground of the city.

An additional length of tramway has still to be laid, making a total length of 13½ miles of single line when completed. This will be vigorously pushed forward, and is expected to be finished by the end of this year.

The results of the working of the lines open have been highly satisfactory.

The one-horse cars are yielding a return of £2 per day, and the steam line to the Herrenkrug has given on special days as much as £20 per engine drawing two cars.

Magdeburg is one of the most important commercial centres of Germany. It is situated at the junction of six railways and upon the navigable river Elbe ; is the head-quarters of the sugar industry, and possesses numerous iron, spirit, tobacco, chocolate, chicory, and other manufactures. It is also the capital and seat of Government of the Province of Sachsen. The population in 1885 was 157,000, and is rapidly increasing, so much so that the Government have found it necessary to level the old fortifications in order that the area of the city may be largely extended.

Its railway and river traffic make it the centre for some 6,000,000 of inhabitants, and it is unquestionably the most improving city on the continent of Europe.

The concessions under which the Company holds its lines are for a period of 39 years, as compared with the 21 years of English tramways.

The lines have been most substantially laid with steel girder rails, and are decidedly superior in their construction and stability to German tramways generally, thus lessening the cost of repairs and renewals.

The equipment of the tramways, which is ample will consist of—
150 Horses.
8 Locomotive steam engines.
16 Steam cars, some of which seat 60 passengers.
30 Horse cars.
1 Freehold depôt, stables, fitting shop, manager's house, offices, &c
1 Leasehold depôt, fitted complete.
1 Large steam depôt, tools, &c., complete.

An older tramway company in the same city, and running through similar thoroughfares, now pays dividends of from 9 to 10 per cent., and its shares are quoted at 90 per cent. premium.

Tramways in Germany have, almost without exception, proved very profitable investments. The Tramways Company of Germany, under English administration, possesses tramways in Hanover and Dresden, which are in the vicinity of Magdeburg. It has paid steady dividends of 7 per cent., and its £10 fully-paid shares are quoted 14½ to 15.

The whole of the lines, the equipment above-mentioned, and the concessions have been obtained by the Company for the sum of £108,000, being at the rate of £8,000 per mile. The contractor receives in part payment of this amount £25,000 of five per cent. debentures.

Copies of the memorandum and articles of association, translations of the concessions and the before-mentioned contract of October 20th, 1886, entered into by the Company, may be seen at the offices of Messrs. Hawkes, Weekes, and Howlett, Solicitors, of 14, Temple-street, Birmingham, and 16, King-street, Cheapside, London.

Applications for shares must be made on the form accompanying prospectus, and be forwarded to the bankers of the Company, together with the deposit of £1 per share, and in the event of no allotment being made the deposit will be returned in full, or if a smaller number of shares be allotted than applied for the surplus will be applied in payment of the amount due on allotment.

Application in due course will be made to the Stock Exchange for an official quotation in the shares.

Prospectuses and forms of application can be obtained from the bankers and solicitors, and at the offices of the Company.

London, October 21st, 1886.

The Times, 26 October 1886.

We have received the prospectus of the Magdeburg Tramways Company (Limited). The nominal capital is £120,000, in 12,000 shares of £10 each, of which the first issue is £85,000, in 8,500 shares. This company, which has hitherto been a private one, was incorporated in 1884, and has nearly completed its routes of tramways, some of which have been worked for 18 months and others for a short period. It being now necessary to raise more capital to pay off the contractor, who is also desirous of disposing of some of the shares allotted to him in lieu of cash, this prospectus is issued.

The Times, 26 October 1886.

THE BARROW-IN-FURNESS TRAMWAYS, LIMITED.

(IN LIQUIDATION).

Directors.
LT.-COL. FISHWICK, *Chairman.*
E. HORTON, ESQ.
E. PRITCHARD, ESQ., M. Inst. C.E.
J. FELL, ESQ.
ALDERMAN TOWNSON, J.P.

Secretary.
MR. WALTER J. KERSHAW, A.C.A.

Auditors.
MESSRS. JOHN LEWIS & Co.

Solicitors.
MESSRS. SLATER & Co.
MESSRS. WILLIAM WEBB & Co.

Registered Office.
34, WATERLOO STREET, BIRMINGHAM.

CAPITAL.	Year ending 30th June, 1895.
4,518 Shares (£10)	£45,180
Debentures and Mortgage	16,433
	£61,613
Total Capital Expenditure	£65,967

Incorporated by Act of Parliament in 1880, to construct and work tramways in Barrow-in-Furness. Extensions were authorised in 1888. [1901, 1909.]

ANALYSIS OF REVENUE ACCOUNT.

		Year ending 30th June, 1895.
Traffic Receipts		£4,538
Other Receipts		208
Total Receipts		£4,746
	Per cent-age of Receipts.	
Total Expenses	100·06	£4,749
Loss		£3
Number of engines		8
Rolling stock (cars)		8
Mileage open		5½
Miles run		142,925
Passengers carried		*892,519

This Company being in Liquidation for purposes of reconstruction no Report is available.

THE DUDLEY & WOLVERHAMPTON TRAMWAYS, LIMITED.

Directors.
JOHN FELL, ESQ., *Chairman.*
WILLIAM BASS NEEDHAM, ESQ.
EDWARD PRITCHARD. ESQ., M.I.C.E.

Secretary.
WALTER J. KERSHAW, ESQ., A.C.A.

Manager.
FRANK HATCH, ESQ.

Auditors.
MESSRS. CALDICOTT, HILL & HARRISON, C.A.

Offices.
34, WATERLOO STREET, BIRMINGHAM.

CAPITAL ACCOUNT.	Year ending 31st Dec., 1897.
22,801 Shares, £1 (fully paid)	£22,797
5% First Debentures	5,000
4½% Second Debentures	17,578
	£45,375
Total Capital Expenditure	£48,717

Incorporated by Act of Parliament, 1880, to construct and work tramways to connect the towns of Wolverhampton and Dudley. [1901.]

ANALYSIS OF REVENUE ACCOUNT.

		Year ending 31st Dec., 1897.
Traffic Receipts		£6,156
Other Receipts		102
Total Receipts		£6,258
	Per cent-age of Receipts.	
Total Expenses	74·48	£4,661
Profit for year		£1,597
Debenture interest		1,041
		£556
Amount brought forward		—
Amount available for dividend		£556
Dividend paid		nil.
Amount written off		£556
Amount carried forward		nil.
Number of engines		6
Rolling stock		5½
Mileage open		5
Miles run		98,978
Passengers carried		611,451

In Liquidation. No Report for 1898 issued.

Madgeburg Tramways Company

1890

1895

NAME OF SECURITY, DATE OF INCORPORATION, ADDRESS, VOTING (**V**), TRANSFERS AND FEES (**T**) AND SHUTTINGS OF BOOKS (**S**).	CAPITAL.					INCOME.	
	Nominal or Authorised.			Called up.		Rate % ⅌ ann. Date of Payment.	
	Total Shares and Loans.	Shares or Bonds.		Per Share or Price of Issue.	Total Shares and Loans and Present Amount.	1888 2nd ½-year.	1889 1st ½-year.
		Number	Amount				
MAGDEBURG TRAMWAYS COMPANY, LIMITED. Registered **3rd September, 1884.** Office .... 95, Colmore Row, Birmingham. **V**.—1 vote for each share. **T**.—Common form. 2/6 per deed. Some of the shares are to bearer.	£120,000	12,000	£10	£10 on 7,671	£76,710	Sce	text
	£25,000 5 % Debs.	....	....	....	£25,000	1 Jan. 5 %	1 July 5 %

Burdett's Guide.

GENERAL DETAILS, INCLUDING PARTICULARS OF CAPITAL, STOCKS, LOANS, RESERVE FUNDS, DIVIDENDS, &c.	DIRECTORS AND CHIEF OFFICIALS.
Magdeburg Tramways Company, Limited.—Formed in 1884 to acquire a concession, granted for a period of 39 years from 1884, for constructing and working tramways in the City of Magdeburg. Contract price, £108,000, of which £25,000 was payable in 5 per cent. Debentures. About 14¼ miles of single line have been completed. No public issue of shares was made until October, 1886, when 8,500 (some of which were held by the contractor) were offered for subscription at par. Accounts made up annually to 30th June, and submitted in November. Reserve Fund for depreciation, £4,975. The contractor guaranteed a minimum dividend of 7 per cent. on the full sum of £10 per share for three years from 1st July, 1886. The guaranteed dividend was regularly paid. The debenture interest is payable by coupon on 1st January and 1st July, and has been paid to date.	*Directors*—Major WILLIAM T. E. FOSBERY (*Chairman*), E. NEHSE, EDWIN HANDLEY, ARTHUR Ll. LLOYD. Director's qualification, 20 Shares. *Auditors*—BAKER, GIBSON & CO. *Bankers*—LLOYDS BANK, LIMITED. *Secretary*—H. F. WOODWARD.
Manchester Carriage and Tramways Company.—Constituted by special Act of Parliament, August, 1880, which amalgamated the Manchester Carriage Company, Limited, and the Manchester Suburban Tramways Company under a new title. Accounts made up half-yearly to the end of February and August, and submitted at Manchester in April and October. Tramways Contract Suspense Account, £32,655. Dividends on A, B, and C Shares since amalgamation (year ended 31st August)—1880-1, 8 and 10 per cent.; 1881-2, 6 and 10 per cent.; 1882-3, 7 and 10 per cent.; 1883-4 and 1884-5, 8 and 12 per cent.; 1885-6, 8 and 12 per cent.; 1886-7, 4 per cent. and 14 per cent.; 1887-8, 4 per cent. and 2 per cent.; 1888-9, nil and 10 per cent. Carried forward at 31st August, 1889, £6,874. The A, B, and C Shares (which rank alike for dividend) are quoted in the *Manchester List.* Prices marked—A, 19¼; B, 13⅛; C, 9⅞.	*Directors*—JOHN KING, Jun. (*Chairman*), WILLIAM TURTON (*Deputy-Chairman*), JOS. WALKER, Sir J. J. HARWOOD, ROBT. NEILL, Jun., JOHN GREENWOOD, DAVID MCGILL. Director's qualification, £1,000 nominal Capital. *Auditors*—JOHN E. HALLIDAY and JAMES A. CARSE. *Secretary*—J. W. BETTENEY.

Stock Exchange Yearbook 1890.

William John Carruthers Wain and the Tramways Institute

This is the man who was, in effect, the Tramways Institute that promised so much. As his power declined, partly after the unpleasantness with the South Staffs Tramway Company, but at an accelerating rate after his conviction for fraud in 1899, so the TI itself went into terminal decline. There are great gaps in this story, reflecting pressures of time and, of course, space, so perhaps another researcher could pick up on this saga and have it published in a suitable magazine, say *Tramfare* or *Tramway Review*. The documents I offer as a taster are more-or-less in chronological order.

A PARABLE (well, really, I do not believe it either but...)

The cast comprises Edward Beall. solicitor. Thomas Lambert a director, Charles Singleton, a financial agent, and W.J.C. Wain. The stage was the Old Court (sometimes shown as the Old Bailey) and the play commenced on Tuesday October 31st., 1899. The programme showed us some really colourful characters, especially Beall who was nick-named 'The Black Prince' as he always moved around in a fancy coach drawn by four black horses. We know Wain for whom I must admit a sneaking admiration as he must have been quite a forceful character to have gained so many directorships. His birth was registered at St. Margaret parish, Westminster in 1854, so he was far too young to have come so unstuck.

The story line centred on the London and Scottish Banking and Discount Corporation Ltd, which was set up in 1893, claiming a working capital of £102,000 and issuing one of those delightful if totally false prospectuses, describing themselves as an international bank of good standing, and offering a variety of investments, all guaranteed to make a good healthy return. Perhaps originally the company was set up with honest plans but whatever they wandered off into the world of 'spin' issuing paperwork showing spurious profits, and paying dividends from capital. One of their 'tame' companies whose plans have a resonance today was the London Refuse Steam Company, which really does seem to

have built a plant, but included an involved and ultimately unworkable patented dust destruction process which would turn street refuse and household garbage into electricity without any coal consumption.

The play's run was 15 days and in the end Mr Justice Channell and a jury of viewers decided

---

Mr. W. J. Carruthers Wain, C.E., chairman of the Southwark and Deptford Tramways Company, has had an interview with the *employés* of the company at the depôt, and told them he had invited them there because there was a good deal of discussion taking place as to the hours of labour and pay of tramway men. It was not an easy thing to manage a line like theirs, which for the last ten years had had a struggle to keep its head above water at all. Fortunately now, however, they would be able to start the new year with a clean sheet and without debt. The company, therefore, wished to hear any grievances stated by the men without the intervention of people who cared nothing for the matter, except that they made a living out of the men's earnings. Without absolutely wrecking the concern the directors were willing to meet the views of the men. The line during its existence had earned £145,000, and of this sum, while £50,000 had been paid in wages, the shareholders had only distributed amongst themselves £5,000. Among the men the average hours of work were 16, or, deducting 2¾ hours relief, 13¼. It did not appear possible, taking into account the circumstances of the line, to reduce the working hours, but he thought it would be best that each conductor and driver should have one day off in 12, with full pay. (Cheers.) He thought also there should be a sort of co-operation between masters and men, and proposed to give at Christmas time a bonus to every man, depending on the success of the company during the year. There was another matter which might well be considered, at that meeting, and that was the desirability of a pension fund for tram men. He was prepared with a scheme for that object, and it would be laid before the next meeting of the Tramways Institute, and, if approved by the companies, something valuable might result from its adoption. Others addressed the meeting, satisfaction being expressed with the chairman's proposals. A vote was taken upon the question whether to have a reduction of hours or one day in 12, and the latter alternative was chosen. The meeting, which lasted an hour and a half, was thoroughly business-like, and cordial relations appeared to exist between the men and the directors, and the proceedings closed with cheers for the chairman and Mr. Pryor, the manager.

The Times, 30 November 1889.

TRAMWAY COMPANIES AND LOCAL AUTHORITIES.

On Saturday afternoon a deputation from the Tramways Institute of Great Britain waited upon Sir Michael Hicks-Beach, President of the Board of Trade, for the purpose of obtaining an authoritative declaration as to the meaning of the 43d section of the Tramways Act of 1870, enabling local authorities to take over the tramways, or the appointment of a select committee upon the subject. The President was accompanied by Lord Balfour of Burleigh, Mr. Courtenay Boyle, C.B., Sir Henry Calcraft, K.C.B., Mr. Ingram B. Walker, and Mr. W. J. Howell. The deputation was introduced by Sir Albert Rollit, M.P., and consisted of Mr. Shaw, M.P., chairman of the Blackpool Electric Tramways Company; Mr. W. J. Carruthers Wain, chairman of the institute; Mr. J. Ebbsmith, chairman of the Birmingham Central Tramways; Mr. S. J. Wilde, South London Tramways Company; Mr. William Turton, chairman of the Leeds Tramways Company; Mr. William Mason, chairman of the Bradford Tramways Company; Mr. S. L. Tomkins, Croydon Tramways Company; Mr. J. Platts, Southport Tramways Company; and Mr. J. G. B. Elliot, secretary of the institute.

Sir M. Hicks-Beach, in reply, said that whatever view the Board of Trade might take, it could not be binding upon the parties in the construction of an Act of Parliament. The position was this—that in 1874 Parliament chose to lay down certain principles upon which compulsory purchase might be carried out, and now that the powers of the Act were beginning to come into force, the deputation came and asked him to give an authoritative interpretation of what Parliament meant. It was absolutely impossible for him to do that. He could not give an authoritative interpretation which would bind anybody as to the meaning of the clause. Then he was asked to support the appointment of a committee to inquire what the clause meant; but such a committee was not the proper tribunal. The proper tribunal was a Court of law, and to that they must go. If the result of an appeal to a Court of law should be that the public were convinced that the law was unfair to the one side or the other, then there might be a case for the intervention of Parliament. As to the difference of opinion amongst lawyers, they could get different opinions of different lawyers on any conceivable subject, and he was sorry to say that he could not see his way to help them at all. As to endeavouring to bring tramway legislation more into accordance with modern ideas, that was another matter, and one which deserved consideration. He did not doubt that there were many points in tramway law which deserved consideration and required amendment, but the period of the Session was now too late to begin such an inquiry, and he could not make any promise with regard to next Session. Looking to the importance of the particular point which the deputation had primarily brought before him, he would like to see how the Courts of law interpreted the clause before making any general inquiry.

The deputation then withdrew.

The Times, 13 April 1891.

the whole thing was a ramp, Beall, said by the judge to be the brains behind the whole operation was sent down for five years penal servitude, Singleton for eighteen months 'in the Second Class', Wain twelve, again 'in the Second Class', while Lambert 'received a good character' and was released. All that destruction of themselves for a measly £30,000.

A few pages from the trial transcript follow, but alas I do not know what happened to Wain after this, although I think Beall who continued with other nefarious schemes seems to have died in prison in 1917. Singleton was already 62, and may not have recovered from his imprisonment.

The following item, dated 28 May 1892, shows how far Carruthers Wain was recognised.

"MR CARRUTHERS WAIN ON TRAMWAYS.

At Wednesday's sitting of Lord Derby's section of the Labour Commission, evidence was taken from Scottish carmen. Mr W. Cuthbertson and Mr R. Lemmon, representing respectively the Glasgow and Greenock branches of the National Scottish Horsemen's Union, said that in Glasgow the wages of carmen were from 21s. to 28s. a week, and in Greenock £1 to 24s. Witnesses were of the opinion that the conditions of agricultural labourers should be remedied by legislation, so as to remove their temptation to compete with town workpeople. Mr Carruthers Wain, President of the Tramways Institute and Chairman of the South Staffordshire Tramways Company, said there had been no strikes in the case of companies connected with the Tramways Institute, while they had been frequent on other lines. Lord Derby: What are the dividends on all the tramways in the United Kingdom? Five-and-a-half per cent. Their concessions are for 21 years only. Do you think there is exceptional discontent among tramway men? It is only part of the general labour movement which has not taken a very deep hold of tramway men. Examination continued: He considered a system of profit-sharing the best remedy for disputes, but the men would not accept it. If a legal eight-hour day were established the present rate of wages could not be maintained without an increase of fares, which had been tried without success on the Deptford and Greenwich [horse] tramways. He was in favour of corporations owning but not working tramways, because they would be likely to yield more readily to the demands of labour agitators, with the result that the population would be carried at the expense of the rates. It would open, moreover, the doors to a large amount of corruption, and put a powerful political engine in the hands of corporations. By Sir H. Beach: If tramways were constructed by corporations they would be made for cash without recourse to financiers, and probably that would enable them to pay higher dividends than 5½ per cent."

Although he was correct in foreseeing that trams would be a drain on rates, it was only after the corporations had spent early profits on "social" activities. This has occurred even on modern tramways where some lines in the UK are built for social reasons rather than following home to work patterns. Where Carruthers Wain got his average 5½% dividend I do not know. At this time the South Staffs paid nothing on ordinary shares.

LIGHT RAILWAYS ASSOCIATION.

A meeting of gentlemen interested in the encouragement and construction of light railways in Great Britain was held yesterday at 17, Victoria-street, Westminster. The meeting was convened to consider (1) what steps should be taken to amend the laws at present governing such enterprises (which laws are at present practically dead letters) ; (2) to appoint a deputation to wait upon the President of the Board of Trade to formulate the views of the conference ; (3) to establish an association to support and foster the movement ; and (4) generally to take all such steps as may be considered desirable in connexion therewith. Among those present were General Hutchinson, Major-General Webber, Mr. P. W. Meik, Mr. W. Rose Smith, C.E., Mr. J. G. B. Elliot (secretary of the Tramways Institute), Mr. W. M. Acworth, Mr. W. J. Carruthers Wain, and Mr. P. A. Scratchley. Mr. Carruthers Wain was voted to the chair.

The CHAIRMAN said that the meeting and the association which it was proposed to form were the outcome of their efforts 12 months ago in connexion with a light railways conference and the formation of a committee subsequently. The result of those labours up to the present was to be found in an exceedingly little Bill brought in by Mr. Bryce at the beginning of last Session. That Bill had died a natural death, due to some extent, he thought, to its own weakness. From that time up to the present little or nothing had been done except that efforts had been made to keep the subject alive by correspondence and the reading of papers. It appeared also that there was some confusion in the minds of gentlemen who had been asked to attend that day. Those who were present at the conference last year, and who also served on the committee, appeared to think that the conference at the Westminster Palace Hotel called for the following day was practically the same as the present meeting. There was no desire on the part of those connected with this movement to act in any way hostile to the association which had summoned that meeting for to-morrow. On the contrary, he understood that that meeting was called at the instance of the parish and district councils. Although their aid was exceedingly desirable, both as an association and independently, yet he thought it would be a mistake for the association itself to promote light railways to be formed distinctly under the auspices of parish and district councils. The body undertaking the work should be an independent one, and the suggestion was that a representative council of men who understood the question should be formed ; it should not consist of men who, however highly placed and dignified by title, did not understand the requirements of railways or of the public. Not only could light railways be constructed, but they could be made to pay, a fact which was evident to all those who had studied the question in America and Europe. He had recently returned from America, and he had seen these light railways working in such a way that convinced him, under proper conditions, they could be made. The question, however, was, "What conditions are reasonable and possible?" In America, for instance, farmers, in order to benefit their property and themselves, did not hesitate to give land. The Secretary to the Treasury of the United States had told him that the districts were allowed to tax themselves within a certain radius for the benefit of a particular line. These facts showed a state of feeling in America with regard to light railways and their utility to which we had not yet attained in this country. It would be premature to discuss details at that stage, but he suggested that a strong committee should be formed, a council of administration, to be guided by the advice of experienced engineers and solicitors ; and with their aid the association might be able to formulate suggestions, or a scheme, which might be useful to the new President of the Board of Trade when he came to submit his proposals to Parliament. Mr. Ritchie had agreed to receive a deputation from the association on December 6, and no doubt the right hon. gentleman would be glad to be informed beforehand of the points to be raised and the names of the speakers. He concluded by moving the resolution— "That a Light Railways Association be formed."

MAJOR-GENERAL WEBBER seconded. If the association accomplished the task of making this question, its difficulties and its opportunities, known to all the authorities throughout the country who were interested in the relief of agricultural distress, he believed that a very good work would be achieved. At the meeting of the British Association at Ipswich he had tried to emphasize the view that light railways could be constructed at a cost, and under conditions, to provide for the sparseness of traffic which was to be found in most agricultural districts, and which hitherto had been looked upon as of a character unable to support the construction and working of a railway.

The resolution was agreed to.

The Times, 28 November 1895.

The following item is drawn from our volume 4 but is inserted here to give readers who do not have volume 4 to hand some salient dates. This particular saga is relatively easy to research as it was carried in the columns of papers as diverse as the *London Times* and the *Midlands Weekly Gazette*.

"SOUTH STAFFORDSHIRE TRAMWAYS CO. v. EBBSMITH AND ANOTHER.

In his summing up his Lordship stated: "The suggestion of the plaintiffs was that this was part of the scheme by which the arrangement for the purchase of the land was carried out, and that it was a fraudulent contrivance to enable the defendants to carry out their fraudulent intent and self-aggrandising programme. The jury must ask themselves whether there was any explanation which occurred to their minds as reasonable, consistent with honour and honesty, in connection with this transaction of the land. Was Ebbsmith fraudulent, and was Wain a party to the fraud, were the questions the jury would have to ask themselves. In conclusion, his Lordship left the following questions to the jury: Did the defendants agree to act in concert together in fraud of the plantiff company and for their own benefit in respect of the sale of land."

The "worthless patents" included the life-saver/guard said to have been invented by Ebbsmith, and also a rail cleaner invented by Alfred Dickinson and sold by him to the Dickinson Appliance Company for £50. Ebbsmith trading under the name of this company then offered each appliance for £900 plus a royalty of £9.10s (presumably per year). William Kenway who had been Secretary and Manager of Birmingham Central Tramways stated: "The rail-cleaner had great disadvantages because if there was dust on the road it would be stirred up to an extent which would cause the public to cry out, and it also scraped the rails. The charge and the royalty was one which he could not conceive any company passing. The Birmingham Central Tramway Company of which the defendants were officers, had used the rail-cleaner, and he believed the North London Tramway Company, with which Mr Wain was connected. He knew of no other company which had used it."

Eventually it transpired that the South Staffs had paid £900 in cash and bought one-thousand £10 shares in the Dickinson Appliance Company. "The negotiations were carried on through Ebbsmith. His Lordship: And evidently the defendant Ebbsmith was the

The Times, 23 July 1897.

Dickinson Company ... A cheque was signed for £500, and bills given for £400 in respect to the cash payments. Charles Henry Preston, an engineer, went into the service of the plaintiff company [South Staffs] in 1884, and remained until 1888. In consequence of instructions, he had a fender made to go in front of the engine. He took the engine, with the fender attached, to Ebbsmith's house for him to inspect it. The fitting of the rail-cleaner to the engine was done by the workmen of the company and paid for by the company. Certain alterations to the wheels of the wagons were done after delivery, and those were done at the expense of the company. John Harvey, examined, said he had been engineer in the plaintiff company for nine years. The rail cleaner was no good. The lifeguard was, in his opinion, no good."

Other patents, not all unsuccessful, included an auxiliary steam-operated trailer car brake, spring or flexible wheels intended to give a better ride over rail joints for which we have a costing when used on both the South Staffs and Birmingham Central companies from the lips of Albert Lewis, the liquidator of the Dickinson Company: "The price at which car wheels were paid for by the Dickinson Company was £24, and sold for £30.6s. for forty-two wheels, which was equal to 11s.5d per wheel bought and 14s.4d and a fraction over sold. Mr Holmes recalled, said the prices were net, and the articles went direct from the manufacturers to the customers of the Dickinson Company. The company [i.e. the Dickinson Appliance Co.] had no premises for storing goods." Other patents were for rail joint chairs (which each cost £5.10s and were sold to the South Staffs for £7.10s), a drainage system, and innumerable parts for cable tramways and, of course, the Dickinson patent swivelling head was used on the cars of the South Staffs tramways. Some play was made over the fact that no tramways unconnected with Ebbsmith and Wain had used these appliances – patent dodging was as rife in the Victorian age as today – many lifeguards used elsewhere look similar.

In the course of the trial other mostly financial matters arose including a suggestion that in one company more debentures were held by Messrs Ebbsmith, Dickinson and Wain than were shown as issued and that some money may have been bled into the Electric Meter Company and the United Dutch Oyster, both Ebbsmith companies. "His Lordship pointed out that there was a suspicion of erasure just at this time in the books. Witness thought that was because he made a mistake. Witness said the book had been in the possession of Mr Wain, and was lost some time ago. Witness got it again a couple of days ago. It was stated that a box was broken open in Mr Wain's office and the book stolen. It was returned to witness by his solicitor, who said it was returned to him by Mr. Wain. (Sensation)."

The third matter was all too reminiscent of the happy O'Hagan days, and one which really vexed the Lord Chief Justice, was recited by Mr Kenway, the ex-Birmingham Central Secretary:

"The next point on which witness was examined was as to the packing of meetings. He stated that meetings were held in 1888, 1889, 1890, 1891 and 1892. At the first of these dates shares were transferred to thirty-four new holders living in London, and these were brought down to the meetings at Wednesbury in saloon carriages, and were supplied with lunch, by instructions from Mr. Wain, who gave witness money to pay for the lunches: but he did not know where it came from. Witness could not trace any payments in the books of the company, but in 1891 and 1892 when the same thing occurred there were cheques drawn by Wain for £100, £50 and £250, for 'expenses of electric traction' and made payable to bearer." His Lordship asked: "With regard to the packing of meetings and the payment of money to the nominee shareholders, was the payment honest and legal, or a dishonest and illegal misappropriation of the money of the company?"

The necessity to pack the meetings with nominee shareholders (some of whom were Ebbsmith's clerks!) was of course to ensure a smooth ride for Ebbsmith and Wain's various manoeuvres; a point not missed by His Lordship.

The jury took just an hour to return with their verdict: "In the matter of the land Ebbsmith and Wain acted in concert, thereby defrauding the company to the extent of £7,313. As regard the patents, they found that there was a conspiracy between the defendants, and in respect of that they found damages to the amount of £1,650, and profits improperly made £500, making altogether £2,150. Then, as to the packed meetings, that the defendants were both parties to the misappropriation of the company's funds to the amount of £362, and they found for these amounts with 3½ per cent interest."

Although one tries to be dispassionate I do wonder how these men felt on that night: did Wain still believe he was innocent and did Ebbsmith regret anything?

The final direct mention was in the newspapers of the 20 February 1896 and was relatively innocuous:

The Times, 23 June 1899.

William James Carruthers Wain aged 40 in 1892

This report of proceedings against Singleton and Wain was transcribed by OCR (computer optical character recognition), but regrettably as we did not have access to the original documents some errors could not easily be identified and thus corrected. Apologies are offered.

"OLD COURT. – Tuesday, October 31st, 1899, and following days.
Before Mr Justice Channell
Reference Number: 18991023-715

715. EDWARD BEALL (47), CHARLES SINGLETON (62), THOMAS HARRISSON LAMBERT and WILLIAM CARRUTHERS WAIN (41), Unlawfully conspiring to defraud the public in connection with the promotion of the London and Scottish Banking and Discount Corporation, Limited.

The SOLICITOR-GENERAL, MR SUTTON, MR H. AVORY *and* MR BODKIN *conducted the Prosecution;* MR ISAACS, Q.C, MR MUIR *and* MR CRAIG *appeared for Beall,* MR GRAIN *and* MR PETER GRAIN *for Singleton* MR MARSHALL HALL. Q.C, *and* MR TURRELL *For Lambert, and* MR A. E. GILL *for Wain.*

GEORGE INGLIS BOYLE. I am a messenger at the Record Office, London Bankruptcy Court, and produce the file in the bankruptcy of Edward Beall in 1892 – the date of the creditors' petition is July 18th, 1892, and the receiving order August 8th, 1892, and the adjudication September 3rd, 1892 – the statement of assets and liabilities shows assets £2,071 16s. 11d., and liabilities £5,534 7s. 9d. – Beall has not been discharged I charged from that bankruptcy – his address at that time is given as "Edward Beall, Tower Chambers, London Wall" – I also produce a second file in the bankruptcy of the same Edward Beall, whose address is "15, Copthall Avenue" – I find that the debtor's own petition was filed on March 23rd, 1899 – there was an adjudication and receiving order made the same day – then there is a statement of affairs showing assets, estimated at £2,300, and liabilities £6,254 19s., – that bankruptcy is still proceeding – I produce a third file in the bankruptcy of a person named Charles Singleton, which shows that a petition at the instance of the Adelphi Bank, Limited, was filed on June 24th, 1884 – the receiving order was made July 10th, 1884, and the adjudication September 5th, 1884 – the summary shows estimated assets £2,405 12s. 7d., and liabilities £627 4s. 5d., showing, therefore, a surplus of £1,778 8s. 2d. – no public examination was held – I find on the file a warrant for his arrest on nonappearance at such public examination, dated in 1884 – that warrant is still extant; he has never appeared – I have no other file there.

HERBERT GEORGE CROSS . I am clerk to Pritchard, Inglefield and Co., solicitors at Painters' Hall – they acted as the London agents for the solicitors to the Adelphi Bank – I remember the bankruptcy proceedings which have just been mentioned by Mr Boyle, against Charles Singleton – I know him as Singleton only.
Cross-examined by MR GRAIN. This bankruptcy was in 1884 – my firm had the conduct

of the proceedings, and it was at my instigation that a warrant for his arrest for nonattendance on his public examination was taken out, no doubt – I had not seen Mr Singleton since 1884 until I saw him at the Mansion House, when I was asked to identifiy him – I have not tried to find him at the address given in the warrant; we are only London agents, and we have to obey instructions – I did not, after obtaining the warrant, attempt to find him at the address which was given by him at that time, and which was in the warrant – I do not think he was living for 10 years at the same address, from 1884 to 1894, or there abouts – we ceased to make inquiries after a few years; from 1884 up to 1890 we could not trace him.
GEORGE INGLIS BOYLE (Re-examined). I have now found the filed document; it recites that Messrs Pritchard, Inglefield, and Co. appeared for the petitioning creditor, and that Beall and Co. appeared for the debtor – the date is July 10th, 1884.
Cross-examined by MR GRAIN. There is no address in this warrant, except 27 and 28, St. Swithin's Lane – that would indicate the place of business where the bankrupt was carrying on his business when he became baukrupt, I believe it does not deal with his private address – I do not know the procedure.
WALTER JAMES MORRIS . I am a clerk in the Copyright Registry at Stationers' Hall – I produce a form of application for registration of what is described on the form as "a book" – this is an application by A. F. Baker: "To the registering officer appointed by the Stationers' Company; A. F. Baker, of 5, Copthall Avenue, B.C., do hereby certify that I am the proprietor of the copyright of a book entitled 'London and Scottish Banking and Discount Corporation, Limited' and I hereby require you to make entry in the register book of the Stationers' Company of my proprietorship of such copyright, according to the particulars underwritten" – then the "title of book" is given as "London and Scottish Banking and Discount Corporation, Limited "; the name of publisher and place of publication, "A. F. Baker, 5, Copthall Avenue, London, E.C."; the "name and place of abode of the proprietor of the copyright," same name and address; "date of first publication," March 24th, 1892. Signed, "A. F. Baker"; witness, "Alice S. Rich" – then there follows the actual document registered in the form of a prospectus.
Cross-examined by MR HALL. Lambert's name does not appear anywhere on that prospectus, so far as I know.
Cross-examined by MR A. GILL. The same observation applies to the defendant Wain.
ROBERT MACGREGOR. I am Chief Clerk of the Exchequer at Edinburgh – I act for the Registrar of Joint Stock Companies – I produce the file, as it is called, of the London and Scottish Banking and Discount Corporation, Limited – the company was registered on

August 18th, 1892 – the memorandum of association was registered on that day; it shows that, amongst other objects of the company, was this: "To confirm and carry into effect, with such modifications as may be agreed upon, an agreement between A. F. Baker and a trustee on behalf of the corporation"; and under Clause 5 of the memorandum, the capital of the corporation, £102,000, is divided into 10,000 shares of £10 each, and 2,000 founders' shares of £1 each, with power, subject to the provisions hereinafter contained, to increase or reduce such capital – the shares are divided into the following classes: 10,000 ordinary shares, 2,000 founders' shares – the,. rights of the shares are stated to be that "the ordinary shares are entitled to a preferential dividend at the rate of £7 per cent per annum, and to share in the remaining profits of the corporation as hereinafter mentioned; the founders' shares are entitled to one moiety of the remaining profits of the corporation after the payment of the 7 percent – interest (non-cumulative) on the ordinary shares, the remaining one moiety of such profits being distributed amongst the holders of ordinary shares, such remaining profits or any part of such profits being subject to the formation of a reserve fund, as the directors or managers may think fit; (6) dividends may be paid in cash or by the distribution of specific assets, shares, stock, or otherwise;" then follows the list of seven signatories – each of the seven signatories subscribes for one founders' share – the witness to all the above signatures is "Oliver R. Mason. Wareford Court, London, E.C., manager to a public company"; then follows: "This memorandum is registered without articles of association. – A. F. Baker, agent for the said bank" – the second document on the file is the duty stamp form; the third is an agreement dated August 19th, 1892, between the London and Scottish Banking and Discount Corporation, Limited, of one part, and A. F. Baker of the other part; that recites certain matters, and then makes over 2,000 £1 fully paid founders' shares to A. F. Baker – it is signed, "For and on behalf of the London and Scottish Banking and Discount Corporation, Limited, Leonard Barker and William Osborne, directors," and also by A. F. Baker – the next document is a return of capital up to September, 1892 – it shows that the seven signatories are still existing shareholders, Braoley, Clark, Cook, Drew, Osborne, Williams, Barker; and in addition to their seven shares there are share warrants to bearer, 2,000, making altogether 2,007 shares issued at that date – that is signed, "A. F. Baker, Secretary" – then there is another return at the end of the year 1892 to the same effect; seven signatories with one share each, and then the 2,000 share warrants in addition; that is made up to January 30th, 1893 – the next document is dated June 16th, 1893, a notice of address – there is another document dated June 16th, 1893, giving the address of the company as 6A, George Street, Edinburgh – so far as I can tell, that is the first address of the company that I had for registration – the next document is a petition filed on February 10th, 1894: in petition to the Right Honourable the Lords of Council and Session; that is the Division of the Court of Session in Scotland – that is presented on behalf of John R. Blackiston, Inspector of Schools, of Peyton Lodge, Sheffield, for rectification of register by the removal of his name from the list of shareholders – the petition itself shows that the ground for that application was the appearance of the name of a Mr Scrafton in the list of governors – "The petitioner has learned, and now avers, that before the said shares were allotted to him the said Robert Scrafton had intimated to the company and to the other governors named in the prospectus that he withdrew his consent to become a governor of the company – on April 10th, 1894, I got a letter from F, J. Baker, the secretary, giving me notice that Mr Blackiston's name had been removed from the list of shareholders; it is dated April 10th; it would be received on the 11th – the next document is a notice of change of situation from George Street, Edinburgh, to 23, St. James's Square, Edinburgh, as the registered office of the company – the next is the summary, showing the number of shares which had been issued and taken up, to December 24th, 1894 – that shows that in addition to the 2,000 fully paid up shares, 2,529 shares had been taken up to that date; the 2,000 being the 2,000 fully paid shares previously referred to, I presume; there are seven subscription shares, and 1,993 others – the summary further shows that the total amount of calls received up to that date was £24,760, and the total amount of calls unpaid £530 – then follows a long list of shareholders; and then I find the very last entry on the return, "share warrants to bearer allotted, 1993" – that would be the 2000 less the seven original signatories' shares – the next document is a petition dated December 13th, 1894, for the windingup of the company presented by Mr M'Gill and Mr Barr; they were the petitioners – among the names mentioned there I find the names of Messrs Davidson and Syme; they were the solicitors for the petitioners, Mr M'Gill and Mr Barr – the Court made an order for the windingup of the company on January 16th, 1895, Mr Richard Atcheson being appointed liquidator.

Cross-examined by MR ISAACS. The memorandum says: "To promote any company or companies for the purpose of acquiring all or any of the property and liabilities of this corporation, or for any other purpose which may seem directly or indirectly calculated to benefit this corporation "; and under letter p.: "To remunerate any person or company for services rendered, or to be rendered, in placing or assisting to place, or underwriting or assisting to underwrite, or guaranteeing the placing or under-writing of any of the shares in the corporation's capital, or any debentures or other securities of the corporation, or in or about the formation or promotion of the corporation, or the conduct of its business" – in Clause 5 it is stated that "the capital of the corporation is £102,000, divided into 10,000 shares of £10 each, and 2,000 founders' shares of £1 each, with power, subject to the provisions hereinafter contained, to divide such shares or stock," and, a little later, "by resolution to increase or reduce such capital"; there is power to increase or reduce – Clause 6 says: "Dividends may be paid in cash or by the distribution of specific assets, shares, stock, or otherwise" – at first, when the registration took place in August, 1892, they were registered without articles under Table A – there was just a memorandum alone; but later I find that on February 15th, 1893, articles were filed with

me, and a special resolution was passed, altering Table A in the shape of special articles according to the resolution.

On December 14th, 1894, the 2,000 shares are referred to there at fully paid – it is quite clear that there are 2,000 founders' shares of £1 – that is 1893, and then the seven signatories' shares make up the rest.

Cross-examined by MR A. E. GILL. This is the winding up petition – it was made by Robert McGill and James Barr – those are the two names printed on the face of it.

Cross-examined by MR GRAIN. The notice of the change of address is 23, St. James's Square – it is sighed "F. J. Baker" – John Macdonald, 23, St. James's Square, Edinburgh, is the name of the man who presented this document to us; it is signed by Baker.

By MR GILL. 1 find among the shareholders the name of Mr Carruthers Wain, 18, Eldon Street, 20 ordinary shares – those are fully paid up – it is put with a call of £10 on them, and assuming that he paid his calls, because there are some unpaid.

ALFRED PHILIP KING. I am an accountant, of Palmerston Buildings, City – in 1891 I was secretary to the Copthall Avenue Office Company, Limited – I own Copthall House – I remember at the beginning of 1891 Hanson applying to me for an office – Charles Singleton is the man; he gave me some references, and amongst them Beall and Co., solicitors – I wrote a letter to that name – this is a copy of it: "Mr J. C. Hanson, of 100, Harrow Road, W., intends renting offices of my company, and has given your name as a reference. Please inform me what you know about him, and if you consider him a trustworthy and responsible person, Thanking you in anticipation of your reply, – Yours faithfully, A.P. KING. [to] Messrs Beall and Co., Solicitors, Tower Chambers" – I got an answer on the 13th – I have not kept it; we sold the property in the following year, and handed over all the books – after I read the answer, I agreed to take Mr Hanson as my tenant at £70 a year, or something like that – after I received the letter from Beall and Co., I wrote this letter (367) to acknowledge its receipt, and then accepted Hanson as my tenant.

FRANCES BERNARDINE STAFFORD. I live at 352, High Road, Tottenham – in 1891 I was the housekeeper in Copthall House, Copthall Avenue – I remember some rooms being taken in that building, in 1891, by a person named Hanson – Charles Singleton is the man – " The Metropolitan Stock and Share Association, J. C. Hanson, Manager," was up – he occupied those offices about 12 months – I know Mr Beall by sight – I have seen him in that building, but not in Mr Hanson's office – I have seen him there during the time Mr Hanson occupied the office – I saw him and Hanson together once – after Hanson ceased to occupy those premises some rent was owing by him, and there were proceedings in the Marylebone County Court to recover such rent – I attended – Beall and Co. acted for Hanson in those County Court proceedings.

Cross-examined by MR ISAACS. It was my business to be about the office a good deal when I was there; I am not there now – I was at that time constantly about, seeing the people go in and out."

...numerous documents irrelevant to us were produced...

"Wednesday November 1st.

JAMES MEEKING. I am a printer – I was formerly employed by a company which printed a paper called the *Financial Critic* which went into liquidation – I became acquainted with Mr Beall at that time – I used to see him in the office of that company frequently – after that company went into liquidation, as the result of some conversation with Mr Beall about another paper, I started the *Financial Gazette* – the arrangement between us was that Mr Beall would supply, without pay, the articles, and I was to do the printing, and pay for everything myself – any profits, of course, would come to me – I had to supply all the printing of it – the leading articles were supplied to me by Mr Beall from time to time, and proofs were submitted in the ordinary way to Mr Beall – I now his writing – the articles when they first came were very seldom in Mr Beall's own writing; they came through him in writing, or typewritten at times – the proofs were corrected mostly by Mr Beall – the paper was sold in the streets, and, as near as I can think, there were about 300 subscribers – I printed per week 1,000 copies, and sent them out for distribution – I used to have five or six men round the City selling them – I sent copies every week to subscribers – the addresses and names of the subscribers came from Mr Beall – he used to have 50 copies or 25, whatever he wanted, sent to him from the office – Exhibits 174 175, and 176 in 1892 and 1893 (Produced)are specimens – I also, at the request of or for Mr Beall, did the application forms, prospectuses, the usual routine of jobbing printing – most of the work was connected with companies – I printed the prospectus of the London and Scottish Banking Corporation on Mr Beall's instructions – I can not tell you the date, but we did all the preliminary work before it went to the public; what are called proof prospectuses; I should think about 1893, it may have been in 1892 – I printed the Exhibits 177, 178,179, and 180, including the inset, a slip that went out with the proof prospectus – the copy was supplied by Mr Beall and corrected from time to time, and it was inserted in the prospectus from time to time: it had nothing to do with the *Gazette* – it is supposed to be a list of agents for the Scottish Bank, and that, I suppose, was got from Mr Beall – I got from Mr Beall the material for that – a 3 in. advertisement of the London and Scottish Bank appeared from week to week in the *Financial Gazette* – they were paid for through the bank, I believe – I received my money when I sent in my bill to the corporation, the bank – they were paid by cheque, so far as I can recollect, from the bank at the end of every month – the cheque was the bank's cheque, I think; I mean a cheque signed by the directors – I never had any cheques from Beall to pay for those advertisements – I have had plenty of cheques from him for miscellaneous printing; all the printing I did – in most cases I sent the bill in and got a cheque for it – I did printing for a firm named Morrison and Co., of Telegraph Street, through the orders of Mr Beall – A. F. Baker was a short, dark man; he used to be one of Mr Beall's clerks – I do not know the difference between F. J. Baker and A. F. Baker – all I got paid for was through Mr Beall, not by the cheques of anybody named F. Baker; not to my knowledge – I printed Exhibit 25; a little article headed "Banks and

Banking," and "Extract from the *Financial Gazette* of July 30th, 1892" – it had previously appeared in the *Financial Gazette*; I should say after the paper had gone to press we lifted it out, and printed the copy of the article from the *Financial Gazette* by Mr Beall's orders – all this time I was carrying on the business simply in my name of Meeking – I tried to form myself into a company, but with no result – I had a good plant and plenty of material, but no work – the name was the Printing Press Agency, Ltd. – I got seven signatures, and I registered myself – I did not have a banking account in the name of the Printing Press Agency, Ltd., nor did the Printing Press Agency, Ltd., have a banking account – I had a banking account myself in the name of Meeking – this is my signature in the signature-book, "James Meeking, Managing Director" – I was supposed to be the managing director if the company went, but the company did not go – this is my signature, but I have forgotten all about it – the account in the bank-book at the bank was, "Printing Press Agency, Managing Director, J. Meeking" – J. Meeking and Son's account was at the London and Scottish Bank – I do not recollect having an account of the Printing Press Agency there – I always signed cheques "J. Meeking and Son" – this account is in 1893, from June to September – I know nothing about the cheques (produced) – I do not know the names down here – I know one Millington; they are the paper people – I paid them money – I used to buy all my paper there, but not through the Press Agency; I never did – some are drawn to J. Meeking – I only drew cheques to myself on my own private banking account – I used to pay it in to J. Meeking and Son, and take it out – I have not got any passbook now – when I failed in business I left everything there – my banking account is closed.

Cross-examined by MR ISAACS. I opened an account when the bank started in my own name of Meeking, and, to the best of my belief, at least I am sure of it all the cheques I signed would be signed "J. Meeking and Son" – I did not call myself the Printing Press Agency before I turned myself into a limited company – the *Financial Gazette* was run entirely for my profit and at my expense – I found the money necessary for the upkeep, and at the same time I took what there was coming in in the way of advertisements, sales, and otherwise – all that Mr Beall had to do with it was that he contributed articles inserted in the paper – everything had to pass through Mr Beall's hands – I cannot tell you who wrote them – I never paid for any of them – a lot of people wrote articles, but they came through Mr Beall and went back to him again – I said at the Police-court, "Very few people wrote for the *Financial Gazette* except Mr Beall, so far as I know" – I always took instructions from Mr Beall as regards the different articles and things to go in the paper – I was not used myself to the editorial department, and he was what I should say was my editor; he used to pass the proofs – I used to get all my instructions from Mr Beall – I knew no one else connected with it – I was examined in the bankruptcy of Mr Beall, on February 17th, 1893, at a private sitting, and by the Assistant Official Receiver in bankruptcy in Carey Street, before Mr Registrar Giffard – I recollect being there, but I do not recollect any question

that was asked me now – I printed the *Financial Critic* for the Rev. Rivington – a man named Boffey was his editor and his managing man – that "then I brought out a paper of my own, the *Financial Gazette*," is quite correct – I had the copyright of the *Financial Gazette* – I had no instructions from anyone else than Mr Beall – I could not have possibly denied that – Mr Mason's time was before I was in business; when I was managing the place for the City and Counties Publishing Company – that was not when I was printing on my own account, or when I printed for the Rev. Rivington – I am referring to the *Financial Critic* – it is so long ago – Mr Mason never had anything to do with the *Financial Gazette* in his life – I did not take instructions from him; I got my instructions from Mr Beall, and not from Mr Mason – "Proof Prospectus" is underlined – I did all the preliminary work until it went to the public – these prospectuses were printed by me; I cannot say about all – in the ordinary course, I suppose a dozen prospectuses would be as much as I should print – I would print one, send it, and get it back, correct the alterations, and then print it – I never worked for Morrison and Co. themselves; the work came through Mr Beall's account – Mr Beall introduced me to Morrison and Co. – I got no introduction; the work came in the usual form, through the usual channel – I did not know Morrison and Co.; I did not know whether there was a company or not; the heading was "Morrison and Co.," and that was all I knew – I got instructions, and did the work – I could not tell you when I was first asked a question about Morrison and Co.; thousands of names passed through my memory – I kept only private books; not a ledger, or anything like that – I do not know about odd printing jobs – I was asked about this question of Morrison and Co., Mansion House, I believe, a few months ago in the Court – I did the work, I suppose, from 1893 to 1895 – I cannot tell you; I have no record of it – since I failed I have had to go back to my case, and I have been working at it ever since, from 1895 to 1899 – nothing has transpired with regard to this matter till the Treasury asked if I had done work for Morrison and Co.; the matter was brought up, and I was asked if I had done work for Morrison and Co., through Mr Beall – nothing was contributed by Beall towards the *Financial Gazette* in the shape of money – I do not think I charged him for the papers he had; he used to pass everything for me, and if he wanted 25 or 50 copies, I do not think I charged him – he would say, "How many copies have you got left?" – I would say, "perhaps 200" – he would say, "Send them round to the office; I can do with them" – 25 or 50 was the general order – sometimes I was sold out, and I would not put them on the machine again; sometimes my 1,000 copies would go by Monday.

Cross-examined by MR MARSHALL I have never had any cheque signed by Mr Lambert, to my recollection – none of the prospectuses I printed had Lambert's name on them, to my knowledge.

Cross-examined by MR A. E. GILL. I do not know Mr Wain; I do not see his name on prospectus No. 179 – on 180 there is no list of governors – these are the names of the governors and directors on No. 179: Trustees: "The Right. Hon. Lord Elibank, Sir Alexander

Armstrong, K.C.B., F.R.S., and the Hon. H, Stanhope"; and the governors: "The Hon. Ashley Ponsonby, David F. Carmichael, Esq., E. T. Gourley, Esq., M.P., Noel Allix, Esq., J.P, D.L., Lieut.-Col. W. Hope, V.C, A. Shoolbred, Esq., and Octavius Stokes, Esq." – prospectus No. 179 is headed "Founders' Issue"; 178 is headed "Founders' Issue" and "Proof Prospectus" as well – that also does not contain the name of Mr Wain – the only one of the documents which I have produced which contains the name of Mr Wain is that headed 'Proposed Officers of the Bank" and "Not for Publication"; also "Proof, subject to Alterations and Additions," – and is simply a list of names and addresses.

[Henry Anson Cavendish, Lord Waterpark then stated why he was upset by the bank misusing his name]

...Cross-examined by MR ISAACS. This letter of February 20th was intended to be the record as it is of the terms upon which I was willing to act – what I intended was that a firm of solicitors should be appointed whose name was to go on the prospectus for the trustees, because before they agreed to have their name on the prospectus they would have investigated the whole thing, and seen as to its *bona fides* and all that – the London and Discount Corporation was to have a separate firm of solicitors to act for the trustees – my own solicitors constantly made inquiries for me – I go to my solicitors and say, "I am asked to join this company; I want you to make inquiries," and I pay them naturally – before I go on a board, or consent to act in this way, I employ my own solicitors, and pay them myself – I was quite willing to become the trustee, but I wanted to advertise a firm of solicitors upon the prospectus as solicitors for the trustees, quite apart from whom the solicitors to the corporation were – I do not know what there was for the trustees to do – in any event I was going to be remunerated, I suppose.

...Cross-examined by MR MARSHALL HALL. I had always found Mr Lambert an honourable, straightforward man – I have never changed my opinion with regard to him in the least – I know his people are just on the borders of Derbyshire and Staffordshire, and I know his family by reputation perfectly – he was connected with some Welsh coal syndicate with me, and other matters of legitimate business, and I saw a good deal of him – from what I knew of Mr: Lambert at that time, I do not think he would willingly have put me into anything, even as trustee, that he did not believe in.

Cross-examined by MR A. S. GILL. I never saw Mr Wain until I visited the offices of the bank on March 17th – my letter addressed to Lambert of February 7th is all the knowledge he could have on the subject – I did not know his connection with the thing; I did not know a single one of the directors, or who they were.

... "That Beall should be appointed financial manager," and he was appointed as such; that I can swear to – I had always understood that he was one of the best financial men in the City of London, and therefore I had confidence – Baker acted as secretary – Singleton or the clerk I looked upon, one as manager and the other as secretary; I do not know how to describe the positions; Mr F.J. Baker I should put as secretary, and Mr Singleton as manager – that is the view I take or it, took of it then –

looking at Exhibit No. 97, I remember Carruthers Wain, Robert Scrafton, Octavius Stokes, Harrison Lambert, and Eden Erskine Greville being appointed governors; I signed that – the document came before us in the same way as the resolutions that we had passed from meeting to meeting, as they were put before us; this was handed to us, and we all signed it, as handing over authority to these gentlemen – I will not swear who was present – I remember prospectuses going out – they were placed before us (copies, proofs) by Singleton; once, I think, we signed them in the same way that we signed this; we took them as read...

EDWARD JAMES KNIGHT. I am accountant to the London and County Land and Building Company, Limited of 31, Lombard Street – there are three owners of 36, Lombard Street; they are the landlords of 31 and 35 I had the letting of both – 35, Lombard Street is about 60 yards up Plough Court-those premises were let by our company to a person described as Alexander Frederick Baker "this is the agreement for seven Years from December 26th, 1892, at a commencing rental of £375 a year, stated that Alexander Frederick Baker is acting on behalf of the London and Scottish Bank – offices, private room, clerk's office, strong room, and lavatory are comprised in the ground floor and basement – the ground floor contains clerk's offices, private room, and what might be used as a board room; and in the basement was a clerk's room, strong room." and lavatory-the bank continued as the tenants, but in 1898 our company took possession for rent, and our solicitors sold the furniture which was left, and handed the proceeds over to Mr Aitcheson, the liquidator of the company-31, Lombard Street is let out in offices – on April 29th, 1893 some offices in that building were let to a gentleman named John Milner, upon this agreement between our company and John Milner of 17, Eastbourne Street, acting on behalf of the London and North British Discount Corporation, Limited – during the tenancy I saw Milner at the office, and he came to see me – I recognise the person I used to see as Singleton – I witnessed Alexander Frederick Baker's signature to the agreement for the London and Scottish Discount Banking Corporation – I saw him sign "A.F. Baker," for and on behalf of that company – the date is November 23rd, 1892 – he took the agreement away and brought it back, signed by Milner, and witnessed by E. Wilson – when I went to 31, Lombard Street, in the first place I went to ask for Mr Milner if he was in, a lady clerk would introduce me to the gentleman I knew as Baker that is Singleton – I said at the Police-court that the North British Company occupied the premises for about nine months – I was trusting to my memory, and unfortunately it misled me – they there nearly 18 months, and when they left they owed nine month rent.

FREDERICK LEVICK. I am a member of the firm of Levick and Plummer, of 7, Drapers' Gardens, office fitters – I recognise Singleton as the Mr Baker who gave me an order for some office fittings at Lombard Street – at the beginning of 1893 I fitted up the bank premises, 35, Lombard Street – the account came to £118 15s. – I was paid, chiefly cash, I think – I had a cheque by Baker – I remember going on one occasion for an instalment of account to the bank premises – I saw the clerk in the first

instance, the cashier – I was referred to Mr Beall – that was at the bank – I asked him for the money for my account – he told one of the cashiers to pay me and debit his account with it – the cashier paid me about £12, I think, of that instalment."

[I feel sorry for the next witness. He was 'conned' by a ruthless man]

"RICHARD JAMES THRELFALL. I am a foreman mechanic at Belgrave Terrace, Gateshead – in 1892 I received a small pamphlet on "Banks and Banking," supposed to be written by a Mr A.F. Baker; it was a little smaller than this (Exhibit 106) – it was written across here, "With the compliments of A. F. Baker" – I read it – at the same time I got a form like a proof prospectus of gentlemen's names, Lord Elibank on the top, and Sir James Carmichael, as far as I can remember; as to the formation of the London and Scottish Banking Company – founders' shares were mentioned – I have sent to the solicitors all the papers I had sent me – I answered this communication, and got this reply (Letter 110) – I sent £2 as a deposit in respect of the £20 for which I was going to buy two founders' shares of £10 each – the letter I got was dated May 7th, 1892 – the heading is "London and Scottish Banking and Discount Corporation. Limited, capital £1,000,000, La Banque d'Escompte de Londres et de L'Écosse (Societe Anonyme), capital 25,000,000 francs. All communications to be addressed to the Secretary. Agencies; Glasgow, Liverpool, Manchester,. Paris, Brussels, etc., etc. – R.J. Trelfall, Esq., 7 Belgrave Terrace, Hexham Road, Gateshead. London Offices: 5, Copthall Avenue, London, E.C., May 7th, 1892. Dear Sir, – I have your favour of the 6th inst., enclosing P.O. for £2 on account of two founders' shares in the above corporation at £10 each. Kindly forward balance, £18, at your early convenience, when provisional scrip will be sent you. I enclose you two more prospectuses and application forms. – Yours faithfully, A.F. BAKER, Secretary pro tem" – I sent the £18; I think by cheque; I cannot be sure – I then received the letter (exhibit 111), with the same heading, "May 10th, 1892: Dear Sir, Thanks for your letter of the 9th inst. enclosing cheque for £18, balance for two founders shares in the above company, I will see that you have provisional share certificates and application forms forwarded to you. – Yours faithfully, A.F. BAKER, Secretary pro tem"; and later on another letter (112), dated June 20th 1892, with the same heading:" July 20th, 1892, – Dear Sir, – I have the pleasure of enclosing you herewith the last proof of the prospectus, and desire to draw your attention to the additional influential names. We are now only waiting for the definite appointment of the Scotch board. As soon as the elections are over it is proposed to publicly advertise the company. Should you desire to take a few of the remaining founders' shares, please let me know at your earliest convenience. I cannot reserve more than 15 or part. Some attempts are being made to secure these shares by brokers and others at far below their value, I hope you will not be influenced by these outside and not quite disinterested people. Personally I am of opinion that the intrinsic value of these shares is nearer £50 than £10. – I am yours faithfully, A. F. BAKER" – I also received a circular

letter about that time. No. 113, undated: "I have the pleasure of enclosing you an advance proof of the prospectus of the above undertaking. The company is to be shortly launched under the best auspices, and will be controlled by influential gentlemen, both in the financial and social world. The yearly increase in almost every branch of commercial business gives evidence of there being ample room for such an undertaking. As has become customary, it is proposed to adopt the usual course of giving the subscribers for the first founders' shares the right of acquiring these shares without the obligation of taking any of the ordinary capital, the first contributions being used to defray the preliminary expenses relating to the formation of the company, and with these objects it has been decided to issue only 100 founders shares at the very moderate sum of £10 each. No other founders' shares will be offered except where the subscriber takes at least £300 in ordinary capital. The advantage of this arrangement will no doubt commend itself to you, and, having regard to the present price of founders' shares in some of the best managed commercial undertakings, it will be seen that the issue price is low, and that within a short time of the public launching of the company they will become of considerable value, and will yield a handsome profit should you wish to realise. As it is only proposed to have 1,000 founders' shares, and in the first instance to issue £250,000 capital, half to be called up, should the profits only suffice to pay 12 per cent., the profits on each founders' share would be equal to 32 1/2 per cent, per annum. If you desire to secure any of the founders' shares on the above terms, your application ought to reach me during the current week on the enclosed form, – Yours obediently, A. F. BAKER, Secretary" – also another letter dated August 29th, 1892, enclosing the scrip for founders' shares – I handed them all over to Mr Davis, the solicitor, and all my other papers – I got another letter of December 29th, 1892 (115): "Dear Sir, – I have the pleasure of enclosing you herewith slip showing the number of additional names we have secured. Bank premises have been taken at No. 35, Lombard Street, which will be opened in the New Year for business. If you or your friends require to secure a few more of the founders' shares without the obligation of taking up any ordinary capital, I enclose you a form, which should be returned to me at your earliest convenience" – this is the printed form that was enclosed: "To Mr A.F. Baker. I herewith send you cheque, value [blank] to procure for me [bank] founders' shares at £10 each in the London and Scottish Banking corporation, Limited, in terms of your letter. I agree to accept such shares or any less number you may procure for me, it being understood that I am under no further liability, or under any obligation to subscribe for or take ordinary shares in the said bank" – a little later on I received this prospectus (Produced) – believing it, I applied for 40 ordinary shares on this application form – this is my writing – it gives the names of the applicants, myself and wife – I was entitled to one founders' share at par – I enclosed with that application form a cheque for £21, and received letter 118: "Dear Sir, – I beg to acknowledge receipt of your application for 40 ordinary shares and one founders' share in the above bank and I beg to hand you cashier's receipt herewith. I also have your cheque, value £21. I beg to enclose you a further prospectus and application form should any of your friends desire to have some shares. Yours faithfully, A. F. BAKER, Secretary"; and another letter (119) dated March 13th: "Dear Sir – As you are a holder of founders' shares in the London and Scottish Banking and Discount Corporation, Limited, perhaps you would like to have an interest in the ordinary capital. I enclose application form, which will be in time if returned to me filled up by Wednesday morning, 15th inst. Yours faithfully, A. F. BAKER, secretary" – then I got letter 120: "Herewith I beg to enclose you letter of allotment in respect of ordinary shares which you hold in the above corporation. – Yours faithfully, A.F. BAKER " – I wrote and sent letter 121: "A.F. Baker, Esq., 36, Lombard Street, London, E.C. Dear Sir, – I beg to herewith enclose draft for £100, as per enclosed allotment form, due for 40 ordinary shares in the London and Scottish Banking Corporation" – I then received letter 122, dated March 15th: "Dear Sir, – I have your favour of 14th inst., enclosing draft for one hundred pounds (£100), being the allotment money on your forty ordinary shares, cashier's receipt for which I enclose herewith. I will see that the scrip is made out in the way that you mention" – that was in the joint names – on April 29th I wrote letter 123: "Dear Sir, – I herewith enclose bankers' receipts for £121, and Bank of England note, value £100, eleven pounds over and above what is required for forty £5 paid-up shares, and one founders' share. The £11 you can place to our credit in your deposit account in the names of Richard James and Elizabeth Hartley Threlfall I will send the remaining half of the note as soon as I hear from you that it has arrived safely. Yours sincerely, R.J. THRELFALL. P.S. – Please give me the name and address of your Manchester agency" – I never got the name and address of the Manchester agency – I did get a letter, acknowledging the receipt of the £124 I sent – I subsequently sent the second half, and in letter 126 got an acknowledgment of it – as far as I can remember, I wrote and asked if I could pay £5 per share up to that time – then I got a letter from the bank, No. 129, saying: "Dear Sir, – Your letter of 10th inst. to hand, and the directors have agreed to your proposal to pay your shares up on August 1st next – Yours faithfully, F. J. BAKER, Assistant Secretary; and in letter 130 I enclosed £200 in cheques, as the balance of £5 on each of the £10 shares I had taken – then I got letter 131, acknowledging the receipt of this sum of £200 – in October 1 got a cheque for £9 28.11d., being the 7 per cent, interest on the shares taken – I returned that cheque, requesting that it should be placed to my deposit account – this letter (134) is from F. J. Baker, of October 10th, 1893: "Dear Sir, – Thanks for your letter and kind wishes of 17th inst., enclosing cheque, value £9 2s.11d. We have placed this dividend to your deposit account". I got no dividend other than the £9 2s.11d. in October, 1893 – I lost everything I paid; £10 for the founders' shares and the 40 ordinary – they charged me £10 for one founders', altogether £430...

...Cross-examined by MR GILL. I took no proceedings against Mr Wain – the correspondence put in has been between me and the bank – F. J. Baker and A.F. Baker have signed all the letters that have been read, that have been sent me – I thought I was dealing with a company newly forming – what influenced me in the prospectus was I thought they were very honourable names at the head as trustees and directors – I refer to 1892, when I took ordinary and founders' shares – that was a great influence for me taking the shares – Lord Waterpark I did not know personally; but I thought they were gentlemen, and they would not see the thing go wrong."

[other witnesses told of bouncing cheques and other peccadillos]

JOHN WILSON HALEY – seems to have fallen for the bank's style of patter hook, line and sinker. In all he was to invest £1,250, his life savings set aside for his old age. He says:

"I am a fish merchant, of Holderness Road Hull – about October, 1892, I received this pamphlet. No. 6, called 'Banks and Banking', by A.F. Baker (Produced) – about the same time I received a prospectus and a document accompanying it; this (Produced) is the prospectus that I received – I read it through – it is headed "Proof Prospectus – Founders' Issue" – this document. No. 25, accompanied it – this is the actual document I received; there is my indiarubber stamp on it – it is a printed paper headed "Banks and Banking' Extract from the *Financial Gazette*, July 30th, 1892" – it begins: "Mr Baker has published a little work on the above subject" – there is a passage: "We understand this gentleman, who evidently has a practical as well as a theoretical knowledge of banking, is associated with a very influential group of financiers who are to be responsible for the London and Scottish Banking Corporation, with branches in Glasgow, Edinburgh, and London,' and a final paragraph: "Both classes of shares in the London and Scottish Bank should prove a remunerative and lasting investment." [He then invested heavily but later grew restless.]

In May it looks like some form of rubber cheque was sent to Mr Haley as "I telegraphed on May 15th, and in answer I got letter 62 from Mr. F.J. Baker: "Dear Sir, – I have your wire, but I cannot get Messrs de Renter and Co. to agree to anything definite, and, therefore, in the meantime I send you our cheque for the amount we have of yours, in case you may desire to take in any of the bills if they are presented. We are to see their representative tomorrow. Yours faithfully, F.J. BAKER, Assistant Secretary" – enclosed in that letter there was a cheque for £430 4s. 9d. – this is it, No. 63 (Produced); the London and Midland Bank's cheque – the heading of the cheque is the "London and Scottish Banking and Discount Corporation Limited; pay J.W. Haley, Esq., or bearer, the sum of £430 48. 9d." – it is signed by Octavias Stokes and T. Harrison Lambert, director, and countersigned by F.J. Baker, assistant secretary – I wrote letter No. 64, and addressed it to Mr A.F. Baker, London – this is a copy of it; "Dear Sir, – I am rather surprised at the tenor of your telegram today, which rather suggests you also decline to renew the other acceptance for me. 'I wrote you in good time, so that same could be arranged before maturity, and not afterwards,

and I never dreamt that my request would be subject to the favour of others, after having written you an honest and straightforward reason why, in consequence of the present labour crisis here, it was not just now convenient to take one up, otherwise I should not have been under any further obligation for your kindness. In plain words, I ask the favour of renewal from our own bank (the London and Scottish), and you will excuse me for observing I do not recognise anybody else to extend such with the security in hand of the whole of the founders' shares (£1,250) in your bank to cover only £430; the consent in writing of E. Haley and S.M. Haley, in addition to mine, for such I can, of course, send you; and to say such is not satisfactory would be to admit a bad state of things for our shares. I should think, however, even if you submitted the same offer to the holders of the bill, they would accept readily, but under the circumstances I consider you should recognise you are dealing with honourable people who have gone into this matter as an investment, and, under the unforeseen circumstances of the present strike, endeavour to oblige, and charge a conscientious discount for so doing. However, I shall rely upon you doing so at three months." – I wrote another – letter next day, No. 65: "Dear Sir, – I am in receipt of yours of yesterday's date, covering cheque £430 4s. 9d., which I return herewith in accordance with my telegram today, in consequence of the two bills having been presented and returned unknown to me by my bankers yesterday. You would also be aware yesterday when writing me they had been sent here, and I am astonished to find you had not retired one of them as directed, and holding cash in hand in full for that purpose. Such a proceeding is most unwarrantable, apart from the injury and reflection cast upon myself as a commercial man in the estimation of my bankers and others, and it is not surprising Messrs Renter declined to renew anything of mine, as you infer, when you failed on my behalf to redeem one of the bills, and my honour and status thus far sacrificed, and you actually held the money for such. If it should resolve itself into anything like a writ by Messrs Renter, then I can only say to the extent of one bill of £430 you must be held responsible, as it is no fault of mine you failed to retire that; but why should Messrs. Renter have any voice or control in any renewal that I ask from you to favour me with, and both bills be presented, when it was your duty to retire one and held payment in hand for the same? However, I am asking you as the London and Scottish Bank, and not others, to renew the one unpaid for three months, to favour me accordingly a: a reasonable charge for the same (which is part of your operations, I believe), and hold security as offered, which I think you should not object to do now, and have my grateful appreciation for" – I got an answer, No. 66. May 16th, 1893: "Dear Sir, – I have your wire and your letter, and you may rely upon my doing all I possibly can to arrange for the bills. I did attend at Messrs de Renter's, the holders of your acceptances, but they point-blank refused to let us retire one bill without the other. Personally I know very little of the matter, as it was an arrangement made by Mr A.F. Baker with Messrs de Reuter. Mr A.F. Baker is not expected at the office until next week. Do not think for a moment it is out of any disrespect to you, and I will do all I possibly can to arrange the matter to your satisfaction, and only regret that personally I am unable to do anything" "

Then in August "I made inquiries as to how the bank was going on; and this is the letter, dated August 29th, which I got in reply from F.J. Baker: "Dear Sir, – In reply to your inquiry, I have much pleasure in informing you that the bank is doing a very satisfactory business, and it is under the consideration of the board to declare a dividend for the first half-year's working next month on ordinary shares. The founders' shares are not freely dealt in at present, but when this announcement is made, it must, of course, increase their value very much" – I did not take any more founders' shares."

Mr Haley, despairing of any return I suppose, and anyway suffering a downturn in his trade due to the lack of fish being landed following to more-or-less continuous strikes then wrote to Baker (who is of course Beall under one of his aliases).

"...Common sense, of course, tells the merest novice what all this means, and that there is something radically wrong, and evidently mismanaged, and you must not suppose people as shareholders to swallow anything you like to write, neither can you be surprised that the whole of your correspondence on this matter is being submitted to the Board of Trade, and further action being taken otherwise. – Yours, etc., J.W. HALEY " – I got a reply dated October 31st (No. 76): "Sir, – I have your favour of the 30th inst. Please don't impute misrepresentation or evasion where it does not exist. If you care to trouble you might see at the office here the auditors at their work, and until this is done, also an important piece of business which is not yet completed and which will materially affect the dividend, I don't suppose the directors in their discretion will call the meeting. – Yours truly, F. J. BAKER " – at the beginning of December I got this directors report and balance sheet (Produced) – I looked at the profit and loss first; the net profit, subject to the realisation of bonuses, was £39,183 17s. 1d. – read the report of the directors and the balance sheet – I believed this statement to be a true statement of account; I could only accept it as it appears here – the report states that a general meeting of the company was to be held at Dowall's Rooms, Edinburgh, on Monday, December 10th, at 11 o'clock; I did not go – one reason I did not go to the meeting was it was called for a Monday, which would have necessitated my leaving on the Sunday, and leaving my business, and that was why I did not attend the meeting – I got after December 10th what purports to be a printed report of that meeting (No. 77) – it is headed "Private: Report of the Annual Meeting of Shareholders of the London and Scottish Banking and Discount Corporation, Limited, held at Edinburgh on Monday, December 10th, 1894" – it is a long printed report – this is the actual thing I got; here are my marks, on it – I got then this letter (No. 78) dated December 21st, 1894: "Sir or Madam, – I am pleased to inform you that the application of the two shareholders for the appointment of a provisional liquidator came

before the Court yesterday and was refused. It has been suggested that you have signed some document addressed to Messrs Davidson and Syme giving your assent to the winding up, and trusting the liquidation to this firm and Mr Gowans, chartered accountant. I need not again remind you of the disastrous result which this would entail to the shareholders, but I shall be glad to have your views if you will kindly signify the same on the enclosed postcard. So far, I understand that very few of the shareholders are desirous of winding up, and the majority of these are associated with others in their attempt to wreck the corporation" – I wrote another letter, dated December 23rd, No. 79: "Dear Sir, – Again I am put off with another evasive acknowledgment of my four letters of the 12th, 14th, 17th, and 21st instant. If you keep a proper share register, it is only a few minutes to refer and answer my requisition of above dates. I now ask you finally to confirm that the £1,250 which I have paid you at various times. All of which you have acknowledged the receipt of by letter, is duly and properly credited in your share ledger to each party named at foot, and in the amount written to each name. It is a simple question, and duty on your part, to comply and if you decline to supply the information, or there is any reasonable cause why you should not, I am the party to know it; if not I shall adopt a course that will soon put me in the possession of your reticence and evasion of the matter, which I am bound to say I have ever met with from you when wanting any information, and to which you have had my strong complaints several times. There is no wonder shareholders are so dissatisfied with such work and treatment like this, and the bank will always be in bad repute under such deliberate and palpable evasion of proprietors looking into their own interests, which, under the present phrase of management, necessitate it. In fact, as a bank it seems to have been brought to that level almost, that it is no bank at all, and only an apology for such, and a convenience for others, and new companies of uncertain prospects. – Yours truly, JOHN W. HALEY.
...Cross-examined by MR MARSHALL HALL. It was in October, 1892, that I first received any communication with reference to this bank – it was in 1892 I received the proof prospectus – the names there are the Hon. Ashley Ponsonby, E. T. Gourley, M.P., A. Shoolbred, Esq., T. G. H. Glynn, Esq., W. Hope, Esq., V.C., and Mr Stokes – they are the directors – I say that I was induced by what appeared in the prospectus to subscribe for those shares whereby I lost my money – the last application I made for founders' shares was for the additional founders' shares; the whole matter was completed on or before March 13th, 1893 – nothing that occurred after that could have affected my application for the shares – I have brought a civil action to recover my money – the only two people against whom I have brought an action are Messrs Beall and Singleton – I cannot say that I should attempt to fix Lambert with any liability in respect of the loss I have sustained, or for the fact that my money was afterwards lost, knowing all I know now.
Cross-examined by MR A. GILL. You may take it from me in a compendious form that what I say with regard to Lambert applies equally to Wain.

RICHARD CHARLES STRACHAN. "As arranged, I send you herewith scrip for 20 fully paid shares in lieu of the ordinary shares" – I got scrip for the founders' shares; so that after that date I and my uncle both held 5 1/2 founders' shares, or thought we did – we never got any dividend or anything on our shares – about the spring of 1895 we began to get anxious about this bank, because we had had no communication from them at all, and we had seen in the papers that an interim dividend of 7 per cent, had been declared – we went up to the offices of the bank; it was shut up; the brokers were in – I ascertained the address of Mr Carruthers Wain, the director – I could not tell you for the moment how I got it; he had an office in Finsbury Circus – I went to see him there; I should think between a dozen and twenty times – I only succeeded in seeing him on one occasion, the last – I had been so many times before, trying to see him, and I was denied every time, and told he was not in; so at last one day I waited about, and saw him go up in the lift – then I followed him up in the lift the next time – when I went in I said I should like to see Mr Carruthers Wain – the man said, "May I ask your name?" – I said Strachan – then he said, "He is not in" – as soon as I gave my name I was told he was not in – I said to the young fellow at the counter, "You are a liar, because I followed him up in the lift" – I ultimately saw him – I daresay we bad a conversation for at least half an hour; he repudiated the shares I showed him altogether – he said that he knew nothing at all about it – I produced my scrip – I wrote him a letter afterwards, and I got an answer to it – (Read): "Dear Sir, – The founders' shares of the London and Scottish Bank were not sold by the directors: they were issued by the founders, and neither I nor any of the directors know how they were disposed of or to whom, and being shares to bearer have no knowledge of the holders or the transfers; consequently also the directors could not communicate with the holders, not knowing who they were. I regret to say that owing to the action taken by certain malcontent shareholders, the company's business has been ruined, and it has been wound up. – Yours faithfully, W. J. CARRUTHERS WAIN"

CHARLES HENRY HAMMOND . I live at 26, Trinity Road, Scarborough – in October, 1893, I received this prospectus by post. No. 83 (Produced); I read it through, and also the heading: "An interim dividend at the full rate of 7 per cent, has been declared on the ordinary shares for the six months ending September, 1893" – then I saw that the governors were Carruthers Wain, Octavius Stokes, Harrison Lambert, and Eden Erskine Greville; but I took very little notice of that, because I did not know any of the parties – I see at the third paragraph on page 3: "The dividend of 7 per cent, per annum just paid as the result of the bank's operations during the past six months is sufficient evidence of the profitable nature of its business"; but I never received anything.

HENRY NORRIS, Licensed Victualler. I am out of business now...
On October 16th, 1893, I received this letter (Exhibit 14) enclosing a cheque for £6 7s., 11d. for dividend – I had seen the name of Mr Carruthers Wain among the directors; I knew

that name by his becoming chairman or being chairman of the North Staffordshire Tramway Company – I was a shareholder in that – in consequence, somewhere about September, 1894, I wrote a letter to Mr Wain himself, and got an answer from him – after that answer I believe I called, and saw Mr Wain at the bank; I cannot be positive, but I believe I did – the date I do not know anything about, but I believe I called on Mr Wain – about the beginning of December, 1894, I went to Edinburgh – I was asked to go by Mr Wain – he said there was going to be a meeting held at Edinburgh, and he wanted me to go down to attend the meeting, to second the resolution – I did not know what resolution it was – I went down prepared to second anything – I was asked to go by Mr Wain, and he said to me it was a shame the company should be wound up, they could pay 125 per cent., and I thought so too, but I do not think so now – I did not know at that time, or did not know it otherwise, that there was any suggestion of winding up the company – I was led to believe from the bank itself, or the officials of the bank, that the bank was in a sound, solvent state, and I was to take no notice of outside statements – they had entered an action against the *Financial Times* – they wrote so to me – I told Wain I could not go, for I could not afford to go – he said they would pay my expenses – that Mr Wain would pay my expenses, or my expenses would be paid to go down – I did go to Edinburgh; I can not say the date; it was on a Sunday night I travelled, to be there on Monday morning – I did not go to any place – when I got to Edinburgh on Monday morning I did not know the place; and I was walking up the square, some place where the meeting was to be held, and I met Mr Wain – I did not know where the bank premises or offices were supposed to be – there were no bank premises there, not of the London and Scottish Banking and Discount Company – I met Mr Wain in the street – he took me to an hotel; I wanted some refreshment, travelling all night – I ultimately got to a place called Dowell's Rooms, where the meeting was held – the room was crammed; there might be 60 people there, or there might be more – Mr Wain, I believe, took the chair – I knew no other officials – I was totally unacquainted with the officials of the bank, except the secretary and Mr Wain: the secretary, F. J. Baker, not A. F. Baker – it was very stormy indeed; you could not hear anybody speak – they made an attempt, a dozen at a time – I have been to a good many meetings, and I never went to one more noisy than that – I cannot tell you what they were speaking about – they were making a noise about the chairman's speech; they would not believe in it; they made all manner of remarks – there was a very great disturbance; I heard that – it was during the meeting that the noise was – it did not begin at once – there was a rush into the room; they broke into the room – they were to be excluded, I believe, but they got into the room by breaking the door open, and they all rushed in pell mell – They said the bank was a swindle and a roguery, and Dickens knows what they did not say – the Scotchmen would not have it at any price, copies of the directors' report and balance-sheet were produced at that meeting; I had one sent me – I will not be positive whether that was, but I think so – I am not very much used to reports,

but I thought it was a very good one – I saw in it that the net profit for the year amounted to £39,183 17s. 11d. – I can not tell you what became of the resolution. [unreadable] had gone down to second – I did second it – I was more towards the door, and the hall was packed full – I was asked to do a certain thing, and I did it according to the best of my ability – I can not say if anybody heard it – I am satisfied I seconded the resolution, but it was on the statement of the profits the bank had made, and people trying to wreck the company; I thought it was a very unjust thing – there was a tremendous row and bother – they closed the meeting the best way they could – I did not come back with Mr Wain: I went alone and I came back alone; the only gentleman I knew by sight was Mr Wain – I got expenses for going up there after a little trouble – a gentleman took me round the corner to a refreshment shop and paid me £3 – he was a gentleman out of the bank, not at Edinburgh – I think it was some time after, the latter end of January or February; I think it was some time in January – I had applied several times for my expenses; about two or three times; the third time I got it, I think; I got £3 – I could not say if it was a clerk in the London and Scottish Bank who paid me; I was totally unacquainted with the officials, but he took me round the corner and paid me three sovereigns – he gave me no reason for taking me round the corner rather than paying me over the counter; he said, "Come along with me round the corner" – there was the usual drink shop round this particular corner; a respectable house."

Here we have the first note I have ever found on how prospectuses were sent out.

"WILLIAM THORNTON . I am manager of the Debenture and Finance Company, at 80, Coleman Street, and in 1893 was secretary of the London Share and Debenture Company, Limited, Union Court, Old Broad Street – a Mr Le Ruey was managing director of that company; he died some three years ago – part of the object of that company was to issue prospectuses of new companies about to be floated – for that purpose the London Share and Debenture Company kept lists of names of possible or even probable investors in London as well as the country – we applied to the companies for those lists – we got them first-hand from the companies, but the companies have to send them in to Somerset House, and we can also get them there – on getting an order to post and circulate these prospectuses it is the practice to send intimations to the person who gives the order as to the number of prospectuses sent out from day to day – I personally did not take the orders for the publication of these prospectuses of the London and Scottish Bank – this (No. 199) is a bundle of intimation notices addressed to "E. Beall, London and Scottish Banking Corporation, 35, Lombard Street, EC," dated March 6th and 8th – the top one of those four shows that the total posted up to March 8th was 123,936 – I do not know who paid our company for that work in March, 1893 – I cannot say whether in June, 1893, our company undertook some further work of sending out prospectuses – this document (No. 200) is an intimation dated June 6th, 1893 – in October and November, 1893, our

company distributed 20,000 further prospectuses for the London and Scottish Bank, of which the documents in the bundle, No. 201, are the intimations – in March, 1894, our company sent out some further prospectuses; document 202 is the intimation notice, addressed to Messrs The Atlas Contracting Syndicate, Limited, 31, Lombard Street, E.C., re the 150,000 prospectuses of the London Refuse Steam Generator Company, Limited; our company published those prospectuses to that number.

DEMETRIUS PAPPADAKI (whose family were bankers in Constantinople). I think it was Mr Beall, as far as I remember – it was in 1894, about a month or so before the company was registered – he told me that I should become a director, as he was going to bring out a refuse destructor – I had studied the subject – this is my signature to the memorandum of association of that company – I was going to have one share when I signed it, but at that time I did not have anything at all – Mr Cooper had given me £2 or £3 when I attended the meeting, but I did not have anything at the time I signed it – I had my fees, £2 or £3, for attending the meeting as a director, as far as I remember – I do not think I had anything before that – I do not remember having a guinea – I made a mistake at the Mansion House; I told Mr Bodkin at the time – I do not quite recollect what I said at the Mansion House – I apologised at the time – I became a director afterwards of the Atlas Contract Syndicate – the offices were at No. 39, Lombard Street – it was not at the same place as the London and Scottish Bank; it was 31, Lombard Street – I believe Singleton used to be in the same offices – I did not know his business at all – I did not know his name; I always addressed him as Singleton – I saw no name there at all – there were three rooms, or two rooms, I think – I do not remember whether the name of the London and North British Discount Company was up there – I know it was the Atlas – there were three doors, or two doors – the name of the London and North British Discount Company was not on the same door as the Atlas Contracting Syndicate – I do not recollect whether it was on the outside door – the business of the London Contracting Syndicate was to bring out this destructor; the letters patent – we did bring it out – I understood the object of the syndicate was to find the money in order to bring out the other thing – there were never more than seven shares taken in the Atlas Syndicate – there was the signatories' £7: that was all the money the Atlas Contract Syndicate ever had, as far as I remember – this company was called the London Refuse Company – I have seen the installation of the "London Refuse Steam Generator and Electrical Power Corporation, Limited" at Westminster, and several other places – I have seen the very furnace itself; the destructor itself, and a splendid thing it was too – the company was brought out, and it did not take – it was issued to the public – the London and Scottish Bank found the money for paying for the advertisements – they were going to get the money back – the arrangement was, allotting to them so many shares in the Refuse Company, as compensation for the money that they advanced – I cannot tell you the exact amount spent in advertising; it was a very large sum, I know – I believe there were some subscriptions which were sent back again – I cannot recollect now, so many years back – it never went to allotment; it did not take – I have seen a Mr John Sheridan come into the bank, but I did not know him personally – he had the patent of the Atlas Syndicate – he was the person who proposed the patent – I am not certain of the man, there were two Sheridans – he had the patent of Levett's [sic] patent Destructor – that is the same destructor as I have been talking about – he proposed to sell it – I believe, as far as I remember, he was going to sell it to the company – I had two or three pounds for my attendances as a director – Mr Cooper, the secretary of the Atlas Contracting Syndicate, paid those; they had a banking account at the London and Scottish.

...The London Refuse Company was to be promoted to work the licence of a patent of Mr Livet, who had invented a process by means of which refuse could not only be destroyed, but could be utilised as a force; that is, as a motive power in generating steam when you burnt it up – that was shown to be a thing which could be done very much more cheaply than it had been hitherto done – there was a trial of that at Halifax; an installation was fitted up there – this is the prospectus – the directors are Mr H. Seton Carr, M.P.; Sir Oriel Viveash Tanner, K.C.B.; George F. Priestley, Wheater White, T. Harrison Lambert, and J. Evelyn Williams; the secretary is Mr Cooper, and Mr Eden E. Greville is the solicitor to the company – that was the gentleman who was a director of the London and Scottish Banking Corporation – the consulting engineer was Mr Edwin Glaskin, and the engineer was Mr Cheesewright – a number of representatives of leading newspapers were invited to Halifax to see the trial, and some of their reports were embodied in this prospectus – I signed the memorandum of the Atlas Syndicate; the Atlas was merely a promotion company – it was promoted for the purpose of launching the London Steam Refuse Generator Company, which was to work under a licence from the British Company, which had general powers – the impression of everyone at the time was that the right we had to work here under Livet's patent was a very valuable thing indeed – there was at that time an installation at Westminster; it is working there now, and it is worked at the present time – there was one at Westminster and one at Shoreditch working at the time this was launched – it was being used by the vestry."

[Some indication of how tangled the web was can be gained from the following]

"Monday, November 6th
JOHN PITMAN . I am a clerk in the Joint Stock Companies Registry Office, Somerset House – I produce the file of the European and Commercial and Industrial Company, Limited – that shows that it was registered as the European Contract Company on April 5th 1892 – the first signatory of the company was Mr Carruthers Wain – the addres the gave in signing the memorandum is 25th, College Hill – that is the registered office of the company – there was a resolution in July,1892, to change the name to the European and Commercial and Industrial Company, Limited, signed by MrWain – then I find on the file a notice that on October 24th,1892, the office of the

company was changed to 18, Eldon Street – on April 1st,1893, I find a resolution for the voluntary winding up, signed by Mr Wain as chairman, and filed October 30th, 1893 – that was registered on June 24th, 1893, by Messrs Brandon and Nicholson, solicitors – it was registered without articles – the first signatory was Mr Eden E. Greville, of 60, Haymarket – the capital was £600,000 in 600,000 shares of £1 each – I find on the file an agreement dated November 9th, 1893, by which 470,000 shares are allotted as fully paid up to Mrs. Livet – that is signed by three persons, including Mr Fordyce Sheridan and George Meadows, the secretary – 1894 the company's offices were registered as at 6, Suffolk Street, Pall Mall, the address of Messrs Brandon and Nicholson – later on, in July, 1894, the address was changed to 60, Haymarket, which is the address of Mr Greville – on the file there is a summary of capital and shares made up to December 29th, 1894, showing that nine ordinary shares had been subscribed for, including the seven original subscribed for by the seven signatories – I have not checked the names – there are nine altogether, dated October 31st, 1895 – I find an order to wind up the company made on a creditor's petition – I find that the liquidator who was appointed was discharged in December, 1897 – the liquidator was the Official Receiver in companies winding up – I also produce the file of the Atlas Contracting Syndicate; that was registered by Jordan on February 9th, 1894, with a nominal capital of £10,000 in 10,000 shares of £1 each – among the seven signatories there was William Cooper, of 31, Lombard Street, and Mr Demetrius Pappadaki, of 157, Fenchurch Street – the registered office of the company was 31, Lombard Street – I find on the file a summary of shares made up to June 14th, 1894, by which it appears that seven shares only had been taken – those were the seven subscribed for by the original signatories – on September 29th, 1895, there is a change of address to 35, New Broad Street, and from that date there has been no further communication from the company – it is the practice on noncompliance with the requirements to send in a summary of capital and shares and so forth, for the registrar to write to the company at its last known place of abode – three letters were sent in this case – they have come back through the post, marked "Gone away" and "Not known" – they appear on the file – those three letters having been written on May 14th, 1897, the company was dissolved by the registration – I also produce the file of the London Refuse and Steam Generator and Electrical Power Corporation, Limited, which was registered on March 16th, 1894, by Jordan and Sons – amongst the signatories there appear Cooper, of 31, Lombard Street, F. J. Baker, Thomas Harrison Lambert – the witness to the signature is Eden E. Greville – the nominal capital was £600,000 in 600,000 shares of £1 each, and the registered office was at 18, Eldon Street, Finsbury – upon the file I find a summary of shares of July 25th, 1894, by which it appears that seven shares were taken, those are the shares originally subscribed for – I also find filed an agreement dated September 11th, 1894, between the London Refuse Company and the Atlas Contracting Syndicate, purporting to transfer 200,000 shares to the

Atlas Contracting Syndicate, fully paid, signed by Cooper, on behalf of the London Refuse Company, and Charles Oram, on behalf of the Atlas Contracting Syndicate – it is not sealed by either company – on November 1st, 1894, the office was changed from 18, Eldon Street, to 25, New Broad Street, and on April 14th, 1896, I find a resolution filed to voluntarily wind up the company, signed by W. Carruthers Wain, chairman – on July 25th, 1898, there is a resolution that the liquidators accounts be adopted, and the liquidator authorised to destroy all books, papers, and documents of the company, signed by Charles M. Grimwood, chairman and liquidator – only seven shares were subscribed for.

WILLIAM COOPER, accountant. *Cross-Examined by* MR ISAACS. I had known Mr Beall before I was employed as secretary, or he would not have employed me; he acted as solicitor for me afterwards – the item for £195 for hotel expenses does not include the special train; it is for hotel expenses – there were perhaps 70 who went down; I cannot recollect at this time – there were three corridor carriages full; I do not know how many a corridor carriage holds exactly; it depends how you pack them – people from the vestries also went down – when we got there a test was made, and an explanation given by Mr Glaskin, the engineer – I believe Mr Cheesewright, the engineer, was also there – the test was perfectly satisfactory; everyone, so far as I knew, came away believing it was a very valuable thing – I cannot say that the articles which were found together in the form of a pamphlet were articles that were written by the Press after having seen it; as comments, and not as advertisements – a certain amount was paid for advertising – I should say they were simply comments written by men who eame down by that special train – I think I can safely say that they were not advertisements at all.

WILLIAM COOPER, Accountant. *Cross-examined* by MR E. GILL Mr Priestly was a director as well as Mr Wain – I believe it was on Mr Priestly's premises that the installation at Halifax was – I cannot say if that installation was provided at his expense – I presume the engineer would be paid, but I cannot tell you who paid for the installation – I rather think he would have paid – he would have paid the furnacemen and that, probably – the cost of patting up the destructor was long before my time – having seen the thing, it seemed to me that it would have cost a considerable sum of money to put up – I cannot remember whether Mr Priestly was interested in the London Refuse Company, because all the money was returned – Wain was never paid any directors' fees in the London Refuse Company – I believe he was paid nothing on account of the fact of his office being the registered office of the company, and the meetings being held there – I do not believe Wain ever got anything out of the London Refuse Company – I think he put in money – that was after it had failed to go to allotment, when the directors returned the money that was subscribed – after that the directors provided the money to keep the company going, and Wain was one of those, like Mr Priestly, who provided what was necessary to keep the company going – there were engineers' expenses always going on – while the company was still going; on after that in that way these negotiations were being carried on with a view to induce the vestries to take up the system."

[As far as I can see, on the evidence of several accountants the bank claimed a profit of £1269.13s.4d despite having not traded]
"Wednesday. November 8th.
FREDERICK JOHN BAKER *(Recalled)* *(Cross-examined by* MR A. GILL). Mr Wain had nothing to do with the issue of founders' shares, to my knowledge, or with the correspondence with the persons who purchased shares – that was a matter between the promoters and the persons who bought – Wain came on other occasions beside the board days – he used to come in occasionally when he was passing in the neighbourhood – I cannot say that Wain never received a shilling of promotion money in connection with this company."

Robert Scott Aitcheson, an accountant of Edinburgh gave evidence on the chaotic state of the financial records which he seems to think were designed to obfuscate the reader although he also states that there had been both inefficiency in their keeping and meddling by different hands. One note is of another of the Bank's ventures, the "Olympic Music Hall (in liquidation), the shares are of no value." He continued:

"When I came on the scene in January, 1895, I found the balance-sheet, which had been made out, and upon which the litigation had arisen which had given me the appointment, and, so far as that was concerned, which had been made out by Messrs Abbott and certified by them, I accepted that as correct; then, as they had only worked up the figures to March 31st, 1894, dealing with the year previous, to it, I set to work to see what the figures showed from March 31st, 1894, to January, 1895 – I found that the interest, discount, and commission amounted to £152 only – the discount, commission, and interest from March 31st, 1894, to January, 1895, were considerably less than they had been after the corresponding period of the previous year, which showed that that part of the business was less from March, 1894, to January, 1895; there was no money to lend – the greater part of the money left had been used with regard to the Atlas Syndicate – £2,885 had been used by the Atlas Syndicate in the promotion of the London Refuse Destructor, and instead of having liquid assets to work with, what they had got were these shares which they had received instead – this item, "Auditor's fees, £126," was paid to Messrs Abbott for writing up the books and preparing the balance-sheet, I understand, then there are other items which bring the figure for that nine months up to £2,739 loss – the loss for the whole period was £11,755, made up of three items shown in the balance-sheet, which give no credit of any kind for the bonus shares, but if I took that £11,459, which was apparently the cash loss for the year from March 31st, 1893, to March 31st, 1894, I show a cash loss of £11,459; with the dividend it makes up the £11,755, which is the loss; that is how I got at it – as to these Buenos Ayres Trams, Abbott's ledger states: "100 shares Buenos Ayres Tram Ways Company and charges on interest on 2,000 shares in the London Metallurgical Company (in liquidation), J. Stewart Boyle,

liquidator, received from C. A. Reeve," and there is another one here: "45 shares £5 paid preference in Buenos Ayres Tram Company, received from J.W. Clarke" – that is the one I was referring to – it is Clarke's account – there are two lots of shares, amongst which there are 45 Buenos Ayres Trams – the whole lot realised £800 – the entry I have just read and some other shares are taken in en bloc without any sum being put to them – some items are estimated, and some are not, and the whole amount altogether is taken in at £1,700, which is composed of the figures which are inserted in the columns against the shares – Messrs Abbott have taken Wallace's acceptance into account at £300 – that is their figure down here – it was they who did that from the books.
Cross-examined by MR MARSHALL HALL. – I tried to realise this estate with my usual judgment, to the best of my ability – the only interest I had was to get the assets in from a professional point of view, to their best advantage – the estate is not wound up yet – I mean there was no immediate hurry – with regard to the 300 Grappler Tyre shares, valued here at £300, I got a valuation on the whole shares – I do not know that the shares which were realised in this liquidation at something like 3s. 6d. a share, sold within twelve months at something like £5 a share in the open market in 1896; free buyers – we believe in Irish tyres – I was not told that these shares were of great value, and ought to be held – I have already said that I know nothing of the shares being freely quoted at £4 10s. and £5 within twelve months of this time – I cannot say that I ever heard that until you suggested it to-day – I will swear I did not – my attention has never been called to the value of those shares – I had heard of it at the Mansion House; I thought you meant, did I know from my own personal knowledge – I did not take up the attitude of treating this thing as a fraud from beginning to end, and refusing; to listen to any advice on the subject at all – if you take the Grappler shares, for example, I got the opinion of a first-class firm here in London on the subject, Messrs Faithfull Begg and Co.; they are members of the Stock Exchange – they valued the whole shares – I could not ask the stockbroker to go and value each thing separately – I have not sold the Grappler shares; I could not, they did not belong to the company – I did not say at the Mansion House that I sold them."

[As the auditors dug deeper into the affairs of the Bank more firms whose shares seem to have been securities against loans came out of the woodwork to appear as credits. They include the District Messenger Company, a newspaper company, Elmore Copper and a second tranche of Buenos Ayres Tramway shares. Even Wulff's Circus appear in the paperwork, but it seems "Wulff's Circus exists only in the imagination."]

"MR WALKER, I am a clerk in the Patent Office, and produce the file relating to certain patents – 726, dated February 9th, 1883, to Mr F. Livet, is for an improvement in furnace bars, and in clinker slicing tools to be used therewith – that patent expired on February 9th. 1896, through non-payment of the fees, £14; in the ordinary course it had got one year to run; fourteen years is the time – if £14 had been paid it would have continued – then 4,872, of July

22nd, 1890, is for an improved steam generator; that is to Livet, too; that expired on July 22nd, 1894, through non-payment of the fees then due – 1,092, of June 13th, 1891, for cremating town dust and like refuse on a new sanitary principle, was also granted to Livet; that expired on June 13th, 1897 – the cause of the lapse of that one was through non-payment of the fees of £7, the sixth year of the renewal fee – then 20,236, December 11th, 1890, an improved setting for Lancashire steam boilers, is one of Livet's patents – that expired on December 11th, 1895 – there is no entry of an assignment of those patents to the British Refuse or the London Refuse Company.
EGERTON SPENCER again. *Cross-examined by* MR HALL. I find no trace of suggestion against Lambert of having had any share in the promotion of this company at all – I do not think that he has had any money out of this company except what he has received by way of directors' fees – I think the account shows that at the date of the liquidation he was a creditor on a balance for £19 due to him – the account shows £69; that is made up by crediting him with a loan of £50 – anyhow, he was a creditor at that time, according to the books – I do not know if the £50 was lent by Mr Lambert on December 5th, and that he had a receipt for it.
Cross-examined by MR A. GILL. £469 5s., which is entered in the minutes as due to Mr Wain, was reduced to £303 13s., by a contra account of £165 12s. – that £303 13s. was paid to Mr Wain – I have not found any vouchers relating to the account – there would be £280 in the first place due from Wain on his shares – of that £280, £10 was paid some time after allotment – then, in December, 1894, £100 was debited to his account for directors' fees – it came out of what was due to him for directors' fees; that would leave £90 still due – if there had been anything due from Mr Wain on account of his shares it would have been the duty of Mr Aitcheson, as liquidator, to have taken proceedings to recover it – I have no knowledge that he did not take proceedings against Mr Wain for any arrears of calls – I looked into the book to see whether this £90 was paid – the first place, I suppose, that anyone would look at would be in the share register – the shareholders' ledger does not give the dates when the moneys were received – there are two payments of £10 and £90 entered – then at a later date, in December, 1894, there is a further £100 – in Wain's ledger account, page 105, I see an item, "October 27th, 1893, London and Scottish Banking and Discount Corporation, Limited: Re shares £90, and the cheque identified, £14,506" – I have now no doubt that Wain paid for his shares; I had overlooked that – the share register shows the amount paid in respect of their shares – it does not act as a shareholders' ledger, because it does not give the dates when the amounts were received.
ROBERT SEAGER *(Detective Inspector, City, the arresting officer).* About half-past five p.m that same day I saw Wain at the Detective Offices in Old Jewry, in charge of Sergeant Willis – I told him that I was a police-officer, and had a warrant for his arrest, and read it to him – he said, "There must be some mistake about that first date, as I was not connected with the company till some time after that" – the warrant put the conspiracy at the date of

March 1st, 1892 – then he was taken to the station, and also formally charged, and made no further reply.

WILLIS (*Detective Sergeant*). I went on June 20th to Wain's address at 39, Hogarth Road, Earl's Court, and inquired for him, and in consequence of what I was told I sent for his doctor – I saw Mr Wain and told him the charge – he said, "This is, I suppose, the outcome of touching pitch and becoming defiled" – I conveyed him to the Old Jewry, and read the warrant to him."

[I have included this item here as it might have given us cheap electricity all these years ago and Wain, as he said, believed in it]

"GEORGE ROBERT WHEELER. I am surveyor to the Westminster Vestry, and have been so for 18 years – in 1891 I saw Mr Livet with regard to this destructor – he was the patentee; I believe he saw me with a view of getting the vestry to adopt it, and in 1894 the vestry adopted it – we are now working it, and have been ever since 1894, with great success – we have gained the whole of the power for lighting our stables with electric light, and doing all the work necessary, cutting blocks, making mortar, cutting chaff, and lifting goods with this destructor, and we have never burnt an ounce of coal since it has been put up – the one we have used has been one made in accordance with the Livet Patent entirely – Livet supervised the first construction of it, but he died, and then one of his representatives saw it completed – the exact invention which Mr Livet patented is on the formation of the flues under the boiler, so that the fumes and smoke are so consumed that there is no nuisance, and the power that is produced by the steam generator is sufficient to do all the work that I think is necessary – the specification was brought to me by Mr Livet some years ago – I do not think I ever knew anything of the prospectus of the London company – I have seen no reports – there has been a saving of £60 a-year, but had they adopted this report, and carried out the building which I proposed, I believe it would have been from £1,000 to £1,200 a-year – it they had burnt all their refuse in this way it would have saved them that – we only consume four loads a day, and they really collect 40 to 50 loads a day – I use it now for generating electric light; not for the streets, only for the stables – I suggested that it should be used for the streets; I think we should then save £1,000 to £1,200 a year – the vestry is a small one – there are between 45 and 50 vestries as large as ours in London.

Cross-examined by the SOLICITOR-GENERAL. This apparatus was put up in 1894 – Mr Livet died soon after it was commenced – I saw Mr Livet in 1891 or 1892 – he had written several letters to my vestry, and asked them to construct such a thing, but, of course, vestries are not very quick in moving, and it took two or three years before they would adopt anything of the kind – then they adopted it on a very small scale; they have considered this larger one, but at the present time they have not adopted it – my suggestion has not been adopted because the barging away of the dust was very much reduced in price; it went from 2s. 8d. a load to 11d. a load – it became cheaper to barge it away even than to destroy it by this process – it

is only for a time, I think – I believe it is a better system to destroy it than to throw it into the river.

Re-examined. I have no doubt as to the value of this process – if you barge away the stuff and get rid of it, you get no benefit from it; if you burn it, you get enough power to light your place with electric light, and if you have a large enough place, you would get enough light to light the streets, and save £1,200 a year – other vestries have not got rivers running through them, and, therefore, it costs them 2s. 8d. to 3s. a load-our vestry adopted it while the patent was going; we did not pay anything by way of royalty; we simply paid them £600 for the construction of the furnace and boiler; that was what we paid Mr Livet or his widow, I do not know which; it was no royalty – if we had to pay any royalty, it would come out of the figures I mentioned as the saving to the vestry – it was put up as a test installation, and also to give us assurance that it was a destructor that was no nuisance to the inhabitants.

FRANK HENRY CHEESEWRIGHT . I am a member of the Institute of Civil Engineers, a Fellow of the Royal Geographical Society, and a Fellow of the Society of Arts – I have been in practice for 30 years – I was introduced to this matter of the British Refuse Destructor about April, 1892 – I did not know Mr Livet before that – I went into the matter, and saw his process – I looked at the specification of the patent – I have no doubt that his invention was then protected by a patent – I know of Mr Aston's opinion – I knew that that patent protected that invention – the peculiar feature of the invention was that as the heat of the furnaces had more energy in them the flues were narrowed, and as the energy got less the flues became larger, and there was a velocity of air through the firebars that was greater than you could ever get except by means of a forced draught – I know all the destructors, and this is the only one where an artificial draught is not created; the flues alter in their size: they expand – they are not elastic – these are constructed to contract or expand as the heat or energy is greater or less – they are larger at one end than at the other – no doubt that was an original idea of Mr Livet's – I formed a very high opinion of it; at that time, I may tell you, an experiment was being tried at a boiler in King's Road, Chelsea; I went there, and I was struck with the novelty and the magnificence of the results; they were burning trade offal, and using no other power to keep the steam going; I asked the Assistant Locomotive Superintendent of the Midland Railway, Mr Wetherburn, to accompany me and see it, and he could hardly believe that such a draught was caused by natural means, and he sent an assistant to the place, and he stayed there for a week to try and find out what was the cause of this draught – Mr Wetherburn put £500 in it with a view of exploiting this patent – the next thing was the installation at Westminster Vestry; that was on a larger scale – I was satisfied with that – it was a practical test on a very extended scale – I have practised in Mexico City, and the municipality there are arranging for it, and £20,000 has been subscribed to make an installation on this principle – I went to Westminster to see this installation, and a large number of pressmen and other people connected with vestries went to see it – the

unanimous opinion, so far as I could judge, was highly favourable – another installation was fitted up at Ira and Ickringill's at Keighley, in Yorkshire – I saw that – that is twice the size – it is working, and has proved an entire success – the installation at Ira and Ickringill's was for burning coal dust and dirt that could not be burnt under any other circumstances – I put a very considerable sum into this; from first to last about £3,000 – all that time I was assuming that this was a patent of Mr Livet's, and that the patent was running – I know Mr Livet entered into arrangements with the British Refuse Company for the purpose of financing this patent – I went all over the country; I saw different vestries, different corporations, with a view of inducing them to put their money into the business; I also prepared and read papers on the subject at different societies, and in that way the money went; I also lent money to Mr Livet – I took some acceptances from Mr Livet for some £2,000 or £3,000, all of which represented money lent – then came Mr Livet's sudden death, and I had to take up those acceptances and repay them myself – the money was sent to my office to pay the fees, and my clerk, who was instructed to pay those fees, took the date of the payment of the fees from the date the patent was granted, not from the time when the patent was applied for: and a private Bill was promoted in Parliament for the purpose of getting the patent prolonged or renewed; it was refused on the ground that they could not take advantage of negligence, and so the patent lapsed – Mr Glaskin was the engineer to the company, and I was consulting engineer.

Cross-examined by MR A. GILL. This document (*Produced*) is a copy of a report made by me, dated January, 1895, to the directors of the London Refuse Company; I find this: "The company has granted certain rights to the subsidiary company for London and the six home counties This company has been formed under the title of the London Refuse Steam Generator and Electric Power Corporation, Limited, with an issue of £300,000, of which this parent company receive 100,000 shares of £1 each for its rights" – that is right – "The London Refuse Steam Generator and Electric Power Corporation, Limited, are on the eve of obtaining many installations on the Livet principles, and mention must be made of the Vestries of Shoreditch, St. Luke's, Croydon, St. George's, Strand, City Commissioners, and Chelsea. The reason of several of these works not being settled is through the vestrymen being elected. As for the prospectus of the company, I can certainly do nothing but express my belief upon my ultimate success, as there is absolutely no other system that produces the same results as the Livet system" – that was my belief, and it is so now – I represented that to the directors.

Cross-examined by the SOLICITOR-GENERAL. I am not active in advertising the merits of this process beyond giving lectures and going to the vestries – I do not know that I have given you a lecture to-day – I was all over the country expounding the merits of the process – the way I made up the £3,000 was not only expenses, but endorsing the acceptances of Mr Livet, which his sudden death made me responsible for – in addition to that, I incurred expenses travelling about the country – that makes up the £3,000 – I had not much success in my tours – they listened to me, but they would not perform – I had a most favourable reception, but no one would take the process; as Mr Wheeler said, the vestries are very difficult to move; I suggest that as the natural history of vestrymen they are very conservative; they have not an old-fashioned prejudice in favour of doing things as cheaply as possible, because had they adopted Livet's system they would have adopted a system cheaper than they are doing now by carting and barging – as to Mr Wheeler stating that barging turned out to be cheaper, and that accounted for its not being taken up, that gentleman must have made a small mistake, because anyone going up the City Road would see an installation, a tremendous one beside a canal, where they could have barged their refuse away, but they do not, they burn it – that is St. Pancras; the City of London destroy their refuse by cremating it, and the St. Luke's Vestry do, but they make no use of it – I suppose the City of London is conservative – I do not think it is due to some other cause, because here is a fact that remains, that they are wasting heat every day by the destruction of the City refuse, and they are making no use of it, whereas if they erected the installation of Livet they would be lighting the City for nothing – I can-not say why they do not adopt this invaluable process; I can only repeat what

I say, that the City of Mexico are going to adopt it – that is governed by a municipality, like the City of London; like our vestries – I do not know whether they are much more enlightened there, they will be, but at home in London, this process has met with very indifferent success. *Re-examined by* MR HALL. The cartage payments have nothing to do with the non-adoption of the process by the vestries; it may be that the contracts for carting or barging have not run out – that may interfere with it."

[The documents mentioned in the text are, regrettably, not available to me. The entries are left in for completeness]

Court Case Wain & Co.

Wain, in his defence, and really he did not have much of one, pointed out that although he had received £200 in directors fees, as his 40 £5 shares were rendered valueless by the collapse of the Bank he hardly gained from his association with it. He claimed to have no knowledge of the *Financial Gazette* which was of course set up as a Beall/Bank mouthpiece to gull the public, and I really cannot believe that a man like Wain would not have had this newspaper delivered, if only out of curiousity. He claimed, and the evidence seems to indicate this was so, that he had nothing to do with the issue of the

founders' shares, as we know he held only ordinary shares, and that he was not a signatory to the Articles of Association. Again he claimed, and was quite vigorous in this, that had it not been for the hostility and generally dirty tricks of certain Edinburgh banks who started what we would call a whispering campaign in Scottish newspapers that the bank really could have traded profitably. This view was echoed by a number of officials involved in rooting around in their papers who considered that with a good accountant (and between the lines, removing Beall) there was some good material in the bank – for example all its loans had good security – apart from the Wulff, which was very odd indeed – and, Wain was adamant that the Patent acquired by the Refuse Company was a good one and would have been highly profitable, especially as they had come to an agreement with the patent holder's widow on his death. In fact Wain held to his belief that he, Lambert and others really had put much of their energies into making the Bank a success. At the end of his speech, probably feeling the latent hostility directed at him by those shareholders who had been bilked and by jury members (who knows – maybe they wanted to see any Wain harvested) he collapsed and had to be half carried out of the Court to recover.

We are pleased to acknowledge the assistance of David Voice in the provision of this item.

1875 and the Way it Was

In the process of tracking down old documents that are vital to the understanding of steam (and other) tramway history certain other items show us all too clearly just what the world really was like during the early decades of the story.

"6 December 1875: SHOCKING TREATMENT OF A LUNATIC BY A SURGEON. At the Notts Assizes on Saturday, before Baron Huddleston, George Goforth Wyer, a surgeon practising at Eastwood [Nottingham] was charged with receiving into his house, which was not properly licensed, and taking charge of a lunatic named Selina Wyer (his sister) without having the requisite medical certificate; and he was further charged with abusing, ill-treating, and neglecting the said lunatic. The prosecution was instituted by the Lunacy Commissioners. On the 29th February, Dr Tate, of the Nottingham Coppice Asylum, in accordance with an order which he had received from the Lord Chancellor, went to the house of the defendant, who, it should be stated, had received large sums of money from his father, a retired army surgeon, living at Whitchurch, Dorset, for taking care of his sister. Dr Tate, producing the order, asked to see the lunatic, and was taken by the defendant upstairs to an attic, the window of which was boarded up, and in which there was no fire. All the furniture the room contained was a box and a trestle, and upon the latter a woman was crouching, with her knees drawn up to her chin. She was quite naked, with the exception of a small vest, which covered her shoulders and breast. She was in a very filthy state, and an old woollen rug which was thrown over her was in a disgusting condition. She was very thin and feeble, and was apparently unable to stand. The defendant roughly told her to get up, and she began to cry. Defendant pleaded guilty. It was urged in defence that he had suffered from sunstroke, and was rather eccentric. He was sentenced to three months' imprisonment."

Alleged Assaults on a Schoolmistress

Any historian digging deep into the past, will suffer from déjà-vu; apart from the far more severe penalty then imposed the following could appear in the columns of the newspapers tomorrow.

25 November 1881

"Alleged Assaults on a Schoolmistress.

Eliza Whyore of St. James road, Goff's Oak, was charged with assaulting Mary Stringer, schoolmistress at the National School, Goff's Oak, on the 18th inst. It appeared from the evidence that on the morning in question five of the scholars played truant. On their return to school Miss Stringer gave them one stroke each with the cane. One of the truants was defendant's brother, and as soon as he had been caned he ran out of the school, and soon afterwards returned with defendant, who commenced using violent language. As her language was unfit for children to hear she was requested to leave the room but refused to do so, and on Miss Stringer attempting to put her out defendant turned round and slapped her face.

Corroborative evidence having been given, defendant was fined 18s, including costs, or 7 days hard labour. She burst into tears as she was being removed in custody, and said to Miss Stringer 'I'll pay you when I am let out of prison'.

Caroline Phipps, of Hammond street, Cheshunt, was summoned for assaulting the same complainant on the 14th inst. On the day in question Edith Phipps, daughter of the defendant, was scolded by Miss Stringer for telling untruths. The girl immediately turned round and left the premises; she returned again and asked for her money, and as Miss Stringer was about to give it her, defendant came into the room and asked for her other child's money. Miss Stringer said she would give it to the child when the defendant left the premises. Defendant then called to the child to come away, when complainant threw the money – four penny pieces – along the floor to defendant, and tried to shut the door, but defendant put her arm inside and assaulted Miss Stringer in the face. Fined 18s, including costs, or 7 days. The money was paid."

The Tramways Institute of Great Britain and Ireland

As we shall show the Tramways Institute comprised the managers and owners of the horse tram operators plus the majority of steam users, although there were surprising omissions. It is not at all clear to what extent the shenanigans of J. Carruthers Wain affected the Tramways Institute's future for they were well in the van of electrical services, but in 1897 the newer electric tramway operators formed the Tramways & Light Railways Association (T&LRA). As a digression here it is worth mentioning the foremost UK tramway modelling society today (2010) has an uncannily similar title – the Tramway and Light Railway Society (T&LRS). The membership of the T&LRA was open to all and drew its support from both private companies and municipal tramway operators, unlike the restrictive TI which purposely prohibited members from municipalities thereby dooming itself to extinction.

Around this time – the late 19th century – an Omnibus Owners Association was formed whose objective in life was to look after the interests of the horse-bus operators, whose membership like that of the tramways companies was under the twin pressures of the nascent and vociferous trades unions and of the public who egged on by the newspapers at last awoke not only to the condition of the horses but also the men involved.

For reasons that are not entirely clear within five years of the founding of the T&LRA the majority of municipal operators formed themselves into a new body, the Municipal Tramways Association leaving the rump of the T&LRA after 1902 to become a mouthpiece for the predominant private operator, the BET group.

After the 1930s both the remaining bodies metamorphosed into two distinctly separate concerns, changing their names to reflect the growth of the motor omnibus and the trolleybus, thus by the outbreak of war the MTA had become the Municipal Passenger Transport Association, and the T&LRA the Public Service Transport Association. A curious spin-off – a sort of transport freemasonry – was the Association of Municipal Transport Managers.

The formation of The Tramways Institute of Great Britain and Ireland occurred at a surprisingly late date. Although the bulk of tramways remained reliant upon horseflesh even in the heyday of steam trams, nonetheless the problems of all operators were not dissimilar. For example, although the smaller horse trams caused far less wear on the rails, there was quite a vociferous following among Victorian ladies for a reduction in the perceived cruelty. This was at least equal to, if not as successful as, the outcry over steam trams' smoke, steam and cinders. And horse trams killed or maimed not a few children and adults albeit the furore was much less than for accidents caused by the steam trams. The pay loads with horses were necessarily smaller, and the cost per mile far higher; although the larger steam cars required a far greater flow of pennies and tuppences per trip to pay for depreciation of the steamer. And both sets of tram operators were plagued by councils niggling away over the condition of what was (in standard gauge) a roadway at least 10' 6" (3.2 m) wide, nicely cobbled and maintained by the tramway company where the rest might well be at best macadamised and at worst, pure mud.

The appointment of the initial tranche of officers for the Tramway Institute seems to have been cut and dried well in advance – it was truly a case of many chiefs and no indians. The first Chairman and President was Robert Hutchinson, the Chairman of the Edinburgh Street Tramways Company. Other officers forming the 'Council' were:

James Fitzgerald Lombard, Chairman, Dublin United Tramways.
A.J. Lambert, Director Hull Street Tramways Chairman, Imperial Tramways Director Anglo-Argentine Tramways

W. Palfrey, Chairman, London Street Tramways
E. Etlinger, Chairman, Sheffield Tramways, Director, Tramways of France

George Richardson, Chairman, North Metropolitan Tramways
Luke Bishop, Chairman, Manchester, Bury Rochdale & Oldham Steam Tramways*

The Vice-Presidents were, if anything, even more awe-inspiring and to see this selection of tramways management together must have been to see many of the 'great and good' of their day:

Alderman C. Barfoot, Chairman, Derby and Leicester lines

Wm. Busby, Director, Liverpool, Birmingham Central* and other lines

Lt.Col. Campbell Walker, Director, Preston and Brighton* lines

David Drimmie, Director, Dublin United

James Marshall Gilkes, Deputy Chairman, North Metropolitan. Chairman, London Street and other lines

Francis James Heseltine, Director Swansea* and Gothenburg lines

Wm Turton, Chairman Leeds* and Bradford* lines. Director Leicester line

Wm James Carruthers Wain, Deputy Chairman, North London* and other lines

J.R. Wigham, Director Dublin United

But, and it is a big but, the omissions were as important and perhaps more eloquent of the fragmentation of the tramways industry. Where, for example, was the Chairman (or even a Director) of the Birmingham Group of Tramways (other than Busby)?

And what of most of the Northern tramways? Out of 44 or so steam tramways only six were represented (and that included Swansea and Brighton!). No Wantage. No Wolverton & Stony Stratford, Huddersfield, Dewsbury and so on. It could not be due to the directors being too busy nor indeed the fees.

If they, The Tramways Institute purported to represent the whole of the industry, then they had one glaring Achilles heel, as "The Members of the Institute shall consist of Tramway Companies, Lessees of Tramways, and Owners of Tramways working their own property, and each such Company, body, or individual may nominate such number of Delegates to attend the meetings of the Institute as they may determine. The Delegates so to be appointed shall

---

*Wholly or partially operated by steam trams.

---

consist of Directors, Solicitors, Engineers, Secretaries, or Managers of Tramway Companies or of such Lessees or Owners who are Members of the Institute. The appointment of all Delegates shall be subject to the approval of the Council."

Council officials were specifically excluded and yet as is shown within this series of books in many ways they held the whip-hand and indisputably could put pressure on the Board of Trade just by waiting until the operating companies (for example) failed to repair the paving, whereas if relationships were amiable such matters could be resolved locally. It will also be apparent that no trades' union officials would be allowed to join or, indeed, any aspiring engineman or inspector. And yet, if we consider para.3 of both the advertisement and the Memorandum of Association it clearly states the Tramways Institute was "to obtain greater facilities for, and to remove obstacles to, the development and prosperity of the Tramway system".

Each Member had to pay two guineas (£2.2s.0d) and an annual subscription of "at least" one guinea (£1.1s.0d) with, quirkily, "Each Member shall be entitled to one vote in respect of each annual subscription of £1.1s.0d)" with each Delegate (as shown above) costing an extra guinea.

In fact the Tramways Institute seems to have had relatively little impact, and from time to time in connection with other matters to this Tramways Institute "...no meetings for two years ... no reply from the registered office". But William James Carruthers Wain was later well involved; and when his shooting star fell perhaps the Tramways Institute effectively went down with him.

On 8 April 1885, Rollit & Sons, Solicitors of 12 Mark Lane, London E.C. wrote to the Assistant Secretary of the Board of Trade forwarding an "Associate Memorandum" and Articles of Association for the Tramways Institute.

These documents were slightly modified by the Board of Trade but at the end was a notation: "I am of the opinion that no objection can be made of these articles ... on behalf of the Board of Trade", and similarly the 'Memorandum of Association' after some modification carries a black ink entry "I have settled this draft on behalf of the Board of Trade".

On 24 April and 2 May 1885 (Daily

Telegraph) and 24 April and 1 May (The Times) an advertisement identical in all cases was carried reading:

"APPLICATION for a LICENCE of the BOARD of TRADE: Notice is hereby given that in pursuance of the 23d Section of the Companies Act, 1867, AN APPLICATION has been made to the Board of Trade for a LICENCE directing an Association about to be formed under the name of the TRAMWAYS INSTITUTE of GREAT BRITAIN and IRELAND to be REGISTERED with limited Liability without the addition of the word 'LIMITED' to its name.

(1) To watch and protect the interests of Tramway Companies

(2) To secure proper legislation in reference thereto

(3) To obtain greater facilities for, and to remove obstacles to, the development and prosperity of the Tramway system.

(4) To acquire and disseminate amongst members and associates of the Institute information relating to Tramways, and to afford such members and associates legal and technical advice and assistance.

(5) The discussion of such questions relating to Tramways and matters pertaining thereto, as shall be proposed by any member and approved by the Council.

(6) And generally to do all such other lawful things as are conducive to the attainment of the above objects or any of them.

Notice is hereby further given, that any person, company, or corporation objecting to this application, may bring such objection before the Board of Trade on or before the 18th day of May next, by a letter, addressed to the Assistant Secretary, Railway Department, Board of Trade, Whitehall, London, S.W.

Dated this 23rd day of April, 1885.

J.H. DUNCAN, F.C.A. Secretary,

ROLLIT and SONS, 12 Mark-lane, E.C. Solicitors for Applicants"

Very oddly and no doubt causing some consternation to the applicants a letter was received from Billearys & Layard, Solicitors, 5 Fenchurch Buildings, London E.C.

"Sir, In reference to the advertisement dated 23rd April last 'R2232' relating to the proposed Tramways Institute of Great Britain & Ireland we as Solicitors for and by the instructions of the West Ham Local Board beg to address you on the subject. The local Board being the Road Authority for and having jurisdiction over an area of some 7¼ square miles which abut upon the Metropolis with a considerable length of tram lines already laid down in their district and with other schemes authorised but not yet carried out are naturally interested in the project and on looking at the objects as stated in the advertisement they are inclined to think that the proposed Institute is not such an Association as is contemplated by the 23rd Sect of the Companies Act 1867. Although it would of course be provided that no profit or dividends will be divisible among the members or Associates yet still the proposal (1) 'To watch and protect the interest of Tramway Companies" such being concerns paying their shareholders dividends, and (4) To afford legal and technical advice and assistance assistance

– presumably in the interests of such companies will constitute an organisation foreign altogether to the spirit of the section. The Board have not yet had an opportunity of perusing the draft memorandum and articles of Association and therefore of course are not in a position to discuss the matter fully but as they observe that the 18th inst is the last day for sending in objections they wish this letter to be treated as such in order that they may not be considered out of time and they would reserve to themselves to make further observations hereafter should occasion require."

Fortunately, someone moved quickly to ensure copies of the relevant paperwork reached the West Ham Local Board as on 29 May 1885 Billearys & Layard wrote to the Board of Trade again:

"Sir, With reference to your letter of the 18th inst, R.2637, we beg to inform you that the West Ham Local Board having now had an opportunity of perusing the draft memorandum and Articles of Association of the proposed Tramways Institute of Great Britain & Ireland do not desire further to press their objections to the grant of the licence of the Board of Trade."

Neatly filed in the Board of Trade paperwork is an admission of a (rare) mistake by this august body, being yet another letter dated 1 June 1985 from Billearys & Layard, the gist of which is that a letter sent to them by the Board of Trade was sent in error but should have gone to The Tramways Institute's Solicitors, Messrs Rollitt & Sons. However, rather loftily they added, "The mistake is easily accounted for as you will recollect that we addressed a letter to you objecting to the grant of a license, on behalf of the West Ham Local Board but we have since withdrawn our objections."

Pure waffle, but it is noticeable that John Fell, W.J.C. Wain, and Norman Scott Russell of the Falcon works, were present.

From *The Times*, 1 August, 1896:

"THE TRAMWAYS INSTITUTE. – The ninth dinner of the Tramways Institute of Great Britain and Ireland took place last night at the Holborn Restaurant. Mr John Fell, ex-mayor of Leamington, presided, and the company included Mr L. Atherley-Jones, M.P. Mr Hugh C. Godfrey, Mr W.J. Carruthers-Wain, Mr William Mason, Mr N. Scott Russell, Mr E. Garcké, Mr R.A. Germaine, Mr J.W. Clydesdale, Mr V.B.D. Cooper, Mr Bassett Hopkins, Mr T.H. Bolton, Mr W. Turton, and Mr J.G. Elliot (the secretary).

Sir J. Puleston, in proposing the toast of the evening, the Tramways Institute, stated it had done much to promote the success of the tramways, an interest the importance of which he fully recognised. The progress made by tramways in this country had been very great, and at no time had that progress been more manifest than it was now. When they next met they would be able to offer their congratulations on the success of a new mode of traction, which would improve still further the tramway service. He hoped that the institute would long

continue to prosper. Mr Carruthers-Wain (past president), in responding to the toast, stated the object of the institute was not merely to promote legislation which would do good to the tramway interest, but also to prevent legislation which might do harm to it. They had done much in this direction already. Mr Alderman Hammersley, ex-mayor of Hanley, proposed "Traction: the survival of the fittest," for which Mr Robert Hammond responded. Other toasts followed."

The Wains travelled far and wide entertaining and giving lectures including the USA. Here is a shipping note:

New York Times, 23 October, 1890:

"PASSENGERS ON THE OCEAN STEAMSHIP ARRIVALS AND DEPARTURES YESTERDAY

…The White Star Liner Britannic's passengers included Mr and Mrs Blaine, Capt. J.R. Brady, Mr and Mrs Bayard Cutting, E.T. Daniels, Dr E. Hausknecht, Capt. J.S. Thompson, **Mr and Mrs W.J. Carruthers Wain**, and Charles Walters…"

En passant, a contemporaneous note:

The Times, August, 1896:

"THE EX-SULTAN ABDULLAH OF PERAK.

It may be remembered that not long ago Mr Henniker Heaton, M.P.,* obtained for the deported ruler of Perak permission to leave the Seychelles and reside at Singapore, and bear the title of ex-Sultan. In consequence of further representations made by the hon. Member for Canterbury, who pointed out the family of an Oriental prince, with more than one wife, was necessarily of considerable dimensions, entailing corresponding expenditure, the ex-Sultan's allowance has now been increased by $100 per month, and a grant of $250 has been made to him to meet the expenses of the circumcision of his four sons."

---

*Later Sir John Henniker Heaton, Bart., Conservative M.P. from 1885 to 1910.

Articles of Association

OF THE

TRAMWAYS' INSTITUTE OF GREAT BRITAIN AND IRELAND.

1. For the purpose of registration the number of Members of the Institute is declared not to exceed These Articles shall be construed with reference to the provisions of the Companies Acts, 1862 to 1883, and the terms used in these Articles shall be taken as having the same respective meanings as they would have when used in those Acts. The Institute is established for the purposes expressed in the Memorandum of Association.

MEMBERSHIP.

1a. The Members of the Institute shall consist of Tramway Companies, Lessees of Tramways, and Owners of Tramways working their own property, and each such Company, body, or individual may nominate such number of Delegates to attend the Meetings of the Institute as they may determine. The Delegates so to be appointed shall consist of Directors, Solicitors, Engineers, Secretaries, or Managers of Tramway Companies or of such Lessees or Owners who are Members of the Institute. The appointment of all Delegates shall be subject to the approval of the Council.

ENTRANCE FEE AND SUBSCRIPTIONS.

2. Each Member of this Institute, shall upon being admitted, pay an entrance fee of £2 2s., and an annual subscription of at least £1 1s.; also an additional £1 1s. for each Delegate appointed. Subscriptions shall be due and payable on the 1st January.

ASSOCIATES.

3. All persons favourable to the objects of this Institute, may, on being duly proposed and elected as hereinafter provided, and on paying an annual subscription of £1 1s. or upwards, become Associates, and shall be entitled to attend all Meetings of the Institute.

NON-PAYMENT OF SUBSCRIPTION.

4. Any Member or Associate whose subscription shall be three months in arrear may be excluded from all benefits of the Institute, and any Member six months in arrear may (subject to the right of the Institute to sue for and recover arrears of subscriptions) be struck off the list of Members.

VOTING.

5. Each Member shall be entitled to one vote in respect of each annual subscription of £1 1s., such vote to be exercised through the Delegate or Delegates representing the said Member.

PROXIES.

6. Votes may be given either personally or by Proxy. A Proxy shall be appointed in writing under the hand of the appointor, or if such appointor is a Company or Corporation, under its Common Seal, or by resolution of its Board.

No person shall be appointed a Proxy who is not a Member's Delegate, and the instrument appointing him shall be deposited at the Registered Office of the Institute not less than 48 hours before the time of holding the Meeting at which he proposes to vote.

ADMISSION OF ASSOCIATES.

7. Any person desirous of becoming an Associate, and who is eligible according to the Rules, shall be nominated in writing by a Member's Delegate, and such nomination shall be seconded by two Members' Delegates and approved by the Council.

TRAMWAYS INSTITUTE

OF

GREAT BRITAIN AND IRELAND.

President.
W. J. CARRUTHERS-WAIN, Esq., C.E. (Chairman, North Staffordshire Tramways Co., Limited).

Vice=Presidents.
JOSEPH EBBSMITH, Esq. (Chairman, Birmingham and Central Tramways Co., Limited).
WILLIAM TURTON, Esq. (Chairman, Leeds Tramways Co., Limited).
A. P. SMITH, Esq. (Chairman, Bury, Rochdale, and Oldham Tramways Co.).

Executive Committee.
ROBERT WHITTAKER, Esq., J.P. (Chairman of the Southport Tramways Co., Limited.)
JOHN WAUGH, Esq. (Director, St. Helen's and District Tramways Co.).
WILLIAM MASON, Esq. (Director of the Bradford Tramways Co.).
JOHN FELL, Esq., Leamington.

Secretary and Offices :—J. G. B. ELLIOT, Esq., Finsbury Circus Buildings, 18, Eldon Street, London, E.C.

This Society was established in 1885, for, as stated in its Charter, protecting Tramway interests, the due advancement thereof, and the diffusion of knowledge specially relating thereto. The interests of Tramway Shareholders have been closely watched, and, wherever possible, safe-guarded by this Institute, and much legislation, injurious to Tramway Companies, has been prevented by it ; while its existence is in itself a warning that their interests will be defended. The advantage to the individual Companies of joining an Association such as this, can hardly be over-estimated, and the more extensive the support given to it the more power it can wield, and the greater its influence and weight. Thirty-two Companies are already Members of the Institute, representing 262 miles of Line, and £4,500,000 of Capital ; but as the necessity for remedial legislation becomes daily more urgent, and the pressure of proposals to damage Tramway Property is becoming severe, the Directors invite the serious consideration of the Shareholders to the urgent necessity for themselves supporting, not by their moral weight merely, but in the manner indicated below, an Institution formed solely for their benefit.

It is urged upon all Tramway Shareholders (1) That they should personally become Associates of the Institute ; and (2) That they should, by personal interview or correspondence with the Member of Parliament representing their particular constituency, induce him to support an enquiry into the operation of the Tramways Act, with a view to its amendment on the large and important matters which experience has proved require alteration and improvement, and the removal from the Companies of the grossly unjust impositions to which they are now subjected ; and (3) To resist the attempts constantly being made to depreciate their property.

Shareholders are reminded that in this case union is strength, and that if they unanimously ask for what is needed they will almost certainly obtain it.

The Association Subscription of half-a-guinea a year, entitles the Subscriber to attend all meetings of the Institute, and to receive a copy of each issue of the official records.

REPORT OF PROCEEDINGS

AT

CONFERENCE

OF

Directors and Officers of Tramway Companies,

HELD AT

"THE GUILDHALL TAVERN,"

Gresham Street, London,

ON THE

19TH APRIL, 1888.

VERBATIM REPORT of Proceedings at Conference of Directors and Officers of Tramway Companies, held at the "Guildhall Tavern," Gresham Street, London, 19th April, 1888.

PRESENT:

NAME OF COMPANY.	BY WHOM REPRESENTED.
Birmingham Central	Joseph Smith, Esq. (Chairman); W. J. Carruthers-Wain, Esq. (Managing Director).
Birmingham and Midland ..	Colonel E. J. L. Twynam (Chairman).
Blackburn and Over Darwen ..	T. Russell Lee, Esq., J.P. (Chairman).
Bolton	Joseph Walker, Esq.
Bradford Tramways & Omnibus	J. C. Chaplin, Esq. (Secretary).
City of Oxford	E. D. Matthews, Esq.
Cambridge Street	S. L. Young, Esq. (Chairman); A. J. Tillyard, Esq. (Director).
Coventry	F. J. Horrocks, Esq. (Director).
Croydon and Norwood ..	J. G. B. Elliot, Esq. (Secretary).
Dublin United	W. M. Murphy, Esq., M.P. (Director).

Leeds	W. Wharam, Esq. (Secretary and Manager).
Liverpool United	James Richardson, Esq. (Director).
Manchester Carriage & Tramways	Joseph Walker, Esq. (Deputy-Chairman), Mr. Alderman John King, (Director).
North London Steam	A. R. Robinson, Esq. (Director); J. W. Newton, Esq. (Engineer); M. Hill, Esq, (Manager).
North Staffordshire	W. J. Carruthers-Wain, Esq. (Chairman).
Sheffield	E. Etlinger, Esq. (Chairman); Walter Webb, Esq. (Solicitor).
South London	S. J. Wilde, Esq. (Chairman); F. R. Bluett, Esq. (Secretary); E. K. Blyth, Esq. (Solicitor).
South Staffordshire	W. J. Carruthers-Wain, Esq. (Chairman).
Southwark and Deptford ..	J. Percy Leith, Esq. (Director).
Stockton and Darlington Steam	Thomas Jervis, Esq. (Secretary).

Letters of Regret for non-attendance, but supporting united action for objects stated in circular received from the undermentioned Tramway Companies :—

Accrington.	Edinburgh Northern.
Birkdale and Southport	Edinburgh Street.
Birkenhead.	Hull.
Birmingham and Aston.	Manchester, Bury, Rochdale
Blackburn Corporation.	and Oldham.
Blackpool Electric.	Newport (Mon.).
Bristol.	Northampton.
Burnley.	West Metropolitan.
Chester.	Woolwich and South East
Derby.	London.
Dublin and Lucan.	

Mr. W. J. CARRUTHERS WAIN (Chairman North Staffordshire Tramways Company) having been voted to the Chair, rose and said :

Gentlemen, as I am responsible for summoning this conference, you may expect to hear a few words from me. Some of you may be aware that I have for a long time past given particular attention to the questions mentioned in the circular which has been issued to you, in fact, so far back as the first meeting of the Tramway Institute, which was held in London three years ago, I then pressed home strongly upon those present three questions: repairs to roads, rates and taxes upon lines of tramways, and license of tramcars. Those questions ought to have been settled long since in a different manner from what they have been, and it seems to me that a very favourable opportunity has now presented itself, of which we ought to avail. Owing to the changes which are likely immediately to take place according to the Chancellor of the Exchequer's Budget proposals, and to the clauses in the Local Government Bill, we have now an opportunity of presenting a fair and moderate statement of our case to the responsible authorities, and of asking for some consideration at their hands. I trust that some good will result from this meeting, and that it will not have been held in vain. There is no doubt that tramway companies are entitled to some relief from the burdens under which they suffer. No organised steps have been taken, to my knowledge, to secure any relief from the burdens under which we groan. These burdens do not affect the flourishing companies in the same degree as they do the struggling ones, yet the flourishing companies, are as compared with the struggling ones—those that can simply pay their way—very rare, and almost like black swans. My experience has been to a large extent with struggling companies, therefore I speak sympathetically on the points I have raised. I am glad to say that this suggested conference has received a great amount of cordial sympathy and support from gentlemen connected with many and important lines. This affords me high satisfaction. Unfortunately, the shortness of the notice convening this conference did not allow many to be present who would otherwise have been glad to be here.

[The Chairman here read extracts from letters from numerous influential gentlemen interested in tramway enterprise, regretting their inability to attend and expressing their sympathy with the objects of the meeting.]

There seems to me to be some misapprehension with regard to the effect of the Budget proposals upon tramway companies, with which I will deal later on. As regards road repairs, no evidence is required to demonstrate the injustice of tramway companies having to bear the burden. The injustice is bad enough in the case of horse tramways, as the horses do help to wear out the tramways. The burden is, however, doubly heavy upon steam, cable, or electric tramway companies, as they do not affect the condition of the roadways which they are required to repair at their own cost. In the case of horse tramways we should not object to contribute something to the repairs. We already pay twice over, and I strongly object to pay for the same thing three times, as we should be called upon to do under the Budget scheme. First, we have to pay for the road repairs (by which the ratepayers are relieved), without getting any return or any allowance from the county funds; then we have to contribute to the highway rates; and, thirdly, under the Budget scheme it is proposed to transfer certain charges to the county councils for the repair of the roads. This would be practically paying three times for the same thing. What we propose is so manifestly reasonable that it has only to be represented in the proper quarter to ensure favourable consideration. With regard to rates and taxes, the principle of railway assessments appears to have been to a considerable extent applied to tramways. That would be a fair argument if the land had been already rated for poor rate and for other purposes, but that is not so. Railway companies are justly charged rates upon their lands because the lands were already subject to assessment for rates and taxes, and these should continue to be paid upon them. But in our case, where we only have a common user of the road, why we should have to pay rates and taxes upon that road is a matter which passes my comprehension. As regards the proposed alteration in taxation, I observe that some companies are under the impression that the alterations will not affect them. I submit that they are entirely wrong. In the first instance, take London alone. We pay £2 a year police license, which is not paid by any provincial tramway company, in addition to two guineas inland revenue license. That is because we come under the provisions of the Metropolitan Stage Carriage Act. A tramway car ought to be considered, if anything, a hackney carriage. It is not a luxury. There is no question about that. We should

siderable extent. The shoe pinches me more than anybody else, as, either as Chairman or Managing Director, I represent one-eighth of the tramway mileage of the United Kingdom, and have consequently looked into this matter very closely.

[The Chairman here read Mr. Goschen's reply to his question 5.]

That was in answer to a question as to what would be done with regard to the goods trucks, which are constructed to run either on the road or rail. You see that these tramway goods trucks will come within the scope of the Budget and be subject to wheel tax, although the truck generally runs upon the Company's own metals without interfering with any other portion of the road. The injustice will again be seen. Gentlemen, it is unnecessary for me to take up your time with any further explanations. I am satisfied in my own mind that we ought not to lose this opportunity of stating a case for the consideration of the Government departments, because if we do not take advantage of the opportunity of making our representations it will hereafter be said that when local government was transferred to the county councils we did not avail ourselves of the chance, and my experience of local authorities is that one has but a poor chance in any representations made to them. They consider we are married to them (so to speak) and unfortunately they are in the position of being the husbands and we are the wives, and have to submit to any treatment they choose to inflict on us. I do hope that the outcome of this meeting will be that we shall join hands, not only in endeavouring to prevent the perpetuation of injustice, but for every purpose in furtherance of the interest of tramway enterprise. I hope we shall unite in organising a strong deputation to present a memorial to the Authorities, so that we may obtain some consideration of our present position, and of the burdens under which we labour. I shall be happy to hear a free and full expression of opinion to aid us this morning. (Hear, hear.)

Mr. MATTHEWS (Oxford Tramway Company): I quite agree with you, Sir, in pointing out the hardships put upon tramway enterprise. I speak for one company for which I feel very greatly, having fostered it to its present position. I would confine my remarks more to the subject of the road repairs. These repairs are a great burden to tramways. I

only pay therefore in all a duty of 15s. a year; and it occurs to me that that point has not been considered by the Government. I will read you a letter from the Chancellor of the Exchequer, dated the 16th instant. I put to him six questions. I find it is as well, if possible, to pin Government departments down closely to facts.

"16th *April*, 1888.
"TREASURY CHAMBERS,
"WHITEHALL, S.W.
"SIR,
"I am in receipt of your letter of April 14th, and now reply to the six questions which it contains:

"1. Horse and steam tramways will not be affected (but "see answer the question 4), by the wheel tax. "Tramcars will pay £2. 2s. as at present under "Carriage Duty. Wheel Tax *does not apply to any* "*vehicles, to which existing Carriage Duty applies.*

"2. It is not proposed to deal with the Metropolitan "Police License of £2.

"3. Whether tramcars should or should not 'come under "hackney carriage provisions,' is a matter of opinion "on which I really cannot give a categorical answer. "As a matter of fact it is not proposed so to deal "with them.

"4. This point, viz., about tramway engines, is a difficult "one and still under consideration.

"5. In the case of tramway goods trucks with two sets of "wheels, both of which cannot be used at the same "time, only one set of wheels will be taxed.

"6. Tramway and omnibus horses will be exempt from "horse duty.

"I am, SIR,
"Yours faithfully,
(Sig.) "A. MILNER."

I think the representatives of the Metropolitan Companies who are here will agree that it is grossly unfair that we in London should be charged the £2 police license, while country tramways are exempt. I don't know whether you have looked at the point, but there is a proposal to put a tax of £5 a year upon street locomotives or traction engines. It is a very serious matter indeed for all steam tramways if they are to have a tax put upon their engines. I maintain, therefore, that we are affected by the Budget to a very con-

am not acquainted very well with the provisions of the new Act proposed for the local government, but I have no doubt there is a way of relieving or getting rid of our local repairs, which are very heavy. In Oxford we maintain ⅓ of the road, and in this way the ratepayers are saved 33 per cent. of their expenditure. When we made the tramways we were forced to bring the roads into the level. In consequence, they are very much improved by our labours. In other parts we were bound by the provisions of the Municipal Council—to pave the road across. The city had new paving at the expense of the tramways. The widening of Merton bridge had to be undertaken. When tramways were proposed therefore we hoped to get something out of the fund. I am sorry to say we were made to pay £2,000. These burdens were put upon us. I would suggest that Provincial tramways should secure some relief from the very heavy cost of maintenance which has to be borne by them. Local ratepayers have their roads improved and ample means of locomotion afforded to them. The poorer classes benefit by tramways and the local authorities should better meet the companies as regards maintenance.

Mr. T. RUSSELL LEE (Blackburn and Over Darwen Tramways Company): I am much obliged to you, Sir, for your exhaustive speech. I have come from Cheshire this morning to attend this meeting. I have often felt the importance of having more gatherings of tramway directors. We don't meet enough to discuss our grievances. I represent, perhaps, the first tram-line in the United Kingdom that was laid exclusively for steam. I hope that the proposed Act for steam tramways will not be so prejudicial to the interests of shareholders as I have been informed. I shall not trouble you with many of our grievances. In the past, our particular Act absolutely compelled the company to pave the whole of the road from kerb to kerb for five miles to Over Darwen. Such an Act will, I hope, never be allowed again. As to the special injustice to steam tramways, I fully endorse what has been said. With our 4 feet gauge, we have, as a matter of fact, to repair 11 feet instead of 7 feet 8 inches. This shows how important it is to the directors of steam tramways to have their grievances represented. I feel very strongly what an injustice the repairing of roads is altogether—how very little injury the steam tramways do to the road and how much the outside traffic makes use of the road. Broad-wheel carts always choose the middle of the road and wear out our paving by coming on from the macadam on each side, and so save expense to the ratepayers. The public use the road as much as they choose, for the moment a tramcar has gone by, the carter comes back again. As to the assessment of tramways, it has always appeared to me an extraordinary enigma how the value of tramway property was arrived at. My line is about five miles; 4 per cent. represents £14,000 or £15,000, but how the property is assessed I am unable to discover. We know that the probable rent of a house is the standard of assessment, but in the case of a tramway average we have never been able to find out upon what we really do pay rates. Then if we calculate for a moment on the basis of the amount paid for repairs we are still at a loss to understand. 20,000 square yards of paving are actually laid, and this, we, of course, keep in repair. I would just make a remark upon the question of licenses. It occurs to me that we are going to be either a carriage or a cart. If a carriage, one horse would pay one guinea and two horses two guineas. I live close to Liverpool, where there has been a loud outcry by the van and cart owners. One grievance is that if they used a less number it would be very unfair to tax each car if they were not all out on the same day. We have eight cars and they are never out on the same day. It is hard to be obliged to pay for every car that is in the sheds. If there is to be a license it ought to be limited to the average number upon the road. I am very glad that the meeting has been called to-day, and I hope that something will come of it. (Hear, hear.)

Mr. S. J. WILDE (Chairman South London Tramways Company): In our case we are a single line in many places, but in some of the parishes we have got to pave and keep in repair the whole of the road to the kerb. In almost every other case it is the rule that wherever there is a single line 3 feet of paving has to be done outside. This is owing to the great powers given to the local authorities, who plume themselves on their right to levy. We cannot do anything without their consent. We must either accept their terms or do nothing at all. Those powers ought to be very largely curtailed, and there should be a power of appeal from them. There should be a power to refer every case to some other authority. In York Road, where the street is very narrow, it was stipulated that we should deposit £750 with the local authorities to pay for the expense of widening

the road. They have had the money five or six years, and have never spent a penny piece upon the work, and have paid no interest on the money. As to the Plymouth Tramway, we presented a Bill to make a line in some of the streets which are very narrow. After our plans had been deposited for a long time, the authorities took no notice of them, and in the result they refused to sanction the construction of tramways in certain parts because the street was too narrow for them. I shall probably loose some thousands of pounds over this case; I hope, Sir, you have drawn up some kind of memorial. I think it would assist us to say whether we concur in it as a whole or in part.

The CHAIRMAN: I have such a resolution, which I will read. (Resolution read, see end.)

Mr. WILDE: Would it be out of place to call the attention of the Government to the Tramway Act? It is rather a side issue but still bearing upon the question.

Mr. RUSSELL LEE: I wish, Sir, to make one suggestion, I am only a representative. I would suggest that if it were possible the assent of shareholders of tramways should also be obtained to anything we do. That would, I think, carry weight with the Government.

Mr. JOSEPH SMITH (Chairman Birmingham Central Tramways Company): Mr. Chairman, while I fully agree with the remarks of the last speaker (the Chairman of the South London Company), I thank you for having prepared the memorial which you have read. I cannot help thinking that if this conference is to be productive of lasting benefit, we must go beyond that resolution. Probably my experience will be that of almost all of you, and I think that it will be productive of much benefit if, as a result of this meeting, some arrangement can be come to by which each company might supply a short statement of the actual and direct grievances which it has suffered in connection with the local authorities. My belief is that if such statements were supplied and properly collated and rendered to the authorities the result would be very startling indeed. However, beyond all that it is highly desirable that in meeting here to-day we should recognize with what we have at present to deal. So far as I am able to understand the Local Government Bill, it does not in any great measure affect us at the present moment, except so far as it transfers certain powers of the Board of Trade to new county councils, and having

regard to the Budget proposals it may be that Mr. Goschen is prepared to alter or modify those special conditions which appear to be more injurious; but what is most important to my mind is the fact that to all intents and purposes this Local Government Bill is the first of a series of measures which will vitally affect us. When it is considered how monstrously unjust the present assessments of tramway companies are, we ought to look critically into the provisions of the proposals. I really do not know which is the greater injustice: the compulsion to maintain the roads which we do not wear or the compulsion to pay the rates and taxes in respect of highways which we ourselves actually maintain. Both appear to be monstrous injustices. What I should like is, that this meeting should not merely authorise certain representations to be made upon the measures now before Parliament, but I should like to see the establishment of an association to watch tramway interests generally. This would enable the weighty and important tramway questions to be properly represented. I became a member of a tramway institute some years ago. Where it is now, what it is doing and who represents it I cannot say, but it does appear to be absolutely necessary that either by an institute or club or in some other way we should be brought into touch with each other for common interest. While I heartily support and would gladly move the resolution which the Chairman has read, I do hope the powers of that proposed committee may be enlarged, so as to consider the best means by which the large interests of tramways may be protected, not merely as to the Local Government Bill, but also as regards their own protection in view of any further legislation. I move the present resolution and trust the meeting may approve of the idea of establishing a permanent institute.

Mr. Alderman KING (Manchester Carriage Company): Sir, we are very pleased you have called this meeting. We think it is a very favourable opportunity for considering the grievances under which we suffer, especially as to the repairing of the roads and with regard to the rates. We have something like 45 miles of single tramways, and on these we have to pay for the repair of the roads. Practically it means this, that although we are not compelled to pave the whole of the road we really do so. The Local Board does not care about the state of the road. It knows there is a good midddle to the road and entirely neglects the rest. We practically pay for the repair of the entire road. We

ought not, at all events, to pay highway rates in this district. The proposals as to steam tramways do not affect us, as we have none. The great questions to us are the repair of the roads, and the reduction of rates. We have no grievances against the local authority who assess the rates, but against the law. I am happy to second the resolution.

Mr. WALTER WEBB (Sheffield Tramways Company): Well, Mr. Chairman, I congratulate you upon the success of this meeting to-day. Having been connected with tramway companies from their introduction into this country, I have experienced what a very great difficulty there has been in bringing together in a concrete form the tramway interest. I am glad to see so large a number of companies represented in this room, as this fact shows me that you have chosen an opportune moment for the purpose of endeavouring to collect together a committee of the tramway interest, so that the voice which has been a very weak voice in expressing itself may gain great strength in parliamentary matters. The real secret of the weakness of tramway companies to protect themselves has been this: we have to compete with the local authority on unequal terms, who saddle upon us conditions which we are obliged to accept. These local authorities are an influential body, not only in their own district but in Parliament. It is almost impossible for the Board of Trade to go against the feeling of the local authorities. We have always had very staunch officials at the Board of Trade—always ready to recognise the unfair position in which we stood—but it has been practically impossible for the Board of Trade to do much. The moment a question has got out of the hands of the Board of Trade and before Parliament, the cheeseparing influence of the local authorities and the weakness of the tramway companies have become apparent. Mr. Joseph Smith has spoken of the Tramway Institute. We all hoped great things from it, but our expectations have been disappointed. It is a pity that that Institute has been allowed to become dormant, for now it would have been a power which would have aided us in the endeavours which we are now making in the promotion of our interests. We have three distinct and difficult matters which we can with reason bring before a Government official. These are something to go upon. I am afraid there has been a general hanging back on the part of many companies, but I am glad to see so many influential companies represented here to-day. There has been a want of co-operation. Some years ago the railway companies co-operated in their own interests. If the example of the railway companies were followed in the case of the tramway companies, we might build up a Tramway Institute to prosecute our cause, and thus good results will have flowed from this meeting, and you, Sir, will have to be complimented for its inauguration. In order to attain the objects we have in view, you must be exceedingly prudent, and shew a certain amount of worldly wisdom. It would be impossible to bring forward at the present moment the whole of the Budget proposals or those of the Local Government Bill affecting tramways. The matters to first engage the attention of the deputation will be those which have been indicated by the Chairman. The unfair provisions of Section 43 of the Tramways Act and other provisions of that Act, should be borne in mind. It may be, Sir, that you will actually get together a sufficiently strong body of representatives to justify you in applying for a Special Parliamentary Committee for the purpose of considering the grievances of tramway companies, and with a view to an amendment of the Tramway Act of 1870. In applying for the relief of tramway companies from many of the grievous burdens under which they groan, we should be careful not in any way to enhance the value of the undertakings so as to encourage the authorities to exercise the powers of purchase under the provisions of the Act. That, however, is a matter which will not frighten us from carrying out the policy we have in hand, but it is a consideration not to be entirely ignored. Upon the question of rates and taxes, I regard Mr. Joseph Smith as a very high authority. He has had immense experience upon that subject, and I would hope that on any committee that is to be appointed, Mr. Joseph Smith himself will be good enough to consent to act.

Mr. WILLIAM MURPHY, M.P. (Dublin Tramways Company): I think, Sir, that no person can find fault with the resolution that you have submitted to the meeting, as it embodies almost the only means by which the grievances of the tramway companies could be brought before the proper authorities and the steps to obtain such redress as is possible. I would suggest, that in order to be practical, it would be better to apply ourselves as closely as possible to the points on which it is in the power of the Local Government Board and of the Chancellor of the Exchequer to give relief. As to the questions of construction,

repairs and maintenance of roads, it must be borne in mind, that the local authorities are very powerful. Those obligations are all statutory obligations which have been accepted by the companies in their special Acts and from which it would now be almost impossible to get any relief. It would rather be better for us to apply ourselves to protection in the future, than to endeavour to obtain relief from past obligations. It is quite possible, that with the extension of local government in this country, and the tendency which prevails of transmitting to the local authorities the various powers which have previously been vested only in Parliament, the opportunity of resisting unfair and unreasonable obligations and claims by local authorities may be lost to us. For instances, it is not an uncommon case for tramway companies to appeal to the Board of Trade. We should see that that appeal is not lost to the companies. With regard to assessments, I think it is very difficult indeed to ascertain the principle of them. It does not appear to me to be a very hopeful prospect, inasmuch as the gas and water mains are assessed to local rates. If these are not relieved, how can tramways expect to be relieved? The question of licenses seems to me the most practical one, but it may be very well to point out the other grievances at the same time. I don't know whether in London the hackney carriages pay the same as stage carriages, such as omnibuses.

The CHAIRMAN: Hackney carriages pay 15s., omnibuses pay £2. 2s.

Mr. MURPHY: That is one of the things in connection with the present movement which to my company is of considerable importance, because we pay in Dublin, under the denomination of stage-carriage, a police tax of £8 for each car. This is in relief of the cost from the Imperial purse. The principle on which the police expenses of Dublin are based is this: the whole of the police are paid out of the Imperial funds, and then a fixed rate on the value of the city, and the guinea extra stage-coach licenses are paid to the Treasury as a re-fund. The Treasury have to pay the first. The whole of the £8 is for the relief of Imperial taxes. We are agitating the question at the present time. I would ask the attention of the meeting to this resolution. I hope that with the other explanations this meeting will be permanently useful.

Mr. WILDE: Between the tramway companies and the gas and water companies there is this difference—the

tramways relieve the parish to an enormous extent by the rating. This makes a vast difference.

Mr. MURPHY: The repairs of the roads are all statutory contracts with the parish authorities.

Mr. WHARAM (Leeds Tramways Company): I don't find any fault with you Mr. Chairman, although the company which I represent had no notice, but we heard of the meeting.

The CHAIRMAN: I am really very sorry, Mr. Wharam, I thought the circular had been forwarded to every tramway company in the Kingdom.

Mr. WHARAM: My Directors thought the meeting of sufficient importance for them to be represented. So far as the road repairs are concerned we have nearly the whole of the roadway to do in some places, where the streets are narrow. We have a 4 feet 8½ inch gauge. All the other traffic in the town makes a very good use of our road. We also suffer in this way: we have so many heavy vehicles engaged in the trade of the town—those of engineering firms and of extensive brewers. Then, again, we have large traction engines with three or four wagons behind them along our tramways; also boilers as long as this room, and great traction engines with them. As a matter of fact, they drag them through the streets. So we have a good deal to complain of in that respect. Then, again, we are, of course, rated for the tramway the same as the rest of the companies. It falls on us to repair the roads. We have about 30 miles of single line, and we work entirely by steam. As to whether tramway engines will come under this license of £5, I don't think they will, because if you notice here [read extract from the London "Daily Telegraph" of the 11th April]; it makes a distinction; it says locomotive or traction engine. There seems to be some relief in the matter of one-horse cars. The license is a guinea. That has been two guineas. There is a relief there. As regards the licenses they ought to be limited to the number of cars daily worked. We have about 76 cars, but we don't use above 40 of them as a rule. These are the only points I notice, except the grounds gone over by other speakers.

Mr. CHAPLIN (Secretary to the Bradford Tramways Company): I have to express to you, Sir, the regret of my chairman at his inability to be present. He feels very strongly upon the matters of the repairs of the roads and of the rates and taxes. I feel sure he would

support the resolution read. I agree with the remarks made by Mr. Lee as to the standard of assessment of the tramways. We have made repeated applications to the authorities, but have never been able to get any satisfaction. It seems to me that the greater the reduction the greater would be the benefit to the public generally.

Mr. RUSSELL LEE: As suggested by Mr. Smith, it also appears to me that now is the time to represent our grievances, because once the principle of the Bill gets settled, although we may have amendments to propose in future years, this opportune moment may be lost. I would suggest that it is a doubtful policy to communicate with every company as to their local authorities. I always find it best to keep square with the local authority. I should deprecate doing more than presenting a memorial. I should like to see the basis of certain charges altered. I look upon this as a very different thing.

Mr. JOSEPH SMITH: I am sorry if I made myself so little clear on the subject. In the first place, I merely sought to point out that the Local Government Bill as now submitted does not materially affect us. It does not assert any principle with regard to the particular matters of complaint under which we now labour. All that the present Local Government Bill does is to settle a scheme of local government as between what we term the local authorities and the larger authority, which will be a county council. The Local Government Bill in its present form affects us very little, except as to the transfer from the local authority to the county council. The present Local Government Bill is but the precursor of one or more bills which must follow with regard to the details of local government, and when that comes it will be Parliament that will deal with the expenditure of local taxes, and it will also deal with the mode of assessment of those taxes and as to the manner in which they shall be collected. Although for the moment we can do no more than see ourselves in evidence upon this Local Government Bill, it is desirable that we should now appear upon 'the Bill and show the authorities that we are watching them, so that we may be prepared when we have hereafter to deal with a further bill. Let us appeal from the local authorities at the present time, and say that although the present Local Government Bill does not seriously affect us, let it be distinctly known that we are already labouring under great grievances, and when they are dealing more particularly in a subsequent bill, we shall have strong representations to make on the subject. I thought it would be an excellent thing in the interval between now and the period when that subsequent bill comes in, if the body to be formed—institute, or what you please—were in possession of the local grievances of the different companies. It seemed to me to be absolutely necessary that the committee whom you may appoint should be not only in possession of a general idea of the grievances, but to show one after the other the particular and exceptional grievances under which the various companies labour. For instance, Mr. Wilde mentioned the fact of the contribution of £750 forced from the tramway company for the widening of the road when the local authorities have done nothing but keep the money. No committee could understand, except from being communicated with. Facts like this would be sufficient from every local district. I am in favor of a policy of action, so far as it can go. With regard to the present Local Government Bill, I desire to point out that our hope of obtaining remedies will be very small indeed. The Supplemental Bill will be a bill, which with due vigilance on our part, ought to enable us to deal with the present grievances under which we suffer.

Mr. MURPHY: I take it there will be power to appeal from the local authority. This is a most serious matter.

Mr. JOSEPH SMITH: That is why the powers of the Board of Trade, with regard to tramways, will henceforth be transferred to the County Council excepting only where the County Council may happen themselves to be promoters of a tramway. The Board of Trade will be over the County Council.

Mr. WILDE: I am of opinion that the resolution should be followed up by another one providing the ways and means. The expenditure should not fall upon any particular company.

The CHAIRMAN: I am very much obliged to you indeed for the expressions of opinion which have been given this morning. I agree with Mr. Murphy entirely. I was quite sure that that point would come out as to the broad distinction between obligations of construction and obligations of maintenance. You have probably had to pay a certain price for your concession, and undertaken to pave the roads to a greater or lesser extent. You cannot get out of your statutory obligations, but there is a broad distinction between obligations of construction and the question of maintenance. I think as to the latter we can get relief. I am of opinion that you have only to appeal to get the relief you seek if the local authorities are unreasonable. There was a company with which I was connected which was very sick, and I was called in as a doctor to attend to it. Having tried in vain to keep the line paved with macadam, as required by the local authority, which, as you know, is a matter of impossibility. For no sooner was the work done than the road was converted by rain into mud, so that the last state of that road was worse than the first. I could not keep my macadam close to the rails. I asked permission to lay granite setts, but the local authority would not give permission, and refused to recognise the Board of Trade as the referee on such subjects. However, the Board of Trade decided against them after the expenditure of much time, labour and money, and I also beat them three times in the courts. But this sort of procedure is much too expensive and laborious to be adopted as a general thing. We ought to have some understanding with regard to repairing, to which the local authority shall be compelled to submit. I perfectly agree with Mr. Smith, as to a general revision of the Tramway Act of 1870. It was passed when tramways were new, and when people thought they were going to be rather a nuisance than otherwise. Now that tramways are a recognized fact, we are practically working under obsolete acts, and I am of opinion that proper representations should be made to the authorities for a revision of the Acts under which we exercise our powers. As to the transfer of the powers of the Board of Trade to the local authority an appeal would mean appealing from one irresponsible body to another. [The Chairman here read the two sections of the Local Government Bill].

As regards the mode of combination among many tramway companies, I was one of the members of the Council of the Tramway Institute. It was not from any want of zeal on my part that its deliberations did not go on up to now. I continued to urge that meetings should be held or that something should be done, but without avail. Gentlemen, I am so much encouraged by the response that has been made to my appeal that I feel we must go forward. I hope one result of this meeting will be that we shall galvanise, and revive the Tramway Institute and make it a useful and responsible body. The railway companies have their trade union for the protection of their property, but there has been no sort of enthusiastic co-operation of those interested in tramway enterprise. Hitherto tramway companies have held aloof from one another, somewhat in the spirit of the rhyme—

Earl Chatham, with his sabre drawn,
Stood waiting for Sir Richard Strachan;
Sir Richard, longing to be at 'em,
Stood waiting for the Earl of Chatham.

As regards the mode of assessment, it is made in a different way in almost every place. That is a matter which ought to be definitely settled. There is no doubt the licenses should be charged only on the average number of vehicles used. The tax presses with extreme hardship in a large number of cases. On one line I have 82 cars, and we have to pay on the whole of them, while our average running is only 50. In another company we have 38: average running 20. Mr. Wharam possibly did not hear what I read from the Chancellor of the Exchequer's letter. There will be no relief in the duty on tramcars. The license on the engines may not affect us, but until the Chancellor of the Exchequer makes up his own mind, I don't see how we can very well know. If anything comes of this meeting, I think we should get the authority of the shareholders in representing our claims and their wishes to the responsible authorities. I also agree with Mr. Joseph Smith as to the necessity of calling upon each company to prepare a statement of the grievances under which it labours. If an institute is formed, these statistics should be collected, as a means to the end we have in view. (Cheers.)

The CHAIRMAN: I have added these words to the resolution:—"And to take such steps for the protection of tramway interests generally as they may think desirable." Gentlemen, I will now read you the resolution :—

Moved by Mr. JOSEPH SMITH, seconded by Mr. Alderman KING (Manchester Carriage Company), and resolved : "That " this conference of representatives of tramway companies " desires to record its sense of the grievances under which " the tramway interests labour in regard to their obligations " for repairs, and the payment of divers rates, taxes and " licenses and other matters. And it is further resolved, " that it is desirable to represent to the proper Government " officials, the Chancellor of the Exchequer, the President of " Local Government Board, the President of the Board of " Trade and others, the views and claims of the above " companies and others, constituting the tramway interests."

Moved by the CHAIRMAN seconded by Mr. JOSEPH SMITH, and resolved : "That the following gentlemen be and they " are hereby constituted a committee for the purpose of " taking the steps indicated and generally of representing " the interests of tramway companies during the progress of " the Budget proposals and of the Local Government Bill " (with power to add to their number, three to form a " quorum), and to take such steps for the protection of " tramway interests generally as they may think desirable, " namely :—

" Mr. W. R. BACON (Chairman London Street Tramways " Company).
" „ E. ETLINGER (Chairman Sheffield Tramway Com- " pany).
" „ C. S. GRUNDY (Chairman Manchester Carriage " Company).
" „ R. HUTCHINSON (Chairman Edinburgh Tramways " Company).
" „ WILLIAM MURPHY, M.P. (Director Dublin Tram- " ways Company).
" „ JOSEPH SMITH (Chairman Birmingham Central " Tramways Company).
" „ WILLIAM TURTON (Chairman Leeds Tramways " Company).
" „ W. J. CARRUTHERS-WAIN (Chairman North " Staffordshire Tramways Company).
" „ S. J. WILDE (Chairman South London Tramways " Company)."
(Carried unanimously.)

The CHAIRMAN: I ought to mention, with regard to the Bill for the examination of persons having charge of steam engines and boilers—a measure of the most absurd character—it met with its deserts, and was rejected by a decided majority.

Mr. JOSEPH SMITH: Gentlemen, I propose that a vote of thanks be accorded to Mr. Carruthers Wain, for his conduct in the chair and for calling us together.

Mr. MURPHY, M.P.: I have much pleasure in seconding the motion.

(Carried unanimously.)

The CHAIRMAN: I am very much obliged, and trust that much good will result from the meeting, and, as you wish, I will try to galvanise the Institute into life.

South Staffordshire Employees

THE SOUTH STAFFORDSHIRE TRAMWAY CO. AND THEIR EMPLOYES.

PRESENTATION TO MR. A. DICKINSON.

The South Staffordshire and Birmingham District Steam Tramway Company entertained their employes, numbering about 150, to dinner at the Anchor Hotel, Wednesbury, on Wednesday night. The host (Mr. Staley) provided an excellent spread, which was well served. The chair was occupied by Mr. W. J. Carruthers Wain (chairman of the company) who was supported by Mr. Davison (director), Mr. Joseph Smith (solicitor), Mr. Byram (contractor), Mr. A. Dickinson (manager), Mr. H. Hatchett (secretary), Mr. Pulden (traffic superintendent), Mr. Partridge and Mr. Jones (members of the office staff), &c.—The toast of "The Queen" was submitted by the Chairman and received with heartiness.—Mr. Joseph Smith proposed the next toast. He remarked that two years ago he asked the men of the South Staffordshire Tramway Company to drink to the prosperity of the company, of which they formed a part and in which their own interests were bound up. He was glad to see a good many that night whom he saw on the occasion to which he had referred. It was a good sign for a tramway company when its old hands stood by it. They gained experience, and experience meant safety. There was a tempering of the old hands among the new ones, whom he was also glad to see. It was an evidence that the company had grown. Now instead of 80 men there were 150. He was very pleased to think that the prospects of the company were improving in other respects as well as in the number of the workpeople. He did not shut his eyes to the fact that the past years had been hard years, not only for those who had invested money in tramway companies but also for those who had worked under tramway companies. Neither did he shut his eyes to the fact that the hours of tramway servants had of necessity to be long, and that the remuneration was not as much as could be desired. But if men were inclined to dwell too much upon that fact, he asked if they worked harder than either the chairman of the company or the manager? Was there any work which they did that Mr. Dickinson shirked—("No.") They knew that all had to work from the top to the bottom if these tramways were to be a success. He called upon them to lend a hand for that purpose. They had every reasonable prospect that it would depend upon themselves as to whether their situations were permanent and remunerative. They had the satisfaction of knowing that a great change had come over the spirit of the people towards them. Some time ago tramways were regarded more or less as a nuisance in the neighbourhood. Now he was glad to say that tramways were regarded as a boon and necessity, and that had been in a very great extent due not only to the admirable management of the company, but also to the care and skill of the drivers, and the watchfulness of the conductors. As a man on the spot, and who had constant opportunities of watching them, he could say that the men of the South Staffordshire Tramway Company would compare favourably with the men of any tramways in the kingdom—(applause). They thoroughly understood that the interests of the company were their interests, and it would be to their benefit to do all they could to enhance those interests. He proposed "Prosperity to the South Staffordshire Tramway Company," coupling with the toast the name of the chairman of the directors (Mr. Wain), than whom there was no more energetic and practical director—(applause).—The toast was drunk with heartiness, after which the chairman responded, thanking those present for the very hearty way in which they had drunk his health. He would not take to himself all the credit that Mr. Smith had been good enough to accord to him. He did his best in the interest of the company, and believed he might say the same of everyone of them. Though he did not see so much of them as Mr. Smith did, yet whether he was in London or Staffordshire he was at all times doing the business of the company. He quite concurred in the remarks of Mr. Smith as to the development of the company, and he believed in its future prosperity. He asked all to unite with the directors in doing the best they could for the shareholders who had built up that line. He was exceedingly pleased to find there was such an unanimous feeling of cordial co-operation between the employers and the Board—(hear, hear.) He should do everything in his power, and his colleagues would unite with him, to promote and assist the personal interests of all the staff connected with that company—(applause). He could only hope that another year they would have as pleasant and cordial a meeting as they were having that night. He had a very agreeable duty to perform, and that was to solicit Mr. Dickinson's acceptance of a substantial mark of the esteem in which as manager he was held by the staff—(applause). He believed it came upon Mr. Dickinson as a surprise, and that they had all conspired together to deceive him—(laughter). It was always very pleasing for a director to be able to speak good words of anyone in the employ of the company; but it was more so when the opportunity was afforded to ask his acceptance of such a substantial token of goodwill. It had been promoted spontaneously, and he believed everyone responded with alacrity to the idea. It was a very great pleasure to be associated with Mr. Dickinson, and singular enough their tenure of office commenced almost simultaneously. He hoped their pleasant intercourse would continue for many years, and he (Mr. Wain) was quite sure he should find in Mr. Dickinson that invaluable assistance, energy, perseverance, and marked attention to his duties which had characterised him in the past—(applause).—The presentation consisted of a handsome marble and bronze timepiece, English gong, and fancy ornaments to match. The time-piece bears the following inscription:—"Presented to Alfred Dickinson, Esq., by the employes of the South Staffordshire and Birmingham District Steam Tramway Company, Limited, on the anniversary of his appointment as general manager, as a mark of their respect and esteem. Darlaston, 17th November, 1886."—Mr. Preston, the locomotive foreman, also added a few remarks, speaking of Mr. Dickinson as straightforward and honourable in his behaviour towards every workman who endeavoured to give satisfaction—(hear, hear).—The "Health of Mr. and Mrs. Dickinson and Family" having been drunk, Mr. Dickinson acknowledged the presentation, and expressed his appreciation of the kindly feeling which had prompted it.—"The health of the officers of the company" was proposed by the Chairman, who coupled with the toast the name of Mr. Hatchett, whom he described as their "popular" secretary.—Mr. Hatchett replied in suitable terms.—During the evening songs were contributed by Messrs. H. Hatchett, W. Robinson, and W. Hill, Mr. Jones acting as accompanist.

The Speed of a Tram

It is a fact of life that every day, justly or not, many drivers will be caught speeding. Even doing 32mph overtaking someone looking for a parking space can cost serious money, whereas a fleet of Jaguars or Fords can overtake the same driver on the motorway doing something over 100mph – they will probably be an MP and his entourage, plus police outriders, or just as likely a footballer, and they won't be prosecuted. If the innocent driver has the time/money/good solicitor he or she could try to defend themselves, but since the photograph will have been taken by a robot and the summons issued by a robot (it will not be long before the case will be tried by a robot) the driver will be just as guilty (or not) as reported in the following case reported in the *Birmingham & Aston Chronicle*, November 29, 1884 under the heading 'Local Chit-Chat'.

"Judging from the proceedings taken at the Birmingham Police Court on Monday, against a driver on one of the Birmingham and Aston steam trams, our energetic P.C.'s are keeping an 'heye' on these convenient modes of conveyances. It was alleged that the driver was running his car at a rate of more than eight miles an hour, the maximum speed allowed by the bye-laws of the Borough. Two police officers and an omnibus driver stated that the car was being driven at from ten to twelve miles an hour, while one of the officers swore that, according to his watch, the car covered a distance of 280 yards – from Aston Bridge to Dartmouth street – in 45 seconds, or at a rate of 10 miles an hour. It appeared that the mechanical indication attached to the engine showed that the time occupied on the journey in question from Aston Lower Grounds to Old Square – a distance of two-and-a-half miles – was 25 minutes or a little over five miles an hour; while an inspector in the company's employ, who in the execution of his duty watched and entered a large number of cars daily, gave it as his opinion that at the time mentioned by the officer the car was only going at about seven and a half miles an hour. It was pointed out very pertinently for the defence that almost the only person who could prove the actual speed of the engine was the defendant, and he, of course, could not be called. Mr Mathews, who appeared for the defendant, urged that the police should summon the company and then Billings, the man alleged to have offended, could give evidence. Mr Mathews also argued that it was absurd to set the evidence of officers who were guided by such watches as they possessed against the mechanical indicator approved by the Board of Trade. Despite Mr Mathew's eloquence and arguments the magistrates fined the unfortunate driver 10s and costs, both of which it is to be hoped the company will not allow the poor man to pay. Mr Mathews was undoubtedly right in his contention that the charge should have been brought against the Company, and in that case I doubt very much whether the magisterial wisdom of Moor-street could have resisted the combined evidence of conductor, inspector and driver, for he also corroborated Mr Mathews. The case only shows the occasional hardship which ensues when the defendant by law is not allowed a hearing. So far as my own experience goes, the Birmingham and Aston cars at times go at a wretchedly slow pace for steam cars allowed to run eight miles an hour – and the stoppages are most tedious. On this occasion my readers will notice the car was only proceeding at five miles an hour. An average pedestrian will go into town in half-an-hour and have a few minutes to turn about in, and in this case the steam car took 26 minutes to do it in. If this sort of thing goes on when we are in a hurry we shall do like the swell in Punch's cartoon – get out and walk."

Concessions gained by TGWU

TO ENGINEMEN AND FIREMEN WHO HAVE NOT YET JOINED US.

"The following list of concessions have been gained by the Union: –

April 10th – The following concessions were gained for 60 Tram Drivers at Rochdale (the men have been working on an average 15 hours a day, previous to this alteration):– They will now work 5 days during the week, 12 hours; on Sunday, 10 hours. Dinner hour and tea is allowed and included in the 12. All hours worked over and above the above-named 12 and 10 will be paid for at the rate of 6d. per hour. All Drivers, after a term of three years' service, to be paid 5/6 per day, as per the new alteration, which comes into effect on May 2nd. …

On June 11th, after a five weeks strike, the Steam Tram Drivers and Guards at Wigan obtained a reduction from 14 hours and 40 minutes to a 12 hours day. The company had been able to fill the whole of our members' positions with knobsticks. We, however, so aroused the public sympathy that they refused to ride in the cars with knobstick drivers. This lever placed the directors in a corner. I then suggested a Board of Conciliation. The directors agreed to this, and signed to abide by the award given by the five gentlemen chosen. They sat on June 11th and the following was their award – 1st, That the 32 old employees of the Tramway Company should be reinstated to their various positions on Monday, June 14th. 2nd, That the 32 present employees should be discharged, and that they be allowed a fortnight's wages as compensation in lieu of notice. Such compensation to be paid as follows – Two-thirds by the Tramway Company, and one-third by the men's Union.

On July 1st, the Steam Tram and Electric Tram Drivers on the Birmingham Central Tram Company obtained a ten hours day, the wages to be paid at the following rate: - New beginners 6d. per hour, to rise according to length of service to 7½d., the length of service already put in to count. …

Birmingham and Aston Tram Co. We have obtained a ten hours day for the drivers without any reduction in wages. Will other steam tram drivers do likewise. …

At Aston, one of the Steam Tram drivers was summoned by the police for excessive speed. This the driver could not help, owing to the sand pipe being broken, and the steam brake would not act. The manager informed the driver he would have to pay fine and costs, if such were inflicted. The driver reported this to the Union. The matter was taken up, which resulted in the Tram Company paying all fines.

Bradford and Shelf Tram Company. On November 1st we were successful in obtaining a reduction in hours to ten hours per day. The men to be paid at the rate of 6d. per hour, all extra trips to be paid at 6d. per hour, which previously have been done for nothing.

Nov. 16 – We obtained for the Steam Tram Drivers on the Birmingham and Midland Tram Company, a ten hours day, to be paid for as follows: - Fresh drivers to start at 5¼d. First year, 5¾d. per hour, second year 6d., third 6½d., fourth year 6¾d. Coupled with this, a bonus of £1 1s a quarter.

In December, at Birmingham, we obtained £60 and all expenses for one of the Tram Drivers, who was injured by a Messrs. White & Co's. Waggon running into the front of his Engine. …

1898. April, – Concessions gained by the Tram Drivers on the Central Tram Co., Birmingham. – Time and a Quarter for Sunday work, where only bare time was paid."

This document is drawn from files held at the Modern Records Centre, Coventry, and is reproduced with permission of the Transport & General Workers Union, to whom we extend our thanks. I would add, personally, I am glad to make this entry – whatever may be said of their perceived faults, the TGWU has long been a staunch supporter of transport workers.

Drunk in Charge of a Tram

DRUNK WHILST IN CHARGE OF A TRAM ENGINE.

At the Wednesbury Police Court on Tuesday, before Messrs. J. H. Pearson and S. Stokes (magistrates), Abraham Earp, engine-driver in the employ of the Birmingham and South Staffordshire District Steam Tramway Company, and residing in Walsall Road, Darlaston, was charged with being drunk whilst in charge of his engine on Saturday night. Mr. Geo. Rose (Messrs. Smith and Co.) appeared on behalf of the Tramway Company, and stated that the defendant, after driving his engine from Walsall to Wednesbury, was taking it to Darlaston. On proceeding down the incline near the tram depot he ran into another car which was standing there, doing damage to the extent of £60. He was fetched off the engine and found to be intoxicated. The manager at once gave him into the custody of the police. The offence was a most serious one, and the company found it necessary to bring such a case before them. Whilst they did not press the charge, they would not, on the other hand, ask the magistrates to deal leniently with it. If the conductor had happened to have been standing on the car which was run into he would in all probability have been killed. The company had found in previous cases that the imposition of a small fine had very little effect, as the men, with that clannishness which distinguished them, clubbed together and paid the fine in that way. It was only fair to Earp to say that he had been a good servant, and was usually very steady. — Alfred Dickinson, manager of the Tramway Company, stated that about half-past eleven on Saturday night he was sent for to the entrance of the tram depot at Darlaston. He there saw Earp on his engine in a state of intoxication. He spoke to Earp and quite convinced himself that he was under the influence of drink. The defendant had been in the service of the company three years, and had been one of their best men. There had been no previous complaint against him.—P.S Curtis stated that the defendant was drunk; he staggered about a good deal, but was able to talk right enough. —Defendant stated that he never took much drink. Having had no tea on Saturday night he drank half-a-pint of ale, and it overcame him. He asked the Bench to deal leniently with him, promising that he never again would touch intoxicants.—Mr. Rose said the company wished to impress their servants with the fact that this was far more serious than an ordinary charge of drunkenness.—Mr. Stokes: Exactly. Those in charge of these engines on the highway must be men of sobriety; that was very essential.—The magistrates imposed a fine of £1 and the costs, or one month's imprisonment in default of payment.

30 July 1887. *West Bromwich Weekly News:*

"A tram conductor had to leave his car by The Dartmouth [Inn] and while he was away his box containing £4 in takings was stolen. 'The conductor was an honest, hard working man and has now to submit to a deduction of a half-a-crown [2s.6d.] weekly from his meagre wages. Hard lines that.' The writer 'Man about Town' went on to say that at very least the company ought to bear some part of the loss, or carry some insurance."

Charge Against a Tramway Manager

"At the Borough Police Court yesterday, William Dinnon (45), tramway manager, Trindle Road, was charged on remand with indecently assaulting Charlotte Bishop, a married women, of Kinver. – Mr William Shakespeare defended. – Prosecutrix said she was the wife of John Bishop, a boatman. On Tuesday week, the 28th ult., shortly after 11 o'clock, she came by the last tramcar from Holly Hall. Defendant and another man were the only other occupants. As soon as she sat down, defendant asked her where she was going. She replied that she was going to Kinver, but was too late, and was returning to her mother's at Gornal. She asked the conductor, in the hearing of the defendant, to stop the car at the corner of the road leading to Gornal. The car stopped before she noticed that it had passed Wolverhampton Street, and asked where she was. She was told she was at Dudley Station, and she said she ought to have got off to go to Gornal. Defendant said, "I'll show you a near way to Gornal," and she went with him across some fields. Defendant pointed to some lights in front, and said, "That's Shaver's End." They passed under a rail, and she said, "I don't like this way: I don't think it's the road to Gornal." He replied, "You needn't be afraid of me, I am a respectable married man," and she replied, "And I am a respectable married woman." When they had crossed the field he put his arms round her waist, pushed her backwards on to the ground, and acted improperly. She struggled with him, and at last got up. While she struggled with him he said what his intention was. He took hold of her, struck her on the forehead, and tried to throw her down again, but she took hold of a rail and prevented him. During this time she screamed "Police" and "Murder", and defendant drew a knife and said "If you scream again, I'll put this in you." She continued screaming, and defendant ran away, and William Fellows came up. She became unconscious, and when P.S. Speake and others came up with the defendant, she identified defendant as the man who had assaulted her. – Mr Shakespeare: How many husbands have you? I have had two. – How many have you now? Only one, sir, – What was your name formerly? Charlotte Thomas. – What was your maiden name? Roberts. Her first husband died in Powick Asylum between seven and eight years ago. – Do you swear that your first husband died at Powick Asylum? Yes, sir. – When? I don't know when it was. – Who told you that your first husband was dead? A policeman at Kidderminster. – What policeman was it? I don't know, sir, but the superintendent told me to get married again – (laughter). – Upon your oath did any policeman ever tell you this? Yes, sir. – Where? In the Bull Ring, against "Baxter," at Kidderminster. – Don't you know that your husband lives at Wolverhampton now? No. – Haven't you seen him within the last two months? No. She went to see him at the asylum once and he told her she was no wife of his. She had not seen him since he came out. She admitted, under great pressure, having been fined four times for using obscene language; and also that on the night in question she had been at Samuel Share's public-house, Holly Hall, and that she had been at Shorthouse's public-house with Share, who was her cousin. – Mr Shakespeare: When you got into the car didn't you go to Mr Dinnon and catch hold of his whiskers and say he was a nice young man? No, I didn't. – Did you fall over Mr Price, who was sitting next to him? No, sir. She did not say she had spent 15s. all but 3d., and ask them to give her a penny to enable her to get a bed in Dudley. The conductor did not tell her at Stafford Street that that was the nearest stopping place to Gornal, or at Wolverhampton Street that that was the only stopping place for Gornal. At the station she did not ask the conductor "Where are you going to, my dear?" nor did she tell him she was going to sleep with him. It was not true that about nine months ago she persuaded William Coley to go along the canal side, and then commenced shouting. Sergeant Head was fetched to her one Good Friday, but it was through the neighbours, and not because she had attempted to commit suicide. She had not lived with a man named Butler, and did not know "Americky" Sam. – William Fellows, stone miner, Kate's Hill, said that between 12 and one on the morning in question he heard screams of "Murder," and ran across the fields, where he found the prosecutrix leaning over a rail. She said a fellow who was running down the side of the hedge, had threatened to kill her with a knife. – David Wiltshire gave similar evidence, and said when he got to her prosecutrix was unconscious. Witness went down the field and had a smoke, and defendant came from under the hedge. Witness said "I believe you're the person that's wanted concerning this woman," and he jumped over the rails. Witness shouted for the police, and they fetched him back. – Sergeant Spoke said that he and P.C. Clarke heard the screams in Fisher Street. Bishop was unconscious. Wiltshire shouted, and they went after the man. Witness said "Hallo, Mr Dinnon, that you." and he made no reply. They took him to the woman, who was just recovering consciousness, and she identified him as her assailant. Defendant replied to the effect that was all stuff, she was drunk. – P.C. Clarke corroborated. – Frank Williams, booking clerk, said he saw the defendant and a "lady" together on the railway bridge on the night in question, but he could not identify the prosecutrix. – Mrs Wigley said she examined prosecutrix, and found her underlinen very much torn and soiled. She had no bruises, except one on the side of her face. – By Mr Shakespeare: As far as she could tell it was a recent tear. – Mr Shakespeare said the Bench would agree with him that this was one of those charges it was most easy to prefer, and most difficult to rebut. An abandoned woman, without any very strong claims of honour or truth, might very easily damage the character of a respectable and straightforward man, if she could induce a Bench of Magistrates to believe her statement, and unless it could be shaken in some way or other. Fortunately in this case he had the means at his command of satisfying the Magistrates beyond all doubt, that if ever there was a wicked untruthful charge, this was one. It would be clearly shown that the woman had committed perjury. This was not the first trick she had played for the purpose of extorting money, but fortunately in this case the accused had the courage and manliness to say he would not submit to the extortion, but would face the wicked charge out in a Court of Justice. – Alfred Price, assistant clerk to the Kingswinford School Board, and the Brierley Hill Local Board, said that the prosecutrix got into the car at Hart's Hill. She was excited, nearly drunk, and caught hold of Mr Dinnon's whiskers, and said "What a nice young man you are." The car stopped at Holly Hall, and she wanted to go into some house, but seeing the lights out she made use of bad language and said she would go on to Dudley. She said she had spent 15s. all but 3½d. and asked for money. – Eliza Shorthouse, publican, Hart's Hill, said that Bishop was at her house from about nine until 11 o'clock drinking with a man with whom she went in. She had since told witness she didn't mind making the case up with the gentleman for the sake of his wife and family. – Martin Cadman, conductor, said prosecutrix told him to put her down at "American Sam's" at Holly Hall, who was her mother's cousin, and who had promised her a bed. She added "He's a widower, and I'm a widow". – (laughter). Finding he had gone to bed, she came on to Dudley, and witness told her both at Stafford Street and Wolverhampton Street the way to Gornal. She replied "I'm going to the station along with you." At the station she said "Ay, my love, I want you." He replied, "All right, my dear, what do you want" – (laughter). She said she was going with him, but he went to the driver, and saw no more of her. – Sergeant Head, of Kinver, said Bishop was very much addicted to drink, and he had sent for to her house. On the 3rd April it was reported that she had jumped into the river Stour, and her husband ordered him to lock her up. – By Mr Barndale: He was not aware she had ever made a charge of this kind before. – William Coley, Kinver, spoke to accompanying prosecutrix part of the way home along the canal side on one occasion. When they got about 30 yards, she shouted "Murder", and jumped three times into the canal. – Without hearing other witnesses for the defence, the Mayor said the Bench had come to the decision that the evidence was not sufficient to convict, and the accused would be discharged – (applause)."

"ACTION BY A TRAMWAY MANAGER – DINNON v THE DUDLEY AND STOURBRIDGE TRAMWAY COMPANY.

An action was brought by Mr William Dinnon, late manager for the defendant company, to recover £45 2s 11d. as commission on transactions connected with his office, and for money paid out of pocket on behalf of the company.- Mr Waldron appeared for the bailiff, and Mr Stubbins (instructed by Messrs Brabazon and Cameron) for the defendants. – In opening Mr Waldron contended that the plaintiff was entitled to a commission of two per cent. on the amount available for dividend, within the meaning of a resolution passed by the company. As to the claim for out of pocket, it was argued that Mr Dinnon was entrusted with a petty cash account, and authorised from time to time to pay certain disbursements. In pursuance of that authority, he paid away several small sums for accidents that occurred on the tramways, and other matters. – Mr Dinnon said he had several sums from the secretary to the company (Mr Woodward) to pay away according to his discretion. Plaintiff presented a book to the secretary, and he balanced it from time to time. The money paid away included an account to Mr G. Matthews for repairs to a trap damaged by one of the company's engines. Other sums were paid for accidents, including a fatal accident to a child, and some sheep. – The plaintiff was subjected to a long cross-examination, with a view to showing that Mr Dinnon did not receive direct authority from the company to pay this money, and was going beyond the scope of his power in doing so.

His Honour asked if there was any reason for saying Mr Dinnon had not acted fairly or honestly with the company, and if he had not, why did they quibble as to the amount? It appeared to him that Dinnon had paid the money and settled the claims to the best of his discretion and in good faith; therefore, the company would have to pay him. Mr Stubbins said there was more behind the affair than a settling up after Dinnon was leaving, but he had no instruction to bring the matter forward.

Finally, His Honour decided that Dinnon was entitled to 2 per cent. on £1,493 and the other items, making a total of £33 18s 11d. with costs on that sum."

This latter item appeared in *The Dudley Herald*, Saturday 3 April, 1886, but unfortunately for some reason the date reference to the other case has been mislaid, and if I am honest I have no idea which date applies, other than he was a 'Manager' in the first case and a 'late manager' in the second. There is obviously a lot more waiting to be studied on Mr Dinnon's life; the only trace I could find was of a William Dinnon being a 'Hotel Manager' in 1888. It is also interesting to note how his title 'Mr' appears early in the case, but changes to a plain 'Dinnon' towards the end. Was some whispering attack going on which affected the reporter?

Charges Against Tramcar Conductors

Dudley Herald, 5 January 1895:
"The charge against a Local Tramway Manager:- Yesterday, at Wolverhampton Police Court, Edward Banner, formerly manager of the Wolverhampton & Dudley Tramways Co., and now of the Talbot Hotel, Wellesbourne, near Warwick, was committed to take his trial on charges of falsification and Larceny, bail being allowed defendant in £100, and four securities of £30 each."

Birmingham Daily Gazette, 10 October 1887:
"West Bromwich – Theft by tramcar conductor
At the Police Court on Saturday [8 October] Joshea Moore, a tramcar conductor, of Oldbury Road, West Smethwick, was charged with stealing a bag and a quantity of cigars belonging to Stephen Cashmore on the 25 September. It appeared that the bag was left on top of a tramcar and the prisoner took it home. He was fined 20s and costs, or in default 21 days."

Dudley Herald, 3 October 1885:
"Editorial Jottings
I don't know whether a fragrant breach of the bye-laws of the D & S Tramway Co has been reported to the management. If it has not, it ought to be. On Monday afternoon, a bibulous looking individual, well-known to the conductor, entered the car, smoking a cigar. Remonstrances from the conductor were of no avail, nor were those of the passengers, one of whom was rudely insulted by the offender. Byelaws, to be effective, must be adhered to, and though I don't object to smoking, I object to the existence of one law for well-known individuals, and another for ordinary travellers."

Suicide of a Tram Conductor

"SUICIDE OF A TRAM CONDUCTOR AT BOURNBROOK: [9 June 1888]

Mr Edwin Docker (Coroner) held an inquiry at the Bournbrook Hotel yesterday morning, touching the death of Stephen Henry Foreman (38) who was found drowned in the canal at Selly Oak on Wednesday morning. William John Greaves, inspector in the employ of the Birmingham Central Tramway Company, said that about a fortnight ago he engaged the deceased as conductor on the Bristol Road route. Deceased told witness on Saturday last that there would soon be a man short, as he did not like the terms. He ceased work the same day, and on Tuesday afternoon last witness accompanied him to the office in the Old Square to ascertain what wages were due to him. It was found that he was £1. 5s. 10d. short in the traffic receipts, and that amount having been deducted, there were 2s. due for wages. This was paid over to him, and he afterwards went to Bournbrook Hotel, and remained there until closing time, when he appeared to be perfectly sober and in good spirits. Thomas Walker, boatman deposed to finding the body of the deceased in the Worcester Canal on Wednesday morning, and Police-Sergeant Holmes, of Selly Oak, produced the property found in his possession. The paper, in envelope shape, was directed to "Mrs. Foreman, 15 Hilda Terrace, Tramway Avenue, Lower Edmonton" and on the inside was written, "For my dear beloved wife, God bless her and the dear children, and may the Lord always look after them. I am pleased to say my Lord has called me from this wicked world. God bless her and all the dear children for my sake". Another piece of paper bore a similar inscription. Amongst other papers found on the deceased was his discharge sheet from the London, Brighton and South Coast Railway, after twelve years service, and also his discharge from the 14th Hussars. These, together with numerous letters, gave him an excellent character. A verdict of "Suicide whilst temporarily insane" was returned."

I feel very great sympathy for Stephen Foreman. Most conductors at one time or another have had to make up 'shortages'; few managements of large companies having any sympathy when, for example, forged coins were passed over, a crowded tram on Friday night gave one precious little time to use a coin tester. For totally different reasons we once had a suicide of a man from our bus garage; he had spent all his wages in the fruit machines at our social club. He was a known gambler and to this day I find it morally wrong that the management acceded to putting temptation in front of a man like that. He could not face his wife but declined our offers of loans.

In the case of Stephen Foreman one can only guess how he felt receiving just 10 pence for probably 120 hours work. Surely an inspector should have found his 'shorts' in the first day or two and helped sort out the causes? This was the downside of steam tram work.

Swansea Tramways Band

BET Gazette, 15 November 1905.

SOCIAL AMENITIES.

—•◦•—

SWANSEA TRAMWAYS BAND.
MAYOR ATTENDS FIRST CONCERT.

We have much pleasure in culling the following paragraphs from the *Cambrian Daily Leader* of October 31, 1905:—

"The first annual concert of the Swansea Tramways Band was held at the King's Hall on Monday evening. Notwithstanding other attractions, the hall was well filled, and a programme of exceptional excellence was gone through. The evening opened with a selection by the band, followed by a glee by the Pentrechwyth Male Voice Party, which went so well that an encore had to be given. Miss Miriam Morgan delighted the audience with a sweet song, and Mr. Griff Lewis was heard at his best in "The Veteran." Mr. Griff Charles sang that pretty ditty of Stephen Adams's, "Blue-eyed Nancy," and Mr. John Mullins proved a fine cornet player. Master Lewis Hart, the sweet-voiced boy contralto, also contributed to the success of the evening; and Mr. W. H.

Jones's elocutionary efforts were perfectly delightful.

"But the tit-bit of the whole programme was the Lauder impersonations of Mr. Alf. Thomas. After rendering a couple of Lauder's old songs, he introduced "The Wedding of Lauchie M'Graw," an excruciatingly funny ditty. To say the least of it, Mr. Thomas went 'strong.'

"The excellent playing of the band was prominent, and a fine combination of artistes had been got together. It is to be hoped that the concert will be an annual event.

"In the course of the evening the Mayor (Alderman Spring) expressed the satisfaction he felt at the advance made by the band. The Swansea tramway system was at present equal to that of any town in the kingdom, and he was sure that there was general recognition of the efforts of their genial manager to meet the needs of the town in every direction. (Applause.) Mr. James was always approachable, and so far as was consistent with the interests of the company, ready to comply with the many requests made to him. It was a capital thing to have such good relations as existed between the manager and the employees. (Applause.)"

Fidelity and Workmen's Compensation

THE GENERAL ACCIDENT ASSURANCE CORPORATION LIMITED

CAPITAL £100,000

AMOUNT GUARANTEED.		PREMIUM.
£ 150	No. G 1674	£ 2:5:

Manager & Secretary—F. NORIE MILLER.

Chief Offices · VICTORIA BUILDINGS · PERTH.

LONDON OFFICES, 4, ABCHURCH YARD, KING WILLIAM STREET, E.C.

Whereas *The Blackburn and Over Darwen Tramways Company*

C19 Queen Avenue, Liverpool

hereinafter called "the Employer," has employed or agreed to employ as *Cashier — Charles Francis Collins*

47 Mill Lane, Blackburn

hereinafter called "the Employed," and hath applied to THE GENERAL ACCIDENT ASSURANCE CORPORATION, LIMITED, hereinafter called "the Corporation," to enter into this Agreement to Guarantee:

And whereas the said Employer has delivered to the Corporation certain statements, and a declaration setting forth, among other things, the duties and remuneration of the said Employed, the moneys to be entrusted to him, and the checks to be kept upon his accounts, and hath consented that such declaration, and each and every statement therein referred to or contained, shall form the basis of the contract hereinafter expressed to be made:

And whereas there has been paid to the Corporation the sum mentioned above, and designated *Premium*, as a premium for one year from the *First* day of *September* 1896:

Now it is hereby declared and agreed that, fully relying on the truth of the said statements and declaration, and on the strict performance and observance hereafter by the said Employer of the contract thereby and hereby created, and subject to the conditions herein contained, and which conditions shall be conditions precedent to the right of the said Employer to recover under this Agreement (except so far as they relate to anything which is not capable of being performed until after payment by the Corporation), the Corporation, during the period aforesaid, and during any year thereafter in respect of which the Corporation shall consent to accept and the Employer or Employed shall pay on the *First* day of *September* 1897, or within Fifteen Days from such date, the aforesaid Premium shall, at the expiration of Three Months next, after proof satisfactory to the Directors of the loss hereinafter mentioned has been given to the Corporation, make good and reimburse to the Employer to the extent of the sum above designated as the *amount guaranteed* and no further, all moneys which the Employed in connection with the duties hereinbefore referred to shall fraudulently embezzle and apply to his own use, and which fraudulent embezzlement shall be committed and discovered during the continuance of this Agreement, or as hereinafter mentioned.

Provided, That on the discovery or the receipt of notice of any fraud or defalcation on the part of the Employed, or of reasonable cause for suspicion thereof, the Employer or other party entitled to make a claim in respect of this Policy shall immediately give written notice thereof to the Corporation at its Chief Office, and the Agreement shall become *absolutely void both as to existing and all future liabilities if such Employer or other party neglect or omit for seven days after making such discovery or receiving such notice,* to forward written notice as aforesaid to the Corporation, and that after such written notice shall have been given by the Employer or other party entitled to make such claim to the Directors the Agreement shall be absolutely void and of no effect with regard to any subsequent act of embezzlement on the part of the Employed.

Provided also, That before any payment shall be made under this Agreement, the full particulars of all claims under it shall be delivered to the Directors, and no claim shall be made for a part only of the liability under this Agreement, but every claim must be complete and final, and must be made within three calendar months of the discovery of any act of embezzlement, and within three months after the death, dismissal, or retirement of the party employed, and shall not be made afterwards, and the Corporation shall be entitled to call for, at the Employer's expense, such reasonable particulars and proofs of the correctness of such claim and of the correctness of the statements made at the time of effecting or deemed to be made at any renewal of this Agreement, as the Directors for the time being may require, and to have the same, or any of them, verified by statutory declaration. And no more than one claim, and that only in respect of acts or defaults committed within the period of twelve months or any lesser period during which this Agreement shall have been in force previous to the date of the receipt by the Corporation of such notice as aforesaid, shall be made under this Agreement, which upon the making of such claim shall wholly cease and determine, and shall be given up discharged on the payment of such claim. And this Agreement is granted on the condition that the business of the Employer shall continue to be conducted and the duties and remuneration of the Employed shall remain in every particular in accordance with the statements, and each of them, and declaration hereinbefore referred to, and if during the continuance of this Agreement any circumstance shall occur or change be made, which shall have the effect of making the actual facts differ from such statements or any of them, without notice thereof being given to the Corporation at its Chief Office, and the consent or approval in writing of the Corporation being obtained, or if any suppression or mis-statement of any fact affecting the risk of the Corporation be made at the time of payment of the first or any subsequent premium, or if the Employer shall continue to trust the Employed with money after having discovered any act of fraud or dishonesty as aforesaid, this Agreement shall be void, and all Premiums paid thereon forfeited to the Corporation.

Provided also, That the Employer shall, if and when required by the Corporation, but at the expense of the Corporation if a conviction be obtained, use all diligence in prosecuting the Employed to conviction for any fraud or dishonesty, as aforesaid, which he shall have committed, and in consequence of which a claim shall have been made under this Agreement, and shall, at the Corporation's expense, give all information and assistance to enable the Corporation to sue for and obtain reimbursement by the Employed or by his estate, of any moneys which the Corporation shall have become liable to pay.

Provided also, That if the Employer shall at the date of this Agreement, or any time thereafter, be guaranteed or hold any securities against loss covered hereby, the Corporation shall only be liable to make good any such loss rateably and in just proportion to the amount of such other guarantee or securities ; and if any difference shall arise as to whether the Corporation is liable hereunder, or as to the amount of its liability, if any, the same shall, before any proceedings are taken, be referred to the Arbitration of two neutral persons, one to be chosen by each party, who may appoint an Oversman or Umpire in the usual way, with power to them to call witnesses, hear parties, and fully determine the matters in dispute, and to give expenses or costs in his or their discretion, and in case the Employer shall not, within fourteen days after request in writing from the Corporation, name an Arbitrator, the Arbitrator of the Corporation may proceed alone ; and the award of such Arbitrators, Arbitrator, Oversman, or Umpire, shall be binding, and if in England, such Arbitration may be made a rule of the High Court, and no action or proceeding at Law shall be brought or prosecuted on this Agreement, except for the sum so awarded, and expenses or costs, if any ; and any sums payable under this Agreement, or any award made in pursuance thereof, shall be payable only at the Registered Office of the Corporation, and upon the delivery up of this Agreement properly discharged.

Provided also, That the Employer or other party entitled to make a claim under the Agreement shall, at his own expense, on being required so to do by the Directors or their Agents, produce all books, accounts, and receipts, and furnish copies of such of them as may be required by the Directors or their Agents, so far as they relate to such claim, or will in any way enable the Directors or their Agents to ascertain the correctness thereof, or the liability of the Corporation under the Policy.

Provided also, That any salary or commission which, but for the act or acts of embezzlement on which the claim shall be founded, would have become payable by the Employer to the Employed as aforesaid, or any other money which shall be due to the Employed from the Employer, shall be deducted from the amount payable under this Agreement, and that all moneys, estate, and effects of the Employed, in the hands of or received or possessed by the Employer, and all sums which may be or may become due from the Employer to the Employed, and also all moneys or effects which shall come into the possession or power of the Employer for or on account of the Employed, after discovery of any act on the part of the Employed, whereupon any claim shall be made on this Agreement, shall be applied by the Employer in and towards making good the amount of his claim under this Agreement, in priority to any person claiming upon such moneys, estate, or effects.

Signed for and on behalf of the Corporation this *Ninth* — day of *September* 1896-.

Entered *R.H.*

Examined *G.*

} *Two of the Directors*
of the Corporation.

Secretary.

L. 1000/2/95.

ENDORSEMENT No. *1031*

It is hereby agreed and declared that the interest in respect of this Policy is now vested in favour of *The Mayor, Aldermen and Burgesses of the County Borough of Blackburn* notwithstanding anything herein contained to the contrary.

Dated at Perth, this *Nineteenth* day of *January* 1899.

Manager and Secretary.

Entd. *E.H.*

Examd. *G.*

The General Accident
Assurance Corporation, Ltd.

Head Offices, - - PERTH.

FIDELITY GUARANTEE AGREEMENT

No. G *1674* —

FOR THE FIDELITY OF

Mr *Charles Francis Collins* —

WHILE IN THE EMPLOYMENT OF

Messrs *The Blackburn & Over* —
Darwen Tramways Co. —

Agency :

William Hilton —

No Receipts for the Renewal Premiums on this Policy are
valid but the Official Receipts signed by the
Secretary of the Corporation.

WORKMEN'S COMPENSATION INSURANCE.

LIVERPOOL OFFICE
6, CASTLE STREET,
THOMAS McPHERSON,
RESIDENT SECRETARY.

THE GENERAL ACCIDENT ASSURANCE CORPORATION LIMITED

CAPITAL £250,000.

BOARD OF DIRECTORS.

PATRICK HUNTER, Esq., J.P., of Waterybutts, Errol, Perthshire, *Chairman*.
ROBERT PATERSON, Esq., C.A. (Messrs. Paterson, Newlands & Co.), Glasgow, *Vice-Chairman*.
Sir ROBERT D. MONCREIFFE, Bart. of Moncreiffe, D.L. and J.P. of Perthshire.
HENRY COATES, Esq., F.R.S.E. (Messrs. Coates Bros., Limited, Manufacturers), Pitcullen, Perth.
A. H. B. CONSTABLE, Esq., Advocate, Edinburgh.
Lieut.-Colonel H. S. HOME DRUMMOND, of Blair-Drummond, Vice-Lieut. and J.P., Convener of County of Perth.
Ex-Bailie GEORGE KYD, Hilton, Perth.
D. M. MACKAY, Esq. (Messrs. Jameson & Mackay, Solicitors), Perth.
D. J. WILSON, Esq., J.P., Banker, Perth.

PRINCIPAL BRANCHES.

LIVERPOOL—50 CASTLE STREET.
MANCHESTER—6 PRINCESS STREET.
BIRMINGHAM—119 COLMORE ROW.
NOTTINGHAM—23 KING STREET.
NEWCASTLE-ON-TYNE—3 NELSON ST.
BRISTOL—2 SMALL STREET.
SOUTHAMPTON—"CLAREMONT," LANDGUARD ROAD.
BELFAST—14 WELLINGTON PLACE.
CARLISLE—38 SCOTCH STREET.
LEEDS—26 AND 27 BOND STREET.
GLASGOW—23 RENFIELD STREET.
EDINBURGH—20 ALBANY STREET.
ABERDEEN—129 UNION STREET.
DUNDEE—1 COMMERCIAL STREET.
CARDIFF—QUAY STREET CHAMBERS.
DUBLIN—39 FLEET STREET.

Policy No. W. 676

Wages, £ 2,300

Due 1st July

Premium, £ 17 : 5 : 0

MANAGER & SECRETARY—F. NORIE MILLER.

Chief Offices · VICTORIA BUILDINGS · PERTH.

LONDON OFFICES. - 115 TO 117 CANNON STREET, E.C.

Whereas Messrs. The Blackburn and Over Darwen Tramways Company, 6 19, Queen Avenue, Liverpool, Steam Tramway Proprietors

hereinafter called the "Employer" by a proposal in writing, signed by or on behalf of the said Employer, dated the twenty-third day of June 1898, has applied to **The General Accident Assurance Corporation, Limited,** hereinafter called the "Corporation," for an indemnity against all such liabilities as hereinafter mentioned, which proposal the said Employer has agreed shall be the basis of this contract, and shall be considered as incorporated herein, and has paid to the Corporation the sum of Seventeen pounds five shillings as premium, subject to adjustment as hereinafter mentioned, for such indemnity for twelve calendar months from noon on the first day of July One Thousand Eight Hundred and Ninety-eight.

2. **Now it is hereby agreed as follows:**—The Corporation shall, subject as hereinafter expressed, during the period covered by the Premium so paid as aforesaid, or any further period in respect of which the Corporation shall accept a Premium or Premiums, pay and make good to the Employer all sums which the Employer shall become liable to pay under or by virtue of "The Workmen's Compensation Act, 1897," "The Employers' Liability Act, 1880," or (subject to the limitation of amount expressed in clause No. 3) at Common Law, as and for compensation for personal injury by accident caused to any Workman in his service, while engaged in the Employer's work in any of the occupations, and at any of the places mentioned in the Schedules hereto, and whether in the immediate service of the Employer or in that of any Sub-Contractor who may have been executing work for the Employer, provided that the wages of such workman shall have been included in the accounts kept by the Employer for the purposes of this Policy, as stipulated in clause No. 5. Such payment to be made immediately upon receipt by the Directors of the Corporation of satisfactory evidence of the liability of the Corporation in respect of which the sum is claimed.

3. **Provided also,** that the Corporation shall indemnify the Employer in respect of any sum he may become liable by the Common Law to pay by way of compensation as aforesaid up to but not beyond the amount of three years' earnings of the injured workman, to be estimated in accordance with the provisions of "The Employers' Liability Act, 1880."

4. **Provided also,** that any weekly compensation payable by the Employer in respect of claims under "The Workmen's Compensation Act, 1897," shall only be paid to the injured workman provided he agrees to accept the payment of such compensation in full of all claims either under "The Employers' Liability Act" or at Common Law; and no weekly payment shall be made without the previous authority of the Corporation, to whose instructions and requirements with regard to medical certificates or to the continuance of any payment the Employer shall conform.

5. **Provided also,** that the premium on this Policy, and on each renewal thereof, shall be calculated on the amount of wages on the classification of the occupations, and on the liabilities of the Company, as stated in the Schedules hereto, or as from time to time declared by the Employer to be the amount estimated by him to be payable during each period of insurance in respect of which the premium is paid, and at the end of each period of insurance the Employer shall furnish to the Corporation an account of the amount of wages and bonuses or other allowances of any and every kind actually paid by the Employer (due regard being had in such account of the classification of occupations and liabilities before mentioned) direct, or by or through persons in his service, or by sub-contractors during the same period; and if the amount differs from the amount for which premium has been paid, the premium on the difference shall be paid by or allowed to the Employer according as the wages and bonuses or other allowances actually so paid as aforesaid may have exceeded or fallen short of the estimated amount on which the premium has been paid. The Employer undertaking for the purposes of this Policy to keep exact account of the wages and bonuses or other allowances so paid as aforesaid to the workmen in the service of the Employer, and of the classification of occupations of the workmen employed in any of the occupations, and at any of the places mentioned in the Schedules hereto; and also particulars of all contracts for work done for the Employer at the places mentioned in the Schedules hereto by sub-contract, and of the specification relating to such work, and also, so far as possible, an account of all workmen engaged in any of the said occupations at any of the said places by any sub-contractor, and the wages paid to them; and shall at all times, but at least twice a year, produce such accounts and documents, to be kept as aforesaid, to the Corporation and its Agents, and give all necessary information and explanation with reference thereto, and vouched in such manner as the Corporation may require. Wages paid by a sub-contractor in respect of work done for the Employer shall be deemed wages paid by the Employer, but if the wages paid by any sub-contractor cannot be ascertained, then for the purpose of this Policy they shall be taken to be a sum equal to sixty per cent. of the sum agreed to be paid to such sub-contractor for such work. In the case of the death or retirement of any member, or the addition of a new member to any firm hereby assured, this Policy shall as from the happening of such event take effect as if it were granted to the remaining or continuing new members, if any, of such firm entitled to carry on business as successors of the former firm.

6. **Provided also,** that notice of any accident causing personal injury to a workman shall be sent by the Employer to the Corporation as soon as possible, and within six days, stating the name of the workman, cause of accident, and the nature of the injuries, and the fullest particulars as to the cause of the accident shall be carefully preserved. If the Employer shall receive notice of a claim, or intention to make a claim, the Employer shall within three days (time being of the essence of this condition) send such notice to the Corporation, and shall further furnish to the Corporation, with reasonable despatch, all such information (upon forms supplied by the Corporation if so requested) as and when the Corporation may require. The Employer shall also in the event of any dispute or question arising in connection with any claim render all possible assistance to the Corporation to enable them to successfully resist such claim, and to act for the Employer in settling any question or dispute so arising.

7. **Provided also,** that the Employer shall not, except at his own cost, pay or settle any Claim or admit liability therefor without the consent in writing of the Corporation, and the Corporation shall have the right to take upon themselves the settlement of any claim, or be entitled to assume during such period as they think proper the absolute conduct and control on behalf of the Employer of any proceedings that may be taken to enforce a claim, or for the settlement of any question arising in connection therewith, and shall, subject to the terms of this Policy, indemnify the Employer against all costs and expenses of and incident to such proceedings incurred while the Corporation retain such conduct and control as aforesaid, and the Corporation shall be entitled to the benefit of all indemnities and other rights given the Employer by the "Workmen's Compensation Act, 1897," or by the "Employers' Liability Act, 1880," or otherwise, and to use the name of the Employer in any action or proceeding in relation thereto.

8. **Provided also,** that if at the time of any injury being sustained any other insurance shall be existing covering the same, then the Corporation shall only be liable to pay a *pro rata* share of the amount payable in respect of such injury.

9. **Provided also,** that this Policy does not insure against liability resulting from injury to or caused by any person while employed contrary to the regulations of the Factory Acts, the Mines Regulation Acts, or any other Act regarding the employment of labour, or of any regulations made thereunder, and if a notice shall be or shall have been given under any Act referred to in this clause of any defect requiring to be remedied, or requiring any practice or method to be adopted, discontinued or altered, the Employer shall not be entitled to any indemnity for any compensation he may become liable to pay in respect of accidental injury caused or sustained after receipt of such notice, and prior to its requirement having been fully complied with.

10. **Provided also,** that if there shall be any mis-statement in, or if a material fact be omitted from the Proposal, all insurances under this Policy shall be void to all intents and purposes, and any premium paid thereon shall be forfeited.

11. **Provided also,** that the Employer shall at all times use all reasonable precautions calculated to mitigate or remove risk of personal injury to workmen, and in particular shall provide all necessary, suitable, and efficient ways, machinery, appliances, plant, and workmen, and shall take all reasonable steps to have the same properly supervised and inspected by competent persons, and kept in a proper state of repair and condition, and shall use all reasonable endeavour to enforce the observance by all workmen and other persons in his employ, or in the employ of Sub-Contractors, of all proper safeguards and precautions against every such injury, and on any defect in the ways, machinery, appliances, or work being discovered shall at once take all necessary steps to remedy such defect, and in the meantime shall cause such additional precautions to be taken as the circumstances may require.

12. **Provided also,** that the Employer shall at such time or times as they may reasonably require permit duly authorised Officials of the Corporation to inspect the plant, ways, works, and machinery.

13. **Provided also,** that the Employer shall from time to time forthwith give to the Corporation notice of the happening of any event, or the existing of any circumstances rendering the employment of any workman more hazardous than it was prior thereto, or of any change in the system of work, and shall obtain from the Corporation their express assent in writing to accept such altered liability, and shall pay such extra premium as may be required, otherwise this Policy so far as regards any accident occurring through such altered employment shall be to all intents and purposes null and void.

14. If the Corporation shall at any time give four weeks' notice in writing to the Employer of their intention to cancel this Policy, they shall be relieved of all liability in respect of any injury sustained after the expiration of such notice. Upon any such determination of this Policy the same method of adjustment of the premium payable thereunder shall be followed as if the Policy had been allowed to run during the whole term for which it was originally issued.

15. **Provided also,** that every notice or communication to be given or made by the Employer shall be in writing to the Chief Office of the Corporation in Perth, or to the Branch Office with which the Employer has been in communication. No notice or communication otherwise given or made shall be recognised for any purpose whatever, and knowledge of an Agent shall not be deemed to be knowledge of the Corporation. Notices given by the Corporation to the Employer shall be deemed to be sufficiently given if sent by post to his last address known to the Corporation, and shall be deemed to have reached him on the day following that on which the envelope containing the same is posted.

16. If a dispute shall arise respecting the amount to be paid to the Employer, or whether these conditions have been complied with or otherwise as to anything herein contained, the matter shall, if required by the Corporation, be referred to the arbitration of two disinterested persons, one to be chosen by each party, or an umpire or oversman to be named by such arbitrators in case of their differing in opinion; and in case the Corporation shall so require, and either party shall neglect or refuse for the space of fourteen days after request in writing from the other to do so, to name an arbitrator, the arbitrator named by the other party may proceed alone; and the award of such arbitrators, arbitrator, umpire, or oversman shall be binding on all parties, and no action or suit shall be brought or prosecuted on this Policy in respect of such dispute except for the sum so awarded and costs if any. The costs of and connected with the arbitration shall be in the discretion of the arbitrators or umpire.

In Witness whereof, the said Corporation have caused their Common Seal to be affixed, and we, the undersigned, two of the Directors and the Manager or Secretary of the said Corporation, have hereunto set our hands, this twenty-eighth day of June in the year of our Lord one thousand eight hundred and ninety-eight.

Patrick Hunter
Henry Coates } *Directors.*

F. Norie Miller *Manager.*

Entered

Examined

L. 2000/5/98.

SEE OVER FOR SCHEDULES.

SCHEDULE I.

Employees to be covered in respect of Liability under Workmen's Compensation Act, Employers' Liability Act, and at Common Law.

Approximate Number of Employees to be covered. (1)	Description and Classification of Occupations. (2)	WAGES, SALARIES, AND BONUSES OR OTHER ALLOWANCES ESTIMATED TO BE PAID. (Insert an Estimate sufficient for Twelve Months.)			Places at which the Employees are to be employed. (6)
		By the Employer.		By Sub-Contractors.	
		To Managers, Clerks, and others not engaged in Manual Work. (3)	To Foremen and Workmen directly employed. (4)	To Foremen and Workmen of Sub-Contractors. (5)	
40	Foreman, Manager, Drivers, Fitters, Conductors, Cleaners, Cokemen, Clerks and Labourers.		£2,300 in all		Darwen and Blackburn.

SCHEDULE II.

Employees to be covered only in respect of Liability under the Employers' Liability Act, 1880, and at Common Law.

Approximate Number of Employees to be covered. (1)	Description and Classification of Occupations. (2)	WAGES, SALARIES, AND BONUSES OR OTHER ALLOWANCES ESTIMATED TO BE PAID. (Insert an Estimate sufficient for Twelve Months.)			Places at which the Employees are to be employed. (6)
		By the Employer.		By Sub-Contractors.	
		To Managers, Clerks, and others not engaged in Manual Work. (3)	To Foremen and Workmen directly employed. (4)	To Foremen and Workmen of Sub-Contractors. (5)	

The

General Accident

Assurance Corporation,

LIVERPOOL OFFICE
6, CASTLE STREET,

THOMAS McPHERSON,
RESIDENT SECRETARY.

Workmen's Compensation Policy No. W. 676

Name of Assured, Messrs. The Blackburn & Over Darwen Tramways Coy.

Premium, £ 17 : 5 : 0

Date, 1st July

Agent :—

Branch Liverpool

Please read the terms and conditions of your Policy, and, if incorrect, return it for alteration.

ENDORSEMENT No. 4082

It is hereby agreed and declared that the interest in respect of this Policy is now vested in favour of the Mayor, Aldermen and Burgesses of the County Borough of Blackburn, notwithstanding anything herein contained to the contrary.

Dated at Perth, this Sixteenth day of January 189 7

Entd. ___
Examd. ___

Manager and Secretary.

The Workmen's Compensation Act 1897

The following item, which first appeared in the *Railway Magazine,* vol. 2 1898 pp38 to 45 and which is reproduced with permission, may at first sight seem hardly relevant to tramways whether steam, cable or electric, but of course it is. After all, our tramways elsewhere would be known as 'street railways' a far more accurate description when one sees 3,000 tons of train trundling along Main Street, US of A., and the tramway workmen suffered exactly the same hazards as their confrères on main line railways. This article seems to me at least to be reasonably dispassionate on the subject; probably more so than your word-smith who has seen too many accidents in employment not to be worried by the miserable meanness of some employers coupled to the crass stupidity of employees. In the case of our steam trams the building of the engines without proper fire-hole doors led directly to many scalding cases, and to this we can couple the inexcusable failure by the operators to retro-fit such fittings. In such matters it is a pity that the Board of Trade was forced to move so slowly as, for example, they did on the subject of continuous brakes on mainstream railways. As to employees how do you protect them against blatant stupidity? Two of us, as engineers, carefully fitted a new guard on a pillar drill, adding the seals etc., only half an hour later finding the operator had removed it and neatly drilled through her own hand in her haste to gain extra bonus. She lost the use of her two middle fingers, our Polaroid (camera) evidence being sufficient for her claim to be disallowed. But at least this Act, the Workmen's Compensation Act of 1897, may be said to be a move in the right direction – and, yes, it did apply to mill-girls and the like, and more especially munitions workers. Even there though the lovable employers tried to claim 'Exigencies of War' as an excuse for their wilful disregard of the safety of these girls, who in real life probably served in a café or a milliner's shop and could not have any comprehension of the dangers they faced from machinery.

The charm of this item lies in its presentation by the author, Mr S.M. Phillp, as a very readable approach to the subject.

"MASTERS AND MEN
THE WORKMEN'S COMPENSATION ACT 1897

EXAMINED BY S. M. PHILLP, General Manager's Department., L. & N.W.R.

FOR good or evil, the Workmen's Compensation Act, 1897, after much strife of parties, and in spite of many conflicting criticisms, is now a fait accompli, and it behoves both sides – the employers and the employed – to sit down with it quietly and try to discern what it really means to them, and how it will relatively affect them. This is the more necessary because it has been assailed from so many points of view, and the workman, if he has attentively followed the controversy concerning it in the newspapers during its passage through Parliament, must have seen such widely differing prophecies as to its scope and effect that, even if he possesses more than average intelligence, he must be in some amount of perplexity as to whether this new charter of his is to be a great benefit to him or the reverse. From one school of critics he has heard that the Act is of no value to him because, amongst a host of other shortcomings, it does not protect him absolutely against "contracting out"; it does not, in terms, abolish the doctrine of "common employment" (although surely it does so in effect); and it does not provide compensation for accidents which do not disable him for more than a fortnight. On the other hand, from another set of critics, he learns that this Act is to impose such a burden upon capital as to cripple all the great industries of the country, and, if it is to take such enormous sums of money out of the pockets of his employers, presumably it must be to put them into his own. So that, on the whole, perhaps, he scratches his honest head and wonders perplexedly whether he has really got "a good thing" or not. Well, time will show; but probably the truth, as usual, lies midway between the extremes and the Act, while far from being without value to the workman, will not necessarily spell ruin to the capitalist. For, after all, when stripped of verbiage and the detail of the machinery for giving it effect, what does the Act do? It provides that when a man meets with injury in following his occupation, and the accident is not due to his own serious and wilful misconduct, he shall receive a payment during disablement, or, if death results from the accident, those dependent upon his labour shall receive a sum equal to

about three years' earnings. Now this is precisely what some of the great railway companies have been giving their men for years past, except that the death allowance has not been quite so large, while the disablement allowance has been on the average larger than under the new Act, and that the men have contributed towards the fund which yielded these benefits a weekly sum so small as to be inappreciable. Yet the great railway companies have not yet ceased to pay dividends, and there does not seem much reason to fear that the colliery proprietors, quarry owners, and contractors whose employees will come under the Act, and who are not commonly understood to be trembling on the verge of bankruptcy, will find it necessary to suspend their operations by reason of the burden which this Act will impose upon them.

For reasons which I will presently proceed to explain, I do not think the Act will prove an unmitigated blessing to the workmen employed by some of the larger railway companies; but to others who will fall within its scope it seems difficult to deny that it involves for them the recognition of a great and beneficent principle, which, sooner or later, was bound to find expression in the industrial legislation of this country, having regard to what has been done abroad. The world is getting to be a small place in many ways, and, when we saw a great system of universal industrial insurance flourishing in Germany and gradually spreading to other European States, it became inevitably only a question of time for some such experiment to be tried in this country. But we are a cautious people, and love to build up our legislation, as our constitution has been built up, piece-meal, rather than in the Imperial and sweeping fashion which we have seen exemplified elsewhere; so that the present measure is rather of an experimental or tentative character, dealing with only certain selected trades and with certain classes of accident.

But the principle of the Act is the vital part of it, and its extension is doubtless only a question of time; so let us see what that principle amounts to broadly. The Employers' Liability Act, 1880, of which the Workmen's Compensation Act takes the place, in effect,

although not in theory, was confessedly a failure, for reasons which were sufficiently obvious from the outset. It provided for the employer paying compensation to an injured workman in cases where the accident was directly traceable to his (the employer's) neglect or wilful default; while every practical man knows that, of the accidents happening during the carrying out of industrial operations, only an infinitesimal percentage would come under this category. Out of the few cases in which the liability of the employer could be called in question at all, there would be in nine out of ten an element of doubt sufficient to warrant the employer in contesting the case, and a legal struggle between a working man, or the poor widow who might survive him in case of death, on the one side, and a powerful railway company or a wealthy colliery proprietor, contractor, or other employer on the other, would be an unequal one indeed. In most cases, the fear of incurring legal expenses and being after all unsuccessful would deter the sufferers from litigation, unless some jobbing attorney could be found to undertake the case on the principle of "no cure, no pay." The proof of this is that the Midland Railway Company, who employ about 48,000 men, and who have never contracted themselves out of the Employers' Liability Act, have had on the average not more than five or six claims per annum under the Act, and during two years only one case came before the Court, this being decided in the Company's favour. Of course, this state of things is explained by the fact that the Company have an admirable Friendly Society for their men, to which they liberally subscribe, and the men prefer the certain benefits of the Society to the very uncertain benefits of the Act.

But now the Employers' Liability Act of 1880 is to all intents and purposes, although not legally, defunct, and the Workmen's Compensation Act, 1897, which reigns in its stead, has a far wider scope. In effect it provides that, where a workman meets with an injury in following his employment, he shall be paid by his employer some allowance not exceeding half his average wages during the period of his disablement, or, if he is killed outright, those dependent upon his labour shall receive an amount equal to his average earnings for three years, or the sum of £150, whichever be the greater, but not exceeding £300. Of course, there are many qualifications and definitions, but this is the main purport of the Act, and the great point is that it covers every description of accident except those due to the wilful misconduct of the workman, and that in the event of any dispute between the injured workman and his employer as to the amount of the allowance to be made, there are to be no ruinous legal proceedings, but the matter is to be settled by an arbitrator, who, if not agreed upon, will be appointed by a County Court Judge and paid by the State.

Now there is no denying that, for the great body of workmen to whom the Act applies — and there is little doubt that its scope will be extended eventually to most, if not all, trades — this is a great charter. In point of fact, what it does is to fully recognise the principle that those who fill the ranks of the great army of industry and serve their country while they earn their bread by carrying on the operations of commerce, are as much entitled to help and consideration when they fall by the way as those other soldiers who serve in the Army of the Queen or the seamen who man our Navy. This is as it should be, because practical men know full well that probably ninety-nine per cent. of the accidents that occur in industrial occupations are such as neither the workmen himself nor his employer can be blamed for. Take the case of a shunter in a railway goods yard. He has been earnestly adjured by his superiors, both by circular and by personal admonition, on no account to risk his own safety or incur unnecessary risks; but the work is perhaps heavy on some fatal night; the trains must be got away, and time presses; perhaps it is foggy and dark; in his zeal he dives between two wagons only a yard apart; an engine backs up unawares, and in an instant he is crushed to death. Who can blame the poor fellow and say he ought to have been more careful and gone round the wagons? Who can blame his employers, who have besought him over and over again not to run such risks? No, these are simply the casualties which will always occur in greater or less numbers where men are engaged in fighting the forces of Nature in carrying on the commerce of the world, and it would be manifestly unfair that the whole burden of the fray should fall upon the individual worker, who possesses nothing but the labour of his hands, and that the capitalist should escape scot-free.

It has been said that the passing of this Act implies the establishment of a great principle in favour of working men, and in this, railwaymen, like others, have their part ; but when we come to consider how the actual working of the Act will affect the employees of the great railway companies, there seems grave reason to doubt whether these men will be as well off as they are under existing conditions, and one may even go further and maintain that the best interests of the service are likely to be impaired by the results of the Act.

In the first place, although a railwayman is in a sense a skilled workman, the conditions affecting his labour widely differ from those which apply to an artisan in any other branch of industry. A carpenter, for instance, who has once learned his business, with his tools upon his back, may reckon upon getting a living anywhere, and if he loses his job he has not far to seek for another. A railway worker, on the other hand, enters the service of a particular company as a boy, works his way up step by step to a certain position according to his industry and abilities, and, with rare exceptions and subject only to good conduct, he may look to remain in the same service until he dies or becomes too old to work and retires upon his pension. To such a man the greatest calamity that can befall him is the loss of his situation from any cause, because there are always hundreds of applicants eager to step into his shoes, and once out of the service, especially after a certain age, it will be a difficult matter to find railway employment, while he knows no other trade. Now let us see how the working of this Act will affect such a man.

Under hitherto existing circumstances, if he unfortunately meets with an injury, he straightway, and without any question, "goes upon the Fund." If it is not a hospital case the Friendly Club doctor will attend him, his mates will come to see him from time to time to cheer him up, and, best of all, when he is well again he goes back to find his old job waiting for him, his foreman shakes him by the hand, and even his superintendent is glad to see an experienced man back again in the ranks. But now suppose that "the Fund" no longer exists: that our friend stands upon his rights under the Act and makes a claim upon the company which they consider to be beyond what the merits of the case demand. An arbitration follows, and, whatever the result may be, a certain amount of friction and animosity is aroused, so that, when our friend has recovered and wishes to resume work, we can imagine the possibility of his superintendent saying : "No; we don't care for people who are so fond of litigation, and, besides, we have unfortunately had to fill your place up, so that there is really no room tor you."

Another undeniably weak point in the Act, when it is compared with the benefits derived from the Companies' Societies, is that it makes no provision for cases of disablement continuing for less than two weeks, and, while the writer does not profess to have much knowledge of other trades, it is an incontestable fact that in the railway service such cases represent between 50 and 60 per cent. of the whole number. Moreover, even in more serious cases, the Act apparently provides no payment for the first two weeks of incapacity, whereas the Societies pay the allowance in the most trifling cases, and even in circumstances in which the Act would give no claim whatever. For example, it is not long since a member of the London and North Western Insurance Society claimed, and obtained, the Society's allowance for temporary disablement on the ground of an illness caused by the sting of a bee whilst the man was walking on the line to his post of duty. But imagine the dilemma of a household of limited means, where the breadwinner is laid aside from the result of an accident, and there is nothing at all coming in for two weeks after the mishap!

And now let me endeavour to justify my assertion that the enforcement of this Act in the railway service is calculated to produce a state of things which will be detrimental to the interests of that service, and, therefore, to those of the public. The railway service, amongst industrial employments, is unique in this respect: that it is absolutely essential that the men occupied in the working of the trains should exhibit the same strict discipline and unquestioning obedience to orders, however distasteful, as are found as a matter of course in the Army and the Navy, while there are not the same means of enforcing them. Why is it that the soldier, when ordered to advance on what seems certain death, as, for example, in the famous Balaclava charge, never hesitates for an instant to obey? In the great majority of cases, no doubt, because he is a British soldier, and devotion to duty is his watchword; but not every private soldier is cast in the heroic mould, and, for those who are not, the compelling influence in the last resort is that he knows that disobedience in the face of the enemy is punishable with death. When the sailor has comfortably turned in for his watch below on a wild and bitter night and is roused from his sleep by the unwelcome cry of "All hands on deck," why is it that he grumbles and swears, but never thinks of disobeying? In some cases, if not in many, it is because he knows that if he refused he would be placed in irons and tried for mutiny. But when the brakesman, on a bitter winter's night, perhaps cold, wet, hungry, and weary, has finished his spell of duty, and is looking forward to his supper and his bed, and his foreman reluctantly says: "Very sorry, Tom, old chap, but you can't get your boots off yet, for I've got nobody else to take out this train," why does he obey without question, for, unlike the soldier or the sailor, he can neither be shot nor put in irons if he refuses? Yet, if he did refuse, the consequences, in disorganisation of the service, delay to goods, claims to be paid, and customers offended or lost, might be most serious, so that blind obedience at all costs is just as necessary as in the case of the soldier or the sailor.

It behoves the railway company, accordingly, by some means or other to attach the men to the service, and foster in them a spirit of allegiance to the company they serve which shall take the place of the iron discipline enforced in the Army and Navy. What the greater railway companies, at any rate, have done, and are doing, is to make the men feel in every possible way that the directors take a keen interest in their welfare, and are anxious by every means to promote their happiness, to meet all their legitimate wants, and to provide for them in health, in sickness, and in old age.

Taking the London and North Western Company, for instance, as a typical case — which one may well do, seeing that they employ no less than 65,000 wage-earners (apart from salaried clerks and officers), that Company has for many years past devoted great care and attention to promoting the well-being of its servants, and has expended very large sums of money with the same object. The directors have established, in the first place, Insurance Societies for the different departments, which provide, in case of temporary disablement from accident on duty, a weekly payment which, on the average, is in excess of the payment fixed by the new Act — a payment of £100 to the widow or other survivors of a man killed on duty, or the same amount to the man himself if he is permanently disabled, and a payment of £10 in case of natural death. These Societies have been paying out in the shape of benefits about £43,000 per annum. In addition there is a Provident Fund which provides a weekly payment in case of sickness, a sum to cover funeral expenses in case of death, and a pension for men who grow old in the service. This Society pays out in benefits about £40,000 per annum. Then the Company has established a Savings Bank for its servants, and, acting as bankers, gives them a much better rate of interest for their savings than they could obtain outside. For the clerks there is a Superannuation Fund, to which the Company subscribes 2½ per cent. per annum upon the salaries of the members. At places like Crewe, Wolverton, and Earlestown, where there are large colonies of railway servants, the Company has built and endowed churches and chapels, institutes and schools, and altogether, in one way and another, for the support of societies and institutions designed to promote the welfare of their employees, the Company has been spending for many years at the rate of about £50,000 per annum. The result of all this is that the utmost good feeling has prevailed between the men as a body and their employers, and that the men, or, at any rate, large numbers of them, cherish almost the same feeling of loyalty to the Company as a soldier does to his flag; but, of course, this state of things is as gall and wormwood to the paid agitators and zealous trade unionists. Their constant mission is to persuade the workman that "Codlin's the friend – not Short," and that he should look upon his employers, not as his friends and helpers, but as his adversaries, and should join the Union, which will back him up against these tyrannous capitalists. Hence their unrelenting opposition to the principle of "contracting out," and their desperate efforts to have it altogether prohibited, in which, for the present, they have not been entirely successful.

The new Act still leaves a loophole for contracting out, for clause 3 enacts that: "If the Registrar of Friendly Societies, after taking steps to ascertain the views of the employer and workmen, certifies that any scheme of compensation, benefit or insurance for the workmen of an employer in any employment, whether or not such scheme includes other employers and their workmen, is on the whole not less favourable to the general body of workmen and their dependants than the provisions of this Act, the employer may, until the certificate is revoked, contract with any of those workmen that the provisions of the scheme shall be substituted for the provisions of this Act, and thereupon the employer shall be liable only in accordance with the scheme, but save as aforesaid, this Act shall apply notwithstanding any contract to the contrary made after the commencement of this Act."

But whatever course the companies may elect to adopt in view of this clause, it is quite clear that the existing societies are doomed and must die a natural death, for clause 9 says :-

"Any contract existing at the commencement of this Act, whereby a workman relinquishes any right to compensation from the employer for personal injury arising out of and in the course of his employment, shall not, for the purpose of this Act, be deemed to continue after the time at which the workman's contract of service would determine if notice of the determination thereof were given at the commencement of this Act."

As most wage servants are paid weekly, and are subject to a week's notice, this means that one week after July 31st, 1898, all existing societies whose rules embrace the principle of contracting out must come to an end.

While upon the subject of contracting out, one may here advert to one clause in the new Act (clause 3, sub-section 3) which is almost amusing in its naïveté. Referring to clause 3, which has been already quoted, this section goes on to say:-

"No scheme shall be so certified which contains the obligation upon the workmen to join the scheme as a condition of their hiring."

It is scarcely probable that any company, in the face of the clause, would be so refreshingly innocent as to insert such an obligation in the rules of any society they might find! Of course, what would happen would be that a candidate for employment would be casually asked whether he would be willing to join the Society, and if he showed any disinclination, he would be found unsuitable for the service, without its being necessary to assign any reason.

What will the great railway companies do in the face of this Act? The writer is not in a position to say, for some of them, at any rate, have not yet made up their minds as to what will be the best policy to adopt, and the question is one which is far from being free from difficulty. They have, as usual, the proverbial three courses open to them. They might re-establish the present societies on the same lines, but without contracting out of the Act, and trust to their men being satisfied with the benefits of the societies without resorting to litigation; but with the paid agitator always in the background urging the men to take all the Society would give them, and then " go for the Company" under the Act, this might, turn out to be a suicidal policy. They might dissolve the societies, and let the Act take its course, setting up an Arbitration Committee, by arrangement with the men, and endeavouring to work the Act with as little friction as possible. This scheme need not present any financial terrors to the companies, because it is questionable whether, under it, they would labour under any greater pecuniary burden than the one they have voluntarily assumed for some years past; but the objection to it, from the men's point of view particularly, would be that more than 50 per cent. of the accidents occurring would not be provided for at all – viz., 'those involving less than two weeks' disablement, and these would have to be met independently by the men themselves at considerable cost. The third alternative would be to re-constitute the societies, so as to make the benefits correspond with those under the Act, and so to satisfy the Registrar; but this would involve either increasing the death payment and decreasing the disablement allowance, which would be very unpopular with the men, or else retaining the present disablement allowance and increasing the death allowance, which would impose a considerably increased burden upon the shareholders.

It will be seen that the solution of the problem is not a simple one to discover. The real question which the railway companies have to decide is how, whilst fulfilling their obligations under the Act, they can best maintain those cordial and friendly relations with their men which have so largely conduced to the efficiency of the splendid railway system of this country.

Accidents

Not only was the steam and smoke of the trams to be a problem, but worse there is no doubt they could, and did, kill children and adults alike and it has always seemed unreasonable to me to expect the driver to keep a keen lookout for passengers, stoke his fire, watch his water level whilst maintaining his boiler pressure, be prepared to sand if the rails were greasy, cope with sulphur fumes, rain, snow, sleet, industrial filth, and at the same time try to watch for small children or fractious horses without any lifeguard whatsoever.

No matter that in all probability the accident rate per mile run was less than with horse transport, and the fact that accidents were a part of life. John Jordan, a blacksmith of Wordsley was found in the local canal due to the thick fog. In Wolverhampton at the same time there was such a dense fog that no-one could see more than a few yards, while in Walsall a man could not see his feet. During this period in that area four girls died or were severely hurt by burning; in each case a paraffin stove or lamp set fire to their frocks. Each got four lines in the paper – as much as John Jordan. Seven years before, a local paper carried a leader on the smoke nuisance: "Day after day, and week after week, our factory chimneys pour out clouds of dense unconsumed smoke, which joined with natural mists and winter fogs to make a compound as nauseous and noxious as the worst London 'pea-souper'."

In 1887 a snow storm in the Bury area bad drifts of up to 6ft (nearly two metres) were reported, telegraph wires were down and so bad were the conditions that trains worked on the 'staff' system, in effect allowing one train at a time to move from signal box to signal box as normal signals were either extinguished, frozen or invisible (incidentally I had this experience many years ago, having to climb signals to ascertain their setting); but somehow, at least until the early evening the trams were supposed to operate. Can you imagine the condition of the drivers? It beggars belief, for while later electric cars were also open fronted, the men rarely worked a 16-hour day and had decent lifeguards.

16 July 1885. "Late on Thursday night a girl called Prudence Evans residing in Dudley Street, Round Oak, was playing with her brother in the street, and ran in front of a tram engine. She was knocked down and received slight internal injuries, and has since been attended by Dr Higgs, of Dudley." Mind you, a couple of weeks earlier a child ran out in front of what was described as a 'ginger-beer cart.' It was said "she ran right into the teeth of danger" and was killed.

15 August 1885. "On Tuesday evening, a married woman, named Martha Brookes (30), residing at Lea Brook Road, was admitted into the West Bromwich District Hospital, suffering from serious injuries about the body, face, and legs. It appears the woman was attempting to get into a tramcar whilst in motion, when she slipped and fell between the car and a coal truck which was attached to it." Although there may have been other instances of this kind of accident, this does seem to be the only report detailing the, albeit indirect, cause as being any form of goods wagon...

14 August 1886. "On Sunday night a man named John Dunn, who is employed at the

692

Stour Valley Works, and resides in West Smethwick, sustained serious injuries in alighting from a tram-car. It appears Dunn and several others were 'larking' on top of the car when his hat fell to the ground. He immediately proceeded down the steps, and jumped off the car while it was in motion for the purpose of fetching his hat. He foolishly jumped in the opposite direction to that in which the car was proceeding, the result being that he fell to the ground with considerable force, cutting his face very badly. He was removed to the Police Station, and was immediately attended to by Dr Jackson, being subsequently taken to his home." (Hatless presumably!)

3 September 1887. King's Heath and one car was turning the corner of Queen's Bridge Road where there was a passing place (the line developed from a single to double set of rails and again runs into a single line across the railway Bridge). The second car involved did not bother to wait but met its protagonist; both travelling so fast neither had time to brake. Damage was extensive but no one was hurt.

26 November 1887. Occasionally one feels that the tramway company were defenceless against accusations, either as their drivers were blatantly in the wrong, or the company itself was at fault. In the case of the former, a carriage proprietor sued the (Birmingham) Central Tramways Company for £24.16.6, being damage caused to one of his broughams. It seems this conveyance (a horse-drawn carriage with a roof, four wheels and an open driver's seat in front) was passing in front of the tramway company's King's Heath depot at exactly 10.37 pm on 23 May when a tram engine backed into it. One of the company's inspectors, Henry Smith, was called to give evidence. He heard a crash, ran and found the brougham's driver lying on the ground. Clayton, the driver, apparently told Henry Smith that his horse had bolted. This far the company may have been winning, but under cross-examination poor old Smith had to admit his tram driver had been dismissed shortly after the accident. Not too unusual a happening in tram companies even until the 1950s, but it seems the driver had collided with a milk float the day after this accident. Perhaps the driver was unnerved by his previous accident, but the coup de grâce for the company came when Smith had to agree that a man was now employed to warn people in the road whenever engines were shunted in or out of the shed. The judge awarded the brougham's owner £21 out of the £24.16.6 he asked for, plus costs. At a guess that late at night the tram driver was probably unwilling to pass from one cab to the other and drove in virtually blind; not to 'change ends' was a practice commonly used on the railways, especially when it was raining, then propelling the engine or unit blind over cross-overs or in sidings. One relied on anyone about on the tracks to hear the engine coming.

13 October 1888. A drayman named Gardiner was leading his horse down Sedgley Hill when it was frightened by the ringing of a tramcar bell and bolted. It does not take much imagination to imagine the scene or why the poor chap eventually fell under his dray which "passed over him, breaking his leg and causing serious injuries to his head, several of his teeth being knocked out." He was, eventually, conveyed home in a passing waggonette. Once again, not to a hospital but home, presumably to die.

1 December 1888. "An accident of rather an alarming character occurred on Saturday night, on the South Staffordshire Tramways, near Dudley Station. Whilst passing the Guest Hospital an engine and car, driven by George Powell, of Darlaston, and conducted by Ernest Reeves, of Bloxwich, struck against the points at the turnout and ran off the line. After running about sixty yards down the incline the car suddenly swerved to the right, and came against a gas lamp. The lamppost was smashed and the car turned right over. The car was full of people, fifteen of whom were more or less seriously injured. They were taken to the Guest Hospital, where their injuries were seen to by the house surgeon. Thomas Mills, manager of the Tibbington Colliery and Thomas Amos, ostler, the Factory Inn, Hurst Lane, Tipton, were detained, but have since been discharged. It is most remarkable that the results of the accident were not more serious as the tram was quite full at the time, and Mills and Amos were riding on the top. It is aid that some time ago a woman was killed near the same place through a tramcar jumping the points."

6 March 1894. Mrs Ann Skidmore of Brierley Hill ran after a car on the Dudley & Stourbridge line at Holly Hall, one mile from Dudley. While the car was waiting at the next passing loop she was taken ill and "she was brought on to Dudley with the view of obtaining medical aid. In Market Place the attention of Inspector Hinde was drawn to her, and he found her dead." She was, however, 83, and "we understand, on her usual round of rent collecting." Clearly an indomitable old lady who at least died in comfort.

9 March 1894. "Edwin Francis Edwards, of 170 Great Lister Street, car proprietor, sued the Birmingham Central Tramways Company to recover £26.14s.9d damages for injuries sustained by a char-a-banc, driven by his son in the Birchfield Road, through the alleged negligence of one of the defendant company's servants ... Plaintiff's case was that on 13 November his son was driving a char-a-banc from a football match at Perry Barr along the Birchfield Road. A grocer's horse and cart stood on the near side of the road, and in passing this the driver had to run on to the tram lines. A tram engine and car was approaching at the rate of five or six miles an hour, and the driver of the char-a-banc and several of his passengers shouted and signalled to the tram driver to pull up, but he did not slacken speed, and a collision followed ... The defence was that the accident was occasioned through the recklessness of the driver of the char-a-banc. His four horses, it was said, were running at a rate variously estimated at between eight and 12 miles an hour, and in attempting to squeeze between the tram-engine – which was either absolutely stationary or merely moving – and the grocer's cart was endeavouring to perform an impossible feat. Eight witnesses were called on each side. The jury, after 40 minutes absence, returned a verdict for £26.10s and costs."

31 March 1894. "If any person who was riding outside the Dudley and West Bromwich tram which left Dudley at 7.45 on the night of 5 December last, and who witnessed the accident which occurred between that tram and a horse and lorry, or any foot passenger who saw the accident, will communicate with Mr George

G. Brown, Priory Street, Dudley, the latter will be obliged."

18 July 1903. A boy, Thomas Groutage from Saltley, was doing as normal boys did until recently inasmuch as he was trying to have a free ride on the front platform of the car. He fell off and his head went under the wheels.

20 December 1904. Boo Hole Farm passing loop, near Prettywood, Lancashire. The driver of a cart ('lurry') carrying coal, one John Rhodes, died following a collision between his vehicle and a steam tram. This accident could not have come at a worse time for Heywood Corporation had only re-started the service on the 12th. Reports on the inquest and the subsequent proceedings in court at Manchester make interesting reading in giving a real insight into a contemporary road accident. The protagonists included in the neutral corner, the Coroner and a full jury. The Town Clerk represented the Corporation, a local solicitor the deceased's family, and E.O. Kay (instructed by the Carters and Lurrymen's Union), for the late Mr Rhodes. The Chairman of the Surveyors Committee and the Borough Engineer were also present. So too was the driver, James Brown, a 50 year-old Rochdale man but no-one, positively no-one, represented him. Details of the case are given elsewhere in this book, the outcome was damages of £550 which had to be paid by the Corporation. For a comparison – James Brown received £1.50 a week for 72 hours work.

2 June 1905. "About three o'clock on Wednesday afternoon a singular accident occurred in Bridge-street. A tram from Heywood was going towards Bury and when passing through the loop, near the Brunswick Hotel, another car was seen coming towards Heywood. The driver of the outgoing car reversed his engine so as to stop in the loop, and the car ran backwards for a short distance. A mail cart containing the daughter of Mr R. Ainsworth, tea dealer, of Benfield-street, was passing behind the car at the time and was struck by it, with the result that the cart was knocked over and the baby went partially under the tram. Happily she escaped in a wonderful fashion without injury but the mail cart was broken. On Saturday evening a man from Castleton was knocked down by a steam engine in Bridge-street. The driver immediately dropped the 'brush' appliance, and fortunately the engine was quickly stopped, the man escaping with a severe shaking." The 'brush' resulting from the safety trials of the 1890s once again showed its value; the man must have indeed been 'shaken', terrified more like! But he survived to tell the tale in his pub.

27 June 1885. "John Robert Jones, aged two and a half years, was killed yesterday morning about ten o'clock by a passing tramcar. The engine and car were proceeding slowly near the turnout opposite the Railway Station, when the child ran in front, was knocked down and pushed about two yards before the engine could be stopped. The child incurred severe injuries to the left shoulder and back, and died in the course of five or ten minutes. The deceased was taken into No.4 Crown Buildings, where his mother resides, and Dr Pearse was sent, but of course could render no assistance."

This was the basic newspaper report but the Coroner's inquest brought to light more detail. Catherine Scott, the mother, stated clearly the child was illegitimate, almost as if this explained matters. It seems he was sitting in his chair in front of the dwelling's front door and about ten o'clock hearing some screams she ran from Meeting Lane, where, she claimed, she had been talking for about 5 or 6 minutes, and saw the child under the tram engine. In the end the engine had to be shunted back before the child could be freed. The inquest report uncommonly blunt, Dr Pearse stating "the deceased's left shoulder was only by a bit of skin, and was as though a rat had gnawed it, and his was also injured." Witnesses all agreed the tram had been moving quite slowly (3-4 mph) "and the driver pulled up with all his might", seemingly in about ten yards. The Coroner then really got to the nub of the matter as he and the jury found it unfortunate that the tram had to be backed off the child before he could be got out. Mr W. Dinnon, the Dudley & Stourbridge Company's Manager, observed that although jacks were carried to lift the cars it was a difficult matter as they weighed nine tons. "The Foreman [of the jury] suggested there might be an arrangement like that in front of locomotive engines, to clear the lines of any obstacles – Mr Holberton [solicitor] said he would take care that the suggestions were brought under the notice of the Company." The verdict, rightly, was "accidental death" after a two-hour enquiry.

The death of children was far from uncommon and many more were hurt to a more or less serious degree. For example on 21 August 1889 a five year-old boy, Robert Gillies (of 4 Court, 5 House, Mansfield Road, Aston – presumably tenements) was admitted to the General Hospital having been knocked down by a steam tram. Said to be in "a very precarious condition" he had two broken legs and serious head injuries.

In 1965 the magazine 'Modern Tramway' published a couple of articles by C. Gilbert entitled 'Memories of Birmingham's Steam Trams." He was there when they were running and had a marvellous memory; mentioning in this context an accident on the Stratford Road around 1904 when a boy of five ran under a tram and was pinned under the engine for half-an-hour before they could be released. The driver and his mate could not find a spanner to undo the engine skirts.

But he also wrote about a girl eight years old who lived in the Moseley Road during 1889 "who had only one leg and used a pair of crutches." She was exhibited as an example of what could happen if one did not stay on the footpath.

3 June 1900. Rochdale and a two year old child who suddenly ran in front of a tram was dragged nearly 15 yards before the driver could stop. Said later "to be progressing favourably", so severe were her injuries the surgeons had had to amputate her right leg.

November 1900. "On Monday afternoon a little girl named Ada Brookes, about two and a half years of age, whose parents reside in the New Terrace, Church-road, was crossing Church-road in front of a tram engine when she was knocked down and severely crushed. On being taken to Mr Fairley's surgery, in the Lichfield-road, it was found that she had received a scalp wound which was dressed, and Mrs Brookes was then able to take the child home. Had it not been that the engines are so constructed as to clear all impediments off the line, the child would undoubtedly have met with instantaneous death."

Trams were not entirely without their allies even when the subject of childrens' injuries and death came up. In an editorial dated 14 April 1883 we read: "I am sorry to hear a child has been run over and injured by a tram car, but considering the tender age at which poor men's children are sent into the streets alone, it is not to be wondered at if they sometimes meet with accidents."

By and large, cyclists did not often get killed by trams; mostly they fell off when crossing the rails at an oblique angle (but wet slippery cobbles may have been as much to blame) or their tyres got caught in the slot of the rails; and although the apocryphal tales of cyclists having to go to the tram sheds to get free from the rails were probably really just fairy tales, it hast to be admitted there was some pleasure to be found by a motorman seeing a cyclist fiddling about ahead of him when a reasonable bell-clanging and air brake application could certainly wake them up! Not so a tricyclist whose tyre got caught in the slot of a cable tramway – he decamped when the car arrived; but somehow in the process of stopping not only was his trike destroyed but the cable became jammed in the gripper, suspending services for a few hours.

On another occasion in 1896 a cyclist hung on the rail of a trailer to 'hitch' a ride. The conductor (who naturally denied it) may or may not have smacked his fingers with his fare box, but certainly the cyclist got badly damaged as he fell off at 10mph.

Another accident in 1904 was an example of a real, genuine 100% accident: "Mrs Mary Ann Wilde (31) of 54 Gooden-street, Heywood, had a narrow escape of serious injury, while cycling in Rochdale Road, Manchester, shortly after one o'clock on Sunday afternoon. She was out for a ride with her husband and another gentleman, and was going along the thoroughfare, following closely at the back of a [tram]car, and when near Nelson-street she turned slightly to the right, quite unconscious of the approach of a car on the opposite line. The carman did his best to pull up, but the vehicle struck Mrs Wilde's bicycle, knocking her down. Fortunately she fell clear of the rails. Suffering from severe bruises on the head and body, she was taken to the Royal Infirmary, and later was able to proceed home."

From time to time cyclists wrote in to papers, some letters were vitriolic, others reasoned, a few ... let this paragraph from a missive explain his viewpoint. "They can make overhead tramways, or they can contrive some means of locomotion along the roofs of the houses, or they can balloon it; or, if they have genius enough, they can develop and work the flying principle. They can do anything they like, but one thing – namely, they must not consider themselves, their comfort, their convenience, or their pocket; but they must consider me and my machine. I therefore warn them not to make a slit of three-quarters of an inch in their own roadway."

In all the sad litany of accidents probably the saddest was reported on 26 March 1887. It is said that some men bear 'the Mark of Cain' on them and if anyone was cursed by the gods it was the unknown man who died under a Birmingham and South Staffordshire District Tramway Company's steam tram. At the inquest held at West Bromwich, Thomas Hall, the tram engine driver concerned "said about six o'clock

on the day named he was driving No.7 engine from Great Bridge to Carter's Green, West Bromwich. As he was going through Swan Village near to the Gold Cup Inn there were several lads playing football with a hard ball on some waste land. The ball was kicked in front of the engine, and a man on a bicycle passed at the time. When about two yards in front of the engine, his bicycle passed over the ball and he fell, and before witness had time to pull up the engine passed over the body, and life was found to be extinct when taken from under the engine. Witness stated that he had been in the employ of different companies for four years, and in that period he had not met with one fatal accident. William Beresford, one of the lads playing at football, said a young man, whom he did not know, kicked the ball into the road. P.C. Bakewell stated that he searched the body, but could not find anything that would lead to the identification of the deceased. On the buttons of the deceased's clothing was a stamp with the name "T. Bennett, Kidderminster". The Coroner said it appeared from the evidence that the driver was not to blame, as he appeared to have pulled his engine up immediately. He believed that the company were willing to do all in their power to prevent accidents. The jury returned a verdict of 'Accidental death' and exonerated the driver from all blame."

As early as 1876, when steam tramcars were really a twinkle in engineers' eyes, 'The Engineer', one of the serious, often thoughtful, magazines of the day, carried an editorial which, although referring to horse trams, was well before its time. "Many street passengers seem to have an idea that, no matter when or where they choose to cross from one side to the other of a thoroughfare – whether crowded or not – any approaching vehicle ought to suddenly stop or steer out of their injudicious chosen and uncertain path. Many of the so-called street accidents are the result more of the thoughtlessness or the carelessness of the causers and victims of such events than of anything else; they to forget that once having started to cross the street, it is much easier for them either to pause or make one or two quicker steps than it is for the driver of a heavy vehicle such as an omnibus or a tram car to avert an accident ... It is not to be expected, however, that everyone will learn to exercise a little judgment in crowded streets, and it is therefore necessary that everything possible should be done to prevent whose who do get under the horses' feet, from whatever cause, from passing under the wheels of the vehicle they pull. This is especially necessary with tram cars, as it is impossible for a limb to pass under the wheels of these without being broken and splintered in the terrible manner, the flanges of the wheels running in the groove acting as very blunt shears. We witnessed this week an accident of this kind, and could not but be surprised that some simple means have not been adopted to keep objects of considerable size from getting under the wheels. A light guard might well be arranged to push a man from the wheel's path, either under the back of the car or into the clear way on either side of the car, according to the position of the fallen person. The 'pitching' of tram cars is not much, so that such guards, the best form, and which will occur to any car builder, could be made to work within three-quarters of an inch of the rails when the rubber springs are compressed under a full load. It is not often that people are seriously hurt by the horses in accidents, so that if they were prevented from passing under the wheels they would in many cases escape without broken bones. The cost of the necessary guards would be but small, and there seems no practical bar to their adoption."

Dudley Herald, 19 November 1887:
"SERIOUS TRAMWAY ACCIDENT
An accident occurred on Saturday night on the Dudley & Sedgley Trmy near the Fighting Cocks, Wolverhampton. A man named Samuel Bradley (38) of Dudley Rd, Sedgley, fell from a car into the roadway, sustaining a compound fracture of the ribs. He was taken to the Wolverhampton Hospital."

Wednesbury Herald, 5 February 1887:
"ACCIDENT AT DARLASTON
Several days ago James Wells, an engine-driver, in the employ of the South Staffs. Tramways Co., and residing at King's Hill, Wednesbury, narrowly escaped serious injury.

Wells was preparing his engine to leave the sheds at Darlaston for Walsall, when the driver of another engine was ordered to move back. He did so, not knowing that Wells was in the way, and the unfortunate man was caught between the two engines with the result his legs were severely cut and bruised. No blame was attached to anyone, the occurrence being purely the result of an accident."

Midland Advertiser, 23 January 1892:
"I caught one of our tram guards while off duty this week sketching in a small note-book he carried with him, and having obtained permission to look it through, was most agreeably surprised at the ability displayed. The numerous sketches evidenced he had a taste for drawing and colouring which if it had been fostered and encouraged in his youthful years would have placed him in a different position, revealing talents which might have been wonderful if developed under suitable conditions. The sketches, both portrait and landscape, are decidedly creditable. I am told, too, by one of his friends, who has watched his work with keen interest, that in his spare time he makes himself perfect in amateur photography, and has already 'taken' several photos of his comrades with their engines and cars, as well as interesting pieces of Black Country scenery, of which he has quite a collection. A mind bent in this direction ought to receive encouragement. Perhaps some of my readers would like to take an interest in his work, and I hope I am not breaking faith when I give his name – Conductor Herbert Hill, who is employed on the cars running between Handsworth and Darlaston.

It is rarely that you find those in humble life, who have to grapple with the stern necessities of existence, taking so deep an interest in art as to devote the whole of their leisure in tracing the beauties of Nature, and in discovering the truths, the pathos, the interest and the charm of that life which has gone on since the world began ... I do not know of a more pleasing instance of self-culture than this of a tram conductor who with constant application has mastered most of the difficult techniques of drawing and colouring, and given vent to his native artistic faculty."

[In our collection of South Staffs photographs there are a surprising number whose provenance is quite unknown – I like to think they came from the hand of Herbert Hill.]

FRIGHTFUL TRAMCAR ACCIDENT AT HUDDERSFIELD.

FIVE PERSONS KILLED AND TWENTY INJURED.

About three o'clock on Tuesday afternoon a fearful accident occurred on the tramway at Huddersfield, resulting in the death of five persons and more or less severe injury to about twenty others. The engine and one car, which was crowded with passengers, several standing on the steps and landing at the back of the car, were coming down from Lindley, and had gone safely until arriving almost at the bottom of West Parade, where the gradient is the steepest on that section. Then, instead of the speed slackening to take the curves and the corners between that point and St. George's Square, several of the passengers noticed that the car increased its rate. This continuing, five or six on the landing and steps at the back, becoming alarmed, jumped off. Soon those left in and on the car became further alarmed by the continually increasing impetus the engine and car acquired, the driver rang his bell violently as a warning to drivers of vehicles, and it is said, shouted to the passengers that he had lost control of the engine. On the engine and car went at a terrific pace, both keeping the rails until reaching the curve at the corner of Westgate and Railway Street, which leads into St. George's Square. On that curve the car left the rails, and fell over on to the outer side of the curve with a crash, and was driven along some distance by the velocity it had acquired. The outside passengers were thrown on the ground with tremendous violence, and the inside passengers in a confused heap. A crowd of willing helpers soon gathered, among them Ald. Walker, Councillor G. H. Hanson, Ald. Denham, and Mr. Green, stationmaster, and the injured were removed, bruised and bleeding, most to the Infirmary direct, and some to the offices and warehouses in the Eastgate Buildings, near, and then to the Infirmary. The first taken to the Infirmary was a dead baby, which remained unidentified for some time, but subsequently was identified as Annie Moore, aged five months, the child of Fred Moore, cotton spinner, East Street, Lindley, and Mary Ann, his wife, both of whom were soon afterwards taken to the Infirmary, and are severely injured. Isabella Woodhouse, about 60 years of age, of Lindley, died soon after being removed to the Infirmary. Several were totally unconscious, and many only partially conscious. There were in all about twenty persons removed to the Infirmary. As soon as the accident became known Drs. Cameron and Irving, Mr. Rhodes, Mr. Knaggs, and Mr. Robinson, of the honorary medical staff of the Infirmary, and Drs. Joll, Wright, McCaskie, Porritt, and Diamond made their way there, and as speedily as possible, with the aid of Mr. Prentis, assistant house surgeon, the injured were temporarily attended to, and those who were slightly injured went home. Mr. Richardson, house surgeon, was out of town at the time.

ACCIDENT ON THE DUDLEY AND SEDGLEY TRAMWAY LINE.

On Saturday evening, about six o'clock, an alarming accident occurred on the Wolverhampton, Dudley, and Sedgley tramway, at a point beyond the Fighting Cocks, and at that steep declivity known as Sedgley Hill. A steam tram laden with passengers was travelling at a good rate of speed in the direction of Wolverhampton, when it suddenly came into collision with a loaded timber waggon going in the same direction. The driver of the tram seems to have been quite unaware of the presence of the timber carriage on the road, and the driver of the latter also does not appear to have noticed the approach of the steam tram. Suddenly the engine, with the car attached, dashed into the pole at the rear of the wagon, with the result that two tree trunks on the latter penetrated the engine doors, and became so jammed that one had to be sawn off three feet from the end before the tram could be released. The sudden impact occasioned a great shock to the passengers, who were naturally much alarmed, and several of the females commenced screaming. Happily, no one was injured, except the driver of the tram, who sustained a slight injury to his left arm. After the occurrence the driver of the tram, which kept the rails, ran his car back to Spring Head, Sedgley, and transferred so many of his passengers as accompanied him to the next car travelling to Wolverhampton.

Earlier in the day a tram ran off the rails opposite SS. Mary and John's Catholic Church on Snow Hill, Wolverhampton, and travelled almost to the edge of the footpath. Nobody was injured.

22 December 1894.

Louth and North Lincolnshire Advertiser, 7 July 1883.

A TRAMCAR OVERTURNED IN THE TIPTON ROAD.

AN ALARMING ACCIDENT.

An accident alike serious and marvellous in its results occurred on Saturday night in the Tipton Road, by which the lives of 50 persons were placed in extreme jeopardy. The tramcars of the South Staffordshire and Birmingham and District Tramway Company, which run from Dudley to Tipton, Princes End, and Wednesbury, are generally crowded on Saturday nights by residents of those thickly populated districts coming to Dudley for marketing purposes and returning by the late trams. At twenty minutes past ten an engine and large car left Dudley for Darlaston with a heavy load of passengers. On reaching a set of points which are near the Guest Hospital in the Tipton Road, the car left the metals and became detached from the engine. The thoroughfare at this point is on a somewhat steep incline, and the huge vehicle at once started down the hill, increasing its speed until it had travelled a considerable distance. Here, swerving from a direct course, it collided with a lamp post and immediately toppled over, falling on the footway with a tremendous crash, the lamp post being hurled to the ground with great force. Many of the passengers, whose alarm had increased with the growing velocity of the car, shrieked with terror, and for a few moments all lay huddled upon the path or within the shattered wreck dazed and unable to realise what had happened. Those who were not much hurt, however, quickly scrambled to their feet, and promptly set about rescuing their less fortunate fellow-passengers. Other assistance was also soon forthcoming, and the injured people were rescued from among the broken glass and woodwork. It was found that fifteen persons had received more or less severe hurts, many of them being cut by glass and bruised and shaken. They were all removed to the hospital, which fortunately was so close at hand, and their wounds dressed, after which most of them were able to proceed to their homes. Two of the injured, who were suffering from more serious wounds, were detained at the hospital. The following is a list of the persons who were injured :—Sarah White, Castle Street, Tipton , Mary Lamer, Bloomfield ; Ann Dudley, Bloomfield ; William Hobson, of Brown Hill Colliery; David Hill, Bloomfield Road ; Martha Mitchell, Sedgley Road ; Thomas Whitehouse, Tipton ; George Whitehouse, Tipton ; Charles Mitchell, Sedgley Road ; Emma Griffin, Church Lane ; Emma Turley, Tipton ; Joseph Royal, Kate's Hill ; Thomas Smith, Princes End ; Thomas Mills, Princes End ; Thomas Amos, Hurst Lane, Tipton. Mr. Mills and Mr. Amos were the two passengers detained, but their injuries were not of a serious character, the main fear being erysipelas if their wounds were exposed to the cold. Mr. Mills, however, did sufficiently recover to be able to leave the institution in the afternoon. Amos remained. Naturally such an extraordinary and serious accident created much excitement and all day on Sunday rumours of all kinds were floating about the district. Such a narrow escape from an appalling loss of life has probably never been known in the history of the district. Our representative called at the Guest Hospital on Monday morning, and had an interview with Amos. He was suffering somewhat from shock, and had a bad abrasion on the left side of his face. Otherwise he was able to converse without effort. He said the car at the bottom was full of passengers when it started from Dudley, and on the top was a great number of passengers. He was amongst the latter, and when the car struck the lamp-post and toppled over he was shot out into the road. He was not aware the car was off the rails when it increased in velocity, and he did not think the passengers were. Asked how he attributed the car leaving the rails, he believed it was because of its going too fast over the points. He described the scene when the car turned over as being awful, the shrieks of the passengers being heartrending. Pedestrians on the road also speak of the accident as most exciting to witness. The car was completely smashed, and it took the exertions of a break-down gang the whole of Sunday to clear away the *debris*. Considerable speculation is rife as to how the car left the rails, and various theories have been suggested. The officials believe that the real cause is the snapping of an axle, and that the heavy gale prevailing at the time assisted in turning the car over. An eye witness, however, states that the engine took one side of the turn-out and the car the other, the sudden jerk snapping the coupling chain. The engine did not leave the metals. The conductor, who lives at Bloxwich, is, it appears, suffering considerably from shock. He was collecting tickets on the top of the car at the time of the accident, and was thrown in the middle of the road with violence, but luckily escaped without injury. Mr. Alfred Dickenson, the general manager to the South Staffordshire Tramway Company at Darlaston, decided to have a minute inspection made of the tramroad from the point where the car left the metals to that where it toppled over. The driver of the engine was George Powell, and he has the character of being an attentive and sober workman.

***Dudley Herald,* 1 December 1888.**

TRAMWAY DEPOT BLOWN DOWN AT DUDLEY.

On Thursday morning a shocking accident, resulting in the death of one man, and the serious injury of another, took place at the new tramway *depot*, being erected near the Dudley Railway Station, at the terminus of the Dudley and Stourbridge tramways. The *depot* is being erected by Mr J. Fell, of Leamington, and is to be a structure of wood and iron, with brick foundations. About half-past ten o'clock on Thursday morning the wind, which had been blowing strongly all the morning increased into a gale, and a bystander observed the framework sway dangerously on one side. He shouted to the workmen that the roof was coming down, but the words were scarcely out of his mouth when down came part of the massive structure with a terrible crash. David Hebblethwaite, and William Woodhall, carpenters, were working on a piece of timber on the side next the Tipton Road when the accident occurred. Hearing the shout, both started to get out of the way, but Hebblethwaite was caught by a piece of falling timber and hurled to the earth. A massive beam fell on his head, dashing out his brains, and killing him instantly. Woodhall was more fortunate for the part of the structure immediately over him fell on the top of a lamp post, and he was enabled to crawl from under it unscathed. A cart being procured, the body of Hebblethwaite was placed in it, and taken to the police mortuary. As this was being done a groan was heard inside the building. Several men went over the place from whence the sound proceeded, and in one of the car pits found a labourer named Michael Connor lying bruised and bleeding. He had been working at the pit, and escaped being killed by falling into it. As it was, he was severely bruised and battered. He was at once taken to the Guest Hospital, where he was detained. His home is in Cross Street, Dudley Hebblethwaite, who lived in Salop Street, leaves a widow and two children.

Mr E. P. Jobson (deputy coroner), held an inquest yesterday, on the body at the Saracen's Head Hotel.—The evidence showed that a violent gust of wind blew down the frame work, a portion of which fell upon the deceased and killed him instantaneously. Mr Bate, builder, said he considered the supports were not strong enough, and other builders alleged that they were quite strong enough for the job.—The jury returned a verdict of " Accidental death."

***County Express,* 22 March 1884.**

COLLISION WITH A STEAM TRAMCAR.

THE DANGERS OF REVERSING STATIONS.

At the Birmingham County Court yesterday, before his Honour Judge Chalmers, John Archer, grocer, Church Lane, Aston, sued the Birmingham Central Tramways Company Limited to recover £8 damages. Mr. Hasell appeared for the plaintiff, and Mr. H. A. Pearson (instructed by Mr. Archibald S. Bennett) represented the defendants.—Mr. Hasell, in opening the case, said that on the 24th March last, about five o'clock in the evening, the plaintiff was driving in a covered cart through the Minories, and attempted to cross the Old Square to get into Corporation Street. He was going almost at a walking pace, and he looked to see if any trams were about, but he did not see one. When he was crossing the rails, without any whistle or signal having previously been given, a tramcar came up and collided with his cart. The car caught the cart about the wheels and Mr. Archer was violently shaken. When he got out of the cart he found that the axle had been bent up and the cart was otherwise damaged. A crowd rapidly collected and three persons voluntarily came forward and gave their names and addresses as being willing to come forward and say that no whistle had been blown. The amount claimed included the following :—Cost of the repair of the cart, £2 15s. ; permanent injury to the cart, £3 ; and 8s., being four weeks' hire of another cart at 2s. per week. The cart originally cost the plaintiff £16, and since the accident he had been obliged to sell it for £8, and to purchase a new cart.—Mr. Pearson submitted that the defendants were in no way liable for the accident. The plaintiff was sitting at the back of the cart, and was driving at a reckless rate across a thoroughfare where it behoved him to exercise more than ordinary precaution. Had he turned either to the right or to the left he would have had plenty of room to avoid the car. Directly the plaintiff's cart was seen the engine was stopped.—A number of witnesses were called on each side, and their evidence was of a conflicting nature. Those for the plaintiff contended that the tram was travelling at the rate of six or seven miles an hour, and that the plaintiff was going at less than walking pace; also that the conductor never gave any signal of the approach of his car. On the other side the evidence was to the effect that the plaintiff was travelling at a furious rate, that those in charge of the car and the engine did all that they could to prevent an accident, and that the plaintiff ran into the car. It was also shown that an old lady was between the car and the cart, and that she had to be pulled out of the way.—His Honour, in giving judgment, said that at the place where the accident occurred the public ran considerable risk. Whether those reversing stations ought to be left unguarded and unprotected he did not say, but they were allowed, and he did not see that under the circumstances the company were guilty of negligence. The Act of Parliament which enabled those heavy engines to be run along the roads did not give them any greater rights than those which other people had who used the streets. He was always inclined to hold the drivers of those engines up to their strict liabilities, but in this case it seemed to him that the accident took place mainly because the plaintiff was not on the lookout. He did not think that the tram was going at an excessive pace, and he very much doubted if the plaintiff had heard the whistle whether it would have made any difference. The plaintiff was not driving very fast, and just in front of him there was an old lady standing in the way. It was to him (the judge) by no means clear that the accident was not caused by the old lady causing the horse to draw up a little. There must be judgment for the defendants.—Verdict accordingly.

***Birmingham Daily Gazette,* 25 October 1887.**

ALARMING TRAMWAY ACCIDENT AT OLDBURY.

Yesterday morning about 9 40 a man named Arthur Thorley, a wagoner in the employ of the Great Bridge Iron and Steel Company, was driving a wagon with two horses and 1 ton 14 cwt of iron through Oldbury. On passing up the Bustle Bridge, past the Oldbury Railway Station, for a long distance it is impossible for a vehicle to pass a tram on the one side of the road. The wagon was half way up the hill when a steam tram came down at a fast rate, and as the tram could not be stopped and the wagon had not time to cross the road a collision took place, the wagon being completely upset on the footpath and crushed. The driver was thrown violently against a pair of gates, which fortunately gave way, or he must have been killed. The shaft horse was thrown to the ground, the other falling on the top of it, but recovering itself. Fortunately there were no passers-by near the spot at the time of the accident, or the consequence might have been even more serious.

***Birmingham Daily Gazette,* 16 January 1889.**

Social Conditions

THE THREATENED STRIKE IN THE BUILDING TRADE

"The notice given by the employers in the building trade of their intention to reduce the wages of bricklayer's labourers one halfpenny per hour terminated on Saturday [12 November 1892]. At a meeting held at the Malt Shovel Inn on Saturday night, it was resolved that the men should turn out on strike on Monday if the employers attempt to enforce a reduction. At a meeting on Monday Mr Keys (general secretary) presided over a large attendance, and it was decided to continue the strike."

[The cut represented about 5% or more. Then the strike was broken by blacklegs and Irish labour being brought in; today it would be Polish or 'Russians'.]

WAGES

From *"The Effects of the Factory System"* by Allen Clarke.

First published 1895-6, but revised 1897-8, this print is, I think, from the 1899 version, but it has entered various prints subsequently, and I understand can still be found in the lists. The material is included to give an indication why work on steam trams was so eagerly sought after.

WAGES

MONEY WAGES

Now, what do the factory operatives get for their toil? What pay for this ruination of themselves and blighting of their children? For this loss of health and brain, this loss of fresh air and sweet recreation, this loss of limb and life, for all this cindery renunciation of the beautiful earth, what are they paid? Let us see.

In 1886, according to the General Report on the Wages of the Manual Labour Class (issued by the Board of Trade, October 1895), the average weekly wage of the adult male factory operative was 25s. 3d., of the adult female, 15s. 3d.; of boys, 9s. 4d.; and of girls, 6s. 10d.; the half-time lads getting 4s. 6d., and the girls, 2s. 3d.

The Board of Trade General Report on Wages, however, does not give a true idea of the real earnings of the factory workers. I fancy that the wages of piecers (adult, though really but apprentices) are averaged with those of the spinners (equal to journeymen). I give the correct wage figures for Oldham and Bolton, the two central towns of the cotton trade :—

OLDHAM

Average spinner's wage	. . .	.	35/-
,, big piecer's wage	. . .	.	17/-
,, little piecer's wage .	. .	.	11/-
,, cardroom hand's (male) .	.	.	26/-
,, cardroom hand's (female)	.	.	18/-
,, half-timer's wage (male) .	.	.	5/-
,, half-timer's wage (female)	.	.	2/6 [1]

BOLTON

Average spinner's wage	. . .	.	38/-
,, big piecer's wage	. . .	.	14/-
,, little piecer's wage .	. .	.	10/-
,, cardroom hand's (male) .	.	.	24/-
,, cardroom hand's (female)	.	.	14/-
,, weaver's wage (female) .	.	.	18/-
,, half-timer's wage (female)	.	.	2/6
,, half-timer's wage (male)	.	.	4/6 [2]

If anything, the average wage is less now. It certainly is not more. In 1832 the adult male cotton operative's wage averaged 31s.; in the same year the adult female (weaver's) wage averaged 12s.[3] It seems the male wage has decreased,

[1] Supplied by Operative Spinners' Secretary, Oldham.
[2] Reckoned from Bolton Spinners' Annual Reports, and checked by personal inquiries amongst operatives.
[3] "The Cotton Trade in England and on the Continent" (Gævernitz, 1895).

---

while the female's has increased. Here are some further figures :—

Yarn Production per Operative.	Cost of Labour per lb.	Annual Wage of Operative.
1819 . . 968 lbs.	6.4d.	£26 13 0
1844 . . 2754 lbs.	2.3d.	28 12 0
1882 . . 5520 lbs.	1.9d.	44 4 0 [1]

The worker thus turns out six times more stuff than in 1819; but does he get six times more wage? Six times the 1819 wage makes £156. But the worker only gets £44. Where goes the other £112? The work is now done in considerably less hours, too. In 1855 the factory hours for adults were 82 per week; to-day they are only 56.

The value of the wage depends, of course, upon its purchasing power, and a shilling to-day will purchase more than it would at the beginning of the century. But there is not much real difference; for a shilling to-day will also purchase more labour than it would in 1801—six times more than it would in 1819; and if food is cheaper it is because the labour is cheaper. A man nowadays does six times more for his shilling than in 1819, though he does not get six times as much value for it—perhaps not twice as much; and he always pays dearly for the cheapness, gaining nothing really. The lords of labour, whose conjuring tricks are

[1] "The Cotton Trade in England and on the Continent" (Gævernitz, 1895).

the most exquisite delusions and bewildering prestidigitation, make it their business to see that the workman never gets anything but at his own expense. While they are making him believe that pennies are growing in his whiskers, they are dexterously abstracting his purse from his pocket; the money taken off the corn to cheapen his loaf is filched from him by subtle, roundabout ways. They pretend to give him gold sovereigns for a shilling; all he gets is a gilded sixpence. The manufacturers agitated against the corn laws because they hoped thereby to get cheaper labour. They were philanthropists when it paid. The Englishman can only get truly cheap bread by growing it himself; or, at least, by seeing that he is not cheated by the go-between party when the produce of his British labour is being exchanged for foreign corn.

REAL WAGES—FOOD, HOUSING, ETC.

THE best way to get at the real value of the factory operatives' wage is to inquire what necessaries and comforts of life it brings them. We have seen the sort of town they get to live in. A brick box with a lid of smoke, which is very unhealthy. "Mr Estcourt, the city analyst, tells us that one ton out of every 100 tons burned in the factories of Manchester remains in the air as soot. This, in fog, is often productive of pain and a feeling of tightness in the chest; very oppressive indeed. All chest affections are made worse by it." This smoke is on all the houses, and even enters them, soiling furniture and clothes.[1] Let us look at the individual houses. They are

[1] Lecture on the Pollution of Air, by Henry Simpson, M.D. (published by John Heywood, Manchester).

mostly small four-roomed (two above and two below) cottages, rents varying from 3s. 6d. to 5s. 6d. They have no baths, as a rule. Each house is one of a long row, like a barracks, divided into so many equal portions. All cooking and cleaning are done in the living apartment; the washing is done in the room behind. On wet days the clothes are dried in the living room, to the discomfort of the husband when he come homes from the factory. The houses have generally scant backyard space; the jerry-builder wishes to squeeze as much property on the land as possible, and tries to cheat the building and sanitary authorities as much as he can.

Internally the cottages are cheaply furnished, though here and there some are set out luxuriously, mainly with intention to display and swagger over less fortunate neighbours. The more furniture a woman has in her house, the greater her social position. The women are proud when they can exhibit a parlour to Sunday visitors; it is shut up six days of the week, and is only kept for brag. Ostentatious superfluity, in the idea of the artisan's wife, is, as with those in higher grades of society, a sign of superiority.

Many of the houses are very meanly furnished. The piecer getting 14s. a week, has to be content with a table, a few chairs, and a bed. Often families of a dozen sleep in two rooms.

Gævernitz (whose book, translated by a factory master, is supposed to be a correct authority on the factory system) makes some very erroneous statements about the prosperity, housing, food, etc., of the Lancashire cotton operatives.

He is taken to visit various houses—selected by the employers or their secretaries, who naturally take him to the exceptional—even rare—specimens; spinners who are teetotalers, co-operators, and have a family of grown-up sons and daughters working. He says nothing of the time during which the families are being brought up; nothing of strikes, lock-outs, and other drawbacks; but makes Lancashire into a little heaven. He speaks of the mule spinner having a yearly trip to the seaside; a house with a garden in front (!); containing a piano (!); "and nowhere is the arm-chair missing for the head of the family."[1] He further describes the "well-nourished, well-dressed operatives," enjoying a holiday at Blackpool, all the males looking strong and healthy, the females fine and strapping; and states that there are no trade disputes, "masters and men working in thoroughly sweet accord."

A pretty picture, if it were only true. I have never seen it, though I have lived in a manufacturing town all my life, and not merely paid an exploring visit of a week or two's duration; neither have I seen the sturdy operatives at Blackpool, as Gævernitz describes, though I have resided there five years, and not got all my

[1] "The Cotton Trade in England and on the Continent" (pp. 173-200).

experience (as he did) on one brief day-excursion. My experience is, that there is one piano in about every hundred of the operatives' houses, and then only got when all the children are growing up and working, and generally on the hire system. Herr Gævernitz does not say whether the musical instruments he saw were paid for or not.

As regards the operatives' holidays at Blackpool, I have observed the factory visitors there for several years; and it is quite easy to single them out in the crowds, not because of their remarkably healthy looks, but the contrary. And I may ask, Is a few days' stifling, jostling holiday, in a town packed with excursionists any commensurate rest after fifty weeks' factory labour? When at the seaside, the factory folks work harder than at their daily toil, rushing to and fro in order to see everything in their brief sojourn, and they generally go home more weary and jaded than they are after a week's work. And most of the factory operatives never get to the seaside for more than one day a year; while a great many never get there at all, even on a day-trip.

Whatever be the wages of the factory operatives, they are mostly barely sufficient. They allow a breakfast of coffee or tea, bread, bacon, and eggs—when eggs are cheap; a dinner of potatoes and beef; an evening meal of tea, bread, and butter, cheap vegetables or fish, and a slight supper at moderate price; a few news-papers, cheap clothes, and sometimes a day or two at the seaside. The factory operatives have small chance of saving a competency for old age. Some few, by sore scraping and hard denial of all pleasures of life, manage to buy a house by the time they are ready for the grave; but most end their working period as poor as they began it. I never yet heard of any operative spinner retiring on the smallest fortune made by his factory work. Most spinners, when they became too old for the mill, used to start small shops or get a donkey and cart and vend greengroceries; but co-operative societies have closed those open-ings, and the worn-out spinner of to-day generally has to be kept by his grown-up children, or spin his last earthly set of days in the workhouse.

A friend of mine, whose employment sends him daily into working-class houses in several towns, sends me the following :—

"The facts which have struck me most forcibly are the following :—

1. The low wages of a large number of factory workers—married piecers earning 13s. per week. I have one family in my mind particularly. The husband gets the wage aforesaid. They have two children already, and a third just appeared. During the whole time of her pregnancy, the wife has almost up to the last moment been engaged day after day in taking in washing to supplement the husband's earnings. She is now lying in bed with a baby at her side, and a tumour in her leg.

The most impressive fact, however, which I have come across is the extent of female labour and its terrible effects on the children and the home.

Female factory labour, whether single or married —but especially married, is the great curse of Lancashire. To take a pistol and shoot a man is moral compared with its effect. I will give you one or two examples.

No. 1. Married woman—works in factory. Up to recently she had one child. This child suffers terribly from fits, and probably will do all its life. Up to within a fortnight or three weeks of the birth of the second, the mother continued her work in the mill. The child is, of course, pining, ailing, sickly, and will probably never be fit for anything. The mother went back to work again two or three weeks after the child's birth. The child is left in charge of its grand-mother, who is nearly worried to death by its perpetual wailing. The house is, of course, a pigstye. Yet they are very respectable people.

No. 2. Married woman—worked in the mill until her marriage—has had six children. Three of them died of convulsions. The last one of the three living is also terribly afflicted with convulsions, and the doctor says it may die in a fit any day.

And so I might go on to any length. There is hardly a house where the mother works or has worked in the factory but the terrible effects of factory life are seen in the physique of the children.

The effects on the home of married women working in the factory are simply awful. There is no home, and no home life. Pegged up in small jerry-built houses destitute of order or comfort. The mother sends or leaves her children to be nursed if young, and if not young, leaves them to look after themselves. At dinner-time she hurries home for a cup of tea and some bread and butter, and after this repast, hurries off back again to the mill. Ill or well, she has to go; children ill or well, she has to go; baby expected, she goes up to the last moment, and back again to the mill soon after it is born. Glorious life—this working in the mill, carrying an unborn baby and coming home to drudge at housework till bed-time.

Finding no home comforts, the natural thing follows. The husband, after his day's work is done and finding his wife helping to keep the home, goes off to the alehouse, and spends in many cases as much as his wife earns—and so the game goes merrily on.

No. 3. Another striking thing is the uncertainty of labour.

To almost every factory worker it happens that one fine morning work is slack, and one or two of the family have to stop at home till times mend. The earnings of the family are reduced, and they can't pay their grocer's bill. Sometimes the case is far worse than this. At Astley Bridge one mill has been stopped nineteen weeks, and has only just started again. During the whole of this time the employés are in a sort of semi-starvation, and running so far into debt for rent, etc., that it will take months or perhaps years to pay off all they owe. Long before they have paid all off the mill may stop again, and then debts will be a drag on them all their life.

Examples of all these I could give galore."

This section was to have been in Volume One of this series but I was unable to obtain a decent copy to work from. At first sight you may well ask what connection there is with steam tramways, and the answer is many, for when the cotton-mill operatives were able to afford to travel they could shift from mill to mill thus ensuring that if the wages were bad at least they could look for another job where a few pennies extra was on offer, and in fact although fifty years later I can still remember the long lists of vacancies outside the mills both in Lancashire and Leicester, vacancies for the weirdest sound-ing jobs! Realistically without the mill traffic many steam tram companies – for example Wigan or Heywood, would have gone under very quickly. I should add the author was a professional writer although as he tells us he came from genuine enough working class stock. " ...my own mother was a winder, and I was born during the cotton panic [1863] when my father was out of work [a self-acting loom minder] and my mother was compelled to become the breadwinner. I was nursed by my grandmother while my mother toiled at a factory a couple of miles distant [from Bolton, where they lived]. During the dinner hour sixty minutes normally, often only forty to forty five in reality, mother would run home to suckle me, get her own meal, and be back at the mill before work started..." However to counter-balance the following quotations a less politically biased version of mill-work can be found in Thomas Armstrong's "Bankdam" series.

Changes in Lifestyle

In the 21st century many people feel a sense of loss as a result of the changes in lifestyle that have occurred and still occur at an accelerating rate. But the wheel always turns and this is a part of a letter sent from Tottenham on 12 May 1890; well over a century ago!

"Sir, Those who have lived in the world many years have seen great changes in society and its ways, but perhaps in no way more than that in which the public streets are used on Sundays. Years ago it was a common thing to see people quietly wending their way to some place of worship, and taking with them the younger members of their family, thus training them as directed in the way they should go, and forming habits which influenced the whole life for good. Even now in country towns and villages the same thing is to be noticed, and the same advantages to some extent realized. But what do we see going on weekly in our public thoroughfares under the name of religion or religious worship. Men and boys beating drums, blowing horns, some of which are horribly out of tune, and singing hymns to song tunes, thus associating the worship of the Almighty with the song of the drunkard, and the tune of the street dancer, and these things are all done in the name of religion. True, there are many engaged in carrying on this sort of work who are themselves good worthy people, against whose character nothing can be said, but surely they are labouring under the great mistake that mere noise, tumult, and excitement, will permanently form and build up Christian manhood; it may stimulate and excite for a time, but a mere appeal to impulse and passion never did yet, and perhaps never will, produce the same good results permanently as appeals to reason, thought, and judgment, and if the good people who promote the street parades with all the discordant noises would reflect in their quiet moments as to results, perhaps they would be led not to relax their efforts but to use the same in another less noisy and objectionable way, with a view to set in motion the thinking and reasoning powers of those they desire to benefit ... An Observer."

This little collection of 'people tales' comes from the Midlands and are included simply because it takes all sorts ...

"A Handsworth working man last Saturday threw away a 15 shilling postal order in one of the streets of West Bromwich, thinking it was waste paper. When he arrived home he found out what he had done, and immediately took the tram to West Bromwich, where to his surprise and intense satisfaction, there was the order just where he had dropped it. It was very dirty, and had been trampled on a good many times but still not sufficient to stop payment. The individual in question must consider himself a fortunate fellow."

"28 April 1894. The three boys who were brought before the Sedgley magistrates on Monday for endangering the lives of passengers on the Midland Tramway Company's line, might have caused serious loss of life. On three nights, during the month the lads placed a chain across the rails, with a view, in their own words "of seeing the tram come off". Fortunately, on each occasion the engine and car passed over the obstruction without leaving the rails, though the passengers were much shaken, and on one occasion the car was nearly being overturned. The defendants who were very young seemed to treat the offence as a "lark", but the Bench reminded them of the serious consequences which might have resulted from their action, ordered them to pay costs and to come up for judgement in six months."

"30 June 1883. A rural or rustic fete, Fete Champetre at Cotwell End Farm [2 miles from Dudley]. This popular pic-nic takes place on Tuesday next. The facilities offered by 'bus and tram to reach the delightful scene of the entertainment will induce many friends to go and spend a most enjoyable afternoon."

"5 December 1891. Football at Stoney Lane. The match today at Stoney Lane is the Albion v Accrington. The kick-off is at 2.30, and the Dudley contingent will have to journey by the 1.45 tramcar to reach the ground on time."

"WELL-KNOWN AT BILSTON. Mary Ann Aston, Birmingham Street, was summoned for importuning passengers in Trindle Road [the junction of three tramway routes]. P.C. Powell proved the case. Mr Chief-Superintendent Speke said the defendant was well known at Bilston. She was sent to gaol for 14 days with hard labour."

We have very few contemporary descriptions of individual men employed by steam tramway companies: although at management level a few obituaries exist. James Sowerby only comes to our notice because he, too, died – in his case from scalds when his boiler protested at its misuse.

"6 January 1891. Shift 5pm to 6am. Middle-aged man, a little over 40, and bore a good character in all respects and especially for sobriety. He had suffered from dyspepsia for some time, and recently he had been absent from the works for two months, having several cysts removed from his head. On his return he seemed in a better state of health. On several occasions Sowerby had, to the knowledge of other drivers, neglected his duties ... on 2 or 3 occasions he had allowed the water in his boiler to get too low, and once he was found fast asleep in his 'cabin'. No-one in authority heard of these defaults ... and [other drivers] did not report them because they did not wish to get Sowerby into trouble."

A curiosity of ladies' dresses was that wearing a crinoline access to the top deck of a tramcar was easy for a lithe young girl but getting down was not as each hoop got caught on the rungs of the steps and had to be freed by the conductor. For short journeys it is recorded they preferred to stand owing to the difficulty in sitting. Unsurprisingly other passengers were known to make barbed comments. Small wonder then that this note appeared on 14 January 1893 relating to the formation of the 'Crinoline League'.

"Henrietta Evie Stannard whose literary name of John Strange Winter is well known in the world of fiction, says 'There is little doubt the unsightly and dangerous crinoline is rapidly coming into fashion. I'm not surprised at the horror with which women of all classes in the United Kingdom regard it; these things are ordered by a small clique of men'".

The Editor of the paper says 'We are quite ready to sympathise with Mrs Stannard in her protests against the revival of the crinoline which likens the female form divine to a pyramidal peramulating gasometer'. What a delightful expression!

"DUDLEY AND STOURBRIDGE STEAM TRAMWAYS COMPANY LIMITED. On Wednesday last, a number of the employees of this company, together with their wives and friends, were provided, by the directors, with a day's enjoyment. In order not to incommode the public any more than absolutely necessary, it was arranged that the outing should be on two separate days, one half being taken on the Wednesday and the remainder yesterday (Friday). Brakes were provided and a start made from the Dudley Arms for Bridgnorth, the scenery on the road being most charming. Arrived at the latter place, the company, to the number of about 35, sat down to a capital repast, provided by Mrs Meads, of the Bandour Arms Hotel. Mr T. Smith (in the unavoidable absence of the Chairman of the company, Mr G. Cattell Greenway) occupied the chair, and amongst others present were – Mr Alderman Bagott, Mr C.A.Edge (directors), Mr H.F. Woodward (secretary), Mr W. Dinnon (manager). Letters of apology for non-attendance from the following directors – Mr G.C. , Mr J.H. Lynde, and Mr E. Pritchard, were read. Substantial justice having been done to the repast, Mr Smith addressed a few words to the men, laying particular importance upon the necessity of the directors and employees working together, and showing how, by the carefulness of the drivers, accidents could be averted, and how, by the willing service of those employed, the company could be made prosperous. In alluding to the long hours of tramway servants, the Chairman stated that from a return just handed to him employees of this company were not so long as those of many others, but the question of shorter hours would always secure the careful attention of the Board. Mr Bagott spoke of the civility and attention of the conductors and bore testimony to the extreme care and caution of the drivers in passing through the Market Place at Dudley on crowded occasions. Mr Edge also spoke, urging the guards to use every energy in looking out for passengers. By so doing they would contribute to the success of the company. A very enjoyable excursion up the river to Apley Hall was then made, the lovely scenery being much appreciated. After tea a start was made for home at six o'clock. Wolverhampton was reached about nine, after a very pleasant drive. The men expressed their hearty appreciation and thorough enjoyment of the outing provided for them, and so ended a most agreeable day. The trip was repeated yesterday, the remaining half of the employees, with their wives and friends, being taken."

"14 December 1885. A TRAM ENGINE DRIVER DRUNK AND ASLEEP ON HIS ENGINE. A CATASTROPHE NARROWLY AVERTED. At the West Bromwich Police Court on Saturday, Edward Jarvis, of 328 Birchfield Road, Handsworth, was charged with being drunk whilst in charge of a tram engine on the 28th ult. Mr Weekes said he appeared to prosecute on behalf of the Central Tramway Company in whose employ the defendant was. The company felt that it was one of the most flagrant offences which it was possible for any of their servants to commit. On the night of the 20th ult information was received at the head office in Birmingham that Jarvis was drunk in charge of his engine. An inspector was sent to Perry Barr, and whilst travelling on an engine along Birchfield Road, where only a single line was laid, he saw the defendant's tram engine coming in the opposite direction at a good rate. The inspector had just time to pull up, jump off his engine, and run and stop this man to prevent a most serious collision. He found defendant asleep with his head hanging over the side of his engine, and he had only just time to strike him to awake him and get the brake applied as the two engines came close together. Thus a very serious accident was averted. The company were very anxious that their servants should conduct their business in such a way as to make it thoroughly safe for the public to travel in their vehicles. Richard Henry Dickenson gave evidence in support of this statement, after which defendant was fined 20s and costs or 21 days' hard labour."

"14 November 1885. DUDLEY AND SEDGLEY TRAMWAYS. On Thursday evening the employees, about forty in number, of the above company, were entertained to a supper, the cost of which had been subscribed for by the public using the tramcars. The repast, which was of a most substantial character, was served up in the large room at Mr Kimberley's Brewery, Sedgley, and was heartily enjoyed by all present. After the withdrawal of the cloth Mr Hill, the company's manager, presided, supported on his right by Mr W.G. Stimpson, manager Wolverhampton Tramway Company and Mr York, Sedgley; and on his right by Messrs Millington, Foster and Hill. Reference was made to the temporary closing of the tram line consequent on the alterations now being made for the introduction of steam, and a hope expressed that when the line was re-opened, as anticipated, on 21 December next, it would be still more extensively patronised and that the coming year would bring with it better trade and prosperity for the district generally. A number of complimentary toasts were proposed, interspersed with song and sentiment, the donors of the feast were thanked for their liberality, and altogether a very pleasant evening was spent."

"3 January 1885. Tipton Local Board of Health. The Rev. S.T. Tozer said there was another kind of nuisance connected with the tramways which the Board should see to, and that was the foul

and filthy language used by the engineers. It was no ordinary curse these men made use of, but filthy and obscene words. He thought the Board might try and stop the use of obscene language in their roads. It was unanimously decided to write to the Manager of the Tramway Company asking for the abatement of the nuisances complained of..."

Pick-pocketing and handbag snatching was as common in 1885 as 2007. The penalties for those caught seem rather better ...

"17 March 1888. POCKET PICKING AT ASTON. Edward Summers (53), rule maker, residing in Pugh-road, Aston, was charged with having stolen at Aston on March 3rd a purse containing a sovereign from Kate Whitby, a married woman. Mr Dorsett prosecuted. The case was heard at the Aston police court on Tuesday of last week when the accused was committed to take his trial. It will be remembered that the prosecutrix and her husband were waiting at Aston Cross for a tramcar, and that when a car came down the hill, and a crowd had gathered round it, the prisoner put his hand into the prosecutrix's dress pocket and abstracted the purse. Mrs Whitby demanded her purse from the prisoner telling her husband at the same time that the prisoner had taken it. Mr Whitby then seized the accused, who at once produced the purse and said the prosecutrix had dropped it and he had picked it up. The prisoner was sentenced to six months hard labour."

"10 February 1889. PICKING POCKETS ON THE TRAMWAY. William Jones (whose abode was unknown) was charged with pocket picking on a tramway car. Elizabeth Hatfield stated that she was getting on a tramcar in Corporation Street on Saturday night, when she felt something touch her dress pocket. She put her hand down quickly and caught hold of the prisoner's hand at her pocket. Her purse was gone. She called out and the man leaped on to the car, where the conductor secured him, and he was given into the custody of Police-constable 24A. There were several people crowding on to the car at the time she felt the hand in her pocket. After the man was arrested the purse was found on the step of the car. When witness accused the prisoner he said "You've made a grand mistake, someone else must have your purse, or it's on the floor". The man was remanded for a week pending inquiries into his antecedents."

"12 December 1885. A VERY DEAR RIDE. Henry Gee, moulder, 104 Lawley Street, Birmingham, was charged with defrauding the South Staffordshire and Birmingham District Tramway Company by refusing to pay his fare; and also with assaulting Walter Edwards, tramcar conductor. The prosecutor said on Saturday night, about half-past 10, he was conductor on the tramcar from Carter's Green to Handsworth. The defendant got in the car in High Street, West Bromwich, and refused to pay the fare. Witness asked him again at Beeches Road, but defendant persisted in refusing to pay. At Handsworth he was asked again but refused, and then kicked witness on the leg. Philip Clair gave corroborative evidence as to the refusal on the part of the defendant to pay at Handsworth. P.C. Gunn

deposed to apprehending the prisoner on Sunday morning, about 20 minutes to one, in the yard of the tramway company at Hansworth. Defendant "who as in beer at the time" would not pay the fare demanded, but at the police station he offered twopence to the conductor, which, however, was refused. The officer searched the prisoner, but did not find a ticket upon him. Defendant: Gentlemen, I paid the conductor twopence, but did not receive a ticket. I would not pay a second time until there was somebody to witness that I did pay. Do you think a man in his sober senses would refuse to pay two pence, and run the risk of getting imprisoned? I paid once, and I reckon I should not be flesh and blood if I did not protest to pay a second time. Mr Underhill: But you had had some beer, and were evidently not in your sober senses. The costs are 9s. and we have decided to reduce them to one-half – 4s.6d in each case – and fine you 6d for each offence, and the costs, total 10s."

This little tale came from a short-lived newspaper, the *Birmingham Leader,* and is dated 11 October 1890. A whole social history is written in this simple (and rather nastily written) tale: shoe-shines are almost gone, the trams are gone and modern plimsolls (sorry, trainers) are never cleaned!

"So Hoppy is a shoeblack, and is said to make a fair income by shining the boots of the tramway passengers who wait at the Aston Cross for the cars, so slow in coming down the hill – when you are in a hurry to get to town ... Hoppy wasn't a 'macaroni', did not wear a 'stand up collar or suck the head of a cane' ... he was polishing brasses in a pub and asked 'that girl' to wed him. 'She wiped her nose with her apron and answered coyly "won't I just – Bli' me". The editor says he doesn't know what Bli' me means but "all Birmingham girls say it". I remind you, gentle reader, this was the newspaper editorial. The wedding day arrived and Hoppy hopped it! "and lazy tramcar passengers went to town with dirty boots".

People, Pleasures and Peccadillos

From time to time in this series we have included reports on various accidents, misdemeanours, and life in general as found in Victorian Britain. Some, by their nature are mildly amusing to our eyes, others deadly serious. Readers have asked me for more of these, which follow but instead of putting them in subject or tramways order they are chronological. As with other 'incidents' and 'happenings' which are written here they are almost in exactly the form they were printed in, and as a generality I have deliberately run them without comment, although I do feel sometimes where any public transport is concerned in the eyes of the legal profession then and now black can become white and vice versa!! So, in the words of my favourite Accrington conductor, 'La's and Gennelmen, for your pleasure herewith, some good reading' – that was as we ran down to the Cemetery turning point. Spoken in pure Lancastrian he never varied the form of the words ... a character himself.

July 18 1903, *Worcester Chronicle*:
"FATAL TRAM ACCIDENT
A fatal accident occurred on the Birmingham to Saltley tramway on Wednesday evening. A boy, named Thomas Groutage, of 26, Bennett's Hill, Saltley, was having a free ride on the front platform of the car, when he fell off, and had his head crushed by one of the wheels."

28 April 1888, *Dudley Herald*:
"HALESOWEN – TRAMWAY RUNNING DOWN CASE"
At the Birmingham County Court on Wednesday, Joseph Coker, farmer, of Ward's End Farm, Ridge Acre, Quinton, sued the Birmingham and Midland Tramway Company to recover £25, compensation due for damage to a horse and cart belonging to the plaintiff, through, he alleged, the negligence of the defendants' servants – Mr Daly (instructed by Mr Brady, Colmore Row) appeared for the plaintiff, and Mr W. Shakespeare for the defendant company. – The case was heard with a jury. – The plaintiff gave evidence that on the date named he had gone to Messrs Mitchells' brewery at Cape hill to fetch a load of grains* and had just left the brewery yard with his horse and cart when he saw a steam tram coming down Cape Hill at an excessive rate of speed. The driver of the car rang his bell to warn the driver of another cart which was on the metals in front of the approaching tram, and the plaintiff's horse, which he was leading by the bridle, being alarmed at the noise, attempted to bolt. Plaintiff retained his hold of the bridle, but the horse overcame him and got on to the metals. The tram was at this time a considerable distance away, and the witness held his hand up to induce him to stop, but he took no notice, and the tram coming on at a high rate of speed ran into the cart, which was overturned, and the grains spilled. The cart was badly damaged, and the horse so seriously injured that for a month it was under treatment, and unable to do any work. The amount claimed included the cost of the repair of the cart, and the expenses of doctoring the horse, the hire of a horse and cart to do the plaintiff's work while his own team was incapacitated, and a sum to cover the permanent deterioration

of the horse and cart. In cross-examination, plaintiff admitted that some of the items which made up the £25 had not yet been paid, and the sum to be paid for the hire of a horse and cart was standing over until the result of the present action was seen. The defence set up by Mr Shakespeare was that the accident was brought about by the plaintiff neglecting to keep proper control of his horse, that, in fact, he was walking on the footpath by the side of his horse until he saw the tram approaching, and that then he suddenly caught hold of the horse's head, and the sharp jerk caused the horse to swerve and so bring the cart into collision with the engine and car. A number of witnesses were called by both sides, and as a result the jury found for the plaintiff, damages £15.

*Now Mitchell & Butler (M&B), with their brewery then at Cape Hill, Smethwick.

11 August 1883, *Louth Advertiser*:
"SERIOUS COLLISION WITH A TRAMCAR
About ten o'clock on Sunday night a serious collision took place near the Golden Cup, Darwen. A waggonette containing about twenty persons was returning from Leyland and when near the Golden Cup it came into collision with a steam tramcar going to Blackburn. The waggonette was completely smashed, and the driver and four of the occupants were seriously injured."

31 March 1894:
"SEQUEL TO THE TRAMWAY COLLISION AT BURNT TREE"
At the Borough Police Court, yesterday, before H.G. Walker and J. Whitehouse Esqs, James Morris, carter Campbell Street, was summoned for furious driving. The case arose out of a collision at Burnt Tree on December 5th between one of the cars of the South Staffordshire Tramway Co., and a lorry belonging to Mr G.G. Brown. The driver of the lorry sustained a fractured leg, and the horse was so seriously injured that it had to be slaughtered. – Mr J.D. Tippett (traffic manager) watched the proceedings on behalf of the Tramway Co., and W. Waldron defended. Messrs A.G. and S. Hooper watched the case on behalf of Mr G.G. Brown.

George Gubbins said he was in charge of the engine of the 7.45 tram from Dudley on the night of December 5th. He saw the defendant's horse and lorry about sixty yards in front, in the middle of the road, and he was driving at a very furious rate, he would say twelve miles an hour. Witness rang his bell, and brought the car to a standstill, but the horse dashed into the car, the lorry was overturned, the driver of it hurt, and the horse's back was broken. The engine was going at three miles an hour.

By Mr Waldron: Defendant's horse was galloping.

Charles Davies, employed by the Netherton Brewery Co., said the defendant was driving at a rate of ten or eleven miles per hour. His vehicle went into the tramcar.

By Mr Waldron: He knew there was a dispute between Mr Brown and the Tramway Company, and that there was likely to be legal proceedings.

William Davies, brother of the last witness, gave corroborative evidence.

Joseph Bullock also gave evidence that the defendant's horse was galloping.

Mr Waldron, for the defence, said the summons was taken out ostensibly by the police, but he was going to say the Tramway Company were the real prosecutors. Was it likely the defendant, who was not alleged to be drunk, would run madly into a tramcar at the risk of losing his life? His idea was that the engine was giving off steam, which frightened the horse. The animal went towards the engine which struck it on the head. He called four witnesses who swore that the defendant's horse had only been trotting. Three of them deposed that he was going no more than five or six miles an hour.

The Bench said the evidence was not sufficient to convict, and dismissed the case.

If any person who was riding outside the Dudley and West Bromwich tram which left Dudley at 7.45 on the night of December 5th last, and who witnessed the accident which occurred between that tram and a horse and lorry, or any foot passenger who saw the accident, will communicate with Mr George G. Brown, Priory Street, Dudley, the latter will be obliged.

31 March 1894, *Dudley Herald*:
"SHOCKING ACCIDENT ON THE SEDGLEY TRAMWAY A BOY'S RECKLESSNESS
On Thursday afternoon Mr A.B. Smith (deputy coroner) held an inquest at the Pig and Whistle Inn, Sedgley, touching the death of George Wise (15) son of Thomas Wise, labourer, of 3, High Street, Sedgley, who was fatally injured by a tramcar on Wednesday night.

Mr E. Banner (manager) watched the proceedings on behalf of the Dudley, Sedgley and Wolverhampton Tramway Co.

Thomas Wise, father of the deceased, gave evidence of identification. He last saw his son alive on Wednesday when he had tea with him. About 8 o'clock he heard the deceased had met with an accident, and on going to Dr Ballenden's surgery he found him dead. He did not blame anyone in connection with the death.

William Richards, grocer, said he carried on business next door to the deceased's house, and deceased was in his employ. At 7.30 on Wednesday night he sent the deceased to the home of Mrs Bull, of Gibbon's farm, on the Wolverhampton Road, with a parcel of grocery. He should think it would take 20 minutes to go there and back. Deceased was perfectly sober when he left the shop. At 20 to eight he heard that the deceased had met with an accident, but he did not see it.

Joseph Henry Moreton, engine driver in the employ of the Midland Tramway Company [successor to the D.S.& W.] said he knew deceased. At 7.20 on Wednesday night he was in charge of an engine from Wolverhampton to Dudley, and when near Springfield House he passed Wise, who was in the middle of the road, on the deceased's right. Deceased was walking towards Sedgley. As soon as the witness passed deceased and that he commenced to run about five yards, and then made a jump as if to get

702

hold of the hand-rail, missed his hold, and fell between the car and the engine. Witness came to a standstill, and found deceased on the rails, between the bogies of the car, unconscious. With the assistance of the inspector and the guard deceased was lifted on the car, and left at Dr Ballenden's surgery. He then appeared to be dead. Men and boys were constantly trying to jump on the front of the cars, and he has often warned them of the danger they were incurring. He had never seen the deceased try to do anything of the kind before. Deceased had no parcel or basket with him. The engine was going at the rate of five or six miles an hour.

Mr Wise said the deceased had always been a nervous boy, and he would like to know if the driver saw his son actually try to jump on the car.

Witness said he was perfectly certain that he saw Wise jump.

James Flavell, miner, said he was a passenger by the tram which occasioned the death of the deceased, and in his opinion the car was going at the rate of six miles per hour. He helped lift deceased from under the car. Deceased did not speak and died before reaching the surgery. Witness who was on top of the car did not see the accident but felt a jerk.

P.C. Wallis said he heard of the accident at 7.45pm. He went to the surgery and saw deceased who was dead (just me to thee: well to be deceased he would be...). His neck was broken, the left ear cut off, and there was a compound fracture of the right thigh. Witness had frequently cautioned boys with respect to jumping on the front of tramcars. He saw the engine driver who was quite sober. The distance from where the boy was first seen to where he was found was 35 yards. He would think the body was dragged about a car's length. The jury returned a verdict of 'Accidental Death' and exonerated the driver from blame."

[I have to add two comments here – how unlucky could a man be, and to read of *a labourer between 70 and 80 years of age* makes me glad to be in that age bracket in the 21st century.]

12 July 1884, *Dudley Herald:*
On Tuesday evening a man named Thomas Haines between 70 and 80 years of age, a labourer, formerly residing at 2, Horseley Heath, died in the West Bromwich Accident Hospital from the effects of injuries received that afternoon. The unfortunate man was walking in the road when he was knocked down and trod upon by a horse which had taken fright at a tram-car. He was immediately conveyed to the District Hospital where it was found his arm was fractured in several places, and he was also suffering from severe lacerations. Death resulted in about an hour and a half. E. Hooper Esq. held the inquest on the body on Thursday at the hospital. Thomas Harper said he was in a tram-car coming from Great Bridge to West Bromwich, and when they reached the Wagon and Horses his attention was drawn to a restive horse attached to a coal cart. He alighted from the tram-car and took hold of the horse, which was entangled in some railings. As soon as the animal was disentangled it dashed across the road, and the shaft caught the deceased, who was standing against the wall, crushing him between the shaft and the wall. Robert Ward, employed by Messrs Sadler Brothers, Oldbury,

said he was in charge of the horse, and when approaching the tram-car the horse became restive, and threw him over some railings. He was rendered unconscious, and saw no more until the horse was quiet. The jury returned a verdict of "Accidental Death".

2 September 1904, *Heywood Advertiser:*
Self-propelled vehicles are increasing in number with great rapidity. According to an official return issued this week 28,073 motor cars and motor cycles were registered in England and Wales up to April 1st. last, as against 12,194 up to January 1st. The number of licences granted to drivers of motor cars was 36,460 as opposed to 14,587. The grand total of cars and motor cycles registered in the United Kingdom to April 1st. was 31,421, as against 13,521 to January 1st., and the grand total of licences granted was 40, 060.

19 January 1905, *Heywood Advertiser:*
[Synopsis] Blizzard from the SE. Slates blown down, and trams stopped. Sleet and snow drifted, but such was the force of the wind that in one place it would be ½" and another 4 feet. ... Southend (Essex) the sea froze 100 yards from the shore ... coldest day in London 'for many years'.

7 October 1904, *Heywood Advertiser:*
The Brixton prison authorities are again resorting to the objectionable practice of moving prisoners to police courts in tramcars ... two men handcuffed and chained together were put on a Westminster car at Brixton among a crowd of work-girls who seemed to take an absorbing interest in their unfortunate fellow passengers. The men and the warden in charge seemed to feel keenly their humiliating position [longitudinal benches so they were exposed – 'the prisoners tried hide the chains'].

24 June 1904, *Heywood Advertiser:*
"EDITORIAL
[This bit of prescience brought me up short]
Preaching at the new Roman Catholic Cathedral at Leeds, on Sunday, the Rev. John Proctor of the Order of Preachers expressed the belief that within a few years there will only be three sects – Roman Catholics, Non-conformists, and Unbelievers. 'One hundred years hence' he added, 'will see only two sects — Roman Catholics and Unbelievers'".

19 November 1885, *Birmingham Daily Gazette:*
[A few examples from many!] Charles Yapp, Dolphin Beerhouse, Steelhouse Lane was fined 40s [£2] and costs for supplying a drunken person with intoxicating drink on the 7th instant. – Julia Woolley, landlady of the Reservoir Tavern, was summoned for permitting drunkenness, and serving two drunken men on Saturday last. The magistrates imposed a fine of 40s. and costs. – Two men, named Green and Cummerford were each fined 1s. and costs for being drunk on licensed premises. – Joseph Thorley, manager of the Engineer's Arms, New Canal Street, was summoned for selling drink during prohibited hours on Wednesday, the 11th inst. Police-Sergeant Roberts saw two men and a woman supplied with a quart of ale by the defendant, for which money was tendered, at about one o'clock in the morning. Defendant stated they were lodgers, whereas on going

upstairs the following morning the officer saw only one room upstairs, and there was no bed in that room. Defendant was fined £5 and costs or a month's imprisonment, and the license ordered to be endorsed.

13 September 1887, *Birmingham Daily Gazette:*
THIRD COURT
Magistrates present: Messrs J.T. Bunce and W.H. Halt.
AN INEBRIATED CAB PROPRIETOR
Joseph Grimley, cab and car proprietor of New Inns Road, Birchfield, was fined 10s. and costs for being drunk in charge of a pair of horse and cart on Saturday night.

UNDUE "SHARPNESS" AT THE TEST-HOUSE.
Henry Perks, inmate of the Test-house, was charged with neglecting to perform his allotted task.– Richard Blakemore, porter at the house, explained that on Saturday he gave the prisoner 4lbs of oakum to pick. Of that quantity he only picked 1½ lbs. The witness, in reply to the Bench, said it was usual to give inmates a second chance, but in this case he had been instructed by the Master to bring the prisoner before the justices.– The Bench remarked that they thought undue sharpness had been exercised in the present case, and the prisoner having been in goal for two days, would be discharged.

November 6 1885, *Birmingham Daily Gazette:*
"FIRST COURT – YESTERDAY
Magistrate present – Mr T.C.S. Kynnersley (Stipendiary)
OBTAINING RELIEF BY FALSE PRETENCES
Elizabeth Anderton (27), Frankfort street, was charged with obtaining relief from the Guardians by means of false pretences.– Warrant Officer Daniels stated that on Tuesday night prisoner went to the Workhouse, said she was destitute and in labour, and asked for relief. Prisoner was continually getting people to fetch cabs for her and take her to the Workhouse on the representation that she was in labour. She had been in the Workhouse as many as fifty times in a year on the same pretence. Several times policemen had paid for cabs to take her to the Workhouse. When witness remonstrated with prisoner for her conduct she replied she could only have a month in prison, and that when she came out any of the police would get her another cab.– (laughter).– Prisoner, in reply to Mr Kynnersley, said Daniels had been telling lies. She had never gone to the Workhouse with such an excuse.– Mr Kynnersley sent her to prison for a month with hard labour.

24 December 1885 [synopsis] was the date for the annual distribution of charity to 50 aged, but honest, poor. They each received a 4lb (1.82kg) of bread, 6lb of beef, 6 cwt (305kg) of coal, plus a length of calico, all to the value of 16 shillings."

29 December 1885, *Birmingham Daily Mail:*
[This one seems a bit upside down as while he was in jail he could not pay for his wife anyway].
"CHARGE OF NEGLECT
John Cornelius, bedstead maker, was charged with neglecting his wife and three children whereby they became chargeable to the King's

Norton Union. Mr Edwin Docker (Clerk to the Board) appeared for the prosecution, and asked the Bench to deal severely with the prisoner, as he put the Guardians [of the Poor] to a lot of trouble. Prisoner was sent to jail for a month with hard labour."

4 July 1903, *Worcester Chronicle*:
"THE CROWN'S IMMUNITY
In a Divisional Court on Wednesday, an appeal was heard against the decision of the Southampton County Justices, by the driver of a traction engine, who had been convicted for driving at a speed prohibited by the Locomotives Acts. Appellant was a servant of the Crown, the engine was Crown property, and the appellant, who was driving only slightly over three miles per hour, was obeying the instructions of his superior officer. The Solicitor-General contended that the Act did not apply, as Acts of Parliament did not apply to the Crown unless so stated in the Act itself. The Court now held that the section did not bind the Crown, and allowed the appeal."

18 July 1903, *Worcester Chronicle*:
"WORCESTER COUNTY POLICE
Before Mr F.J.A. Wood.
DRUNK – Ellen Neale, married woman, of no fixed abode, was charged with being drunk on the highway, at Stoulton, on July 15th. P.C. Cook said he saw the prisoner lying asleep on the side of the road. She was drunk. Fined 5s. or 7 days [imprisonment. The danger was literally that she might have 'spooked' a horse]."

17 February 1883, *Handsworth Chronicle*:
'WIT AND HUMOUR
'Why do you suppose Mr Johnson is always taking the tram over to Smithbury?' asked one gentleman of another. 'His wife says he goes over there to admire the beauty of the place' was the reply – 'Yes but does she know the beauty of the place is a young widow?'
'Goods at half price' said the sign. An elderly lady asked a constable to accompany her to the stall. Mystified he does so. 'How much is that tea-pot' the old lady asked the stall-holder. 'A shilling, mum,' was the response. 'I'll take it 'says she, throwing down sixpence. The officer watched. The tea pot was handed over and the sign taken down [1 shilling equals 12 pence].
[I cannot resist this awful pun]
'Carriage people'. – There is a law in Denmark which enacts that all intoxicated persons are to be taken comfortably home in carriages at the expense of the publican who sold them the last glass. Thus, while we in England can tell when a man is intoxicated by observing his gait, the good people of Denmark are able to do exactly the same thing by noticing his 'carriage' "

6 July 1889, *Handsworth Chronicle*:
WEST BROMWICH POLICE COURT
YESTERDAY (FRIDAY)
Before Alderman Farley and Mr Williams
THEFT OF A WATCH.– John Howell, Mallin Street, and William Ingram, George Street, both of West Bromwich were charged with stealing a watch and chain belonging to E. Hodgetts, of Smethwick. Howell was ordered to receive ten strokes with a birch rod, and three days' imprisonment, and Ingram discharged

with a caution. [Mr Hodgetts was a CBT Inspector – perhaps this was a 'Company' watch]"

4 December 1885, *Birmingham Daily Gazette*:
"NATIONAL DOG SHOW
[Not quite an orthodox item but included as a contrast with men's wages on the tramway]
Admissions 19,356 Receipts £666.15.6d Sales of dogs £363.4s.0d
A Clumber spaniel fetched £32.10s., a Bedlington Terrier £15, a retriever £15.
Airedales which were also shown as 'Waterside Terriers' and Otterhounds also fetched 'good money'."

3 January 1885, *Dudley Herald*:
[synopsis] Two inquests on children.
"Ellen Danks, 7, Simm's Lane, Netherton aged nine.
...Elizabeth Boot, next door neighbour, said she was in the habit of looking after Mrs Dank's children when she went out, and on Friday last Mrs Danks asked her to keep an eye on the children ... [she went in, no problem until] ... a quarter of an hour later she heard screams. She rushed to the house to find the unfortunate child in flames. A paraffin lamp was on the table, bursted, and the child said she had been lighting the lamp. [She threw water over her to put her out, and 'oils were used'] ... Ellen died in the Guest Hospital on the Monday, and the verdict was 'Accidental death'.
William Kendrick, no address given, aged 3.
...he died from the effects of scalds received on the 30th November last. On that day the deceased's mother was pouring out a cup of tea, when her thumb slipped, and the contents went over the deceased. He was dressed with oils, and the doctor sent for, but sickness set in, and the poor child died on Monday last. – a verdict of "Accidental death" was returned..."

29 July 1882, *Dudley Herald*:
[This is an interesting case. The hand-nailers were having a terrible time as foreign machine-made nails over-ran the country. With one well between 14 houses and only 2 privies I assume the girls, famously dirty in that trade, were scrubbed up but clearly the reporter had problems with their thick accents here and there! A noticeable absence in the report were the parents, they would close ranks against 'them lot'. I should add here that the area around Gornal Wood, in the Black Country, had a ferocious reputation even in my youth; my RAF colleague from a nearby town, Kingswinford, advised me never to go there in uniform. I assume it has changed now...]

"SEDGLEY POLICE COURT
INDECENT ASSAULT
On Monday, before F.W.W. Boughey Esq., Stipendiary, Benjamin Flavell alias "Stunner", nailer, Spills Meadow, Upper Gornal, was charged with indecently assaulting Annie Porter. – complainant, who is 15years of age said she was a nailer, and worked with the defendant. Whilst in the pantry on Tuesday defendant behaved indecently, and when she resisted him he knocked her down, and gave her "a good smack". He then told her not to tell anyone. Two or three weeks ago he similarly assaulted her. – By the Stipendiary: I did not tell my mother anything about it, but

someone else did. Pollie Hickman saw me coming up the garden road crying.– Defendant in reply to the charge said: I acknowledge what she says is pretty near correct. I didn't do the girl any harm, nor wish to. This is the first time I have ever had a summons. – Hannah Evans (14) said she saw the complainant come out of the defendant's house, crying, on Tuesday morning. Witness asked her what was the matter, and she accused the defendant of assaulting her. The girl Hickman having given evidence, the prisoner expressed contrition. – The Stipendiary: When a person like yourself is in a position to have a servant, it is your duty to serve her as you would serve your own family. That girl of only fifteen was at your mercy. It is your duty to have protected her. A person at your time of life and a married man too knows more of the moral law than perhaps I do; but I also know the criminal law, and now you should have a taste of it. I fine you 40s [£2] and costs, or one month's imprisonment with hard labour.
[The spelling of Pollie is exactly as printed – along with the rest. Given nailers' lives – they died in their 30s – prison was probably quite pleasant. Gornal Wood was still hairy 20 years ago – I'm told there is a nailer's museum from there in the black country museum.]

3 June 1904, Heywood Advertiser:
"SERIOUS TRAM ACCIDENT AT
CASTLETON
A GIRL SHOCKINGLY INJURED
A tramway accident attended by a serious result, occurred at Castleton on Saturday evening.
One of the cars belonging to the Middleton Electric Traction Company was proceeding through Castleton in the direction of Sudden at six o'clock when it knocked down and ran over Annie Fletcher, the two-year-old daughter of Austen Fletcher of 283, Manchester Road, Castleton, who suddenly ran from the path in front of her home into the road.
The driver of the car was Joseph Dyson, of 4, Amy Street, Middleton. He states that at the time of the accident the tram was travelling at the speed of eight miles an hour, which is the usual speed for that locality. As soon as he noticed the child run on the road he applied both the electric and chain brakes and rang his gong. Unhappily this did not have the effect of averting the evil, as the girl Fletcher, who was running across the road, did not notice the tram, and was therefore knocked down by it.
After throwing her down the car proceeded nearly 15 yards before stopping. The driver promptly went to the assistance of the child whom he transferred into the care of Sarah Davies, of 281 Manchester Road. She conveyed Fletcher to her home.
The girl had received shocking injuries to the lower part of the body. Dr S.T. Lord was at once sent for, and in accordance with his directions the child was taken to Rochdale Infirmary in the ambulance carriage. [2 miles].She went in the care of P.C.'s Wilson and Bennett.
At the Infirmary it was found that the girl was suffering from a fracture of the right thigh and that her right foot had nearly been cut off. Consequently it was found necessary to amputate the right leg.
The operation was successfully performed, and on inquiry at the Infirmary afterwards we

were informed the child's condition was satisfactory. Ernest Heath of 294 Oldham Road, Middleton, was the conductor of the car. He says he knew nothing of the accident until the tram was stopped.

This morning the injured child was reported to be progressing favourably."

---

30 September 1904, *Heywood Advertiser:*
"TRAMCAR MISHAP
On Saturday morning a trap, driven by Mrs R.A.L. Hutchinson of Greenbooth, Norden, collided with an electric car in Edenfield Road, Norden. Mrs Hutchinson was accompanied by Miss Baren Crumble, and a groom was seated at the back of the conveyance. Fortunately none of the occupants of the trap was injured. The trap was, however, badly damaged. At the place where the accident occurred the roadway is rather narrow.

---

2 June 1905, *Heywood Advertiser:*
"NARROW ESCAPES
At about three o'clock on Wednesday afternoon a singular accident occurred in Bridge-street. A tram from Heywood was going towards Bury and when passing through the loop, near the Brunswick Hotel, another car was seen coming towards Heywood. The driver of the outgoing car reversed his engine so as to stop in the loop, and the car ran backwards for a short distance. A mail cart containing the daughter of Mr R. Ainsworth, tea dealer, of Benfield-street, was passing behind the car at the time and was struck by it, with the cart was knocked over and the baby went partially under the tram. Happily she escaped in a wonderful fashion, without injury, but the mail cart was broken. – On Saturday evening a man from Castleton was knocked down by a tram engine in Bridge-street. The driver immediately dropped the "brush" appliance, and fortunately the engine was quickly stopped , the man escaping with a severe shaking.

---

28 March 1885, *Dudley Herald:*
[This is one example of a letter which appeared in most decent newspapers at the time, and it is pleasing to record that gifts from £100 to as little as one penny (all a girl had) were recorded and as far as I could check came to around £500 – at 5% in Government stocks this would give the widow £25 per year. Bravo, say I].

"Sir.– Allow me through the columns of the Dudley Herald to appeal to the sympathies of the charitable, on behalf of the widow and three children of the late Police-Constable James Davies, who was brutally murdered while in discharge of his duty at Alvechurch last month. This brave, warm-hearted, generous fellow now lies in his grave. Tributes of respect, and acts of loving remembrance have been paid to the memory of the dead, by friends and comrades, and an effort is now being made to mark the public sense of the courageous conduct of this officer, by raising a fund as will provide of permanent benefit to the widow and orphans. Contributions to this fund from friends in Dudley will be gratefully received by your obedient servant,

H.BURTON,
Chief-superintendent
Chief-superintendent's Office,
Dudley, 26th March, 1885."

---

7 July 1884, *Louth & North Lincs. Advertiser:*
"TRAGEDY AT SEA
The Italian vessel Teresa Oliver, which arrived at Queenstown on Monday, reports that early in August a seaman named Antonio attacked the chief officer while asleep in his berth with a razor, inflicting a fearful wound. He rushed at the captain who, in defending himself, received several wounds. The chief officer, recovering himself, fired his revolver at Antonio but missed him. A second shot, however, passed through his heart, killing him instantaneously."

[same issue, but this is a synopsis]
"THE DWELLINGS OF THE POOR.
Daniel Smith, 120 High-street, Poplar [London] the owner of the houses Nos 1,2 and 3, Brook's Court, was summonsed at the Thames Police-court on Saturday ... to show why an order should not be made upon him to close the premises concerned... William Atherstone Shadrake, Sanitary Inspector to the Poplar Board had visited the premises, the approach to them was up a small entry or alley leading fromn High-street. The alley was unpaved, and was nearly always in a state of mud and filth. ...The houses themselves had their ground floors some eighteen inches [457mm] below the level of the front, and in consequence the downstairs rooms were continually damp and wet. The walls and ceilings of the house were in a horribly dirty condition, and very much dilapidated, the plaster being decayed and reeking with an unwholesome moisture. The windows and roofs were defective, the rain pouring continuously through them during bad weather. There are no sanitary offices ... no drains ... Close adjoining the houses upon one side were some slaughterhouses, and on the other cattle lairs ... the air locally was awful... The three houses were, in the witness's opinion, utterly unfit for human habitation. [The landlord had been told to sort himself out but he did not] ... in one of the houses there was a man and his wife and five children and in another a widow with two children who earned a living mangling. ...there was no fresh water supply ... nothing could be done to make the houses inhabitable. ...Mr Lushington [Magistrate] said that upon the evidence which had been adduced to him ... he had no alternative but to make an order upon the landlord to close the houses forthwith."

---

7 July 1884, *Louth and North Lincs. Advertiser:*
"STEALING DUCKS
Two boys, named Frederick Scrimshaw, aged 11, and George Howis, aged 10, were charged with stealing one live duck, value 1/- [12 old pence], the property of Mr W.O. Parr, of Well. It appeared from the evidence that Mr Parr has for some time missed ducks off his farm, and as these boys were caught with the duck in their possession it was necessary an example should be made of them. The boys pleaded guilty. Scrimshaw was ordered to receive six strokes with a birch rod, and Howis two."

---

17 January 1889, *Birmingham Daily Gazette:*
"DENSE FOG
CASUALTIES IN BIRMINGHAM
[Synopsis] The volumes of vapour which had been hanging over the country for several days descended upon Birmingham during Wednesday night and yesterday, and up to an early hour this morning enveloped the city and surrounding district in a thick fog. During the whole of yesterday Birmingham had the aspect of a city of permanent night. Business could not be conducted in any of the offices or emporiums without the gas being lit, and to add to the depressing effect the street lamps, which were necessarily lighted, dotted the streets with dismal yellow lights, emphasizing rather than dispelling the density of the clouds which rolled through the streets all day long. Vehicular traffic was considerably interfered with, and an effort was made to avoid accidents by many horses carrying bells ... a heroic attempt was made to continue the tramway traffic, but after struggling through the day with prolonged journeys, the tramway people found the fog too much for them, and between five and six o'clock in the evening running was ceased on all routes. [On the railway] no main line trains were delayed more than half an hour, and the local service was kept up with commendable punctuality. [One accident was to a newsboy who slipped off the platform at Smethwick and went under a train. He lost a hand and was, incredibly even for then, only 12 years of age.]"
[Similar dense fogs impeding traffic etc were reported from Walsall, Redditch, Kingswinford, Wolverhampton, West Bromwich, Dudley etc – in other words almost the whole of the industrial Midlands was affected for about a week]

[It will be noticed that in this series much material is based on Dudley and its environs. This is simply because, situated in the centre of industrialised England it was the great melting-pot where industries sucked in working men when times were good and left them destitute at the sniff of a slump. The great, but outmoded, ironworks were well in blast at the beginning of our tramway saga, but dying quickly by the time of this cutting. Collieries were susceptible not only to natural problems (firedamp, flooding and the like) but to trade fluctuations with the price of coal, to which wages were tied, rising and falling almost on a daily basis. Certain trades required an apprenticeship – particularly those in chain and nail making, which left no chance of employment for offcomers, and unlike Birmingham, 'the greatest toyshop in the world' there were little or no outlets for a day's casual labour to be found. It was said that the best or safest occupation, if you could withstand the sheer brutality of it, was to work on the canal, whether labourer or boatman. Certainly some continuity of work was to be found from the 'company' boat operators – L&NWR, Bantocks (for the GWR) and the chemical and oil processing companies. A lucky labourer if he was not too weakened by hunger could get a job shovelling out the boats – I don't know what the rate then was, in 1950 we paid 6d. a ton – hardly generous, but men queued for the work. But in times of dreadful weather during the late Victorian period life was a grindingly hard one. The 'soup' in this article was probably made from good beef and root vegetables – the RAF provided something of the kind during the Canvey Island floods. Most of all, note the late date of this item.]

---

16 February 1895, *Dudley Herald:*
"DISTRESS IN THE TOWN AND DISTRICT
VERY SERIOUS CONDITION OF AFFAIRS
The giving of the frost seems – at the time of writing – as remote as ever, and the distress in

the town and district consequent thereon, have now reached a point which must be considered as alarming to a degree. Practically the whole of out-door work has been suspended for about eight weeks, and even those who were able to put a little by for the proverbial rainy day could hardly be expected to hold out for so lengthened a period, whilst those who were unable to make the slightest provision for the hard times must of necessity be absolutely helpless. Those who have taken up the work of finding where the distress exists, tell heartrending stories of the privations the people are suffering. There can be no doubt that a great deal of genuine distress exists – probably more than has been known in the town for very many years – and whilst we have unbounded praise for the exceptionally hearty response to the appeal which has been made, we sincerely hope that the flow of charity will not cease, for, of our own knowledge, we know there is plenty of room for it. We shall be glad to receive subscriptions to the General Relief Fund, or for any means that has as its object the relief of the distress.

...collective and individual charity has been nobly forthcoming. There must be a score or more of soup kitchens in the town. At the Parish Church Guild Rooms, in Stafford Street, 400 are fed every day except Sundays, and many more are sent empty away. The Reverend A.M. Gardiner is distributing soup and bread to about 250 people each week, and a soup kitchen has been established in connection with the Dixon's Green and King Street Wesleyan Chapels for several weeks. Watson's Green Football Club have set a capital example to other football clubs. Two gifts of ten tickets have been sent by them to the Reverend H. Soames for distribution in St. John's Ward, each ticket representing a 4lb loaf, ¼ lb of tea, 1lb of sugar, and ½ lb of bacon [The cost of these tickets was met by the football club members and were usually drawn on the Co-op Store, as they gave fair, honest weight – as ethical as they are today]. The vicar of St. Edmund's has been giving away soup ... the Quakers collected a good sum. ...The children attending Baylies' and Parson's Charity Schools have also been provided with dinners by the trustees. Councillor Richards, of Hall Street, has for some weeks been giving away bread and soup...

A meeting of the Dudley Relief Committee was held on Thursday night at the Town Hall ... the Secretary reported that since the last meeting 2,175 tickets had been distributed, absorbing £172. 3s.9d of the funds ... [various collections were to be made in churches] ... Mr Challingsworth intimated that the Licensed Victuallers Association would increase their donation from two to four guineas [£4.4s.0d] ... the Dudley Volunteer Band had offered to play round the streets on Saturday, and to solicit subscriptions in the Market Place on Sunday. ...it was decided to issue 25 books of tickets value 1s 6d and 1s 0d. [ie, married or single men or women] for distribution this week...

The children attending Kate's Hill Board Schools are being provided for by Mr A.G. Hooper, solicitor, who generously offered to give 140 dinners daily for ten days.

During the last three weeks soup and bread have been distributed in connection with the King Street Wesleyan Church, and last Sunday morning 100 children were given breakfast, and tomorrow this will be repeated."

September 20 1890, *Handsworth Herald:*

"THE STONE THROWING NUISANCE
The stone-throwing season has set in with a vengeance, and has attacked the youth of Handsworth with a particular virulence until now it is scarcely safe to walk through the streets. Hansworth seems to be the happy hunting ground too of juveniles from Birmingham [who rode the cable cars] ... and who want a little practice in the art of shying. Perhaps they know policemen are rather scarce, and take advantage of this knowledge. However, the youthful delinquents are sometimes caught, and yesterday four of them were summoned at the police court and fined. We hope these cases will come as a warning to others similarly disposed. [The fines were required to be paid by the parents, in another similar case before a stricter magistrate yobs were given a sound thrashing and two sent to the Reformatory]"

August 20 1893, *Dudley Herald:*
[The cause of the hand nailers was a lost one, especially when foreign horse shoe nails undercut their prices, and their masters who provided the raw material and took away the finished products wanted to be paid a higher rate for the one, and a lower for the other. The following is part of a report on a Primitive Methodist meeting held in Dudley in a field. I think I would have liked him!]
"...the Rev. T.S. Bateman (Primitive Methodist minister) delivered a sermon, having special reference to the strike in the nail trade in Dudley. He remarked that, as the result of enquiries he had made, he was convinced that the strike was a justifiable one, and deserved the practical sympathy of the general public.

He understood that a really clever workman in the nail trade of that district, provided he had strength and energy enough to throw his whole soul into his occupation for fifteen hours a day and six days a week, could manage to take home about 15s. on Saturday night. He was told by two operatives on the ground that by working from nine to eleven o'clock each day from Monday to Saturday they could only earn 7s. Since he had arranged to take part in that service he had been told that ministers of religion should not dabble in such matters. He was going to dabble in such matters, if asked, without consulting friend or foe."

30 April 1887, *County Express:*
"IT IS ALL COMPARITIVE
Robert Sheldon, ironworker, of Netherton was charged with 'committing a filthy nuisance' in Stafford Street. Defendant pleaded it was caused by a sudden illness. Fined 2s 6d plus costs

John Taylor (53), no abode, stole 16 growing turnips 'for food'. Said to be out of work. Fined 2s 6d or 7 days' imprisonment.

A child died from enteric fever. They had only one bedroom and that had a collapsed floor. In bed were found the woman (not said to be the wife), a baby three months, the dead child 12 months old (they thought) and five other children aged between 6 and 15 years. The man slept downstairs. Called as a witness a neighbour stated 'she was not in the habit of visiting the house because of its dirty condition and the smell'. The Coroner giving his verdict added it was a 'terrible state of things'."

[A little light relief – I cannot imagine a journalist reporting this exchange in today's papers]
24 March 1898, *South Wales Echo:*

"CABS COMMITTEE
A SCENE BETWEEN COUNCILLORS LEWIS MORGAN AND CHAPPELL.
A meeting of the Cabs Committee of the Cardiff Corporation was held this morning, when a controversy with the Tramways Company was renewed upon an application made for forty additional licences, in respect of drivers and conductors, for the replacement of men who were ill. An application was also made to run twelve additional 'buses to Ely in Easter week in connection with the races.

Councillor Lewis Morgan remarked that it was a wonder to him that not more were laid up, having regard to the nature of their occupation.

Councillor Good observed that the whole twenty-two (reported absent) were not absent through illness. The letter from the company mentioned "illness and other causes"...

The Chairman said it was a question whether they could refuse the application. He was of the opinion that if the man's character was satisfactory they were obliged to grant the licences.

Councillor Chappell did not concur with the Chairman's view

Councillor Lewis Morgan ... Each member has a right to express his opinion without being "jumped upon" by certain distinguished members of the committee.

Councillor Chappell ... [stated] ... the number of men already engaged was much in excess of the last licensing day in July. On the occasion named the total number was *380* and it had now gone up to *430*. [presumably for 'buses, cabs and trams]...

[The Chief Constable was asked his opinion and thought the number asked for quite reasonable]

Councillor Lewis Morgan moved the licences be granted. Alderman R. Cory seconded.

Councillor Chappell moved the licences be not granted, and Councillor Good seconded.

The vote of the chairman in favour of the licences decided the application in the affirmative.

[After further argy-bargy]

Councillor Chappell observed the council might be proposing to licence shoe-blacks.

Councillor Lewis Morgan said the question of the ability of the men was for the committee to consider.

Councillor Chappell: You would licence any cad.

Councillor Lewis Morgan: I would not licence you for anything respectable.

[The report then effectively grinds to a halt – one has to wonder if the reporter was sent out of the room, later he did observe that the men applying for licences had left the vestibule!]"

Section 16

PERMANENT WAY AND CONTRACTORS

From The PWC, Birmingham, Minutes:

Letter from Councillor Toller to J. Price, City Surveyor, 21 January 1899:

"...The Tramway men also refuse to accept the 1/- a week increase as settlement to their case, and I am instructed to ask that the following be granted:

That the minimum rate of wages for all men employed on the Tramway system be 22/- per week [22 shillings for a six day 60 hour week], rising after two years of service to 24/-, viz., after one year's service 23/-, rising to 24/- after two years' service.

That the leading hands [gangers] be paid 27/- a week with the privileges of rising to Foreman when vacancies occur.

Flagger's labourers are happy with the extra 1/- a week.

Rammermen ... very dissatisfied that their case has not been settled, and I have promised them that it will be before the Committee immediately. [he adds 'please reply as soon as possible as the men seem very determined'] They would accept 2/- a week [rise] or 4d. per day.

At this point three tramway labourers appeared before the Committee, to explain their wishes. A compromise was met whereby the leading hands would receive 26/- a week, and new men starting in the post would receive 25/- rising to 26/-. The logical move was to rename 'Rammermen' Improvers and place them in that grade.

The Committee could not see their way to granting a rise to unskilled Tramway labourers and this should be referred to the Joint Committee as it would have implications to all the labourers employed by the Corporation."

What we should note here is how conciliatory the PWC Tramways Committee were – a far cry from a decade before – and Councillor Toller appears to be one of two representatives within the Committee appointed by the men, or their Trades Union.

Tramway Construction

THE

INSTITUTION

OF

CIVIL ENGINEERS.

SESSION 1876-77.—PART IV.

Sect. I.—MINUTES OF PROCEEDINGS.

April 24, 1877.

GEORGE ROBERT STEPHENSON, President, in the Chair.

No. 1,518.—" Street Tramways." By ROBINSON SOUTTAR.

PART I.—TRAMWAY CONSTRUCTION.

Foundation.—Where a tramway is likely to be subjected to heavy traffic, it will generally be desirable to excavate about 7 inches under the lower surface of the longitudinal sleeper, and to lay a bed of Portland cement or bituminous concrete over the whole width of the tramway. Some doubt has been expressed as to the value of cement concrete as a tramway base, from the fact that in many cases where tramways have been taken up, the concrete is found to have perished; but this is probably owing not so much to the vibration of the tramway as to the poverty of the concrete in the first instance. Tramways have frequently (from causes beyond the engineer's control) to be hurried to completion, and the concrete is attacked by paving beaters and street traffic before it has thoroughly consolidated. A bed of concrete 7 inches thick requires from two to three weeks to set throughout, whereas it is afforded sometimes hardly as many days. When it is necessary to hurry the work, it would mostly be wiser to use bituminous concrete, and this concrete will also be more suitable where the thickness is less than 6 inches.

Cross sleepers should be imbedded in the concrete, as they are of great value in preserving the level of the rails. The rails of the Birkenhead street railway, laid twelve years ago with cross sleepers, preserve their level better than some lines laid at a comparatively recent date without. Objections have, however, been

[1876-77. N.S.]   B

2   MINUTES OF PROCEEDINGS.

urged against the use of cross sleepers on tramways. It is said that they injure the concrete by their vibration, and that the paving setts will not bed firmly over them. This is true, to some extent, of rectangular cross sleepers, but the objections will be overcome if cross sleepers with slightly bevelled sides are used, measuring, say, 5 inches on the top and 7 inches on the underside (Plate 1, Figs. 7–10). The concrete cannot fall away from bevelled sleepers, and if they are soundly bedded, and the concrete well punned round them, vibration would appear to be impossible. This being so, the paving will bed perfectly if care is exercised in selecting stone of a depth that will allow of a thin cushion of sand lying between the stone and the wood, and especially if the paving joints are grouted with pitch.

Longitudinal Bearing.—Tramways with rigid iron bearings have been constructed, and mention will be made of these hereafter. It is generally conceded, however, that a continuous timber bearing is an essential element in a perfect tramway. It forms a cushion which absorbs some of the sound and jarring, and renders tramway travelling agreeable and noiseless. It is also of service to the rail, doubtless increasing its life considerably as compared with what that would be if the rail was fixed on an iron bed. It is likely, too, that the elasticity of the timber bearing neutralises in some measure the vibration and hammering to which a tram rail is subject, and which but for the presence of this elastic medium would injure the concrete.

With regard to the life of the timber great misapprehension exists. The Author has taken up pitch pine, spruce, and memel, after it has lain five, six, and eight years, and found it to all appearance as good as when laid. He has also taken up timber which had been lying twelve years, and found it, where the line had been paved, in very fair condition. The timber referred to had carried a rail spiked through the groove, and the timber was in good condition only where it had not been injured by spikes or transverse saw cuts. In constructing tramways a pernicious practice still prevails of sawing the timber and driving wedges into the saw cuts so as to bend it round curves. When this is done the timber splits and rots quickly. Where the curve is so sharp that the longitudinal cannot be sprung round it, the timber should be sawn to template. If care is taken in these respects, the longitudinal will last fifteen to twenty years, even with the spiked rail. If the box rail (*i.e.* a rail having side flanges and fastened on the sides with wrought-iron dogs) is used, there will hardly be a limit to the life of the timber. As a matter of fact, however, it will be

707

advisable to change the bearing when the rail is changed, as the timber will get torn in the operation, and the price of the longitudinal being insignificant, it will be better to have a fresh one with the fresh rail. If, therefore, the rail is calculated to last twenty-five years, the timber, if sound, intact and properly creosoted, may be depended on to bear it as long.

Rail and Fastener.—When tramways were inaugurated in England by the laying of the Birkenhead street railway, the American section of rail was used (Plate 1, Fig. 1). Being unsatisfactory, however, it was removed, and a grooved rail, spiked through the groove, substituted. The grooved rail has been laid on every subsequent system, although alterations have been made on the underside and in the manner of fastening the rail. The spiked rail, as laid on the Birkenhead and other tramways (Fig. 2), has certain advantages. It can be taken off and changed when worn out without the paving being in any way disturbed. The plate-laying is done very readily, and the rails can be cut and scarfed with great ease. Where, therefore, cheapness at first is the chief consideration, a tramway laid with flat spiked rails will answer; but these have many disadvantages which render them unsuitable where there is much car or street traffic to contend with. The spiking is the weakest point. At first it was feared that the timber would not grip the spikes, and they were made in some instances to go right through and be screwed up with nut and flanged washer beneath. This was speedily found to be superfluous, as the spike-head wore away first. The spike-heads are worn off by the working of the rail, or are knocked off by the car, so quickly that this form of rail requires respiking once a year, or more frequently where the traffic is considerable. The spike-holes weaken the rail, and the spikes act as wedges, so that the rail is split in a few years; a rail ¾ inch thick under the groove lasting six years and upwards.

The spiked rail has been superseded by the box rail (Fig. 3). This has flanges on the underside, punched with holes 18 inches apart, alternately on the right and on the left. Through each hole one end of a stout clip is driven, the other end, which is jagged, being driven into the longitudinal sleeper. This rail answers well. The groove is no longer weakened by the fastener, neither is the fastener in any danger of getting injured or worn. Care must be taken to check the sleeper so that it will exactly fit the rail, to press the sleeper well home into the rail by hand-screws, and to see that the fastener is not cracked at the neck in driving. If these points are attended to a rail fastened in this way will never work loose. These clip fasteners, however, if applied to the

B 2

ordinary form of rail, by projecting keep the stone immediately adjacent away from the rail, and as they occur very frequently, there being ordinarily fourteen thousand fasteners per mile of double way, the evil is a substantial one. It is found, besides, that every wheel which strikes a hole helps to extend it, until by degrees an interstice is formed along the side of the rail, down which water soaks, washing the bedding from under the stone, and permitting it to sink beneath the rail-level. Anything therefore which prevents the stone from coming dead up to the rail is highly objectionable.

The Author has introduced a rail which seems to meet this difficulty (Plate 1, Figs. 7–10). The flanges are brought in beneath ¾ inch, that is, the thickness of the clips; and if a bit of the longitudinal sleeper is gouged out where the hole in the flange of the rail comes, the fastener can be driven in flush with the sleeper and the side of the rail. The paving setts can then be got dead up to the rail, which will thus be firmly gripped, and the tendency to form ruts alongside, which this fastener, excellent in every other respect encourages, is abolished. Not only so, but whereas there has been heretofore an inducement to keep the fasteners widely apart, so as to diminish the number of these holes in the paving, there is now no such inducement, and the number of fasteners can be increased to any extent without the introduction of a single disadvantageous feature.

The changing of tram rails when worn out is such an expensive matter, and a few lbs. per yard is of so little consequence in first cost, that it is always better, whether the traffic to be sustained will be little or much, to lay a good stout rail at the outset. The first tramway rails laid in this country weighed rather more than 40 lbs. per yard; but the weight has been increased, and 60 lbs. is now considered the best weight for rails where the traffic will be great. At present prices it will be more economical to use Bessemer steel instead of iron for the rails. In Liverpool it is proposed to use a rail having a centre groove. Whether experience will justify this departure from precedent remains to be seen. It is to be feared that the friction will be greater, owing to there being no escape for mud and gravel; that the tendency of cars to run off on curves will be greater, and that the centre flanges on the car wheels will be weaker, and more liable to chip off than the side flanges.

Paving.—The paving of a tramway is a most expensive item, amounting to about one-half the entire cost; but it is impossible to avoid this expense. The stone abutting against the rail supports and protects it, and without it the rail would be shaken loose,

forced out of gauge, and hammered to pieces by the ordinary street traffic. The attempt has been made to provide this protection economically, by placing a row of setts on each side of a rail, and filling between with macadam. It is, however, impossible to maintain the narrow strips of macadam at the same level as the setts, and the road soon gets into a rough state. The inconvenience to the public is equalled by the inconvenience to the tramway company, whose horses, running upon the uneven road with one foot on stone the other on macadam, will stumble and fall lame daily. On this point engines would have the advantage over horses. Asphalt has been tried as a pavement for tramways, but has proved a complete failure, and has in most instances been replaced by stone. Superficially speaking, it would appear to have advantages. It can be laid with neatness and uniformity from rail to rail, and makes at first a very close joint with the rail. The slight vibration to which a tram rail is subject soon frees it from the asphalt, which then exposes alongside each rail two edges, and as asphalt seems to be specially weak at its edges, it is soon ground into holes and ruts. So far as wooden pavement has been tried it has scarcely given more satisfaction. The wear along the rail side is so great that nothing but hard stone will support it. If any other material is used it should be looked upon as an expensive luxury, and the cost of repair should be borne by those for whose benefit the luxury has been provided. Looked at in this light, the Improved Wood Pavement Company's system is probably the only one at all suitable, as the longitudinal sleeper could be fastened to the boarding in a way which would keep the setts and rail at one level until the former were fairly rubbed away. Where the gradient of the street renders hard stone unsuitable for the traffic, it will sometimes be best to let the rows of setts immediately abutting on the rail be of a hard nature, and to pave between with a less slippery stone. The joints of the paving should be racked with dried shingle and grouted with pitch. This impervious pavement is of special value on a tramway, as the rain-water flows down the rail, and (unless the joints are sealed by pitch) sinks down by the rail side, causing the setts to present a ragged appearance, and washing away racking and bedding. Excessive ramming should not be permitted where the tramway has been well concreted, as the concrete will be greatly injured. It will be necessary to tap the stones lightly with the rammer, so as to shake the shingle into the joints, but nothing beyond this should be allowed. The stones alongside rails should be picked, care being taken to see that they can come

dead up to the rail, that they are exactly the depth from rail to concrete, so that they may never sink beneath the level of the rail, and that they break joint well with one another.

Points.—Points were at first made wholly of cast iron, flat, about 6 feet long, and spiked through the groove. Soon side flanges were introduced, and gradually it has been found desirable to lengthen the point, so as to make it easier, until 9 feet has come to be the favourite length where the rail is 4 inches wide. The points wear rapidly at the end of the tongue, where the wheel of the car bears only upon a small portion of the tread. Under heavy traffic a point will wear greatly in this place in twelve months; but the point will not thereby become unworkable, and where appearance is not much object it will last two years. Chilled iron gives somewhat better results, but there is not much difference. A good plan is to insert two pieces of cast steel, one in the tread and one in the tongue. These are securely riveted to the cast iron, which has a recess for the steel, and a projection, which, serving as a back, prevents the steel from being knocked out of position. A point so constructed should last three years. The same idea may be ingeniously varied, by making the steel in one piece, bevelled in front and secured by a pin behind, so that it may be taken away when worn out and replaced by a new piece, without the point being disturbed (Fig. 14). This last is probably the best point yet designed. In movable points the tongue should be made of one piece of steel, and not of steel and iron welded together.

Crossings.—Crossings were at first made flat and spiked in the groove. They were found to wear out and snap across quickly. They were then cast with side flanges, and in this form they wear better, but are still unreliable. Besides, curves in tramway work are so various, and sometimes of necessity so sharp, that it is far from easy to keep a stock of crossings in hand sufficient to maintain an existing tramway, and very troublesome to model with sufficient accuracy patterns for a new one. Consequently, where cast-iron crossings are used, curves have frequently a broken-backed appearance. It is better to lay the rails throughout with all necessary curves, and then, having marked the places where the rails cross, cut or saw them with the proper bevel. In laying crossings the longitudinal timber and rails should be made to break joint, the scarfed timber being bridged by a continuous rail, and the scarfed rail lying on a continuous timber. Thus, in Fig. 11, it will be better to lay the straight timbers A A than the curved timbers A B, scarfing these at crossings. The curved rails should then be laid running continuously through and bridging the scarfed timber; and, finally, the straight rails should be cut and laid on the continuous timber A A. This method entails extra labour, but it is impossible to keep the scarfed rails and the continuous rails at the same level unless it be so carried out.

Curves.—The question of curves is still misunderstood in tramway work. It having been found that cars can be hauled round almost any curve, little care is taken to lay easy curves. This is a great mistake. On a sharp curve the cars will get wrenched, the horses strained, and the passengers occasionally injured. Where there is any choice the curves should not be sharper than from 150 to 200 feet radius. The Author was surprised to see plans for an important system of tramways where it was proposed to construct passing places with curves of 60 feet radius, and room for one car only; whereas all experience shows that passing places should have room for two cars at least. Cast-iron rails have been used for sharp curves, but they wear and break quickly. Flat rails are also used, the idea being to let the wheels take their natural course, one slightly outside the other. But on very sharp curves, where flat rails would appear to be most necessary, they, having no groove wherewith to catch the flange of the wheel, permit it to leave the rails. On sharp curves, where cars had the habit of running off, the Author has frequently had to take up flat rails and lay grooved rails. The proper course would be to roll rails with greater grooves for use on curves; but this would be expensive, and is unnecessary. Wrought-iron rails can be bent to any curve over 30 feet radius by the "Jim Crow." Steel rails had better be at least partially bent at the rolling mill.

Single Line.—Single line may be loop line, whereby the up car traverses one street the down car another, or single line with passing places. Where the streets traversed by loop lines are more than a trifling distance apart loop lines are most objectionable, as it is found that though the through traffic from the point where the lines diverge to the place where they again meet is secured, the local traffic along either single line remains undeveloped. If residents can only depend on a car one way, they will not depend on the car at all. It is easier to develop local traffic upon a single line with passing places, than upon a loop line; nevertheless, the former still labours under grave disadvantages. The ideal tram car will glide along swiftly and noiselessly, a constant temptation to the foot passenger. On a double line this may be, but on a single there is inevitably so much delay that the cars, instead of being a

[1] *Vide* "Tramways: their Construction and Working." By E. Dowson and A. Dowson. 8vo. London, 1875, pp. 9 and 10.

temptation, will occasionally be a source of ridicule to the foot passenger. It is also hard to keep single lines in repair. Compared with double lines, a single line will not wear half so long, and the passing places, with their points, crossings, and curves, are expensive to maintain, and a nuisance in the road. Excepting under peculiar circumstances, for instance, where the line is intended for goods, or where only cars at great intervals are proposed to be run, it is generally unwise to lay a single line if the street is wide enough for two lines. Where cars run frequently, the greater revenue and the lesser wear and tear of roads, cars, and horses, quite counterbalance the interest on extra capital. Where, however, single lines are necessary the passing places should be numerous, lengthy, and with easy curves.

There is an art in laying the points of passing places of great importance. Generally a main line is run through the centre of the road, and the passing places are laid on one side, the points being arranged so that the cars will run forward in the straight line, unless dragged over into the passing place, or the lines are in similar positions on opposite sides of the road, and the points equally divided, so that the cars have to be pulled across into either road. Now, as by the rule of the road vehicles should always pass by the left, it is evident that if the points are cast straight on the left hand, and that straight groove is laid exactly in the line of the rail immediately preceding the passing place, the car will run, without the horses being required to use any effort whatever, along its proper road (Fig. 12). The advantage is evident. Cars no longer miss the points, and pushing back, and confusion, so irritating to the passengers and injurious to the popularity of the tramways, are avoided, as well as much of the delay hitherto considered incidental to single lines. Collisions with cars and other vehicles, caused by the car getting on its wrong side, are minimised, and there being no longer any need for straining, the saving in horse-flesh is great. The same system is applicable to cross-overs (Fig. 13), and by carrying it out thoroughly, movable points and pointsmen can frequently be dispensed with.

Suitable Roads for Tramways.—Tramways have practically conquered the fierce opposition that was directed against them some time back in this country; but they are still regarded as an inconvenience by owners of private vehicles, and there can be no doubt that they always will to some extent injure the surfaces of the streets through which they are laid. This is particularly true in streets where the breastwork beyond the 18 inches of paving pre-

scribed for the tramway is macadam, owing to the difficulty experienced in keeping macadam and stone at a uniform level. It is better when a tramway is laid to pave from rail to channel; and if the paving along the entire width of the street, as well as the formation of the concrete bed beneath, can be carried out simultaneously with the construction of the tramways (sufficient care being taken with the manufacture of the concrete and with the selection of the paving sets), a surface should be arrived at which will interfere very little with the ordinary street traffic.

It may be roughly understood that a single line of tramway should not be laid in a street of less width than 24 feet; a double line in less than 32 feet. When it is desirable to lay a tramway in a street of less width, it may be more convenient to keep to one side. The question of gauge does not affect that of street width, as the width of the car is not ruled by the gauge of the line, but by the amount of room required for the convenience of passengers. Tramways will generally be found to facilitate instead of hindering the traffic even in narrow streets, as the cars compel or induce drivers of other vehicles to drive in regular lines.

Iron Tramways.—Though a timber longitudinal is most in favour, still various descriptions of iron bearings have been invented, and the question of wood *versus* iron, settled long since in railway construction, has been revived to a certain extent in connection with tramways. In a book written lately on tramway construction[1] the arguments generally used against a timber bearing are stated as follows:—"For tramways, it appears to us worse than useless to provide an elastic bed for the rails; for when the bed of the rails is elastic, and that of the contiguous paving is inelastic, there is an unequal settlement of these two important parts." But it will be evident, especially to those who have had to keep tramways in repair, that in this argument the elasticity of the timber bearing is entirely overestimated. It is not to be imagined for a moment that a sound longitudinal timber will ever be compressed by either street or car traffic, so that the rail will be appreciably lowered. In practice the difficulty is to keep the paving up to the rail, not to keep the rail up to the paving, and where rails are occasionally depressed it is entirely owing to the settlement of the foundation under the sleeper, and never in a single instance to any compression of the timber.

The second argument is, timber "decays rapidly, and requires

to be often renewed." Though the timber bearings first laid in this country were, from inexperience, laid under a spiked rail, and often in a way which did not give the timber a fair chance, the Author is not aware that the timber of any tramway in the kingdom has been or is being renewed from any fault in the timber. He is connected with the two oldest tramways in the kingdom—severally eight and twelve years old—and can certify that the timber of neither has been renewed. The Authors of the book in question have perhaps been deceived by having observed the work of laying box and discarding flat rails, which is now being proceeded with by degrees wherever tramways had the disadvantage of being laid with flat rails in the first instance. As these wear out, box rails with side fastenings are substituted; and as the deep flanges of the box rail require a corresponding rybat on the timber, it is evident that the timber must be changed with the rail. Mr. George Hopkins, an authority on tramway construction, says: "I have frequent occasion in the course of alterations to take up sleepers that have been in use seven years, and I find the timber perfectly sound."

The third argument is, "owing to its (timber) yielding nature, and to the fact of the sleepers being frequently deflected by passing loads, the fastenings of the rails work loose, and the difficulty of securing them is much increased." The Author admits this with regard to the old spiked rail, but he has not known any instance of a box rail properly side-fastened working loose. Where he has found a loose rail it has been because the sleeper had not been pressed into the rail, or the side fastenings had been omitted or been broken by careless driving. It is evident that the firmness of this rail is simply a question of the number of fasteners, and, confined and kept tight to the sleeper as these are by the paving, it will be seen that they cannot possibly work loose. If the hole punched in the rail flange be slightly larger than the head of the fastener, it is evident that the rail will work up and down under varying pressure without the fastener being disturbed in the slightest degree.

So far, therefore, experience in tramway construction seems to prove:—1st. That the timber sleeper, by its elasticity, acting the part of a cushion for the rail and a buffer for the concrete, occupies a valuable position, but that this elasticity is not so great as to
. . . .
with proper precautions, neither decays nor requires renewal, but will last whatever reasonable time the rail may be estimated to serve—say, from twenty to twenty-five years; 3rd. That the rail

may be secured to any desired extent by simply increasing the number of side fasteners, and that these may be fixed in such a manner that they will neither wear nor break, but hold good as long as the rail endures.

The experience of iron tramways in this country is limited to one system, which has been laid in various provincial towns. The rail is supported on cast-iron chairs placed 3 feet apart (Figs. 5 and 6). The earlier specimens were spiked through the groove, the spike going into a hard wood pin in the top of the chair. An improvement was made by the introduction of a side fastener somewhat similar to the one already described, the lower end being driven into a hard wood plug in the side of the chair. This system lacks advantages in fastening which the timber sleeper possesses. In the latter case both ends of the fastener penetrate into the wood, and the fastener therefore never springs out; in the former the upper end simply catches the rail, and must be apt to spring out. All the power of screw and lever are used to press the timber into the rail before the fasteners are driven home; and the wood, when relieved from this pressure, has a tendency to spring back, and thus the fasteners are made doubly tight. Of course this cannot be done where wrought and cast iron are in question. Further, the fasteners must be opposite one another, with iron chairs, instead of alternately as in timber, and the number of fasteners cannot be increased unless the chairs are increased.

It is proposed to construct the Manchester tramways with a continuous cast-iron bearing, to which the rail is held by iron pins (Fig. 4). It is to be feared that the difficulty of constructing this system (entailing as it does getting the holes in the castings and the holes in the rails to correspond with delicacy) will be great, especially at curves and crossings; and that the rail will wear away more quickly on an iron bearing than on timber. Though it is possible that in a foreign country, where timber might be subjected to the ravages of insects, the iron tramway would be the only alternative, it is not easy to see what good purpose can be served by laying one in this country. An iron tramway must be expensive in the first place, troublesome to lay with accuracy, and most unmanageable when out of repair. It is not at all likely that an iron bearing, such as that proposed for Manchester, will last as long as a timber bearing, as there will be great wear at the fastenings; and even if it could be proved to be everlasting there would be little advantage, as the first cost would provide a fresh timber bearing every few years.

PART II.—MECHANICAL MOTIVE POWER.

In the year 1873 a Select Committee of the House of Commons took into consideration the working of Locomotive Engines on Roads, and in their report recommended the following (p. x):— " That self-contained locomotive carriages (or engines), not exceeding 6 tons in weight, making no sound from the blast, and consuming their own smoke, be classed as light, and that they be permitted to travel at the ordinary speed of vehicles drawn by horses, and only subject to the same restrictions as such vehicles." Before this date a law limiting the rate of speed to 2 miles per hour in towns was in force; and though various engineers had worked at the subject, and had discovered many of the difficulties that would have to be overcome in applying steam to tramways, practical men had generally hardly considered it worth while to spend time and money in working out an invention of which the legislature practically prohibited the use. Latterly, however, great energy has been shown in several cases with most encouraging results.

The difficulties which have to be surmounted in the invention of a tramway engine are so numerous that the railway locomotive is a simple affair in comparison. In the latter case power and endurance are the principal features; in the former much beside that is necessary.

Messrs. Hughes, of Loughborough, the inventors of a steam car which is at present regarded with favour, put the peculiarities of a tramway engine very fairly as follows:—1st. It must possess sufficient power to draw one or more loaded cars up steep gradients; 2nd. While possessing sufficient weight to grip the rails, especially on steep ascents, it must at the same time not be so heavy as to press injuriously on the rails; 3rd. It should possess very powerful brakes, so that it can be stopped almost instantaneously in a crowded thoroughfare; 4th. It must be so contrived as to take the curves which exist on all tramways easily; 5th. It must not emit its exhaust or any steam into the air; 6th. It must be smokeless; 7th. It must not produce any noise in working calculated to alarm timid passengers and horses; 8th. Its machinery must not be visible, and yet must be easily accessible; 9th. Its fire must be concealed, especially at night; 10th. It must not present an unsightly appearance; 11th. It must not require more than one attendant to work it; 12th. It must be reversible,

i.e. capable of going backwards or forwards with equal safety; and 13th. If possible, it should be so simple in construction and working that it can be driven by an unskilled man.

When these, which may be termed the external difficulties, have been met, then many internal difficulties, at present only guessed at, will arise, and though it is not contended that these difficulties are insuperable, still there is much to be accomplished before other than animal power can be used extensively on tramways. Neither is it desirable that the change, if change there is to be, should be unduly hastened, lest by the introduction of imperfect engines public prejudice, at present dormant, should be again aroused.

The tramway engines hitherto experimented with at all successfully have been of three classes:

1st. Steam engine and car in one, as Grantham's.
2nd. Steam engine separate from car, as Hughes' and Merryweather's.
3rd. Pneumatic car and engine in one, as Scott Moncrieff's and Mékarski's.

There is some difference of opinion as to whether it is more desirable to have the engine and car combined or separate, and substantial arguments may be urged on both sides. It is argued, on the one hand, that with a detached engine there must be a great deal of shunting at the beginning and end of the journey, and with tramways as at present laid this argument is very forcible; the Author having witnessed experiments where the changing of the engine from one end of the car to the other was a most tedious process. But the difficulty could be overcome to a great extent, in some cases by laying a circular line at the terminus, in others by a V shunt up a side street, and where neither is practicable by double cross-overs. Again, with a detached engine the difficulty of passing round quick curves is increased. It is likely that on a curve, say of 40 feet radius, the car would be occasionally pulled off the line. This objection is valid where quick curves are essential, but in many cases tramway curves are unnecessarily quick, and if mechanical motive power is introduced the tramway constructor must meet the difficulty by making the curves as easy as practicable. In the matter of adhesion, the detached engine is evidently inferior to its rival. Where the car and engine are combined it will not, probably, matter much how great the load on the car is, as the adhesion will increase in proportion; whereas

if the engine is separate, the weight it can pull after it will be a known quantity, and will be just that portion of the whole tractive force which is more than sufficient for itself.

On the other hand, the detached engine entails less alteration to rolling stock, and permits of two cars being drawn by one engine on special occasions. The design of engine and car combined must be greatly cramped; the separate engine can be designed with greater freedom, and in it the experience gained in connection with railway locomotives can be more fully taken advantage of. Though it is claimed for the Grantham steam car that the boilers are perfectly safe, and that the passengers experience no disagreeable sensation from the heat, it is to be feared that this state of things will not improve as the car becomes older, and it will be a long time before timid passengers will sit beside a boiler with complacency. Where detached engines are employed a smaller stock of engines will do the work, as in case of accident to the car, it can be unhooked and another attached. Where engine and car are combined a trifling accident will cause £800 to lie idle. In the matter of repairs generally the detached engine will be greatly superior to the combined. In the former case the engine can be removed at night and cleaned or repaired in a suitable engine shed; in the latter, the fittings of the car will be quickly soiled and damaged by the smoke and dirt incidental to engine repairs and cleaning.

From these considerations it is likely that detached engines will be used more generally than combined. At least this will be the case where steam is used. With compressed air the case is different. The machinery necessary to drive a car by compressed air is comparatively simple, and can be accommodated under a passenger car in a manner neither dangerous nor disagreeable to the passengers. This seems satisfactorily proved by Mr. Scott Moncrieff's car. If heating is resorted to, as in M. Mékarski's, it becomes a question whether the detached engine will not again be more suitable.

1. *Steam Engine and Car combined.*—The steam carriage designed by the late Mr. John Grantham, M. Inst. C.E., is slightly longer than an ordinary car, and has two boilers, so placed on each side in the centre of the car, that a continuous passage is maintained throughout for passengers. The driving wheels are of a larger size, and there are four smaller wheels on a bogie frame. The car can be driven either way and from either end, and is well under the driver's control. It complies with the Board of Trade regulation, which renders it necessary that the speed should be limited

by automatic machinery to 10 miles per hour. A stoker is required, and the objection caused by the escape of smoke and steam is not entirely abated. A Grantham steam car is at work on the Wantage tramway. It weighs empty 6½ tons, and when fully laden with fuel and passengers over 12 tons. It cost £800.

2. *Detached Engines.*—Messrs. Merryweather and Co. have many engines at work, chiefly on the Continent. Those used in Paris weigh, when laden with fuel and water, about 3¼ tons. The boilers are multitubular, 6 feet long and 2 feet 6 inches in diameter. The two cylinders have a diameter of 6 inches, with a length of stroke of 10 inches. The working pressure is about 100 lbs., and the consumption of fuel 20 lbs. per hour. Each engine has ordinarily attached a car containing, when full, forty-eight passengers, which it draws up various ascending gradients, the steepest being about 1 in 30. The engine is perfectly under control, and can be propelled at any required speed at the will of the driver. The brake power is a foot brake, which acts on all the wheels at once with rapidity and effect. Various ingenious contrivances can be applied to these engines for increasing adhesion and power on heavy inclines. The exhaust steam from the engine is disposed of partly by condensation, viz. by mixture with dry air, by passing through diaphragms of wire gauze, and through a surface condenser; the residue is led into the smoke-box, and escapes in a superheated state. The speed of the engine is controlled by a governor, driven by the rotation of the wheels and acting upon a throttle valve. In the course of experiments on the Vale of Clyde tramways, it was found that, notwithstanding the apparent completeness of the methods for getting rid of the smoke and steam, the escape was still somewhat objectionable. The manufacturers believe they will be able to improve the engine in this respect, and it is to be hoped they will be successful, as no engine has a chance of succeeding in this country which renders outside travelling impossible or even disagreeable. In Paris a stoker accompanies the engine, but as it seems that his chief duty consists in blowing a horn, Messrs. Merryweather think his services might be dispensed with in this country. It is desirable that, on a tramway engine, not only the stoker, but the operation of stoking during the journey should be unnecessary.

The steam tramway engine designed by Messrs. Henry Hughes and Co., of Loughborough, is at present giving great satisfaction. It is heavier than Messrs. Merryweather's, weighing 4 tons 15 cwt. empty, 6 tons loaded. The cylinders are 7 inches in diameter,

with a length of stroke of 12 inches. The wheels are 24 inches in diameter, and coupled. The exhaust steam is got rid of by condensation. The condenser is subdivided by horizontal perforated partitions, down which a stream of cold water gradually falls, condensing during its descent the ascending currents of steam from the exhaust ports. The water of condensation is allowed to flow on to the road; or when this is objectionable, to accumulate in a tank under the tramway carriage, from which it is discharged at the end of the journey. Coke is used as fuel, and the amount of smoke and steam that issues from the roof of the engine is trifling, certainly not enough to annoy passengers. The firing of this engine is completed before it starts on its journey, and is not disturbed until the journey is complete. In this way much nuisance is doubtless saved, and the services of a stoker are rendered unnecessary. Messrs. Hughes endeavoured so to arrange their engine, that all the work requiring technical knowledge could be done before the engine started on its journey, and thereafter the engine could be driven by one, and he an unskilled, man. This principle has certainly been carried out, the engine being so constructed that the driver can perform every required service on ordinary occasions without moving from his seat in front. On the level, and on gradients as steep as 1 in 30, this engine can do all that would be required of a tramway engine sufficiently well; but on gradients of greater inclination than 1 in 30, the Author thinks that neither this nor any other engine he has seen could be trusted to stop with a laden car behind it, and to start again without trouble and delay. Still it is not right to draw absolutely adverse conclusions from this opinion. In actual practice it would not be necessary to stop an engine on a stiff incline unless it was a long one. On a well-managed tramway the horse cars would not be stopped under similar conditions. Though there are tramways that could not, owing to their gradients, be worked successfully by steam power, there are in a majority of cases no insuperable engineering obstacles. At the same time, it will probably be longer than some imagine before steam engines will be allowed to run to any considerable extent in towns.

3. *Pneumatic Cars.*—A pneumatic car, designed by Mr. Scott Moncrieff, has been at work on the Vale of Clyde tramways for some time. The car is in appearance like an ordinary passenger car, but the floor is more elevated. Under the ends of the floor three reservoirs, 6 feet long and 2 feet in diameter, are placed, and these, when charged, contain 100 cubic feet of air at a pressure of

350 lbs per square inch. The machinery lies between the reservoirs, under the middle of the car. Mr. Scott Moncrieff says, in a description of the car, "The principal obstacle with which inventors have had hitherto to contend in utilising compressed air at high pressures is the excessive cold that is produced in the exhaust, and this has proved fatal to all applications of compressed air for locomotive purposes up to the present time. In any mechanical arrangement, such as a locomotive carrying a definite quantity of compressed air, and absent from time to time from the original sources of supply at the pumping stations, it is absolutely necessary that the fullest advantage should be taken of the limited power stored in the receivers. The only way in which this can be done is by using the air expansively, and as the pressure is always decreasing towards the end of the journey, this expansion must vary correspondingly.

"By an arrangement of valve gear suited to these requirements, the air is always exhausted in the Scott Moncrieff system at the atmospheric pressure, the effect of which is not merely to obviate the difficulties arising from excessive cold, but also to propel the car in silence, and utilise to the utmost the available power."

It is impossible to judge fairly of the value of Mr. Scott Moncrieff's car under the circumstances presented on the Vale of Clyde lines. The car there is the first, and is, as might be expected, roughly constructed and unnecessarily heavy. The pumps for compressing the air are of a temporary character, and there is no proper storage for the air, so that the process of charging is exceedingly tedious, occupying an hour each journey. Under these circumstances it is rather remarkable that the car should have achieved even a degree of success, and been able to compete not discreditably with steam cars. Mr. Moncrieff is now building a new car of a larger size, and with greater capacity for storing air, and as he will be able in this car to take advantage of the improvements that experience has suggested, it is likely that even more satisfactory results will be arrived at.

M. Mékarski, of Paris, is the inventor of a tramway engine and car combined, driven by compressed air heated before admission into cylinders.[1] The reservoirs, thirteen in number, are cylindrical, and lie crosswise under the floor of the car. They contain when charged 70 cubic feet of air at a pressure of 375 lbs. On the front platform stands a vertical vessel filled with water at a high tem-

---

[1] *Vide* Minutes of Proceedings Inst. C.E., vol. xliii., p. 383, and vol. xliv., p. 254.

perature. The compressed air enters at the underside of this vessel, and bubbles up through the water, thus becoming charged with vapour. By a reducing arrangement the air can be admitted into the cylinders at any required pressure. From this car very good results are said to be obtained. The method, however, appears complicated, and the position of the hot-water vessel makes it necessary that the car should travel one way only. The weight of the car must be considerable, and it is possible that when compressed air is proposed to be used in this way, it will be found better to have a detached engine.

PART III.—FINANCIAL.

The cost of tramways is affected by so many circumstances that it would only be misleading to attempt to give an estimate. The price will vary from £1,500 to £6,000 per mile of single line, according to the design recommended for the particular road to be traversed and the price of materials at the time and place. A Table is annexed (p. 24) showing, as fully as practicable, the present position and progressive development of nine tramway companies. This Table attests the remarkable success achieved by tramways in this country within a few years. From it almost any information that can be desired on the subject of working expenses may be easily procured.

It is not easy at present to make any reliable comparison between the relative cost of horse and steam power on tramways. If attempted, it would be sure to err in favour of steam, from the fact that while experience has taught the worst that can be learned about horses, as yet the best only has been seen of engines. Where steam is introduced there will probably be a substantial saving, but less than the advocates of steam locomotion predict. The wear and tear to engines by mud getting amongst the gearing, sudden stoppages, collisions, jerking over stones in the groove, and running off lines, would be enormous. The repairs will entail the services of a staff of engine-fitters, and after a few years, when the engines become worn, workshops with expensive machinery and manned by expensive men will have to be erected. The nightly cleaning of the engines will be formidable, and can only be satisfactorily accomplished by skilled men. Horse-driving requires little skill, and it is easy to find drivers who will work long hours at a low rate of wages; but engine-drivers will require high wages, and will most likely decline to work twelve to thirteen hours per diem. Indulgence granted to drivers in this respect would have to be extended to conductors, and in this way complication and expense would arise. It is to considerations such as these that the hesitation to recognise the value of a change from horse to steam power is to be attributed, rather than to prejudice.

In the following memoranda the actual cost of working a car by horses is contrasted with the probable cost of working by steam and air. The cost of fuel for steam power is taken from recorded experiments. The cost of fuel and fixed machinery in the third estimate is taken from Mr. Moncrieff's statement. In such matters as wages, repairs, cleaning, spare engines, &c., the Author has followed his own judgment, and the figures are somewhat higher than ordinary, but in practice they would probably be low enough. The wages of the engine-driver are taken as higher than the car-driver's wages. Most inventors claim that their engines can be driven by an unskilled man, and though this may be correct, it would be none the less extremely injudicious to trust unskilled men with them. One cleaner is allowed to every three engines. Such expenses as management, rent, interest on outlay, &c., are not included, as these would be about the same in any case. The spare engines are taken at 25 per cent., and, considering accidents and periodical overhauling, this number would not be excessive. It is always to be remembered, however, that whilst the cost of horse power has been ascertained with absolute certainty, the cost of mechanical motive power is, to some extent, an unknown quantity.

ESTIMATE No. 1.—COST OF HORSE POWER PER DIEM.

	£.	s.	d.
Forage for ten horses and one spare horse at 2s.	1	2	0
Veterinary attendance and shoeing	0	2	2
Depreciation of horses	0	6	3
Harness maintenance, renewal, and cleaning	0	1	1
Horsekeeper 3s. 6d., car-driver 5s., conductor 3s. 6d.	0	12	0
Per diem	2	3	6

Or assuming 60 miles per car per diem = 8¾d. per mile.

ESTIMATE No. 2.—COST OF STEAM POWER PER DIEM.

	£.	s.	d.
Fuel, oil, and water, 1d. per mile	0	5	
Renewal of engines, 10 per cent.	0	3	3
Repair of engines, 1d. per mile	0	5	0
Interest on 25 per cent. spare engines	0	0	4
Engine cleaner (⅓) 1s. 6d., driver 6s. 6d., conductor 3s. 6d.	0	11	6
Per diem	1	5	1

Or at 60 miles per diem = 5d. per mile.
Where a stoker is necessary the rate would be 5¾d. per mile.

c 2

ESTIMATE No. 3.—COST OF PNEUMATIC CAR PER DIEM.

	Pence per Mile.
Enginemen and firemen for fixed engines	0·125
Depreciation of fixed machinery	0·125
„ „ cars	0·625
Fuel, oil, &c.	0·500
Contingencies	0·272

	£.	s.	d.
1·647 × 60 =	0	8	3
Repair of car engine 1d. per mile	0	5	0
Interest on spare engines	0	0	4
Cleaner (⅓) 1s. 6d., driver 6s. 6d., conductor 3s. 6d.	0	11	6
Per diem	1	5	1

Or at 60 miles per diem = 5d. per mile.

Part IV.—TRAMWAY CARRIAGES (Plate 1, Figs. 15 to 20).

The cars for the New York and Harlem street railway were built in 1832 by Messrs. John Stephenson and Co., of New York. These cars had the features of ordinary road coaches, viz. a carriage part independent of the body, elevated driver's seat, side-doors, and leather springs.

Springs.—The wear of the lower part of this description of vehicle proved to be so great, that it was soon found necessary to unite the carriage part to the underframe, to place the springs under the body, and to substitute steel for leather. At first the axle-box was fixed to the spring on the underside; but this was unsatisfactory, the adjustment of wheels and axles not being positive; and the single pedestal, which permitted the car to move in a vertical plane only, was introduced. In 1858 a further improvement was made; a yoke being placed on the axle-box, each end of which yoke sustained a spring, thus giving two springs to each journal. At the same time steel spiral springs were introduced; and these, in turn, gave way to india-rubber, which last are now almost universally used. The rubber is prepared in a way which makes its elasticity practically independent of temperature, and increases its power of sustaining burdens. The india-rubber springs are cheap, durable, easily changed, not liable to sudden failure like metal springs, and give ease and delicacy to the motion of the car.

Wheels (Figs. 21 to 25).—Much ingenuity has been expended in

designing car wheels. Solid wooden wheels, with steel or wrought-iron tires, were popular in England; but they are complicated; the tires are liable to work loose, and the endurance of the wheels does not justify their cost. Wheels with wooden spokes were attempted, but speedily abandoned. Light wheels, with cast hub and rim and wrought-iron spokes, are made and used in America, but they require great care in manufacture, and are costly. Crucible-steel wheels, cast in one piece with arms, are made in Sheffield. They are light, and seem to give good results. Wheels made of American chilled iron are, however, perhaps the best for the purpose. Where lightness is an object, as in the case of one-horse cars, openings are left between the arms. Of the American, the waved-plate wheels, manufactured by the Lobdell Car Wheel Company, give great satisfaction (Fig. 21). The difficulty in the manufacture of chilled wheels is, to combine strength in the plates, with sufficient depth of chill in the tread to insure durability. If the plate is flat, it is frequently injuriously affected by the sudden cooling of the outside rim; but the waved plate can give slightly, and is not left in a state of tension. The average life of chilled cast-iron wheels in America is from sixteen to eighteen months; but in England it is not more than ten to fifteen months, owing to the section of the rail. In America there is no groove, and the flange of the wheel has always plenty of freedom, and can only wear on one side. In England the groove is so narrow that the wheel flange is continually rubbing either on one side or the other. Stones are also caught by and forced into the groove, and the wheels get jerked and chipped. Nothing of the kind can happen with the American rail.

It is not an uncommon theory that wheels on the same axle, having the freedom of independent motion, will operate better than wheels fast on the axle, and practically forming a cylinder, and that the free wheels will have special advantages in passing round curves, because the wheel on the outer rail can rotate to accord with the longer length. This theory is fallacious, for the axles are held parallel, and cannot form radii of the curve; therefore the wheels, when passing curves, must necessarily be forced round by a sliding process. If, for illustration, the front axle of an ordinary road carriage be lashed so that it cannot swing round, and the attempt be then made to drive round a street-corner, it will be seen that the looseness of the wheels will not make the operation less impracticable. The loose wheels are therefore useless, and experience shows them to be absolutely detrimental.

An ingenious wheel is used in America, having a second rim or tread on the inside, of a lesser diameter than the other. On coming to facing points this second tread strikes on an inclined plane, the car runs up out of the ordinary groove, and is led over on this elevation into its proper line, when it falls to the same level. By fitting the cars with or without this additional tread, movable points and pointsmen may be entirely dispensed with. The system works well in America, but the elevation in the points would be objectionable in this country.

Brakes.—At first brakes were applied to the treads of car wheels, as on railways; but it was soon seen that the circumstances were different. On railways a deep flange is necessary, and this is not in any way injurious to the rail. On tramways a very slight flange is adequate, and a deep flange would be positively injurious, as it increases the resistance and splits the rail. The tread of the wheel has evidently a tendency to wear more rapidly than the flange, and it is, therefore, necessary to wear down the flange proportionately, so as to keep it off the bottom of the groove. This work is best done by chilled iron brakes. The system of using wood for tramway brakes, with the view of saving the wheels, is therefore fallacious, the wheels being saved at the expense of rails and horses.

Timber.—The peculiar construction of cars with short wheel base and great overhang, coupled with the immense loads they constantly have to carry, renders it necessary that unusual care be taken in their construction, and in nothing more than in the seasoning of the timber. Oak is the best timber to choose for the substructure, and ash for the superstructure.

Endurance.—Cars worked constantly on roads having heavy gradients should last about ten years. It is doubtful if any car in this country will last, even with much renewing, over fifteen years. Some of Messrs. Stephenson's cars have been known to last nearly twenty years in America; in fact, some of that age are certified to be still at work in New York, on "Commodore Vanderbilt's Road."

Size.—The size of the cars may be to some extent ruled by the expected traffic and gradients; but two-horse cars accommodating forty-two passengers are generally useful. Some thought has been expended in arriving at a medium weight, which, while it permits of the car being constructed in a sufficiently substantial manner, is yet not so great as to unreasonably distress the horses. Where steam is used as the motive power, it will probably be prudent to increase the weight and substantiality of the cars. One-horse cars are used freely in America, and to a limited extent in this country. They may be of use where the road is level and the traffic light. The gearing, wheels, &c., of the cars, whether two-horse or one-horse, must be to a great extent similar; so that, in the latter case, the horse has more dead weight to pull.

Mr. HUNTINGTON said the question of tramways had taken such a footing in English construction that it was quite time to have a fair and deliberate discussion concerning it. Tramways would in future form an important part in conveyance, especially in situations where the cost or the site of a railway might be inexpedient, and that not only in England, but also in the Colonies and in other places where English skill might be called for. He regretted that the Author had given so little information as to the cost of the different systems in relation to the actual construction. The statement that the cost varied from £1,500 to £6,000 a mile was very vague. He had been interested, as a shareholder, in undertakings of that kind, and had found the information given at public meetings to be of an unsatisfactory character. In London certain tramways might be said to be in full working condition, such as the North Metropolitan and the London or South system; in Dublin also they had been at work for a long period. Some were worked by horse contract, like the North Metropolitan, and others horsed themselves, like the London and the Dublin. The capitals of the companies varied considerably, as also did the results of working the roads. In making a comparison, in addition to the tramways, he had thought that it would be instructive to join thereto the railway system and the omnibus system, for which purpose he had selected the Metropolitan, the Metropolitan District, and the North London railways, as a group approaching the nearest to the tramways for conveying passengers. The length of the North Metropolitan tramway was 30½ miles, of the London, 20¼ miles, and of the Dublin, 15 miles: the length of the group of railways was 32 miles; and the General Omnibus Company covered a range of 58½ miles. The cost for six months to the 31st of December, 1876, of the North Metropolitan had been £22,447 per mile; of the London, £20,697; of the Dublin, £17,125; of the group of railways, £578,320; and the capital of the General Omnibus Company was equal to £10,264 per mile. To put the North Metropolitan on a fair level with the others, the cost of horse stock and equipments (on the London scale) should be added, or £3,040 per mile, making that system cost £25,487 per mile, or about £6,000 per mile dearer than the London. The item "Tramways," which included the roads, paving, engineering, extra works, preliminary

and parliamentary expenses, cost on the London £15,005 per mile, which might be analysed thus:—

	£.
Double line of tramways	3,000
Paving, 6 yards wide	8,000
Engineering	1,000
Extra works, &c.	2,000
Parliamentary, &c.	1,000
	15,000

Besides these expenses the London cost £2,177 per mile for horse stock, also £1,959 per mile for cars and other plant, and £1,555 per mile for land and buildings; while the cost of the North Metropolitan for the last two items only was £1,077 and £1,345 per mile respectively. Taking the single passenger as the unit, the North Metropolitan carried 2,457 per mile per day; the London, 2,070; the Dublin, 1,150; the railway group, 7,735; and the General Omnibus Company, 2,450. The receipts per passenger were: North Metropolitan, 2·08d.; the London, 2·10d.; the Dublin, 2·88d.; the railways, 2·57d.; the General Omnibus Company, 2·53d. The horsing of the North Metropolitan was done by the General Omnibus Company, and the contract amounted to 0·88d. per passenger; the London horsed itself, and the cost, including renewal of horses, was 0·81d. per passenger, and the Dublin cost for horsing and renewal, 0·88d. The locomotive cost on the railways was only 0·35d. per passenger. The cost per passenger for the horsing of the General Omnibus Company was 1·31d. With regard to the railways, the returns contained the gross receipts for goods and the total gross receipts, so that the gross passenger receipts could be ascertained; but, as far as expenditure was concerned, the returns combined both, and a separation therefore had to be made by computation and approximation. The total cost under each system respectively was: North Metropolitan, 1·51d.; the London, 1·57d.; the Dublin, 1·88d.; the railways, 0·88d.; and the General Omnibus Company, 2·11d. per passenger. The general results showed that the railway system had at all events the advantage of economy. The probable cost of steam on tramways had been stated by the Author as 25s. 1d. per car per day, which nearly agreed with his own calculation. He had not taken into account, what the Author had included, the renewal of engine, &c.; in the Tramway reports he found it

as renewal of horses, plant, and other matters, and left it to stand as the equivalent of the new form of renewal.

	s.	d.
Fuel, 7 cwt. (during eighteen hours)	7	11
Engineman and stoker at 6s. per day above the present wages of driver	6	0
Sundries, oil, waste, tools, materials, assistance, &c.	1	10
Interest on capital for reforming road and stock	2	10
Contingencies	1	5
Renewals, now charged for horses ¼d. per passenger	5	2
Total per car per day	25	2

Therefore, withdrawing the renewals from this estimate as being elsewhere included, and taking the steam alone, he calculated the amount to be as nearly as possible £1 per car per day. Thus the cost on the North Metropolitan, running one hundred and forty cars per day, would be £140; and applying that to 14,000,000 passengers in the half-year, the amount was 0·44d. per passenger; also in the case of the London it was 0·45d. That gave a bonâ fide gain of about 0·4d. in favour of mechanical motive power, which was equal to an increased dividend of 8 per cent. or more. By comparing the tramways with the railways in the subjoined table it would be seen that, although the system by steam had great advantages in large cities, where passengers were numerous and distances short, the cost of steam was considerably augmented in country districts, where there were fewer passengers and longer distances to travel. During the six or seven years that tramways had been working, roads, cars, plant, and horses had been more or less subject to renewals. The roads cost about £4,000 per mile, double line, including engineering and other matters exclusive of the paving. Up to the present time the total renewal from the 1st of January, 1871, of the tramway upon the North Metropolitan had amounted to £601 (or £777 including the contractor's outlay) out of £4,000, and on the London to £936. If renewals went on at that rate previously a considerable period would elapse before the tramway was thoroughly worn out; but there was a slow annual increase in this item, which in 1871 was about £88, and in 1876 became £220 per mile on both tramways. With regard, however, to the cars and other plant, the original outlay was £1,133 per mile on the North Metropolitan, and the company had already spent in renewal £1,311. On the London the original cost was £1,919 per mile, and up to the present the repairs had amounted to £1,442, so that the American statement of a ten-years' life did not appear to be borne out. For horses the original cost per mile on the

London amounted to £2,480, and the renewal to £1,540. The actual reserves in hand to meet the renewals exclusive of these annual outlays were for the North Metropolitan £738, and for the London £595 per mile; insufficient sums, seeing that the annual outlays were already £250 per mile for roads, cars, &c., and £142 per mile for horses. With regard to the tramway itself, he had received the following particulars three or four years ago from a gentleman connected with the construction of the line. The price of iron, timber, and labour was constantly varying at the time, so that the figures could not be taken as an accurate estimate of what the real cost had been :—

	Per yard.	
	s.	d.
Rails, ties, spikes, bolts, dogs, fishes, &c. (rails 50 lbs. per yard at £10 10s. delivered)	10	6
Timber creosoted and shaped	2	0
Fixing and laying, including crossings	1	0
Maintenance for one year	0	6
Contingencies, cartage, lights, watching, waste, and cutting	1	6
Risk and profits 10 per cent.	1	6
Total	17	0

1,760 yards at 17s. = £1,496, say £1,500 per mile of single line.

Paving with 7-inch cubes of granite for a double road with concrete bottom cost :—

	Per square yard.	
	s.	d.
Granite paving set to tramways, 18 feet wide, materials and labour	11	0
Concrete, averaging 6 inches thick, including excavation and removal of road	1	6
Contingencies, grouting, carting, watching, removing materials, and sanding	1	0
Maintenance for one year	0	3
Risk and profit 10 per cent.	1	3
Total	15	0

1,760 × 6 × 15s. = £7,920, say £8,000 per mile of double line.

He had also obtained the following particulars :—Gauge, 4 feet 8½ inches with a 4-feet midway. Rails, dogged on kyanised longitudinal bearers 21 feet long, with four transverse bearers bolted with ¾-inch bolts and nuts to the gauge, the weight being, as computed after measurement, 45 lbs. per yard. The gauge was kept by the paving. The dogs were 4 inches long, ⅝ inch in diameter, and were driven into drilled holes on both sides of the rails, slightly angular, about 3 feet apart, one side dividing the space with the other. The dogs were driven into the timber after being well screwed down by a double-sided square-threaded cramp. The joints were fished with plates 9 inches long, ⅜ inch thick, let

into the longitudinals. The timbers were bedded in Portland cement concrete 6 inches thick, and the paving was laid upon the same. The sifted rubble of the road was used for grouting, and fine red sand was laid above all. The paving extended 1 foot 6 inches on each side of the outer rails, 7-inch granite cubes being used. Extra works, crossings, and sidings, were not included in the above estimates. The following table illustrated the foregoing remarks more exactly :—

DETAILS of the COMPARATIVE COST of CONVEYING ONE PASSENGER by TRAMWAY, OMNIBUS, and RAILWAY; the TWO FORMER SYSTEMS for ONE YEAR ENDING the 31st of DECEMBER, 1876, and the RAILWAY SYSTEM for ONE YEAR ENDING the 31st of DECEMBER, 1875.

Item.	Tramways.			Omnibus.	Railways.[1]	
	North Metropolitan.	London (South).	Dublin.	London, General.	North London, Metropolitan, and District.	Nine great trunk lines from London.
	d.	d.	d.	d.	d.	d.
Horsing (net)	0·897	0·808	0·761	1·139	..	..
Renewal of horses	..	0·156	0·099	0·215	..	..
Locomotive, passengers only	..	..	..	..	0·348	1·745
Wages	0·358	0·349	0·182	0·490		
Miscellaneous	0·066	0·091	0·083	0·019		
Repairs of cars	0·067	0·090	0·101	0·136	0·076	0·476
" road	0·060	0·072	0·157	..	0·123	1·286
" plant	..	0·016	0·027	0·062		
Rents, rates (net)	0·047	0·127	0·095	0·058	0·076	0·275
Duties	0·006	0·009	..	0·006	0·094	0·500
Compensations	0·007	0·025	0·026	0·012	0·015	0·228
Law and parliament	0·023	0·026	0·034	0·031	0·151	0·804
General (net)	0·010	0·013	0·041			
Total cost	1·541	1·782	1·906	2·168	0·883	5·314
" receipts	2·078	2·076	2·895	2·552	2·576	13·031
Gross profit	0·537	0·294	0·989	0·384	1·693	7·717
Capital expended per passenger, adding horses	6·856	6·420	10·382	2·800	31·160	99·520
Passengers per mile per day	2,105	2,101	1,106	2,400	7,735	117
Cost per mile (£)	25,487	20,697	17,125	10,264	578,320	58,245
Miles open, all as in double line	30½	20¼	15	58½	32	5,875

[1] The cost of goods is eliminated from the railways.

Mr. HEAD had not studied the subject very much, but he had had a great deal to do with traction engines on roads.[1] In considering the application of steam to tramways, it should be remembered that the gradients could not be altered, so that the engine had to work upon a variety of gradients according to circumstances. Two kinds of engines—separate and combined—had to be constructed for tramway cars. There were many advantages in the separate engines constructed by Mr. Merryweather and Mr. Hughes. The companies using those engines could employ their present rolling stock; the passengers had not the same fear of being blown up if the boiler should burst as when the engine and car were combined; and the public had an idea that the system was the right one from association with railway trains. At the same time, looking at the gradients of the lines in London, Edinburgh, Liverpool, and other places, he thought there would be a good deal of difficulty in getting an engine weighing from 4 to 5 tons up some of the inclines in wet, foggy weather. It was difficult, however, to bring data forward of what could be done under such circumstances. The experience with traction engines on roads showed that in damp weather adhesion was small. Horses could always haul the cars, for, if two would not suffice, a third, and even a fourth could be added; but if an engine could not get on in wet weather the whole traffic might be blocked. With an engine on the principle of Mr. Grantham's there was the whole of the adhesion from the combined weights of the engine and boiler, the car, and the passengers. It was unnecessary to say that adhesion was practically the keystone to the propelling power of the car, and that an engine of great weight had more power to propel itself than one of light weight. These important matters must be cleared up before tramway companies could decide upon the best engine to be employed. There might be one or two level lines on which a separate engine could be used with advantage, but he thought there were many lines in London which could only be worked safely with a combined engine and car.

Mr. LONGRIDGE said it was evident that separate engines could only be employed where there were easy gradients. He had seen an engine of Mr. Merryweather's at Vienna, and it struck him at the time that there would be considerable difficulty with a steep gradient. It weighed 3½ or 4 tons, and, including car and passengers, the total weight would be about 10 tons. With a gradient of 1 in 20 that weight would require a tractive force of

¹ Vide Minutes of Proceedings Inst. C.E., vol. xxxvi., p. 36.

about 1,482 lbs. He took the friction of the engine at 20 lbs., and of the car at 15 lbs. The insistent weight was the weight of the engine itself, 4 tons, and he believed that in ordinarily slippery weather the adhesion would be not more than one-tenth, or 896 lbs. Under those circumstances he did not think it possible to work with any satisfaction. Much the same thing applied to Mr. Grantham's car, which he also saw at Vienna. It went very well on level ground, or on a moderate inclination, and there was no nuisance from blast, sparks, or smoke; but in that case the engine was placed at one end of the car, and the driving wheels beside the engine. About two-thirds of the way towards the other end there was a bogie with four wheels, and the only adhesion that could be obtained was the adhesion upon the driving wheels of the engine, which would not amount to more than one-half of the total weight. The same difficulty therefore arose as in the case of Mr. Merryweather's car, and he knew that considerable trouble had been experienced at Vienna with a gradient of 1 in 24 when the rails were at all out of order. It was not only the slipperiness of the rails that affected the tramway, but their inequalities. The constant passage of heavy traffic made it impossible to keep the rails in the same order as on a railway, so that one wheel would perhaps bear scarcely at all on the rail, and the other would bear very heavily. For steam traction it would be necessary to devise some means of utilising the whole of the carrying wheels of the car, and that might be readily accomplished with Mr. Grantham's car. Another difficulty in the way was the great variation in the work to be done at different times. In the case of Mr. Merryweather's car, running nearly empty on a level, at 8 miles an hour, a tractive force was required of 2½ HP., whereas on a gradient of 1 in 20, a tractive force of 19 HP. was needed. With the small boiler necessarily used in such cases, he considered it would be difficult to regulate the fire and the generation of steam so as to meet those varying conditions. The steam would sometimes blow off with violence, which would be objectionable, and would perhaps be experienced with almost all steam engines. No doubt many objections would be avoided by the use of compressed air, but that was an extravagant mode of getting power. Compressed air was not itself a motive power, but only a method of applying it, the power being in the steam engine which compressed the air. M. Mékarski found that for every horse-power, effective, obtained in compressed air, an amount of 5 steam HP. was needed, so that the power actually used was only 20 per cent. There appeared to be an error in the Author's comparison of the pneumatic car with steam power. He estimated, for instance, the fuel by steam power at 5s. per day, and in the pneumatic car at 2s. 6d., whereas if M. Mékarski was right, it should be five times as much. A combination of compressed air and steam had been brought under his notice, the power being obtained by the explosion of ordinary coal gas. It seemed ingenious and likely to prove of value. It avoided all the difficulties arising from noise, smoke, and the like, and was always perfectly at command, since it could be varied almost at any moment from 2 HP. to 20 HP. Although gas, as fuel, was expensive, he thought the expense would be far more than counterbalanced by the great advantages that would be obtained.

Mr. A. M. FOWLER said, in Salford 22 miles of tramway were being laid down, and great anxiety had been felt as to the best mode of construction. He was surprised to find that the Author had come to the conclusion that a timber foundation was the best for large towns. With regard to side fastenings, he agreed with the Author, that unless the paving stones were brought close to the iron the necessities of the case in regard to heavy traffic in large towns could not be met. In Salford a system had been adopted (Fig. 1) to

FIG. 1.

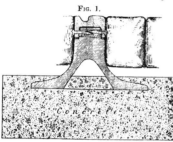

which the objections raised in the Paper were not applicable. There was a deep flange under the rail, a close joint to the iron, and by having a fastening every 3 feet it was impossible that the traffic could produce any detrimental effect upon the surface of the street. The paving setts were bedded in ashes on the top of the concrete. The first portion of the line had been laid about two months, and although the traffic had been heavy there was no crack or break in the joints of the paving. Before the Salford committee decided upon that plan, they had visited almost every town in

England where the best-known systems of construction were employed, and, after his report, they came to the unanimous conclusion to adopt that system. The Author had stated that, by having the timber foundation set back from the face of the rail, the fastening was made flush with the side of the rail. That allowed for the width of the dog, or the fastening, and it allowed for the sett to come close to the rails. In tramway construction the object was to preserve the foundation, and if it was preserved by keeping out the water, vibration was to a great extent prevented. He did not suppose that the setts were grouted, as in London, with lias lime, or, as in Lancashire and Yorkshire, with asphalt concrete; the space would require to be filled up, otherwise the water would get in, and so it would work loose. He thought the asphalt or concrete would not adhere so well to timber as it would to iron, and that a continuous bearing was objectionable. If the vibration of the rail was to be reduced to a minimum, the bearings should be about 2 or 3 feet apart. In the old plan of railway construction, with longitudinal timbers, the vibration in the foundation had been so great, that transverse sleepers had been resorted to. If such sleepers were laid solid throughout, the structure would not be so good. With a rigid longitudinal foundation, packed hard in the centre, it must necessarily tilt, just as a flag in a street would when not bedded well at the corners. He did not wish to say anything against a continuous iron bearing, or a foundation of iron under a portion of the setts; but he maintained that if there was not a uniform foundation for the setts they would tilt. He had found that to be so in tramways already constructed on that principle. Railways were generally level, as compared with tramways, the latter having to be regulated according to the inclination of the streets; and he did not think it would be safe to construct tramways of steel where the gradients were as steep as 1 in 20. On that ground he had adopted the old iron rail. He did not agree with the Author that the fastenings of timber should be more numerous. If the fastenings by dogs were numerous, there would be a tendency to split the timber, and the wear would not be so permanent.

Mr. LIVESEY described a road that had been largely used in South America, composed entirely of iron and steel. Seven years ago he designed for Buenos Ayres a tramway in which the rail was of steel, and the channel dovetailed, so that the fastening would not project and interfere with the stones. More than 100 miles had been sent to South America, and laid down in the interval. In Buenos Ayres the timber roads were being taken up and relaid with iron

roads, which were much more durable, and in the end more economical. He greatly preferred steel rails to iron rails whenever the capital could be afforded, as the former did not wear so soon; indeed some of the iron rails had already been renewed. He believed that an iron permanent way would ultimately supersede the use of timber, and that an iron road with a steel rail would last thirty or forty years, if not longer.

Mr. J. H. LYNDE remarked that the traffic on tramways was different from that upon railways, and that the pavement abutting upon the rail was subjected to much extra wear and tear by the ordinary traffic. Thus it was important that this part of the pavement should be provided with such a foundation as would prevent the subsidence of the setts, which had proved to be the great objection to the introduction of tramways. As the pavement was practically rigid, so the materials used in constructing a tramway should be rigid; moreover the materials should not be liable to decay. The tramway adopted in Manchester fulfilled these conditions. The foundation was a continuous series of cast-iron bearers provided with side flanges for the support of the adjacent setts, and a deep groove on the upper surface for the reception of the tongue of the steel rail, which was keyed down by means of wedge cotters passing through the cast-iron bearer and the tongue of the rail. No difficulty had been experienced in laying the tramway, and as much as 220 lineal yards complete had been executed in one day by a gang of sixteen men. The cost of this system, which was known as "Barker's Patent," varied from about £2,000 to £2,300 per mile, according to the weight of metal and depth of pavement used. The Manchester line consisted of 212 tons of cast-iron bearers and 63 tons of steel rails to the mile of single line. One great advantage of this tramway was, that the rails could be renewed with but little interference with the cast-iron bearers, or the pavement, and, also, that the delay and difficulty of using concrete were avoided, except in rare instances of soft foundation.

Mr. LAWFORD agreed with the views of the Author, with one or two exceptions. He had stated that asphalt and wood paving had always proved failures. On the south side of London there was a tramway the first 400 yards of which were paved with asphalt. There were stone setts on each side of the rails, and also at 18 inches outside the rail where it joined the macadam; and it was as good a piece of tramway as could be seen. The mischief arose where the asphalt joined the macadam, and there there was a series of ruts. The same remark applied to

wooden pavement. About 200 yards of similar tramway, near Clapham Rise, were paved entirely with wood, for the purpose of deadening the sound in front of the Home for Incurables. Whatever the pavement was, it should, he thought, be carried across the road; and in that case as good a job might be made with wood or asphalt as with stone. The only other matter on which he disagreed with the Author was with regard to cost. He should like to see a street tramway made for £1,500 a mile. He had made the Duke of Buckingham's tramway, which was not, strictly speaking, a street tramway, but it crossed wide public and turnpike roads. It was 8 miles in length, and had been in existence nearly seven years. The rails, weighing 30 lbs. to the yard, were laid on longitudinal sleepers, and the gauge was 4 feet 8½ inches. For the first twelve months it was worked entirely with horses, and since then it had been worked by steam, which had proved more economical. Two of Aveling and Porter's traction engines had been built for the purpose, fitted with flanged wheels, and they had acted extremely well. The speed was from 4 to 8 miles an hour, the average being about 6 miles. Within the last six months a small four-wheeled coupled locomotive, rather lighter than a traction engine, had been introduced. The manager of the line had informed him that the cost of haulage by horses was £1 12s. 11d., as against £1 by steam; adding, "in my desire to be impartial, I think I have rather underestimated the cost of horse haulage." The maintenance of the line, exclusive of renewals, was £63 7s. 6d. per mile per annum. The steepest gradient was 1 in 45 for about ¼ mile; the others were easy, practicable gradients. It was a single line with sidings, and was made at a cost slightly under £1,400 per mile, when rails were rising considerably in price. No mention had been made of the internal dimensions of the cars. On the south side of London the directors tried to pack eleven people inside. He thought there should be a division into two classes, as on the continental tramways. A premium had been offered by the General Omnibus Company for the best method of checking the fares. He did not know whether a mechanical mode of checking the takings of the conductors was possible; but a move had been made in that direction on the south side of London; one uniform fare was charged for any distance, and as each ticket was punched, a little piece of paper fell into a box (not under the conductor's control) with the operation.

Mr. RAPIER said, several years ago Mr. Deas, M. Inst. C.E., consulted him as to the best way of obtaining some easement to the traffic along the Broomielaw, Glasgow. At the time he referred

Mr. Deas to the tramways for ordinary street traffic at Ipswich, and in the Devonshire Street goods yard, which had been worked for twenty years without repairs, not, however, subject to such incessant traffic as that of Glasgow. The result was the construction of the tramways on the principle shown by Figs. 2 and 3, in which

Fig. 2.

Cast-iron Tramway for dock purposes for flanged vehicles, or ordinary street lorries, as laid on the Glasgow Quay.

Fig. 3.

Tramway for flanged vehicles only, as laid at the Glasgow Gasworks.

it would be seen that the bottom flange was discarded. These tramways had been in constant work for seven years, and had not cost sixpence a mile for maintenance or renewal, or repair of any kind. At first it seemed desirable to have a bottom flange at the outside of the blocks, but it was found inconvenient in fixing the paving setts. The bottom flange was then put on the inside; that did very well, but, economy being the order of the day, it was cut away altogether with the most satisfactory results. The blocks, which were adapted both for flanged and unflanged vehicles, were cast with recesses at the ends to receive fish-plates, which were bolted in the ordinary manner. The blocks were entirely filled with concrete composed of 1 part of Portland cement and 7 parts of gravel and sand well punned in, and allowed to lie three or four days to set. The road was made like an ordinary first-class street or dock road, with the bottom in dry rubble, and a base of concrete was prepared for the tramway blocks, 1 foot 10 inches wide and 6 inches thick. The tramway blocks were then turned over and were fixed with Portland cement to the concrete bed. In a few instances, where the blocks had to be raised for laying water or

---

gas pipes, it was found that they had stuck to the concrete beneath, and had to be actually cut away.

The cost of these two sections was—

	Fig. 2.			Fig. 3.		
	Cwt.	qrs.	lbs.	Cwt.	qrs.	lbs.
Weight of cast-iron blocks, per lineal yard	3	2	14	2	3	0
	£	s.	d.	£	s.	d.
Cost of cast-iron blocks, per lineal yard	1	5	4	0	19	0
Cost of concrete for filling and foundations, per lineal yard	0	4	8	0	3	3
Cost of laying blocks, per lineal yard	0	2	6	0	2	3
Total cost per lineal yard	1	12	6	1	4	6

Such a road was, of course, contrary to all preconceived notions. Though elasticity had been constantly advocated, this road was thoroughly rigid. The blocks, once laid, remained there. At first tie-bars were used, but it was found that they were not necessary, because the blocks could not be got to stir even when it was required to move them. The first part of the tramway had been laid seven years. Shortly afterwards the price of iron rose so rapidly that he ceased to think about the matter; but when the subject was about to be brought before the Institution he wrote to Mr. Deas, and received the following particulars:—From one hundred to one hundred and forty railway trucks went over the busiest part of the tramway daily, which was equal to a vehicle twice the weight of a tramcar passing every five minutes. He had inquired whether any regular railway locomotives had passed over the line. The reply was that none had done so; but that contractors' locomotives constantly passed, often dragging heavy loads upon bogies to the 60-ton crane. The highest speed of the railway vehicles was about 5 miles an hour, and of the street lorries 6 miles an hour. The tramway was chiefly designed for street or dock lorry traffic, which in Glasgow was very heavy; and it was a noteworthy circumstance that, if horses had to turn off the tramway, they always went back again of their own accord. The tramway was made of cast iron; he had therefore asked Mr. Deas how many blocks had been broken, and the reply was, "Not one." The blocks were ordinarily cast in 5-feet lengths. It was originally expected that in order to get them to lie steady 10-feet lengths would be required; but it had been found unnecessary to increase the lengths, because the blocks never showed any signs of motion. About six years ago 3 or 3½ furlongs of the same kind of tramway, for flanged vehicles only, had been laid in the Glasgow Corporation gas yard, and the manager reported that it had worked very well

---

and occasioned no trouble. The edges had little notches ½ inch wide cast in them, at intervals of 3 or 4 inches, for the use of vehicles crossing the road; and he feared that there might be fractures from that cause, but none had occurred. The only thing beginning to need repair was the granite horseway between. In addition to the tramway along the street, two double lines were laid across the thoroughfare, to obtain access to a railway yard, and the whole of the ordinary traffic along the river-side passed over them, but no complaints had been made of horses falling down. The cost of the tramway had been £3,500 per mile, or £1,000 more than ordinary tramways, if made so as to accommodate unflanged, as well as flanged, wheels. For flanged wheels only, the cost was about £100 per mile more than that of other types of tramway. The latter, however, were now costing £250 a year per mile for repairs, although they were only beginning to get rickety, and no one could say what their condition would be in three or four years. He might add that the traffic on the Broomielaw tramway was incessant.

Mr. C. H. BELOE thought the subject of street tramways had not received the attention which it deserved from the profession. Their construction had been in the hands of comparatively few engineers in England, but the time was coming when works of that kind would be greatly extended. The hurried manner in which street tramways were generally constructed was a matter deserving serious consideration; and it was a wonder the roads stood as well as they did. An effort should be made to obtain from the Board of Trade some relaxation of the rule limiting the amount of roadway to be opened at one time to 100 yards. Local authorities were very severe in enforcing those restrictions upon tramway companies. Companies were often blind to their own interest in urging engineers to push forward their works so rapidly. To assist in rapid work the Author recommended the use of bituminous concrete. He had tried it, but it had not answered his expectations. The Glasgow tramways were laid almost exclusively upon bituminous concrete, and the paving had sunk there to a greater extent than he had observed anywhere else—certainly more than it did upon cement concrete, if time were given for it to set. If any material could be found which would set more quickly than cement concrete, a great advance would be made in the construction of tramways. He agreed with the Author in his approval of cross sleepers. He had recently laid a road with tie-rods. It was a macadamised road with hard rock pitching underneath; cross sleepers would have involved excavating the hard rock

---

pitching, and then the foundation of the road would have been seriously weakened. Under those circumstances he was induced to use tie-rods; but though the expense was considerably reduced, he regretted that he had not taken out the old pitching, and laid a substantial bed of concrete. The box rail was certainly a good one; but having regard to the probability of increased weight on tramways in the future, and to the introduction of steam locomotives, he was inclined to think that the T-shaped rail was the best. He did not object to the use of the rail with the central groove, because he thought it the best form for tramway purposes. The waste of the guard rail, carrying no traffic, was saved, and the whole surface of the rail for the tread of the wheel was utilised. Nor did he think that the flange was weakened, or that the car was more liable to leave the rail. In his opinion a simple form of construction would be two ordinary flat bars set on edge, and secured to cast iron chairs, resting on cross sleepers. If necessary the chairs could be cast to receive wooden cushions under the rail to deaden vibration; but he believed that by the use of the central groove the width of the rail could be diminished and many other advantages be obtained. He should watch the use of it in Liverpool with great interest. He agreed in the recommendation of tar grouting, which was extensively used in the North of England. The principal objection to it was the impossibility of applying it in wet weather. Borough engineers could stop up a whole street and cover it with a roof under which to carry on grouting operations; but the ordinary tramway engineer was not so fortunate; and hence tar grouting, though most effectual, was useless unless a continuance of fine weather could be insured; because the grouting must proceed as rapidly as the rest of the work, and a few days' rain would spoil the whole operation. He did not agree in the disapproval of cast-iron crossings and preference for cut rails. Cast-iron crossings were not as durable as could be desired, but no doubt in a short time steel points and crossings would be cast, though hitherto he had failed to obtain them. It was difficult to make a neat crossing by cutting iron rails, but it was much more difficult to do so with steel rails. He believed that iron tramways would supersede wooden ones. He had watched the process of laying the tramway in Manchester, and noticed that the workmen had no difficulty in pinning down the rail to the cast-iron sleeper. With regard to the cost of tramways, he thought that a single line, including paving, but without any contingent expenses for engineering or company's affairs, might be set down at from £4,000 to £4,500 a mile. It was difficult to estimate the cost of repairs, although it seemed that there had been a great increase in the cost of renewals and of repairs of late years. He hoped that the new tramways now being laid would show a better result in that respect than their predecessors.

Mr. W. MARTINEAU said his connection with a large tramway car building firm had given him opportunities for becoming acquainted with what had been done in the construction of tramways in England and abroad. In England and Scotland the ordinary 4-feet 8½-inch gauge had been almost universally used. In Ireland the Irish railway gauge of 5 feet 3 inches had been followed, but he thought it was a little too wide for the convenient working of tramways. In a few other countries a narrower gauge had been adopted. Thus the Madras tramway was on the métre gauge, and the same gauge had been laid in Rome. In the Isle of Man and in one case in Ireland the gauge was 3 feet. He thought there was no objection to the narrower gauges; but whatever the gauge might be, it was of the utmost importance that it should be maintained throughout the whole length of the tramway. Nothing contributed more to the destruction of tramway wheels than a line being a little out of gauge; and wherever wheels were found to wear unduly, the engineer might be almost certain that some part of the line had not been truly laid. He thought that cross sleepers were advisable, and indeed necessary for the preservation of the width throughout.

The weights of the cars and wagons employed on different systems were shown in the following table :—

WEIGHTS of CARS and WAGONS CONSTRUCTED by the STARBUCK CAR and WAGON COMPANY, LIMITED.

Carriages—

						Cwt.	qrs.	lbs.
London car to seat 22 in and 24 out			weight	49	3	0
Hoylake	„	22	„	24	„	46	3	7
Birkenhead	„	22	„	24	„	47	1	14
Oporto	„	20	„	20	„	40	2	0
Middlesbro'	„	16	„	16	„	34	0	0
Naples open car, with 5 transverse seats to seat 20			„	21	1	20
„ car to seat 12 inside only (with partition)			„	26	3	14
„	„	16	„		„	34	0	0
Brussels	„	16	„		„	34	0	0
Middlesbro'	„	14	„		„	24	1	0
Sheffield	„	16	„		„	29	0	0
Leeds	„	18	„		„	34	0	0

Tramway goods trucks—

					Cwt.	qrs.	lbs.
Pernambuco wagon				weight	29	2	11
Oporto open goods				„	27	1	0
„ covered goods				„	32	1	0

N.B.—The weights given above include wheels and axles.

It would be seen that the weights varied from 2½ tons for a full-sized car carrying forty-six passengers, to as low as 24 cwt. for a light one-horse car carrying fourteen inside. Some heavier cars weighing over 3 tons (not mentioned in the table) had been made for Russia. They had wrought-iron under-framings, iron panels, and elliptic springs. The Author had stated that india-rubber springs might be got to endure every climate, but it had been found that they would not bear the extreme and lasting cold of a Russian winter, for which steel springs were indispensable. The Russian engineers also preferred screw brakes. These things, of course, rendered the car much heavier. Fortunately, St. Petersburg, where tramways were largely developed, was level, otherwise great difficulty would be experienced in dragging the cars. Light one-horse cars had been introduced in England, principally at Sheffield, Leeds, and Leicester; and abroad, in Naples, Oporto, Antwerp, and Brussels; and he thought they would be brought into extensive use. An eminent French engineer, in reporting to the Municipality of Paris about a year ago, stated that the essence of a tramway was to keep up a continuous flow of traffic, so that, as far as possible, a car should always be in sight; and that could often be much more economically attained by a light one-horse car than by heavier cars with two horses. With regard to the duration of cars, the Author stated that cars had run in the United States for twenty years. It should be known that those cars had no top seats, for there could be no doubt that the heavy weight of a top seat, with a number of people on it, did, in starting and stopping, strain the framework of a car, and that therefore cars without such seats lasted the longest. American wheels combined extraordinary hardness in the tire with great toughness in the body of the wheel. There were not many wheel-making firms in America, and the procedure of each firm was to a certain extent secret. A quality of iron was secured which admitted of crystallisation and chill entering a remarkable distance into the fibre of the iron, and a careful system of annealing was adopted after the wheels were cast. The question of the construction of tramways had long since been discussed. He had a plan for tramways for the whole of London, dated January 1851; also a sheet of tramway sections dated 1854, in which most of the points as to the structure of the permanent way of tramways were laid down. He had attended several trials of steam tram-cars, and it appeared to him that on a level line little difficulty was experienced. The limit of incline, which the Author had put at 1 in 30 for tramway rails laid in England, was probably reached much earlier than that. An

engine was required which would start without hesitation on the gradient, whatever it might be, in all states of the weather; and in order to secure that result, in any particular case, the amount of adhesion was an absolutely known item in the calculation. If the amount of adhesion implied a weight on the wheels greater than the rails would properly and economically carry, the limit was reached, and either heavier rails must be laid or the use of steam be abandoned. The use of steam in each case must be determined by the strength of the line to carry the weight of an engine necessary to work on the steepest incline.

Mr. E. A. COWPER was surprised that an opinion should have been expressed in favour of iron rails over steel rails for tramways. Not only were steel rails stiffer and stronger, but they were harder. A great deal of grinding or wearing of the rails was caused by the grit and sand on the road; and a soft rail would necessarily suffer from that action more than a hard one. Any one who had observed the grinding action of emery would have noticed that it made a much deeper cut into soft iron than into steel. Steel, therefore, was undoubtedly the right thing for tramway rails.

Mr. E. PERRETT observed that the Author had not mentioned what he considered to be the immediate cause of the rapid loosening of the spiked rail from the sleeper. It was impossible to suppose that the mere passage of a 5-ton car over a 30 or 40-lb. rail spiked down could loosen it. The cause was rather to be sought in the extremely unmechanical construction of the car. An ordinary London street car weighed when loaded about 5½ tons, was 22 feet in length, and was balanced on a 5½-feet or 6-feet wheel base in order to get round a sharp curve. Oscillation was soon set up, which this wheel base was unable to control; and that had been the chief cause of the withdrawing of the spikes, and the abandonment of a rail which was otherwise cheap and good. He did not think that any rail would long remain secure without a more extended wheel base to the cars running over it. He was aware that cars with six wheels had been tried, but the additional weight was too much for the already overtaxed horses. When steam was introduced, together with suitable rolling stock, that difficulty would be overcome. In the cars with six wheels the wheel base was made flexible, the central pair of wheels having power to travel sideways across the car. He disagreed entirely with the conclusion of the Author that detached engines and cars were superior in nearly every respect to combined engines and cars. Leaving out of consideration such qualifications as absence of smoke, steam, or noise, which both kinds of machines might or

might not have, the great requisite for a tram passenger car for use in and about towns was handiness. In this was included, power, to run either end first without turning or bringing the engine round, to ascend a steep gradient, to stop quickly in going down, to take sharp curves, and also, what had apparently been lost sight of, power to steer. The detached engine failed in all these important particulars, the combined engine need not fail in any one of them. In the case of some combined cars the driver had only to walk from one end to the other on the return journey. With reference to ascending a steep gradient, it might be all very well to increase the weight of an engine from 3 tons to 5 tons to give the necessary adhesion, but that was not the proper way of overcoming the difficulty. A heavier engine than was otherwise necessary to do the work was a faulty machine. A detached engine of 3 tons was not sufficient to draw a car of 5 tons up a moderate gradient. To drag cars on ordinary lines 20 or 30 lbs. was necessary, and on curves the traction amounted to 50 or 60 lbs. to the ton, so that the limit of gradient was soon reached by a detached engine and car, and to connect the moving parts of the engine to the car wheels to gain adhesion was making a combined car of the worst kind. The disadvantage alluded to by the Author, of an engine drawing a 22-feet car with 8 feet overhang round a curve, was obvious. Suitable cars could be made to be pulled by an engine, but that did away with the argument for the use of detached engines, namely, the possibility of using up existing stock. As regarded steering power this was of no moment with horse cars as the horses gave the necessary list to the cars, but a locomotive must have points and attendants at the branches, whereas with the number of wheels necessary for a combined car, steering could be easily effected. The alleged advantages of a detached over a combined engine were: the power of using up old stock, the power to take two cars on an emergency, greater safety to passengers, and cheapness or facility of repairs. The first was no advantage in new tramways; and in the case of old tramways, especially where outside passengers were carried, he had been informed that the existing cars broke up so rapidly, owing to their unmechanical construction, that no company would care, even if it could afford, to replace the existing stock by steam stock any faster than the existing stock broke up. Independently of that, the existing stock was not fit for steam traction, being far too light. The power of drawing two cars was not peculiar to a detached engine; a combined engine and car was still more capable of taking an additional car. A detached engine was considered by some safer for passengers, but he did not remember any instance in which a locomotive boiler had exploded whilst running. The Author stated that when a combined engine was under repairs £800 would lie idle. That might be so for slight repairs, but it amounted only to this: the cost of a detached engine was about £600 and of an ordinary car about £200; the cost of an engine and car combined was £700; so that there was a saving on the original cost; and in the case of repairs to the engine the difference in the value laid up was only that between £600 and £700, or £100. But if a combined engine and car were properly made, for extensive repairs the engine could be easily detached and another substituted, in which case the amount lying idle would only be £200 or even less. He had constructed a car for experimental purposes, with a fixed wheel base of 4 feet, to which the power was attached, set on a frame that could be easily removed from the main frames of the car. A two-wheeled Bissel bogie at either end gave a 17-feet wheel base. It was capable, nevertheless, of running round a curve of 35-feet radius, and by a steering arrangement at each end, it could be taken on to the road or off the road, or on the branches, without the slightest difficulty; and was free from oscillation. There was a small boiler at each end, connected together, the object being to distribute the weight, and also that the driver might stoke the boiler behind him, whichever way he was going, the two boilers being connected, he knew what was going on in both. The weight of the car when loaded was 8 tons, of which 5 tons were on the driving wheels and available for adhesion. He believed the car fulfilled all the conditions required in a passenger car. Where a tramway was like a light railway, the vices of a detached engine were less apparent, and it might be made suitable for the work, but for ordinary passenger traffic he thought a combined car possessed every advantage.

Mr. C. B. KING considered that the car just described would not satisfy the requirements of the public. In Paris, one line of tramways, 5 miles long, was worked entirely by an ordinary locomotive engine, with a special arrangement to prevent the emission of steam and smoke, and it did its work well. He was informed that the cost of steam, as compared with horse traction, was at present 5½d. to 7½d., but this was subject to variations as coal and fodder altered in price. The advantage of a combined car in obtaining adhesion had been mentioned. He, however, preferred a light detached engine. In order to increase the power of adhesion of such an engine many arrangements had been tried, the most effective of which was Holt's system adopted by

Messrs. Merryweather. The engine was coupled to the car by an endless chain, passing round a chain pulley on an axle of the engine, and likewise round another chain pulley on one or both axles of the car. These pulleys were disengaged on the axles by self-acting gear when the extra adhesion was not required; in some cases this chain was driven by an independent auxiliary cylinder, which only worked when going up inclines. This cylinder had a much higher piston speed than the locomotive cylinders, so that a 5-ton engine could work an ordinary car up inclines of 1 in 12 and 1 in 14 in all weathers with ease. He had seen an engine of 3½ tons weight, on one of the North Metropolitan tramways, ascend an incline of 1 in 27, and go round a curve of 35 feet radius, with a car and fifty passengers. He was afraid that Mr. Perrett's car would not pass the regulations of the Board of Trade, one of which was that passengers were not to pass and repass the motive power. He had been informed that on the Paris line the public were at first much terrified at the prospect of an engine going along the road at a speed of 15 miles an hour; but after an experience of six or eight months the idea of returning to the old modes of conveyance had been abandoned. It was found that ordinary vehicles never got on the line, always carefully avoiding it.

Mr. E. PERRETT explained that the Board of Trade officials had seen the drawings of the car he had described, and offered no objection to the arrangement.

Mr. WALTER HANCOCK remarked that his uncle (whose pupil he had been) had worked at the subject of steam carriages continuously from 1824 to 1836, and had made eight or nine carriages designed to compete with carriages on common roads. He was obliged to allow for the enormous tractive force required, and for the vicissitudes of the roadway, so that the power of his engines was greatly in excess of that required on tramways. The engines were of three classes. One was a small engine, with 3¾-inch cylinders, making 150 strokes per minute, for a carriage conveying four persons; another was a 9-inch cylinder engine, with 100 lbs. pressure of steam per square inch, making 100 strokes per minute, for a carriage conveying ten or twelve persons; and another was a 12-inch cylinder engine, with a length of stroke also of 12 inches, for a carriage to take twenty-four to thirty passengers. This was prior to the great improvements in steam engines, so that the consumption of fuel would now be considered enormous. In twenty weeks' continuous working of the "Automaton," the largest engine, when making

100 revolutions per minute, to go 10 to 12 miles an hour, over a distance of 4,200 miles, 700 journeys, and carrying 12,700 passengers, 55 chaldrons of ordinary gas coke were used, equal to 20 lbs. per mile. The total cost was 2¼d. per mile for carrying only half the number that an ordinary tram carriage would carry at a cost of 1d. per mile. The engines were made, as all old engines were, with defective valves, it being long before the improvements by Dewrance and others in 1837 and 1838, by which the consumption of steam had been much diminished. Not only was it necessary to carry more coke and more water, but the strength and weight of the carriage were increased, its weight when loaded being from 4½ to 5 tons. In consequence of these experiments a parliamentary committee was appointed, and in their report in 1831 the belief was expressed "that the substitution of inanimate for animate power, in draught on common roads, is one of the most important improvements in the means of internal communication ever introduced. Its practicability they consider to have been fully established; its general adoption will take place more or less rapidly, in proportion as the attention of scientific men shall be drawn by public encouragement to further improvements."[1] Here were none of the timid fears and cautions to be found in the reports of the more recent committees.

Mr. E. CHADWICK, C.B., thought that sanitary science might put in an appearance in connection with the subject of tramways. It had long since been apparent that every means of cheapening transit, and facilitating the distribution of the population, tended to diminish overcrowding in urban districts. If things had remained as they were, there might now have been in the metropolis and other urban districts a double and even a threefold population heaped up on the old areas; and however good the sanitation might have been, there would certainly have been increased death rates. His colleagues on the Metropolitan Sanitary Commission had before them the evil of overcrowding. Stone trams were suggested, of which various examples existed, reducing the horse traction more than one-half; but there were obstacles in the way, chiefly administrative, arising from the fact that all the radii out of London were split up into different parochial jurisdictions, there being one for almost every mile of road. This division had added largely to the expenses of all the tramways, and one director had informed him that the dividends of his line had been almost

[1] Vide "Report from Select Committee on Steam Carriages; with the Minutes of Evidence and Appendix." Folio: London, 1831.

taken away by the exactions of the separate jurisdictions. He would suggest that accounts of the expenses of different lines should not only contain the engineering costs per mile, but the cost per vestry. It would be seen by the evidence given before the recent Tramway Committee, that in that respect there was an enormous difference in favour of Paris, in consequence of the unity of management and scientific administration existing in that capital in having only one authority to work through, and that a scientific authority acting with knowledge, instead of obstructive from ignorance and prejudice. He still thought that the granite tram, as adopted in Italy, possessed a prodigious advantage; but a well-laid asphalt might take its place, being only half the expense, and double the wear. The asphalt tram had the advantage over the granite tram, and indeed over the iron tramway, in the absence of joints, and when properly laid there were no jolts. Being, as it were, in one piece from end to end, there was little or no resistance, so that it was more favourable to the use of lighter locomotive machinery and carriages, than granite or iron. The tenacity of the Neuchatel asphalt, as displayed in Cheapside, with its traffic of sixteen thousand vehicles daily, was marvellous. It had been laid down about seven years, and had apparently lost little weight, and was only compressed by about one-third, and might have a wear as long as that in Paris, which was seventeen years. The wear of the ordinary granite trams at the East of London, with much less traffic, was stated to be about 1 inch a year. Much of the first asphalt roadway was defective in being wavy and undulating from being badly laid. He had been led to believe that the saving of tractive force on asphalt roads was about the same as that on granite tramways, or about one-half, as against common macadam roads, but he had later assurances that the saving on well-laid asphalt was fully two-thirds of the tractive force required on the common roads, enabling a proportionate saving of engine power on them. The obstacles that stood in the way of the application of the principle of the tramway were chiefly the divided jurisdiction of the roads and the want of science, some additional outlay, and no interest, created by a monopoly, such as was given by the iron tramway; the asphalt tramway being like the granite tramway in Northern Italy and this country, open to all private vehicles, which was, in reality, its recommendation. He had been at pains to ascertain the comparative wear of the road by the wheel and the horse, and he thought he could state it as a constant, that whilst the wear by the horse foot was as one, the wear by the wheel was as two.

[1876-77. N.S.]   E

Hence the tram he proposed would take away two-thirds of the common road wear. But it would have great importance in saving the wear of common carriages, as well as of locomotive machinery of all sorts. Locomotive machines were at present excessively heavy, as were carriages, to withstand the roughness of the roads. He did not mean to say that for roads of slight traffic, and for bye-ways, wheel tracks of cheaper construction than those he proposed might not be had. But a great object, as he conceived, for the attainment of economical transit was to get hardened wheel tracks open to all traffic.

Mr. HOPKINS believed the time was not far distant when some mechanical power would be introduced on tramways. At present the only motive power at all complying with the requirements of the Board of Trade was steam and compressed air. Steam engines, made by Messrs. Merryweather, were running in Paris at the present moment; steam engines were also running in Brussels. Mr. Hughes had also succeeded in producing an engine which had given great satisfaction; and he had likewise seen an engine by Mr. Perrett which had considerable merit, but it had not been brought before the committee of the House of Commons. Mr. Scott Moncrieff's engine, worked by compressed air, had been running successfully at Glasgow; and M. Mékarski's compressed-air engine in Paris had worked admirably. They worked generally with a pressure of 4 atmospheres, and could run easily at 20 miles an hour, stopping within a short distance. In ascending gradients the action was perfect; the engine was stopped purposely, in the middle of an incline, about 1 in 20, and then ran down and ascended it again. The authorities were labouring under great disadvantages with regard to charging the cylinders, because they had only temporary engines for compressing the air.

Mr. SOUTTAR, in reply upon the discussion, said, with regard to the complaint that his Paper contained no estimates, in the first place he had felt that estimates were to some extent misleading, and in the second place he had written a chapter on the subject, but had eliminated it as the Paper was getting so long. He regretted, however, he had not mentioned that a tramway would cost practically the same whatever system was adopted, and that it was a question of condition and not of system. In every well-constructed tramway there were three constant quantities, the concrete, the paving, and the rails, making more than three-fourths of the total expenditure, the remaining fraction being represented by the longitudinal bearing, fastener, &c. Comparing

tramways with timber bearings together, the cost would be practically the same, or a little more where cross sleepers were used instead of tie-rods, and comparing these with tramways having iron bearings the latter would naturally be more costly. In Mr. Kincaid's system, with chairs 3 feet apart, the cost was, at the present price of iron, about the same as that of timber. The longitudinal bearing for the Manchester tramway was in the proportion to a timber bearing of 256 lbs. of cast iron to 6 lineal feet, by 6 inches by 4, of timber, with an allowance for cross sleepers and fastenings, the ratio being practically as 3 to 1. Mr. Lynde had stated that "the cost of this system varied from about £2,000 to £2,300 per mile, according to the weight of metal and depth of paving used." The remark illustrated what the Author had said about the misleading nature of estimates. For, taking the amount of metal required for the work, at market prices it would be found that the margin could only cover the labour of excavating, laying the line, and reinstating old paving. The estimate neither included concrete under the tramway nor paving, and the rail was only 40 lbs. to the yard, instead of from 50 lbs. to 60 lbs., as usually adopted. Mr. Beloe had fairly set down the price of a properly constructed tramway at £4,500 per mile, and with this price Mr. Lynde's system would appear to contrast most favourably; the fact being, however, that Mr. Beloe gave the price of a complete tramway, whilst Mr. Lynde gave the price of half a tramway. It could not be too clearly understood that the cost of a tramway was only slightly affected by the particular system under which it was laid, but materially by the weight of rail and quality of paving and concrete that the circumstances rendered advisable. Mr. Fowler's preference for a rail supported on a series of hard points, instead of on a continuous bearing, seemed incomprehensible, as well as his preference for iron over steel. Mr. Cowper's remark, that the grinding of the rails caused by grit or sand was better resisted by steel than by soft iron, was justified by experience. Mr. Fowler was under a misconception with regard to the rail which the Author had introduced. There was no space between the fastenings, the timber was the extreme width of the rail, and a little piece was gouged out into which the fastener sank. The sinking of the pavement on the Glasgow tramways, noticed by Mr. Beloe, was probably due to the fact that an unnecessary quantity of sand, 2 inches, was laid under the paving, and not to any failure on the part of the bituminous concrete. The tramway described by Mr. Rapier would be useful as a means of reducing the friction of heavy vehicles,

travelling at a slow pace, just as rows of flat stones were useful for that purpose. There were, however, points in the system which would render it unsuitable under ordinary circumstances, where a quick, rattling motion had to be endured; and there was nothing in its design calculated to diminish the cost of repairs, as compared with other tramways. Mr. Lawford disagreed with the conclusions on the subject of asphalt, and quoted an instance of asphalting in London. The piece referred to was done under the Author's superintendence, and he would therefore gladly defend it; but the fact mentioned, that it had been found necessary to put stone on each side of the rails, spoke for itself. Mr. Lawford said he should like to see a street tramway laid at £1,500 per mile, and then gave details of a tramway he had laid for less than £1,400 per mile. Of course a tramway could only be laid at the price mentioned under exceptionally favourable circumstances, and in the lightest possible manner. Mr. Perrett would find that "the immediate cause of the rapid loosening of the spiked rail from the sleeper" was the breaking of the spikes at the neck. Perhaps the construction of the car had something to do with this; but the Author thought it would generally happen when the rail became so worn that the wheel flange could touch the bottom of the groove. Mr. Perrett had contrasted some of the arguments in favour of a combined engine with some of the arguments in favour of a detached. For the former he claimed adhesion, handiness, and steering capacity. There could be no doubt that the combined engine was superior in the matter of adhesion. On the second point, the detached engine would be made handier to work than the combined engine in everything except shunting. On the question of steering there was little to say. Steering gear would complicate the car, and would be useless at night. It was questionable if the power of steering would be of any practical value. In dealing with repairs, Mr. Perrett had misunderstood the Author. In saying that a slight accident would cause £800 to lie idle, an accident to the car was meant, not to the engine. Whilst the Author felt that the question might be still more fully tested with advantage, he thought that every day showed more clearly that the detached engine was the tramway engine of the future. On the question of pneumatic cars, whilst recognising the difficulties in the way, the Author was scarcely so hopeless as some of the speakers. He was sorry that Mr. Scott Moncrieff had found it impossible to be present at the discussion, especially as he believed an arrangement had been concluded which would enable the method to be fairly tested in the course of the next year.

Mr. STEPHENSON, President, had hoped that more distinct information would have been elicited in regard to a better class of engine. The improvement of the rail would take place in the course of time. Some years ago he had occasion to examine the details of one of Mr. Grantham's engines, and he was strongly of opinion at the time that a separate or detached engine would be the best. He had carefully watched the progress of the engines, and although he was not prepared to give the cost of working, the more he had gone into the subject the more satisfied he was that a detached engine would ultimately come into use. He had no interest in any of the engines, and his opinion was, therefore, an unbiassed one. Mr. Longridge had objected to the detached engine on the ground that it had only its own weight to deal with for adhesion; but if he had looked at the matter more closely he would have seen that a detached engine could be made to take certainly half the weight of the carriage. It might be placed in the middle of two carriages, one-half of each carriage resting upon it, by a joint devised for the purpose. He was not prepared to admit that the old stock could be guaranteed for the proposed new tramways. He was glad that the subject of tramways had been discussed; and every one would desire that the sufferings of the horses might be relieved, even if the pockets of the shareholders were not filled to the extent they were at present.

Mr. DEACON remarked, through the Secretary, that for many years he had given attention to the subject of street tramways. Before making any recommendation with respect to the proposed reconstruction of the existing lines in Liverpool, he had visited all the more important tramways in this country and many of those on the Continent, and had studied the available literature on the subject. He had endeavoured to approach the question with a mind unbiassed by railway practice, or by the particular forms of street tramway which had in some degree grown out of that practice. His investigations had been completed with a strong conviction that no existing system of laying street tramways was entirely suited to the exigencies of the irregularly built and crowded streets of the principal cities and towns of this country. He thought inventors had not apprehended the true nature of the difficulties to be overcome before municipal authorities and the owners of ordinary vehicles could fairly be expected to approve of tramways. The inconvenience to ordinary vehicles, caused by cars having no power to move aside, was very great, and though not inevitable in a mechanical sense, it must be admitted as a necessary evil when street tramways were allowed at all, for nothing but confusion would arise if ordinary vehicles had the power to cause heavy tramway cars to leave the rails. But the evils of street tramways were due not only to the inevitable tramway car, but to the existence of the permanent way. This permanent way involved, for each line of tramway, four longitudinal joints between materials of different hardness. It was well known to be impossible, in the ordinary mode of paving, to prevent the formation of a groove wherever a longitudinal joint existed, even when the materials on both sides of the joint were the same. It was still less possible when the materials were of different natures. If, however, a course of setts were sawn in halves parallel with the street, and the setts were so bedded that the sawn joint remained close, the bearing surface of the setts was not reduced and no greater wear took place at the joints than elsewhere. Again, if near the line of such a joint the upper edges of adjacent setts touched each other at the transverse joints, there would be more bearing surface at and near the longitudinal joint than elsewhere, the intensity of pressure from traffic would be reduced, and instead of a groove forming, the wear would be actually slower than elsewhere. Having applied the same principle to the courses of setts immediately adjoining tramway rails, his expectations had been completely realised, after seventeen months' trial, under the most severe conditions.

During the reconstruction of the tramways in Liverpool the streets in which they were laid were being repaved and provided with new foundations from curb to curb. The vehicular traffic was entirely suspended, the old foundation was removed, and a bed of Portland cement concrete was laid and finished with a perfectly smooth surface, which was allowed to stand for ten days or more before the paving was commenced. Directly upon this the longitudinal sleepers rested. The rails were held down by bolts passing through the sleepers to plates beneath the concrete at every 3 feet, and these bolts could be tightened at openings in the sides of the sleepers. The setts next the rail were of durable stones, and were carefully dressed in such a manner that, unlike the other setts which were bedded upon ½ inch of sand, they rested firmly upon the concrete, while their edges touched the edges of the rails, and their sides near the rails touched, or nearly touched each other. Being laid alternately, and accurately gauged in all dimensions, they could be drawn and replaced with similar setts without disturbing the surrounding pavement. The joints of all the setts were filled with gravel from ¼ to ⅜ inch in diameter, among which a mixture of boiling pitch and creosote oil was poured.

It was generally known that in streets of moderate traffic the wear of a tramway rail, caused by the tram-cars, was insignificant in comparison with that due to the ordinary traffic. In the rail now in general use, 4 inches wide, a breadth of 1⅞ inch was covered by the tread of the wheel, 1¼ inch being occupied by the groove, while the remaining width of ⅞ inch was only useful for strength and as a guard for the flange of the wheel and the pavement of the horse track; but this extra metal gave only lateral strength, which was not required, while the whole surface, whether superfluous or not, was constantly being worn down by the ordinary traffic. It was therefore obviously important to make the rail as narrow as possible. A reduction of width would also lessen the danger to horses, and the incentive which the drivers of ordinary vehicles felt to occupy the rails, and thus wear them and the adjoining pavement unduly. If the groove were placed in the centre of the rail and the tread on both sides, not only would the pressure be better distributed, but the whole surface might be utilised, and with the same total width of tread the width of the rail might be reduced from 4 inches to less than 3⅛ inches. Where, therefore, as in the case of street tramways, a groove was desirable, it was difficult to understand why it had never been placed in the centre. Mr. Souttar had referred to the central groove which Mr. Deacon had adopted, but had not stated the reasons for its adoption, though he had expressed fears that the friction would be greater, owing to there being no escape for mud or gravel; that the tendency of cars to run off on curves would be greater; and that the centre flanges on the car wheels would be weaker and more liable to chip off than the side flanges. The mud difficulty was common to all grooved rails. In the side-grooved rail, if there was enough mud to be pressed out, part escaped on the free side, part under the tread of the wheel. In this case it had twice as far to travel before it was liberated from the rail as in that of the central groove, where it all passed beneath the two half treads; so that for the same quantity of mud the two cases were almost similar. It was usual to remove mud periodically by an instrument designed for the purpose, and in order to avoid friction due to the squeezing out of mud during the intervals there was no objection to the groove being made deeper than usual. The Author of the Paper had given no reasons for his belief that the cars would run off the line more readily because the grooves were central; and as the flanges of the wheels were not altered in depth there was no mechanical reason why they should do so. The Author thought a side flange would be stronger than a central

flange; but this was opposed to the known conditions of strength in projecting portions of castings. In cast-iron wheels the central flange with fillets on both sides would certainly be stronger than the side flange with a fillet only on one side; while any method adopted in the case of the side flange, to prevent it from becoming brittle by too deep chilling, was available in the case of the central flange.

In straight lines the central groove might with advantage be reduced in width. The flanges of tramway wheels were generally only ½ inch wide, while the groove of the rail was more than 1¼ inch. He believed that great extra friction, due to transverse motion of the car, resulted from this; but the wide groove was stated to be necessary to hold mud. This might be a good reason for deepening the groove, but it could not, he submitted, be a good reason for widening it. Some allowance must be made for defective gauging of wheels and rails, but his own observations had led him to believe that ¾ inch for the width of a groove was ample. With such a central groove a rail 2½ inches wide would have greater bearing surface than the present rails 4 inches wide.

Among the most expensive parts of a tramway to maintain were the points. Their chief cause of weakness arose from the want of sufficient area of tread when a wheel approached the point and bore upon its narrow surface only. This surface was rapidly worn down, and the wheel, on coming in contact with the tread of the rail beyond the point, had to mount on to it, and thus produced the inclined plane noticeable in all tramway points after a short period of use. The central groove and flange with the double tread obviously removed this difficulty. In Liverpool he had, unfortunately, had to consider the fact that the side-flanged wheels on the old lines must at first run upon the reconstructed portions also, and the width of the rail had therefore only been reduced from 4 inches to 3¼ inches.[1] For rails of the usual width the recessed dog-hook fastenings used by the Author had obvious advantages over the projecting dog-hook fastenings; but if used with the narrower rails, which he thought desirable, they would involve a greater reduction of the base of the rail and of the width of the sleeper than was consistent with stability. Another objection to such comparatively light

[1] Since this was written a length of about 1,000 yards of the most recently constructed tramway has been opened to traffic in Liverpool. The side-flanged wheels are now running in a perfectly satisfactory manner on the central-grooved rails, as well as upon the old side-grooved rails; but these wheels are being rapidly replaced with central-flanged wheels which, until the lines are entirely reconstructed, will also run on both kinds of rail.—G. F. D., Aug. 4, 1877.

fastenings was their greater number and consequent interference with the pavement before they could be reached.

Mr. H. Hughes observed, through the Secretary, that the locomotive designed by his firm had been tried against a compressed-air engine at Glasgow. The former engine had two cylinders, each 6 inches in diameter, with a length of stroke of 12 inches; the average pressure in the cylinders being 50 lbs. per square inch; the distance run was 31 miles; the time occupied in the run five hours and one quarter, and the speed 6 miles an hour. The compressed-air engine had two steam cylinders for pumping, each also 6 inches in diameter with a length of stroke of 14 inches. The air was compressed to 350 lbs. per square inch; the average working pressure was 50 lbs. per square inch. The distance run was 12 miles, and the speed 6 miles an hour. The steam engine was nine hours in compressing the air.

He thought the reason why some engineers were favourable to an engine placed in a car was, that they underestimated the power required. It had been found that the weight of a well-constructed locomotive engine, with all proper appliances, and to be safe for a tramway journey, without taking in fuel or water, would be 6 tons, a sufficient weight for adhesion. But if such an engine were placed in the car, the total weight on the four wheels would be 10 tons, a load too great for many tramway rails. The separate locomotive was a simpler way of distributing the weights on the rails, and of extending the wheel base without diminishing the facility of passing round curves. Moreover, in all cars containing their own engines which had yet been designed, the wheels were not coupled, thus dispensing with the merit to which their inventor laid claim.

Mr. A. O. Schenk remarked, through the Secretary, that in trying to find out the soundest mode of construction for the permanent way of street tramways, the probable substitution of mechanical for animal power, at no remote date, should be prominently kept in view. If this were effected, any defects in existing arrangements would be intensified, when the traction was obtained by the adhesion due to a concentrated load on two or more pairs of wheels. Under these conditions, the system, in which the rail was a mere bar laid flat, dependent for its stability on the permanence of the connections that united it with its continuous longitudinal support, must give way to a mode of construction better adapted to the new method of traction. In this arrangement the rails, under the action of passing loads, tended to slide upon the upper surface of the timber, but were resisted by the fastenings, these being thrown into direct shear, in the course of time, and under the frequent repetition of this action worked loose. If this was the case now, what might be expected when a thrust of considerable magnitude was exerted along the rail, dependent on the weight on the driving wheels and the state of the rails? Further, the longitudinals had little lateral stiffness; and when it was borne in mind that heavy vehicles came on and went off at all angles, it would be seen that the paving adjoining the rails stood a poor chance of maintaining its position, being constantly under the action of severe shocks. The breadth, too, of the longitudinal being limited to 4 inches or thereabouts, the load was distributed over a small area. This also tended to shorten the life of the road. The system known as "Barker's," in which the longitudinals were of iron, possessed no advantage over wood in this respect, and, being of a harder material, would be more injurious to the foundation; while it also appeared to have disadvantages peculiar to itself—such as the impossibility of getting a uniform bearing between rough surfaces of wrought and cast iron over a continuous length, and the want of surface in the cotters which secured the rail to the support. It would seem, then, that the system which would be permanent must be one in which the above-mentioned defects were avoided or overcome. Mr. Beloe suggested that a good road might be made by a rail of common bar-iron section attached to cast-iron chairs, fixed in their turn to cross sleepers. Such an arrangement had been devised by him some months ago. To this plan the following advantages were attached:—(1) A rail was used which had vertical stability enough to carry the load without continuous sleepers. (2) The load was distributed through a broad-based chair over an area which was limited by considerations of expense. (3) A rail could be taken out and replaced without interfering with a single paving sett. (4) No iron fastenings were employed, and the evils of corrosion and enlargement of holes were avoided. (5) Less smooth iron was exposed on the surface of the street than in any other system. (6) The form of rail was adapted to the formation of points and crossings, and was well fitted for bending round curves limited in radius by the width and angles of streets. (7) It compared favourably in first cost with the best of existing systems, while in subsequent maintenance a considerable reduction might be looked for.

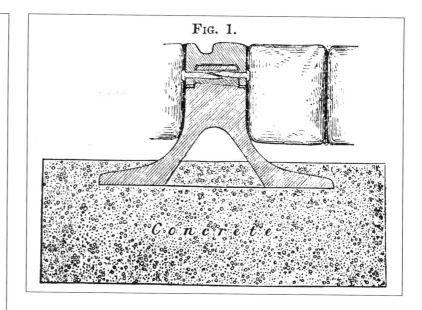

FIG. 1.

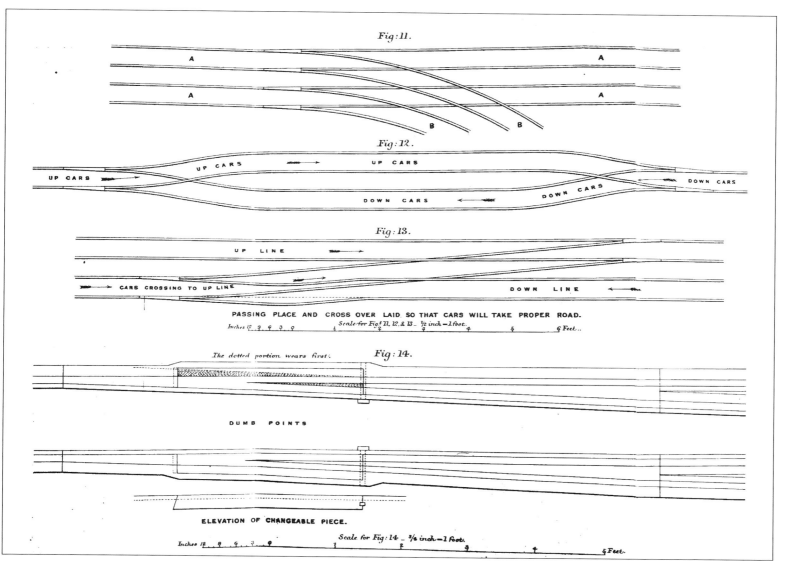

Fig: 11.

Fig: 12.

Fig: 13.

PASSING PLACE AND CROSS OVER LAID SO THAT CARS WILL TAKE PROPER ROAD.

Inches 12   9   6   3   0   Scale for Figs 11, 12, & 13 – ½ inch=1 foot.   4   5   6 Feet.

The dotted portion wears first.   Fig: 14.

DUMB POINTS

ELEVATION OF CHANGEABLE PIECE.

Inches 12   9   6   3   0   Scale for Fig 14 – ¾ inch=1 Foot.   4   5   6 Feet.

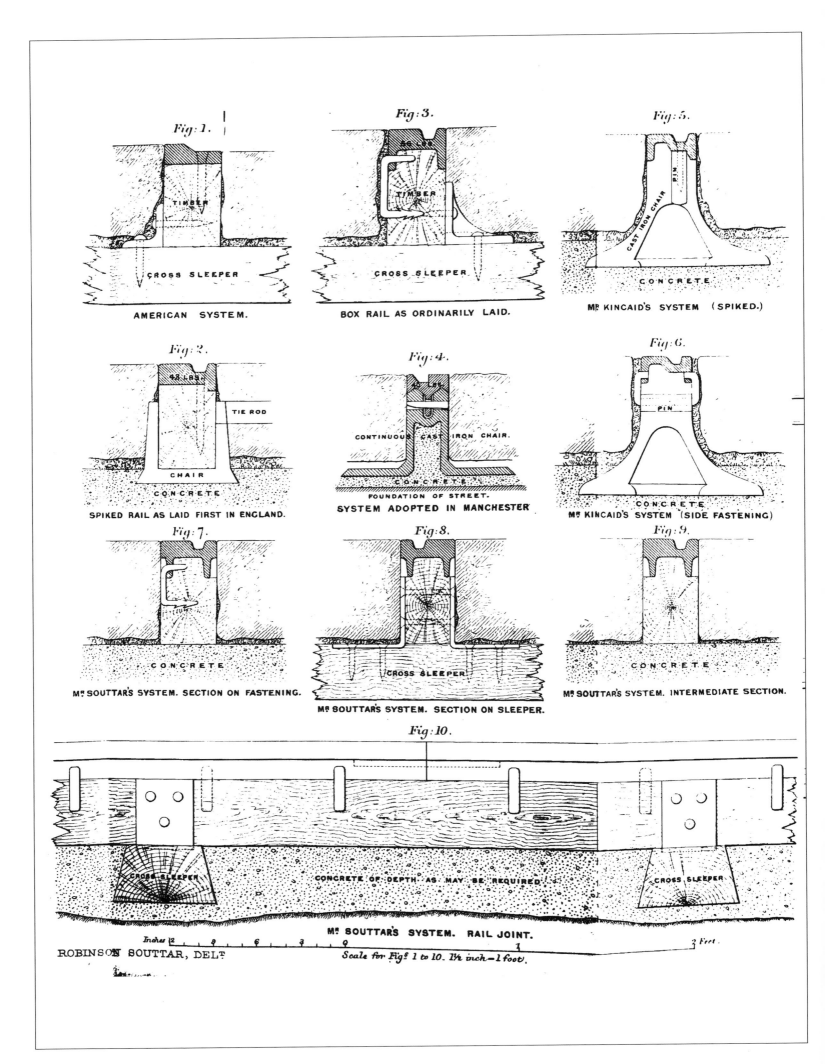

Fig: 1.

AMERICAN SYSTEM.

Fig: 3.

BOX RAIL AS ORDINARILY LAID.

Fig: 5.

M.ʳ KINCAID'S SYSTEM (SPIKED.)

Fig: 2.

SPIKED RAIL AS LAID FIRST IN ENGLAND.

Fig: 4.

SYSTEM ADOPTED IN MANCHESTER.

Fig: 6.

M.ʳ KINCAID'S SYSTEM (SIDE FASTENING)

Fig: 7.

M.ʳ SOUTTAR'S SYSTEM. SECTION ON FASTENING.

Fig: 8.

M.ʳ SOUTTAR'S SYSTEM. SECTION ON SLEEPER.

Fig: 9.

M.ʳ SOUTTAR'S SYSTEM. INTERMEDIATE SECTION.

Fig: 10.

M.ʳ SOUTTAR'S SYSTEM. RAIL JOINT.

ROBINSON SOUTTAR, DEL.ᵗ

Scale for Fig.ˢ 1 to 10. 1½ inch = 1 foot.

Permanent Way Miscellaneous Cuttings

On a Steam Tramway from the Hague to Scheveningen.

(Glaser's Annalen für Gewerbe und Bauwesen, 1879, p. 346.)

This tramway is about 3 miles long, and connects the Hague with the flourishing watering-place of Scheveningen. The Haarmann system was selected for the permanent way, on account of its great facility for laying on sharp curves, of which there are a large number on the line. The sleeper is longitudinal, and its section is that of a bridge rail, very much enlarged and opened out, and with the feet slightly bent over at the edges. The top is broad and flat, with a light feather along each edge; between these a Vignoles rail rests, and is held down by dog-headed clips hooked at the bottom. These clips are set opposite each other, and the hooks at the bottom are inserted in holes in the feet of the sleeper. A bolt passing through both clips and both sides of the sleeper tightens all up. The vertical sides of the sleeper of course enable it to be bent to a curve without difficulty, which is not the case with the gutter-shaped section of Hilf and others. On the Scheveningen line the dimensions of the rail and sleeper were adapted for a load of 5 tons on each wheel. The rails are jointed with steel fish-plates and bolts. The joints of the sleepers coincide with those of the rails: the ends of the two sleepers rest on a cross-sleeper, of the same section, but turned on its back, and having the bent edges of the feet cut away, where it passes under the longitudinals.

Memoirs Institution of Civil Engineers Vol. L X 1879

A cast-iron junction-piece fits under and is bolted to the feet of the longitudinals, and also bears on the cross-sleeper, thus conveying the load from one to the other. In addition to these cross-sleepers, a tie-bar, passing through the vertical sides of the longitudinal and tightened up with a nut at each side, is introduced in the middle of each rail length of 24 feet 7 inches. On curves this tie-bar is replaced by a second cross-sleeper. Where the tramway is laid along paved streets, a guard rail is laid along the inner side of each rail, leaving an interval of $\frac{7}{8}$ inch, and secured to it by bolts and cast-iron distance pieces. As the height from the top of the rail to the upper surface of the sleeper foot is 6 inches, the first row of paving stones rests conveniently on the sleeper foot, and there is thus no possibility of their sinking below the level of the rail.

In laying the line the rails were supplied from the works ready bolted to the sleepers, and both bent, where necessary, to suit the curves, of which the sharpest has 92 feet radius. The rails weighed 39 lbs. per yard, the sleepers 32 lbs.; and the total weight of the track was 162 lbs. per yard on the open road, and 190 lbs. in paved streets.

The engines used are Merryweather's tramway locomotives, 7-inch cylinders, 11 inches stroke, working pressure 120 lbs. Twelve of them are now working with success. The rolling stock consists of long double-bogie carriages, ordinary four-wheeled carriages, and light open goods wagons. Drawings of all these are given. The tramway has been open since June 1879, and has been very largely used, running at the busiest season sixty-four trains daily.

W. R. B.

(Paper No. 1809.)

"Extension of the Dundee Street Tramways."

By Andrew Greig, Assoc. M. Inst. C.E.

The Dundee Police Commissioners accepted tenders for the extension of the tramway system in December 1878. The first section was for 1 mile 1,140 yards of double line of tramway, and 1 mile 5 yards of single line, according to the designs of Mr. William Mackison, Burgh Surveyor. The double lines have been constructed between Dundee and the village of Lochee, along the Lochee Road. The single line is the Perth Road extension. The lines are laid to a gauge of 4 feet 8½ inches, with a 4-foot way; and the rolling surface of the rails is 1½ inch. The rails are of steel, made by the Bessemer process from a mixture of the best English Hæmatite brands and Spiegeleisen, cast into ingots of sufficient weight, and have the web perforated according to Gowans'

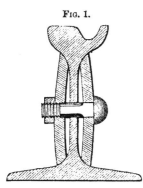

Fig. 1.

system (Fig. 1). They weigh about 80 lbs. per lineal yard, are 7 inches high, and in lengths of 24 feet and upwards. An allowance of 10 per cent. was made for lengths of 18 feet and upwards. The bed of the rail, being 6 inches broad, gives a bearing of fully 1½ inch on each side for the paving setts. This section of rail never having been previously rolled, considerable trouble and delay were experienced, especially in forming the grooves. After many experiments and much expense, caused by the necessity for the adoption of specially prepared rolls, the sections were satisfactorily completed. Formerly this kind of rail was made by rolling the head solid, and then planing out the groove. But this process was costly and tedious; and, besides, it broke the skin of the steel, and caused irregularities in the width of the lip and bearing surface. The perforations of the web are 4½ inches wide, the space between them being 3 inches, and they are intended

Minutes Institution of Civil Engineers Vol LXVII 1881.

to add stiffness to the tramway, by allowing the concrete and grouting to pass through the rail, and bind it and the paving setts together. All the rails were sent to the ground straight, those required for curves being bent to the proper radii by strong cramps. This was easily accomplished notwithstanding the peculiar section of the rail.

The ground was excavated to the depth of 12½ inches below the finished surface of the roadway. The bottom of the track was cleared of soft and unsuitable material, and then levelled and beaten to secure a solid and uniform bed. On this was laid a foundation of concrete 6 inches in thickness, composed of 1 part of Portland cement, 2 parts of clean sharp freshwater sand, and 4 parts of clean whinstone metal, broken to pass through a 2-inch ring. The rails are so laid that the upper surface of the bottom flange is flush with the top of the concrete foundation, and they are carefully levelled and solidly bedded underneath with cement mortar. They are joined at the ends with fish-plates 18 inches long, 5 inches broad, and ½ inch thick. Each pair of fish-plates is secured by four bolts and nuts, the bolts being 2¾ inches long, ⅝ inch thick, and square under the head. The paving setts laid between the rails and on the outside are of whinstone, 6 inches deep, 6 to 12 inches long, and average 3½ inches in thickness. While the paving was going on, gauges were kept on the rails to maintain them in proper position, there being no tie-rods. The setts next the rails are bedded on cement mortar and sand, and the top of them is left as nearly as possible flush with the top of the rail. The other paving stones are bedded on a ½-inch layer of clean coarse freshwater sand, and well beaten down. Before the setts were laid, the sides of the rails were packed with Portland cement mortar. The setts were grouted with best bitumen manufactured from pitch, pure coal-tar, and creosote oil, in the proportions of 1 ton of pitch to 80 gallons of tar, and 20 gallons of creosote, or such other proportions as the engineer approved, these substances varying considerably in quality.

The steepest gradient is 1 in 18·5. The inclinations vary from 1 in 52 to 1 in 138. In the centre of the town a portion of the tramway is almost level.

The second section, from the Post-office to the East end of the town, is double for a considerable distance. Its length is 2 miles 742 yards, taken as single line. At Victoria bridge a branch begins, and runs along Victoria Street and Arbroath Road to Baxter Park. The rails used for the lines leading northward are similar to those already described, but as the web is not perforated, they are much stronger. They weigh about 82 lbs. per lineal yard, and were called "heavy rails" to distinguish them from Gowans' rails.

The branch is 847 yards in length, measured as single line, and has been constructed according to Mr. Mackison's system (patent No. 2894, dated 20th July, 1878). This system consists of two parts :—cast-iron tee sleepers and rolled rail fastened on the top. The sleepers weigh 120 lbs. each, are 3 feet 11 inches long, 11¼ inches broad across the bed-plate, 6 inches high, and are laid 1 inch apart at the ends (Fig. 2). They are of open make, the

Fig. 2.

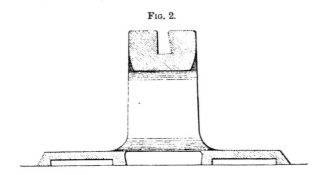

rail-bed at the top being connected by vertical supports. The underside of the bed-plate is cast with recesses in it for the purpose of gripping more securely the cement mortar on which it is bedded (Fig. 3). The open spaces in the bed-plates, those between the vertical supports connecting the bed-plate with the rail-bed, and those between the paving setts next to the rail on each side, are packed with concrete. The greater part of the sleeper is therefore embedded in the concrete, and is held firmly in position. The rail-bed of the sleeper has a dovetailed groove for receiving the dovetailed tongue on the underside of the rail, and has inclined and slightly dovetailed recesses for fixing the keys (Fig. 4). The rails, weighing about 36 lbs. per lineal yard, are of rolled steel, and shaped at the bottom so as to fit exactly to the side of the groove of the sleeper, and have slot-holes pierced through the grooves at intervals for the insertion of the fixing keys. These keys are of wrought iron, 4 inches long, 1½ inch broad, average ⅜ inch thick at the centre, and are tapered and bevelled. They can be easily removed, so as to allow of the rails being taken off and replaced without disturbing either the paving setts or the cast-iron sleepers.

The experience gained in rolling the other section of rails enabled the makers, Messrs. Brown, Bayley and Dixon, of Sheffield,

Fig. 3.

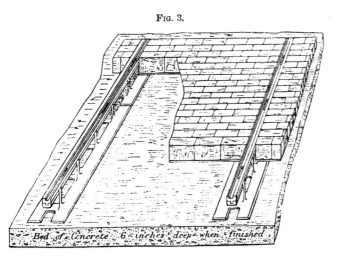

Bed of Concrete 6 inches deep when finished

Fig. 4.

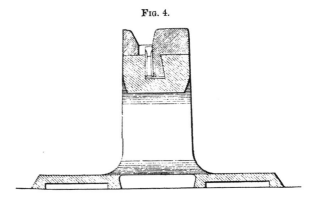

to manufacture this section with dovetailed tongue successfully, after a few trials. When the rails are fixed, that part of the grooves in the rail-beds of the sleepers not occupied by the tongues of the rails is filled with plastic British bitumen to keep out water and mud. The lengths of the rails are 20, 24, and 28 feet, less ¼ inch for expansion. An allowance of 10 per cent. was made for lengths of 16 and 20 feet, less ¼ inch. The gradients vary from 1 in 23 to 1 in 517.

The cost of the tramways laid with Gowans' rail was about £2 6s. 5d. per lineal yard of single line, or £4,085 1s. per mile. That of the tramways laid with the heavy rail was about £2 3s. 11d. per lineal yard of single line, or £3,867 2s. 4d. per mile. The cost of the tramway laid along Victoria Street to Baxter Park, according to Mackison's system, was about £2 8s. 10d. per lineal yard of single line, or £4,299 2s. per mile. This being the first contract for Mackison's system, and the quantity small, the rates were proportionately higher, special rolls having to be prepared. But a material reduction has recently been made in the manufacture of the sleepers and rails, as in the case of the contracts for Oldham, where a length of 7 miles has been laid.

The following are the rates for the various items in the contracts, arranged to show the cost per mile of single line :—

1. GOWANS' SYSTEM.

—	Quantity.	Rate.	—
		£ s. d.	£ s. d.
Lifting and carting away macadam, &c.	522 cubic yards	0 1 9	45 13 6
Excavation, &c.	1,108 „	0 2 0	110 16 0
Portland cement concrete 6 inches thick.	782 „	0 17 0	664 14 0
Laying tramway, &c.	1,760 lineal yards	0 1 8	146 13 4
Paving, &c.	2,836 sq. yards	0 7 3	1,028 1 0
Paving on cement and sand next rails	1,564 „	0 7 7	593 0 4
Grouting joints of setts with bitumen	4,400 „	0 1 3½	284 3 4
Steel rails	125¾ tons	8 14 0	1,094 0 6
Wrought-iron fish-plates	4¾ „	8 0 0	38 0 0
„ bolts and nuts	9 cwt.	0 11 0	4 19 0
Royalty at £75 per mile	..	..	75 0 0
Cost per mile of single line (exclusive of points and crossings)	..	..	4,085 1 0

2. Heavy Rail.

—	Quantity.		Rate.				—		
			£.	s.	d.		£.	s.	d.
Lifting and carting away macadam, &c.	522	cubic yards	0	1	6		39	3	0
Excavation, &c.	1,108	„	0	1	6		83	2	0
Portland cement concrete 6 inches thick	782	„	0	14	0		547	8	0
Laying tramway, &c.	1,760	lineal yards	0	1	6		132	0	0
Paving, &c.	2,836	sq. yards	0	6	10		968	19	4
Paving on cement and sand next rails	1,564	„	0	7	0		547	8	0
Grouting joints of setts with bitumen	4,400	„	0	1	3		275	0	0
Steel rails	129	tons	9	10	0		1,225	10	0
Wrought-iron fish-plates	4¾	„	9	0	0		42	15	0
„ bolts and nuts	9	cwt.	0	13	0		5	17	0
Royalty		..		..				0	0	0
Cost per mile of single line (exclusive of points and crossings)		..		..			3,867	2	4

3. Mackison's System.

—	Quantity.		Rate.				—		
			£.	s.	d.		£.	s.	d.
Lifting and carting away macadam, &c.	522	cubic yards	0	1	4		34	16	0
Excavation, &c.	1,108	„	0	1	7		87	14	4
Portland cement concrete 6 inches thick	782	„	0	14	6		566	19	0
Laying tramway, &c.	1,760	lineal yards	0	2	2		190	13	4
Paving &c.	2,836	sq. yards	0	6	10		968	19	4
Paving on cement and sand next rails	1,564	„	0	7	0		547	8	0
Grouting joints of setts with bitumen	4,400	„	0	1	3		275	0	0
Sleeper (cast iron)	141½	tons	7	0	0		990	10	0
Steel rails	56½	„	9	10	0		536	15	0
Wrought-iron keys	19½	cwt.	1	6	0		25	7	0
Royalty at £75 per mile		..		..			75	0	0
Cost per mile of single line (exclusive of points and crossings)		..		..			4,299	2	0

The tramways have now been in operation for some time, and are giving great satisfaction. The wear and tear, however, of the stones next the rails, where the vehicular traffic is great, have been considerable, which seems to indicate that harder materials are required next the rails, and that it is not good to have these stones too rigidly bedded. Where these setts have been seriously cut by the carriage and cart wheels, they have been replaced by others of the same kind, with Gowans' chilled-iron plates in the joints; or with creosoted beechwood blocks, with similar chilled-iron plates in the joints, bedded and stuffed with gravel not larger than common peas. The wooden setts give little frictional resistance to the ordinary traffic, and promise to answer well. Mackison's system is found to be smoother, more elastic, and more pleasant to run over than the other rails, which are very rigid.

ON PERMANENT WAY FOR STREET TRAMWAYS, WITH SPECIAL REFERENCE TO STEAM TRACTION.

By Mr. J. D. LARSEN, of London.

ON PERMANENT WAY FOR STREET TRAMWAYS, WITH SPECIAL REFERENCE TO STEAM TRACTION.

By Mr. J. D. LARSEN, of London.

If we dismiss from consideration Mr. Train's attempts in 1861, the failure of which arose from the unsuitable section of rail adopted, we may fairly say that the introduction of Street Tramways, so far as London is concerned, dates only from 1869. In that year three lines were authorised, viz. (1) the North Metropolitan Tramways, embracing the Whitechapel, Mile End, and Bow roads; (2) the Metropolitan Street Tramways, for the Kennington, Brixton, and Clapham routes; and (3) the Pimlico, Peckham, and Greenwich Tramways, from Pimlico to Greenwich. The two latter companies, which had powers over some 25 miles of streets, have since been amalgamated, and are now known under the title of the London Tramways Company.

Some idea of the success of tramways, and of the increasing estimation in which they are held by the public, may be formed from the fact that in nine years, up to 30th June 1878, there had been authorised by Parliament no less than 65 miles 58 chains of line, of which 56 miles 50 chains were completed and open for public traffic. The greater portion of this was double line; turned into length of single line it gives 124 miles 46 chains authorised, and 107 miles 29 chains finished. These lines, necessitating a paid-up capital of as much as £1,326,054, refer to the metropolitan district only.

The growth of the system has been no less widely developed in the provinces. The total mileage of road for the United Kingdom was at the same date 346½ miles authorised, and nearly 269 miles finished and in use. This, turned as before into length of single line, gives 526½ miles, and 408½ miles respectively, with a paid-up capital of £4,035,464.

The extensive patronage which tramways receive from the public (nearly 150 millions of passengers being carried annually) is by no means due to the superior accommodation of the vehicles, as is evidenced by the fact that the business of the London General Omnibus Company, contrary to all expectation, is not adversely affected by them. In the author's opinion their success is mainly due to the reduction in fares, and to the increased service, these two innovations having been sufficient to create a traffic which before was non-existent.

Street tramways are now so firmly established, and have proved so great a boon to the masses, that the opponents to the system, on the score of its spoiling the roads, are daily being ousted from their position. Any improvements in the facilities for intercommunication in large towns are of such vital importance to the industries which have created such towns, that the opposition of the few must inevitably succumb to the rapidly increasing wants of the many.

The objections to a tramway on a public highway are being grappled with and overcome one by one as experience is gained; and if ten years hence the best constructed tramway is as far superior to the best of the present day as this latter is to the original road of ten or more years ago, we shall have so far progressed that opposition on the ground of interference with other interests will not be tenable.

The author's present object is to point out some of the defects in the different systems of permanent way for tramways, and some of the steps that have been taken to overcome them. It may be observed at starting that many lines in this and other countries have been unfairly handicapped, by being called upon for duties they were never designed or constructed to perform, notably in the matter of steam traction in lieu of horse-power. Here, in addition to the rails having to carry perhaps three times the load originally intended, all the tractive force is transferred from the roadway to the rails; and

when it is considered that this is an entirely new and very heavy duty, which these lines were never expected to perform, the only matter for surprise is that they should have stood so well. A tramway that would serve admirably for heavy horse traffic, might be so constructed that to use steam traction on it would be to destroy it immediately. An illustration may be found in the original way or track laid for the running of coal-wagons, otherwise trams, whence the derivation of the word "tramway." These tracks were made, and are so still in some places abroad, of hard wood scantling, about 4 in. square, faced with light flat bar iron spiked on. These do good service with horse or mule traction; but to transfer the tractive force from the road to the rails themselves would ensure their total failure.

Early Systems of Laying Tramways.—The first form of rail used in London is shown in Fig. 2, Plate 15; it is the same as had previously been used in Liverpool and Birkenhead by Mr. George Hopkins. The method of construction was also the same, except that in London trenches for concrete, about 9 in. deep, were dug under the longitudinal sleepers, as shown in Fig. 1. The Whitechapel section of the North Metropolitan Company, and the Brixton section of the London Tramways Company, were laid in this manner. The rails weighed 45 to 48 lbs. per yard, and were spiked to the longitudinal sleepers by vertical spikes, through countersunk holes made in the bottom of the groove. The longitudinals were laid in cast-iron chairs, or shoes; and the gauge was secured by 1½ in. × ⅜ in. iron tie-rods, the ends of which were upset of a dovetail form, as shown in Fig. 3, and dropped into sockets of corresponding shape, cast on the shoes. There were many objections to these tie-rods: in the first place, the slightest variation in the angle of the bevelled ends, or of the sockets, would affect the gauge; in the next place, after the road was finished the tie-rods would occasionally work up above the surface of the stones; and last, but not least, in some instances it was found that when the pavior came upon a rod that did not lie conveniently for a joint in the paving, he would, if he had an opportunity, solve the difficulty by lifting it out, dropping it into the bottom of the trench, and paving over it, in which position it was

possibly quite as useful as in any other. In the reconstruction of some of the North Metropolitan lines in 1877, the tie-bar shown in Fig. 4, Plate 15, was substituted, which did away with many objections to the former system. In some places the author has used the forms of tie-rods shown in Figs. 5 and 6, that in Fig. 5 having a cottered end, and that in Fig. 6 being simply split, turned back, and punched for the nails. Where however the rail is mounted on a longitudinal timber sleeper of a width not exceeding the rail, transverse sleepers should be used if possible instead of ties. At the same time it would be bad policy in dealing with a road previously paved, and where the substratum under the setts is in good condition, to destroy this for the purpose of putting in cross sleepers; and as a matter of fact it will generally be found that the municipal authorities will not allow it to be done. In all such cases the best practice is to increase the base of the longitudinal sleeper.

The original method of securing the rail to the sleeper, as shown in Fig. 2, Plate 15, was also very objectionable. The vertical countersunk-headed spikes were apt to work loose, and the water, percolating through the hole in the rail, so softened the timber round the spike that it had no hold. In some instances the heads of the spikes would fly off, probably quite as much from the percussive action of the ordinary road traffic as from that of the tramcars. From these causes the vertical spike fastening proved wholly inadequate as an effective method of securing the rails; on lines so laid, after a few months' work, loose rails were the rule and not the exception. Irrespective of the defect itself, this in wet weather formed so great an eyesore that it was an unanswerable argument in the hands of the opponents to tramway extension. Each passing vehicle created a continuous line of little mud fountains, bespattering the adjacent roadway and everything near it with slush and filth, while this same action was rapidly destroying the foundation and substructure.

Again it will be seen that this section of rail, Fig. 2, is practically a flat bar of iron with a groove rolled in it near one edge; its inherent weakness under a load will thus be evident. To obviate this defect the author had rails rolled with flanges about ½ in. in depth

depending from the under side of the rail on each side. This made a considerably stronger rail without increasing the sectional area; and with this section the first portions of the Pimlico, Peckham, and Greenwich, and also of the London Streets Tramways, were laid. One part of these was laid with 60 lb. and another part with 50 lb. rails, the two sections being as shown in Figs. 7 and 8, Plate 15. The author then proposed to deepen the flanges still further, but was met by the assertion that it was not possible in rolling the rails to get the metal down to fill so narrow a flange. By degrees however they were deepened to 1 inch, and ultimately to 1⅛ in. and 1¼ in., a large delivery of these latter being accompanied by an intimation that the author could have them rolled to any depth he chose. The North Metropolitan Company are now using a rail with flanges full 1½ in. deep on either side, as shown in Fig. 9.

As soon as rails were obtained with depending flanges an inch in depth, the author commenced the use of side fasteners, attaching the rail to the sleeper in the manner shown in Figs. 10 and 11, Plate 15, which are an elevation and section of what have since become known as "Larsen's rails and side fasteners." This system was brought out in 1871, and from that time has been the method of attachment universally used for this section of rail when mounted on wood sleepers, and in some instances when mounted on iron sleepers also. The flanges are rolled of a sufficient depth to enable holes to be pierced through them below the upper surface of the sleeper. The sleeper is rabbeted down on its upper edge, to fit accurately the under side of the rail, and the latter is then secured to it by means of a half staple. Of this the portion A, passing through the rail flange into the sleeper, is round, while the other part B, lying against the rail and sleeper, is flat, of say ¾ in. × ⁵⁄₁₆ in. section, and has a hole or holes punched in the end, for a nail or nails as may be desired.

The introduction of this rail and fastener abolished completely the old form of rail with vertical spikes, and proved a marked improvement over former practice. The greater portion of the London Streets Tramways, and of the Pimlico, Peckham, and Greenwich Tramways, were laid by the author on this method.

This fastener has no tendency to draw the rail and sleeper into close contact. The author therefore designed a screw cramp, Fig. 12, Plate 16, to hold the rail and sleeper together while fixing the side fasteners; and found that with the aid of this tool a very sound and close attachment of rail and sleeper was obtainable. This tool was first used on the Greenwich lines, but so universally has it come into use that it may be seen wherever a tramway is being constructed or repaired.

Since these side fasteners were first introduced, many modifications of them have been attempted. Figs. 13 and 14, Plate 15, represent a form designed by Mr. H. T. McNeale, and used at Rouen. The author considers this form a good one; but, unless considerable play be allowed to the pins of the fastener within the holes in the rails, trouble will be caused by the expansion and contraction of the rails under varying temperatures.

The greater portion of the Pimlico, Peckham, and Greenwich lines were laid with transverse sleepers of the same section as the longitudinals—4 in. by 6 in.—laid on the flat and secured to the longitudinal sleeper by means of brackets, as shown in Fig. 15, Plate 16. The principal objection to these brackets is that they necessitate the cutting back of the side of the paving stones wherever they occur, to enable the upper surface of the stone to come close up to the rail. Hence the stone is more or less pyramidal in form, and, standing on its apex, is very liable to rock; the result is that every here and there there is a loose stone adjoining the rail, giving an unsightly appearance to the road, and admitting water to percolate through to the foundation.

In Paris the author laid some miles of rail to the section in Fig. 16, which is still weaker than Fig. 2, and perhaps the worst section he has ever seen. By persistently advocating a change, he ultimately induced the municipal authorities to use a rail of the section shown in Fig. 17; and these, in steel, are the rails now in use. It would scarcely be supposed that the section in Fig. 16 would have been adopted after the section in Figs. 10 and 11 had actually been in use; but so it is, and the former section is even now down on one road, where steam traction is used. While such is the case, but little surprise need be felt if bad accounts of the

success of steam power reach us from Paris. In this instance some at least, if not all, of the blame may be laid to the permanent way. Even the section of steel rail, Fig. 17, is light to run locomotives over; but the author was limited to 42 lbs. per metre run.

One unavoidable element of weakness, on every road along which a tramway runs, lies in the fact that there is everywhere a continuous unbroken joint between the rail and the pitching, lying in a line with all the traffic of the highway. This has been the cause of one of the most irritating inconveniencies yet met with in connection with street tramways, so far as they affect the ordinary traffic of the road. In spite of the greatest care in paving, the stones immediately adjoining the rail sink in places, allowing the rail to peep up above the surface of the road. Now the slight sinking of one or a dozen stones from their normal level, in the middle of a wide paved street, is in itself of comparatively little moment, and would only show a slight depression in wet weather; but when a straight and level iron rail runs through the centre of such a depression, every carriage or vehicle crossing the spot, at any angle short of a right angle, will be most unpleasantly skidded or slung more or less out of its course. This occurs, however small the difference between the level of rail and stones may be, a quarter of an inch being quite sufficient to constitute a grave fault.

Larsen's improved System for Steam Traction.—The time has now come when tramways about to be constructed will have to be designed for the possible contingency of using steam traction on them, even where at present its use may not be contemplated.

In view of this necessity the author in his latest practice has adopted the system of construction shown in Figs. 18 and 19, Plate 16, which are an elevation and section of a rail and of a continuous wrought-iron girder sleeper. The rail A is of the ordinary section known as Larsen's rail, the side flanges being punched precisely as when first introduced for use with timber sleepers. This rail is secured to the top of the sleeper by a side fastener in the form of a hook-bolt B, having one end simply turned over at a right angle, and the

other end screwed for a nut. Between the web of the rail and the central web of the sleeper there is a filling piece of cast iron I, made with a slot or groove down its outer side, in which the hook-bolt lies. The hook-bolt is first inserted through the rail flange from the inside; this filling piece is then slipped up behind it, and a lock nut screwed on; and the rail is thus secured to the girder in a manner as rapid and easy of accomplishment as it is secure and effective.

The base-plate D may be made as wide as desired; but by making it wide enough to form a good broken joint with the first paving sett, ample base area will be secured for the stability of the tramway rail, being in fact nearly three times that of the earlier systems. The continuity of the rail and sleeper is secured by making rail, sleeper, and base-plate all break joint. Fish-plates are unnecessary, inasmuch as the base-plate forms an effective fish-plate for the girder sleeper, and this again for the rail; so that, due attention being given in first construction, a faulty or loose joint is impossible, unless the rail, girder, and base-plate should all be broken completely through. Loose joints at the ends of rails are common faults with the light sections used in Paris, and are due to the difficulty in fishing, and also to the fact of there being no concrete substratum.

It will be seen by Fig. 19 that the paving, or road metalling, can be laid close to the rail throughout the whole length, there being no projection, however trifling, such as exists in the case where shoes or brackets are used. The advantage derived from having nothing projecting outside the rail is a substantial one; the evils resulting from having to cut the under side of the stones have already been noticed, and are also dwelt upon by Mr. Robinson Souttar in a paper read before the Institution of Civil Engineers (Proceedings, vol. L., p. 4) when criticising the author's side fasteners and the method of securing them. Mr. Souttar proposes to remedy this defect by having the rail rolled with the flanges set back towards the centre $\frac{3}{8}$ in. on each side, or by a distance equal to the thickness of the side fastener. This method however practically makes the under side of the rail $\frac{3}{4}$ in. less in width than the top. Now although it is very possible that this would make no great difference to the stability of the rail,

nevertheless it is at least a step in the wrong direction. It is removing one evil by substituting another, perhaps a little less objectionable. Other conditions remaining equal, if the base of the rail could be made $\frac{3}{4}$ in. wider than the top, a decided advantage would be gained.

The wide base-plate in the author's system keeps the paving alongside the rail quite sound, and prevents that deposit of mud and slush which is now so commonly seen on either side of the rail, and which is continually working down, and rotting or injuring the foundation of the road. Between the rail and sleeper a piece of tarred felt or similar material is inserted throughout the whole length, to give a little elasticity, and make a good joint. Iron bearing against iron is always objectionable, unless the pieces be riveted together, as in the case of the base-plate.

In the author's opinion the arguments used in support of a timber longitudinal sleeper, on account of its superior elasticity, rest upon wrong premises. It has often been urged that all experience with railways has proved the superiority of an elastic over a non-elastic road, and that a tramway being really a railroad, the same necessity exists. A moment's consideration will show the absurdity of the comparison. A railroad has frequently an engine weighing 30 to 40 tons dashing over it at 50 or more miles per hour; while an excessive weight and speed on a tramway would be 8 tons and 8 miles per hour. Now assume the case of a completely non-elastic road, and on it a sharp inequality, such for instance as would be produced by the end of a rail being packed up $\frac{1}{4}$ in. above the adjoining rail. Then the heavy and fast engine would either beat down the obstruction at one blow, or else would leap clean off the rails; while the light and slow engine would pass it with a slight shock or jolt and nothing more. The author holds on the contrary that a tramway should be more rigid than a railroad, for the reason that it should approximate, as nearly as may be, to the condition of the highway adjoining it.

The author's system is particularly adapted for steam traction, as the girder sleeper most effectually fishes the rails, and a good junction of rail to rail is a *sine quâ non* for any mechanical method of haulage. With the section of rail under consideration, and with timber sleepers, a good fishing of the rail-ends is not easily accomplished; and this is one of the weak points in most existing lines. The advantage of having no perishable material buried underground is so evident as to require no comment. When the rails require renewing, they alone will need to be disturbed; the concrete, if good when first laid, will be better twenty years afterwards.

Figs. 20 and 21, Plate 16, show other rails and sleepers, differing in section, fastenings, &c., but each embodying the same system of construction, namely a continuous rail and a wrought-iron or steel girder sleeper, with wide base-plate extending underneath the adjoining paving.

Barker's System.—Figs. 22 and 23, Plate 17, represent the system of tramway construction introduced by Mr. B. Barker. This, like the author's, has an extended base beneath the adjoining paving, but the sleepers are of cast iron and are necessarily in shorter lengths. They are specified to be " of such lengths compared with the lengths of the wrought-iron or steel rails as will ensure the joint in the rails always occurring in one of the castings. Thus if all the castings are three feet in length, the rails may be nine, twelve, fifteen, eighteen, twenty-one and twenty-four feet in length, and in this case a rail joint will always occur in the centre of a casting." By this it appears that three feet is considered a convenient length for the sleepers, and this would especially be the case on curves, since separate castings would otherwise have to be made for each radius. The use of cast iron, and the necessarily short lengths, are the only apparent objections to this otherwise excellent system.

The section, Fig. 23, shows the method of securing the rail to the sleeper. The taper key or cotter C passes through a hole cast in the sleeper, and through a corresponding hole in the central web of the rail.

Gowan's System.—Figs. 24 and 25, Plate 17, show Mr. Gowan's system. This consists of a simple flat-bottomed rail, with the web deep enough for the foot or base to reach below the paving, and with this foot rolled wide enough to constitute a foundation for the concrete or

paving setts on either side of the rail. The web is perforated at intervals, Fig. 24, which, in the case of a tramway laid in cement or concrete, enables the cement or concrete to be filled into the openings, thereby binding the whole together, and keeping the rails both in line and level. No method of fishing is shown, as it is obvious that with this section a most perfect junction of rail to rail can be easily obtained. Mr. Gowan describes several methods. The only apparent objections to this system are the great first cost, due to the difficulties of manufacture, and the fact that when the rail surface is worn out the whole requires renewing. The rails seen by the author had the grooves planed out of the solid, and the perforations through the web drilled out; consequently the cost for labour in manufacture could not but be large. With regard to the second objection, not only must the whole substructure be renewed, but the taking it up necessitates the disturbance of the concrete foundation in which it is embedded.

Aldred's System.—Figs. 26 and 27, Plate 17, show the construction introduced by Mr. Aldred. The rail is made in two pieces, not riveted together, but of such a form that, when keyed in the chairs A, they may be said to be dovetailed together, the combination forming a reversible or double-headed rail. These rails require no punching or drilling of holes for fishing; their peculiar shape enables them to be dropped into their place within the jaws of the chair, and on the wooden key B being driven securely home they are firmly held in position. The rail is laid on timber cross sleepers, and is so far open to the objection of being laid on a perishable material; there is also no base-plate to support the adjacent paving stones. At each chair the paving stone on either side of the rail has to be cut or dressed, the objection to which has been previously pointed out. Whether the advantage of a double-headed rail is sufficient to compensate for the extra weight of metal to be laid down in the first instance is a moot point. For railways, at all events, the double-headed rail is not looked upon so favourably now as it was some years ago.

Winby's System.—Figs. 28 and 29, Plate 18, represent Mr. Winby's

system. It is somewhat similar to Mr. Gowan's, but some of the difficulties of making are successfully grappled with; the base or foot is not so wide, the rail being mounted on a base-plate. This system has also been used without a wide base-plate, the rail being laid on cross sleepers and spiked down with dog spikes, like an ordinary contractor's road. The inner edge of the rail A, Fig. 29, is rolled flat in the bar, as shown dotted, and is afterwards turned up while hot, as shown full. This saves planing out the groove, but it may be a question whether it does not tend to weaken the rail in what is already a weak part. It is a common cause of failure for a rail to split along the bottom of the groove, and this tendency is augmented by the action of the tramcar wheel.

The flange of a tramcar wheel, having to travel continually round sharp curves, becomes worn, by friction against the sides of the groove in the rail, to the shape shown in Fig. 30; while the tread of the wheel and the top of the rail are also worn down, till the flange bears on the bottom of the groove. The flange then acts in a similar manner to a revolving cutter in a tube-cutting wrench, especially with chilled wheels. The author has taken up many rails split along in this manner. To delay the operation of this cause, the brake-blocks on tramcars are now made of iron, and so arranged as to bear on the flanges as well as on the treads of the wheels, and thus to wear the flanges down also; but if once the top of the rail is worn down in any part sufficiently to allow the flange to bottom the groove, a very short time suffices to destroy the rail in the manner indicated.

Mackisson's System.—Figs. 31 and 32, Plate 18, show one form of Mr. Mackisson's construction. This consists of a cast-iron longitudinal sleeper, with broad base-plate, the principal novelty being in the method of securing the rail to the sleeper. It will be seen that the rail has a central web of a dovetail shape, which is secured in a groove cast in the sleeper, by means of keys driven at intervals along its length. Mr. Mackisson describes several other sections, and methods of fastening them to the sleeper, but the general construction is the same. In Figs. 31 and 32 the keys A are dropped into the groove in the cast-iron sleeper, through slots B

cut in the bottom of the groove in the rail, and are then driven home with a drift. The long slot necessary to drop the key through must, in the author's opinion, weaken the rail in what is already its weakest part. Figs. 33 and 34, Plate 18, are different sections of reversible rails, so arranged that the surfaces in and out of use are at right angles to each other or nearly so. The manufacture of such sections seems likely to present much difficulty; and with regard to the sleepers there is the objection before alluded to, namely that being in cast iron they are necessarily in short lengths.

General Conclusions.—The author has now briefly noticed the latest methods of tramway construction, having for their object the removal of various defects indicated by experience, and also designed to meet the requirements of steam traction. There are many other systems which are better known than those selected, but they do not so well meet these latter requirements, and therefore need not be dwelt upon. None of the methods described in this paper have been long enough in use as yet to enable a complete comparison to be made of their merits. They all possess good qualities in different directions, and no doubt will in each case be found to remedy some of the defects with which experience has made us acquainted.

The author has throughout referred to steam alone as a motive power for tramways; and for the reason that according to our present knowledge it is the only available power. Compressed air answers admirably in every way except one, but that one most effectually shuts it out from all competition with steam. Where compressed air is used as a motive power, principally in underground operations, it has been found by experiment that the resultant efficiency of the working engine, as compared with the air-compressing engine, rarely exceeds 30 per cent. Consequently the difference in cost, under the most favourable conditions, will be as 3 to 1 against compressed air. This difference is sufficient to justify us for the present in discarding the idea of compressed air, as a motor for tramway purposes. The same objections apply, though not perhaps to the same extent, to the hot-water or fireless engine, invented by Dr. Lamm of America. Several modifications of this type have been tried with varying success. The chief reason that its use has not been extended is doubtless the financial difficulty; and even with steam traction, it must first be satisfactorily demonstrated that it is cheaper than horse-power, and it will then become practically universal.

At no very distant date, in the author's opinion, horse tramways will be the exception and steam tramways the rule; and for this reason, amongst others, namely the superiority of steam as regards safety to the ordinary traffic. The author is aware that just the converse of this is now urged by many persons; but in this, as in everything else since the beginning of time, the majority of to-day becomes, by the spread of knowledge and the light of experience, the minority of to-morrow.

The following is the comparative net cost of the different systems described, each taken per mile run of single line. These figures are estimated for permanent-way materials only, and do not include cost of laying, or of paving, concrete, &c. :—

	£	
Ordinary line, timber longitudinal and cross sleepers .	1150	
Larsen's system, wrought-iron sleeper, and base-plate .	1400	(¹)
Barker's system, cast-iron sleeper, ...	1556	
Gowan's system, wrought-iron, ...	1760	
Aldred's system, chairs, and timber cross sleepers .	1100	(²)
Winby's system, wrought-iron, with base-plate . .	1550	(³)
Mackisson's system, cast-iron sleeper, with base-plate	1600	

With respect to the comparative cost of steam and horse-power, the first has not been in operation long enough to give reliable and accurate data respecting the cost of maintenance of tramway engines; and moreover this is an item which, with improved permanent way and engines carefully designed, will be

(¹) 78½ tons rails (50 lbs. per yard) at £7 = £549 10s.; 95 tons sleepers and base-plates at £7 10s. = £712 10s.; small materials, &c., £138; total £1400.

(²) 94 tons rails (60 lbs. per yard) at £7 = £658; 30 tons chairs at £5 10s. = £165; 1760 sleepers at 2s. 6d. = £220; keys, spikes, &c., £57; total £1100.

(³) 121 tons rails (77 lbs. per yard) at £9 15s. = £1179 15s.; 47 tons base-plates at £7 = £329; small materials, &c., £41 5s.; total £1550.

T

continually decreasing. The author believes that, if the roads had been better in the first instance, steam traction would have come more prominently to the fore than it has as yet; but so many men of ability and experience are now devoting their energies to the solution of the problem of applying mechanical power to tramways, that its ultimate success is assured.

According to Mr. D. K. Clark (Railway Machinery, 1855), the resistance to traction on a railway may be as low as 6 lbs. per ton. If this is the case, the haulage of tramcars over grooved rails can never be accomplished at so cheap a rate as those prevailing on railways. In 1870 the author made a series of experiments on the New Cross tramways, using a dynamometer to register the resistance to traction; and on a level and straight road in good condition, and under favourable circumstances, the resistance was as much as 18·2 lbs. per ton, or about three times the force necessary on a railway under similarly favourable conditions.

This great difference in the traction on a tramway, as compared with a railway, may be in some measure due to the build of the cars, inasmuch as they have a very short wheel-base, and considerable overhanging weight at either end. Engines for tramways, especially the earlier ones, have also been made usually with a short wheel-base; but latterly they have been fitted with a pair of small leading wheels, and with very good results. Doubtless some modification in this direction will take place in the wheel-base of the cars, and a lower resistance to traction will probably then be observed.

The author has thus brought finally into view what, among the defects and objections admitted or supposed to exist in tramways, is the greatest of all, namely, the necessity of having a grooved rail, level with the surface of the road. The exigencies of the highway however render this condition an absolute necessity; and all our energies must be devoted to minimising the inconveniences which it inevitably entails.

————

Discussion.

Mr. J. G. LYNDE said there was one point in this very exhaustive paper to which he should like to direct attention, namely the estimates of cost. From the figures given at the commencement, it would appear that the cost of tramways, when they were first started, was something like £7000 to £10,000 per mile; but the estimates at the end of the paper varied, at present prices, from £1100 to £1760 per mile. Those last estimates did not of course include the paving &c., while the first estimates did. But, as far as he knew, the cost of paving with granite was about £2000 per mile; and when that was added to the latter estimates, it would still be found that the tramways cost originally something like double what they did now. Formerly, no doubt, a great deal of money was spent in the promotion of companies, which was not the case at present.

He quite agreed with Mr. Larsen that tramways should be laid, not on the elastic principle, like railways, but on the rigid principle, as in the systems which were now being adopted. Continuous iron bearings, whether of wrought or of cast iron, should be adopted throughout, and no perishable material should be laid beneath the surface of the ground. But one point, not touched upon in the paper, was the tendency to torsion in the rail when a great weight came upon it on one side of the centre line, as was the case when an engine was used on tramways. Therefore it was necessary that some support should be placed directly under the part of the rail upon which the weight was thrown. That was one of the reasons why he had himself adopted Barker's system, of which he had laid many miles in Manchester and its suburbs, Leeds, Derby, Edinburgh, Wallasey, Patricroft, and other places. In that system, Fig. 23, Plate 17, there was a cast-iron wall under the table of the rail; and this carried the weight fairly down to the bottom flange, and so on to the foundation; thus there was no tendency to torsion, and no vibration when the weight came on, such as occurred with rails having a web in the middle. Again, with the middle web

T 2

the top of the rail, being only 3 in. or 3¼ in. in width, had an overhang of something less than 1½ in. on each side, to be filled under with concrete. But a wall of concrete 1½ in. thick was not worth much, and the vibration of the centre web against it would prevent its ever forming a strong support for the rail, which was very essential if steam was to be used on tramways.

A base-plate beneath the paving stones he thought was essential, in order to form a continuous bearing throughout for the first course of paving stones alongside the rails. In one of the busiest streets in Manchester the rails and paving stones had thus been laid perfectly level at first, and they had never cost a penny in repairs: they had been down three years, and were as good now as when they were first put down. This was at the foot of the approach to the Victoria Station, where there was an immense cross-traffic, and only a single line of rails. He regarded that as a very important point, because the repairs of the paving constituted one of the great nuisances in connection with tramways. If stones could get away from their work, they would; but with Barker's system there was an upright wall of iron for the paviors to pave up to, instead of loose concrete or whatever else might be used. With Gowan's system, which was now being tried in Manchester, they were putting in tar to fill up the 1½ in. space on each side the web, as they could not manage the concrete. That system had an advantage in being one entire steel rail, but had the fault that the weight came entirely on one side of the centre web.

There was another advantage in having a continuous cast-iron sleeper, as in Barker's system. The hollow centre of the sleeper was filled with concrete, merely however to add weight, not strength; but that weight absorbed the vibration, and the consequence was that the trams ran very easily and smoothly on it. The short length of the sleepers was objected to in the paper; but he himself found it an immense advantage, as the lines could thus be easily laid round curves, while the steel rail formed a complete backbone to the system. It was keyed down well to the sleepers at intervals of 18 inches, so that they formed one continuous piece with it. In making a connection two months ago, a portion of Barker's tramway, in

Deansgate, Manchester, had to be taken up; and it was so solid that the sleepers and the foundation, which was a thin bedding of concrete, came up in one mass.

In the estimate on page 201, nothing was said about steel rails in Barker's system, but these were put down in every case; and it was hardly fair to compare that system with Gowan's, in which wrought iron, not steel, was used. An estimate could hardly be regarded as affording a fair comparison, unless the same material were used in both cases. It was of great importance to look forwards to the future repairs of tramways, as even a steel rail would eventually wear and require renewal. If the weight of the rail bore only a small proportion to the total weight, then the expense of renewal was reduced to a minimum. This was the case in Barker's system; but in Gowan's and similar systems, whether wrought iron or steel were used, the whole of the material would necessarily become scrap when worn out, and thus entail a cost for repairs nearly equal to that of relaying the line.

He might mention that, in the tramways he had laid down, the grooves were 1 in. wide, and the tyres of the wheels were chilled cast-iron. The use of timber beneath the rails was quite out of date; and the simpler and fewer the parts in tramway permanent way the better. As to the bearing of the steel rails on the sleepers, the paper mentioned a layer of tarred felt as being inserted; but in Manchester they just took a tar brush and brushed over the groove in the sleeper before the rail was slipped into it, and they found that no other bedding was necessary. The holes for the bolts were squared, and were made slightly oblong to allow for expansion. The length of the sleepers was 2 ft. 11 in. instead of 3 ft., which gave an inch play for the rail at the ends. It was then very easy to key the rails to them.

In conclusion he would give the prices that were now being paid for Barker's system. The figures given in the paper were about correct, but they varied of course with the price of iron and steel. The prices at present were as follows:—

Cost of one mile of single line of Tramway.

	£
53 tons steel rails (34 lbs. per yard) at £11 10s., say	610
180 tons cast-iron sleepers (114 lbs. each) at £4	720
Wrought-iron keys	15
1760 lineal yards, laying line—including opening out and removing roadway, preparing concrete bed 1 inch thick, and filling underside of sleepers with concrete—at 3s. 6d.	308
Cost without paving	£1653
4400 square yards best Welsh granite paving, 6 inches deep, on 2-inch bed of gravel, racked with broken granite, and run with asphalte complete, at 10s. 3d.	2255
Total Cost, including paving	£3908

Mr. R. C. RAPIER, referring to Mr. Lynde's remarks on the cost of tramways, would venture to suggest that the first cost of the permanent way for a tramway was an item of the least possible consequence. The *best* construction for a tramway was of great importance; but whether it cost £1000, £2000, or £3000 per mile was of no importance at all. Mr. Lynde had drawn a comparison between the cost of permanent way, given at the end of the paper, varying from £1100 to £1760 per mile, and the whole capital account, given at the beginning of the paper as being £10,000 per mile, ten years ago. But the capital of a tramway company included not only the cost of its permanent way and paving &c., but, what was much more important, the cost of the vehicles, the horses, the stables, the depôts, and, what must not be forgotten, the Parliamentary charges; so that if £10,000 per mile was the average capital expended for tramways, the cost of the permanent way was not more than one-fifth of the whole cost of the undertaking. He believed that some tramways in London cost as much as £17,000 per mile of road; but of course the great bulk of that £17,000 must be connected with items of expense other than the permanent way.

He would suggest for the consideration of engineers whether they were not altogether wrong in one or two points with reference to tramways. A great effort had been made for several years past to get

the rail as narrow as possible, the idea being that horses were apt to slip upon iron rails. It was a great pity that such a fallacy should have been so implicitly believed for so long a time; but it was incumbent on engineers to endeavour to get rid of such erroneous ideas. It was clear that a tramway in any town was made for the benefit of the inhabitants of that town; and the more the tramway could be used, the better for those inhabitants. If the tramway was only used as at present by about one vehicle out of thirty-five, while the road was made simply abominable for the other thirty-four vehicles, he maintained that that was not first-rate engineering. Why was the road thus spoilt for all other vehicles? Firstly, because the rail was so narrow; and secondly, because the inevitable joint between the stones and the rails, described in the paper, happened to be so near the gauge of the wheels of the other vehicles, that one wheel was always hugging the groove on the one side, while the other wheel rattled about somewhere near the joint between the paving stones and the rail on the other side. If any one would carefully examine the condition of the paving adjacent to the rails of the tramways in London, he would find that there was a subsidiary groove worn in the paving stones, alongside the rails, by the wheels of the ordinary traffic. The remedy for both these evils, in his opinion, would be to make the rails wider. He had himself laid down some rails of considerable width, as described in Proceedings Inst. C.E., vol. L., page 38. The principle he went upon was this: that, whatever the surface of the tramway was made of —whether of steel, wrought iron, or cast iron—the wearing surface ought to be wide enough to take the wheels of any vehicles that at all approached the gauge of the rail. The gauge of the rail was 4 ft. 8½ in., and the gauge of almost all other vehicles was comprised between 4 ft. 7 in. and 4 ft. 10 in.

Reference had been made to the fact that the success of steam traction had been very much delayed by the imperfection of the permanent way. He submitted that the permanent way should be improved by having more of it in quantity, but in fewer pieces. For that reason he approved of Gowan's system, because it was in one continuous girder; and although originally the grooves had to be planed out, he believed he was right in saying that that was no longer

necessary, and that the rails were now rolled with the groove in them. With reference to Mr. Lynde's objections to the 1½ in. wall of concrete on each side of the rail web, he did not apprehend that Mr. Gowan supposed his rails to get any very great support from the concrete. It was simply necessary to fill in the space with some impervious material, so as to make a fair joint with the paving stones.

He thoroughly agreed with what had been said in the paper, that it was useless to go on opposing tramways. He himself hated them, and suffered from them greatly, especially on account of the roughness and severe shaking in driving along a road laid with tramways. That state of things was discreditable, because engineers ought to do something better. But as regarded the eventual success of tramways, and of steam power on tramways, he thought an engineer must have very little faith in his profession, if he had any doubt as to that point.

With respect to the cost of compressed air on tramways (p. 200), he thought the author had overlooked the fact that a small tramway steam engine was not itself a very economical motor. It was therefore an open question whether the compressed-air system or the hot-water system might not compare favourably with the steam-power system, inasmuch as their lower efficiency might be compensated by the greater economy of the stationary boilers in use at the depôt. With regard to the necessity or desirability of making the tramway in fewer pieces, he might mention that the tramway which he had before referred to, as being made of wide plates upon concrete, was practically in one piece from end to end, i.e. for a length of 2¼ miles.

Mr. JOHN ROBINSON pointed out that Mr. Rapier had after all given no reason for his somewhat surprising statement that there was no difficulty in a horse passing over tramways without slipping, provided the metal was not too narrow. As far as his own experience went, wherever there was a large surface of metal, especially if wet, or covered with grease or mud, there was the greatest danger to a horse of slipping upon it. With regard to what had been stated in reference to the improvement of tramways, he had been delighted with the experience which a few weeks' driving in Manchester had lately given him; for at the present time he could not even find out where the tramway was, unless he saw it. He thought one of the greatest successes yet achieved in tramways was that in Manchester there was now a tramway which was almost imperceptible. That tramway was, he believed, on Barker's system.

Some time ago, when the Corporation of Manchester was proposing to lay down tramways in the streets, he was called upon by Mr. Lynde to give his opinion—not as having had experience in tramways, but as to the general construction of a road which should be most economical in the first instance, and (what, as Mr. Rapier had observed, was of far greater importance) should afterwards require the least amount of repair. Nevertheless he did not quite concur in Mr. Rapier's idea, that, because a rail could be got in one piece, therefore the facilities which Barker's composite system seemed to give should be thrown away. First of all, in Barker's system there was a very easy mode of paving up to the side of the tramway. It would be seen by Fig. 23, Plate 17, that the system consisted of a flat rail with a central rib, connected with a series of cast-iron sleepers, the whole presenting a very square side, up to which the paving stones could be brought quite close; and the result was that in Manchester the rail was, as he had said, almost imperceptible when driving over it. There was besides the great advantage that if the steel rail became cut and split, in the way described in the paper, by the action of the wheels, it was possible, by simply removing the adjacent blocks, to take away the rail and replace it with a new one. If, when a rail had to be changed, it was necessary to take up the whole road, disturbing the concrete and the pavement, that was a much more serious affair; and practically a road made in that way would be left to go very much longer after it needed repair than a road made on Barker's system, because of the greater ease with which the latter could be taken up and the rail changed. He was by no means disposed to say that in Barker's system they had arrived at something which was final, for he hoped they would still go on with improvements; but he thought for the present it met the general requirements of the public.

He was surprised to find from the paper how inadequate the Paris tramways had been to the requirements of steam traction. The tramways had been treated, as Frenchmen were liable to treat things,

by bringing them down to the very minimum of requirements. Nothing could be worse for a steam tramway than the shape of the rails which had been laid down in Paris. He therefore hoped that the difficulties which had been experienced in Paris by Mr. Lyster Holt, whom he was glad to see present, and by others, in regard to the use of tramway engines, would be very much lessened when they began to be used on such rails as had been laid down in Manchester. They would then have a very good and substantial road, and there would not be any necessity for doing what the author had described with approval, viz. adding a pair of small trailing or leading wheels on the engine. He thought any locomotive engineer would say that this would have a very bad result; not because it did not relieve the weight upon the other part of the engine, but because it added so materially to the friction of the engine in working along the streets, and passing round curves. On the contrary, a short wheel-base was needed; but it should always be remembered that the limit of the weight upon any pair of wheels was not determined by the engine, but by the carrying power of the road; therefore, if they had as good a road as that which he believed Barker's to be, they could probably do without the third pair of wheels, working the traffic with a four-wheeled engine, which facilitated getting round curves, and availing themselves of the whole weight of the engine to give adhesion for drawing the tramcar, which, with a greasy surface like that presented by street tramways, was a most important point.

He observed that the proportion of the frictional resistance upon tramways to that on railways, according to page 202 of the paper, was very much what he had himself anticipated when discussing the question in Glasgow last year (Proceedings 1879, p. 402). Looking at the very much higher amount of friction on tramways, he felt sure that, whenever in country places it was possible to establish railways with raised rails, instead of tramways, that course would be permanently economical; but in towns it was of course necessary to have tramways.

Mr. RAPIER explained that by a wide rail he meant a rail at least wide enough for a horse to plant the whole of his shoe upon. He was

not alone in the opinion he had expressed about horses not slipping upon iron surfaces if sufficiently wide. He had lately had some conversation with Mr. George Hopkins, who had had very great experience in tramways, and he was very much mistaken if that gentleman was not of opinion that an iron surface was less slippery than granite.

Mr. A. PAGET said it so happened that he had in his works a granite surface over which horses had to pass. The blocks were about 9 in. wide and 3 ft. long. On fine days he should say that a horse would stand as good a chance of keeping his footing on ice as on that granite. He also had some experience of iron plates about 9 in. wide; and he was sure that on a fine day, when the surface was bright with constant traffic, it was more slippery than ice. It was not the same when it was covered with mud, as it was then gritty, and there was not so much slipping. The iron was more slippery than the granite. The granite pitching in ordinary use was not a flat surface, but a number of narrow irregular edge surfaces with grooves between; and this did not cause horses to slip so much.

Mr. RAPIER said that on the wide tramway he had alluded to, which had been in use for nine years, there was no instance on record of a horse ever having fallen. The traffic along it was continuous, and the horses sought the tramway of their own accord; in fact in one place a chain had to be put up to prevent their going upon it where they were not allowed. This was the Quayside tramway, Glasgow: the rails were of cast iron, 10 in. wide, with a central groove; and it was worked by horse traction, not by steam power. Figs. 35 and 36, Plate 18, were illustrations of the two forms in use: the broader one, Fig. 35, was on the public quays, and was chiefly used by ordinary vehicles without flanged wheels; whilst the narrower type, Fig. 36, was used when the tramway was intended for flanged wheels only. The cost of the broad tramway was about £500 per mile more than that of other tramways, but its cost for maintenance, during nine years of incessant traffic, had been nil. The cast-iron blocks were about 9 in. deep, hollow on the underside, and chilled on the top. They were cast in

lengths of 5 feet, and a few days before they were fixed they were filled with concrete; the ends of the castings also were not entirely closed, so that when the blocks were fixed and cemented to their concrete bed, the concrete in adjacent blocks also became united, and this together with the bed really formed one continuous piece. There was no difficulty from expansion and contraction: it would appear that the great extent of surface in contact with the earth passed off the heat of the sun as rapidly as the exposed surface absorbed it.

Mr. T. R. CRAMPTON observed that the Institution had previously discussed the tramway question with regard to engines, and his impression was now, as it was then, that the matter of the engine was extremely simple; what was wanted was a solid road to put it on. If the road was sufficiently solid to stand the wear and tear of the ordinary street traffic running upon it, it would be strong enough for any locomotive. To obtain that strength and solidity, the principal thing was a solid bottom, taking care to have the stone pitching set closely and solidly against the iron structure, and to keep all the strains in a vertical direction, preventing all vibration along the lines of junction between the rails and the stones. Looking at Barker's system, Fig. 23, Plate 17, from that point of view, it seemed to offer many advantages as compared with Mr. Larsen's system, Figs. 20 and 21. The side action of the traffic, which was of a tremulous nature, must tend to force apart all the connections in the latter system; and he should imagine that it would soon disintegrate the inch or two of concrete placed there. If something more elastic were put in, e.g. concrete mixed with tar, possibly it might not disintegrate; but the road would be much better without it. In Barker's tramway there was simply a solid wall of iron, which could not get away from the adjacent paving stones. The solid concrete filled in between the two sides of the sleeper would become one mass with them, and would be as firm as if of one solid piece. Again, to get a strong road, the strains must be brought vertically on to the foundations; there must be no side action producing a tremulous vibration in the web, as there would be in the case of Larsen's system, Figs. 20 and 21.

Whether the road cost £1000 a mile or £2000 was not a very serious matter. There were so many other expenses connected with tramways that they could afford to spend almost any amount of money in getting a solid foundation. With regard to the estimates however, no information was given as to what was put underneath the base-plates. When a new road was to be made, was it intended to run steam rollers over the road and consolidate it, for two or three months, and then to put down some concrete and consolidate that? He mentioned this because in making the calculations everything ought to be taken into consideration; and in making comparisons the same elements and the same materials should be used. He believed that a great mistake had been made in using the 4 ft. 8½ in. gauge for tramways. A 3-ft. gauge was ample for all purposes. With that gauge everything was more simple, and it was possible to get round the curves more easily.

Mr. W. LYSTER HOLT had no doubt all were unanimous in believing that, sooner or later, steam, or some other mechanical power, would supersede horse traction. He had had great difficulties in Paris with regard to steam traction; but on looking at the rail that was there used (Fig. 11), and the sleeper, which was the same as in Fig. 2, it would be seen that it was practically the same as if a house wall were built without any footings, or as if the old bridge-rail had been laid with a sleeper of exactly the same width as the rail itself. No doubt the permanent way used in Paris would have been far stronger if the sleeper had been turned at right angles, with its width downwards, so as to give greater base, which was what was wanted, whether for horses or for steam.

In Paris it was found that the rail often sank, and the tyres of the engines, being wider than the rail itself, used consequently to ride upon the stones and wear away rapidly; and the jolting also seriously affected the valve-motion. Mr. Robinson had advocated a very narrow rail; but for steam traction, where all the force of the traction was transferred to the rails, there would then be a serious wear and tear of the tyre, which could be only 1 inch or 1¼ in. wide. For horse traction the narrow rail might do very well; but for steam

traction a wider rail was wanted, or else they would still have what had been the great difficulty with steam tramways—the engines being constantly in the shops for repairs.

He agreed that Barker's system was a very good one; but for himself he should prefer Gowan's, for the simple reason that this had in one piece what Barker's had in three pieces. Again, if Mr. Gowan's system was good, Mr. Winby's must be better, because he rolled his rail with the groove in, and so preserved the skin on it, besides effecting a saving in cost. The paper gave a comparison of the cost of various systems, but unfortunately in some cases no figures were given as to the weights; it was therefore impossible really to compare the costs of those systems with others.

Mr. JEREMIAH HEAD observed there was one point which might be further discussed with advantage, namely the question of elasticity. In the early tramways timber sleepers had been almost universally adopted, because it was taken for granted that elasticity was necessary, and could only be secured in that way. But they were now coming to the point when engineers asserted either that sufficient elasticity could be gained with iron, or that elasticity was not wanted at all. Now, during the last two years, he had very frequently walked up and down a part of the North Eastern Railway, where the permanent way was laid upon wrought-iron sleepers—cross sleepers of inverted trough section, known as Mr. Charles Wood's system, and described by him to the Iron and Steel Institute (Journal 1878, p. 83). These iron sleepers had been laid down about two years ago, and had endured an extremely heavy mineral traffic. When they were first laid, and the ballast was fresh, he had observed a decided undulatory action across the sleeper as the wheels passed over it, as well as a torsional movement, giving evidence of considerable elasticity; in fact he thought quite as much as with the wooden sleepers that were laid on the adjoining lines. The ballast had now become packed pretty solid, and there was not so much of that motion to be seen; but the sleepers seemed to be standing well. There was no looseness about the fastenings, and no weak points that he could observe.

It seemed to him that elasticity was not so much a question of wood versus iron, as a question of form. With the deep girder type, as in Fig. 19, he should suppose the rail would be pretty rigid, because of the great depth; but much must depend on what the ballast was composed of below the bottom plate, and how it was packed, which, as Mr. Crampton had pointed out, was not shown. He was rather inclined to think that, whatever was done, there would be sufficient elasticity, even with wrought iron or steel girder rails, and that that elasticity would not of necessity tend to disintegrate the substratum. The conclusion he had come to certainly was that wooden sleepers might be advantageously abandoned, whether for railways or tramways, not only on account of the perishable nature of that material, especially when spikes were driven into it, but also because a far better construction could be made exclusively of iron.

Mr. F. C. WINBY said that, when he had first turned his attention to the different sections of rails used on tramways, he had found it difficult to see the object of using a channel section such as Fig. 7, Plate 15; it could not be for the purpose of strength, because, though there was plenty of metal in the head for compression, there was next to nothing at the bottom for tension. But he soon saw that that rail had been designed, like many others, mainly to facilitate the rolling of the groove in the head of the rail. But a tramrail had to do a certain duty as a girder, to support a rolling load; and he had therefore sketched a rail after the section of a rolled girder, like Fig. 25 or 29, but he saw directly that he could not get it out of the rolls. Then it occurred to him that he might roll the lip A straight, and have it simply turned up in the last groove. He had a trial rolling, and it was successful the first time. There were other features however to be looked to. The ordinary street vehicles were driven over the tramrails on account of their smoothness; but not being of the same gauge, and having no flanges, the wheels of these vehicles ran on the stone setts which were laid next the rails, and forced them below the level of the heads of the rails. Then the wheels of ordinary vehicles, in crossing the tramway, were skidded against the rails; and it was this defect that made street tramways a nuisance. It was therefore

necessary to keep the rail and the adjacent stones strictly to the same level. His first design was to roll a broad bottom flange to the rail, as in Fig. 25, in order to give a bearing surface for the adjacent stone. Those however who were accustomed to rolling deep sections would know the difficulty of rolling a flange 7 or 8 inches wide, and also the difficulty of bending such a section to go round sharp curves. He accordingly preferred to use a longitudinal base-plate, which broke joint with the rail, and which would give a larger bearing surface than could be got with a rail alone. He had now laid about 30 miles of this line.

He could not see any advantage in Mr. Larsen's rail, Figs. 20 and 21, from its having the head separate from the web and foot, since a grooved rail could now be rolled solid; it was all very well to use a combination of the kind before that could be accomplished. The head could, of course, be easily changed; but the stones at each side would still have to be removed, and therefore there would be very little extra difficulty in moving the rail altogether, as in his own system. But the life of a rail was in fact so long that the extra amount of weight in the compound system would more than balance the saving in renewal.

He had had some experience of Barker's system. He had seen it laid in Manchester, where the Corporation had now arranged to lay his own line in preference to Mr. Barker's, simply because the latter had not the vertical strength required to distribute the weight longitudinally. In fact he very much questioned whether that rail would of itself carry more than 2 tons on 3-ft. bearings without serious deflection; whereas his own rail, as in Fig. 29, weighing 58 lbs. per yard, and 6 in. deep, had carried 20 tons without any perceptible deflection, and 30 tons without any permanent set, and with slight deflection. It was necessary to have a rail of something like that strength, in order to carry locomotives. Barker's system was really a series of cast-iron shoes, only 3 ft. in length, and simply fished by the rail; hence, like a chain, they would follow all the undulations of the road. With regard to the cast-iron bottom flanges, which were ½ inch thick, it might be true that they would suffice to carry a reasonable weight; but a ½-inch flange that could be broken with a hand hammer would surely not do for Manchester traffic. Heavy loads coming across it, such as boilers or locomotives, would break off such a flange very easily.

It had been suggested that the width of the gauge should be less than that of ordinary vehicles. He was now laying down generally a 3-ft. gauge, which was quite sufficient, and gave room to put the wheels under the seats of the tramcar, while admitting of a good passage, nearly 3 ft. wide, along the middle of the car.

As to elasticity, this appeared to him to be unnecessary. Elasticity could only be for the purpose of smoothing down inequalities; but in a tramway it might be the means of bringing two inequalities together, and make matters worse. A tramway should have a good bearing surface on a strong base-plate, carefully and truly laid; then with wheels perfectly concentric and balanced, the tramcars would run perfectly smooth. He did not mean to suggest a road so unyielding and rigid as would break before it bent; but the idea of having an elastic rail, where there was a solid pavement, seemed to him to be very absurd.

Mr. Rapier had stated that he had laid a line which formed one solid piece $2\frac{1}{4}$ miles in length. In his own practice he generally reversed the rail, laid the base-plate upon it, riveted it up, and turned it over into its place; and he had turned over 200 yards at a time in that way. He thought that was very good work, and formed quite a sufficient length to have in one piece.

With regard to the flanges of the wheels wearing down to an acute angle, as represented in Fig. 30, according to his own experience the angle was much more obtuse than that shown. He had had cars running with a flange not more than $\frac{3}{16}$ inch deep, and they had taken the curves and ran round splendidly; there was not a single case of their running off. That showed clearly that there was no necessity to have such large grooves or such large flanges. He generally made the head of his rail about $2\frac{3}{4}$ in. in width. With so narrow a rail the wear and tear of the tyres, in locomotives, would certainly be very heavy; but it did not take up so much of the road, and was scarcely seen. In Nottingham, where he had laid 12 miles of line with this rail, he ventured to say that a stranger going there

u

would never know from simply driving over it that there was a tramway there at all. It had been down two years; and on one curve of 35 ft. radius, where not fewer than 180,000 cars passed every year, there was not the slightest perceptible wear. He had not used any concrete, but had simply consolidated the ground underneath: owing to the rail having such a large bearing surface there was no necessity for concrete in any case. The space under the rail-head was filled in with one part Portland cement to five parts sand; and having had occasion to take up a piece of line that had been down two years, he had had great difficulty in getting the cement away from the side of the rail. The strength of his system was so far beyond what it had to do, that there was no tremulous motion upon it.

Mr. R. PRICE WILLIAMS said it would be of great value if, from the author's experience of eleven years, he could give the average annual cost of maintenance for some of the systems referred to. He had been very much struck with what Mr. Lynde had said with reference to the Barker rail at Manchester, namely that there had been practically no repairs at all for two or three years. Of course if that were generally the case, it would be a very important point in its favour. The main part of the question, at least as set forth in the title of the paper—the endurance of the permanent way under steam traction—had been scarcely referred to. From his experience in railway permanent way, and looking dispassionately at this subject, he thought a great many of the designs now shown would meet with the same fate that many early forms of railway permanent way had met with, e.g. on the Liverpool and Manchester line. Directly these designs—at all events those that were composed of so many parts— were subjected to the action of a locomotive, his notion was that they would give way. With all deference to Mr. Robinson's preference for the Barker system, he must say, judging from his own experience and looking forward to the necessary advent of steam locomotion, that the more simple form of rail, such as that of Gowan or Winby, supplied those elements of permanency which he did not see in the others. Engineers were now feeling their way with regard to the permanent way of tramways, just as they did in the case of railways.

Many members could remember, as he did, the time when Mr. Bridges Adams gave an exhaustive paper on the permanent way of railways (Proceedings Inst. C. E., vol. xvi. p. 226). A great variety of designs for permanent way were then discussed, all of which (Mr. Adams's included) had since disappeared.

He had recently been giving a good deal of attention to the subject of train-resistance, and he was certainly much surprised to find that Mr. Larsen's experiments with a dynamometer should give such a large amount of resistance as $18 \cdot 2$ lbs. per ton on a tramway. He dissented entirely from the reason stated for this in the paper (p. 202)—that it "may be in some measure due to the build of the cars, inasmuch as they have a very short wheel-base, and considerable overhanging weight at either end." On the contrary, Mr. Fisher, the chief engineer of the Taff Vale Railway, had always maintained, and it appeared to him with much reason, that the very short wheel-base used on that line was the very cause why the train-resistance was so small: therefore he thought some other reason than that assigned in the paper must be found. It should not be forgotten that in the groove of a tramway there was a *dirt* resistance, which might in a great measure account for the higher friction; and he thought there ought to be a disposition to deepen the groove on that account.

He could not agree that with the advent of steam locomotion elasticity could be done away with. It was now found in the case of railways that, with a more perfect substructure, a very much more solid road could be laid than formerly; and that weight as weight in the rail itself had, as Sir John Hawkshaw had said, a decided value. He thought therefore that with road tramways engineers ought not to go to the other extreme of having too light a rail; nor could they do entirely without elasticity. It might very well be, as Mr. Head had maintained, that an iron sleeper supplied in itself sufficient elasticity; but elasticity as an element in a durable road could not in his opinion be done away with.

Mr. JOHN ROBINSON would ask Mr. Larsen what was the section of the tramway rails which in his experiments of 1870 gave a resistance

u 2

of $18 \cdot 2$ lbs. per ton; because that was an important item in the question.

Mr. C. E. COWPER asked whether, with regard to the newer systems which the author had so well described, he could mention where they had been in use, and with what success. With regard to horses liking to trot on iron rails, if wide enough, even if that were true, it must be remembered that, on a road where a tramway was laid, the traffic was generally considerable, and horses could not always be on the iron, but only stepped on to it now and then, when crossing the tramway at various angles, in passing other vehicles. Hence it appeared to him that the effect was the same as when, in walking on a good pavement, a person suddenly stepped upon a piece of orange-peel or an ice-slide; he would then be much more liable to fall than if walking across a frozen pond. If the rail must be made wide enough for the horses' hoofs to be always fully upon it, as had been suggested by Mr. Rapier, he did not see how that could be accomplished unless the rail was the full width of the road.

Mr. W. SCHÖNHEYDER asked what was the actual practice in paving close up to the rail, as shown in Figs. 19 or 23; whether the paving setts were dressed to the exact depth necessary, so as to rest on the iron, or were packed up with concrete or cement underneath.

Mr. WINBY said in the 30 miles of tramway that he had laid on his system, he had always packed up the setts underneath with about $\frac{3}{4}$ in. of sand, which had been rammed down to about $\frac{1}{2}$ in.

The PRESIDENT observed that good setts properly dressed were very accurate in point of depth; and of course they would be properly made to fit the height of the rail. He partly agreed with what Mr. Crampton had said in reference to the severe shocks that tramrails received from the ordinary road traffic. He did not think that the weight of a light locomotive running along the tramway would produce anything like the same stress upon the rail, as a heavy weight passing *across* it. In the latter case the whole weight came suddenly upon one point, whereas with a tramway engine the weight would be more distributed, and there would be nothing like the same shock.

Reference had been made to the rails being wide or narrow. He himself complained of the *grooves* being so wide, which he thought was one of the greatest reproaches to the present tramways. Many of those who designed tramrails did not seem to care anything about the carriages and other vehicles that would pass over them, but only about the wheels of their own cars. If some of those wheel-flanges wore to such an extreme thinness as shown in Fig. 30, why could not very thin steel flanges be used to start with—say $\frac{1}{4}$ in. or $\frac{5}{16}$ in.—and new ones be put on when they were worn out? The rails could then have narrow grooves, and the ordinary wheels would not drop into them. He threw out that suggestion because some of the grooves now in use seemed exactly designed to tear the wheels off a carriage; and that was in fact a thing which constantly happened.

Mr. LYNDE asked leave to mention that some very heavy loads had gone over Barker's rails in Manchester, but he was not aware of any of the flanges having ever been broken off.

Mr. LARSEN said, in reply, that little fault had been found with the paper, in regard to the different modes of construction mentioned; but he wished to make an apology to several gentlemen who had desired to have their systems described. As the paper was limited in extent, he could only refer to those methods which he thought most to be recommended in point of construction and of first cost. He was sorry he had not been able to obtain sufficient information to lay before the meeting as to the places where the different systems were in use, and the length of time they had been down. In regard to Mr. Barker's system, on his last visit to Manchester he came to the conclusion that the tramways there were the best he had ever seen in any city (and he had been nearly all over Europe); but nevertheless the sleepers were of cast iron, and he thought, if the paving stones were rammed there as they were in London and in many other cities, the cast-iron sleepers would be smashed continually; whereas a rolled

plate would stand any blow. That was the only objection in reality to Mr. Barker's system. The placing of the support directly under the load, as described by Mr. Lynde, was all in the right direction; but he considered that the single-rail systems were equally strong, being on just the same principle as the ordinary Vignoles rail.

The President and others had referred to the depth and width of the groove. He might mention that the Board of Trade had now adopted a rule that no groove should be more than 1 in. wide and $1\frac{1}{8}$ in. deep. That might be admirable from the point of view that a tramway should be so laid as not to be noticed; but he pitied the horses that had to drag the cars along such a groove. Mr. Robinson had asked what kind of rail was used in his experiments at New Cross. It was the rail shown in Fig. 7, Plate 15; and the cars had American wheels, which had deep and broad flanges. No doubt the fact of the wheels being new and the gauge tight had something to do with the high resistance; and also the fact that the rails deflected considerably. Since that time a great many improvements had been made in wheels.

With regard to the question of first cost, it was all very well in the case of such towns as Manchester or Liverpool to construct tramways in the very best way without reference to expense; but in outlying districts, and in lines worked by a company, the question of economy in first cost was a very important one, because it was necessary to make the lines pay.

With reference to the use of steam, the section of rail in Fig. 17 was that on which most of the steam traffic in Paris had been carried; but, as he had stated in the paper, he was limited as to weight with that rail; consequently it was made hollow underneath, and thereby its stiffness was diminished. With reference to the observations of Mr. Holt, he could only repeat that the lines on which steam had been tried had never been originally constructed for it.

With regard to the number of wheels for tramway engines, he might point out that most of the engines now used had four driving wheels and two uncoupled leading wheels; and that was a great improvement, because the leading wheels took any blow that might

be given by a joint, and bent the joint down so that the centre wheels followed easily over. They also prevented the great oscillation caused by the overhang, where so short a wheel-base was used as was generally the case in both tramway engines and cars: with both of which this oscillation was very serious, wherever a slight fault existed in the permanent way. Of course the two uncoupled wheels were capable of taking a radial position.

Mr. Crampton had enquired about the foundations usually employed below the sleeper. With the systems shown in Figs. 19, 20, and 21, Plate 16, he used 6 inches of concrete, and that was the usual depth. As to the setts, the arrangement simply was that, if the road was to have a 6-in. pavement, the girder was rolled accordingly to suit that depth.

He could not admit that Mr. Winby's rail was superior to that in Fig. 20. If the latter was worn out, and had to be renewed, all that was necessary would be to take out the bolts and replace the rail with a new one; whereas in Mr. Winby's or Mr. Gowan's rail, the whole would have to be cast away as scrap. Mr. Gowan's rail, Fig. 25, was 92 lbs. per yard; whereas the whole structure in Fig. 20 would be something like 72 lbs. per yard. That was a great consideration in the first cost, and also in regard to maintenance. Mr. Price Williams had asked a question as to cost of maintenance; so far however the maintenance of tramways had really not been gone into. The matter was a great deal mixed up with other expenses, and there was great difficulty in getting at the actual results.

The PRESIDENT proposed a vote of thanks to Mr. Larsen for his paper.

The vote of thanks was carried.

———

The Meeting was then adjourned till the following evening.

———

The Adjourned Meeting of the Institution was held at the Institution of Civil Engineers, London, on Friday, 23rd April, 1880, at half-past seven o'clock, p.m.; EDWARD A. COWPER, Esq., President, in the chair.

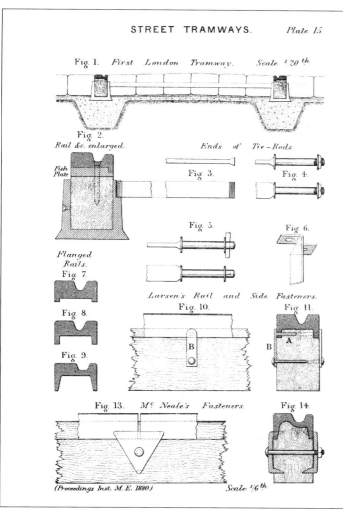

STREET TRAMWAYS. *Plate 15.*

Fig. 1. *First London Tramway.* Scale ¹⁄₂₀th

Fig. 2.
Rail &c. enlarged.

Ends of Tie-Rods.

Fig. 3.

Fig. 4.

Fish Plate

Fig. 5.

Fig. 6.

Flanged Rails.

Fig. 7.

Fig. 8.

Fig. 9.

Larsen's Rail and Side Fasteners.

Fig. 10.

Fig. 11.

Fig. 13. *Mc Neale's Fasteners.*

Fig. 14.

(*Proceedings Inst. M. E. 1880.*) Scale ¹⁄₆th

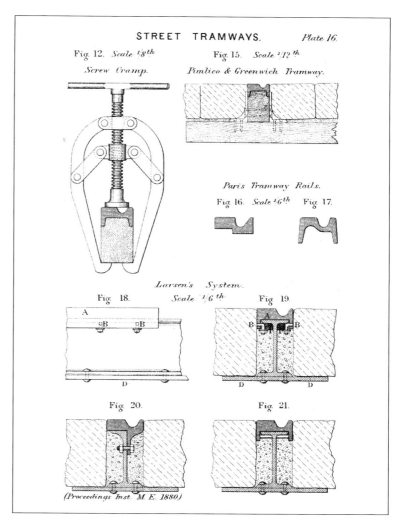

STREET TRAMWAYS. *Plate 16.*

Fig. 12. Scale ⅛th

Screw Cramp.

Fig. 15. Scale ¹⁄₁₂th

Pimlico & Greenwich Tramway.

Paris Tramway Rails.

Fig. 16. Scale ¹⁄₆th

Fig. 17.

Larsen's System.

Fig. 18. Scale ¹⁄₆th

Fig. 19.

Fig. 20.

Fig. 21.

(*Proceedings Inst. M. E. 1880.*)

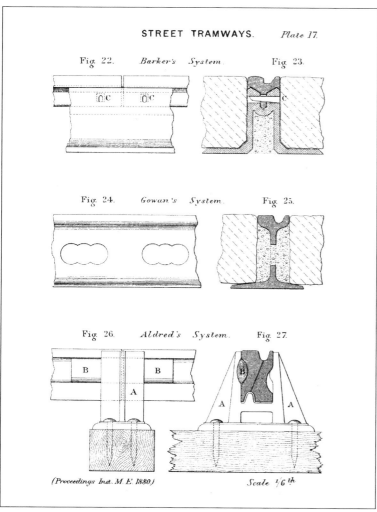

STREET TRAMWAYS. *Plate 17.*

Fig. 22. *Barker's System.* Fig. 23.

Fig. 24. *Gowan's System.* Fig. 25.

Fig. 26. *Aldred's System.* Fig. 27.

(*Proceedings Inst. M. E. 1880.*) Scale ¹⁄₆th

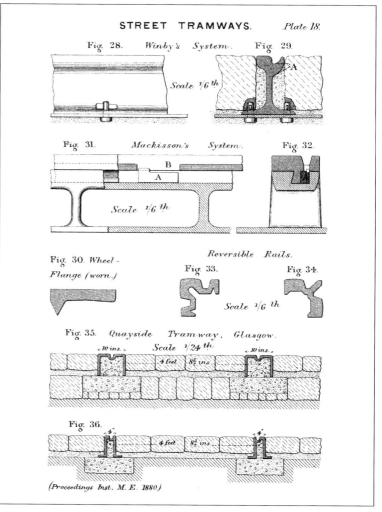

STREET TRAMWAYS. *Plate 18.*

Fig. 28. *Winby's System.* Fig. 29.

Scale ¹⁄₆th

Fig. 31. *Mackisson's System.* Fig. 32.

Scale ¹⁄₆th

Fig. 30. *Wheel-Flange (worn.)*

Reversible Rails.

Fig. 33.

Fig. 34.

Scale ¹⁄₆th

Fig. 35. *Quayside Tramway, Glasgow.*

Scale ¹⁄₂₄th

10 ins. 4 feet 8½ ins. 10 ins.

Fig. 36.

4 feet 8½ ins.

(*Proceedings Inst. M. E. 1880.*)

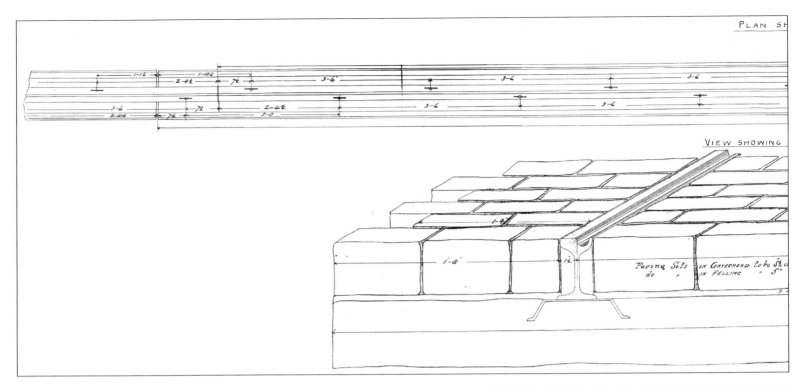

VIEW SHOWING

Kerr's Patent Rail Formation

Any form of trackwork had to be tested, but for financial reasons this was often not before it was in service. Pricing had to be competitive – often by open tender – and each different profile had to be approved not only by the tramways' engineer, but finally by the Board of Trade representative – usually our old friend, Major-General Hutchinson R.E. The handwritten note tells us what could happen after a few years running.

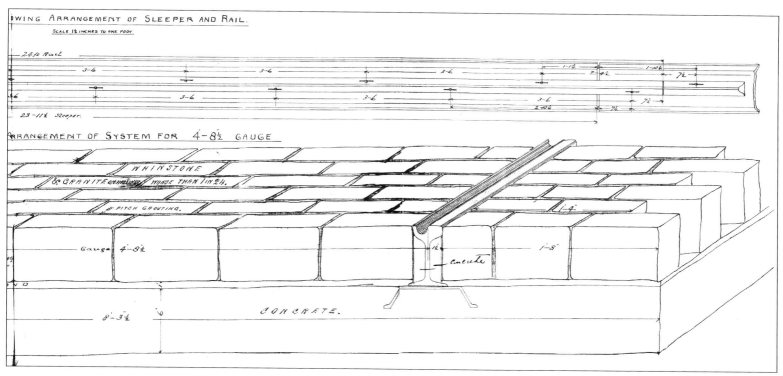

DWING ARRANGEMENT OF SLEEPER AND RAIL.

SCALE 1½ INCHES TO ONE FOOT.

ARRANGEMENT OF SYSTEM FOR 4-8½ GAUGE

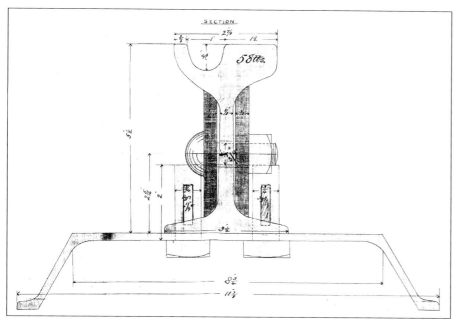

**Plan and Section for Kerr's Patent
form of trackwork.**

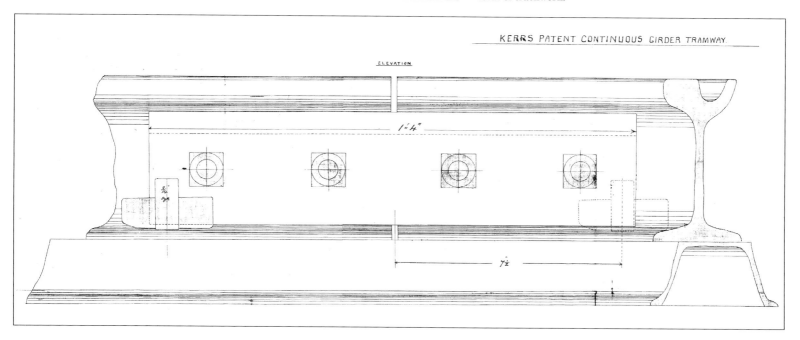

KERRS PATENT CONTINUOUS GIRDER TRAMWAY.

ELEVATION

Debates – Accrington

Although strictly speaking the following belongs within the story of the Accrington Tramways nonetheless it also deserves to be here as a stand-alone item; the debates within councils over when, where and how to build tramways were almost invariably acrimonious and given the hours and hours the Councillors spent debating the matter amid political and social struggles (typically, when one Councillor asked for a ruling his 'colleague' was reported to have replied "(with a sneering laugh): Th' old song". That is a literal quotation and many meetings were punctuated with cries of "Humbug", "You are a liar and a cad Sir" "You altered the balance sheet" and similar items.

The type of oblique comment that turned up and was faithfully recorded included in January 1885: "Councillor Sprake said Alderman Hindle had referred to his not pointing out that Mr Sharples tender was the lowest. Alderman Hindle could not have forgotten that at the General Purposes Committee he pointed out that Mr Sharples' tender was less and that at that meeting there was not one got up and contradicted it, because it was impossible to do so. Alderman Hindle had further said that Mr Sharples never asked to attend the meeting. Mr Sharples did ask, and attended, in the vestibule of the Town Hall on two occasions, and he was refused admission, though Mr Plowden [a partner in Green & Burleigh, the chosen contractor] was on one occasion paid £5 for attending."

However we must remember many Councillors were shop-keepers, builders and the like; even an iron-master or colliery owner might only employ 30 or 40 men.

The James Moorby who wrote the letter which ends this item to the *Accrington Gazette* was a Councillor of the Conservative flavour; the Town Clerk, a Liberal who at one time boycotted the Gazette. They reacted by giving plenty of space to their friends. Two quotations may explain why it is sometimes difficult even using Minute Books to understand the internal machinations of 1880s politics. This is from a *Gazette* editorial: "During the late Town Clerk's time the *Gazette* was frequently ignored, and when Mr Aitken succeeded him we inquired from that gentleman if he intended to pursue the same course. Mr Aitken was at first very testy; our opposition to his appointment had nettled him, and when he was first seen he said in the course of his remarks that he neither knew where the Gazette was printed, nor who were the proprietors, nor did he care. It was clear that Mr Aitken had been displeased with us because we had advocated the appointment of a local solicitor as Mr Whittaker's successor to the Town Clerkship in preference to an inexperienced young man – and a stranger too – whose principal recommendation was that he was the son-in-law of Mr John Eastham."

Next came the question of corruption and in one form and another (often only innuendo) this seems to have bedevilled the whole story of steam tramways not only in towns like Accrington, but cities including Manchester where the bribery was blatant: "... it is equally improper and it ought to be illegal, for a gas director or shareholder to occupy a seat in the Council and sell gas to the Corporation. On that ground Alderman Rhodes ought not to be in the Council, and on the same ground Mr John Eastham, of Clitheroe, as the solicitor to the Gas Company, ought not to be the adviser of the Corporation. We may go further, too, and say that on the same ground Mr A.H. Aitken, who is connected with Mr Eastham as a partner in business, ought not to occupy the position of Town Clerk. Alderman Rhodes has, perhaps, neglected to attend the Council meetings for above 2½ years because of this. But he has taken care to keep possession of the seat, and he took care to attend the Council meeting to vote for the appointment of Mr Aitken to the Town Clerkship, which we say was a most improper thing to do."

Nowadays when a loaf of bread costs over £1 and the Government blithely budget for zillions of pounds expenditure to enrich railway companies (would we railwaymen had had Government subsidies like that in BR days before we had profit-takers) then £32,000 is nothing, but a comparison lies in the fine for drunk and disorderly at 12½p, a big bowl of hot pease pudding cost 1p, a meal 2½p and for stealing 12½p from a trader this was so great a sum that a 12 year-old boy was taken to Court: "P.C. Hodgson said he apprehended prisoner at his residence, 35 Dowry-street, on the same night. He brought him to the police station, and after searching him found the half-crown in his possession. In answer to the charge prisoner replied 'Yes, I stole it'. Mrs Dawson, who appeared in court, said she had had a great deal of trouble with her son, and he was always staying away from school. She hoped the bench would punish him severely. Prisoner was ordered to receive eight strokes with the birch rod." A condign punishment reflecting the seriousness of the crime.

"ACCRINGTON TRAMWAYS

Sir, – During the last week in October last, there were issued for electioneering and other purposes, two statements attempting to show which of two tenders were the lowest, and that would give the lowest cost for the construction and equipment of the lines and depot, and for leasing the same for five years, the said cost to be computed at the end or termination of the said lease, the said two tenders being those of Messrs Green and Burleigh and of John Sharples. One statement being issued by Alderman Hindle and Councillor Thomas Whittaker, and which sets forth that Messrs Green and Burleigh's tender has a balance in their favour, as compared with Mr John Sharples' of £1,876.14s.9d., whilst the other statement issued by John Sharples and D.L. Sprake, claim to have a balance in favour of the tender of John Sharples of £123.5s.3d., making together a difference of say £2,000. Now, sir, this large difference together with the matter appearing again in the Council Chamber on Monday last, induced the writer, who is a member of the General Works Committee, and who attended most of the meetings when the two tenders (amongst others) were being considered, discussed and finally decided upon – to again review the matter in dispute. After having done so, and found as he thought both statements incorrect, he prepared a statement of the facts as he conceived them, but upon rising in the Council for the purpose of giving his statement, he was ruled as being out of order. I will therefore venture to ask leave through year paper to make known to the public the true state of the matter, and for this purpose it will be necessary that I should put in four letters from Green and Burleigh, and two from John Sharples. Most of the said letters having been read at the Council meeting, and so having become public, I have not hesitation in giving them."

1st letter dated September 8th, 1883. – "8, Suffolk Lane, London. To the Chairman and members of the General Works Committee, – Gentlemen, – Herewith we have pleasure to hand you tender for construction of your tramway line and depot for the amount of £51,176, also tender to lease same at 6 per cent on above amount for five years, it being understood that the tender for leasing is contingent on your acceptance of our tender for construction. We may, however, mention that we would be willing to construct the lines and depot, but without equipping and leasing same, for the sum of £336,000. We are, &c, GREEN AND BURLEIGH."

2nd letter. – "September 17th, 1883. – 8, Suffolk-lane, London. – To the Town Council. – Gentlemen, – In further reference to our tender to you for the constructing and leasing of your tramways, we beg to state that we hereby agree in the event of our tender being accepted to hand over to you at the expiration of the five years lease the whole of the rolling stock and equipment, in good condition and efficient working order, free of cost to you (and should any of the engines and carriages not be in working order, we will replace same with new). We will furthermore agree to do all the necessary repairs, and keep the permanent way and paving in good condition to the satisfaction of your engineer, during the same period, we agreeing, as per tender, to pay you interest at the rate of 6 per cent per annum, we paying rates and taxes; and we are further willing, in case of the line paying a higher dividend that this, to agree to hand over to you such increase, the same to be verified by inspection of our traffic books and documents by your Borough Accountant. We shall, if you accept our offer, put on as large a service of cars and engines as can work the line to the greatest profit. P.S. – If we can offer any further explanation, our Mr Burleigh, who is now in Accrington, will be pleased to attend upon you either this evening or anytime to-morrow up to three o'clock. – Signed, &c, GREEN AND BURLEIGH."

3rd letter. – "October 9th, 1883, 8, Suffolk-lane, London. To the Chairman and members of the General Works Committee. Gentlemen, – Referring to our previous correspondence in regard to our tender for tramway, we find, on going through the quantities, that our Mr Burleigh had based his calculations on a 4ft. 8½ in. gauge instead of a 4ft. gauge, and we are now therefore enabled to submit you the following proposal: – 1. We are willing to construct and equip your lines and depot as per specification for the sum of £40,500, and to lease same, guaranteeing you 4 per cent interest on above amount for the space of five years, and in addition pay to you 4 per cent on initial cost of your obtaining the Act for same, and for a like period, it being understood that the equipment shall be your property at the end of lease, and be handed to you worth £6,000 for working purposes, any value above or below that sum to be ascertained by valuation, and shall be allowed between us and the Corporation as such valuation may determine. 2. We will construct your lines and depot as per specification for the sum of £29,850. – Signed, &c, GREEN AND BURLEIGH."

4th letter. – "October 9th, 1883. 8, Suffolk-lane, London. Re-amended tender. The Chairman of General Works Committee. Dear Sir, – Referring to our amended proposal of even date, we omitted to state therein that in the event of same being accepted we would, at our own expense, apply for powers to extend the line into Oswaldtwistle, our powers to revert to the Corporation at the expiration of five years, subject to the provision of the Act or order. We also omitted to state that we would be willing to relieve you of the expense of maintaining the tram lines for which you have obtained the Act during our five years' lease, instead of same being maintained by you, as mentioned in the specification, and that our guaranteed percentage will date from the signing of the joint contract. – Signed, &c, GREEN AND BURLEIGH."

1st Letter, from John Sharples. – "Accrington, September 13th, 1883. To the Chairman and members of the General Works Committee. Gentlemen, – I will undertake, for the sum of £16,500, in addition to my tender, viz., £31,995 for the construction of the tramways, to fully equip and work the lines for five years, and pay you 5 ½ per cent on the total cost, and find you satisfactory security. – Signed, JOHN SHARPLES."

2nd Letter, from John Sharples. – "Accrington, September 17th, 1883. To the Chairman and members of the General Works Committee. Gentlemen, – Will you please allow me to withdraw my last letter, and substitute the following: – I will agree in accordance with your specification and form of tender, to lease the tramway and pay you 3½ per cent on my tender for constructing the same. Should any explanation be required, I shall have pleasure in meeting your committee. – Signed, &c., JOHN SHARPLES."

Now, Sir, in the preceding six letters lies the proof of which of the two contracts was most favourable to the Corporation, in point of cost for the same materials and other advantages. Alongside you have the result: –

	£ s. d.	£ s. d.
Messrs Green and Burleigh's tender for construction of lines and depot, And equipping with rolling stock and working plant		49,500 0 0
Agreed to pay as rent on £40,000, and also on the initial cost of obtaining the Act (£1,800), £42,500 at 4 per cent, as per letter, would give a yearly rent of £1,692, or for 5 years	8,460 0 0	
agreed to apply for Act or order for running into Oswaldtwistle £1,500, say it would cost them	1,000 0 0	
Agreed to repair the permanent way and paving for four years, at a cost say of	500 0 0	
Agreed to pay in advance six months rent, say	847 0 0	10,807 0 0
Take £10,807 from £40,500, and it would leave a balance		29,693 0 0
Mr John Sharples's tender for construction of lines and depot		31,995 0 0
Add a similar amount for cost of equipping and furnishing with working plant to be paid by Corporation		10,000 0 0
Would make a total cost as per John Sharples 41,995 ... 0	0	
Agreed to lease and pay 4 per cent on £31,995 would give a yearly rent of say £1,120, or for 5 years		5,600 0 0
Would leave a balance of cost on John Sharples's tender		36,395 0 0
Take Green and Burleigh's balance off		29,693 0 0
Would leave a balance in favour of Green and Burleigh		6,702 0 0
Or if we take off the three disputed items, viz, £1,000, £500, and £847		2,347 0 0
Balance still in favour of Green and Burleigh's tender		4,355 0 0

Ratepayers examine for yourselves the above, as the writer feels confident that they will be found correct, barring £5.17s.6d. loss through omitting calculation of shillings. – Yours truly,
JAMES MOORBY
5, Hyndburn-terrace, Accrington
January 8th, 1885.

12

SPECIFICATION OF WORKS AND MATERIALS.

35. The Contractor to excavate and remove the present pavement or macadam as the case   Excavations. may be, for a width of 8 feet 6 inches along each Tramway track to the depth of 13 inches below the finished line shown upon the sections.

The limestone or granite and also the setts taken up to be carefully kept seperate from any other kind of material, and stacked for use at the sides of the road in such manner and in such positions as may be directed by the Engineer or his Clerk of Works. The underbedding to be used (after being washed as hereinafter specified) by the Contractor in the preparation of concrete. The Contractor to remove any earth, clay, or other excavation necessary to a tip to be provided at his own expense.

36. The bed thus excavated to have 7 inches of concrete put in for the whole width.   Concrete.
The concrete shall be composed of broken stone, coarse sand, or fine gravel, and Portland cement, mixed in the following proportions :—

           Broken stone..................Four parts.
           Coarse sand or fine gravel...Two parts.
           Portland cement..............One part.

37. The Contractor may use the underbedding excavated as above named, which must be   Stone. thoroughly washed if necessary, to remove all dirt or earthy matter, and broken to pass through a ring 2 inches in diameter.

Any underbedding left, to be the property of the Contractor.

38. The sand or gravel shall be clean, sharp, Altham river, or Duckworth Hall sand, properly   Sand. screened, and free from all impurities.

39. The whole of the cement shall be the best quality Portland cement, weighing   Cement. not less than 112 lbs. to the imperial striked bushel, and shall not leave more than 10 per cent. residue on a No. 50 sieve. The cement shall be capable of bearing a tensile strain of 350 lbs. on a sectional area of one square inch, eight days after being made in a mould, and immersed in water during the interval of seven days. The tests to be made by the Engineer, out of at least every tenth two bushel sack. The cement is to be brought on the works in a fit state for use from special stores provided by the Contractor, and under the control of the Engineer, but it is not to be used until sanctioned. Such cement to be applied as soon as mixed, and unless so applied shall be rejected and removed. The Corporation will provide a proper machine and moulds for testing the cement.

40. The concrete shall be mixed on clean portable mixing boards, formed of planks tongued   Mode of Mixing. and grooved together, and provided with ledges one foot high round three sides. Separate boxes to be employed to measure each ingredient of which the concrete is to be composed, such boxes to be made to hold the exact proportions of each material.

Not more than half-a-yard of concrete is to be mixed at one time on each board. The materials to be turned over twice in a dry state, and twice with a sufficient quantity of water, which must be applied through a finely perforated rose, and provided by and at the expense of the Contractor.

The concrete to be thoroughly well pounded with a heavy beater after it has been placed in position, and the top surface shall be carefully formed to the required curvature and floated over with fine concrete and a smooth surface obtained with a flat implement specially made for the purpose.

13

No traffic shall be allowed upon the concrete, or any paving setts placed upon it until four days after the concrete has been finished. The Contractor shall also during such time protect the concrete from rain or wet.

Extra Concrete where sewers are put in.

41. In those parts of roads where sewers have been lately put in the Contractor shall excavate an extra depth of six inches, to fully eighteen inches either side of the trench, and fill up such space with concrete.

Paving.

42. After the time specified above has elapsed, and the sleepers, rails, &c., have been properly fixed, the Contractor shall provide and lay upon the concrete a layer or bed of clean river sand or very fine gravel not exceeding one inch in thickness to receive the paving.

The Tramway lines to be paved between the rails, and for a width outside each rail of eighteen inches, ~~making... as heretofore specified~~

The setts to be laid in regular and straight courses at right angles with the lines of Tramway, the joints to be crossed not less than one third the length the sett.

All setts abutting upon the rails are to be guaged to depth and are not to be more or less than the depth shown on the respective sections. These setts shall be most carefully and properly laid with each course truly at right angles to the rail, and having a bond of at least four inches or half the length of the sett.

Paving at Crossings.

43. The setts shall be neatly and carefully filled up and trimmed at all crossings, points and junctions, the stones being carefully picked and properly dressed, so as to closely fit and fill up between the rails, and where directed the angles shall be filled with special castings.

Racking.

44. After the paving, the joints of the setts shall be filled with perfectly clean and dry granite chippings, free from dust, and passed through a ¾ inch riddle and retained by a ¼ inch mesh; the setts shall be well rammed, and new chippings applied until the joints are full. The ramming to leave the paving so finished as to present a regular curved surface throughout, not exceeding ⅜th of an inch above the rails.

Grouting.

45. The joints to be thoroughly run with a mixture of boiled tar pitch and creosote oil, of such a consistency as shall be approved by the Engineer. No partially filled joints will be allowed, and the pitch is to be poured out of buckets and not out of vessels with spouts.

Tarpaulins.

46. A sufficient quantity of tarpaulin sheets must be provided by the Contractor to protect the paving from wet before it is grouted, and he will not be permitted to grout any paving that is in the slightest degree wet.

Binding Pavement.

47. After the pavement has been grouted it shall be blinded with a layer of sharp granite chippings half an inch thick.

Bonding with other Pavement.

48. When the rails are laid through those portions of the road shown on the plan as intended to be paved the whole width of the street or where crossings are shown, the paving is to be [*with the rest of the carriageway as the case may be*] of the carriage-way properly bonded, &c. applies equally to these portions and crossings.

Setts.

49. The setts to be 5 in. by 3 in. and of mixed lengths, in order to secure cross joints when laid. They are to be of true and uniform shape, squarely cut, and not tapering towards the base. None will be accepted that are less than 4¾ in. or more than 5¾ in. deep. They are to be of a quality approved by the Engineer, and from either Newhall's Dalbeattie Quarries, Welsh Granite Co, Cumberland Road Metal Co, Robinson's, Belfast, or Brundrit's Pwllheli Quarries, and in such quantities and put in such part of the route as shall be directed by the Engineer.

14

Laying of Tramways.

Keys and Keying.

50. The Contractor to provide wrought iron keys of the best quality, and such only will be approved by the Engineer; the keys to be of various sizes as may be required. After fixing they are all to be tapped with a two pound hammer, and if loose, larger ones are to be driven in place of them. Every keyway is to be keyed.

Bed for Sleepers.

51. The Contractor is to prepare the bed for, and to bed and lay the cast iron sleepers to a true and even line, and to the proper guage, and in the exact positions shewn on the drawings, and to such levels as will ensure the paving setts when fixed being at the proper height. The hollow of every sleeper must be filled with fine concrete, and every sleeper must be bedded completely solid in a layer of the same material. The Contractor is to punch or drill all holes rendered specially necessary during the laying of the lines, he is also to fix all such special castings and other material necessary for the due completion of the work. He is likewise to dress off, straighten or otherwise rectify any irregularities that may be found in any castings, that may in the opinion of the Engineer be necessary for the better fitting and finishing of the works.

The Contractor is to fix the steel rails in their places after having first tarred the grooves for their reception, he is also to cut all rails that may be required, also bend all rails that may require it to make them fit the curves, to put in all points and crossings, and to take care when it can possibly be done not to have the joints of the rails opposite to each other on the same track.

Cast Iron Sleepers, Parker's Patent.

52. The Contractor to provide all cast iron sleepers, points, crossings and special castings necessary for the due completion of the works in accordance with the forms, weights and dimensions shewn on the drawings.

The castings must not be hard or brittle, and are to be made from re-melted iron of a quality and mixture to be approved by the Engineer, containing not less than one sixth part of scrap, they are to be finished true, with clean and even surfaces free from sand and air holes and all other imperfections.

Great attention must be paid to the top surfaces of the sleepers, they must be finished without any roughness or uneveness and perfectly straight, every casting to be true and out of winding, so that the rail may bed exactly on them for the entire length, and each casting not corresponding with the above requirements will be rejected

Tests.

53. The Contractor to state in his Tender the description and proportions of the different kinds of iron he proposes to use in the castings. Test bars are to be cast at such times as the Engineer may require, 3ft. 6in. long, 1in. broad, and 2in. deep. The Engineer will then see them tested by being placed edgewise on bearings three feet apart; the load is then to be placed on the middle of the bar, and should it break with any weight less than 27 cwt. all casting from that metal will be rejected The Contractor is at his own expense to perform the tests, in the presence of the Engineer or his authorized assistant, who is also to have the power to reject any castings which he may consider of insufficient quality or workmanship.

Holes.

54. The holes for the keys must be of the exact size and shape shewn on drawing No. and no hole shall vary more than one-sixteenth of an inch from the position shewn on the drawings. The holes must be left quite clean and of full size throughout.

Weight of Sleepers.

55. The weight of each sleeper of 2ft. 11in. in length must not be less than 110lbs; any sleeper that may be required of less length must be of the same proportionate weights.

All special sleepers necessary during the construction to be made to the details furnished by the Engineer.

62. The 30 inch random wall in Hyndburn Road to rest on a concrete foundation 4 feet wide and 15 inches deep The 27 inch foundation walls to rest on concrete beds 3½ feet wide and 12 inches deep. The 18 inch foundation walls to rest on concrete beds 3 feet wide and 12 inches deep. The 14 inch foundation walls to rest on concrete beds 3 feet wide and 12 inches deep.

The boundary walls and outside walls for Offices, Lamp Room, Shed, Coke Shed and Gateway to rest on concrete foundations 2½ feet wide and 10 inches deep. The bottom of the pits to be covered with concrete 6½ feet wide and 10 inches thick, after being well levelled and rammed. *(Concrete foundations.)*

63. The whole of the concrete foundations above specified to be equal in quality and to sample to that specified for the Tramways, and to be finished level and straight on the upper surface, to receive the wall courses. *(Quality of Concrete.)*

64. The end wall abutting on Hyndburn Road to be faced outside with Yorkshire shoddys from Messrs. Brookes' Quarries, Hipperholme, to be not less than 6 inches wide on the bed, dressed full and lean to a template of ¾ of an inch to one foot, to be not more than 3 to 5 inches thick, and of equal width throughout. Provide and fix at the height of the floors a base course 12 by 9, clean tooled and splayed 3 inches. This wall under the base to be backed to the required thickness with strong local random walling, to have two throughs in each superficial yard of walling, all to be set on quarry bed, knocked down and pointed off outside. This wall above the base course to be lined inside with pressed bricks, laid with close joints, perfectly straight and neatly pointed on both sides. Provide and fix a stone through for every superficial yard of walling, punched off clean to the length required, squared and well set up at the back. *(Stone Walls.)*

65. The whole of the stone, bricks, lime, sand, sewer pipes and other building materials required and used in these buildings and premises to be equal in quality and finish to the samples at the Borough Surveyor's Office. *(Quality of Materials.)*

66. The front boundary wall to be built 18 inches thick, to the height shewn on plan, faced outside with Yorkshire shoddys, lined inside with pressed bricks, and throughed and pointed as specified. The remaining boundary walls to be built of pressed bricks, neatly walled in English bond and pointed. These walls to be covered with 18 in. by 4 in. tooled coping Yorkshire stone, to be set perfectly straight, with clean joints and pointed in cement. *(Boundary walls.)*

67. The whole of the remaining 14in. walls to be built to the heights shewn on the plans with hard burned pressed bricks in English bond, all to be set in good beds of mortar, and pointed neatly on both sides, and to have close and straight joints. Build the projecting heads as shewn, and fix all wooden lintels and iron girders.

The 9in. brick walling to be built to the heights shewn on the plans with hard burned pressed bricks, to have headers every fourth course laid in good beds of mortar, and well pointed neatly on both sides. Build the projecting heads 14in. by 4½in. as shewn, all to be firmly bonded to the main walls. Turn arches over the doorways 9in. deep, and provide all centres required. *(Brick Walls.)*

68. The walls on each side of the pits to be built from the present ground level to the required heights on the concrete foundations before specified, with pressed bricks, to be 18in. thick to within 2½ ft. from the top, and from thence to be 14in. thick, to be walled in English bond, each brick to be set in cement, knocked down, and neatly pointed. *(Pit walls.)*

56. The crossings and points are to be cast to the forms and dimensions shewn on the drawings; the points and top surfaces are to be of chilled cast iron, made in such manner as shall be approved of by the Engineer. The surfaces of the rails and points must be quite smooth and even. *(Crossings and Points.)*

57. The Contractor to provide Barker's patent rails of Bessemer steel to the forms, weights and dimensions shewn on drawing No.

The rails are to be made from a mixture of the best English Hematite brands and Spiegeliesen cast into ingots of sufficient weight to make one or more rails, which are to be heated and rolled to the required section. No ingots of less weight are to be used. The bar so rolled must be of sufficient length to allow all defective metal at the ends to be cut off to ensure the soundness at both ends of the rail.

The rails are to be accurately rolled to the sections shewn on the drawing. The weight of each rail must not be less than 40lbs. per yard. The rails to be 21 feet and 24 feet each in length, with not more than five per cent. of 18 feet lengths. *(Rails. (Steel))*

58. Keyways are to be punched to the forms and in the positions shewn, and a guage pin to the holes is to be provided by the Contractor, and supplied in duplicate to the Engineer; no hole must vary more than one sixteenth of an inch from the position shewn on the drawing. *(Keyways.)*

59. The Contractor is at his own expense to test such of the rails at the works as may from time to time be selected by the Engineer, in his presence, and in such manner as he may direct, so as to ascertain the suitability of the materials for the purpose intended, and the Engineer is to be at liberty to reject any rails he may consider of insufficient quality and workmanship. *(Testing.)*

Any or all of the following tests may be applied :—a drop test; a weight of 20 cwt. to fall from a height of 10 feet upon the centre of a rail supported on bearings 3 feet apart, without fracture.

Tensile Test. Pieces cut from rails to have a tensile strength of from 28 to 31 tons per square inch, with an elongation of 20 per cent. in a length of 6¼ inches.

Hot Bending Test. Strips of rails heated to a cherry red heat to bend double round a curve of which the diameter shall not exceed three times the thickness of the piece tested.

Deflection Test. Rails supported upon bearings 3 feet apart and loaded at the centre to have an elastic limit of 7 tons of load.

DEPÔT.

60. Excavate trenches for the walls as shewn on the foundations plan to the levels shewn on the sections, all to be dug out to a thoroughly hard and approved bottom, and to be well rammed. The trenches for the longitudinal walls and cross walls where required to be excavated in steps as shewn, and levelled to receive the concrete foundations. The pits in Sheds and alongside the Coke Shed to be excavated 6½ feet wide and 6 feet deep from the levels of the Shed floors. The whole of the trenches for the walls of all buildings and boundary walls to be not less than 18 inches below the Tramways rail level. *(Excavating.)*

61. Lay down salt-glazed earthenware pipe sewers in the directions indicated, and according to the sizes marked on the plans, to be laid on a solid bottom to an even incline the joints to be packed carefully with tough clay. Provide traps and grates where marked on plans and also the requisite junctions and bends. Provide and fix bends at the foot of each fall pipe to receive the roof water and connect the same. Carry the trunk sewer from the site and connect the same to the Hyndburn Road main sewer. Make good the street after connecting. *(Sewering.)*

Foundation Walls.

69. Build brick walls under the entire lengths of the rails, and the cross tie walls as shewn in the foundations plan to be built of pressed brick on concrete foundation before specified to the thickness marked on the plans, all to be well mortared and pointed off where seen.

The whole of the walls shewn on the foundations plan to be built from the present ground levels to the floor levels with pressed bricks, well bonded and mortared, and pointed off where seen.

Steps to pits.

70. Provide and fix at the ends of the Pits, where shewn, five steps of Enfield stone, 12in. by 9in., punched off clean, and fixed on a 14in. cross wall, built from the present ground level to the underside of the top step.

Filling in on site.

71. Provide and lay down dry sound, and clean material to fill up the entire site of the Depot from the present ground level to within 13ins. of the upper surface of Tramways rails, to be thoroughly rammed down and levelled to an even surface.

Tramways rails and Foundations.

72. The Tramways rails, foundations, concrete beds, crossings, and everything appertaining to the same inside the Depot and Yard, to be subject to the same specification in all respects as those on the outside. The remainder of the Yard between the 18ins. outside the rails already specified, to be paved with 5in. Brinscall setts, on a similar bed as specified for Tram lines.

Offices and Coke Shed.

73. The Coke Shed to be built of 9in. brickwork, 3½ft. high from the floor, and prepared for the timber work above.

The Offices' outside wall facing Taylor street to be 18in. thick, faced with Yorkshire shoddys, and lined inside with bricks as before specified, throughed every superficial yard. The remaining outside walls to be 14in. thick, of bricks as before specified. All ashlar to be from Haworth, near Keighley, to be clean wrought to the detail drawing, and stroke tooled, and to have all the necessary weatherings, drips, and rebates.

Fireplaces, and Flues.

74. The Fireplaces to be built as shewn, and to have a range in each room, on both floors, value £5, fixed complete. The flues to be 14in. by 10in. carried to the end chimneys as shewn, to be well parquetted and made good. The inside walls to be built to the thicknesses shewn on the plans.

Lamp room, Stable, & Shed.

75. The outside walls of Lamp Room, Stable and Shed to built to the thickness shewn, pointed on both sides as before specified. Fix a fire-place in the Lamp Room value £3, complete. The Stable to be 7½ feet wide, paved with 6 inch Witinell setts on a 6 inch concrete bed, and run with pitch. Lay sewer to same, and fix stone dish with 12 in. by 12in. wrought iron grate over gully. The Ashlar for these buildings to be clean wrought, as specified for the Offices and the sizes according to the details.

Conveniences.

76. Build the petties in yard where shewn, and cover with 3in. Rossendale landings, dressed on the edges, and laid with sufficient lap. Build the screen wall 8 feet high of 9 inch bricks, and cover with 12 in. by 3 in. tooled coping, set straight with close joints. Provide and fix urine stones and slate divisions for the urinal, fixed with iron holdfasts to the walls, and grooved into a 12 in. by 8in. channel stone, hollowed 2 ins. and laid firmly on a solid foundation. Fix at the end a 12 in. by 12 in. stone dish and grate connected to the sewer.

Sand Ovens.

77. Build the two Sand Ovens at each side of the Engine Shed, as shewn, with wrought iron plates on the top, bars at the bottom and furnace doors complete, set in firebricks and connected to the flues.

Smithy Hearth.

78. The Smithy Hearth to be provided and fixed where shewn, to be Steven's patent, with bellows, air trunk, grates, doors, and fire guards complete, set in firebrick, the ashes hole to be dug out, walled round, and flagged at the bottom. Connect properly to the flue.

Chimneys.

79. The Chimneys to be built 8ft. high, of pressed brick, with projecting collars.

Beam filling.

80. Properly perform all Rake Cutting, Beam, Butt and Spar Filling.

Ashlar to Sheds.

81. Provide and fix clean tooled Gable Coping on each gable, 14in. by 4in., with kneelers, bondstones and terminals, as shewn in the drawings, all to be set straight with joggled joints, and neatly pointed off in cement.

Entrance Gateway.

82. The Entrance Gateway to be wrought to the drawings and details, all to be clean tooled work and set as shewn.

Floors.

83. The whole of the Platforms inside the Car Shed, Smithy, Petties, Coke Shed, Cart Shed, Lamp Room, the Platforms in the Engine Shed and the Store Room to have a floor foundation of broken stones 10in. thick, broken to pass through a 2in. ring, rammed down solidly, finished on the top with Wilkes' patent concrete, 3in. thick, finished perfectly level, straight, and to a smooth surface.

The bottom of the Pits also to be covered 3in. thick with Wilkes' patent concrete, to have a 9in. by 7in. channel formed on one side in the concrete, and rebated on the top to receive a continuous wrought iron grate ½in. thick to be fixed along the top of the channel. Build a small manhole at the end of each pit, and fix a trap, stone dish, and iron grate at the bottom of the channel, and connect the same to the sewer.

Lay down a bed of concrete 12in. thick, along the whole length of the traversers, finished to a smooth surface.

The floors of the Joiners' and Fitters' Shops to have a bed of concrete 6in. deep, and covered on the top with wood paving, formed of creosoted beech 6in. long, 9in. wide, and 3in. thick, laid firmly and straight on one inch boarding upon the concrete bed, and the joints to be filled in with hot pitch. Make good at the junctions with the concrete floors.

IRONFOUNDER.

Quality of Iron.

84. The whole of the wrought iron required for these buildings to be of the best Lowmoor. The rolled iron for girders and roofing purposes to be of satisfactory quality and finish. All bolts to be of the best quality Lowmoor wrought iron. Cast iron for gutters, fall pipes and angles to be equal in quality and finish to Mc. Farlane's.

Roofs and Gutters and Fall-pipes.

85. The whole of the iron roofs to be framed according to the plans and detail drawings, the sizes of the various parts as marked thereon. Fix the louvre frames over the Engine Sheds, Fitters and Joiners' Shop as shewn, to be framed as per detail drawings, fitted with zinc louvres, and glazed on the top with Hartley's patent rolled glass 3/16 of an inch thick. The flashings on each side of the louvre frame to be of 6lbs. lead, 14 inches wide, fixed in groove of woodwork under the first louvre, and flashed carefully into the slates. The ribs to be formed of channel iron, filled in solidly with clean Baltic timber, and bolted securely to the principal rafters as shewn. The whole of the roofs (except the Fitters' Shop) from the eaves gutters to the louvre frames to be covered with the best St. Petersburg redwood boarding, 7 inches by 1½ inch, dressed, tongued, grooved and v jointed on both sides, screwed securely to the ribs, and fied at each end to the ironwork. The centre eaves gutters to be of clean cast metal 3/8ths of an inch thick, fixed on a 9in. by 3in. redwood wallplate, laid on the top of the wall the full length of the gutter. The joints of the eaves gutter to be put together with red lead, and secured with 3/8th bolts firmly screwed up, and to be provided with the requisite stop and return ends, nozzles and angles. Provide and fix fall-pipes from

the centre gutters in every alternate bay, 4 inches diameter, plugged securely to the walls against the projecting heads, and to be connected to the top water sewers. Provide and fix the requisite offsetts and bends. The eaves gutters for the outside walls to be 7in. by 5in. clean cast metal supported with iron holdfasts, the joints to be put together as specified for the centre gutters, and provide the necessary stop and return ends, angles, nozzles, etc. The fall-pipes for these gutters to be 3in. diameter, fixed in every alternate bay, plugged securely to the walls, and connected to the top water sewers.

The whole of the roofs above specified and shewn on the drawings to be left perfectly water-tight, and in perfect order throughout.

Stable fittings.

86. The Stable to have an iron rack and manger from the St. Pancras Iron Company, fixed complete.

Eaves Gutters & Fall-pipes.

87. The eaves gutters for the Offices, Lamp Room, Stable and Shed to be 6in. by 4½in., screwed to the wall-plates, the joints made good as before, and provided with the requisite angles, ends and nozzles.

The fall-pipes to be 3in. by 2½in., plugged securely to the walls and connected to the top water sewers.

Provide and fix over the pits in the two Engine Sheds sheet iron smoke troughs, 4½ feet wide, and 15 inches deep, with sheet iron or zinc funnels 12 inches diameter, fixed in each bay of roof, flashed outside, and surmounted with Boyle's Patent Extract Cowl. The smoke troughs to be hung from the rafters with iron rods.

JOINER AND CARPENTER.

Quality of Timber.

88. The whole of the timber used in these buildings and premises to be of the best St. Petersburg redwood, to be free from sap, shakes, large, loose or unsound knots or other imperfections, and to be thoroughly seasoned.

Shutters, Beams and Uprights.

89. Provide and fix five 14 in. by 11 in. upright posts at entrance to Sheds and Shops where shewn, to be 15 feet long, fixed on a concrete bed, and tenoned to the cross beams above the openings. Provide and fix cross beams above the entrances to the Sheds and Workshops, 14 inches wide, 12 inches deep, one 35 feet long, three 26 feet long, laid level on the uprights and brick heads, and dressed off. Fix behind each beam Stones' wood revolving shutters, ¾in. thick, with balance weights, pulleys, chains, rods, holdfasts, and eyes complete, value 1/9 per foot superficial. Provide and fix wood runners up the sides of each opening, of birch, plugged securely to the walls. Fix boxes of 1 inch stuff, with bars screwed on the same, round the shutter coils at the top. Provide locks for the shutters, with catches complete.

Roof to Fitter's Shop.

90. The roof over the Fitters' Shop to be framed in timber as shewn, tie beams 12 in. by 6 in., principal rafters 12 in. by 5 in., kingpost 12 in. by 5 in., struts 5 in. by 5in., to be strapped and bolted together to detail drawings. Fix two ribs on each side, 9 in. by 4in., and on these, from the eaves gutters to the louvre frame fix 7 by 1½ in. tongued, grooved, and v jointed planks, securely nailed. Louvre frame to be similar to that specified for Sheds and fixed according to detail drawings. Fix 2 inch sheets on the top, glazed with Hartley's rolled glass three-sixteenths of an inch thick.

Roofs to Offices, Coke Shed, Lamp Room, &c.

91. The hip rafters for the Office roof to be 12in. by 3in., bolted together at the top; rooftree 7in. by 3in., one rib on each side and ends 9in. by 4in.; Wallplates 4½in. by 3in.; Spars to be 3in. by 2¼in., nailed securely to the roof timbers, not more than 12 inches apart. Trim properly for chimneys, and lay ¾in. gutter boards round the same. The roof to

Coke Shed to be carried on six 6in. by 6in. pillars, wall-plate 6in. by 9in., to have framed spars 4in. by 2½in. with tie piece 4in. by 1½in. halved together, fixed 12in. apart, and securely nailed. The roof of Lamp Room, Stable and Shed to have a rooftree 9in. by 3in., two ribs on side 11in. by 3in., wall-plate 4½in. by 3in., wall-plate for shed, two 11in. by 3in. planks bolted together; spars to be 3in. by 2¼in., not more than 12in. apart, securely nailed to roof timbers. Provide and fix a 12in. by 4in. beam over pillar, to Shed roof, let into the wall at the top and supported with a 5in. by 4in. strut as shewn.

Ceilings.

92. The ceilings of Offices and Lamp Room to be formed of 3in. by 2in. joists nailed to the spar feet, 12in. apart, and slung from the roofs. Provide and fix manhole frames and doors.

Floors.

93. The ground floors to be formed of 7in. by 2½in. joists, not more than 13in. apart, covered with 7in. by 1½in. dressed, tongued and grooved flooring boards. The first floor to Offices to have 9in. by 3in. joists, fixed and covered as before. Perform all counterflooring to hearths.

Doors.

94. The front doors of Stable, Lamp Room, and Offices, and small door in entrance to be 2½in. thick, framed and lined, hung to 4in. by 3in. rebated cheeks, with 5in. butt hinges, and furnished with 9in. rim locks and brass handles and snecks, with catches, complete, value 2/6 per set. The large door to entrance to be 3ins. thick, with framed styles and rails, and 4½in. by 2in. bars behind, 20ins. apart, lined with 5½in. by ⅞in. dressed, tongued, and grooved boards, to be fitted with Kenrick's patent sliding gear, with guides, pulleys, brackets, and lock, complete.

The inside doors to be 2in. thick, panelled and double moulded, hung to 6in. by 2in. rebated casings, with 4in. butts, and furnished with Tonks' 8in. rim locks, and 2in. ebony furniture.

Windows.

95. The windows to have 1¾in. sliding sashes in double cased frames, double hung, fitted with iron weights, brass bushed axle pullies, and sash fasteners.

Stairs.

96. The stairs to Offices to have 10in. by 1½in. treads, nosed, 8in. by 1¼in. risers, and 9in. by 1½in. moulded and trenched string boards, with landings, and 3in. by 2½in. baywood handrail fixed on iron holdfasts.

Casings.

97. The whole of the windows and doors to have ⅞in. plain casings inside, finishing on 1¼in. bottoms, tongued into the window sills, and to have rounded projecting nosing.

Skirtings.

98. The skirting for all the Offices and passsages to be 9in. by 1in., moulded and plugged securely to the walls, and scribed to the floors.

Moulds.

99. Fix 4in. by 1¼in. moulded architraves round all doors, windows, casings, cupboards, &c. in Offices, neatly mitred.

Cupboards.

100. Provide and fix the three cupboards as shown 9ft. high, fitted with 12in. by 1in. shelves 18in. apart, boarded at the back and sides with 6in. by ½in. stuff. Framing and doors to be 1¼in. thick, panelled and moulded, hung in two widths, with 3in. butts, and furnished with locks, hooks and eyes, and turns complete.

Provide and fix wood lintels where required.

Shed Doors.

101. The small doors in the Sheds and Shops to be 1½in. framed and lined doors, to have Kenrick's patent sliding pullies and bars fixed thereon, with handles complete.

Petties.

102. The petties in yard to have doors 1in. thick, hung to 3in. by 3in. cheeks, with bands and gudgeons, and furnished with Norfolk handles. Fix seats 1¼in. thick, with faceboards.

W. C's.

103. The watercloscts to be fitted in pitch pine, framed front and cover, 1¼in. thick, seats to have clamped ends. Covers hung with 2½in. butts, and skirting carried round the same.

Lavatories.

104. The lavatories to have 1¼in. birch covers, & boarded round with 5in. by ⅝in. dressed tongued and grooved boards, fixed to 3in. by 3in. corner posts, and screwed fast.

Plumbing work.

105. Provide platform, cistern and pipe covers for plumbers.

PLUMBER AND GLAZIER.

Material.

106. The whole of the Service Pipes for the water supply, gas fittings and pipes, and other material connected therewith, used in these buildings and premises, to be in accordance with the regulations of the Accrington Gas and Waterworks Company.

Water Service.

107 Provide and lay a main supply pipe from Taylor Street to the Sheds, and from thence fix branches on the roof tie-beams along the whole lengths of the seven platforms in the Sheds, 1in. diameter, and from thence at every alternate bay in each platform hang ½in. vertical branches, 7½ft. frcm the platform level. Fix to each branch a ½in. flexible pipe, 6½ft. long, fitted with brass nozzle, and Sutcliffe's patent taps. On one of the offsets in each pit lay one inch pipe, with flexible hose connections and branches every 12 feet, each flexible branch to be 5 feet long, and fitted as before specified. The supply pipes above specified to be iron, the sizes and weights to be in accordance with the Gas Company's rules.

Provide and fix two extra wall taps, as above specified, in the Fitters' and Joiners' Shops, and one ½in. supply pipe in the Smithy, with Sutcliffe's taps complete.

Fix an ½in. supply pipe to the Lamp Room, and to each Lavatory in Offices, and to the Water Closet Cisterns, all fitted with Sutcliffe's screw and ball taps respectively. Fix ⅜in. branch and tap in Stable.

Fix two 2in. branches from the main to the eaves of the Coke Shed, and an ½in. flexible branch with brass tap, and hose with brass nozzle.

Gas Fittings and Service.

108. Provide and fix supply pipes of iron along the tie-beams over the central platforms in each Shed, & from thence hang two-light pendants at every alternate bay along the whole length of the same to within 7ft. from the floor. On the side platforms, at every alternate bay, fix common double brackets, 7ft. from floor, along each length. Provide and fix iron supply pipes along each pit, and to these at every bay fix double brackets with joints to fold close against the walls.

Provide and fix three double brackets in Joiners' Shop, three ditto in Fitters' Shop, two in Smithy, and one pendant as before specified, one bracket each in Lamp Room and Stable, eighteen brackets in Offices value 6/- each, and three pendants value 30/- each. The whole of the above fittings to have supply pipes, pateras, screws, &c., complete, according to the Gas Company's regulations.

Glazing.

109. The whole of the roof and window glazing for the Sheds & Workshops to be glazed with Hartley's patent rolled plate glass ³⁄₁₆in. thick. The windows to Lamp Room, Offices, and Stable to be glazed with 21oz. sheet glass. The whole of the above to be well back-puttied, sprigged in, and pointed off in good oil putty.

W.C's.

110. Fix two Cisterns, Guest and Chrimes 73X, in Waterclosets, supplied with ½in. ball taps and service as before specified. Provide and fix two of Woodward's patent wash-out Closets with 1½in. flush, and supplied with the requisite chains, cranks, and levers, and connect the soil pipe, 5in. diameter, to the sewer.

Lavatories.

111. Provide and fix two Lavatory Basins value 20/- each, with plug and chain, and ½in. service and taps, neatly fixed, with 1½in. waste pipes, trapped, and connected to the sewers.

Lead work.

112. The flashings along the sides of the louvre frames, and round the smoke trough funnels on the Shed roofs, to be done with 6lbs. lead of approved width. The chimneys to be flashed with 6lbs. lead, 12in. wide, stepped with under flashings of approved width.

Flash the gable copings at the kneelers, terminals and bondstones, and round the nozzles of the fall pipes. Provide and fix 3lbs. lead flashings under each course of slates at the hips of the Offices roof to be of approved width. Flash the roof of the Shed, Lamp Room and Stable with 6lbs. lead, 12in. wide, grooved into walls, flashed into the slates, and pointed off with good oiled mastic.

Closets,

113. Provide and fix Guest and Chrimes' patent cistern and closet apparatus, with seat motion to petties in yard, to be connected to the sewers.

Painting.

114. The whole of the outside wood and iron work to have two coats oil paint, finishing brown. The woodwork inside the Offices to have two coats oil paint, grained, and twice varnished. All the remaining inside wood and ironwork in Sheds, Lamp Room, Shops, &c., to have three coats oil paint. The material to be cleaned down, stopped, knotted, and puttied before being painted.

SLATER.

Slating.

115. The whole of the slating to be done with seconds Vellenheli blue, 18in. by 9in, fixed on 1½in. by ¾in. Baltic laths, with two 2in. galvanized nails to each slate. Laths to be secured to roof timbers with cut nails. Each slate to have not less than 3in. of side and tail lap. Properly perform all cutting and mitreing to hips, and work in all flashings supplied by the plumber. Point in all flashings and the slates under the gable coping with good oiled mastic.

Ridging,

116. The ridging for the Sheds, Offices, Coke Shed, &c., to be Thomas' patent 2½in. slate roll ridging, with ½in. wings, neatly fixed in good oil putty. The roll to be screwed on in putty and made perfectly tight. Provide and fix one finial to the Office roof, value 10/-.

Take out all broken slates and replace with sound ones.

PLASTERER.

Ceilings.

117. The ceilings of all the rooms, passages, and closets in the Offices to be three coat work. The ceiling of Lamp Room to be two coat work.

Walls.

118. The walls of Offices on both floors to be three coat work. Lamp Room walls to be two coat work. All to be laid perfectly straight, with clean and true angles.

Slate pointing.

119. The Offices, Lamp Room, Stable, Shed, & Coke Shed roofs to be pointed under slates and at sides of spars with well haired mortar.

Cornices, &c.

120. Run cornices 18in. girth round passages and ground floor rooms of offices with clean and true mitres. Fix four centre pieces 30in. diameter.

Pointing.

121. Point all windows round frames and under stone sills with good oiled mastic.

Tarring walls and washing.

122. The Shed and Workshop walls to be tarred 5ft. high, two coats, and the remainder of the walls to have two coats limewash.

E. KNOWLES, Borough Engineer.

TOWN HALL, ACCRINGTON,
August, 1883.

Witness to the signature of the said Charles John Eastlake

This is the annexed specification referred to in the signature of this one.

745

AN IMPROVED TRAMWAY POINT.

Since the first introduction of tramways there has always been more or less difficulty experienced at the passing places. This was not so much felt when horse-power was alone used, as by pulling the horses sideways the car could be turned in the proper direction, but on the introduction of steam-power the difficulties were considerably increased. It is impossible for a locomotive car, depending entirely upon the rails and points for guidance, to have the divergence given it unless by making the point so that the engine or car will be prevented from proceeding on the wrong line. The system now in use is generally known as the "drop off" point. The left-hand facing point is an "open" point, and the right-hand point is a "turning" or "drop off" point. The groove of the rail being filled up turns the engine and car in the right direction, but when returning they have to ride upon the flanges of the wheel over that portion of the rail, the groove of which is thus filled up, instead of riding on the tread, and after passing the point they drop suddenly on the head of the wheel again. The depth of the groove is ⅜in., therefore an engine weighing eight to nine tons and travelling about 70 miles per day must drop about ⅜in. about 600 times per day. The damage thus occasioned to springs, axles, and boxes, and the general machinery under these circumstances must be palpable to any one.

A new point has, however, been invented by Mr. Clifford E. Winby, C.E., of Rochdale, which obviates all this. "The Patent Vertical Action Automatic Safety Point"—as Mr. Winby's invention is called—consists of a steel bar acting as a point, and cut partially to the section of the groove part of the rail, and presenting a face to an advancing engine when returning in the opposite direction; the flanges of the wheels press the bar gradually downwards in a vertical direction, the weight of the engines and cars being thus borne on the tread of the wheels instead of (as with the dummy point) on the flanges; the drop, jolting, and knocking being thus done away with. When the engine or cars have passed, the point returns to its normal position, being pressed vertically upwards by a spring or other mechanical arrangement. This ingenious invention is one which has so far commended itself that the Bradford Corporation, after thoroughly testing the "patent points," instructed Mr. Winby to take up all the ordinary points now in use on their tramways, and to replace the same with his patent system.

The Railway Times, 8 November, c.1884.

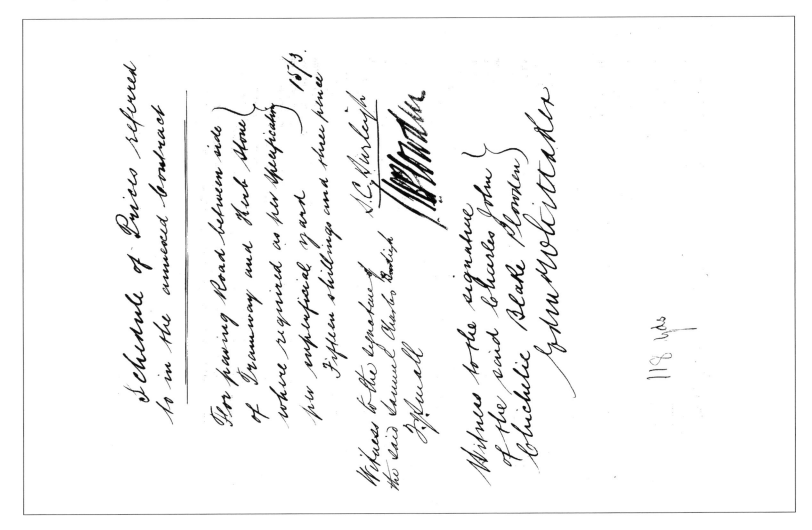

Railway Chemistry

Railway Magazine, Vol . 2, Januray-June 1898, with permission.

RAILWAY CHEMISTRY

By GEORGE E. BROWN, *Fellow of the Institute of Chemistry, Great Western Railway*

Chemical Laboratory, Swindon Works

MOST people are surprised to find that practically all our great railway companies have a well-equipped laboratory for analytical chemistry, and retain the services of a staff of analysts. It is a common remark of visitors to a railway laboratory: "What does a railway company want with chemistry?" and at first sight there seems but little connection between the silence of a chemical laboratory, with its array of shining glass vessels and delicate balances, and the roar of the express as it thunders through the night with its living freight. Yet, as the writer hopes to show, there is a very intimate connection, and the one has a good deal to do with the safe, efficient, and economical working of the other.

Consider for a moment the vast quantities of all kinds of materials which a railway company purchases for the construction of its rolling stock. In the first place, steel is one of the most important articles entering into the construction of locomotives, carriages, and wagons. The metal—or, more strictly speaking, the alloy—is used for axles, tyres, boiler and frame plates, springs, etc, and in America largely for fire-boxes; its quality varies according to the particular purpose for which it is to be employed. For example, the steel used for engine tyres is harder than that used for wagon or carriage tyres, whilst all these are harder than the steel of which axles are constructed. These differences in the physical character of steel are due to the different proportions of other elements which are introduced or allowed to remain in it.

The chief elements occurring in steel in such quantity as to affect its properties are carbon, silicon, sulphur, phosphorus, and manganese; carbon, in particular, affects the character of steel, an increase in its proportion rendering steel harder. Thus, steel from which tools, such as drills, etc, are constructed contains upwards of one per cent. of carbon, whereas a boiler plate, which is a comparatively mild steel, contains only one-fifth or so of one per cent. Silicon, sulphur, and phosphorus all act prejudicially on steel when present in excessive proportion. The relative quantity of these elements which may be present in steel without detriment depends to a great extent upon the percentage of carbon. Without going further into the question, it will be readily understood that a knowledge of the chemical composition of steel is of the greatest importance to the engineer in ensuring that materials of proper

---

quality, as laid down by specification, are being supplied.

The literature dealing with the chemical analysis of steel is very voluminous, and many different processes exist for the determination of the elements occurring in steel. These

THE BALANCE ROOM IN THE CHEMICAL LABORATORY, G.W.R. WORKS, SWINDON

different processes do not, as may be imagined, give absolutely concordant results, and the desirability of certain standard methods, the use of which could be agreed upon by buyer and seller, has long been discussed. Dr. Chas. B. Dudley, the chemist of the Pennsylvanian Railway, has taken a very active interest in this question, and when laying down specifications is accustomed to state the methods by which the respective constituents shall be determined. Dr. Dudley has done a good deal of work for the American Section of the Committee on the International Standards for the Analysis of Iron and Steel, and as a practical result of the labours of the Committee it seems probable that an international laboratory for the investigation of analytical methods will be established in Switzerland, under the superintendence of Baron Hans Jüptner von Jonstorff, an eminent Continental steel analyst.

Next to steel the question of copper used in making fire-boxes and boiler tubes has engaged the attention of railway chemists of late years. These Engineers have complained that the refined copper obtainable at the present time does not stand the wear and tear of working so well as the copper supplied twenty or more years ago. At the present time copper is very highly refined for electrical use, and does not contain such appreciable proportions of other elements—arsenic, lead, bismuth, etc.—as were present before the rise of electricity necessitated the supply of a pure metal. It is difficult to say whether the lack of resistance to wear and tear exhibited by modern copper is due to the absence of these impurities, or to the much higher temperatures and greater strain to which the metal is subjected, through the increased pressures now used in locomotive boilers. It is probably due in part to each. The problem of ascertaining which of the impurities in copper are beneficial and which deleterious is a difficult one, as may be seen from the elaborate series of analyses communicated not long ago to the Institution of Mechanical Engineers by Mr. Wm. Dean, the Loco. Supt. of the G.W.R. Although it is difficult to draw definite conclusions from analyses in which the number of constituents is so great, the figures show that comparatively high percentages of arsenic—from three-tenths to five-tenths of one per cent.—do not prevent a copper fire-box attaining a high mileage. It used to be the custom of engineers to ask for copper containing iron pyrites, which by oxidation in presence of moisture had given rise to sulphur compounds capable of attacking the iron.

Next, perhaps, in importance to the analysis of constructive material stands the chemical examination of lubricants. Railway engineers have not been slow in seeing that the efficient lubrication of locomotives and carriages, as well as of the numerous installations of stationary machinery in all parts of the system, is a very important factor in economical working. The selection and control of the supply of lubricants adapted for various classes of work is naturally relegated

INTERIOR OF CHEMICAL LABORATORY, G.W.R. WORKS, SWINDON

containing not more than about one-tenth of one per cent. of arsenic; but at the present time there seems to be a disposition to place the proportion of arsenic in fire-box copper at about two-fifths of one per cent. The examination of other metals and alloys, such as brass, bearing metals, phosphor-bronze, etc., also comes within the chemist's province. The way in which these various materials behave under trying circumstances, and investigations into the causes which promote their wear and tear, also occupy the chemist's attention and time. We illustrate a nut and bolt of a hydraulic main which, after four years' burial in the ground, was found to be corroded to the extent shown. Experiments showed that the mains had been laid in ashes

A NUT AND BOLT CORRODED THROUGH LYING IN ASHES CONTAINING SULPHUR

(The upper bolt shows size of original bolt)

to the chemist. For it must be remembered that it is not only the body or viscosity of a lubricant which has to be taken into account

dry up with the formation of a more or less tough skin, whereby much of its lubricating value is lost, is indicated by several chemical reactions; whilst the various adulterations practised by merchants, by which an inferior oil may be doctored to counterfeit a genuine sample, so far as answering to a few rough and ready tests, like specific gravity, colour, and so on, is concerned, can hardly remain undiscovered

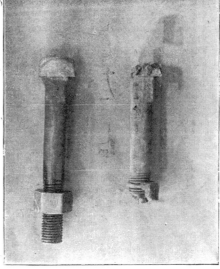

TAKING THE "VISCOSITY" OF A LUBRICATING OIL, G.W.R. CHEMICAL LABORATORY, SWINDON WORKS

when judging of its suitability for a given purpose—this is, of course, one of the main considerations—but the chemical qualities of lubricants are of hardly lesser importance, and cannot be neglected without incurring the risk of damage being done to the machinery on which the oils are used. The percentage of free fatty acid in an oil or grease derived from animal or vegetable sources becomes, when excessive, a serious drawback to the employment of the lubricant, in consequence of the action of these acids on the bearing, the metal of which not only becomes corroded, but forms with the fatty acid a species of metallic soap, which is deposited as a coating on the bearing surfaces and prevents efficient lubrication. The corrosion of the seat of the regulator valve-box so frequently noticed on locomotive boilers which come in for repairs is no doubt caused by the use of a saponifiable lubricant, like tallow. The superheated steam with which it comes in contact causes the decomposition of the fat, the liberated acid attacking the metal. The tendency also of an oil to "gum," or

TAKING THE "FLASH-POINT" OF BURNING OIL, WITH ABEL'S APPARATUS, AT G.W.R. CHEMICAL LABORATORY, SWINDON WORKS

by a complete chemical examination. Oils used for burning—rape oil and petroleum—are also submitted to examination by the chemist. The restrictions enforced on the supply of petroleum by railway companies are much more stringent than those sanctioned by the Legislature for public sale. Most companies require an oil which does not give off inflammable vapour below 100 degrees Fahr., the minimum flash-point allowed by Government being 73 degrees Fahr. The very great immunity from accidents through using petroleum enjoyed by railway employés should be a strong recommendation for the legal adoption of a much higher flash-point.

Another exceedingly useful service which

A LOCOMOTIVE BOILER TUBE WITHDRAWN FROM SERVICE, TO CLEAN OFF THE SCALE

(The dark portions show where the scale has been removed)

the chemist renders the locomotive engineer is in the testing of water used in the boilers. Anyone who has chatted with the **driver of a locomotive** knows that he has certain favourite places on his route for taking up water, and though, perhaps, he cannot say why, he knows that he is able to raise steam better with these waters than with others, which he avoids as far as possible. The difference, of course, lies in the quantity of lime and magnesia salts which the waters contain, and which are deposited on heat being applied. Waters containing a large proportion—that is to say, hard waters—cover the boiler tubes with an incrustation which is an extremely bad conductor of heat, and consequently lessens the steam-raising capacity

LOCOMOTIVE BOILER WITH SEAT OF REGULATOR VALVE-BOX. CORRODED BY FATTY LUBRICANT

of the boiler. Some incrustations are powdery and are easily washed out, but others are hard and strongly adherent, and have to be removed with a chisel, or even a machine specially designed for the purpose. The chemist can, from an examination of a water, predict its behaviour in a locomotive boiler, and thus makes it possible to select the most suitable waters available for use on the system. A slight incrustation in a boiler is desirable rather than otherwise, and an ideal boiler water may be said to be one containing lime and magnesia equivalent to about five grains of calcium carbonate per gallon. Unfortunately such waters are not generally obtainable, and where tenders have to be filled from a very hard supply it is often desirable to resort to artificial softening processes. Here, again, the chemist's investigations indicate which of the various softening processes is best adapted to a particular water, what amount of, and expenditure in, chemicals will be necessary, and what degree of softening may be expected.

Besides analysing water intended for boiler purposes, the chemist is constantly analysing water used for drinking and other domestic purposes in waiting or refreshment rooms, and for consumption by the company's employés. The benefit derived by a railway

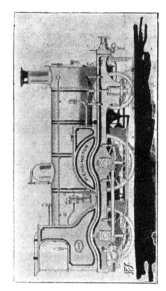

company from thus supervising the supply of a commodity the purity of which is so necessary to the health of its servants is none the less valuable because it is impossible to express it in pounds, shillings, and pence.

One other way in which the chemist plays a useful part—and one which the Goods Manager is not slow in recognising—may be mentioned in conclusion. Those who have studied that volume, sacred—or perhaps otherwise—to all who are constantly despatching goods by rail, the "General Railway Classification of Goods," know that goods are carried at rates dependent on their value, fragility, dangerous character, and other qualities. New traffic is constantly being offered for conveyance, and the chemist's aid in classifying new goods and in drawing up regulations for their safe transport is constantly forming additional evidence of the usefulness in every-day commerce of a science which at the time of the birth of railways was hardly thought of, except in connection with pretty experiments, or with the malodorous atmosphere of alkali works.

For permission to utilise the accompanying illustrations the author is indebted to Mr. Wm. Dean, the courteous Locomotive and Carriage Superintendent of the Great Western Railway Company.

Rail Wear

This article is from the Memoirs of Proceedings of the Institution of Civil Engineers, Vol CXLII, session 1899-1900.

For obvious reasons we cannot include the 60 odd pages of this item, especially as at first sight it appears peripheral to the story of steam trams, but the fact is that until air in cities and industrial areas got a lot cleaner the 'acid rain' that came down from the sky was really acid – my wife's normally clear skin always deteriorated badly when we were working on the canals in the Black Country and Birmingham. Add to this the incredible filth found on roads during the late 19th century and – as any gardener knows – the acid in raw horse-muck, it is small wonder the relatively porous joints in setts led to the destruction of tramway rails' bases. And again, the author dwells upon the effects of magnetism on rails; this was reported as 'one of those odd things' in steam tramway days as points (switches) filled up with magnetised horse shoe nails, and other bits of scrap iron, but when the overhead came into use, there was a study in Norwich where the trams ran through the Market Place which pretty well corroborated Mr. Andrews' findings. The magnetic effect plus the acid changed the whole of the rails' structure; while famously all the surface contact (stud) systems suffered from the assortment of old iron that gathered under the skates, leading to, as a writer put it rather poetically, 'coruscating fountains of fire along the route.'

"...It has been observed that the action of acid vapours and the products of combustion is chiefly noticeable on the bottom flange of the rail where its surface sits in the chair. This is illustrated by Fig. (6) which is a typical instance of this corrosive effect ... [the author then refers to a study in magnetism. The rails he studied were by coincidence laid due north and south] ... the Author observed indications that magnetization exerts an influence tending to increase the corrosibility of steel in certain situations; and as is well known, steel retains more or less permanent magnetism after having been magnetised. It may therefore be possible that steel rails gradually become magnetic from the influence of the earth's magnetism, when laid in a direction bearing a suitable relation to the direction of the magnetic meridian, and hence the corrosion in rails when so situated may be somewhat increased...*

...The rail studied had weighed 84 lb per yard, and after seven years was reduced to 64½ lbs per yard which represented a loss, from wear and tear and corrosion, of about 2.8 lb per yard per annum. This is comparatively an excessive annual loss. [This study may also explain the wild discrepancy between the expected life of tramway rails and the reality]. By and large Mr Andrews' rails showed only normal cracks and flaws Fig. 5.

Table I.—Chemical Analyses of the Steel Rail.			
—	Head.	Web.	Foot.
Combined carbon by colour	0·410	0·420	0·410
Silicon	0·063	0·057	0·062
Manganese	0·778	0·828	0·784
Sulphur	0·115	0·110	0·120
Phosphorus	0·051	0·048	0·048
Iron by difference	98·583	98·537	98·576
	100·000	100·000	100·000

The combined carbon was satisfactory and as high as is desirable for rail-steel, and the silicon, Manganese and phosphorus were present in normal proportions. Sulphur, however, was present in great excess – nearly double the proportion that ought to obtain in a good steel rail. As the carbon and other elements were satisfactory, the excess of sulphur is to some extent responsible for the considerable wearing down noticeable in this rail.

The typical normal micro-crystalline structure of this rail, in places free from micro-segregation of the impurities, is seen in longitudinal section near the rail-face. It is shown in Fig. 3 from which it will be seen that some of the grey carbide-of-iron areas were of comparatively large size ... owing to the large excess of sulphur present in this rail, the micro-flaws (apparently chiefly due to sulphide of iron and sulphide of manganese) were found to be very numerous, and in many places they were massed in areas of micro-segregation. The individual sulphur micro-flaws were also of considerable size. A typical illustration of these internal micro-flaws is given in Fig. 4 [These micro-flaws, which are fully detailed in the original study, varied between longitudinally 0.0006 of an inch to 0.0036, most being in the 0.0025 area, and transversely between 0.0004 to 0.0008 of an inch, averaging 0.0006, the rail was badly worn underneath] ... the under surface of the rail-bottom, where it had rested in the chair, was much weakened by excessive transverse depressions and corrosion-cavities, although there were no actual fissures. These transverse depressions, or indentations, resulted from

mechanical wear and the cold hammering which the rail received in the chair, caused by the rolling stock passing over it. Another feature manifested in the bottom surface of this rail was the considerable extent to which the bottom of the rail, where it had rested in the chair, had been widened by mechanical shocks ... see Fig. 6. [There is then a discussion on the chemicals found in the rail] ... The chemical analyses show the general composition of the steel was excellent, the chemical elements being well balanced, with the exception of the sulphur, which latter constituent was present in considerable excess – nearly twice as much as ought to be present in a good rail-steel. ...this impurity, being present in such excess, has micro-segregated (as sulphide of iron and sulphide of magnesium) as shown in the high-power micrograph Fig. 4. The presence of these innumerable minute areas of segregation has greatly facilitated (for mechanico-physical reasons easily understood) the disintegration and wearing down of the rail, under stress of wear, though the distribution of the sulphide micro-flaws throughout the mass was such as not to affect the physical strength of the rail as a mass ... [The author then refers readers to a series of papers on fatigue deterioration of rails published in Engineering 1897 and 1898.] ...To ensure that a reliable composition and structure of rail is obtained, it is of advantage for railway companies [and, obviously tramway concerns!] to have their new finished rails (apart from the maker's test of the ingot) chemically and physically tested.

[After this a discussion followed, Mr Inglis, for example, bringing up a matter most pertinent at the time for railways to be built under a Light Railway Order as did Sir Benjamin Baker]

Engineers often talked learnedly about the quality of the steel when the fault was in fact inefficiency in maintenance, and he believed that particular cause of fractures would increase instead of decrease as manufacturers went on making rails heavier ; at any rate, he felt sure it would so far as the joints were concerned, because the more unbending and rigid the structure became, the more likely it was, if there was a deflection in the rail, to get at certain points very severe twists and reciprocating stresses which would produce fracture. It would appear from Sir Lowthian Bell's Paper that the Board of Trade now absolutely refused to certify a new line for passenger traffic if that line was laid with rails which had been in use in other parts of the line. He hoped the Board of Trade would never get to that advanced stage of consideration for public safety. He thought if they did they would be somewhat illogical. At any rate, he would be a sinner in the matter, if the Board of Trade took it into consideration. His Company were now making a railway for passenger traffic and goods traffic – it was true it was a light railway – and there the Board of Trade had inserted a

---

*Three observations: ships had to be degaussed during the war to make them less attractive to magnetic mines. Corrosion on any steel vessel was always greatest 'twixt wind and water, and particularly noticeable on fixed draught shipping, and on canals (which are not normally salt corrosive) modern practice is to fit sacrificial anodes fore and aft, thus having something in common with oil-rigs! These anodes are normally a zinc/magnesium/aluminium compound matched to the hull's requirement (more-or-less, but cost comes into it!). Technically, it is accepted the corrosion cannot be entirely halted in steel hulls (although copper-bonded iron hulls lasted a century or more), and the anodes provide a more negative electrochemical potential. And thirdly I was shown at the RTB works that some rails coming off the rolls were themselves magnetised by the action of passing and re-passing through the rolls.

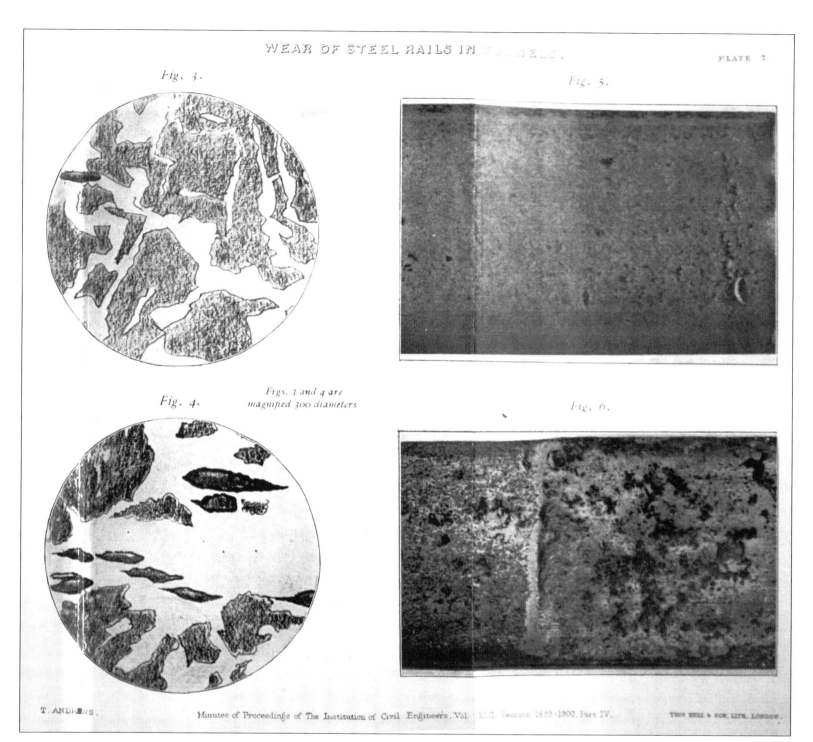

Fig. 3.

Fig. 4.

Fig. 5.

Fig. 6.

Figs. 3 and 4 are
magnified 300 diameters

T. ANDREWS.　　Minutes of Proceedings of The Institution of Civil Engineers. Vol. XLII. Session 1899-1900. Part IV.　　THOS. KELL & SON. LITH. LONDON.

clause in the Bill providing that worn rails might be used if they were not lighter than 60 lb per yard when laid. That was an indication of what the views of the Board of Trade might be about light railways; but he did not think such a regulation as that mentioned by Sir Lowthian Bell would be quite fair. He had a case now, for instance, where, on the main line, with very heavy traffic, the spacing of the sleepers was perhaps wider than he would like it to be. The ballast was not quite satisfactory, and would have to be taken up, and the sleepers required to be re-spaced. The rails were 7 years old, and were almost at their best, or, at any rate, in quite good working-order. A railway company might desire to put down a type of road which was adjacent, and might take up those perfectly good rails and the sleepers, and move them to another line less frequented and carrying lighter traffic than the main line ; and if the Board of Trade prevented such an operation as that, he thought they

would only perpetuate the jolting of the British public in express trains ; because, if the Board of Trade would not allow it, the simple result would be that the company would have either to leave the rails until they were considerably more worn, and so perpetuate the unsatisfactory running for a series of years, or to take up the whole at a greater cost, re-space the sleepers, shift their old beds, and produce an unsatisfactory road – at any rate, for the first 12 months after it was laid. He thought the Board of Trade ought not to be encouraged in any such very safe method as was suggested in the Paper.

Sir BENJAMIN BAKER, K.C.M.G., Past-President, thought he Baker, might reassure his friends Mr McDonald and Mr Inglis on the point which had been raised about the views of the Board of Trade on the question of using old rails. One of the first remarks that he had made when he was on the Light Railway Commission of the Board of Trade was to

protest against what might be called the definition of a light railway as a railway which had a certain limited weight on the driving-wheel or which had light rails. He said if there was to be any extensive introduction of light railways it could only be through the help and assistance of the leading railway companies, and questions of economy would be the first consideration. Therefore, one of the very first conditions would be that the railway companies should be able to take out their old rails and use them for light railways, and should be able to take their old rolling stock and engines which were obsolete for mainline service and put them on light railways. There was not a word of protest from any of the Board-of-Trade officers present, and he did not think any fear need be felt about putting the old rails of main lines on light railways. It would be regarded as a common-sense matter which all Englishmen, including the Board of Trade, would accept as proper."

When electric tramcars entered service engineers had to learn a whole raft of new methods of working. Here the solutions to one problem are offered.

BONDS.

In order to keep within the Board of Trade limit, that in no part of the rail return shall the drop in volts be less than 7, it is important to pay great attention to the way the bonding is done, as the resistance of joints would make considerable difference in the drop of a line when high currents were passing. From three to four volts drop is all that is allowed in the best practice, and this is achieved by the negative booster, described by Major Cardew in his paper read before the Institute of Electrical Engineers. In England and on the Continent the troubles due to electrolysis are reduced to a practically negligible quantity compared with those experienced in America, where a larger drop is allowed. In dealing with this most important subject the author will treat bonds in the following order: Continuous Rail—Electric Welded, Cast Welded (Falk, Milwaukee). Fish Plate Joints—Edison Bond, (a) Cork Plastic, (b) Solid with Plastic Alloy, Chicago type.

CONTINUOUS RAIL.

That a continuous rail is entirely feasible mechanically now admits of no dispute. It makes the best electrical bond when well constructed. Expansion does not and cannot take place longitudinally when rails are firmly embedded in paving; whatever yielding there is, it is taken up in a lateral direction and the track is not sprung out of line; the life of the rail is thus also increased.

ELECTRIC WELDED.

This process in its latest development consists in making a weld from a boss on the fish-plate instead of from a flat bar as in the old system. The boss is the only portion of the bar which comes in contact with the rail, therefore all the heat is concentrated at that point (see Fig. 13). As soon as a welding heat is reached the current is cut off, a heavy pressure is exerted on the weld and artificially cooled while under pressure. The effect is exactly the same as hammering or working the steel. A strain of 350,000 lb. did not shear off a weld made in this way.

On making a joint, a bar 1 inch by 3 inches, having three bosses, is used as shown in Fig. 13, and one bar is welded to each side of the rail web. The centre weld is made first, then the end welds. The bars, when cooling, exert a powerful force to bring the rail ends together, making a perfectly tight joint. The intimate union of steel to steel, and the increased carrying capacity due to the bars at the joint, make the joint the place of least resistance. An electrically welded track is, if properly made, of lower resistance than the rail itself. By this process the head of the rail is heated but slightly, thus avoiding the danger of annealing and softening it, which is apt to be the case where the whole rail is raised to a red heat when forming the joint. The cost of first outlay prohibits the adoption of this system in most cases.

CAST WELDED FALK.

This type (Fig. 14) has been used in Norwich, Coventry and Liverpool. It consists in casting an iron sleeve round the sides and bottom of the rail joints, the rail ends being first placed firmly together. In cases where they do not absolutely touch, thin plates of steel called "shims" are driven in between the heads of the rails before casting. Before fixing the moulds, which are of cast iron, the sides and bottom of the rail are cleaned, and this is generally done with an emery wheel or a sand blast. The probable cupola is shown in Fig. 15.

The cast iron running into the iron moulds cools rapidly on the outside surface, thus causing an enormous pressure to be exerted on the metal which is still in its molten state in contact with the web and foot of the rail. As the metal is poured in from one side and comes in contact with the web or thinnest part of the rail at its greatest temperature, this part of the rail is brought to a white heat, and owing to the enormous pressure exerted on the molten cast iron, by the shrinking and cooling of the outside surface of the metal, it is practically forced into the interstices of the steel, thus not only making a thoroughly good mechanical joint, but also ensuring a good electrical one, 80 to 103 per cent. conductivity of the solid rail. The author has tested this joint extensively; its only drawback seems to be the first expense.

While carrying out these tests the author found the main switch got very hot with 460 amperes, and he found there a drop of 15 millivolts. He used some plastic alloy and amalgamated the contacts of the switch, after this the drop at

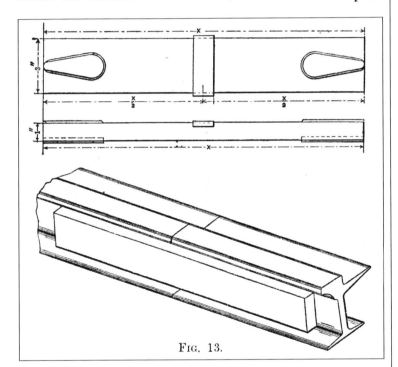

FIG. 13.

FIG. 14.

460 amperes was reduced 1·3 millivolts. He used the plastic alloy to make contact on the rails he was testing. The following table gives the results of the worst joint he tested, other readings are given in Mr. Dawson's pocket-book.

Solid. 5-foot Solid Rail.		Joint. 5-foot Rail, "Falk" Joint.		Solid. 5-foot Solid Rail.	
Amperes.	Millivolts.	Amperes.	Millivolts.	Amperes.	Millivolts.
342	17·2	344	18·9	345	17
376	19	380	21	378	19·2
460	23·1	462	25	452	23·5

Cast Welded Milwaukee.

This process is somewhat different from the Falk (see Fig. 16). A casing or jacket, formed of two L-shaped pieces of rolled steel, is placed under and at the side of the joint, and is temporarily fastened to the rails by clamps. The metal is then poured round the joint inside this jacket, after which the clamps are taken off and the jacket remains in position, giving additional strength to the cast iron which it encloses. The rivets at the end of the metal case shrink on cooling and draw the outside metal of the casting close up to the rail web, thus making an almost watertight joint. Joints of this kind have been used on exposed rails on inter-urban tracks in America, between Milwaukee and South Milwaukee. Slip joints are provided, every 500 feet, and the contraction and expansion of the track has been found to amount to about 1¼ inch per 100 feet. At the slip joints the rails are sometimes 6 inches apart. The roadbed consists of a 56 lb. T-rail, 4¼ inches high, rolled in 60 feet lengths, and laid on broken stone or gravel ballast.

Fish-Plate Joints.

The Edison bond (a), cork type plastic bond (Figs. 17 and 18) is composed of two portions; namely, a plastic alloy or putty-like metal compound which makes contact between the rail and the splice-bar or fish-plate, and a flexible, elastic cork case to hold it in position as near the end of the rail as possible. The thickness of the cork case is nearly double the distance between the web of the rail and the inner surface of the fish-plate. It is therefore compressed about 40 per cent. when in place, and after pressure has been applied it adheres to rail and plate, completely sealing the plastic alloy. The cork case is made of a compound of cork and oxidised linseed oil. It is elastic and will maintain the seal even when the plate has loosened a quarter of an inch, but it is doubtful whether this quality will last after years of use.

Fig. 15.

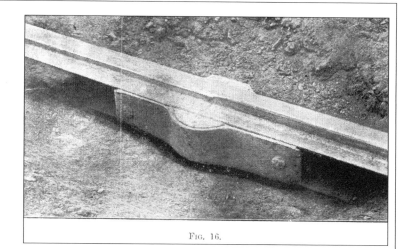

Fig. 16.

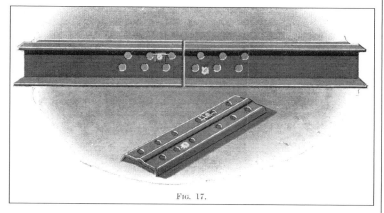

Fig. 17.

The current passes from one rail (Fig. 18) through one plug to the fish-plate, then through the second plug from the plate to the next rail. Contact spots, about two inches in diameter on both rails, and fish-plates are cleared of scale and rust and treated with the Edison solid alloy, which silvers the surfaces and prevents them from rusting. This fills the surface irregularities and penetrates the metals for a perceptible distance, leaving a surface to which the plastic alloy adheres.

In these bonds of Edison type 1000 amperes per square inch contact surface can be reached without the bond heating more than the rail. The following table shows some tests which will prove of interest.

Tests made February 15 to 17, 1898, at the Power House of the Boston Elevated Railway Company, by their Electrical Engineer, Mr. Roger W. Conant.

90-lb. Rail Joint with Plastic Rail Bonds under both Fish-plates. 12 inches between centres.		90-lb. Rail Joint with two West End Type No. 0000 Copper Bonds. Rails and plates new and rail ends touching. 12 inches between centres.	
Amperes.	Millivolts.	Millivolts.	Volts with fish-plates removed and rails separated.
500	..	..	25·0
600	..	..	30·0
650	..	..	33·0
750	..	13·8	
800	..	13·8	
850	5·8	..	45·0
900	6·3	16·0	49·5
1000	..	16·6	53·0
1100	..	..	64·0
1200	..	..	70·0
1400	..	..	81·0
1500	11·8	28·4	86·0
1600	12·8	30·0	95·0
1700	..	32·5	Bonds too
2200	17·5	43·0	hot to per-
2300	18·5	45·0	mit further
2400	19·0	47·0	tests.

Major Cardew expressed doubts regarding the lasting power of this bond and of the surfaces in contact with it. The author has found, after careful enquiries, that this bond does not deteriorate with time, as can be seen from the historic samples exhibited. Its weak point seems to be that it is liable to harden under pressure and to make a bad joint should the fish-plate get loose, but the author may be mistaken. The following type seems to eliminate the possibility of this trouble.

The Edison solid bond (*b*) is made in a different form, and consists of a solid copper strip 3 inches long, $\frac{1}{8}$th of an inch thick and $1\frac{1}{2}$ inch or more high. A cup-shaped projection is pressed at each end of it so as to give a contact against the rail web close to the end of each rail. Inside the cup is a strip of steel supporting a pair of steel springs; this steel keeps the springs from wearing into the copper. All the pieces are held together by a small iron strap or staple until the bond is applied, when the sharp web on the outside of the spring cuts it away and enters the fish-plate, thus aiding the conductivity of the bond. The metal parts of the bond are amalgamated to prevent rusting, and the contact surfaces are covered with plastic alloy. The springs are proportioned to

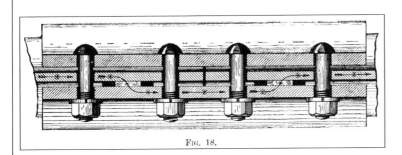

FIG. 18.

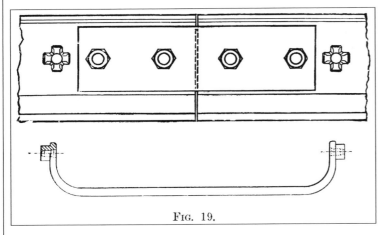

FIG. 19.

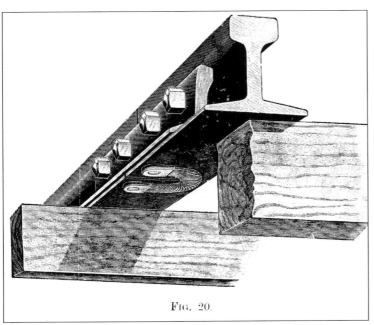

FIG. 20.

give a pressure of 1000 lb. per square inch when the fish-plates are bolted up.

When in service the springs serve merely as distance pieces so long as the joint is tight. If the nuts loosen or the plate wears, the springs still hold the bond in contact. The use of spring lock washers is advised on track nuts to keep them fast; the spring will then take up the wear of the plate. Fixing is executed as in the former type. The lubrication afforded by the plastic alloy permits the rails to move in any vertical direction without wearing the bond metal away.

Two gangs of three bonders and six track men can work at the rate of 125 joints or 250 bonds per day for each gang. On a covered track in wet or alkaline soil, where steel is apt to rust rapidly, both the springs and the sheet steel base should be treated with a petroleum compound which will permanently protect them. This, however, will prevent the fish-plate from taking any portion of the current through the bond contacts. The following table shows the resistance of bonded rails compared with solid rails :—

	Resistance in ohms.	Smallest Area in inches.
30 feet 85-lb. unbroken rail..	·000294231	8·5
30 feet of same, including joint, with four flexible copper bonds of the best type ..	·000296348	·96
Ditto, with two Edison solid ($3'' \times 1\frac{3}{4}'' \times \frac{1}{4}''$), one under each fish-plate..	·000296438	·875

CHICAGO TYPE.

This bond (Fig. 19) should be generally designed so that the current density per square inch of surface contact should not exceed 25 amperes. Care should be taken in adopting this type to have plenty of flexibility in the body of the bond itself, still keeping the terminals firm so as to allow for any vertical motion should the joint or fish-plates have any "give." The great advantages of this type over the others of similar design have been fully dealt with by other engineers. The losses due to the resistance can be divided into three, namely: (*a*) contact resistance of copper bond expanded into a hole in the web of the rail by a steel drift-pin is practically negligible; (*b*) the resistance due to gathering is also very small, and this can be got over by spreading the bond when double bonds are used, placing one on top of the web and the other lower down; (*c*) the resistance of the bond proper is brought to a minimum by using copper of 98 to 100 per cent. conductivity, and by reducing its length. With short bonds, of course, a special flexible type should be adopted. That shown at Fig. 20 is built of two solid terminals, connected by flexible strands.

Some engineers object to place the bond along the centre of the web, which is the general practice in England; they say that a torsional force is exerted on the bond, which in time will tend to get loose. They place the bond in the foot of the rail, as shown in Fig. 20. It is quite true there is only a bending strain here, but there is necessarily more movement. Summing up, the author would observe that the principal thing besides the bond-conductivity, is the lasting power of the contact surface of the bond with the rail against mechanical and heating effects, produced by the wheels passing over the joints and loosening them, and by sudden large currents inherent to electric traction.

The author desires to acknowledge his indebtedness to Mr. Philip Dawson, Mr. Harold Brown, The Westinghouse Company, The British Thompson-Houston Company, The Chloride Company, Messrs. Dick, Kerr and Co., and Mr. R. W. Blackwell, who have afforded him valuable information in the preparation of his paper, Mr. Blackwell having kindly lent him the models and apparatus.

[A discussion then followed, but only the relevant part of this is reproduced below]...

Mr. BINYON, in replying upon the discussion, said that with regard to the flexible bonds, personally, he did not think they would last as long as other bonds, because there was always a tendency on the part of the metal to crystallise. That happened in a bond just the same as in ordinary fuses. There were several types of bond which would illustrate what he meant. The circular section, for some reason or other, gave a far better result than the parallelogram section or the section with parallel sides. The flat ribs were supposed to take up all the vibration, but it was found that they always snapped off, and the middle was found to be highly crystalline.

In America, the working expenses of traction had been thoroughly investigated, and it had been found that the cost per car-mile when using electricity was $1\frac{1}{4}d$. less than that of steam. If electric traction was adopted on the suburban railways in London, there would be a saving of cost, even if the traffic did not increase. But traffic was increased by electric traction, and that was an important point. Electric traction gave a higher speed between the local stations than an ordinary steam locomotive, and the time between the stations was reduced. A maximum speed of about fifty or sixty miles could be obtained by electric traction. A person living near Sloane Square would highly appreciate getting to the Mansion House in ten minutes, or a quarter of an hour less than the time now occupied on the District line.

Mr. MORISON said he thought the introduction of electricity on the Underground would be a great improvement.

Mr. BINYON said that in America electricity was used overground, and it effected a considerable saving. Germany and France had railways working by electricity.

As to the combination of traction and lighting, it was perfectly true, as Mr. Bernays had said, that the same steam boilers could be used for both purposes. That was the case, and there was no reason whatever why the same boilers should not be used. Personally, he was in favour of the combination on a large scale; but the dynamos should be separate, because the fluctuations were so large; and the switch-boards should be entirely distinct.

Mr. Nursey had spoken about the continuous rail. The first experiments on that point were carried out in America. The rails were entirely imbedded right along, and the ends of the rails were opposite each other. There were thermometers underground and above ground, and the temperatures were taken, and the expansion of the rails was taken. It was found that the expansion was a practically negligible quantity. As to lateral expansion, the head of the rail would expand because the head was not imbedded in the earth. The road-bed in England was far better than in America, and therefore there was not so much heard about the trouble at the joint as in America.

Mr. NURSEY asked what the length of the rail was which was experimented with.

Mr. BINYON said that the length was about 100 feet.

With regard to the casting of the joints, Mr. Nursey was perfectly right in saying that there was a chill put on the metal as it came into the mould. On the table there was a sample which would show that result. The actual welding only took place in the centre. When the joint was broken off, the rail broke away with it. The electric contact practically took about $3\frac{1}{2}$ square inches. To obviate the effect of the chill the rail was heated before the joint was formed. Blow-lamps were used, and the rail was made very nearly red hot. There was, of course, a disadvantage in this process, as the rail became soft and lost some of its carbon.

With regard to the woodite bushes which Mr. Skinner had described, he would like to ask that gentleman what the cost of them was.

Mr. SKINNER said that they were 18s. each.

Mr. BINYON said that he thought that was a very high price to pay just to prevent leakage.

Mr. SKINNER said that leakage was a very important point.

Mr. BINYON said that it was an important point; but there was double insulation, and it seemed to him that the appliance which Mr. Skinner had spoken of was not quite necessary.

Mr. SKINNER said that at Blackpool it was difficult to maintain insulation at all.

Recent Tramway Construction – Demerbe System

Recent Tramway Construction

BY

WILLIAM DAWSON,

DEPUTY CITY ENGINEER,

BRADFORD.

———

PAPER READ BEFORE THE MEMBERS

OF THE

BRITISH ASSOCIATION,

MECHANICAL SCIENCE—(G) SECTION.

———

Bradford, September 5th—12th, 1900.

———

PRESIDENT :

SIR ALEXANDER R. BINNIE, M.INST.C.E., F.G.S.

———

BRADFORD:
H. GASKARTH, PRINTER, SUNBRIDGE BUILDINGS.
1900.

RECENT TRAMWAY CONSTRUCTION.

WITH SPECIAL REFERENCE TO THE

DEMERBE SYSTEM.

BY

WILLIAM DAWSON.

———

It is about thirty-five years since the introduction of Tramways into the large towns of Europe, and an account of the changes and developments which have been made in this means of transport would be very interesting from an historical point of view, but of little technical or industrial interest. The principles of construction, the different systems formerly in use and the mode of traction have all been revolutionised in the comparatively short time which has passed since the introduction of Tramways into this country—so that there is little to learn from the past. It would take up too much time to enumerate and investigate all the systems of Tramway construction which were successively tried when Tramways were generally worked by horse traction, and which have now given place to other methods more suitable for mechanical or electric traction. The first tram-rails were laid on either longitudinal or transverse wooden sleepers, but it was found that the wood soon rotted; the sleepers, were therefore discarded, and experiments made with Tramways constructed entirely of metal. The Vignole's rail was adapted for this purpose, and finally rails of the Brocca (or girder) and the Demerbe (or trough) type were manufactured.

The Brocca rail was afterwards adopted in Germany and England under the name of the Phoenix or Girder rail. This form of rail was a modification of the Vignoles rail, as the foot or bottom flange was merely widened and laid direct on the soil or on a bed of concrete. It is now generally adopted throughout England, but in my opinion has not proved a success. When animal traction only was used, very little attention was given to the fishing of the joints of the rails, but on the introduction of steam and electric traction it was soon found that the joints were unable to stand the increased strain. The fishplates were increased in length and thickness until in some cases they were three feet long and one inch thick, eight one inch fish bolts were used, sole plates were placed under the ends of the rails, narrow steel strips were placed on the top of the bottom flanges of the rails at the joints, and the whole securely bolted together with six ¾ inch bolts. The joints still worked loose, and it is now recognised that all it is possible to do in this direction is insufficient to make a perfect joint. In Germany the ends of the rails were cut obliquely, afterwards they were halved on to each other or the ends were notched and a fishplate placed in the recess. All possible methods have been tried to prevent the joints working loose and numerous patents have been obtained for different ways of strengthening the fishing—all costly and not completely satisfactory in spite of the extra outlay. The girder rail joint is undoubtedly defective, and the trouble which arises is to be attributed partly to the fact that the top and bottom of the fishplates corrode, as also does the under side of the head of the rail; the fishplates then occupy a less space and are less in depth than they were when new. The head and bottom flange of the rail is not firmly gripped by the fishplates,

and as their proper work is to maintain the level of the ends of the rails under the action of unequally distributed forces, the joint soon becomes loose. It is not therefore surprising that the consideration of the best means of fishing the joints of tramways has brought to the surface numerous, complicated, and often very remarkable methods of dealing with this branch of tramway construction.

The Demerbe system of Tramway differs entirely from all other types, and possesses in many ways some of the chief attributes of a perfect Tramway. It consists of a hollow trough rail (A. Fig. 1) and the fishplate (B. Fig. 1) is placed inside under the ends of the rails and exactly fits its contour, the point of application being immediately under the head of the rail. When this system was first introduced the fishplate was pressed into the rail by means of bolts, but it was soon found that this was not satisfactory and cotters (E. Fig. 1) were used. As the holes in the fishplates and rails are cut at different depths, when the cotters are driven in the fishplate is forced close up to the underside of the rail. The ends of the cotters are then clinched against the side of the rail and are thus fixed and prevented by any possibility from working loose. The rail when laid in position in the carriageway is completely filled by means of specially designed tools with concrete composed of 4 parts of ½ in. unscreened granite shingle to 1 part of Portland Cement.

The tie bars (G. Figs. 2 and 3) used in the Demerbe System are flat, and the use of screw ends, nuts and bolts is avoided. The rail is inserted into two oblique grooves one of which is cut so as to exactly fit the outer side of the rail, whilst the other is wider so as

to facilitate the introduction of the inner side of the rail. In the space which is left a wedge of soft steel (D. Fig. 3) a little smaller than the opening it has to fit, is inserted and driven up. This arrangement of the tie bar enables the rails to be fixed to gauge with almost mathematical exactitude.

In England, as a rule, a concrete foundation is laid the whole width of the carriageway to receive the paving, and when the Demerbe rail is filled with concrete in the manner above described, it becomes attached to the concrete foundation and is practically part and parcel of the carriageway. It is therefore capable not only of withstanding the strains caused by the cars, but also all the strains and vibrations caused by the ordinary vehicular traffic, without any loosening of the joints or displacement of the paving.

The girder rail is laid direct on the concrete foundation, and the oblique strains brought to bear on the head of the rail by the tram cars and other traffic causes the extremities of the foot or bottom flange of the rail to have a tendency to crush the concrete and so allows the rail to oscillate on its base. As soon as the rail is subjected to the least movement or vibration, a narrow fissure is produced alongside, which increases in width as the foot becomes more moveable. Water penetrates between the paving and the rail, and in frosty weather the paving is uplifted. The joint of the rails is also partly responsible for these defects, as the water finds an easy passage between the rails and fishplates.

It is necessary to take into account another factor which contributes to the grinding away or pulverisation of the concrete. The ends of the rails rest on a sole plate,

which is intended to maintain the ends of the rails at one level. When the cars pass over the track the shock is harder at the joint than on the rest of the rail where the movement caused by the car is more elastic, because the sole plate and the concrete do not support the rail with the same rigidity, and the rails become dented at the joints even when they are in perfect alignment. It follows then that the same rigidity should exist at the middle of the rail as at the joint. In the Demerbe system this is so, as the concrete becomes perfectly attached to the rail and the ridge of armoured concrete becomes part and parcel of the foundation itself. The same resistance is offered to the weight of vehicles for the whole length of the rail, no part being found to be weaker or more elastic than another.

In 1894 a short experimental length of the Demerbe rail was laid in Leeds Road, Bradford, end to end with a similar length of Girder rail. Both portions have been subjected to a five minutes' service of steam locomotive cars since that time. About three weeks ago a Demerbe rail was removed, in the presence of the Tramway Committee, to ascertain its condition. The rail, joint and gauge were found to be in every way perfect, and it was only after repeated blows with heavy hammers that the rail could be detached from the concrete foundation, and when raised it dragged up with it part of the foundation.

No money whatever has been spent in repairing this portion of Demerbe tramway, but the adjoining portion of Girder rail has been several times repaired during the six years it has been laid down. The setts used alongside the Demerbe rail are splayed to fit the sides of the rail, and laid directly against it, the rail thus serving as a support for the paving ; and there is no tendency either for the setts to rise or fall as is the case with the Girder rail.

There are in Bradford 40½ miles of Tramways, of which 36½ miles are laid on the Girder system, with rails weighing 105 lbs. per yard, and fishplates weighing 80 lbs. per pair. There are 4 miles of Demerbe tramway, constructed of rails weighing 70½ lbs. per yard, and fishplates weighing 51½ lbs. each, and the Corporation have further in course of construction an additional 10½ miles of Tramway, which they are putting down on the Demerbe System.

The detailed cost per yard of single track, on the two Systems, based on the price of materials delivered at Bradford is as follows :—

DEMERBE SYSTEM.

					s.	d.
Rails	...	...	...	...	10	7.9
Fishplates	...	...	...	...		9.4
Tie-bars	...	...	...	...	1	6.8
Wedges	...	...	...	...		1.4
Cotters	...	.	...	...		7.1
Track labour, including curve	...		...	...	2	6.0
Rails, &c., Carting	...	...	...	...		1.1
Packing Rails (Labour)		...	...	...		11.0
Half-inch unscreened Granite shingle		...	...	1	0.0
Cement	...	...	...	...		11.5
Team Labour	...	...	...	...		3.2
					19	5.4

GIRDER SYSTEM.

				£	s.	d.
Rails	...	...	...		15	11.2
Fishplates	...	...	...		1	8.8
Marshall's Patent Joints	...	...			9.9
Bolts and Nuts	...	...	...			5.4
Soleplates	...	...	...		1	0.3
Tiebars	...	...	...	...		2.8
Unscreened Granite Shingle	...		...			4.0
Cement	...	...	...	...		5.1
Labour (packing rails)	...	...			3.6
Road Scrapings (for plastering rails)	...			0.6
Track Labour	...	...	...		1	3.0
Team Labour	...	...	...			1.6
Soleplates Punching	...	...			1.9
Blacksmith's Work	..	...	...			1.3
Repairs to Punches	...	...			1.9
				1	3	1.4

Although it will be seen from the foregoing tables that the first cost of the Demerbe track is cheaper than the Girder track, this point is not the most important. There is the cost of maintenance to consider, and judging from the condition of the Demerbe track in Leeds Road after six years' wear and tear, it does not appear that any repairs will ever be necessary during the life of the rail once it is properly laid. This life I should estimate to be about twenty years, whilst the Girder rail has to be renewed in sixteen years.

The opponents of the Demerbe System when they compare these rails with the Girder type state that the latter rail when laid on two supports will carry a heavier load than the Demerbe rail under the same conditions. This is quite true, but the Demerbe rail does

not act, nor is it intended to act, as a girder. It is supported throughout its entire length by a ridge of concrete and the rail merely acts as a metallic covering.

The advantages of the Demerbe System of Tramway over other Systems may be summarised as follows :—

1. The system is simple, being composed of very few parts. It is also cheaper, and can be laid more quickly than the Girder System.

2. The rail and concrete resist the heaviest loads without displacement, depression or other alteration of the track.

3. The cost of maintenance of rails and paving is reduced to a minimum.

4. The tiebars are constructed without rivets or nuts. No punching or drilling of the rails is therefore necessary, as the tie bars can be fixed to any part of the rail by means of the slots.

5. Curves of quick radii are made at the works, and are laid as quickly as straight-track.

6. The concrete support effectually prevents water finding its way under the rail.

Having regard to the very large sums spent annually on Tramways maintenance, it is of the highest importance that lines should be constructed on a system which promises the longest working life, with a minimum of cost for repairs. The writer, after a considerable experience in Tramway construction and maintenance, has no hesitation whatever in affirming that the Demerbe System possesses points which place it far before the

Girder and other Systems, and he can confidently commend it to the consideration of those having in any way to do with the development and extension of facilities for public transport by means of Tramways. And as Bradford is the only City in the United Kingdom which has tested the Demerbe System, it is perhaps not unfitting that this paper should form a contribution to the British Association when it holds its meeting in that City.

Pointwork

Although we have used some material on the basic types of trackwork, I have not, up to now, ventured into the field of pointwork (switches) for which there was a requirement in steam tram days that they were absolutely reliable. This was never quite attained, despite some marvellous designs brought forward, but iron (cast or chilled) was always prone to wear, and it was not really until manganese enriched steel arrived that some degree of permanence could be attained. Many of the designs which follow, culled from a booklet published by Edgar Allen & Co., Ltd Imperial Steel Works and entitled *'Tramway Evolution'*, had at their heart the understanding that parts would wear and require constant renewal – for example Dickinson's design.

Volume 2, page 98, shows the conditions that points worked under.

POINTS AND CROSSINGS.

EVOLUTION.

THE " IRON AGE."

The seventies was the " Iron Age." Originally, chilled iron points were used, consisting of a movable and open point at junctions, such movable point having frequently a tongue of only 1 in. deep, and from 3 to 6 feet long. At passing places, dummy and open points were used, the dummy point being one through which the cars could *not* run, and merely consisted of one groove raised ¼″ to ¾″, which sent the car to the left hand, and in running out the car " dropped off " into the running track.

In many places both points were open, and the drivers pulled the horses halfway across the road until the car wheels had taken the correct road. In fact, anything was good enough, upon some lines so long as the car could run *on or through* the point, and weird and wonderful were many local examples I have seen scrapped.

The first points used for steam trams were on the same principle of dummy and open, but in many cases the dummy portion was a renewable Insert fastened in by cotters (and not run in with Spelter). These were the forerunners of Insert work (*nearly twenty years before the American type was used in this country*).

In some cases the fishplates were cast into the points, necessitating cutting off when being taken up or a long rail had to be taken out.

STEEL ERA.

In 1882 my old firm (Askham Bros. & Wilson, Ltd.) placed on the market a crucible cast steel point, which, while dearer, was tougher and more durable, and the first steel points used in England were laid upon the North Staffordshire Tramways and the North London Tramways, both of which concerns were constructed together. Then came the Manchester, Bury, Rochdale and Oldham Tramways, the St. Helens, Wigan, Darlington and Stockton, Middlesbrough, and West Metropolitan Tramways, followed by others.

Nearly all points for the main track were then made straight, 7′ 6″ and 8′ 6″ long, radius points only being used upon sharp junctions and at depots, the curve being a true radius from the toe of the points.

Crossings also, were all straight, but always of the Frog type, whereas now they are chiefly " leg " ends, to ensure better joints. Where required for junction work they were made the angle of the radius, and being short, worked well.

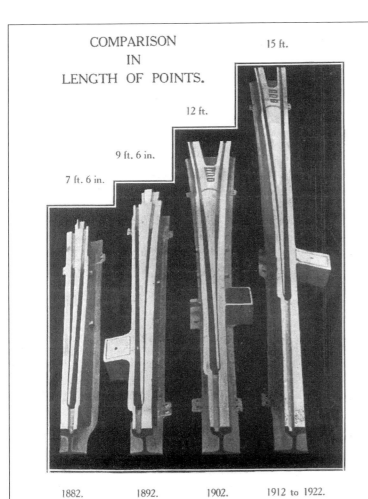

COMPARISON IN LENGTH OF POINTS.

15 ft.

12 ft.

9 ft. 6 in.

7 ft. 6 in.

| 1882. | 1892. | 1902. | 1912 to 1922. |

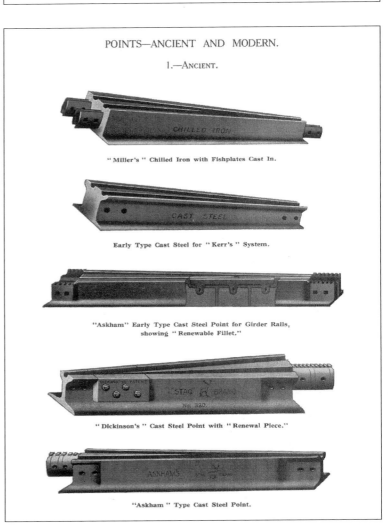

POINTS—ANCIENT AND MODERN.

1.—ANCIENT.

" Miller's " Chilled Iron with Fishplates Cast In.

Early Type Cast Steel for " Kerr's " System.

"Askham" Early Type Cast Steel Point for Girder Rails, showing " Renewable Fillet."

" Dickinson's " Cast Steel Point with " Renewal Piece."

" Askham " Type Cast Steel Point.

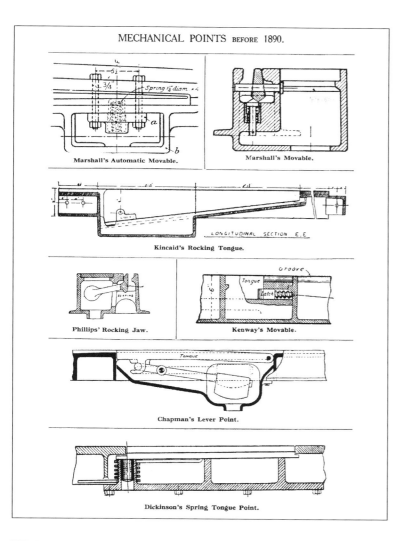

MECHANICAL POINTS BEFORE 1890.

Marshall's Automatic Movable.

Marshall's Movable.

Kincaid's Rocking Tongue.

Phillips' Rocking Jaw.

Kenway's Movable.

Chapman's Lever Point.

Dickinson's Spring Tongue Point.

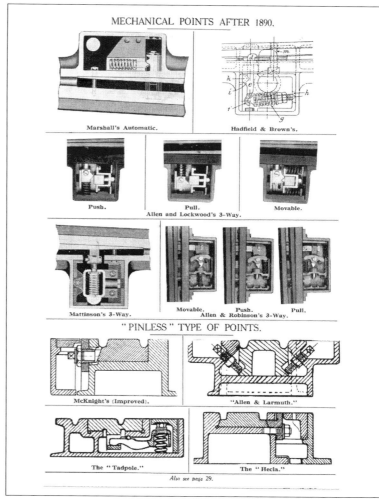

MECHANICAL POINTS AFTER 1890.

Marshall's Automatic.

Hadfield & Brown's.

Push.

Pull.

Movable.

Allen and Lockwood's 3-Way.

Mattinson's 3-Way.

Movable.

Push.

Pull.

Allen & Robinson's 3-Way.

"PINLESS" TYPE OF POINTS.

McKnight's (Improved).

"Allen & Larmuth."

The "Tadpole."

The "Hecla."

Also see page 29.

TYPES OF CROSSINGS.

Chilled Iron with Fishplates Cast in.

Crossing with Renewal Piece (Kenways).

Cast Steel "Frog" Crossing.

"Cast Steel" Crossing with "Manganese" Insert.

Iron Bound Crossing with "Manganese" Insert.

"Manganese" Leg Crossing.

AUTOMATIC POINTS.

Now came the day of the automatic point. The dummy point was found unsatisfactory, and the Board of Trade stipulated that an automatic point should be used upon all single lines of Tramways where mechanical traction was to be used. After various experiments the "Marshall" Patent Point was produced, and laid upon several lines. Other companies were induced to try these (frequently under free conditions), and the point was found to be so reliable that it was made the standard point, and was the father of all automatic points since that day, and still holds its own.

Wm. Marshall.

The patent rights were purchased, a great trade followed (as the demand grew, extensive alterations were made in the old works, which were then adapted to the production of points and crossings, as apart from constructional work), and some thousands were turned out per annum.

As stated, "Marshalls" was high over others.

W. E. Kenway patented a movable point, with a spring inserted in the toe end, but this "jammed" frequently. He also patented a Swell Point, which had the side of the R.H. tread swollen out to throw the Cars to the Left, and alternatively had a recess for a "Jumper" to be inserted, but these were not successful. "Phillips' Rocking Jaw" point had a short life. "Chapman's" point had a brief life, and worked well, but was more expensive. The principle was a weighted lever—the tongue being depressed when the car ran over it—as against the Winby point, with a leaf-spring lever.

(A dispute as to patent rights took place between these two patentees, lasting over two years, and costing a good round sum of money. Askhams, as manufacturers, were the defendants. The first trial was won by the plaintiff. Then the appeal was given against them, with an order for a new trial at the County Palatine Court, Liverpool. Final result, a verdict for the manufacturers. Nett result, no more points used of either kind. The late Justice Lord Moulton was counsel for Askhams at the second trial, and many leading engineers of that day were subpœnaed on either side).

Mechanically Controlled Points.

It is astonishing how this idea cropped up during the past 35 years. Over 100 different patents have been taken out for a point to be worked mechanically from the tramcar ; there was a perfect wave about 1900, when Glasgow invited inventors to submit their designs for this type, and " all sorts and conditions of men " imagined there was a fortune in prospect. Many were ingenious, few were worth experimenting with, although a fair sum of money was spent, with no practical results.

A mechanically controlled point is absolutely out of date, being superseded by electric point controllers. The first was the " Turner," well known throughout the country, then came the Tierney-Malone, then Collins, and these to-day hold the market.

As Tramway Tracks advanced further mechanical points were produced. The Tadpole, Marshall, Allens 3-way, Hadfield 3-way, &c., which are now in use.

Recent years have seen very notable improvements in the design of the mechanisms for controlling Single Points, and also for the Centre Connecting Mechanism for controlling Double Tongue Points, etc.

Silencers, or Silent Points.

In 1901, Mr. McKnight (a Liverpool merchant) had the idea of producing a silent point, and spent a considerable sum of money in experimenting, the result being what is now known as the " McKnight Silencer." This was adapted for both " push " and " pull " points, to suit the requirements.

Later, according to market terms, " silencers were quiet," and the demand has been intermittent since. The idea was to reduce the noise at passing places where a spring point was constantly working, and there is no doubt that the comfort is worth the extra expense.

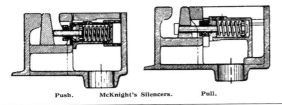

Push.　McKnight's Silencers.　Pull.

Terms "Right and Left Hand."

If the observer stands at the toe end of the points the running tread is on either the right or the left hand, independent of whether points are straight or curved, but foreign terms " Left and Right " always mean curved to Right or Left, and mean a pair in all cases.

" Open," " Neutral," " Dummy," or " Mate," are terms for the Point working with a movable, irrespective of curve or hand. " Dummy," however, was the term for the R.H. Point, which had a high groove as against the Open with two grooves.

Grooves are now usually raised in both the Mate and the Crossings, to ⅝" deep, New British Standard. In Diamonds, Curved Junctions, or Level Crossings, the groove should be raised throughout, and should end " square " to obtain the best working results.

Loops and Turnouts were also different to the present systems. Where possible the loops were laid with a perfectly straight run in at each end, and always with straight points and crossings, and this loop is still easiest to work. Now the loops are either diamond or lateral loops, with curved points.

Crossovers were frequently laid both right hand and left hand, but are now chiefly left hand, the Dublin Southern was laid right and left alternately at very short distances. *En passant*, this line I think is the only one that ran express cars morning and night with three stops in nine miles, the earlier cars being shunted to let the express pass.

For Crossovers :—At first, the movable was the right-hand point, either automatic or a movable, but we substituted the left-hand movable point, thus ensuring an easier run through, and this is now the standard practice, although some still use right-hand points, while in some cases both points are movable and connected together.

Where these crossovers are for emergency use only, a through rail is often used, with wings bolted on, thus saving cars and giving easier running. When the crossovers are used, then the cars mount the through rail and pass through as usual.

Junctions.

In the early days all tracks were laid by contractors, and one had to deal both with the contractor, his engineer and resident engineer, who, if they did not work together, made matters very uncomfortable.

A very great improvement has now been made in the laying of special work. Everything is set out and curves spiralised, and principally built up at the works, so that everything can be tested before laying.

In the " good old days " the majority of layouts were constructed on site and a great deal was left to the ideas of the local ganger, or platelayer, who, without any technical aid, made the best of the material with which he was supplied. To-day, no such latitude is allowed, as the new special work has to align correctly with the existing tracks, and in many cases to connect to existing joints in those tracks. In all cases it is essential to get the correct alignment for renewal work, which is frequently laid in sections, thus the exact positions of the various joints must be very accurately defined. Renewing Special Work is often complicated by the fact that there must be no interruption of the car service. Thus the time at the disposal of the Engineer is limited, frequently one night only being allowed for the laying of a difficult Junction.

Curves.

Originally upon sharp Curves a high lip was used on the outside from ³⁄₁₆" to ¾" high, either as part of the rolled Rail or riveted on the side. The Board of Trade later on objected to these, and many were taken out. There are now several types, but the best are :—

1. A Solid Cast Manganese Rail curved to radius.
2. A Rolled Manganese Guard bolted on, either as a flat bar, or preferably a " section bar," known as the " Holt Guard," fastened with Chairs and Bolts.
3. A Cast Guard, known as " Bulfin Lip," bolted on to the Rail.
4. The L.C.C. section of Guard, also rolled in Manganese Steel.

Curves—continued.

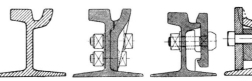

Solid Manganese Rail.　"Bulfin Lip."　"L.C.C."　Flat Guard.

" Holt's " Rolled Manganese Guard Rail.

Tram Car Wheels.

America first used rails and flanged wheels in the streets, and when Electric Tramways were introduced here it was thought that the best thing was to adopt American cars, American wheels, and American track. Now English cars are used, American wheels are abandoned, and English manufacturers can hold their own against American track material.

Using American wheels of chilled iron was a retrograde movement (which has been proved by the general adoption of steel tyred wheels), because under steam traction all the engine wheels had steel tyres, and if chilled wheels were unsuitable for steam they were doubly so for electric cars, but America used chilled wheels, consequently we had to do the same. The writer was always opposed to these, and supplied the first steel tyred wheels that were used—viz., in 1894, to the South Staffordshire Tramways Company, Limited—and in looking over some old papers I found a letter written on March 26th, 1895, by Mr. Alfred Dickinson, who was then engineer to the South Staffordshire Tramways, and I have ventured to give an extract as a prophecy since fulfilled :—" When the use of steel tyres for electric cars is more fully appreciated I feel sure that they will be exclusively used."

Steel Tyred Wheels were supplied to Bristol in 1898, Halifax and Bradford in 1899, and in 1900 the question was discussed with Sheffield, because of the numerous fractures of chilled wheels in entering the points, which was one of the reasons for tyred wheels being adopted.

In this series of books I have alluded to the writings of R. Bickerstaffe Holt who is, in tramway terms, an almost unknown hero. He was the man on whose shoulders fell all the manifold problems inherent in 'dodgy' trackwork, awkward, often inflexible rolling stock and the sheer grind of day-to-day traffic on his precious rails. As a permanent way man it was upon his shoulders there fell the sins of drivers in a big city whose techniques and indeed abilities varied enormously. A good electric tram driver would, as far as it was possible, brake reasonably gently, and accelerate 'by the book', where a bad one would brake roughly and skid along the rails and accelerate so strongly that the breakers would need resetting, and we know from reports there was precious little difference between steam and horse tram drivers (except the latter would practice cruel tricks when they thought no one was looking), and electric tram drivers and today's car drivers. All 'controllers of vehicles' from the steam buses of 1835 to those of the latest 4x4 suffer the same frustrations, likes and dislikes as one another. Below them all was and still is here and there a man like Mr Holt trying to maintain his patch of the road.

The Foreword from his book is quoted in full, as it represents the perceptions of a man facing innumerable problems in a big city, Leeds , in the early part of the 20th century.

WHAT'S WRONG WITH THE TRACK?

"So much has been written about tramway permanent way during the past ten years that one might feel tempted to apologise for again introducing this subject, were it not for the fact that, speaking generally, all is not well with the permanent way. The managers of overburdened systems will aver that there is nothing permanent about their way but its appetite for assimilating what would otherwise be handsome trading profits. One must sympathise with those gentlemen who are struggling hard to meet the expenditure on the maintenance of tracks which they did not design, and in the maintenance of which, in many cases, they have no say. It is truly a case of bearing the other man's burden.

Engineers and managers throughout the country will tell you that they have spared no expense to secure a really permanent way; every modern improvement has been tried, and yet one regrets to relate that the report from many of the sources — too many — is that the cost of maintenance is still high, and shows an alarming tendency to increase each successive year. It cannot be wondered at, therefore, that these people are all unanimous in their condemnation of the "rigid" form of construction, attributing to it all the evils the track is heir to. It is frequently stated that the rigid form of construction has been proved to be unsatisfactory. It has also been alleged that the rigid

form of construction has a deleterious effect upon the rolling stock, one writer having gone so far as to assert that "the rigidity of the track has shortened the life of the rolling stock to such an extent that tramway cars, for this reason, have only one quarter the life of railway coaches." Such a sweeping statement would obviously not bear critical analysis, even if the railway coach and the tramway car were at all comparable. There is obviously a vast difference between the work performed by the fast, but regular travelling, drawn bogie coach, running on easy grades and curves, and the work done by the driven tramway car, particularly of the single-truck type, travelling as it does over routes through tortuous streets, with cambered tracks, steep grades and sharp curves; to which must be added the enormous strain caused by constant use of powerful brakes on grades, at stopping places, and in avoiding collision with the ordinary vehicular traffic. It may be readily admitted that imperfections of the track are the cause of a considerable amount of damage to, and expenditure on, the rolling stock; but this is by no means due to the rigidity of the track; but to the failure of those responsible for its construction and maintenance to obtain a rigid track. It is the looseness and irregularities in the track that damage the rolling stock and in turn react through the car upon the track itself.

It must be granted that where the subsoil renders it possible to lay a flexible track, such a method of construction would be in many ways superior to the rigid form of construction; but it must be borne in mind that the subsoil and local conditions and the requirements of the vehicular traffic in this country in regard to the surface of the paving, in addition to third party risks, are such, in the majority of places, as to prohibit the use of a flexible track. The rigid method of construction in one form or another is the standard form for this country; but it is by no means a failure, and tracks have been and are being constructed on rigid lines on which the expenditure on maintenance has been reduced to a minimum.

To parody a recent literary catch phrase, "What's wrong with the track?" There are

usually three things wrong with a defective track. (1) Either the design was unsuitable for the locality, or (2) the materials were defective in quality or application, or (thirdly and generally) the supervision of the construction and maintenance has been inadequate and defective. The supervision of track construction is an almost unknown art, and the lack of it is responsible for most of the present day track troubles.

A track may have been well and suitably designed, the materials and workmanship may have been the best procurable, and still the track may fail to sustain the burden of the frequent service of heavily-laden, high speed tramway cars without correspondingly heavy maintenance charges.

It is not intended to reflect upon the skill and professional integrity of the engineers responsible for the work, but the fact remains that much of the tramway permanent way in this country has been constructed by engineers and contractors who, although skilled in the construction of roads and paved streets, had nevertheless little or no experience in the requirements of a modern electric tramway track, whilst their knowledge of track maintenance was nil. Knowledge of track construction was never acquired in the drawing office, nor in the actual construction of new track work alone. The actual requirements for first-class work are only to be found during a daily and almost hourly attention to the maintenance of an existing track. It is only by the constant observation of the phenomena of track movements that the cause of track troubles can be traced. It has been declared that "any competent street contractor can lay a tramway track; that the work presents no difficulties; that it consists merely in laying two steel rails above a bed of concrete, packing the same, and finally paving up in the usual manner." This is, of course, quite true, but these are the tracks that very soon "speak back to you," to borrow the expressive phrase of one of our prominent tramway managers. The same applies to the supervision — no expense has been spared in providing assistant engineers, foremen, and gangers — the surveys and levels may have been accurately prepared, and the curves well set out, and each of the gangs well watched; but the whole has been spoiled by the lack of knowledge of maintenance and of the subsequent behaviour of the track in operation. Here, then, is the chief cause of high expenditure on maintenance, and the pity of it all is that these men may continue to lay track after track without ever gaining any knowledge of the working conditions of the track beyond what they see during the ridiculously short period of maintenance. They undoubtedly become adepts (sic) at quick construction, but they are unaware of incipient flaws in their work, which are certain to develop to an amazing extent long after they have completed the work.

There is no question of the work having been scamped; but there are a hundred and one small items which require constant attention if the rigid form of construction is to be made a success from a maintenance point of view. The cause of the present day track troubles lies not in the rigid method of construction, but in the failure of those responsible for the construction of the track to lay a rigid track.

It is not intended in these pages to review the various methods of track construction which have been adopted in this country since the advent of electric traction. Such a review would no doubt be interesting from an historical point of view, but it would not serve the present purpose, which is to deal with the construction and maintenance of tramway track in a practical manner in the hope that it may be of some little service to tracksmen and tramway men generally."

I have mentioned elsewhere how I got enlisted to help relay a crossing one appallingly bad (freezing and snowing) night where the engineer was sweating (our!) blood and his tears that the 'black' cement used would set, only on completion for a Corporation steam-roller to chug its way diagonally across the newly laid track.

All too often when old trackwork is dug out the hole looks something like our illustration alongside where the hole in the left foreground was 15 inches (38cm) below the road surface.

"It is obvious that there is but one thing to do with such cases of fractured concrete foundations as those shown in Figs. 1 and 2, and that is to take them up and replace them.

Of course these are bad examples, but no fractures, however small and indistinct, can be neglected during the reconstruction of the track; they must be traced, cut out, and the concrete renewed in wide trenches. As previously stated, such fractures generally occur beneath or near to the rails, and are not discernible until the rails have been removed; but they will frequently be found to occur where the track has previously required much attention in the way of "patching."

In addition to the larger fractures, the more pronounced of the finer cracks referred to may be clearly seen in Fig. 1. There are several reasons for these fractures. In the first place, on almost every tramway system, everything was sacrificed for speed in construction, so as not to inconvenience the general public. This led to (1) hurried mixing of the concrete, (2) careless watering, and (3) either the cars or vehicular traffic were permitted to run over the new work

Fig. 1. Fractured and sunk concrete foundations.

Fig. 2. Showing settlement of fractured concrete foundations..

before the concrete had had reasonable time to mature.

Upon examination, many of the old concrete foundations show signs of being short of cement in some places and possessing too much in others. This fact is eloquent of the method adopted in mixing the mass; one can almost picture the banker, and the material being turned over "twice dry and twice wet," a man with a bucket sluicing a plentiful supply of water over the whole, and the wet cement flowing off the stage on all sides. This is what undoubtedly occurred, and the result is evident in the concrete referred to. Most of the cement was precipitated, and some of the aggregate at the bottom got more than its share of the matrix, and the remainder simply got a covering of cementy water.

In order to avoid a recurrence of such costly defects the following method of mixing the concrete has been adopted on the Leeds and

other tramways, which has the advantage of being simple, and effectually preventing overwatering. The cement and sand are first of all mixed dry on a stage having sides about 4in. high, and are then spread round the stage in the form of a basin, water is added, and the mixture is turned over until a plastic mass of the nature of floating or mortar is prepared, and spread over the stage. No further water is used, and the broken stone, having been previously wetted, is spread over the composition in a layer, and then the whole mass is turned over twice, and thoroughly incorporated before being laid in the bed. It takes very little more time to mix the concrete in this manner, and the results will certainly justify the extra cost of the work. Without doubt many fractures have been caused by the unloading and handling of rails upon concrete which is merely hard enough to walk on, and this consideration alone ought to settle finally the question as to whether the concrete should be laid before the rails or afterwards. When the concrete is laid before the rails it is practically impossible to maintain a uniform space between the rails and the concrete foundation for the packing. In such cases the interspace varies between 2½in. and actual contact with the rail flange, and it is obvious that where the concrete is close up to the rail flange it cannot be packed solidly. In such cases cement grout has been run beneath the flanges, but such a procedure cannot be condemned too strongly. One can never be certain that the grout has entirely filled up the voids. This can be clearly seen when the tracks are being reconstructed; and, again, at the best it is but a thin layer of material between the hammer and the anvil, as it were, which is liable to crack and become pulverised."

Mr Holt then alludes to the worst problem: that of traffic, "In regard to the weight and density of vehicular traffic, these are factors having a direct bearing upon the design of the track, particularly in our busy industrial centres, where extra-ordinarily heavy loads of goods are hauled by mechanical power along and across the tracks. These heavy loads, it must be remembered, are not rolling smoothly along the rails, but are jolting over the rough surface of the paving, and slipping on and off the rails with deleterious effect. Our illustrations alongside show, respectively, tread and cheek wear on two rails which, although six years old, had never had a tramcar pass over them. The wear is entirely due to other road traffic."

The age-old division of thought between the running or traffic men who want every vehicle to be available for service 24 hours a day, at least 6 days a week, collides with the demands of engineering who, however, are always mindful of their budgets. Their cause was never helped by the baleful eye of the General Manager as he wondered loudly to his secretary why 'they' put an old rattletrap on his route, being all too well aware that the latest tranche of vehicles (chosen by said GM over a round or two of golf) were horribly unreliable. Meanwhile the permanent way man is jumping up and down, vociferating loudly over his problems, "There can be little doubt that the wear of the rails is influenced to some extent by the condition of the wheel tyres.

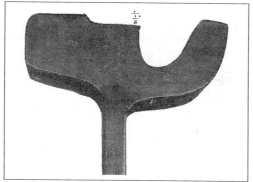

Head of rail worn by street traffic alone.

In many instances the tyres are allowed to run too long before they are either turned up or replaced, the effect of badly worn tyres being to cause uneven bearing on the rails, which results in the deformation of the rail tread and loss of metal by extrusion."

Very few of the photographs used by Mr Holt show electric overhead equipment, with some being taken in 1904 when steam tram track albeit bonded for electrical circuitry was still the norm, and some of the profiles shown in our illustration are strange to our eyes but not to his.

"...tramway rails, unlike railway rails, have either flat level treads or flat coned treads when new; but these treads ultimately become convex after a certain period in service ... at the same time it must be noted that the wheel tyres wear concave. It is obvious that it is not possible for a partly worn wheel to make perfect contact with a new flat topped rail; and in like manner it is not to be expected that a new tyre will make a suitable contact with a worn rail. In the latter case, the wear on the wheel [tyre?] being local, it is worn to a fit with the rail in a very short time, but it takes some years under an ordinary service of cars to bring a flat-topped rail into proper contact with the wheels, and during this period much irregular wear takes place. The detrusion of the metal in the tread commences immediately the rails are put into service.

This is due to the unequal contact between the wheel and the rail treads, which concentrates immeasurable pressure on a limited area, thereby causing an unrestrained flow of metal. The writer [R.B. Holt] has observed

Cheek wear due to street traffic.

frequently where new rails have been laid that quite a substantial beading of extruded metal will form on the gauge line after about forty-eight hours in service. This beading is ultimately shorn off by the wheel flanges, but the same action continues until the rails have assumed a convexity of about 12in. radius." [It is worth noting here that our British Rail permanent way men were well aware of this action on their lines, particularly where either 4-wheeled cars were used or sinuous trackwork was present; on my patch it was called 'bacon slicing' from the little curls of metal we would find].

If we refer back to our allegorical meeting before the GM of the men who matter the next speaker would probably be the Overhead Line Manager, as he would complain about rotten trackwork causing his poles or bow collectors to bounce and give an irregular electrical contact with deleterious effects on his wires and that he really must have a 6 hour occupation of the line to replace the burnt overhead wire. "Otherwise ..."

"Ah, but" would answer Mr Holt, " the irregular wear referred to takes place on new systems as well as upon those which have been in opera-

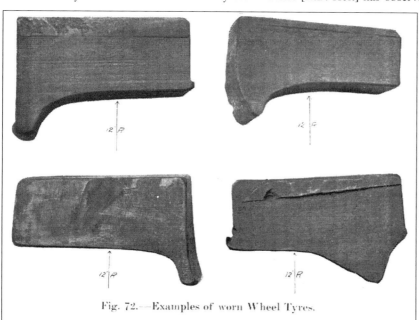

Fig. 72.—Examples of worn Wheel Tyres.

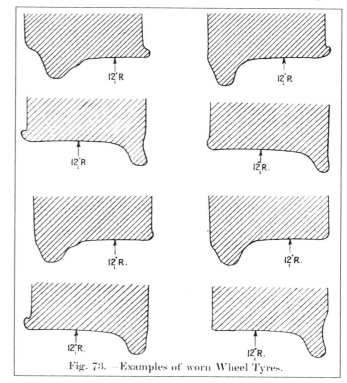

Fig. 73.—Examples of worn Wheel Tyres.

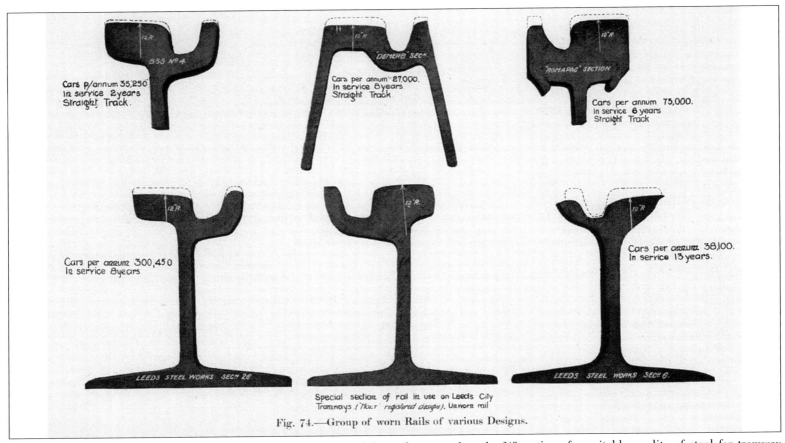

Cars p/annum 35,250
In service 2 years
Straight Track.

BSS Nº4

Cars per annum 27,000.
In service 8 years
Straight Track

"DEMERB" SECT.

"ROMAPAC" SECTION

Cars per annum 75,000.
In service 6 years
Straight Track

Cars per annum 300,450
In service 8 years

LEEDS STEEL WORKS SECT 26

Cars per annum 38,100.
In service 13 years.

LEEDS STEEL WORKS SECT G.

Special section of rail in use on Leeds City
Tramways ("Holt" registered design). Unworn rail

Fig. 74.—Group of worn Rails of various Designs.

tion for some time. The wheel contact in such cases is near the edge of the groove. This is indicative of the irregular wear that is taking place, and which continues until the rail tread is moulded under the car traffic to the shape required by the car wheels. With coned wheels and tyres it is obviously impossible to maintain a uniform contact with the rail when the wheels are in motion, seeing that the wheels are endeavouring to ride upon varying diameters at the same time. The result is that there is a constant tendency for that part of the wheel tread nearest to the flange to advance, and for the outer edge to lag, or else both movements to occur simultaneously, thus increasing the friction and abrading the rail, causing noisy running and loss of energy."

This problem was of course mentioned time and time again by early writers. Necessarily a gauge width will vary even on new rail, it being normal practice to slightly widen the gauge on sharp radius turns, and when the rails are worn (abraded as Mr Holt would say) 'wide to gauge' was a common report even on Blackpool's tramways in the 1980s. (It may be so elsewhere even now, but no-one will admit it!)

Throughout the story of first horse, secondly steam, and thirdly early electric tramways one underlying theme has been the terrible variation in the quality of the rails provided, although most were made in Britain, much was imported, but in all too many cases there seems to have been little more than lip service paid to the consistent quality of the metal. This was inevitable particularly as prices fluctuated so wildly. If I may give a relatively modern example of this in relation to the building of a new tug in the 1960s to Lloyds highest classification. This was expensive, well-built and every sheet of metal had to meet the required specification for quality. Now all these sheets came from the same stockholder but I noticed the pile of discards was growing. The foreman showed

me how on an eighteen-foot run plate the ¾" nominal thickness tapered to 9/16". This he said was nothing unusual for as the metal processed through the rolls they cooled and then 'chattered' causing undulations on the length of steel. These poor ends of roll were supposed to be sold as 'boiler reject sheets' and used, probably, for non-commercial boat building, where inspection was suborned to a low price. Would most tramway companies even have a strong enough Inspectorate to have a man available to test the metal at the steelworks or even on site?

"Tramway engineers have not, until recently, paid much attention to the relation between the composition and manufacture of the steel and the wear of the rails. Consequently they have not been in a position to give to the manufacturers such information as would enable them to produce steel suitable for the purpose. At the same time, it is evident that metallurgists and steel experts have not exactly conceived the necessity for a superior quality of steel for the purpose of rail manufacture. The following excerpt from "Steel, its Varieties, Properties, and Manufacture," by Messrs Greenwood and Sexton, conveys a fairly accurate idea of the esteem in which rail steel is held. The authors refer to the growing popularity of the open hearth steel for all purposes, "whilst the Bessemer process is falling back, and is likely in future only to be used for rails and similar articles where the output required is very large, the price low, and absolute uniformity of composition is not essential." Quite accidentally the authors of this excellent little treatise have expressed the prevailing opinion in regard to the quality of steel which is suitable for rails in general, and tramway rails in particular.

As the wear of tramway rails is so unsatisfactory, and they are subjected to so many different influences which are conducive to excessive rail wear, it is evident that the ques-

tion of a suitable quality of steel for tramway purposes should receive an early and exhaustive investigation. At the recent conference of the Municipal Tramways Association at Glasgow, Mr H. Mattinson, in his report on "Tramway Track Construction and Maintenance," referred to the quality of rail steel, and observed that "the percentage of the cost of the rail, allowing its scrap value, is only about 20 per cent of the cost of reconstruction, yet the rail alone is the determining factor in the life of the track. Too much attention cannot, therefore, be given to this question, and the very best steel procurable for this purpose is the most economical." Mr Mattinson further stated that the "composition of the steel given in the British standard specification cannot be classed as a high quality steel, and is by no means of a grade suitable for electric traction." Actual experience on heavily worked systems bears out the accuracy of these statements. It will be generally admitted, however, that the preparation of a standard specification for tram rail steel, suitable for the various ores, processes, and works, is a very difficult matter to arrange. Over 40 years ago the late Sir John Fowler stated at the Institution of Civil Engineers that "no rule could be laid down for the manufacture of rails which would be applicable to all localities." In 1889, at the same institution, the late Sir Lowthian Bell said "that he had tabulated many hundreds of specimens according to the quantity of metals and metaloids contained in the rail, and there was no kind of harmony between weakness and great purity, and, on the other side, there was no harmony between great purity and great strength. He had come to the conclusion, therefore, that great care was necessary in forming any decision too rapidly on all subjects connected with rails." He further stated that "with regard to manufacturers aiming at any particular constitution of rails, that was a much more difficult question. When it was conceived that into a great cauldron about 15 tons of metal were poured, and that in 15 minutes the whole of that metal had been converted into Bessemer steel, it would seem that it was almost impossible to calculate with any degree of nicety the character of the product."

So recently as the Engineering Conference of 1907, such eminent engineers as Mr Alex Ross, Mr R. Price Williams, Mr C.P. Sandberg, and others, were unanimous in their remarks to the effect that a universal specification or composition for rails which will suit all cases cannot be satisfactorily arrived at. "The varying conditions, such as ores available, processes of manufacture, weight of the rails, climatic and traffic conditions, differ to a great extent in every case, and all of them should be taken into account in order to obtain the best results." Notwithstanding these convincing statements in regard to the impossibility of preparing a standard specification for rail steel, many thousands of tons of tramway rails are purchased annually on the understanding that they are manufactured in accordance with the requirements of the Engineering Standards Committee, it being considered that the steel is the best obtainable for the purpose. This is not so, however, and it is not to be expected that steel of a uniform and high-grade quality, suitable for withstanding the extraordinary effects of tramcar and vehicular traffic, will be obtained from the meagre metallurgical data given in the standard specification, which merely consists of a hypothetical analysis suitable for Bessemer steel of ordinary quality, but which in no way guarantees the production of a steel of equal quality and hardness by the other "approved processes" referred to."

However, poor quality of rail steel could only aggravate wear and tear, and other great engineers were exploring other causes, some of which can be found elsewhere in this section. In a paper contributed to the Journal of the Tramways and Light Railways Association, Mr W. Thom, described as the General Manager of the Potteries Tramways [P.E.T., by then] he draws attention to the fact that the wear of the rails is not directly proportionate to the number or even weight of the cars which have passed over the rails, but instead the bulk of the extra wear is due to corrosion, and that in any event the speed of the cars can be ignored. From the measurements he had taken Mr Thom infers that the wear of the rails due to the passage of 10,600,000 car-tons was to the order of 0.2279in. and the loss of metal due to corrosion during the same period was 0.0846in. It should be borne in mind that for many long years almost every newsagent in Stoke and the general Potteries area proudly sold postcards black on one side with various comments on the other. One I remember in the early 1950s said this was a grand sight for a working man, another 'Summertime in Stoke' inferring that black smoke indicated full employment. Corrosion was therefore a fact of life in the area, mainly from 'acid rain'. How far Mr Thom's measurements were accepted by his peers I do not know but it certainly seems a reasonable factor.

Among the many matters raised by Mr Holt in his book we come to that always vexing question of setts or other paving.

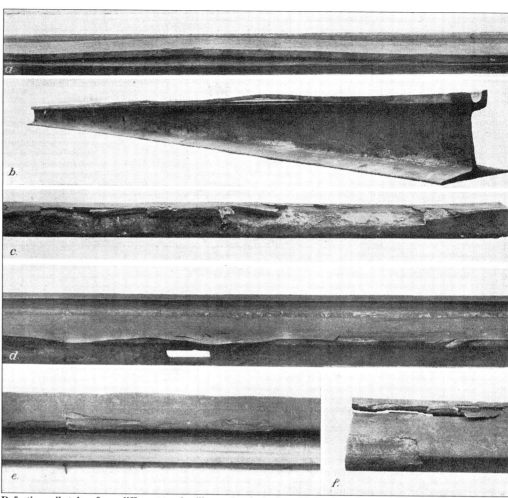

Defective rails taken from different tracks, illustrating faults found in Basic Bessemer Steels of Standard Quality. (a and b) show the entire stripping of 20ft 0in. rail, due to being made from a badly-piped ingot. (c and d, f) show the battering, extrusion, exfoliation and total collapse of the heads of two rails.. In (c) the presence of slag is easily detected. (e) shows a case of scabbing which is very common.

"It is not to be expected that the promoters of a tramway should be freed from their obligations to reinstate paving setts which have been disturbed by the looseness or vibration of the rails, and which may be readily traced. But it is reasonable to anticipate an amendment of the archaic Tramways Act of 1870, which insists that the rails shall be kept level with the surface of the paving. In the days of the horse-drawn tramcars there was a certain amount of justification for this provision, but to-day it is not reasonable to insist that the promoters should bear the cost of the wear and tear of the sett paving which is caused by the ordinary vehicular traffic.

Notwithstanding the injustice of the existing legislation, the prospect of any alleviation appears to be remote, and taking into consideration the amount of wear that takes place on the paving of all tramway tracks, it is necessary that the closest attention should be given to the quality of the granite, the size and dressing of the setts, and the manner of laying the same. It is false economy to execute the track paving with roughly dressed setts of inferior quality. So long as there are rails in the road, and in the absence of statutory powers limiting the use of the track by other vehicles, the track paving will be subjected to more than its share of the ordinary street traffic on account of the decreased tractive effort offered by the surface of the rails. In many instances it may not be possible for more than one pair of wheels on a four-wheel vehicle to make use of the rails, and in the case of some two-wheel carts perhaps

only one wheel may ride on a rail, but no doubt a certain advantage is gained in each case, and in the course of a short time the other wheels form for themselves a smooth path alongside the rails, as may be seen in Fig. 100.

Roughly-dressed setts very soon accomplish their own destruction, for the constant passage of heavy vehicles, which pound along from one sett to another, rapidly pulverise soft setts of this type, and split the harder varieties (see Fig. 101). For tramway purposes where there is any vehicular traffic worthy of note, it is necessary that well-dressed setts of good serviceable granite should be used. Such may be obtained from Bonawe, Trevor, Aberdeen, Mount Sorrell, Enderby, Llandbedrog, Dalbeattie, Newry, Penniaenmawr, and other quarries. These granites vary in hardness, and should be selected after due consideration of the weight and density of the vehicular traffic and the gradients and other local conditions. For instance, Mount Sorrell, Trevor, and Aberdeen are each capable of sustaining very heavy traffic, but on appreciable gradients with tight-jointed setts they would become too slippery to afford a satisfactory foothold for horses drawing heavy loads. For steep gradients an excellent foothold is afforded by Dalbeattie and Newry granites, which are of large grain and contain plenty of white mica which crumbles away, leaving the sharp edges of the quartz and spar crystals exposed, but in consequence of which they are not so durable as the other varieties mentioned.

Again, where exceptionally heavy loads are to be borne by the paving, it is necessary that the granite should combine great hardness with toughness and non-slipperiness. These qualities are rarely found in one stone, and so far the writer has obtained the most satisfactory results in such places from the use of Bonawe granite. This is a grey granite of fine texture, containing just sufficient white mica to keep the edges of the crystals exposed and the surface of the setts sharp.

Fig. 104 shows a track paved with Bonawe granite, which has carried heavy road traffic for four years. Particular attention should be paid to the dressing of the setts. Badly-dressed setts are not so durable as well-dressed setts, and it will be found to be more economical eventually to pay the difference in the cost of the better-dressed ones. Setts should be dressed so that they may be paved with a tight joint, and without the use of racking. The setts should be free from bulges, and at the same time they should not be wedge-shaped or undercut to any extent, as shown in Fig. 105. Each sett should be dressed and squared on all its faces, its ends should be parallel and square, and the top and

bed should be level (see Fig. 106). Setts should not be less than four inches in width, and no variation greater than one-quarter of an inch under or over the specified sizes should be allowed. For tramway purposes the length of the setts should vary between 6in. and 9in. If the setts are made longer than this it is not possible to pave them with the half-inch of camber which is necessary to free the paving of standing water. Again, long setts are liable to rock when cambered between two rails. The depth of the setts will depend entirely upon the form of construction adopted. The writer has invariably obtained the best results from the use of setts not exceeding 5in. in depth, paved upon a half-inch bed of cement and sand composition."

This article can only represent a taste of Mr Holt's erudite and dare I say it, fascinating book, and unusually at the back are a set of contemporary advertisements, one or two of which I used in volume 1, two other charming examples (opposite).

Wear of tramway rail entirely due to ordinary street traffic.

Fig. 101.—Showing Track Pavement crushed by heavy vehicular Traffic.

Fig. 100.—Showing Wear due to vehicular Traffic alongside of Rail.

Fig. 106.—Showing Square-dressed Setts.

Fig. 107.—Nidged Granite Setts (Unpaved).

Fig. 108.—Nidged Bonawe Granite Paving, Leeds Tramways.

Fig. 109.—Nidged Granite Setts (Unpaved).

Fig. 105.—Showing Wedge-shaped Setts.

Fig. 110.—Showing Nidged Bonawe Granite Sett Paving.

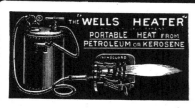

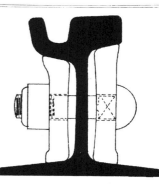
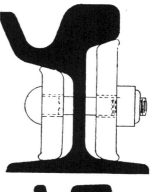
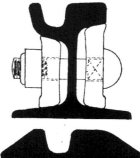

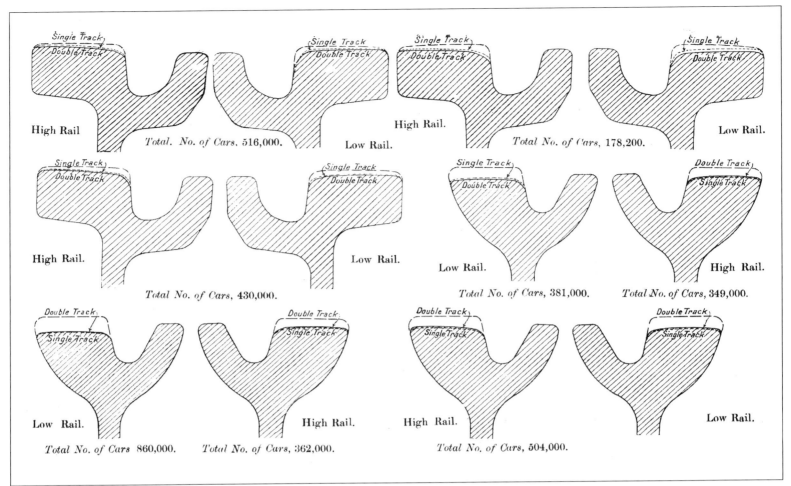

High Rail.   *Total. No. of Cars, 516,000.*   Low Rail.

High Rail.   *Total No. of Cars, 178,200.*   Low Rail.

High Rail.   *Total No. of Cars, 430,000.*   Low Rail.

Low Rail.   *Total No. of Cars, 381,000.*   *Total No. of Cars, 349,000.*   High Rail.

Low Rail.   *Total No. of Cars 860,000.*   *Total No. of Cars, 362,000.*   High Rail.

High Rail.   *Total No. of Cars, 504,000.*   Low Rail.

Comparison of wear on double and single track rails.

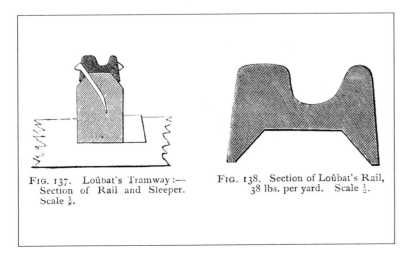

FIG. 147. Lille Tramways :—Section of Rails and Chair, for Passenger Traffic. Rail, 21·7 lbs. per yard. Scale ⅙.

FIG. 148. Lille Tramways :— Section showing arrangement of Rails for Railway Waggons. Scale ⅕.

FIG. 137. Loûbat's Tramway :— Section of Rail and Sleeper. Scale ¼.

FIG. 138. Section of Loûbat's Rail, 38 lbs. per yard. Scale ½.

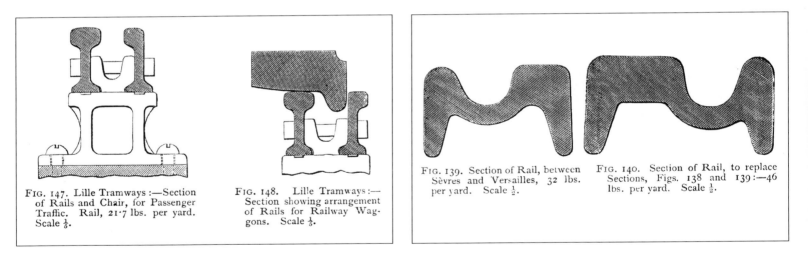

FIG. 139. Section of Rail, between Sèvres and Versailles, 32 lbs. per yard. Scale ½.

FIG. 140. Section of Rail, to replace Sections, Figs. 138 and 139:—46 lbs. per yard. Scale ½.

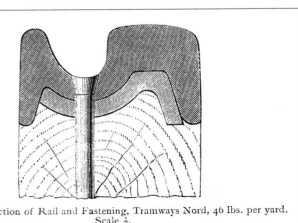

FIG. 141. Section of Rail and Fastening, Tramways Nord, 46 lbs. per yard. Scale ½.

Permanent Way for Tramways

Proceedings of the Rugby Engineering Society

Session 1904-1905
Vol. 2

PERMANENT WAY FOR TRAMWAYS.

By CHAS. T. TAYLOR (*Member*).

An essential feature of a well-equipped tramway or light railway is a good track. This is a fact that has been brought home with force to most managers of electrically operated systems, so that to successfully design the permanent way will require the most careful consideration of a multiplicity of small detail. While great strides have been made in this direction since the advent of electric traction, it can hardly be said that perfection has been attained in this any more than in other phases of our mundane existance. A well-designed track, therefore, which is the outcome of practical experience, will be a large factor in lengthening the life of the track and subsequent saving in capital outlay. It is, therefore, advisable that every possible means should be adopted (consistent with reasonable expense), to ensure that the permanent way shall be perfect, both in design and construction; for in addition to the first cost, which is about £6,000 per mile of single track of 4′8½″ gauge (which is approximately one-third of the total outlay), its proportion of life is far lower than any other portion of the traction plant. This may be taken anywhere from 10 to 14 years (all depending on the service), which, if we accept a generous average of 12 years, means that every year the sum of £500 per mile of single track must be earned over and above the fixed charges for maintenance and sinking fund. It will be seen, therefore, that every year added to the life of the track means a very considerable saving in capital outlay, and consequently increased dividends to the proprietors.

As the most important part of the track is the rail, a few words on its design and composition will, no doubt, be of interest. Experience of the last 14 or 15 years has shown that the section should be one that will provide maximum vertical and lateral stiffness, that the profile of the head should be one that will not interfere with the general traffic, and that its total width should be as narrow as possible. The width and depth of groove allows a thicker and therefore stronger wheel flange, and is desirable at curves, as it

allows free passage of the wheel flange without excessive friction, it has the disadvantage that it also allows more dirt, grit and larger stones to enter, as well as having a far greater reservoir capacity for surface water, which will be splashed by the passing car into the bearings and resistances. As the width and depth is practically controlled by the wheel flange, and it being hardly safe to use a less than ¾″ flange, in the writer's opinion, the width of groove best suited to the climatic conditions of this country is 1⅜″. This allows the use of a wheel flange ¾″ thick on straight work and curves with a greater radius than 75ft, and also reduces the capacity for grit, etc. On curves of less than 75ft. it is advisable to use rails having a wider groove so as to reduce the friction and flange wear.

The rail lip should be strong enough to support vehicular traffic, and should, on straight work, be lower than the tread, which naturally wears away much faster. It has now become nearly general practice to increase both the height and strength

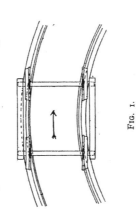

FIG. 1.

of the lip on curves, as there is a greater tendency for the wheels to ride, and consequently increased friction and wear from the wheel flanges. This is particularly noticeable were single truck cars are employed, and why it is so will be clearly seen by reference to Fig. 1. This shows clearly the position a four-wheel rigid base truck assumes in traversing a curve. The portion of each wheel flange below the head of the rail is shown shaded, and that part of the flange in contact with the rail in black, the arrow indicating the direction. It will be seen that the truck is guided almost entirely by the inner front wheel, which is all the time trying to climb the lip, and that the flange of its mate is in contact only where the gauge of track and truck permit. It has been definitely proved that were the rear wheels not retained by the flanges they would follow the forward pair in the manner shown in Fig 2, viz., with the rear axle on a radial line. Thus with a 6ft. wheel base on a 35ft. curve the distance of the rear wheels from the gauge line would be about 7″, and on 100ft. curve 2¼″.

This will be recognised as a fact beyond dispute by any who have had the opportunity of seeing a partially derailed car on a curve.

It is apparent, therefore, that the duty imposed on the rear wheel flanges is simply to keep that portion of the truck a few inches out of its normal position, thereby necessitating an increase in the height of lip to prevent derailment. Naturally this tendency of the wheels to climb produces greater friction and wear, thereby supplying the need of a heavier and stronger lip.

The web should be so placed that its centre is as near as is practicable below the tread so that the resultant of the forces from the rolling load of the car and the lateral pressure of the flange shall fall well within the base so as to reduce the tendency to tilt. The base should be sufficiently wide to resist this tilting, and to spread the weight over as large an area of concrete as possible without interfering with the paving. In the

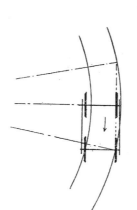

FIG. 2.

author's opinion, the design of existing rails is far from perfect, and an important fact that has been generally overlooked is one that will be seen in practically all worn tramway rails, this is the decided inclination of the top surface of the head from the gauge line outwards. Figs. 3 & 4 attached show this. This, no doubt, comes from the coning of the wheels. It has up to quite recently been almost general practice to have the rail rolled flat on the tread so as to facilitate rolling, but that it is not impossible to make rails having an inward slope of the head will be seen by referring to some of the more recent sections; aside from all questions of better electrical contact, better traction, etc., to be obtained from a full bearing of the wheel tread, the rail head is bound to assume this shape early in its career, and if made so in the first instance, it is manifest that the life of the rail is increased thereby. Within the last few months, the British Standards Committee have recommended British Rail Makers to adopt five standard sections of various weights for both straight and curved work. They recommend that the groove shall be 1⅛" wide and deep for straight rails, and 1¼" wide and deep for curved rails; that the lip of the latter should be brought up level with the highest point of the rail head, and the weight of the same increased 6lbs. per yard; also, that the head of all rails should have an upward slope of 1 in 21 from the gauge line outwards, and that car wheels be made of corresponding slope. The chemical composition of tramway rails is an interesting problem, as the specifications vary very much. During the last 10 to 15 years there have been as many changes in the chemical composition as there have been types of rail. Ten years ago rails contained only .35% of carbon: this gave a very soft rail, much too soft, in fact, as has been found out by those employing it. This has been gradually increased, until, at the present time rails contain from .5% to .65% of carbon: this gives a much harder and more durable rail. This steel will stand an ultimate tensile stress of 45 tons to the

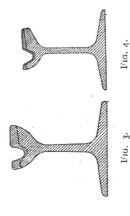

Fig. 3. Fig. 4.

square inch, with an elongation of 15%, and a contraction of over 40% in a 2" test piece ¾" diameter.

This, of course, varies considerably with the weight and percentages of the other elements employed. The effect of varying the proportions of these are—

Manganese in excess causes
Increase in resistance.
Softening of metal.
Flow of metal under traffic.

Silicon in excess causes
Increase in density.
Smooth and close surface when rolled.

Sulphur
Gives a long fibrous and seamy metal.

Carbon and Phosphorous in excess
Gives brittleness and hardness.
Shortness of grain to the metal.
Liability to fracture under severe temperature.

The following is a fair average percentage of the elements in steel rails of from 90 to 110lbs. weight per yard:—

Carbon	.5% to .65%
Manganese.. ..	.8% to 1.0%
Phosphorus not more than ..	.06%
Sulphur " " ..	.05%
Silicon " " ..	.15%

The length of rails until quite recently, seldom exceeded 36ft., but as it became recognised that the provision for expansion and contraction usually allowed was unnecessary owing to the small proportion of the total rail area exposed, the remainder being buried in practically a non-conductor of heat, and the variation of temperature in this country covering such a small range, the length has been increased until it is now quite common to employ rails of 45ft. and 60ft. Whether the latter or whether one of 45ft. is the best length to employ, is a matter of opinion, but from observation and experience the author prefers 45ft. rails, as the cost of handling and carriage is much less, and far less work has to be expended in straighten-

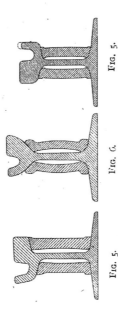

Fig. 5. Fig. 6. Fig. 5.

ing after shipment. The British Standards Committee recommend three lengths, viz., 36ft., 45ft., and 60ft., for straight work, and 36ft. for curves.

As there must be some good connection between the individual rails when laid, to ensure a continuity of track surface, the question of joints comes forward as one of the greatest moment. As a matter of fact the joint has received fully as much consideration as the rail since the advent of electric traction, if not previously. What constitutes a good joint? Simply a fastening, which, when properly applied to the abutting rail ends, will hold them in as good line and surface as the body of the rail. As before explained, the fact of the rail being laid in paving and being practically buried, no provision has to be made for expansion, and they can be butted, *i.e.*, laid without a gap for expansion.

This simplifies to a great extent the problem of making a good joint, for any opening, however small, will cause the wheels to pound, the resulting jar eventually causing the nuts and other fastenings to loosen, consequently producing a weak

or defective spot in the track. The most common form of joint is made with two plates, called "fish plates," placed one on either side of the rail, and taking a bearing on the inclined surfaces of the head and flange. From very early days until quite recently, fish plates were rolled with a much too obtuse angle at the shoulder, this allowed the rail to act as a wedge, thus gradually bending the fish plates outwards, eventually causing a bad joint. This has now been greatly reduced and a more acute angle adopted, thus giving a much better and stiffer support for the rail head and eliminating the tendency of the rail to spread and bend the fish plates. Fig 5 shows a good type of seating and fish plate; a bad type being shown in Fig. 6.

At the same time the weight and length have greatly increased, and it is now common practice to use six 1" bolts to each pair of fish plates, instead of the four used a few years back. This, undoubtedly, adds considerably to the stiffness of the joint, but the author can see no advantage in putting in more, as is sometimes done.

In order that the fish plates shall not bend under the strain of these bolts and reduce the amount of bearing with the rail head, they are made convex. This is a proper feature, but if not of sufficient thickness they buckle, and the bearing, instead of being distributed over a surface, is consequently concentrated along a line. The effect of this is to rapidly wear away the parts of the plate and rail in contact, and thus loosen the joint. Great care should therefore be exercised to see that the fish plates are of sufficient strength to prevent buckling. They have during the last few years been composed of tougher and softer steel than the rail, but the British Standards Committee now recommend that they be made of the same mixture as the rails.

It is questionable whether fish plates should be relied on as the principle means of connecting tramway rails, or whether they should only be considered as an auxiliary to a more efficient form of joint piece. With fish plates only it has been found that the wear on the rail for a distance of 12" from the rail ends is nearly double the remaining portion. It will be seen, therefore, that the joint governs the life of the rail and consequently of the track. It remains, therefore, to find the best means of augmenting the fish plates. Numerous devices have been designed to meet the demand, all of which give more or less satisfactory results. The majority of these are modifications or additions to the fish plate, and all more or less depend for their success on the accuracy of the profile of the rail.

The employment of a flat joint or sole plate bolted to the rail flange is one that is not recommended, as it does not give much increased vertical stiffness, and being broad does not allow of good tight, solid packing with concrete, the bottom being broken with nut heads.

In the author's opinion, the ideal thing to aim at is vertical stiffness with a good solid concrete bed. So far, the most satisfactory joint piece the author has seen is described below. This, in addition to providing a thoroughly rigid and efficient connection between the rail ends, makes reliable electrical contact between the abutting ends, and it has the additional advantage that no bolts are employed and it can be solidly packed.

The joint piece mentioned above consists of three parts, a large curved bar A, Fig. 7; a small curved bar B, and a wedge C. A and B are made of cast steel, and C of martin steel. This joint is assembled in the following manner: The small curved piece B is driven on to the rail flange, so that the joint of the two rails lies in the centre of the curved bar. The large curve bar A is now inserted in a red hot state under the rail from the opposite side and pressed into position; the wedge C is then driven in between A and B. In consequence of the driving in

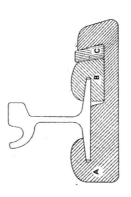

FIG. 7.

of the wedge, and the contraction on cooling of the bar A, the ends of the rails are gripped by the bars so strongly that there is secured a firm mechanical coupling, and a nearly perfect electrical contact of the two rail ends. The shape of the wedge and the nose piece of bar A causes both bars A and B to press strongly against the under surface of the rail, and at the same time prevent A slipping back.

It will be seen that all rails fresh from the mill are covered more or less with a thin coat of black oxide of iron. Much of this undoubtedly falls off during the process of loading and unloading, but there is always some adhering to the rail when placed in position. This, in the author's opinion, is one of the greatest enemies of the joint, for after the latter is fixed and the track put into service this scale is reduced to a powder by the jar of passing car wheels. This powder works its way out from between the rail and joint plate, and leaves the latter loose, or well started in this direction. This coating is also found on the joint plates. Therefore, the first thing to be done

is to remove this scale from the bearing surfaces of both the rail and joint plates: this is a matter of considerable importance, and yet is often, if not generally, overlooked. The next step is to place the plates in their proper position with the bolts screwed up sufficiently tight to see that the plates bed evenly; the bolts should then be tightened up carefully. This can be accomplished by tapping the bolt head with a light hammer while putting on the wrench.

Special Work.—It is safe to assert that there has never been built a tramway that has not had a section of track that required some special consideration other than that given to straight track before it could be laid in position. Most systems have a large percentage of their track made up of curves, crossings, etc., and in most cases these have to be made up to suit given locations, hence the term "special work." It is usual on all curves over 500ft. radius to spring in the rails as

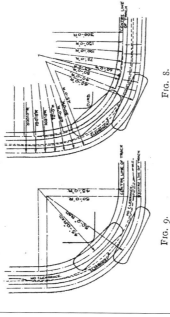

FIG. 8.

FIG. 9.

the work proceeds, as they can be relied on to retain their position, but with curves of less radius it is advisable to employ a "jim crow." The author thinks it is better to employ the jim crow on all curves and not trust to the rails retaining their position. In the early days all curves were "simple" or curves built from one centre, but since the advent of electric traction and higher speeds it has become nearly general practice to compound the curves, i.e., commence with a long radius, and gradually reduce same until the desired curvature is reached for the centre portion of the curves. This is done from each end so as to make a curve that is symmetrical about the radial line at the centre. Theoretically, the most satisfactory curve is the spiral, with gradually increasing curvature; but practically a compound curve as described above gives just as satisfactory results, while being much easier to figure out. It will be found quite impossible to detect any difference

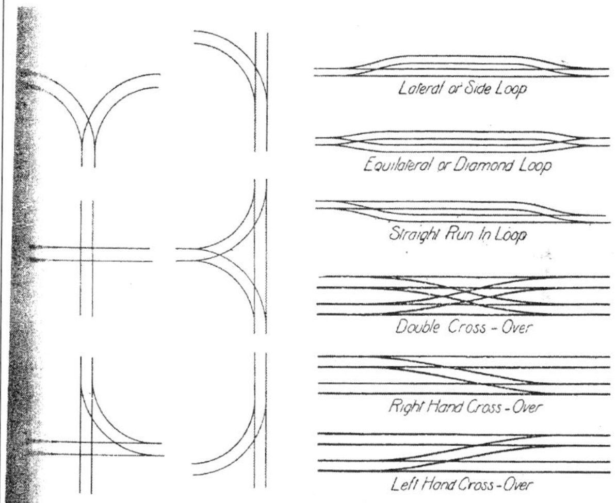

Lateral or Side Loop

Equilateral or Diamond Loop

Straight Run In Loop

Double Cross-Over

Right Hand Cross-Over

Left Hand Cross-Over

FIG. 10.

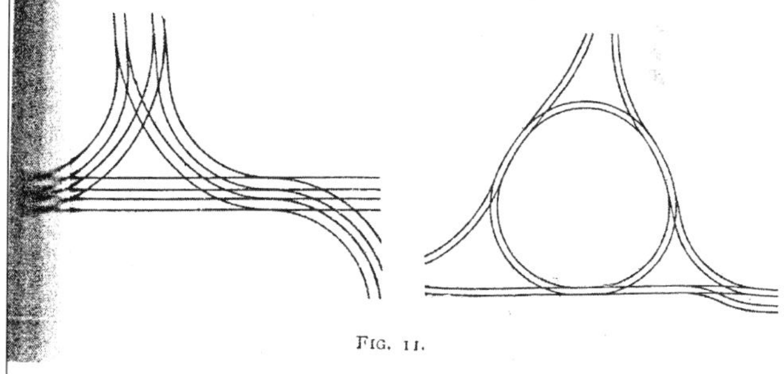

FIG. 11.

771

in the motion of a car when rounding such a curve if a sufficient number of centres has been employed and the arcs kept short. It will be found advisable to keep the arcs made from the different radi less than the car wheel base, otherwise a jerky motion will be given to the car when passing round such a curve. As it is desirable for all cars to clear and pass one another on curves, the advantage compounding gives will be clearly seen by reference to Fig. 8 & 9 which show the overhang and clearances on a simple and compound curve round a given corner. As special work covers such a vast amount of detail, and both space and time is limited, the author has prepared drawings illustrating the various simple layouts, giving the names most generally used. (Fig. 10.) There are many other peculiar and complex arrangements of track work to which no specific name can be given other than "special work." Several examples are given. (Fig. 11.) Outside the curves the pieces that go to make up a section of special work are :—Moveable and spring points. Fixed points and crossings.

These have been greatly improved during the last few years by the introduction of manganese into the steel, thus giving a much harder and more durable steel. Points and crossings, owing to their short length, are especially liable to work loose, and great care is required in the design of the joints with the rails. Their bases should be wide and well supported, and the grooves reduced so as to help the wheel over that portion where it cannot ride on the tread. Their lead off from the straight should be as easy as possible so as to prevent undue racking of the cars and discomfort to the passengers. Many of the points and crossings now installed are fitted with renewable wearing pieces, but it is doubtful if they will last as long as a good sound steel casting. Considerable trouble is experienced in renewing these pieces on account of wear on the rest of the point; this does not allow the new piece to bed down sufficiently, and thus a jar is given to the car when passing these points. All moveable points should be provided with side boxes, so as to permit of easy removal of the tongue without interference with the paving. The greatest care should be exercised in the laying of points and crossings, as if they are badly laid their life is shortened, cars are liable to jump the points and become derailed, and the force of impact is frequently such as to cause discomfort and possible injury to passengers. Care should always be taken not to lay points so as to turn out towards the inside of a curve, as this involves an increased angle of deflection with its consequent jerk. The angle of any crossing should not exceed 1 to 9, and the tops of all crossings outside the tread should be chequered.

The usual length of point employed is 7′ 6″ with a 1 in 3½ lead off, but longer points are sometimes employed, these, however, have to be specially manufactured. Crossings vary in length according to the angle, and in nearly every instance "except in the case of turnouts and cross over roads," have to be made to suit the requirements.

Drain rails are not recommended, as their short lengths necessitates joints close together: a better arrangement is to drill several holes in the bottom of the groove, or cut away a short length of the rail lip and insert a drain box or special gulley.

Rail Bed or Foundation.—In preparing the road bed for the concrete, care should be taken to see that sufficient superelevation is allowed for the outer rail on curves, and that the camber of the roadway is maintained.

All tramway permanent way should have a foundation of portland cement concrete not less than 6″ deep. This should be composed of one part of cement to six of broken stone and sand.

There are several methods of laying this foundation; probably the first method was to lay the 6″ layer as nearly as possible to the required level with a smooth top, and when the rails were laid to ram in cement grout in the spaces left between the hollows in the concrete and the rail flange. This is a bad method as it cannot be done tightly enough; another method is to pack the rail to the required level, and then pack in the 6″ layer of concrete in one mass and finish it off. This has the disadvantage that it is impossible to pack a mass of plastic concrete 6″ thick so as to take the weight of the rail, and consequently the rails are only bearing on the original support; and further, if it were possible, the slightest vibration would cause the still plastic concrete to sink away from the rail flanges. The method the author considers best, is to put the 6″ layer of concrete in as truly to level as possible, but from ½″ to 1″ lower than the finished level of the rail flange. After this has set, the rails should be put in position, and brought to a true level by cement packing at the joint and two or three intermediate places on a 30ft. rail, two men should then be set to work, one on each side, to pack the space between the rail flange and concrete bed. This packing should be composed of one part granite chips or shivers that will pass a ½″ mesh, two parts sand and one part Portland cement. The whole to be slightly damped before packing, and well watered afterwards through a rose or nozzle.

Paving.—It is essential that the paving used for tramways should be as imperishable as possible, and at the same time give a safe and firm foothold without the use of sand, under all atmospheric conditions.

Granite or other stone blocks are usually employed, the type depending on the district. These usually are from 5″ to 6″ in depth, laid on a sand bed varying in depth from ¾″ to 1″, and finished from ¼″ to ½″ above the rail tread. It is now usual to make this bed of a mixture of dry cement and sand, as when this becomes damp and sets it gives a firm and rigid support, and undoubtedly adds to the life of the paving. Pitch grout is now generally used, and is undoubtedly the best of all groutings for tramway purposes. Its superiority over cement grout is due to the fact that it is more elastic, and instead of breaking, yields to the vibration of the rails and remains watertight. One of the chief drawbacks to the employment of pitch on electric tramways is the trouble it gives in very hot weather, when it bubbles up, fills the rail groove and insulates the car. This has been overcome in many instances by grouting the setts for ¾ of the way up in pitch and filling in the remainder with cement grouting and fine chivers. All setts are now laid as closely as possible, as this reduces the amount of repairs and the cost of maintenance. For this reason it is necessary to see that they are well dressed, they should also be of various lengths from 5″ to 9″, as if setts of one length are employed the cutting of closers wastes from 10% to 15%.

Where the margins of a tramway abut on a macadamized road, they should be finished straight, and not toothed, as this greatly facilitates the maintenance of the macadamized road and the marginal paving itself, as the macadam can be rolled right up to the paving; whereas with toothed margins there is always trouble as the macadam can only be rolled to the outside of the long tooth, and the space between the long and short tooth is left loose. This allows surface water to get in, and the result is loose setts and increased maintenance. Wood paving is on account of its noiseless character often called for in busy thoroughfares; but there are so many attendant disadvantages, especially with soft wood, that a tramway engineer seldom lays it from choice. It should not in any case be laid on grades exceeding 1 in 18. One of the chief troubles with wood paving is due to its expansion and contraction. It contracts with the cold as well as from excessive dryness. This allows surface water to penetrate to the underbed and wash the sand from the joints, thus causing the blocks to rock and tilt and the surface to wear unevenly, and in very wet and snowy weather it expands and either lifts bodily in the centre from the underbed or forces the rails out of gauge.

It is impossible with the time and space at disposal to go thoroughly into all the details of permanent way construction, but it has been the object of the author to draw attention to the importance that permanent way bears to the success of an electric operated tramway, and to impress upon all interested how essential it is to have the best possible material and design, and in construction, to pay the most careful individual attention to each and every part.

DISCUSSION.

Mr. R. H. SIMPSON : Referring to the life of the track, I should like to ask whether Mr. Taylor has any reliable data as to the amount of wear on the track in relation to the number of cars passing over a particular portion, say, on the level.

In one of the technical papers lately there were particulars given of the Sheffield track, where the wear was about 1/16" to about 40,000 to 50,000 cars passing over a particular point, and the life came out at roughly nine years. As Mr. Taylor gives about 14 years as the average life of the track, perhaps he would give the composition of the rail.

As regards the shape of the rail head, has he any reasons why the type of rail head used on railways should not be used. It seems to me that in many points tramway engineers do not follow railway practice sufficiently.

One reason why car wheels are coned is, that it helps to keep the car to the centre line of the track, and prevents the tendency to ride the rail. I notice that the British Standards Committee recommend that this coning of the track and wheels should be 1 in 21, although it has been the English railway practise for some years to use 1 in 20.

Mr. Taylor mentions three lengths of rails, and I agree with him that the 45 foot length is the best. There are not many places in the country where the 60 foot rail is used. This rail has shown a tendency to "hogback." This means that the rail will rise from the ground in the centre, especially if the track has not been laid very well. For this reason the 45 foot length is preferable.

Mr. Taylor says that the wear at the centre of the joint is about four times greater than that at the centre of the rail. At Sheffield careful notes were made, and it was found that the wear on a certain piece of rail was about ¼" at the centre, and 5/16" at the joints. In the paper we are not told anything about wave wear, at which I am not very much surprised, as it has been the subject of much discussion during the last few years.

I notice that nothing is said about the length of the joint shown in Fig. 7. Also no mention is made of the anchor joint, which is used practically throughout the country in all tramways.

With regard to draining the rail, I believe in a portion of the lip being cut away and a drain box being put in, as this is much better than drilling holes in the bottom of the groove.

I should like to know what rule Mr. Taylor follows with regard to superelevation in relation to the radius, which is a point often omitted in electric traction. In the case of laying out a cross grade where two streets meet, what is the best way out of the difficulty, where it is practically impossible to superelevate the outer rail?

It would be interesting to know his objections to laying the rails on a sleeper bed, as is done on railways. It has been done in some parts of the country, and it would seem to give far better riding than rails laid on a concrete bed.

On a curve, should the rails be laid to a light or wide gauge, that is, one less or more than the normal? I myself believe in the latter.

In Mr. Taylor's chemical analysis, he is not in accordance with the latest practise advised by the Standards Committee. He gives the maximum amount of carbon as .65%, whereas the Committee advise that it should not be more than .55%. Also in his proportions of phosphorus and sulphur he gives .02 to .03 per cent. less than the B. S. C.

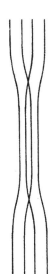

FIG. 12.

Mr. WILSON : Mr. Taylor says that water is splashed into the bearings, I should like to know how this is, as I understood that all tramway motors are totally enclosed.

Mr. DONALDSON : It seems to me that the statement Mr. Taylor makes on the first page is rather a serious one. He practically assumes that when the rails are in such a condition that they have to be re-laid, it is necessary to spend as much money as when putting down the track. Although the rails are very much worn for tramway purposes, they have a considerable value as scrap iron. The scrap value must be something, and, further the wear of the setts would be less still than that of the rails, and the outlay on granite setts is usually more, I believe, than the cost of the rail itself. Furthermore, I suppose that if the concrete work were put in well to begin with, it would still be serviceable when re-laying the track, and it seems to me that to saddle the earnings with £500 per mile for maintenance is rather wide of the mark.

So far as I am aware, the use of wood sleepers is universal in the States, and I think it makes better riding and less noise. On the other hand, I suppose that the wood would wear and in the course of time the rails would get much below the setts and

trouble would ensue. It is obvious, of course, that it is much cheaper to use wood sleepers. I have also seen iron sleepers used for this purpose, taking the form of shallow channel irons which are bolted underneath the rails. I do not think this would be conducive to easy and quiet riding.

With regard to the special work, there is a type of construction one often sees but which is not given in Mr. Taylor's paper. I do not know the technical name of it, but it is required when running with double track, but owing to the width of the street being insufficient, single track must be used. The advantages appear to be that only two crossing pieces are needed and the four frogs which are required for the ordinary turn-out can be dispensed with. Naturally the construction is somewhat more expensive, as four rails are used instead of two, but for short lengths, the saving by omitting frogs would counter-balance this. The running is much easier than with the ordinary turn-out, as there is no special work and the curves can be made more gradual.

Mr. HUGHES-CALEY : The question of the gauge at curves is a very much debated point. Mr. Simpson thinks it better to spread the gauge a little there. Recently I had occasion to discuss the subject with an engineer who had laid his own track, and who took a directly opposite view. He thought the gauge at the curves should be precisely similar to that on the straight. But his experience was a sad one, the flanges of the wheels being knocked completely off; but whether this was due to the wheels or the setting of the track is difficult to say.

In the paper the Standards Committee are mentioned as recommending that on the straight the groove should be 1⅛" wide and on curves 1¼". This would probably get over the difficulty. Personally, I do not believe in spreading the curves.

Mr. E. R. BRIGGS : The author objects to the staggering of the sets, in cases where the full road width is not paved, owing to the difficulty of making up the road at the joint. There is, however, a decided advantage in the system of staggering the sets in the effectual prevention of the skidding of the vehicular traffic when passing across the track. The skidding of buses and other vehicles has been the direct cause of several fatal accidents, and the prevention of which, as far as possible, is a duty of the track engineer. It may be pointed out that the road is no worse off, since, if rolled, there is always a portion near the sets in a state of muddy puddles in wet weather.

Mention has been made of wave wear on the rails ; perhaps Mr. Simpson would say whether the car wheels are balanced in the same way as ordinary car wheels are balanced on railways, as, if not, the centrifugal force of the unbalanced mass may have an appreciable effect towards wave wear.

Mr. WHARTON said that he would like to ask Mr. Taylor why it is that railway work differs so very much from tramway practice. On page 4[1] it is stated that no allowance has to be made for expansion. He believed that on railways it was usual to allow at the joints quite a considerable amount of clearance for expansion, and even though the railway track is more exposed, still, he would have thought that the maximum difference in temperature must in the long run be the same for tramway as for railway track.

He had an idea that in certain instances where tramway tracks had been laid without any clearance they had buckled in warm weather and lifted part of the roadway.

He would also refer to the point already raised by Mr. Briggs that according to the methods described by Mr. Taylor it was the practice to make tramway joints as rigid and stiff as possible, while on railway tracks a certain amount of elasticity was allowed. The former practice certainly seemed to be the most desirable, and he would like to know what led railway engineers to employ an elastic joint.

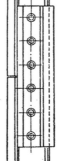

FIG. 13.

Mr. H. GUSTERSON: Pounding of the rails can be eliminated in a simple manner by employing a joint of the continuous rail type as shown in Fig. 13.

This is a combination of a vertical fish plate and a sole plate, and has all the qualities of a sole plate without decreasing the section of the rail flange by bolt holes, whilst losing none of the vertical stiffness of an ordinary fish plate.

This method was recently used by Messrs. J. G. White & Co. on the Derby Corporation Tramways. The plates are each 2' 3" long and weigh 11olbs. the pair; six 1" diameter bolts, three per side, secure them to the rails. In some cases the sole plate extension is only on one of the fish plates forming the pair.

Mr. WATSON: I should like to ask the author why he has not mentioned the Thermite process of welding rails, nor the so-called cast iron weld poured in place.

Mr. SIMPSON: With regard to Mr. Briggs' question as to the balancing of tramway wheels, I can inform him that they are not balanced, and this may have something to do with the

MR. SIMPSON.

wave wear of the rails. However, it seems hardly necessary to balance them because of the slow speed of the tram car. I have found it impossible with two standard 30 H.P. motors to get a single truck car up to 20 miles an hour.

Tramway wheels are of two types; these are the chilled iron wheel with no spokes, and the steel tyred wheel of wrought iron or cast steel with spokes.

Where high peripheral speed is obtained, balancing is necessary. A short time ago I had occasion to inspect some wheels for electric locomotives. They were of the railway type with steel tyres, the centres being of cast steel of the disc pattern, the diameter was 36" and width of head 5½". On testing sixteen of them I found that the amount out of balance was from ¼ to 3½ lbs. at 12' radius, although the tyre and rim were machined all over.

The idea of swivelling axles is not new, and has been used in this country and in Germany. From the diagram in the paper of a truck on a curve, it is seen that it is advisable to have the wheels as close together as possible; with single truck cars they cannot be brought nearer than 5' 6", but on bogie trucks this distance can be lessened to 4' 0". Consequently, the latter run round curves easier than single truck cars.

The first trucks built on the swivelling system are now running on one of the Birmingham lines; in these the axle itself radiates through the axle box. This method has been used on steam rail roads for some years, and in Germany another method has been used in which the axle swivels on the centre of its length.

Mr. C. T. TAYLOR: I might say that when writing the paper, owing to the fact that the length was limited, I undoubtedly omitted a large amount of detail, but tried to cover those points of most importance and interest to the Society.

With regard to the life of the track, I presume that Mr. Simpson was referring more particularly to the wear of rails. I have some results as to the wear of rails, but whether they are reliable I very much doubt, as the life does not depend only on the number of cars passing over it, but principally on the hardness of density of the steel.

Leeds.—Weight of rail 92lbs. to the yard. This was one of the first installed for electric traction, and in 8 or 9 years at a point 2¼" from the joint had worn about 9/16"; the number of cars passing being 7 to 8 per hour.

Norwich.—Weight of rail 65½lbs. to the yard. With 15 cars per hour in three years on the straight at a point midway between the joints has worn nearly 7/16". This means a life of 15 to 16 years for this rail.

In the case of Sheffield mentioned by Mr. Simpson, the

MR. C. T. TAYLOR.

wear given was, I think, on a particularly busy part of the system, and also as the track was one of the earliest laid down, the rail employed is much softer than that laid down now.

I think an average life of 12 years will be found to be a fair one, but in systems where there is a light service this may be exceeded.

The one principal reason why the rail head should not be similar to that used on railways is that a bearing must be provided for the paving, and if setts were undercut so as to bed against the rail web, water and dirt would accumulate in the groove left, they would be more difficult to remove, and they would be much more readily split by vehicular traffic.

In many points I agree that tramway engineers could follow railway practice with advantage, but in the case of the track, there are entirely different conditions; for while the elasticity of the railway track is one of its best features, in a tramway track it is impossible owing to the continual repairing that would be necessary.

If the joint is solid the wear there should be the same as on the rest of the track, but after the joint has sprung a little the wear increases owing to what is commonly called the pounding of the wheels.

Wave wear has been the subject of much discussion for some years, but no satisfactory conclusion has been arrived at.

I think there are two distinct causes for this wear. One is the lack of uniformity in the qualities of the metal due to the work done upon the rail in the rolls. This could also be caused by straightening the rail, the Glasgow Corporation have found such corrugations, which although not noticeable on inspection showed up under wear. The other cause is looseness on the foundation, through which a passing car would cause vibration, and therefore uneven wear, the corrugations corresponding to the lengths of the vibration waves. Superelevation of the rail on curves should be commenced from 50 to 300 feet on either side of the curve.

The superelevation in inches is given by $E = V^2/1.25R$ where V is velocity of car in miles per hour, and R the radius in feet.

Where it is impossible to superelevate, the only way is to install a guard rail on the inner side of the curve, rising about ¼" to ½" higher than the head of the rail.

The gauge on curves of 30 to 40 feet should be made 1/16" to 1/8" light and to standard gauge for a large radius when fixed wheel base cars are employed.

I think that the statement, doubted by Mr. Donaldson, that it would cost as much to renew the track after 12 years as it did originally, will be found to be not far from the mark. The material excavated will have some value, but against

MR. C. T. TAYLOR.

this must be set loss from closing the track, cost of removing old track, and possible changes in the manner of laying the rails.

The original cost of the track would be roughly £6,000 per mile. After twelve years wear credit might be allowed as follows:—

	£	s.	d.
158 tons of rail, fish plates, and bolts, @ £3 per ton	474	0	0
Scrap copper from bonds	20	0	0
975 cubic yards concrete @ 14s. ...	682	0	0
	£1176	0	0

The old setts will be found to cost as much to clean and dress as new ones, also from 12 to 15 % will be completely shattered, and all will be reduced in height to such an extent as to be useless.

Against this we have:—

	£	s.	d.
Cost of lifting old setts 5426 yds. @ 1s.	271	6	0
„ rails 158 tons @ 11s.	86	18	0
Cartage of setts at 9d.	204	0	0
„ „ rails, 158 tons @ 1s.	7	18	0
Cleaning bed, 5426 yards @ 3d.	68	0	0
Cartage of rubble, &c., 300 cub. yds. @ 2s.	30	0	0
Watching and lighting...	80	0	0
New concrete, 200 cub. yds. @ 14s.	140	0	0
Loss through closed road, 120 car miles per day for 14 days... ...	84	0	0
Cleaning fish plates	102	0	0
Anchor plates, 12 tons	8	10	0
	£1082	12	0

In answer to Mr. Wilson's remark, I may state that I was referring to the bearings of the track, and not of the motor.

Mr. Wharton asks why no gap is left at the joints for expansion of the rail. On a railway track the whole rail is exposed to wide ranges of temperature, whereas the tramway rail has only the top surface thus exposed, the ground protecting the rest, so that the range of temperature in the two cases will be quite different.

The minimum curvature employed on 4' 8½" gauge is 32 feet, for although it is possible to go to 28 feet radius with bogie tracks, it is very seldom that bogie cars only are employed on any system.

MR. C. T. TAYLOR.

The difference in the weight of rails when new and when scrap varies with the type of rail used, but generally speaking a 100lb. rail would weigh about 85lbs. when scrap.

In answer to Mr. Watson, I would say that I omitted rail welding as I did not think there would be time to deal satisfactorily with so interesting a subject, and further, I have had no practical experience of this class of joint.

Rugby Engineering Society.

17th November, 1904.

THE FOURTEENTH ORDINARY MEETING of the Society was held in the Benn Buildings on Thursday, 17th November, 1904, at Eight p.m. The President in the chair.

The Minutes of the previous meeting were read and confirmed. A motion was brought forward by the Council to amend Mr. Briggs' resolution on the Metric System of October 6, 1904, by rescinding the latter part reading from the words, "and the Hon. Corresponding Secretary be instructed, etc." This was put to the meeting and carried unanimously.

It was announced that a black-board had been presented to the Society by the students of the B.T.H. Co.'s Technical Classes; also that donations had been given to the Reading Room and Library Fund of £1 1s. from Mr. C. W. Phipps and 15/- from Mr. J. T. Irwin, and also of four numbers of the Transactions of the American Institute of Electrical Engineers by Mr. W. J. Larke. A vote of thanks to the donors was passed by acclamation.

The President announced that, in deference to the wish of several members, the Council had decided that in future it would be optional for members to read their own papers.

There followed a discussion on "The Relative Advantages of Electric and Steam Traction for Railways," opened by Mr. F. W. Carter.

There were 65 Members present.

Mechanical (Branch) Department

Not the Birmingham Tramways Committee or even a sub- or sub-sub-committee, instead a sprout from presumably the PWC or one of its relatives, but I cannot trace this body whose existence seems to be wholly to do with tramway track maintenance. I have asked for these items to be under the generic Permanent Way and Contractors section as, at least, we have a clear illustration of properly audited tramway maintenance costs.

1901-1902

The Bristol Road line was adapted to electric traction on the overhead principle by the City of Birmingham Co., and inspected by the Board of Trade on the 10th of May, 1901, and opened for public traffic on the new system on the following day. The length between Bromsgrove Street and Smallbrook Street was relaid with new metals, the tracks spaced a further distance apart, and the poles for carrying the overhead wiring placed in the centre of the roadway. On all other parts of the route the old rails were merely bonded at the joints. Between Bromsgrove Street and the City boundary the rails being only 6in. deep proved to be insufficient to carry the increased service, and it was therefore determined to replace them by others 7ins. deep; the cost thereof is part of the cost of repairing and maintaining the tramways leased to the City of Birmingham Tramways Company.

In the Parliamentary Session of 1901, the City of Birmingham Co. obtained an Act authorising the construction of tramways in Coventry Road between the existing terminus and the City boundary; in John Bright Street from the Horse Fair to Station Street; and a connecting line into Navigation Street. The Act also authorised the lines in Navigation Street, which had been constructed in 1889 without Parliamentary powers, and therefore had not been brought into use. Following the usual course the Corporation became promoters of these tramways, and in December, 1901, commenced the construction of the tramways in John Bright Street from Horse Fair to Station Street, and from the northern end of John Bright Street into Navigation Street, a single line only being laid in each case. The southern track in Navigation Street was also partly relaid, and the curve turning into Suffolk Street improved; the lines in John Bright Street and Navigation

1900

MECHANICAL (BRANCH) DEPARTMENT.

The ordinary work of repairs and maintenance of tramways has been carried on during the year at a total cost as follows :—

	Dec., 1900.			Dec., 1899.		
	£	s.	d.	£	s.	d.
Birmingham and Aston Co. ...	710	5	11	957	15	0
(Exclusive of loop, Old Square.)						
Birmingham and Midland Co....	852	1	3	797	2	0
City of Birmingham Co.	...8,361	19	4	9,473	5	11
Birmingham and W. Districts Co.	15	8	0	37	18	2

The triangle in the Old Square, which had been used by the Companies since the opening of the line in 1882, was taken up in the early part of the year, and a circular loop constructed instead thereof. The cost of this work amounted to £525 3s. 6d., which sum is repayable by the Tramway Co.

1901-1902

MECHANICAL (BRANCH) DEPARTMENT.

The ordinary work of repairs and maintenance of the tramways has been carried on during the fifteen months at a total cost as follows :—

	£	s.	d.
Birmingham and Aston Co.	853	16	1
Birmingham and Midland Co.... ...	1,112	14	0
City of Birmingham Co.	24,662	16	10
Birmingham and Western Districts Co.	15	8	0
Total	£26,644	14	11

MECHANICAL (BRANCH) DEPARTMENT.

The ordinary work of repairs and maintenance of the tramways has been carried on at a total cost as follows:—

	1903-4.	1902-3.	1901-2.*
	£ s. d.	£ s. d.	£ s. d.
Birmingham and Aston Co.	336 11 9	1,842 10 3	853 16 1
Birmingham and Midland Co.	1,988 4 9	1,680 13 8	1,112 14 0
City of Birmingham Co. ...	10,524 4 1	22,369 6 7	24,662 16 10
Birmingham and Western Districts Co.	...	15 8 0	15 8 0
Birmingham Corporation (Aston Route)...	241 17 9	...	...
	£13,090 18 4	£25,907 18 6	£26,644 14 11

* Fifteen months.

The lease of the lines in Corporation Street, Aston Street, and Aston Road, held by the Aston Manor Corporation, expired on the 30th December last, and traffic from Aston to the Old Square ceased. Arrangements were made with the City of Birmingham Tramways Co. to continue their traffic from Gosta Green and from Lancaster Street into the Old Square until the termination of their lease in 1906.

The line in Steelhouse Lane, authorised by the Birmingham Corporation Act, 1903, was laid, making a junction with the main line in Aston Street. Land fronting to Elkington Street and Miller Street was purchased for a tramway depôt, and a tramway connecting it with Aston Road was laid along Miller Street. The lengths of these new lines were as follow:—

Steelhouse Lane 22.56 chains, double line.
Miller Street ... 23.20 ,, single line.

The joints of the old lines in Aston Street and Aston Road were bonded, and the whole equipped for electric traction by the Tramway Repairing Staff, at a total cost of, for permanent way and bonding, £5,757, and for poles and overhead equipment, £2,449. The line was opened for traffic by the Corporation on the 4th January, the outer terminus being the City boundary, pending the reconstruction of the lines in Aston Manor. The old tracks in Aston Street and Aston Road proved to be unsuitable for electric traction; the work of reconstruction was put in hand, but was not complete at the end of March.

The tramway in Coventry Road, between Dora Road and the City Boundary, being No. 4 of the City of Birmingham Company's Act, 1901, has been completed, and leased to the Company until the end of the lease of the other lines in 1906. It is 45.50 chains in length, all double line; the cost was £7,910 17s. 3d., on which the

Company pay 10 per cent. as rent during the term of the lease. It was inspected by the Board of Trade, and opened for traffic on the 29th of March. The electrical equipment was provided by the Company, and is to be purchased by the Corporation at end of lease.

The agreements with the Birmingham and Midland Tramway Co. for the reconstruction of the tramways on the Dudley Road route and in Heath Street have been completed, and the works commenced; at the end of March the expenditure upon them was £12,648 6s. 8d., and they were still incomplete.

In August the King's Norton and Northfield Council paid the sum of £3,000 provided for in their Act of 1901 in respect of the tramways in Pebble Mill Road and Pershore Road authorised by that Act. The works were commenced, but not completed at the end of March, the expenditure to that date being £2,655 7s. 10d. In connection with these works, a strip of land has been given up by Lord Calthorpe for widening Pershore Road between Pebble Mill Road and the City Boundary.

In November, the only Parliamentary Plans affecting the City were deposited by the Great Western Railway Company. They provided for the acquisition of certain lands at Winson Green and for a diversion of the River Cole at Small Heath. Satisfactory arrangements have been made with the Company for the protection of the public rights in the water-way.

The Bristol Road line was adapted to electric traction on the overhead principle by the City of Birmingham Co., and inspected by the Board of Trade on the 10th of May, 1901, and opened for public traffic on the new system on the following day. The length between Bromsgrove Street and Smallbrook Street was relaid with new metals, the tracks spaced a further distance apart, and the poles for carrying the overhead wiring placed in the centre of the roadway. On all other parts of the route the old rails were merely bonded at the joints. Between Bromsgrove Street and the City boundary the rails being only 6in. deep proved to be insufficient to carry the increased service, and it was therefore determined to replace them by others 7ins. deep; the cost thereof is part of the cost of repairing and maintaining the tramways leased to the City of Birmingham Tramways Company.

In the Parliamentary Session of 1901, the City of Birmingham Co. obtained an Act authorising the construction of tramways in Coventry Road between the existing terminus and the City boundary; in John Bright Street from the Horse Fair to Station Street; and a connecting line into Navigation Street. The Act also authorised the lines in Navigation Street, which had been constructed in 1889 without Parliamentary powers, and therefore had not been brought into use. Following the usual course the Corporation became promoters of these tramways, and in December, 1901, commenced the construction of the tramways in John Bright Street from Horse Fair to Station Street, and from the northern end of John Bright Street into Navigation Street, a single line only being laid in each case. The southern track in Navigation Street was also partly relaid, and the curve turning into Suffolk Street improved; the lines in John Bright Street and Navigation

Street were also equipped for electric traction. The total cost of these works (exclusive of the electric equipment) amounts to £1,139 2s. 9d., on which the Company pay a rental equal to 10 per cent. until the termination of the lease of the lines in John Bright Street in 1906. The new lines were inspected by the Board of Trade on the 3rd of February, 1902, and opened for regular traffic on the following day; the electric cars taking John Bright Street on the "up" journey, returning *via* Navigation Street and Suffolk Street.

In July an improvement was made at the junction of John Bright Street and Hill Street, the corner of the street set back, and the tramway relaid with a larger radius; in Hill Street the line was relaid close to the footpath alongside the Railway Station wall for a length of about 100 yards, and with the consent of the City of Birmingham Tramways Co. the unused lines in the other part of that street were removed altogether.

MECHANICAL (BRANCH) DEPARTMENT.

The ordinary work of repairs and maintenance of the tramways has been carried on during the year at a total cost as follows:—

	£	s.	d.
Birmingham and Aston Co.	1,842	10	3
Birmingham and Midland Co. ...	1,680	13	8
City of Birmingham Co.	22,369	6	7
Birmingham and Western Districts Co.	15	8	0
Total	£25,907	18	6

The lease of the Birmingham and Districts Co., which relates to the tramways in Heath Street only, having been assigned to the Birmingham and Midland Co., the cost of repairs will, in future, be included with the costs of the other lines leased to this Company.

An Agreement between the Corporation and the Birmingham and Midland Tramway Co. has been entered into, providing for the electric equipment of the lines leased to them on terms similar to those applying to the work in the Bristol Road. In order to provide for cars of greater width than those at present in use, negotiations were entered into with the Company as to a supplementary agreement, providing for a reconstruction of the tramway so as to admit of such wider cars; the discussion on the proposals of the Company for a fresh lease, however, caused delay, and at the end of March the agreement was still uncompleted.

The lines belonging to the Aston Tramways Co., outside the city, have been purchased by the Aston District Council, as from the 30th June, 1902. The lease of the line from the City Boundary at Aston Brook to the Old Square, which does not expire until 30th December, 1903, has therefore been assigned to the District Council until the end of the term.

Birmingham & Midland Contract

THE BRITISH ELECTRIC TRACTION COMPANY, LIMITED.

BIRMINGHAM AND MIDLAND TRAMWAYS:

TRAMWAYS NOS: 3, 4, & 5.

CONTRACT NO: 3.

September, 1903.

Gauge 3'-6"

Route	1 Mile	6 furlongs	1.30	chains
Equivalent single	3 "	4 "	2.60	"

Schedule of Quantities and Prices referred to in the Specification and Agreement.

NOTE. These quantities are furnished for the convenience of the Contractor and Engineer and are believed to be correct, but they are not guaranteed in any way; the Contractor must satisfy himself as to their correctness.

All the items in the Bill of Quantities and Schedule of Prices are to be priced, if any be omitted a reason must be given for such omission. It is particularly requested that this note be borne in mind when tendering for the above Tramways construction.

SECTION NO: 1 (TRAMWAY NO: 3)

Route length		4 furlongs	4.20	chains
Equivalent single	1 Mile	0 "	6.40	"

Quantity	Description	Rate	£	s	d
1756 C.Y.	Excavation	5/-	453	12	8
778 C.Y.	Concrete 6 to 1 (Portland Cement)	16/-	622	8	0
33 C.Y.	Concrete under rail joints 4 to 1 (Portland cement)	19/-	31	7	0
4456 S.Y.	Granite nett paving 4" x 5" netts complete	13/-	2895	8	0
1944 L.Y.	Labor laying single line	1/-	97	4	0
	Carried forward.		4099	19	8

PERMANENT WAY MATERIALS.

Quantity	Description	Rate	£	s	d
	(Carried forward)		4099	19	8
972 L.Y.	Making good to margins	6d	24	6	0
972 L.Y.	Fencing lighting and watching	6d	24	6	0
7776 L.Y.	Cement pad to rails (3 to 1)	1½d	48	12	0
164 tons	Girder tram rails 94 lbs per yard	6/16/-	1048	10	0
6 tons 10C.	Fishplates as specified	7/10/-	48	15	0
1 " 8 C.	Fishplate bolts as specified	18/-/-	18	4	0
4 tons	Soleplates	9/7/6	37	10	0
1 ton 1 C.	Soleplate bolts	15/15/-	16	10	9
1 " 1 "	clips	21/-/-	22	1	0
5 tons 5 C.	Tie-bars	10/-/-	57	10	0
540 No.	Joint bonds 30" long	3/-	75	13	0
20 No.	Single track cross bonds 48" long	3/6	3	16	8
10 No.	Double track cross bonds 54" long	4/2	2	1	8
6 No.	Crossing bonds 84" long	5/9	1	14	6
6 No.	Point (long) bonds 150" long	9/6	2	17	0
3 No.	Sets of points and crossings	340/-	97	10	0
	Allow for alterations to sewers, manholes, lamp holes, gas, water telephone, mains, and all underground pipes, &c. *to be Reported.*				
	To SUMMARY.		5625	19	3

South Staffordshire Staff Outing

This article, which appeared in the *Midlands Advertiser* 30 July 1898, depicts that rarely recorded event, an outing for the staff, rather than 'the men'; logistically it would have been almost impossible to transport the drivers and guards to Kinver, whereas the twenty or so involved here would have fitted in two brakes or omnibi. Their innocent pleasures make a contrast with the Alton Towers or the Safari Park amusements required today.

"SOUTH STAFFORDSHIRE TRAMWAYS CO.

On Tuesday last the office staff of the above company had their annual outing, the place selected this year being Kinver. The following accompanied the trip: Messrs J.J. Robins (general manager), H. Hatchett (Secretary), G.J. Robins, W. Jukes, F.H. Bridgwater, H. Wilson, Marlow, Williams, Gilbey, W. Timmis (locomotive), H. Chamberlain (permanent way), E. Griffiths. The headquarters for the day at Kinver was the "Plough and Harrow". All places of interest were visited including "Nan's Rock". Dinner was provided by Host J.W. Stone, of the "Plough and Harrow", in a very able manner, to which every one of the party did ample justice. After the dinner was over Mr J.J. Robins presided and proposed "The Queen". Mr Hatchett proposed "The Board of Directors", and spoke of the good work done by the directors and of the manner in which they carried on the Company. He was pleased to be with them and trusted he would meet the same faces many years to come. Mr Bridgwater proposed the health of Mr Robins and Mr Hatchett, their manager and secretary, and said how proud all were in having two such capable men at their head. They had made the tramway blade of grass grow where many others had failed, and how was that accomplished? By looking after the interests of the shareholders and the Company, and he hoped that they would have them as their manager and secretary for many years to come, in fact as long as they were in the Company's service. – Mr Timmis supported and the toast was drunk with musical honours – Mr J.J. Robins in a very able speech replied, and spoke of the work of the Company and also its present success. He thanked them for the manner in which they had received the toast, and trusted the good feeling existing at present would continue. – Mr Hatchett also replied, and heartily supported all that Mr Robins had said. – The party then adjourned to the river, where much enjoyment was found and fun created by dodging the trees over-growing the stream. A most enjoyable day was spent and Darlaston was reached about 10-50p.m."

Birmingham and Midland Guards

Smethwick Telephone, 27 February 1892

"BIRMINGHAM AND MIDLAND TRAMWAY GUARDS

To the Editor of the *Telephone*

Sir,–I have gathered a few particulars of the hard lot of the above men and I should be glad if you will permit me to make them public through *Telephone*.

I am told that their working hours average 15 per day, that it is often from one o'clock to half-past one in the morning before they can get away from the shed, a considerable delay being caused by their having to wait to pay in &c. Every man is expected to be on duty fifteen minutes before he is due out of the shed, and to keep himself clean and tidy all day. They very naturally ask: 'How can we do this when we have to get water and fuel every trip at the depot?' It is said that the passengers complain about the guards being uncivil, and it is noticed that by seeing fresh faces they are continually being changed. Well, as regards incivility, I have noticed one or two instances, not lately; but I can also testify to their general courtesy, which, I think, under the pressure of their long hours and other trying circumstances, is exemplary. Now as to wages. These men are paid the munificent (?) sum of *eighteen shillings per week* and if they behave well they may, in the course of time, rise to a *guinea per week*. I ask, sir, is this not putting a premium upon honesty with a vengeance?

Now, sir, this company paid a dividend, last year, of *one per cent*. Anyone who travels by their cars as often as I do knows that they are always crowded. Where does the money go to? Certainly not in excess wages to the guards, and as certainly not into the shareholders' pocket. What are the shareholders thinking about? I would advise them to make enquiries of the Central Tramways Company; [but]...

I believe they treat their guards well; they do not use thief-catching contrivances to collect the fares; and they certainly do not put notices inside the cars to the effect that 'In no case must the fare be given to the guard.'

Yours, &c,
P.B.P."

Railways & Tramways Monthly, Vol.1 No.1, 1 January 1908:

"Birmingham – The Digbeth and Moor-street tramway ... has been opened for traffic. The Corporation Tramway Committee have come to the conclusion, after various experiments, that the watering of street curves on the tramway system is the most satisfactory way of overcoming the screeching difficulty." [These so called 'water fountains' also tried on steam tramways, were not entirely popular as the water displaced from the grooves by the tram's wheel flanges could freeze with unfortunate results for horse and pedestrian traffic.]

Railway & Tramways Monthly, 1 February 1908:

"Rawtenstall: The Town Council have accepted the tender of W.T. Glover and Co. for supplying electric lighting and tramway cables." [and so another steam tramway succumbs]

SELECT COMMITTEE MINUTES

MINUTES OF EVIDENCE.

Thursday, 23rd June 1870.

MEMBERS PRESENT:

Mr. Armitstead.
Sir Thomas Bazley.
Mr. Birley.
Mr. Cawley.
Mr. Joshua Fielden.
Colonel Gray.
Lord John Hay.

Mr. Hermon.
Mr. Hick.
Mr. Lancaster.
Mr. McClure.
Mr. Pim.
Mr. Platt.
Dr. Lyon Playfair.

JOHN HICK, Esquire, in the Chair.

Sir WILLIAM FAIRBAIRN, Bart., called in; and Examined.

1. *Chairman.*] YOU are a Member of the Institution of Civil Engineers?—I am.

2. Have you had considerable experience as a practical engineer?—Yes.

3. For how many years?—I have been engaged since I was 14 years of age up to this time, more or less, in engineering.

4. That would be how many years?—Upwards of 60 years.

5. And you have had considerable experience in the investigation of steam-boiler explosions?—Yes, I believe I was one of the first who took anything like an interest in boiler explosions, from the circumstance that I was frequently called in by the coroner in cases of accident when high pressure steam was first introduced, in order to investigate the causes; that was for some years previous to the establishment of the Association for the Prevention of Explosions.

6. Will you be kind enough to give the Committee your early experience of the causes of some of the steam-boiler explosions as well as your later experience?—Boiler explosions were almost unknown a quarter of a century ago, and from the days of James Watt to about the year 1835 it was a rare occurrence to hear of boiler explosions; about that time, when the principle of high steam worked expansively came into use the most disastrous consequences ensued, chiefly from ignorance and the want of knowledge of the properties of steam at a pressure exceeding 10 lbs. per square inch. At that period, that is to say, before the introduction of high-pressure steam, we very rarely had a boiler that was worked above 10 or 12 lbs. per square inch; indeed the Boulton and Watt rule was 7 lbs. on the square inch; so that when the pressure was increased up to 30 lbs. and 40 lbs., they

were using that in boilers that were only calculated to stand a pressure of 10 lbs. or 12 lbs. On these occasions I was frequently called in by the coroners of the different districts round Manchester to investigate and explain the causes of those catastrophes. For a number of years I was occupied with these inquiries, so much so as to trench seriously on other duties. It was at this time, and for several years afterwards, that I suggested and advocated the principle on which the present association was founded. These suggestions were submitted to some friends and gentlemen interested in the use of steam, and it was proposed that the millowners and others employed in manufactures should establish themselves into a voluntary association for the protection of property, and the lives of those who worked and lived in the vicinity of boilers and of mills worked by steam. That was about the year 1833–34, I think, and before that time, probably from the year 1830, commenced the working of steam at a much higher pressure than had been usually done before. The suggestion was cordially responded to, a committee was formed, and a public meeting was held in the Town Hall, Manchester, which fully confirmed the principle on which the association was founded. It will not be necessary that I should describe in detail the rules and regulations of this institution, as copies will be handed to each Member of the Committee; and should further information be required, it can be easily obtained from the engineer-in-chief. I would, however, observe that the association is strictly on the voluntary principle, and for a small sum per boiler; the members are not only secured from accidents by the only means applicable for that purpose, but they are guaranteed, should an explosion occur, to the full value of the boiler exploded. Such is the principle on which the

0.109.

A

Sir *W. Fairbairn*, Bart.

———

23 June 1870.

the association I have the honour to represent is founded, and I have only to refer to the services it has rendered to the community, and the lives and limbs it has saved since the commencement in 1855, to recommend it as a model for adoption. I have a very strong impression in favour of this association, which is strictly voluntary, and that has worked so well for the last 15 or 16 years; and I do not know of any other association, or any other insurance company, which has worked so well and so satisfactorily as this has done. I do not think that a single life has been lost from the commencement to the present time from boilers in charge of this Association, and that is entirely owing to this careful periodical inspection. If you compare that with the number of accidents which have occurred in other parts, you will find that this association has been much more satisfactory than any other in the kingdom. I have already stated that the voluntary system was adopted in the first instance, and it has worked well ever since. We make no money, divide no dividends, and what surplus arises from the rates is employed in scientific research on subjects connected with the construction of boilers and the use of steam. From this it will be seen that in case all other associations and companies had acted on the same principle, boiler explosions would be almost unknown. Now I am decidedly of opinion that with a very careful periodical inspection, and a thorough inspection of the boilers once a year, we should very rarely hear of any such thing as a boiler explosion, or loss of life or property in that way. I believe the evil chiefly arises from want of careful inspection, and if this was properly carried out there would have been no occasion for my honourable friend in the Chair to have asked for a Committee to investigate a subject which we know thoroughly well can be done without Parliamentary assistance. These views are, however, not popular. It is considered an unsound principle to work for nothing, as we have been doing for the last 15 years; and, in order to show that such was the case, in less than two years after the association was founded, companies, on the principle of insurance, were formed, and are now in operation in different parts of the country. I have always contended against this principle, as it will be seen that the shareholders in these companies are most of them steam users; and although they enter their boilers at a much higher rate than those of our association, they nevertheless prefer it, as a considerable amount of the money subscribed returns again to their pockets in the shape of dividends. Now I maintain that the principle on which boiler insurance companies are founded is not the one calculated to prevent boiler explosions but to a very limited extent, as the natural working of such companies is to make money at the least possible cost, and to enlarge their dividends at the cost of a comparatively limited number of inspectors. The tendency of an insurance company, in a case of this kind, is to make a dividend in the first instance, and that probably at the expense of neglecting that duty which is the most imperative and important; that is to say, very careful periodical inspection. In fact, judging from the number of efficient inspectors employed by the first and largest insurance company in Manchester, where more than 10,000 boilers are enrolled; the number of inspectors are probably in the ratio of one to about 1,000 boilers, perhaps. We have about 2,000 boilers, and seven inspectors;

I think the insurance company, which was the first company that was formed, has upwards of 10,000 boilers; and it is a question with me whether they have any more inspectors than we have for the 2,000 boilers. From this it will be noticed that thorough inspection is out of the question, and so long as the practice of making money at the expense of human life remains prevalent, we shall never, in my opinion, be relieved from boiler explosions. On this subject I have just received from Mr. Fletcher, our chief engineer, a document in the tabulated form, giving a statement of the number of persons killed and maimed from boiler explosions since the Association was established 15 years ago; and from this it appears that nearly 1,000 persons have been killed and about 1,100 injured. At the present time he states that we have, on the average, about 50 explosions per annum, and about 160 persons killed and wounded.

7. Mr. *Cawley*.] Is that within your own inspection?—No; it is the number of people that have been killed by boiler explosions in one year, and from that it appears that nearly 1,000 persons have been killed and 1,100 injured during a period of 10 years, according to the table to which I beg to refer.

8. That is in the whole of England?—Yes, in the whole of England for the time given in the table; but Mr. Fletcher will give the Committee full particulars. Allow me now to direct the attention of the Committee to the causes of boiler explosions which, in most cases, will be found to arise from, 1st, undue or dangerous pressure. The remedy for this is a sound and perfect boiler, made of the best material, and on the best principle of construction; also double safety valves well and properly adjusted, water gauges, blow-off cocks, &c., all to be kept in good and efficient working order. In this case the pressure of steam should never exceed one-fourth of the pressure that would burst the boiler; that will give a large margin above that which would absolutely burst a boiler. The next cause is the collapse of flues. There are a number of boiler explosions which take place from the collapse of flues. This is prevented by the introduction of two or more hoops of T or angle iron round the flues, equi-distant in the length of the flue. This is a very important point; it has only been discovered more than ten years ago, and it arose from experiments that I was engaged upon to ascertain the cause of the collapse of tubes. I found out, after repeated experiments, that with the boiler flue which is in use in what is called the Lancashire boiler, the double-flued boiler, two or three feet in diameter, and probably 30 feet in length, that boiler would burst without the hoops with probably a pressure of 100 lbs. per square inch; but if you rivet two hoops and divide the length into 10 feet, and make it stiff, it would then stand a pressure of 400 lbs. on the square inch. Hence I have had myself, and so have others, an impression that a collapse would scarcely occur in a perfectly true circle; but this is not the case, as we find that it follows a certain law, namely, that it is inversely as the length. If, for example, you shorten a flue 30 feet long by means of a perfectly rigid hoop, you double its powers of resistance and so on for the number of hoops that are employed. The next is corrosion; this is a fruitful cause of explosions, and more particularly since the introduction of high steam. The cure for this evil is careful periodical inspection, sound and perfect workmanship, and to see that the boiler is tight and free from

from leakage. I can give the Committee some samples of that (*producing some samples of corrosion*); that is not more than the 32nd part of an inch thick, and it was originally three-eighths of an inch thick. In this case there was one person killed and four others injured. We have had many examples of this; I also produce some specimens of hoops.

9. *Chairman.*] Those hoops are put at the junction of each plate, are they not?—Yes.

10. The section of the hoop being an angle or T iron?—Yes.

11. *Mr. Cawley.*] The important point is this, that you have found the theoretical laws confirmed experience, that the strength is in the inverse ratios of the length?—Yes.

12. And you found that confirmed in that case? —Yes, from external pressure; if you take double this length (30 feet), it collapses, which with a pressure of 100 lbs. to the square inch, and you put a hoop round it and shorten the distance one-half, it will just double the strength, the hoop being outside and perfectly rigid.

13. *Chairman.*] Then the plate might be bent, as shown in the drawing you produce?— Yes.

14. That is the same thing, in fact?—Yes.

15. *Mr. Fielden.*] The flue becomes four times as strong in that case, does it not?—Certainly, if the flue is sufficiently rigid to keep its form, it is not necessary to do any more.

16. *Chairman.*] At what distance should you consider that sufficient rigidity would be obtained if the strength of the plate were sufficient?—Ten feet is amply sufficient.

17. *Mr. Lancaster.*] In other words, a flue 10 feet long would not require strengthening?—No; if you made it 20 feet long, one hoop would do.

18. *Mr. Pim.*] That is to resist the external pressure on the flue?—Yes; any Member of the Committee who wishes to pursue the subject will find the whole of the experimental researches in the "Philosophical Transactions."

19. *Mr. Cawley.*] By putting those hoops around it (which are from their shape of so much greater strength to resist that particular pressure) you practically reduce the boiler into so many short lengths, and the tendency to collapse is then reduced as affecting each short length?—Yes; the fact is, that collapse follows the same law as girders; if you double the length of a girder or beam you will lessen its strength one-half; we did not know that before, but now we do know it, we ought to apply a remedy for it. If, for example, we take a boiler of the ordinary construction, 30 feet long and 7 feet in diameter, with one or more flues, 3 feet or 3 feet 6 inches diameter, we find that the cylindrical external shell is from three to four times stronger in its powers of resistance to the force tending to burst it, than the flues are to resist the same force tending to produce collapse. This being the case in boilers of ordinary construction, it is not surprising that so many fatal accidents occur from the collapse of the internal flues, followed immediately by the explosion and rupture of the outer shell. To remedy these evils, and to place the security of vessels so important to the community upon a secure and certain basis, it is essential that every part should be of uniform strength to resist the forces brought to bear upon it. The equalisation of the powers of resistance is the more important, as the increased strength of the outer shell is absolutely of no value so long as the internal flues, as at present,

0.109.

liable to collapse at a pressure of only one-third of that required to burst the envelope by which they are surrounded. (*Vide* "Useful Information for Engineers." Second Series.

20. *Mr. Hermon.*] You have stated that the boiler plate was reduced to that thinness by corrosion?—Yes.

21. Had the corrosive substance any local or other peculiarity about it?—We are unacquainted with the nature and the causes of corrosion; on many occasions we are quite at sea about it; the real fact of the matter is, that we have corrosion in a great variety of forms. I believe that we have had the assistance of almost every able chemist upon the subject; and among them, I think, Dr. Lyon Playfair has paid attention to that subject; my opinion is that it has both a chemical and mechanical action. If there is any acidity in the water, or carbonate of lime, forming incrustation, or anything that tends to corrosion, it requires careful attention; if, when you knock the plates with a hammer, you bring off a small scale of oxide of iron, then you expose a fresh surface to chemical action, and corrosion is the result.

22. *Chairman.*] I should be right in saying, that that corrosion takes place generally in places that are out of sight, except it is by some special action?—Yes, the most fruitful cause of corrosion and explosion is that if there is any leakage in the boiler the water begins to ooze out among the brickwork; it gets wet and dry alternately, and it is just as if it was exposed to the atmosphere, and corrosion takes place very rapidly.

23. But it is, generally speaking, out of sight? —Yes, and hence the necessity for constant inspection.

24. Careful inspection will enable such deterioration and corrosion to be found out, you think?—Yes; but there are other examples of corrosion for which we have not found a remedy; we do not know the cause of it where it joins the plates, particularly where at the end of a boiler there is very rapid corrosion going on, like grooving as if with a tool. I have seen that groved all round for half the diameter of the boiler, to the depth of about three-eighths of an inch, leaving nothing but a mere thin shell about the thickness of a shilling.

25. Have you formed any opinion with regard to the cause of that?—With regard to locomotive boilers, I have a very strong impression that, independently of the chemical action that may be taking place from the water that contained in the boiler, there is a mechanical action going on from the change of temperature in the plates; it keeps on longitudinally backwards and forwards, and though it is scarcely appreciable, it always has a tendency to work off any oxide of iron that may be formed, and that more particularly at the riveted joinings of the plates.

26. *Mr. Cawley.*] Is the groove you speak of between the two plates?—No; it is on the solid plate.

27. *Mr. Platt.*] The point is, that the corrosion of which you speak is one of the great causes of the explosion of boilers?—Yes.

28. Is there any other means of detecting this except by regular periodical inspection?—I think there is no other means whatever.

29. *Mr. Armitstead.*] Is corrosion easily detected?—No, it is very difficult to find out sometimes; a great deal of it takes place in the

A 2   interior

interior of the boiler. In many cases it will leave a grooved circle of not more than the thickness of a sixpence.

30. You say that the groove is immediately outside the junction of the two plates and not between the two plates?—Yes, it is inside; and the only cure is to examine the inside of the boiler.

31. Mr. *Lancaster*.] But in locomotive boilers it is difficult do it, is it not?—No, you can see it through the man hole in locomotive boilers. I should state that I might multiply those causes, such as enumerating all the different mountings and appendages appertaining to a boiler, but I will not trouble the Committee with these details, as they can be obtained from other witnesses. Suffice it to observe, that the great secret of security is inspection, and where that is duly and properly performed, malconstruction and all other imperfections will be discovered, the dangerous symptoms removed, and the boiler restored to a safe working condition. That certainly is my opinion. Then there is another subject connected with steam-boiler explosions that I am anxious to direct the attention of the Committee to; that is to say, the present unsatisfactory state of the investigations conducted by coroners into the causes of violent and unexpected deaths arising from boiler explosions. On these occasions a jury is empanelled, not composed of men competent to understand the nature of these occurrences, but of persons such as the coroner can find; and in these cases the almost universal verdict is accidental death. Want of intelligence on the part of the jury is, however, not the only evil, as most of the witnesses examined on these occasions are even more ignorant on these questions than the jury, and what appears to me to be wanted is, that the Government, by enactment, as the conservators of human life, should not only supply the means, but should compel the attendance of some scientific well-informed person to undertake the duty of inspection, thoroughly to sift the question in every case of accident, and bring home to the authors the full responsibility of the catastrophe. This officer, whoever he may be, should be perfectly independent and thoroughly conversant with boiler construction and the properties of steam. He should, moreover, be a person of strict impartiality, in whom the public have confidence, and he should be well paid. That is my opinion, so far as the verdict of coroners' juries is concerned.

32. *Chairman*.] You are of opinion, as I gather from you, that most boiler explosions should not be put down as accidental circumstances, but that they are all of them to be accounted for from some definite cause if they are properly investigated?—Yes.

33. You think that we have no business to find coroners' verdicts of "accidental death" given so often as we have them, at all events?—No. I am decidedly of opinion that, with proper inspection and making the owners of boilers responsible (and the inspection should be carefully undertaken, and pursued regularly and periodically, there being a thorough inspection once a year) you would very seldom hear of boiler explosions, and a great number of useful lives would be saved.

34. Mr. *Fielden*.] Do you often find the grooving that you spoke of just now to occur under the water alone, or also where the steam is?—It is more in the water.

35. Do you ever find it where there is only steam?—Yes; I have seen it all round the boiler, but not so intense in the steam as in the water.

36. Mr. *Hermon*.] Do you find this corrosion in any particular district more than others, so that it might be accounted for by any peculiarity in the water?—Yes, in some cases where there is hard water, and there is carbonate of lime, it is much more extensive, or where there is any acidity.

37. Do you employ any remedy by using negative chemical appliances?—I do not know what effect they have. I have not experienced them. There are a great many nostrums which are recommended, but I believe the best thing is careful inspection.

38. Who would you recommend should make the inspection?—I would recommend that it should be at the expense of the owner of the boiler, and I would make it compulsory by law, that they should employ such an association as I I have the honour to represent, or some other.

39. *Chairman*.] Have you such confidence in the sufficiency of a competent periodical inspection, that you think if it were generally adopted throughout the country boiler explosions would practically be prevented?—Perhaps not entirely prevented; but I think they would be very much diminished, and that instead of having to record 50 lives lost every year, we might very likely reduce them to five, and, after further experience, some years none.

40. Would you see any objection to a law to compel every steam user to have his boilers inspected?—No, certainly not. I apprehend that is the object of this inquiry, that the Government should be requested to make it compulsory that every person using a boiler should have it regularly inspected.

41. But not by a Government officer, I suppose?—Certainly not, but by committing it to competent authorities for inspection.

42. Mr. *Birley*.] Suppose this inspection were made obligatory as a universal law, and an explosion took place, would you make the liability of that explosion fall on the owner of the boiler?—If there were lives lost, and it could be proved that he was the cause, I would then make him liable.

43. I am assuming that the boiler had been properly inspected?—I think that should exonerate the owner from the responsibility.

44. Would you make the liability fall on the company in that case?—No, I think not; unless it could be proved that the company had neglected their duty.

45. Then would you look upon it as an unforeseen accident?—Yes; suppose there was a company entrusted with the inspection of your boiler or mine, and they neglected to inspect it periodically, and to see that it was in good working condition, I should say that the consequences would fall on the company.

46. You would have a Government inspector to inquire into the cause of every explosion, and if he found that the boiler company had neglected to inspect the boiler properly, the liability would fall on that company; would that be your view? —No; I am against Government interference at all, if you can possibly do without it. I think it is a very important question who is to be responsible in case of accident, and my opinion is that a person having a boiler should enrol it in an association (I do not like an insurance company, as I think the principle is wrong); he gets it enrolled and

and pays so much a year for its being inspected; and if the association neglects to inspect it, I think the responsibility would fall upon them; but if the owner of the boiler neglects to enrol his boiler, and to see it is regularly inspected, I think the responsibility ought to fall on the owner of the boiler.

47. Suppose an explosion occurs, and that the owner has not neglected his duty, and that the association has not neglected its duty, then you would not cause the responsibility to fall on either, I presume?—Then the boiler ought not to explode.

48. But you have already said that explosions may be expected to occur through unforeseen circumstances, though they may be a very small number?—Yes; some may occur from unforeseen occurrences, such as engineers or stokers interfering with the safety valves, or neglect of duty.

49. Mr. *Hermon*.] You spoke of making certain persons responsible, namely, the owners of boilers and others; I suppose you would not include in that, accidents arising from the carelessness of an employé; for instance, neglecting the water gauge, or the pressure gauge, or a safety valve; if a man who was accustomed to superintend the working of a boiler produced accident himself, it would be rather hard, would it not, that the owner of the boiler should be liable to compensate his family for the loss of that man's life?—I have known a man tie down the safety valve, and tamper with the works; but the responsibility would not be entirely removed from the owner, because you would infer from that that he had not employed a proper person to look after the boiler; but it might arise even with a person who ties down the safety valve; it might be from ignorance; but he runs the risk of being blown up along with the boiler, and he naturally would not do it intentionally for his own sake. Under those circumstances, it would have to be left to the jury to say who was the responsible person.

50. Of course you find more accidents arising from boilers at a high pressure than boilers at a low pressure, do you not?—Certainly. It is the same as kitchen boilers. I believe that during the days of James Watt, when he worked at a pressure of 7 lbs. on the square inch, we never heard of a boiler explosion at all unless it was from gross neglect or being stopped outright, because the moment the steam got up to a pressure exceeding 7 lbs. on the square inch, it forced the water out of the boiler; but that is not the case now with high pressure.

51. Mr. *Fielden*.] Would you test boilers up to four times the pressure at which they work?—I would not exceed one-fourth of the bursting pressure.

52. To what extent would you test a boiler above the working pressure?—Suppose a boiler to burst with a pressure of 400 lbs. on the square inch, I would only work it at 100 lbs. to the square inch.

53. Suppose you work a boiler at 40 lbs. pressure, what would you test it up to?—Not more than double the working pressure; certainly not.

54. Is it your opinion that over-testing a boiler tends to injure it?—There is no doubt of it.

55. Take a piece of iron, for example; if you apply one-half of the weight that would pull it asunder, you injure that iron very considerably?—Yes.

56. Is it not better if you are working a boiler

at 40 lbs. pressure, to test it up to 60 lbs. with cold water than to test it up to 80 lbs.?—Yes, perhaps, it is; unless the boiler is new, and then you may double the working pressure.

57. Do you think that a boiler may be considered safe if it is tested at 60 lbs. when you work it at 40 lbs.?—A case might happen where a boiler had been injured by some unforeseen corrosion; it might burst with 80 lbs., and it would not be safe to test it up to 80 lbs., but you might test it up to 60 lbs. A boiler in such a condition would be on the point of explosion even at 40 lbs. pressure, and ought to be removed.

58. It might be dangerous to test a boiler up to 60 lbs. when you could work it at 40 lbs.?—Yes; if you test it up to 60 lbs., and still go on until in a very short period of time, perhaps, it would burst; then comes the question of inspection, which is a very important one, namely, to find out whether the boiler has not been worked so long as to reduce its power of resistance to the extent of one-half the working pressure, and even then it would be unsafe.

59. At what periods should the boilers be inspected; that is to say, what is the longest period that you would propose a boiler should go without being inspected?—I would have it inspected every quarter, and thoroughly inspected once a year to ascertain the state of the boiler.

60. By inspection, do you mean an inspection of the interior of the boiler?—Yes, an inspection of the interior of the boiler and the exterior, too; in other words, a thorough inspection of every part of the boiler.

61. You would have an inspection every three months, you say?—Yes, every three months; but not into the interior of the boiler, unless it were absolutely necessary from incrustation, or something of that kind.

62. What would the quarterly inspection consist of?—You would examine all the valves, and so on, to see that the boiler was in good working order, and give a certificate to that effect.

63. I think that you are in favour of a voluntary inspection rather than a Government inspection?—Yes, certainly.

64. Now suppose this association were appointed, and that everybody was obliged to have his boiler inspected by the officers of that association, how would you create control over them; what machinery would you devise to take care that the association should perform its duty of inspection?—Supposing the association were to employ inspectors, the association would look after those inspectors.

65. But who would look after the association?—They must look after themselves; they are responsible to the public, and they would be of very little value if they wanted to be looked after.

66. But associations do not always do all that they should do, and the difficulty is how to ensure that any voluntary association will do its duty thoroughly?—I am only judging from my experience in our own association; for 15 years it has worked exceedingly well, and if it requires attention, there is an executive committee, and that executive committee not only has a chief engineer who does his duty, but he has a large staff of inspectors under him, and it is the duty of the members of the association who enrol their boilers, to see that they are inspected thoroughly and periodically.

67. From what you state about your association,

Sir *W. Fairbairn*, Bart.

23 June 1870.

▲ 3

785

tion, it appears you have a very efficient executive; but suppose from change of time and from necessary changes of persons from death, and so on, in the executive, the executive became apathetic, or that the persons were not energetic, then it seems to me that the association might not do the duty which you depute to it, and for the sake of doing which, you give it arbitrary powers to compel an inspection, is not that so?—I think the Government should deal with that question, as also the members to see that the associations were kept up to the mark.

68. Do you think if we relied upon an inspection by a voluntary association there should be Government control over that association, not to interfere with the minutiæ of their arrangements, but to take care that they did their duty?—There is a circumstance connected with it, and that is this, that any person on enrolling his boiler in such an association would have to pay for it, and very few people will pay for a thing unless they get some return for it to the value of the money they pay; under those circumstances it would naturally work well; but, suppose the association, either from want of care or from leaving to others what they ought to do themselves, was to allow the superintendence of the staff to get out of order, the time would come when something should be done to rectify it; a change of the committee, or something of that kind.

69. Persons subscribe their money in the belief that this inspection would be efficient, and we do not know that it is not efficient; and, of course, the officers would never neglect to go round; but I am supposing a case where they do go round and nominally inspect, though they really do not inspect, the boilers; do you not think, in such a case, that if a voluntary association were allowed to be used as a means of inspection, it would be necessary to have some Government control in the shape of a chief inspector or sub-inspector, to keep a check on the inspectors of the voluntary association?—I think, with regard to the association to which I belong, that their object is that the Government should establish a general principle, not going into detail at all, but leaving that to the associations and to the members of the associations. I think it would be very obnoxious to millowners and those who had factories and boilers, to have a Government inspector overlooking them; it is only in certain cases that I should wish for Government interference.

70. What I gather from you is this, that you think the Government should lay down certain broad principles which must be followed in all cases, and leave the carrying out of the detail of those principles to voluntary associations?—Yes, certainly, as I think a well-organised association, with an energetic committee, and an active superintendant engineer, would be quite equal to the task of managing their own business.

71. You think that would be more effective, and tend more to what we are all aiming at; that is to say, the prevention of explosions, than having a Government inspector to go round?—We cannot foresee the working of a law which does not exist; and very likely any enactment that might be passed by Parliament for the general supervision of boilers, might require after that law had passed, and had been tried, some amendment; at all events it is probable.

72. Colonel *Gray.*] You have had an associa-

tion in Manchester for 15 years, I think, you say?—Yes.

73. Can you tell the Committee at all, what the proportion of the whole of those who have steam boilers in the district have enrolled themselves in the association?—Only a fraction of them. I think there is probably one-eighth or one-tenth of them. The number of boilers in Manchester and the district would very likely be 50,000, and we have only 2,000.

74. If something could be done to induce more persons to join the association, probably explosions would be very much more prevented?—Yes. There is a great many more boilers insured in insurance companies than there are in associations; one insurance company has 10,000 boilers while we have only 2,000. But although I could not from memory say what the strength of the staff of the insurance companies may be as compared with the staff of our association, I know it is considerably less. If for instance we have as large a staff for 2,000 boilers as they have for 10,000, the result would be a very imperfect inspection on the part of the insurance company.

75. I suppose there is no difficulty in obtaining good, efficient inspectors?—Certainly not; but they must be well paid, and must be intelligent men, and men who understand their work too; they ought to be mechanical engineers, in my opinion, of a superior class.

76. I daresay the reason of more men not joining the association is that they do not see any advantage in it?—They do not like to pay the rates. A great many people have boilers who belong neither to an association nor an insurance company, but they take the responsibility upon themselves.

77. Mr. *Cawley.*] Will you be kind enough to state in a few words what is the particular action which you think the Government could beneficially take in this matter, apart altogether from the voluntary question?—In simple terms I would say that all that is wanted on the part of the Government would be to enact a law that every person having a boiler should be bound to have it inspected by some competent authority; either an association or a company.

78. Would you have the Government take any active means to ascertain and certify the competency of those parties?—No. The fact is, that I think the less we have to do with the Government in a case of this kind the better, excepting that they should establish some general principle that steam boilers should be carefully inspected.

79. Would you leave that without the imposition of a penalty in case it were not done?—I must leave that to the Committee to determine in their Report; but I think that it ought to be under a penalty.

80. Mr. *Lancaster.*] You begin the inspection first by certifying that the boiler is a properly constructed one, I suppose?—Yes.

81. That would be the foundation?—Yes, or we would not accept it. If a boiler is defective in construction, and it is not satisfactory with regard to its powers of resistance, we object to it, and we will not have it.

82. You would retain that power to reject any boiler that did not come up to the standard of the inspector's rule, I suppose?—Yes, certainly. And then having once got a satisfactory boiler into the association, we have to take care that is kept in that state, and in good working order.

83. Any

83. Any neglect of inspection, whether by the owner or by the association, would now come under Lord Campbell's Act, and the owner would be liable for damages, would he not?—Certainly, but I never heard of penalties being exacted.

84. You have already stated that coroners' juries invariably give verdicts of accidental death, and that verdict excludes a case of that kind from the operation of the Act, does it not?—I do not say that in every case the verdict was brought in accidental death; as in several cases the causes have been fully ascertained by inspection. What I complain of is this: that witnesses are examined who are not competent to give an opinion, either from general ignorance or from want of knowledge of the particular subject, and they give evidence that induces the jury to return a verdict of accidental death, when the cause of an explosion might have been known by the examination of competent persons.

85. Mr. *Platt*.] I think we may take for granted that a periodical inspection is necessary, and we are agreed that it would be a very desirable thing?—No doubt.

86. But the means by which that inspection should be carried out is really the important point that we have to consider; now, as far as I understand the answers you have given, you appear to have a decided objection to Government inspection; would that objection be still the same if it was municipal instead of Governmental?—I think that a municipal inspection would not succeed at all, and it would not be much better than a Government inspection. What I want to do with regard to inspection is, that the owners of the boilers themselves should be the inspectors through some association that would really do the thing well.

87. You have been the president of this voluntary association for 15 or 20 years, have you not?—Yes.

88. During that time you have reached only a very small proportion of the boilers in the country, I suppose?—Yes, a very small proportion.

89. Now, I should like to know if, after that 20 years' experience, you do not think the voluntary system has failed?—No, I think not, quite the contrary; I think that a voluntary inspection is safer than any other inspection.

90. But would you not say that you had only got about 2,000 boilers out of about 50,000 in your district?—Yes.

91. Therefore, I ask you, should you not call that a failure in point of numbers?—Yes; but we have reasons for it, and here is a very excellent example set; we have gone on for 15 years without a single person being killed; and if you take the number of 50,000 boilers, how many out of that 50,000 have been killed during that time for want of inspection.

92. We are entirely agreed that great good is done by your association, but how are we to reach the 50,000 that are still left out of your association?—By multiplying the number of associations, but I must leave that to the Committee to determine.

93. But, esteeming highly your opinion, the Committee want to get a suggestion from you, if you please, as to what would be the best means of reaching those people?—I have already stated that the Government ought in my opinion to establish a law to make it imperative that every person having boilers should have them inspected,

either voluntary, or as they please; let them agree among themselves how it should be done.

94. That would be, practically, a Governmental inspection, would it not?—No; I do not mean that the Government is to employ inspectors, quite the reverse; I only want the Government to make it compulsory that they should inspect, and leave the owners of the boilers to make the inspection as they please; I have already stated the number of visits that should be given, and a thorough inspection besides, once a year; and it remains with the Government to entertain it or not, as may be expedient.

95. I take your answer with regard to the Government, that you object to their having the inspection of the boilers, and I suggested whether you thought a municipal inspection would answer, and you said "No"; but the Committee are still without an answer with regard to who is the proper party to overlook the inspection, because there must be some authority to whom that must attach, must there not?—I think I said that I was extremely anxious that the Government should make it compulsory that boilers should be inspected; I did not mean that they should inspect the boilers, or that they should appoint a corps of inspectors at all, as in case of accident, either the association or the members would be responsible.

96. But you did not say who should be the parties to appoint those inspectors, and to whom they should be responsible; that is the question, is it not?—I must leave that in the hands of the Committee to say whether a Government inspection is necessary or not. My opinion is, the law of inspection should be compulsory, and inspection would follow as a matter of course.

97. *Chairman*.] I understood you to say that the Government should make it compulsory on the parties to place themselves under inspection, and then you think that the association would appoint their own inspectors?—I do not know whether the Committee understood what I said; but what I said was this: my opinion is, that the Government should compel every person who has a boiler to place himself under inspection.

98. But under whom?—Under the associations, which may form themselves under their own voluntary arrangements.

99. Lord *J. Hay*.] You do not mean that they are to be compelled to form an association?—I do not want the Government to force them to form an association; but I think it would naturally arise, if they were compelled to have the boilers inspected, that they would soon create an association for that purpose.

100. Mr. *Platt*.] I think you said, in the first part of your evidence, that there were two or three kinds of associations, one of which was an assurance association, and you thought that it was a very objectionable one?—Yes.

101. Would you be satisfied that the inspection should be thus: that if the Government said that all boilers should be inspected, certain parties might say, "We prefer to have it inspected by an insurance company"; or have you thought that that would be a very objectionable association for them to go to?—My opinion is, that it is immaterial whether the inspection takes place by an assurance society or by an association; that is a matter of no moment; but the inspection ought to be effective, and fully up to the mark with regard to the nature of the inspection.

102. Mr. *Armitstead*.] Do you think that if

0.109.

▲ 4

any

any accident occurs, the parties in fault should be liable to the parties injured?—I think that people neglecting to put boilers under inspection should be liable. An Act of Parliament would be of no use without that condition, where loss of life and serious injuries are the result.

103. Mr. *Pim.*] You said that there were about 2,000 boilers in the neighbourhood of Manchester under your inspection?—Yes, we have 2,000 boilers in the neighbourhood of Manchester under the inspection of our association, and there are two or three insurance companies in Manchester besides our association.

104. But if in the 15 years that the association has been in existence there have been no accidents, are not the owners of the 2,000 boilers some of the most carefully and respectably managed concerns in the neighbourhood; and do you not think that from their general character, even if there had been no inspection, there would have been no accidents, or very few accidents, in concerns of that kind?—You see the number of boilers that we have under inspection in the association to which I belong is comparatively small with regard to the number of boilers in the United Kingdom. If a law was established to make it penal, that any person having a boiler should neglect to employ some company or association to inspect his boiler in order to prevent explosion, I think it would be a good thing. What that penalty should be, I am not prepared to say. As regards the class of subscribers to the association, they are not a selected class, but the general run of steam users.

105. But if the parties in connection with your association are among the best managed concerns in the kingdom, the experience you have had of there being no accidents is not at all a proof that the inspection would have the same result if you go to a lower class of concerns; would not that be so?—If it were established on the same principle, and carried out with the same interests and perseverance as ours, it would have the same effect.

106. You think that the Government should make a general law that every boiler owner should be forced to submit his boiler to inspection, do you not?—Yes.

107. I suppose your association only extends to Manchester and its neighbourhood?—Just so, and to other parts of the three kingdoms.

108. It does not go over the whole of the kingdom?—I daresay there are many gentlemen who have boilers, some of them more than a dozen boilers perhaps, and they say, "We will inspect our own boilers, and we will do it carefully." Under those circumstances, they take the whole of the responsibility.

109. But the point I wish to raise is this: your association exists in a district in which there are a large number of boilers?—Yes.

110. It is very easy to get up an association of owners of boilers, who are anxious that everything should be well managed, and who are well pleased to have them inspected; but how will your idea work out in places where there are perhaps two or three boilers in the neighbourhood, with no others near them; you would not propose to have a single association all over the kingdom, with a series of local associations; your plan may be easily worked in Lancashire, but how would it be in the remote districts of Ireland?—I think it would work equally well, and

we have proved that it works as well in Ireland as in England.

111. But you cannot form an association where there are perhaps only a dozen boilers within a hundred square miles, can you?—In our association, we have boilers in all parts of the kingdom, including Ireland, at a very great distance apart, and our association is contending with regard to the boilers, that they should be inspected, but by whom they should be inspected is immaterial. If the Government were to establish a law to say that no person should use a boiler but what must be regularly inspected on a certain principle (I do not say that ours is the best), there would be no difficulty in working an association, provided you compelled every one to have his boiler inspected.

112. How are the inspectors to be paid?—By the owner of the boiler.

113. So much per horse power?—Yes; if you have half-a-dozen boilers, and enter your boilers into our association, you have to pay 31 *s.* 6 *d.* every year for it, and you obtain proper inspection. That would remove from the owner, to a certain extent, the responsibility of employing proper persons to carry out the instructions of the inspector.

114. You would compel the user of every boiler to pay an annual sum or tax for the inspection?—Yes.

115. Dr. *L. Playfair.*] Would you be satisfied with the private inspection of an engineer?—Yes, I would, if he was a qualified man.

116. But how would you determine his competency?—From a knowledge of his actual experience.

117. But who is to be the determiner of that competency?—The party employing him.

118. Supposing, then, a person in a distant part said, "I will take a local engineer," whose competency nobody knows, would that satisfy your idea of a proper inspection?—Persons at a distance being in communication with a number of persons employing boilers, and enrolling a boiler in an association, are sure to obtain competent inspection.

119. But I am not supposing the case of an association; I am supposing persons employing private engineers of their own; suppose I am a boiler user, and am willing to pay you, as a distinguished engineer, a large fee to inspect my boiler, is there any reason against that?—None whatever.

120. Suppose I am not able to employ a distinguished engineer, and I employ an engineer of far less mark, what is to be the proof of his competency?—You would not be justified in employing an engineer who was incompetent.

121. But you would leave it entirely to me, would you?—Yes, I would leave it entirely to you to take the responsibility; but that is a very rare occurrence; it would be much better for you to enrol yourself in an association.

122. We know that your association is well conducted, but if these associations arose all over the kingdom, what is to be the evidence of an engineer's competency?—You can have no other evidence, but by employing a competent engineer who thoroughly understands his business.

123. Mr. *Fielden.*] With regard to these associations, would you have them registered, and authorised to act by the Government?—Yes, I think so.

124. And

124. And that no association that was not registered should be held a competent association?—I think they ought to be registered, and that they should obtain the authority of Parliament as to their competency to examine boilers.

125. You would not allow any examination to be made by an association that was not registered?—No, I think not; I see no difficulty in having them registered.

126. Mr. *Hermon.*] In the proposed periodical examination by the inspector, would you recommend that the boilers should, at those periodical examinations, be tested at about 40 or 50 per cent. above the working power?—The practice in our association is this; that we test boilers occasionally, when we have any doubt with regard to their security, to something above the working pressure.

127. When a boiler has been declined or condemned, would you not make it imperative that that boiler should cease to be used? — Yes, certainly.

128. That is not the case at present, is it?—No.

129. *Chairman.*] Have you any further remarks to make to the Committee?—No.

Mr. LAVINGTON E. FLETCHER, called in; and Examined.

130. *Chairman.*] YOU are Chief Engineer to the Manchester Steam Users' Association?—Yes.

131. I believe that you have had considerable experience in the investigation of explosions that have taken place in the country generally?—I have paid considerable attention to the subject of steam-boiler explosions, having investigated all the most important cases that have occurred throughout the kingdom since the commencement of 1861, and reported thereon to the president and executive committee of our association. The results of these investigations have been given in the association's printed monthly reports circulated amongst its members, and sent to the public press gratuitously; so that the association has been at considerable pains to acquire information on the cause of these sad disasters, and to disseminate that information as widely as possible.

132. Will you be good enough to make a short statement to the Committee of the number of explosions that have occurred during the last several years, and the results that have attended them?—The records of the Manchester Steam Users' Association show that steam-boiler explosions are both frequent and fatal; I have selected from those records a few leading particulars that will, I think, prove of interest to this Committee. On one occasion as many as 29 persons were killed by a single explosion that occurred at the Millfields Ironworks, near Bilston, on Tuesday, the 15th of April 1862; the wreck caused by this explosion is illustrated in two or three of the photographs now shown (*handing in photographs*). In another case 13 persons were killed by an explosion at an ironworks at Masbro', on Wednesday, the 3rd of December 1862. In another case again 13 persons were killed at an ironworks at Aberaman on Wednesday, 17th February 1864. On this occasion two boilers exploded simultaneously; the wreck is shown by three of the photographs now handed in (*handing in photographs*), while these two plates (*producing iron plates*), cut from the boilers, are illustrations of their corroded state, to which reference will be made shortly. A further explosion, killing 12 persons, occurred at an ironworks at West Bromwich on Tuesday, the 1st of March 1864; the wreck in this instance also is illustrated by two of these photographs (*producing the same*). Another explosion may be named which killed 15 persons and injured 33 others at a bobbin turnery at Bingley, last summer, on Thursday, the 9th of June; the wreck in this instance also is illustrated by these four photographs (*producing the same*). A more recent one, resulting in the

death of 13 persons, at the Kidsgrove Ironworks, Staffordshire, on Thursday, the 26th of May last, will be fresh in the memory of all; the ruptured boiler is shown in two or three photographs, which I produce (*producing the same*). These might be regarded as somewhat special cases, but explosions are by no means of occasional occurrence. They recur with the greatest regularity year by year; thus there have occurred already, since the commencement of this year, as many as 20 explosions, killing 44 persons and injuring 34 others; of these, I will hand in a tabular statement, giving the killed and injured in each case (*tabular statement handed in, see Appendix*). From that table it will be seen that since the Kidsgrove explosion, which occurred on Thursday, the 26th of May, that is to say, precisely this day four weeks, there have been six other explosions, killing six persons and injuring three others; so that, during the last month, including the Kidsgrove, as many as 19 persons have been killed. Last year, that is to say, in 1869, there were 58 explosions, killing 86 persons and injuring 126 others. Going further back still, as shown in this tabular statement (*handing in a Table*, vide *Appendix*), the Manchester Steam Users' Association has recorded since its formation in the year 1854 up to the close of 1869, as many as 539 explosions, by which 909 persons were killed, and 1,081 others injured. Adding to this those killed during this year it brings the total up to 559 explosions, killing 953 persons, and injuring 1,114 others. The total number of persons injured, including those killed, is 2,067. This, however, is by no means the whole number of lives sacrificed, as, in the earlier years of the association's operations, such complete records were not obtained of all the explosions occurring throughout the United Kingdom as is now the case; so that many escaped its notice. It may be stated that at the present time, on an average, 50 explosions occur every year, killing about 75 persons, and injuring as many others, so that, in round numbers, one explosion occurs every week, and one life is sacrificed every fourth working day in the year. Last year this estimate was exceeded, as many as 86 persons being killed, and already this year, although we have scarcely got half way through, as many as 44 persons have been killed. Thus it will be seen that explosions are not occasional, but that they recur with the regularity of a fixed law; and, judging from the experience of the past year, it appears absolutely certain that, if nothing is done to prevent these fearful catastrophes, by this time next year 50 more explosions will have occurred,......................................

0.109.

B

Chairman.

3558. I think you are an Engineer in the City of London?—I am.

3559. And you have been turning your attention to the application of steam for conducting traffic on tramways?—I have.

3560. The Committee wish to direct your attention to the points in which the use of engines upon tramways differs from their use on roads; you have, I believe, constructed what may be called a steam omnibus for use on tramways?—I have.

3561. Is that ready for use?—Yes, it is a common tramway carriage, and you would hardly perceive any difference between that and a carriage which had not an engine at all, except for the chimney.

3562. It is a common car with two small engines?—Yes.

3563. They being one on each side of the carriage in the centre of its length?—Yes.

3564. Do they work independently?—No; they could be so worked, but I prefer not to do so.

3565. Are you likely to try this carriage upon any public tramway soon?—Yes, a place is preparing for it, but as it is against the law, we can only do it upon sufferance, but a tramway is offered us, and a siding and all is now preparing.

3566. And that within a reasonable distance of where we are sitting?—Yes, within a mile.

3567. And you expect to be able to have it tried there, within what time?—I am in great hopes of its being tried there within a fortnight.

3568. Now, looking to the special point of difference between the use of horses and steam power, so far as you have been able to come to a conclusion, what should you say is the difference

Chairman—continued.

in the power of stopping?—We have an opportunity of trying that feature where the engine is built, and I think it indicates a much quicker stoppage than you can obtain by horses, I think in half the time.

3569. What speed are you able to get up to in the yard?—Not a great speed; it is an indication, that is all I can say.

3570. It is an inference drawn from a slower speed?—Yes.

3571. Do I understand you correctly that your impression is that, in going at seven miles an hour, you could stop in less space with your engines than they could with horses?—I think it is probable that we can stop in half the space, or thereabouts, for this reason: that we have the usual break which is always used to stop the carriage, because the horses at present do not stop it; it is always done alone by the break, but we have that break in addition to our engine, which is of great power in assisting to stop; in fact, we do stop quickly.

3572. Are you able to stop by reversing the engine?—Yes, upon emergencies. We should not resort to that, except upon emergencies.

3573. Ordinarily, you would shut off the steam and apply the break?—Yes; which is done by the foot in our case, that the man's hands may be both at liberty to manage his engine.

3574. The carriage at present being stopped by the break, and not by the horses?—No tramway carriage is stopped by horses; so that we have the same power of breaks that they have, and, in addition, the power of the engine.

3575. In constructing your engines, have you paid any attention to the question of the blast?—Yes; that is our principal point.

3576. Have

3576. Have you done away with the blast?—No; I have never professed to do away with the blast. What I profess to do is this: that it shall not exceed the ordinary noise of the streets; there will be at times, but only occasionally, a little noise; but so low that the ordinary hum of the streets will entirely deaden it; that I expect, as regards working in towns.

3577. Is the blast very much less than that which is produced by the road-rollers?—Very much less; there is no comparison whatever. We do not employ the power required by the steam-rollers; the noise would be scarcely anything; and then we can make the white steam almost disappear, because we inject the steam into a hot chamber, and it is scarcely visible at all.

3578. Do you produce smoke?—No, we use smokeless coal or coke; either entirely prevents smoke; we never have any smoke.

3579-80. Each carriage would be, so to speak, working itself; that is to say, the motive power would be confined within each separate carriage?—Yes; and I may say upon that point, I believe a traction engine in the street is inapplicable, and altogether unsuitable; it must be self-contained in order to be used for passenger traffic in a crowded street.

3581. Whether upon a tramway or not?—Almost; of course I do not speak of common road engines now. On the common roads, I believe a traction engine is absolutely essential; it must to some extent draw things after it.

3582. But upon a tramway you would have it self-contained?—Yes.

3583. That gets rid of any difficulty in stopping an engine upon a rail, as compared with on a road, because it is the break which stops in both cases?—Yes; the photograph shows the handles of the steam-engine; those handles are taken up, and the driver shifts them to the other end when he returns, so that the man is always just in front of his load, wherever he is.

3584. Have you taken any special precautions to prevent the temperature of the carriage being more than is agreeable to passengers?—We have had the steam up for many hours together, and I invite any honourable Members of the Committee to come in and try it for themselves. Numbers have passed through the carriage, and have pronounced it quite without any objection. So much is it below any objection that there are mirrors at the end, just to set off the end of the chamber where the boiler is confined, and those are always cool to the touch; you never feel them the least warm.

3585. Have you taken special precautions with regard to that?—There are special precautions in the way of air chambers, and felt, and what we call lagging; there is a double quantity of that, and it is perfectly successful.

3586. I believe I am right in saying that what is done with very high temperature in heating apparatus, cooking apparatus, and other matters of that kind, shows that the heat can be shut out?—Yes.

3587. There it is done by vegetable charcoal, I think?—Yes, we do it in two ways; the part of chamber next to the passengers is of wood, and then there is an air chamber about as broad as your finger, and then sheet-iron applied within that again; we have also felted and lagged it with thin wooden sheeting, so that there is all that for

0.88.

the heat to be passed through; then round the boiler it is lagged in the usual way with wood and felting, and the air is admitted all round, so that this entirely prevents the heat; you cannot perceive it at all; there is no annoyance to passengers whater in any shape from the engine.

3588. I presume, so far as your experiments have gone, that the conclusion you have come to is that self-contained carriages worked by steam would be less objectionable in a street than if drawn by horses?—I think they are very much less objectionable, being much more under command, and there is one thing with regard to curves which is a great trouble with tramways; horses going in front pulls the carriage off; there is a tendency that way; they constantly run off upon the curves. Now, an engine being self-contained, there would be much less liability to do that, because the wheel which drives it is almost underneath the centre of the carriage.

3589. Then, supposing the absolute prohibition upon the use of engines to be removed, what would you say are fair and proper regulations or restrictions which should be imposed to protect the public?—In the first place I heard questions put with regard to proving and testing the engines; that upon the tramway would not be difficult; I think the boilers should be tested and watched; then I think that something corresponding with the surveys now adopted in vessels by the Board of Trade, or some other body, might fairly be required, certainly at first; that seems to be thorough protection in the case of ships, and some modification of the same system might be fairly applied I think upon tramways.

3590. You would not object to it?—I should not object to it; I went through the whole system in regard to our ships; I always felt that it was a great protection and a great comfort to the owners and everybody else, to have the Board of Trade authorities to say yes or no to the state of a ship.

3591. With regard to the use of these tramway engines, what power would you give to the local authorities?—I think it should be a police regulation. I think that seems to be the best plan, the same regulation should apply that they have for preventing smoke and other nuisances of that kind; it is all done by the police I believe at present.

3592. I presume you mean the power of regulating the entire traffic of the streets, that their power over a tramway should correspond with whatever power they have upon the street generally?—That is what I mean, but I thought probably your question went further, and applied to the noise or smoke or any other nuisance which it might occasion.

3593. I was rather assuming that to have been covered by the inspection of the engine in the first instance, but with regard to that, how would you ensure obtaining the results which you say would be obtained from your arrangements?—I think the police should give notice and information as they do at present of any great nuisance, and that there should be a controlling power, whether in the Board of Trade or magistrates, or whatever it might be, to stop it.

3594. In point of fact, you would have a penalty for breach of the law by committing a nuisance?—Yes, I think the magistrates deal with all those questions from information given by the police. I think the same may be done

X

here,

here, because the police become informed with reference to the limit to which certain things may be carried, and when they see that they exceed that limit, then they give information.

3595. I need hardly ask you as a London man, whether you remember the time when the same thing was done upon the Thames above London Bridge with regard to smoke. I presume you would have some similar regulation with reference to these carriages?—Yes, I went through the whole question of the smoke 28 years ago in Liverpool, and I was called upon to give evidence, but I saw that it resolved itself into a very simple question, and the public have submitted to it very well, and I do not see any difficulty about it. There is one further observation that I would make. This carriage under these circumstances is adaptable to the wants of the public in this way, that this peculiar carriage allows the system at present existing with tramways being carried on, that is to say, the tramways carriage goes both ways without being turned, and there is a passage right through the carriage, that is the only plan of a steam carriage in which this has been done, they have always interfered with the passage.

3596. The engine does not interfere with the passage, I believe?—No, the engines are under the seats, and I find that one boiler answers the purpose. I have two, one on each side at present, but in my next carriage I shall only place one. I can get a boiler quite sufficient upon one side. I was timid in my first carriage about the point of balancing the weights, but I find there is nothing in that.

Mr. F. Stanley.

3597. Were those experiments of yours with reference to stopping the carriage made upon a level or upon an incline?—The rails where the carriage stands at present are upon a slight incline.

3598. Do you know what level the incline is?—No, but the water-gauges, of which there are two, one at each end stood at a considerable difference; there was a difference of about three inches in 18 feet.

3599. But still you would guard that, would you not, by stating as you did in your previous remark that the carriage was not tried under ordinary conditions?—No, the man would start it, and then run it to the wharf, and then stop it, and run back, and so on, but it showed a command which horses could never have accomplished.

3600. You stated that you had diminished the blast to a considerable extent; when you reverse the engines for the purpose of stopping, would you not increase the blast?—Just for a jet or two, and I think that would be no nuisance.

3601. Probably there would not be more noise than by horses pulling up in the ordinary way with their heels?—No.

3602-3. Are the Committee to understand that you contemplate keeping the car and the mechanism within the ordinary limits of the size of a tramway car?—Yes, it is exactly the same in length and everything, only that I have got longer platforms for another object; the object of that is to have a better mode of collecting the money, to collect it outside instead of inside, but that has nothing to do with the steam question.

3604. With regard to the steam question, the car is constructed upon the same principle as an ordinary tramway car?—Yes, the mechanism is all concealed.

3605. What speed do you contemplate travelling at?—The usual speed of all carriages, seven or eight miles an hour.

3606. You spoke of a survey; would you apply that survey to the engine and boiler only, or to the carriage generally?—I suppose the public would be satisfied with the engine and boiler being surveyed; it might extend to the whole; I have hardly thought of that question.

3607. Am I right in supposing that you would have one advantage besides that of which you spoke just now, of being able to drive end foremost, namely, that you do not require when you come to the end of the line to unhook the horses and take them round?—That is so; the handles are taken up; the little gate is shut across the end; the handles are shifted to the other end, and the driver stands in front.

3608. Then at the end of the tramway there would be a very considerable saving of space?—It would be a very great comfort to the streets, and a saving also to the carriages, I think.

3609. Does the limit which you have been obliged to impose upon the space for your engines limit your convenience for the supply of fuel?—The new carriage will have the fuel upon the top; it is not at present so, but it will be upon the top, a simple feeding apparatus lets the fuel into the fire upon the top of it; if you are constructing an engine going a distance of 10 miles, you would have rather a larger coal-box, but for five miles an hour you would have rather a smaller one on the top; so that it does not interfere with the passengers, it is merely making rather a larger or smaller coal-box.

3610. How many persons would be required to work your car?—Only an engineer and a conductor; no other.

3611. And a stoker?—No; the stoking is all done by the engineer; it is all done upon the platform.

3612. With regard to that last question, is the driver supposed to drive and stoke as well?—Yes.

3613. So that the stoking is done in the middle of the car?—The stoking will be done while it is going on; there is an apparatus to let the coal on to the top of the fire, and when he gets to the end of his journey, the driver will get off and see that the fire is all right.

3614. And with regard to all the other minor matters which require attention, the engineer is sufficiently able to look after that?—Yes, the steam gauge is just over his head, and the water gauge is also close at hand, and he has rods to lead to the different cocks and works.

3615. In point of fact, it would not be further from his control than the gear of a locomotive engine is from the man who now drives?—Some part of the gear is further from him, but it is a very differently-shaped thing.

Mr. W. Wells.

3616. I understand you that there is only one man in charge of the engine?—Yes, there is one man in charge of the engine.

3617. And one man besides?—Yes, the conductor, just as we have at present. The engineer takes the place of the driver.

Mr.

3618. I do not wish to ask you any question with regard to the working of the tramway, but I only wish to ask you the difference that will be made by the substitution of steam power for horses; with regard to that, I would ask you if any of the accidents which occur upon a tramway, arise from the horses which draw the present carriages?—No, except perhaps that there is a tendency to drag the cars off at the curves; the horse certainly has that tendency, being ahead of it drawing at an angle.

3619. When the weight is in the carriage, when the carriage is loaded, would it not increase the difficulty of stopping it very much?—Just to the extent of its own weight, the weight of the engine.

3620. Will not it increase the difficulty with regard to the weight of the people who ride in the carriage, that is to say, that it is much easier to stop an empty carriage than a full one?—Yes.

3621. Your experiments have been made with an empty carriage, have they not?—Yes, they have, but I do not know that our experiments are worth more than just as an indication.

3622. Is your engine self-feeding?—It is not exactly self-feeding; the boiler is upright, and we put the fuel in through a little funnel at the top of the boiler, dropping down upon the furnace.

3623. Is that fed of itself?—No, it is regulated by a handle which is led to each end of the carriage, and a little wheel is turned which drops it down in a certain measure, something like the old powder-flask which gave it charge; this is a thing which lies horizontally, and not vertically, and in that way it gives you an idea.

3624. I think you stated that the advantage of an engine in a tramway carriage over a locomotive with an omnibus on the road, would be that you could stop so much more easily?—Yes.

3625. Or was it rather, that you thought that you could work a locomotive omnibus upon a tramway, but that you could not work a locomotive omnibus upon a road?—I did not mean to say that.

3626. I understood you to state, that a road engine could not carry passengers, but must draw trucks behind it?—That is the general tendency; I will not say that it cannot be, but it would be very difficult to construct a carriage which should carry a complement of passengers; that is to say, 40 or 50 passengers in addition to its engine upon a common road, you could only carry a few passengers.

3627. I want to know what would be the difference, if your carriage was put upon an ordinary road, what pace would it go, because you say that there is a want of power in an engine to drag passengers in an omnibus like yours upon a road?—No; that is not exactly the point; the point is this, that upon a self-contained engine and on a tramway, the power required is so small, that we can do with much smaller engines

than you could if you dragged that carriage by another engine, especially upon a common road.

3628. What I ask is, do you think that this engine as it is now, could drag that full of passengers upon an ordinary road?—Not with the power I put into it; because I intentionally put a smaller power, not requiring so large a power for the tramway.

3629. Could you put a larger power on than that?—Yes.

3630. I did not understand you to say, that it would be impossible to make an omnibus like yours, self-contained, working upon an ordinary road; the advantage of the tramroad is, that you get with the same proportion of engine power greater facility for carrying passengers?—Yes, I think that is what it resolves itself into; it is well known that a carriage of that sort must have a large number of passengers to make it pay, therefore you are obliged to make a very large carriage, and if in addition to that, you are obliged to put the power requisite to draw a large carriage upon a common road, it becomes altogether too massive, too heavy, and too lumbering, that it is inapplicable to the ordinary traffic; one of the great advantages of a tramway locomotive is this, that requiring so little power comparatively, it can take its large complement of passengers within itself. A traction engine may weigh three or four tons, whereas my engine weighs a ton.

Chairman.

3631. Your engine weighs about one ton?—Yes.

3632. That is to say, that your tramway carriage is about one ton heavier than a corresponding one drawn by horses?—Yes, there is one little difference; I think I shall make the frame of the carriage a little stronger than at present, and so on, but the engine itself is only about a ton. I think the carriages are known to be too weak; they do not like to add to their strength, because that would make them too heavy for their horses.

3633. With regard to stopping, I understood your point to be this, that by making it self-contained you get rid altogether of the time within which an engine as such could stop?—Yes.

3634. And you stop by a break?—Yes.

3635. And the only difference between a steam carriage, the same as is drawn by horses, and this one, with a self-contained engine, is the difference of the effect of the momentum of the heavier one as compared with that of the lighter one?—Yes, that is it.

3636. I gather that that would not be found to be much measured by distance?—No, very little. I may add that in going up the little incline which we have in the yard, we can hardly perceive any difference in starting the carriage whichever way it goes.

3637. That is about 1 in 72?—Yes, the difference is perceptible to the eye, and very perceptible in the water gauges.

Major General C. S. Hutchinson, R.E., called in; and Examined.

Major
Gen. *C. S.*
Hutchinson,
R.E.
——

Chairman.

99. You have been for ten years Inspector of Railways of the Board of Trade?—I have.

100. And the tramway work connected with the Board of Trade has principally passed through your inspection and hands, has it not?—Not entirely, but principally so.

101. You have given considerable attention, I understand, to the new systems for locomotion upon tramways that have been recently proposed?—I have.

102. I think you visited Glasgow a short time ago?—Yes.

103. When was that?—It must be, I think, two years ago now.

104. And you were present at the trial of the Moncrieff system?—Yes.

105. Will you kindly describe the result of your inspection of that experiment?—The experiment was made upon a short piece of *railway*, not upon a tramway or a highway, near the Govan Station; I think it was about three quarters of a mile long.

106. The motive power is compressed air, is it not?—It is; and it was applied to the car itself in which the passengers ride. The air was compressed in reservoirs at the station from which the car started, and was supplied to the car by hose, and stored up under the car, and it was then used for the purpose of driving the car

Chairman—continued.

backwards and forwards along this piece of railway which it seemed to do very successfully. There was nothing particular to notice about the mode of transit. It was noiseless, and there was nothing objectionable in the way of escape as there might be sometimes with steam; there was no smoke, or steam, or any fire visible. The speed was never very high; I do not think it exceeded eight or ten miles an hour, and the means of stopping the car appeared to be ample and expeditious.

107. What was the length of the railway on which it was tried?—It was a short piece of line, I think about three quarters of a mile in length, upon which it went backwards and forwards. It was a piece of line of easy gradients; about one in 100, if I recollect aright, was the maximum rate of gradient.

108. Has it been running regularly since that time?—No, I think not; I believe it was merely being tried experimentally.

109. I take it that the advantages of that system would be that it is free from noise, smell, and smoke, and many of the difficulties which attend steam?—Quite so.

110. On the other hand, what are the disadvantages?—The disadvantages would be, that you can only store the receiver under the car with a certain amount of air, which must become

become exhausted in a longer or shorter time, and it might be very awkward to get your store of motive power exhausted when the car might by chance be at the middle of its journey, as then it would stick fast. That, I presume, is one of the principal objections to the arrangement, that there is only a certain amount, and necessarily a small amount, of motive power contained in the car itself.

111. You are not aware whether that system has been further developed, or not?—I believe that it has been gone on with, but I cannot tell you anything further about its history; I think it has been since used on the Vale of Clyde tramway.

112. I understand that you have also visited Birkenhead, and were present at the trial of the Grantham steam car?—I was.

113. Upon what length of tramway was that tried?—It was upon the tramway running from Woodside Ferry to the Holylake railway station near Birkenhead. The length of the tramway I think would be about three miles; but I will not speak positively as to that.

114. Will you give the Committee the result of your observation of that experiment?—The experiment was a very successful one. First of all the car surmounted a very steep incline, which adjoins the Woodside Ferry, before getting up to the higher level, and it was a serious matter to get up this incline of which the gradient is something like 1 in 14; it managed, however, to get up, and then it ran along the road very successfully, and attained a very high rate of speed—as far as one's judgment could tell, from 25 to 30 miles an hour. It was early in the morning, and there was nothing along the road to interfere with the experiment, and it was desirable to ascertain what speed really could be attained under favourable circumstances. Shortly afterwards an accident happened to the car from some defective work underneath it, which prevented the experiment being continued further at that particular time. But the experiment was, I think, a very successful one as regards the power of transit.

115. I understand that the passengers and the motive power in that case are in the same vehicle?—Yes, they are.

116. Is there any inconvenience to the passengers in consequence of that?—I think that unless the break handle, and the steam handle, and the reversing lever are very well indeed shut off from the exit and ingress of passengers, they may be sources of danger from persons tripping over them or meddling with them, and so on. It is provided for in the rules of the Board of Trade that in similar cases these different parts of the machinery should be carefully shut off from the passengers, and of course that is not so easy in a steam car which contains the power, and in which also the passengers are carried; it has not been yet done in any car that I have seen.

117. Can you describe the arrangement of the car?—At either end of the car where the passengers go in and out, there were handles on a gangway outside, viz., the handle for shutting off and applying the steam, a break handle for applying the break, and the reversing lever for altering the direction of the motion. Those were all much in the way of people getting in and out of the car, and in the dark a passenger might run against them, or they might be tampered with, and interfered with improperly by passengers going in or out. Then, if I remember rightly, in this car

0.74.

the boiler was vertical and carried in the centre of the car, and the steam cylinders were, I think, underneath in the centre also; so that there was a kind of central division in the car, which enclosed the boiler, and past which the passengers would go in moving from one part of the car to another. There was no danger, of course, attending that. That was a car that had been constructed for the Vienna tramways.

118. How many wheels had it?—I rather think it had eight wheels on two bogie frames, with four wheels each, but I am not quite certain.

119. I suppose that there were no outside seats for passengers?—I do not remember whether there were or not; there was nothing to prevent it; there might have been.

120. Were the arrangements with regard to the escape of steam and smoke and with regard to noise satisfactory?—They were tolerably satisfactory; there was nothing particularly objectionable in this respect.

121. What arrangements were made for stopping?—The break power was very efficient; there was perfect control over the car, and it was stopped very rapidly even when going at the high speed I mentioned.

122. Assuming a car to be going at the rate of 10 miles an hour, in what distance could it be stopped?—It could be stopped practically in its own length, or very little over it.

123. Is that system still at work, or has it been further developed?—There was one of the cars running upon the Wantage Tramway when I was last down there, and, as far as I know, it may still be running there; I am not aware of any other car being actually in use in England upon Mr. Grantham's system.

124. Did it not continue to run at Birkenhead?—No, that was only an experiment; it was merely sent down there before going to Vienna, and whether it is in use at Vienna now I cannot say; but I know that the company who have taken up Mr. Grantham's patent are engaged in constructing similar cars.

125. Do you know the weight of that car?—I think it is somewhere about six tons, but I am not quite certain.

126. I think that you also visited Wantage?—Yes, I visited Wantage.

127. What system did you see at work at Wantage?—They had at Wantage, when I went down on the occasion referred to, one of Grantham's cars, and also a Merryweather's car.

128. Merryweather's system is quite different from Grantham's, is it not?—It is.

129. Whereas Grantham's engine is contained in the car itself; the power in the other case is a steam horse or traction engine?—Yes.

130. What have you to say about the system of the traction engine?—In the first place it avoids the difficulties attaching to the arrangement where the motive power is in the car itself by keeping the passengers perfectly separated from the machinery; and in that point of view it is more favourable to my mind than the one in which the machinery is contained in the car itself. On the other hand, without a special arrangement you do not get the benefit of so much hauling power owing to the engine alone being lighter than the combined engine and car necessarily are. I believe there is an arrangement by which that is to some extent overcome by connecting

B

Major Gen. *C. S. Hutchinson,* R.E.

7 March 1877.

Major
Gen. *C. S.*
Hutchinson,
R.E.

7 March
1877

Chairman—continued.

necting the engine and the car together for ascending heavy inclines by a special means and obtaining the benefit of the weight of the car as well as of the engine. With regard to other matters, the engine seemed to answer fairly well. It was not in very good working order and emitted more exhaust steam and smoke than was desirable, but this was said to be merely owing to some fault in construction which would be easily overcome. The engine in that case was fitted with a means by which steam was cut off when the speed exceeded 10 miles an hour, and in consequence the speed never attained a greater height than 10 miles an hour. The break power in this case appeared to be amply sufficient.

131. I suppose that the system of limiting the speed to 10 miles an hour is one which you would strongly recommend, is it not?—Yes, that is a very important point.

132. I understand that when you saw Merryweather's traction engine, it was not in such a condition as to be suitable for work upon roads? —I would not say that, but I merely say that it was quite a new engine which had been hastily prepared, and that it probably was not in nearly as good working condition as it would have been a few weeks afterwards; it was emitting more steam and smoke than was desirable, but that probably was a difficulty which would have been overcome.

133. Are you aware whether it has been overcome or not?—I can only say that in some of Merryweather's engines which I saw in Paris, I did not observe the same emission of steam and smoke.

134. I think you have also been to Edinburgh, and have seen Hughes' steam traction engine? —I have. That is like Merryweather's as regards the power traction being separate from the car.

135. Was that satisfactory with regard to the steam and smoke and noise?—Yes; so far as I saw, it emitted no objectionable steam and smoke, and appeared to do its work very well.

136. Was there much noise?—No, there was no particular noise, but it did not at that time possess the means of shutting off its own steam, which power, I believe, has since been applied.

137. Was the brake power sufficient?—Yes, the break power was quite sufficient.

138. I forgot to ask you whether the brake power of Merryweather's engine was sufficient? —Yes, the brake power in that was sufficient. With regard to Hughes' engine, I understand that since I saw it at work in Edinburgh, Mr. Hughes has nearly or quite perfected engines possessing both the power of cutting off steam and applying brakes.

139. In fact, the system has been improved since you saw it?—Yes.

140. How long is it since you were at Edinburgh?—I think it was last autumn.

141. Do you know whether that engine is running in Edinburgh now or not?—I cannot tell whether it is running now or not; what I saw was an experiment.

142. I think you have been to Paris?—Yes, I went to Paris last June.

143. Whose system did you see at Paris?— There it was Merryweather's system.

144. What part of Paris was it in?—It was along the Boulevard Mont Parnasse, from the bridge of Austerlitz to the Luxembourg, or thereabouts.

Chairman—continued.

145. Is there much traffic there?—It is a very wide road, and there did not appear to be any large amount of traffic; I think the principal things we passed in going backwards and forwards were some troops of cavalry exercising or going from one station to another, and it was curious to observe the different way in which the horses behaved as they passed. The troop horses were, as a rule, very little attracted by the engine; the non-commissioned officers' horses were certainly more restive than the troop horses, and the officers' horses were exceedingly restive; it seemed that as the mettle of the horse improved, so its dislike to the steam tram-car increased. The car did its work very well indeed; there was nothing particular to notice with regard to it; the motion was easy, and there was very little escape of steam or smoke, and very little noise, and it altogether seemed to be very successful. At that time the lines were not open for public traffic; they were simply waiting for some formalities to be gone through, I believe, with the Prefect of the Seine, and therefore this was merely a kind of experimental trip which was made for my information.

146. Do you know at all what has become of it since?—I believe that it is now in full work along certain of the tramways of Paris.

147. And you found that it was easy to stop? —Yes, there was plenty of brake power. The Paris authorities, I understood, intended to allow a maximum speed of nearly 12 miles, or 20 kilométres an hour, and that the engine should work up to a pressure of 150 lbs. to a square inch. That was the maximum pressure that they were allowed to work at, but there are no other restrictions, as regards speed or as regards working pressure.

148. In what distance would it stop travelling at a speed of 12 miles an hour?—I should think probably in about the length of a car and a half.

149. Have you visited any other places to see experiments?—No; those are the only places.

150. Can you tell the Committee in what places in England steam power on tramways is being now regularly used?—I do not think it is being regularly worked in any places.

151. Is it not regularly worked at Wantage?— That I cannot tell you. I know that they have been working there; but whether regularly or not I do not know. When I was down there I saw this Grantham car apparently regularly at work, but whether it is so now or not I do not know.

152. Is there any place that you are aware of where it is in regular and continuous work?—No, I am not aware of any place where it is regularly at work.

153. I suppose you have had a good deal to do with advising the Board of Trade with respect to the bye-laws that they should adopt?—Yes, I have. The reason why I went to Paris before the thing was really completed was that the Board of Trade were very anxious to get their bye-laws framed before the end of last Session; and as soon as I had returned, I put together in a report the experience that I had gained from what I had seen at Paris and elsewhere, and I framed what I thought would be some suitable bye-laws for the Board of Trade to enact. My report was referred to the inspecting officers of railways, and we met together to consider these bye-laws, and with one or two alterations, the suggestions that
I had

I had made were adopted; those suggestions were afterwards embodied in the form in which you have them in the bye-laws which the Board of Trade framed in the case of the Wantage Tramway.

154. Will you shortly tell the Committee to what points you particularly directed your attention?—The all-important point seemed to be that the control of the speed of the appliance, whatever it might be, steam or other mechanical power, after it reached a certain velocity, should be out of the control of the driver. Of course a driver could, without such controlling power, if he chose to be reckless, proceed at a very high speed along a piece of level road, and it would be a very great danger to expose both the passengers in the car and the public to, without having some means of neutralising it. We therefore came to the conclusion that it was highly desirable that every tram car propelled by steam or other mechanical means should have a self-acting arrangement, by which the steam or motive power should be cut off, when some maximum velocity should be attained; I put it down myself at 12 miles an hour, but after consideration it was reduced to 10 miles an hour, which was considered the maximum speed that it would be safe to allow. Then in the case of tramways running down hill, although you could cut off the steam at, say 10 miles an hour, yet still, if a driver neglected to apply his brakes, a very great velocity might be attained in going down steepish gradients, and we considered there should also be a means by which a tram-car could apply its own brakes in case of negligence on the part of the driver. We also considered it desirable that every tram-car so propelled should have a speed indicator attached to it by which the driver might be informed as to the rate at which he was actually running, because we know that drivers are, as a rule, exceedingly ignorant of the speed at which they go; they generally very much underrate it; but with a good clock dial, or some similiar arrangement close to him, he would be always reminded of the speed at which he was going, and would have no excuse for exceeding the maximum speed allowed. We also considered that it would be desirable that the car should record its speed, which would be very useful for police purposes, or in questions of dispute as to speed in case of accident, and so on; it being a matter not very difficult to arrange, and one which no doubt will soon be accomplished. Another source of danger in the use of mechanical power is the passing over facing points. I had myself recommended that a dead stop should be made at all moveable facing points, but it was thought that that would be perhaps rather too stringent a rule to adopt, and therefore the speed was altered to four miles an hour, which should not be exceeded.

155. With regard to noise and the escape of steam and smoke, what provision has been made? —That is provided for by the rule that every engine shall be free from noise produced by blast or clatter of machinery; and shall not emit steam or smoke, and no fire in, on, or under it shall be visible.

156. To sum it up, I suppose I may take it that the most important points upon which you think general rules should be laid down are the following: limit of speed, indication of speed, escape of steam or smoke, noise and brake power? —And I think you should also add the separation

of the machinery so as to prevent its being interfered with, or being in the way of the public entering or leaving the car.

157. For the convenience of the public?—It is not only a matter of convenience, but also of the prevention of danger. With regard to the limit of speed, we think it a most important point that it should be placed out of the control of the driver, that the driver should not be the man to limit the speed, but that the machine itself should limit its own speed by some governor principle.

158. From the experience which you have had, and from the inspections which you have recently made at different places, how far has modern invention approached the rules that you have laid down for the safety and convenience of the public?—The only engine which I have seen yet fitted with any of these appliances is the Merryweather engine, which I before alluded to as being used at Wantage; but from what I understand, both Merryweather, Hughes, and Grantham's successor have engines nearly completed which will comply entirely with the requirements of the Board of Trade.

159. You think that there are engines now in the course of construction which would comply with the requirements that you would advise the Committee to adopt?—Yes.

160. Have you had much experience with regard to the use of locomotives on roads?— No, I have not. That simply comes before us sometimes with regard to bridges being too weak to bear the locomotives passing over them.

Dr. *Lyon Playfair.*

161. Do you attach much importance to the complete separation of the machinery from the car containing the passengers?—No, I do not think it is of much importance if you thoroughly screen off the driver's appliances from the passengers, and prevent their coming in contact with them in getting in or coming out of the car.

162. You used the expression that in the first car, you saw where the passengers sat round the boiler there was no danger, but if an explosion had taken place what would have happened?— No doubt there would be danger then, but I do not think it would be much better if the steam-engine was separated from the car.

163. Would it not give them a better chance? —Perhaps slightly so.

164. If the cylinders of compressed air are below the seats occupied by the passengers and not outside, in the event of an explosion the consequences must be serious, must they not?—No doubt.

165. In the trials that you saw on the Portobello Road in Edinburgh with Hughes' engine did you meet much traffic?—Not a great deal.

166. Were the horses that you met startled? —To a certain extent; and I perhaps ought to have stated that, so far as my experience goes, I have always seen horses more or less startled and frightened by the passage of those vehicles.

167. They would gradually get accustomed to them, I presume?—Yes, no doubt horses that are continually meeting them would get accustomed to them, but strange horses would, I think, always be more or less frightened.

168. Is that from the size of the whole thing, or is it from the escape of steam and smoke?—I do not think it is from the escape of steam and smoke; I think it is from the unusual mode of locomotion.

Major Gen. *C. S. Hutchinson,* R.E.

7 March 1877.

Major
Gen. *C. S.*
Hutchinson,
R.E.

7 March
1877.

Dr. *Lyon Playfair*—continued.

locomotion. Captain Galton in his paper made, I think, the reasonable suggestion that the horses imagine that the vehicle which they see is being backed against them. It is something unusual which they cannot account for. I do not think myself that their fright is attributable to either the smell of the steam, as some people think, or to the sight of the steam, or to the sight of the fire; but under all circumstances I think you will find strange horses more or less restive at meeting such vehicles.

169. In Paris were the ordinary cab horses more or less startled?—Slightly so; we did not meet many, but I do not think we passed a horse that did not show some signs of disturbance at something unusual passing him.

Colonel *Loyd Lindsay.*

170. With regard to the Grantham steam car, I suppose the machinery which you describe, which is open to the public at the two ends, might be boxed off by some mechanical contrivance?—I should think so, certainly; it would of course require a little more room in the gangway to thoroughly screen it off.

171. With regard to the advantage of the Merryweather steam engine over the Grantham steam engine, should you say that the Merryweather steam engine, being in the nature of a steam horse, might be applied not only to drawing carriages for passengers, but also to drawing railway trucks?—No doubt there would be an advantage in that; that especially applies to the Wantage Tramway, because railway trucks can run on it.

172. You say you think it necessary to be able to cut off the steam, and also to have a speed indicator, and also to record the speed?—Yes.

173. So far as you are aware, is there at present any invention which will accomplish all these necessaries?—Yes; speed recorders have been used in America, I believe, for many years past, and there is a speed recorder in use on the Brighton Railway. Of course it is a more difficult thing to get it applied to the high speed of a railway than to the low speed of a tramway; I have no doubt in my own mind that those requirements will very shortly be met by the mechanical talent of the country, if they are insisted upon.

174. May I take it that you are favourable to the use of mechanical power on tramways?—If it is used under proper restrictions, I see no objections to it; and I should think that it would be a very great gain to the public.

175. Do you consider that by using mechanical power instead of horse power, a great saving of cost might be effected?—I have no doubt about it.

176. Would you say roughly that the cost of steam traction would be about one-half that of horse traction?—From what I have gathered on the subject, I should think that it would be somewhere about one-half; it is not a point upon which I should like to give a decided opinion, but I know that it would be very much cheaper.

177. May I ask you whether, in your opinion, the public would get the benefit of any economy that was effected?—I can hardly answer that question.

178. They would share the benefit, would they not?—I suppose it is probable that they would. I

Colonel *Loyd Lindsay*—continued.

do not know whether any rates might be laid down.

179. Do you think that there would be any inconvenience to the public generally from the use of steam on tramways?—The disadvantage of tramways generally is to people who are in the habit of driving and using their own carriages; and I think probably that disadvantage may be slightly increased by the use of steam on tramways, owing to some additional frightening of horses, which will no doubt to a certain extent take place.

180. Then I understand by your evidence that you see your way by mechanical contrivances to reduce these inconveniences to a very great extent?—Not the frightening of horses; I do not think that would ever be reduced; I think that will always exist, more or less. Of course the more perfectly you shut off your steam and smoke, and screen your fire, the more you reduce this difficulty; but I think there will always be a certain amount of terrorism produced in the horses which are not used to passing steam cars.

Mr. *Floyer.*

181. I think among the regulations proposed by the Board of Trade, there is one, that when a driver saw that a horse was frightened, he was to stop his car?—Yes, that was one of the regulations.

182. If these carriages were proceeding on a road that was very much frequented, it would very much interfere, would it not, with the progress of the carriages along that road if the driver of a steam tram-car had to stop every time a horse was frightened; would it not almost prevent the use of steam for the purposes of tramways?—I do not think you would find the stoppages so exceedingly frequent as to interfere seriously with the traffic.

183. Not in such frequented roads as those near London?—It is a question of course, whether in very frequented thoroughfares you would sanction the use of steam; that would perhaps be a question to consider in each particular case.

184. You do not think that the suggestion of one ingenious gentleman that something should be made in the shape of a horse in front of the tram-car, would overcome the difficulty?—I do not know; I see that that suggestion was made.

185. You have no great faith in that remedy?—No.

186. Was it a very broad road upon which you saw the trams running, in Paris?—Yes, it was on one of their new broad boulevards.

187. You said that the troop horses were not very much affected by it; do you not suppose that that might have arisen from the fact of their being accustomed to act in such large numbers together, and that, therefore, they felt encouraged by one another, whereas that would not be the case with the officers' horses?—I really cannot say, but that was the fact.

188. The officers' horses, which were no doubt apart from the others, and which proceeded separately, were much more affected by the tram than were the others?—Yes, they were, certainly.

189. You do not know, I think you said, the circumstances attending the two places in this country where steam is used for propelling the tram-cars?—I did not know that there were two places where steam is used regularly.

190. We

190. We are told that at Wantage and in the Vale of Clyde, it is so?—I have no doubt that it may be so, but I do not know.

191. Do you know the line of road upon which the Wantage Tramway runs?—Yes, I know it very well.

192. Is that an ordinary turnpike road?—It is, perhaps, rather a narrow ordinary turnpike road.

193. I think it was said that it ran alongside a line of railway?—Not the Wantage Tramway; it runs alongside of the highroad; it runs into the Great Western Railway yard, at Wantage-road Station.

194. This is an ordinary turnpike road which is used in the ordinary way by carriages?—It is rather a narrow turnpike road.

195. Is it a road upon which there is much traffic?—Yes, it is the high road from Oxford to Wantage, with an ordinary amount of country traffic upon it.

196. Do you know at all what sort of traffic the other turnpike road has upon it?—No, I could not speak as to that. I think that that would be more a suburban traffic, but I do not know the Vale of Clyde well.

197. You concur in the provision which is contained in the regulations suggested by the Board of Trade, that when the driver sees a horse frightened by the tram he shall stop?—Yes, it was one of our own recommendations.

198. You think it is necessary for the safety of the public?—Yes, I think so.

Mr. *Mitchell Henry*.

199. It is some time since you visited Paris, is it not?—It was; last June.

200. When did you visit Wantage?—I was last at Wantage in November.

201. And when did you visit Edinburgh?—Somewhere about September; sometime in the autumn.

202. And the Vale of Clyde?—I have not visited the Vale of Clyde.

203. In all those cases, except in Paris (and perhaps even in Paris), the engines were by no means perfected, as I understand?—They were not; the thing is quite in its infancy now.

204. You have not seen any engine which comes up to the requirements of the Board of Trade, as they at present exist?—No, I have seen none that completely comes up to them.

205. Do you think that you could obtain for the Committee, if it was desired, information from those various places in which there are engines running on tramways as to the present condition of them?—I have arranged to go down on Tuesday next to Loughborough to see one of Mr. Hughes' engines, which, save and excepting a speed recorder, in all other points, he informs me, completely fulfils the Board of Trade requirements; that is to say, it cuts off its steam, it applies its breaks, and it has a speed indicator attached to it.

206. If you have not visited Paris since June last, and the thing has been in operation during the last winter, would it not be desirable to obtain information as to the actual condition and working of the tramway there; if the Committee desired it, the Board of Trade could obtain that information, I presume?—No doubt; they may have received some information that I am not aware of. Paris and Brussels, I suppose, would

0.74.

be the two best places, being tolerably near at hand, from which to obtain information. You can hardly say that the system has begun in England yet. The Wantage bye-laws, I think, were only sent to the Wantage Company last month, and that is the first instance in which steam has been authorised to be used on tramways.

207. Do you generally concur in the paper which Captain Galton has communicated to the Society of Arts?—It appears to me a very valuable and well-written paper, and I think I may say that I generally concur in it.

208. It contains nearly all the information that is at present obtained upon the subject?—It does.

Viscount *Holmesdale*.

209. I may take it that you do not think that there is any mechanical improvement that will do away with the frightening of horses on public roads by steam tram-cars?—I do not think so. As I have already stated, I think that is in the nature of things, and cannot be entirely eliminated.

210. In Paris it appeared to you that as the horses were more or less spirited, so they were more or less frightened by the cars?—Yes.

211. So that the use of these steam carriages upon roads where there was a good many carriages passing would be dangerous?—Yes, it would be; I would not say absolutely dangerous, but, of course, it will require great care upon the part both of the tram drivers and upon the part of the coachmen.

212. But if the horses were so much frightened, no amount of care on the part of coachmen or drivers could prevent accidents?—I would not say that the horses become uncontrollable.

213. My honourable and gallant friend talked about the advantage to the public; you have also the disadvantage of the risk of spoiling your carriages by the wheels getting wrenched, have you not?—Yes.

214. And if this steam power were used you would have the additional disadvantage of having the horses frightened?—You would have that additional disadvantage, no doubt.

215. And those horses which you saw in Paris showed their terror; that is to say, that every horse that had a kick in him gave a kick?—Well, I think that was pretty much the fact.

216. Do you think there is any possibility by any mechanical contrivance, such as an imitation horse, or anything of that kind, of doing away with this fright on the part of horses?—I do not think you would ever entirely eliminate it; nothing that I have seen would do so. Of course I have not seen the imitation horse of which you speak.

Mr. *M'Lagan*.

217. Do you think that the inconvenience to the public by the startling of horses is so great as to prevent the use of mechanical power on tramways?—No, I think the advantages largely outweigh the disadvantages.

218. You have some doubts, I believe, as to the desirability of the use of steam power in crowded thoroughfares?—I think it is open to question, whether in the streets of London or of other large towns or cities it might be desirable.

219. You said that the Board of Trade knew very little about the use of locomotives upon highways

Major Gen. *C. S. Hutchinson*, R.E.

7 March 1877.

B 3

highways except in matters relating to the strength of bridges; have you had many applications made to you about the strength of bridges where those locomotives have been used?—Personally speaking, I have only had one case; I do not know whether the Board of Trade have had any more; that was simply to report upon the strength of a bridge which was to be used by locomotive engines. There is a provision in the Locomotives Act for the course to be taken under such circumstances.

220. From your own experience and observation, do you think that bridges generally on parish roads are strong enough to admit of the use of locomotives?—I should think there are grave doubts whether they are. There was a case last week where a bridge on the North of Scotland Railway was broken down by a locomotive, and it fell on to the railway.

221. Would not that be an objection to the extension of tramways in country districts?—I suppose the surveyor of roads would look out for the strength of his bridges, and see that nothing was permitted to come over them that would endanger them.

222. The loss would fall upon the trustees in that case, would it not?—I think that it is provided that it shall fall upon the owners of the locomotives; but, as a rule, the weight upon the wheels of those tramway engines would not be very great; not like the large locomotives which are used for dragging steam machinery about.

223. I think those engines which you mention, such as Merryweather's and others, would weigh about six tons?—About that; about a ton and a half on each wheel.

224. I should think very few bridges on parish roads would be constructed to carry such a weight as that?—I can hardly say; certainly the bridge which I looked at last year was a very weak one, but that might have been an exceptional case.

Mr. Samuelson.

225. Do you think that horses which are in the habit of approaching railway stations, or crossing bridges under which railways pass, are as much alarmed by the trains as those that are quite strange to railways?—No, I think not.

226. You think that there is a tendency for them to become accustomed to them?—I quite think so.

227. Do you think that the same would occur in regard to mechanical power on tramways?—I think so; I think that when horses got used to them they would cease to regard them.

228. The more mechanical power there was used on tramways the less danger there would be to horses in that sense?—Yes, of course it would be in a diminishing ratio.

229. And you think also that the frightening of horses is not so much due to the emission of steam or smoke, or even to the noise of blowing off the steam, as to the unaccustomed form of the car?—That is my opinion, although, of course, it is only given for what it is worth. I have no doubt that if there is a great emission of steam, and a sight of fire, and a quantity of smoke, it increases the fright which the horses experience.

230. Still you do not attribute it principally to that?—No; I think that whatever precautions you take for preventing the escape of steam or smoke, or the sight of fire, you will still have the frightening of strange horses, although the

frightening would, of course, be increased if those were allowed to be visible or a nuisance.

231. But you do not attribute it chiefly to that?—Not entirely.

232. You would think it necessary, however, to prescribe that there should be no noise from the blast?—Yes.

233. And that there should be no escape of smoke allowed?—Yes, we think so.

234. So far as you have told us in reference to these engines, none of them, I think, have been satisfactory in that respect?—Perhaps not entirely so. I think that the most satisfactory that I have seen were those which are working in Paris. There seemed to be very little objectionable escape of steam or smoke there, and in the engine which they use at Wantage, Grantham's engine, I do not think that there was anything particular to complain of, nor in the Hughes' engine that I saw at work in Edinburgh. I have no doubt that as the construction is improved they will entirely get rid of these matters.

235. But up to the present time are you aware of any engine that is absolutely free from these drawbacks?—I should say that Hughes' engine, as I saw it in use at Edinburgh, and Grantham's engine, as I saw in use at Wantage, might be said to be practically free from these disadvantages.

236. Have they any special appliances for the purpose?—Yes, they have special appliances. I cannot tell you exactly what the mechanism which they employ is, but they have special means for avoiding the escape of the exhaust steam and for consuming the smoke; of course the screening off of the fire is a very simple matter.

237. You would expect, of course, that when these engines were subjected to your inspection they would take special pains to avoid these objections?—No doubt that might have been so.

238. Do you think, then, that in the present state of the art of construction the time has arrived for requiring that there should be absolutely no escape of steam and no emission of smoke under any circumstances?—Yes, I think it has. It is not a point which any of the engine constructors have objected to; they all hope and believe that they will be able to meet it.

239. Still they have not yet succeeded in meeting it, have they?—I should have no hesitation, I think, on the part of the Board of Trade, in passing such engines as I have described; I think they might be fairly said to comply with our requirements.

240. If that question were brought before a bench of magistrates might not their opinion be somewhat different from yours?—It is quite possible that it might be.

241. Then do you think it would be quite safe to make the rule so stringent as you propose to make it under the bye-laws, seeing that you would not be always there to interpret it?—I do not see how you can make it at all elastic; I should think it would be better to have the rules stringent, and then if cases came before the magistrates they would deal with them, I suppose, according to their merits. If it was a continual evasion of the requirements, or simply an accidental one, the circumstances would be taken into consideration.

242. Referring to the Locomotives on Roads Act, are you aware that magistrates have said that they thought it was very difficult to comply with the special provisions as regards the escape of
steam

Mr. *Samuelson*—continued.

steam and the creation of smoke, but that the law was so stringent that they had no option but to insist upon the absolute avoidance of both?—No, I was not aware of that.

243. With respect to the gauge, do you think that any advantage arises from adopting the 4ft. 8½in. gauge?—I do not think that there is any advantage in the ordinary mode in which tramways are constructed with the grooved rail, because it will not admit of railway carriages running on it. In the case of the Wantage Tramway, the rail is an ordinary flat-bottomed rail, and railway trucks and carriages can run upon that tramway and trucks do run upon it; but as a rule the 4 feet 8½ inch-gauge has no particular advantage one way or the other that I can see.

244. It would be rather a disadvantage, I suppose, in some cases, on account of the greater expenditure which it might involve?—Yes. There was one tramway authorised some few years ago in a narrow country road on a gauge of three feet; that was a case in which a 4 feet 8½ inch-gauge was inapplicable.

245. You would not go so far as to prescribe by Act of Parliament the rate of speed or conditions affecting the emissions of smoke, or of steam; I suppose you would wish only that the Board of Trade should have the power, or that the Standing Orders should have the power to prescribe these matters, and that they might be varied from time to time?—Yes, I think so.

246. In reference to the Locomotive Acts of 1861 and 1865, the fact of these conditions being prescribed would rather stand in the way perhaps of the development of the art of the construction of road locomotives?—I should imagine that it would.

247. You would not think that in any fresh legislation these conditions should be left absolutely binding, but you would prefer that the cases should be judged on their merits by some authority?—I should certainly think that it would be desirable to review those Locomotives Acts in conjunction with the inquiry of this Committee.

248. Do you think that there should be a certain elasticity with regard to the question of speed?—I should think it might be desirable, at all events, to prevent a conflict of jurisdictions, the Board of Trade sanctioning a speed of one kind upon a tramway, and a speed of another kind being enacted by the Locomotives Acts upon a road.

249. You have not recommended any restriction as to the steam pressure which may be employed?—No, we have left that open.

250. Do you consider that there would be more or less danger in using steam at considerable pressure?—No, I think that might be left to the tramway companies themselves. We have always tried as much as possible to avoid interfering with details of that nature.

251. If you were called upon to give an opinion upon that, you would not say that it was desirable to limit the pressure to 150 lbs. per square inch, or to any other amount?—Practically, I think the pressure would generally be limited to something within a moderate compass. Of course, that is very much the case with locomotive engines; you very rarely find them exceeding a certain recognised pressure.

252. But if some 10 or 15 years ago a pressure of 150 lbs. had been talked of, it would not have

Mr. *Samuelson*—continued.

been considered to be practically attainable; the pressure used now in engines of various kinds is very much greater than was formerly considered to be practicable, is it not?—I do not know about the distance of time to which you refer; I should have thought it had been much longer ago than that, but no doubt the working pressure has increased very much during recent years.

253. And therefore it is not unreasonable to believe that it may be still further increased in the future?—It may be, of course.

Mr. *Pell.*

254. Were you in the Crimea?—No, I was not.

255. I suppose that in common with others who have been in the Army, and who know anything of the history of the horse, you know his horror of the camel?—No, I have never had anything to do with camels, and I did not know that.

256. Should you say that a horse is very readily educated to become composed when he meets these engines on the road?—I should think he would be easily educated to that.

257. You do not think that that is an insuperable objection to the scheme of applying mechanical power to tramways?—I do not think so; I merely bring it forward as what I have seen in my own experience.

258. Should you say that it was a great difficulty to be got over at all?—I do not see how it would ever be got over. There it would be constantly; whenever strange horses met those cars they would be frightened.

259. Might it not be a positive advantage as regards the horse that he would receive his education gently by the process of tramways, and so become accustomed to the more violent operation of the steam when he sees it on a railway?—I suppose that the more horses are accustomed to see these things the less they would become frightened at them.

260. Should you agree with me in supposing that steam tramways might be really of service in educating the horse?—I suppose they would be of service in educating the horse, if the horse was in the habit of meeting them.

261. Horses must meet them if they are on the highways, must they not?—If they become very general, of course horses must meet them.

262. At all events, would you go so far as to say that the advantage derivable from the education so received would be so great and so valuable as to counterbalance any inconvenience to which the public would have to submit by occasionally finding their horses scared by meeting these cars?—I think the gain to the public by the use of steam on tramways would far outweigh the comparative disadvantage of frightening horses.

263. But is it really a valid objection to this system to say that the horse and people drawn about by horses are likely, taking a general view of it, to suffer inconvenience?—I think they are certainly; it is only to my mind, a balance of advantages and disadvantages, in which the former preponderate.

264. Have you never heard that it is a very usual thing to put young horses into fields near railways in order to accustom them to the passage of the steam engines?—No, I have not heard that.

B 4

265. There

Major
Gen. *C. S.*
Hutchinson,
R.E.

7 March
1877.

Mr. *Pell*—continued.

265. There are certain objections, some of which have been already admitted, to the introduction of tramways in populous places and in crowded roads?—Yes.

266. But are not the objections common to cars drawn by horses and to cars driven by steam; supposing the steam-engine to comply with all the requisites which you, representing the Board of Trade, say are desirable?—The point, as I think, is that in introducing steam into crowded thoroughfares, you run the risk of frightening horses to a certain extent; and the more crowded the thoroughfare the more danger there is from the frightening of the horses.

267. Omitting that objection, can you name any other peculiar to steam-driven or steam-drawn cars as compared with horse-drawn cars on tramways?—No, I do not think I can, provided proper appliances are insisted on.

268. I think you have stated that these engines can be drawn up in their own length?—Yes, they can be very rapidly stopped.

269. A startled horse sometimes cannot be drawn up in its own length when he is drawing a tram car, can he?—No, I should think with a properly contructed steam tram there would be very little difference between running it in a crowded thoroughfare and running a horse tram in a crowded thoroughfare.

270. Are there not certain rules laid down by the Board of Trade with reference to the form of rail that is to be used?—None; it is left entirely to the company.

271. And to the local authority with whom they have to deal?—Yes.

272. And the local authority I think, as a rule, have insisted upon the grooved rail, and not upon the elevated rail?—Yes, upon the sunk rail.

273. There are very great objections, I think, to that rail, inasmuch as it entails serious inconvenience and expense to the company from their having to clean it out constantly?—Yes, it requires to be kept constantly clean.

274. And there is also another serious objection, that the same wheel is not suited to run over this and over railway rails?—No, it will only admit a very shallow flange.

275. With regard to a question which was asked you by an honourable Member as to the objection that might be raised against these engines in making use of the bridges in the country; I think you said that, as they are at present constructed, they do not exceed something like six tons in weight; are you acquainted with the weight of a Fowler's steam ploughing engine?—No, but I think it is considerable.

276. Should you think that I am exceeding the mark when I say it weighs from 15 to 20 tons?—I thought it was over 10 or 12 tons at any rate.

277. If the Quarter Sessions, having jurisdiction with regard to county bridges, and the surveyors with regard to parish bridges, are prepared for the passage of these engines which are now very generally used, their bridges would of course be strong enough for these engines?—That is my own opinion.

278. I should like to have your opinion as to whether you would place the trams by the side of the road or in the middle of the road?—It depends a great deal, I think, upon the width of the road. In a wide road I should always place it in the middle, but in a narrow road I think it

Mr. *Pell*—continued.

is necessary to place it along one side of the road so as to leave the rest of the road free.

279. Is there any objection to placing the tramways in the middle of the road, if the road is of a fair width?—No, not if it leaves sufficient passage on each side.

280. Have you ever considered the applying of the grass sides, the unused part of turnpike roads to tramways, before they are inclosed?—That has been done in some cases. This Wantage Tramway is one instance of it; and in the case of the Neath Tramway in Wales, it runs along the unused side of the road.

281. Do you know whether the use of traction engines for drawing carts over the common roads is excessively destructive to the highways?—That I cannot answer.

Major *Beaumont.*

282. With reference to the probable fright of horses, you are acquainted no doubt with the road rollers which are in common use in London?—I am.

283. When the road rollers are at work in the thoroughfares with which I am acquainted, in Westminster, not far from this House, have you ever noticed that the omnibus horses and cab horses pass those road rollers without taking any notice of them at all?—I think I have noticed the cab and omnibus horses pass them without taking any notice of them.

284. And could you at all inform the Committee whether you have ever known a case of interruption to the traffic by a road roller?—No, it has never come before me. I have never noticed that the traffic was interrupted, but the road rollers which I have seen used are generally on very broad thoroughfares; for instance, in Whitehall. I have not often noticed them in narrow thoroughfares.

285. But you never happen to have noticed any serious fright on the part of the horses from passing those road rollers?—No.

286. Would you as a matter of judgment think that a road roller was a less terrible object than a tram engine constructed according to the provisions which you suggest?—It is hard to know what is in horses' minds, but one would certainly think that a road roller ought to frighten them more than a tram-car; but then a road roller is a very slowly moving affair.

287. As to the point of safety, you have stated that a tram engine running at 12 miles an hour can be brought up in about a car and a half's length?—I would not bind myself absolutely, but it is somewhere about that.

288. Do you not think that a steam car can be stopped absolutely more quickly than a horse car?—Yes, I suppose it can; because you can communicate the wish of the driver at once, as it were, to a steam car, and perhaps it takes some little time to stop the horses.

289. Is it not the fact that out of the number of people who have unfortunately lost their lives under tramway cars, about four times as many have been killed by the horses as by the cars?—That is a point which I do not know.

290. If you arrange the car with cow catchers in such a manner that a man tumbling in front must necessarily be shovelled on one side, do you not think that the introduction of steam, as against horses, would be absolutely more advantageous

tageous as a matter of safety to the public?—In that point of view, certainly it would be safer.

291. You mentioned a point with reference to the storage of air upon Moncrieff's system, and you stated that the main objection to that system consisted in the fact that if the supply of air ran out the car was helpless?—Yes.

292. Would it not be the same thing as if an engine has neither fuel nor water?—Yes; but of course an engine can carry a supply of fuel and water which will drive it far greater lengths than any supply of air which you could give to a car like Moncrieff's. You leave a much larger margin in any supply of fuel and water that you give to a steam engine than of air that you could give to an air engine.

293. Assuming that an air engine could be constructed that should run a distance of 10 miles and still have a margin of power left, then your objection to the use of air on that score would vanish, would it not?—Of course the larger the supply that it can carry the less becomes the objection.

294. And if it could carry a sufficient supply of air to run 10 miles, you would think that that left a sufficient margin of safety?—Yes, for most tramway purposes.

295. Putting aside mechanical questions, as a matter of convenience to the public you would prefer Moncrieff's carriage to any steam carriage that you have seen?—No, I do not think I could say that; in those steam cars in which the mechanical power is separate from the car, I do not think that the public sustain any inconvenience from the use of the steam car, further than perhaps from the occasional emission of steam and smoke.

296. But that you have stated is inadmissible according to the terms of the Act?—Yes, but there may be in the best constructed engines an occasional escape of steam and smoke which you would not have in the air engine.

297. You think that it is possible to construct an engine which shall absolutely and perfectly comply with the Act at all times?—I think in the nature of things there must always be some occasional emission of steam or smoke in a steam engine which of course any air engine would be free from.

298. As to the gradients; what is the greatest gradient which in your opinion could be mounted by a tram-car carrying its motive power within itself; it is of course the limit of the adhesion of the wheels; but what would that be practically on tram-roads?—I should imagine about 1 in 15, speaking roughly; but I should not like to commit myself to the statement.

299. And that would be somewhat flatter in the case of an engine that was drawing the car?—Yes, unless there was some means of obtaining the benefit of the adhesion of the wheels of the passenger car.

300. Would 1 in 20, or 1 in 24, be about what you would consider to be the gradient which under the last circumstances might be successfully worked by a tram engine drawing a load?—Of course very much would depend upon the weight of the tram engine.

301. Bearing in mind the existing state of the tramroads with which you are acquainted, what is the greatest weight per wheel that you think ought to be put upon them?—I do not think that the weight ought to exceed two to three tons on each wheel.

302. Do you think it would carry as much as that?—I think so, at a moderate speed, of course.

303. What is the weight per wheel of the ordinary tram-car itself, when loaded?—I am not sure.

304. If a loaded car, which is about 4 tons, is carried on four wheels, that would make a weight of about one ton per wheel; consequently you think that the tramroads made to carry one ton per wheel could with safety carry two or three tons?—Many of them would, I think, but I cannot speak as to all.

305. Could you inform the Committee what sort of a speed indicator you allude to; because, so far as I know, no speed indicator has ever yet been constructed that could be put on a tram-car, and that would show the rate at which the tram car is travelling?—I have not seen one myself; I have only been informed that there are several speed indicators.

306. The speed indicator has never been invented yet, has it?—It has been applied, as I have already stated, to some engines which I hope to see next week, and then I shall be in a better position to inform the Committee about it.

307. I believe that a prize was offered by the Society of Arts for the best speed indicator, and it was gained by an instrument called the Stropometer; but it is impossible to attach it to anything that jars, and it is consequently inapplicable to a railway?—I cannot speak practically, but, as I have before said, I shall see one next week, and I could then let the Committee know if they wished to do so.

308. Will you explain the nature of the instrument that you stated was in use upon the Brighton Railway?—That I have not seen, and I cannot tell you about it; I said, I think, that a speed recorder was in use on the Brighton Railway, and a speed indicator and recorder are, I believe, in use on some of the American railways.

Mr. *Hick.*

309. With regard to the speed recorder (which I would rather call a speed governor), as I understand you, you say that one of the conditions should be that the regulation of the speed when it gets up to a certain limit should be out of the control of the driver, and that there is some such machine in America?—No, I did not say anything about America with regard to that; it was the speed recorder that I alluded to.

310. That simply indicates the speed at which the carriage has gone?—Yes, it is, or ought to be, an infallible register of the distance and speed.

311. But I understood you to say that it ought to be one of the conditions to have a means of cutting off the steam when the carriage got to a certain speed, say 12 miles an hour, such means being out of the control of the driver?—Yes.

312. We have an ordinary governor in land engines and marine engines, but I have never heard of any such thing being applied to a road engine. I understand that another condition would be that the brake should work in the same manner, because the steam might be shut off altogether when going down an incline, and then you would be dependent altogether upon the brake, which would be also automatic?—Yes, as I have already stated, I have seen an engine which has an appliance by which the steam is cut off when the speed reaches a certain point.

313. Have

0.74

C

Major
Gen. C. S.
Hutchinson,
R.E.

7 March
1877.

Mr. *Hick*—continued.

313. Have you seen the apparatus?—I have.

314. Can you describe it at all?—I should not like to undertake to describe it. I probably should not make myself intelligible; but such an apparatus does exist, and was at work at Wantage when I went there. As I have already said Hughes' engine, as I understand, is supplied with the means of cutting off the steam, of applying the brakes, and of registering the speed.

315. You are quite satisfied that an engine propelled by steam or compressed air could be stopped in less time than one drawn by horses? —Yes, if the brake power is in proper order.

316. But you are aware that you can turn the propelling power in the opposite direction and get the benefit of that as well as of the brake, and you cannot do that with horses?—Quite so; by reversing the engine you would, of course, stop it still more suddenly.

Chairman.

317. I think you spoke of the use of a speed recorder, not so much for the purpose of providing for the safety and convenience of the passengers as for the sake of proving infallibly whether the driver had broken the law?—Yes, for police purposes more than for any purposes of safety.

318. The speed indicator, whenever it is invented, will be for the safety of the passengers? —Yes, the speed indicator will be for the driver's information.

Major Beaumont.

319. I want to get quite clearly your opinion upon these three points, of the governor, the speed indicator, and the recorder; the governor serves automatically to cut off the steam, and so to prevent the engine from going at a greater speed than it ought; that I understand you to say there is no difficulty in doing, and it consists in taking the governor of an ordinary engine and putting it on the car?—Yes, or some equivalent arrangement.

320. And there is no difficulty in doing that, simply because the oscillations of the car do not produce any specially great variation in the governor. Then we come to the speed recorder, which is an automatic means by which you count the revolutions of the wheel, and consequently know what has been done; and that again is a simple mechanical arrangement which is in every day practice, and there is no difficulty about it. Then we come to the speed indicator, which has for its province to show the speed of the car at any particular minute; that enters upon an entirely different problem in mechanics, and it is one that presents particular difficulties, and as a matter of fact, one which has not yet been solved in this country?—Yes; I ought to have stated what escaped my memory just now, that this car of Merryweather's, which I saw at Wantage, had a speed indicator upon it, which appeared to faithfully indicate, so far as I could judge from passing objects, the speed at which the car was travelling.

Dr. Lyon Playfair.

321. Is it not the case, that if you put clearly before the public wants that are not scientifically impossible, inventors soon work up to those wants in order to satisfy them?—That is my opinion.

322. And that is the motive that induced you to put these conditions into the rule?—Yes; the motive we had was that we thought it highly im-

Dr. *Lyon Playfair*—continued.

portant that this question of steam on tramways should be started in a way which would provide, as far as possible, for the safety of the public; and we thought it therefore advisable to impose requirements which might, perhaps, be a little stringent as the thing was new, but which would no doubt be soon met by the mechanical skill of the country.

Chairman.

323. Is it one of the requirements of the Board of Trade under the rules which have been put in, that the speed indicator should be applied?— Yes.

324. And brake power?—Yes.

Major Beaumont.

325. Brake power that should be automatically controlled?—Yes.

326. Then the Board of Trade have asked for conditions which have never yet been complied with in this country?—That is so; but there is no doubt that they will be complied with.

Colonel Loyd Lindsay.

327. Would it not be sufficient for the purposes of the Board of Trade that there should be a means of cutting off the steam when a certain speed is reached, without requiring a speed indicator, which, as far as we know, has not yet been invented?—According to my information, it has been invented; it was on that Merryweather car at Wantage.

328. Neither the speed recorder nor the speed indicator are we yet able to say has been efficiently invented, and as I understand, they have sent to America to try one which they have heard of there?—I was under the full impression that I had seen a speed indicator on the Merryweather car.

329. And a recorder combined?—No; simply a speed indicator on the Merryweather car which was running at Wantage; I may, of course, have been mistaken.

Viscount Holmesdale.

330. An honourable and gallant Member drew a parallel between a steam roller and this tramcar; I think the steam roller is much smaller than the tramcar?—It is.

331. It is the great bulk of the tram-cars moving themselves apparently automatically which frightens the horse, as far as we know?— It is a moot question as to what it is that frightens them, but there is no doubt that something frightens them.

Major Beaumont.

332. Is it the speed indicator or the recorder to which you attach the most importance, and which you have seen?—The indicator.

333. That is a thing which, as I understand, has never been made in this country, but the recorder has. There are plenty of apparatus that tell you the speed at which an engine has gone, but there is no instrument yet made that tells you the speed at which it is going?—I may be mistaken about its being in Merryweather's engine, but in some engine which I have seen there was a small dial in the engine driver's box which gave apparently a very fair indication of the speed at which the car was travelling.

334. Do I rightly understand you to say that one

Major *Beaumont*—continued.

one of the requirements of the Board of Trade is, that the brake power is also to be automatic?—Yes.

Mr. *M'Lagan.*

335. Is it not the fact that you can tell the speed at which a railway train is going when sitting in the train by looking at the telegraph poles and counting them?—If you are skilful in doing it, no doubt you can do so. I do not think it at all beyond the mechanical genius of the country to invent such a thing as a speed indicator.

Mr. *Samuelson.*

336. Do I correctly understand you to say that you have only on one occasion seen this speed indicator at work?—Only on one occasion.

337. And you have not adopted any means of ascertaining whether this might not be one of those things which is very beautiful as an experiment, but which is scarcely available in ordinary practice?—I was in the car for about half an hour, and I watched the indicator move, and, as I say, it seemed to be a faithful record of the movement of the car.

338. With respect to the automatic apparatus for putting on the brakes, is your experience of that of any very great length?—I have not yet seen any apparatus for doing that.

339. You also prescribe that, do you not?—Yes.

Mr. *Pell.*

340. I think you said that these little delicate instruments which do not appear yet to be perfected were to guard against furious driving?—The cutting off of the steam and the application of the brakes were to guard against furious driving.

Mr. *Pell*—continued.

341. What is the precise object of this instrument which is to show the rate at which the carriage is going?—To enable the driver to know at what speed he is running. For instance, there is a rule that facing points should not be passed over at a greater speed than four miles an hour, and it would give the driver the means of knowing the rate at which he was going.

342. On the railways we see "speed not to exceed 10 miles an hour," but are the engine drivers assisted by one of those instruments to know at what speed they are going?—They are not.

343. Then can you explain why it should be required upon these tramways?—It is all with relation to attaining and insuring a moderate amount of speed, which is so much more important according to our ideas upon tramways than upon railways, because in case of excessive speed upon tramways there is a double danger; you have the people riding in the car endangered and the public using the highway endangered.

344. Your desire would be that the steam-driven car should not go at any greater rate of speed than well-bred horses would go at; but do you not think that the human brain and human intelligence on the part of the drivers, supposing them to be sufficiently educated men, would secure that without having this mechanical appliance, subject of course to penalties for offending against the laws regulating the speed?—We thoroughly considered the matter when we met together about it, and we thought that the speed indicator was a very important matter to place before the driver, so that he might have a perfect knowledge of what speed he was going at.

Chairman.

345. Have you any other observations to make?—No.

Major Gen. *C. S. Hutchinson,* R.E.

7 March 1877.

Mr. HENRY MERRYWEATHER, called in; and Examined.

Chairman.

1127. I THINK you are one of the firm that is connected with the invention of an engine of which we have heard a good deal in the Committee-room?—Yes.

1128. I believe you have been good enough to send to the Committee some photographs of your engine?—Yes.

1129. You have engines running in Paris, have you not?—Yes.

1130. How long have they been running there?—About 14 months altogether; nine months regularly, and the rest experimentally.

1131. Fourteen months from the time when they first began to run?—Yes.

1132. Are they now running regularly from day to day?—Yes.

1133. Carrying ordinary traffic?—Yes.

1134. Have you made many improvements in your engine since you first began?—Yes, a great many.

1135. What is the average speed at which they run in Paris?—About 8½ miles per hour, including stoppages and starting.

1136. What is the maximum speed allowed?—I am not sure as to the speed allowed at some parts of the journey; I think they sometimes attain a speed of 12 or 14 miles an hour.

1137. Have you on your engines an indicator which shows the pace at which the tram is going at the moment?—Yes, on the English engines, but not on the French engines.

1138. Can you describe that indicator?—Yes; it indicates the speed in miles per hour every half minute, and it makes a diagram to one-eighth of an inch scale. It is driven direct from the engine, and the highest point the hand reaches every half minute is then recorded. It would be rather difficult to describe it.

1139. What is the form of dial on which it records?—It is a plain plate with the miles marked on it, and a hand which points to the numbers.

1140. Do you attach much value to the use of the indicator?—I think it is useful for a man to refer to.

0.74

Chairman—continued.

1141. Is the steam shut off when an engine attains a certain speed?—Yes.

1142. At what speed is the steam shut off?—It can be put to any speed you like with the apparatus which we have. On the English engines it is now put to eight miles per hour.

1143. I assume that your engines show no steam or smoke?—They do not now.

1144. And that the fire is concealed?—It is.

1145. Is there any noise?—No; practically, there is none.

1146. With regard to the brake power, in what distance can the engine be pulled up?—An engine and car proceeding at say eight miles an hour, would pull up in about half the length of the car; perhaps in 10 feet.

1147. I need hardly ask if the egress and ingress of the passengers from and to the car are quite convenient?—They are not interfered with at all.

1148. What is the weight of the engine?—Our present engines in Paris weigh about three tons; they were made light to reduce the wear and tear upon the roads.

1149. Is it capable of driving more than one car?—Not on an incline. It would drive two on a fairly level road.

1150. Are your engines at work anywhere in England?—Only experimentally. We have run them at Portsmouth and Batley for a few weeks, and we are at work now at Leytonstone.

1151. But they are not in regular work?—Not conducting regular traffic. One is conducting the regular traffic, or part of it now, I believe, at Wantage.

1152. Have you had any accidents since you have been running in Paris?—No, I do not think that there have been any accidents there. A little while ago an omnibus ran into the tram engine, but it was more malice on the part of the omnibus driver. No one has been hurt.

1153. Are you under contract to carry the Paris traffic at a certain rate per mile?—No, we supply Messrs. Harding & Co. with engines;

G   I believe

Chairman—continued.

I believe they have an arrangement with the tramway companies.

1154. You simply sell your engines in the ordinary way?—Yes.

Mr. Hick.

1155. Can the speed be regulated independently of the governor?—Yes, by the ordinary steam regulator.

1156. That is under the maximum speed?—Yes.

1157. Can it be interfered with at all, supposing that you wish the engine to go at more than the maximum speed; could it be disengaged?—The engineer could not interfere with the governor.

1158. Would it be desirable, in your opinion, to have the means, in case of emergency when it was desirable to get out of the way of any other carriages, to, go at a greater speed than the specified maximum?—I hardly think so, or else the men might be tampering with it.

1159. So far as I can judge from the photograph which you have placed before the Committee, the rails upon which these carriages run in Paris are raised on chairs like the ordinary railways?—No, that is photographed in the yard at the depôt. They run on sunk lines like our ordinary London lines.

Mr. Samuelson.

1160. You say that in the French engines you have no speed indicators, but that in the English engine you have speed indicators?—Yes.

1161. But your English engine has only been worked by way of experiment?—That is all, except at Wantage.

1162. What is the nature of the speed indicator which you have at Wantage?—It is an apparatus called the strophometer; it is not such a complete apparatus as the one which we have on the engine at Leytonstone. This is the last apparatus which we have invented, and which is intended to act up to all the Board of Trade requirements.

1163. Then you have not yet an indicator in practical working which comes up to the Board of Trade requirements?—Not in conducting regular traffic; we have it now on an engine at Leytonstone.

1164. What is that engine doing?—It is running experimentally.

1165. How many miles is it doing a day?—We have not had it there many days; we have only had it running just to show people who are interested in it.

1166. It has not been put to any severe test as yet, has it?—No, not as yet. I have here a record of the speed of every day (producing the same).

1167. This is the recording part; I am speaking now of the indicating part?—The indicating part moves the hand; and you can see at any time, when the engine moves the hand, the speed at which the engine is running.

1168. In what way have you ascertained that the indication is correct?—It is driven from the wheels, a mile being indicated by a certain number of revolutions, and, unless the engine slipped, it is practically correct.

1169. What is it that is driven by the wheels?—The apparatus, which combines the recorder and indicator.

Mr. Samuelson—continued.

1170. Then in what way does the number of revolutions show the speed at any given moment?—It moves a ratchet one tooth every revolution, or seven revolutions in half a minute equal a mile; and at each seven revolutions a pencil moves one division, representing a mile.

1171. That is the recorder?—The indicator moves a ratchet, and at each revolution or seven revolutions in half-a-minute, the pencil moves one division, which, as I said before, means a mile, and when it moves 14 revolutions the hand moves up to "two miles." The indicator being driven direct, points its hand to a numbered plate, and the speed is recorded on a paper band.

Major Beaumont.

1172. It is not in connection with the governor, is it?—No, it is driven direct from the engine.

Mr. Samuelson.

1173. You say that your engines both in France and in England do not emit any steam?—The French ones, in very bad weather, show a little, but the means of condensing the steam there is not with water; it is by superheating the steam; of course that is a simple method, and you can do away with the annoyance of carrying a lot of water.

1174. In what way does the superheating of steam prevent the emission of steam?—It does not prevent the emission of steam; it hides it.

1175. You do not see it?—No.

1176. Do you hear it?—No, not at all.

1177. In the English engine, what is your provision for preventing the emission of steam?—We partly condense with water now, so as to hide it altogether.

1178. What becomes of the rest?—The rest is condensed with air.

1179. What is the nature of your air condenser?—The exhaust steam is split up into a lot of little sections, and it passes through a tube-condenser, and it is condensed in part, and the rest is led into the water-tank, and circulated round with the water, and that finishes it off.

1180. Where is there an engine of this description at work?—At Leytonstone.

1181. Not at Wantage?—No; the one at Wantage is merely superheated, and it shows a little.

1182. In what way do you prevent the emission of smoke?—We burn good Welsh smokeless coal.

1183. If you were obliged to burn north country or midland coal you would have smoke, I suppose?—Yes.

1184. Do you know any means by which smoke could be prevented if you were obliged to use north country or midland coal?—It could be prevented to a great extent, but I am afraid that in a tram-engine which carried outside passengers you would get a little smoke.

1185. Do you stoke during the journey?—The man can stoke; the firehole is close to his hand; but it is not found to be wanted.

1186. In Paris do they stoke during the journey?—Sometimes the man may put on a shovelful of coke, but it is found that they can run to the journey's end without wanting it.

1187. Even if you were using good coal it would emit a little smoke at the moment that
that

that shovelful was being put on, would it not?—Not with good Welsh coal.

1188. But you would not expect to get good Welsh coal all over the world, I presume?—No; but you would get coke at most civilised places.

1189. Have you made any calculation as to the cost of steam traction as compared with horse traction?—Of course, in comparing the two, you must remember that the cost of horse traction at every place varies a good deal.

1190. In Paris, do you know what is the difference between the contract price of Messrs. Harding and the previous cost of horse traction?—I do not know it exactly, but Mr. Harding will give the figures.

1191. Do you apply the brakes automatically to your engines in Paris?—No.

1192. Do you do so in the engine which is at work at Wantage?—Yes, partially. At Leytonstone it is applied according to the requirements of the Board of Trade.

1193. That is to say, when the steam is shut off, the engine without the intervention of the conductor, puts on the brake?—Yes.

1194. What advantages do you consider would be derived from that, as compared with having an apparatus by which the power of the engine could be put on by the driver?—It acts a little more quickly.

1195. Is it not a little more complicated?—Yes, it causes a complication, because every increase of the machinery causes a complication.

1196. As an engineer, which of the two plans would you prefer?—I should always have a brake that the man could put on himself as well as the others.

1197. That is to say, not an ordinary brake, but a steam brake?—If you have a steam brake, I should always have the foot or the hand brake that the man could put on.

1198. But would it not be a good thing if the man could put on the steam brake?—The Board of Trade require that the steam brake should be affixed.

1199. But there is a difference between the man putting on the steam brake and the engine putting on the steam brake; which do you prefer?—I think the automatic arrangement is the better of the two.

1200. You do not think that an automatic brake is more likely to get out of order than a hand-worked brake, both being steam brakes?—No; practically, I think not.

Mr. *Floyer*.

1201. It has been suggested that looking at this indicator would interfere with the attention of the driver to other matters; do you think that would be the case?—I think it might distract his attention a little.

1202. The driver would only have to look at it very rarely, would he, when he was running, because he would from his own judgment see when he was running very close to his maximum?—Yes, and then the automatic brake arrangement would prevent his running any faster.

1203. Still it would be an assistance to the driver, would it not, if he was in doubt as to the speed at which he was going?—Yes, it would assist him a little, if he looked at it; but practically, perhaps, he would very seldom look at it. Of course the dial would be placed in some very convenient position where he could almost see it

sideways, or in such a position that he ought not to have to turn his head to look at it.

1204. That would be a matter of arrangement, I presume?—Yes; that would be a matter of arrangement.

1205. And in that case it would not take off his attention from his other work?—No, but all these arrangements complicate an engine.

1206. Would it affect the working of the engine in any way?—Not at all.

Colonel *Loyd Lindsay*.

1207. Of course you are very much interested in turning out an engine which shall be perfectly safe so far as the public are concerned?—Yes.

1208. Do you think if you could have an apparatus which would cut off the steam when a certain speed had been reached, that would provide all that would be necessary in the interests of the public?—I think so.

1209. This invention, I presume, would prevent the engine going beyond the particular speed which might be settled by the authorities?—Exactly.

1210. In that case, if it could not exceed that pace, that would meet all that the Board of Trade, or the authorities who were watching the interests of the public could require, would it not?—Of course they do require more than that.

1211. But, as I understand, this apparatus prevents the engine going beyond 10 miles an hour?—Yes, it does.

1212. If it goes at a less speed than that, of course nobody can complain?—No.

1213. Are you also interested in the Grantham car as well as your own?—We manufactured the first Grantham car, the original Grantham car, for the late Mr. Grantham.

1214. Have you heard any complaint about an escape of steam at Wantage?—No; they have mentioned that the steam does show a little in bad weather.

1215. You are aware, are you not, that it does show a good deal?—Yes, in bad weather.

1216. In fact, when the engine rises up an incline at all the steam escapes?—It is more likely to do so when the engine is going up an incline. The more work it has to do the more likely the steam is to show.

1217. There is a funnel out of which the steam comes, is there not?—Yes.

Mr. *Hick*.

1218. Under any circumstances, when the weather is bad and the rails are greasy, have any of your wheels ever slipped?—I think they have slipped once or twice in the light engines going up the Avenue Josephine in Paris, in very greasy weather.

1219. In that case how does the recorder act?—With a recorder driven by a band it would not be much good, but the recorder which we have is not driven by a band.

1220. But it is actuated by the wheel axle, is it not?—Yes.

1221. If the wheel was running round without advancing, it would give an incorrect record, would it not?—It would.

Major *Beaumont*.

1222. Would you say that you have sufficient adhesion for ordinary purposes?—Yes.

1223. Have

Major *Beaumont*—continued.

1223. Have you not tried some experiments, with a view to increasing the adhesion of the engine, by putting the weight of the car upon the engine ?—We have not tried the experiments; we have several methods of doing it, and also some methods of coupling up the car as well.

1224. That is on the assumption that the adhesion which you have is insufficient ?—Yes.

1225. Do I correctly understand that these proposals have never been carried out because you have always found the adhesion to be sufficient ? —No, hardly that. Of course the engines which we have sent to various places have been sufficiently powerful to work the roads on which they have been used. If we had to go on heavier roads, we should have either to employ heavier engines or some different arrangement. We consider that we have power enough, but not adhesion enough.

1226. Up to the present time you have had no want of adhesion ?—No.

1227. What kind of boiler do you use ?—The ordinary tubular boiler.

1228. For your fire engines you use the Field boiler, do you not ?—Yes.

1229. In reference to condensation you said, if I rightly understood you, that you now use partly air and partly water condensation ?—Yes.

1230. The air condensation consisting in blowing the steam into tubes, in which it gets mixed with cold air, and the residue being condensed by water; in what way is it condensed ?—It is conducted into cones. There is an inside and an outside cone; the steam is in the inside cone and the water is in the outside cone, and there is a continuous circulation round the tanks until the water is so hot that we cannot use it any more. We can work up to about 200°, and then we let it loose.

1231. Are you aware of the way in which the steam is condensed in the Metropolitan locomotive ?—Not exactly; I think that they merely conduct the steam into the tank.

1232. So that the steam, after it has passed

Major *Beaumont*—continued

through the air tubes, is then delivered into cones which are surrounded by water, keeping the water in constant circulation; what happens as soon as the water has got so hot that it will condense no more steam ?—We have to let it pass away until we get to the end of the journey, and then we take up fresh water.

1233. Do you let it into the furnace or up the chimney ?—We can let it into the furnace.

1234. What result did you find, as regards the killing of the steam, when you were blowing the steam off into the fire ?—We found that it kept the firebox clean, and that it did not use more fuel.

1235. Had it no tendency to put the fire out? —No, not at all, if you blow plenty of air in with it, but it did not do in very bad weather.

1236. Do you consider that this combined arrangement of air and water condensation effectually prevents the emission of steam ?—Yes, it effectually prevents it.

Mr. *Samuelson.*

1237. The condensing water becomes less and less efficient as you proceed on your journey ?— Yes.

1238. But that you do not find in practice to be any drawback ?—No; at the end of the journey we can load up with fresh water.

1239. But just before you get to the end of your journey, we will say, do you find the condensation still as efficient ?—If our water gets too hot before the end of the journey, we can use our old method by opening a valve.

Chairman.

1240. Are you acquainted with the proposed regulations of the Board of Trade ?—Yes.

1241. Do you think they are reasonable ?— I think they are fairly so.

1242. They are not more than inventors can with tolerable ease comply with ?—No; I think inventors can comply with them.

101. You say that you have never had any application to have two or more tram carriages coupled together?—The cases are so very few that we really have had no experience as yet. Except the cases of the Vale of Clyde and Wantage tramways, there are no steam tramways that we have inspected; but I know that in Paris they have been running for two years, and they have only one carriage attached to the engine.

102. Do you not think it very likely that if tramway companies are allowed to use steam power they will put more than one carriage on?—It is possible.

103. Then do you not think it will be necessary to impose some limitation on the number of carriages; because, in going down hill, for instance, a large weight behind must operate upon the engine power?—Yes; I suppose that they must put brakes to all the carriages; but I can conceive that it would be desirable to make a rule against their running long trains in the streets.

104. At Paisley, the other day, where the engine was mastered by the weight of the carriages, there was an accident, and they could not stop it; if they had four or five carriages behind one engine, as a matter of course there would be great danger?—A long train of carriages following one another with no interval between them is always a nuisance in the streets.

Mr. *Pemberton.*

107. I suppose the difference between tramways and railways generally is in the formation of the iron rail, is it not; one is a hollow rail or tube, the wheel running in the groove instead of running, as railway carriages do, on a flat surface with a flanged wheel?—Yes; but I am not sure that that applies to all tramways and all railways; I do not know that there is any absolute line to be drawn between them.

Major General CHARLES SCROPE HUTCHINSON, R.E., called in; and Examined.

Chairman.

114. You have been for 11 years Board of Trade inspector of railways, have you not?—I have.

115. A report has been laid before the Committee on the Vale of Clyde Tramways; we should be very glad to hear your own observations and comments upon that Report, if you feel competent to give them; our object being to ascertain whether anything new has occurred which modifies your views in reference to tramways since you gave evidence before the Committee of 1877?—I was directed by the Board of Trade to visit the Vale of Clyde Tramway, and report to them upon the working of the steam engine or engines which had been sanctioned provisionally for use there. I went down

Chairman—continued.

and paid an unexpected visit, and I watched pretty narrowly the working of the engines during three periods of the day; and I found that there were seven engines running altogether, and that they were behaving fairly well, although there was more noise and more emission of steam than was perfectly right. I also found that their average speed was exceeding what had been permitted by the bye-laws.

116. What is the country through which the Vale of Clyde runs?—It runs along a street the whole way, lined on each side by houses and shops.

117. Where is the Vale of Clyde?—It is a suburb of Glasgow; the street runs parallel to the river Clyde.

Major Gen. *Hutchinson*, R.E.

B

118. What

Chairman—continued.

118. What is the length of the tramway?—The length of the tramway which is worked by steam is a mile and a half.

119. Is steam the only motive power used?—Steam is the only motive power used at present.

120. I believe last year there was another motive power used?—They tried for a short time, I believe, the Moncrieff compressed air engine, but I never saw it working on the Vale of Clyde Tramway.

121. Is it a double or a single line?—It is a single line.

122. What is the width of the street?—It varies from 30 feet down to 22 feet, or 20 feet perhaps in places, but I cannot speak quite accurately. It is not what you would call a very narrow street, nor is it a very wide one. As I was saying, I found that the rate of speed somewhat exceeded, viz., by about a mile and a half an hour, that laid down by the bye-laws. That was the rate of the average speed running from one end to the other. Of course there might occasionally have been a higher speed than that to maintain that average; and I understood, although I did not see it myself, that on Saturdays, when the traffic was very heavy and a more frequent service was required, the speed was even still further in excess of that permitted by the bye-laws, because there were only a given supply of engines, and they were obliged to be run more quickly in order to carry the traffic that presented itself.

123. How were these bye-laws drawn up?—They were drawn up by the Board of Trade.

124. Did they include the regulation as to the rate of speed?—Yes.

125. Is there anything about the rate of speed in these bye-laws?—The rate of speed is left blank in these bye-laws. On the Vale of Clyde, I think it was eight miles an hour; and from the observations which I made, the speed was up to $9\frac{1}{2}$ miles an hour; and I was told by the officials of the company without any concealment, that they were obliged to exceed that speed still further on Saturday.

126. What are the gradients?—There are no gradients at all; I think it is almost flat. It is parallel to the Clyde, and there are no hills occurring. The speed was not to exceed eight miles an hour; and on passing through moveable facing points, it was not to exceed four miles an hour.

127. When were these bye-laws drawn?—On the 1st of February 1877.

128. Upon what experience were they founded?—There was no experience to found them upon; they were tentative more than anything else. I should mention that these cars are fitted with a self-acting mechanical appliance for controlling the speed and applying the brakes, which, as far as I could gather, appeared to be acting well. There were no complaints about it. The cars were also supplied with a speed indicator, a kind of clock face which showed by a hand the rate at which the car was travelling; that also appeared to be acting with tolerable exactitude. The cars were not supplied with a speed recorder as they had been originally, for it was stated that it had been found very difficult or impossible to make the speed recorder work satisfactorily.

129. I was under the impression that the speed indicator was the more difficult mechanical contrivance?—So one had understood; but the engine builders apparently do not find the same difficulty with the speed indicator that they do with the speed recorder. At any rate, these engines have had the indicator all through the time, and with tolerably satisfactory results. The recorder, as I said before, was abandoned, after about a month's trial, on the plea that they could not get it to work.

130. Which would be the more valuable safeguard in the public interest, the indicator or the recorder?—The indicator is a tell-tale to the engine driver, whether he is exceeding the proper speed; the recorder is more particularly for the use of the police, that they may have a record of the journeys in the case of accidents occurring, and be able to ascertain the speed at which the tramway car was running at or about the time at which the accident occurred. These engines had also been ordered to be fitted with a special bell for warning persons or vehicles to get out of the way, but the use of this bell had been strongly objected to by the inhabitants, and the company had taken it upon themselves to fasten the bell up, and were using merely a whistle in the ordinary way that tram-cars give notice of their approach, and which was found sufficient for the purpose.

Mr. *Pemberton*.

131. Was the bell continuous?—The bell was intended only to be rung to clear the road, but they had fixed it badly, and it was always jingling, and no doubt it caused a great nuisance along the road. This is not a point of any very great importance; it was only thought desirable, when the rules were framed, to have something more special for steam cars than an ordinary whistle, which might not be recognised and attended to. Then I observed, also, that these steam engines were running with the door enclosing the engine open, and not closed, so that the fire might, under certain circumstances, especially at night, be visible; this was not according to rule. I suppose that they could not get sufficient draught if it was closed.

Chairman.

132. That was, of course, contrary to the bye-laws?—It was. Those are the principal things which, I think, occurred in the running of the engine. I also had an interview with the police authorities, and obtained from them a record of the accidents which had occurred on the tramway since the steam cars had been running. There had been altogether nine accidents.

133. In what period?—That was, I think, from August to February. Of those accidents, two had not then been investigated. Of the remaining seven, in three cases the drivers had been convicted of careless and reckless driving, and in the other four cases the parties injured had been themselves held blameable. The superintendent of police told me that, in his opinion, for police purposes, a speed recorder would be a most valuable addition to the engine, because in almost all these cases there had been great dispute as to speed, the public contending that the speed had been, perhaps, 15 miles an hour, and the servants of the company saying that it was not more than five miles an hour. He also told me that shortly after the cars had first started running, there had been great trouble with them, owing to want of proper attention;

Major Gen.
Hutchinson,
R.E.

18 March
1878.

attention; but the superintendent had been changed, and they were in a much more satisfactory condition at the time I visited the Vale of Clyde than they had been previously. That is the result of my experience of the Vale of Clyde tramways.

134. Have you visited any other tramways with steam upon them since the last report?—I have, but the result of my observations was included in a paper which was appended to the evidence last year; that was as to Paris, Wantage, and Loughborough, and also Leytonstone on the North Metropolitan Tramways.

135. I suppose your experience of the Paris tramways gave you a good opportunity of coming to some conclusion as to the bye-laws?—It did.

136. I believe there has been a temporary suspension of the use of steam on the Paris tramways; but that was owing to something quite independent of the working of the company?—That I was not aware of.

137. It is stated on good authority that the differences were only some difference between the contractors and the tramway company; and that the suspension does not arise from any objection on the part of the authorities?—I think the use of steam was only sanctioned tentatively and provisionally when I was there. I do not know that it has definitely sanctioned.

138. For what period of time were they sanctioned?—I do not know what the period was, but the authorities had not given their final sanction when I was there; the use of steam was still considered, as far as I understood, as an experiment.

139. What length of tramway was being run over with steam?—They were then running over a length of three miles.

140. And the tram companies were willing to apply steam simply for a limited period, subject to an entire revocation of their powers?—Yes, I imagine so; I am pretty sure that the authorities of Paris had not given a final sanction, although they had expressed themselves well satisfied with what had been done.

141. As the material which we have before us are chiefly the bye-laws laid down by the Board of Trade, I think it would be useful if you would go through them shortly, and state your opinion as to whether any alteration should be made in them, or whether you think them generally fairly applicable. The first point that arises is the difficulty of making a distinction between a street and road; do you think that the conditions could be framed in such a way as not to be too general, but to be applicable, subject to modification in particular instances, so that a fair distinction could be drawn between a street and a road?—I am afraid it would be a very difficult matter. It is a definition the want of which we have felt very frequently, and I have often called attention to it; but I have never seen my way to be able to frame a Parliamentary distinction between a street and a road.

142. Do you think that the distinction which is drawn in the first, second, and third paragraphs of the bye-laws is one that could be practically acted upon, and would be useful when schemes come before you? I think it is a question more of width than of anything else, except in certain cases where there are no houses or shops along one side of a street or road there might be some exception made.

143. The width, of course, would be only one of the elements?—It is only one of the elements; but that again is a very difficult matter, because it is impossible to say that a frontage which now exists without any shops or houses will not in the future have some. For instance, in laying a tramway along the side of a road where there is such a frontage, it might be very hard upon the owner in future, because it might prohibit him from erecting houses on the frontage if he wished to do so.

144. That applies to existing tramways too?—No doubt; but in some cases where tramways are carried by consent along a frontage which does not at present possess any houses or shops, it does not follow that in the future it may not possess them, and it might be a hardship.

145. Should you lay down any condition as to the tramway being in the middle or at the side of the road if steam is applied?—I think if steam is applied to tramways, the general condition should be that the tramway should be in the centre of the street or road if it is a single line. In the case of a double line, the centre of the space between the two lines should occupy the centre of the street or road.

146. Is that stated or implied in the bye-laws?—It is not stated; it is in the General Tramways Acts of 1870. But although that would be the general rule, I think it might be well to give a certain power deviating from that rule under specific circumstances, and not to lay down a perfectly hard-and-fast line.

147. In fact, I imagine that there would be none or very few of these regulations which you wish to see established as a hard-and-fast rule?—No; but as a general rule of course the centre of the street is the most suitable place.

148. I think you stated in evidence in 1877, that there were three things of great importance as mechanical appliances in reference to the engines and the cars; and those were a speed governor, a speed recorder, and a speed indicator?—Yes.

149. You lay great stress, do you not, upon the necessity of having the governor out of reach of the manipulation of the engine driver?—Yes, out of his ordinary reach. It must be able to be reached by the man when the engine is in the sheds, of course, but it should be out of his ordinary reach. The idea the inspecting officers have about the matter is, that if you have a drunken or a reckless driver, he should not be able, without great difficulty, to tamper with the speed governor.

150. The object of that speed governor would be to let off the steam by an automatic process, if a certain speed were exceeded, would it not?—Yes, either to cut it off, or to let it off, and to apply the brakes.

151. Would you not allow the engine-driver to apply the brakes?—He would either be able to apply the brakes himself, or they would be applied automatically. I think I had better state that I have received a communication from an experienced firm of locomotive builders, who are now engaged in tramway engine construction, and to whom I referred the question as to whether they anticipated any serious difficulty in applying speed governors to tramway engines. I will read what they state, if you will allow me to do so. There is a preamble with regard to clause 2, specifying that an engine should possess a speed governor, and they remark as to this: " This presents no insuperable difficulty, and we have

Chairman—continued.

complied with its terms by designing an arrangement of governor on one of the axles working a friction clutch, a chain from which shall engage a lever on brake and regulator shaft. It is at the same time impossible for a driver to render this inoperative, but he can increase the brake pressure at will. The apparatus is adjustable to any desired speed." Then they go on to say: "We have never been able to see any actual necessity for this principle being carried out in practice, or any advantage justifying the additional complication and cost involved, simplicity and non-liability to derangement being leading considerations."

152. That is, as regards the governor?—That is, as regards the governor; so that I have no doubt, from what they state here, that they consider it perfectly feasible; in fact, they have done it; and they are a very eminent firm of engine-builders, who, I am sure, would not state that they could do it if they were unable to do it. Then they go on to say: "Working arrangements as to time, and where there is much single line, accuracy at passing places, as well as police supervision, all tend to make excess of speed difficult, and, so far as the crowded portion of streets are concerned, the speed will in all cases be greatly below the maximum at which the apparatus takes effect." Of course that is perfectly true; but it seems very desirable to guard against any recklessness on the part of the driver. One knows that occasionally, even on railways, you get drivers who are not quite what they should be, getting drunk, or becoming reckless from other causes, and the men who would be employed on tramway engines, I apprehend, would be an inferior class to those employed on railways, so that there will be all the greater need, I think, for introducing, if possible, some mechanical means of guarding against improper conduct.

153. Am I right or not in saying that the danger from the recklessness of the drivers would be considerable enhanced by very steep gradients? —It might be, no doubt.

154. What is the steepest gradient on which a tramway exists in this country?—I think the steepest gradient is about 1 in 14.

155. Is that in Edinburgh?—No. I think there is a steeper gradient, though only a short one, at Birkenhead, leading from the Woodside station up to the road which runs from it.

Mr. *Pemberton.*

156. That, at present, is not worked by steam, is it?—It is not. Steam has been used upon that tramway experimentally, but it is not used there regularly. I am not sure whether any of the Edinburgh gradients exceed that, but I do not think they would. It is a very severe gradient.

Chairman

157. Would it be necessary, in drawing up these conditions, to have in our mind any gradient of exceptional severity going either up or down? —In going down, if the speed was over the allowed speed, the governor would come into play and apply the brakes if the driver did not do it himself.

158. These are rules of general application; can we lay down general rules which should be applicable in the case of excessively steep gradients, or do you think that in those cases special regulations would have to be made by the

Chairman—continued.

Board of Trade?—It should be left, I think, to the Board of Trade, in all cases, to decide at how much in excess of the maximum speed to be allowed on the tramway the governor principle would come into force, and there might be a greater margin in the case of steep gradients than in those cases where the lines are tolerably level; but I think that is a matter of detail.

159. You think that need not be included in these general regulations?—No; I do not suppose that it would be desirable to include that. If the governor principle were adopted, it would probably be better left to be decided by the Board of Trade according to the merits of each case, at what extra allowance over and above the maximum speed on the tramway this restrictive power should come into operation.

160. You think that the exceptions are so general as not to be able to be covered by any rule that we could lay down?—I do not think it would be necessary. With regard to the point as to the speed recorder, this firm of locomotive builders do not go into that; they do not seem to anticipate any difficulty in constructing it, only they do not think it necessary.

161. You do think it necessary?—We think that in the interests of the public a speed recorder is a most desirable appliance to have attached to these engines, and that the speed indicator is desirable for the purposes of the engine drivers.

162. Are you able to state whether there is any tramway or railway where both a speed indicator and a speed recorder are in use?—No, there is not. The only case in which a speed indicator is in use is on the Vale of Clyde tramway, and there it works tolerably satisfactorily.

163. I think on the American railways they have both those appliances?—I cannot speak personally as to that. They have, I know, a speed-recording instrument, but whether it is largely used or not I am not aware. With regard to the speed-recorder on the Vale of Clyde tramways, that was given up after what was to my mind a very insufficient trial, and was allowed to fall into disuse; it was not properly looked after, I am informed, and it fell into decay. After my visit to the tramway, last month, the inventor was sent down to look at the speed recorder, and it was again put in order, and seemed to have worked satisfactorily for some time; but it has again got out of order, simply, as he informs me, from the want of being properly attended to. This particular contrivance requires a clock-maker to observe its proceedings once a day, and to look to it to see that it is going all right; and the inventor says that if that is done he has no doubt in the world that its working will be perfectly satisfactory. Before the cars go out in the morning a mechanician (a clockmaker, as he expressed it,) ought to see that each recorder is in proper order; and if that is done, he says, there will be no difficulty about it.

164. Do you think that an unreasonable precaution to impose?—I do not think it is.

165. I understand that the speed indicator shows the speed at which the tram car is travelling at any given moment, and that the speed recorder shows the space traversed and the speed maintained during the journey; why should there be any more necessity for ascertaining, by mechanical appliance, the speed of a tram car than there is for ascertaining the speed at which an omnibus is going when there is an accident? —It seems to me that no reasonable means should

be

be neglected for controlling the use of so powerful an agent as steam, &c., when used in our streets or roads.

Mr. *Pemberton*.

166. Does it record the speed at each particular period of the journey?—Yes, at intervals of so many seconds. These (*producing a speed record, and explaining it*) are registered every ten seconds, and the number opposite represent the rate of speed, and by dividing this by six, you get the number of miles per hour. It is done by a clockwork management, combined with electricity; this was the record of the journeys of the car after the recorder had been put into order.

Chairman.

167. Then virtually this would answer both purposes?—Except that it does not show the driver the speed at which the car is going, which is very important.

168. At all events, it is your opinion that the use of the speed indicator and the speed recorder should be conditions laid down in any general regulations that might be made?—That is the opinion of the inspecting officers of the Board of Trade. Of course I do not speak for myself alone, but it is my opinion, and the opinion of my colleagues too.

169. I am asking you these questions as representing the engineering department of the Board of Trade?—I hope it will be understood that the bye-laws with regard to these mechanical matters were drawn up at a conference of the four inspecting officers of the Board of Trade.

170. We have touched, I think, upon all these conditions except the one that an engine shall be free from noise produced by blast or clattering of machinery, and that the entrance to the carriages shall be separated from the machinery; have you any remark to make with reference to that?—No, I do not think I have any remark to make with reference to that bye-law; it is a very reasonable one, I think.

171. These are the conditions as distinguished from the bye-laws. Turning to the bye-laws we see that certain spaces are left blank; do you think it would be possible to fill up the spaces by specifying a rate of so many miles an hour in a town, and so many miles an hour elsewhere?—No; I think it would be preferable to leave that to be decided according to the merits of each particular case.

172. The next paragraph is as to the speed at which the engines may pass through moveable facing points; would you have a rule laid down as to that?—I would have a rule laid down as to that, because otherwise you might have very serious accidents. You cannot manage steam-engines, in the same way as you can manage horses, so as to turn them one way or the other.

173. I understand that it was once contemplated that when the cars came to facing-points they should stop altogether?—Yes; but that was thought to be rather too onerous.

174. Those are the only remarks that you have to make upon the conditions and the bye-laws; if there is anything else that occurs to you, we shall be very glad to hear it?—I have nothing further to remark.

175. There are tramways which you have not specially inspected with regard to the scope of this Committee's inquiry, but I understand that you would be willing, for the convenience of the

0.68.

Committee, to inspect those tramways if the Committee thought it necessary?—I shall be most happy to do so.

176. I think I may say that the Committee would think it very advantageous if you would examine the Leith, Leicester, Wantage, and Belfast tramways, with reference to any particular points which arise in these schedules and bye-laws, and as to what conditions it is necessary to impose in the interest of the public safety?—I will endeavour to do so. We do not always hear of these trials of steam at the Board of Trade; you are much more likely to hear of them in the Committee than we are at the Board of Trade. I did not know that steam was being used at Belfast. I will endeavour to find out, amongst other things, what accidents have occurred there.

177. Is there steam at Paisley?—No, there are are no tramways, I think, at Paisley.

Mr. *Bates*.

178. What was that accident which occurred the other day between Govan and Paisley, where the engine of the steam tram-car was mastered by the carriage, and the driver lost all control of it, and it ran down an incline?—I did not see the account of that; it could hardly have been on the Vale of Clyde tramway, because there are no ascents there. I do not think there is any tramway at Paisley; the nearest tramway to Paisley is this very Vale of Clyde tramway which runs through Govan.

Chairman.

179. I observe that in the bye-laws which the Board of Trade have drawn up, they have retained some clauses which had not been recommended by the Committee of 1877?—Yes, they are these mechanical appliance clauses, I think.

180. Do they only refer to the mechanical appliances?—I think so principally, but I have not compared them seriatim.

181. The Committee would like to know why those appliances have been retained though they are outside the recommendations of the Committee of last year?—The only ones I had anything to do with was the retention of the clauses relating to restrictive mechanical appliances; I think if they could be carried out without any great difficulty or any great expense, they would be very valuable from the point of view of safety to the public; and my feeling is that if they are not imposed, or endeavoured to be imposed, now, they never will be; if steam is now allowed on tramways without any restrictive appliances they certainly will never be got in the future, and therefore it is now or never.

Mr. *Bates*.

182. With regard to this speed indicator you say that it would be valuable for the police?—Yes, that is what they themselves think; I give you their own experience.

183. You say it gives the speed every ten seconds?—It can give it every ten seconds, or at any short interval.

184. Supposing that one of those engines was going 10 miles an hour, and supposing that they saw that an accident was likely to take place from some one crossing the road, would they not be going at the rate of three miles an hour within five seconds?—They might be.

185. What, in that case, would be the value of the

B 3

Mr. *Bates*—continued.

the indicator?—It would not record such minute points as that, but it would show you a very faithful record of the whole journey.

186. Then it would give you the speed at which they had been going ten seconds before?—Yes; it would give you the average of the ten seconds.

187. You named Woodside Ferry; do you know what the gradient is at Woodside?—My impression is that it is 1 in 14.

188. Do you think it is possible for an engine to go down that steep incline to the gates of the ferry?—Yes, I have seen an engine go up and down; it was Grantham's engine that did that.

189. Of course it would make a wonderful difference with a number of cars attached to an engine going down these inclines?—They could get down if all the cars had brakes on them, but they could not get up with one engine. It was as much as the engine could do to haul itself up, it was a self contained engine, the engine being contained in the car.

190. If each car had a break, you think going down an incline would make no difference?—If each of the cars had a brake they might go down with safety, supposing the brakes to be applied; but I do not think they could get up without more than one engine on.

191. You said that there would be a hardship in making a tramway along one side of a road where the opposite side was not built upon; do you not think that it would be rather the other way, and that it would make the land much more valuable?—No, because it is such an obstruction to the frontage.

192. Do you think that if a tramway went along a street, whether on that side or not, it would not make that vacant land more valueable?—Not in the way that I was thinking of it. It is often customary in tramways, along roads with no houses fronting, to carry them close alongside the pathway or the hedge as the case may be; then of course if that land is ever built upon afterwards, the tramway would obstruct the entrance to the doors of the houses or shops.

193. But you might put them further back?—Then you would require to widen the road to give access to them, otherwise, whenever a tram-car was running, any vehicle which was standing at the door of a house or shop would have to move out of the way to let the tram-car pass, and that becomes a great nuisance.

Mr. *Denis O'Conor*.

194. With reference to these accidents on the Vale of Clyde Tramway to which you have referred, do you know whether any of them occurred from horses being frightened by these engines?—No; I was not told they occurred from that reason.

195. I suppose there have been no records

Mr. *Denis O'Conor*—continued.

kept of accidents of that kind?—Not unless they have led to personal injury.

196. Supposing that an accident led to personal injury, but that the tramway rules had been carried out so that the person in charge of the tramway had not been in fault, would it be treated as a tramway accident?—It would depend upon whether the person injured brought an action against the tramway company or summoned the driver.

197. You do not know as a matter of fact whether horses have been frightened by these engines?—When I was making these experiments, I myself saw one or two horses frightened, and some accidents very nearly occurred, but not quite.

198. I see in your evidence last year that you expressed a very strong opinion that horses will always be very likely to be frightened by steam tram-cars?—No doubt strange horses will be frightened by them; but when horses get used to the tram-cars they do not notice them.

199. Is there much traffic in those streets where the steam tram-cars run?—Yes, a great deal of traffic, but it is more cart traffic than carriage traffic. I do not know whether the Committee want any foreign information in addition to those tramways which have been mentioned.

Chairman.

200. The Committee will be glad to have any information that you think may bear upon the question, whether general conditions should be imposed in the interest of the safety of the public. If, in the course of your inquiries, you find that any new matter, which you think important, has arisen since your last report, we shall of course be glad to hear it?—I will do my best to get what information I can for the Committee.

201. In your last year's evidence you stated that, in your opinion, it was not necessary to impose any general condition as to steam pressure; do you remain of the same opinion still?—It has not been customary to impose such a condition for locomotive engines in this country. In France they do it, and they require the engines only to be worked up to a certain pressure.

202. You do not think it is advisable to introduce such a rule?—No; I think it would be better not to enter into it. I see that a speed recorder has been invented by a firm in Hanover; this a railway engine builder writes to me to say is simple, and that he has ordered one. I may be able to give the Committee some account of that.

Mr. *Maurice Brooks*.

203. Have you heard that the steam-cars have been taken off the line at Paris within the last 12 days?—The Chairman was mentioning that, but I had not heard it myself.

REPORT.

BY THE SELECT COMMITTEE appointed to inquire into the Regulations which it may be desirable to impose in relation to the construction and use of TRAMWAYS, and to Report to the House.

ORDERED TO REPORT,

THAT the Committee have met and have examined several Witnesses, and have agreed to the following Report, viz. :—

1. The Committee, in considering the subject referred to them, have had the advantage of having before them the Reports of two Committees of the House of Commons, which sat in the years 1877 and 1878, and the Evidence taken before those Committees ; and they have themselves heard such further evidence as seemed to them required to supplement that already given, and to bring the information in their possession down to the present time.

2. The Order of Reference, under which the Committee was appointed, directs them to inquire into the regulations which it may be desirable to impose in relation to the construction and use of Tramways, whatever may be the motive power employed upon them ; but the circumstances out of which the appointment of the Committee arose, and the intrinsic importance of the subject, have naturally led them to turn their chief attention to the questions connected with the use of steam or other mechanical power on Tramways.

3. The evidence given before the Committee shows that there is a growing tendency, both in the United Kingdom and on the Continent of Europe, to substitute mechanical for horse power, although one witness stated that in the United States the use of steam, after having been adopted for some time, had lately been almost entirely discontinued on account of the wear and tear of rails and engines. There is, on the whole, reason to believe that if legal sanction were given to the employment of mechanical power, it would be made use of at once in many places, and that its adoption would extend considerably in the future both in towns and in rural districts.   *Mr. Small, Q. 338.*

4. Under these circumstances the Committee agree with the two Committees of the House of Commons in the opinion that the use of mechanical power on Tramways should be permitted on conditions calculated to afford due protection to persons using the streets or roads, through which the Tramways may pass, for the purposes of ordinary traffic, as well as to those whose interests may be in any other way injuriously affected.

5. The novelty of the whole matter, and the fact that the employment of mechanical power on Tramways can scarcely at present be said to have advanced beyond the experimental stage, make it desirable that while the conditions imposed should be of sufficient stringency to give reasonable security for the public safety, and for the freedom of ordinary traffic, they should be elastic enough not to throw needless impediments in the way of the development of the system in the form which experience may show to be practically the best. It is upon this principle that the Committee have based their recommendations.

(15.)   a 2   6. One

6. One of the most important questions which has engaged their attention has been the minimum width of street or road on which Tramways, whether using horse or mechanical power, should be permitted to be laid down. Qs. 185 and 186. Major General Hutchinson, one of the Inspectors of Railways under the Board of Trade, gave it as his opinion that, where steam power is used, there should be a minimum width of certainly 9 feet 6 inches between the edge of the tramway and the kerb, and that the width of the street should in no case be less than 24 feet from kerbstone to kerbstone, and, as a general rule, that opinion appears to the Committee to be correct; but cases may often occur in which it would be unadvisable to prevent the establishment of a Tramway of considerable length, whether for horse or mechanical power, because for a short portion of its course it might have to pass through a street or road of somewhat less width; and the Committee, therefore, think that it should be left to the Board of Trade to decide, in each case which comes before it, whether, looking to the local circumstances, the construction of the Tramway should be permitted, although for some part of its length it may pass over a narrow roadway.

7. It appears that in many cases the permanent way of existing Tramways upon which horse-power alone is used, is in a very unsatisfactory condition, and that much inconvenience to ordinary traffic is the result. This evil would be increased if mechanical power were to be employed, and the Committee think that it is important that measures should be adopted to secure that the permanent way should, in the first instance, be of a sufficiently solid character, and should be afterwards maintained in a satisfactory manner. With this view they recommend that the Board of Trade should instruct their inspectors to pay particular attention in their inspection of Tramways, before they are opened for use, to the solidity of the permanent way, and that the Board of Trade should also, in the case of existing Tramways, satisfy themselves, before sanctioning the use of mechanical power, that the permanent way is constructed in a sufficiently solid manner to bear the increased wear and tear. These measures ought to secure the original construction of a proper Tramway; and in order to give greater security than at present exists for its after-maintenance in good condition, the Committee think that it would be advisable to embody See Appendix. in all Provisional Orders relating to Tramways, Section 8 of the Stoke-upon-Trent Orders, which imposes a penalty not exceeding 5 l. a-day upon a Tramway Company which fails to keep its rails and its own part of the road in good condition and repair, in accordance with the requirements of Section 28 of the Tramways Act, 1870.

8. It may fairly be expected that these provisions will be adequate to prevent the streets and roads used by Tramway Companies from falling into the bad state of repair in which they are at present too often found to be; but the Committee are strongly of opinion that, wherever it is possible, it is most desirable that Tramways, especially in towns, should be constructed and maintained, though not worked, by the Local Authorities. In this way the repair and management of the whole of the roadway is kept in the same hands, and the interests of the general traffic more certainly secured.

9. The Board of Trade have inserted a clause in their recent Provisional Orders giving them power to put a stop by Order to the use of steam or mechanical power on Tramways, in case the Regulations of the Board are not complied with. Stoke-upon-Trent Order, sec. 15. See Appendix. The Committee feel that this is a very large power to entrust to any Government Department, and under ordinary circumstances they would hesitate to recommend that it should be granted; but there is at present so little experience of the use, on ordinary streets and roads, of engines moved by steam or other mechanical power, and the possible danger and inconvenience of any neglect of the conditions imposed for the security of the public are so great that, for a time, at all events, at the first introduction of the system, they are of opinion that it would be wise to embody a provision of this kind in all Provisional Orders. The Board of Trade should be required to make annually to Parliament a Return of the cases in which they have found it necessary to exercise the power thus conferred upon them.

10. The

10. The evidence given before the Committee shows that in many cases it is advisable to establish Tramways with a narrower gauge than 4 ft. 8½ in., and the Board of Trade have sanctioned such gauges in several of their recent Provisional Orders. The Committee are of opinion that in any revision of the Tramways Act, 1870, Section 25 should be so altered as to give no preference to a 4 ft. 8½ in. gauge, but to leave the width of the gauge to be settled freely, according to the circumstances of each case.

11. There are at present two modes by which Promoters of a Tramway can obtain power to carry out their undertaking: they may proceed either by Private Bill or by Provisional Order. The Committee feel that there is a danger that under this double system, some relaxation of the restrictions required for the safety and convenience of the public may creep into practice. The Board of Trade may lay down regulations strictly in accordance with what seem to the Committee to be the requirements of the case, but Committees of either House might be more inclined to indulgence, and Promoters who disliked the strictness of the Board of Trade, might be tempted to see whether they could not obtain easier terms by means of a Private Bill. If this should to any degree be found to be the case, the whole system of restrictions would soon be broken down, and it is important to prevent this from taking place, except after due trial, and as the result of the deliberate judgment of Parliament. There are of course cases, such as those in which it is desired to take any land compulsorily, in which the powers required by the Promoters can only be obtained through a Private Bill; and even in cases in which the objects sought could be secured by Provisional Order, the Committee are not prepared to go the length of recommending that Promoters should be debarred from applying for a Private Bill; but they are decidedly of opinion that it is most desirable that the Standing Orders of both Houses should enforce the same restrictions and conditions as those which they have recommended for adoption in the case of Provisional Orders.

12. The Committee think that notices ought to be served on railway companies in all cases in which it is proposed to cross their lines upon the level; and that the attention of the Board of Trade should also be called to such cases in order that they may be specially reported upon by their Inspectors. Similar notices should also be served on railway and canal companies respectively in all cases in which it is proposed to lay Tramways over any of their bridges.

13. The Committee are of opinion that the Tramways Act, 1870, should be amended in accordance with their suggestions; but as it would be impossible to pass an amending Bill in the present Session in time to enable the Private Bills and Provisional Orders now before Parliament to be afterwards carried through both Houses, they recommend that if those Bills and Orders are so altered as to bring them into harmony with the views expressed in this Report, they should be allowed to be proceeded with without further delay.

14. The Committee agree with the recommendations contained in the Report of the Committee of the House of Commons of 1878, except in so far as they are modified by the suggestions made in the preceding paragraphs, and the following summary exhibits in one view the Regulations which the Committee consider that it would be desirable to impose at the present time in relation to the construction and use of Tramways :—

    i. It is desirable that, wherever it is possible, Tramways should be constructed and maintained, but not worked, by the Local Authority.

    ii. The preliminary consent of the Local Authority to the construction of Tramways by private Promoters should be required as at present, with the exception that where the proposed Tramway passes through the districts of more than one Local Authority, and those authorities differ as to whether it should be sanctioned or not, there should be an appeal to the Board of Trade.

    iii. There should be freedom of contract between the Local Authority and the Promoters as to contribution to local rates, fares, tolls, and general charges, subject to an appeal to the Board of Trade.

Report, House of Commons, 1878, Suggestions, p. ix.

(15.   a 3   iv. The

Report, House of
Commons, 1878,
p. iv.

Report, House of
Commons, 1878,
p. iv.

iv. The periodical revision of fares and tolls should be provided for.

v. The use of steam or other mechanical power should only be conceded for a limited period not exceeding seven years.

vi. Notices should be served upon any Railway Company across whose line it is proposed to carry a Tramway on the level, and upon any Railway or Canal Company, whose bridges are intended to be used for a Tramway; and the attention of the Board of Trade should be called to all cases of level crossing, and they should require a special Report from one of their inspectors in every instance of the kind.

vii. No absolute minimum width of street or road should be laid down, and the veto conferred, under certain circumstances, by Section 9 of the Tramways Act, 1870, upon one-third of the frontagers, should be done away with; but as a general rule there ought to be a space of at least nine feet six inches between the edge of the Tramway and the kerb, and a minimum width of 24 feet from kerbstone to kerbstone; it should, however, be left to the Board of Trade to decide, according to the special circumstances of each case, what width of roadway is required to provide adequately for the safety of the public and the convenience of ordinary traffic.

viii. No preference should be given to one gauge over another, but the width of gauge should be settled freely, according to the circumstances of each case, Section 25 of the Tramways Act, 1870, being altered accordingly.

ix. The Board of Trade should instruct their inspectors to pay particular attention, in their inspection of Tramways, before they are opened for use, to the solidity of the permanent way; and should also, in the case of existing Tramways, satisfy themselves, before sanctioning the use of mechanical power, that the permanent way is constructed in a sufficiently solid manner to bear the increased wear and tear.

x. The Board of Trade should have power to regulate the width of groove to be used in the rails, so as to protect the wheels of carriages, or other vehicles, as far as possible, from being caught in the grooves.

xi. A Tramway Company which fails to keep its rails and its own part of the road in good condition and repair, in accordance with the requirements of Section 28 of the Tramways Act, 1870, should be made liable to a penalty not exceeding 5 l. a day.

xii. The Board of Trade should have power to make regulations which should be of general application on the following points :—

a. The general speed to be permitted.

b. The speed on passing through narrow streets or roads, or approaching facing points or other places where a low speed is desirable.

c. The pulling up of cars at the intersection of cross streets or roads, or at other places where such a precaution may be advisable.

d. The stoppage of cars in case of horses becoming alarmed or of impending danger of any kind.

e. The provision of efficient self-acting break-machinery regulated to the satisfaction of the Board of Trade.

f. The use of bell, whistle, or other warning apparatus.

g. The provision with every engine of a fender, and also, as far as possible, of an indicator.

h. The freedom of engines from noise, smoke, and the emission of steam.

i. The

> *i.* The concealment of fire in engines.
>
> *k.* The safety of passengers in their ingress and egress to and from the cars, and their protection from machinery.
>
> *l.* The posting of Regulations and Bye-laws in conspicuous places.
>
> *m.* The numbering of engines.
>
> *n.* The position of the engine-driver, who should be placed in front of the engine, so as to command the fullest possible view of the road before him.

Report, House of Commons, 1877, p. v.

xiii. The penalties for breach of these regulations should be of moderate amount.

xiv. The Board of Trade Regulations should be applied to all Tramways, whether established by Private Bill or by Provisional Order.

xv. In the event of the Promoters of any Tramway failing to comply with the Regulations having reference to the preceding points, the Board of Trade should be empowered to suspend the use of steam or other mechanical power on the Tramways belonging to such Promoters, until the Board has reason to expect that the Regulations will be obeyed for the future. The Board of Trade should make annually to Parliament a Return of all the cases in which they have exercised this power.

xvi. The Board of Trade should be at liberty to inspect engines and boilers, whenever necessary, and to prohibit the use of those which may be found to be unsafe.

xvii. The Board of Trade should be permitted to grant special licenses, to be in force for a limited time, for the experimental use of steam or other mechanical power on Tramways not otherwise authorised to use such power.

And the Committee have directed the Minutes of Evidence taken before them, together with an Appendix, to be laid before your Lordships.

31 March 1879.

Chairman.

426. SINCE your examination some days since I believe you have, at the request of the Committee, made several inquiries as to the working of steam upon tramways, both abroad and at home?—Yes.

427 You went to Paris?—Yes.

428. To Rouen?—Yes.

429. Liege?—Yes.

430. Portsmouth?—Yes.

431. Batley?—Yes.

432. And Edinburgh?—Yes.

433. Do they comprise all the places you have visited?—Those are the places I have visited.

434. We have heard it stated that steam upon tramways has been disused at the present moment in Paris, is that so?—I found that that was the case.

435. Will you explain why?—I was informed that one reason of it was that there had been a dispute as to terms between the providers of the engines and the tramway company.

436. Did that arise from any objection on the part of the corporation?—I understood there was no objection on the part of the municipal authorities. I saw some of the municipal authorities, and they stated that they only wished that the engines had been able to do their work more satisfactorily; that they had been weak and not up to their work; but they did not at all regret sanctioning the use of steam on the tramways of Paris, but, on the contrary, were about to sanction the extended use of it.

437. Will steam power be recommenced shortly on the Parisian tramways?—The concessionnaire of the tramways, Mr. Harding, informed me that steam traction would recommence on the route on which it had been previously employed in the course of a fortnight or three weeks, and that it would be commenced on a new route from the Arc de Triomphe through Neuilly to Courbevoie, a distance of about 2½ miles, in about two months' time.

438. Anywhere else?—I have been informed that there will shortly be steam traction upon the

Chairman—continued.

tramways in the north of Paris. That I was merely told incidentally.

439. The two last instances that you are speaking of are additions to the existing trams?—The two last are additions to the existing trams.

440. Has any inquiry been made by the municipality of Paris as to the comparative results of the working of tramways with horses as compared with steam?—I was informed that that had been the case, and that the comparison was very favourable with regard to the use of steam; in fact that was one of the reasons, or the main reason, why the use of steam was for a time given up, because there was a great anxiety on the part of the tramway company to use horses for a time upon absolutely the same route on which steam had been hitherto employed, and then to compare the results of the two systems of working. Although I could not obtain these results, the concessionnaire informed me that the results were very favourable as regards steam power. He promised to send me the particulars, but he has not done so yet.

441. That was merely as regards the steam power as compared with horses?—On the route from the Place de la Bastille to Mont Parnasse.

442. You mean that steam compared favourably, in a financial point of view, with horse power?—Yes. I find I made a slight mistake about the new routes. Steam is to be first commenced from the Arc de Triomphe through Neuilly to Courbevoie. That is to be commenced in two months. Then there is another route from St. Denis to la Chapelle, which is a distance of four miles, where steam traction is to be employed, in three months.

443. So that there will be three new routes?—Yes; I omitted one.

444. What length of tramway, upon which the use of steam is sanctioned will there be in Paris, added to the existing tramways?—I cannot state what the length of the northern tramways is;

is ; but the existing route and the two new routes will make a length of about 10 miles. I think a witness who will be called will be able to give the former distance.

445. You went to Paris, I believe, at the request of the Committee of last year ?—I did.

446. Had any accident occurred up to the time when you went to Paris last year at the request of the Committee on Steam Tramways ?—That was up to March last year. There had been some accidents, which are referred to in my report.

447. Have there been any accidents since that date ?—I have ascertained that there has been no accident of importance since that date.

448. But we must take into account, must we not, that during a certain period of the time steam had been discontinued upon the tramways ?—Steam had been discontinued since the month of February for about a fortnight.

449. Are we to understand that during the 11 months there had not been any fatal accident ?—So far as I could ascertain there have been no accidents of any importance.

450. I believe you also went to Rouen ?—Yes; there I found steam traction in use.

451. In what part of the town are steam tramways at work ?—The steam tramways are running from the bridge over the Seine along the quays through the suburb northward, a distance of about four-and-a-half miles.

452. Does that pass through any populous part of Rouen ?—No, not through any populous part of Rouen.

453. In no part of Rouen is there a steam tramway running in the populous part ?—No.

454. Are there any horse tramways in Rouen ?—Not at present ; they are under construction, but I was informed that, at any rate for the present, it is not intended to use steam through the narrow streets or centre of Rouen, but that a horse-service tramway was to be instituted in the centre of Rouen, which would connect together the different steam tramways which it is proposed to construct.

455. Speaking generally, is Rouen a town of broad or narrow streets ?—Some of the streets are narrow, one in particular. The high street, as it were, of Rouen is, I think, only 22 feet in width between the kerbs.

456. Do they run cars daily upon the tramway that runs from the quays to the suburb that you mention ?—Constantly ; there is a frequent service.

457. Do they increase the service on Sundays or holidays ?—They increase the service by letting the engine draw two cars along the level part of the line as far as the Octroi barrier, and from that point the engine carries one car to its destination.

458. What is the nature of the gradient on that line ?—The worst gradient beyond the Octroi barrier, where there is only one car taken, is 1 in 28. Upon that gradient two cars have not been worked.

459. The whole of that runs along a road which is comparatively wide, does it not ?—Yes, all the road is wide. There is no narrow road except a little bit at the Octroi barrier. The tram runs by the side of the road, except for a short distance, a space of nine feet being left between the nearest rail and the kerb.

0.68.

460. Is that a regulation of the authorities of the town of Rouen ?—Yes.

461. There is no general Act, I suppose, to that effect ?—No, there is no general Act ; the circumstances are special.

462. There is no bye-law of the municipality ?—No ; the tramways have to be authorised both by the municipality and by the Ponts et Chaussées.

463. The central government reserve to themselves a right of appeal ?—The project itself has been approved of by the Minister for Public Works in Paris. The details of carrying out the project are settled by the Ponts et Chaussées and the municipal government.

464. Would the director of the central government have under his care such regulations as are dealt with by our Board of Trade ?—Hardly so much in detail ; he has to give his approval to such projects generally.

465. A great deal would be left to the discretion of the local authority ?—Yes ; the local officer of the Ponts et Chaussées representing more or less the central government.

466. While the steam power was being tried upon the tramway in Rouen, was there much traffic upon the road ?—A few carriages passed, but no great number.

467. Did you observe the effect of the passing of the steam tram-car upon horses ?—There was the usual effect of a small number, more or less, being frightened. There were no horses badly frightened, but a great many noticed the tram-car ; they jibbed as it were, but there were no horses of any great mettle went past upon that occasion.

468. Is there any rule laid down now by the local authority, to use our English word, of Rouen, as to the speed which the tram-car should travel at ?—The restriction is 15 kilomètres per hour, or about nine miles per hour ; that was the only restriction, except the restriction that was imposed with regard to the pressure at which the engine should work.

469. Have you formed any opinion as to the necessity of a regulation as to the pressure on the engine ?—I have been thinking that it might be desirable that there should be some cognisance taken of the strength of the boiler. If the Board of Trade are to be called upon to certify that engines are fit to run, I think it would be reasonable to require a certificate that the boilers have been submitted to a certain test, such as the ordinary test which is considered adequate in locomotive engines, viz., a pressure of 280 lbs. or 300 lbs. to the square inch.

470. Is anything of that kind in use with reference to railways ?—Railway companies give no certificate to the Board of Trade or anyone else ; but the Board of Trade does not certify that locomotives on railways are fit to run. They have no responsibility with regard to that.

471. But you would introduce some supervision of the kind you have mentioned in the case of locomotives upon tramways ?—I do not mean any supervision ; but it has struck me that it would be desirable before an engine was certified as being fit for running, that a certificate should be given to the Board of Trade that it had been submitted to a certain test pressure, and that the working pressure should not exceed a certain definite proportion of that test pressure ; because

c 4

it

Chairman—continued.

it would be a very awkward thing if a boiler were to blow up a few days after it was certified and there had been no provision taken to ensure that it had been properly tested. What I submit is, that the tramway company should give a certificate that their engine had been tested.

472. I find nothing in these proposed regulations about an inspection of boilers?—No.

473. That is a point which has recently occurred to you then?—It has occurred to me that that would be only right; I did not mean to suggest that there should be any inspection of boilers by the Board of Trade, because I think that would be launching the Board of Trade into a very large affair. I think if the company were to furnish a certificate in an approved form, that the boilers had been subjected to a certain pressure, and they were to give an undertaking that they should be worked only at a certain pressure, that would meet the necessities of the case.

474. In that case there would be no need of the periodical report as to the state of the boilers?—There might be a periodical report required; that would be quite another matter. I do not wish to recommend an inspection of boilers on the part of the Board of Trade, because it would almost involve the creation of a new department to carry out such an inspection properly.

475. Is your recommendation founded upon the danger arising of a boiler exploding in a narrow and populous street?—That would be a very serious matter.

476. Is it contemplated to extend the tramway system in Rouen?—Yes, very largely; I am informed that it is in contemplation to extend it to several suburbs. One of the longest lines will be a line of 12 miles to a suburb called Elbœuf where there is a great cotton factory. They anticipate a large traffic from Elbœuf to Rouen.

477. It is not contemplated to have steam upon those tramways?—Yes; and to have a horse-tramway connecting the different steam tramways together.

478. Are you able to speak to what is the width between the kerbs in the narrow streets of the city of Rouen, where they propose to make a horse tramway?—Yes; 22 feet is the narrowest.

479. Would that width allow of a horse tramway to be taken through it?—Yes. They are not all so narrow as 22 feet; 22 feet is the narrowest, and that is in a very busy part of Rouen.

480. Is that inclusive or exclusive of the foot pavement?—That is the width between the kerbs of the pavement, the part available for carriage traffic.

481. It is a very important matter to know the width of the street between the houses?—I should say, at a rough guess, that the pavement is six feet wide; they are narrow pavements. That would make the total width of the street 34 feet.

482. Did you hear of an accident having occurred at Rouen?—No; no accident of any importance whatever had occurred, as far as I could ascertain.

483. During what period?—Steam had been used since September last.

484. You went to Liege, did you not?—From Rouen I went to Liege, understanding that steam was in use upon the tramways there.

485. How long had steam traction been in use at Liege?—It had been in use since September, but it had been discontinued from about the middle of March, owing to a steam traction engine having run into a cart. There was only one engine, which was employed in conjunction with the horse tramway. The engine had met with a collision. I was told that an obstinate carter persisted in driving zigzag across the road in front of the steam tram engine, and the driver of the engine lost his temper.

486. Then that was not an accident fairly incidental to the working of steam on the tramway?—No; it was an accident owing to the obstinacy of the carter, and the temper of the driver of the engine.

487. Did the steam tramway go through the heart of the city?—It did, through very narrow streets indeed.

488. I suppose Liege is a town of exceptionally narrow streets?—A great many of the streets are exceedingly narrow. The tramway was carried through these narrow streets on a single line close to the pavement, only leaving more than a foot or 18 inches between the kerb and the tram-rail. The street I allude to was only 18 feet in width between the kerbs, and 26 feet wide from house to house.

489. Did not that cause any disturbance to the local traffic?—The local traffic passed to one side when the tram-car was coming. I did not see the steam tram-car running, but the horse-cars were running, and the traffic seemed to accommodate itself to the horse-cars. The streets are wretchedly kept in Liege; both the pavements and the carriage-way are in a miserable state, and the tramway itself is also in a very bad state.

490. The pavement on each side would be about four feet wide?—Yes; it is a very narrow pavement. I never saw a large city with streets so badly maintained.

491. Did you have any conversation with the chairman of the tramway company at Liege?—Yes, I had.

492. Did he tell you anything that you think worth communicating to this Committee?—He told me that they had found by experiments at Liege, that if one-horse cars were sufficient to carry the traffic, there was no economy in the use of steam. He also told me that he had found, from his experience, that a tramway engine painted yellow was much more terrifying to horses than if some neutral colour, such as brown or mahogany was used. I believe that is not borne out by the experience of other people, though that was his experience, decidedly. He said there was no question but that the yellow colour is exceedingly frightening to horses.

493. As a rule, the horses would be colour blind; it would make no difference to the horses unless it was a very staring colour, such as a coat of yellow?—Yellow is a very staring colour. They are not at all strong on the use of steam in Liege, because single horse cars can do their work very adequately.

Mr. *Pemberton.*

494. Do the tramways run on the hilly part of Liege?—No; they have a tolerably level road. The worst gradient they have is 1 in 20. Through the main parts of the town it is tolerably flat. The gradient of 1 in 20 occurs in the suburban part.

Chairman.

495. I think that exhausts your experience of steam tramways in foreign countries?—Yes. I am

am sorry I had not time to go further into the matter, but I thought the Committee were going to meet last Monday, and I wanted to get back.

496. I believe you then went to Portsmouth?—I did, on my return.

497. There is a steam traction engine at work at Portsmouth, is there not?—Merely experimentally, not regularly. It was working, in fact, as an experiment, on the day I saw it.

498. It goes through the High-street of Portsmouth, does it not?—Yes; they had permission to try it experimentally.

499. Do you know during what time the experiment has been practised?—I think it was the second time only that the engine had run when I saw it.

500. You saw it in operation?—Yes.

501. Therefore, it was a comparatively novel sight, both to the people and to the horses?—I believe they had been trying steam engines experimentally there before, but only occasionally.

502. With what effect upon the horses?—They were more or less frightened. Some horses shied on to the footpath, but, as a rule, only a very small per-centage of the horses were frightened.

503. Was that engine built to comply with the regulations of the Board of Trade?—No. It was built for sending to Bilbao, in Spain. It made no pretence to comply with the regulations of the Board of Trade.

504. Was there any emission of steam?—No. It was very perfectly condensed. There seemed to be an excellent arrangement for that purpose, and also for getting rid of the products of combustion. I travelled on the top of the engine, with my nose over the funnel, for two miles, and I did not perceive the least atom of noxious vapours coming out. The way it is managed is this. The act of putting on steam closes a valve in the funnel, and throws the products of combustion downwards on to the streets, instead of upwards into the air.

505. Therefore, we cannot take that engine as exemplifying, in practice, any of the appliances which are thought to be necessary by the Board of Trade?—No, except the condensation of the steam, and the getting rid of the noxious vapours, so as not to annoy passengers.

Admiral *Egerton.*

506. Was there any noise?—The noise was nothing more than absolutely necessary; there must be a certain amount of noise.

Chairman.

507. It caused a certain amount of fright?—Yes. I have never seen one that did not.

508. Was there any fire visible?—No.

509. Have you any further remarks to make upon the Portsmouth steam tram?—No. There is nothing else that is special that I observed. If the use of steam is introduced at Portsmouth, I know the tramway company very much wish that they should be able to run two cars together. It is the idea of the tramway company at Portsmouth that it will be a great help to them if they are allowed to take two cars at once.

510. I believe you have visited Batley, near Leeds?—Yes.

511. How far is Batley from Leeds?—About 12 miles.

0.68.

512. What did you see going on at Batley?—A tram-car had been running for three or four days with an engine which had been sent from Leeds, for the purpose of trying an experiment. It appeared to be doing its work well as regards its power of traction. There are some severe gradients at Batley.

513. Was it working through the suburbs or through the town?—It worked through the towns of Dewsbury, Birstal, and Batley. They are three towns, which form a continuous street.

514. Is it a wide street?—Part of it is wide, and part narrow. On the narrow portion in Dewsbury, towards the end of the tramway, it becomes very narrow, it is not more than 24 feet wide.

515. You saw steam in operation throughout the line?—Yes, the engine was drawing a car backward and forward. That engine is provided with a novel mode of condensing the steam by passing it through a series of pipes at the top of the engine, and it appeared by that means to be condensed very fairly, although now and then there was an emission of steam visible.

516. Then this was different from the last instance, because the products of combustion were carried through a funnel?—They were carried in the ordinary way upwards into the air.

517. How did the engine work?—The engine worked very well indeed.

518. There was occasionally an emission of steam?—There was occasionally an escape of steam visible.

519. You saw the usual effect upon the horses?—Yes. The horses we met were principally of a superior description of drayhorses carrying the produce of the mills about, and a few of these were somewhat frightened.

520. Was that engine fitted with any of the appliances recommended by the Board of Trade?—No, it was not.

521. You then went to Edinburgh?—I went to Edinburgh after that.

522. I believe there is a special form of engine in use there?—It is a combined engine and car at Edinburgh, that has been working there for some time.

523. Under what sanction?—Under no sanction that I am aware of. I fancy it is against the wishes of the municipal authorities, though they have not formally interdicted the use of it. The requirements of the Locomotive Act are to a certain extent complied with by sending a man on horseback in front of the steam-car with a red flag.

524. Through what streets?—It was through the whole of Edinburgh. In the experiment I made with it, we started from the Post Office, and it went along Princes-street through a number of other crowded streets, making a detour, and coming back into Edinburgh to the same point from which we started.

525. Had the rails been specially laid for that engine?—No.

526. Did it run upon the ordinary rails used by the horse trams?—Yes.

527. Do I understand rightly that the boiler is in the same compartment with the passengers?—The boiler is at the right hand side of one of the entrances. It occupies, perhaps, the space of

Major Gen. *Hutchinson,* R.E.

4 April 1878.

D

Chairman—continued.

of two passengers in the right hand corner of the entrance on one side of the car.

528. Speaking from your experience, would it be a safe thing for the passengers to have it in their immediate proximity?—There would be no danger, except in the case of an explosion of the boiler; of course that would be an objection to a boiler anywhere.

529. But I suppose it would intensify the danger?—It would to a small degree.

530. I want to know the extent to which it would; would it make a difference?—It might.

531. If a boiler were to burst, you would sooner have it in a separate car than in the passenger car?—Yes, but I do not think that ought to be a ground of objection to the system.

532. Had that engine got any of the appliances which you have spoken of?—It was provided with a governor for regulating the speed, and applying the brakes, but unfortunately it was not at work when I saw the engine running. I suppose it was not in proper working order, but I saw that the appliances had been provided. The inventor of the engine said there was no difficulty in making it work, although they had unfortunately not got it working when I saw it.

533. How are the products of combustion disposed of in that engine?—The products of combustion were emitted from a hole just under the roof. Of course, to a certain extent, they would be felt on the roof by the outside passengers. The steam seemed to be perfectly condensed; there was no emission of steam.

534. I suppose in Edinburgh it went up a steep incline?—Yes.

535. What was the steepest gradient?—There was a short one of 1 in 13, aggravated by the existence of two sharp curves. The engine went up it without much difficulty.

536. For the purpose of ascending a steep incline, did they put on any extra cylinder?—Yes, they had a provision in this car for using either two or three cylinders, and when they were rising up the steep incline they used the additional cylinder.

537. Was there any danger apparent to you in descending those gradients?—The car was fairly manageable. It being a combined engine and car, there was extra ease in stopping on the gradients from the fact of the car being heavier than usual, and from there being no pressure from the carriage behind on the steam engine. The whole being self-contained, the brake power was applicable to the wheels of the combined car. The car was stopped with tolerable facility, but I do not think the brake arrangements were as good as they might have been.

538. You mention, as an element of safety, the brake power being contained in the carriage?—Yes.

539. I suppose if there were a continuous brake extending from the engine to all the carriages, you might extend the number of carriages with safety?—Are you referring to the case of an engine separated from the car?

540. Or in stopping and preventing pressure from behind?—Yes.

541. I suppose you attach great importance, do you not, to the brake power of those engines?—In those that I have hitherto seen I do not think there has been enough attention paid to giving the driver sufficient immediate control

Chairman—continued.

over the brake-power. That is a point which can readily be attained if it is attended to.

542. Was there any exceptional effect produced on horses in Edinburgh?—Many of the streets that we went through were much crowded with a superior description of horses, drawing carriages. It was in the middle of the afternoon, from three to four o'clock, when the fashionable people in Edinburgh were out. I never saw so little effect produced on carriage horses as by this particular engine and car combined. I do not remember noticing one horse of a superior description frightened. But the strange thing was, that the tramway horses were those that were the most frightened. We passed a number of tram-cars, and the drivers had apparently great difficulty in keeping their horses on the road at all.

543. Those horses of course were the nearest?—They were close to the engine. No doubt it was from the unusual fact of seeing a tram-car passing near them without any apparent means of being moved. Otherwise the ordinary traffic horses were very little frightened. The cab-horses on the cabstands next the tramway cars were those that were the next most frightened. They showed signs of restiveness as the steam tram-car passed them.

544. As far as Edinburgh is concerned should you gather that there is security to the public from the steam engine and the car being in one?—As regards the frightening of horses I think so, certainly.

545. I meant generally with reference to the safety of passengers in descending or ascending inclines?—I do not know that there would be any additional safety if a tram engine separate from a tram-car were provided with continuous brakes in the way alluded to. I think in all cases, where there are bad gradients on tramways, it will be very necessary that the driver should have some means of controlling by continuous brakes the brakes of the tram-car which is attached to his engine, or else in descending inclines the tram-car will press forward on the engine, and be very likely to cause an accident.

546. The brake power is probably an important element in the case; will you kindly look at the proposals of the Board of Trade, in which it is recommended that every car should be fitted with a self-acting mechanical appliance, placed beyond the control of the driver, and operating when the engine attained a certain speed?—That is to guard against recklessness or carelessness on the part of the driver.

547. That is to guard against excessive speed?—Yes.

548. Where is the regulation that deals with the brake power necessary for the purpose that you have been speaking of?—That is a point which has occurred to me since I was last before the Committee.

549. Then you would think it important in the interests of the public, that some regulation should be laid down as regards the brake power?—I think so. I think that the driver of the steam car should have the control of such brake power as would cause the car to be stopped within a certain prescribed distance.

550. I think all that is only consistent with the repeated recommendation of the Board of Trade in the case of railways?—Yes. I do not think it would be advisable to lay down a rule
that

that the car should be capable of being stopped within its own length. I think that it is hardly possible; but I think some reasonable distance should be laid down, such as 10 or 15 yards.

551. There is no provision for that in these proposals?—No.

552. You do not think it desirable to insert a provision to the effect that it should be stopped within its own length?—I think that is more than could be complied with.

553. Would you put in any regulations?—I think it is desirable to put in some, but I am not prepared to say exactly what form it should take. I think a certain distance, say of 10 or 15 yards when running at the maximum speed allowed.

554. Such as that which is recommended by the Railway Commissioners when they said that a train travelling at 45 miles an hour should stop within a distance of 500 or 600 yards?—Yes.

555. Who would be the judge of the brake-power. That would be referred to the Board of Trade, I presume?—Before certifying that an engine was fit to run, it would have to be seen that there had been provision made for enabling a steam engine and carriage, or a combined engine and car, as the case may be, to stop within a certain distance.

556. Speaking generally, as you are at present advised, you think it would be possible to put in some general regulation to say that there should be some sufficient brake-power, without specifying the extent?—I think that would meet the case. It is a subject which should not be lost sight of. In many of the experiments, the engine would not stop in 30 yards.

557. Besides those two new points, which I gather you have raised in this examination, namely, the strength of the boiler and the sufficiency of the brake power; is there any other point that occurs to you as the result of your experience, from your recent inspection, and what you saw last year?—No. I think I have brought before the Committee the points which strike me as being most important.

558. Would you attach much importance to laying down in the regulations an absolute limitation of width between which there was to be a single or double line?—I think it would be desirable not to make a hard-and-fast rule, but to leave it to be dealt with by the Board of Trade upon the merits of each particular case.

559. Would you agree to the proposal that was made that a large latitude of discretion should be allowed to the local authority?—In such a matter as that, they ought to know what was best, having regard to the facts connected with each town, and the feelings of the people.

560. You think it would be necessary for the sake of the general public to take such precautions as might be imposed by the central department?—I think the public would be protected, perhaps, to as great an extent as might be necessary by the General Tramway Act. Presuming that the General Tramway Act would not be over-ridden by any new regulations, and that the same rule as to frontagers' objections would exist as heretofore, I think that the question of the relaxation of the 10 feet 6 inches distance might be considered. The limit of 9 feet 6 inches is in the case of tramways being laid out of the centre of the road.

561. You think, in all cases where a tramway

0.68.

is laid out in the centre of a road, that there should be 9 feet 6 inches between the kerb and the outer rail?—No. I think that in that case again there might be a dispensing power given to the Board of Trade under certain circumstances.

562. In short, you think that those regulations should be made as elastic as possible?—I think they should be made as elastic as possible.

563. Is there any point upon which you wish to stand with more absolute firmness than upon others; with regard to the indicators and governors, are you still of opinion that it is absolutely necessary to insist that these engines should be fitted with indicators and recorders?—I see no reason to alter the opinion I have already expressed. I think it would be very desirable to lay down a rule that they should be so fitted. Of course, if experience further on shows that it is an impossible requirement, then it might be relaxed.

564. Your further experience has not shaken your belief as to the necessity of requiring there should be an indicator and recorder on each engine?—No. I heard what the chairman of the Leicester Tramway Company said, namely, that they had been running at a speed of 20 miles an hour experimentally. That is a very dangerous speed on a road, and it is very desirable that a driver should not have it in his power to run at that speed. It shows what can be done with these tramway engines, and the desirability of not putting such a very dangerous power into the hands of the drivers.

565. Is it necessary, do you think, to lay down bye-laws on the part of the Board of Trade, or would you leave that to the local authority; would they or would they not be the best judges of deciding what bye-laws, as distinguished from the conditions which should be imposed upon tramway companies, are desirable; I observe in these proposals that there is to be a record of the speed; that the speed is not to exceed so much per hour, and there is to be the use of a bell and whistle, and that it is to stop in the event of a horse being frightened, and so on; are those matters which you think would be advisable to specify on the part of the Government?—Yes, I think most of these are important bye-laws to be prescribed on the part of the Government.

Mr. *Bates.*

566. What is the width of the streets in Paris where these tramways are laid?—The road is very wide; it is, perhaps, 50 feet.

567. They have double lines of rails there, have they not?—Yes.

568. I think you said that at Rouen they only ran alongside the quays?—No; they commence running alongside the quays, and then they go along the ordinary country roads.

569. Then in the town they only go along the quays?—At present they only go along the quays, they do not go into the crowded part of the town at all.

570. What is the width of High-street, Portsmouth?—It is a narrow street; I cannot tell you precisely, but I should think some of it would be as narrow as 22 feet between the kerbs.

571. Is it a street of much traffic?—Yes.

572. Are there shops?—Yes, all the way along.

D 2

573. The

Mr. *Bates*—continued.

573. The streets in Edinburgh are very wide, are they not?—The principal streets are.

574. Throughout the town?—Many of the streets through which the tram runs are very narrow.

575. What is the width?—I suppose in some cases not more than 18 feet wide. The principal streets are wide, but there are some exceptionally narrow. I am, in all cases, speaking of the width between the kerbs.

576. You have stated that, in the case of the Edinburgh tram, the boiler is in the carriage?—In this particular car.

577. Do you think there is any more danger in its being in that position than if it were outside?—I do not quite say that.

578. Suppose a boiler were to burst in this room, would you rather be in the room, or in the lobby?—I would rather be in the lobby.

579. If a boiler were in this room and it were to burst, would it not do a great deal more damage than if it were in the lobby?—There is a great difference between the boiler of an engine bursting in a car were there are passengers, and the boiler of an engine bursting in the lobby with thick walls between.

580. I am referring to the injury which would arise from scalding, which, of course, is the greatest danger?—Danger will arise from fragments.

581. The fragments may touch one or two, but the steam might touch everybody; you do not approve of the boiler being inside the car?—I think if it came to a question of saying whether a certificate should be granted for a self-contained steam-car, one would not feel justified in refusing it on account of the boiler being in the car.

582. For instance, we do hear of cases of boilers bursting?—Yes.

583. What would be the effect if a boiler were to burst inside a car full of passengers; would it not be very dangerous if it were enclosed in a car with passengers?—No doubt the results would be more serious than if it were otherwise.

584. Do you think it is possible to have a steam-car, with more than one carriage attached to it, on an incline of 1 in 13?—No, I do not think that would be right.

585. Do you think it might be done?—It might be done with continuous brakes, but it would be absolutely necessary to have continuous brakes.

586. You think it might be done?—I think it might be done, but I do not think that it would be a place in which to recommend that it should be done. It would require an exceedingly good brake arrangement; but the thing would cure itself, because it would never contemplate carrying two cars up a steep; in fact, they could not be got up. It would be difficult to get one up, to say nothing of two.

587. But still, with extra power, they could get up two?—It would not be worth while to use such extra power as would be requisite.

588. You think there should be power to stop these steam-cars, at all events, in 10 or 15 yards?—That is my opinion.

589. Then you do not agree with the former witness, when he said that you could stop a steam tram-car in a less distance than you could stop a horse tram-car?—I do not know about the comparison; I have never seen steam tram-cars stopped within the short distance that has been

Mr. *Bates*—continued.

spoken of; my experience is that they require 10 or 15 yards in which to stop.

590. You have seen horse-cars stopped?—Yes; but I have never made notes of the distance in which they are stopped; it depends upon the speed at which they are going, &c.

Sir *Graham Montgomery*.

591. Who was the maker of this steam tram-car that you have referred to?—Robertson and Henderson, two young engineers of Glasgow.

592. Where did you commence and end your journey?—We began at the Post Office, or close to the Post Office, and then went along Princes-street, turned to the left past the Lothian Road station, and then made a detour, and came round across Canongate, over the bridge, and so back to where we started from.

593. In the afternoon?—We started about three o'clock, and got back about four o'clock.

594. Besides the company's officials, had you any of the corporation officials with you?—There were some.

595. Did you hear them express any opinion as to the practicability of applying steam on the tramways in Edinburgh?—I think it was the first baillie who expressed himself very much pleased with the result, and that it was much better than he had anticipated, or words to that effect

596. You yourself were very well pleased with the trial in Edinburgh, were you not?—Yes; it was a very satisfactory trial.

597. The gradients there being probably steeper than in any of the other places you had visited?—Yes.

598. Great complaints have arisen in consequence of the cruelty to horses, owing to the incline?—Yes.

599. Do you think if steam could be used in Edinburgh, it would obviate that to a great extent?—Yes; I should have said that, after returning to the Post Office, we went down to Portobello. In returning from Portobello there is a very long incline; it is not a severe one as regards gradients, but it is a very long one; it is a very trying pull, it being one in 22 for a mile or a mile and a half.

600. The engine came up that incline very successfully, did it not?—Yes, without any difficulty.

Mr. *Denis O'Conor*.

601. In France the tram-cars always run by the side of the road, and not in the centre, do they not?—Not always; at Rouen they were running on the side of the road because the side of the road was paved, and the tramway company had got authority from the road authorities to lay a tramway along the paving; had they gone in the centre of the road it would have been more expensive to them.

602. Do you see any particular objection to their running on the side of the road in country districts where there are no houses?—At Rouen there are wide roads.

603. I mean on either narrow or wide roads?—In some cases, on roads where there are no houses, I think it is an advantage to carry the tramway on the side of the roads.

604. They are more out of the way of the traffic there, are they not?—Yes; there is very often spare or waste ground on the side of the road

road where it is desirable to carry the tramway, that is, where there are no houses to be interfered with.

605. If the rule with regard to having 9 ft. 6 in. between the outside of the rail of the tramway and the footpath were to apply to country districts as well as to towns, you would be precluded from having them on the side of the road in the country districts?—With regard to that, it might be well to make these rules elastic, so that they might be modified, to meet the requirements of any particular case.

606. You would have it so arranged that the local authorities might give power to them to run at the side of the road?—Yes.

Mr. *William Holms.*

607. And the frontagers?—The frontagers should have their present powers of objecting.

Mr. *Maurice Brooks.*

608. You spoke of the danger of committing to the hands of the driver the power of travelling at the rate of 20 miles an hour?—Yes.

609. Is danger in that respect likely to arise on suburban roads?—There would be no danger at certain times of the day when the road is tolerably clear, but the danger is in putting into the hands of the driver a power he may use very improperly at certain times.

610. It might be a great advantage on a suburban road which is clear early in the day?—I do not know about the advantage.

611. I want to know whether you apprehend any mechanical danger?—Mechanical danger would arise from the nature of the tram rails not being sufficiently good to allow of such a rate of speed being maintained with safety.

612. Then, besides the risk of collision, there would be danger from the lightness of the rail?—Undoubtedly.

613. Your experience will enable you to inform the Committee whether you think there is any difficulty in the education of horses to confront the steam-tram?—I have no doubt that if steam is used largely on tramways that horses will be less frightened than they are at present; but there will be always a number of strange horses who will not be used to steam, and who will be frightened when they see it for the first time.

614. As in the case of artillery horses, it is simply a matter of education, is it not?—No doubt; but there are always fresh objects being brought under the notice of horses.

615. They may be educated in other places than on the public roads, where they would cause danger to others?—The fresh horses will be always frightened. Those that are habituated to the sight of the steam tram-cars will cease to notice them. But you will always have fresh horses cropping up.

Mr. *William Holms.*

616. May I ask you what engine is used in Paris?—The engines that have been hitherto used are those made by Merryweather.

Mr. *William Holms*—continued.

617. And at Rouen?—Merryweather, and Fox and Walker.

618. What engine is used at Liege?—At Liege they use the Varssen engine.

619. With reference to a combined engine and car at Edinburgh; how long had it been working there?—I think about a month; it had run about 2,000 miles.

620. In your experience, have you ever seen a combined engine and car working anywhere else than in Edinburgh?—I have only seen it experimentally at Birkenhead; that was the Grantham car.

621. In travelling in a combined engine and car, have you observed any difference in the amount of oscillation and vibration when compared with riding in a car drawn by a locomotive?—I think there is rather more oscillation in a combined engine and car than in a car drawn by a locomotive. But it is quite a new thing, and, no doubt, great improvements will be made in the construction.

622. So far as regards the length of the combined car and locomotive with the separate locomotive and car, is there not a considerable advantage in the former occupying less space, and therefore being pulled up more quickly?—Certainly, the combined engine and car is just the length of the ordinary car, whereas, the other is the length of the car plus that of the engine drawing it.

623. Has your attention been at all called to the difference in cost between using steam *versus* horse-power?—No; I cannot give the Committee much information on the subject beyond what I have stated.

Admiral *Egerton.*

624. Do you think the extensions that you mentioned in Paris and elsewhere, are likely to furnish this Committee with any very valuable data as regards tramways?—I am afraid they would hardly be in time for your purpose.

Mr. *William Holms.*

625. From your experience in connection with railways, can you give the Committee any idea what proportion of all the people killed in any given time upon railways are killed by the bursting of boilers?—No; the bursting of boilers is a very rare occurrence upon railways.

626. Exceedingly rare, is it not?—Yes; I do not remember the case of a passenger having been killed by the bursting of a boiler upon a railway for a very long time.

627. Do you know any case at all of a boiler bursting on a railway within the last three or four years?—Yes; as a rule they are about two per annum, or something like that. The number of boilers that have burst has very much diminished within the last 15 years. The construction of boilers has been much improved. I think the records of the Board of Trade give an average of two per annum.

628. Out of about how many locomotives?—I do not remember the number.

LORDS PRESENT:

Marquess of RIPON.

Earl of DERBY.

Earl of DEVON.

Earl COWPER.

Earl REDESDALE.

Viscount CARDWELL.

Lord COLVILLE OF CULROSS.

Lord HARTISMERE.

Lord CARLINGFORD.

Lord NORTON.

THE MARQUESS OF RIPON, IN THE CHAIR.

MR. HENRY GEORGE CALCRAFT, is called in ; and Examined.

1. *Chairman.*] You are, I believe, Assistant Secretary of the Railway Department of the Board of Trade?
I am.

2. That is the department which deals with tramways, is it not?
It is.

3. Will you be so good as to give the Committee a short statement of the recent course of proceedings with regard to tramways in that department, and in Parliament?
Your Lordships are no doubt aware that previous to 1870 there were several tramway Bills ; and at that time the Government thought it was necessary that some steps should be taken which would lead to those tramways being dealt with on certain fixed principles. Mr. Lefevre in 1870 for that purpose brought in a Bill for facilitating the making of tramways, which Bill was referred to a Select Committee of the House of Commons, and the result was, the Tramways Act of 1870, 33 & 34 Vict. c. 78. That Act was divided into three parts :—The first part provided for the facilitation of the making of tramways by means of Provisional Orders, and provided certain conditions with which the Promoters were to comply ; it did not take away from Promoters the power of proceeding by Bill rather than by Provisional Order, and the Board of Trade, and the authorities of both Houses of Parliament have endeavoured to make the Standing Orders and the practice of the Board of Trade as similar as possible. In fact, when the Houses of Parliament make a new Standing Order, the Board of Trade have incorporated that Standing Order with their rules. The second part of the Act relates to the construction of tramways ; and the third part of it to the working of tramways. These two parts of the Act are always incorporated in all Provisional Orders. After 1870 there were a great number of applications to the Board of Trade for Provisional Orders, and there were also a great number of Bills for the construction of tramways. Up to 1876 the power which was contained in the tramways Act of 1870 to authorise tramways to be worked by power other than animal power was never conferred upon any promoters, but in the year 1876 the Wantage Tramways Company, who had already obtained authority to make a tramway about two miles and a-half in length, from the town of Wantage, in Berkshire, to the Wantage-road station, succeeded in inducing the Board of Trade to make an additional Provisional Order conferring upon them the right to work their tramway by steam. The application for power to use steam was the first of its kind, and it was not granted until very careful consideration had

Mr.
H. G. Calcraft.

27th February
1879.

(15.)   A 2   been

been given to it by the Board of Trade; and in order to call the special attention of Parliament to the case, this particular Order was introduced into a special confirming Bill, and a special Report was made to Parliament upon the subject. In the same year Parliament, in the case of the Vale of Clyde Tramway, which was a tramway between Glasgow and Govan, authorised that company to work by steam. In both the Wantage Tramways Provisional Order and the Vale of Clyde Tramways Bill clauses were introduced providing that the tramways should not be worked by steam, except under regulations to be made by the Board of Trade; and very stringent regulations were drawn up requiring the companies under rather severe penalties to work the tramways in such a way as the Board of Trade might think necessary to secure the public safety. The bye-laws prescribed by the Board of Trade required that the steam engines used on the tramways should be fitted with various mechanical appliances, which the inspecting officers of the Board of Trade advised them were practicable and reasonable; and they also limited the rate of speed, and provided for the stoppage of the engines at certain places where they crossed roads. In the following Session, that is to say in 1877, in consequence of the decision of Parliament and the Board of Trade to allow the use of mechanical power on tramways, there were a great number of applications to Parliament and to the Board of Trade for authority to use steam upon tramways; some upon tramways which had already been laid, and some which were entirely new schemes; and the Government thought it such an important question, that a Committee of the House of Commons was appointed to consider how far, and under what regulations, the employment of steam, or other mechanical power, might be allowed upon tramways and public roads. That Committee took a great deal of evidence, and eventually made a Report, in which they stated that they thought that the use of mechanical power on tramways should be generally permitted, and that any Order or Bill granting the necessary power should contain clauses, imposing certain conditions specified in their Report. They also recommended that a short Bill should be introduced that Session to enable the Board of Trade to grant to certain tramway companies power to use steam as an experiment. A Bill for that purpose was introduced into the House of Commons, but was subsequently withdrawn. It was subsequently introduced into your Lordships' House, and was again withdrawn; and the result was that in that Session no tramways were authorised to use steam. That brings the case up to the end of 1877. In 1878, after communication with the authorities of the Houses of Parliament, some clauses were drawn, which it was proposed to insert in all Tramway Bills and Provisional Orders. Subsequently, however, it was considered desirable that another Committee should be appointed, and a hybrid Committee was appointed in the House of Commons to consider the whole question of the use of steam upon tramways, and all the Bills of that Session, with regard to tramways, and also all the Provisional Orders, were referred to that Committee. That Committee, after considering the subject generally, and also going into the particular circumstances of each individual scheme, drew up some clauses, which they inserted in all the Bills and Orders; and they also made a Report, stating the principles on which they thought tramway legislation should be conducted in future. The result was, that those clauses were inserted in all the Bills and Orders, and they came down to the House of Commons, where there was a debate and a division, and they were carried by a large majority. They subsequently came up to your Lordships' House, where there was a debate; and eventually it was agreed that all the steam-power clauses should be cut out in the schemes of that Session (with the exception of one, which I will mention afterwards), and that a Committee should be appointed early this Session. The one exception to which I refer was the case of a tramway which was made in connection with the Vale of Clyde Tramway; I think it is called the Glasgow and Ibrox. That was allowed to go on, because it was not proposed to work it by steam, but by a system called the Scott-Moncrieff system of compressed air. It was hoped that that tramway would have been speedily finished, and that by this time there would have been some experience gained from its working. However, owing to the severe frost and other circumstances in the neighbourhood of Glasgow, the tramway has never been completed, and the result is, that there is at the present moment no further experience than there was at the end of last Session.

4. Of

4. Of the Scott-Moncrieff system?

Yes, neither the Scott-Moncrieff system, nor that of steam. With regard to the present moment, this Session there have been a great number of applications for tramways, both by Bill and by Provisional Order; in fact, there are 33 Bills before Parliament this Session relating to tramways, proposing the construction of 209 miles of new tramway, and the raising of a capital of 2,752,000 *l.*

5. Lord *Norton.*] With steam clauses?

Some of them. And by Provisional Orders there are also 32 applications to the Board of Trade, involving 147 miles of new tramway, with an estimated capital of 901,000 *l.* I am not enabled to give your Lordships the number of applications for power to use steam by Bills, but by Provisional Order there are 19 cases of steam out of the 32. In dealing with those Provisional Orders the Board of Trade have acted as was arranged in the debate in the House of Lords, that is to say, they have considered each scheme upon its merits, and have in such schemes, as they think it desirable, authorised the use of steam; but the promoters have been informed that those powers have only been given them subject to any decision which your Lordships' Committee may come to, or at which the Government may arrive after your Lordships have reported. As I said before, there are 32 applications for Provisional Orders to the Board of Trade, 19 of which are for steam; and as far as the Board of Trade has at present decided, out of those 19 schemes they propose only to allow steam upon four. The course which they have adopted is in every case to send down one of their inspecting officers to inspect the locality, and to look at the place generally, as to whether it is suitable for steam. This they have done in cases even where the local authorities have themselves applied for powers to construct the tramway, and to use steam; and in consequence of the unfavourable report of their inspecting officers, in many cases the Board of Trade have declined to entertain the application, so far as regards steam; in some cases in consequence of the narrowness of the streets, and in some cases because of the steep hills that the cars would have to go up, or from the very sharp corners they would have to turn. But upon these details Major General Hutchinson, who will be before your Lordships presently, will be able to give you more detailed information, as he has visited all the spots himself.

6. Lord *Carlingford*] Are any of those cases in country districts?

Some of them; in one case, at Burnley, the proposed tramway is seven miles in length between country towns

7. Earl of *Redesdale.*] Are any of these tramways in competition with railways?

That I do not know. Railway companies have not opposed in any way except with regard to clauses to preserve their rights as to bridges, and so forth; they have not opposed on the ground of competition.

8. What has been the ground on which permission to use steam-power has been refused in the number of cases in which you say it has been refused?

Principally on the ground of the streets being too narrow.

9. Do you consider, from the statements that have been made to you, that the inhabitants of the streets through which the tramways are laid generally consider them advantageous, or nuisances?

I do not think we have more opposition from the people who inhabit the houses where steam is proposed to be used on tramways than where there are ordinary tramways.

10. I mean with regard to tramways generally?

I think, certainly, in some places they are very much disliked. For instance, at Portsmouth, or rather Southsea, the opposition is very great; but, again, in the North of England the opposition is very small.

11. Are the oppositions chiefly in places where the streets are very narrow? Certainly.

12. Do you think that in some cases tramways have been allowed where there was not a proper width of street to admit of such a thing?

(15.)　　　　A 3　　　　Yes;

Yes; I think that it is possible that in some cases tramways have been authorised where they would not be authorised now.

13. What width of street do you consider necessary for a tramway?
Where steam is proposed, the Board of Trade consider necessary that there should be nine feet six inches from the outside of the rail to the pathway.

14. On each side?
On each side.

15. Lord *Colville of Culross*.] Do I correctly understand that at the present moment there are only two tramways in the United Kingdom worked by steam?
That is all; the Wantage Tramway and the Vale of Clyde Tramway.

16. Lord *Norton*.] Are there none worked by steam without the authority of Parliament?
That I cannot give a decided opinion upon; I have heard of such a case.

17. Is there not the case of Leicester?
They did work by steam at Leicester, but I do not know whether it is going on or not; they certainly tried experiments at Leicester, and I believe in some parts of Ireland, and in Scotland; but as to whether they continue to work, I have no information.

18. *Chairman*.] Practically then there is no change in the situation since last year?
None whatever.

19. There is no farther experience so far as you know?
None whatever.

20. Lord *Carlingford*.] That is to say in this country?
In this country.

21. Lord *Norton*.] In the cases where opposition has arisen, as at Portsmouth, did the tramway originate with the local authority?
At Portsmouth the tramway was originally promoted by the General Tramways Company of Portsmouth.

22. Without the consent of the local authority?
No; if the local authority do not consent, the Board of Trade have no power to grant a Provisional Order.

23. Then the opposition made to the tramways must have been contrary to the view of the local authority?
Yes; the local authority consented.

24. Earl of *Derby*.] Have you any means of saying from what class of persons the opposition to tramways has mostly proceeded; has it been mostly from those who use their own carriages, or from persons in other classes?
I should say that, to a certain extent, it has proceeded from those who use their own carriages, but to a very much greater extent from the owners of cabs and omnibuses.

25. That is to say, it is a matter of trade competition?
Exactly.

26. The objections being, that the tramway gives greater conveniences at a cheaper rate than the cab or the omnibus?
Yes; in fact it drives the omnibus off the road.

27. *Chairman*.] The Committee of last year made certain recommendations and suggestions with regard to bye-laws to be made by the Board of Trade, and also with regard to general regulations and restrictions; do you concur in those suggestions of the Committee of last year, or would you recommend any modifications of them?
I have brought down one Provisional Order that we have already settled, which contains the recommendations of the Committee of last Session (*handing in*

in the same). It is for the Stoke-upon-Trent, Fenton, Longton, and District Tramways.

Mr.
H. G. Calcraft.

27th February
1879.

28. Is this a Provisional Order of the present year?
Yes.

29. The principle, I think, upon which the Committee of last year went was, that certain matters should be settled between the local authority and the promoters of the tramway, subject to an appeal to the Board of Trade; and that other matters should be settled by bye-laws of general application, to be made by the Board of Trade?
Yes.

30. Do you consider that the division so proposed is the best that could be suggested?
I think so; on the whole it slightly alters the provisions of the Tramways Act of 1870, because some of the matters which the Committee of last Session proposed, should be settled by the Board of Trade, are matters which, in ordinary tramways, are left to the discretion of the local authorities. It is taking a little of the power out of the hands of the local authority, and placing it in the hands of the Board of Trade.

31. Will you mention to the Committee the points in which that is done?
They are "for regulating the speed at which engines and carriages may be driven or propelled along the tramways; for limiting the speed at which engines and carriages may be driven; for regulating the use of the bell, whistle, or other warning apparatus fixed to the engine; for regulating the emission of smoke or steam from engines; for providing that engines and carriages shall be brought to a stand at the intersection of cross streets, and at such places as the Board of Trade may deem proper for securing safety; for regulating the use of the bell or other warning apparatus fixed to the engine for regulating the entrance to and exit from, and accommodation in, the carriages and on the tramways, and for the protection of passengers from the machinery; and for providing for the due publicity of all bye-laws in force for the time being in relation to the tramways." Those points with regard to horse tramways are matters which would be ordinarily settled by the local authority. The wording is a little different from the recommendation of the Committee of last year.

32. Those, I understand, are points which, under the Act would have been left to the local authority; but which it was proposed last year by the Committee, and which you propose in this Provisional Order, to leave to the decision of the Board of Trade?
Exactly.

33. Lord *Carlingford*.] Has the Board of Trade power under these Orders to put a stop to the use of steam altogether, if they think necessary?
Yes. At the bottom of page 4 of the Provisional Order I have put in, you will see that the Board of Trade "may by Order direct the promoters, or such persons, to cease to exercise the powers aforesaid, and thereupon the promoters, or such persons, shall cease to exercise the powers aforesaid, and shall not again exercise the same, or any of the same, unless with the authority of the Board of Trade."

34. *Chairman*.] Is that in the entire discretion of the Board of Trade?
In the entire discretion of the Board of Trade.

35. Lord *Carlingford*.] Has much local objection been raised to the proposed use of steam upon these tramways?
No, I think not. It is in such a tentative condition that a great number of people are hanging back until they know what kind of regulations or restrictions will be imposed by Parliament; but I do not think in any case we have any, or, certainly, not many objections, simply on the ground of steam.

36. There is not much local alarm about the use of steam?
I think not. It has only been allowed in two cases; and there has not been as yet much practical experience of steam.

37. I mean in these new cases?
No, they do not object on the ground of steam. Some of the people whose

(15.)   A 4   houses

houses are passed by very often object until arrangements are made to give a little more space in front of their houses.

38. *Chairman.*] Would your inspector have heard of any objections on the part of the inhabitants generally, on the ground of danger, when he made those inquiries?
I should think so. He walked over all the streets where it was proposed to lay tramways.

39. You have no very strict rules as to *locus standi*, or anything of that sort, I suppose, in those inquiries?
No; at our public inquiries we hear everybody.

40. Lord *Norton.*] Must not there have been ample opportunity for objections being made before the applications came to you at all?
Yes; notices are required by the Standing Orders, as for Bills in Parliament.

41. And notices are given locally, are they not?
Yes, they are posted up locally, and are given in the local newspapers, and it is necessary to serve a notice upon all frontagers.

42. So that everybody has had an opportunity of making an objection?
Yes.

43. Have many objections been made in those three cases which you have passed?
No. One is a very large case; it is the town of Liverpool, where steam power is to be used. We do not propose to grant it exactly as it was applied for, as Major General Hutchinson, who went down there, will explain to you. He thought some portions of the streets were not fitted for steam power, and that portion of the scheme is proposed to be cut out, unless the road is widened.

44. Earl *Redesdale.*] Have you framed any bye-laws which you intend to propose in addition to those regulations to which you have already referred?
Yes; if your Lordship will look at page 10 of this Provisional Order, in Schedule A., you will see the bye-laws.

45. Lord *Carlingford.*] Is the case of Burnley, which you mentioned just now, a case of a really rural tramway; a tramway running along a rural road?
I should imagine that it was. There are two actually rural tramways with which I am acquainted; one is the Wantage Tramway, which is entirely rural, running along the side of the road for about two miles and a half from the town of Wantage, and there are no houses at all there; and again, there is a tramway that runs from the camp to the station at Aldershot, which is completely rural; it passes one house, I believe a public-house, on the way.

46. The Wantage Tramway, I suppose, was made upon the green strip of waste along the roadside?
I believe it was.

47. *Chairman.*] I observe that in this Schedule A. there is no requirement of what I see in the previous Committee was called a "Recorder"?
No; both Committees of the House of Commons thought that the regulations of the Board of Trade were rather stringent, and relaxed them; they thought that we required too much, and that was one of the things which was cut out by the second Committee, Mr. Peel's Committee.

48. With respect to the first article of the Schedule, is that intended to provide a self-acting means of preventing the engine from going beyond a certain speed?
It is.

49. Lord *Norton.*] What is the meaning of the clause in this Provisional Order for Stoke-upon-Trent, which says that no carriages or trucks adapted for use on railways shall be used on the tramways?
That Clause 23 is cut out.

50. I suppose it was to prevent trains from being run on the tramways?
Exactly.

51. Earl

51. Earl of *Redesdale.*] But such a clause would be unnecessary in this Order, because I see that the gauge of the tramway is to be four feet?
It is.

52. Therefore railway carriages could not come upon the tramway?
They could not.

53. Lord *Norton.*] Is it the view of the Board of Trade that there should not be trains of more than one carriage upon tramways?
That is a question that has not been settled yet. On the Wantage Tramway they run, I believe, two or three carriages. In the evidence that was given last year, I think that, in regard to Edinburgh, it was stated that it did not interfere so much with the traffic to have one short train, or two or three carriages, as to have the constant running of an engine and one carriage.

54. Earl *Cowper.*] In the case of all these Bills and Provisional Orders, has the consent of the local authority been obtained?
Yes.

55. Have you any power, in case the local authority should object, to make a Provisional Order in spite of them?
Yes, in the case of tramways running through the districts of several local authorities, if two-thirds of the length of the tramway is agreed to, the Board of Trade have the power of dispensing with the consent of the remaining one-third, but they have to make a special report to Parliament, stating their reasons.

56. Earl of *Redesdale.*] I see that you insist upon an indicator, but not upon the recorder?
That is so.

57. Why do you object to the recorder?
These requirements were founded upon the recommendations of the Committee of the House of Commons last year, and the recorder was cut out by them.

58. Lord *Hartismere.*] Are there any tramways of the same gauge as railways?
Yes, 4 feet 8½ inches is the usual gauge.

59. But the gauges of the tramways vary very much, do they not?
Not very much. The usual gauge is 4 feet 8½ inches; in this special case it is four feet, but as a rule it is the same as the railway gauge.

60. *Chairman.*] The Board of Trade do not feel bound to require that tramways shall be of the same gauge as railways?
No; we should put in the 4 feet 8½ inch gauge, unless there were special reasons why it should be less; of course, if the streets are very narrow, a narrower gauge does not take up so much of the road.

61. Earl of *Derby.*] Is there any special advantage in that identity of gauge; I presume tram cars would not be employed to run upon railways, or railway carriages upon tramways?
No, not as a general rule; of course in a case like Southampton, where you go from the station down to the pier, the railway train and the carriages run over the tramway on to the pier.

62. Earl of *Redesdale.*] Is the Wantage gauge a 4 feet 8½-inch gauge?
Yes.

63. I suppose, in that case, coal, and so forth, is brought in the railway trucks from the railway to Wantage?
I should imagine so, but I cannot say.

64. *Chairman.*] You spoke just now of notices given to frontagers; what is your definition of frontager for the purpose of notice?
I think we take an objection from every house on either side of the street that has less than the statutory space of 9 feet 6 inches for a distance of 30 yards.

65. But in the case of a tramway in the country you would not give notice to the landowners adjoining the road, would you?
No.

66. Earl of *Redesdale*.] Why not?

Because it is not required by the Standing Orders.

67. *Chairman*.] Are there any other observations or suggestions that you would wish to make to the Committee?

No, I think not. I do not know whether it is desirable to point out that the law in Ireland is a little different from the law in England. Both Ireland and Scotland obtained Acts facilitating the construction of tramways about the year 1860, before there was any such Act in England. The Scotch Act has never been made use of, but the Irish Act of 1860 gives power to make tramways, after approval by the grand jury, or the principal authority, and by the Lord Lieutenant, and the Order which the Lord Lieutenant makes upon the subject has to be confirmed by Parliament. There is also another case in which the Lord Lieutenant can make an Order by himself, so that practically it is in the hands of the Lord Lieutenant of Ireland to grant the use of steam upon tramways without coming to Parliament.

68. Is Scotland now under the same law as England?

Yes.

69. Lord *Colville of Culross*.] In granting Provisional Orders or Bills for tramways in streets, is it compulsory that the tramway should be in the centre of the street, or is it permitted to pass along the sides?

It is not compulsory that it should be in the exact centre.

70. Are they permitted to run alongside the footpath?

No; where steam is proposed there must be 9 feet 6 inches between the rail and the kerb.

71. So that they cannot block up the approach to a shop for a carriage?

No, they are not always in the exact centre of the street, but they must be 9 feet 6 inches from the kerb.

72. Earl of *Redesdale*.] And you would insist upon the same in a rural tramway?

I should not say that, because in this case of Wantage it was not done.

73. Do you not consider it a great injustice to the owners of the property in front of which the tramway is carried, that such a requirement should not be insisted upon?

It might be desirable to do so, but I think the practice of Parliament has been not to insist upon that.

74. Do you not think that in justice to the owners of property it ought to be insisted upon?

I see no reason why a landowner should not have the same notices as frontagers.

75. But do you not think that the law ought to be as imperative in the one case as in the other, so as to enable a man to protect his property from such an invasion?

I see no objection whatever to that.

76. Lord *Norton*.] Do you think it would be advisable that Parliament should pass an Act enabling the Board of Trade to license experiments, as has been attempted in the years 1877 and 1878, or do you think that it would be better to proceed at once to lay down definite rules with regard to steam traffic on tramways?

I think that is almost a question for the Committee to decide. It is one upon which the Government would scarcely wish to express an opinion.

77. Is it a decided point whether the Locomotive Acts apply to tramways?

No; in the case of the Wantage Order, it was necessary to repeal a part of those Locomotive Acts, because all the regulations connected with the Locomotive Acts would have made a steam tramway impossible (one of them was that a man should walk in front with a red flag); those parts of the Acts were repealed.

78. *Chairman*.]

78. *Chairman.*] And they would have to be repealed in any similar case, I presume?

In any similar case.

79. Earl of *Redesdale.*] Do you think the tramways pay sufficiently for the advantages granted to them of having the land upon which the tramway is to be laid given to them for nothing?

No, I think it would be only fair, that if they get this right to occupy so much of the road with steam cars they should be called upon to contribute in some way to the local funds; and also it is a question whether they should not be called upon to contribute more to the imperial taxation. In fact that was felt so much, that Clause 35 of this Order was specially put in; it says, "Notwithstanding anything in this Order contained, the promoters or any persons using the tramways shall be subject and liable to the provisions of any general Act now in force or which may hereafter be passed during this or any future Session of Parliament relating to tramways, or by which any tax or duty may be granted or imposed for or in respect of tramways or the passengers or traffic conveyed thereon, and to any condition, regulation, or restriction which may be imposed upon the use of tramways or upon the use on tramways of animal power, steam power, or any mechanical power." That was put in specially to show that the Government thought that it would be a very fair subject to consider what additional taxation should be imposed upon tramway companies if they got the privilege of using steam.

80. *Chairman.*] The Committee of last year recommended that contracts relating to the maintenance and repairs of streets and roads, contribution to local rates, &c. between the promoters of tramways and the local authority, should be subject to an appeal to the Board of Trade; do you think that that is a desirable arrangement?

I think, on the whole, it is the best that could be adopted.

81. Have you had any cases of that kind to decide?

No; these clauses have never become law. Under the General Tramways Act, the Board of Trade have power, in the case of any difference arising between a tramway company and the local authority, to appoint a referee, and we have had some few cases of that kind.

82. Lord *Norton.*] Does any confusion arise in consequence of some of these cases proceeding by Provisional Orders and some by Bills?

I think not. The Board of Trade endeavour, as much as they possibly can, to conform their practice to the practice of Parliament; and, I think, with some success.

83. Viscount *Cardwell.*] The Provisional Order requires Parliamentary sanction, does it not?

Yes, it requires to be placed in a Confirming Bill.

84. Lord *Norton.*] It is only by continually consulting the Parliamentary authorities that you keep the Board of Trade action running parallel with that of Parliament?

Yes.

85. Unless there was constant consultation, you might go on different principles?

Yes; of course there is a revision by Parliament.

86. But, practically, that is not very rigid, is it?

The Board of Trade always consult with the Parliamentary authorities in the event of their proposing to make any change in the principle of dealing with Bills.

87. Lord *Hartismere.*] With regard to the nine feet six between the trottoir and the rail, you always follow out that rule, with very few exceptions, I believe?

Yes, as regards steam.

88. In point of fact I may say that you always do so, except in a case like Wantage, a very exceptional case, or where, perhaps, in a broad road at some particular point the road may narrow for a short distance?

Exactly.

(15.)   B 2   89. *Chairman.*]

89. *Chairman.*] If you were not to make some deviation from the rule last alluded to, a sudden contraction of the road or street might make many miles of tramway impossible, might it not?

Yes, exactly. There were some clauses drawn making a hard-and-fast rule that no tramway should be laid down for the use of steam, except in a street, say, 35 feet wide; but in going over the schemes of that Session it was found that those clauses would practically prevent steam being used upon any tramways at all, because at some one spot there was a less width than 35 feet.

90. Earl of *Redesdale.*] Do you not think that it would be reasonable that the tramway company should, in such cases, be called upon to widen the street?

Generally speaking, I think it would; but any hard-and-fast rule like that would make it very difficult to work the system.

91. Do you not think that it would be impossible to obtain the widening of the street unless you had the hard-and-fast rule?

I think not; for instance, there is a scheme this Session before the Board of Trade for tramways in the town of Derby, which the local authority, although not promoting, are very anxious to obtain. One of those streets is too narrow, and we have declined to sanction the tramway being made until the street is widened. There is no difficulty in doing that.

92. Then you do not allow the tramways?
Not until the street is widened.

93. That is to say, the street must be widened; is not the proper party to widen the street the tramway company?
It may be so. In this case the local authority are doing it for public improvements.

94. Lord *Hartismere.*] Would not a hard-and-fast rule with regard to widening the road be very inconvenient in a purely rural district?
Yes, I think it would.

95. Earl of *Redesdale.*] In a rural district the widening of a road would be a much cheaper operation than it would be in a town, would it not?
No doubt it would be an easier thing in a rural district to obtain the land.

96. Viscount *Cardwell.*] But the traffic is much smaller, and therefore the inducement to do it is less?
Yes.

97. Lord *Carlingford.*] The Board of Trade does not, I suppose, agree with some of the witnesses before Parliamentary Committees, who say that, in their opinion, steam is safer in a narrow street than horses?
The matter is in a very tentative condition.

98. The Board of Trade has not ventured to go so far as that?
Not quite so far as that.

99. *Earl Cowper.*] Do you know any cases in which tramways pass over bridges?
A great number.

100. Is there any rule about the width of a bridge?
There would be the same kind of rule with regard to a bridge as there is now with regard to a street, but you cannot always get the width, because bridges are very often made narrow. Your Lordships may be aware of the bridge at Oxford; there is at this moment a proposal for tramways for Oxford; Magdalen Bridge there is decidedly narrow. The Board of Trade propose that there shall be a single line instead of a double line, but all the local authorities and engineers there have pressed upon the Board of Trade that much greater inconvenience and danger would arise from a single line of tramway there than from a double line.

101. In most cases of bridges you have to relax the rule?
Yes, to some extent.

102. Have

102. Have you any complaint of bridges being injured by the weight of the tramway car?

None; and there are always clauses protecting those who have to keep the bridges in repair. The tramway companies have to pay towards keeping the bridges in repair.

103. Lord *Colville of Culross.*] There is a Government inspection before you open a tramway, as in the case of a railway, is there not?

Yes, before you open it, but not afterwards.

104. I suppose the Committee may infer that you concur with Mr. Farrer in his evidence given at page 4 of the Evidence of last Session, that steam tramways and railways should be put upon the same footing as regards Imperial taxation?

Yes; I see no reason whatever why a tramway which has the privilege of using steam should not be put on the same footing, with regard to taxation, as railways.

105. *Chairman.*] Is it your opinion that steam tramways are likely to be extensively used in this country in the future?

Judging by the very considerable number of applications that have been made to Parliament since these two schemes were allowed, I think steam is likely to be very largely used on tramways.

106. Earl of *Devon.*] You spoke of the difference between the law as regards this subject in Ireland and England; are you aware whether many tramways have been constructed under the Lord Lieutenant's authority in Ireland?

No; I cannot say for certain that there have been; there is a Return on the subject which has been presented to your Lordships' House.

107. Are you aware whether the Lord Lieutenant, in giving any sanction to tramways, introduces the same, or similar, restrictions and provisions to those which you impose?

I am not aware whether that has been so in times past; recently the Irish Government have been in communication with the Board of Trade as to the regulations which they impose with a view of imposing similar ones; the Warrenpoint and Rostrevor Tramway, as your Lordship will see, is granted by the Lord Lieutenant, and that appears to be the only one.

108. Lord *Carlingford.*] Is steam to be used upon that tramway?
No.

109. *Chairman.*] To what extent have the local authorities a power, practically, of veto upon the establishment of tramways?

No tramway can be granted unless the local authority in whose district it is proposed to run gives its consent; they have an absolute power.

110. I think there is a provision in the case of a tramway passing through the districts of various local authorities, is there not?

Yes; where two-thirds of the tramways are agreed to, the tramway may be granted.

111. Viscount *Cardwell.*] Do you mean two-thirds in number, or in the distance passed over?

In the distance passed over.

112. *Chairman.*] Of course in a district in which there is no highway authority, the local authority is the parish or township?

It is.

113. And therefore a very few miles of tramway might pass through the districts of a very great number of local authorities?

Yes; and that is frequently the case.

114. But in that case the consent of two-thirds, in distance, would enable you to disregard the dissent of the other third?

It would.

115. Earl *Cowper.*] Have you ever had to exercise that power?

Yes; I should think on an average once or twice each Session, and we always then make a report to Parliament, giving the reasons.

116. *Chairman*.] Do you think it desirable that the local authority, subject to that proviso, should have an absolute power of veto?

The whole principle of the Tramways Acts is to give the power to the local authority, and I think, on the whole, it is the only authority that you could have, unless it was placed entirely in the hands of the Government, which would not be desirable.

117. Lord *Norton*.] Would you state, generally, in cases in which you have over-ruled the opposition of the one-third, what has been the nature of their opposition?

Either there have been some competing schemes, or they thought they would have a scheme that was more suited to them in future Sessions of Parliament, or they were indifferent, or simply refused to consent.

118. Has the opposition ever been to the thing as a dangerous thing?

No, I think not; I never heard of opposition on that ground. I may, perhaps, mention that with regard to the local authorities, they have, by the Tramways Act, very stringent power to compel the tramway company to keep the tramways in proper repair. I am not, however, quite sure that that is a duty which has always been quite satisfactorily performed. Even in London, recently, there have been complaints, both from the north and from the south of London, as to the very bad condition of the tramways, and although the local authorities who, in that instance, are the vestries (because the roads in London are not under the control of the Metropolitan Board), have those very large and powerful means of compelling tramway companies to repair the roads, they have never exercised them. At the present moment, in Camberwell, the tramway is in a very bad condition indeed. Whether it would be possible to suggest any other means of compelling the tramway companies to keep their road in order, is a matter I think worthy of consideration.

119. *Chairman*.] That observation applies particularly to the peculiar arrangements of the metropolis, does it not?

I think it applies throughout the country; not in very large places where there are well organised municipal bodies like Liverpool and Manchester, and similar places, where the tramways are kept in very good order; but when you come to small towns with small local authorities, the tramways certainly are not kept in such good repair as they might be.

120. Do I correctly gather from your evidence generally that you think the whole system of steam tramways is in its infancy, and that on the whole it is desirable that any regulations laid down should possess a considerable amount of elasticity?

I think so.

MAJOR GENERAL CHARLES SCROPE HUTCHINSON, R.E., called in; and Examined.

121. *Chairman*.] You are an Inspector of Railways under the Board of Trade?

Yes.

122. And you have had the special duty of inspecting proposed tramways, have you not?

Proposed and constructed tramways.

123. Have you inspected the tramways which are proposed for construction for which Provisional Orders or Bills are now before Parliament?

Not Bills, Provisional Orders. I have examined a great many of the routes along which tramways are proposed, but not the whole of those which are before the Board of Trade. There are three or four on which it is proposed to use steam, which have not yet been inspected; there has not been time to do it.

124. I believe it was on your report that the permission to use steam-power on a considerable number of tramways applying for it was refused?

Yes, it was, I believe.

125. Would you give the Committee a general account of the reasons which induced you to report unfavourably upon most of those cases?

Mr.
H. G. Galcraft
and
Major General
C. S. Hutchinson,
R.E.

27th February
1879.

In most of the cases it was in consequence of the narrow character of many of the streets along which the routes of the tramways were proposed to run. One bad case was Chatham and Rochester, where the streets are 13 feet and 14 feet wide. In other cases the widths were greater; but I took this rule as a general guide, that whenever there would be less than 9 feet 6 inches intervening for any considerable distance between the tram-rail and the edge of the kerb, I thought in no case ought the use of steam to be allowed. Another circumstance that guided me was the crowded nature of the traffic in some wide and important streets, where there was no question of the width being insufficient. Newcastle, for instance, was one of those. It was proposed to have the use of steam sanctioned through some of the important crowded thoroughfares of Newcastle, which it seemed to me was a very objectionable proposition, and I reported in that case that I thought the use of steam should not be allowed in the heart of Newcastle.

126. Was there any local opposition in that case?

No, there was no local opposition in that case. It was a corporation tramway in Newcastle.

127. Lord *Carlingford.*] Do you mean that in those cases you did not report against the tramway itself?

No, only against the use of steam power; I was not called upon to report upon the tramway itself. Then there were other cases where there were very sharp turns, perhaps, occurring in tramways running through tortuous streets where the turns seemed objectionable and dangerous.

128. *Chairman.*] That was mainly a case of danger to the persons using the tramway, rather than to the public using the street, was it not?

Both, I think; there was the danger of running into cross traffic. The foregoing were the reasons which mainly guided me in reporting, as I did, to the Board of Trade.

129. And the result of that was, that out of 19 cases, in only three has the use of steam been allowed?

I think that out of the 19 there are four or five which have not yet been visited, so that out of the remaining 14 you may take it that the use of steam has been allowed upon only three.

130. Still, as a matter of fact, in the majority of instances, you reported against the use of steam upon the grounds that you have stated?
I did.

131. There has been, I believe, no further experience of the use of steam in this country since last year?

Not that I am aware of in this country. I believe that in Nantes, in France, compressed air has been in use for some time for moving tram cars, but I have not any personal experience of the matter.

132. You have not visited Nantes?
I have not.

133. Is it upon the Scott-Moncrieff principle?
It is, no doubt, upon the same principle, but it is not his system; it is compressed air, but probably manipulated in some rather different way?

134. You visited Paris last year, I think?
I did, while the Committee was sitting last year.

135. Do you know whether the use of steam is still going on in Paris or not?

I have not any information since I was there; I have not been there since last year.

(15)   B 4   136. Then

Mr.
H. G. Calcraft
and
Major General
C. S. Hutchinson,
R.E.

27th February
1879.

136. Then you have no more recent information or practical experience in the matter than you had when you gave your evidence last year?

I have not, with reference to steam.

137. Earl of *Derby*.] We understand that there are two cases in which steam has been allowed to be used upon tramways; can you describe what precautions have been taken in those cases to prevent alarm to horses, or danger to passengers?

The ringing of a bell to warn approaching vehicles has been one means of guarding against danger; the enclosing of the apparatus to a certain extent, so that fire shall not be visible to approaching horses; precluding as far as possible the emission of steam from the funnel of the engine; and also the adoption of a governor to regulate the speed if the driver becomes reckless, and a speed register to show the driver the rate at which he is running; those are the means that have been used in the Vale of Clyde. At Wantage, there have been no precautions except the use of a bell or whistle, and the enclosing of the apparatus, so that it shall not be seen.

138. That I presume is a much more thinly populated district?

Yes, it is a mere country road, along one side of which the steam cars run.

139. *Chairman*.] Is there any limitation of the maximum speed?

At Wantage, as far as I remember, it is eight miles an hour, and I think the same on the Vale of Clyde.

140. Is anything done to prevent alarm being caused by noise from the engine?

The engine is ordered to be made as noiseless as possible. One of the bye-laws is that there shall be no clatter of machinery, and, practically speaking, there is no great amount of noise, though it is not practically silent, but there is no very objectionable amount of noise; in fact, for my own part, I think a little noise is desirable. Too noiseless an engine would be rather a source of danger.

141. Earl of *Devon*.] In the case of accident, is there any provision or regulation requiring that a report shall be sent to the Board of Trade by the tramway company owning the line?

I think not; I am not aware that there is.

142. Lord *Carlingford*.] Are the engines on the Wantage Tramway satisfactory from the point of view of safety; do they come up to the requirements which the Board of Trade now think necessary for the purpose of preventing alarm to horses?

Yes, I think they are sufficient in that respect. They were some of the first tramway engines constructed, and no doubt future ones will be made more perfect; but there were no particular objections in that respect.

143. Have you any means of knowing how the Wantage Tramway goes on, and whether there is much complaint from the people who use that road?

No; I have not been to Wantage for some length of time, and I have not heard any particulars recently.

144. In the course of those inquiries that you have made lately, did you find that the people using the road were afraid of the use of steam?

I had no means of ascertaining that; I simply examined the roads without having any intercourse with the inhabitants.

145. You had no means of knowing what the neighbours thought of it?
No, none.

146. *Chairman*.] Was any public notice given of your visit?
No, no notice. I made private visits in all cases.

147. Viscount *Cardwell*.] There is very little experience in this country of the use of mechanical power on tramways, is there?
Very little.

148. But

Mr.
H. G. Calcraft
and
Major General
C. S. Hutchinson,
R.E.

27th February
1879.

148. But there is a good deal if you take all the foreign countries put together, is there not?
There is.

149. What would you say is the result of that foreign experience?
I am not in a position to state that; I do not know what the experience of last year may have brought with it.

150. Can you suggest any person by whose experience we might be guided in this matter?
I do not suppose there is anybody who could collate or bring together the experience of foreign countries with regard to the matter.

151. But that is one of the most important elements in the matter, is it not?
No doubt.

152. (To Mr. *Calcraft.*) There is a very great deal of experience in America upon the subject, is there not?
Yes. That I think you can obtain from Mr. Small, whom your Lordships are, I understand, going to summon. But with regard to Paris and Germany, if your Lordships thought it desirable, General Hutchinson could go and visit the tramways there and report to your Lordships.

153. Lord *Norton* (to Major General *Hutchinson*).] Has steam been used anywhere?
There have been several experiments, but I do not know to what extent they have gone.

154. Lord *Hartismere.*] I remember being on a joint Committee of the House of Lords and House of Commons some six or seven years ago on this subject, when it was proposed to put tramways worked by animal power in the narrow streets of London, and there it was said that these tramway-cars could be pulled up more quickly than ordinary vehicles; in regard to steam on the Wantage Tramway, how soon can a tramway-car be pulled up?
I do not think you can say in less than twice its own length, but, of course, it depends upon the gradient.

155. What is the length of a tramcar?
You can pull it up in from 20 to 30 yards. A good deal depends upon the state of the rails.

156. *Chairman.*] A good many of the witnesses said that the cars could be pulled up within their own length?
It may be done under favourable circumstances, but I do not think it could be done, taking it as an average.

157. Earl of *Devon.*] At what pace do you take the car to be travelling?
Eight miles an hour.

158. Earl *Cowper.*] Is there such a thing as a speed register that can be thoroughly depended upon to tell you the exact rate at which the tramcar was running at any particular moment?
To a very fair extent.

159. I think, in your former evidence you said that you were rather doubtful about how far it could be trusted?
I have not seen any further experiments, but from what I have seen of the register used on the Vale of Clyde, it seemed to be giving a very fair indication of the speed at which the tramcar was running.

160. *Chairman.*] It appeared from the previous evidence that there was likely to be more difficulty in getting what is called a speed indicator than in getting a speed recorder; but I observe that in Schedule A. of the Order which Mr. Calcraft has put in, a speed indicator is required and not a speed recorder; what is the reason of that?
It was, I think, taken from the recommendations of the Committee of last Session. (Mr. *Calcraft.*) It was; they cut that out.

161. (To Major General *Hutchinson.*) The object of the speed recorder is in fact to afford security to the public, is it not?

(15.)   C   Yes,

Mr.
H. G. Calcraft
and
Major General
C. S. Hutchinson,
R.E.
_____
27th February
1879.

Yes, it is more for police purposes, so that in case of disputes arising and accidents occurring, some idea may be obtained of the speed at which the car was then running.

162. If you have self-acting machinery for the purpose of preventing the engine from going beyond the prescribed speed, is there very much use in having an indicator which tells the driver at what speed he is going?

It is a help to him in driving. For instance, there is a regulation that drivers should not approach moveable facing-points at a speed of more than four miles an hour. Then there would probably be police regulations laid down with regard to the speed at the crossings of streets. There again it would be useful to the driver to know at what speed he was running.

163. But still you would mainly rely upon your self-acting machinery?

Yes, but you would always place the action of a governor at a rate above that speed at which the engines would ordinarily be permitted to run, so that for emergencies there might be a little extra power of quick movement; the indicator would tell the driver when he was exceeding the regulated speed at which he was permitted to run by the bye-laws.

164. Your regulated speed being eight miles an hour, what margin would you give?

I should think 12 miles an hour would probably be the speed at which the governor would come into play.

165. Earl *Cowper*.] I suppose from your experience of railways you would say that a man very soon gets to be a good judge of the speed at which he is going?

No; my experience is that very few people are so ignorant of speed as drivers.

166. *Chairman*.] As you go along a railway you see directions, "Speed not to exceed ten miles an hour," or something of that sort; do you believe that those directions are not carried out?

They are generally framed so that the drivers should not go more than double the rate indicated on the boards.

167. Earl *Cowper*.] Does not the engine driver find it very difficult to keep his time at the different stations if he does not know how fast he is going?

He has a general knowledge, no doubt, of the time he must take between the stations; but if you ask him his speed at any particular point, he will not, as a rule, be able to tell you it within a reasonable limit.

168. Lord *Hartismere*.] In reference to the answer that you gave just now, in the evidence before the Committee of last year, at p. 46, Question 1015, a story is told of a tramway which is worked by steam, and where the car came almost in contact with a cab driving down a cross street, and was pulled up immediately, although if it had been drawn by horses they could not have pulled it up, and there was no damage done. Then Question 1017 is as follows: "Then, from your experience of the engines, you think they are more readily stopped than horses can be?" And the answer is, "We are satisfied from actual experiments that they can stop within a shorter distance than horses." Do you agree in the answer which is there given?

I should have thought that that answer was a little strained.

169. My question was founded upon the evidence given before the former Committee of the House of Lords and House of Commons by some of the most experienced engineers, who said that tramcars with steam could be pulled up more quickly than a carriage; does not this answer confirm that opinion?

I have not seen any of those exceedingly quick stops that have been mentioned, although I have often tried stopping with steam-cars.

170. *Chairman*.] I think you went through the streets of Edinburgh upon a tramcar, did you not?

I did.

171. Had you upon that occasion any opportunity of judging how quickly the cars could be stopped?

Yes;

Mr.
H. G. Calcraft
and
Major General
C. S. Hutchinson,
R.E.

27th February
1879.

Yes; there my recollection is, that within one and a half to two cars' lengths were the best stops that we got. I do not think that any stop was within the length of the car, which is sometimes stated to be possible.

172. I think you stated in your evidence that you pulled up upon the ascent of a rather steep gradient?
Yes, I think we did.

173. Did you find any difficulty in that case?
No, I do not think there was any difficulty. There is no difficulty in stopping, but I do not think you must take it that the stops are quite so quick as are held out by the advocates of steam.

174. On the whole, did that journey in Edinburgh give you a favourable impression of the system of steam cars as regards their safety, to the traffic of carriages and passengers?
Yes; I think there was nothing to the contrary; they were very manageable.

175. Lord *Carlingford.*] But there is a great deal of alarm caused to horses by those cars, is there not?
More or less, horses are frightened; they no doubt get educated to the passage of the cars, but there will be always in all towns fresh horses coming in from the country and taking their turn of town traffic, and those of course, until they get accustomed to it, are frightened.

176 Viscount *Cardwell.*] Are you now speaking of tramways generally?
No, of steam tramways.

177. *Chairman.*] Horses are ordinarily more or less frightened by horse tramways, are they not?
Possibly so.

178. Lord *Carlingford.*] Do you suppose that horses would be more or less frightened on country roads, as compared with streets in a town?
That again would be a question of use; I suppose they would less frequently meet the tramcar on country roads, and therefore would be longer in getting accustomed to the sight of it.

179. *Chairman.*] I think you recommended that they should always be obliged to stop, in case of the horses becoming restive, or of there being any danger of that kind. I do not observe any such provision in Schedule A. of this Order?
I think that was one of the original recommendations, but whether it has been put in the Order or not, I do not know. (Mr. *Calcraft.*) That was one of the relaxations which the House of Commons insisted upon; they thought the provision was unnecessary. It is in the Vale of Clyde Tramways and the Wantage Tramways bye-law, but it is not in the new ones as settled by the House of Commons.

180. (To Major General *Hutchinson.*) Do you know whether any practical inconvenience has arisen from that provision in those two cases?
I never heard either one way or the other.

181. You, I think, went upon the Vale of Clyde Tramway, did you not?
Yes; I have been there several times.

182. When you were there, was there any case of stopping, in consequence of the restiveness of horses?
Yes, I think we had to stop two or three times; principally at crossings, I think. There was once very nearly an accident I remember; a horse got frightened and ran across the path of the tramcar, but the car was pulled up without any bad results.

183. Would you recommend the adoption of that regulation?
I think it is only a reasonable one.

184. Lord *Colville of Culross.*] Are tramways subject to the provision of what is called Lord Campbell's Act?
That, I do not know. (Mr. *Calcraft.*) Certainly they are, I should think.

(15.)   c 2   185. *Chairman*

Mr.
H. G. *Calcraft*
and
Major General
C. S. Hutchinson,
R.E.

27th February
1879.

185. *Chairman* (to Major General *Hutchinson*).] Are there any other suggestions which you would wish to make to the Committee as to the general regulations which it would be desirable to establish in regard to the use of steam on tramways?

I do not know whether the Committee would think it well to lay down any minimum widths of streets or roads in which steam should be allowed, or to leave it as a matter of discretion with the Board of Trade. That is one point that strikes me, whether the Committee might say that they think that in all cases there should be a minimum width of certainly 9 feet 6 inches between the edge of the tramway and the kerb, as provided for in Section 9 of the Tramways Act. It is relaxed in many cases of ordinary tramways. If there are no frontagers' objections to tramways being carried through narrow spots, then they are frequently sanctioned in streets of a much narrower width than 9 feet 6 inches on each side of the tramway would give.

186. Would you recommend the adoption of an iron rule of that kind?
I think that it is very inexpedient to allow the use of steam in streets where the general width is less than, say, 24 feet for a tramway of ordinary gauge, because, in the case of restive horses, it gives them so little room for escape.

187. *Earl of Redesdale*.] It would be dangerous for the foot passengers, and other people too?
No doubt; I think it is a question deserving of consideration, whether it should be left elastic, or whether an absolute minimum width should be insisted upon.

188. *Chairman*.] You would recommend an absolute minimum width throughout the whole length, so that a single narrow gut, if I may so say, would prevent the establishment of a tramway at all?
An accident might occur at the narrow gut.

189. Earl of *Devon*.] Would not that be met by requiring that at the narrow gut they should slacken speed, and go at half speed, for instance?
To some extent it might, no doubt.

190. Lord *Carlingford*.] I suppose that the Board of Trade does not relax that rule, or dispense with the observance of that rule in the case of ordinary tramways for any length of way, but only at particular points?
So long as there are not objections raised on the part of the frontagers, as a rule the Board of Trade have not objected to the construction of tramways along narrow streets; of course the frontagers have the power of raising objections which are fatal to the construction of a tramway, if their number exceeds a certain proportion of the whole of the frontagers; and I was going to ask your Lordships whether it might not be possible to frame the 9th Section of the General Tramways Act in a somewhat clearer way than it is now framed, for it gives rise to a great many points of discussion as to its interpretation.

191. *Chairman*.] Would you be so good as to read the clause to which you refer?
The section is this: " Every tramway in a town which is hereafter authorised by Provisional Orders shall be constructed and maintained, as nearly as may be, in the middle of the road; and no tramway shall be authorised by any Provisional Order to be so laid that for a distance of 30 feet, or upwards, a less space than 9 feet and 6 inches shall intervene between the outside of the footpath on either side of the road and the nearest rail of the tramways, if one-third of the owners, or one-third of the occupiers, of the houses, shops, or warehouses, abutting upon the part of the road where such less space shall intervene as aforesaid, shall in the prescribed manner, and at the prescribed time, express their dissent from any tramway being so laid." Now, two or three points arise there.

192. Earl of *Derby*.] Is there anything to show where a town is supposed to begin or end?
No, there is not. One of the points that arises with regard to streets is this: that, say King-street, ends at a certain point, and Princes-street commences where King-street ends, without any visible break in the continuity; the difficulty is as to how the 30 feet is to be taken in that case. The question is

is whether, if there is no break of continuity in the narrow space, the street is to be taken to end at the end of King-street, or whether it is to be taken right through King-street and Prince's-street, from one end of the narrow space to the other. That is a point which frequently arises, and causes difficulty of interpretation. The narrow space might commence in King-street, and there might be three frontagers, perhaps, in King-street, two of whom might object, and that would be fatal to the construction of the tramway in King-street, whereas there might be perhaps 30 more frontagers in Prince's-street adjoining it, only five of whom, or three of whom, dissented; and therefore there would not be a statutory objection, if the two streets were taken as one, whereas taken sectionally it might be fatal to the scheme, which would be a hard case.

Mr.
H. G. Calcraft
and
Major General
C. S. Hutchinson,
R.E.

27th February
1879.

193. Lord *Carlingford.*] It would be a mere accident of name?

Precisely. Then another question which arises is this: In some cases the tramway is placed out of the middle of a street; it leaves on one side of the street a clear interval of 9 feet 6 inches between the edge of the tramway rail and the edge of the kerb; on the other side it leaves a less space than 9 feet 6 inches. A great deal of argument frequently occurs as to whether, in that case, the frontagers on both sides, or only one side, are to be heard in objection to the tramway. It would be desirable that that should be clearly defined. A case turned up the day before yesterday at Ipswich in a local inquiry there. There were two frontagers on one side of the street, and the tramway was to be carried to within about five feet of their frontage; on the other side of the street there were four or five frontagers, and the tramway was carried more than 9 feet 6 inches from the edge of their kerb. One of the frontagers on the side to which the tramway was close dissented, and it seemed to me that his dissent was fatal to that part of the scheme, because he was one of two frontagers affected by the narrow width. But the view taken by the promoters was, that the five or six other frontagers on the other side had a right to be counted, and that therefore his objection was not fatal.

194. The frontagers on the other side having no ground of complaint?

Quite so; but according to the wording of this clause, they all required notices on both sides of the street, and consequently it was held that they ought all to be heard as assenters or objectors.

195. *Chairman.*] Is there any other point upon that clause to which you wish to draw the attention of the Committee?

This case also occurred at Ipswich: two streets, King-street and Prince's-street, are continuous, but between King-street and Prince's-street there is a large opening from another street running in; I think that in that case the continuity of the narrow space, although it continued both along King-street and along Prince's-street, should be held to be interrupted by the running in of the intervening street. If the clause could be made clearer, so as to include these points, it would save a great many difficulties, which now frequently arise.

196. Do you require the space of 9 feet 6 inches in the case of passing places, as well as in the case of the ordinary line of tramway?

I think in a single line it may be very often dispensed with, or otherwise it would be fatal to the construction of many lines of tramway; they are for very short distances, and therefore are very little obstruction to the traffic; the frontagers can object, of course.

197. You would hold that under that clause, if they objected in a sufficient proportion, their objection would be fatal?

Yes, I think so.

198. Earl of *Devon.*] In the case of turnings where you pass out of one street, at right angles, into another, you would want a curve with a longer radius, would you not, for the use of steam than you would with horses?

Perhaps slightly longer; but there is a very short distance between the wheels, and the engines can go round very narrow curves.

199. They are bogie carriages, I suppose?

Perhaps, in some cases. With regard to the question of the repair of tramways, to which Mr. Calcraft alluded, going about the country as I do, I see the very bad

(15.)   c 3   state

Mr.
H. G. Calcraft
and
Major General
C. S. Hutchinson,
R.E.

27th February
1879.

state into which, in many cases, the tramways are allowed to fall by the laxity of the local authority, causing a serious impediment to all the vehicular traffic that runs along the roads; of course there is a provision for the local authority to repair those tramways, but in very rare cases do they appear to exercise it; and if your Lordships' Committee could devise some mode of fortifying the provisions of the repairing clause of the general Tramways Act, it would be an exceedingly valuable thing to the public generally.

200. *Chairman.*] Would any person suffering therefrom have a right of action, either against the local authority, or against the tramway company?

They have a right of action, and they very often exercise it, but still, for all that, the state of the streets is, in many cases, very deplorable indeed.

201. Would it be an action against the local authority, or against the tramway company?

Against the tramway company, I should imagine.

202. Lord *Carlingford.*] Then the local authority has full power to compel the tramway company to repair, if it chooses to exercise its power; is that so?

It has power.

203. But it does not exercise it?

As a rule, it does not exercise it.

204. Earl of *Redesdale.*] Is there any penalty for leaving the tramway for any number of days without repair?

There is a power, I think, on the part of the local authority to take the repair into their own hands, and to charge the tramway company with the expense.

205. But there is no penalty?

I am not sure. It is Clause 28 of the General Act of 1870.

206. Do you not think that a penalty, with a daily payment until the thing was done, would be a very good thing?

Anything would be good, I think, that secured the streets being kept in good repair.

207. *Chairman.*] The process here laid down is that the local authority have a right to do the repairs themselves, and recover the expense?

Yes; in some cases the local authority hold money of the tramway companies in their hands from which they can execute the repairs. But the state of bad repair into which the streets have been allowed to fall has become exceedingly serious in many cases, and it is getting tramways into very bad repute indeed.

208. Lord *Carlingford.*] Do you remember where those cases are?

I remember numbers of them. Camberwell is the worst. I was called upon to inspect the tramways there, and the state of the streets is horrible. Almost throughout the entire length of the tramways in Camberwell, the rails are loose, the spikes have given way, the crossings are in a very bad condition, and the paving is very bad. In cases where asphalte has been used, the asphalte is all broken up and in holes, and so dangerous, that the local authority have had to fill it up with gravel to try and get rid of the nuisance as far as they could. Now I believe that they are likely to enter into some arrangement to improve matters, but in the meantime, and for some time past, the public in Camberwell have been suffering very grievously from the state of the tramways.

209. Do you know of any similar case in other cities?

Not so bad; but in a great number of cases the pavement is not kept up to the level of the tramway, and the consequence is that in endeavouring to cross the tram-rail, the wheels of vehicles get wrenched, and go skirting and skimming along the rail.

210. Earl of *Redesdale.*] In those cases are the shareholders in the tramway companies receiving good payments?

In many cases they are paying good dividends.

211. Is

211. Is that the case in Camberwell?

There it is the London Tramways Company, and I do not think that has been in quite so good a financial position as some of the others.

Mr.
H. G. Calcraft
and
Major General
C. S. Hutchinson,
R.E.

27th February
1879.

212. *Chairman.*] Do you know whether the local authority complain that this clause does not give them sufficient power, or is the state of things which you have described simply owing to their neglect?

I think it is simply owing to their disinclination to put the power they have into operation.

213. Earl of *Redesdale.*] Would it not be a good thing to have a penalty upon the local authority?

A penalty is very much wanted somewhere; I do not care upon whom it is put.

214. *Chairman.*] In the case that you mentioned in Camberwell, are the rails intended to be level with the road?

Yes, in all cases of street tramways, except in very rare instances, the tramways are level with the road. In the case of the Wantage Tramway the regular railway rail is employed because it is on the side of the road, and is not crossed by the ordinary vehicular traffic.

215. But there would be no difficulty in applying steam with the level rails?

No; it is so applied in the Vale of Clyde, and at all the other places where experiments have been tried. There is one other point which I should like to mention, and that is, whether in any future Act where tramways are to be sanctioned for the use of steam, the mode of construction of the tramway should not be first of all submitted to the Board of Trade for approval.

216. Do you inspect the tramways now before they are opened?

We do.

217. But you would have the plans submitted to you?

I think the proposed method of construction to be adopted should be submitted to the Board of Trade.

218. Lord *Carlingford.*] The permanent way?

The permanent way.

219. Lord *Redesdale.*] But you can order anything you please?

I do not think we can.

220. Surely in every case they are bound to adopt any new scheme of improvement that the Board of Trade may order?

They are; but so long as the tramway has been satisfactorily constructed when it is inspected, it would be going very far to order its re-construction.

221. But you could object to anything being done, and give them notice from the beginning that only one sort of railway will be approved of?

Yes; but you do not know when they are constructing, and, therefore, I think that if before construction the tramway company were called upon to submit the mode of construction which they intended to adopt for approval, or otherwise, it would be a very salutary thing. That is the case in one of the London Tramways; they are bound to submit for the approval of the Board of Trade the mode of construction that they intend to adopt, and I think that it would be a very healthy rule to apply to all cases, particularly where steam is proposed.

222. *Chairman.*] What do you mean precisely by the "mode of construction"; do you mean that they should lay plans and sections of the whole line before you?

I mean a section of the permanent way, so that we might know the character of the rail, the mode of fixing it, and the nature of the paving.

223. Are there any other remarks that you wish to make to the Committee, either upon the General Act or upon any other point?

No, nothing further strikes me.

(15.)   c 4   224. I think

Mr.
H. G. Calcraft
and
Major General
C. S. Hutchinson,
R.E.

27th February
1879.

224. I think you are in favour of requiring a certificate in regard to the efficiency of the boilers to be used in tramway engines, are you not?
Yes. The inspection of the boilers might be too big a matter to be undertaken, but a certificate of efficiency might very well be called for.

225. Earl of *Redesdale*.] Who is to give the certificate?
The tramway company, I suppose.

226. They are to certify that their own engine is a good one?
They would have to certify that it had been tested up to a certain pressure.

227. *Chairman*.] Do you attach much importance to that suggestion?
Yes, I think it is an important point.

228. I think the suggestion was made before the Committee of last year that the Board of Trade certificate should be given to the drivers of these tramway engines; has the Board of Trade any opinion upon that point?
I have not heard that question discussed. (Mr. *Calcraft*.) I think the Board of Trade was very strongly against it.

The Witnesses are directed to withdraw.

Ordered, That this Committee be adjourned to Monday next, at Two o'clock.

Die Jovis, 6° Martii, 1879.

LORDS PRESENT:

Marquess of RIPON.
Earl of DEVON.
Earl COWPER.
Earl of REDESDALE.
Viscount CARDWELL.

Lord SILCHESTER.
Lord HARTISMERE.
Lord CARLINGFORD.
Lord NORTON.

THE MARQUESS OF RIPON, IN THE CHAIR.

MR. GEORGE STEVENSON is called in; and Examined, as follows:

506. *Chairman.*] I BELIEVE you are the Engineer of the Wantage Tramway?
I am.

Mr. G. Stevenson.

6th March 1879.

507. How long has that tramway been open?
Since October 1875.

508. Has steam been used upon it ever since it was opened?
No; we commenced using steam in August 1876.

509. Before that time, did you use horses upon the tramway?
Yes.

510. Can you tell the Committee what number of passengers have made use of the tramway during the last year?
Thirty-two thousand odd.

511. What is the length of the tramway.
Two-and-and-half miles from the Wantage terminus of the tramway to the Great Western Railway station.

512. What comparison does that number of passengers bear to the number of passengers along the road before the tramway was established?
We estimated that the present travelling population is about two-and-a-half times what it was under the old omnibus system. The omnibus used to average three passengers each journey, and we average seven.

513. Do your cars carry more passengers at a time than the omnibus did?
Four or five times as many. We have one car that will carry 60 passengers.

514. Do you run more than one car at a time?
Sometimes we do on special occasions.

515. What amount of heavy goods have been brought up by the tramway?
We have not been in working order for heavy goods until about Christmas. During last month we brought up about 600 tons of heavy goods, and 133 tons of light goods, such as grocery and ironmongery.

516. Is the gauge on the tramway the same as that on the Great Western line.
Precisely the same; the narrow gauge.

(15.)   G 2   517. Can

517. Can trucks from the Great Western line run along your tramway?
Yes, we bring up as many as 14 in a day.

518. Do you consider that an advantage?
Very great indeed.

519. I suppose that that requires your tramway to be constructed more solidly than would be necessary if you did not take railway trucks?
I do not consider that there is very much difference, because the passenger engine travels at a rather higher rate of speed, and requires about an eight-ton engine; and goods require about a 14-ton engine, which travels at a less speed; so that I consider that the strength of the tramway would require to be about equal for either.

520. You consider that an equal strength would be required to convey the passenger traffic, under all circumstances, as to convey railway trucks?
In using steam I should consider so.

521. At what speed do you travel?
At a speed not exceeding 10 miles an hour, but sometimes in a straight course we attain a speed of 10 miles.

522. Are you limited by Act of Parliament, or otherwise, to that speed?
We are limited to a speed of 10 miles per hour.

523. Have you any self-acting brakes on your locomotives?
Yes; on each of the passenger engines. We do not find that those are so operative as we should like, but we have never found any difficulty in coming to an almost immediate standstill owing to having steam. The appliances are not so operative as we should like. We have tried hard to get them, but it seems a great difficulty.

524. What is your locomotive?
We have Grantham's combined car, that is with the steam engine and boiler all combined in one car; we have Hughes' detached steam car, which is a locomotive of itself, which we attach to the train passenger cars; and we have also a goods engine enclosed round, made by the London and North Western Railway Company. We have tried also Merryweather's steam engine car.

525. That is a detached engine, is it not?
It is, and Hughes' also.

526. Which of those do you consider the best?
Merryweather's engine, which we had, was not sufficiently heavy to give adhesive force to bring up a good load under unfavourable circumstances, such as snow and frost, and when there were obstructions on the line. The engine which we had of Messrs. Merryweather was about six tons when loaded, and that did not give sufficient adhesive force to bring up a full load of passengers. It is a passenger engine. Hughes' engine, which weighs about eight tons, is very successful in that respect, and we have never had any difficulty in bringing up one or two loaded cars with that. In that respect Hughes' engine, as we have tried it, is the best; but I believe that Messrs. Merryweather make a heavier engine, which we have not tried. The Grantham combined car is by far the most economical in working, owing to the weight of the passengers giving the additional adhesive force when there is a heavy load, the adhesive force being all combined in one car; and we can work with much less fuel than we can with the detached engine. There is one other advantage with regard to the Grantham engine, and that is, that it is all combined in one, and if you want to stop immediately there is no butting of the cars behind; you bring the thing to a complete standstill in its own length, or thereabouts. Those two things, I consider, are the great advantages of a combined car.

527. In what length can you stop the Merryweather, or Hughes' detached car?
We can stop on our heaviest gradient in about 12 yards.

528. What is the heaviest gradient?
One in 44. On a level we can stop in about six or seven yards.

529. In what distance can you stop with the Grantham car?

We

We can stop with the Grantham car in about the same, or rather less, length.

6th March 1879.

530. Lord *Carlingford.*] Are you likely to adopt one of those cars exclusively in future?

We have had such difficulty in getting the thing that we really want, that we have not definitively decided. We are using them daily. Hughes's car is running alternately with Grantham's six or seven journeys a day; we are using them constantly and with great satisfaction.

531. But you have not come to a final choice between them?

They are expensive things to buy, and our company being limited as to its means, we are doing with what we have. We are not likely to require fresh engines, I think, for some little time.

532. Lord *Norton.*] Do you mean that you can pull up within the distance you mentioned when the cars are travelling at full speed?

When they are travelling at the rate of 10 miles an hour.

533. *Chairman.*] What is the relative cost of steam power, as compared with horse power, according to your experience?

I worked it out some months ago, and I found that our horse cars cost us 8 *d.* a mile, reckoning all expenses. The steam car I made to come to 5½ *d.* per mile, but since then we have had practical experience. We broke an axle in the frost, and we were reduced to horses for a fortnight, and we found that we had to pay for the hire of horses 2 *s.* 6 *d.* per journey, which amounted to 17 *s.* 6 *d.* a day; and when we came to compare that with the cost of fuel, we found that the difference between 17 *s.* 6 *d.* and 9 *s.* 6 *d.* was the actual difference, so that it works out more favourably than it did in the first instance.

534. That was a case where you had not a supply of horses of your own?

Yes; but we found that to hire horses was cheaper than to keep them. We found that they cost us nearly 3 *s.* per journey when we kept them ourselves.

535. What are the other advantages of steam, in your opinion?

The principal advantage is the convenience that it offers under pressure when there is a great amount of traffic. On the occasion of His Royal Highness's visit to Wantage last year, we carried 1,500 passengers in a few hours, whereas if we had been reduced to a horse tramway we could not have carried 500. We can, when occasion requires, adopt railway carriages on our line, and on several occasions, such as reviews, and specially on the occasion of His Royal Highness's visit, we carried the traffic and moved along when the road was lined with vehicles of all descriptions; even the carriage in which His Royal Highness rode, came along immediately by the side of it, and we carried the traffic without any accident or mishap, and we have generally done so. There have been one or two slight mishaps, but we have never had an accident of any consequence.

536. Supposing that your driver sees that horses are becoming unmanageable, is he directed to pull up or not?

Yes, he is under most imperative orders to stop at the slightest signal.

537. Lord *Carlingford.*] Do you mean at a signal from a person on the road?

If a person is driving a vehicle or riding a horse, and if he holds up his hand we are bound to stop, and we always do so. There is always a guard with the car, and if there is a horse that is restive he leads it by.

538. *Chairman.*] He gets off the car and helps the coachman or person in charge of the horse?

Yes.

539. Does that often happen?

Not once in a week, I think, I may say.

540. You do not find that it interferes with your traffic materially?

We practically do the traffic; there is but very little other traffic.

(15.) G 3 541. But

541. But you do not find that the fact of having to pull up on those occasions, is any inconvenience to you?

Not the slightest.

542. Lord *Norton*] What means have you for giving warning to anybody who is in the way?

We have a bell and a whistle, and the driver must ring the bell when he sees anyone coming.

543. *Chairman.*] Have you either a recorder or an indicator upon your engine?

We tried a recorder, but we found it to be inoperative, and we have no recorder in use at present. We only keep very strict watch upon the driver. We know the time at which they start and the time at which they arrive, and we constantly give them strict orders to keep within the 10 miles an hour, and we have never had any complaint of furious driving or over driving.

544. Is it a single line of rails?

It is a single line of rails, with three turnouts or passing places.

545. Can you state what, if any, has been the reduction in the freights of goods, such as coal, corn and stone, and matters of that kind, on the tramway?

Previous to the introduction of the tramway we were paying 2 *s.* 3 *d.* per ton for large quantities, and 2 *s.* 6 *d.* for small quantities of coal. Those quantities we bring up now at 1 *s.* wholesale, and 1 *s.* 3 *d.* retail. In the case of stone and timber, the reduction is from 3 *s.* 6 *d.* to 2 *s.* 6 *d.* Road-stone is brought up at the low rate of 1 *s.* 3 *d.* The ordinary rate for merchandise, such as drapery and grocery goods, used to be 4 *s.* 6 *d.*, for grocery we now charge 3 *s.* The rate for ironmongery was 4 *s.* 6 *d.*, and we now bring it at 3 *s.* 6 *d.*

546. Can you tell us what number of parcels you carry?

Last year we carried just over 15,000.

547. Lord *Norton.*] What are your heavy goods?

Our heavy goods consist of stone, coals, timber, corn, and general heavy traffic.

548. What is the length of the whole line?

Two and a half miles.

549. Is it necessary in so short a distance to have the means of replenishing either fuel or water on the road?

Not at all.

550. All that is done at either terminus?

Only at the Wantage terminus; we never require it elsewhere; we have a supply of water there under pressure.

551. *Chairman.*] Have you ever tried the Scott-Moncrieff system, or any other mechanical appliance?

We have never tried any mechanical means, with the exception of steam.

552. Lord *Carlingford.*] Do you find that horses get used to the engines?

We find that after the first time or two they almost invariably get used to it, and take very little notice of it. Young horses will look at it, and perhaps will show some signs of being frightened, but after they have been by it a few times we find they take very little notice of it. I noticed the other day that whilst horses were greatly terrified at a traction engine on the road, they passed our engine scarcely noticing it.

553. Lord *Norton.*] Have you had any accident at all?

I do not know that we can say that we have been perfectly free. Our doctor, who is one of our managing directors, was down on the line; he got off for the purpose of inquiring as to a passenger who was travelling; he left his man in the trap, and, while he was doing so, the horse, by some means or other, we are not quite sure what, took fright at the tramway, and run into a miller's cart, and broke the shafts and wheel. It did not do any injury to the man, nor anything beyond the mere accident; I do not know exactly whether the accident might be attributable to the tramcar, which was very near at the time.

544. Lord

554. Lord *Carlingford.*] Then you find your engine and car less alarming to horses than the traction engines are?

Much less alarming. I should like to state another circumstance. While we were reduced to running with horses for a fortnight during the frost, we had two mishaps with our own horse cars. In one case a horse which is constantly going by our engines day by day met the horse car coming, and seeing, I suppose, an alteration from the steam, he took a slight fright and backed into it, and took the wheel off. Then, very strange to say, on the Saturday following a man was coming along with a load of crockery ware, and his horse did exactly the same thing; so that we had two mishaps in one week while using the horse car, and for six months, I think, there has not been a single accident with the steam car.

555. Lord *Carlingford.*] The horse looked upon the steam-engine as the natural mode of locomotion.

I only mention that as having positively occurred.

556. Have you found any difference in respect to frightening horses between those two or three sorts of engines that you used?

I think that the more quiet the engine is, and the less clatter there is, the better; it is the clatter that is likely to frighten the horses. But we have had so few accidents, that I think there is not much difference between them.

557. Lord *Norton.*] What is the width of the whole road?

It averages rather over 35 feet wide; but there is a space for about four chains, which is only about 24 or 25 feet wide.

558. Are there houses on both sides?
Very few, scarcely any.

559. Lord *Carlingford.*] Is the rail on one side of the road?

The rail is on one side of the road, and we find that that is a great advantage over having it in the centre.

560. In what respect?

We are always out of the way of the public traffic. We take up about six feet of road, which is 30 feet wide on the average, and we are always out of the way of the general traffic.

561. Lord *Norton.*] What do the people say who have houses on the side nearest to which your tramway passes?

We have never heard any complaint, and I think the public who live in the neighbourhood find it a very great boon, because they use it as well as other passengers.

562. Lord *Carlingford.*] Are there many houses having a frontage to the road on the side nearest to which the tramway passes?

Very few indeed, not more than a dozen in the whole distance.

563. *Chairman.*] Do you pull up to take people in at any time?

At any point, and in that respect it is very much more convenient than a railway. Whenever passengers signal the tram, we pull up and take them up.

564. Lord *Carlingford.*] Supposing that any number of houses were to be built upon the frontage, would not your rails be found very inconvenient?

There are various outways into the farms and farmsteads, and we never find any inconvenience. Our rail is the ordinary bridge section; it is rather distinct from ordinary tramways in that respect; it is the same section as the Great Western Railway rails, so that in radiating the curves we have no groove, but we have a lateral play, which eases us round the curves very nicely.

565. Lord *Norton.*] What is the average time taken in running the whole distance?

From 16 to 20 minutes.

566. How often do you run?

We meet every train on the Great Western Railway, running seven times on ordinary days, and eight times on market days.

567. Earl *Cowper.*] You say that the recorder has been given up. Do you

(15.)   G 4   find

find that the speed is regulated entirely according to the judgment of the driver?

According to the judgment of the driver and the conductor. We make a strict charge to them not to exceed 10 miles an hour.

568. Do you find that the driver and conductor get to be pretty good judges of the speed at which the car is travelling?

Yes, we check them every journey.

569. Lord *Norton.*] How do you check them?

By the time of leaving and the time of arrival.

570. Earl *Cowper.*] And they get to know how fast they are going?

Yes.

571. Earl of *Devon.*] How many stoppages do you make on an average between the two termini?

I should think the average would be about two.

572. Have you little waiting boxes, or anything of that sort, where people wait?

No, nothing whatever; they wait until we come, and simply they step on the step of the car. Sometimes they go the whole distance, and sometimes they go part of the way, and anywhere they wish us to put them down we do so.

573. Are there any side roads which come into the main road between the two terminal points?

Yes, several.

574. Is it your practice to go at the same pace across the points of junction as you do when there are no such side roads?

Where we come to facing points in the turnouts we always slacken, and in going over a bridge or coming round a curve we always do the same thing. We travel at about four miles an hour when there is any impediment in the way. When we come to a straight line with nothing before us, then we increase the speed to some extent.

575. Earl *Cowper.*] Do you find that you can prevent all escape of steam?

We can with the exception of a very small amount. In the Grantham car we condense, and the remainder of the steam we burn in the furnace. In the Hughes's car it is condensed entirely by condensing tanks, and we can travel for the distance without showing any steam under favourable circumstances. If it is a very rough day the probability is that we might show some, but never enough to inconvenience any one.

576. Lord *Norton.*] Is there any smoke?

There is no smoke; we use coke, which prevents that.

577. Earl *Cowper.*] Is the fire completely concealed?

Completely. I may say that we have never had the slightest mishap in darkness of any kind; every mishap that we have ever had has been in broad daylight, but never that I remember have we had any mishap whatever during the night.

578. Lord *Norton.*] Should you call the engine noiseless?

It is not perfectly noiseless, but it does not make one-fourth of the noise of a traction engine. Of course the cars being light they glide along with very little clatter indeed.

579. Is there much wear and tear of the engine?

I think I may say that the wear and tear is of about the ordinary amount. It costs us about 100 *l.* a year to keep our engines going.

580. We have evidence from the United States that they gave up the steam traffic on account of the wear and tear of the engines; your experience is different from theirs?

I think our line is peculiar in that respect. Owing to our being able to get lateral play, we do not get half the wear and tear we should if we had grooved rails; because in radiating curves where one wheel requires to radiate faster than another, it is a great strain upon the engine; whereas if you have a little lateral

play,

play, you get round much more easily; and I think also that where the rail is

sunk it comes more in contact with the road than ours does. There are more obstructions in putting down material and things of that kind, and the wear and tear is much greater than in our case.

581. *Chairman.*] Is the top of your rail level with the metalling of the road?
It is level with the surface of the road.

582. Earl of *Devon.*] Have you any physical junction with the Great Western Railway?
Yes.

583. So that you can transfer trucks from one to the other?
Constantly, day by day, we may transfer many trucks. We have a goods junction. Our passenger line comes to a terminus, but we have two junctions with the goods sidings of the Great Western Railway Company.

584. One up and one down, I suppose?
One up and one down.

585. And in that way you do a good deal of business?
We are doing a very considerable business. The traffic seems to be very rapidly developing. I may say that if it had not been for our tramway at Wantage this year, we should have had a coal famine, for there was not a single hundredweight of coal on the wharf, and it was only on the tramway that we could get coal.

586. Earl of *Devon.*] The canal was frozen, I suppose?
The canal was frozen.

587. Lord *Norton.*] Was economy your chief reason for coming for a second Act to enable you to use steam?
We tried with horses, but the strain on the gradients was so great that we found it impossible to carry on the traffic, hauling up the railway trucks with horses; and, in addition to that, we always considered that steam was a very great advantage over horse-power in every respect.

588. Lord *Carlingford.*] Was your tramway got up by the inhabitants of the neighbourhood, or by the Great Western Railway Company?
By the inhabitants of the neighbourhood, and principally of the town; but we are greatly indebted to the aid of Colonel Loyd Lindsay, who is a large land-owner in the neighbourhood, and who generously took an interest in it, and took a considerable number of shares. We carried it through entirely by local assistance.

589. Lord *Norton.*] How was it that you never thought of steam when you got your first Act?
The tramway was originally constructed with a view of steam power being used.

590. Then how was it that you had to incur the expenses of a second Act?
I can hardly say. We put down a strong line of the same gauge as the Great Western in the hope of having steam. I think this was the reason: that at that time steam was contemplated, and we hoped that a general Steam Act would have been introduced.

591. *Chairman.*] When you changed from horses to steam, had you to alter your permanent way at all?
Not the slightest. The great advantage with steam is that in using steam we have not to keep up the metalling between the rails. If we use horses and steam too, we have both to do; whereas if we use steam the wear and tear of the tramway by the horses is done away with; that is a very important point.

592. That is all very well when you are practically off the road, but that would not apply to the case of a tramway in the middle of a road, would it?
No.

593. Lord *Carlingford.*] How was the ownership of the green strip along the road which you have made use of treated, when you obtained your Bill?
We had to obtain the consent of the road authorities, and of the turnpike trustees, and then the whole road was incorporated within the limit of our deviation on our plans, and we had permission to put down our tramway either in

(15.)   H   the

the centre of the road or on one side of the road. But it appeared to me to be very plain that it would be a great advantage to have the tramway out of the road, and the consequence was that we selected the route along the side of the road, and I should very strongly recommend in the case of any further tramways of this kind that the same course should be adopted. If we had our tram rails in the centre of the road, with scores of traction engines passing over them, the probability is that they would be battered, and the road would suffer very considerably. The wear and tear would be much greater, and the inconvenience to the travelling public would also be very much greater.

594. Have you scores of traction engines in these parts?
We have, I think, more than 20 in a radius of eight miles.

595. Were there no claims of ownership on the part of the owners of the frontage on the side of the road along which you pass?
We only run by the side of the road on public property; we purchased all the private property over which we pass. The first 600 yards of the line from the town is over private property, which we purchased.

596. Earl of *Redesdale.*] Did you give any compensation to the owners of the land whose frontage you occupied?
We did where compensation was sought, where there was any damage; but that was only in one or two instances.

597. What do you mean by damage?
There was one instance only in which we passed close to a man's stable. His stable was on a lower level than our tramway. We raised our tramway a certain amount to get a proper level; he thought he was injured by that, and we then, as a compensation, raised his building, and filled up his stable to the proper level. That was the only case I know of where we had any compensation to make.

598. Lord *Carlingford.*] Was the green waste by the roadside generally treated as the property of the road authorities, or as the property of the owner of the adjoining land?
Entirely as the property of the road authorities. We do not go into any adjoining land.

599. But was not the green waste claimed in any case as the property of the owner of the adjoining land?
Not in any case. We consider that we have been of very great advantage to the road authorities, because we have taken off half, or more than half, the heavy tonnage of the road. We did not get any claims for compensation.

600. *Chairman.*] Have you any liability for the repair of the road?
We pay the road committee 20 *l.* per annum for repairing the road 18 inches outside the rail.

601. Earl *Cowper.*] Do you go over any bridges?
One bridge.

602. Did you make the bridge?
Yes, and we had to make an iron bridge.

603. Lord *Norton.*] In whom is the property in the roadside vested?
In the turnpike trust.

604. Are you aware that it was the property of the trust?
It was at that time. The trust has just expired. I may say that the major part of the way was the public footpath. The tramway was put down where the public footpath was. There were two footpaths, one on each side of the road, and we occupy one. We never had any application for any compensation.

605. I suppose it has checked the extension of the town in that direction; no houses will be built upon that side where your tramway is?
There has not been very much building, but we anticipate a considerable addition to the buildings on that particular side; we think that it is a great advantage. At the village of Grove, one mile off, building has been more going on.

606. Earl of *Redesdale.*] In estimating the difference of cost between carrying coal or other goods to Wantage from the station by road and by your tramway, have not the people, after getting the articles to your station at Wantage, to cart them to their own houses or places?

In

858

In some cases they have, but as our wharves are on the tramway, the major part of the coals are deposited in the wharves; and our gasworks also are so situated that we empty the coals on to the gasworks, so that a large proportion of it is done without cartage. There is a small proportion of household coals which have to be carted; but even in that case there is a saving of at least 6 *d.* per ton.

607. Earl of *Devon.*] What was your cost of construction per mile?
As nearly as possible, 2,000 *l.*

608. The country is flat, is it not; there were no hills to go over?
We have one gradient of one in 47 for 600 yards, and another of 1 in 44 for about 100 yards.

609. What weight do you take up the steeper gradient?
We never take more than three trucks of coals.

610. How many tons would that be?
They would average about eight tons net weight besides the trucks.

611. Lord *Carlingford.*] I suppose the inconvenience caused to the adjoining houses in your case is very much less on account of the small number of trains that you run in the day as compared to the tramways in cities?
I have never had the question of any inconvenience raised at all. I think that everyone who lives on the tramway thinks it a very great convenience to be able to get up and ride to the town. In every case there is room enough for two carriages to pass besides the tram.

612. Earl of *Redesdale.*] Is that a hard road?
It is all hard road.

613. You have hard road on both sides of your tramway?
Not on the outside; our tramway keeps the outside of the road everywhere.

614. Then no carriage can stand between your tramway and the fence?
No.

615. *Chairman.*] There is no space of road between your tramway and the hedge upon the side upon which your tramway is?
No, we are not more than three feet from the outside of the road. There is no space for any carriage to stand on the outside of the road, but we are singularly fortunate in that respect, as there are not many houses that require it.

The Witness is directed to withdraw.

677. *Chairman.*] You are a locomotive manufacturer residing at Loughborough, I think?

I am.

678. You gave evidence before the Committee of the House of Commons as to the use of mechanical power on tramways in 1877, did you not?

I did.

679. Did you give evidence before the Committee of last year?

I did not.

680. Have you since that date been actively engaged in improving the engines which you had previously manufactured for tramways?

I have.

681. What is the character of the engines which you manufacture; are they Merryweather's or Grantham's engines, or of what kind are they?

They are of my own invention. If you will allow me, I will hand in a drawing of them (*handing a drawing to the Committee*).

682. Are they separate engines not combined with the car?

Separate engines.

683. I think Mr. Stevenson told us that one of them was used upon the Wantage Tramway?

There is one used upon the Wantage Tramway, but it does not act so perfectly as those which they use in the public streets, because there is no water supply in Wantage, and it is necessary, in order for our engines to work perfectly, that there should be a water supply. With a water supply and the use of coke we show no steam and no smoke.

684. In what places have your engines been in use?

Our engine is mostly in use in Glasgow, where we are travelling about 2,500 miles per week, and have been for the last two years on the Vale of Clyde Tramway, which is through a very populous district. During the last few weeks we have been running in Paris very successfully. We have run in Bilbao, Hamburg, Cologne, Hanover, Dublin, Belfast, Sheffield, Leicester, and several other places.

685. In a good many of those cases your engines were only running experimentally, I suppose?

Only experimentally. Our principal work is in Glasgow, where we have been running for two years.

686. Are you running in Paris again?

Yes. Steam is being extensively used in Paris now, and other engines are being used in Paris now. Ours is an experimental matter for the present. We are running for a month to convince the authorities and the tramway directors as to our engine being a useful one.

687. In what part of Paris is it at work?

I cannot say exactly; but it is running along the side of the Seine through a populous district, and up a steep gradient of about 1 in 35.

688. I believe that one of your engines ran for some time in the streets of Leicester, did it not?

It did.

689. Are those streets wide or narrow streets?

They are narrow streets. I should think one of them is about 26 feet wide.

690. From kerbstone to kerbstone?

Yes.

691. What is the width of the tramway in Leicester?

It is a 4 feet 8½ inch gauge.

692. Had

692. Had you any personal experience of those engines when they were running in Leicester?

Yes, I was continually with them; I live in Leicester.

693. Can you tell the Committee whether they were found to be inconvenient to the public traffic in the town?

No, they were not at all; indeed people have wondered why we do not use them now in the streets. I have never heard a word against them from anybody in Leicester.

694. For how long did they run?

For about two months on and off; but of course as there was no Act of Parliament, and we were running against the law, we did not run oftener than we could help.

695. As a matter of fact, did any accident happen during that time?

None at all.

696. At what rate did they run?

At 10 miles an hour, I think, and sometimes perhaps 15 miles an hour. We were running against the law then.

697. Did they run at that speed in those narrow streets?

In those narrow streets.

698. Have you powerful brakes upon them?

Yes, very powerful brakes, steam brakes and foot brakes.

699. Within what distance can you stop your engines?

It depends entirely upon the state of the road. Running at the rate of 10 miles an hour on a level road, we could stop in about 20 feet.

700. What is the whole length of the engine?

The length of the engine is about 10 feet, and the length of the car is about 22 feet.

701. You could stop in twice the length of your own engine on a level?

We could. In going down a gradient, if we had no special means, we could not stop so quickly, but there being a governor on the engine to regulate the speed, we cannot run down a hill at too great a speed, so that we can stop almost as quickly going down hill as on a level.

702. Have you self-acting brakes?

We have self-acting brakes, according to the Board of Trade regulation.

703. Lord *Carlingford.*] What patent brake is it?

It is an invention of my own, patented by myself.

704. *Chairman.*] You have brakes upon your cars as well as upon your engines, I suppose?

We very seldom use the car brake.

705. Lord *Norton.*] Was it the main street of Leicester through which your engine worked?

Yes, it is the main street of Leicester.

706. Earl *Cowper.*] Are your engines fitted with a recorder?

We have tried a good many recorders, but I do not think the recorder will answer in the long run. It is like driving a watch with an engine strap; it is obliged to be an intricate piece of machinery, and I should think we have spent 400 *l.* upon recorders, but they have not answered. We have some on our engines at Govan now, but they certainly would not be good evidence in a court of justice in case of accident.

707. *Chairman.*] Do you use an indicator?

Always; that is very necessary for police purposes.

708. And with that you have not found any difficulty?

None at all.

709. Would you give the Committee your opinion upon the requirements of the Board of Trade?

(15.)   I   I think

I think that the requirements of the Board of Trade are very good indeed, and that we ought to try and comply with them. I do not know any requirements except that of the recorder which we cannot carry out.

710. You approve of the self-acting brakes?
I do.

711. And of the indicator?
And of the indicator.

712. What is your opinion of the regulation under which the drivers are required to stop if they see any horse becoming restive; do you see any difficulty in that?
I think they should stop, certainly; but they always do. We should not think even of passing a horse that threw his ears up. We know directly a horse that will shy from a long distance, and the driver is obliged to be cautious; he does not run into anything that is likely to be frightened, and from practice they know a timid horse when they meet him. I may tell you that in Glasgow the first year we had a few accidents, but the last year we have had but one. The horses on the road get quite used to the engine, and I never have to reprimand a man now, and we have no accidents. At first we had. There is a practice in Scotland of leaving one horse behind a cart, there being one driver to two horses and two carts, which is a very awkward thing for tramways, and sometimes the horse will turn round and touch our engine and damage it.

713. Lord *Norton.*] You are aware that 10 miles an hour is beyond the speed laid down in the Board of Trade requirements?
Eight miles is the speed allowed by the Board of Trade.

714. So that your speed in Leicester was excessive?
Certainly.

715. *Chairman.*] The trial at Leicester was wholly experimental, was it not?
Wholly. Our average speed, I suppose, is about five miles an hour on the Vale of Clyde Tramways.

716. To what is your self-acting brake set?
It is set to eight miles an hour on the Vale of Clyde Tramway.

717. Does it act with sufficient accuracy to keep the speed down to that limit, or must you allow something beyond?
It acts with sufficient accuracy, but we have to be very careful in keeping it in repair. We have had several visits from General Hutchinson, and we are afraid of his coming, so we keep it all right.

718. Lord *Norton.*] Can the engines be made noiseless?
Quite noiseless.

719. And so as to emit no smoke or steam?
No smoke or steam. We now take our smoke down to the ground; we do not even use a draught in the chimney upward.

720. Lord *Carlingford.*] The road upon which the tramway is laid in the Vale of Clyde is a crowded one, I suppose?
Very crowded in parts.

721. *Chairman.*] You have been frequently on your engines down there, I suppose?
Yes, I have been months there.

722. Lord *Carlingford.*] Probably horses are less frightened in such a crowded street as that than they would be on a quiet country road?
They might be. A horse will be frightened at anything unusual.

723. *Chairman.*] Have you any experience of running your engines upon tramways in rural districts?
Not except at Wantage. We have had an engine there for some two or three years.

724 In

724. In these towns abroad, Bilbao, Hamburg, Cologne, Hanover, and Paris, the tramways are all in the town, I suppose?
In the streets of the town.

725. Have you been to Hamburg?
I have.

726. How long have they been in use there?
They are not running there now. Those were all experimental trials.

727. Lord *Norton.*] Why were they given up?
It is often a question of money with a tramway, and the fact is that tramway companies do not know at present which is the best engine to use, and they do not know how it would pay them; so that they often try four or five different engines, and then do not make up their minds after all.

728. Do they go back to horses?
It is a very difficult thing to change a tramway from horses to steam. All the people connected with it are horsey people; people who have been accustomed to horses; so that it is a serious question.

729. But do they change back from steam to horses?
They have never adopted steam, except as an experiment.

730. Then the experiment has been considered a failure?
No, it has been considered successful, but it requires a large sum of money to have the engines. The experiments have been made at our own expense. In Paris they have spent a great deal of money in engines, and they have purchased different engines from different persons.

731. *Chairman.*] In the case of changing from horses to steam, is it necessary to strengthen the permanent way?
No, unless the permanent way has been laid badly in the first instance, which in a great many cases it has been. I should say that that would not be necessary. The rail is as heavy as most of the rails upon which we run our colliery engines.

732. Lord *Norton.*] What is the price of one of those engines?
About 600 *l.*

733. *Chairman.*] What is the greatest number of cars that you use with your engines?
We never take more than two; we take two at Govan on Saturdays.

734. How many people does a car hold?
About 40, inside and out.

735. Lord *Norton.*] What is the probable life of one of those engines, working them constantly?
It is a question of keeping them in good repair; they do not wear out if you keep renewing the parts. Engines are generally only put off the road because there are better engines made, and not because they are worn out.

736. They are lightly constructed, I suppose?
They must be very heavily constructed. That has been the great mistake in making these tramway engines; you must make them strong, and very good indeed.

737. *Chairman.*] What does one of your engines weigh?
From 6½ to 7 tons; but we make them according to the work to be done, and the gradient to be surmounted.

738. What is the heaviest gradient that you have ever had to work with your engines?
One in 20 is the greatest that I have worked upon in Edinburgh, up the Calton Hill.

739. Did you find any serious difficulty there?
Not at all.

(15.)   I 2   740. Lord

740. Lord *Norton.*] We have had evidence that the use of steam in the United States has been given up on account of the wear and tear to the engines; how does that strike you?

I should think it quite possible, because the roads are so bad that I should think they would almost give up their carriages.

741. But these are on rails; how does the fact strike you that the general use of steam trams in the United States has been abandoned, because they find the wear and tear of the engines too great on the rails?

I cannot say unless they were lightly made; they must have been lightly made.

742. You do not happen to know anything about the kind of engine used in America?

I do not; we are quite willing to enter into contracts for the maintenance and also working them by mechanical power.

743. *Chairman.*] Is there anything more that you wish to state to the Committee?

Only that we have spent a very large sum of money on this matter, and we should be very glad to come to some conclusion soon; it will be a very large trade, and I am quite sure, from my experience, that there need be no difficulty with horses. When I was a boy I used to see the animals rushing across the fields away from the locomotive, but they have now become used to it, and they stand quietly looking on; and if you hear the witnesses from Glasgow you will see that in a crowded narrow thoroughfare we are able to work with perfect safety.

744. Lord *Norton.*] Supposing that Parliament was to allow experiments to be made in the use of steam for a certain number of years, do you think any experiments would be made with the risk of having to abandon the use of steam?

I think it would be considered that sufficient experiments have been made already.

745. But it would apply differently to different kinds of places, would it not, according to the nature of the traffic along the road?

We should not require to make any further experiments as far as the engine goes.

746. But the circumstances of the different towns would make it a different question in different places, would they not?

Yes; I should like to mention that I would not introduce steam upon all the tramways in the country at once; I think it would be a most injudicious thing; Parliament might allow the Board of Trade to authorise certain tramways which they considered would be suitable for the use of steam.

747. What sort of conditions are in your mind when you make that suggestion?

They are these: that you have not managers or drivers, or people to do it all at once; and I think if you had large numbers of tramway engines put into the public streets they would be so badly managed for a time that they would not be successful.

748. Is the width of the street an element in your mind?
I should not put them in very narrow streets.

749. What sort of minimum width would you recommend?
I think that 26 feet might be the minimum.

750. *Chairman.*] Would you put the tramway in the middle of the street?
Whenever I could I would make a double tramway, certainly.

751. Viscount *Cardwell.*] We were told by some very eminent railway gentlemen that it was a mistake to think that all tramways ought to be of the same width as railways, but that, on the contrary, there might be many cases where it would be much more convenient to make tramways much narrower, and to
make

make the engines much lighter, and, in short, to accommodate the wants of different localities; do you think that is a wise suggestion?

I quite think so; tramways have, in my opinion, been made much too wide, and I think that the guage should not be 4 feet 8½ inches, but that if you had two lines of three feet it would be much more convenient.

752. In short, as a gentleman from Wantage told us, one thing might be very good at Wantage and another thing might be very good at Camberwell?
Quite so.

753. Therefore in applying this system to the wants of the whole country, it would be very expedient that the regulations should differ very much according to the different characters of the localities?
I think so; where railway trucks have to go over the lines you must have the 4 feet 8½ inches gauge; but I anticipate that most of the lines would be merely tramways, and the less the gauge the better.

754. Lord *Carlingford.*] It is a question of cost, is it not?
It would not cost very much less to make a narrow gauge than to make a broad gauge tramway, except when the land had to be purchased.

755. What is the advantage of a narrow tramway, except that it is cheaper to make and to work?
Other carriages would be much more likely not to come into contact with the tramway or tramcar. The cars would be narrower, and would occupy less space in the street; I think the present cars are far too wide.

755*. Viscount *Cardwell.*] One of the great objects now is to accommodate very crowded places, and if you could accommodate that traffic in a narrower vehicle than you now do, you would of course attain a greater advantage to the public?
Quite so. I think it should be a minimum width.

756. Lord *Carlingford.*] That of course does not apply with the same force to a country road?
I think in most country roads it would apply. Wantage is an exceptional case.

757. Why so?
Because I do not think you would generally take your heavy goods in railway trucks over the road from a station; I think it would be better to transfer them into lighter vehicles. Then again, you would not get many roads like the Wantage road, where you could take so great a width.

758. As between the side of the road and the centre of the road, as the place for the rails to be laid, have you any decided opinion?
It would entirely depend upon the width of the road. In most country roads I should think it would be best to have the tramways at the side, but in towns it must depend entirely upon the width of the street.

759. Earl *Cowper.*] What is the advantage of a double line?
The turns-out, where you have to pass other cars, wear the wheels very badly, and the one car must wait for the other; whereas if you have a double line, you may run right through, without stopping till the other comes up.

760. *Chairman.*] Is it your opinion that if the use of steam upon tramways were authorised under reasonable conditions, steam tramways would increase much?
Yes, I think they would. The engines would be brought to perfection by practice, and in the end all the cars would, I think, be driven by steam, but not for some time.

761. Do you think that a power on the part of the Board of Trade to stop the use of steam by its own authority, if it should be found to work to the disadvantage of the public, in any case, would very much interfere with the use of steam upon tramways?
I should almost think it would. No one would enter into a contract on those terms, at so much per mile.

(15.)   I 3   762. Not

762. Not if they were subject to an arbitrary power?
I think not; I think no one would invest his money under such conditions.

763. You think that would seriously interfere with the introduction of steam?
I do; because it would be done by contract at first. The management would be left in the hands of the engineer rather than in the hands of the tramway companies.

764. Still it is possible that the use of steam might be found in some cases to work injuriously to the public interest or safety, and in such cases some power would be required to put a stop to it?
Certainly.

765. How would you meet that case?
I think the Board of Trade would have the judgment not to authorise it where it would be likely to be stopped; still they should have the power to stop it, I think.

766. Viscount *Cardwell.*] In short, they would proceed tentatively and gradually?
That is the best plan.

767. Lord *Hartismere.*] Would you be able to make narrower cars so convenient for passengers that went by them, as the broader ones are?
There may be a difference of opinion about that, but I think so, for I have just made them of a 3 feet 6 inch gauge for New Zealand, and they are very elegant, nice cars, and occupy very little space.

768. Do you make them longer than the old ones?
We have made some longer for steam to hold 60 passengers inside, and I think it will come to that. For the colonies at all events it will, because no doubt these tramways will be used in the colonies instead of railways very largely, and we have numerous inquiries from the colonies.

769. *Chairman.*] Have you sent any engines to the colonies?
Yes, we have sent some 7,000 *l.* worth to Dunedin, New Zealand.

The Witness is directed to withdraw.

Mr. STEPHEN ALLEY, is called in; and Examined.

770. *Chairman.*] You are, I believe, a consulting engineer in Glasgow, and a member of the Institute of Engineers?
I am a member of the Institute of Mechanical Engineers.

771. And you are employed by the Vale of Clyde Tramway Company to inspect their engines?
Yes; my position is this: Messrs. Hughes & Co. have rented these engines to the Vale of Clyde Tramway Company at so much per mile, and I look after the Vale of Clyde Company's interests, if anything should go wrong with the engine.

772. Then are Messrs. Hughes' engines the only engines used now?
There were some others tried, but those were selected.

773. And they are at present in use?
Yes, we have at present, I think, nine of them altogether.

774. Do you consider that they work satisfactorily?
In the beginning they did not work satisfactorily; some parts of them proved rather light for the road, and some details went wrong; but for the last 18 months they have worked very satisfactorily indeed.

775. Have there been any accidents during the time?
That is a little out of my department, but I have heard of some two or three; there was a small child killed upon one occasion.

776. Mr.

Die Jovis, 13° Martii, 1879.

LORDS PRESENT:

Marquess of RIPON.	Earl of REDESDALE.
Earl of DERBY.	Lord SILCHESTER.
Earl of DEVON.	Lord CARLINGFORD.
Earl COWPER.	Lord NORTON.

THE MARQUESS OF RIPON, IN THE CHAIR.

MR. DUNCAN WILKIE PATERSON, is called in; and Examined,
as follows:

Mr. *Paterson.*

13th March 1879.

1070. *Chairman.*] I BELIEVE you are a Solicitor in Edinburgh, and Secretary to the Edinburgh Tramways Company?
I am.

1071. Have you filled the office of secretary as well as solicitor to that company from their outset?
I have.

1072. And you have had the arranging of all the details with the various local and road authorities?
I have.

1073. Will you, in the first place, be good enough to give us information with respect to the experimental use of the steam engine upon your line?
I will. We have a route within the system of the Edinburgh Street Tramways, than which, of all routes of which I am aware, nothing could be better adapted for mechanical power. It is a section of from $3\frac{1}{4}$ to $3\frac{1}{2}$ miles from almost the heart of Edinburgh to the adjacent small town of Portobello, with a population of between 5,000 and 6,000 in the vicinity, with very bad gradients; some of the gradients are as bad as 1 in 21 or 1 in 22. On the whole section of $3\frac{1}{4}$ miles we have got sections put together equal to nearly one mile of from 1 in 22 to 1 in 24; and from the very outset we have looked forward with great interest to alleviating the suffering to horses by substituting some other power for horse power; and we have looked about to see what power we could get. We have tried Hughes' engine; we have had two or three of his engines running on that section; we have also had a composite engine and car, or combined engine, Robertson and Henderson's, and both of those appear to do remarkably well, excepting that they have not yet been constructed with sufficient power to work the traffic continuously with loaded cars. We put them to very severe tests. We applied the maximum tests for the purpose of ascertaining whether they would come within our requirements; and Mr. Hughes has said over and over again that he could overcome the want of power. We have endeavoured to get the necessary sanction from the local road authorities, but we have failed; so that every time we have run there we have practically run without the authority of the various bodies.

1074. How often have you tried steam?
We have tried steam continuously for several weeks, and we have also, I may say, run both Hughes' engine and Robertson and Henderson's through the most crowded parts of Edinburgh, along Princes-street, which is in the centre of the

(15.)   N 2   city,

city, about a mile in length; and we have got round what we call the circular route, which is about five miles in extent; and the engines, so far as disturbance of traffic is concerned, and otherwise, appeared to be quite unobjectionable.

1075. Did you observe horses to be much frightened by the engines on those occasions?
The horses were not so much frightened as the drivers. That is a very curious thing, to which I paid very particular attention, attending almost all the trials, and especially on the Portobello-road. If the drivers of the vehicles paid no attention to the horses the horses themselves, as a rule, passed the engines quite quietly; but the drivers I noticed often on seeing the engine coming would pull the reins and direct the attention of the horses to it; and the horses in this way came to look at the engine, and it was, I may say, almost only on those occasions that any of the horses showed signs of fear, sympathising with the fear of those in charge.

1076. Did any accident occur on any occasion?
None.

1077. Can you state upon how many days you made those experiments?
We had various trials extending continuously over ten days at a time, and we ran alternately with a horse car. I may also state that on one occasion we passed some 200 or 300 horses, with rough riders, belonging to the cavalry regiment in Piershill, and, I may say, none of those horses shied, although the engine passed without stopping. We found the same horses shied when a tramway car was allowed to run down a declivity without engine or horses.

1078. Have you found those engines easy to stop in a short distance upon your steep gradients?
Very easy, surprisingly easy; in fact they almost anticipated all our fears. We had no accident; I myself repeatedly saw the engine stopped in a much shorter time than a car could have been stopped.

1079. On one of the steep gradients?
The case to which I particularly refer was not on one of the steep gradients, but they have stopped as well on the steep gradients. The instance to which I refer was in Princes-street, where I saw a carriage coming down a cross street, we having taken care to see that there was no vehicle in the way, and it came right in before the engine, and I thought there would have been a smash; but the engine was drawn up, I should say, within a few feet and stopped dead.

1080. Was the engine furnished with any bell, or had you a horn, or any other mode of indicating its presence?
We had no bell; we trusted to a whistle. I may state that all the drivers of the Edinburgh tramway cars are furnished with whistles. We trust a whistle rather than a bell.

1081. Do you have whistles with your horse cars as well?
We have.

1082. Have you ever had any complaints made against your company on the ground of cruelty to the horses?
Very many; and at the present time we have complaints now and again. In fact, what may be called cruelty to horses must exist to a greater or less extent on account of our gradients, although we supply as many horses as we can put to a car; we have four horses to almost every car. In fact, we have not a route without having four horses at particular places. We put two additional horses on at the foot of the gradient, and still the horses are very much distressed; and that is evidenced by the fact of their lives being so short.

1083. What is the average length of the life of one of those horses?
From three to four years. To show the enormous waste that there is in the stud of the Edinburgh Streets Tramway Company, I may state that on a capital sum, representing about 20,000 *l.*, there is as much depreciation in the year sometimes as from 7,000 *l.* to 8,000 *l.*

1084. What number of horses do you keep on an average?
About 520 to 540; the number varies with the season of the year.

1085. May I ask what is the average price that you pay for your horses?
The

The average price is about 40 *l.* now. We get the best horses we possibly can.

1086. At what age do you generally buy them?
From five to seven years old.

1087. If you obtain the necessary power, would you entirely abandon the use of horses, and substitute steam?
That would be a question for consideration. What we feel and say is, that there is no tramway system with which we are acquainted where it would be more desirable to have other than animal power applied.

1088. During the time that you were making these experiments with the engine (without any proper authority, I imagine), were any complaints made against the company for using it?
No complaints were made on the part of the public or frontagers, or of any of those persons; but we were repeatedly threatened with interdicts; in fact, we were warned now and again, but still we thought that it was a matter of such importance that we ran the risk of running without authority.

1089. Lord *Norton.*] By whom were you warned?
By the city authorities, and by the road authorities.

1090. Was the experiment made without their consent?
It was.

1091. *Chairman.*] Have you had any accident with your tram cars when you have been using horses?
We have had a great many accidents.

1092. Of what nature were they?
I am sorry to say that a great number of people have been killed. I think that out of from about 8,000,000 to 9,000,000 people carried, we have had one fatal accident. That is about the average. We carry over 10,000,000 people in a year out of a population of between 200,000 and 300,000. At first, serious accidents were more frequent than they are now. People have got into the way of observing that there are tramway cars in the streets, and that they ought to get out of their way. I could give several instances where the accidents have been occasioned more by the horses than by the cars. The horses get frightened when they find anything about their feet, or anything unusual.

1093. You mean the tram horses?
I mean the tram horses. Supposing one unfortunately happens to fall, the horses, when they feel anything about their feet, get restive, and as a rule bolt off, beyond the control of the driver.

1094. Were the fatal accidents of which you speak accidents to foot passengers crossing?
Wholly; or to parties entering the car at the end next to the driver, instead of at the proper end.

1095. Is it your intention to lengthen your tramway, and to enter fresh districts?
We have made various attempts on the earnest solicitations of various parties in the suburbs to extend the system, but we have failed. We have been unsuccessful in two attempts that we have made to get the necessary consent from the local and road authorities, and in consequence of that, notwithstanding the fact that the people in the district desire the extensions, we have failed to get them carried out.

1096. Those are objections which would not, I suppose, be removed if you used steam?
They would not; or at least, I assume not. But there would be this difference with regard to steam, that we might apply to Parliament without the consent of the local or road authority; and the question as to whether the use of steam-power should be permitted or not, would be a question for the Committee before which the application came. But at present we are required before we can extend a yard of tramway to get the consent of the local and road authorities, whether we proceed by Bill or by Provisional Order.

1097. Lord *Norton.*] Are the local authorities and the road authorities different, or are they the same?

In some districts they are the same, and in other districts they are different. There is a local authority in each instance, and there are in some of the districts separate road authorities.

1098. Are they both annually elected?
No.

1099. How often are they elected?
The local authority is elected every three years, although there is an annual election; that is to say, there are three representatives for each ward, so that each representative remains in office during three years; then one retires every year. The county road trustees remain in office after being elected.

1100. Are they also elected annually?
They are not elected annually.

1101. How long do they remain in office?
I am not aware of the provision in the Act with regard to that, but practically they are permanent; they are the county gentlemen, as a rule.

1102. Who appoints them?
I am not sure. I think the Commissioners of Supply. They are appointed under the Turnpike Act.

1103. They are not elected by the same electoral body as appoint the others?
I think they are appointed by the Commissioners of Supply.

1104. Which is the opposing body, the elected body or the nominee body?
The last attempt which was made was last year. We were very anxious to comply with the petitions from the various parties, and the road authorities objected to give their consent.

1105. But not the local authority?
The local authority did not object. In fact, when we were informed by the road authority that they would not give their consent, we withdrew the application to the local authority as being useless; as the year before we had been thrown out before the Standing Orders Committee, on account of not having had the necessary consents in regard, practically, to the same sections as those for which we applied; that is to say, a doubling of the line between Edinburgh and Portobello, and a short extension.

1106. Earl of *Redesdale.*] I suppose the objection of the road authority was because they considered the thing a nuisance on the road?
They gave no reason; they simply declined to give their consent; and we felt it all the more hard, because in our Act of 1871 we had got authority to make a double line; we believed that the traffic on that section would not require a double line, and we subsequently applied to Parliament and got power to make a single line. After a year or two's experience we found the traffic so great that we desired to have a double line; and they have declined, notwithstanding the fact that we had previously the authority to make a double line, to allow us to change the present single line into a double line.

1107. I suppose they considered that the single line was as much as the road could take without inconvenience to the other traffic upon it?
Quite the contrary, because that road is a very wide road all through.

1108. But what do you suppose was their reason for objecting?
I can give you the reason given by one of the trustees, and that was that they were afraid that mechanical power would be introduced if we had a double line.

1109. Lord *Norton.*] Why do they dislike that?
That is beyond our comprehension, because it is only the road authorities who appear to object; certainly it is not the public.

1110. *Chairman.*] Have you had complaints with respect to injuries sustained by private carriages or cabs, from their wheels getting locked in your rails?

We

We have had such complaints occasionally; but, on the whole, the complaints have not been very serious, although we have had to pay damages now and again on account of injuries sustained.

1111. Are you bound to keep up any part of the road over which you run?
We are bound to keep up the width originally laid down by the Company, which is 17 feet in the case of a double line; and we are obliged specifically to see that the stone is perfectly on a level with the rails, so that the street might be used without danger.

1112. Lord *Silchester*.] But do you do it?
Practically we do it. Sometimes the stones are out of order, and get down. We think now, however, that we have hit upon a system by which that would be overcome to a great extent. The objection hitherto has been that from the continual traffic of heavy vehicles passing along the rails, the stones get pressed down.

1113. *Chairman*.] Not by your carriages?
No, not by our carriages; they run on the rails. It is the ordinary traffic with broader wheels that grind away the edges of the stone next the rails; it is the other heavy traffic that does it. All the traffic, as a rule, seeks the tramway line, as being much more easy for drawing; and we think now that having got a rail with a broad base, so as to allow the edge of the stones to rest upon that, the objection is entirely overcome. I may state that we have got the whole of Princes-street laid with the new rail, and there is not the slightest evidence of the stones giving way, although they have been down more than six months. There is a small section of the rail in the room which your Lordships might see (*producing a part of a tramway rail*). That is a piece cut out of a tramway rail (*describing it*). Hitherto the tramway rails have always been laid down upon a longitudinal beam and spiked down, but from the continual traffic the spikes have got worn, and the nut works into the wood, and one great objection to tramways has been the loosening of the rail; but there is no probability of that now with such a rail as that.

1114. The top of the rail is flush with the street, is it not?
It is flush with the street.

1115. That you think will reduce the inconvenience to the other traffic to a minimum?
Very much; and in point of fact you may drive and cross and re-cross, and not feel that there are tramway rails there at all. I may state also that that rail is so solid that there is no probability of its giving way whatever weight may pass along it or over it.

1116. Earl of *Derby*.] Do you consider that a rail of this construction would prevent the wheel of a carriage catching in it?
Absolutely; the wheel of a carriage cannot get in there.

1117. So that the wrenching and twisting, which have been complained of, would be impossible?
Practicably impossible.

1118. Lord *Norton*.] Does not that groove get choked with mud, or ice, or snow?
We have an average of three men to every mile of line who are continually passing and repassing, and some of them have got an instrument by which they scoop out any mud or dust or stones that may collect in the groove.

1119. *Chairman*.] Supposing that you were to neglect your duty in maintaining the road, whose business would it be to enforce the performance of that duty upon you?
It would be the business of the city surveyor, or of the surveyor of the county road trustees; and I may state to your Lordships that, as a rule, we find that they do attend to their duty, and on their giving us notice we immediately put matters to rights.

1120. Lord *Norton*.] If you did not do so, what would the authorities do?
They are able to put it to rights themselves and charge us with the expense.

1121. Can they do that by Act of Parliament?
They can do that by Act of Parliament.
(15.)

1122. *Chairman*.] Has that ever taken place?

It has never taken place, because when a complaint has been made we have immediately put our men to work upon the particular section complained of.

1123. Is this rail that you now produce more expensive than the rail which you formerly used?

The expense is practically the same within 100 *l.*; I understand that the cost is 1,500 *l.* or 1,600 *l.* a mile; and the other rail, with spikes and chairs and timber, comes to between 1,400 *l.* and 1,500 *l.* a mile. The saving, we believe, will be in the maintenance, and there will be greater convenience to the public, and no obstruction to the streets. One great objection which has been often stated is the continual breaking up of the street, but that we believe will be very much lessened by the use of that rail.

1124. Does your company pay local rates?

They do.

1125. Upon what do you pay?

We pay upon income, and we pay upon property, and we pay upon the assessed value of the undertaking, just as railway companies do, as well as proprietors of heritages. Our rates are serious.

1126. But you pay no special highway rate; you have no other obligation, except the maintenance of that portion of the highway that you have spoken of?

Our annual obligations are the laying and maintenance of the highway, and the local and Imperial taxes.

1127. Have you any observation to make to the Committee with respect to the requirements at present enforced by the Board of Trade with regard to tramways?

On the whole, we think that the requirements of the Board of Trade are reasonable. If I might be permitted to make a suggestion (and it is borne out by actual experience), we think there ought to be an appeal to the Board of Trade on all matters of difference between the authorities and any tramway company, but more especially in cases where extensions are desired. That arises from the fact that local and road authorities may very often be influenced by other considerations than those merely relating to the merits of the particular undertaking. We feel that it would be of very great importance if the Legislature were so to arrange that we should have some dispassionate party to come in and say what should be done.

1128. Lord *Norton*.] Are you aware that the Board of Trade can overrule local opposition now if it is only to a certain amount?

They cannot overrule opposition in reference to an extension, but there is an absolute veto to any undertaking being promoted without the consent of the local and road authorities being first obtained. That was not so at first.

1129. If only two-thirds oppose, the Board of Trade can overrule the opposition, can they not?

That is so. But still we consider that if an undertaking is promoted by private Bill, instead of by Provisional Order, it would be only reasonable that the question of consent should be made a matter for the Committee than one of Standing Orders. Formerly we did not require the consent of the local and road authorities in promoting a Bill in Parliament; but now we do require it always, a Provisional Order being permissive legislation.

1130. Lord *Carlingford*.] Are the same consents required both in the case of a private Bill and a Provisional Order?

That is so; and that is the hardship which we feel, and which I have illustrated with respect to this particular section at Portobello. I omitted to mention that upon that section, although it is only three miles in length, we carry over a million of people a year; and I am perfectly certain that, if we had a double line, we should double that traffic. Portobello is a very desirable suburb, and a very great number of people doing business in Edinburgh reside there, while on Saturdays and holidays the ready access to a fine sea-beach makes it a very popular place of resort.

1131. You desire that upon a Report of the Board of Trade the Committees of Parliament should have a power of overruling the local authorities?

I would not say that it should be put in that way, but rather that whether the consents should be given or not should be matter for the consideration of the Committee on the Bill.

1132. *Chairman.*] And in the case of a Provisional Order you would wish that if there was a difference between the company and a local authority, there should be an appeal to the Board of Trade?

That might be. Still proceeding by Provisional Order is purely permissive, and it implies consent; but if an undertaking is desirable at all they may proceed by Bill, and then it should be considered upon the merits.

1133. Would you have any objection to the requirements of the Board of Trade with respect to having self-acting brakes and regulation of speed, and so forth, in the case of the use of steam?

No, with the exception probably of a recorder; and I am by no means sure as to a regulator of speed as well; one reason in regard to the regulator is that speed implies power in operation. At particular points, for instance in going from one line to another, very often greater power is required to be exercised than the speed would indicate, because they require to put on particular power just to get over a little difficulty. Therefore I am not quite sure that it would be a desirable thing to cut off the steam to a power, say, that would give 8 or 10 miles an hour, because that might prevent the vehicle passing over an obstruction, or passing from one line to another. There are points and crossings which sometimes may come in the way of the wheels, and a little more power may be required than would be ordinarily requisite.

1134. You are not using steam now, are you?

We are not. We are very anxious that your Lordships should consider the question favourably.

1135. Lord *Norton.*] In what year was your experiment made?

This last year and the year before.

1136. When it was made did the local authority take any part either in opposing or in approving of the experiment?

The local authority, as a body, never deliberated upon the matter. We, as a rule, gave an intimation to the superintendent of police that the experiments were to be made, and we endeavoured to get as many members of the authorities to see the experiments as possible, and a number of them did see them. I am not aware of any one occasion on which objections were stated. In point of fact there was a concurrence of opinion that the day would come when mechanical power would be allowed.

1137. Did the subject arise at all at the next election of one-third of the local authority?

I rather think not. The question whether steam should be allowed, or not, did not arise.

1138. Do you think that the notices given were such as to call general attention to the subject?

Yes; because almost every day after the trial had been made a paragraph appeared in the newspapers; and thousands of people looked on while the experiments were proceeding.

1139. What is the width of Princes-street?

It is about 50 feet wide, I think; it varies.

1140. Is the tramway in the middle of the street?

Quite in the centre of the street.

1141. *Chairman*] Have you two lines of rails in Princes-street?

We have.

1142. What is the distance between them?

Four feet. They are of the ordinary gauge, 4 feet 8½ inches. I may state that we have had a good deal of experience in reference to the effect of a single and a double line, and the result is that a double line of tramways, as a rule, is preferable to a single line, especially where there is a large amount of traffic; inasmuch as the two lines, instead of being objectionable, regulate the traffic,

(15.)	O	whereas

whereas a single line in a street of, say from 20 feet to 22 feet wide, is very inconvenient. We have one case of a double line where the street is only some 21 or 22 feet wide, and we find it not only no inconvenience, but a matter of great convenience that there are two lines. We have got a cross-over at short distances; so that in the event of carriages or vehicles standing before any door, the cars have simply to move on to the other line; and then they get on their own line again a few yards further on.

1143. Lord *Norton.*] What is the village that the tramway goes to? Portobello.

1144. Lord *Carlingford.*] Are those cross-overs very frequent? Wherever they are required we put them in; we have put them in over and over again in order to obviate any inconvenience whatever in that particular street to which I refer; they are put in quite conveniently.

1145. But are they frequent enough to enable the tramcar to avoid a shop-front with a carriage standing at it? They are put in at such places as convenience suggests. The principal streets of Edinburgh are fortunately wide.

1146. Lord *Norton.*] What is the width of the road at Portobello? Some parts of it 60 feet, 50 feet, and 40 feet; and in the villiage of Portobello itself, where we have only a single line, it is about 20 feet in some places.

1147. What space does that leave on each side? That leaves about 8½ feet on either side, outside the outer edge of the rail.

1148. *Chairman.*] Beyond the edge of your cars? The car is about 11 inches over the rail, so that the car leaves about a foot less than that.

1149. I do not understand what you mean by the double line of rails regulating the traffic of the street? I mean this; when two lines are in a very narrow street (and I may state that we have long sections with very narrow streets only about 21 or 22 feet in width), vehicles passing and re-passing on the two lines of a tramway, as a rule, follow the car; they know which is the up line and which is the down line, and in that way you have one line of traffic going one way and the other the other way; and it is much more convenient than it would be supposing the vehicles were attempting to pass on either side of the car, the car being in the centre.

1150. On a country road would you prefer to have the rails in the middle or on the side of the road? Undoubtedly in the middle.

1151. Why? Simply because of the convenience to traffic.

1152. Lord *Norton.*] For the purpose of keeping the up and down traffic on each side. For the purpose of keeping it on each side, or following the car. I may state that in a very crowded street in Leith we had only a single line. We had not so much experience at the outset as we have now, and we thought a single line in a very narrow street would be the best. Since that time we have very much regretted that we had not a double line; and the probability is that should we ever be permitted again to apply to Parliament, we may apply for power to make a double line in such places; in fact, it has been suggested to us over and over again that there should be a double line there.

1153. Lord *Carlingford.*] But with the tramrails on the side of the road, is it not the case that the other traffic will generally be able to keep more away from the tramcars than it would with the line in the middle of the road? No doubt; but to the exclusion of the traffic practically being on the side of the road on which the tramcars are.

1154. *Chairman.*] I understand you to say that the traffic generally goes along the tramway? Invariably, and especially the heavy traffic; and to such an extent that during the

the past few years the vehicles have been made so that the wheels should be on either rail fitting the 4 ft. 8½ in. gauge.

1155. So as actually to use your rails?

So as actually to use our rails, and especially where there are gradients, and that is particularly the case between Leith and Edinburgh, where there is very heavy traffic in machinery and heavy goods; and it is a great convenience to the general public apart altogether from the carriage of passengers.

1156. Lord *Norton.*] What was the cost of your steam engine?

The cost of the steam engine that we were to have got, if we had had the authority to use it, was 750 *l.*

1157. Was that the cost of the one you used in your experiment?

We have used several. The second one was to be 750 *l.*

1158. Was the experiment long enough to show you whether the wear and tear would be very considerable?

We did not see very much difference in the condition of the engine at the end of the experiments from what it was at the outset.

1159. How long do you think an engine would last in common use?

Of course an engine would require to be continually overhauled; but I am not engineer sufficient to answer that question.

1160. Lord *Carlingford.*] When I put my question I was not thinking of the use of the tram line during the absence of the tramcar, but of the case of vehicles meeting the tramcar; in that case there would be more space for other vehicles if you had the tram line upon one side of the road, would there not?

No doubt; but that would not give the general traffic the advantages of the tramway lines which are, in the way of the traction of heavy goods, very great.

1161. Lord *Norton.*] I suppose the kind of horses that are met with on the road to Portobello are omnibus horses and cart horses, and not carriage horses?

There are carriage horses.

1162. There are not many carriages on that road, are there?

A great many; that is one of the principal county roads; in point of fact I have seen very spirited horses passing along it.

1163. Earl of *Devon.*] Have you ever had accidents in Princes-street?

Yes, we have.

1164. Of what nature were they?

Unfortunately one passenger got in before a car and there was a fatal accident.

1165. I rather referred to accidents to be met with by carriages or horses meeting your cars?

We have had none of that nature.

1166. Of course along Princes-street a great many private carriages go, and a good many gentlemen probably are riding there at times?

A good many. There is probably more riding between Edinburgh and Portobello than along Princes-street, that being a country road.

1167. *Chairman.*] Is there anything else that you wish to state to the Committee?

No further than to repeat what I said in reference to tramway enterprise as a whole, that when it is proceeded with by way of Bill the consents should form part of the merits and be for the consideration of the Committee; and also in reference to the alleviations to horse flesh in the event of our being allowed to use mechanical power. These are very important considerations; and the fact of the immense traffic that the Edinburgh Tramway Company is now carrying shows the advantages of the system; I may also state that the assessable area of Edinburgh is being very much extended in respect of the extension of the system. These are reasons of course that I take the liberty of simply referring to, as reasons why the enterprise should not be retarded.

1168. Is it then your opinion that in the event of Parliamentary sanction being

(15.)   O 2   given

given to the use of steam upon tramways, it would be extensively used in large towns?

We have not the slightest doubt about it; and instead of there being an objection to steam as compared with horses, we think that the objections are against horses. I have myself seen the traffic in streets nearly as crowded as those in Edinburgh, between Paisley-road toll and Govan, where Hughes's engine is being worked continually; and the engines work there in quite an unobjectionable manner.

1169. Earl of *Redesdale.*] Do you consider that working by steam would be more economical than working by horses?

I am not aware that any one is able to form an opinion upon that yet; but we consider that the wear and tear of horse-flesh, and the expenses, are so great that surely mechanical power could be got at a less expense.

1170. *Chairman.*] Can you tell us what is your present cost of working by horses per mile?

About 8 *d.* per mile.

1171. Earl of *Derby.*] You say that the cost of the working is 8 *d.* per mile; how do you calculate that?

Eight pence per mile per car per day. Each car runs from 60 to 70, or 75 miles a day, and we calculate it in that manner. In fact, we check it in both ways, because we have got the expense of each individual horse, as well as of the whole; and we are able to check that with the number of miles run, and in that manner we can tell decidedly.

1171.* Lord *Norton.*] Do you know anything of the working of the Vale of Clyde Steam Tramway?

Yes, I know the particulars of the contract, and I am also aware of the manner in which generally they have worked.

1172. Has the Vale of Clyde steam tram worked satisfactorily?

Very satisfactorily, in so far as I have been able to ascertain. I myself am seldom in Glasgow without going down to see how they do work; and they certainly work on the whole, I should say, very satisfactorily.

1173. Do you know of any complaints having been made?

I am not aware that there have been any. I know that some parties objected to the emissions of the hot air to begin with; but that, I suppose, was incidental to the enterprise not having got into proper working order.

1174. *Chairman.*] Was there any emission of hot-air with the engine that you employed?

It was scarcely perceptible. We tested them very severely, as I have stated, and sometimes with very heavy loads, the uncondensed steam appeared; but there was no such emission of hot-air or steam as to be objectionable.

1175. Lord *Carlingford.*] Do you think that there would be any danger or serious difficulty with horses on country roads if steam were allowed to be used on tramways?

I do not think so, after a little time. I may state that we observed repeatedly that where we were passing the same horse for the first time, it did shy a little; but after two or three times the same horses pass without taking any notice; and as I stated, what occasioned their shying is more the driver's directing the attention of the horse to the engine than the horse itself taking notice of it.

The Witness is directed to withdraw.

Mr. WILLIAM DUNDAS SCOTT-MONCRIEFF, is called in ; and Examined,
as follows :

Mr.
Scott-Moncrieff.

1022. *Chairman.*] You are, I believe, an Engineer residing at Glasgow?
Yes.

1023. Have you had considerable experience in the science of practical
mechanical engineering ?
Yes.

1024. And especially in connection with prime movers ?
Yes.

1025. You have yourself, I believe, invented an engine, if it may be so called,
which works by a system of compressed air ?
Yes.

1026. Would you, without going into the scientific details of the question, explain to the Committee the results of the experience that has been had with
that engine?
This drawing (*producing a drawing*) will give your Lordships' Committee
some idea of the general arrangement of the engine.

1027. What are the results of the practical experience that has been had with
this machine of yours ?
In 1875 I made experiments upon the line of railway where I was first allowed
to run, and I was then allowed to run afterwards upon the Vale of Clyde Tramways ; and, I think, I may say that it was the success of those experiments which
led the Vale of Clyde Tramway Company to become the pioneers in the use of
mechanical power on tramways. They applied to Parliament in the Session of
1876 for power to use mechanical appliances upon their line, and this was
granted to them. They then advertised for competitors and after a series of com-
petitions I retired from the competition on the ground of expense, that is to say,
that the contract was taken on the Vale of Clyde line at a price that I did not
care to compete with. The Ibrox Tramway Company promoted a Bill in the
following year, and applied for the use of mechanical power, and in doing so the
local authority of Govan, which was the same local authority as the Vale of
Clyde Company had to deal with, confined their sanction to the use of my
invention. This was after they had some experience of the use of steam. In
the last Session of Parliament a power was given to use mechanical power upon
the Ibrox line ; and it was also understood between the promoters of that
tramway and Parliament that your Lordships' Committee should have the
benefit of any experiment that would be made in order to assit in this inquiry.
Unfortunately, however, as your Lordships are aware, it has been a very hard
winter in Scotland in more respects than one, and the frost retarded the formation of this line for about 13 weeks. I think I am justified in pointing to the
case of Pall Mall, where a similar obstruction took place, which may almost be
said to have interfered with the business of the country during the long continued frost. It is, however, the endeavour of the promoters of the Ibrox Tram-

(15.)   M 3   way

way to have their line completed as soon as possible, and that no doubt will be done in the course of a few weeks. At the same time, Messrs. Neilson & Co., who are my licensees, acting under my patent, are using all their endeavours to have an apparatus ready for the purpose of proving the invention upon that line.

1028. But, practically, there has been no experience of your machine upon the Ibrox Tramway?
There has not.

1029. Where has it been actually tried?
It was actually tried, under an agreement with the Vale of Clyde Tramway Company, in 1876.

1030. For how long was it used there?
It ran for a fortnight, carrying passengers at stated times according to a time bill.

1031. Did the company then return to the use of steam?
There is an explanation of the negotiations which took place at that time at page 59 of the Report of the Select Committee of the House of Commons of 1877, in which, for the reasons which I have already stated, they adopted the steam-engine.

1032. Has your system ever been tried in America?
I believe it has. I think that was stated in evidence by Mr. Small.

1033. He did not know whether it was your system or not?
I think there is very little doubt of its being my system, because it was conducted by a draftsman who was formerly in my employ in Glasgow. I have noticed in the English newspapers that it has been spoken of as the invention of two Scotch engineers of the name of Hardy and James. Mr. Hardy was my draftsman for two years.

1034. Will you state to the Committee what you consider to be the advantages of your invention over a steam-engine?
It is simple, efficient, and suited for traffic in crowded thorougfares, inasmuch as it is self-contained, and really takes up less room than an ordinary tramcar with horses attached to it. There is an entire absence of noise, smoke, or smell. The air which is used in this machine escapes as pure as it went in, so that there is no possibility of its making smoke or smell. There is a greater immunity, I believe, from explosion, because of the absence of all the elements of corrosion and of the weakening of the parts of a boiler which arise from the contraction and expansion of the parts from changes of temperature, and so on. In other words, an air vessel has no inherent causes of decay whatever.

1035. What is the longest distance you have ever run with your machine without refilling?
Four miles was the distance with the original car which was tried in the experiment to which I referred; but the car, of which there is now a drawing before your Lordships, will go six miles with one charge of air; and, as I stated in my evidence in 1877, if the principle which is advocated by such authorities on the subject as Sir Joseph Whitworth, were adopted, it would go a very much longer distance.

1036. Your pressure is not so great as that, is it?
It is only about one-third of that which is used in torpedo practice at Woolwich.

1037. The car is situated on the top of the engine, is it not?
Yes, everything is on the level of the floor.

1038. Earl of *Derby.*] Is there any noise?
No noise.

1039. *Chairman.*] Do you require a separate engine for each car, or would you draw two cars with one engine?
If it was arranged in that way, we could. I think it a disadvantage myself, on account of the additional room taken up in the street. It has been also pointed out to your Lordships' Committee, I think, by the manager of the
Metropolitan

Metropolitan Railway Company, that there was a considerable disadvantage at termini from the passage of the locomotive from one end of the vehicle to the other.

1040. Earl of *Derby*.] Does your car travel backwards and forwards?
Either backwards or forwards.

1041. *Chairman*.] Is it furnished with self-acting brakes?
It is to be furnished with self-acting brakes.

1042. There would be no difficulty in applying them to it, would there?
I expect no difficulty; I think it is a matter of great importance.

1043. Lord *Silchester*.] Is there an apparatus in the carriage to charge it, or does it require a fixed engine at certain stages to re-charge it?
It requires a fixed engine.

1044. The same as in the case of the electric light?
It is analogous to that.

1045. *Chairman*.] How long does it take to charge?
The time that I contemplate for large traffic is two and a-half minutes. It depends, practically, upon the arrangement of the pumping station whether the air is allowed to escape from large reservoirs, in which case the filling would be practically instantaneous, or whether it is supplied from the engine during the process of pumping. In America, I believe, the difficulties have been entirely overcome.

1046. Lord *Norton*.] Have you a fixed engine every four miles?
Every three or four miles in the case of a four-mile car, and every five miles in the case of a six-mile car, so as to allow a margin.

1047. Earl of *Redesdale*.] Has the thing ever broken down in working?
During that fortnight, which was the last occasion of its being on the road, it did not break down. The chief constable of Govan gave evidence before your Lordships on Thursday last about its having very nearly killed him, I think. That arose, I may say, from a fault of the rails: it was coming upon facing points which were not properly adjusted, and it ran across the pavement into a wall.

1048. *Chairman*.] Would that accident have occurred with a steam engine?
Quite so. It might no doubt have resulted in a serious accident, but, as it was, we were upon the rails, and running a short time afterwards.

1049. What is the weight of the engine and car?
I think one of the witnesses, Mr. Hughes, a gentleman connected with a steam-engine, spoke of his new engines being eight tons. The weight of this last car, which is capable of carrying 42 passengers, and going a distance of six miles, is 7 tons 15 cwt.; rather less than a single locomotive without a car.

1050. In a paper which I have before me, Mr. Hughes says that the weight of his engine is 7½ tons; that would be just about the same?
Yes, practically, about the same.

1051. I believe there has been a system of mechanical power in operation at Nantes?
I know nothing of it.

1052. It is not on your system?
No.

1053. Is there any other point which you wish to mention to the Committee.
I am interested in the construction of tramways, and I think that in the evidence which has come before your Lordships' Committee, it is made pretty clear that the tramway companies themselves would lose nothing at all by being required to construct their lines in a very thorough and efficient manner; and also on the question of maintenance, I should think that they would lose nothing in the long run by being called upon to maintain their lines in a very efficient manner; I think it would be well in the long run for tramway companies if the Board of Trade insisted upon some standard of construction which should be incumbent upon them; and I would say that the more power the local authority

(15.)   M 4   had

879

had to keep the tramways in a condition of thorough repair the better it would be for the tramways themselves in the end.

1054. Viscount *Cardwell.*] What do you mean by "insisting upon a standard of construction"?

The tramways that were constructed in the strongest manner in the earlier days of tramways failed from certain faults of construction, which have been discovered since; and the Board of Trade are in possession of a great number of facts with regard to that, and would no doubt be able to state whether or not a certain form of construction would in future be advisable or inadvisable in the case of new tramways.

1055. But would it not almost inevitably happen that if we had, we will say, to-day settled a standard of construction, you and other gentlemen would make such discoveries, that the next day there would be improvements, which everybody would think ought to be adopted?

But that is for the future, I think.

1056. Supposing that we desired, and the Board of Trade laid down, a standard of construction, would not that be merely laying down for to-day this thing that we knew of to-day, and to-morrow, as I suggested, might not other improvements be introduced which would cut at the root of that which was settled to-day?

Still for the time, I think, at which the proposal was made it would be the best thing in the interest of the public.

1057. I am assuming that you have hit upon the best thing that is known to-day; but you cannot positively lay that down as a standard without also preventing the march of improvement from suggesting better things to-morrow, can you?

I still think that there should be some standard. The Board of Trade might judge of what was not sufficient at any rate without perhaps saying what was.

1058. Then you would reduce your standard to a negative?

Perhaps so.

1059. Lord *Carlingford.*] Have you any opinion as to the part of the road upon which the train line had best be laid, whether on the side or in the middle?

I have seen the Wantage Tramway and travelled upon it; and it is perfectly clear that where there is such a margin as that it is the most suitable place for a tramway or any other such obstruction to be placed upon; because the margin is an addition to the road which is not practically used every day, and therefore it is the part of the road which would be practically available for such a thing as a tramway.

1060. But take the case of a road without a green margin, upon which part of the road would you prefer to lay the tramway?

I am not in a position from experience to say what I would advise in the country. In the town certainly I should think the centre of the road would be the most advisable part.

1061. Do you think that the danger of accidents to horses will prove to be any serious objection to the use of steam on tramways?

I think not.

1062. *Chairman.*] In your experience are horses frightened at your machine?

I did not notice much difference. I think that a horse is naturally timid at what it does not know, and has not seen before; it does not matter whether it is a steam engine or an air engine. Anything that is self-moving, and that is new, is startling to a horse. I noticed in the most crowded thoroughfares in Glasgow that horses were not in any way taken up with anything in particular.

1063. In what distance can your engine be pulled up?

In its own length?

1064. Earl *Cowper.*] We have heard of the tendency of the road to sink away from the rails; have you noticed that?

I have; and I think the only remedy for that is great insistence on the part of the

the local authority to see that the whole thing is kept up ; and I do not think the tramways will lose anything by doing that.

1065. Can you suggest a practical remedy that is not used now?
In the case of Govan, the local authority have paved from the part of the road which is kept up by the tramway company in to the kerb, so that that is, practically, the way of getting over any such difficulty as that; but where the road is partly macadamised and partly paved, which is not unfrequent with tramways, I know no practical remedy except constant repair and care.

1066. It would be better, then, that that part of the road should be paved ? No doubt.

1067. *Chairman.*] Do the local authority exercise control over the Vale of Clyde line in that respect?
They have laid out road trustee money upon paving right across, as they had the means to do so. I do not know if it is yet finished.

1068. But do the local authority keep the company in order; do they make them do their part of the work?
The Vale of Clyde line was a very well-constructed line, and I do not think it has yet been subjected to the test of wear.

1069. You are not aware that any inconvenience to other traffic has arisen there from the want of repair?
No, I should think not yet. That is a question of time.

The Witness is directed to withdraw.

Ordered, That this Committee be Adjourned to Thursday next,
Half-past Two o'clock.

Section 18

STATISTICS

Tramway Statistics 1875 to 1876

Name of Company.	Miles of line open.	Capital received.				Capital expended.			Number of Horses.	Number of Cars and Omnibuses.	Passengers carried.	Traffic.			
		Ordinary Shares. £	Preference Shares. £	Debentures and Loans. £	Total. £	Construction, Equipment, and Buildings. £	Horses. £	Total. £				Miles run.	Traffic Receipts. £	Receipts per Mile of Tram. £	Receipts per Mile run. £
NORTH METROPOLITAN.															
Half-year ending June 30, 1875	29¼	600,000	...	69,700	669,700	682,662	Horsed by L.G.O.Co.	682,662	...	164	13,488,354	1,714,917	112,372	3,809	15·73
" Dec. 31, 1875	30¼	600,000	...	80,200	680,200	684,566		684,566	...	168	14,267,563	1,841,767	121,894	3,996	15·89
" June 30, 1876	30¼	600,000	...	85,000	685,000	684,632		684,632	...	166	13,065,184	1,768,559	113,231	3,712	15·37
" Dec. 31, 1876	30¼	600,000	...	85,000	685,000	684,632		684,632	...	166	13,783,270	1,800,441	119,468	3,917	15·92
LONDON TRAMWAYS.															
Half-year ending June 30, 1875	20¼	250,000	80,000	94,700	424,700	362,116	50,208	412,324	1,209	139	7,583,400	1,224,272	67,661	3,399	13·50
" Dec. 31, 1875	20¼	250,000	80,000	99,750	429,750	368,957	49,708	418,665	1,157	145	8,207,567	1,273,371	70,389	3,543	13·51
" June 30, 1876	20¼	250,000	80,000	101,050	431,050	372,575	44,093	416,668	1,060	147	7,881,537	1,192,542	67,454	3,331	13·57
" Dec. 31, 1876	20¼	250,000	80,000	101,050	431,050	375,033	44,093	419,126	1,060	147	7,713,999	1,137,161	68,033	3,359	14·35
LONDON STREET TRAMWAYS.															
Half-year ending June 30, 1875	4½	90,490	...	37,300	127,790	132,925	16,308	149,233	400	48	2,575,320	330,174	20,714	4,602	15·05
" Dec. 31, 1875	5½	94,900	...	42,000	136,900	134,826	16,308	151,134	400	48	2,778,761	367,167	23,233	4,224	15·10
Year " Dec. 31, 1876	5½	100,000	...	40,750	140,750	137,028	16,538	153,566	400	48	5,620,880	772,598	46,829	8,514	14·55
GLASGOW TRAMWAYS.[1]															
Half-year ending June 30, 1875	15	287,644	...	...	287,644	235,599	25,950	261,549	865	139	...	845,306	54,744	3,649	15·54
" Dec. 31, 1875	15	287,644	...	...	287,644	239,324	32,375	271,699	925	149	...	913,536	63,010	4,200	16·55
" June 30, 1876	15	287,654	...	...	287,654	272,410	43,563	315,973	1,180	182	...	1,074,528	67,579	4,505	15·09
" Dec. 31, 1876	15	287,654	...	...	287,654	288,981	51,177	340,158	1,368	197	...	1,235,832	75,006	5,000	14·56
EDINBURGH TRAMWAYS.														Including omnibus receipts.	
Half-year ending June 30, 1875	13	149,060	...	40,450	189,510	195,053	12,979	208,032	407	43	Special circumstances.	352,738	26,030	2,002	17·71
" Dec. 31, 1875	13	149,540	...	45,500	195,040	198,317	16,017	214,334	478	41		415,031	29,603	2,277	17·11
" June 30, 1876	13	149,550	...	40,262	189,812	200,761	17,834	218,595	482	48		...	28,904	2,223	..
" Dec. 31, 1876	13	149,720	...	40,130	189,850	203,883	16,903	220,762	457	48		...	31,622	2,433	..
DUBLIN TRAMWAYS.															
Half-year ending June 30, 1875	15	239,956	...	15,000	254,956	235,827	17,258	253,085	486	79	2,734,807	495,137	33,152	2,210	16·06
" Dec. 31, 1875	15	240,000	...	15,000	255,000	235,827	16,088	251,915	456	85	3,049,925	543,587	36,738	2,449	16·22
" June 30, 1876	15	240,000	...	15,000	255,000	235,827	17,971	253,798	500	79	2,904,592	...	35,120	2,341	..
" Dec. 31, 1876	15	240,000	...	15,000	255,000	235,827	17,364	253,191	486	81	3,160,045	...	38,129	2,542	..
CARDIFF TRAMWAYS.									Special circumstances.						
Half-year ending June 30, 1875	2½	35,000	...	...	35,000	32,747	1,680	34,427	56	12	490,627	59,992	4,088	1,635	16·35
" Dec. 31, 1875	2½	35,000	...	...	35,000	32,847	1,680	34,527	55	12	632,159	66,874	5,667	2,106	18·90
PORTSMOUTH TRAMWAYS.															
Half-year ending June 30, 1875	3	42,514	...	...	42,514	40,624	1,890	42,514	63	12	489,282	76,045	3,440	1,146	10·86
" Dec. 31, 1875	3	42,625	...	...	42,625	40,735	1,890	42,625	63	12	432,448	82,160	3,994	1,331	11·54
PLYMOUTH TRAMWAYS.															
Half-year ending June 30, 1875	1¾	33,833	...	...	33,833	31,483	2,400	33,883	76	12	836,863	63,002	4,748	2,713	17·13
" Dec. 31, 1875	1¾	35,921	...	...	35,921	33,521	2,400	35,921	82	12	734,489	68,427	5,469	3,125	19·18

[1] Under special arrangements.

TRAMWAY STATISTICS—*concluded.*

Name of Company.	Working Expenses. Working and General Expenses including Track Repairs.	Working Expenses. Per Mile of Tram.	Working Expenses. Per Mile run.	Working Expenses. Track Repairs.	Working Expenses. Per Mile of Tram.	Percentage of Working Expenses to Gross Receipts.	Dividends, Ordinary Shares. Per cent.	Dividends, Ordinary Shares. Total.
	£.	£.	d.	£.	£.			
NORTH METROPOLITAN.								
Half-year ending June 30, 1875	84,748	2,872	11·85	2,362	80	73⅔	8	24,000
,, ,, Dec. 31, 1875	91,194	2,990	11·91	2,387	78	73⅛	8½	25,500
,, ,, June 30, 1876	88,604	2,905	12·02	2,467	81	76⅓	8	24,000
,, ,, Dec. 31, 1876	89,269	2,927	11·89	4,271	140	73	9	27,000
LONDON TRAMWAYS.								
Half-year ending June 30, 1875	60,702	2,975	11·81	1,063	52	..	nil	..
,, ,, Dec. 31, 1875	63,109	3,116	11·89	1,549	75	87¾	..	..
,, ,, June 30, 1876	66,192	3,268	13·32	2,919	144	96⅓	..	..
,, ,, Dec. 31, 1876	51,597	2,548	10·88	1,694	84	75¾	3	3,750
LONDON STREET TRAMWAYS.								
Half-year ending June 30, 1875	16,171	3,593	11·75	550	122	..	7½	2,892
,, ,, Dec. 31, 1875	18,689	3,308	12·21	518	94	..	7	3,321
Year ,, Dec. 31, 1876	37,081	6,742	11·51	1,246	226	80¼	6	5,936
GLASGOW TRAMWAYS.[1]								
Half-year ending June 30, 1875	44,469	2,964	12·62	..	..	..	nil	..
,, ,, Dec. 31, 1875	49,422	3,294	12·98	..	..	76½	3	4,375
,, ,, June 30, 1876	52,164	3,477	11·65	..	..	75	3	4,375
,, ,, Dec. 31, 1876	56,530	3,768	10·97	..	..	74	4	5,833
EDINBURGH TRAMWAYS.								
Half-year ending June 30, 1875	19,522	1,501	13·28	664	51	..	6	4,500
,, ,, Dec. 31, 1875	22,499	1,730	13·01	1,031	79	..	6	4,500
,, ,, June 30, 1876	24,601	1,893	..	708	54	82½	4	3,000
,, ,, Dec. 31, 1876	22,498	1,730	..	1,689	130	70	8	6,000
DUBLIN TRAMWAYS.								
Half-year ending June 30, 1875	24,741	1,649	11·99	1,137	76	73½	6	7,200
,, ,, Dec. 31, 1875	25,079	1,672	11·07	1,404	93	67	8	9,600
,, ,, June 30, 1876	23,919	1,593	..	1,740	116	67	8	9,600
,, ,, Dec. 31, 1876	25,492	1,699	..	2,243	149	66	9	10,800
CARDIFF TRAMWAYS.								
Half-year ending June 30, 1875	3,320	1,328	13·28	67	26·8	about 68	10	750
,, ,, Dec. 31, 1875	3,360	1,344	12·05	113	45·2			1,750
PORTSMOUTH TRAMWAYS.								
Half-year ending June 30, 1875	3,077	1,025	9·57	57	19	about 83	3	350
,, ,, Dec. 31, 1875	3,122	1,040	9·11	17	5·6			650
PLYMOUTH TRAMWAYS.								
Half-year ending June 30, 1875	4,330	2,474	16·49	57	32·57	about 85	4½	400
,, ,, Dec. 31, 1875	4,567	2,617	16·01	53	30·30			800

[1] Under special arrangements.

[MR. HUNTINGTON

Steam Tram Costings in 1880

The majority of locomotives (27 from 29) used on the Strasbourg (Strassburg) standard gauge lines came from the Swiss locomotive works at Winterthur, and were built to Brown's Patent from 1877 to 1886, most surviving until electrification by 1904. In 1880 the operational costs were remarkably favourable towards steam compared with horse traction, but this was claimed to be more due to the nature of the traffic (6-8 engines required during the week. 12 on Sundays) and the ability of the company, having 40-50% of the fleet spare in the week, to keep up maintenance standards.

The costs in percentages per day were:

Depreciation and interest on loan	24.1%
Repairs and cleaning	19.1%
Coke and coal	25.2%
oil, tallow and packing	7.5%
Drivers' wages	24.1%
Total	100%

In 1880 this was roughly the equivalent of £1 for 50 miles or 5d per mile.

The equivalent figures for a year's horse working on the Hamburg and Wandsbeck Tramway are interesting, partly for the proportions of the expenditure:

Stable staff	13.32%
Stable, cleaning materials etc.	1.80%
Oats	17.56%
Maize	21.85%
Hay	12.42%
Sundry forage	6.61%
Straw	4.84%
Sawdust	2.79%
Shoeing	5.57%
Harness	1.11%
Depreciation of horses	8.56%
Depreciation of stables	0.79%
Interest on money expended on horses	2.78%
Total	100%

Although the sales of manure reclaimed 2½% of the total.

In daily terms steam cost 29.50 shillings, horse 40.70, thus in theory the horse tram cost 38% more than steam, but steam power had a far greater haulage capacity, so if the trailers were full (100-120 persons) this figure rose to around 65%, an argument which must have weighed heavily with English steam tramway promoters.

Statistics Can Tell the Truth

Obviously, as this series of books relates to, and is about, steam trams so accidents mentioned tend to involve steam trams. But as most were pretty horrible this can give an entirely wrong impression; much as today an accident on the railways gets publicity all out of proportion to the daily deaths on motorways.

The town is Birmingham,* where there was a strong caucus in favour of the abolition of steam trams (or sometimes it seemed, any form of public transport) and on 4 October 1887 in a laudable attempt to quantify the number of accidents the Council agreed under Minute 14529 *"That the report of the Public Works Committee be approved, and that it be an instruction to the Watch Committee to present to the Council a Quarterly Return, as complete as possible, of the Casualties incidental to Street Traffic occurring in the Borough a distinction being made between those in connection with Steam Trams and General Accidents."* This motion was carried. Unfortunately it has not proved possible to obtain a complete set of these figures, but enough have survived to give a good idea of just how dangerous Birmingham streets were – and how few accidents involved tramcars of all types.

The descriptions used need a little clarification. Steam trams included the Birmingham and Aston, Birmingham and Midland and Birmingham Central tramcars etc working an intensive service. Cable covered only the line to and from Hockley while electric, initially at least, referred to the accumulator (battery) cars running from Bournbrook to the City centre.

---

*Birmingham became a city when this was agreed to by Queen Victoria in a letter dated 10 December 1888.

On 19 March 1889 the Chief Constable first reported that, "In compliance with Council Minute 14529 ... casualties coming to the knowledge of the police are as follows:

1888		Quarter ending September 30	Quarter ending December 31
Accidents by steam trams		12	8
Accidents by cable trams		1	-
Accidents by other vehicles		80	87
Totals		93	95

1889	Quarter ending 31 March	Quarter ending 30 June	Quarter ending 30 Sep.	Quarter ending 31 Dec.	1889 Total
Steam	7	9	9	7	32
Cable	-	2	1	3	
Other	51	78	81	70	280
Totals	58	87	92	78	315

1890	Quarter ending 31 March	Quarter ending 30 June	Quarter ending 30 Sep.	Quarter ending 31 Dec.	1890 Total
Steam	8	13	11	11	43
Cable		2	2	-	4
Electric		-	-	-	-
Other vehicles	68	85	82	82	317
Totals	76	100	95	93	364

Accidents involving trams, not necessarily fatal

In 1890 there were demands by a couple of councillors who, as it were, were getting their feet under the table, for more details showing the companies concerned. However for some reason after 1891 either quarterly figures were not reported or cumulative statistics were acceptable.

		Steam	Electric	Cable	Others	Totals
1891	B&M	14				
	Central	34	5	1	290	346
	B&A	2				
1892	B&M	6				
	Central	23	2	3	300	337
	B&A	3				
1893	B&M	1				
	Central	20	3	1	353	380
	B&A	2				
1894	No figures available					
1895	B&M	2				
	Central	26	2	6	387	425
	B&A	2				

"Two of the accidents by steam trams and eleven of the accidents by other vehicular traffic proved fatal"

		Steam	Electric	Cable	Others	Totals
1896	B&M	4				
	Central	21	2	1	510	539
	B&A	1				
1897	B&M	7				
	CBT*	29	2	10	529	579
	B&A	2				
6 months ending 31.3.98	B&M	6				
	CBT	16	0	13	248	287
	B&A	4				
12 months ending 31.12.90	B&M	10				
	CBT	34	1	16	554	621
	B&A	6				
9 months to 29.9.99	B&M	5				
	CBT	25	1	6	397	437
	B&A	3				
9 months to 30.6.00	B&M	2				
	CBT	25	1	8	347	384
	B&A	1				
6 months to 31.12.00	B&M	3				
	CBT	5	2	6	323	340
	B&A	1				

*Central became City of Birmingham Tramways from 15 October

Date	Location	Loco No.	Builder	Persons Hurt	Damage & Notes
16 June 1889	near Royton Depot	88	Beyer Peacock horizontal boilered engine W/no. 2738 1886 (not Wilkinson	None	Thin tube (1/32") ruptured and collapsed. Rupture 6" long by 1" wide. "The driver says the engine was working well, and he did not observe any escape of steam until the tube burst, when at once he applied the engine-brake and leaped from the car. Fortunately the car was open at both sides and thereby afforded ready means of escape from the contents of the boiler. Had the car been closed at the sides, and glazed in a similar manner to some belonging to the Tramways Company, it is almost certain that the driver would have been severely scalded, seeing that the dimensions of the fracture in the tube were such as to admit of a large volume of steam and water to escape."
14 October 1889	Heywood Market Place	72	Beyer Peacock Wilkinson Patent W/No. 2722 1886	None	Thin tube (1/16") ruptured and collapsed. Rupture 4¾" long x 1¾" wide which put out the fire. "The driver and the public were fortunate in having escaped without injury, but, seeing that these tramway engines traverse the public thoroughfares, it is especially important that every precaution should be taken to prevent the recurrence of such explosions."
28 December 1889	Ashton Road, Oldham	91	Beyer Peacock 4-cylinder compound horizontal boiler. 1887. Note: withdrawn 1900 and sold to tea plantation in Rangoon	Driver Jospeh Bond "slightly scalded in the face"	Thin tube ruptured. Rupture about 5" long. Not a popular engine and had only travelled 38,215 miles in three years. Joseph Bond, the engine-driver, said: "I left Royton depot in charge of No.91 engine at 8.25am on the 28th December last. At 9.15am I heard the report of a tube bursting, and at once turned on the blower and applied the steam-brake. I then went to the smoke-box end of the engine and applied the hand-brake, thus stopping the engine. When the explosion occurred the furnace door was shut, but the steam and flame came up from the ashpan and scalded my face. The engine was pushed on to Royton depot by the car which followed about half an hour afterwards, when I went to the Tramway Company's medical officer and had my face attended to. The pressure of steam on the boiler when the tube exploded was 150 lbs."
17 February 1892	Manchester Street, Oldham	87	Beyer Peacock horizontal boilered engine W/no. 2737, 1886 (not Wilkinson)	None	Thin tube ruptured. Rupture about 4" on the fire side of the tube. Tube collapsed. "Tubes in boilers of this description commonly fail from the cause assigned in the prsent instance. The action upon the metal of the sulphurous gases produced by the combustion of the coke is well known, and, if of soft quality, brass tubes cannot resist this action for a very lengthened period, especially when subjected to the intense heat produced by a coke fire. From this point of view it would be well to employ metal of a harder nature, which would also be more able to resist the abrasion due to the passage of pieces of fuel, &c. Such tubes most frequently give way when the engine is standing, for the pressure then generally rises, and it is often found necessary, if other means of regulating it are not fitted, to check the draught by opening the fire-door; the cold air which is thus admitted causes a change of temperature, which is detrimental to the tube."

	1888	1889	1890	1891	1892	1893	1894	1895	1896	1897	1898	1899*	1900	1901
Accidents involving steam trams	20	32	43	50	32	23	-**	30	26	38	50	44	37	51
Accidents involving cable & electric trams	1	3	4	6	5	4	-	8	3	12	17	9	12	21
Accidents involving other road vehicles	167	280	317	290	300	353	-	387	510	529	554	582	563	636

*1899/1900 estimates based on 9-months' figures. All other years drawn from Public Works Department or from 1900 Tramway Committee Minutes, and/or figures reported to and by the police. ** 1894 – no figures available.

Date	Location	Loco No.	Builder	Persons Hurt	Damage & Notes
9 September 1892	Gigg Lane, Machester Road, Bury	8	Wilkinson engine, rebuilt by Thos Green, Original Wilkinson boiler. 1883.	None	Field tube ruptured 1" from the bottom. "One of the Field tubes at the bottom, or hemispherical end allowing the water and steam to escape and put out the boiler fire... The explosion occurred in consequence of the tube having become too thin to sustain the ordinary working pressure to which it was subjected... As previously stated the engine was standing when the explosion occurred, therefore it may be assumed that the steam within the boiler had risen to the maximum pressure to which the safety-valves were loaded, and, having regard to the wasted condition of the tube it is not surprising that the explosion occurred."
29 October 1892	Market Place, Heywood	75	Beyer Peacock 1886. W/no. 2725, 1886. Wilkinson Patent.	None	Field tube burst "with a report of a gun". Rupture 4½" x 1¾"."The explosion was caused through the lower part of the tube having been reduced by the action of the fire and corrosion from the original thickness of 1/8" to about ½" in the locality of the opening and in that condition it was unable to withstand the pressure of steam at the time in the boiler... The tube which had exploded had wasted more or less from the top to the bottom, but most at the lower part in the locality of the rent where, as before stated, its thickness was no more than ½", and on weighing this tube its weight was found to be 3 lbs. 14oz., and that of a similar tube but, new, was 6lbs. 2oz., thus showing that a great amount of wasting had been going on during the three years it had been in use."
28 November 1892	Hathershaw Bank	52	Manning-Wardle W/no. 850. Built 1883. Entered service 1885. Horizontal boiler.	David Richardson, driver, slightly injured by jumping off engine.	Brass tube ruptured 4" from fire-box end; water and steam drowned out fire. This is another case in which one of the smoke tubes in the boiler of a tramway engine became so thin from wear at the fire-box end as to be unable to resist the ordinary working pressure. The tube in question collapsed and ruptured, but no bodily injury resulted except to the driver who hurt himself slightly by jumping from the engine. The results, however, might have been serious, as the engine ran down an incline and collided with a car which was standing at the terminus situated about 300 yards from the place where the explosion occurred.
21 May 1893	Whitefield Terminus	8	Wilkinson engine, rebuilt by Thos Green, Original Wilkinson boiler. 1883.	Thomas Simpson, driver, was scalded on the face, legs and hands (had recovered two weeks later)	One Field tube gave way at the bottom and the whole of the tube end was blown out, putting out the fire. The explosion was due to the deterioration of the metal resulting from the overheating and burning of the tube end, owing to the pressure of a deposit of hard scale in the bottom of the tube.
18 October 1893	Ashton Road, Oldham	84	Beyer Peacock, W/no.2734, 1886. Wilkinson Patent. 1905, sold after tramway closed, to Ince Forge Co. Ltd. Became their "Ant". Semi-preserved at NTM, Crich	James Greenwood, driver, died from injuries received by scalding and falling down on the road between the engine-carriage and tramcar	One of the iron screwed and riveted stays supporting the fire-box, and situated in the lower back tier, decayed in the body and got broken. It then became defective in the screwed threads at the plate in the fire-box and was forced out of its position by the internal pressure, thus leaving a hole ⅞" in. diameter in the plate. The escaping water and steam, along with the coke fire on the bars, were blown out through the firing hole where the unfortunate driver was standing... According to the evidence, the conductor and the driver were both on the engine-car at the time of the explosion, the driver being close to the firing hole of the boiler. The conductor, being on the opposite side of the boiler, put on the engine-brake to endeavour to stop the engine and the car, and then managed to jump off without sustaining injury. The driver, in attempting to escape from the cloud of steam in which he was enveloped, seems to have fallen down on the road between the engine-carriage and tramcar. Seeing that he had received very serious injuries he was removed to the infirmary at Oldham, where he died about two days afterwards.

St. Helen's & District Tramways Company,

LIMITED.

Incorporated under the Companies' Acts, 1862 to 1886.

Issue of 15 First Mortgage Debentures of £1,000 each.

Interest payable half-yearly, 13th Nov. and 13th May

No. 3

DEBENTURE. £1,000.

1. THE ST. HELEN'S AND DISTRICT TRAMWAYS COMPANY, LIMITED (hereinafter called "the Company"), will pay to *the Law Guarantee and Trust Society Company Limited* to whom this Debenture is issued, or other the Registered Holder or Holders for the time being hereof (all of whom are intended to be included in the expression "the Debenture Holder" when used herein), the principal sum of ONE THOUSAND POUNDS upon the 24th July, 1900, or upon such earlier day as it may become payable in accordance with the Conditions endorsed hereon. And also until payment of such principal moneys will pay to the Debenture Holder interest at the rate of FOUR POUNDS FIVE SHILLINGS per cent. per annum on the said sum by half-yearly instalments on the 13th day of November and the 13th day of May in each year.

2. And the Company hereby charges with such payments the undertaking of the Company, and all its property, present and future, for the time being; and also charges with such payments the net proceeds of any sale to be made under section 43 or section 44 of the Tramways Act, 1870, or any statutory substitute therefor, or modification thereof respectively.

3. And it is hereby declared that this Debenture is issued upon and subject to the Conditions endorsed hereon, which are to be deemed part of it.

GIVEN under the Common Seal of the ST. HELEN'S AND DISTRICT TRAMWAYS COMPANY, LIMITED, this 13th day of May, 1895.

Rev. J. P. Gross }
W. P. Withnell } Directors.
L. F. Butler — Secretary.

D9194

GUARANTEE.

THE LAW GUARANTEE AND TRUST SOCIETY, LIMITED (hereinafter called "the Society"), acknowledges that the within Debenture was subscribed for on condition and in part consideration that the Society would give the guarantee following, and accordingly the Society hereby guarantee to the Registered Holder of the within Debenture (which expression in this guarantee means the person or persons within named, or other the Registered Holder or Holders for the time being of the within Debenture), the payment of the principal moneys and interest to become due under the said Debenture in manner following, that is to say :—

1.—If the Company makes default in the payment of the principal moneys or any part thereof, or if the Company makes default in payment of any interest and the Debenture Holders or Debenture Holder shall give to the Society notice requiring repayment of the principal sum and interest due under the within Debenture, the Society will pay the amount upon whichever of the days following shall first happen, viz. :—(a) six calendar months after the date of the above-mentioned notice (b) on the 24th day of July, 1900, within mentioned, or (c) on the day after the security for the Debenture Holders of the series to which the within Debenture belongs shall have been enforced and completely realised and distributed, so far as regards the holder of the within Debenture.

2.—At any time after the Company shall have made default for more than fourteen days in the payment of any of the said principal moneys or interest, the Society may, by notice in writing to the Debenture Holder, call on him to transfer to the Society the within Debenture and all his rights thereunder, and the Debenture Holder shall be bound to comply with such demand on payment of the full amount of the principal moneys and interest then owing in respect of such Debenture.

3.—If the Company makes default for more than thirty days in the payment of any principal moneys or interest secured by the within Debenture, the Debenture Holder must give notice in writing of such default to the Society, as to interest, within six calendar months after the default, and as to principal, within twelve calendar months after the default.

IN WITNESS WHEREOF the Society have caused these presents to be signed by two of the Directors and the General Manager this day of 1895.

For and on behalf of THE LAW GUARANTEE AND TRUST SOCIETY, LIMITED,

Directors.

General Manager.

The principal sum of One thousand Pounds due under this Debenture with all interest thereon has been paid.

Dated the 11th day of May 1894.

THE COMMON SEAL OF THE LAW UNION & CROWN FIRE & LIFE INSURANCE COMPANY, affixed in the presence of

J. W. Watney }
Scott } Directors.

Section 19

Higher Fares

HIGHER FARES.

A careful observer will have recognised that at the present time many signs are pointing to the fact that a great deal of good work is being done and a great many useful services rendered either for a very inadequate return or else for no return at all.

The published figures of the Imports and Exports show large expansion and this is seized upon as a fact in their favour by those whose political interest it is to maintain that trade in the country is booming, but the traders themselves look in vain for the corresponding increase in the profits which such expansion ought to show. The fact is that there is a sort of mad desire passing over the country for getting things cheaper than it is commercially possible to supply them.

The statistics of the Post Office show that the number of letters and parcels handled has enormously increased and yet the profit has not expanded to any extent. This in a Government monopoly, where other trades are not affected, may not be a bad thing in itself, but the example has its effect upon the municipalities who carry passengers on their tramways at unremunerative fares. The consequence of this is that carriers of passengers who have to work their undertakings on commercial lines are prejudicially affected, outrageous claims are made on behalf of the working classes that railway companies shall be compelled to carry them at fares which do not cover working expenses.

If this vicious principle is allowed to extend it means that the effort required to produce a given effect has now to be doubled or trebled with the absolute certainty that the machine, human or otherwise, putting forward the effort will be worn out in a correspondingly shorter time. Cheapness may be purchased too dearly.

There are signs, however, of an awakening to the necessity of resisting the modern tendency and that a determined effort will be made to insist upon the purchaser paying such a price for the article or service as will yield the provider a fair return upon his work and money, and it behoves the B.E.T. Companies to be amongst the first to take advantage of this movement.

Given that a tramway company has been fairly and moderately capitalised and that the management is brought as near to perfection as is possible, which ought to apply to all the Associated Companies, then if a fair return is not being earned upon the capital invested it follows that the fares charged are too low. There is no getting away from it; and the fares must be increased. There are objections, no doubt, local and otherwise, but they can in most cases be got over.

Mr. Garcke has put the case with great force when he points out that if the 300,000,000 passengers now carried by the Associated Companies could be made to pay one farthing more per journey each, the result would be a net increased profit of over £300,000. The average fare per passenger in what may be called the horse period of tramways was 1·84d., this fell to 1·23d. in the steam period and is now, under electric traction, down to 1·10d. So that, in spite of the increased capital cost of providing a service better in every way than that given in the horse or steam days, the fare charged has been greatly reduced.

A determined attempt should be made to bring this average fare up, and although it may not be possible in every case to increase the fare on each stage, it can be increased on some of the stages; in other cases the stages can be shortened, and again long stages can be sub-divided. Each case must be carefully considered, and it is hoped in a short time to have a full discussion of each company's proposals for dealing with this urgent matter.

Birmingham Post, 1 December 1884:

"THE TRAMWAYS – WAITING ROOMS.

Dear Sir, We are all exceedingly thankful for the extensive provision made for our wants by the tramway system ... But will you allow me to call attention to a serious want, which I know is felt by a great many of the public? This is of a waiting room at the tramway terminus at Old Square. If the companies would be good enough to provide this, I have no doubt they would be rewarded by an increase of passengers, many of whom still prefer using the 'buses, simply because the accommodation of a waiting room is connected with them.

Yours etc. VIATOR"

Timetables

The use of single-line working always inhibits fast movement of traffic – anyone faced with 'temporary' traffic lights blocking one lane of a two-lane highway will concur with this!

In many cases, particularly on tramways geared to horse-drawn tramway characteristics, loops or passing-places were so badly laid out that neither driver could see the other and then strict adherence to a timetable was required, although tales abound of an ensemble waiting for another only to find that for whatever reason his 'mate' was cancelled. Had he known, time and much passenger grief could have been obviated. In the early days one advantage put forward in the retention of horse tramways was their ability when faced with an obstruction to 'jump' the car out of its grooves and to drive along the setts stating, rightly, that this cannot be done with a steam tram and trailer. But in the same magazine it was (almost casually) mentioned that out of the London General Omnibus Company's 8,000 horses, 1,000 were destroyed annually and another 700 were 'broken down'.

Where loops were placed at reasonably equal distances, and as the engines grew more reliable, so closer timings became possible and after a few years service some (although not all) councils proved amenable to passing loops being relocated or supplemented. A twist on the tale of this traffic management was commonplace in tramway days whereby although there might be two sets of rail, extra points (switches) could be required by the Councils or the Board of Trade so that the engine and trailer could pass from the 'up' to the 'down' line and back again in order to clear market or traders' carts or wagons which, although a useful manoeuvre for a rail bound vehicle (and one commonly used in old British Rail days to pass permanent way works or a failed train) was nonetheless time consuming.

And, of course, we must never forget that where a tramway was always steam operated, without horses as predecessors, the company secretary, already knee deep in paperwork had to, in effect, take a guess what kind of service he could maintain ... if the engines did what they were supposed to do ... if nothing broke ... if the engineman was 'on his toes' ... and without fixed stops (other than those required by the Board of Trade) in the hope passenger flows were as they ought to be ... then maybe a timetabled service could be run. Two letters from the Wolverhampton Express & Star show how the hapless Dudley, Sedgley and Wolverhampton came unstuck, although they had at least published a timetable. However, alas, I have not been able to trace a copy of this.

"14 January 1886. Dudley, Sedgley, and Wolverhampton Tramways. Sir, I understand the steam trams will commence running upon

DUDLEY, SEDGLEY, AND WOLVERHAMPTON
TRAMWAYS.
TIME TABLE.

	WEEK DAYS.	SUNDAYS.

Tram Cars leave Dudley as follows :—

Morning : (8.0 on Wednesday and Saturday mornings only) 9.0 10.15 11.30

Afternoon : 12.45 2.0 3.15 4.30 (5.45 and 7.0 Workmen's Cars) 8.15 9.30 (10.45 Saturdays and Mondays only) | 2.0 3.15 4.30 / 5.45 7.0 8.15 / 9.30

Leave Wolverhampton—Morning : 7.0 Workmen's Car—8.5 on Wednesday and Saturday mornings only—9.0 10.15 11.30

Afternoon : 12.45 2.0 3.15 4.30 — 5.45 and 7.0 Workmen's Cars — 8.15 9.30 — 10.45 on Saturdays only | 2.0 3.15 4.30 / 5.45 7.0 8.15 / 9.30

FARES :

DUDLEY	to	Tram Depôt at Sedgley	2d.
,,	,,	Bull Ring, Sedgley	3d.
,,	,,	Fighting Cocks	4d.
,,	,,	Wolverhampton	5d.

this line on Saturday or Monday next; but at present no official time-table, or list of fares, and stopping stations are before the public. The management of this line now steam is introduced is a matter which concerns all the inhabitants of Wolverhampton, and the Blakenhall and Goldthorn-hill section in particular. Is it right or just that the company should carry men from Sedgley and back (six miles) for threepence, and charge others sixpence for two and a quarter miles? There is no first and third class carriages or accommodation. Blakenhall, and Goldthorn-hill, and Fighting Cocks district are practically boycotted by such unfair charges, and unless some alteration is made I, along with others, shall agitate for stopping the traffic at the Fighting Cocks when the six months granted by the Corporation terminate. Why should not the interests of Wolverhampton be considered as well as that of Sedgley, Gornal, and Dudley? Why should we have steam trams in the borough at all, if we are to derive no benefit? Is there any valid reason why the line should not be conducted upon the penny stage principle? It is so conducted upon nearly all lines that are paying. Surely the directors must be very simple to suppose people will pay just what they like to demand, or that by charging the uttermost farthing, and cutting off hundreds of passengers day by day, they will ever secure a profit, or make the line a benefit to others? What is wanted are cheap fares, punctuality, and civility; and if this is not the motto of the company, the sooner the line is closed the better. C.J.DAVIDSON, 16 Shaw-road."

And on 19 January 1886 when the temperature in Wolverhampton never rose above 40.5°F (4.8°C) and dropped for most of the day and night to a max of 30.3° F (−1°C), the wind was Northerly, fresh (and they say Wolverhampton is the next stop for the winds from the Urals) and 0.2" of rain had fallen, one really cannot blame the next writer for his acidulous attack. Dudley to Wolverhampton is to the order of 6 or so miles (10km).

"DUDLEY, SEDGLEY, AND WOLVERHAMPTON TRAMWAY COMPANY. Sir, At last we have got the steam trams running on this line, but if they are to be really a boon to the people of the district, I am afraid the company will have to show a little more consideration towards their passengers than was shown to myself and six or seven more of my fellow travellers last night. The company's time table (issued on Saturday) announced the last tram to leave Dudley on Sunday nights for Wolverhampton at 9.47. On leaving the car at Dudley, on Saturday afternoon, I asked the conductor if that was correct, and was informed that it was. Accordingly I reached Dudley last night in time for this tram, and, after waiting 'til the time of starting was passed, and no tram having made its appearance, I started to walk towards Wolverhampton. The tram passed me by the Dudley Union, and I waited for its return at the Green Dragon. I was then informed that it would only run to the depot, and was charged 2d for about three minutes' ride. Then I, with others, had to walk to Wolverhampton. I think, sir, it is high time this company told the public what they intend doing. If this is to be the kind of treatment the passengers are to receive, then the sooner the rails are taken up the better. We should know then what to depend upon; but, as it is, we know neither one thing nor the other. If the company's time table cannot be depended upon, then what is the use of having one, as it only puts people to a vast amount of inconvenience? I am, Sir, yours &c. J.T.M. January 18th, 1886."

DUDLEY, SEDGLEY, AND WOLVERHAMPTON
TRAMWAYS.
TIME TABLE.

	WEEK DAYS.	SUNDAYS.

Tram Cars leave Dudley as follows :—

Morning : 9.25 10.15 11.5 11.55

Afternoon : 12.45 1.35 2.25 3.15 4.5 4.55 5.45 6.35 7.25 8.15 9.5 9.55 (10.50 on Saturdays and Mondays only.) | 1.35 3.15 4.55 6.35 8.15 9.55 | 2.25 4.5 5.45 7.25 9.5

Leave Wolverhampton—
Morning : 6.0 9.0 9.50 10.40 11.30 12.20 | 2.0 3.40 | 2.50 4.30

Afternoon : 1.10 2.0 2.50 3.40 4.30 5.20 6.10 7.0 7.50 8.40 9.30 10.30 (Saturdays 10.20) 11.5 on Saturdays only | 5.20 7.0 8.40 10.10 | 6.10 7.50 9.30

Extra Cars leave Gornal on Saturday evenings only, at 6.25 7.25 8.15 9.5 10.5

Extra Cars leave Dudley on Saturday evenings only, at 6.50 7.50 8.40 9.45 10.35

FARES :

DUDLEY	to	Tram Depôt at Sedgley,	2d.
,,	,,	Bull Ring, Sedgley,	3d.
,,	,,	Fighting Cocks,	4d.
,,	,,	Wolverhampton,	5d.

Trams for the Working Man

The majority of tramway companies were obliged, by their Board of Trade Orders, to make provision for the carriage of working men (and to some extent women) at certain specified times and at an agreed low fare – usually half (i.e. return for single), and exceptionally four trips for three, thus enabling men to travel home and back for their midday 'snap', although this was far more common in electric tram days.

However, there were many reasons why steam tram companies failed to run these cars; they were financially quite a loss, the crews hated them as, leaving the depot at, say, 5.30am they could then be out until 10 at night, whereas normal services started an hour or more later – the pay was the same.

In this particular quotation taken from a report of a Dudley Council meeting early in August 1887 we have the other side of the coin – the tramways referred to are the Dudley, Sedgley & Wolverhampton, Birmingham Central, South Staffs & Birmingham District, Birmingham & Midland and Dudley & Stourbridge. It is quoted in full as throwing a light on a normal council's appreciation of tramway's problems.

"COUNCILLOR MATTHEWS AND THE TRAM COMPANIES Councillor Matthews moved:

'That, in consequence of the various tramway companies not replying satisfactorily to the applications made to them pursuant to the resolution passed on the 7th ult by the Council, a representation be made from this Council to the Board of Trade requesting them to compel all tramway companies whose lines run into or through the borough to carry out forthwith the clauses directing that two cars shall be run each way every morning and evening, for the benefit of the labouring classes at reduced fares".

He said the companies were required by law to run not less than two carriages each way in the morning and evening, viz. not later than 7am or earlier than 5pm for the benefit of the working men, at charges not exceeding ½d per mile. There were five tramway companies running into or through the borough, and up to that morning only two replies had been received to the resolution of the Council, and one was altogether unsatisfactory. Hence his reason for moving the resolution. The letter from the South Staffordshire & Birmingham Company, which was the altogether unsatisfactory one, said they had experimented with early workmen's cars, and they had not been patronised. They would be glad to issue workmen's tickets for the cars now running. In his opinion the great object of tramways was that cars should be run for the benefit of the labouring class. They had taken up the best part of the roads, which were given to them on condition that they gave something back to the working class, and his contention was this that it was intended that they should run workman's cars whether they paid or not. The Council had not to consider whether they would be remunerative to the companies or not, but to look after the interests of the working men, and to see that they carried out the article. He, however, argued that not only would the cheap cars be a

boon to the people, but they would also pay, as was shown by figures he had obtained of the experiment on the Dudley and Stourbridge line.

Alderman Bagott pointed out that the South Staffordshire and Midland companies only run about half-a-mile into the borough. He ventured to say that every tramway company was anxious to meet the requirements of the Town Council. Mr. Matthews had no right to jump on to their tramcars and ask the guard for information. If he or any other gentleman of the Council wished for information he should go to the office. The information was not got in that dignified manner in which the Town Council should get it.

Councillor Matthews said he had no right to go and inspect the company's books.

Councillor Hancox said that whilst he felt in harmony with Councillor Matthews in principle, it was only in the details that he took exception to the resolution. He should not like the Council to hamper the companies by compelling them to run two cars, when perhaps there would not be passengers, and one would be sufficient. He would rather see if one car could carry the passengers before he went further.

Alderman Garrat asked if this order was imperative, the companies were not bound to carry it out under some penalty?

The Town Clerk: No, there is no penalty, but a representation can be made to the Board of Trade on it, and there is no doubt the Act of Parliament says they shall run two cars each morning and evening.

Alderman Bagott said the Dudley and Stourbridge Company had no desire but to carry out the law.

Alderman Billing said it seemed to him a very simple question. The tramways were in full work, and the question was whether this was one of the provisions entered into by the tram companies and the Council. Were they carrying out part of the arrangement which should be carried out? It was a matter of paramount importance to working men when, as had been very fairly stated by Councillor Matthews, the tram companies took up the best part of the road, and the Town Council should look after the working class and see that those things were carried out which were in their interest. For his part he said they ought to run the cars, and the Council was not doing its duty if they did not see that they did so. He, therefore, seconded the resolution.

Councillor Turner said the question was whether the cars were wanted by the working men. If so he thought they should all support the resolution.

Alderman Bagott promised to lay authoritative information as to the patronage of the cars before the next meeting.

Alderman Smith asked if the Dudley and Stourbridge Company were running two cars or only one.

Alderman Bagott: Only one.

Alderman Smith said it seemed to him the question was whether they could redeem the companies in any way in the event of it being a loss. He thought they might call their representatives together to confer with the committee and have the whole thing discussed with the

view of seeing whether any modification could be carried out in the stipulations.

Councillor Millington said there was not an early car from Stourbridge to Dudley to bring working men to the intermediate works.

The Ex-Mayor thought the thanks of the town were due to Councillor Matthews for bringing this matter before the council (hear, hear). He thought it was a very great pity that it had been allowed to go on for three years without the companies introducing the workingmen's car. The Town Clerk had written to the companies, and they had promised to do all they could to meet the requirements of the Town Council. He therefore appealed to the mover and seconder of the resolution, whether it would not be better to let the matter rest for a month or two to see whether they would carry out what they promised. The tramway companies should carry out the letter of the law as far as was necessary.

Alderman Bagott said if the Dudley and Stourbridge Company had a depot at Stourbridge there would be no difficulty because they would run a car from Stourbridge at the same time as they ran one from Dudley.

The Mayor said the working classes should have the boon of cheap cars, and the matter should not be allowed to rest, but to take the step suggested by Councillor Matthews was perhaps going a little too far. It seemed to him advisable that they should wait and see the course of events. The companies had stated that they were willing to meet the council, and he thought they should let the matter stand over until the next meeting.

Councillor Matthews said he could not see his way clear to withdraw the resolution, he was prepared to stand or fall by it. He took it that he had done a public duty in bringing it forward (hear, hear). The companies had had sufficient opportunity to carry out the stipulations – they had had three years – but they never intended carrying them out until the matter was brought before the Council. He would withdraw the word 'forthwith' and would give them six months in which to carry out the stipulations but could not concede more.

Councillor Bridgwater said he should like to know if the course Councillor Matthews proposed – to call on the Board of Trade to interfere in the matter – would incur any expense. He (the speaker) would like to avoid expense if they possibly could.

The Town Clerk said that was a new question, but his view of it was that the town would incur no expense whatever (hear, hear).

The Ex-Mayor said he was very sorry that Councillor Matthews would not agree to withdraw his motion for the present, but they did not wish to bring the Board of Trade and the tram companies into collision, and he thought they should be doing a wise thing, the companies having expressed their willingness to carry out the wish of the council, if they waived the matter for a time. He proposed that the resolution be postponed until the January meeting.

Councillor Hancock, in seconding the amendment, complimented Councillor Matthews on the calm, able, and reasoning manner in which he had handled his brief (laughter). He appealed to him to postpone the matter.

Councillor Matthews still declined, and the amendment was carried by 13 to 4."

The following correspondence which appeared in the *Dudley Herald* on 10 November 1887 requires no comment but does show the thin line between 'workmen' and 'others'.

"Sir, I enclose a copy of correspondence upon this subject. To fight the question out with the company is no business of mine, but others may be more interested in the matter, and to them I now leave it. My objections to the company's claim were: 1. That the charging of two fares is unreasonable. 2. That the company have no authority for making two charges and distinguishing between their customers. 3. That their 11th bye law is repugnant to the 43rd section of their order, and consequently void. 4. That an analogous case is the running of Parliamentary trains. The company's last letter is no reply to these objections. Evidently they tend to continue their present practice until it is declared by a court of justice to the illegal.
Yours truly,
JAMES F. ADDISON"

"Dudley and Stourbridge Steam Tramways' Company Limited
95, Colmore Row, Birmingham
Dear Sir, We are informed that you are in the habit of using the workmen's cars, and that you refuse to pay the legal fare demanded. I am desired to call your attention to bye law No.11 (enclosed) and to give you notice that if you continue to commit a breach of this bye law measures will be adopted which will be very unpleasant to you.
Yours truly,
H.F. WOODWARD,
Secretary To Mr. Addison"

"To H.F. Woodward Esq.,
Dear Sir, I beg to acknowledge receipt of your letter of yesterday's date. You are misinformed as to my being 'in the habit of using' the workmen's cars. It is true I have travelled by the car which is called the workmen's car on several occasions when the time at which it runs has happened to suit me, and I have then on each of those occasions declined to pay more than the reduced fare. I have done so on principle and because like many I thought the company were putting a wrong construction on the clause of their Tramway Order (section 43) under which they run cheap cars; and I may say that that Order is the only statutory reference to the running of these cars that I have seen until favoured with a copy of the company's bye laws by you. Nor can I admit that the bye law you refer me to altogether settles the question. Comparing it with section 43 of the Order its terms appear to be repugnant to those of the section, and, therefore, even though confirmed by the Board of Trade, to be void and unenforceable under section 46 of the Tramways Act, 1870. The charging of the two fares has given rise to considerable irritation, and I have never ridden in the car without hearing many passengers express their annoyance at the differences made between one party and another and at the conductor being placed in the delicate position of making distinctions among those travelling on the cars. The company have been commended hitherto for their prompt and ready attention to the wants and comforts of the public, but in this instance a most unfavourable impression has been created. Either a car should be run expressly for "artisans, mechanics and daily labourers" from which people of other occupations should be excluded – though I doubt if this would be a compliance with the requirements of the statute, or if all are to ride on the so-called workmen's cars, all should be charged the same fare. I have no wish to make a difficulty, but I think your bye-law might have been shown to me at the time I objected to pay; at all events I submit that I should have been asked the grounds of my objection before you were instructed to threaten unpleasant measures. As this is a matter in which the public are cheated, unless you offer any objection I propose to hand your letter of yesterday, this one, and any reply you may send me to the local press.
I am, sir, yours truly
JAMES F. ADDISON"

"Dear Sir, Your letter is to hand, and in reply I must call your attention to the fact that our bye-laws are placed in each of our cars and can be seen by any passenger. I trust that this correspondence may have the effect of inducing you to conform with our regulations. I am, dear sir, yours truly,
H.F. WOODWARD, Secretary To: J.F. Addison Esq."

Central Tramway Season Ticket Holders

On 24 October 1892 in the *Birmingham Daily Mail* there appeared a report of a court proceedings which in the light of the ill-fated attempts by British Rail and subsequently the local companies to enforce payment of so-called 'Penalty Fares' proves there really is nothing new under the sun! But it is an interesting document on its own; the reply from J.H. Dean is curious and shows some laxity in fare collection on the trams:

"THE CENTRAL TRAMWAY CO. SEASON TICKET-HOLDERS
At the Birmingham Police Court today, before Messrs Middlemore and Ludlow, John Henry Dean, High Street, was summoned for unlawfully avoiding the payment of his tram fare. Dr Showeil Rogers who appeared for the Central Tramway Co. said the defendant had been a season ticket holder, and travelled on the small Heath route. His ticket expired on September 30, but between that date and October 17 he travelled in the company's cars sixteen times without paying his fare. Defendant was asked by three separate conductors for his ticket and to such he stated that he had sent a cheque to the office but that his new ticket had not been forwarded to him. Dr Rogers added that as a matter of fact the defendant had not sent either a cheque or money to the office. On Saturday last when the summons was served the defendant tendered a cheque but it was refused. The proceedings were taken because so many season-ticket holders took advantage of the company, and it was intended that they should see that they could not cheat the company with impunity. Mr Tanner, for the defence, said that a more outrageous prosecution of a respectable Birmingham tradesman never took place. He did not wonder at the Central Tramway Company being on the verge of bankruptcy, or having to send round the hat, if they chose to carry on their business in this way, and wasted their money by such prosecutions. Dr Rogers: My friend has no right to make such a statement. It is a libel. The company is not on the verge of bankruptcy. If every customer acted as Mr Dean has done the company might soon be on the verge of bankruptcy. Mr Tanner: At any rate, the company has been obliged to send round the hat to assist them in carrying on. He added that he thought it was ridiculous to suppose that Mr Dean had any intention to defraud. Before the magistrates could convict it would have to be shown unmistakably that this was not a mistake but that the defendant intended to defraud the Company. Mr Dean never understood that the money should be paid regularly. Mr Middlemore said they were advised that intention to defraud must be proved, and they did not think any such intention has been proved in this case. The summons would therefore be dismissed."

"To the Editor of the *Birmingham Daily Mail*. Sir, I shall feel obliged if, in justice to me, who, unfortunately had my mouth closed, you will kindly correct the announcement you made in yesterday's Mail. 1st That it was not proved in evidence that Mr Dean did on three separate occasions state that he had sent the cheque, but that he did on the 4th, 6th, 8th and 10th simply quote his number, which he has held all along. 2nd. That when asked for his ticket on the 17th he then said, I have not renewed it, but it is written out and will be sent in due course. At the same time I offered to pay my fare, which the man did not deny in evidence, but said he 'could not remember'. My past custom has been to pay the cheque some time after due, and the ticket post dated back. The Company have always held in hand 5s deposit, which would have amply repaid them for the fortnight's travelling. Trusting you will insert this, in justice to myself. I am, yours respectfully, J.H. DEAN, High Street, Birmingham."

John Henry Dean was a solid business-man, having in 1892 three premises in the centre of Birmingham – 88 High Street, 53 Snow Hill and 76 Digbeth, although by 1894 he seems to have given up the Snow Hill address, the Head Office of his tailoring and outfitting business now being 87/88 High Street.

Smethwick Trams

Smethwick Telephone, 16 June 1892:

"SMETHWICK TRAMS
To the Editor of the Telephone

Sir,– It has been said that the manager of the Birmingham and Midland Tramways Company strives to provide the best accommodation possible for the public, with respect to the running of the cars. Let us see how far he succeeds. First, with regard to the 'Workmen's cars.' At holiday times they are discontinued for a week or more, although the actual holidays seldom exceed more than two days; there is never any notice given when they will recommence running, and what is more, if you make enquiries, none of the officials seem to know anything about the matter. On Thursday evening, the 30th, two men enquired at the depot, Bearwood Hill, when the 6 o'clock tram, from Windmill Lane, would begin to run again, and they were told 'Not before Monday.' It was started the next morning (Friday), with the result that the greater part of the passengers, having walked on, had the pleasure (?) of seeing it pass them near to town, and, of course, the shareholders were minus their fares. Until very lately there has not been nearly enough accommodation for would be passengers by the

early tram. I know that scores of fares (during the week) have been lost on that account, the people preferring to walk rather than run the risk of being shut out. I have known the tram to run past Windmill Lane without stopping because of its being full, and it was a common occurrence to do so at Aberdeen Street. I believe it is better now, as the first tram does not go to Dudley; but still, I feel quite sure that, if properly managed, there would be enough passengers to make two trams pay between Smethwick and Birmingham, say at 6am and 6.30am, even charging ordinary fares for one of them. I am quite aware that an extra tram was put on as an experiment some time ago, and it was taken off 'because it did not pay.' But what effort was made to make it pay? Nothing but what was done by a few of the passengers, who were interested in it; and I am told by one of these that the tram men did what they could to get it taken off again. I wonder if it was extra work for them without extra pay. *If that were so* I cannot be surprised, for they are none too well paid for the hours they have to make. Again, there is the 'workman's car' from Birmingham, timed to leave at 6pm. Forsooth, what an hour to be sure to start a Workman's Car! What time must they leave work to avail themselves of it?

The 5 o'clock men must wait nearly an hour, and of course the 6 o'clock men cannot catch it. What is the class of passenger who patronise it, pray? Now with reference to the tram from Birmingham to Smethwick. Note the 'alterations during the winter months, every 15 minutes to Windmill Lane, and every 7½ minutes to Aberdeen Street' – what a delusion! I venture to say, sir, that the arrangement has never yet been carried out, at least after 6pm; it is a common occurrence to find two, and even three Aberdeen Street trams without one for Windmill Lane. There is another matter: some time ago several of the cars were fitted with curtains at the top, now if one of these could be used for the early car, it would confer a great boon upon those passengers who are obliged to ride outside. Perhaps, some one else may have something to say on the matter; I know there are very many who are very dissatisfied with the present arrangements. May I ask, sir, if you could give us in an early issue the text of the Board of Trade regulations, *re* the above. I am quite aware that the primary object of the Company is to make their undertaking pay, but they owe a duty to their patrons, the public.

Yours truly,
P.B.P."

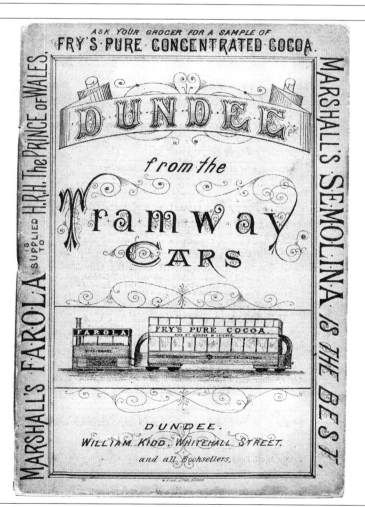

Dundee was Scotland's most successful operator of steam trams between 1885 and 1902. They proved a boon on the steep gradients which beset all routes except the Perth Road line which ran parallel to the River Tay. That the steam trams were highly appreciated is shown by the cover of the official publication 'Dundee from the Tramway Cars' of 1888. Published in several editions until c1910, this has a vignette drawing of the first tram engine – even with its name 'STRATHMORE' correctly displayed. For this and the material on the next two pages we thank Alan Brotchie.

Dundee from the Tramway Cars
(courtesy Alan Brotchie)

Advertisement indicating improved services from June 1888.

DUNDEE

FROM THE

TRAMWAY CARS.

TRIP THE FIRST.

HIGH STREET TO WESTPARK ROAD.

TOWN HOUSE.

THE tourist who sets foot in Dundee for the first time is generally at a loss how to gain a general idea of the extent of what has been justly called the second commercial centre of Scotland. He may be advised to ascend the Law Hill, which overlooks the town and the river, or he may set himself to study some dry plan. As to ascending the Law Hill we have no objections, but the tourist is not always ready to take a long walk and climb at the beginning of his visit, and he is more inclined to view the streets and mark their architecture and other characteristics. It is because we believe this is his mind that we beg to advise him to take advantage of our tramway cars, which now run along our principal thoroughfares. In respect to these modern convenient and public con-

veyances, Dundee is before her sister towns in as much as she has utilised steam-power in place of horse-power. It shows the enterprise of Juteopolis, and although from an artistic point of view they do not commend themselves, yet when we consider the steep places of the town where painfully the horses used to pull the cars, we may consider them a decided improvement. Steam tramway cars! Could even the most prophetic in 1746 have even conceived such things as running along the principal thoroughfares of Dundee in 1888? We trow not. Yet to such facilities have we arrived; and now we pay our coin and get quickly drawn along, whereas a hundred and fifty years ago such a mode of progression was never dreamed of.

With these introductory remarks we start on a round of sight-seeing such as can be had from the top—or even for that matter the inside—of a tramway car.

We will take the car then on the High Street and proceed at first westward. As we take our place, and before the car starts, the tourist may observe what a fine square the High Street is. Yon building to the east is the Clydesdale Bank, a very handsome edifice. That street to the left of it is the Murraygate, and the one to the right the Seagate, where stands at the top St. Paul's Episcopal Church, and further down Her Majesty's Theatre and Opera House.

This building, in front, with the fine vaulted arcade or loggia of seven arched openings, is the Town House, familiarly known to the inhabitants of Dundee as "The Pillars." It is a very old building, and a great many years ago used to be the Tolbooth of Dundee as well as the Townhouse.

That street behind you is Reform Street, of which we will have more to say by and bye; and that other street running westward from it off the High Street, the Overgate, a thoroughfare having many historical memories, for an account of which we would recommend Mr Kidd's complete Guide to Dundee.

But our car has started, and we go off along the Nethergate, which is to Dundee what Princes Street is to Edinburgh, and Sauchiehall Street to Glasgow. The handsome new street—Whitehall Street—on the south side, after it is completed, will be

by common consent, the finest street in Dundee. The buildings in it are of a massive and ornate style, and well justify the title which has been given—the Regent Street of Dundee. The first buildings erected on it were the Palace Buildings, belonging to Mr Wm. Kidd, bookseller and stationer. At the top, on the east, stands Whitehall House, occupied by Mr J. B. Hurrie; and on the west are the handsome new warehouses of Messrs T. S. Blakeney & Sons. Further down, on the east side, is Mr Mathers' Temperance Hotel, and at the foot is the Gilfillan Memorial Church. In the Nethergate, opposite Whitehall Street, is Mr W. H. Melville's drapery establishment.

OLD STEEPLE.

The next street on the south side is Union Street, at the top of which stand the Albion House and Russell's Royal Hotel. The objects of interest at this point, however, are the Town Churches and the Old Steeple. A full description of this fine old tower will be found in Kidd's larger Guide to Dundee, already referred to. It is one hundred and fifty-six feet high, square, and the walls are said to be about eight feet in thickness A fine view is obtained from the top, which can be reached by a stair inside, on payment of one penny to the keeper. The surrounding country can be seen to full advantage, and the town lying at its base with its pigmy people and houses. Opposite the Old Steeple, at the corner, is the premises of Dr. Stewart, the well-known East of Scotland Dentist.

The car now takes us along pretty swiftly, and we pass in succession St. Paul's Free Church on the south side, St. Enoch's Established Church on the north side, and then opposite Tay Street St. Andrew's Roman Catholic Pro-Cathedral. The round jutting building on the north side is Morgan's Tower (an ancient building), the basement of which is now occupied as the Pharmacy of Mr J. W. Russell, Chemist, who is a manufacturer of several

well-known Pharmaceutical preparations, and nearly opposite the large fine building is the Queen's Hotel.

The car now passes from the Nethergate to the Perth Road, and almost at the connection on the north side is the Harris Academy, the University College, and Airlie Place (see Kidd's Guide to Dundee for particulars). The next opening of importance is the Magdalen Yard Road, which gives access to the Magdalen Green and the Esplanade, the former a fine large pleasure ground, and the latter a promenade. At this point a fine view is had from the car of the new Tay Bridge and the opposite shores of Fifeshire. Opposite is Belmont House, in the ground of which is the "Tree of Liberty," for an account of which we again refer the curious to Kidd's Guide.

Further along the Perth Road is new Free St. John's Church, the Established Church of St. Mark, opposite is Springfield, St. Peter's Free Church, M'Cheyne Memorial Church, Manor Place, and then we come to Windsor Street, a fine thoroughfare, leading to the Magdalen Green and the Esplanade, as well as to the Caledonian Station. The tourist may alight from the car here if he so selects, and walk townwards again by the Esplanade, or he may continue with the car to West Park Road, which will lead him into Balgay Hill Park, a fine wooded pleasure ground, and from thence he may take the steam tramway car to Dundee.

TRIP THE FOURTH.
THE BAXTER PARK, &c.

BAXTER PARK ENTRANCE GATE.

WE left the tourist to enjoy himself a while in that fine public recreation ground known after its donor as the Baxter Park. It was presented to the community by the generosity of Sir David Baxter, Bart., and his two sisters, as a place of recreation for the inhabitants in all coming time. The Park, which is 38 acres in extent, cost about £50,000. It is splendidly laid out, from a design by Sir Joseph Paxton, the well-known architect of the Crystal Palace, and, as the tourist will observe, is kept in admirable order by the gardeners. The interest of an endowment provided by Sir David and the Misses Baxter is used for the purpose of defraying the expense of keeping up the Park. The upper part of the Park is wooded and laid out into charming winding walks; the lower portion is one large lawn, whereon the public disport themselves in various games. The lawn lies in front of a long Pavilion, having an extensive piazza, wherein is a fine marble statue of Sir David Baxter, executed by Sir John Steell.

It is more than likely that the visitor to Dundee will spend half a day, or even a whole one, in the delightful precincts of this charming spot; but as we are intent upon showing him as much as possible in the brief time we have at our disposal, we will conduct him out of the south-east gate, and on to the Arbroath Road.

Within the limits of a short walk eastwards will be found the Eastern Necropolis, one of the "God's acres" of Dundee. It is

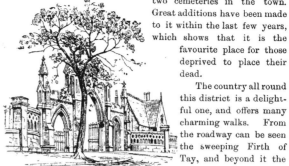

EASTERN NECROPOLIS ENTRANCE GATE.

at once the larger and finer (laid out by Mr M'Kelvie) of the two cemeteries in the town. Great additions have been made to it within the last few years, which shows that it is the favourite place for those deprived to place their dead.

The country all round this district is a delightful one, and offers many charming walks. From the roadway can be seen the sweeping Firth of Tay, and beyond it the shores of Fife. Should the visitor be inclined to continue his walk, he might do so, when by and bye he would pass the old Castle of Claypotts, which was formerly a seat of the Abbot of Lindores. It must have been along this road that Jamie Gair, the fisherman, in Grant's novel of "The Yellow Frigate," journeyed to Dundee, for it is said he passed the old Castle of Claypotts, and reverently said a short prayer in the little Chapel of St. Rocque of Narbonne, which stood without the Cowgate Port, on the east side of the Butter-burn.

Beyond Claypotts is one of the most delightful roads to Broughty Ferry. Trees, in which are embowered mansion-houses and villas, line the roadway, and speak mutely of the great change that has taken place where once there was nothing but wild wooded land, and no sign of Dundee's increasing greatness or importance. Dundee's merchants used then to live in houses over their shops and business premises in the town; now increased profits and the progress of enterprise enable them to live in handsome villas in the suburbs.

Another walk in this direction is to proceed out the road until the Strips of Craigie are reached. A long wooded and winding lane here conducts you to what is called the new Ferry Road,

whence the first watering-place on the East Coast—viz., Broughty Ferry—may be reached by a different though as charming a road. The roadway runs along the sea side, and from the Stannergate onwards is a most delightful walk.

But we must return, for the car is about to start from the Baxter Park gate. It will be noticed that the land about the Park is already being feued, and in a few years more it will be surrounded by houses. This neighbourhood, better than any we have seen yet, shows how Dundee is extending. Along the Arbroath Road, out as far as the Strips of Craigie, and even beyond that, has long been a favourite walk with Dundonians. Here on a fine Sabbath evening they will be seen in crowds enjoying the pleasant prospect of field, trees, and river.

But the car has started, and we with it. There is little to be seen in the road west of the Park. There are no buildings of any interest save large works and warehouses, chief among which are Craigie Works (Gibson, Robertson, & Co.) and Taybank Works (Storrier, Brough, & Co.)

Reaching the end of the Arbroath Road, we pass over into Victoria Street. On our left is Princes Street leading townwards, and Albert Street leading to the Morgan Hospital and that district. In Princes Street are the extensive linen and jute mills and factories of the famous firm of Baxter Brothers & Co. These works are the largest in town, covering upwards of nine acres, and yielding employment to over 4000 persons. This firm now spin and weave jute to a large extent, a lofty range of buildings, fitted up with machinery with all the latest improvements, having been lately erected for that purpose. The portion of the main building fronting Princes Street presents a striking appearance from its massive proportions. It is surmounted by a statue of James Watt. The Messrs Baxter are honourably distinguished for their attention to the education of the young people employed at their works. There is a large and efficiently conducted school, with a play-ground in front, in which the half-timers during the day, and all who desire to attend in the evenings, receive a gratuitous education.

There are no buildings of importance to point out in Victoria Street through which the car rapidly passes. The Victoria Bridge,

which spans the old Dens Burn, was a much needed improvement. The bridge as it is now forms a connecting link between the eastern and western thoroughfares, forming them into one.

We now pass again into the Victoria Road, as the route of the Baxter Park car lies the same way as that to the Morgan Hospital.

It will be difficult to convince the stranger that this fine broad street was, not so very long ago, a narrow, sinuous, dirty lane, a daily source of trouble to all who had business in it, or in its direction. From its old name, the Buckle-makers' Wynd, it was at one time inhabited mainly by buckle-makers, but that trade has long ago been annihilated. There are yet a few houses lying on green banks on the north side of the street, and these serve to show that there were even then among the miserable erections some very good ones.

We now traverse the same route as we did coming, and therefore the visitor can utilise his time by noting the characteristics of the Dundonians as they present themselves in the streets. There is doubtless not much difference between them and those of other large towns and cities.

We reach again the High Street, and thus, as far as we are concerned, for the last time. We hope, in the brief space given us, that we have made the various trips on the tram-cars interesting and edifying. But our information cannot be anything more than slight. The great body of the town has been passed over, and only its general characteristics pointed out and commented upon. To those who desire a thorough acquaintance with old and modern Dundee no better book can be recommended than Kidd's Guide, which has been referred to more than once throughout these pages. This little work is intended only as an introduction to the fuller knowledge which will be found in the larger Guide. It is full of information, which is exact and interesting, and is written in a style that is free from dulness and pedantry. With these recommendations, we beg to bid farewell to our reader.

Kaye's Fare Box

In Volume 2 of this series some mention was made of Kaye's Fare Box as a system for collecting fares. As long as fares were basic, in our case 1d and 2d but later, elsewhere, 'flat fare' schemes were tried whereby the passenger paid 6d for any length of journey, the box worked fairly well, albeit rather clumsily and indeed there are around twenty patents relating to 'Improvements' on the basic system.

My favourite is a relatively late patent (25662 29 December 1899) from G.H. Green an accountant in Unley, Province of South Australia.

"My invention relates to certain improved mechanism to be used in connection with that class of portable and other fare boxes such as are usually provided for the reception of tickets and fares in tramcars, omnibuses, and similar passenger conveyances. Hitherto fare boxes have been provided with two distinct compartments, the upper part being for receiving the fares, and the lower chamber for their general storage. Further improvements in such boxes have been made so as to comprise in combination an externally hinged receiver or lip, an announcing bell, and an enumerated recording or totalling device, these several parts acting in combination for the purpose of receiving fares, announcing their reception, and recording the total number of fares so received. … From an intimate knowledge and close connection with this and somewhat similar fare boxes, I find in actual practice that it is objectional to allow a slow or gradual opening of the receiving apparatus as in the case of the invention specially above referred to, because after several hundred fares have been received the various parts (which are subjected to considerable wear) can be so manipulated that fares can be abstracted from the box. I also find that the bell can be caused to ring without altering the totalling mechanism, thereby enabling unscrupulous officers to defraud their employers of monetary and other takings."

Unfortunately he replaced simplicity with a cat's-cradle of gears, pawls and the like. The two drawings will show what I mean.

But however ingenious a man, someone somewhere tries to circumvent the system; in this case not the conductors but the clerks.

"AT WESTMINSTER, WALTER BOUGHTON, a clerk in the office of the London Road Car Company, Wilton-road, Victoria-station, was charged before Mr. Partridge with embezzling 1s., the moneys of his employers, on the 21st of August, 5d. on the 22d, and 1s. 5d. on the 24th; and JAMES BOUGHTON, his brother, another clerk was charged with similar offences as to 7½d. and 1s. 1d. on the 27th and 28th of August respectively. Mr. Greenip prosecuted for the company. The informations charge the defendants with a serious fraud. Mr. Ernest Henry Poulter, the assistant manager, had received information from two of the conductors, and, accordingly, with another gentleman, travelled in the cars on the dates in question. The process was for the conductor to take in his money in a box, pay it to one of the prisoners, and receive a way bill, a corresponding entry being made in the cash book. Deficiencies were found as charged, and that the way-bills and cash books had been falsified. They were both remanded for a week, bail in £80 each being required."

It appears they received three months in gaol with hard labour.

South Staffs Service Alterations

Midland Advertiser, 16 July 1892:

"The South Staffordshire Tramways Company have made several alterations in their service of cars which will be very acceptable to the public. A late car will now leave Darlaston at 10pm, arriving at Handsworth at 11 o'clock, and on Sundays extra cars will run between Carter's Green and Handsworth. On Sundays the last car will leave Darlaston for Walsall at 10pm, and on week-days the first car from Wednesbury to Dudley will leave at 8.20am. There are also alterations in the early weekday service from Handsworth and Dudley to Wednesbury and Darlaston.

The contractors are pushing forward with the alterations and equipment for the electric car service between Bloxwich and Walsall and Wednesbury and Darlaston, having a large body of men employed in the work. It is hoped to have the electric cars running on Bank Holiday or shortly after, and no doubt under the improved conditions later cars will run between Wednesbury and Walsall."

---

1 May 1900: Approval of the Corporation

The Company undertake to run a minimum five minutes service of cars between 8 a.m. and 8 p.m., with a minimum fifteen minutes service between 8 and 10·30 p.m., to continue their present line into Selly Oak, to divide the whole journey between Selly Oak and the City terminus into two penny stages, and to run four workmen's cars each way before 7 a.m. and after 6 p.m. at a penny for the whole distance.

Your Committee are of opinion that the proposals of the Company are reasonable, and that their acceptance, by providing a cheap, efficient, and frequent service on this route, in place of the present inadequate, irregular, and inefficient service, without any extension of the present lease or contribution from the Corporation, and without committing the Council in any way as to the motor which it should ultimately adopt, would be advantageous to the City; and they therefore recommend that the Company's offer be accepted, and referred to your Committee to see that it is properly carried into effect.

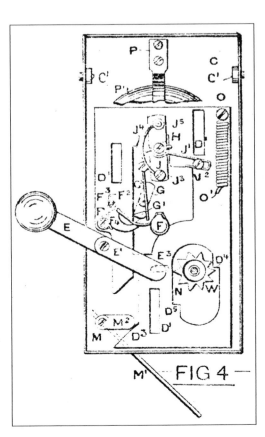

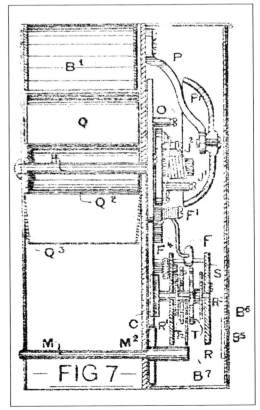

Bradford Tramways & Omnibus Company Ltd

The problems of single line working on railways are well known to those who have to rely on railway services from as an example Hereford to Paddington where two bottlenecks exist, plus the complexity of Oxford station working. Any delay, however caused, and the whole pack of cards collapses. Neither of the bottlenecks existed in the days of the Great Western Railway, but 'economy' demanded that the lines were singled, partly to eliminate signal boxes, certainly to eliminate freight, and overall there was the theory of reduced maintenance. Many lines not expected to carry much traffic were built as single road, as with only an anticipated three or four trains a day the economies in first cost were very high indeed; in many cases these lines adopted what we know was to prove a suicidal practice of running 'mixed' trains with perhaps only one or two carriages, and a raft of trucks to be put off (and added to) as the train made its very leisurely way across the countryside. We stopped at a station on one now long closed line and after the usual bashing and clashing of buffers everything went quiet until the guard opened the door and asked in a rising tone, "did we not want a drink and bite before we go on?" We did and it was worth the price of a round to hear the men's craich. Afterwards the train positively galvanized itself and perhaps unsurprisingly we eventually arrived somewhere near time.

But when the fog, be it the Welsh mist, the haar or an honest pea-souper comes in, often when least expected then the weight falls as much on the signalman's shoulders as on that of the driver, for the signalman still has to allow his 'mixed' or pick-up goods train to carry out the requisite local shunting, while trying to give priority to a through – maybe express – passenger train. And the driver has to observe his signals, wait for the fireman and/or guard to be advised by the signalman over his actions and then try and see a dim red or green lamp in the distance requiring him to set back or draw up as appropriate All too often in these conditions on a winter's night it may mean setting back, leaving half the train in no.1 sidings and drawing forward into the loop while an express passes by, the shunt move being completed afterwards into no.2 siding. All this called for teamwork and precision timing.

It could all go 'pear-shaped' too easily. We had a job where the empty passenger train was placed in a carriage shed for cleaning; the shortness of the shed roads laid, I suspect, in the days of four-wheeled carriages meant our eleven carriages had to be split with five in the one road already containing a buffet car for the next days working and six on the other line, this being the maximum that could be accommodated. Working was incredibly slack as I was told that the signalman having laid out the shunt did not bother with the controlling ground signals and toddled off to the Staff Club. Meanwhile the shunter had been 'on the weed' as usual but called us back with his green lamp past the red

signals (a very odd procedure but ratified unofficially as 'local working') then detaching the first tranche of carriages. We moved forward, the shunter 'nobbed up' the points and we again set back ... and back ... and back still with the shunter bouncing up and down frenziedly waving his green lamp. As our diesel note changed to a growl my mate threw the brake in, and told me to go and see what was happening. The shunter was cursing us wanting to know why we had stopped. The twit had, in fact, called back our remaining six coaches on top of the buffet car, proving that seven coaches do not fit a six-coach road for the buffet car was neatly parked up the end wall of the shed at an angle of 45 degrees to the rails. My mate and I filled in remarkably similar report forms, had an interview over the matter with the Area Manager and were told to go away. The shunter was moved away, and the signals suddenly started working. The buffet car was scrap.

You may wonder quite reasonably what this has to do with steam tramways and the answer is

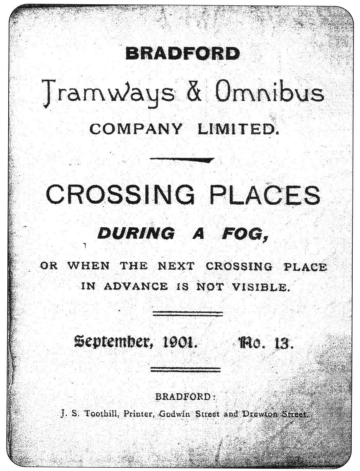

almost everything, for the bulk of tramways were single-line working with passing loops, but there were neither signals or signalmen to advise the tram drivers. The onus was entirely on their shoulders. Where the distance between two loops was very short, albeit because of a bend in the road or the forward one was invisible in the dark or fog, it appears drivers would send their guards forward as human pilots; on arrival advising the driver of an oncoming tram that his mate was on his way. Where a passing loop was long we know from photographic evidence that three

or four engines and trailers might be lined up waiting for an oncoming tram to clear the road. In the days of single-bore canal tunnels it was decreed that whoever met the white line indicating the halfway point within the tunnel had the right of way and I understand something similar was arranged for the long loops. We must never forget that these steam trams did not have headlamps as we know them, and street lights were normally doused at 10pm, leaving only the moonlight to serve as illumination for the drivers. But then we get back to the fog and in fact where a spring-loaded single-blade point existed it was not easy to propel a trailer back into the loop the driver had just left. One elderly gentleman told me that in electric days it was not uncommon for them to go 'bang road' into the loop, run through and come back to their proper line, although he did mention they did this one murky night and failed to see their proper line was blocked by another tram that had – as he put it – 'snuck up on them', so until they reached the terminus the two drivers took one another's times.

Another problem with single-line working with only passing loops is that making timetable changes is quite an algebraic puzzle; for some years the 'trams start at 06.00 and run at approximately 20 minute intervals' was the norm, covering the management if not the hapless passenger against such happenings as a Wilkinson engine swizzling to a halt and taking two or three attempts to get going, even when assisted by the next engine running on his 20-minute interval. A dirty fire or poor coke can delay departure from the terminus or a damaged point blade requiring the attendance of a Regulator or Inspector – if the company has one – to bar the thing over for each tram or where the loop is unusable to treat two loops as one long extended one. There again even where double track existed in a number of locations clearances did not allow two trams to pass so this had to be treated as single line without the points. Elsewhere point (switches) were installed between the two sets of rails 'to accommodate the traffic of the locality'; thus a tram would enter Mill Street, change from one line to the other to bypass a dray, then return to his own set of rails, which his mate would then want to use to bypass another dray on the other side of the road. All this and a million other pin-pricks wrecked timekeeping.

Here is reproduced a document of a type I have never seen elsewhere, which appears to be the 13th issue presumably reflecting timetable changes. Although a few pages were used in an earlier volume we have re-used Roger Smith's Bradford map to show how this would work, which have greatly clarified these workings. The manager is showing the new professionalism that was sweeping through the industry, and in this booklet was showing his men were supposed to be literate. The publication in date seems to have been a last fling by the private company before municipalisation.

CROSSING PLACES.

Engine out at 4-30 a.m

Wakefield Road Section.

4-30 a m out meets none to Tong

Return Journey and Remainder of Day.

Meets 1 at Tong Street End

1 at Street House

1 at Lorne Street

1 at Hall Lane

Engine out at 4-40 a.m.

Wakefield Road Section.

4-40 a m out meets one at Tong Street End.

Return Journey and Remainder of Day.

Meets 1 at Tong Street End

1 at Street House Crossing

1 at Lorne Street

1 at Hall Lane

Engine out at 4-55 a.m.

Wakefield Road Section.

Meets 1 at Street House Crossing

1 at Tong Street End

1 at Street House

1 at Lorne Street

1 at Hall Lane

Engine out at 5 a.m.

Saltaire and Undercliffe Section.

From Saltaire to Undercliffe.

Meets no Cars on the Undercliffe Section (going or returning). Return journey meets 1 at Grammar School. 6-0 a.m. from Saltaire, and 6-15 a.m. at Park Gates, Manningham. Must pass carefully over crossing at Well Street and Harris Street on Leeds Road Section, and keep bell ringing, keeping a sharp look-out for Cars going to or from Thornbury.

Engine out at 5-10 a.m.

Leeds Road & Thornton Road Section.

To Allerton.
Meets none to Allerton.

On Return Journey.

Meets 1 on Double Road Thornton Road	out at	5-40
1 ,, ,,	...	5-50
1 ,, ,,	...	6-0
1 on Sunbridge Hill	...	6-10
1 at Mechanics'	...	6-20
1 Near Harris Street on Double Road		6-30
2 at Level Crossing	...	6-40
1 at Oak Inn	...	6-45
1 at Greenhill	...	6-50
1 at White Bear	...	6-55

Engine out at 5-10 a.m.

Wakefield Road Section.

Meets 1 at Lorne Street

1 at Street House Crossing

1 at Tong Street End

Return Journey and Remainder of Day.

1 at Tong Street End

1 at Street House Crossing

1 at Lorne Street

1 at Hall Lane

Engine out at 5-20 a.m.

Leeds Road & Thornton Road Section.

To Four Lane Ends.
Meets none to Four Lane Ends.

Return Journey.

Meets the 5-30 a.m. out on Double Road, Thornton Road

Meets the 5-40 a m do, do.

Meets 5-50 ,, do. do.

Meets the 6-0 a.m. out at Mechanics" Institute

Meets 6-10 ,, ,, Well Street

Meets 6-20 ,, ,, Oak Inn

Meets 6-30 ,, ,, Greenhill

Engine out at 5-25 a.m.

Wakefield Road Section.

Meets 1 at Hall Lane

1 at Lorne Street

1 at Street House

1 at Tong Street End

Return Journey and Remainder of Day.

1 at Tong Street End

1 at Street House

1 at Lorne St

1 at Hall Lane

Engine out at 5-30 a.m.

Leeds Road & Thornton Road Section.

To Four Lane Ends.
Meets the 5-20 out at Young Street

Return Journey.

Meets 1 at 5-40 out, on Double Road, Thornton Road

1 at 5-50 ,, ,,

1 at 6-0 ,, ,,

1 at 6-10 ,, at Mechanics' Institute

1 at 6-20 ,, at Well Street

1 at 6-30 ,, at Oak Inn

2 at 6-40 ,, at Greenhill

1 at Croft and Perkins, out at 6-45 a.m.

11

SALTAIRE.

Engine out at 5-30 a.m.

Saltaire Depot to Thornbury.

From Saltaire to Forster Square.

Meets one in Forster Square from Thornbury, out at 5-45 a.m.

Meets 1 at Harris Street, out at 5-50 a.m., to Four Lane Ends.

Meets the 6 o'clock Workman's Car from Thornbury, at Oak Inn.

Meets the 6-10 a.m. out at Croft and Perkins.

12

Engine out at 5-40 a.m.

Leeds Road & Thornton Road Sections

To Allerton.

Meets 1 on Double Road, Thornton Road,
out at 5-20 a m

| 1 | ,, | ,, | ,, | 5-30 a m |
| 1 | ,, | ,, | ,, | 5-10 a m |

Return Journey.

Meets 1 at Lady Royd	...	out at 6-10 a m
1 on Double Road, Thornton Road,	}	6-20 a m
1	,,	,,	6-30 a m
1	,,	,,	6-40 a m
1 at Mechanics' Institute		6-50 a m

The 6-55 from Thornbury passes down Well Street before seeing the 7-0 a.m.

Meets 1 at Well Street	...	out at 7-0 a m
1 at Oak Inn	...	7-10 a m
2 at Greenhill	...	7-20 a m

13

Engine out at 5-45 a.m.

Leeds Road and Midland Station.

From Thornbury to Midland Station.

Meets one at Midland Station ; the 5-30 a.m. from Saltaire.

After leaving Midland Station meets one at Park Gates, 6 a.m. out at Saltaire.

6-15 a.m, at Frizinghall.

15

SALTAIRE.

Engine out at 6-0 a.m.

Saltaire and Undercliffe Section.

From Saltaire to Forster Square.

Meets one at Park Gates, 5-45 from Thornbury.

Meets one at Grammar School ; the 5-0 a.m. from Saltaire.

Meets 6-15 a.m. from Saltaire at Boys' Grammar School

Meets one at Branch Hotel ; the 6-55 a.m. from Saltaire

16

Engine out at 6-0 a.m.

Leeds Road & Thornton Road Section.

To Four Lane Ends.

Meets 1 the Midland Workman's Car at Oak Inn, Leeds Road, 6-0 a.m., from Forster Square

1 Mechanics' Institute	...	out at 5-20 a m
1 on Double Road Thornton Road	}	5-30 a m
1 on Double Road	}	5-10 a m
1 on Double Road Thornton Road	}	5-50 a m

Return Journey.

Meets 1 at Sunbridge Road	...	6-10 a m
2 at Sunbridge Road	{	6-20 a m and 6-30 a m
1 at Mechanics'	...	6-40 a m
*1 at Well Street Junction	...	6-50 a m
1 at Harris Street	...	6-55 a m
1 at Oak Inn	...	7-0 a m
1 at Greenhill	...	7-10 a m

* Pass very carefully and slowly over Well Street. Points as the 6-45 out for Saltaire is due to pass over this JUNCTION about same time as the 6 o'clock out is returning to Depot from Mechanics' Institute.

17

Engine out at 6-10 a.m.

Leeds Road & Thornton Road Section.

To Allerton.

Meets the 6-0 a m from Forster Square at Croft and Perkins

1 at Well Street	...	out at 5-20 a m
1 at Mechanics'	...	5-30 a m
1 at Sunbridge Hill	...	5-10 a m
1 on Double Road, Thornton Road	}	5-50 a m
1	,,	,,	6-0 a m
1 at Lady Royd	...	5-40 a m

Return Journey.

Meets 1 at Lady Royd	...	6-40 a m
1 on Double Road, Thornton Road	}	6-50 a m
1	,,	,,	7-0 a m
1	,,	,,	7-10 a m
1 at Mechanics'	...	7-20 a m
1 at Well Street	...	7-30 a m
1 at Level Crossing	...	7-40 a m
1 at Oak Inn	...	7-45 a m
1 at Greenhill	...	7-50 a m

18

Engine out at 6-20 a.m.

Leeds Road and Thornton Road Section.

To Four Lane Ends.

Meets 1 at Oak Inn	...	out at 5-20 a m
1 at Well Street	...	5-30 a m
1 at Mechanics'	...	5-10 a m
1 on Double Road, Thornton Road	}	5-50 a m
1	,,	,,	6-0 a m
1	,,	,,	5-40 a m

Return Journey

Meets 1 on Double Road, Thornton Road	}	out at 6-30 a m
1	,,	,,	6-40 a m
1	,,	,,	6-50 a m
1 at Mechanics'	...	7-0 a m
1 at Well Street	...	7-10 a m
2 at Level Crossing	...	7-20 a m
1 at Greenhill	...	7-30 a m

19

Engine out at 6-30 a.m.

Leeds Road & Thornton Road Section

To Four Lane Ends.

Meets the 5-20 a m out at Greenhill
Meets the 5-30 a m out at Oak Inn
Meets the 5-10 a m out at Harris Street
Meet the 5-50 a m out at Mechanics
Meets 3 on Double Road, Thornton Road, out at 6-0, 5-40, and 6-20 a m

Return Journey.

Meets the 6-40 a m out on double Road
Meets the 6-50 a m ,, ,,
Meets the 7-0 a m out on Sunbridge Road, near Sun Hotel
Meets the 7-10 a m out at Mechanics
Meets 2 out at 7-20 a m at Well Street
Meets the 7-30 a m out at Level Crossing
Meets the 7-40 a m out at Greenhill Crossing
Meets the 7-45 a m out at Croft and Perkins

SALTAIRE.

Engine out at 6-40 a.m.
Thornbury to Undercliffe.

Wait at Depot until 5-20 a m out arrives
Meets the 5-30 a m out at Greenhill
Meets the 5-10 a m out at Level Crossing
Meets the 5-50 a m out at Well Street
Meets no more to Midland Station, and then forms the New Car, 7-5 to Undercliffe—Meets none to Undercliffe.

Return to Undercliffe.
From Thornbury

Meets 1 at Cock and Bottle	...	out at 6-55 a m
1 at Midland	...	7-10 a m
1 at Manor Row	...	7-25 a m
1 at Manningham Lane	...	7-40 a m
1 at Grove View	...	7-55 a m
1 at Branch Hotel	...	8-10 a m
1 at Ring of Bells	...	8-25 a m

Return from Saltaire and remainder of Day
From Thornbury.

| Meets 1 at Ring of Bells | ... | 7-45 a m |

From Saltaire.

1 at Branch	...	6-55 a m
1 at Grove View	...	7-10 a m
1 at Manningham Lane	...	7-25 a m
1 at Manor Row	...	7-40 a m
1 at Midland Station	...	7-55 a m
*1 at Cock and Bottle	...	8-10 a m
1 at Cemetery	...	8-25 a m

*Up Car must stand in Barkerend Rd. until arrival of Down Car.

21

Engine out at 6-40 a.m.

Leeds Road and Thornton Road Section.

To Allerton.

Wait at Depot until 5-20 a m out arrives.

Meets 1 at Greenhill ...	out at 5-30 a m
1 at Level Crossing ...	5-10 a m
1 at Well Street ...	5-50 a m
1 at Mechanics ...	6-0 a m
1 on Double Road, Thornton Road,	5-40 a m
1 " "	6-20 a m
1 " "	6-30 a m
1 at Lady Royd ...	6-10 a m

Return Journey.

Meets 1 at Lady Royd ...	7-10 a m
1 on Double Road, Thornton Road,	7-20 a m
1 " "	7-30 a m
1 " "	7-40 a m
1 at Mechanics ...	7-50 a m
1 at Well Street ...	8-0 a m
1 at Level Crossing ...	8-10 a m
1 at Greenhill ...	8-20 a m

22

Engine out at 6-45 a.m.

Saltaire and Undercliffe Section.

From Thornbury.

Meets 1 at Croft & Perkins out at 5-30 a m	
1 at Oak Inn out at 5-10 a m	
1 at Harris Street out at 5-50 a m	
*1 at Well Street Junction which leaves Town at 7-0 a m and which is the 6-0 a m out. To see each other at Well Street.	

To Saltaire

Meets 1 at Manningham Lane ...	out at 6-55 a m
1 at Grove View ...	7-10 a m
1 at Branch Hotel ...	7-25 a m
1 at Ring of Bells ...	7-40 a m

Return Journey and remainder of Day.

From Thornbury

Meets 1 at Ring of Bells	6-55 a m
1 at Branch Hotel	7-20 a m
1 at Grove View ...	6-40 a m
1 on Manningham Lane	7-45 a m

From Saltaire.

1 at Manor Row ...	6-55 a m
1 at Midland Station	7-10 a m
1 at Junction Otley Road and Barkerend Road ...	7-25 a m
1 at Cemetery ...	7-40 a m

* Pass very carefully and slowly over Well Street points as the 7 o'clock from Town Hall passes over this junction about this time. Drivers to ring bell continuously at this place.

23

Engine out at 6-50 a.m.

Wait arrival of 5-30 out

Leeds Road and Thornton Road Section.

To Four Lane Ends.

Meets 1 at Greenhill ...	out at 5-10 a m
1 at Level Crossing ...	5-50 a m
1 at Well Street ...	6-0 a m
1 at Mechanics' ...	5-40 a m
1 on Double Road, Thornton Road	6-20 a m
1 " "	6-30 a m
1 " "	6-10 a m

Return Journey.

1 on Double Road, Thornton Road	7-0 a m
1 " "	7-10 a m
1 " "	7-20 a m
2 at Mechanics'	7-25 a m / 7-30 a m
1 at Well Street	7-40 a m
1 at Harris Street	7-45 a m
1 Level Crossing	7-50 a m
1 at Greenhill...	8-0 a m

24

Engine out at 6-55 a.m.

Saltaire & Undercliffe Section.

From Thornbury.

Meets 1 at White Bear	out at 5-10 a m
1 at Oak Inn ...	5-50 a m
1 at Harris Street ...	6-0 a m

To Saltaire.

From Saltaire.

Meets 1 at Manor Row	out at 6-55 a m
1 at Manningham Lane ...	7-10 a m
1 at Grove View ...	7-25 a m
1 at Branch Hotel ...	7-40 a m
1 at Ring of Bells ...	7-55 a m

Return Journey and remainder of Day.

From Thornbury.

Meets 1 at Ring of Bells ...	out at 7-20 a m
1 at Branch Hotel ...	6-40 a m
1 at Grove View ...	7-55 a m

From Saltaire.

Meets 1 at Manningham Lane ...	out at 6-55 a m
1 at Manor Row ...	7-10 a m
1 at Midland Station ...	7-25 a m
*1 at Junction, Otley Road and Barkerend Road...	7-40 a m
1 at Cemetery ...	7-55 a m

* Down Car must wait opposite Mr. Stephenson's, Chemist, until arrival of Up Car at Barkerend Road.

25

SALTAIRE.

Engine out at 6-55 a m

From Saltaire.

Saltaire & Undercliffe Section.

Meets 1 at Branch Hotel ...	out at 6-0 a m

From Thornbury.

Meets 1 ot Manningham Lane...	out at 6-45 a m
1 at Manor Row ...	6-55 a m
1 at Midland Station ...	7-20 a m

To Undercliffe.

Meets one at Cock and Bottle ...	out at 6-40 a m

Return Journey and remainder of Day.

Meets 1 at Cemetery...	out at 7-10 a m
1 at Junction of Barkerend Road and Otley Road	7-25 a m
1 at Midland Station ...	7-40 a m
1 at Manor Row ...	7-55 a m
1 at Manningham Lane...	8-10 a m
1 at Grove View ...	8-25 a m
1 at Branch Hotel ...	8-40 a m
1 at Ring of Bells ...	7-55 a m

Down Car must wait opposite Mr. Stephenson's, Chemist, until arrival of Up Car in Barkerend Road.

26

Engine out at 7-0 a.m.

Leeds Road and Thornton Road Section.

To Four Lane Ends.

Wait at Depot until 5-10 arrives.

Meets 1 at Greenhill ...	out at 5-50 a m
1 at Oak Inn ..	6-0 a m
1 at Well Street ...	5-40 a m
1 at Mechanics'...	6-20 a m
3 on Double Road, Thornton Road ...out at 6-30, 6-10, and 6-50 a m	

Return Journey.

Meets 1 on Double Road, Thornton Road ...	out at 7-10 a m
1 do. do.	7-20 a m
1 at Double Road ...	7-30 a m
1 at Mechanics'...	7-40 a m
1 at Peel Place ...	7-48 a m
1 at do. ...	7-50 a m
1 at Level Crossing ...	8-0 a m
1 at Greenhill ...	8-10 a m

27

Engine out at 7-10 a.m.

Leeds Road and Thornton Road Section.

Wait at Depot for 5-50 a.m. to arrive.

To Four Lane Ends.

Meets 1 at Greenhill Crossing ...	out at 6-0 a m
1 at Oak Inn ...	5-40 a m
1 at Well Street...	6-20 a m
1 at Mechanics' ...	6-30 a m
3 on Double Road, Thornton Road, out 6-10, 6-50, and 7-0 a m	
1 at Lady Royd...	out at 6-40 a m

Return Journey.

Meets 1 at Lady Royd...	out at 7-40 a m
3 on Double Road, Thornton Road out at 7-50, 8-0, and 8-10 a m	
1 at Mechanics' Institute ...	out at 8-20 a m
1 at Well Street ...	8-30 a m
1 at Level Crossing ...	8-40 a m
1 at Greenhill ...	8-50 a m

28

SALTAIRE.

Engine out at 7-10 a m

Saltaire and Undercliffe Section.

From Saltaire

From Thornbury

Meets 1 at Grove View...	out at 6-45 a m
1 at Manningham Lane ...	6-55 a m
1 at Manor Row ...	7-20 a m
1 at Midland Station ...	6-40 a m

From Saltaire.

1 at Cemetery ...	6-55 a m

Return Journey and remainder of Day.

From Saltaire.

Meets 1 at Cemetery ...	out at 7-25 a m
1 at Junction Otley Road and Barkerend Road ...	7-40 a m
1 at Midland Station ...	7-55 a m
1 at Manor Row...	8-10 a m
1 at Manningham Lane ...	8-25 a m
1 at Grove View...	8-40 a m
1 at Branch Hotel ...	8-55 a m
1 at Ring of Bells ...	8-10 a m

* Down Car must wait opposite Mr. Stephenson's, Chemist, until arrival of up Car at Barkerend Road.

29

Engine out at 7-20 a.m.

Leeds Road and Thornton Road Section.

To Four Lane Ends.

Wait at Depot until 6-0 a m arrives.

Meets 1 at Greenhill ...	out at 5-40 a m
1 at Level Crossing ...	6-20 a m
1 at Well Street...	6-30 a m
1 at Mechanics' Institute ...	6-10 a m
3 on Double Road, Thornton Road out at 6-50, 7-0 and 6-40 a m	

Return Journey and Remainder of Day.

Meets 3 on Double Road, Thornton Road out at 7-30, 7-40 and 7-50 a m	
1 at Mechanics' Institute ...	out at 8-0 a m
1 at Well Street ...	8-10 a m
1 at Oak Inn ...	8-20 a m
1 at Greenhill ...	8-30 a m

30

Engine out at 7-20 a.m.
From Thornbury.
Saltaire & Undercliffe Section.

Wait at Depot until the 6-0 a m out arrives
Meets the 5-40 a m out at Greenhill
Meets the 6-20 a m out at Level Crossing
Meets the 6-30 a m out on Double Line near
Harris Street

To Saltaire		From Saltaire
Meets 1 at Midland Station	... out at	6-55 a m
1 ot Manor Row	...	7-10 a m
1 at Manningham Lane	...	7-25 a m
1 at Grove View	...	7-40 a m
1 at Branch Hotel	...	7-55 a m
1 at Ring of Bells	...	8-10 a m

Return Journey and remainder of Day.

Meets 1 at Ring of Bells	... out at	6-40 a m
1 at Branch Hotel	...	7-45 a m
1 at Grove View	...	6-55 a m
1 at Manningham Lane	...	7-10 a m
1 at Manor Row	...	7-25 a m
1 at Midland Station	...	7-40 a m
*1 at Junction of Otley Road and Barkerend Road ...		7 55 a m
1 at Cemetery Crossing ...		8-10 a m

* Up Car must stand in Barkerend Road until arrival of the Down Car.

31

SALTAIRE.
Engine out at 7-25 a.m.

Saltaire & Undercliffe Section.
From Saltaire

	From Thornbury.
Meets 1 at Branch Hotel	... out at 6-45 a m
1 at Grove View	... 6-55 a m
1 at Manningham Lane	... 7-20 a m
1 at Manor Row	... 6-40 a m
1 at Midland Station	... 7-45 a m
	From Saltaire.
*1 at Junction of Otley Road and Barkerend Road...	out at 6-55 a m
1 at Cemetery ...	... 7-10 a m

Return Journey and remainder of Day.

	From Saltaire.
Meets 1 at Cemetery ...	... out at 7-40 a m
*1 at Junction of Otley Road and Barkerend Road...	... 7-55 a m
1 at Midland Station	... 8-10 a m
1 at Manor Row	... 8-26 a m
1 at Manningham Lane	... 8-40 a m
1 at Grove View	... 8-55 a m
1 at Branch Hotel	... 9-10 a m
1 at Ring of Bells	... 9-28 a m

* Up Car must stand in Barkerend Road until arrival of the Down Car.

32

Engine out at 7-30 a.m.

Leeds Road and Thornton Road Section.

To Four Lane Ends.

Meets 1 at Depot	...	... out at 5-40 a m
1 at Greenhill	...	6-20 a m
1 at Level Crossing	...	6-30 a m
1 at Well Street	...	6-10 a m
1 at Mechanics' Institute	...	6-50 a m
1 on Double Road, Thornton Road	...	7-0 a m
1 ,, ,,	...	6-40 a m
1 ,, ,,	...	7-20 a m

Return Journey and remainder of Day.

Meets 1 on Double Road, Thornton Road	... out at 7-40 a m
1 ,, ,,	... 7-50 a m
1 ,, ,,	... 8-0 a m
1 at Mechanics' Institute	... 8-10 a m
1 at Well Street	... 8-30 a m
1 at Oak Inn	... 8-30 a m
1 at Greenhill	... 8-40 a m

33

SALTAIRE.
Engine out at 7-40 a.m.
Saltaire & Undercliffe Section.
From Saltaire to Undercliffe.

	From Thornbury.
Meets 1 at Ring of Bells	... out at 6-45 a m
1 at Branch Hotel	... 6-55 a m
1 at Grove View	... 7-20 a m
4 at Manningham Lane	... 6-40 a m
1 at Manor Row	... 7-45 a m
	From Saltaire.
1 at Midland Station	... out at 6-55 a m
*1 at Junction of Otley Road and Barkerend Road ..	7-10 a m
1 at Cemetery Crossing ...	7-25 a m

Return Journey and remainder of Day.

	From Saltaire.
Meets 1 at Cemetery Crossing ...	out at 7-55 a m
1 at Junction of Otley Road and Barkerend Road ...	8-10 a m
1 at Midland Station	... 8-25 a m
1 at Manor Row	... 8-40 a m
1 at Manningham Lane	... 8-55 a m
1 at Grove View	... 9-10 a m
1 at Branch Hotel	... 9-25 a m
1 at Ring of Bells	... 9-40 a m

* The Up and Down Car must see each other at this point.

34

Engine out at 7-40 a.m.
To Allerton.

Leeds Road & Thornton Road Section.

Meets 1 at Depot	...	... out at 6-20 a m
1 at Greenhill	...	6-30 a m
1 at Level Crossing	...	6-10 a m
1 at Well Street	...	6-50 a m
1 at Mechanics' Institute	...	7-0 a m
1 at Double Road, Thornton Road		6-40 a m
1 ,, ,,	...	7-20 a m
1 ,, ,,	...	7-30 a m
1 at Lady Royd	...	7-10 a m

Return Journey and remainder of Day.

1 at Lady Royd	...	... out at 8-10 a m
1 at Double Road, Thornton Road	{	8-20 a m
		8-30 a m
1 ,, ,,	(	8-40 a m
1 at Mechanics' Institute	...	8-50 a m
1 at Well Street	...	9-0 a m
1 at Oak Inn	...	9-10 a m
1 at Greenhill	...	9-20 a m

35

Engine out at 7-45 a.m.
From Thornbury.
Saltaire & Undercliffe Section.

Meets 1 at Croft & Perkins	... out at 6-30 a m
1 at Oak Inn	... 6-10 a m
1 at Harris Street	... 6-50 a m

To Saltaire.

Meets 1 at Midland Station	... out at 7-25 a m
1 at Manor Row	... 7-40 a m
1 at Manningham Lane	... 7-55 a m
1 at Grove View	... 8-10 a m
1 at Branch Hotel	... 8-25 a m
1 at Ring of Bells	... 8-40 a m

Return Journey and remainder of Day.

Meets 1 at Ring of Bells	... out at 6-55 a m
1 at Branch Hotel	... 7-10 a m
1 at Grove View	... 7-25 a m
1 at Manningham Lane	... 7-40 a m
1 at Manor Row	... 7-55 a m
1 at Midland Station	... 6-10 a m
*1 at Junction of Otley Road and Barkerend Road	... 8-25 a m
1 at Cemetery Crossing ...	8-40 a m

* The Up and Down Cars must wait to see each other at this point.

Engine out at 7-50 a.m.

Leeds Road and Thornton Road Section.

Wait at Depot for the 6-30 a m out to arrive.

To Four Lane Ends.

Meets 1 at Greenhill	...	.. out at 6-10 a m
1 at Level Crossing	...	6-50 a m
1 at Peel Place	...	7-0 a m
1 at Mechanics	...	6-40 a m
3 on Double Road, Thornton Road	{	out at 7-20, 7-30 and 7-10 a m

Return Journey and remainder of Day.

Meets 3 on Double Road, Thornton Road	{	out at 8-0, 8-10 and 8-20 a m
1 at Mechanics' Institute	...	8-30 a m
1 at Well Street	...	8-30 a m
1 at Oak Inn	...	8-50 a m
1 at Greenhill	...	9-0 a m

Engine out at 8-0 a.m.

Leeds Road and Thornton Road Section.

Meets 1 at Depot	...	... out at 6-10 a m
1 at Greenhill	...	6-50 a m
1 at Level Crossing	...	7-0 a m
1 at Well Street	...	6-40 a m
1 at Mechanics	...	7-10 a m
3 on Double Road, Thornton Road	{	out at 7-10, 7-30 and 7-30 a m

Return Journey and remainder of Day.

Meets 1 on Double Road, Thornton Road	{	out at 8-10 a m
1 ,, ,,	{	8-20 a m
1 ,, ,,	{	8-30 a m
1 at Mechanics' Institute	...	8-40 a m
1 at Well Street	..	8-50 a m
1 at Oak Inn	...	9-0 a m
1 at Greenhill	...	9-10 a m

Engine out at 8-10 a.m.

Leeds Road and Thornton Road Section.

To Allerton.

Meets 1 at Depot	...	... out at 6-50 a m
1 at Greenhill	...	7-0 a m
1 at Level Crossing	...	6-40 a m
1 at Well Street	...	7-20 a m
1 at Mechanics' Institute	...	7-30 a m
3 on Double Road, Thornton Road,	{	out at 7-10, 7-50 and 8-0 a m
1 at Lady Royd	...	... out at 7-40 a m

Return Journey and remainder of Day.

Meets 1 at Lady Royd	...	... out at 8-40 a m
3 on Double Road, Thornton Road	{	out at 8-50, 9-0 and 9-10 a m
1 at Mechanics' Institute	...	out at 9-20 a m
1 at Well Street	...	9-30 a m
1 at Oak Inn	...	9-40 a m
1 at Greenhill	..	9-50 a m

39

Engine out at 8-20 a.m.

Leeds Road and Thornton Road Section.

To Four Lane Ends.

Meets 1 at Depot ...	...	out at 7-0 a m
1 at Greenhill ...	...	6-40 a m
1 at Oak Inn ..	...	7-20 a m
1 at Well Street ...	...	7-30 a m
1 at Mechanics' Institute ...		7-10 a m
3 on Double Road, Thornton Road	{	out at 7-50 a m 8-0 a m 7-40 a m

Return Journey and remainder of Day.

Meets 3 on Double Road, Thornton Road,	{	out at 8-30 a m 8-40 a m 8-50 a m
1 at Mechanics' Institute ...		9-0 a m
1 at Well Street	...	9-10 a m
1 at Oak Inn ...	...	9-20 a m
1 at Greenhill Crossing ...		9-30 a m

40

Engine out at 8-30 a.m.

Leeds Road and Thornton Road Section.

To Four Lane Ends.

Meets 1 at Depot ...	...	out at 6-40 a.m
1 at Greenhill ...	...	7-20 a m
1 at Oak Inn ...	...	7-30 a m
1 at Well Street ...		7-10 a m
1 at Mechanics' Institute ...		7-50 a m
3 on Double Road, Thornton Road	{	8-0 a m 7-40 a m 8-20 a m

Return Journey and remainder of Day.

Meets 3 on Double Road, Thornton Road	{	out at 8-40 a m 8-50 a m 9-0 a m
1 at Mechanics' Institute...		9-10 a m
1 at Well Street...	...	9-20 a m
1 at Oak Inn ...	...	9-30 a m
1 at Greenhill Crossing ...		9-40 a m

41

Engine out at 8-40 a.m.
To Allerton.

Leeds Road & Thornton Road Section.

Meets 1 at Depot ...	... out at	7-20 a m
1 at Greenhill Crossing ...		7-30 a m
1 at Level Crossing ...		7-10 a m
1 at Well Street ...		7-50 a m
1 at Mechanics' Institute ..		8-0 a m
3 on Double Road, Thornton Road	{	7-40 a m 8-20 a m 8-30 a m
1 at Lady Royd...	...	8-10 a m

Return Journey and remainder of Day.

Meets 1 at Lady Royd...	... out at	9-10 a m
3 on Double Road, Thornton Road	{	9-20 a m 9-30 a m 9-40 a m
1 at Mechanics' Institute...		9-50 a m
1 at Well Street	...	10-0 a m
1 at Oak Inn ...	...	10-10 a m
1 at Greenhill ...	...	10-20 a m

42

Leeds Road and Thornton Road Section.

(10 Minutes' Service).

CROSSING PLACES DURING A FOG.

Ten Engines Running.

- 1 at Depot
- 1 at Greenhill Crossing
- 1 at Oak Inn
- 1 at Well Street
- 1 at Mechanics' Institute
- 1 at Double Road, Thornton Road
- 1 at do. do.
- 1 at do. do.
- 1 at Lady Royd

43

Leeds Road and Thornton Road Section.

CROSSING PLACES DURING A FOG.

Thirteen Engines Running.

(7½ Minutes' Service, or 8 Minutes' Service).

- Meets 1 at Depot
- 1 at White Bear
- 1 at Victooia Crossing
- 1 at Level Crossing
- 1 at Peel Place
- 1 at Mechanics' Institute
- 1 at Double Road, Thornton Road
- 1 at do. do.
- 1 at do. do.
- 1 at Kensington Street
- 1 at Four Lane Ends
- 1 at Lady Royd

44

Leeds Road and Thornton Road Section.

CROSSING PLACES DURING A FOG.

Fourteen Engines Running.

(7½ Minutes' Service—*Saturday Afternoon*).

- Meets 1 at Depot
- 1 at White Bear
- 1 at Victoria Crossing
- 1 at Level Crossing
- 1 at Peel Place
- 1 at Mechanics' Institute
- 1 at Double Road, Thornton Road
- 1 at do. do.
- 1 at do. do.
- 1 at Kensington Street
- 1 at Four Lane Ends
- 1 at Lady Royd
- 1 at Wood's Mill, Allerton

45

Saltaire and Undercliffe Section.

CROSSING PLACES DURING A FOG.

Nine Engines Running.

- Meets 1 at Cemetery Crossing
- 1 at Otley Road Junction with Barkerend Road
- 1 at Midland Station
- 1 at Manor Row
- 1 at Manningham Lane
- 1 at Grove View
- 1 at Branch Hotel
- 1 at Ring of Bells

In the morning the Pointsman at Harris Street must not allow the 8-0 a.m. from Mechanics' Institute to leave Harris Street Points until the whole of the Saltaire, Frizinghall, and Wakefield Road Cars, also the 7-50 a.m. from Thornbury, have passed him. **The 7-30 will bring down the Staff from Depot.**

46

Leeds Road and Thornton Road Section.

SUNDAYS.

CROSSING PLACES DURING A FOG.

Seven Engines Running.

- Meets 1 at Croft & Perkins
- 1 at Oak Inn
- 1 at Mechanics' Institute
- 1 at Double Road, Thornton Road
- 1 at Kensington Street
- 1 at Lady Royd

47

Wakefield Road Section.

CROSSING PLACES DURING A FOG.

10 Minutes' Service.

SEVEN ENGINES RUNNING.

- Meets 1 at Croft Street End
- 1 at Barley Mow
- 1 at Lorne Street
- 1 at Bellet's Arms
- 1 at Holme Lane Hotel
- 1 at Tong Street Terminus

Wakefield Road Section.

Crossing Places during a FOG.
Weekdays and Sundays.
15 Minutes' Service.

Tong Street Terminus

Street House Crossing

Lorne Street

Hall Lane

48

Special Precautions

TO BE TAKEN DURING A FOG.

Cars coming off the Undercliffe and Saltaire Section at any time and returning to the Depot, at Thornbury, during a Fog, must wait **inside Well Street,** and those off **Wakefield Road at Town Hall,** and there stand clear of Leeds Road up line, and be piloted up to the Depot by a Leeds Road Car.

In all cases of dense fog, Conductors must walk in front of Engine with a lighted hand lamp.

49

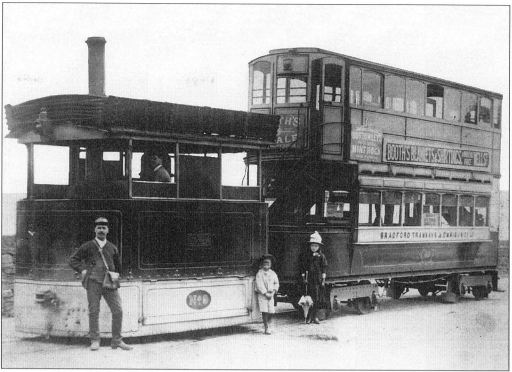

Locomotive No.8 of the Bradford Tramways & Omnibus Company was an odd-one-out built by Kitson & Co. as T104 of 1884. All BT&O rolling stock was built to the Bradford standard 4' 0" (1219mm) gauge.

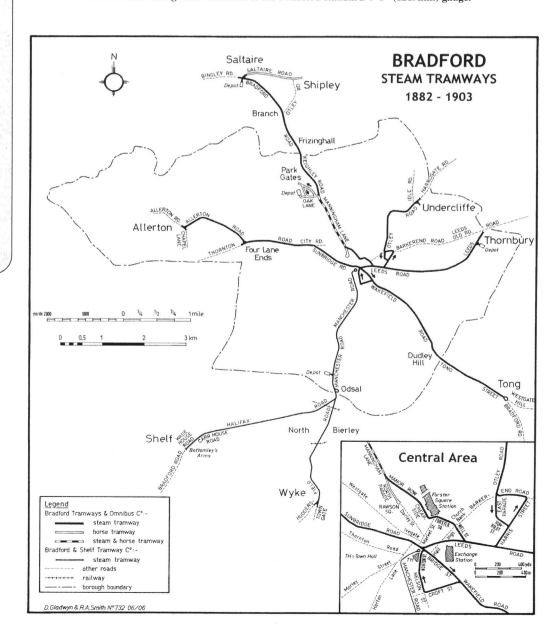

Limit of Liability

LIMITATION OF LIABILITY.

In connection with the circular of the Advisory Committee of June 15th (which appears in full in another column), it may be useful to point out that the attitude which it is proposed that Associated Companies should adopt in this matter is distinctly different from that which has been taken up by the municipalities, more especially by the Corporations of Sheffield and Huddersfield.

The municipalities contend that they are under no obligation to carry passengers, and that it is sufficient "consideration" if they are carried at all, even if the maximum fares authorised are charged. Consequently, at Sheffield and Huddersfield the passenger who is unwilling to accept the principle of the limitation of liability has no alternative but to leave the car or be ejected therefrom.

The legality of this contention is about to be contested at Sheffield by a town councillor, who has addressed the following letter to the town clerk :—

54, Bank Street, Sheffield,
May 12th, 1904.

DEAR SIR : I desire to notify the Tramways Committee through you that I decline to receive any more tickets from any conductor on the cars so long as they have printed on the back the condition seeking to limit the Corporation liability to £25.

I hope that other ratepayers will similarly decline. Please bring this letter before the Committee at their next meeting, and acknowledge its receipt.

Yours faithfully,
A. MUIR WILSON.

At the Council meeting which followed the receipt of this letter it was stated that the regulation to which objection was taken had been made upon the advice of the town clerk, whose opinion had been confirmed by counsel, and the Chairman of the Tramways Committee succeeded in obtaining a majority in favour of his scheme.

The following letter has been since received by the town clerk from Councillor Muir Wilson :—

June 11th, 1904.

DEAR SIR :
MYSELF AND THE TRAMWAYS COMMITTEE.

You will be saved considerable trouble in this matter with reference to your evidence.

Please take this letter as an unqualified admission by me of the following facts :—

This morning I rode outside a Nether Green car, arriving at High Street at 9.30. The conductor was No. 126. I paid my fare to him, and he tendered me ticket Fd3,255, which I refused to accept on the ground of there being printed on the back the condition limiting the Corporation liability. He dropped the same on the roof of the car, where it remained until Inspector No. 13 boarded the car on Sheffield Moor. He asked me for my ticket, and I told him I had not got one. He then called the conductor and requested him to demand a second fare from me, which I declined to pay. I told both the conductor and the inspector that I was prepared to accept a perfectly clean ticket without this endorsement.

If you require me to make any further admissions I shall be glad to do so. I subsequently took the ticket from the roof of the car, and have it in my possession for production.

I should like to state that both the conductor and the inspector were very courteous.

Please consult me as to the date of the hearing of the summons.

Yours faithfully,
A. MUIR WILSON.

Acting on the advice of Mr. Morse, the Advisory Committee do not propose that the Associated Companies of the B.E.T. should take up the attitude of the Sheffield Council. The Advisory Committee are informed that tramway companies, provided they give "consideration," *are* entitled to limit the amount of their liability to their passengers for any injury that may be caused to them whilst riding upon the cars. Consequently, passengers travelling on the cars of the Associated Companies who may not wish to have the company's liability limited in respect to them, can demand a non-limited liability ticket, for which they will enjoy the luxury of paying the full statutory charge.

BET Monthly Gazette, July 1904.

Sovereigns and Tram Fares

SOVEREIGNS AND TRAM FARES.

The "contrariness" of human nature is responsible for many petty annoyances in the daily round and common task of the tram conductor. What conductor does not know the garrulous old dame who prods him with her umbrella and insists upon being set down opposite some particular corner or shop; the captious old gentlemen who abuses him because of the draught or the lack of air; the poverty-stricken young mother who will only pay one fare for herself and her two children, and who appeals passionately to the other passengers for protection when he dutifully insists that the children do not come under the category of "infants in arms"; and last, but not least, the dirty and derisive little urchins who "snatch" surreptitious rides on the step? As a rule, an indifference born of experience, combined with a sense of humour or a thick skin, enables the conductor successfully to resist these inroads on his civility, patience, ingenuity and good temper. But occasionally the unreasonable conduct of a passenger places the man in uniform in a very awkward predicament. Mr. Walklate, in a letter which we publish in this issue, draws attention to the problem presented by a passenger who tenders a sovereign for his fare. The conductor may or may not be permitted to accept gold. If he accepts it, he takes the risk of its being bad. If, on the other hand, he refuses it and the passenger is honest enough to leave the car, the Company loses the fare for the distance travelled. But, usually, the passenger emphatically declines to leave the car. Mr. Walklate suggests that the path of least resistance and the path of least expense, also, is to allow the passenger to ride free ! The problem is one which lends itself to discussion, and we shall be glad to hear the views of other managers on the subject.

A tramcar passenger who was summoned recently for refusing to produce his ticket pleaded that the ticket had blown out of his hand and that this constituted an "act of God." Evidently unaware of the legal phrase, the magistrate expressed his horror at such appalling "blasphemy" and fined the man heavily.

Steam tram services in a nutshell!

Birmingham Daily Post, 27 August 1892

"To the EDITOR of the DAILY POST

Sir,— May not the unsatisfactory state of the Central Tramways compared with the success of the Aston Company be partly attributable to the following facts? The Central Company is much hindered on the journeys to Moseley, Sparkhill, and Small Heath by the indirect route from the centre of town to Bradford Street. The Aston Company's route is a direct road, and passengers often avail themselves of the cars to travel for only short distances. A great part of the Central Tramway is worked by single line. Cars on the Newtown Row route are very often kept standing for five minutes at a time, but not only is much annoyance caused to passengers, but the timetable is thereby considerably thrown out. Instead of the Perry Barr and Aston Newtown cars running at an equal time from each other, and thus giving a better service to Newtown Row, one invariably follows the other at a short distance. Many people who would otherwise travel on this route two or four times a day make a practice of never waiting for a car. If they catch one handy, well and good; if not, they walk on, and generally reach their destination before the tram. The Aston route is all double line, and no delay is caused in the working.

The Central steam trams are built to carry forty passengers. The Aston can carry half as many again, and yet there does not seem to be so much strain on the engines. The Central service on some routes is very bad. The only route that pays – viz. the cable to Handsworth – is the only one that has a really first-class service. The Aston Company's service (especially between Corporation Street and The Vine, Lichfield Road) is all that could be desired, cars following each other at an interval of only three minutes. The Central are so much hindered by Board of Trade stops. There are nine between John Bright Street and Rea Street, whereas on the Aston route, between Corporation Street and The Cross, there are only two Board of Trade stops going, and only one on the return journey.

[signed] Latton
Birmingham
August 26"

Section 20

TRACTION IN TRANSITION

This item is drawn from the *St. James's Gazette,* 19 January 1883, and is surprisingly out of date, for by then Kitson had supplied around 70 engines, Merryweather were nearing the end of their life as a tramcar builder, and poignantly Hughes had come and gone. The problem with articles like this in an influential paper, read by tea-planters in Malaya, mining engineers in Australia and men working the African diamond fields as much as the bien pensant in London, is that many who might have invested no doubt had second thoughts and those who had shares in the steam tram companies would have plagued their brokers. A curious left-over from the 1860s!

THE FUTURE OF TRAMWAYS.—What are the advantages, mechanical or otherwise, which the tramway is calculated to offer? By the correct appreciation of these we shall be able to form a sounder judgment as to the probable development of the system than seems to be common just now. The mechanical advantage obtained by the use of tramways consists solely in the diminution of the running friction—or, in other words, of the draught—as compared with that of such a vehicle as an omnibus on the common road. On a perfectly level line the draught of the tram-car is just half that of a carriage of equal weight on a road in good order. But perfectly level roads are rare, and as soon as a hill, however slight, intervenes, the advantage derivable from the use of tram-plates becomes proportionately less. On an incline of one in a hundred, which is hardly to be detected by the eye, the gain is reduced to one-third; and on a rise of one in thirty, which is considered moderate for a main road, the gain is reduced to little more than one-eighth. These mechanical facts limit the saving to be effected by the use of tramways, and explain how it is that the financial outcome of the system does not compare more favourably with that of the ordinary omnibus. There may be said to be three classes of persons, representing different and, to some respect, conflicting interests, who are mainly affected by the introduction of the tramway—namely, passengers, neighbours, and investors. It cannot be denied that to the passengers a tramway offers a gain in comfort, almost amounting to luxury. The contrast between a trip in a thoroughly well-appointed tramway car (such as those which ply over forty-two miles of line in Manchester) and the London omnibus is almost as great as that between a brougham and a tax-cart. There is more room, more ease of motion, and far greater quiet. These are very great advantages; but though it may be said that they are enough, they are all that the passenger obtains. There is no gain in economy, no gain in speed, and perhaps loss rather than gain in convenience of access to the carriage. We have, therefore, to place on the credit side of the account the increased comfort of about 430,000 passengers. We arrive at that number by allowing two journeys, for 300 days in the year, to each of the 257,600,000 passengers returned for the year ending June, 30, 1882. It is true that this is rather more than one-third of the number of railway passengers in a year; but then it must be remembered that the distances traversed by the latter are at least five times as much as those covered by the tramway passengers, the mean receipts on the tramways being 1·8d. per trip against 9·5d. per trip on the railways. Against the gain in comfort, then, of less than half a million of passengers have to be set the cost, inconvenience, and even danger, which are caused to the owners and users of all kind of vehicles, as well as of all horsemen, that use the roads on which the tramways are laid. To this item has to be added the great increase in noise occasioned by the tram-plate. As far as the tram-cars themselves are concerned, indeed, the noise of their wheels is much less to the neighbouring residents, as well as to the passengers, than is that of the wheels of the omnibus. But the vehicles using the tramway form but a small number in proportion to those using the road. And the addition to the noise made by these other vehicles, especially at corners or crossings, is deafening. Balancing gain and loss, then, it may appear that more annoyance is caused to a much larger number of people by the tramways than is saved to the 430,000 persons who use them for conveyance. And as to national gain, while the average return for 1881-82 did not allow a nominal net income of 5 per cent. (with no allowance for sinking-fund) on tramway capital, the losses incurred in depreciation of house property, in extra wear and tear of carriages and horses, and in compensation due for accidents, have to be considered. On these grounds it appears probable that the 444 miles of tramway open in England will not witness an increase at all corresponding to that which has taken place with our railway system. The main advantage offered by the railway—gain of time—is absent in the case of the tramways. And when all is said and done, nothing tells on passenger traffic like gain in time.—*St. James's Gazette.*

History Compressed

The Railway World April 1894 contained four items on one page that really give us a true snapshot of the world of tramways in 1894. First of all there was a view of the sickness within a steam tramway company, the South Staffs., then a note on the Isle of Man Tramways, who were expanding following their Act of 1893, then came 'Electric Traction in New York' covering a line proposed by Siemens & Halske, similar to that 'employed with considerable success in Buda-Pest.' The fourth, shortened here, tells of the tribulations of a horse-drawn tramway concern who, as we have shown in volume 2, turned their faces against steam traction, despite their lines being horse-killers.

"POISONING OF BRISTOL TRAMWAY HORSES

The malady which attacked with disastrous results the stud of the Bristol Tramways and Omnibus Company has now abated, and investigations into the cause of the sudden epidemic have apparently revealed the fact that the animals were poisoned by some foreign substance in the food. The company has long enjoyed the reputation of having a stud equal to that of any company in the country, and their fine appearance has always been indicative of the skill and care of those in charge ... animals that had left the stalls in apparently good health were brought back in a dying condition. The reports of the men were generally of the same character, and showed the animals in almost every case suddenly commenced to stagger, to pant, and to roar distressingly, and that gradual loss of strength supervened, followed by a rush of blood from the nose and mouth... [It seemed suspicion fell on a certain food] ...it appears that in the latter part of last year the company were supplied with what purported to be a parcel of Indian peas. [a form of maize] which were mixed with food ... the 'peas', however, proved to be the seed of an Indian vetch, well known in that country as a cumulative poison, and deadly to horses, although it is said sheep and cattle do well on it. The poison is not an immediate, but cumulative, one which accounts for the effects taking so long to manifest themselves. [similar problems were found on Glasgow and Liverpool tram horses]

Altogether one hundred horses of the Bristol Company have been affected, nine of the cases terminating fatally."

Given the thousands of cases recorded of cruelty to tram horses, one can only imagine how they suffered being whipped as 'being lazy' or 'lying back' when the poor devils were in reality dying.

In the Beginning

Birmingham and Aston Chronicle, Saturday, 30 December 1882.

"THE TRAMWAY PROPOSED

On the 1st of November, 1879 we announced in the columns of this Journal that a Tramway was projected to start from the corner of Bull Street, Birmingham passing through Stafford Street and along the Aston Road to Aston Cross, where the line, instead of continuing double, was to divide into two single lines, one running along Park Road and the other along Lichfield Road and both meeting near Aston Parish Church. On Tuesday the 4th of November the Aston Local Board was waited upon by a deputation representing some gentlemen who intended shortly to apply to the Board of Trade for a provisional order for laying down the proposed Tramway and the Board, after the interview, passed a resolution which, while favourable to the Promoters, did not commit the Board to any definite Policy.

On Saturday the 22nd November in the same year we printed the requisite notice of Application to the Board of Trade for "A provisional order pursuant to the provisions of the Tramways Act 1870" to authorise and empower the Promoters to lay down and work a number of Tramways of which the most important were almost identical with those which were opened on Tuesday the 26th December, 1882. Much newspaper correspondence following, some favourable to the project, some opposed. While opinions were also divided both on the Aston Local Board and the Birmingham Town Council, but it is worthy of notice that before the latter body Mr Coun. Mathews read a memorial signed by 2,400 residents of Aston in favour of the proposal to lay down lines both in Birmingham and Aston, the assent of the local authorities of both places was practically almost indisputable and in both cases some discussion arose but ultimately no objection was offered and on the 24th April, 1880 the provisional order of the Board of Trade authorising the construction of the Tramways specified was issued to the public. The Promoters therein mentioned were Mr C.L. Browning, Mr F.D. Bannister, Mr E. Harold Carter, Mr Charles Dudley, Mr C. Allerton Edge, Mr T.M. Hopkins, Mr Alfred Southall, Mr H.G. Smith and Mr H.E. Wallis but it was stipulated that the Corporation of Birmingham and the Local Board of Aston should have the option of substituting themselves in the place of the Promoters, subject however to the necessity of granting to the Promoters a lease for the term of 21 years.

The provisional order also imposed upon the Promoters the furnishing of a Guarantee amounting in the case of Aston to £5,000 and in the case of Birmingham to £4,800, which sums were to be deposited with the Union Bank of Birmingham and with the Birmingham Bank respectively, before they proceeded to break up any road for the purpose of laying the lines. The only other point that need be here mentioned was the stipulation for the provision of artisans cars in the morning and evening at fares not exceeding one halfpenny a mile.

One course suggested by the Promoters to the effect "that the Tramways should be working by animal or other motive power" the Board of Trade was unable to admit, but this inability was remedied by a bill brought in by Mr Joseph Chamberlain in May, 1880 and when in August 1880 the Royal Assent was given to the bill for confirming the provisional order in reference to the Birmingham and Aston Tramway it became possible that steam should be used to draw the car instead of horse-power.

It now lay with the Corporation of Birmingham at one end of the proposed line and the Local Board of Aston at the other to decide definitely within the next three months whether they would saddle themselves with the risks and responsibilities involved in taking over the construction of the tramways from the Promoters. On the 1st November a Public Meeting convened by the Ratepayers Union was held in Aston at which a motion in favour of leaving the whole undertaking in the hands of the Promoters was unanimously carried and on the 3rd November the Local Board came to the same decision. In Birmingham, however, Public feeling ran the other way, the Corporation resolved to keep the tramways in their own hands and the next seven months were occupied in protracted negotiations by the Promoters and the Corporation and thus it was not until June 1881 they were able to announce that the Promoters had effected an arrangement with each of the local authorities concerned.

THE TRAMWAYS COMPANY FORMING

On the 9th July, 1881 we published the Prospectus of the Birmingham and Aston Tramways Co. Ltd and to show the terms obtained by the Promoters we cannot do better than quote the contents of this Prospectus.

This Company is formed to lay down, work and maintain a system of Tramways between Birmingham and Aston, authorised by the "Birmingham and Aston Tramways Order 1880" which was confirmed by an act which received the Royal Assent on the 26th day of August in that year. The Tramways will commence in Stafford Street at its junction with Aston Street and the main line will terminate opposite the Chief entrance to the Aston Lower Grounds. The Directors have reason to believe that when the new street between New Street, Birmingham and Aston is in a more forward state, facilities will be afforded to the Company for extending the line as far as Bull Street. The Company will have power to construct branch lines in Park Road, Witton Road and Bevington Road.

The Company will acquire all the Rights of the Promoters and "Birmingham and Aston Tramways Provisional order 1880" and the undertaking thereby authorised, together with all Rights incidental thereto and, subject to the consent of the Board of Trade be transferred to the Company after the opening of the line to traffic.

The Promoters will receive from the Company the sum of £4,500 in consideration of the transfer of all Rights under the provisional order and this amount will include all the Barristers and other costs and are incidental to the obtaining of the Provisional order and no other promotion money will be paid, in any shape or form.

The line will be part double and part single; will be about 4 miles in length of which ¾ of a mile is in the Borough of Aston and 3 miles and ¼ in Aston. By the terms of the Provisional order both the Corporation of Birmingham and the local Board of Aston have the option of becoming Promoters of that part of the line within their respective districts and in case of their exercising such option are bound to grant leases to the Promoters on terms to be agreed upon or, failing Agreement to be settled by the Board of Trade. The Local Board of Aston have declined to exercise the Right reserved to them in the Provisional order. Consequently, the Company will leave this portion of the line and obtain the Freehold interest of it. The Corporation of Birmingham have availed themselves of the option and the terms of a Lease have been arranged which are shortly as follows:

1. The length of lease to be 21 years.
2. The Corporation to construct at their own cost that part of the line which is within the Borough.
3. The Corporation to keep the line in good and efficient repair.
4. The Company to pay the Corporation a rental of £300 a year during the first 14 years and £450 during the last seven years of the term, as interest upon the outlay incurred by the Corporation of £150 a year towards the cost of repair and maintenance of the line in the Borough.

By the terms of the Provisional order and in order to secure the due completion of the Tramways a security fund of £4,000 has to be deposited with the Corporation and £5,000 with the Local Board of Aston. Half of the £4,000 deposited with the Corporation, with interest thereon, is to be repaid to the Company at the end of two years from the opening of the line and the remainder is to be retained and invested by the Corporation till the end of the term as a security for the payment of the rent and performance of the Covenants in the Lease, the interest to be paid out to the Promoters during the progress of the work.

The prolonged negotiations had rendered necessary on application to the Board of Trade for extension of time fixed for the completion of the lines but had apparently no effect upon the Public confidence in the success of the undertaking for all the capital required was immediately taken upon.

THE TRAMWAYS LAID

In consequence of the alterations resulting from the Birmingham Improvement Scheme, it was for some time uncertain what would be the exact course taken by the Tramways but, when at last operations were commenced in April 1882 it was decided that the line should run in through Dale End as had been suggested but straight up the newly constructed Corporation Street as far as the Old Square; at the other end the plan of dividing at Aston Cross into two lines which converge at the Church was adhered to, the tramway terminating in a single line running from Aston Church to the Witton Arms.

The gauge of the lines was 3' 6" the rails being thus known as "Barker's, Patent" in which the groove is only ⅜ of an inch wide, an improvement which to a great extent removes the objections of carriage owners and is therefore one of no slight importance. The rails, it may be mentioned, were supplied by the Darlington Iron Company while the Smethwick Patent Nut and Bolt Company manufactured the sleepers which were placed upon a substantial bed of concrete, and granite pavement to the breadth of 8ft where the line was single and 16ft where double, was laid down along the whole length of the Tramway.

The work was finally completed in October 1882 having been supervised from first to last by Mr C. Allerton Edge, the Company Engineer.

THE CHOICE OF MOTIVE POWER

Meanwhile there had been no discussion as to whether the Company should be permitted to use steam power on the tramways instead of horses. As before mentioned, Mr Chamberlain's Bill had rendered this possible, but it was still necessary to obtain the consent of both the local Authorities through which district the Tramway passed.

The question came before the Birmingham Town Council in July and before the Aston Local Board in August 1882, the usual arguments were adduced to the effect that steam engines would be dangerous because they would frighten the horses and also be difficult to stop; the usual irrefutable replies were made that on the one hand many horses are never frightened at the engines while almost all soon become accustomed to them, and on the other that engines can be by means of strong brakes pulled up with far greater ease than vehicles drawn by horses. To these reasons may be added the more unimportant fact that the use of engines prevents a large amount of inavoidable cruelty incurred in starting and stopping heavily laden tramcars as these operations constantly necessitate severe strain upon the powers of an ordinary tramcar horse. The Company were naturally desirous of obtaining permission to use steam power as being considerably less expensive than horsepower, and on several occasions in the columns of this Journal we supported a provision which seems to us in every way, and from every point of view, altogether desirable. Fortunately, both for the Company and the Public, the Local Authority very liberally gave their permission and the Company anxious to procure the best engines resolved to order them from two of the best known Makers, Messrs Kitson and Company of Leeds and Messrs. Wilkinson and Company of Wigan.

THE TRAMWAY INSPECTED.

Everything being now ready it remained for the lines, cars and engines to pass successfuly through the ordeal of an Official inspection before the Company could actually commence operations. Accordingly on Friday the 22nd December 1882 Major-General Hutchinson, the Official Inspector appointed by the Local Government Board made a through and searching investigation along the whole route. Many Gentleman interested in the Tramway otherwise were present among others being The Mayor of Birmingham and Councillors Payton, Lawley,

Parker, Brinsley, Baldwin and Barker. Mr Orford-Smith (Town Clerk), Mr Till (Borough Surveyor), Mr Ferndale (Chief of Police), Mr Arthur Keen, Mr R. Williams, Mr Joesbury (Chairman of the Handsworth Local Board), Messrs Millward, Reeding, Wragg, Bloor, Darrell and Nightingale, Members of the Aston Local Board, Mr Browning (Chairman of the Tramway Company) and Messrs. Pritchard, Southall, T. Smith and H.G. Smith and Wilson (Directors), Mr C.A. Edge (Engineer) and Mr E. Harold Carter.

About half past twelve o'clock a tramcar containing about 50 passengers and drawn by one of the Kitson engines darted from the Old Square, General Hutchinson however walked as far as Aston Cross and subjected the lines to a close examination. It will be enough to point out that the only points on which any anxiety could possibly be felt were as to the behaviour of the engines at sharp corners and upon steep gradients and accordingly the severest tests were applied at every possible place of difficulty. The engines were driven at a higher speed round several of the most formidable curves up and down the steep gradients in Park Road and in the course of their being driven at high speed were in fact always stopped instantaneously by the powerful brakes. The quiet working of the engines, the smoothness of their motion and the freedom from steam and smoke were especially noticeable and appeared to satisfy the requirements of the Engineers who witnessed the trial and of General Hutchinson, the Inspector.

The lines also gave full satisfaction as regards the general traffic and the running of the tramcars. The whole length of the line has been constructed under the personal supervision of Mr Edge and measures 3 miles, 2 furlongs, 7 chains of which 2 miles, 1 furlong 6 chains are in Aston and 1 mile, 1 furlong 1 chain in the Borough; the steepest inclines 1 in 11 and 1 in 23 being in Park Road, Aston; the length of the longest incline 5 furlongs with an average gradient of 1 in 48 in Aston Road. The sharpest curve is 40ft radius. The gauge of the rails from the outer edges of groove is 3ft 6in. and the width of Bessemer steel rail on building surface 3ft with ⅜in grooves.

The cars were built by the Metropolitan Carriage Company, Saltley and weigh about two tons 3 cwt. each. They are constructed to carry 20 passengers inside and 24 outside. The engines can be worked from a pressure of 75 lbs. up to 150 lbs. per inch. Their length is overall 11ft. and width 6ft. The cars and engines are fitted with steam brakes and will be lighted with Muller's Patent gas.

THE TRAMWAY AT WORK

With the express sanction of General Hutchinson the Company were allowed to begin running their cars on Boxing Day and to judge by the great crowds who since then availed themselves of the new means of locomotion there can be little doubt that a prosperous and useful existence is before the new undertaking and that both the Public and the Shareholders will look back with complete satisfaction to the starting of the Birmingham and Aston Tramways Company at the Christmastide of the year 1882.

You gentlemen of Edgbaston

You gentlemen of Edgbaston,
Who loll in broughams at ease,
You'd better on this tram question
Just mind your Q's and P's.

You've set your face against steam trams
Upon the West End routes,
And proved, by this, your nothing but
A lot of selfish brutes.

The greatest good unto the great—
Est number must be done,
And in my case I'm glad to say,
That number's number one.

What's it to me if you object
To live in steam and smoke,
Why we must ride through Edgbaston,
Though you may have to choke.

What if your flowers and plants decay,
To your disgust intense;
Pooh! what are these when placed beside
Our great convenience.

And if they will to property
Its value soon abate,
Be thankful you have property,
It can depreciate.

The sulphur, too, you rave about
Which in your rooms they pour,
It's not a grain a minute each,
He says it can't be – Moore.

And if the bell will jangling go,
From morn till eventide:
Put up with it - we don't object,
Who off the route reside.

Not everyone fancied the new trams! More of this and similar sagas will be found in our Volume 1. I suppose, ultimately it depends where you stood – ladies and gentlemen, disliking and fearing the hordes moving out of city centres, artisans seeking to better their dwellings by moving a 'penn'orth of tram-ride' away from the city centres, the shareholders and those who sought employment, and omnibus operators – all had an axe to grind. But no-one could foresee how Edgbaston is now...
The Town Crier, March 1884.

Success ... and Failure

There are a number of viewpoints on exactly why urban steam tram companies were, in the main, unsuccessful or, at least, just viable. The concerns were undercapitalised to the extent that there was little spare cash to buy new locomotives; the ground-level managers were far too busy just running the lines day-to-day to be able to evaluate any improved models the steam tram manufacturers offered (and they were precious few); many had half an eye on the forthcoming electrical systems, and those which might have done well found themselves lumbered with either 'wrong' engines, trade slumps, or faced such incredible and articulate vituperation that the steam tram protagonists deliberately stayed low-key, just collecting their meagre dividends. Finally there was the inescapable difficulty that licences for steam trams were always issued for short periods, giving little security.

If we take an individual and relatively successful company, the Birmingham & Aston Steam Tramway Company, the problems can be encapsulated. They never built their promised extensions but bought 28 engines, three in 1882, nine in 1883, four in 1885, and twelve in 1886. Twenty-four were by Kitson and quite orthodox, two by Wilkinson were regarded as scrap after seven or eight years, and their one experiment, no.27 of 1886, a Kitson compound, was regarded with disfavour: "The engine is rarely in service, the ordinary engine preferred". Although repaired, their bogie trailers (built 1882-86) were only noticeable inasmuch as four of them were made from eight four wheelers, and two – the most advanced design – were single-ended. But nothing in their fleet was less than sixteen years old when the B & A was sold out to Aston Manor UDC. And yet this tramway had started with such high hopes and many good wishes from influential people.

In this context it is worth quoting from an editorial leader in the *Birmingham and Aston Chronicle, Nechells Gazette,* and *Saltley Courier* of Saturday, 30 December 1882, which occupied virtually the whole of one page.

The article began with stating "Now that this long-promised addition to the means of a communication between Birmingham and Aston has been fully and successfully effected, it seems desirable to place on record some account of the successive steps in the execution of such an important scheme; by so doing we feel that we shall add greatly to the interest with which our readers must naturally regard the latest of our public improvements." Rhetorically, the editor asked why trams, precursors of railways that they were, had not arrived sooner, and answered himself that engines would consume vast amounts of fuel "dragging heavy loads up the steep gradients of many high roads", and just as importantly there were not then the "thickly populated suburban districts round most of our great towns" which would make tramways "exceedingly lucrative". In the intervening 50 years, towns had expanded as labour moved from country to city, locomotive engines had advanced and, says our Editor, "it seems impossible to place any limit upon the advantages which may eventually be enjoyed throughout the length and breadth of the land when tramways come to be universally adopted."

He was, sadly, both right and wrong, for electric trams proved to be the means adopted to expand "throughout the length and breadth of the land". He admitted there were objections to tramways – "Objectors by the score may be found" – but shot them down one by one. One claim was that they injured the road, "nonsense" was his robust answer. "Now whatever may be alleged by unreasonable grumblers, there can be no fear that the lines of the Birmingham and Aston Tramway Company will tend to deteriorate the roads on which they are laid. On the contrary, in Aston, the Company is actually bound under the regulations of the Tramway Act to keep a large portion of the road in thorough repair, and in this manner the ratepayers are relieved very considerably at the expense of the company".

"In some cases, it must be admitted the lighter and fancier classes of carriages" could get damaged due to their narrow tyres dropping into the slot of the tram rails, but the Birmingham & Aston "has shown all reasonable forethought by adopting an unusually narrow groove." It was true that as new the slot was narrow at seven-eighths of an inch (22.225mm) but the points or switches were ever a problem.

The company had even turned a disadvantage into a pat-on-the-back. Where there was not sufficient road width to allow double track they had either to use single, or interlaced lines, or operate on a one-way system, but "As the cars ran on lines carefully laid for the purpose, there is an immense decrease in the friction encountered by the wheels as compared with those of a vehicle running upon the ordinary surface of the road. As a result of this ... it also follows that less power is required to move any given weight on the tram-cars, than would be necessary to move the same weight upon the road."

The mechanics of 'friction' were covered mentioning for readers to whom this was a new concept, that the rolling resistance of a wheel on steel rails must always be less than that of an iron tyred wheel on cobbles or other road surfaces. "Another point in which the superiority of tramways is incontestably established is the easy and quiet motion by which a tramway journey is pleasantly distinguished from the rough and tumble jogging inseparable from travelling by omnibus or even carriage, and in these days of high pressure and nervous exhaustion, such a consideration should by no means be lost sight of." The pre-history of the line (see our volume 2) took up a column or so, giving the passage of the Tramways Act through Parliament, mileage, and the agreement with the two relevant councils, the Corporation of Birmingham and the Local Board of Aston, later Aston UDC, (in passing having just two councils to deal with was a great advantage – other companies were bedevilled with difficulties and local rivalries. If council A liked it, council B would always say no!) There was some degree of pride in the announcement that the sleepers and fixings were manufactured by the Smethwick Patent Nut and Bolt Company, and the rails were of course British, being rolled by the Darlington Iron Company in best Bessemer steel.

The company then had to decide which form

of motive power to use, and it is worth quoting the whole of the relevant paragraph in order to contrast the relative ease with which they passed various hurdles, without the shenanigans practised elsewhere. "Meanwhile there had been much discussion as to whether the Company should be permitted to use Steam Power on the tramways instead of horses. As before mentioned, Mr Chamberlain's Bill had rendered this possible, but it was still necessary to obtain the consent of both the Local Authorities through whose district the tramway passed. The question came before the Birmingham Town Council in July, and before the Aston Local Board in August, 1882; the usual arguments were adduced, to the effect that steam engines would be dangerous because they would frighten horses, and also be difficult to stop: the usual irrefutable replies were made, that on the one hand many horses are never frightened by the engines, while almost all would become accustomed to them, and on the other the engines can by means of strong brakes be pulled up with far greater ease than vehicles drawn by horses. To these reasons may be added the not unimportant fact that the use of engines prevents a large amount of unavoidable cruelty incurred in starting and stopping heavily-laden tram cars ... Fortunately both for the Company and the public, the Local Authorities very liberally gave their permission and the Company, anxious to procure the best engines, resolved to order them from two of the best-known makers, Messrs Kitson and Co. of Leeds and Messrs Wilkinson and Co. of Wigan."

Everything being ready, Major-General Hutchinson, the appointed Inspector, arrived on Friday 22 December 1883 (roughly four years after the application for a Provisional Order to build the tramway was announced) and he made a "thorough and searching" inspection of the whole route. "Many gentlemen interested in tramway enterprises were present, among others being the Mayor of Birmingham and Councillors Payton, Lawley Parker, Brinsley, Baldwin and Barker, Mr Orford Smith (Town Clerk), Mr Till (Borough Surveyor), Mr Farndale (Chief of Police), Mr Arthur Kean, Mr R.Williams, Mr Joesbury (Chairman of the Handsworth Local Board), Messrs Millward, Reading, Wragg, Bloor, Darrall and Nightingale (members of the Aston Local Board), Mr Broughton (Chairman of the Tramway Company) and Messrs Pritchard Southall, T. Smith, H.G. Smith and Wilson (directors), Mr C.A. Edge (engineer) and Mr E. Harold Carter".

We presume that around this time the menfolk (and the omission of ladies is noticeable compared with electric tramways twenty years later when some Lady Mayoresses actually drove the first cars with great aplomb) had some refreshment as then "About half-past twelve o'clock, a tramcar containing fifty passengers, and drawn by one of Kitson's engines, started from the Old Square. General Hutchinson however walked as far as Aston Cross, and subjected the line to a close examination; it will be enough to point out that the only points on which any anxiety could possibly be felt were as to the behaviour of the engines at sharp corners and upon steep gradients, and accordingly the severest tests were applied at every possible place of difficulty. The engines were driven at a high speed round several of the most formidable curves, up and down the steep gradients in Park-road, and in the course of their descent at high speed, were checked almost instantaneously by the powerful brakes. The quiet working of the engines, the smoothness of their motion, and the freedom from steam and smoke were especially noticeable and appeared to satisfy the requirements of the engineers who witnessed the trial and of General Hutchinson the Inspector."

Described as three miles two furlongs and seven chains long, the steepest gradients were noted by the Inspector as being 1:11 and 1:23 in Park Road, Aston, where compulsory stops were to be made at the top! There were regrettably no fixed stops as we know them today, drivers having to stop when and where required. The sharpest curve was of forty feet radius, the gauge of the rails "from the outer edges of the grooves" was the later-to-be Birmingham standard of 3' 6" (1067mm) while (and as this is mentioned three times one feels there was still some element of doubt) the groove was only seven-eighths of an inch against a bearing surface of three inches width.

The trailers (or 'carriages') were tiddlers, weighing two tons three cwt each, carrying forty-four passengers. It was claimed the engines (a mere eleven feet long and six feet wide) and the trailers were fitted with steam brakes (although no trailers were known to be so fitted) and lighting was by 'Muller's patent gas'. "With the express sanction of General Hutchinson, the Company were allowed to begin running their cars on Boxing Day, and to judge by the crowds, who have since then availed themselves of the new means of locomotion, there can be little doubt that a prosperous and useful existence is before the new undertaking, and that both the public and the shareholders will look back with complete satisfaction to the Birmingham and Aston Tramways Company in the Christmastide of the year eighteen hundred and eighty-two."

Mechanical problems reared their heads very quickly, but failings in both trackwork and the actual performance of the rolling stock could have been overcome. It is however an inescapable fact that the very existence of steam trams running on public roads left them open to attack. People today, other than those directly affected, are seemingly quite blasé when details of another accident killing two, three, four or five people is read out in the course of a television news bulletin. How does it go? Blah, blah, "two people, a boy and girl killed", blah, blah, "when their car was hit by a lorry", blah, blah, "lorry driver taken to hospital with bruises", blah, blah, "today's total of dead on the roads twenty-two" blah, blah, and then we watch the weather forecast.

But it was not like that in the 1880s. There was no TV, no radio, just newspapers which appealed primarily to the middle class ratepayers – the people who voted for, and stood for, the local council; the people who could, would, and did, influence the success of a tramway. Some councillors hated tramways with virulence that is difficult now to comprehend, while others took every opportunity to disparage them.

We have a cameo of this in November 1884.

"The Surveyor [of the Rowley Regis Local Board of Health] reported that the Birmingham Western District Tramway Company were posting notices to apply for a provisional order for the construction of a line from Oldbury boundary to Blackheath, thence through the village of Rowley, and along the Rowley Road to the Dudley boundary at Dixon's Green.

The Chairman: "I have to ask what is your proposition with regard to the proposed line?"

Mr Taylor: "I should say dead against it."

Mr Barker: "I should keep them out of the parish."

Mr Taylor: "They ought not to be allowed."

The Chairman said he was very strongly prejudiced against the tramways when he saw how they were coming into the roads in all directions, and endangering people's lives and limbs. But before saying anything about it at the Board he felt disposed to call a parish meeting and see whether the inhabitants wished for the tramways or not.

Mr Taylor: "If the tramways come through Blackheath there will be one killed every day."

The Chairman: "I must confess I am dead against all tramways. I hate them, they're the ruin of our roads.

Mr Round: "Are the roads sufficiently wide for them?"

The Chairman: "Nothing like sufficiently wide..."

Continuing, he said it was no joke to drive up Dudley Street with that beastly thing (the tramcar) elbowing one up. If his horse had not been staunch on a recent occasion he should have been knocked over, as there was not six inches of room all the way up. Mr Round considered the tramways should not be allowed where the roads were not wide enough.

If this wasn't enough, further discussion then ensued in which the Chairman expressed his regret that they could only oppose the tramways after calling a public meeting, but the Clerk informed him that as it was only a Provisional Order the Board could decide against it without the sanction of the ratepayers. It was fairly obvious from the reports, if not expressly said, "Whoopee" and "hurrahs" were in the air at the thought of being able to hinder progress.

"If the Board were unanimously of opinion that they ought to oppose the obtaining of the Order they might do so at once, and he had no doubt that the mere show of opposition would make the promoters do as was done in a previous instance, [and] withdraw the application at once. He [the Chairman] moved that the application for a Provisional Order for the extension of the tramway system to Rowley be opposed by the Board. Mr Taylor seconded, and the motion was unanimously carried."

Did the members of the Local Board ever guess the furore they were to cause? The local, very influential newspaper (not one to wholly back tramways) inveighed against them. "*Dudley Herald*, Saturday, 20 November 1884: We much regret the necessity for again advertising to the policy pursued by the Rowley Local Board of Health with reference to tramways projects; and we do so now because we believe that their policy, if successful, must necessarily be most injurious to the interests of those the Board profess to represent ... Tramways have

become as essential to the prosperity of populous places as railways; and those districts whose governing bodies take an enlightened view of their duties will do all they can to encourage the formation of steam tramways, which cannot fail to be beneficial to the traders, inhabitants and property owners, and to be a great convenience to the public. Those, on the contrary, who opposed tramway schemes show that they are not alive to the value of the progress which is going on around them; their districts will decline and prosperity vanish, and soon the value of the property and the number of inhabitants, which are now sufficient to constitute a guarantee of success to a tramway project, will have become so reduced as to render such an undertaking impracticable."

The Birmingham Western District Tramway Company proposed to make this new line from the main line at Oldbury, through the heart of the old manufacturing area of the Black Country, thus going via Blackheath and Rowley Regis to Dixon's Green, Dudley. "The Rowley Board appear to be inclined to oppose this scheme, as they did the one to connect Cradley and Netherton with Dudley; and one member of the Board expressed himself as 'dead' against tramways generally. In his representative capacity he should remember that it is possible in being 'dead' against this particular scheme, to be acting 'dead' against the interests of his constituents, whose welfare he is bound to make his first consideration. The pleas about danger to the public is scarcely worth noticing, in view of the fact that steam tramways have proved to be less dangerous than the same amount of traffic conducted by ordinary vehicles. The tramcars take up a less width of road than an ordinary wagon, are far more under control, and are always in care of responsible men. The feeling of the Rowley Board is in strong contrast with that of Sedgley who, after the tramway had been in operation for some time, stated publicly, that 'it had conferred a boon on the parish', and had given to its inhabitants 'the greatest benefit the Sedgley people had ever had'. A public meeting of the ratepayers and inhabitants of the parish of Rowley would probably very much alter the views of their representatives as to tramway enterprise."

The minutes of the prosaically named Streets & Gas Committee, whose members were drawn from the Dudley Borough Council General Purposes Committee, followed an (almost) neutral stance until 3 January 1883 when "The ex-Mayor reported that owing to the action taken by the Rowley Local Authorities, the Promoters of the above Tramways had decided not to proceed further in their application for a Provisional Order for the construction of these tramways."

Nearby Brierley Hill was another relatively small area but lay athwart the line of the Dudley & Stourbridge Steam Tramway; at meeting after meeting the Local Board scritched and scratched at the subject; it does seem a fact if only some truth was spoken the tramway company brought many of their problems on themselves. In a typical example reported on 10 April 1886, "The Chairman said he had several complaints about the smoke and steam issuing from the tramway engines. Mr Roberts, of Church Hill, said it was a very great nuisance to his house. The Tramway Company were of course under certain regulations which they were bound to obey. Mr Fereday said that if there was extra smoke it should be allowed to emit before the populous places were reached. Mr Grove said he had been struck with the want of facility to get in and out of the tramcars. Twelve months ago he understood the Company applied to the Board for leave to enlarge the cars and engines six inches. If that six inches additional had been made to the cars, travelling would be much more convenient. The Chairman said the increased width only applied to the engines, and only one he believed had yet been enlarged. The directors of the Tramway Company however were not very obliging in other ways. Several gentlemen, himself included, having sons who went to the Stourbridge Grammar School, had applied for season tickets for them between Brierley Hill and Stourbridge. He had himself written two or three times, and the only answer he could get was that if the boys wanted season tickets they must pay the full price of one between Dudley and Stourbridge – nearly £4 a year. The directors said that was cheap enough, and as low as they could afford it. He however did not see why Dudley should have an advantage over Brierley Hill. He had offered £2 for a season ticket for his son – that being half the price of a ticket from Dudley to Stourbridge – and thought it a fair sum, seeing that it was only 2d. from Brierley Hill to Stourbridge, and 3d. from Brierley Hill to Dudley. The company however refused to do anything of the sort." The railway, for the same journey, allowed Grammar School children a season ticket at the cost of £1.17.6 but "The Tramway Company would not take £2 for the same distance (interjection – Oh!). He considered the Company had treated him in a rather cavalier spirit. It was not for him to tell them how to conduct their business, but his opinion was that they were not looking after their own interests."

Another councillor (Mr Guest) said he had approached the chairman of the Tramways Company to ask to help "but he positively refused ... with respect to the inconveniences of travelling, Mr Guest thought the Board had only to ask for better accommodation – more regularity in starting and stopping – to get it. It would be for the benefit of the shareholders and of the public who used the trams."

After some further discussion Mr Guest then seems to have got carried away, declaring "The times kept by the trams were bad, the convenience was bad, and the conduct of the conductors was very reprehensible and careless." One in three of the trams passing "the lamp in the centre of High Street" did not stop at all, with the conductors looking neither right nor left. He agreed the engines had slackened their speed, "but the wheels never ceased revolving." He then seems to have back-tracked and admitted "No doubt the public are somewhat to blame, as people sometimes stood twenty yards on either side of the proper stopping point, and caused the tram to stop sometimes by Mr Marsh's shop, and again at the Horse Shoe Market. That was a cause of complaint for the company."

After a discussion over whether the track should be doubled to make matters better ... (it should, but a Mr Freeth added that a double set of rails would serve but to block the way)...the Chairman added that the steam and smoke alluded to earlier (Mr Freeth, again, "he had frequently seen as much emitted between Round Oak and the Level as would come from a railway engine") could be avoided if the engine ran more regularly. "Owing to prolonged stoppages, and the consequent loss of time, the drivers sometimes exceeded the speed allowed by the Act of Parliament. Were the speed uniform the smoke and steam would not be emitted."

And then the Chairman stated his Board should have received better treatment "...at Oldbury, Moseley, and Balsall Heath he found the tramway companies had to pay a large sum of money to the Boards for the privileges of laying down the lines ... The Brierley Hill Board had pressed for no such payment."

Even when it was obvious that steam tramways could be perceived as a problem many councils fully understood that both the employers and (in the main) employees were doing their best to operate as well as they could. Birmingham Council set its face against steam and tried to bully all the local area councils to support them in "Suppressing the Steam Tram Nuisance."

Early in May 1888 the Town Clerk of Dudley read a communication from his opposite number in Birmingham stating that a conference of local authorities was to be held in Birmingham "to consider the best means to abate the nuisance arising out of the emission of steam from tram engines..." The council members agreed that the Town Clerk might attend but, and it was a big but, "they might agree to do something to abate the nuisance, but they must not countenance anything that would have a tendency to interfere with the public convenience which tramways undoubtedly gave. They may be a great nuisance and danger, but the beneficial element predominated, and, therefore, they must not do anything likely to check their usefulness – (hear, hear)." The Tipton Local Board agreed with Dudley but made an away-day of it, sending three councillors plus the Chairman!

The end result of the conference was, inevitably, a fudge, and worth quoting to show how attitudes could vary from town to town. "A conference of representatives from local bodies of the district to consider what steps may be taken to prevent the nuisance arising from steam trams was held on Wednesday at Birmingham – Mr Weekes (Clerk to the Aston Local Board) read a resolution as follows: 'That this conference of representatives of local authorities of districts through which the tramways of the Central Company, the Aston Company, and Midland Company pass, is of opinion that the use of steam as a motor ought to be abolished unless the dangers and nuisance arising therefrom in the shape of smoke, steam, and offensive odours are minimised so as to cease to be a cause of reasonable ground of complaint by passengers or the public. And inasmuch as the law for breaches of the Board of Trade regulations in these respects cannot be enforced against the real offenders – namely the tramway directors and managers of the companies, but only against engine drivers, whose stereotyped defence is that they are entrusted with defective engines – there is no alternative for the local authorities but to make the further use of steam absolutely dependent on their own regulations being complied with. And the members present undertake to respectively recommend their authorities, when the existing licenses for steam-user expire, to regrant them for a limited period only (say twelve months), with the understanding that they will not be renewed unless in the meantime the escape of smoke and steam is brought within proper control, and the foul stenches prevented by the use of suitable 'fuel'. The Mayor said he would accept that resolution, but not for adoption by the conference. Mr E.M. Warmington (Town Clerk of Dudley) said if the companies would only meet the objectors in the matter of the fuel they used, the consent to burn North-country coke, the bye-laws of the Board of Trade were sufficient to keep down all the other evils complained of; and if the companies would remedy that one matter, they should not attempt to hamper the carrying on of the tramways, which were undoubtedly a great public convenience. Mr Wright (Rowley Regis) and Dr Underhill (Tipton Local Board) expressed sympathy with the objects of the conference, and the latter gentleman drew attention to the fact that the engines of the South Staffordshire Company in his district travelled at a highly dangerous rate, and not only emitted steam and sulphur, but also fire, which at night was a grave source of danger to the drivers of horses. A lengthy discussion took place on the matter."

Inspection of the Birmingham Central Tramways

Birmingham Daily Post, 29 October, 1884:

"THE INSPECTION OF THE BIRMINGHAM CENTRAL TRAMWAYS

The Mayor's prescience.

The inspection of the lines of the Birmingham Central Tramways Company was completed yesterday by Major-General Hutchinson, of the Board of Trade. The northern section of the lines were inspected on Monday, and yesterday the southern portion, commencing in Station Street and going by way of Bradford Street and the Moseley Road, to Moseley, was traversed. Major-General Hutchinson will report the result of his inspection to the company, and until his certificate has been received the lines cannot be opened.

After an inspection a luncheon was provided at the Queen's Hotel. Mr J. Christopher James, chairman of the company, presided; and there were also present the Mayor (Alderman Cook), Councillors Lawley Parker, Baldwin, Moore, Barker; and Messrs Lake, Bishop, A. Handiside and C.E. Davison (directors of the company) ; the Hon. R.C. Parsons of the firm Kitson and Co., Leeds, makers of the tramway engines; W.S. Till (borough surveyor), C.E. Mathews, J. Slater, J. Avins, J. Bigwood, T. Parsons, W.B. Wilkinson, B. Weekes, T. Milward, T. Wragge, J. Ansell, W.J. Davis, E. Pritchard (engineer of the company), J. Smith, (solicitor), B.S. Biram (manager) &c. There was a large attendance.

After the usual loyal toasts, the CHAIRMAN proposed "The Inspecting Officer of the Board of Trade", and regretted Major-General Hutchinson was unavoidably prevented from attending that meeting. – The MAYOR next proposed "Tramway Enterprise." He wished the directors of the company success in their great undertaking. He believed the company had undertaken to lay down something like twenty miles of rails in and near to Birmingham, representing about thirteen miles of road. The company had, he was told, a subscribed capital of £170,000, a large amount of which was raised in Birmingham. He believed that in future tramways would be the means of locomotion for people from and to their workshops. He was very glad to learn the company proposed to use steam power upon their lines. If they were to have penny stage fares they must have steam as the motive power of the trams. (Hear hear.) It would not be long, he predicted, before steam was superseded as a motive power. At the present time steam was very much preferable to horseflesh, and he believed that in time to come even steam would be superseded. (Hear hear). So far as he had heard the trials which had taken place had been very satisfactory.

The CHAIRMAN acknowledged the toast, after which Mr BISHOP gave "The Local Authorities", and said that from the first he had been impressed with the fact that the Birmingham Corporation was in favour of the tramway enterprise. They had very much to thank the authorities for in the carrying out of the enterprise.

Mr LAWLEY PARKER, in acknowledging the toast on behalf of the Birmingham Town Council, cordially welcomed the new tramway facilities. He mentioned that as soon as the system was in working order an inspector would be appointed on behalf of the Corporation to see the engines were in proper working order, and that there would be no danger to the passengers. He hoped that the company would not be governed by a desire to pay large dividends; but that they would be vigilant in seeing that the regulations of the Board of Trade would be properly carried out. (Hear hear.) He hoped that the company would at once start running workmen's trams, and suggested the penny fare system should be taken into consideration. The lines were in every way suitable for such a system. (Hear hear.)

[Mr MILWARD (Aston), Mr JOSBURY (Handsworth), Mr BOWEN (Balsall Heath), Councillor BALDWIN, and Messrs AVINS and WILKINSON (King's Norton) all acknowledged and added to the toasts.]

Mr J. SMITH submitted "The Engineers", and this having been replied to, the company separated.

A fairly serious, if to our eyes whimsical, project of the 1870s.

Trams and Tramways in Birmingham

TRAMS AND TRAMWAYS IN BIRMINGHAM.

THE development of the tramway system in Birmingham and the neighbourhood during the last sixteen or eighteen years, is one of the most salient marks of the immense progress of the town during that time. Those who can look back thirty or thirty-five years, can remember the time when five or six omnibuses were sufficient to meet the wants of the suburban residents. These were, as a rule, largish vehicles, drawn by four horses, and the drivers and conductors of them were well-known on the road, and seemed to go on from year to year without change. There was a long green one, drawn by four horses, which used to ply between Handsworth and Birmingham, the conductor of which was one of the best known men in the district. He knew all his customers, who almost claimed their respective places in the "'bus," and who were generally to be found waiting at a certain spot to the minute. There was an equally well-known one on the Bristol Road, generally drawn by four greys. It was the property of a firm of the name of Russell, and was driven by a member of that firm whose fair hair and whiskers earned him the sobriquet of "yellow Russell" among some of the passengers.

The first tramway put down in Birmingham was that to Handsworth; the Bristol Road followed, and, after a long interval, came in quick succession the immense enterprises of the Central, the Birmingham and Aston, and the Birmingham and Midland Tramways Companies. As an example of contrast, we may compare the expenditure of the Birmingham Central Tramways Co. in their undertaking, with the old-fashioned 'bus days before mentioned. On September 3rd, 1887, the Company issued the following statement of expenditure to Midsummer of the same year:—

ANALYSIS OF THE EXPENDITURE OF THE BIRMINGHAM CENTRAL TRAMWAYS CO., LIMITED, UPON CAPITAL ACCOUNT TO JUNE 30TH, 1887.

	£	s.	d.
Permanent Way	122,181	18	6
Depôts	82,932	2	1
Engines	59,961	9	9
Steam Cars	17,839	16	5
Horse Cars and Omnibuses... ...	17,746	10	10
Horses	27,321	12	3
Harness	4,403	13	7
Machinery and Tools	3,650	18	11
Office and Waiting Rooms' Furniture, &c.	853	18	11
Miscellaneous Stock...	2,605	5	9
Cable Engines	2,707	10	0
Parliamentary Acts and Orders, Engineering Fees, Legal Costs, Preliminary Expenses, and other Payments representing the cost of various concessions held by the Company	115,720	17	3
	£457,925	14	3

Our illustration represents a scene at the King's Heath depôt of the Central Co., and the day will come when no doubt this picture will be looked at with curiosity, and when motors of a less cumbrous description will have taken the place of the somewhat unwieldy engines represented there. Beside the King's Heath depôt, which is one of the smallest, the Company have six others, some of them covering acres of land, and finding employment for hundreds of workmen.

If a procession of tramway rolling stock were inaugurated, the Central would lead the way with 70 engines, 64 steam cars, 23 horse cars, 50 omnibuses, and several hundred horses. The Birmingham and Aston would follow with 27 engines and 26 cars; while the Birmingham and Midland would bring up with 24 engines, and a similar number of cars.

After all that can be advanced against the steam tramcar in the way of objections to its large bulk, its smells, its ugliness, its noisiness, and its alleged dangerousness; it must be allowed that it is a great convenience to an immense number of people; and that it has abolished a very large amount of cruelty to horses. The iron steed does not stand panting, perspiring, and exhausted at the end of its run, so that humane people actually feel conscientious scruples as to mounting the vehicle he has again to start away with in a few moments. There was plenty of that sort of voiceless, brute suffering in the old times, and there is plenty now. The tram-rider, however, is free from any qualms of conscience on that score, as in company with forty or fifty companions he buoyantly travels up Snow Hill, Summer Hill, Bradford Street, Spring Hill, or the hill on Coventry Road. The horse of science and mechanics is untiring, and as soon as he has got to the end of his "trip," as his driver calls it, he is quite ready to start back again, and it must be conceded that great credit is due to the drivers of these immense machines, that, considering the enormous numbers of people they carry, the accidents have been so rare.

Democratic in its tendency, the tramcar brings together various sorts and conditions of people, and it is sometimes a motley and various group that stands waiting at the terminus for its latter-day chariot to approach. Here is a mother with six or seven bundles and four or five children; there a bank-clerk, whose collars are a credit to his laundress and whose pious carefulness as to the cut of his clothes is a joy and a support to his tailor; while on the right hand a pretty Board School teacher carries her half-dozen books in a strap, and looks thankful that she can get to her home in the suburbs for the small expenditure of one penny. There is sure to be an assemblage of three or four giggling girls; for living in the suburbs seems to be conducive to progenies of daughters, and, of course, everyone lives in the suburbs. The girls usually come out in twos or threes, and a run into town, in the tramcar, and back is an immense pleasure to them. The female sex is gregarious, so that, in addition to the three or four giggling graces, a pretty and pleasant group, the observer may rely on seeing—especially on Mondays—a coterie of matrons; young and otherwise; who talk quietly, but incessantly and confidentially; for what with husbands, children, and servants they have much to talk about, and in some of the talk they display the air and the mysteriousness of conspirators. Quite a contrast to these is the tall middle-aged bachelor, whose well-brushed hat is evidently the recipient of constant personal attention, whose solicitude is principally devoted to himself, and who hasn't a word to say to anybody; while another phase of humanity is presented by the very stout gentleman who carries himself as though he thought that the accumulation of adipose tissue was a meritorious and excellent work, for which he ought to receive credit and respect, and who, when the tramcar comes up, occupies the room of two people with an equanimity of temper which almost makes one long to grow fat too. Make way there for the red-faced motherly woman who keeps a small greengrocery shop in the outskirts, her bundles of leeks and onions are odoriferous, and we will be thankful if she has not been investing a moderate outlay in "fresh" fish. "Now mother, be careful," says a good-natured man, supporting the steps of a very very old lady, who walks with a stick and who looks every day of ninety years old. She looks out for the tram-car with as much interest as if the last journey of all was scores of years in the future. If it is the time for leaving off work at the factories there will be a crowd of the better class of artisans, with dirty hands and pipes in their mouths, waiting to clamber up into the top storey of the car, with as much alacrity as schoolboys. The monster on wheels comes up, the crowd presses into it and fills it, a touch of the valve by the driver, and it glides away with fifty passengers as easily as a nursemaid pushes a six months old baby in a L'Hollier perambulator. Now, nobody can deny that there are some nuisances connected with the steam trams. Everybody will welcome the motor of the future, which will do away with the foul and noxious fumes, the unsightliness and the danger of the present tram-way engines. But so great are the numbers carried, and so great is the convenience of penny tram fares to the general mass of the population of Birmingham, that it seems improbable that the use of steam tram-cars will be abolished, and horse-traction again resorted to, until some new system is discovered and perfected which will have all the merits of the steam tram-car without any of its disadvantages.

From *Birmingham Faces and Places*, Vol.1, No.1, 1 May 1888.

Central Tramways Company and its Prospects

THE CENTRAL TRAMWAYS COMPANY AND ITS PROSPECTS

The shareholders of the Birmingham Central Tramways Company will muster in large force, and with considerable misgivings, at the ordinary general meeting at the Queen's Hotel on Wednesday next. The subject for consideration is the directors' report, of which we gave a gloomy forecast a few days ago. The most dismal anticipations are confirmed. The concern is indeed in a parlous state. Profits are diminishing at an alarming rate, owing, as the directors say, to the constant increase of the charges for maintenance of the lines; the electric system, of which so much was expected, has proved a financial failure; the steam cars, notwithstanding the enormous extent to which they are patronised, are swallowing up the profits in working expenses, and the only hope for the Company lies, we are told, in the substitution of the cable for the existing systems of traction. There is manifestly something radically wrong with the concern. The figures speak for themselves. There has been during the year a material increase of business, and yet the working profits show a remarkable shrinkage. Last year the company over its various lines carried 24,381,323 passengers, and its working profits were £43,579. This year the passengers number 25,718,282, and the profits have fallen to £37,028. The cable line, despite its occasional breakdowns, has proved the backbone of the concern. It has carried something over one third the number of passengers that are claimed by the steam trams, and yet the balance of receipts over charges almost equals that set down to the credit of the steam department. So strongly impressed are the directors with the success of the cable as a source of profit that they recommend the conversion of the Stratford Road service into a cable line. How is this to be done? Those who remember the costliness of the cable experiment at Handsworth will want to know how the limited financial resources can meet the demands involved in the extension of the system to Sparkbrook. The directors hold out the hope that the Public Works Committee of the City Corporation will allow the sum of £68,580, which they hold as security to be applied for the purpose of extending the cable system to the Sparkbrook route. Application has already been made to the Public Works Committee for their consent to this disposal of the money. Whether the Public Works will view the situation in the same light remains to be seen. They can do nothing without the consent of the Council, and the Council is at present taking a holiday. There is this to be remembered, the Corporation must have some security for the money that has been sunk in the tramways. The question is, what alternative security can the company offer in the event of the money being released?

But is there a reasonable chance of pulling the company together on its present basis? Some of the most sagacious business men, who do not as a rule take a doleful view of things, have their doubts on this point. The concern is, beyond all dispute, hopelessly overburdened with capital. Hope for the ordinary shareholder is, we fear, at vanishing point. The directors throw out a significant remark that some of the largest shareholders are of opinion that the time has arrived for reducing the ordinary share capital from £10 to £5 per share. No definite view is expressed by the directors as to the advisability of wiping off one-half of the ordinary share capital. They admit that opinions among the shareholders differ upon the subject, but they go the length of suggesting that the whole question of capital be referred to the Committee of Shareholders. If the Public Works Committee do not yield to the solicitation of the directors in regard to the money locked up as security, it is difficult to see what there is for the company but a sweeping reduction of capital and the re-constitution of the business on a basis which will permit of its being profitably worked. It is certainly the queerest of anomalies to find a thoroughly popular concern like the Central Tramways Company, carrying over twenty-five millions of passengers a year, and yet hardly knowing how to struggle along for money. The increase in the passenger traffic has been something phenomenal. During the last five years it has very nearly doubled. And yet the concern was never in a more deplorable financial fix than it is to-day. The explanation is the persistent swelling of the working expenses which have increased by £45,000 in five years. And yet we hear dismal descriptions of the rolling stock on some of the lines, and the lines themselves are naturally getting the worse for wear. Bad as is the present prospect, worse remains behind. If new engines are to be bought, and the cars put spick and span, and the permanent way brought up to date, an enormous sum of money will have to be found somewhere. But the directors do not foreshadow an expenditure of this description on the steam lines. Are we to assume from this that steam as a motor is doomed in Birmingham, and that by-and-by we shall have nothing but the cable all over the town? That is certainly a legitimate inference to draw from the report.

We do not know that there will be any conscientious laments over the disappearance of the steam tram. To look at the sulphurous monstrosities as they rumble along our narrow streets compels a feeling of wonderment how they ever got there, and how the patience of the people tolerated them. There is not likely to be much further development of steam traffic for two reasons—first, because some of the engines have a weary, worn-out look, and can barely struggle through the work they are called upon to do; and, secondly, because in view of the conspicuous success of the cable system, and its probable application to other parts of the town, the directors are not likely to launch out any more than is absolutely necessary in the equipment of their steam department. As for the unfortunate Bristol Road line, it would be interesting to know how much money has been sunk on that ill-starred electric experiment. The working account shows a dead loss of nearly £2,000 on the year, but this, we are told by the directors, is chiefly due to the heavy charges for renewal of batteries, an incubus which is likely to be removed by an advantageous contract which is now under consideration. But is there any reasonable hope of a substantial profit on the line? The cars that run along the Bristol Road are not sufficiently numerous to ensure a remunerative business. Now, the great advantage of the cable is that when the steel rope and apparatus are in working order any number of cars can be run without additional cost. Birmingham is celebrated for its hilly roads, and, as everybody knows, no system of traction can hold its own with the cable over uneven gradients. There is a big hill in Bradford Street on the Sparkbrook route which would afford almost as good a scope for the cable as Hockley Hill. Some day or other public sentiment might sanction the extension of the cable system even to Harborne, which, beyond all question, has its hills and plenty of them. There is only one point upon which the public may feel some apprehension. The cable, as probably some of the residents at Handsworth are aware, has an unfortunate habit of going wrong at the wrong time, and this is apt to irritate the tired business man who wants to get home sharp to his tea. But as more is known about the cable system and its peculiarities these accidents will become rarer, until the risk of a stoppage or breakdown will be almost infinitesimal. Experience has certainly shown that upon populous routes with steep gradients the cable is the only system which admits of being profitably worked, and with that knowledge it remains for the shareholders of the Central Tramway Company to work out their own salvation. The steam trams, beyond being ugly and in every way offensive, cost too much in the wear and tear of engine power, and as for the electric trams—well, the directors have hardly the heart to speak of them. Possibly science may in process of time reduce the heavy cost of renewing the batteries, but companies, in want of money, like the Central Tramway Company, cannot afford to wait.

Birmingham Daily Mail, **17 August 1892.**

Transition

Towards the end of their lives it is obvious that the steam tram companies tried to avoid spending more money on trackwork renewal than was absolutely necessary. The engines were, mainly, quite well maintained although any that suffered from a serious, but repairable, defect were laid aside to see how matters went. The reason? Section 43 of the Tramways Act 1870, part of which reads:

"Where the promoters of a tramway in any district are not the local authority, the local authority, if, by resolution passed at a special meeting of the members constituting such local authority, they so decide, may, within six months after the expiration of a period of 21 years from the time when such promoters were empowered to construct such tramways and within six months after the expiration of every subsequent period of seven years ... with the approval of the Board of Trade by notice in writing, require such promoters to sell, and thereupon such promoters shall sell to them their undertaking, or so much of the same as is within such district, upon terms of paying the then value (exclusive of any allowance for past or future profits of the undertaking; or any compensation for compulsory sale or other consideration whatsoever) of the tramway, and all lands, buildings, works, materials, and plant of the promoters suitable to and used by them for the purposes of their undertaking within such district, such value to be in case of difference determined by an engineer or other fit person nominated as referee by the Board of Trade on the application of either party, and the expenses of the reference to be born and paid as the referee directs."

It therefore became fashionable for councils who had their eyes on tramways in their districts to ask an 'independent' surveyor to report on their condition. Such takeovers were often the result of a surge of local pride for the period around the end of the 19th century was one when it really did seem the sun shone on Britain – epidemic diseases were becoming controllable as the new drains and sewers came on stream, main streets were commonly gaslit, some (the worst) slums were being eradicated, industry seemed to be booming and that great source of civic pride, the electric tram, was clearly feasible. Theoretically, these surveys were carried out confidentially but few of the experts would not, at least, have the courtesy to ask the help of the tram company's engineer.

In 1900 the Aston Manor Urban District Council (Aston Manor only became a Borough in 1903) Electric Lighting and Tramways Committee asked a London based surveyor, Reginald P. Wilson, to report on the steam tramways within Aston. Their basic question was, however, slightly different to most inasmuch as:

"It is probable, the tramways in the district are at some future date purchased by the Council and reconstructed (so far as may be necessary), and electrically equipped and then leased to a Company, the Birmingham Corporation or others, at what price could the Council supply current to such lessee, having regard to the cost of generating such current and to the capital expenditure incurred in the purchase, reconstruction, electrical equipment, and maintenance of the tramways?"

Mr Wilson in his own words attacked the question "with some diffidence" as without a close inspection of the rails it was impossible, "and indeed unfair" to predict how long a life remained in the rails, and because, inevitably, there would always be a wide difference of opinion on the worth of the tramway between the tramway companies as vendors, and the Council "in their capacity of prospective purchasers".

However, he did examine the lines carefully and equally carefully thanked the Company's engineer, J. Pritchard, "for a great deal of information". Exit, one would have thought, any element of confidentiality.

"Value of Car-sheds, Engines, etc. In the following estimate no definite figure has been taken as representing the value of any of the Companies' properties other than the track, and I think it is better that they should not be included, because there will be little or no difficulty in ascertaining their values accurately when the time comes, and further because it is not unreasonably sanguine to expect that these properties would realise, if sold, the price paid for them within a very little, always assuming that such valuations are properly made."

So far very matter-of-fact but further in the preamble to his report we have a clear idea of the thinking of a Victorian engineer.

"I do not propose to discuss the broad principle involved in the acquisition of the tramways by the Council, because I take it there is no doubt in the minds of any of the members that the Council should be the actual owners of the lines if not of the cars, and that the entire control of the streets and the regulation of the traffic should remain in the hands of the local authority, in whom it is already nominally vested."

Aston Manor U.D.C's problem was that their big neighbours, Birmingham, were already casting covetous eyes on them, seeking a 'merger' – the Aston councillors quite violently opposed this seeing it rather as a takeover, and it has to be said when the Birmingham City Council was enlarged the Aston Manor representatives were swamped under the influx from the south and west of Birmingham and rarely had any impact thereafter.

Mr Wilson, who seems to have been quite a diplomat, continued:

"Lease of Tramways – Whether the lines after purchase are leased to the Birmingham Corporation, or to a trading Company or Companies, the fundamental principle remains the same, and the Council have nothing to gain by disposing of their birthright; but on the contrary, by doing so they put themselves in a somewhat equivocal position, more especially if they consent to the sale of the lines to a neighbouring local authority."

He also laid down one axiom:

The price for supplying current to whoever leased the lines should be based on, and to some extent would vary according to the mileage actually run. The actual number of units of power consumed was the variable especially as even the coal and water consumed at the power station would vary. Conversely the actual cost of reconstructing the line was fixed – when it was done it was done!

The price of obtaining power where they did not control supply was one of the banes of future electric tramway companies; on the one hand the council wanted to recover cost plus 5% in the actual power output, plus 6½% to 8% to cover the cost of purchase and reconstruction of the physical elements of the tramway including the power station. Typically, the money would have to be borrowed by the Council at 4% or so over 25 or 30 years, so 6½% to 8% was on the face of it not an unreasonable return; although 1½% of the 'profit' would, inevitably, be absorbed by repairs to the roads, permanent way, and electrical equipment. A sinking fund of around 1% was also desirable to cover renewals or new work. Sadly though many small councils found themselves still paying for municipal tramways long after the trams and the lines themselves had been scrapped.

The lines with the Aston Manor U.D.C's remit and then being used for steam trams were neatly tabulated:

Description of Line	Length	Length of Double TrackTrack	Total for Single
Gravelly Hill	1½ miles	1 mile	2½ miles
Aston Lower Grounds	2 5/16 miles	/8 mile	2 7/16 miles
Perry Bar	9/16 mile	7/16 mile	1 mile
Witton Road	5/8 mile	1/16 mile	11/16 mile
Lozells Road	½ mile	1/16 mile	9/16 mile
Wheeler Street	5/8 mile	1/16 mile	7/16 mile
	5 5/8 miles	1¾ miles	7 5/8 miles

[Conversion: 1 mile = 1.609 km]

Incorporated within the report were the costings of a couple of extensions to existing lines; as we are solely concerned with steam trams I would only mention these totalled 1 3/16 miles at a total cost of £6,280.

How much of a shock to the Council the total costing of the conversion work was is not clear, but as it had no doubt been 'leaked' and Minutes are only dispassionate records we may never know.

The figures are most impressive especially as we know the figures for the original tracklaying in 1882 were not far short of £5,000 per mile; although this estimate does include re-use of the concrete underlay and most of the granite setts.

"Estimated Cost of Putting those Lines on

which the Rails are already worn out into Proper Order for Electric Traction.

The total length of such lines considered as single track, 5$\frac{15}{16}$ miles; gauge, 3 feet 5 inches.

The Concrete and 90 per cent of the Granite Setts may be used for the new line, but all the rails will have to be replaced. For this purpose I propose to use 6 inch rails, weighing 92 lbs to the yard. The rail joints to be made to sit on channel iron."

	£	s.	d.
Unlaying Existing Rails at 1s.3d. per yard of track	653	0	0
Laying New 6-inch Rails at 2s per yard of track	1,045	0	0
Cost of New Rails at £7.10s per ton	6,438	0	0
Cost of Channel Iron for Joints, at £7.15s. per ton	290	0	0
Cost of Tie Bars at £14 per ton	266	0	0
Cost of Fish Plates at £7.10s per ton	350	0	0
Cost of Bolts, Nuts and Washers	170	0	0
Unlaying all Setts and relaying 90 per cent of same	3,415	0	0
Supply and Laying 10 per cent of New Setts at 9s.6d per square yard	1,156	0	0
Special Work for Turnouts, etc.	1,825	0	0
Electrically Bonding Rails at £200 per mile	1,188	0	0
Lighting, Watching and Fencing during reconstruction	700	0	0
Turnouts to deal with Traffic during reconstruction	500	0	0
	£17,996	0	0
Less by sale of existing Rails, Fish Plates, etc., as old iron, at £2 per ton	1,500	0	0
	£16,496	0	0

Where the rails were still in good order, only electrical bonding was necessary, the 1$\frac{11}{16}$ miles being costed at £498 making a total of £16,994 to convert the trackwork from steam haulage to electric. The next page quoted here no doubt rubbed salt in the Council's wounds, as this brought the cost to, roughly, £37,000 to buy and renew the rails:

"The following is an Estimate of the Expense the Aston Manor Council would be put to in Purchasing those Portions of the Tramway Companies' Lines that run in their district.

BIRMINGHAM & ASTON TRAMWAYS COMPANY, LIMITED

The lines belonging to this Company as far as they run in Aston are in a most deplorable state as far as the rails are concerned, and new rails will have to be laid down throughout. The total length of the lines belonging to this Company in the Aston District is roughly 3$\frac{5}{8}$ miles double and single track, or considered as single track nearly 5 miles.

5 miles at £2,000 per mile = £10,000.

CITY OF BIRMINGHAM TRAMWAYS COMPANY, LIMITED

The lines belonging to this Company are partly in good condition and partly in bad condition as far as the rails are concerned. The total length of single and double track belonging to this Company in Aston Manor is about 2$\frac{1}{16}$ miles, or considered as single track about 2$\frac{11}{16}$ miles, and of this 1 mile requires new rails, the rails of the rest of the track being in good condition.

Say 2$\frac{3}{4}$ miles at an average price of £2,500 per mile = £6,875

The total sum for repurchase will, including cars, etc. etc., be approximately £20,000".

One also feels that the Birmingham & Aston Tramways Company were probably somewhat unhappy as they had spent quite an amount of money on track renewals and "deplorable state" is not what they wanted to read, neither would they be too pleased at the detailed examination. For example on the stretch between Aston and Lichfield Roads although the permanent way was well looked after with good rail joints and granite setts, "The rails are very much worn and required renewing at once, as the flanges of the car wheels are running on the bottom of the groove in the rails...", a similar report for the stretch near Aston Lower Grounds including a comment that one turnout leading to Trinity Road is so worn that the guard rail had turned over. The 'Perry Bar Tramway' was in good condition, the rails not appearing to have had more than four years wear; the Witton Road (where the tram museum now stands) trackwork was no more than three years old, but along here wood block paving was used instead of setts. Lozells Street was not in at all good condition "...the rails on this line appear to have had some six or seven years' wear at the least, and probably more, as the traffic on this line appears to be rather light ... rails are badly worn, especially at curves and turnouts ... [the work to be done] should be done before new cars are placed on the line..." a comment echoed on the line between the Lozells Road line and the bottom of Wheeler Street. All in all, not a pretty sight one fears!

The earliest the council could compulsorily purchase the tramways within their area was 31 December 1903 (i.e. 21 years after the beginning of the Company's lease, 1 January 1883) but in the event they purchased the lines of the Birmingham & Aston Tramways Company from 1 July 1902, with a neutral arbitrator, Sir Frederick Bramwell, to decide a fair price. In the meantime the company was asked to continue with the service as "the agents for, and on behalf of, and for the benefit of the Council". Interest at 4% was to be paid to the Company on the eventual purchase price paid as from 1 July 1902. The arbitration hearing, rather protracted, took place from 16 October and 24 November.

Granted it is rather unfair to R.P. Wilson to compare voluntary purchase with compulsory purchase figures but nonetheless he did say £20,000 for the Council to acquire the lines of not only the B & A but also the BCT within their territory, this sum to "include cars etc." The company for 27 locomotives, 21 tramcars, 31 horses and 6 omnibi asked £80,000. The council's reposte was to offer £50,000. Sir Frederick Bramwell awarded the one £61,175 against the other.

In 1902 the British Electric Traction Company took over the City of Birmingham Tramways Company. On 27 May 1903 a special meeting of the Aston Manor Tramways & Electric Light Committee discussed what agreement could be reached with BET. On 9 June (suspiciously quickly, one suspects it was all cut and dried) a formal agreement was reached between the BET (or rather the City of Birmingham Tramway Company) and the Council allowing the former to lease the old steam tram lines, after they were relaid for electric traction for a minimum sum of £1,000 per annum, plus whatever profits might accrue from the Aston section, CBT (BET) having plans for further expansion outside the immediate area. Eventually, the lease was ratified to commence from 1 January 1904, but it was not to be long lived as on 9 November 1911, the Borough of Aston Manor was enveloped by the City of Birmingham, the lines within Aston being sold to Birmingham Corporation Tramways by the CBT, their last cars running on 31 December 1911, little more than seven years after the last steam car.

Retrospect

It is a salutary thought that it is nearly fifty years since the last 'real' tramways were scrapped, and the only survivor when we started this series of books, Blackpool, is no more, but just another of the continental-style caterpillars that drift through various cities. Efficient movers of people, but no longer representing the loyalties of the local Corporation or company that operated their predecessors.

How different was it in 1902, when on 2 August the *Aston News* could report that at the meeting of the Aston District Council, "The committee reported that they were of the opinion that the overhead trolley system is the most suitable for the tramways in the district when acquired and electrically equipped by the Council and accordingly recommended that this system be adopted" All these modernised tramways were built on the back of money borrowed via the Board of Trade from Government sources at 3, 3½, or 4%, this charge to be met from the rates. The report continues "Tramways (Electrical Equipment) – The committee were informed by Mr Wilson that the Board of Trade desired the present application for sanction to the loan of £24,516, part of the tramway works, should be supplemented by an estimate of the cost of the overhead equipment of the tramways. Mr Wilson has accordingly prepared the following estimate:

	£
450 poles, including the necessary bases, finials, brackets etc	5,850
15 miles of trolley wire	1,360
Suspension wire	220
Guard wire	300
Overhead material, insulators, etc.	1,050
Section boxes etc.	440
Bonding etc.	600
Safety devices	500
Contingencies, engineering fees etc	1,032
Total	£11,352

The committee recommend that this estimate be approved, and that an application be made to the Board of Trade for their sanction to the borrowing of this sum." Elsewhere in the report a cost of £6,000 overall per mile is quoted.

Birmingham Tramways Electrification

THE TRAMWAY MUDDLE

During the interregnum between horse, steam, and electric traction the Tramway Committee in Birmingham vacillated between their choices of the new traction. Horse haulage was never considered after 1899, steam continued about its business but there was absolutely no chance of its expansion, and cable cars had proved expensive to install and inflexible which left an electric system. This in turn divided the Council, newspaper proprietors, politicians, and The Public, and it was this latter who were incredibly vociferous.

OLE (Overhead Line Equipment) was the obvious choice if only for the country districts, but the conduit was seductive, leaving the landscape clear and unsullied, but should this be the London County Council system with electric pick-up from the centre conduit returning the current through the running rails, or a side rail conduit where current is picked up from a slot in one running rail and returned through the other? And then of course, the 'new vastly improved' accumulator cars had their protagonists.

The following quotations are a tiny, indeed microscopic, percentage of the letters and editorial comments that appeared in the local papers. My favourite is that sent to the Daily Post by R. Armond and published on 4 January 1896 'and when the wires are suspended and covered with hoar-frost and dirty accumulation of smoke and dirt they will be as thick as 1½" ropes...'. No doubt a genuine enough belief, but let us take a quick look at what was happening in the world in one year, 1900: The Boer War ended and in the concentration camps set up by the British women and children died of hunger and fever. There was a fire at Buckingham Palace, and 8 March Queen Victoria made a rare visit to London, Mayor van Wyck of New York City dug the first sod of the new "Rapid Transit Railroad"

between Manhattan and Brooklyn. Sydney suffered an outbreak of bubonic plague and was forced to clean the city – 1,000 tons of 'filth' was removed.

In March it was stated India was in crisis as millions starved. 1900 was of course the year the old Labour Party was formed, with Ramsay MacDonald as secretary, and the Boxer Rebellion began in China. These put worrying about tramway current collection methods rather in the shade, but throughout Britain it was a local matter, and then anything local that affected the ratepayers was properly inspected, top, bottom, sides and ends.

We must apologise for the dreadful condition of these cuttings (despite our designer's best efforts at cleaning them up) but in balance we thought it better to include them in what is, after all, a giant scrapbook. Incidently – these were the good copies!

OVERHEAD TRAM WIRES FOR NECHELLS.

To the Editor of the Daily Post.

Sir,—I was very pleased to see a letter from Mr. T. A. Baylis, of Edgbaston, protesting against the above system, as showing that the same objections will be raised against the introduction of it in that neighbourhood.

I also notice in to-day's *Post* that the employés of the Electric Tramway Company on the Bristol Road route had their annual dinner, and judging from the remarks of Councillor W. Davis, the chairman—who, I should think, was a shareholder—that the tramway company claim the whole of the rights of doing with the roads as they think proper, simply because they pay a rent for the use of running tramcars, irrespective of any rights which the residents may have. Will Mr. Davis please tell me by what rule the tramway company claim the right to erect unsightly poles in the pavements in front of property, and detrimental to it by its depreciation? The tramways are big monopolists by the objectionable rails we have to contend with in driving along the roads; and if they want electric traction, let them do the same as other companies, such as the Telephone and Electric-lighting, do, and put them underground, and not depreciate private property.

Take the street I live in as an example. Opposite my property the road is only 22ft. 6in. wide. The road by Saltley is only 21ft. 6in. wide. It is impossible for two conveyances to pass one another at the same time. The roads are not so wide as the poles they propose to erect are long, and when the wires are suspended and covered with hoar-frost and dirty accumulation of smoke and dirt they will be as thick as 1¼in. ropes. This will have a depressing influence and depreciate my property, and as a private citizen I object to being over-ridden by a public company for the sake of a bigger dividend to the shareholders at my expense.

Am I to take it for granted that the gentlemen who also attended the dinner by their presence gave their consent to adopt the overhead system for the Bristol Road? as I know a greater portion of them are residents in that part. It gives one the opinion of the "lion and lamb" sitting down together, especially after the opposition that was shown when the overhead system was proposed to be laid down there. Surely, sir, if the Bristol Road is unsuited for it, I am sure the narrow roads in this district are, and I for one shall strongly object to it.

Duddeston Row.   R. ARMOND.

Birmingham Post, 4 January 1896.

TRAMWAY OVERHEAD ELECTRIC TRACTION.

To the Editor of the Daily Post.

Sir,—I see that the subject of overhead electric tramways is still being discussed in your paper. One writer, who claims to have no interest in the matter, gives his experience as unfavourable of the Walsall tramways, which run on this system. I should like to say that though the Walsall tramways may be either disagreeable or dangerous, and found to "emit a shower of sparks," it by no means follows that properly constructed, properly-worked overhead electric tramways need do so. I travelled by such a tramway some years ago in France: a short line runs from Clermont Ferrand to Royat, a French watering-place in the Auvergne, much frequented by English people. Many of them used this tram line daily to go up and down to Clermont, a distance of from 2½ to three miles (if I remember correctly). Remembering, as we did with much distinctness, our huge, hideous, smelling, smoky, and dirty trams at home, we congratulated ourselves on finding such a quick, airy, easy-travelling car. As for the posts, I cannot recollect that they were obtrusive or numerous, or dangerously high; nor do I see how they could have come in contact with overhead wires. I certainly never saw sparks as we travelled, nor was there particularly much noise. The only danger seemed to be that too great a pace was allowed down an extremely steep gradient; but the road was much steeper than most of our suburban roads. I am quite sure if the majority of the Nechells people had ever used the overhead electric tram, as constructed by the French engineer, they would not clamour against it, but agitate for it. If the Walsall people do not know how to manage them properly, do not lay the blame on the system, but get someone who does for Nechells. As for the steam trams, they are everything that is detestable, both as to noise, dirt, smell, and stuffiness; no one can ride outside with comfort owing to combined smell and smuts, and inside the smell is not much superior, though the smuts are absent. Moseley Road, once green and pleasant to the eye, is now fast showing the signs of a decaying residential suburb, not yet, transformed into a shopping district; the change is largely due to the vacant houses, caused by the annoyance of the steam trams.

    A TRAVELLER.

January 10.

Birmingham Post, 11 January 1896.

PROPOSED OVERHEAD-TRACTION.

The Public Works Committee of the Birmingham City Council have received a letter from the Birmingham and Midland Tramways Company, asking whether the Corporation would consent to them replacing the present steam traction on their route within the city of Birmingham (that is, from Lionel-street, Parade, along the Dudley road, to the city boundary at Winson Green) by an overhead system, without attaching any conditions, and without any extension of the lease. The letter was not discussed by the committee at their meeting on Thursday, but was referred to the Tramways Sub-committee to report, with a view to the application being considered in connection with any future arrangement that may be made with the Corporation of Smethwick. The lease has about six-and-a-half years to run, and the proposed overhead system is intended to be part of a general overhead system in South Staffordshire, in which district many of the lines are controlled by the British Electric Traction Company, who have recently acquired a great proportion of the shares in the Birmingham and Midland Tramways Company. The Tramways Sub-committee will consider the matter at their meeting on Tuesday next.

Alderman Cook, the chairman of the Tramway Sub-Committee, in conversation with our representative this morning, spoke in warm terms of this offer, which, he says, is much more favourable to the City than that relating to Bristol-road, for the reason that it is entirely unconditional, although the lease has only six and a half years to run, compared with eleven years on the other line. The reason the British Electric Traction Company are able to make such an offer is because, having overhead plant all over the country, they could easily make use of the poles and wires if Birmingham does not choose to finally retain them. Some members of the committee favour this offer in preference to the Bristol-road one. But he is prepared to strongly support both.

Daily Argus, 7 February 1900.

A NEGLECTED SUBURB.
To the Editor of the Daily Post.

Sir,—It is many months since the last note of dissatisfaction was heard from the long-suffering inhabitants of the roads between Calthorpe and Bristol Roads, as St. James's, Charlotte, and Gough Roads.

Is there no owner or company of owners with sufficient enterprise to start some means of public locomotion whereby the above population may be benefited? The electric trams, which might be some help, though very inadequate, are far too irregular.

It is a common occurrence, when wishing to return from town in the middle of the day or early afternoon, to find no tram in Suffolk Street or near it, and to meet near Sun Street two or three cars on their way to town!

There is great need of direct communication between Edgbaston and Moseley. Surely a service of omnibuses might be established that would be profitable, and immensely useful, to the inhabitants of both suburbs, as well as to the locality from which I write. MATER.
Charlotte Road, October 17.

Birmingham Daily Post, 18 October 1899.

THE TRAMWAY MUDDLE.

[To the Editor of the "Daily Argus."]

Sir,—I am very pleased to see that there is a likelihood of the question of the overhead system for Bristol-road being brought forward. If the Tramways Committee treat the Tramway Company in an enlightened and business-like manner, there should be not the slightest difficulty in arranging terms. It is very remarkable how apathetic the general public appears to be about this tramway question. I suppose it is because they do not know what a really good service is. If they did, they would wonder, as I do, why we put up with the present apology for a service on all routes except the cable.

In the first place, we should insist on having the overhead system, as this is far the cheapest, and it is possible to give a much longer ride for a penny with this system than any other. The absurd resolution passed by the City Council when they pledged themselves against the overhead system is on a par with the ignorance displayed by people who years ago opposed the making of railways as smoky substitutes for canals. The objection on account of looks is altogether farcical in a town which was formerly supposed to be progressive and practical, and the experience of Dudley clearly proves that it can be easily worked in the midst of the heaviest street traffic, as the cars work there through the Market-place and High-street with the greatest ease.

Let the people of Birmingham realise that it is entirely their representatives in the Council who are standing in the way of a better service, for it is quite certain that nothing can be done till they are prepared to adopt the overhead, which they will be bound to do sooner or later.

The tramway question is the one question at the present time, and all municipal candidates at the next elections should be elected or otherwise, according to their views on this question.

I am not a shareholder or in any way interested in the C.B.T.C., but I do think the Council are pursuing an ignorant and dog-in-the-manger policy about the tramways. E. J. MORRIS.
35, Vaughton-street South, March 15, 1900.

Daily Argus, 16 March 1900.

THE BRISTOL-ROAD TRAMS.

OVERHEAD SYSTEM RECOMMENDED.

At the meeting of the Public Works Committee, yesterday, it was decided to recommend the City Council to consent to the adoption of the overhead system on the Bristol-road tramways. The voting was 6 to 3 in favour of the recommendation, the three dissenters being Alderman Hallam, and Councillors Balden and Lane.

The committee sat for nearly three hours.

The absence of any mention of the Bristol-road tramway question from the agenda of the City Council meeting on Tuesday next

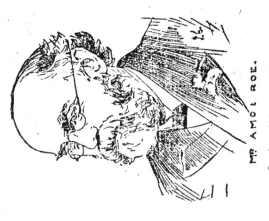

MR AMOS ROE.

Leader of the opposition.

TRAM LINES AND WORKMEN'S DWELLINGS.
To the Editor of the Daily Post.

Sir,—As Mr. Roe says, your correspondents were surprised to find that 217 persons living in Bristol Road had signed a petition against improved tram traction in that quarter, and still more so to see that sixty-three of them were full-grown. One would have thought they were all children. I think we may presume that the sixty-three full-grown signatories were all very old women, although they may have belonged to both sexes. In reply, I say there are 63,000 ready to petition the opposite way, who own property in the centre of the town. Mr. Roe objects that Mr. Holmes (the only man who voted right on the question) owns property at Bournbrook. If he has, it is as slightly as safe, and as sanitary as that owned by Mr. Roe in the centre of the town. It will be well for the Bristol Roaders, including Mr. Roe and the city councillors, to know that, whether they like it or not, the working classes mean having healthier homes, and better surroundings in the suburbs. There is a surging stream of opinion in favour of better homes for the workers, and if Mr. Roe and his Bristol Road friends and the city councillors are stupid enough to stand in front of it, there is no help for it. They will certainly be drowned out. J. W. CLARKE.
75, Irving Street.

To the Editor of the Daily Post.

Sir,—Your correspondent, Mr. Amos Roe, makes a great point of the fact that I am the only resident on the Bristol Road who advocates the overhead wires, although he admits that only sixty-three adult residents have signed a petition against it. I venture to assert, and if necessary prove, that I could get a petition signed by 600 adult residents on the Bristol Road (between Wellington Road and the top of High Street, Selly Oak), in favour of the overhead or any other system which would be more efficient, and would provide cheaper fares for the people.

Mr. Roe insinuates that my advocacy of a better system of trams and cheaper fares is prompted by selfishness, because, as he learns, I am the owner of small house property in Bournbrook. Allow me to inform both Mr. Roe and his tutors that five-sixths of my property is situated on the Bristol Road, the road which the overhead system (as he and his friends say) is not only going to deface but also to ruin. I fail to see where the selfishness comes in, when, according to Mr. Roe's own showing, I am advocating a system prejudicial to my own interests. My reasons for advocating the adoption of the overhead system are—

(1) Because I think it a better service at cheaper rates would be obtained ; (2) because the congested parts of Birmingham would soon be relieved, and the great question of the housing of the poor be solved, if a cheap and reliable communication between the city and suburbs was established ; (3) because the working classes of Bournbrook and Selly Oak look upon the question of cheap trams as one of the greatest necessity, and whatever I can do to forward in any way the interest of the class to which I belong I shall do not only as a pleasure, but as a duty. WILLIAM HOLMES,
219, Bristol Road, April 4.

Birmingham Daily Post, 5 April 1900.

shows that, contrary to expectation, the offer of the City Company will not be discussed at this meeting. It was originally intended to consider the matter, and to facilitate this a special meeting of the Public Works Committee was held after the Council meeting on Tuesday evening. As a decision was then found impossible, the matter could not appear on the agenda, and no notice of motion having been given, it is by the standing orders excluded from the consideration of the meeting. The Council will devote itself to the new rates and a report of the Markets and Fairs Committee, and it is understood that the tram question will be considered at the May meeting of the Council

Daily Argus, 6 April 1900.

THE TRAMWAY TURN.

At last daylight begins to appear through the tramway deadlock. The movement referred to in the *Argus* yesterday for replacing the cumbrous and cripple vehicles which toil along the bristol-road by a service of modern trolley cars propelled by overhead traction is an evidence of common sense emerging victorious from a long struggle with prejudice and obfuscation. Before the end of 1900 we shall probably have a tramway service to Bournbrook to which the name can be applied without irony. The same result might have been gained four years ago if wisdom had reigned in the Council Chamber. An immense boon to the travelling public has been obstructed by a policy which it is using the mildest language to call parochial, unbusinesslike, and narrow-minded. It has been hard work recommending common sense to the members of the Public Works Committee. But we hope soon to be as proud of them as a missionary of his first convert. The first step is half-way in matters of this kind. When the overhead system has been working for a month on the Bristol-road, the question will have settled itself as regards the other lines. There will be no need for more deputations to go abroad and return to mislead Birmingham. The advantages of quick and cheap travelling will be first-hand evidence for everybody. There will be no more wild-goose chasing after conduits which Birmingham cannot afford or self-contained motors which only Birmingham councillors dream about. Now that all the nonsense has been cleared out of the way the introduction of the new order of things should not be tarried over. Time has been frittered away too long. May we implore the City Council not to waste any more?

Daily Argus, 16 September 1900.

OVERHEAD AND UNDERGROUND ELECTRIC POWER IN AMERICA.

TO THE EDITOR OF THE DAILY GAZETTE.

Sir,—I have been much interested in the discussion of the tramways question in the City Council and the newspapers, from time to time; but, looking upon myself as merely a sojourner within the gates of Birmingham, I have taken no part in it. However, as reference is made continually to American method and proceedings, I may, perhaps, be permitted a few words, not about the merits of the question, but upon one of its phases.

I find there is an impression that American cities are replacing overhead wires—known with us as the overhead trolley—with the conduit system—which we call the underground trolley. So far as I am aware, this has not been done in any of our cities. The mistake must have arisen from the substitution in Washington and New York of the underground system for the cable. In the National capital—largely a show place—where the streets are very wide—Congress has declined to authorise overhead wires, and the conduit has succeeded cable power.

In New York, within the limits of the original city, the cable has been the mechanical power employed on surface roads. This was put in on two through lines eight or ten years ago, but has now either been displaced or is in process of displacement by the underground system. The shape of New York is so unusual, its traffic so large, and its down town streets so narrow, as to make the overhead system impossible. These elements will be the more easily understood when it is known that the Island of Manhattan—upon which is built the original city of New York—contains upon an area only equivalent to that occupied by Birmingham, above two millions of people, or four to one.

On the other hand, Baltimore, Boston, and St. Louis, each with a population approximately the same as that of Birmingham, have overhead wires for lines aggregating from 250 to 438 miles in length, while Cincinnati, Buffalo, Cleveland, Detroit, and like cities, ranging from 200,000 to 300,000 in population, each have in their streets from 150 to 250 miles of lines operated by overhead wires. In none of these, or in any others, so far as I am advised, has there been any proposal to change from the overhead to the conduit system.

It is not my purpose to discuss, in any way, this question so far as it relates to Birmingham. I merely desire to correct an evident misapprehension as to the trend in a country where 16,000 miles of electric tramways and railways are already in operation.—I remain, very truly yours, GEORGE F. PARKER. Elmwood, Arthur Road, Edgbaston, April 9.

Daily Gazette, 10 April 1900.

THE CITY COUNCIL AND THE TRAMWAYS

The tramway schemes for the Bristol-road and Winson Green sections of the Birmingham Tramways were further considered by the Tramway Sub-committee of the Public Works Committee yesterday. The press were subsequently informed that the Committee had decided to recommend to the City Council at the May meeting the adoption of the overhead wire system on the Bristol-road section, on the terms already published. With regard to the lines made by the Midland Company to equip the Winson Green route with the overhead system the Committee felt they were hardly in a position to seriously consider this at present. It was a simple offer accompanied by no conditions whatever. The Committee would want cheap fares and workmen's cars with other concessions, and on these they would require information before the matter could possibly come before the Committee for serious consideration. The transfer of the line to the British Electrical Traction Company was a circumstance also to be taken into consideration. Alderman Cook expressed the opinion, in reply to a question, that if the required conditions were met, it would be favourably entertained.

Daily Post, 10 April 1900.

BRISTOL ROAD TRAMWAYS.

TO THE EDITOR OF THE DAILY GAZETTE.

Sir,—The opponents to the scheme for propelling the tramcars along Bristol Road by electric overhead motion base their objections on the alleged unsightly appearance of the apparatus. One is inclined to think that they protest through ignorance, not knowing that there are other methods than that adopted at Coventry by which the means adopted may be made attractive. The standards may be ornamental, certainly more so than the lamp posts which line the footpaths, and they might also be used for lighting purposes (electrically).

I have travelled in many places on the Continent where the overhead motion is used without noticing any eyesore, and in one instance (in Spain) a journey of about eight miles was made in a delightful manner, along a tree-bordered road. If the inhabitants cannot have the conduit system, by reason of excessive expense, they should put up with the other method, which in a short time would be accepted by them as not destroying the beauty of the prospect which strikes the coup d'œil so agreeably, but having regard to the standards adding to the attraction of the road.—Yours truly, IMPARTIAL. April 9.

Daily Gazette, 10 April 1900.

THE CITY COUNCIL AND THE TRAMS.

FURTHER IMPORTANT PROPOSALS.

OVERHEAD FOR BRISTOL AND DUDLEY ROADS.

"Having once admitted the principle of the overhead electric traction, I really don't see how the Council can reasonably stop at the Bristol Road route." Such was the remark made to a "Mail" representative thus morning by a gentleman who, though not a member of the City Council, has perhaps a closer acquaintance with the "inner workings" of the tram question in Birmingham than any one. The City of Birmingham Tramway Company is not the only tramway company in the city; and it will be interesting to observe how the Council, should they adopt the present recommendations of the Public Works Committee with regard to the Bristol Road line, will act with regard to proposals which may come before them shortly concerning the adoption of the overhead system on another important route. As a matter of fact, the Midland Tramway Company, whose lines run from Lionel Street to Smethwick and beyond, have through representatives of the British Electrical Traction Company, which practically owns the Midland Tram Company, approached the Lord Mayor with proposals concerning the re-equipment of the

PARADE AND DUDLEY ROAD LINES

similar to those made by the City of Birmingham Tramway Company in relation to the Bristol Road. The proposals were brought up before the Public Works Committee yesterday, and as far as we can ascertain it would appear that the majority of the members were prepared to recommend their acceptance by the Council if Smethwick Town Council has no objection. It is, we understand, not likely to raise any objection if Birmingham is disposed to grant the concession, and consequently there is, if the Public Works Committee has its way, the prospect of the overhead wire being sanctioned not only for the Bristol Road route, but also for the Dudley Road line as well. The lease granted to the Midland Tramway Company has yet about six and a half years to run, and though we are not fully acquainted with the proposals concerning this line we have reason to believe that, in the main, they are identical with those brought forward by the City of Birmingham Tramway Company and adopted yesterday by the Public Works Committee. The lease held by the Birmingham and Aston Tramway Company has not so long to run, but if concessions are granted to the other two tram companies, whose lines run through the city, there is nothing to prevent them, if they so desire, seeking similar privileges; and it is this possible extension of the application of the principle of the overhead system that makes yesterday's decision of the Public Works Committee one of such importance and one likely to have far-reaching results.

"Mail", 6 April 1900.

Birmingham Central Tramways Company

Plots and Schemes

We must apologise for the condition of some of the pages in this report. A now deceased colleague supplied it ten years ago presumably from his original which I have been unable to trace. On the other hand it is too valuable to omit. Eventually the whole scheme fizzled out.

7th July, 1896.

17,078. Mr. Alderman White presented the following Report from the Public Works Committee :—

REPORT.

BIRMINGHAM CENTRAL TRAMWAYS COMPANY.

Public Works Committee's Report.

Your Committee report that they have received an application from Mr. R. Harding Milward, acting on behalf of Messrs. William Mackenzie, of Toronto, and James Ross, of Montreal, the President and Vice-President respectively of the Toronto and Montreal Street Railway Companies, for the consent of the Corporation to an assignment to them and a Company to be formed by them, of the Leases now held by the Birmingham Central Tramways Company from the Corporation, to the subsequent surrender of such Leases, and to the granting to the new Company of new Lease or Leases of the Tramways for a fresh term of twenty-one years.

Your Committee have ascertained from the Solicitors to the Birmingham Central Tramways Company, that this application is made with the concurrence of the Directors of the Company.

The following are particulars of the Leases referred to in the application :—

Route.	Length in Miles of Single Line.		Certified Cost.			Deposits made with Corporation (for securing fulfilment of Leases.			Rent First Fourteen Years.			Rent Last Seven Years.			Annual Sinking Fund Payment during whole Term.		
	Miles.	Chains.	£	s.	d.	£	s.	d.	£	s.	d.	£	s.	d.	£	s.	d.
Albert Street to Nechells Park Road (Horse); Aston Street to Salley Road; Corporation Street to New-town Row; Station Street to Moseley Road; Fazeley Street to Moat Row; Kyott's Lake Road; Bradford Street to Camp Hill and Stratford Road; Rea Street to Coventry Road (Steam)	15	40·5	80,697	18	4	38,765	12	6	3,227	18	0	4,034	18	0	2,311	6	0
Station Street, Hill Street, Hurst Street, Bromsgrove Street, Lower Hurst Street, Sherlock Street, and Gooch Street; Sherlock Street and Benacre Street; John Bright Street and Station Street (Steam)	2	68·8	16,357	0	9	7,196	17	6	654	6	0	817	17	0	474	7	0
Colmore Row to Hockley Brook (Cable)	2	53·6	13,648	1	0	6,691	0	0	545	18	0	682	8	0	390	18	0
Navigation Street to Bournbrook (Electric Accumulators)	·5	45·6	26,593	1	10	13,942	4	9	1,063	14	0	1,329	13	0	761	13	0
Great Hampton Row and Wheeler Street (Steam)		66·2	4,301	1	11	1,984	7	6	172	1	0	215	1	0	123	4	0
	27	34·7	£141,597	1	11	£65,580	2	3	£5,663	17	0	£7,079	17	0	£4,061	8	0

NOTE.—In addition to the payments above specified, the Company pays the actual cost of repairing its Tramways, as certified by the City Surveyor.

7th July, 1896.
Public Works Committee's Report.

A sketch map showing these Tramways and the other Tramways within the City, and also showing their connection with Tramways outside the City, accompanies this Report.

After correspondence and several interviews with Mr. Milward and his clients, the Town Clerk was requested to put the application and the several points upon which your Committee thought it necessary to have a definite understanding, into a letter, which was forwarded to Mr. Milward.

The letter was as follows :—

"Town Clerk's Office,
"3rd June, 1896.

"Dear Sir,

"CITY TRAMWAYS.

"Referring to our previous correspondence, and to the interviews which you and your clients have had with the Public Works Committee on this subject, I am requested now to put into writing what the Committee understand your application to be, and to submit the following points as the basis of an agreement, if the Council should accede to your application.

"We understand your application to be (*vide* your letter of to-day's date) :—

"(a) The transfer of the existing undertaking of the Central Tramways Company from that Company to your clients, and a Company to be formed by them.

"(b) The approval of the Council of the surrender of the existing Leases, and the grant of new Leases for a term of twenty-one years.

"(c) The approval of the Council to the discontinuance of the use of steam, horses, and of the electrical system now in use on the Bristol Road, and the substitution of some approved means of mechanical traction to be decided upon with the consent of the Council.

"The Committee understand that if the Council accept the principle involved in this application, your clients are prepared to accept the following conditions :—

"1. To pay off all outstanding balances of Sinking Fund, &c., against the Central Tramways Company.

"2. To deposit such a sum, as evidence of *bona fides* and security for fulfilment of Lease, as the Corporation may reasonably require.

"3. To construct any new lines or alterations of lines that may be approved of by Corporation, and authorised by Parliament, to satisfaction of Corporation; or to pay cost of same if Corporation shall determine to construct same.

"4. To adopt such motive power or mode of traction in lieu of the present horse, steam, or electrical power as Corporation may approve.

"5. To pay a rental or wayleave at the rate of £185 per mile of single line per annum during term of Lease,

"6. On termination of Lease the whole of the lines *in the City,* whether constructed by Corporation, or constructed or purchased by Syndicate, to become the absolute property of the Corporation, together with all posts, wires, cables, or other appliances used in connection with the Tramways, except rolling stock. The Syndicate also to transfer all licenses, and allow Corporation to use all patents granted or belonging to Syndicate.

"7. To reduce the long-distance fares, and to provide for halfpenny fares for short stages.

"8. To maintain, repair, and renew the Tramways to satisfaction of Corporation, or, if Corporation shall themselves maintain, repair, and renew, Syndicate to pay cost as certified by City Surveyor.

"9. To accept a Lease on lines of existing Leases, subject to foregoing alterations.

"10. The existing Tramways in Corporation Street and Old Square to be removed if required by Corporation, and an alternative route, to be approved by Corporation, to be adopted.

"11. To undertake not to employ their drivers, conductors, or other workmen more than ten hours a day.

"I shall be glad to hear not later than 10 a.m. on Monday next, that your clients will accept the foregoing conditions.

"Yours faithfully,

"E. O. SMITH,

"Town Clerk.

"R. Harding Milward, Esq.,
"Solicitor,
"Waterloo Street."

To this letter your Committee received the following reply :—

"Birmingham,
"June 6, 1896.

"Dear Sir,

"CITY TRAMWAYS.

"My clients have considered your letter of the 3rd instant, and the various heads of points therein set forth as the basis of an agreement upon our application as therein set forth under the heads (a), (b), and (c), and I am directed to say :—

"As to Clauses 1, 2, 3, 4, and 5, my clients accept them as they stand, but with reference to new lines and the method of traction, my clients ask that the Corporation Engineer may be at once placed in communication with their Engineer, so that a report may be presented as quickly as possible to the Council, both as to the scheme of the new lines and of the method of traction to be adopted, so that these matters of supreme importance may be agreed upon directly after the principle has been accepted by the Council,

"With reference to Clause 6, I am to say that whilst my clients quite recognise that at the expiration of the Lease they are bound to yield up the now existing permanent way, they do not consider that they should be asked to forfeit to the Corporation all the assets acquired by the expenditure of their own capital in return for a further Lease for ten years only, and in respect of which they are asked to pay an annual rental. The case would be different if the term of the Lease were sufficiently long to enable the outlay to be recouped by any ordinary sinking fund, but under the terms as proposed, the sinking fund necessary to recoup the capital expended would be crushing.

"As to Clause 7, my clients are quite in accord with the Council as to the principle of the reduction of fares, and the establishment of halfpenny stages; but as the adoption of this principle will undoubtedly cause a considerable reduction in the earning capacity of the Company,—in consenting to it, it must be considered in connection with the requirements of the Corporation, both as to the cost of the method of traction to be adopted, and of the value of the surrender required by the Corporation at the end of the term.

"As to Clause 8, my clients would enter into the usual repairing covenants, and execute the necessary repairs.

"Clause 9 follows as a matter of course upon the acceptance of the other clauses, the terms of the lease being adapted to the altered circumstances.

"As to Clause 10, my clients could not consent to withdraw the tramways from that part of Corporation Street where they now stand, unless they could see some equally satisfactory position.

"As to Clause 11, my clients readily consent not to compel any drivers, conductors, or other workmen in their employ to work more than ten hours in a day.

"You will remember that at the meeting on the 3rd inst. it was arranged that, if during the term of the lease the Council should determine to construct new lines within the City, my clients should have the first offer of leasing and working them.

"I am,

"Very faithfully yours,

"R. HARDING MILWARD.

"E. O. Smith, Esq.,
"Town Clerk."

The Town Clerk immediately replied, as follows :—

"Town Clerk's Office,
"6th June, 1896.

"Dear Sir,

"CITY TRAMWAYS.

"I am in receipt of your letter of to-day's date, which will be submitted to the special meeting of the Public Works Committee which will be held on Monday morning next, the 8th inst.

" With reference to Clause 6, I think the Committee will expect that at the expiration of the lease your clients shall yield up everything connected with the Tramways, the removal of which would necessitate the disturbance of the surface of the street or roadway. This is the case with regard to the existing Cable Tramways, although the Company themselves paid the full cost of the underground apparatus. This precedent will have to be adhered to.

" With regard to Clause 10, the Tramways in Corporation Street are leased to the Aston Company until the 31st December, 1903, and at the expiration of that time the Corporation have power to remove them. I feel quite confident that the Committee will not enter into any arrangement that would involve a continuation of these Tramways beyond the term I have indicated. I do not think, at present, that it is necessary for me to make any observation upon the other clauses; but I think it may be convenient for you to hold yourself in readiness to see the Public Works Committee on Monday morning, if they should desire it.

" Yours faithfully,

" E. O. SMITH,

" Town Clerk.

" R. Harding Milward, Esq.,
" Waterloo Street."

" As regards the lines into Corporation Street, it is clear that passengers must be brought at least as near to the centre of the City as they now are, or else the Tramways would not be worth working at all, as passengers will not get into a tramcar to be landed a long distance from where they want to go.

" This matter, however, can be arranged later, when it can be seen what (if any) alternative route can be adopted, as at present we are not dealing with the Tramways of the Aston Company.

" I would only add that my clients are most desirous of making an arrangement which will be satisfactory to the Corporation, but it must be one which will give fair interest upon their own capital, and also provide for the return of that capital during the currency of the lease.

" I am,
" Yours faithfully,
" R. HARDING MILWARD.

" E. O. Smith, Esq.,
" Town Clerk."

The foregoing correspondence was laid before your Committee on the 8th June, after which the Town Clerk addressed the following letter to Mr. Milward :—

" Town Clerk's Office,
" 9th June, 1896.

" Dear Sir,

" CITY TRAMWAYS.

" I thank you for your letter of the 7th inst., which I submitted with my letter of the 3rd inst., your reply, and my letter of the 6th inst., to the Public Works Committee yesterday.

Mr. Milward, who was away from Birmingham, wrote on the 7th June :—

" Knowle Hotel,
" Sidmouth,
" June 7th, 1896.

" My dear Sir,

" CITY TRAMWAYS.

" I have received here a copy of your letter of the 6th. I am sorry I cannot attend a meeting of the Public Works Committee to-morrow, as I am compelled to take a few days' rest, but I could attend any meeting with the Chairman or the Committee on Monday, the 15th, if it should be desired. With reference to the points raised in your letter I would remark that the terms of the present lease to the Central Tramways are such that at least £150,000 of the shareholders' money will be forfeited to the City at the expiration of the present term of the leases, and if these terms are extended even to the existing lines, when converted, at least £350,000 would be confiscated, whilst for every additional mile of tramway which is authorised and constructed, not less than £10,000 would be lost for the benefit of the City. The Committee will at once see that, to provide a sinking fund for so large an amount, the greater part of the net earnings of the lines, as they now stand, would be swallowed up, and very little would remain for interest on capital.

" I am sure that the Committee will recognise that this business must be conducted on sound principles, and that both the Corporation and the Company must have fair and equitable treatment.

" A slight alteration was made in the wording of Condition No. 4, which now reads :—

" ' 4. To adopt such motive power or mode of traction in lieu of the present horse, steam or electrical power on the existing tramways, and to adopt such motive power or mode of traction on any new tramways to be constructed by or for them as the Corporation may approve.'

" The Committee approve of my letter of the 6th inst., with respect to Condition No. 6. It involves a principle upon which they have acted in relation to all their tramways, and they cannot depart from it.

" The Committee will consent to the words ' on such routes as the Corporation may reasonably require ' being added to Condition No. 7.

" With reference to Condition No. 10, the Committee approved of my letter of the 6th inst. They feel certain that the Corporation will not consent to the continuance of the lines in Corporation Street, after the expiration of the present lease to the Birmingham and Aston Company, viz., December 30, 1903. At the same time, they will give every consideration to any suitable alternative route which your clients may submit.

" With respect to the last paragraph in your letter of the 6th inst., the Committee have no recollection of having arranged to give your clients the first offer of leasing and working any new lines which the Corporation may construct. They feel that this is a matter upon which, for many reasons, they could not bind the Corporation, who must consider each case as it arises, and as it affects the public interest. At the same time, the Committee recognise that a Company which was giving satisfaction to the Corporation and the public would have a strong claim to favourable consideration.

"It is, of course, impossible now for this matter to come before the Council on the 16th instant, but I am directed to ask for a definite acceptance of the conditions contained in my letter of the 3rd inst., as now modified, by 10 a.m. on Monday next, when the Committee will meet again. In that case the Lord Mayor will call the Council together for the 23rd June, to receive the Committee's report.

"Yours faithfully,
"E. O. SMITH,
"Town Clerk.
"R. Harding Milward. Esq.,
"Solicitor."

On the 15th June Mr. Milward and his clients had another interview with your Committee, and subsequently the following correspondence was exchanged between the Town Clerk and Mr. Milward :—

"Town Clerk's Office,
"16th June, 1896.
"Dear Sir,
"CITY TRAMWAYS.
"I understand from what you stated at the interview which you and your clients had with the Public Works Committee yesterday that the only

---

condition contained in my letter of the 3rd instant, as modified by my further letter of the 9th instant, which your clients could not accept, was Condition No. 6.

"After hearing the statement made by you at yesterday's interview, the Committee agreed to recommend the Council to make the following concession, as an addition to Condition No. 6, viz. :— Provided that if the Corporation require the Syndicate to lay more than 8 miles of single line of underground electric conduit out of the existing 24 or 25 miles of tramways (exclusive of cable lines), leased to the Central Company, the Corporation will at the expiration of the lease pay the then value of so much of such underground conduit as shall be in excess of such 8 miles, less the estimated value at that time of a corresponding length of tramway if constructed on the overhead electric system. In case of dispute as to such value the amount to be settled by open arbitration—the basis of arbitration to be the fair market value at the time of purchase, due regard being had to the nature and condition of the materials and apparatus and the state of repair thereof, to the suitability of the same to the purposes of the undertaking, and to the then existing conditions of electric or other traction. No addition to be made in respect of compulsory purchase or any other considerations.

"It must of course be understood that the Corporation do not by this concession in any way pledge themselves to the approval of the overhead or underground or any particular system of traction.

When the time arrives for settling this, the Corporation will consider any proposal which your clients may make to them, and will exercise their power as the Local Authority, and if they give their consent will do so for such period, and subject to such terms and conditions of working, as they may be advised are necessary or desirable.

"Yours faithfully,
"E. O. SMITH,
"Town Clerk.
"R. Harding Milward Esq."

———

"London, June 17th, 1896.
"Dear Sir,
"CITY TRAMWAYS.
"I have to thank you for your letter of the 16th inst., which shall at once be considered by my clients, and I will communicate with you at the earliest possible moment.

"I take it that it is understood that all reference to the Tramways in Corporation Street is to be excluded from the present negotiations

"I am,
"Yours faithfully,
"R. HARDING MILWARD.
"E. O. Smith, Esq.,
"Town Clerk."

"Town Clerk's Office,
"19th June, 1896.
"Dear Sir,
"CITY TRAMWAYS.
"On my return from town this morning I have your letter of the 17th instant.

"It is quite understood that as the Tramways in Corporation Street are leased to the Aston Company they cannot come into the present negotiations. The Corporation, desiring to deal perfectly fairly with your clients, wished them to understand that at the expiration of the present lease those Tramways will in all probability be taken up, and the running powers of the Central Company or your clients over them will cease. That being understood between us, I see no reason for including it in the conditions to be accepted by your clients.

"Yours faithfully,
"E. O. SMITH,
"Town Clerk.
"R. Harding Milward, Esq."

———

"41, Waterloo Street,
"Birmingham,
"June 22nd, 1896.
"Dear Sir,
"CITY TRAMWAYS.
"My clients have carefully considered your letter of the 16th, together with the terms of the

modification of Condition 6 as proposed by the Public Works Committee.

"My clients, in accepting your conditions as set forth in the letter, do so understanding that the maximum amount of underground electric conduit which will be required by the Corporation, including central connections, will not exceed 10 miles.

"With reference to the method of traction, as mentioned in the last clause of your letter, my clients have only in view the adoption of either overhead or underground electricity, which experience has proved to be perfectly successful.

"My clients desire to emphasise the necessity of instructions being given to the Engineer of the Council at the earliest possible moment to place himself in communication with their Engineer.

"I assume that the whole matter will be considered and disposed of at the meeting of the Council to be held on the 7th July, as time is now of great importance.

"Yours truly,
"R. HARDING MILWARD.

"E. O. Smith, Esq.,
"Town Clerk."

It will be seen from the particulars of the Leases given in the earlier part of this report, that the Leases of about 18 miles of the tramways, all of which, with the exception of the tramways from Albert Street to Nechells Park Road, are at present worked by Steam Traction, have 10½ years

longer to run, and those of the remaining 9 miles or thereabouts (principally Cable and Electric) have 15 years unexpired.

The first and chief point which your Committee had to consider had relation to the desirability or otherwise of renewing the Leases for a term of 21 years, and so postponing for another 10½ years in the one case and 6 years in the other, the time when the tramways would revert to the Corporation, especially having regard to the probability of the Corporation desiring themselves to work the tramways at the expiration of the existing Leases.

At present the General Tramway Act forbids (except under special conditions and by license of the Board of Trade) the working of tramways by municipalities. A few towns, however, have obtained such power by special legislation. These are Glasgow, Huddersfield, Leeds, Plymouth, and Blackpool.

From a report of very recent date made by a Special Committee of the Manchester City Council, your Committee find that the Corporation of Leeds are only working the tramways temporarily pending a reconstruction of the lines; that Blackpool, which has only 2 miles of single line on the esplanade, makes a profit, but the line is so short, and the circumstances so different to those which prevail in this City, that it affords no data of any value to your Committee; that in Huddersfield, where 20 miles of single line have been worked by the Corporation for 13 years, the Corporation have sustained a loss of over £40,000; and that in Plymouth, where the Corporation work 4 miles of single line, after paying interest and sinking fund no profit is made.

In Glasgow it was not until *after* the failure of the negotiations between the Corporation and the Lessees for a

renewal of the Lease on terms satisfactory to the Corporation that the Council decided to work the tramways themselves. The Tramways have been worked by the Corporation since 1st July, 1894. During the first 11 months of working, for which period alone the accounts are available, it would appear that the "profit" resulting from the working of the 32 miles of double line, or, rather, the net payment to "common good," was £8,260. From the report of the Glasgow Tramways Committee, however, it appears that during the period included in the accounts no payment had to be made for sinking fund, and that in future a Sinking Fund of 2 per cent. per annum on the amount borrowed for capital purposes will have to be provided. Moreover this payment of £8,260 appears to have had no relation to the income or expenditure in connection with the tramways, but to have been a proportionate part of a sum of £9,000 which the Council determined should be paid into the "common good" in lieu of the net revenue derived from the former Lessees.

Your Committee have applied to the Town Clerk of Glasgow for the report and accounts relating to the working of the Tramways during the twelve months ending 31st May last, but are informed that the accounts have not yet been printed, and they have been unable after repeated applications to obtain any official information with respect to them.

It must also be borne in mind that in Glasgow the population is much more dense than in Birmingham, the streets are generally level, and in consequence the tramways can be—and have been—worked with horses. There is therefore, no large capital charge such as would be required for mechanical or electric traction. Your Committee

understand that the Glasgow Council are now considering the question of electric traction, and in case of its adoption there will have to be a large capital outlay.

Your Committee, therefore, came to the following conclusions :—

(1) That they have not sufficient experience of the working of Tramways by municipalities to guide them as to the probability of the Corporation desiring to take the Tramways into their own hands at the expiration of the existing leases.

(2) That the experiments being made in methods of traction, auto cars, &c., render it desirable that for the present the Tramways should continue to be worked by Lessees, under such covenants for ensuring cheap and quick transit and the safety, comfort, and convenience of the public, as may be thought necessary.

(3) That the Corporation would not be justified in rejecting the immediate and prospective advantages which they and the public would derive from the acceptance of the present offer.

The principal advantages to be derived from complying with the request of Messrs. Mackenzie and Ross, upon the conditions which your Committee have provisionally arranged, are :—

(1) The *immediate* abolition of steam traction, and the substitution of overhead, or underground, electric or other improved system of traction to be approved by the Corporation, with smaller and more sightly cars, and a quicker and improved service,

(2) The introduction of halfpenny fares for short distances, and the reduction of fares for long distances.

(3) A reduction of the working hours of the men.

(4) An immediate increased rental to the Corporation.

The profit of the Corporation upon the existing Leases is estimated during the remaining portion of the first fourteen years of the Leases, after paying capital charges, at ½ per cent. per annum on the cost of construction, or about £700 per annum, and during the last seven years of the Leases at 1 per cent., or about £1,400 per annum.

Under the proposed terms the Corporation would at once receive £5,000 per annum, and a proportionately larger sum if any new lines are constructed, all the capital charges being borne by the Lessees.

It will be seen from the correspondence that the chief contention between your Committee and Messrs. Mackenzie and Ross had regard to Condition No. 6 in the Town Clerk's letter of 6th June, under which—while the new Company were to pay off the balance of capital charge on existing lines, to purchase the lines in the Balsall Heath district, and to pay the cost of altering existing lines and constructing any new lines that might be authorised—the whole of the lines within the city, together with any underground conduits and apparatus required for working the Tramways, were, at the expiration of the Lease, to become the absolute property of the Corporation.

only be effected by the Corporation purchasing the existing leases, and expending a very large capital sum in addition for re-construction, in a similar manner to that proposed by the Syndicate. This expenditure your Committee could not recommend to the Council, nor in their opinion would the Council accept such a responsibility. The alternative then remained of leaving the existing leases in the hands of the present Company until their expiration. The adoption of this course offers the prospect of a comparatively limited improvement in the present services and no reduction of fares or of working hours to the men.

Your Committee believe that by the acceptance of the offer of Messrs. Mackenzie and Ross upon the conditions which have been provisionally agreed, the Corporation and the public will derive all the advantages which they could reasonably anticipate from the working of the Tramways by the Corporation, while they will run none of the risks which are inevitably associated with such an undertaking.

By adopting the scheme now recommended by the Committee the use of steam will be at once abolished, the tramways will be reconstructed without increasing the Corporation debt, a reduction of fares will be secured, a reduction of the working hours of the men will be obtained, and a substantial annual contribution will be made in relief of the rates.

These advantages will be at once secured, at the cost of deferring the possibility of the municipalisation of these lines for a period of ten years. The balance of advantage to the City seems to the Committee clearly to lie in accepting the scheme now proposed.

As will be seen from Mr. Milward's letter of 7th June, Messrs. Mackenzie and Ross declined to commit themselves to the provision of a Sinking Fund for so large an amount as would be required if the whole or the greater portion of the existing Tramways had to be reconstructed on the underground electric system. They were, therefore, anxious to ascertain what proportion of underground conduit the Corporation would probably require; and after a long interview with Mr. Milward and his clients, your Committee, recognising the force of the argument adduced, consented to the compromise contained in the Town Clerk's letter of 16th June, viz., that if the Corporation require more than eight miles of the existing Tramways to be converted to underground electric system, they will, at the expiration of the Lease, pay the difference between the then value of so much of the underground system as is in excess of eight miles, and the then value of a corresponding length of overhead wire system.

Mr. Milward in his letter of 22nd June stated that his clients accepted the terms, understanding that the maximum amount of underground electric conduit which the Corporation would require should not exceed ten miles. Your Committee, whilst unable to pledge themselves to any maximum amount of underground conduit, think it probable that not more than ten miles will be required. They have so informed Mr. Milward, who has expressed himself as satisfied.

It must not be assumed that the Committee are opposed to the principle of municipalisation. They gave full consideration to this aspect of the question, but inasmuch as the present leases do not expire till 10½ and 15 years hence respectively, present municipalisation could

Your Committee therefore recommend that, subject to the conditions which they have provisionally arranged, the Corporation should consent to an assignment by the Central Tramways Company to Messrs. Mackenzie and Ross and a Company to be formed by them of the existing leases, to the surrender of such leases, and the granting of a new lease or leases for the term of 21 years, and that your Committee should be authorised to take such steps for ensuring the carrying out of such conditions and generally for the protection of the Corporation and the public as they may consider necessary or advisable.

It was moved by Mr. Alderman White, and seconded by Mr. Councillor W. Wilkinson,

That the arrangements now reported by the Public Works Committee, with respect to the Tramways leased to the Birmingham Central Tramways Company, be approved; that the said Committee be authorised to consent to an assignment by the said Company to Messrs. William Mackenzie and James Ross and a Company to be formed by them of the existing leases of such Tramways, and to the subsequent surrender thereof, and to grant to Messrs. Mackenzie and Ross and a Company to be formed by them upon the conditions provisionally arranged with them, a new lease or leases for a term of twenty-one years; and that the said Committee be authorised to take such steps in the name of this Council—and where requisite under the Corporate Seal—for ensuring the carrying out of such conditions, and generally for the protection of the Corporation and the public, as they may consider necessary or advisable.

Whereupon it was moved by Mr. Councillor Stembridge, and seconded by Mr. Councillor Dexter, as an Amendment,

That in the opinion of this Council it is not desirable to bind our successors by entering into any new Agreement with reference to the leasing of Tramway lines within the boundaries of the City, and that the General Purposes Committee be instructed to take the necessary steps to procure such Parliamentary powers as are required to enable the Birmingham Corporation to work the Tramways for the public benefit, if such a policy be found expedient on the expiration of the current leases.

It was moved by Mr. Councillor Randall, and seconded by Mr. Councillor Hennessy, as a further Amendment,

That the recommendation of the Public Works Committee to the City Council for an assignment of the leases of the Birmingham Central Tramways Company to Messrs. William Mackenzie, of Toronto, and James Ross, of Montreal, be deferred for the further consideration of the above Committee and the public at large.

During the discussion on the preceding Motion and Amendments,

It was moved by Mr. Alderman Baker, and seconded by Alderman Dr. Barratt,

That this Council do adjourn till this day week.

The Motion for adjournment, on being put, was negatived, and the discussion continued.

Upon the second Amendment being put it was negatived.

The first Amendment was then put, and was negatived.

Hereon a poll having been demanded and taken, the votes were as follows:—

FOR THE FIRST AMENDMENT (23).

Mr. Alderman Barratt	Mr. Councillor	Jephcott
" " Fallows	" "	Johnstone
Mr. Councillor Allen	" "	Jones
" " Baker	" "	Lancaster
" " Bayley	" "	Martineau
" " Berkeley	" "	Nixon
" " Coombs	" "	Reynolds
" " Dexter	" "	Stembridge
" " Edwin Fletcher	" "	Stevens
" " Green	" "	Waters
" " Haines	" "	Wilson
" " Hunt		

AGAINST THE FIRST AMENDMENT (35).

The Lord Mayor	Mr. Councillor	Davis
Mr. Alderman Ash	" "	Thomas Fletcher
" " Bowkett	" "	Holloway
" " Clayton	" "	Hughes
" " Cook	" "	Lane
" " Edwards	" "	Samuel Lloyd
" " Hallam	" "	Marsh
" " Manton	" "	Murray
" " Pollack	" "	Osler
" " White	" "	Price
Mr. Councillor Adie	" "	Rogers
" " Balden	" "	Arthur Smith
" " Ball	" "	Tonks
" " Barber	" "	Wm. Wilkinson
" " Beale	" "	John Wilkinson
" " Bishop	" "	Winkles
" " Bradley		

Mr. Councillor Randall did not vote.

Hereon a poll having been demanded and taken, the votes were as follows:—

FOR THE SECOND AMENDMENT (14).

Mr. Councillor Baker	Mr. Councillor	Hunt
" " Berkeley	" "	Jephcott
" " Coombs	" "	Jones
" " Dexter	" "	Randall
" " Edwin Fletcher	" "	Reynolds
" " Haines	" "	Stevens
" " Hennessy	" "	Waters

AGAINST THE SECOND AMENDMENT (41).

The Lord Mayor	Mr. Councillor Thomas Fletcher	
Mr. Alderman Ash	" "	Green
" " Barratt	" "	Holloway
" " Bowkett	" "	Hughes
" " Clayton	" "	Johnstone
" " Cook	" "	Lancaster
" " Edwards	" "	Lane
" " Fallows	" "	Samuel Lloyd
" " Hallam	" "	Marsh
" " Manton	" "	Murray
" " Pollack	" "	Nixon
" " White	" "	Osler
Mr. Councillor Adie	" "	Price
" " Balden	" "	Rogers
" " Ball	" "	Arthur Smith
" " Barber	" "	Tonks
" " Bayley	" "	Wm. Wilkinson
" " Beale	" "	John Wilkinson
" " Bishop	" "	Wilson
" " Bradley	" "	Winkles
" " Davis		

Councillors Allen, Martineau, and Stembridge did not vote.

The original Motion was then put, when it was

Resolved—

17,079. That the arrangements now reported by the Public Works Committee, with respect to the Tramways leased to the Birmingham Central Tramways Company, be approved; that the said Committee be authorised to consent to an assignment by the said Company to Messrs. William Mackenzie and James Ross and a Company to be formed by them, of the existing leases of such Tramways, and to the subsequent surrender thereof, and to grant to Messrs. Mackenzie and Ross and a Company to be formed by them, upon the conditions provisionally arranged with them, a new lease or leases for a term of twenty-one years; and that the said Committee be authorised to take such steps in the name of this Council—and where requisite under the Corporate Seal—for ensuring the carrying out of such conditions, and generally for the protection of the Corporation and the public, as they may consider necessary or advisable.

It was moved by Mr. Alderman White, seconded, and

Resolved—

17,080. That the Report of the Public Works Committee be approved.

The Council then dissolved. (7-30 p.m.)

JAMES SMITH, Lord Mayor,

Chairman,

14th July, 1896.

Birmingham Association for Suppressing Steam Tram Nuisances

from *Birmingham Daily Gazette*, 16 November 1887

BIRMINGHAM ASSOCIATION FOR SUPPRESSING STEAM TRAM NUISANCES.

A meeting of the promoters of the "Birmingham and District Association for the Suppression of Nuisances arising from Steam Trams" was held last night at the Birmingham Restaurant, Lower Temple Street. Mr. C. C. Smith presided, and there were present Messrs. Henry Brown, A. T. Powell, T. W. F. Newton, H. C. Taylor, F. Taylor, H. Satchell, Rev. N. M. Hennessey, George Kendrick, G. T. Smith, and C. Osborne. Apologies for absence were read from the Rev. H. Sims, Messrs. G. F. Lyndon, H. H. C. Horsfall, and F. H. Cartland. The association was formally brought into existence in September by a few gentlemen who met in the offices of Mr. G. T. Smith. The association has for its object—so runs the prospectus—the protection of the health, persons, and property of the inhabitants of Birmingham and its suburbs from the injuries and unhealthy nuisances arising from the steam tram traffic as at present carried on; and its efforts are to be directed in the presentation of memorials to the local authorities and the Board of Trade in enforcing regulations, and, if necessary, in the prosecution of offenders and in obtaining injunctions. The experience of the past three years' working of steam trams, it is stated, is that the nuisances arising therefrom have been practically continuous and unchecked. The emission of steam has been pretty general, but the emission of sulphurous fumes from bad fuel has been intolerable, and should have been most sternly dealt with by the authorities, but in the absence of proceedings on their part the necessity for the association is shown. The nuisance of noise arises from clatter of defective engines, also from the length of the car on bogey platforms with small steel wheels, which, being driven on steel rails at great speed, make an excessive number of revolutions and create great noise. Bell ringing is done offensively and dangerously. Instead of using it in cases of need as a warning the bell is often rung furiously, and so with their ponderous engines the drivers unduly turn other vehicles out of the track. In the matter of danger, the steam trams have not only been the direct cause of many deaths, injuries and shocks to the nervous system, but they have made the general traffic of the streets and roads much more dangerous than heretofore, and the association will work in the direction of lessening existing risks. The ugliness of the engines and cars quite detracts from the appearance of the streets and roads, and it is hoped an improvement in that respect will be effected. The destructive tendency of the steam tram promoter as regards the horse roads is shown by the announced intention to have a goods traffic worked along some of the lines, and if this be accomplished in one direction the strong probability is that the other lines will want to do similar work. This conversion of main roads into makeshift railways is much to be deplored from every point of view except that of the company speculator, and it behoves the community to provide the necessary safeguards against such unwarranted encroachments.

The Chairman said he had for some time sympathised with the efforts his brother had been making for the abolition of steam trams. Until lately, however, as a member of the Town Council, which had the control of the tramways in its hands, he had not cared to appear in public opposition to the Tramway Companies, although in the Town Council he had taken an opportunity of expressing an opinion that the steam trams were a decided nuisance. He still held that opinion. Steam trams were objectionable on three or four grounds. They were, to begin with, highly dangerous. The accidents that occurred—the crushing and mangling of invalids and children by the trams—were appalling and heartrending. Such accidents were unknown in Birmingham until the steam trams were introduced. In the next place they were unhealthy on account of the vapours and odours issuing from them. It was subject for surprise that the Health Committee of the Town Council had not interfered to put a stop to this nuisance. In the third place, the trams were extremely ugly. New streets had been opened, grand new buildings erected, and much preaching done with the object of beautifying the town, and yet the most hideous piece of machinery in the world had been allowed to take possession of the streets. The glaring green eyes of an approaching train on a dark night in a dark road had a depressing and terrifying effect. Finally, the steam trams were not necessary. The principal reason urged in their favour was that penny stages would be useful to the working classes, and that penny stages could only be made to pay by means of steam trams. They had yet to learn that steam tram penny stages did pay. One did not gather from the reports of the Central Tramway Company that it was in a very healthy condition, or that it was likely to pay very big dividends on penny stages. But, anyhow, there might be penny stages without steam trams. For a penny passengers were carried to Bordesley Green, a distance of two miles—twice the distance of a steam tram penny stage. In other directions similar enterprise was being displayed, and people were beginning, and he hoped they would continue, to prefer the 'bus to the steam trams. During the recent elections his canvassers had been told that voters could not support him, because he had opposed steam trams. But he did not oppose cheap fares. He believed, on the contrary, that the working classes were entitled to have cheap means of locomotion provided for them. This was provided—without the introduction of steam trams—in other towns. Excepting Birmingham, Coventry, and Leeds, and perhaps one or two other towns, cheap rides were afforded by 'buses and horse trams, and cheap rides would be possible in Birmingham even though the steam trams were abolished altogether. In Manchester, Liverpool, Sheffield, and London, and some of the most important cities in the Kingdom, the Corporations carefully eschewed steam trams, and would not have anything to do with them. There was no reason why Birmingham should not hold a similar position.

Rev. N. M. Hennessey asked whether the association would as soon as possible direct its efforts to abolishing steam trams altogether.

Rev. N. M. HENNESSEY asked whether the association would as soon as possible direct its efforts to abolishing steam trams altogether.

Mr. G. T. SMITH replied that some people who were anxious that nuisances caused by the traffic should be put down were not quite prepared to abolish steam trams. The association was formed to do away with the nuisances; and his own impression was that if the association succeeded in putting down the nuisances the steam trams themselves would be put down.

Mr. HENNESSEY said that if the association could abolish the steam trams and the steam tram monopoly he would not put up his hand in opposition. He did hope, however, that the permanent way would not have to be taken up. A better kind of car, propelled by a better motive power, with cheap stages, could be managed by any company that chose to cater for the public. In Manchester the horse cars were now running long stages for a penny, and, it was said, the receipts were larger than when the charges were higher. Probably, if Birmingham had had the advantage of seeing steam trams at work in a neighbouring town before they were introduced into our streets, they would never have been allowed. He would be very glad if this association could bring pressure to bear upon members of the Town Council touching this matter. As to the ugliness of the trams and the horrible accidents to children, he heartily concurred in all the Chairman had said. It was monstrous to say that the poor children, say of Aston, were not to be allowed to leave their courts and alleys for a glimpse of sky and a breath of fresh air in the streets. The streets were their playground and drawing room. As to 'bus traffic, what had been done in Bordesley Green might be done elsewhere, and if the smaller 'bus companies chose to join hands they could strangle the monopoly.

Rules for the government of the association were then considered, and the following officers elected:—President, Mr. G. F. Lyndon; vice-presidents, Messrs. S. B. Allport, N. H. C. Horsfall, J. O. Holder, J. P. Lacy; hon. treasurer, Mr. Lister Lea; hon. secretary, Mr. George T. Smyth; hon. auditor, Mr. A. T. Powell; and a committee.

THE EMISSION OF STEAM AND SMOKE FROM TRAMWAY ENGINES.— In the Queen's Bench Division, on Monday, the case of Davis v. Leach came before Justices Matthew and A. L. Smith, sitting as a Divisional Court. It was an appeal from the decision of the West Bromwich Bench of Magistrates, who had convicted the appellant of having permitted smoke and steam to be emitted from a tramway engine, at Handsworth, contrary to the bye-laws of the Tramway Company, framed by the Board of Trade. Mr. Blower appeared in support of the appeal, while Mr. Darling, Q.C., opposed it.—Mr. Blower said the point raised in this case was whether the justices were right in convicting the appellant of two offences on one information. The appellant was convicted of having permitted smoke and steam to be emitted from the engine, and fined 20s.—Mr. Justice Matthew pointed out that the justices had found that the smoke and steam were mixed.—Mr. Blower submitted that the conviction ought to be quashed, because, under the 10th section of Jarvis's Act, appellant ought to have been charged on two informations, there being two offences alleged against him.—Their lordships, without calling on counsel for the respondent, held that the justices were right in convicting the appellant, and dismissed the appeal, with costs.

Handsworth & Smethwick Free Press, 27 March 1886.

Birmingham Daily Gazette Editorial

FOR a long time now the conversion of our public thoroughfares into miniature railways has excited the indignation of a portion of the populace. Now and then a mild protest has been raised against the ploughing down of infants and the emission of sulphurous fumes, but at last the opponents of the system have determined to organise. Last night there was a first meeting of the members of the "Birmingham and District Association for the Suppression of Nuisances arising from Steam Trams," and a President, Vice-Presidents, and Committee were appointed. The aggressive campaign against the steam tramways may, therefore, be regarded as having begun, and from the tone of the speeches delivered last night these offenders against public comfort may expect no mercy. It is complained that the cars are not of that ornamental nature which would render more attractive the appearance of the streets and roads, and it is further objected that the "ponderous engines" and "furious bell-ringing" disturb the public peace. The obnoxious odour emitted from the funnels is sufficient to cause one of a sensitive organisation to think unkind things of the system, but the most tangible grievance is to be found in the number of accidents which street-railways occasion. The requirement of the age is cheap and speedy locomotion, and the steam-tram is cheap and speedy. Does the new Association offer anything in its place? So far as its specified objects are explained (in half a dozen paragraphs so oddly framed that a member of the Industrial Schools Committee might have been the writer) it seems that the Association limits its work to suppressing nuisances by means of prosecuting offenders and obtaining injunctions. This is to be the first step towards abolishing steam tramways altogether, and then the point to be determined will be whether the nuisances are of such a character as to make the whole system intolerable. We could willingly dispense with the evil, but if the sacrifice of the good is also involved the subject is not to be so easily settled.

Smoke Abatement

The Handsworth Chronicle.

OCTOBER 26, 1889.

THE STEAM TRAM NUISANCE.

We notice the Association of Handsworth Ratepayers, which recently came into existence for the protection of their interests against the steam tram nuisance, summoned one of the drivers at West Bromwich last week, and after hearing the case the magistrates found the defendant guilty, and he was fined 5s. and costs. In looking over the report of the case, however, we were rather sorry to notice that Mr. Elliott, defendant's solicitor, implied that the members of the Association were actuated by a malicious and vindictive spirit, and that their real and only object was to "oust" the trams from Handsworth altogether. We do not know what grounds this gentleman had for such an assertion, but from enquiries we have made we are enabled to tell the public that there is not the slightest truth in the statement, and that the accusation on the part of Mr. Elliott was most unjustifiable and uncalled for. We, ourselves, happen to know as a positive fact that one of the members of the association only a very short time ago offered to lend to the South Staffordshire Tramway Company £10,000 or £20,000, to provide electrical cars in place of the present steam engines, if satisfactory security could be given. Surely this does not look as if the members of the association were desirous of stopping the trams entirely. We think what the association requires, and what they have a perfect right to demand, is that so long as the steam trams continue to run in Handsworth, that they should comply with the Act of Parliament. We have heard it said by the officials as well as the drivers that it is impossible to do this. If such is the case, then we say that those who promoted and got the Bill passed through Parliament, obtained the consent of our legislature through misrepresentation, and we are confident these powers would never have been granted if the Government had known it was im-

....

....

the Government had known it was impossible to comply to the very letter to the Act passed for the regulation and working of these trams.

We fully recognise the great convenience of the tram system, and should be very sorry to see any one attempt to stop their running, at the same time we must say that those living in or near the steam tram route in the Holyhead Road are great sufferers, and we do not at all wonder that a large number of residents have formed themselves into an association to see if they cannot stop the nuisances caused by the emission of sulphur, smoke, steam, &c., contrary to the Act of Parliament. All frequent travellers from Handsworth to West Bromwich on the steam trams must often have noticed the discharge of noxious fumes from the engines, and many have time after time had to place something over their mouths to prevent their inhaling objectionable as well as unhealthy fumes. No longer ago than last Saturday morning we went to West Bromwich in one of the South Staffordshire Trams, and all the way the engine kept suddenly stopping, whilst volumes of black smoke kept constantly coming from the engine. We made enquiries as to the cause of this from the conductor, and were informed the engine was not in good order. About an hour after this we got on a tram to return to Handsworth. The engine attached to this car was also out of order, and before we reached our destination all the travellers had to get out and walk as the driver was unable to proceed any farther. Can the public wonder at the nuisances seeing such engines as these are brought out for use? The company states that the complaints are unreasonable, but to our certain knowledge there are three or four large houses void in Holyhead Road because people will not put up with the nuisances caused by the steam trams. In addition to that several residents state they will leave the district altogether rather than tolerate it any longer. We hardly wonder at it. Some of the gardens are entirely spoilt by the poisonous nature of the fumes emitted from the engines, and the residents are unable to open their windows in consequence of the unpleasant odours which immediately fill the house if they do so. Why is it the Handsworth trams bear so unfavourable a comparison to the steam cars in Birmingham? We seldom ever see smoke or any other matter coming from their engines, and if they can run in Birmingham without committing these nuisances they ought to do the same in Handsworth. We are confident if the steam trams in the city created the same nuisances as the South Staffordshire Companies, the authorities in Birmingham would soon compel them to make better arrangements or else stop their running powers altogether. Our Handsworth authorities have the power to do likewise if they will only use it. Let them compel the South Staffordshire Company to provide engines equal to those in Birmingham or otherwise place electrical cars on the route. The latter would certainly be the best cause to adopt as then all possible cause of complaint respecting noxious fumes and smoke must necessarily disappear. There is little doubt but that those residents who have formed themselves into an association have very strong grounds of complaint, and we do hope something will be done to remedy what at the present time is nothing but a palpable and gross injustice.

STEAM TRAM NUISANCE.

TO THE EDITOR.

Sir,—The Smoke Jacks were much wanted here on Sunday last. The trams were frequently running at the rate of 16 miles an hour, giving off steam, smoke, and sulphur in large volumes, to the great annoyance of the residents.

I know the emission of steam and smoke are under the control of the drivers, who can emit them from the chimney at their own will or pleasure, well knowing by emitting them they are doing wrong, and violating the Act of Parliament, therefore, I think they ought to be severely punished for creating such abominable nuisances.

As regards sulphur and noxious fumes, the drivers have not the same control over them as they have over steam and smoke, but these would be very considerably reduced if the Company would use the best coke instead of the very inferior coke they are using.

If the South Staffordshire Tramway was better managed, and good experienced men employed as drivers (instead of inexperienced young men), and compelled to work without violating the Act of Parliament, there would be very few complaints, which would be very much to the interest of the shareholders.

Is it not time our Local Board gave their attention to the numerous complaints that have been made about the many and great nuisances created by the working of the steam trams. Surely it is their duty to protect the ratepayers from having forced upon them such intolerable nuisances.

What is the Association doing? If they want to punish the drivers by getting them fined they will have no difficulty in getting cases against them. I could take many cases, day and night, and in this shall be happy to assist the Association.—Yours, &c.,

ENGINEER.

Handsworth Chronicle, 2 November 1889.

Two views on the way forward

DUDLEY AND WOLVERHAMPTON TRAMWAYS, LIMITED.

The eighth ordinary general meeting of this company was held on Tuesday, the 15th inst., at No. 1, Victoria Street, Westminster, S.W.; Mr. WM. BASS NEEDHAM, in the absence of the chairman, Mr. John Fell, presiding.

The SECRETARY (Mr. Walter J. Kershaw) read the notice convening the meeting and also the minutes of the last meeting, which were confirmed.

The CHAIRMAN in submitting the report and balance-sheet of the company for the past twelve months remarked that he had not very much to say. He regretted that there was such a small attendance of shareholders, and that their chairman, Mr. Fell, had found it impossible to be present. As the report stated, they showed a profit this year of £556, that was after paying interest on the first and second debentures. Last year the profit amounted to £588, therefore, on this occasion, their accounts were pretty satisfactory. There was, however, very little doubt that that sum would have been considerably increased, and that this company would have been a paying concern had they had additional rolling stock — additional engines, and additional cars. The line passed through a district that was very badly served with the means of locomotion. It was a largely-peopled district, and was daily increasing in population. The people there were entirely dependent upon the tramway which connected Wolverhampton on the one side with Dudley on the other. Unfortunately the company had no means of raising further capital, and therefore they must work on patiently and do the best they could under the circumstances to increase the receipts. The directors proposed that with the balance available they should this year apply it in reduction of the expenses and costs of the proposed extension. Two years ago they had been put to considerable expense in trying to make some extensions which it was thought desirable, and it was now thought best to write these expenses off, a procedure which he hoped would meet the wishes of the shareholders. He concluded by moving, "That the report and accounts be received and adopted."

Mr. H. H. CROFT said the directors proposed that £555 be applied in the reduction of the expenses and costs re proposed extension account, upon which they said in the report there would then remain a balance of £136 to be written off next year. He should like to ask whether, instead of adopting that course, it might not be advisable to apply the money towards the purchase of a new engine, because he saw the share capital was not completely exhausted, and neither did the debentures issued represent the whole amount that was authorised. It therefore seemed to him that a little money might still be squeezed out of the concern in order to provide one more engine. It was obvious that the providing of another engine last year had been a very good thing for the company. It had enabled a greater mileage to be obtained, more passengers, and, in fact, his suggestion seemed to be the only way really of resuscitating the concern. He supposed it was hopeless to expect the bank to advance any more money, as they already held debentures to the amount of £5,000, and he further presumed there was no means of applying to the public, because they could not, he took it, issue more shares without going to Parliament for the proper authority. He would, therefore, be glad to know if it was feasible to devote the £555, which it was proposed to apply in the reduction of expenses and costs, as stated, to the purchase of a new engine.

Mr. H. B. FRANCIS said Mr. Croft was right in his contention that a new engine should be procured, but he must remember that of the second debentures only £423 remained unissued, and that would not be sufficient to purchase another engine.

The CHAIRMAN said that unfortunately they had been put to considerable expense in relaying the line, and that was put to capital account, therefore, though they showed a profit, they had practically spent it in necessary work.

Mr. CROFT : Then, in fact, there is no available cash, and I take it, there is no means of applying to the public.

The CHAIRMAN said they did not require to go to Parliament or take further powers. They were in a position to issue preference shares, but the question was, how far they would be taken up by the public or the present shareholders. The directors had that question under consideration at present.

Mr. CROFT then seconded the adoption of the report and accounts, which, on being put to the meeting, was unanimously adopted.

The CHAIRMAN moved the re-election of Mr. John Fell as a director.

Mr. CROFT seconded the motion, which was carried.

Messrs. Caldicott, Hill and Harrison were reappointed auditors, and the proceedings then terminated.

THE PROPOSED ELECTRIC TRAMWAYS AT DUDLEY.

IMPORTANT COMMUNICATION.

Yesterday, the Railway, Tramway, and Electric Lighting Committee of the Dudley Town Council issued a report, containing a copy of a letter just forwarded to the Light Railway Commission, setting forth the views of the Corporation in reference to the question of electric tramways in the borough. The communication, signed by the Mayor (Mr. G. H. Dunn), stated that they desired to lay before the Commission the views of the Corporation, more especially as a suggestion was made at the recent enquiry at Dudley that the applicants on behalf of a trading company for an order to lay tramways within the borough might meet their lordships in private conference, to see if it were possible that a middle course might be found which, satisfying the reasonable claims of the borough, would yet permit of the promoters (the British Electric Traction Company) having a continuous service over the whole of the proposed system. The population of the several districts affected, as given by the promoters at the enquiry, were as follows: Dudley 45,000, Brierley Hill 12,000, Amblecote 3,000, Wordsley 5,400, Kingswinford 3,400, Pensnett 8,600; total 77,400. He (the mayor) had omitted Stourbridge and Rowley Regis, because the proposed tramway would run a few yards only into Stourbridge and a comparatively short distance into Rowley Regis. Dudley represented considerably more than one-half of the population of the affected districts, and was the only corporate body. The Corporation considered that their right of purchase under the 43rd Section of the Tramways Act was a valuable asset, for the following reasons: (a) The present Dudley and Stourbridge Steam Tramway Company were now paying about 3 per cent. upon an issued capital of £58,000.; (b) the actual value within the meaning of the 43rd Section would be a very much smaller sum ; (c) the traffic was an increasing one, and the stages within the borough they believed to be the best patronised ; (d) by running smaller cars driven by electricity at more frequent intervals the traffic would enormously increase, and the cost of traction would be much less than steam. The right of purchase by the Corporation accrued in about four years, and, as at present advised, the Corporation intended to exercise this right. The Corporation had cause to complain of the condition of their highways over which the present tramways ran, and they considered it important that no other trading company should have the right to interfere with their roads. The tramway lines and the power to repair must be vested in the Corporation. With regard to the construction of proposed tramways by the promoters from Cradley through Old Hill and Netherton to Dudley the Town Council objected on these grounds: (a) It would seriously prejudice their right of purchase of the Dudley and Stourbridge Tramways, as it formed a junction therewith, and it would result in the tramways in the borough being vested in two authorities, which would be objectionable. (b) The application ought not to be made under the Light Railway Act, as it was an extension of the present tramway. The Light Railway Act did not repeal the Tramways Act, and corporate bodies ought not to be deprived of the valuable provisions of the Tramways Act in their favour. (c) The Corporation of Dudley proposed to construct this proposed line either to Bishton's Bridge or to the borough boundary, 580 yards beyond. The extension to Cradley could either be made by the Rowley Regis authorities or by the Corporation, as might be determined. The Corporation had recently obtained a Provisional Order for supplying electric light and power within the borough. They were advised that it was important to the success of this undertaking that they should find a customer to take electric power in the daytime. They looked to the tramways to do this. To permit a trading company to supply electric power within the borough would be very prejudicial to the interests of the town. The same committee report that they had had laid before them the notice on behalf of the Midland Electric Corporation for Power Distribution, of their intention to apply to the Board of Trade for a Provisional Order to supply electricity for public and private purposes within, amongst other places, the county borough of Dudley; and they had instructed the town clerk to oppose such application.

Trial of the First Elwell-Parker Birmingham Tram

Birmingham Mail, 7 November 1888:

"ELECTRIC TRAMWAY MOTORS IMPORTANT TRIAL IN BIRMINGHAM

Yesterday the Directors of the Birmingham Tramways Company afforded to the Public Works Committee of the Corporation, and to a number of eminent men who are interested in electrical engineering, an opportunity of witnessing the trial of an electric tramcar of the type recently produced by Mr Thomas Parker (Elwell-Parker and Company Limited), of Wolverhampton, in conjunction with Mr Alfred Dickinson, M.I.C.E., the consulting mechanical engineer of the company. The car in question is the same, which has been the subject of one or two previous trials lately noticed in our columns.

Yesterday it was run from Station Street to the Sparkbrook Depot and back with a full load of passengers, and in the course of the journey ascended the long and severe incline of Bradford Street, a feat the like of which, the engineers allege has never been performed by any self-contained tramcar.

The company which assisted at the trial included the Mayor of Birmingham (Alderman Barrow), Sir Saul Samuel (Agent General for New South Wales), Sir Daniel Cooper, G.C.M.G., Sir R. Fowler, Bart., M.P., Sir Henry C. Mance, C.I.E., Sir Douglas Fox, M.I.C.E., Adlerman Powell Williams, M.P., Mr J. Spencer Balfour, M.P., Mr T.P. O'Connor, M.P., Colonel Twynam (Chairman of the Birmingham and Midlands Tramway Company), Alderman Johnson (solicitor to the Central Tramways Company); Councillors Lawley Parker (Chairman), J.J. Smith, and Granger (members of the Public Works Committee); Mr W.R. Highes (City Treasurer), Mr Farndale (Chief Constable), Mr T. Arnall (from the Borough Surveyor's Office); Messrs Martyn J. Smith, William Neale, and W.J. Carruthers Waine, Assoc. Inst. C.E. (directors of the company); Messrs. Joseph Ash, James Balfour, J. Irving Courtenay, L.M. Bronsson, G. Dibley, Francis Fox, J.E.H. Gordon, D.S. Hasluck (Chairman of the Birmingham and Aston Tramways Company), F. King, F.H. Lloyd (Wednesbury), H.G. Wright, W. Wiley, and E.B. Tonks; a number of journalists, and the following officials of the Central Tramways Company: Mr J. Kincaid, engineer; Mr W. Holmden, secretary; Mr Alfred Dickinson, consulting mechanical engineer; Mr C. Harvey Herring, traffic manager; Mr R.H. Dickinson, locomotive superintendent.

The party was too large to travel by the electric car alone, since it carries no more than 50 persons, and a steam-driven car of the ordinary pattern preceded it during the trip, to carry the surplus passengers.

The trial was regarded as eminently satisfactory. It is true that the ascent of Bradford Street was accomplished at a rate of only four miles an hour, and that steam-driven cars make it a little more quickly. The engineers state, however, that the gearing is designed for journeys on the level route in Bristol Road, that the experiment of yesterday was meant only to demonstrate a possibility in electric propulsion hitherto doubted, and that by merely altering the gearing, the pace might have been increased.

The car ran very smoothly, and with less noise than even the cable system makes, except when the brake is applied. This latter has been imperfectly adjusted, and gave forth a jarring sound; but as it is a common mechanical contrivance, it may be easily set right. A slight hiss proceeded from the motor when it was at work, but was not audible to the inside passengers. The car was driven by Mr R. Dickinson, and its journey was watched with much interest by curious crowds, who were kept in order by a special force of policemen stationed along the route.

The car may now be more fully described than has hitherto been possible. It has much the appearance of the cars on the New Inns route, for one sees no sign of the machinery which propels it.

There is no rack and lever on the driver's platform at each end, and, as the mechanism by which the switches are actuated is contained in a small box beneath the steps which lead to the roof, the platforms are smaller, and the car, though but 10" longer than a cable car (26ft) has seats for six more passengers.

The electric motor is carried on the front bogey, within a frame, distinct from that which bears the weight of the car, and not subject, therefore to the fluctuations of that weight which take place in the course of traffic. The effect of this immunity from depression and elevation, and of a further bit of ingenious adjustment, is that the "pitch-line" is constant in all circumstances, and that helical gearing, which is safer and stronger than the chain gearing formerly suggested, can be used to connect the motor with the four wheels of the bogey. In this adjustment, and in the helical gearing, the real novelty of the car may be said to lie, and much of the credit of it is due to Mr Dickinson.

It need hardly be nowadays explained that a self-contained electric car, is a car in which the driving force is stored in accumulators or batteries, which have been charged by steam power at a fixed station from such a dynamo as those which are now to be seen at Bingley Hall. The so-called "charging" consists simply in this – that the electric energy generated by the dynamo spends itself in working a chemical change in the constituents of the battery. The change is of a nature which tends to undo itself as soon as opportunity is given, and this reversal of the process gives out again the electric energy which the dynamo passed to the battery.

There is some waste in both processes, but Mr Thomas Parker affirms that the net result in energy is 70 percent of that generated by the stationary engine, which drives the charging dynamo. The economical results of using electricity as a motive power are, if this be true, remarkable. It takes 15lb of coke, at 24s. per ton, to run a steam engine and car a mile, and it will take 3lb or 4lb of slack coal, at 8s. a ton, to propel an electric car the same distance. These are theoretical figures, and it will be remarked that the chairman of the company, in speaking to his guests, made a prudent and considerable allowance upon them.

The accumulators, twelve for each car, are carried beneath the seats, and are put in and taken out from the outside, being shut off from view by sliding doors. They make an automatic connection with the motor. Their present form is not likely to be long retained, for they are enclosed in boxes of unnecessary weight and cumbersomeness, made up of teak and lead. Glass or vulcanite would be preferred if manufacturers could be induced to make the kind of box required. Even as it is however, a set of exhausted motors can be replaced in three minutes with a set of newly charged ones, and their disadvantage consists mainly in the fact that they add very largely to the burden which has to be carried.

A car without its compliment of passengers weighs 9 tons, and with it 12 tons. One charge is sufficient to propel a loaded car 60 miles; but in practice no charge is allowed to get exhausted. The accumulators undergo some wear and tear, but it is said to be doubtful if their maintenance will cost more than that of steam engines.

It is likely that two or three months will yet

930

elapse before the Bristol Road route is furnished with electric cars, even if the Public Works Committee and the City Council should presently give their sanction for the new system. Mr Joseph Smith states that if the order for twelve cars were given at once, it could not be executed in less than two months.

The Public Works Committee on their part, still hold to the requirement that the tramways company should demonstrate the trustworthiness of the Elwell-Parker motor by running a car with it for a month. With reference to this proposal, the company's engineers point out that in order to comply with it, they must perforce put down the plant, which, in any case, will be needed at the generative station. The station as designed by them, will be furnished with large engines, and with the most modern appliances for handling the accumulators.

It will probably be suggested, therefore, that the Council should be asked to grant to the company provisional running powers for a month, and only to make them absolute if at the end of that time electric traction should become a proved success. If this concession were granted, the hands of the directors would be materially strengthened. They can hardly be surprised however, at the firmness of the committee when they remember that at least one other local authority has been induced to sanction a system of electric traction which belies the hopes of its promoters, and that the Central Company itself not long ago pressed hard for the adoption in Birmingham of a motor, which is now admitted to have had grave mechanical defects.

It was doubted, moreover, by a mechanical specialist who saw the tramcar which made yesterday's trial trip, whether the brake attachment in use would prove of permanent value. If Messrs Elwell, Parker, and the company's motor does not establish its claim to be safe and efficient, its success will be attributable to the combination in one inventor of both mechanical and electrical skill, and to his regards for a consulting engineer's knowledge of the actual requirements of tramway work.

After the trial a luncheon was held at the Queen's Hotel, at which Mr Joseph Smith presided. The health of "The Queen" having been drunk, Mr Smith proposed the toast of "Success to the system of electric traction." He said that among the buried treasures of wisdom in the east, he believed there was a maxim that he who shot at the sun would strike higher than a bush. He hoped that that maxim would not encourage the Corporation of Birmingham to strike too high or too hard, if he acknowledged that the result of that day's experience in electric traction was in no small degree due to the absolute determination of the Corporation of Birmingham in general, and of the Public Works Committee in particular, that nothing less than the best illustration of electric traction would be good enough for the City of Birmingham. (Hear, Hear).

Mr Lawley Parker had that day seen a distinct advance upon anything which had before been shown in this country or on the continent of Europe. The improvement in mechanical details in the car upon which they had travelled was most marked and most satisfactory, and so far as the car itself was concerned, he ventured to state that it would

give satisfaction both to the Corporation and to the travelling public. As to the commercial aspect of the experiment, which was interesting to the shareholders of the Central Tramway Company, it was one of the features of electric propulsion, and of the self-contained car in particular, that power must be lost at the fixed station in changing mechanical energy by dynamos into electric energy in the accumulators, and in again that electric energy into mechanical energy in the car motor.

Taking the average of opinions which had been given to him from the highest sources, it appeared that probably 40 percent would be placed as mechanical energy upon the wheels; but he preferred to calculate the cost upon the supposition that they would only preserve 25 percent of the original energy, and with that loss electric traction emphatically justified itself as the coming power of the near future. He was speaking in the presence of men who would be able to check him when he said that one ton of ordinary coal consumed at the generative station, meant as much efficient work as three tons of coal expended in a steam locomotive. More than that, the cost of hard coke was nearly three times the cost of the coal which the company would use, and thus the cost of generation at a fixed station was only one sixth; possibly less than that of the cost of steam locomotives. What cared he, therefore, as a tramway man, if he got only 25 percent of the power generated, when he could generate six times as much for the same expenditure of money, representing a 20 percent profit upon their expenditure upon electric trams? Working expenses would be less and the wear and tear upon the roads would be less.

The average weight of a steam locomotive and car is 16 tons, the weight of an electric car is only 9 tons. The economic results of electricity were of course still better than those of horse traction, and at the same time the electric car was only 26ft long whereas a steam engine and its car were 51ft 6in. long (Hear, Hear). He would call upon nobody to respond to the toast, because on that showing he thought that electric traction was able to answer for itself (Laughter and applause).

Councillor Lawley Parker proposed the toast of "The Visitors" and said that the occasion was a very interesting one to the members of the Corporation and to the public. They had witnessed a most successful and interesting experiment. Birmingham had not been afraid to venture upon several important experiments connected with tramways, and now they saw another experiment which he believed, and hoped, would prove to be practical on other tramlines in the borough.

He desired, however, that they should first see the electric car at work continuously for, say, a month. It was the desire of the Public Works Committee that that should be required in order that they might see the system thoroughly and fairly tried. As they did not know much about electricity themselves, they were bound to consider that the proof of the pudding lay in the eating, (Hear, Hear) and if the month's work was satisfactory, he was sure that the City Council and the Public Works Committee would be very much disposed to favour electric motors on other lines in the borough (Hear, Hear).

It was of course unfortunate that when the

Bristol Road line was completed the company would not at once be able to put electric motors at work; but he hoped that they would be able to make some temporary arrangements for a service of horse cars. As to the use of electric motors on other lines, it was not for him to say what the company should do; but if he might express a hope, it was that they would boldly attack their depreciation fund, and write off their steam engines pretty rapidly. They might depend upon the Council dealing fairly and properly with their shareholders. (Hear, Hear).

Sir Saul Samuel responded on behalf of the visitors and said that his interest was the greater in the experiment which had just been tried, because the people of Sydney, whom he represented, were extremely anxious to get rid of their steam cars, which were the same pattern as the Birmingham cars. (Laughter). The trial had been a perfectly successful one, and he regarded the system as the best form of electric traction yet devised. He ended by giving the toast of "The Mayor and Corporation of Birmingham". (Applause).

The Mayor responded, and said that he hoped the Corporation would soon be able to get rid of the smoky engines, which now traversed the streets of the City. (Hear, Hear). Birmingham was smoky enough without having smoke emitted in its thoroughfares. The electric car was an immense improvement on the system of steam traction, and, for the sake of the promoters, as well as of the public, he hoped it might prove a success. He concluded with some remarks on the importance of penny fares as a great advantage to the working classes, and by proposing the health of the chairman.

Mr Joseph Smith, in replying, welcomed the proposal that electricity should be used on other routes than Bristol Road, and said that if he had not been satisfied that the enhanced profit of electric traction would pay for the abolition of steam engines, he would never have advocated it. (Hear, Hear).

The proceedings closed when the health of Mr Thomas Parker had also been drunk.

The regular running of electric tramcars on the Bristol Road route, began on Friday, 25 July, 1890."

———

This was one of a very few experimental 'modern' designs to enter service, and unlike those designs for whom notes follow, it was a true precursor of the trams that, here and there, were to last at least another fifty years, the last of all, Blackpool, finally closing 8 November 2009.

Connolly Gas Tramway Motor

Variants upon a theme, whereby town gas was substituted for coke, appeared in Blackpool, Neath and Trafford Park but many and bitter were the complaints about the fumes mainly owing to problems in obtaining gas tight seals on 'rock'n'roll' trackwork. This gas-motor using oil as a basic fuel should have worked, and was essayed on the lines of the Deptford and Southwark (LCC) but on 29 June 1892 Major General Hutchinson refused to allow its use eventually repenting (after many alterations were met) on 12 December. Use on the Rotherhithe New Road line it plodded up and down until some time in 1896, covering a mere 5,348 miles and carrying 41,000 passengers. Hardly a ringing endorsement.

From *The Engineer*, 30 September 1892

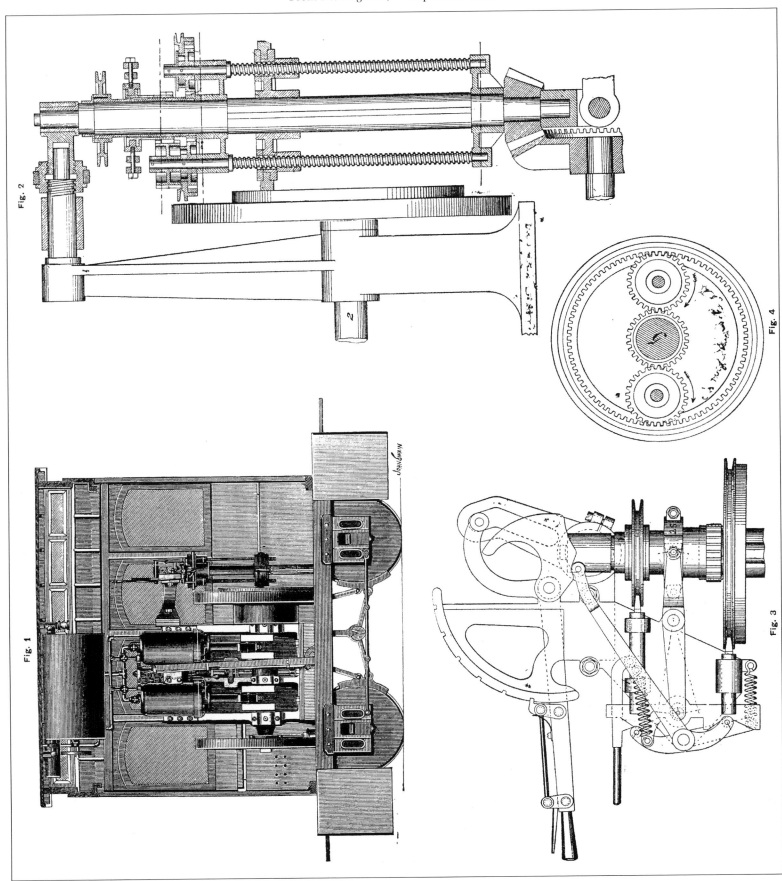

A TRAMWAY GAS ENGINE LOCOMOTIVE.

THIS motor was brought before the English public last year, but since then improvements have been effected in it, and a new one constructed by Messrs. Weyman and Company, of Guildford. The motor is independent of any central station or stationary plant, as it carries its own supply of fuel for a day's run, in the shape of oil contained in a strongly-made closed tank fitted to the inside of the roof of the car. This oil is vapourised to supply to the engine.

The action of all gas engines is such that their speed cannot be varied like the steam engine, but must run at a nearly uniform rate, therefore special mechanism is required for transmitting power to the axle at any desired speed. The mechanism employed for this is almost noiseless, and the wearing part, a thin, cast iron disc, is easily, quickly, and cheaply replaced. It prevents giving shock or jar to the car when starting, and transmits maximum propulsive power when driving a car at minimum speed. In the transmission of power by friction it is necessary that the contact pressure should vary in proportion to the power transmitted. This is accomplished automatically by means of a right and left screw nut, Fig. 2, operated by an excentric extension of the hand lever, Fig. 3, so that any movement of the lever in either direction, to vary the speed, changes the pressure of contact correspondingly, thus securing maximum pressure on grades or curves, and minimum when running at full speed. This is one of the most important features of the device, as it would be impracticable to run at full speed with the same contact pressure that is required when starting on grades or curves.

The method of transmitting power from the engine to the axle is illustrated by the several engravings which we now publish, and is as follows:—The main vertical shaft is set parallel with a disc, 30in. in diameter, placed on the face of the fly-wheel. On the shaft is a loose friction pulley 12in. in diameter that engages with the face of the disc. In Fig. 2 this friction pulley is shown in section, an outside view is given in Fig. 1, which shows the Weyman double-cylinder motor mounted in the dummy car. This loose pulley is prevented from revolving on the shaft by a tongue and groove, but is moved up or down on the shaft at the will of the driver, by means of two screw rods which pass through the pulley and revolve with the shaft. When it is required to slacken speed or stop, the friction pulley, still in contact with the disc, is run down to near its centre, and at this point can be slightly moved from the disc. The engine requires no attention after being started, and regulates its own speed whether the car be running or standing still. To start the car the contact of the pulley with the disc is always made near the centre, so that the car is started at slow speed. When the hand lever seen in Figs. 1 and 3 is pulled over to the position shown in Fig. 3, it pulls up the slotted lever which grips the right and left-handed nut seen in section in Fig. 1. It will also be seen that by the cam on the

same lever spindle, movement is given to a lever which pushes one or other of two friction fingers into the lower or upper of two grooved pulleys, the rotation of one of which is thus stopped. If the large one be stopped, the small cog pinions on the screws, as seen in Figs. 1, 3, and 4 are quickly rotated for bringing the pulley rapidly back to the centre of the disc wheel. When the small grooved wheel is stopped, by a movement of the hand lever through short range, the screws move slowly, and the friction pulley is moved from the centre and pressed up to the disc.

In rounding curves, or in ascending steep gradients, the contact is also generally made near the centre. The friction pulley has a loose band that revolves slightly when the contact is first made—see Fig. 2—thus avoiding all danger of flattening the friction pulley.

The motor developes 12 actual horse-power and weighs 4½ tons, having a 5ft. 6in. wheel base. The engine is quite different to that in the old motor. For the one working cylinder in the latter—which, when the engine was working, had an impulse every revolution—a pair of cylinders have been substituted working on the four cycle, by which means an impulse is still obtained every revolution; but the impulse is taken alternately in each cylinder, with the advantage, that on running up a long grade the motor cylinders do not become hot. In the old motor the thrust of the transmission motion was taken through the crank shaft, setting up considerable strain and undue friction. A fresh arrangement has therefore been adopted, whereby the solid framework of the engine next the fly-wheel takes the thrust through a large radial roller bearing, relieving the crank shaft and bearing of all crank-closing thrust, some power being thereby saved. Other improvements have also been effected, not the least of which is the silencing of the exhaust. For the ignition of the charge a small dynamo is now used, which charges accumulators, and from these cells the spark for the ignition is obtained, and also electricity for lighting the motor and passenger car.

The motor, which is built to the Board of Trade regulations, has a length of 11ft. over all, with the platform at either end, and is capable of hauling a heavily-loaded car up grades of 1 in 20, or on roads having grades not exceeding 1 in 50 it can easily handle two cars. The gearing is arranged for a maximum speed of twelve miles per hour. The Connelly Motor Company estimate the cost of working the motor per day of 14 hours, say 70 miles, with everything supplied to the motor, including driver, to be 15s. 6d., made up of the following items :—10 gallons oil, 6s. 8d.; fitter—having charge of 10 motors—8d.; repairs—wear and tear—10d.; lubricating oil, 4d.; drivers, 7s.; making a total of 15s. 6d., or 2·35d. per car mile. The driver's wages at 7s. may appear excessive, but one man would have to be relieved at the end of about 10 hours, so that part of another's wages have to be estimated for.

The Messrs. Connelly have, during the past year, made improvements in their motor, quite independent of those made by Messrs. Weyman and Co., in this country. The motor is now very largely used in the States, and arrangements have recently been made for working several of the Chicago lines with it. The motor in this country was a short time ago shown at work on the Deptford and Greenwich tramway, and may be seen at that company's depôt, Lower-road, Deptford.

933

Narrow Gauge Self Propelled Tramcar

"HORSELESS CARRIAGES

AMONG the vehicles exhibited in the Imperial Institute Exhibition is a narrow-gauge tramcar for carrying about a dozen passengers on longitudinal seats, as shown in the accompanying engravings. It has a light canopy over it, and is propelled by a Daimler motor placed in the case shown at one end. At the same end is the seat for a driver, within whose reach are placed the two levers necessary for controlling the movements of the car, the arrangement of the motor, the gearing, and the brake and gear levers. The motor we have already described (in The Engineer, 20 December, 1895) as to its oil or benzoline, and air-supply arrangements. It has two cylinders, and is connected to the driving axle by strong gearing thrown in or out of gear by a flat bar connected to the brake-lever M. On this bar is a projection having an inclined surface. This passes through a slotted head projecting from the end of the hollow continuation of the crank shaft at K, the head being connected to the friction clutch by a rod through the hole in the shaft up to the clutch at L. Thus when the lever M is pulled to put the brake on the driving wheels, the driving power is simultaneously cut out by the separation of the friction clutch surfaces, the which are pressed together by a spiral spring which is seen between the outer bearing and the small pinion E. When the latter is in gear, as shown with the wheel G on the intermediate shaft, the slowest speed is made, and by pulling the lever N out, the pinion F is put into gear with the wheel H, a higher speed being obtained. From the third wheel on this shaft the wheel I is driven. At D D are the two cylindrical exhaust boxes. The exhaust from both cylinders passes into the box nearest the engine, and from this it passes by a pipe to the bottom of the second box, from the top of which it passes into the air by a pipe which turns over from the top and leads it to near the ground. The oil vessel is not shown in our sketch, but provision is made for about a day's working. The arrangement of the car and its motor is very neat, and it gives a good idea of what may be done for vehicles for light narrow-gauge tramways or tramroads."

The Engineer, 12 June 1896

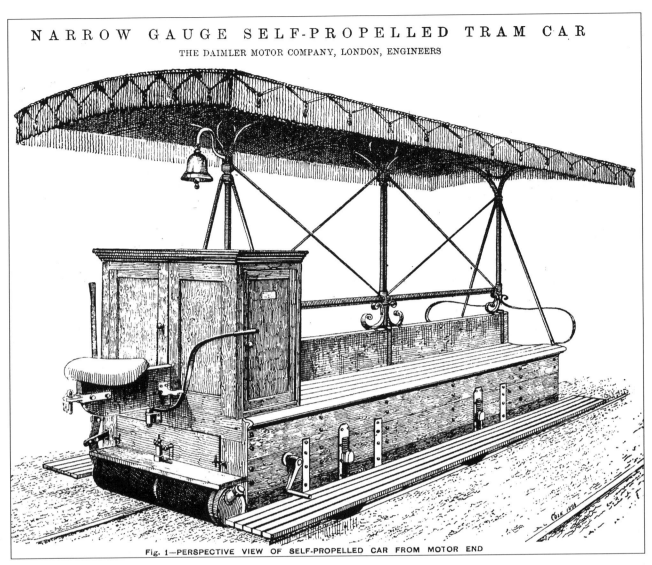

NARROW GAUGE SELF-PROPELLED TRAM CAR

THE DAIMLER MOTOR COMPANY, LONDON, ENGINEERS

Fig. 1—PERSPECTIVE VIEW OF SELF-PROPELLED CAR FROM MOTOR END

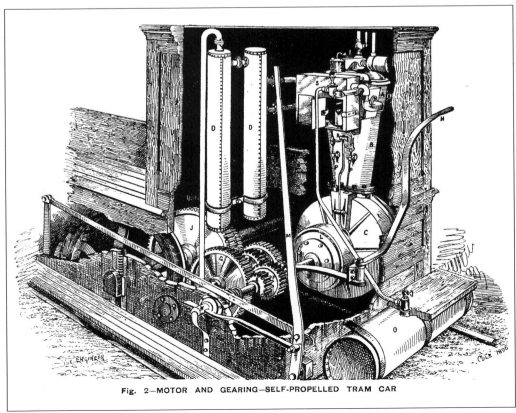

Fig. 2—MOTOR AND GEARING—SELF-PROPELLED TRAM CAR

The Mékarski System

For reasons not entirely clear (at least to me) some readers have found the Mékarski system to catch their imagination, when all along I thought I was the only one! These drawings are really a continuation of the text and drawings in our volume 5 and are drawn from both Engineering and the Memoires ... de la Societé des Ingenieurs Civils. Our only example ran at Wantage, but there were plans for others – the big problem was that a tight headway service was called for to compensate for keeping the boilers and compressors ready for use 24 hours a day. I think perhaps as far as the UK market was concerned the 'moteur' was perfected as far as could be far too late. These drawings should help modellers.

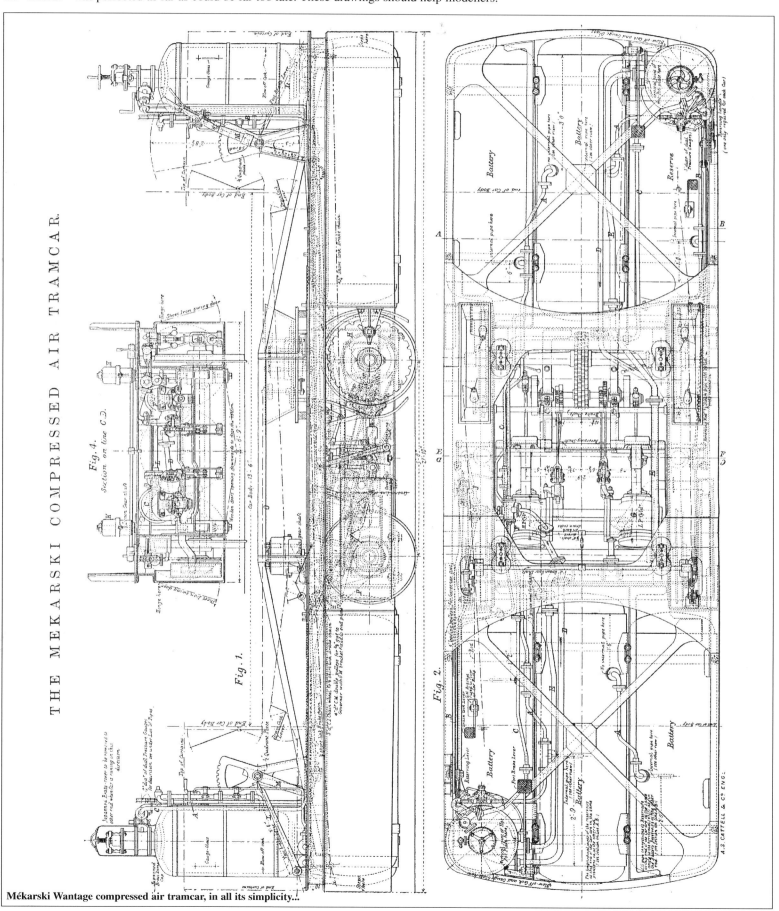

Mékarski Wantage compressed air tramcar, in all its simplicity...

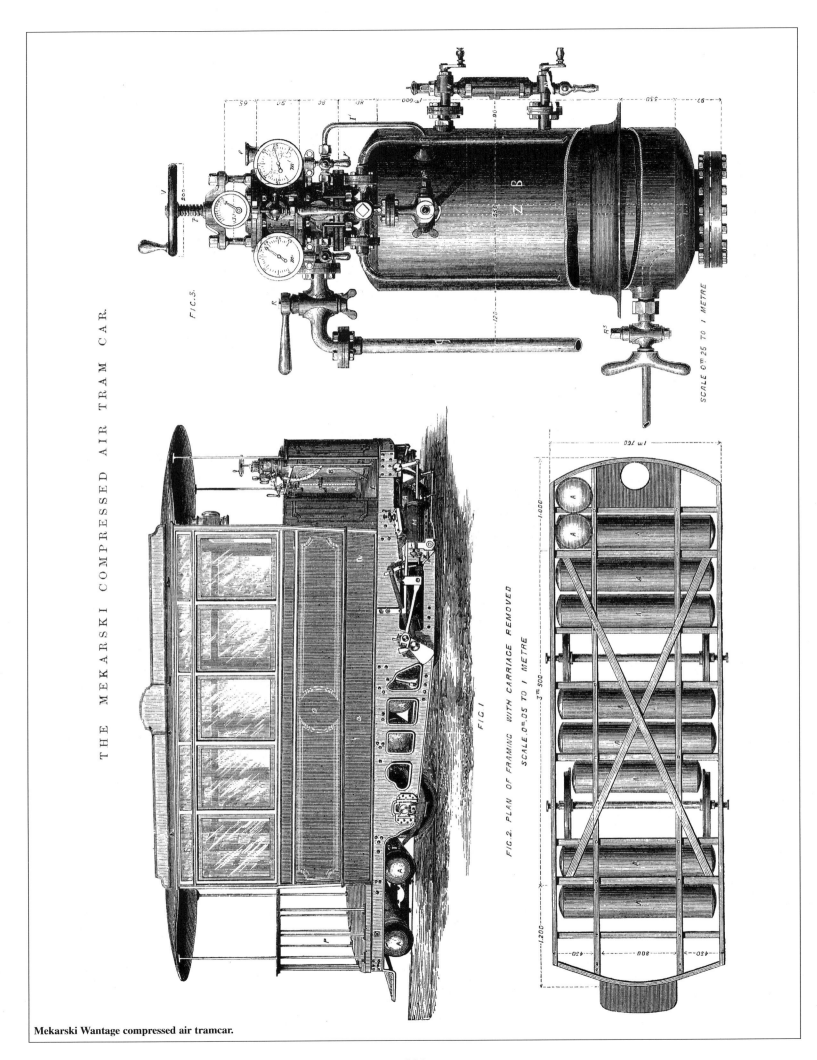

THE MEKARSKI COMPRESSED AIR TRAM CAR.

FIG. 3.

SCALE 0ᵐ·25 TO 1 METRE

FIG 1

FIG. 2. PLAN OF FRAMING WITH CARRIAGE REMOVED

SCALE 0ᵐ·05 TO 1 METRE

Mekarski Wantage compressed air tramcar.

This 1888 drawing shows the compressor room at Maltournée depot on the Nogentais system. It is typical of those used by the earlier Mékarski tramways. The compressor set was installed at Maltournée depot where there was a charge point. Two boilers fed two 55 horsepower steam engines which were connected by line shaft to two compressors. Each compressor had low and high pressure cylinders delivering air compressed to 6 and 45kg respectively. The air was then stored in twelve reservoirs. Extra charge points were at Vincennes and Bry-sur-Marne, fed from Maltournée. All three charge points had their own steam generators to reheat the water in the bouillotte. This was done by a jet of steam and each charge took 15 minutes. The air consumption was said to be 10kg per car kilometre.

The compressor sets in the CAG works at Billancourt. The works at Billancourt was in its day the largest installation for the production of compressed air in Europe. It used 3-stage compression at 4.3 atmospheres, 18 atmospheres and 80 atmospheres. There were 16 Babcock and Wilcox multi-tube boilers, supplied with purified Seine river water, feeding 7 compressor sets which in turn charged a battery of 500 litre tanks. It was said to use about 2kg of coal per car/kilometre. Each compressor set had a horizontal triple-expansion steam engine driving the compressor. The low pressure cylinder of the compressor had water injected to cool the air. Between the second and third cylinders there was a tank containing serpentine copper tubes. These two cylinders and the tank were cooled by circulating cold water.

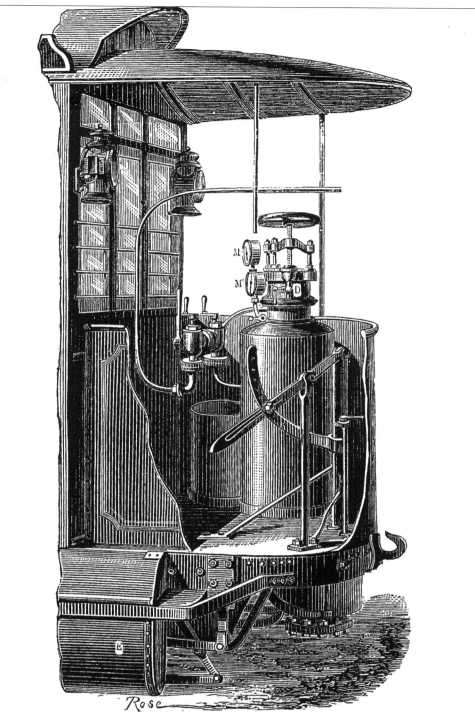

FIG. 97. — APPAREIL RÉGULATEUR DE LA PRESSION DE LA LOCOMOTIVE MEKARSKI

Appareil régulateur de la pression de la locomotive Mékarski.

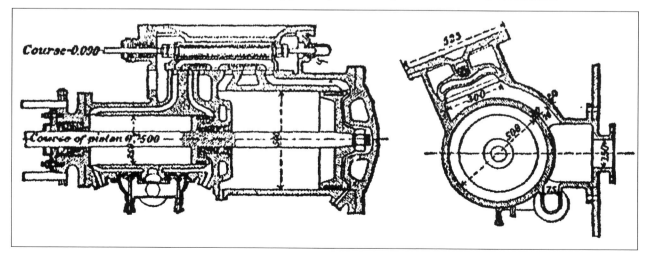

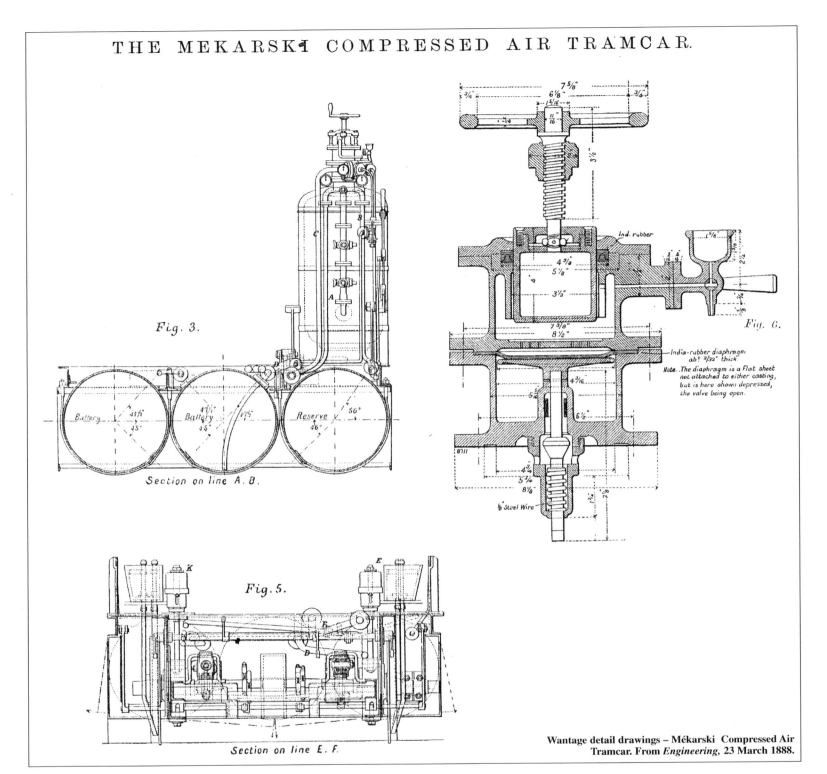

Fig. 3.

Section on line A. B.

Fig. 6.

India-rubber diaphragm abt. 3/32" thick

Note. The diaphragm is a flat sheet not attached to either casting, but is here shown depressed, the valve being open.

Fig. 5.

Section on line E. F.

Wantage detail drawings – Mékarski Compressed Air Tramcar. From _Engineering_, 23 March 1888.

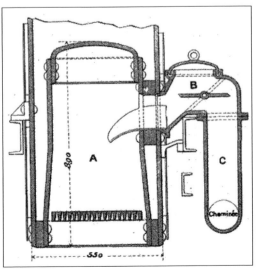

A drawing of 1903 shows the Bonnefond firebox as fitted into the bouillotte of later Mékarski cars. The fire was at A. The flap valve at B closed off the flue C, when coke was being added. The regulator, placed between the air reservoirs and the bouillotte, was controlled by a wheel in the usual position. on top of the bouillotte. For normal running the cylinder pressure was 8-10 atmospheres. The low pressure of the air fed to the bouillotte was raised by about 2 atmospheres by the water vapour formed there at a temperature of 130 degrees centigrade.

ELECTRIC TRACTION.

CHAPTER I.

ELECTRIC POWER AS APPLIED TO TRAMWAYS.

THE only available source of electrical energy was until comparatively recently the galvanic battery, and attempts have been made, since the beginning of the century, to apply that force for obtaining and transmitting power. The hopelessness of the attempts is obvious. A pound of zinc is produced by the combustion of from 15 lbs. to 20 lbs. of coal, and while a pound of coal in burning gives out 12,000 heat-units, a pound of zinc in burning gives only 2,340 units. Thus zinc gives in burning only one-fifth of the effect in energy that coal does, and taking the cost of zinc at fifty times that of coal, it follows that the cost of energy in the case of a galvanic battery is approximately two hundred and fifty times greater than in a steam boiler.

For the purpose of mechanical traction on tramways, electric-power may be transformed into mechanical power, with a large percentage of efficiency. The dynamo is the source with which, principally, electricity has been associated. The current produced is known as inductional electricity, as it is magnetically induced by the revolution of the armature of the dynamo. The motor is connected to the wheels of the car, for the purpose of propulsion, by direct gearing or by reducing gear. Self-contained motor trucks comprise a rigid framework resting on the axle-boxes.

The body of the car rests on and is fastened to the frame. Thus may be provided an elastic gear connection ; the axle-journals are maintained parallel; and the gear-wheels may be properly proportioned to reduce the speed of the armature from, say, 2,500 revolutions per minute, for a suitable speed of the car on the rails. In order to secure a sufficient degree of adhesion for propulsion, it is expedient to provide two motors to each truck, geared to independent axles.

To transmit current from the dynamo, or generator, to the motors on the car, it is necessary that a complete metallic circuit should extend from the generator to the car, and return to the generator. "Positive" current is conveyed over that part of the circuit which leads out from the generator. "Negative" current is the return current leading back to the generator.

It is readily seen that an electric motor can be connected by reducing gear to the wheels of a tram-car to cause them to revolve : in the manner of a turning-lathe, for instance. But the peculiar difficulty in dealing with electric traction is to convey the electricity produced at the supply station to the electric motor on the moving cars :—properly to locate these conductors, with the best means of securing a continuous movable contact.

(1.) On some early tramways, a third rail was laid, on insulating material, through which positive current was transmitted, and from which, by means of a brush or wheel, the current was taken up, passed through the motor, and thence, by means of the car-wheels, to the rails of the way, through which it was returned to the generator.

(2.) Underground communication by two wires or metal rods, one for positive current, the other for negative current, in a shallow conduit laid between the rails or at one side of the way. Contact with the conductor is effected by means of brushes or ploughs, supported by a thin iron plate or finger hung to the truck, and moving along a narrow longitudinal slot in the top of the conduit. One brush takes up current from the positive wire and conveys it to the motor, whence it is returned to the negative wire through the other brush. The conducting wires must be carefully insulated from the sides of the conduit, and from contact with the slot-rails.

(3.) The overhead system of connection is the system most generally employed. It includes the methods of (1) supporting one or both conductors on trolleys, and (2) making contact with them above the car. Of these, the single-wire under-contact arrangement is the more popular. The positive wire is supported over the centre of the way by means of cross wires attached to poles at the side of the street, or by means of cross-arms on poles placed between the ways. For single lines of way, side poles with brackets are used. The trolley wires are braced on curves.

In the single-trolley system, the rails are utilised for the return or negative current ; and for this purpose the ends of the rails are wired together, and are usually supplemented by one or more return wires which are buried beneath the pavement, to which each section of rail or casting is connected by means of branch wires. The bonds are riveted to the rails. Galvanised iron wire is recommended for rail-bonds and way wiring. Copper wiring deteriorates rapidly by electrolysis.

The way connections should return the current to the generator in a direct path—having a minimum of resistance in the return circuit—and resulting in economy of power, and efficient service from the motors.

In some soils the resistance of the rail-return may be reduced and leakage avoided, by driving metal rods or pieces of gas pipe 10 or 15 feet down into the ground and connecting these rods with the rails or a supplementary wire.

In place of rods, copper ground plates, having from 30 to 40 sq. ft. of surface, may be placed at intervals of 1,000 feet, and at a depth sufficient to insure their being always in moist ground.

For supporting the overhead wire, poles of wood, iron, or steel, from 26 to 30 feet long, may be employed. The best timber is chestnut, cedar, or Georgia pine. Wooden poles on straight lines should be from 7 to 8 inches in diameter at the top, and at least from 10 to 12 inches at the base ; but iron or steel poles are more desirable than wooden poles. The poles are usually placed 125 feet apart, and they should be set at least 6 feet deep in the ground in a foundation of concrete. Near the top of the pole a device should be provided to secure the most perfect insulation for the suspension wire. The trolley wire is supported from above without obstructing the passage of the under-running trolley wheel.

The trolley wire should not be smaller than No. 0 (·325 inch) of hard drawn copper wire or silicon bronze wire.

Feed Wire.—The trolley wire is usually not large enough to transmit the power to a long distance without undue loss ; and it is advantageous to supply the current to the trolley wire at intervals, by means of auxiliary insulated feed wire. By this means a nearly uniform potential can be maintained at all points of the line. Subways, or electric conduits for feed wires, should be of non-conducting tubing, through which the bare conductors can be laid ; and the tubing should be enclosed in a creosoted plank casing. Contact of the moving car with the overhead wire, for the purpose of conducting the current through the controlling mechanism on the car to the respective poles of the motor, is made by means of a trolley pole and stand. The relation of the cars to the circuit is illustrated by diagram, Fig. 340, showing that the current seems to start from the positive brush of the generator, G, and along the overhead conductor in the line of the arrows until it reaches the trolley, T, of one of the motor bars, which is in contact with the conductor. Here a portion of the current passes down through the trolley to the motors M, M, as shown by the dotted line. The current having done its work in the motors goes on the rails through the wheels and by the rails return wire, W, back to the negative brush of the generator. The main portion of the current, which divides at T, passes on to feed the other cars upon the line in the same manner, each car taking from the conductor only the necessary amount of current to develop the required power, while the entire return current is carried by the rail and a supplementary wire.

The trolley-stand consists of an upright, firmly attached to the roof of the car, and a long wooden or iron arm mast, pivoted near

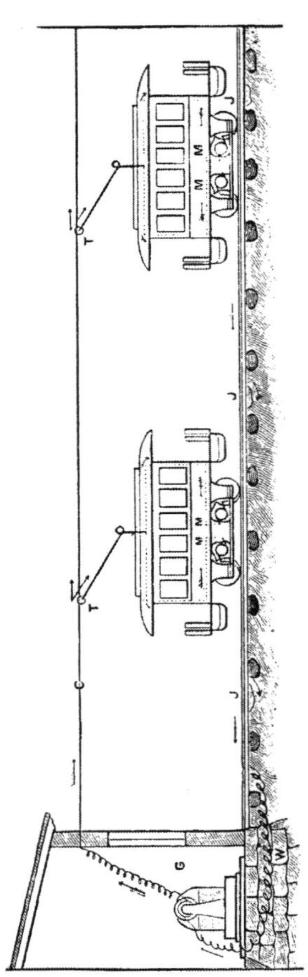

FIG. 340.—Electric Traction: Overhead Conductor System. Relation of the Cars to the Circuit.

one end upon the top of the upright. The long arm of the mast carries a metal trolley wheel which is held firmly up against the under side of the conductor by strong springs attached to the short end of the arm and connected with the base of the standard. The mast springs and attachments are all free to swivel upon the upright.

An insulated wire embedded in the mast conducts the current from the trolley wheel to the controlling switches on the car, but in place of a trolley wheel, a sliding contact may be obtained by means of a carbon-lined metal brush at the end of a trolley pole.

Two overhead wires, 5 inches or 6 inches apart, are, as already stated, sometimes employed instead of the single overhead wire and rail connections to form the necessary metal circuit. Two trolley wheels, or two masts, each carrying a wheel, are required, one wheel in contact with the positive wire and the other with the negative wire. The current is thus conducted from one wire to the motors and back to the other wire.

As to the wiring of the car, and how the wires are connected with the switches and with the poles of the motors. Usually a switch on each platform directs the current to both motors, and controls the speed and the direction of the car. In addition, the flow of current through the motors is controlled :—according to *one system*, by a peculiar winding of the field magnets ; by *another system*, current is controlled through a " rheostat," or resistance box, by which any abnormal flow of current through the armature is prevented, and the motor is enabled to start gradually. It is in the form of a half circle, mounted under the floor of the car. Resistance is produced by small pieces of thin sheet-iron, side by side, separated by mica, so arranged that they are connected in series throughout the rheostat. At proper intervals, contact pieces of heavy sheet-iron are provided. The whole is secured in a semi-circular iron case thoroughly insulated with mica throughout.

Storage Batteries, Accumulators, or Secondary Batteries, belong to a class of *chemical batteries,* in which chemical action, primarily induced by the application of a current of electricity, supplied from a primary battery or from a dynamo, enables a strong current to be given back any time after cutting off the charging current. This derived current is the product of chemical reaction.

The accumulator system of storage batteries, or secondary batteries, is the simplest and most convenient method of conveying the electricity produced at the supply station to the electric motor on the cars. The stored energy is carried in accumulators, which are placed under the seats of the car, and connected by wires through a regulating switch to the motor. But there is an unavoidable loss in the use of current taken from accumulators, and there is a loss in addition due to the additional weight of the accumulators to be drawn.

ELECTRICAL TERMS AND UNITS.

It may be useful to recapitulate these here :

Volt.—Unit of electro-motive force (E.M.F.) : *Electric Pressure.*

Ampere.—Unit of current; *rate* at which electric current is transmitted through the conductor forming the circuit.

Ohm.—Unit of electric resistance in the conductor. *Resistance* is that which tends to stop the flow of electricity.

Watt.—Unit to express rate at which electric power is absorbed or developed in an electric system, stated in terms of any two of the other units. It serves as a means of comparison between electrical and mechanical power.

Thus, to measure the power exerted by a current in a wire, the *volts* of electro-motive force and the *amperes* of *current* are measured. The two numbers are multiplied together. Or, the same result is obtained by multiplying the square of the current in *amperes* by the resistance in *ohms*. Products are the same, and give the rate of doing work, or the watts.

A Watt is $= \frac{1}{746}$ th part of a horse-power.

Resistance of Conductors (say, a wire), is, 1st, proportional to its length ; 2nd, is inversely proportional to the area of section ; 3rd, depends on the material of which it is made.

	Conducting power.	Resistance.
Silver	100	·2421
Copper	99·55	·2106
Iron	16·81	1·2425
Lead	8·32	3·236
German silver	—	2·652

$\frac{\text{Volts}}{\text{Ohms}}$ = Amperes of current. $\frac{\text{Volts}}{\text{Amperes}}$ = Ohms.

The United States of America are conspicuously in advance of the United Kingdom in the application of electrical traction to tramways. In nearly every town in America, horse traction has been either totally or in part superseded by electrical traction. In the year 1892, the number of electrical tramways in the United States was 436, with 3,532 miles of track and 5,851 motor cars, travelling in the aggregate 50,000,000 miles and carrying 250,000,000 passengers annually. On the Continent, many important city tramway systems are now worked electrically. (For a list of electrical tramways in Europe, compiled by Mr. R. Hammond, see Appendix.) On the other hand, the British and Irish electrical tramways, aggregating 22 miles of way, have been reduced, during the past five years, by three on account of the abandonment of electrical working on those lines, whilst only six new lines have been added to the list, making $33\frac{1}{4}$ miles of way in all.

ELECTRICAL TRAMWAYS IN THE UNITED KINGDOM, 1893.

Year of opening.	——	Miles.	System.	——
1883	Portrush and Giant's Causeway	8	Side conductor . .	Water-power
1883	Brighton Beach .	1	Rails	Gas-engine
1885	Bessbrook and Newry Tramway.	$3\frac{1}{4}$	Central conductor .	Water-power
1886	Ryde Pier . . .	$\frac{1}{2}$	Side conductor . .	Gas-engine
1886	Blackpool . . .	2	Conduit	Steam
1889	Carstairs	$1\frac{1}{4}$	Side conductors .	Water-power
1890	Birmingham . . .	3	Accumulator . .	
1890	City and South London . . .	$3\frac{1}{6}$	Side conductor . .	Steam
1891	Southend Pier . .	$\frac{3}{4}$	Central conductor .	,,
1891	Guernsey	$2\frac{3}{4}$	Overhead conductor	,,
1891	Leeds	$3\frac{1}{4}$	,, ,,	,,
1893	South Staffordshire	$7\frac{1}{2}$	,, ,,	,,
1893	Liverpool Overhead	$6\frac{1}{3}$	Central conductor .	,,

Different Kinds of Power for Tramways

Minutes of the Proceedings of the Institution of Civil Engineers 1898-1899

"The Relative Advantages of Different Kinds of Power for Tramways, Light Railways, and Motor-Car Traffic, both Heavy and Light." [1]

By Thomas Parker, M. Inst. C.E.

(Abstract.)

Horse traction upon tramways had many disadvantages besides its costliness. The average cost per mile, with a car weighing 2·75 tons empty and seating 26 passengers, might be taken at 7·78 pence, made up as follows :—driver's and conductor's wages 2·50 ; horses, forage, renewals, attendance, harness, &c., 4·53 ; management and general expenses 0·75d.

Steam traction, though quicker and less costly in proportion to load, had yet greater disadvantages for street tramways. Practical working had shown that the cost per mile, with a car weighing 12 tons empty and seating 54 passengers, might be taken at 8·99 pence, made up as follows:—driver's and conductor's wages 3·50 ; locomotive repairs 1·75 ; car 0·50 ; fuel 1·65 ; lighting 0·33 ; management and general expenses 1·26d.

Compressed air had better prospects of success than steam ; the proportion of dead load per passenger was in its favour, and it appeared to be more economical than the use of steam direct.

Endless-rope traction had many high merits ; but also serious drawbacks, including heavy initial outlay and heavy cost of working. So few tramways were now being laid for rope traction that it might be regarded as having ceased to compete successfully with other plans.

Gas engines working on tramcars were being tried ; but no trustworthy practical data were yet to be met with.

Electricity was generally selected at the present time as the best power for tramways. Besides many other advantages, it admitted of great variation in the power exerted at different points on the line. Its disadvantage lay in the conductors being carried overhead ; nevertheless overhead wires were at present generally accepted for their attendant practical advantages. Accumulators on the cars had not realised the expectations formed of them ; the loss of capacity in the cells during use was a great difficulty. The power required per car-mile with accumulators was about 4·6 E.H.P.-hours ; and with overhead conductors about 2·15 E.H.P.-hours, with higher speed and heavier gradients. With overhead conductors the average cost per mile, with a car weighing 4·3 tons empty and seating 30 passengers, might be taken at 3·16 pence, made up as follows :—driver's and conductor's wages 2·49 ; expenses of generating station 0·46 ; car 0·04 ; lighting 0·02 ; management and general expenses 0·15d.

For railways, whether light or heavy, electricity was employed under the most favourable conditions on long runs, and under the least favourable where the stoppages were frequent. For railways on which few trains ran, electricity did not compare with steam locomotives, because the capital outlay for the generating station, dynamos, and conductors, was the same for a few trains as for a number. But for a long run of 50 miles with sufficient traffic, electricity could work trains of 100 tons at intervals of 15 minutes, doing the distance in 40 minutes, at a cost of 2½d. per train-mile, and carrying as many passengers as steam trains of 140 tons. On the Liverpool Overhead Railway, which had now been working for nearly seven years, electricity was under its worst conditions in comparison with steam, owing to the number of stoppages and the shortness of runs. In this instance the average cost per mile, with a train weighing 31 tons empty and seating 140 passengers, was 4·32 pence, of which 0·42d. went for management and general expenses, and the remaining 3·90d. for driver's and conductor's wages, expenses of generating station, cars, lighting, &c.

For motor-cars, steam had been early in the field, followed by oil ; with both there was still much room for improvement, with prospects of ultimate success in comparison with horses. For electric motor-cars the weight of accumulators had recently been reduced to ½ cwt. per H.P.-hour, or 5 cwts. of cells for a car which two years ago had required 16 cwts. The following data were from one of the best examples the Author had had the opportunity of testing :—weight of car without batteries 9 cwts., weight of batteries 5 cwts., total weight with four passengers 20 cwts. ; discharge 12 amperes at 80 volts, giving speed of 9 miles per hour on level ; power about 1½ E.H.P. ; safe length of run 40 miles ; one motor, making 1,200 revolutions per minute, with double-reduction gear.

---

[1] *The Engineer*, vol. lxxxvii. p. 565 ; *Engineering*, vol. lxvii. pp. 740 and 756 ; *The Electrical Engineer*, vol. xxiii. p. 723 ; *The Electrician*, vol. xliii. p. 234 ; *The Electrical Review*, vol. xliv. pp. 964 and 998.

Bradford Daily Telegraph, 11 February 1902:

"KILLED BY A CAR

BRADFORD WOMAN'S TRAGIC END

This was the heading to the report of a Coroner's 'investigation' regarding the death of a very old lady of 75 (and in 1902 75 was a very old age), Hannah Sykes, who was run over by an electric tramcar in the Manchester Road. She apparently went out to do some shopping on the Friday night, when goods were at their cheapest, and was described as being 'hard of hearing but having good eyesight'. Witnesses saw the tramcar coming down the hill, the driver 'ringing his bell vigorously and shouting' while another only a few yards away who tried to grab Mrs Sykes stated the driver called out 'hey up, missus'. Sadly for her she had a heavy shawl over her ears and had kept her head down. The body, which had gone under the lifeguard and her clothes had then been entangled in the wheels 'had been mutilated in a very shocking manner'.

There then followed a slightly surreal (at least to us) conversation:

"The Coroner: Did you see any signs of electric burning?

Dr Lodge [who had dealt with the body]: No, there were no signs of any escape of electric fluid whatsoever

Mr C.J. Spencer [tramways manager]: That was an absolute impossibility.

The Coroner: But the public want satisfying. I asked the doctor to make the examination, as some people think that there is a danger in front of the cars...

The Jury returned a verdict of 'Accidental Death' and did not attach the blame to anyone.

The Coroner said that he called the doctor to satisfy the public that the woman had not been electrocuted.

Mr Spencer explained that the metals under the cars were all electrically dead..." "

One can understand their fears for electricity was this new unseen product that was not hot like a paraffin fire, or a steam tram, nor was it smelly like gas, but something that might sneak up and catch you unawares – the municipalisation of Bradford's tram services had only taken place on 1 February 1 1902.

Tramway Traction

TRAMWAY TRACTION.

RÉSUMÉ OF PAPER

READ BEFORE THE ROCHDALE LITERARY AND SCIENTIFIC SOCIETY, 18th MARCH, 1898,

BY

S. S. Platt, M.Inst.C.E.

Borough Surveyor, Rochdale.

Reprinted from the "Rochdale Observer," 23rd March, 1898.

TRAMWAY TRACTION.

THE BOROUGH SURVEYOR'S VIEWS.

THE SYSTEM FOR ROCHDALE.

At a largely attended meeting of the Rochdale Literary and Scientific Society, held at the Higher Grade School on Friday evening, Mr. S. S. Platt, M. Inst. C.E., the borough surveyor, read an interesting and valuable paper on "Tramway traction." Among those present were several members of the Corporation. The lecture was admirably illustrated by about sixty lantern slides, a number of them specially prepared for the occasion. In the absence of the president of the society (Mr. James Ogden), the chair was occupied by Alderman J. R. Heape, who said Mr. Platt had made a careful and exhaustive enquiry into the subject.

Mr. Platt, who spoke for close upon an hour and a half, expressed the opinion that the days of haulage by horses were numbered, and passed on to steam traction, which though convenient, cheap, and reliable, was, he said, rapidly losing ground on account of the objectionable steam, smoke, fumes, dust, and noise, which were a nuisance to passengers and persons using the roads and living along the sides of them. The system invented by M. Serpollet to mitigate these objectionable features by instituting a new method of generating steam, while having certain advantages, had many disadvantages, and did not appear to be recommended by several English deputations which had inspected it. Of haulage by gas the Luhrig system appeared to be the one most in use, but it had a highly objectionable smell, and there was also incessant vibration, the difficulty of ascending steep gradients, and the noise and rattle of machinery. Its advantages were very low cost of traction and absence of any overhead apparatus or conduit. The system was only in its experimental stage. Similar objections were applicable to the oil haulage system of Connelly. Compressed air motors had also been tried, but hitherto their success had not been great. Turning to electric traction, Mr. Platt shortly described

how the use of electricity as a motive power necessitates the change of electrical energy into mechanical energy. On every electrically propelled vehicle it was necessary to have one or more electric motors which were geared or connected to the wheels of the vehicles in some suitable way, generally through cog wheels provided to give a less speed than that of the motor, and so gain power. Describing the system of supplying electrical energy by means of storage batteries or accumulators carried under the seats, he said its great advantage was that it entirely obviated the necessity for overhead wires or conduits or alteration of the track, but it was nevertheless a system not generally looked upon favourably on account of the great weight of the cars, the liability of the accumulator to get out of repair, the great expense of maintenance and repairs, the constant recharging which was necessary, the smell, and the possibility of injury to passengers' clothing. At Birmingham, where it had been tried, it was far from a financial success. At Hanover the centre of the town was worked by accumulators, and the remainder by the overhead system, and the company were decidedly in favour of converting the entire system to propulsion by accumulators. But the English deputations from Leeds, Glasgow, Sheffield, Birmingham, Liverpool, and Douglas could none of them recommend the adoption of the system. The

GREAT DEVELOPMENT OF ELECTRIC TRACTION

had been due to the system by which the vehicle derived its supply of electric energy from an external source as it passed along on its journey. This might take several forms — overhead wire or conduit in the middle or side of the track, but either system would require a central power station, where electricity could be generated and delivered from thence into the overhead wire or conduit, as the case might be. This involved interference with the existing tramway track or the erection of poles and wires. The underground cable haulage system, like the electric conduit, necessitated considerable alteration to the track. Describing the cable system, Mr. Platt said it consisted of the employment of a continuously moving wire rope carried within a continuous tube, either concrete, brick or iron, constructed below the surface of the street between the tram rails. The cable maintained its proper position by passing over small pulleys fixed within the tube at intervals of about 30 feet apart, and it received its requisite motion from the stationary engine, which might be fixed at either terminus or at some suitable central position on the system, the power being transmitted from the engine to the cable by means of a large driving drum. Midway between the tram rails at the road level was a narrow longitudinal slot, about three-quarters of an inch wide, communicating with the continuous underground tube to allow the passage of the cable gripping appliances attached to each car. These appliances were worked by the driver by means of levers. The speed at which the cable travelled varied in different places from six to nine miles per hour. By gradually closing the gripper on the cable the car was drawn forward without jerking until it travelled at the same speed as the cable, and in order to stop the car the gripper was opened and the brakes applied. The system was exceptionally applicable where severe gradients were encountered, and it had been found in practice that any gradient could be negotiated without difficulty by a cable tram. A special advantage in descending a steep gradient was that the car could only travel at the rate at which the cable was run. Other advantages were the absence of overhead apparatus, regular speed and freedom from accidents, the adaptability of the cable line to the demands of increasing traffic, economy of working, practical noiselessness and cleanliness, and absence of unpleasant smells. The disadvantages were that if time was lost, it could not be regained, the speed of the cable limiting the speed of the car, the impossibility of reversing the car, the necessity for more iron work on the surface of the street than was desirable, the fact that any breakdown of engines at the power station or of the cable stopped traffic entirely on that particular section, the heavy initial cost, about double that of the ordinary tramway track, and the great disturbance of traffic and interference with business during construction, and with sewers, drains, gas and water mains, telegraph and telephone wires and cables. In the British Isles only a few of the cable lines had been a financial success. The working cost of the cable and overhead systems was equal at between a two and three minutes' service each way. If the frequency of the service exceeded this the cable would be the cheaper; with a slower service the overhead would be more economical. Coming to

THE OVERHEAD SYSTEM,

the lecturer said the electrical energy was conveyed from the central station to the car by means of an overhead wire supported on poles or on wires spanning the street. The current passed through the overhead wire to the motors underneath the cars,

and by means of gearing to the wheels of the car, causing it to travel in either direction as desired. On this point and on the way in which the electric current propels the car, Mr. Platt went into considerable technical detail. He pointed out that the cars could be one storey or two storeys high, as the circumstances of the case required, and that in the newest cars carrying outside passengers the seats were of the garden type with reversible backs. In case of specially busy traffic what were called "trailer" cars could be attached to the trolley cars, and still steep gradients could be ascended. The interior of each car was lighted by electricity from the same current running along the trolley wire that supplied the electric motive power, and in some instances, notably at Bristol, some lamps were lighted in series from the trolley wire, and some from a small storage battery carried at one end of the car, so that in the event of any stoppage of machinery at the power station, or the trolley is jerked off the wire, all the lights would not be extinguished on the car. Referring to the great objection often taken to the overhead system on the ground that the poles supporting the wires which convey the current render the streets ugly, he showed illustrations where they are of exceedingly neat appearance and an ornament to the thoroughfares where they are placed. In some of the latest installations, at Bristol, Dover, Leeds, and Dublin, for instance, they had claims, he said, to a very elegant appearance. In regard to the arrangement of the overhead wires there was great variety—wires carried on poles with single arms for single lines, others on poles with double arms for double lines, and in both cases the poles lent themselves admirably for utilisation as electric lighting standards, and would remove the necessity for gas standards in the streets. There were also longitudinal wires carried by transverse wires spanning the streets from building to building, being fixed to the buildings by rosettes. This prevented the obstruction to the footpath and roadways by poles, and in many instances was preferred by shopkeepers. In all overhead wire systems guard wires had to be placed to protect telephone and telegraph wires crossing them in case of the latter breaking and falling on the trolley wire with the current in it. This would be obviated where telegraph or telephone wires were arranged to be laid underground, as would shortly be the case to a great extent in Rochdale. The special advantages of the overhead system as compared with all other forms of electric traction were, cheapness and simplicity...

the latter allowing any necessary repairs to be effected with the minimum of trouble, delay, and expense; the rapidity with which the lines can be constructed or converted—in Rouen the conversion was made from the horse system in about ten months; and the comparatively small interference with the surface of the streets and traffic as compared with the conduit system. The chief objection urged against the system was the appearance of

THE POLES AND WIRES

in the streets, and this might have been maintained with regard to some of the earlier installations. But with reference to the perfected and best equipped lines in typical cities abroad and at home in Bristol, Dover, Leeds, and Dublin the prejudice could only be transitory, for people soon became reconciled to their appearance. In most of the places mentioned the poles were considered ornamental rather than otherwise, and when they were utilised for electric lighting, and the ordinary gas lamps were removed the effect was remarkably pleasing. Turning to the conduit systems, the idea of which is to place the conductor of electricity in a conduit in a similar manner to the underground cable system, Mr. Platt said they were innumerable, and all of them expensive, their use being chiefly confined to city thoroughfares where overhead wires were prohibited or impossible. The sole advantage seemed to be that the overhead wires and poles were removed. The chief objections were the great expense, from 40 to 50 per cent. more than overhead; the prolonged interference with the streets during construction and repairs; the difficulty in locating any defect in the underground part of the system, the difficulty and expense of carrying out any sewerage works in the streets in which there were conduits; the danger to traffic through the presence of the exposed slot in the track; the difficulty of keeping the conduit clean and maintaining satisfactory insulation, and the liability to stoppage through storms. Some of these objections had been met by what was called the "simpler" or inverted trolley system, which was said to work well. In the closed conduit system the distinguishing feature was the absence of either overhead wires or slots in the roadway. Among the several objections to the delicate system was the danger caused by the apparatus of the electric distribution box, for if it failed to work a horse stepping on to one of the projecting electric studs might be killed. There was also considerable leakage in wet weather.

George Train

The Engineer, 22 April 1870:

"A TRAMWAY EVIL

SIR,– Will you allow me to ask one question through your columns ? I remember – and the reminisence is sufficiently horrible – that it was my fate to reside in ill health, near one of the tramways laid down by that eccentric individual, George Francis Train. The establishment of this tramway was a boon to all the idle little "gamins" of the district. Their favourite amusement was to collect a pile of granite chips from a neighbouring stoneheap and adjust them at regular intervals on the rails. The car came rumbling along with quite sufficient noise of its own, but when it came to the stones, bumping, crash continually repeated, supplemented by the cheers of the admiring youngsters, was anything but soothing to disordered nerves. What I want to know is, whether the new cars cannot be furnished with guards to remove such obstacles before the wheels reach them.

PETER"

Mr. Platt: I should say the overhead system. I don't think there is any question about it.

Mr. S. Turner, in moving a hearty vote of thanks to Mr. Platt for his paper, said the address was very opportune seeing that the Council were just on the point of considering the introduction of electric traction here. He thought the overhead trolley system was the one likely to be adopted here. It was cheap and was not at all to his mind an eyesore. (Applause.)

Councillor Dunning seconded, remarking that the system for Rochdale was the overhead system. Electric trams it must be remembered would not knock the roads about so much as the present heavy cars. (Hear, hear.)

The Chairman supported the motion, also favouring the overhead system.

The motion was cordially adopted, and Mr. Platt replied, endorsing Mr. Dunning's remark as to the less damaging effect of electric traction upon the roads.

The electric studs of iron projected above the paving and where the pavement was of wood the uneven wear of the two materials was liable in time to make the studs dangerous to ordinary street traffic. Mentioning the cost of working Mr. Platt said steam averaged from 10d. to 1s. 2d. per mile, 63 to 90 per cent. of the receipts, the cable system cost 5½d. to 6d. per mile, or 45 to 50 per cent., the electric accumulators in Birmingham cost 117 per cent., the overhead cost 5½d. per mile, and generally about 50 per cent. of the receipts. He pointed out how rapidly electric traction was being taken up by municipalities, and almost in every case it was on the overhead system. Birmingham had, however, reported against it. The

OVERHEAD SYSTEM HAD CERTAIN MERITS

not possessed in so great a degree by any of the other mechanical systems—the power of the cars to accommodate themselves to the state of traffic by running slowly or quickly or reversing; in case of accident on any part of the system only that section immediately affected was thrown out of use and even if the engines should break down, accumulators could be brought into use and would keep the traffic going for some time; every car could be used in case of emergency instead of being dependent on the number of horses as was the case with horse cars; much less space was taken up by the cars than by horse and steam trams, the interference with traffic being consequently less; and there was greater cleanliness of the cars and streets. The last three advantages were also common to the cable system. In cities or towns with a large suburban population improved facilities of communication had brought the residential suburbs much nearer the centre in point of time. If people could live further away from the centre of the town building operations would be developed and land would accordingly increase in value. Over-crowding would decrease and public health would be improved. This had been exemplified at Bristol which was visited by a Rochdale deputation twelve months ago. It was manifest from the experience of other places that taking all the circumstances into account electric traction was the only method within the range of consideration calculated to satisfactorily meet local necessities. (Loud applause.)

THE SYSTEM FOR ROCHDALE.

Councillor Rushworth asked which system Mr. Platt considered the best for Rochdale?

Proceedings of the Rugby Engineering Society

Session 1903-1904
Vol. 1

THE DESIGN AND CONSTRUCTION OF THE ELECTRIC TRAMWAY CAR.

BY R. H. SIMPSON, *Member.*

With the increasing necessity of travelling both quickly and cheaply at the present time, it may be of interest to describe the electric street tramway car which is now an important competitor amongst the older forms of traction. It will not be possible to deal with this subject at any length as the ground it covers is wide and contains much detail. Horse traction will not be discussed, but for purposes of first comparing modes of traction by power and to show the advantages gained by adopting electricity, the case of a town will be taken, whose system was steam and which has been converted to the overhead system, having been in operation for two years. This comparison will be seen to be extremely fair, as the steam line was owned and worked by a private company, whereas the electric service is controlled by the Corporation. Again, the latter system shows up well when taking into consideration that the power is supplied from the electricity department, and that the employees' wages have been materially advanced with the usual shortening of the hours of labour. The original rolling stock consisted of 16 steam locomotives and one spare, weighing 10½ tons each loaded, each hauling one bogie car weighing 4¾ tons light and seating 64 passengers. The overall length of the locomotive was 13′ 0″ and of the car 26′ 7″, making thus a total combined load of 15¼ tons, and taking up a street space of 39′ 7″ if close coupled. The new electric stock consists of 24 bogie cars weighing 10½ tons each light, having a seating capacity of 68 passengers and an over all length of 32′ 6″, this shows a saving in street space of 7′ 0″, a passenger increase of four and a saving in dead load to be hauled of 4¾ tons. Although it will be seen that the new cars are longer, the small increase in passenger capacity is due to the gauge being reduced to 4′ 0″ from 4′ 8½″. The total expenditure with steam per car-mile averaged 11·86d. and with electricity 8·61d., the least expenditure with steam was 9·26d. with a proportion of expenses to receipts of 65·51% and the highest 14·46d. with a proportion of 79·13%, the period of steam taken being from 1885 to 1900 inclusive, the company paying a dividend of 5% for the last eight years and previously never less than 3%, though the length of line still remained the same. There has been an increase of passengers carried equal to 154% and of receipts 88% against the best of three years' working by steam. The proportion of expenses to receipts is 68·55%. The car-miles have shown an increase of 161% due to the higher speed attained, *i.e.*, from 8 to 12 miles per hour. This steam line was the most successful one in the country, as it was under the first-rate management of railway educated men, hence some idea can be drawn of what this line would pay if controlled by a private company. The cost of working here given is not the lowest obtainable with electric driving, some towns falling to as low as 4·4d. per car-mile and others as as high as 9d. This figure depends upon the features of the district, the layout and upon the degree of efficiency the stock is kept in. The maintenance in the case given comes out practically the same for both systems, and this again is shown in the case of a Scotch town, where steam cost 12·96d. and electricity now costs 7d. per car-mile. The amount of power consumed naturally varies according to the district served and the type of car in use, the case before us being 1·53 B.T.U. per car-mile, some of the highest being 1·88 and the lowest ·88 B.T.U. per car-mile. The lighting of the cars is responsible for about 0·15 B.T.U. per car-mile. It is of interest to learn that if rolling stock is left to run itself, that is without a definite periodic inspection, the consumption of power increases some 25%: this has been deduced from actual experiment; it has therefore been found that generous maintenance pays best, besides, the exact state of the stock is then known, and it can be relied on accordingly.

The type of car most generally adopted in this country is the double decker, mounted on either a single four-wheel truck or on a pair of bogies: this type can be further amplified by changes in interior seating accommodation, the design of staircase or by the addition of vestibuled ends. The single deck car, which does not obtain such favour, is built in various types on both single and double trucks. It may be well to touch on a few points to be considered in choosing a car for a new line and a given service.

In deciding the type and size of car it is necessary to consider several points, amongst others the most important are: the gauge of the line; the traffic to be catered for; the contour of the line (which two latter usually decide as to whether single or double truck cars are to be used); the wheel base admissable due to the curves, this point only entering into the question with single truck cars; the length, height and width suitable. The first consideration is the gauge, and this should always be the standard or 4′ 8½″ if at all possible, so as to get the advantage of as great a carrying capacity as can be obtained. There are practically three gauges in use, *i.e.*, 3′ 6″, 4′ 0″ and 4′ 8½″. The gauge is settled by the width of street and the Board of Trade Regulations, which are that there shall be not less than 15″ between the side of a car and the kerb, and also the same distance between cars on a double track; if possible, it is of advantage to obtain 9′ 6″ between rail head and the kerb, to allow of standing traffic not stopping the service The wheel base is dependent on the curves with single truck cars and is generally 6′ 0″, with 4′ 0″ for bogie trucks. The length of car is settled by the wheel base in the case of single truck cars and has devolved on a standard length of 16′ 0″ over the body, and 26′ 6″ over platforms. Bogie cars should not be less than 22′ 0″ over the body, which is also a standard length, otherwise the inner pair of wheels would practically touch one another and no advantage would be gained in carrying capacity by the extra length of body obtainable when supporting same on a pair of trucks. The height inside for standing room is usually 6′ 9″ in the clear, but sometimes this has to be reduced on account of low bridges to be run under; the lowest car in this respect running in this country, to the best of the author's knowledge, has 6′ 2″ standing height. There should be at least 6′ 4″ standing room on the top of car when passing under bridges, and if this cannot be obtained, the road must be lowered; this is sometimes impossible due to sewers, etc., and in this case the single deck car must be resorted to, but it must be a last resort on account of its low carrying capacity. The principal dimensions of double deck single and double truck cars for 4′ 8½″ gauge are as given in the table herewith:—

	Single Truck.	Double Truck.
Gauge	4′8½″	4′8½″
Passengers inside	22	32
Passengers outside	35	47
Length of body outside	16′ 0″	22′ 0″
Length over platforms	26′ 6″	32′ 6″
Length over fenders	27′ 6″	33′ 6″
Width over side pillars	6′ 9″	6′ 9″
Width over all	7′ 0″	7′ 0″
Height from floor to ceiling	6′ 9″	6′ 9″
Height from rail to top of roof	9′10″	9′10″
Type of staircase to give seating capacity on roof	Reversed or Improved Ordinary.	
Approximate weight of body	3¾ tons	4¾ tons

The total weight complete ready for service of a 16′ 0″ body single truck car is approximately 8½ tons and of a 22′ 0″ body bogie car 10½ tons. Before taking up various points of construction it will be well to point out the most important to be looked well after. No pitch pine whatever should be permitted in the underframe. No countersunk headed bolts are to be let into wood that may have to take an end strain, otherwise they will work loose. Truss rods should not have a palm at their ends and then be bolted to the side of the sole bar. The sides of the trap doors in floor, as well as the opening, should be plated. Collision fenders should extend sufficiently far to protect projecting parts on the ends of the cars when butted together on the straight or on a curve. There should also be sufficient space left for passengers' hands between handrails and adjacent parts of the car. All pins that have to stand tension should be bolts. Headlights should be of substantial construction. Trolley planks should be extended the whole length of the body and firmly fixed to the roof. The roof to have alternate carlines of steel to withstand the strains of the trolley. The roof seat legs should be arranged so that the fixing screws should not all come in the same grain of the roofing planks. No sharp points should be left on the grilles. Cushions on inside seats should not be entertained as they harbour filth. Sand tubes should be brought as near to wheels as possible. All timber should have two years' natural seasoning. For leading particulars as to details we may take as follows :—The underframe is constructed of oak and rolled steel sections or entirely of oak with the sills trussed by adjustable rods, all mortices and tenons are covered with white lead before being driven in. The floors are of Norway pine boards, tongued and grooved with openings for access to the motors. Slats of hard wood are laid on the floors for wearing purposes. The platforms are provided with a step on one side, which is now being arranged to fold up when not in use, so as not to strike a person when knocked down under the car before being caught by the pick-up guard. Some lines prefer the platform to be vestibuled or closed in as a protection to the driver from the weather; this is glazed and provided with dropping lights. A collapsible gate is fitted to the platform if required. Staircases can be of several types, the Ordinary, Improved Ordinary, Reversed and the Double staircase. The platforms are provided with brake gear, draw-bars, sand gear and gong pedals. All pillars, etc., are of ash with panels of mahogany and whitewood. The roof is constructed of bent ash and flat or angle steel carlines, the external roof is boarded with Norway pine, the internal with red deal covered externally with white leaded cotton duck canvas, and the ceiling is in bird's eye maple veneer. The roof seats are of the garden type with reversible backs. The doors are either single or twin as required, glazed, and hung by rollers at the top. The roof railing is usually 3′ 6″ high, and is of iron tubes with sometimes a top rail of brass, all supported on iron stanchions. The interior is panelled in oak and ash with embossed mouldings over the doors. The inside seats are usually longitudinal and are either of perforated veneer or slats of oak. The space allowed per passenger is from 16 to 17 inches. The side windows are constructed as large as possible and are of plate glass, there being three each side in single truck cars, and four in bogie cars. The ventilators are of the swinging pattern over the side windows. A signal lense is fitted in opposite corners with interchangeable coloured signals. The destination indicators are either lettered boards or, as is now more general, of a type that can be illuminated at night. There are four sand boxes, one in each corner of the car with rake valves connected to the pedal gear on platforms and provided with down tubes to the rails. All material should be of first class quality, and the painting and varnishing to a carefully detailed specification.

Truck :—Trucks are designed in three types, viz. :—The single four-wheel truck, which does not swivel under the body; the maximum traction bogie; and the equal wheel bogie truck. The first mentioned is used under car bodies from 14′ 0″ to 18′ 0″ over the body, or from 24′ 6″ to 28′ 6″ over the platforms. The 16′ 0″ body with reversed stairs should not have a truck under it with less a wheel base than 6′ 0″, otherwise pitching will result. The maximum traction truck is so called by reason of it being arranged for about 75% of the load being taken by the driving wheels, the remaining two wheels called pony or trailing, being of smaller diameter, viz. :—20″ or 22″ so that they may clear the underframe of car when the truck swings over, and at the same time allows of the car being carried lower. The shortest car that can be used with these trucks is 18′ 0″ over body. The last type of truck has four equal wheels, and is generally used for four motor equipments, two motors per truck; this type can also be used as a maximum traction truck by shifting the bolster over from the centre towards one pair of wheels, if one motor per truck only is required. Truck side frames should be perfectly square one with the other and remain so in service, besides being well braced and stayed, otherwise the truck, and especially the wheel flanges, will suffer. Frames should consist of as few parts as possible, and all bolts provided with a locking device. The spring base must be long to ensure easy riding, and two types of springs preferably used, viz., elliptical between body and frame, and coil between frame and axle boxes. The axle boxes should drop out of the horns without dismembering the truck and must ride easily in the guides. The brasses, which should easily be brought out at the front of the box, must be long and have ample lubrication as well as being dust tight; a collar should be provided for taking up end thrust. The horns should have renewable wearing strips on one side at least.

The following tables give leading dimensions :—

Single Truck for 4′ 8½″ Gauge.

Wheel base	6′ 0″
Length over top plate	15′ 7″
Width over top plate	6′ 0″
Width over all	6′ 6¾″
Diameter of wheels	30″ to 33″
Diameter of axles	4″
Diameter of journals	3½″
Weight	2 tons.

Maximum Traction Truck.

Wheel base	4′ 0″
Width over all	6′ 6¾″
Centres of frames	5′ 9¼″
Diameter of driving wheels	30″ to 33″
,, ,, trailing wheels	20″ to 22″
,, ,, driving axle	4″
,, ,, trailing ,,	3½″
,, ,, journals	3½″ and 3″
Weight	1½ tons.

Wheels :—Careful consideration should be given to the question of wheel diameter, especially if it is decided to fit steel tyred wheels. In the U.S.A. the standard diameter is 33″ and the wheel is of chilled cast iron. In England the diameter is usually 30″, this diameter is practically a relic of horse traction, and an effort to keep the step as low as possible. With 30″ wheels there is a clearance between motor and top of rail, of about 2¾″, but this clearance is not maintained in the centre of the track, due to the crowning of the paving. With chilled wheels it is not possible to wear them down to a less diameter than 28¾″ or 28¼″ on account of getting beneath the chill. With steel tyred wheels the diameter should be greater as the tyres are 2½″ thick and allow a wear of 1½″ to 1¾″ radially, if a 30″ wheel is used the motor will be down on the track before the full life of the tyre has been obtained. A steel tyred wheel should therefore not be less than from 31¾″ diameter up to 33″. The smaller diameter is obtained thus: take 28¾″ as worn-out chilled wheel, and add twice 1½″ for steel tyre wear. Though dearer at first cost the steel tyred wheel comes out cheaper after a two years' working. This saving is entirely effected by reason that the wheel centre never requires renewal. Whichever type of wheel is used the conditions should be considered and a section chosen to suit the rail on which it will have to run. Chilled iron wheels should be made only from the best grades of charcoal iron, should be balanced and carefully ground true to 1/64″ in a special machine, and to prolong their life should be re-ground as soon as a difference in diameter appears between the two wheels on one axle. The guaranteed life is 30,000 miles, but there are records of obtaining 40,000 and even close on 60,000 miles with these wheels. The weight of a 30" chilled wheel is from 300 to 325 lbs. Steel tyred wheels are of two types, the cast steel centre as made by Hadfields and the pressed centre as supplied by Bakers. The first type is of the spoke pattern and is of toughened cast steel of a special grade. They are capable of withstanding a test load of 50 tons applied to the centre of the boss without producing any permanent set, and will withstand 100 tons before breaking up. The second type is forged from selected scrap iron to the disc shape by hydraulic press. All centres are turned up perfectly true for the reception of the tyre and the boss bored and faced on both sides. The tyres are 2¼" thick on the tread and are of the best quality English Siemens-Martin Steel. The percentage of carbon is very high, at least 0·6 per cent, and consequently the tyres are exceptionally hard, but very tough and ductile. The tyre is heated and shrunk on to the centre and secured there, by set screws or retaining rings, from side movement. The complete wheel is then pressed on to the axle by hydraulic pressure of not less than 30 tons, after which it is turned up perfectly true on side and on the tread. The guaranteed mileage is usually 60,000 miles, the wear is usually ⅜" on the radius for every 5,000 to 6,500 miles run; this has run to 10,000 miles in some districts. The weight of a 31¼" diameter steel tyred wheel is 330 to 370lbs. The axles are of similar material to the tyres but milder in temper, they are cold rolled on the wearing surfaces after being machined and polished so as to compress the surface and cause longer life; the diameter is usually 4".

ELECTRICAL EQUIPMENT :—The equipment for a car consists of the following :—

2 25 or 35 H.P. Motors.
2 Controllers.
1 Set of resistances.
1 Automatic circuit breaker.
1 Main switch
1 Fuse.
1 Lightning arrester.
1 Set of cables.
1 Trolley standard with pole and head.

The motors are of the four-pole enclosed type, hung on the axle by two bearings, and from the truck by a bar supported by draw and recoil springs; the gearing is single reduction.

The control is that known as Series Parallel.

The trolley standard is provided with an internal spring under compression and the trolley head is of the swivelling pattern.

The current supply is from trolley through main switch at one end of car, to circuit breaker at the other, then to fuse (with tap off to lightning arrester) and into the common supply to both controllers; from the controllers the necessary connections are made to the resistances and motors.

The lighting is generally by two or three circuits of five lamps in series, distributed as follows :—

2 Dash.
2 Canopy.
2 Signal.
4 or 6 Inside as required.

The remainder to make up a 12 or 17 light equipment arranged in roof lights and destination indicators. The bell installation is usually:—one bell on each platform, one conductors push on each platform, one push at the head of each staircase and four or six pushes inside, one two-way switch and one battery of three cells.

The trolley earthing has generally been effected by connecting the non-current carrying part to earth through two 250 volt red lamps, in series, which will therefore light up when a ground is on the standard, thus drawing the attention of the driver or conductor to the fact. A later method, much in favour by the Board of Trade, is to earth the standard direct through a switch which is closed by the blowing of a light fuse, a connection at the same time being made so that the battery current actuates the driver's bell, which again causes attention to be directed to the earth on the car.

It is hoped that the above short description may have some few points of interest for the younger members of this Society who may not have had the opportunity of gathering such information as is given. The author here wishes to express his thanks to those firms who have so kindly supplied him with illustrations, amongst these being :—Messrs. Milnes, The Brush Co., and the B.T.H. Co.

DISCUSSION.

THE PRESIDENT said he was sure the members would all agree with him that they had had a most interesting paper from Mr. Simpson on a subject with which the majority were not familiar. This makes the paper interesting because we are obtaining information all the time.

There were one or two things which he would like to ask the author. What is the minimum radius of track double bogie trucks, and also the single truck cars can take.

With regard to the electrical equipment which the author gives at the end of the paper, he noticed it was not said what size of car this is for. The author says there are two motors of 25 or 35 H.P., but it would be interesting to know whether in the double motor cars, where there are only two motors on a car, what the minimum and maximum H.P. is in general practice, and are cars built of sufficient capacity to warrant four motor equipments, and if so what is the size of the motors in this case.

He asked members to put on record, by acclamation, their thanks to the author for his paper, and also to pass a hearty vote of thanks to Messrs. Fell and Cubitt for their assistance with the lantern.

MR. E. S. CONRADI said that the author, on page 70, in mentioning truss rods says they should not have a palm at their ends, and then be bolted to the side of the sole bar; by sole bar does he mean the headstock, that is, the cross bar which joins the two side sole bars of the car at their extremity, and if so what is the correct method of fixing them.

On page 71 some mention is made re the position of the pony wheels on maximum traction trucks as trailing and in the illustrations some were shown as leading. He believed both the Brush Company and Messrs. Hurst Nelson fit their maximum traction trucks with the pony wheels leading. What are the causes of the variation of the position of the pony wheels on the trucks; one advantage the leading pony wheels possess is, that a double step at the car entrance is avoided, but there seemed to be greater risk of the car jumping the track with the pony wheels leading than with them trailing.

Do track cleaners in any way affect the life of car wheels?

On page 74, re trolley earthing, mention is made of a direct system which appears to be favoured by the Board of Trade. He would like to ask the author if he would explain the merits of this system so approved by the Board of Trade,

MR. E. S. CONRADI.

as there are obviously many great disadvantages to such a scheme. On a contract where he was recently engaged, this device was put on by a Consulting Engineer and taken off by the Resident Engineer.

No mention was made about brakes; he would have thought that we should have had some notes on them in this paper. Would the author give some information on system, particularly track brakes. In the case of a system having heavy gradients, and the lines being in a more or less greasy condition, which would be the more efficient and reliable, the ordinary track brake or a magnetic brake.

MR. STANNARD CUBITT remarked that on page 68 the author says "the gauge should be always 4' 8½', if at all possible, so as to get the advantage of as great a carrying capacity as can be obtained." He would like to suggest to the author that the motor is also a great consideration when setting the gauge. He believed that the design of a motor for a small gauge is a great deal more troublesome than that of a motor for a broader gauge.

On page 69 the author gives a table comparing a single and double truck car. He would like to see added to the table a figure comparing the increase of weight with the increase of passengers in a double truck car over a single truck car. He found roughly an increase of about 38% in passengers with an increase of only about 26% in weight. It is a point worth noting.

With regard to the curious names given to parts of the car, he would like to ask the author, subject to the approval of the Council, to insert a diagram of a car with the parts named, when the paper was printed in the "Proceedings."

On page 71 the author says "the horns should have renewable wearing strips on *one side at least.*" The italics were the speaker's. Why on one side only, surely the wear would be equal on both sides.

On page 72 with regard to renewing chilled iron wheels was it not a fact there was a limit to the number of times wheels can be pressed on and off the axles, this was also an item in favour of steel tyres.

With regard to the Blackpool car with the double stair-case at the back, which the author stated as being unique, it might be interesting to recall the old horse cars which used to run to Moorgate street station from over the river. These cars had just such a double staircase.*

* (Communicated). Mr. Simpson objects to my bringing in these cars—he says he calls them busses. As a matter of fact they were officially known as "Road Cars."—A.S.C.

MR. W. E. W. MILLINGTON remarked that the author says at the bottom of his paper that he hopes it will contain some few points of interest to the younger members of the Society. Why he excludes the older members he did not know. It must be admitted that it contains a great number of points of great interest, but unfortunately the majority of them are merely points, and very nearly approached the definition of Euclid. He would say with regard to the comparisons in the first case that it was difficult to see why the author had simply taken steam traction and altogether ignored horse traction. Was this because steam traction is so far superior to horse traction, and thus forms a better basis of comparison. If this is so he could hardly see why, because we only saw the hideous steam car in a very few places, whereas we saw so much of the horse cars. He should be glad if the author would give his reasons for this comparison even though it is rather wide of the title of the paper.

There are two other points which he would have mentioned, namely, the question of brakes, and that of pick-up arrangements. All knew that the co-efficient of statical friction, or as he had heard it called, the co-efficient of "stiction," was greater than that of moving friction. If pressure be applied to the brake blocks such that the wheels do not skid, then the braking effect is nearly that due to the co-efficient of "stiction" between the wheels and the rails. Now, if a little more pressure be applied on the blocks, so as to make the wheels skid, then the braking effect is considerably less as it is only that due to the co-efficient of friction between the wheels and the rails. This shows pretty clearly that there is a maximum pressure which should be applied to the brake blocks. He would be glad if the author could give any figures regarding this maximum load.

As regards the question of track brakes he had seen these applied on cars and they seemed very effective, especially as emergency brakes. Could the author say why these are not used more, as it seemed to him that they would considerably reduce the wear on the tyres.

MR. W. R. WATSON (*Member of Council*), said he should like to ask one question of the author, and that was—that "the axles are of similar material to the tyres but milder in temper." What does this mean? Are the axles made of a milder steel or are they toughened in "temper"?

MR. E. B. TUPPEN said the author referred to the loss with the double truck cars when they are not sufficiently lubricated on the guides which support the car. Has it ever been tried to use rollers or some other similar arrangement to reduce this loss. He would like to know the radius from the centre-pin of the truck to centre of guides.

MR. J. SUGDEN said he had noticed that in London busses the drivers are always seated on the top, whilst in tram-cars they are always at the bottom. It seemed to him that the tramcar driver had much to obstruct his view especially on cars with closed ends. If the driver could be hoisted on to the upper deck he would have a much wider range of view and at the same time it might offer a larger accommodation for passengers on the lower deck.

MR. J. MUIRHEAD said he would like to ask the author if it was not the case that 30" wheels were more suitable in some cases than 33" wheels. He thought that for certain services, with frequent stops and high acceleration, 30" wheels have an advantage due to the higher tractive effort obtainable at starting. Perhaps the author would say if this was one reason why the 30" wheel is still standard in this country, where tramways have hitherto been principally confined to city service, while in the U.S.A., where a large portion of the tramway work is of an interurban nature with long runs and high speeds, the 33" wheel is general.

The author had shown very few cars with seats arranged transversely inside. He thought that all cars should be designed with transverse seats having a centre aisle and seats for two passengers on each side. For a comfortable arrangement this would require an overall width of almost 8ft, and on a 4' 8½' road this should be attainable. Such an arrangement besides increasing slightly the seating capacity would add much to the comfort of the passengers, especially as we are having a gradual increase of speed and length of run.

There is a point to which a speaker has already referred to, namely the method of earthing the trolley standard. The author had pointed out that the disadvantage of the second method mentioned, is that it puts a dead short on the line.

The first method, namely, the one in which the leak is detected by the lighting of two 150 volt lamps placed between the trolley standard and earth, has several disadvantages. Owing to the resistance of the lamps they will not light up very brightly if the leakage is small, and so the leak may not be noticed. A bell connection, however, will get over this difficulty. There is also the possibility of one of the lamp filaments getting broken, in which case the leak would not be detected.

MR. KENNETH F. KINGWELL asked if it was not possible to use electro-magnets on the bottom of the car in series with the brake coils, so that the act of using the brake for an emergency would, by attracting plates on the back end of the lifeguard, cause the front end to drop on to the track. The conductor only having to turn his controller handle to apply the brake and drop the life guard.

Mr. CHAS. T. TAYLOR said there were several items to which he would like to call attention, viz., on page 68 the author stated that if cars were left without periodical inspection, the consumption of power increases 25%. Does this extra consumption only occur with bogie trucks, and not with single four wheel trucks, as the author pointed out previously that this increase was largely due to the want of grease on the pivots and guides?

As there are no guides or pivots on a single four wheel truck, should not this 25% be greatly reduced, or an explanation given showing how the extra power is expended?

On page 72 the author stated that with 30″ wheels the clearance between the motor and the rail is about 2¾″ but that this is not maintained in the centre of the track due to the camber of the paving. To what type of motor does he refer, is it the "B.T-H" or the "Dick Kerr" motor? Would a "Dick Kerr" motor of the same rating allow the wheels to wear down more than the "B.T-H" motor or not?

On page 73 the author stated that the axles are cold rolled after being machined and polished. Would not the wear of the bearings be materially reduced if the axles were burnished, instead of being polished, as in polishing, emery or crocus has to be used and some is bound to be left in pores to give trouble afterwards. It is usual railway practice to burnish and not to polish the axles for this reason. He would therefore like to have the author's reason why polishing and rolling is employed instead of burnishing.

Mr. F. W. COOKE asked the author if he could give some particulars with regard to installations for electric heating, and include the comparative cost for equipment per passenger, and of operation and maintenance per car mile.

Mr. R. H. SIMPSON, in replying to the discussion, said in answer to the President's remarks as to the minimum radius of track that single truck and bogie truck cars will take, for tramway work the minimum radius met with in practice is usually 30ft., a single truck car with 6ft. wheel base will negotiate this without trouble if not to be continually run over throughout the day; this radius is generally met with at the entrance to car sheds and at sidings off the main line. Where a single truck car will travel a bogie car with trucks having 4ft. wheel base will naturally follow. For running continuously over 30ft. curves the wheel base for a single truck car should not be more than 5' 6″.

With regard to the horse-power of motors for the various types of cars, this is a very misleading rating to those not accustomed to tramway or railway work, as it only expresses the capacity of the motor for one hour's continuous load with a given temperature limit. The size of motor required for

MR. R. H. SIMPSON.

any given line is entirely dependent on the contour of the line, more so than on the weight of the car loaded. For instance, a single truck car may be equipped with two 20 or 25 H.P. motors, and rarely, with the most severe conditions met with in this country two motors of 30-H.P. each; again, a bogie car with two motors of 30-H.P. each, has sufficient power to cope with traffic on a fairly level line and never requires more than two motors of 35 to 40-H.P. each under the most severe conditions; that is a bogie car mounted on maximum traction trucks, which type of car is not satisfactory if used on grades of 10%, on account of insufficient adhesion. A bogie car, on grades of this magnitude, requires a four motor equipment with all wheels drivers to obtain sufficient adhesion between wheels and track, under these conditions four motors of 20 to 25 H.P. each are usually capable of dealing with the service.

In reply to Mr. Conradi, the sole bar is not the headstock but the timber, or channel iron, forming the sides of the underframe. The most suitable form of truss rod fixing is by taking them through the headstock with the nuts bearing against a heavy washer or plate. The Brush Company and Hurst, Nelson and Company both fix their maximum traction trucks with the pony wheels leading. There is a great diversity of opinion in this connection as to the correct method to be adopted. One reason for using the pony wheels leading is, that the trucks can be arranged with their swivelling centres further apart, thus giving a better support to the platforms. The point of a double step does not affect matters as there are plenty of cars running without, having the pony wheels trailing. As to the effect of track cleaners on the life of wheels, it has not been possible as yet to collect any date on this matter. It is a very tall order to explain why the B.O.T. favours the direct earthing system, and shows that Mr. Conradi cannot have had much experience with the B.O.T. vagaries. The author is in agreeance with the remarks as to the resident engineer discarding the consulting engineer's devices and may say that this is an everyday proceeding. With regard to brakes, a paper of great length could be written on this subject alone, and it must be remembered that this paper does not claim to be a treatise on the whole subject of electric traction. The author would refer Mr. Conradi to a very complete paper on this subject, published in the *Tramway and Railway World*, for December, 1903, on pages 573 to 576. In the case mentioned in the question the magnetic track brake would be most reliable.

In reply to Mr. Cubitt on the matter of gauge and motors for same, there has been no difficulty in providing a motor suitable for a narrow gauge, i.e., 3' 6″ by any of the leading manufacturers. The author cannot see what value a table

MR. R. H. SIMPSON.

comparing the increase of weight with increase of passenger capacity for both types of car would be in practice and Mr. Cubitt appears to have been able to compare this for himself without much trouble. As to the names used in our construction, the author has prepared a diagram with the various parts named as requested. The horns should have a wearing strip on one side at least for the reason that the purchaser may think himself well off if he gets this from the truck builders, especially with the cutting in prices which prevails; generally if you require luxuries you have to pay for them.

There is no stated limit to the number of times a wheel may be pressed on and off a single axle for this reason: it entirely depends upon how the wheel is pressed on and the solution used as to the way it comes off. If white lead is used this disappears after a time and the wheel seat rusts to the wheel hub, some railway companies use a solution which does not lose its rust preventing qualities. In the first case it will take about twice the pressure to press a wheel off as it did to press it on, but in the second usually not more than 10 tons extra pressure is required. Sometimes a great deal of trouble is experienced in getting a wheel off and in doing so the axle is badly scored or seized, may be so much that there is not sufficient metal left to turn away, or if so done, the diameter will be too small for safe working. As a rule the axle wheel seat is not touched, but the wheel is bored to suit the axle in every case after the old wheel is pressed. As to staircases, Mr. Cubitt must remember that the subject of the paper was tramway cars not horse drawn road vehicles, which are generally known and spoken of as busses, though the word car crept in in the case mentioned when a certain London Company had to find a name for itself differing from another old established rival company; anyhow Mr. Cubitt's stairs had to be climbed up whereas those illustrated can be walked up.

Replying to Mr. Millington, steam traction was taken as a comparison, as both forms were mechanical and the author had full particulars at his command. As to brakes, reference may be made to the reply to Mr. Conradi, the first portion of which will apply to life-guards.

In reply to Mr. Watson, the expression "milder in temper" with respect to axles is a generally accepted term with wheel and axle makers, it is not intended to convey the meaning that the axles are "tempered," which would simply have ruinous results, but only of a softer quality. The steel used for tyres has usually a tensile stress of 50 to 55 tons, whereas for the axles it is 32 to 35 tons. Below is given the chemical analysis for tyres and axles of the above tensile strength.

MR. R. H. SIMPSON.

TYRES.

Carbon not less than .600 and not more than .650%
Manganese ,, .900 ,, ,, ,, 1.100%
Silicon ,, .900 ,, ,, ,, 1.100%
Sulphur ,, .045 ,, ,, ,, .055%
Phosphorus ,, .045 ,, ,, ,, .055%

AXLES.

Carbon not less than .23 and not more than .30%
Manganese ,, .70 ,, ,, ,, .80%
Silicon ,, .08 ,, ,, ,, .12%
Sulphur ,, ,, ,, ,, .05%
Phosphorous ,, ,, ,, ,, .05%

In answer to Mr. Tupper, the loss mentioned is chiefly attributable to the use of a certain type of truck, and no arrangement other than good lubrication will get over the difficulty; in all other types the design eliminates the trouble, unfortunately the country is pretty full of the former type. The radius from centre pin to centre of side bearings for a 4' 8½" gauge is usually about 2' 2" to 2' 10½" according to the make of truck.

Replying to Mr. Sugden, this proposal is impracticable; with the driver situated on the roof, the roof would have to be very much stronger and heavier, to take the weight of controller and brake gear, also to stand the strains due to the braking. All cables, brake gear, sanding gear and pedal gongs, would have to be brought up and connected from the platform to roof, making a costly job, with no benefit accrued, no extra seating accommodation either could be arranged for on the platforms as this space is required in any case for access to the roof, the controller and brake gear taking up very little room at present which could be used for seating. Experience on the road at the controller handle would soon prove to Mr. Sugden that there is a little or no trouble as to a sufficient view as things are.

The author does not think Mr. Muirhead's reason for 30" wheels is a correct one. The small difference in speed gained and the correspondingly smaller tractive effort obtained with 33" wheels does not affect the practical running of cars in this country, the current consumption, of course, will be slightly higher but this will not weigh much against the other benefits gained. There are several roads in this country through busy streets which are equipped with 32" and 33" wheels with which the author has been connected, and no difficulty has resulted. The author was sorry that he was not able to show

types of every kind of car in existence, and with respect to transverse seats agrees with Mr. Muirhead, but it is not possible to build a car 8ft. in width as the B.o.T. would not sanction it, the maximum width allowable being 7' 1" for a gauge of 4' 8½". Newcastle certainly have some cars arranged in this way but the seating space and walking passage is very restricted and to effect this the cars have to be built with straight sides which gives them the appearance of a box. The earthing device mentioned in the paper has a bell connected and does not require lamps in circuit with it.

The device mentioned by Mr. Kingwell is useless as it entirely depends for its success on the presence of mind of the driver to switch off if an accident is feared, and it is the rule rather than otherwise that the human element breaks down; the present life guards are automatic in their action and rarely fail if kept in proper order. The best a life guard can do is to save a person from getting under the truck but it cannot save him from being damaged in some way or other. A great many accidents have resulted before even the person has got as far as the guard, such as the fender, dash, step, or headlight striking him.

In answer to Mr. Taylor, it should have been stated in the paper, that the 25% extra current consumption was found to be with bogie cars mounted on maximum traction trucks of a type that have not an ideal swivelling action when lubricated inefficiently. The 2¾" clearance was taken as a mean dimension embracing all the leading firms motors. The wear on the bearings would not be materially reduced if the axles were burnished, as they very soon burnish themselves after a short period in service; no trouble is found after polishing, the emery being very fine. Railway practice cannot be compared with tramways as the speeds obtained on each differ so widely, necessitating on the part of the Railway Companies more attention and better work.

As to the electric heating of cars, mentioned by Mr. Cooke, little has been done in this country, as the extremes of temperature met with does not require it, but some isolated cases do exist: in these cars, whether for a 4 wheel or a bogie car, the equipment has consisted of four Consolidated Car Heating Company's heaters, two under the seats at each side of the car, each heater has two coils, each coil being of different resistance, the four coils of same resistance are connected in series in each case, and three different intensities of heating are obtained by either switching on the high resistance coil, the low resistance coils, or both together. The cost of this equipment per car is about £8, the cost of operation can easily

MR. R. H. SIMPSON.

be figured when knowing the charge for current supplied, as with the switch in the three positions, the amperes flowing are 3, 4, and 7, respectively. This size equipment is suitable for the average conditions of weather in this country and will heat the car to a considerable degree, of course this is dependent on the number of times the door is opened. As to maintenance the author has no figures available, but the makers guarantee the coils for 5 years and they have been known to last as long as seven years without being replaced.

Rugby Engineering Society.

PROCEEDINGS.

21st January, 1904.

THE SIXTH ORDINARY MEETING of the Session was held at the Lower School on Thursday, 21st January, 1904, at Eight o'clock p.m. W. J. LARKE, Esq., President, in the Chair.

The Minutes of the previous Meeting were read and confirmed.

The following paper was then read and discussed :—
"Notes on Cupolas and Cast Iron," by Mr. C. MOREHEAD, Member of Council.

The following gentleman was reported as a member :—
FREDERICK AGUSTUS YERBURY, Kingston-on-Thames.

About 120 Members were present.

Accident on the Electric Tram Route

Inevitably, there were accidents on the new electric tramway. There must have been a certain temptation on the part of the driver to test the power he had so easily to hand, but also we do know that sometimes the tramcars were not entirely well designed, build quality at the works could be 'iffy' and assembly at the tramway depot was not easy. But both of these accidents were due to conditions beyond reasonable control, to maximise revenue trams were kept going where today the road would be closed for weeks.

Birmingham Post, 1 April 1902

"ACCIDENT ON THE ELECTRIC TRAM ROUTE

An accident which placed the lives of several people in grave peril happened on the Bristol Road tram route last evening. Tram no 154* was being driven in the direction of Bournbrook when, just as Sir Harry's Road was reached, the front wheels jumped the track, and before the driver knew what had occurred the hind wheels followed suit. The reel was immediately pulled from the overhead wire by the conductor, but so great was the momentum of the car that it forced the heavy vehicle across the road on to the kerbstones. A heap of sand into which the car ran itself helped, probably, to reduce the shock against the kerbing, and the five passengers who were on the car at the time escaped without injury. The tram, being partly on the footpath, stood at a rather ugly angle, and had obviously narrowly missed falling over. Frederick Taylor (409) [His Hackney Carriage Licence number], the driver, states that he had pulled up in Speedwell Road just previously to set down a passenger, and the car jumped the rails at a time when no electric current was being used to propel it. The permanent way is being repaired at the spot where the accident took place, and the fact that a large quantity of mending material lies by the side of the road suggests the theory that a pebble may have got into the track and thus caused the car to leave the metals. Owing to the small number of passengers, too, it is thought the car would be particularly liable to jump the track. A complaint is made as to the speed at which the car travelled, it being alleged that it was excessive."

[I have placed this under Traction in Transit because engineers and manufacturers alike were finding their way in to this new form of power. I do not think the driver could have been speeding, as there is insufficient speed for him to get into top notch between Speedwell Road and Sir Harry's Road, and as I remember there was a circuit breaker at Sir Harry's Road, so as the driver says he would have been coasting.

*154 was one of a set of open top cars (151-165) delivered to the CBT Company by the Electric Railway & Tramway Carriage Works, Preston, in 1901, and was therefore almost new. Fitted with Peckham 9A Cantilever trucks which did not prove entirely successful, 154 was fitted with

Accident at Small Heath

... But modernisation brings its own problems.

The Weekly Mercury, Saturday 27 August 1904:

"TRAMCAR UPSET.
ALARMING ACCIDENT ON THE COVENTRY-ROAD. PASSENGERS INJURED.
Since the preparations for the electrification of the Small Heath tram route commenced the ordinary steam traffic on the line has been conducted with great difficulty, and, as is being demonstrated, with a considerable amount of risk to passengers. Only a month ago the overturning of a car in Hurst-street shook the confidence of the public in the safety of the service during the operations of relaying, etc. The feeling of uneasiness had to some extent been allayed.

On Tuesday night, however, another alarming smash occurred just at the point where the cars turn out of Bordesley on to the Coventry-road, but by a miracle, as it seemed, no one was killed, although between twenty and thirty passengers received more or less serious injuries.

It was about eleven o'clock that the accident took place, and the car, which was bound for Small Heath, was well loaded, forty-seven passengers altogether being carried.

In order that the new electric cars may pass under the Great Western Railway bridge at the city end of Coventry road it has been found necessary to lower the roadway to the extent of between two and three feet, and while this is being effected the traffic has to be conducted on a single line. Between this and the excavation there is very little space, and cars passing in and out have been controlled by signals, the speed naturally being slow.

FELL WITH A CRASH.

As the car to which the accident occurred last night was negotiating this corner the back wheels jumped the metals. The wheels ploughed into the narrow strip of roadway, which gave way, and almost before the passengers realised the danger the car overturned with a crash into the excavation below.

The shrieks of the passengers, the smashing of glass, and the crash of breaking wood and ironwork were heard for some distance, and speedily a large crowd collected. One of the first on the scene was Inspector Batchelor, of the city police, who had been on duty at Bordesley Theatre. He promptly telephoned to the Central Station, and in a short time Deputy Chief Constable McManus and a staff of officers were rendering assistance.

At the time the car overturned there were no fewer than nineteen persons seated on the top, and it was feared that some of these might have lost their lives. When the breakdown gang had finished their labours, and the injured had been extricated, it was a great relief to all concerned to find that no fatality had attended the accident.

The excitement for the time was intense, and the screams of one injured woman who feared her baby had been killed were heart-rending. The injured passengers were despatched in all directions to the nearest doctors, the Fire

Brigade Ambulance rendering assistance where necessary. News of the occurrence soon reached the hospital and preparations were made for the speedy treatment of the patients, but fortunately only the following four injured passengers attended for treatment.

TREATED AT HOSPITAL.
Detective-Sergeant Whitehouse, cut hand and thigh.
John Foster (32), a butcher, Old Know road, Small Heath, contused leg and back.
John Trewrall (34), Green-lanes, cuts to the face.
Beatrice Owen, (25), Albert-street, Small Heath, cut eyebrow.

None of these, however, were detained after treatment. Other passengers treated by doctors in the neighbourhood numbered about twenty. They were found to be suffering from shock and injury.

The following complained of the injuries named:

Alfred Gibbs, 62, Eversley-road; shock.
Mrs. Jeffrey, 32, Mansell-road, internal injuries.
Evelyn Mosedale, 830, Coventry-road; shock.
Mrs. Frances Bennett, 4, Bordesley Green; shock.
Mary Jane Hughes, 189, Cattell-road, shock.
Percy Pearce, 5, Charles-road, cuts about the face.
Rose Morgan and Edith Morgan, 50, Eversley-road; shock.
Peter Debney, Wordsworth-road; shock.
Annie Jeffries (20), Arthur-street, injuries to the back.
Miss Eales, Arthur-street; injury to shoulder.
Miss Innes, Coventry-road, shoulder and elbow injured.
Miss Hartwell, Bordesley Park Tavern; scalp wound.
Miss Hughes, Cattell-road, injuries to hand and head.

OFFICIALS' VIEW

The car itself was completely smashed. Part of it fell on a heap of stones, and this caused a good deal of glass to be broken and wood to be splintered. The top of the car had to be sawn away.

A prominent official of the tramway company, in a chat with a 'Weekly Mercury' representative stated that he was informed that at the time the mishap occurred the car was merely "crawling along" at a speed of about two miles per hour, it having just previously pulled up at Bordesley station.

It was in charge of Driver Richard Bradley, he said, "a most capable and careful servant" who had been in the employ of the company for some sixteen or eighteen years.

The actual cause of the accident was the leaving of the points by the back bogey and was almost identical with that of the accident in Hurst-street.

Asked if, during the process of relaying the lines, it was not possible to take further precautions against accident, he replied that the only real safeguard was the cessation of the service of carts."

The B.E.T. Gazette, **15 March 1905.**

No Electric Conversion for Birmingham

Birmingham Public Works Committee Minute 1499 reported 2 January 1894:

"...That the Central Tramways be informed that your committee cannot accede to their request to be allowed to substitute overhead electric traction on the Bristol Road route..."

The idea was to adopt the Ewell-Parker system as used on the South Staffs and to extend the lines outwith the Birmingham boundary down to the King's Norton UDC area. Until a few years ago manhole covers existed with King's Norton & Northfield UDC Tramways Committee cast in the iron. I have to assume the accumulator cars were already proving unsatisfactory, but it was also the time when various 'interested bodies' discussed whether to extend the cable car network or use the less unsightly conduit system.

Birmingham Post, **2 March 1894.**

End of the (steam tram) line

Railways & Tramways Monthly:

"Rossendale Valley Tramways Company – Mr A. Love, the chairman, presided at the annual meeting of the Rossendale Valley Tramways Company held in London, and moved the adoption of the report. The report stated that there had been a decrease in the traffic and other receipts of £47. Owing to extensive repairs to the permanent ways the expenditure in that department was much higher than usual. The balance available for distribution was £2,083, which admitted of the usual dividend on the preference shares, and 5 per cent. on the ordinary shares, with £500 to reserve. The local authorities have given notice to purchase the tramways, and negotiations are proceeding. The Board had had the undertaking carefully valued by an expert, which had somewhat increased the professional charges. The report was adopted."

From time to time a misleading notice can appear in a magazine – had this been a decade or two earlier one might have taken it at face value. *Railway & Tramway Monthly,* 1 March 1908. "The Government have sanctioned the construction of a steam tramway from Wallsend to West Wallsend. The estimated cost of the line is £37,075 exclusive of land, and has a length of eight miles inclusive of loops".

Brush AGMs

"An extraordinary GM was held on 14th January 1901 to confirm an agreement between Brush and BET in which they had made an offer for the ordinary shares of the Brush Co., which would enable BET to become majority shareholder. In return BET agreed to place the whole of its orders and those of its associated companies with Brush for a 5% rebate. The financial terms of the share offer was one £10 ordinary share of BET for 7½ £2 ordinary shares of Brush. The market value of BET shares was about £13.5.0d and of Brush about £1.15.0d. The offer of 7½ to 1 placed a value of about £1.18.0d on the Brush shares, a premium of three shillings below par value of £2. Issued share capital increased by £65,000 to £424,600 of which about £100,000 was held by BET."

At the AGM of 10th April 1902 it was stated that the £2 shares were quoted at £1.

Extracted from a summary of Brush AGMs, 15th AGM (1903/4) held on Tuesday 10 May 1904.

One (shareholder) said that profits were illusory until the item for Patents and Goodwill, which stood at £181,397 was drastically reduced. Another stated that British Electric Traction which now held more than half Brush shares, had secured half the Company's assets at something less than one-third the price it cost shareholders, because of the fall in share prices. So long as the shares remained at a discount on the market, the Company could not get fresh capital by a new issue. Consequently bank and other loans amounted to some £125,000. The Company was paying higher interest on this than it was receiving for invested securities.

Our thanks to George Toms for finding these items.

Aston Tramways Completed

Weekly Mercury, 5 November 1904

"ASTON TRAMWAYS COMPLETED
The whole of the Aston tramway system is completed as far as the laying of the metals is concerned, and the contract has been finished thirteen days before the specified time, which was November 12th. During the period of construction there have been 39 days when the work has been stopped owing to the bad weather, which the contractor could claim for, so that Aston may be congratulated on the promptness with which the work has been brought to a conclusion.

One satisfactory feature is that no accident has occurred to the public, nor have they been seriously inconvenienced, as a service of the cars has been maintained in its entirety from start to finish of the work."

Railway & Tramways Monthly, 1 March 1908:
"Accrington: The Corporation has completed the conversion of its tramways, comprising 11¾ miles, to the electric system, and each section has received the sanction of the Board of Trade."

PETER HAMMOND'S MODEL TRAMS

Wantage Tramway car no.3, Hughes no.4 (1877), Matthews no.6, c.1880. Fine scale, 12 volts 2-rail. (P. Hammond)

Hughes no.4 and trailer car no.3 (Milnes 1890). O gauge. (P. Hammond)

Trailer car no.4 (ii) ex Hurst Nelson double deck exhibition car of 1900. To Wantage as single-deck 1912.

The genesis of this story is a longer article in *Modern Tramway,* May 1962, pp165-168, and we are grateful to both the editor and Peter for assistance in its provision and usage.

Some decades ago tramway modellers were few and far between whereas now the hobby is going forward, with new kits and parts being made available, especially in Continental outline 'Hailing' products and their ilk, and some rather marvellous kits coming over from Russia. Conversely in Britain, although we have lost a number of manufacturers, others have arisen to take their place – a fact easily established by the purchase of a copy of *Tramfare,* the Journal of the Tramway and Light Railway Society. My own impression is that due to downsizing of houses and apartments tramway builders' scale sizes have followed suit, with HO and OO gaining ground at the expense of the larger O, S, and 1 scales. The exception to this are some marvellous garden tramways which at night look incredibly realistic as they flash and spark their way between the buddleias, begonias or (seen once in Cornwall) bougainvillea but such lines require a good space and virtually bottomless pockets.

"My main interest is in ¾" scale, or ¹⁄₁₆th full size; a scale which has much to commend it. To my mind, the smaller scales do not give the correct atmosphere and running qualities for which the full-sized tramcar was noted. In ¾" scale you can incorporate all these features by making the model heavy and well-sprung, adding all the fine details a tramcar bristles with.

My own models come into what one might call the 'operating' kind as distinct from the 'glass case' kind and as such have some of the finer details left off. My first model, a Birmingham bogie car No.512, had just about everything working, including track and wheel brakes, but as these features affected the running qualities of the model, I have since removed many working parts, leaving only the components that are visible."

"Many people ask me "Why model tramcars?" I find it very difficult to answer in a direct way, though it may be summed up as follows. Imagine a line late summer evening; the garden layout has been running well all day and the time has come for the "last car in". The car, No.512, cannot be seen from the controller position (lying flat on one's front for an eye-level view) but with each successive notch of the controller one can hear the "tick-tack-tack-tick" of the wheels and the hiss of the trolley on the overhead. No.512 soon swings into view about 30 yards away, rolling over the points of a passing loop where there is a compulsory stop. Immediately after this there is a short 1 in 12 gradient which requires "full parallel". Being last car in, No.512 only slows down at

Hughes no.4 and Matthews no.6, showing Peter Hammond's detail even in O (7mm to the foot) gauge.

No.7 (Manning Wardle W/no. 1057 of 1888 to Wantage 1893) and no.4. O gauge, 12 volts, 2-rail, fine scale.

this point and then storms the incline. Motors humming, trolley flashing, she comes over the top, gaining speed at every rail joint. The controller is eased back for a slight right bend, and then top notch for the terminus. The view of No.512 bearing down on one like this does bring on a feeling of nostalgia – happy memories of riding the last car from Rednal, or just walking along the Bristol Road reservation and watching the cars go swinging by – happy memories indeed!

The main object to me, then, is a model tram which runs and has "atmosphere", a very difficult feature to incorporate in a model. I have no wish to condemn glasscase models – tram or otherwise – but so often one sees highly-detailed well-painted models which completely lack the atmosphere of the original prototype."

In 1960 the TLRS held a Tramway Centenary Exhibition in London and it was suggested by a group of modellers that to have a working model steam tram and trailer would enhance the displays. Peter then paid a visit to the fabled 'Whitcombe Collection' at South Kensington, and after this was to produce his working drawings for a 'Kitson' locomotive and 'Falcon' trailer to be built in ¾" scale. "It was a foregone conclusion that the locomotive would have to be electrically powered, as the local government regulations ruled out steam propulsion at exhibitions".

The underframe was possibly the simplest part of this model, being a simple inside-framed box structure of robust proportions, fully sprung.

"The first big problem was how to propel the model quietly and at the low speed necessary for realism, especially as the locomotive had to be self-contained. This latter point indicated that it would have to carry batteries. Experiments started with just the chassis, wheels, motor and batteries in the form of a test rig. The initial results were not very encouraging, to say the least. Transmissions tried were rubber band, friction disc, and worm gears, both single and double reduction. The double

Hughes no.4, O gauge. Detail. (P. Hammond)

Mathews no.6. 7mm scale, O gauge. (P. Hammond)

No.7.

reduction gears were eventually found the most satisfactory and reliable.

The next snag was power. The locomotive would propel itself along quite well, but balked at pulling anything else. Also, the two six-volt batteries ran down very quickly. As time was running short, it was finally decided that "stud contact" was the answer – a long collector shoe would not be too conspicuous under the locomotive, as the body side and end plates would be within ¼in. of the track. A short length of track was fixed up with studs – spaced at about 4in. centres – and the locomotive and trailer were placed on it and coupled together. On with the power and away they went like the wind – success at the eleventh hour! The batteries, however, were left in the locomotive for adhesion purposes; this accounted for the half boiler arrangement, an unfortunate detail which will be rectified in the near future (the second model has the correct floor height). An oval of track was constructed for the stand by my friend Leo Gibbs, and both track and models behaved very well indeed for the duration of the show, where they clocked 40 hours running time or 15 actual miles.

Both locomotive and trailer car bodies are constructed on orthodox lines – that is, of obechi wood framework with thin plywood and Bristol board skin, the windows being of glass (old photographic plates cleaned off). The whole structure was glued and pinned together in the normal way. The painting and livery called for some special research into the actual colours used by the C.B.T. around 1886. The colours finally established and thus portrayed were a deep crimson for the lower panels that is, rocker panel and waist panel – with a deep cream for the window frames and surrounds. The lining out was in the conventional manner – gold with "Greek fret" treatment in the corners. A point of interest here regarding the lining out was that trouble was experienced with the gold paint used in the ruling pen – the

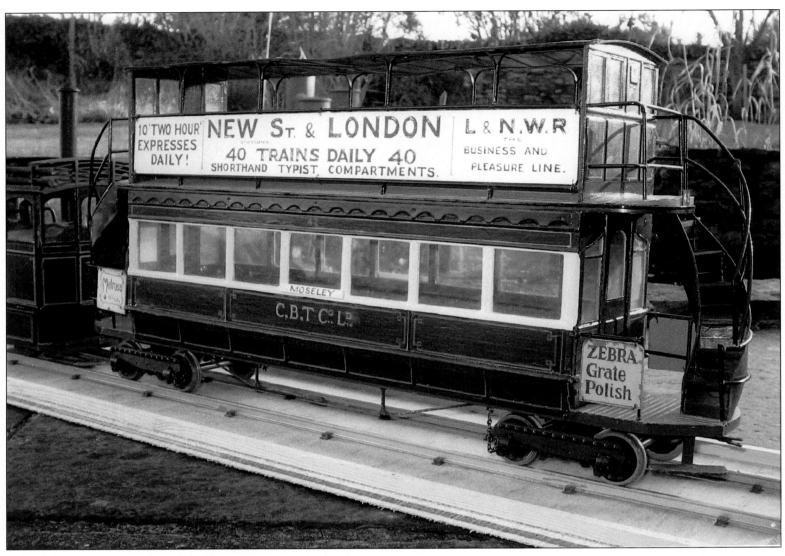

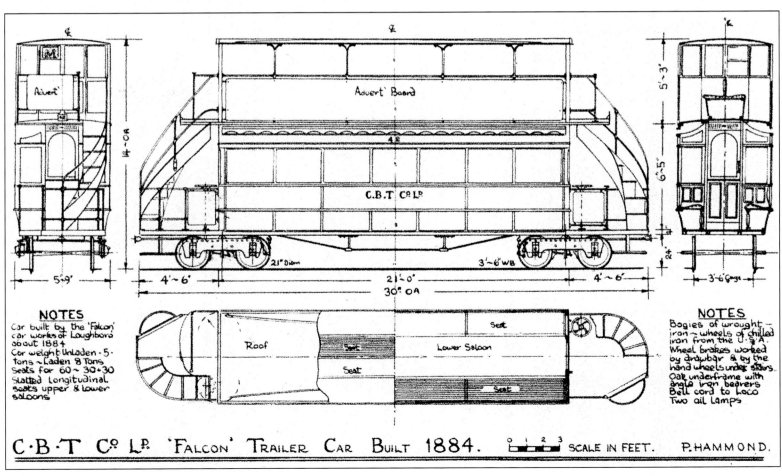

NOTES

Car built by the 'Falcon' car works of Loughboro' about 1884
Car weight Unladen - 5 Tons ~ Laden 8 Tons
Seats for 60 ~ 30 + 30
Slatted longitudinal seats upper & lower saloons

NOTES

Bogies of wrought iron ~ wheels of chilled iron from the U.S.A.
Wheel brakes worked by drawbar & by the hand wheels under stairs
Oak underframe with angle iron bearers
Bell cord to loco
Two oil lamps

Advert Board

C.B.T C⁰ L⁰

21" Diam.   3'-6" WB

5'-9'   4'-6'   21'-0'   4'-6'   3'-6' Gauge
30' OA

Roof   Seat   Lower Saloon   Seat   Seat

C·B·T C⁰ L⁰. 'FALCON' TRAILER CAR BUILT 1884.   0 1 2 3 SCALE IN FEET.   P. HAMMOND.

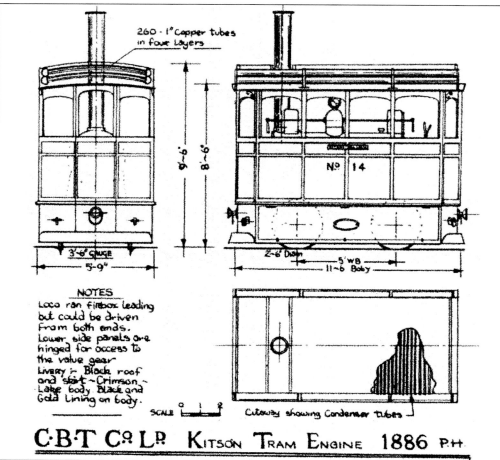

260 - 1" Copper tubes
in four Layers

9'-6"
8'-6"

Nº 14

3'-6" GAUGE
5'-9"

2'-6" Diam
5' WB
11'-6 Body

NOTES
Loco ran firebox leading
but could be driven
from both ends.
Lower side panels are
hinged for access to
the valve gear
Livery :- Black roof
and stairs - Crimson -
Lake body Black and
Gold Lining on body.

SCALE

Cutaway showing Condenser tubes

C·B·T Cº Lᴰ KITSON TRAM ENGINE 1886 P.H.

paint would not flow evenly. After some thought
into the matter it was decided that the cause of
this was the varnish solution in the paint, so
when the paint had settled overnight the
residue was removed from the top of the paint.
The almost pure gold dust was then thinned
with some normal white spirit and applied to
the model, with reasonable success."

Since then Peter Hammond has proceeded to
make a range of trams of various outlines and
gauges, some for his own amusement and many
commissioned, a few of his steam variants are
shown photographically with a note of the relevant scales alongside.

These models put him far above the level of
people like myself working in plastics and wood
for as can be seen this is true engineering of the
highest class – a standard which once put the
'Great' in Great Britain. One of the very pleasant facets of tramway modelling and most
noticeable at the annual shows at either Kew or
Manchester is the air of co-operation between
tram enthusiasts and a remarkable willingness to
share 'secrets'; almost without exception
exhibitors will be pleased to show you their own
'gizmos'. Long may this continue.

SOME REMARKS ON WORKING

STREET TRAMWAY LINES

BY

STEAM POWER,

WITH

DESCRIPTION OF VARIOUS ENGINES.

———

LEONARD J. TODD,

ROAD LOCOMOTIVE CONSULTING ENGINEER,

LEITH, SCOTLAND:

———

MAY 1874

CONTENTS

OF THE ANNEXED NINE SHEETS OF DRAWINGS.

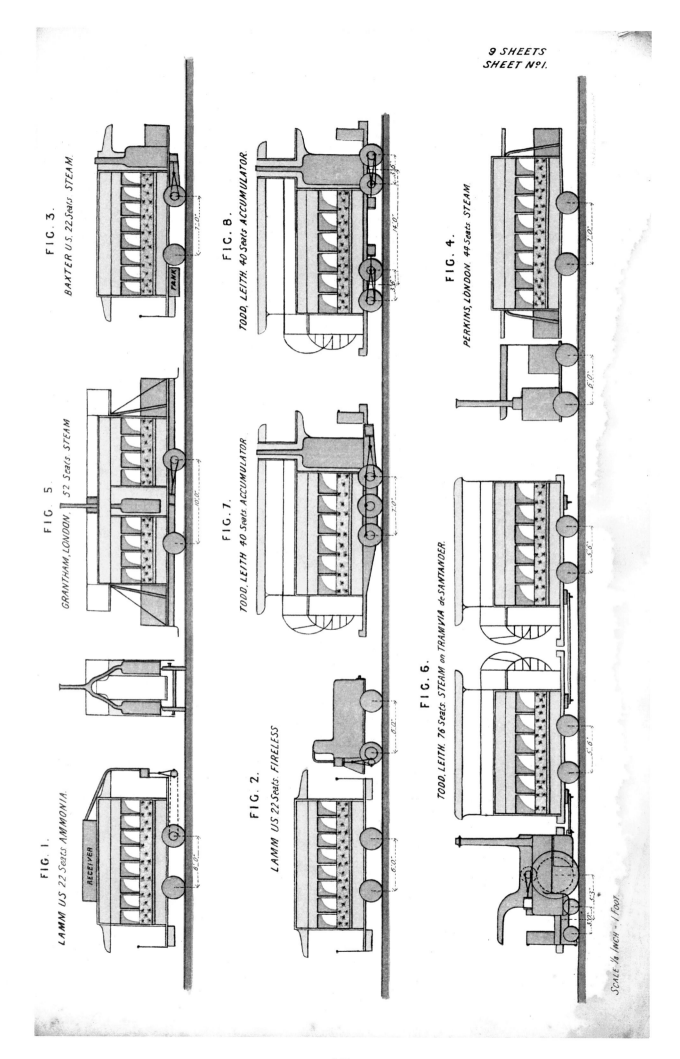

FIG. 3.

BAXTER U.S. 22 Seats STEAM.

FIG. 8.

TODD, LEITH. 40 Seats ACCUMULATOR.

FIG. 4.

PERKINS, LONDON. 44 Seats STEAM.

FIG. 5.

GRANTHAM, LONDON. 52 Seats STEAM.

FIG. 7.

TODD, LEITH. 40 Seats ACCUMULATOR.

FIG. 6.

TODD, LEITH. 76 Seats STEAM on TRAMVIA de SANTANDER.

FIG. 1.

LAMM U.S. 22 Seats AMMONIA.

FIG. 2.

LAMM U.S. 22 Seats FIRELESS.

SCALE ½ INCH = 1 FOOT.

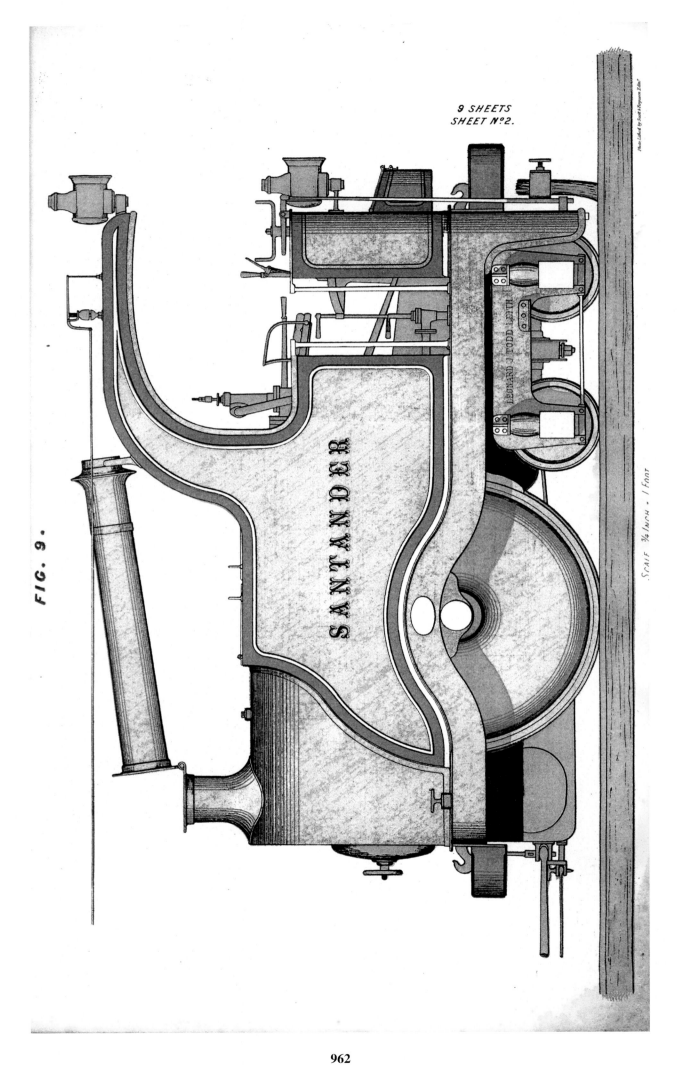

FIG. 9.

9 SHEETS
SHEET Nº2.

SANTANDER

LEONARD J TODD LEITH

SCALE ¾ INCH = 1 FOOT

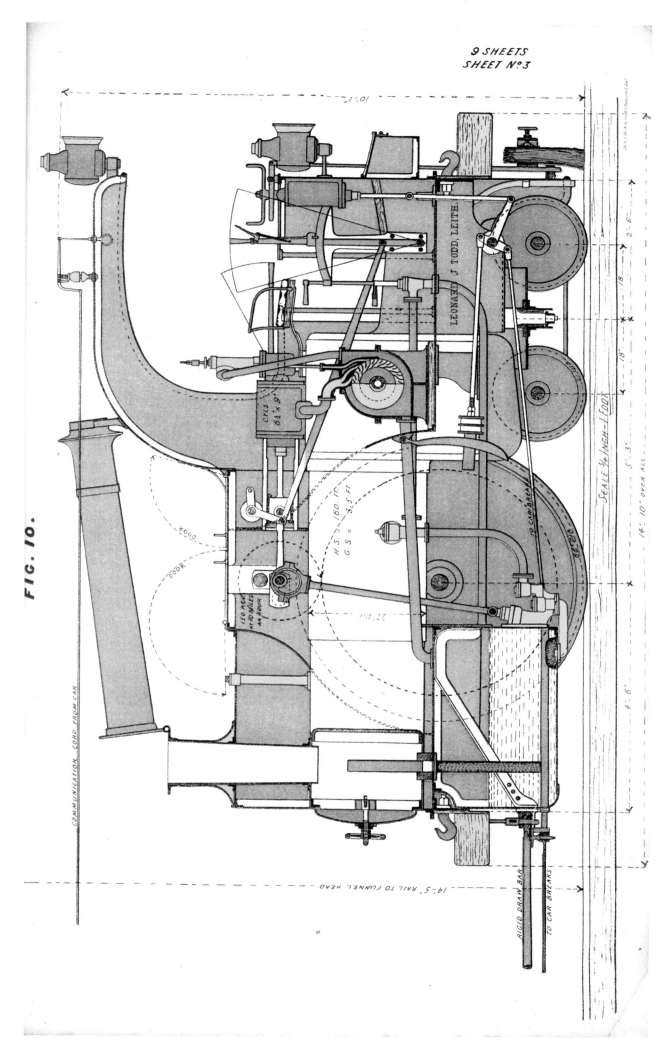

FIG. 10.

COMMUNICATION CORD FROM CAR

RIGID DRAW BAR

TO CAR BREAKS

14'-5" RAIL TO FUNNEL HEAD

SCALE ¾ INCH=1 FOOT

14'-10" OVER ALL

4'-6"   5'-3"   18"   18"   2'-6"

LEONARD J TODD, LEITH.

CYLS
6¼ x 9"

H.S. = 160. FT.
G.S = 3.5 FT.

150 REVS
AT 40 MILES
AN HOUR

DOOR

TO CAR BREAKS

FIG. II.

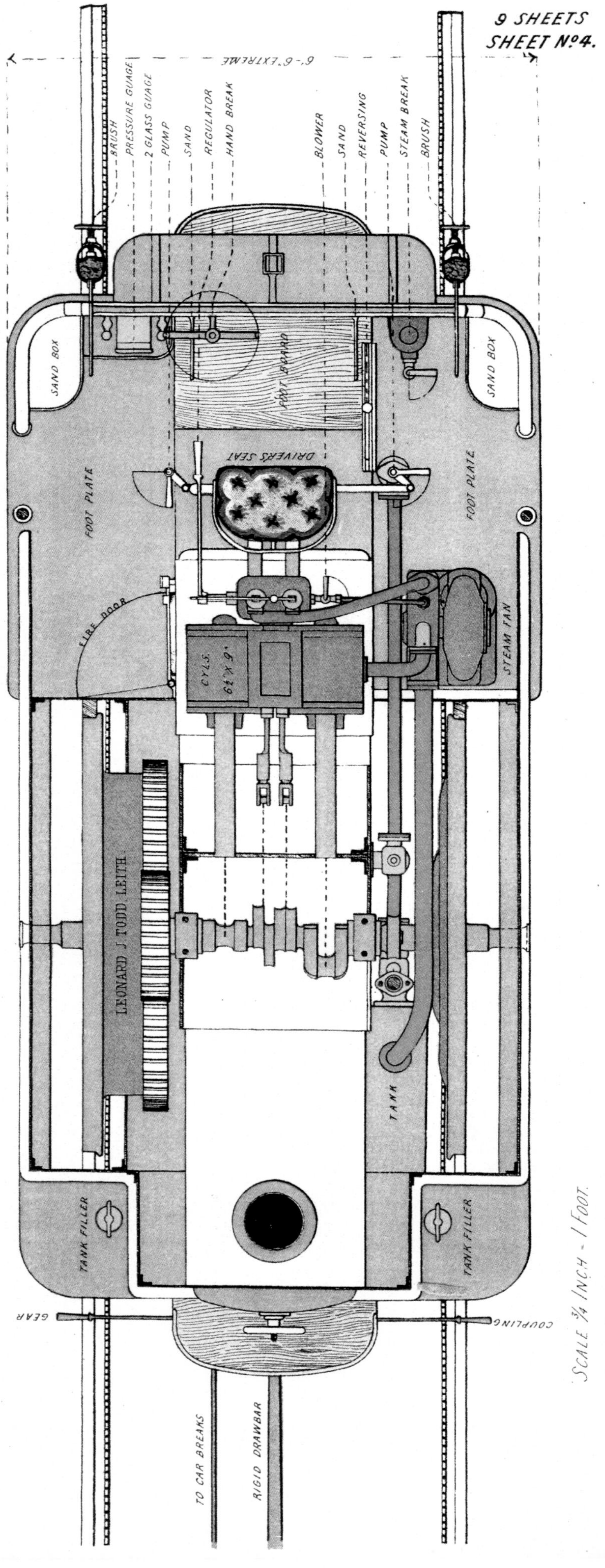

6'-6" EXTREME

BRUSH
PRESSURE GUAGE
2 GLASS GUAGE
PUMP
SAND
REGULATOR
HAND BREAK
BLOWER
SAND
REVERSING
PUMP
STEAM BREAK
BRUSH

SAND BOX
FOOT PLATE

FOOT BOARD

DRIVERS SEAT

FIRE DOOR

CYLS.
6½ X 9"

STEAM FAN

SAND BOX
FOOT PLATE

LEONARD J TODD LEITH

TANK

TANK FILLER

TANK FILLER

GEAR

COUPLING

TO CAR BREAKS
RIGID DRAWBAR

SCALE ¾ INCH - 1 FOOT

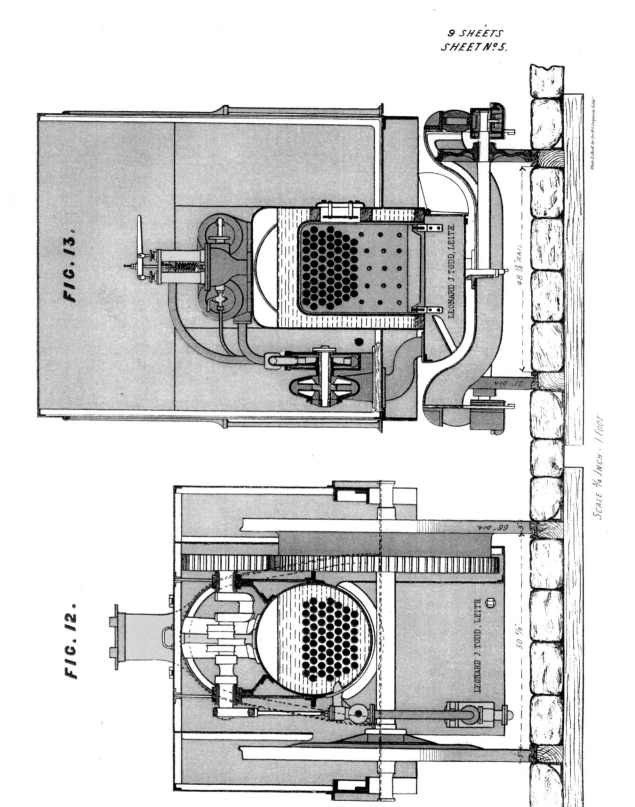

FIG. 13.

FIG. 12.

LEONARD J. TODD, LEITH.

LEONARD J. TODD, LEITH.

SCALE ¾ INCH = 1 FOOT

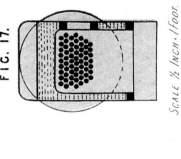

FIG. 15

LEONARD J. TODD, LEITH

FIG. 14

LEONARD J. TODD, LEITH
Level when capacity 45 cub. ft.
Level after 6 cub. ft. of evaporation - 20 I.HP for half an hour.
Level after 12 cub. ft. of evaporation - 20 I.HP for an hour.
Boiler 42 in. dia. X 84 in.
G.S. .... 1·5 ft.
H.S. .... 60·
Water Capacity - 45·
Water area - 9·
WATER GRATE
FAN BLAST
CLOSE ASH PAN

FIG. 16.

FIG. 17.

9 SHEETS
SHEET No. 6.

SCALE ½ INCH - 1 FOOT.

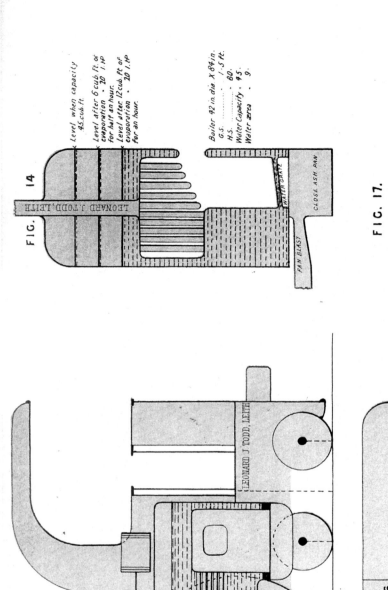

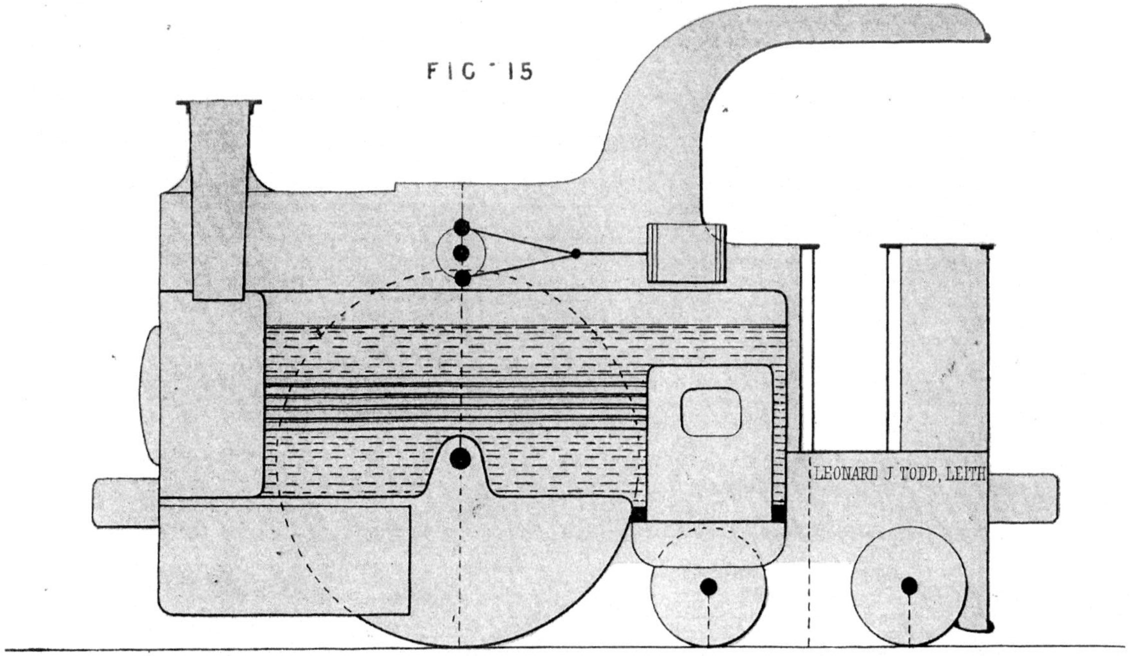

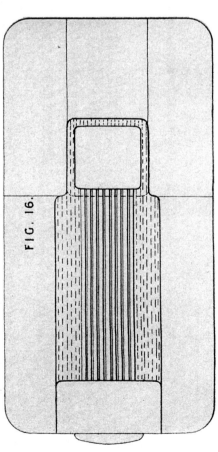

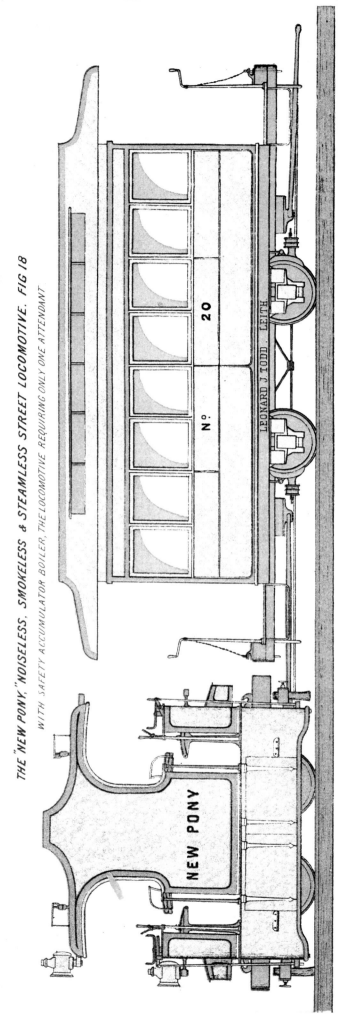

THE "NEW PONY," NOISELESS, SMOKELESS & STEAMLESS STREET LOCOMOTIVE. FIG 18

WITH SAFETY ACCUMULATOR BOILER, THE LOCOMOTIVE REQUIRING ONLY ONE ATTENDANT

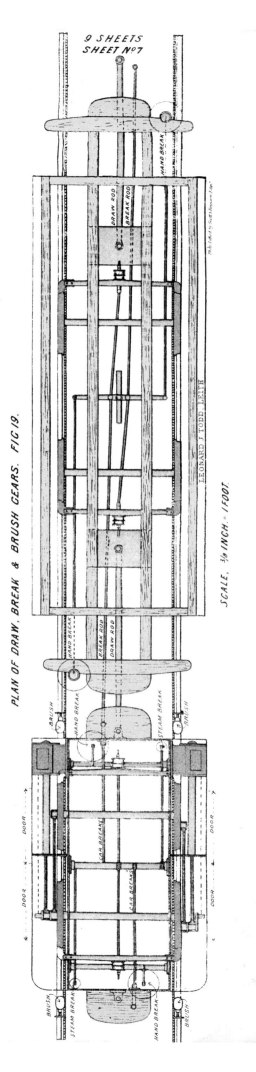

PLAN OF DRAW, BREAK & BRUSH GEARS. FIG 19.

SCALE, 3/8 INCH = 1 FOOT.

967

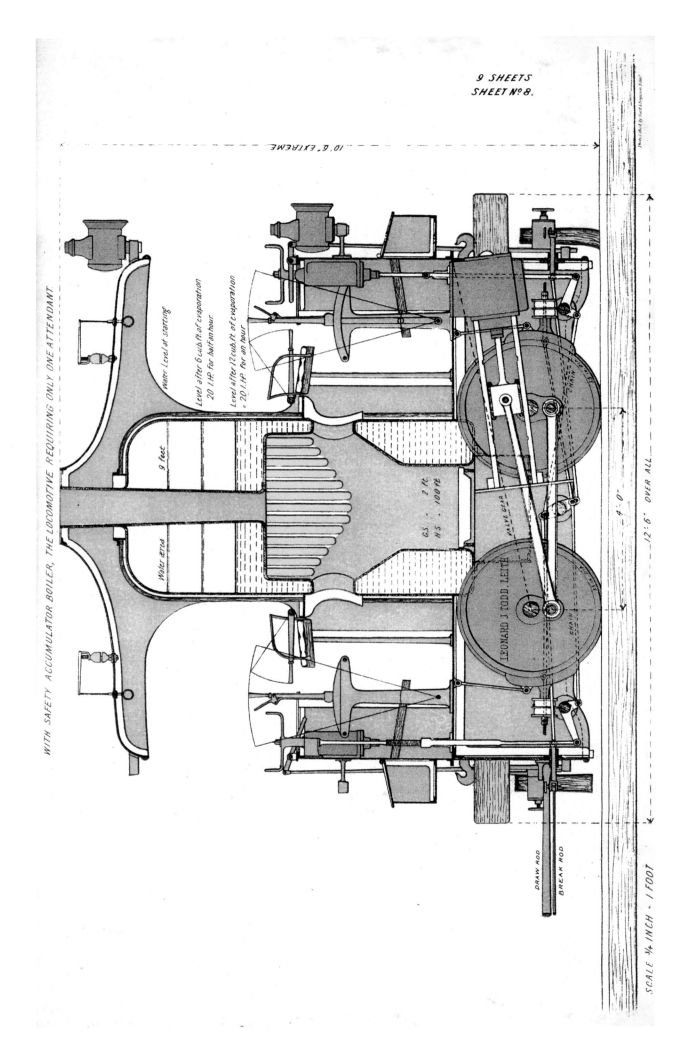

WITH SAFETY ACCUMULATOR BOILER, THE LOCOMOTIVE REQUIRING ONLY ONE ATTENDANT.

Water Level at starting

Level after 6 cub.ft of evaporation
20 I.H.P. for half an hour.

Level after 12 cub.ft. of evaporation
= 20 I.H.P. for an hour

9 feet

Water area

G.S. - 2 Ft.
H.S. - 100 Ft.

LEONARD J TODD, LEITH.

CHAIN

CHAIN

VALVE GEAR

DRAW ROD

BREAK ROD

10'.6" EXTREME.

4'.0"

12'.6" OVER ALL.

SCALE ¾ INCH = 1 FOOT

Photolithd by Scott & Ferguson Edinr

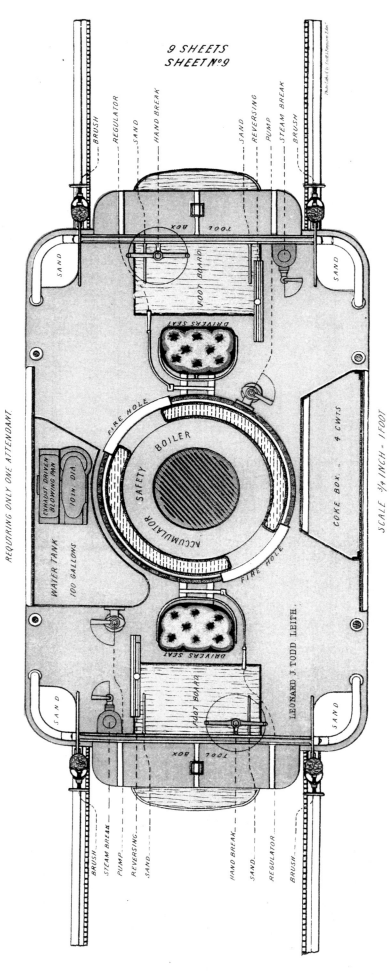

PLAN OF "NEW PONY" STREET LOCOMOTIVE

REQUIRING ONLY ONE ATTENDANT.

9 SHEETS
SHEET No 9

BRUSH
REGULATOR
SAND
HAND BREAK
SAND
REVERSING
PUMP
STEAM BREAK
BRUSH

SAND
TOOL BOX
FOOT BOARD
DRIVER'S SEAT
SAND

FIRE HOLE
EXHAUST DRIVEN BLOWING FAN
10 IN. DIA.
SAFETY
BOILER
ACCUMULATOR
WATER TANK
100 GALLONS
COKE BOX - 4 CWTS
FIRE HOLE

SAND
DRIVER'S SEAT
FOOT BOARD
TOOL BOX
SAND

LEONARD J TODD LEITH.

BRUSH
STEAM BREAK
PUMP
REVERSING
SAND
HAND BREAK
SAND
REGULATOR
BRUSH

SCALE ¾ INCH = 1 FOOT

969

CONTENTS

ON WORKING STREET RAILWAYS BY STEAM POWER.

(1.) THE opinion is now generally gaining ground that many if not all street railways could be more cheaply and efficiently worked by some mechanical power than by the present animals; and it is now proposed to consider this subject at some length, in order that the solution of the problem may be rendered clearer. And the production of a locomotive suitable for working street railways should not be a very difficult matter, if, in the first place, we could only clearly understand the various features and capabilities which such an engine must possess, and which are very considerably different from those which experience has proved to be well suited for ordinary railway traffic. The problem is also one that will well repay the task of solving it, and amongst the various branches of engineering there are few that now offer such an unoccupied field as does this. Already millions of capital are invested in tramways in Britain alone, while the lines already laid on the Continent, India, the Colonies and South America, and even Japan, almost eclipse our home lines, and yet in addition to all these is the enormous mileage of street lines laid in the States. But few of the companies working these lines run less than 50, while many of them run 100, and some more than 200 cars daily. And as each car must have a propelling power, whether that consist of a detached locomotive or of other combination, it will be seen what a field for a suitable engine already exists, and one which also, from the continual opening of new lines, is very rapidly increasing; for at the present moment the only known means of regularly working these street lines is animal power, either that of horses or mules. **General opening remarks.**

(2.) In the first part of this article several points of the subject will be considered, and therefrom be deduced a series of main features and capabilities which all street railway locomotives must possess; in the second, some of the very few locomotive cars which have yet been built will be considered; and in the third part, some general idea will be given of the apparently best manner in which locomotives for street railways should be constructed and worked. **Three divisions of subject.**

(3.) In connection with horse haulage, it may be remarked in passing that it may at times fail altogether, as in the case of war or a horse epidemic, but without laying much stress on these extraordinary considerations, we may at once pass to the ordinary objection to it, which is very simply that it is too expensive. It is true that street lines succeed very well so long as the roads are nearly level, as the draught is then so small that two, and in many cases one horse can manage a car; but the case is widely different on hilly roads. On all lines the one great item amongst the working expenses is that of horsing the cars, and yet this item, from the increasing cost of horses and of feeding and keeping them, is very steadily increasing. So although it is easy to enumerate many advantages that a suitable mechanical motor would possess over horses, as that it would not raise dust, wear the stones, make animal droppings, &c., yet the main point of all most unmistakeably is that it would cost very much less than any system of animal haulage, and it is almost this consideration alone which excites any interest in the subject. **About horse haulage.**

On level lines a tramway car effects a considerable saving in draught over a road omnibus, but on inclines of about 2. or 2.5 per cent. the draughts are equal, while on all steeper roads the draught tells heavily against the car. On straight level lines the rolling resistance of .5 per cent. of the tram rail is so small that the great weight of the car hardly signifies, but on inclines the gain from reduced rolling resistance is quickly swallowed up by the great increase of resistance due to gravity, which is shown in the accompanying Table No. 1.

TABLE No. I.

Resistance of 'bus and car.

		Horses.	Passengers.	Passengers per horse.	Weight, total.	Weight with passengers.	Weight per passenger.	Weight per horse.	Resistance of street and tram.	Pull required on level.	Pull on grade of 2·5 per cent.	Pull on grade of 6·25 per cent.	Pull per horse on level.	Pull per horse on grade 2·5.	Pull per horse on grade 6·25.
					Cwts.	Lbs.	Cwts	Cwts.							
I.	EDINBRO BUS.	3	28	9·33	28	6272	1·00	18·6	2·0	125·4	282·2	517·4	41·8	94·0	172·5
2.	EDINBRO CAR.	4	38	9·50	42	8960	1·105	20·0	Straight .5	44·8	268·8	604·8	11·2	67·2	151·2
									Curve 1·0	89·6	313·6	649·6	22·4	78·4	162·4
3.	ORDINARY CAR.	2	44	22·0	50	10528	1·136	47·0	Straight .5	52·6	315·8	too steep.	26·3	156.	too steep.
									Curve 1·0	105·2	368·4		52·6	184·2	

Owing to this great resistance of gravity all cars run too slowly on hilly roads, and this, notwithstanding that extra horses are attached on inclines. And that these extra horses must tell very seriously upon the profits of a line can be seen when it is stated that on one line 4 horses are required to work cars carrying only from 30 to 38 passengers, and that from time to time these poor animals actually fall dead from the strenuous efforts they require to make to draw the unwilling cars up 1 in 16. Even with equal draughts it is much more fatiguing to an animal to draw a carriage rigidly running on rails, than it is to work an ordinary road vehicle in which the horse can naturally shoulder to its work, and, by swaying the lock carriage from side to side, can take a purchase from first one wheel and then the other, and thus materially lighten its labour. And thus the mere difference between the calculated draughts of the 'bus and car in Table No. 1 does not nearly represent the extra fatigue that the car horses have actually to undergo. Compared to level lines cars on inclines have many disadvantages besides that of the increased horsing; they must then be smaller, and thus the drivers' and conductors' wages are charged against a smaller number of passengers than usual, and more cars must also be used to accommodate a given amount of traffic; and the wheels, break-blocks, break-gear, and harness, all suffer much more than on level lines. On the Copenhagen level line Swedish chilled 30 in. wheels run 70,000 miles, while on some steep roads they are worn out in 20,000 miles, as the breaks are constantly used running down the long inclines. The break-blocks also wear out proportionately as fast, and owing to the way they are hung they rack the framing very severely, as from the small diameter of the wheels and long blocks the action of the bearing springs is completely arrested when the breaks are hard up; and the tremor sent through a car when thus suddenly running on to the sand, that must be constantly used in damp weather on lines of more than 2 or 3 per cent., rapidly starts all the joints and fastenings. Indeed, all things considered, horse-worked tramways compare very unfavourably with ordinary omnibuses for working inclines. For then each horse only draws about as many passengers as an ordinary omnibus, whereas a tram horse should draw at least twice as many passengers as does one working an omnibus, as it has not only to earn interest on the cost of the carriage, but also on the great capital sunk in the line, from which the omnibus is quite free. Thus in the table the No. 1 omnibus horse, working on inclines of 1 in 40 to 1 in 16, draws 9·3 passengers, and the No. 2 car horse only takes 9·5 passengers on the same road, whereas the No. 3 car horse on a nearly level line takes 22 passengers, and thus is twice as profitable as the No. 2 animal; but it will only be more profitable than the No. 1 omnibus horse if the difference of the 12 passengers it draws is more than sufficient to pay interest on the great cost of the line. This is neglecting some minor considerations. In reference to the horse draughts in the table, which exceed 160 or 170 lbs., it may be remarked that these severe strains are only kept up for very short distances.

The danger also of working street railways of more than 2 or 3 per cent. by horse power is not inconsiderable, as in certain very frequent conditions of the weather the cars cannot be stopped in less than 20 or 30 yards, and they will frequently on such roads run several yards with both wheels skidded. And so, in short, on all street railways, but especially on those with inclines, there is abundant room for the introduction of a suitable mechanical motor, which shall reduce the working expenses, safely increase the speed, and give the driver greater control in working and stopping his car.

Different motive powers.

(4.) Of course there are several mechanical means by which it is possible to propel light carriages along rails, as by hot air, compressed air, carbonic acid gas, ammoniacal gas, steam, or even other means. The hot air engine we may at once dismiss as far too cumbersome for the object in view. The compressed air engine working from a reservoir may also go, although it is a favourite project with those who for the first time turn their attention to this subject. It is extremely difficult to store air above 100 lbs. for any length of time in a reservoir, as it leaks with ease through joints which are perfectly steam-tight, and small leaks are also difficult to discover, as they cannot be seen. Even could the air be worked from 100 lbs. down to 20 lbs. yet still a very large receiver would be required, and, indeed, for hilly roads, the design may be called impracticable. Quickly charging the receiver at the end of each run would also be a very difficult matter. The carbonic acid gas engine may also be dismissed, as one of those schemes that are in the last degree likely to be brought into commercial use. The ammoniacal gas engine may be classed with the preceding, although Dr Lamm of New Orleans actually ran a car by this means for a considerable time. Finally, then we come to the only mechanical means which appears to be in the least degree likely to become commercially practicable and profitable for working street railways, viz.,—steam, or rather the heat evolved from evaporating water. This heat for the particular purpose in view may possibly either be stored up at the end of each run in a "boiler" holding a quantity of water, as proposed by Dr Lamn, and thus constitute a "fireless" steam engine; or it may be communicated directly to the water of the car boiler by a fire, and so become an ordinary steam engine. Either of these plans is quite practicable and may be safely and cheaply worked, but whether a street car should be driven by the heat of a fireless boiler, or of one with a furnace, depends entirely upon the road and situation, and other things to be afterwards considered.

On steam omnibuses.

(5.) It may here be remarked that if determined to adopt steam power in streets, why not use steam omnibuses, instead of cutting up the road with rails and running steam cars. For it may be said that if a steam 'bus costs £1000 that it must pay double or treble the profits of a steam car; for the 'bus has merely to earn an interest on this £1000, the road on which it runs costing it absolutely nothing, while the car must not only earn an interest on the same amount, but also from the same number of passengers must earn interest on the enormous amount of capital sunk in laying the line. Now, although the rolling resistance of a street will be, say 4 times that of the tram, and, consequently, the fuel and repair charges of the 'bus be 4 times those of the car, yet this statement may be taken as passibly true, and might be attended to were it only possible to work an engine as safely on a common road surface as it is on rails, and could the road engine be made something like as durable as the rail locomotive. Unfortunately, however, on neither of these points can the road locomotive for one moment compare with its rail rival; and, indeed, to run road locomotives at high speeds may be taken both to be commercially impracticable and to be dangerous in streets from the risk of defective steerage. For, judging from the opinions of those who have had most experience with road locomotives and steam 'busses, it seems now to be generally allowed that, although, road engines may in many situations do good service in hauling goods at 2 or 3 miles an hour, yet that to run these engines at the high speed of, say only 10 miles an hour is commercially impracticable, as they literally knock themselves to pieces in a very short time from jolting over the rough surfaces. And although an individual road locomotive may, and indeed has often been driven at even 20 miles an hour, yet to work great numbers of such fast running engines in streets would be to introduce a most imminent source of danger, as any accident to the steering gear or driver would instantly cause some disastrous collision. And amongst the few high speed road locomotives that have from time to time been made, although all driven by the best obtainable picked men, yet many more serious accidents have occurred from defective steering than is generally supposed. And with steam power, were it for no other reason than this, rails should most certainly be laid in streets, that so the locomotive could then be automatically guided. Steam omnibuses might perchance be allowed to be steered by hand at high speeds along country roads, but most certainly not along streets. And so we may dismiss the consideration of steam omnibuses for working street traffic and return to that of carriages guided by rails along a given and certain track.

(6.) Work on street railways may be divided into three classes, viz.,—Country, Suburban, and City. The first being work on purely country lines where the roads are for the most part clear, and which extend 5, 6, or even 10 miles from one town to another. The second, suburban lines, being where the streets are mostly wide and the traffic light. And the third, city lines, being purely intramural work, where the streets are mostly of but very ordinary width and the usual traffic severe. **Three kinds of street railway work.**

(7.) Now for working classes 2 and 3 it has been abundantly proved in practice that the way to draw most money and make most profit is to keep the ground constantly covered with cars, not to run a few large cars, but rather a very great many small ones; indeed, on many routes cars should start every few minutes. And the necessity for this is obvious when it is considered that on most city routes people only ride a short distance, say 10 or 15 minutes' walk, so that if a car is at hand they take it, but if not they walk, and then, having gone half their distance before the car passes them, they think it not worth their while then to ride, and thus their fare is lost. On such routes cars must always be passing along, so that no one may be allowed to walk, but they must all be enticed into either one car or the other, and thus every available penny be brought in. As a striking instance, showing the necessity of this, it may be mentioned that in a certain town in South America cars were at one time run at intervals of 20 minutes or so, and the shareholders lost money by the work; but by rearranging the cars to run at intervals of only a few minutes, they straightway earned over 20 per cent. These remarks, however, do not apply to lines of the No. 1 class, where the distance is too great to be walked, as then the cars may start at even half hour or hour intervals, and yet not a passenger be lost. In short, street railway cars should in all cases be run at such an interval of time apart as will not allow an appreciable number of fares to escape, and that interval on many city roads is not more than a few minutes. **City cars must run frequently.**

(8.) As then, in cases 2 and 3, the roads must be worked by a great number of small cars, it necessarily follows that with steam power only 2 men can be afforded to work each car, viz., a driver and a conductor; a special fireman cannot be allowed, as the extra cost of his wages would go far to neutralise the gain from the use of steam. In short, whatever combination of steam engine be used for cases 2 and 3 it must be of such a kind that one man can both safely attend to the boiler and also to the driving of the car. But as the driving alone is quite sufficient while engaged in to occupy one man's whole attention, it follows that the boiler of such a car must be so constructed that it can, with perfect safety, be left to take care of itself while the car is running, although at the end of each run it may require and receive attention from the driver, who is then, and then only, at liberty to look after it. **Different kinds of boilers.**

Now, of all boilers, most unquestionably the one requiring least attention, is that from which the fire has just been drawn; it then requires no safety-valve, as its pressure cannot rise, but must gradually decrease from that which it bore when the fire was extinguished; nor does it longer require a guage glass, as the height of the water is not then of any consequence. Indeed, such a boiler, while giving off it may be the considerable amount of heat remaining stored in the water after the withdrawal of the fire, requires absolutely no attention at all; and of this class is Lamm's "fireless" boiler. The boiler next to this in requiring little attention, or attention only at long intervals, is one that contains a very great quantity of water in proportion to its grate surface. It then takes, it may be, several hours to raise steam, and again a long time to lose pressure or water, and only requires feeding at lengthened intervals, for serious fluctuations of pressure or water level cannot with it rapidly occur. Of this class of boiler are most of the egg-end kind, which often contain 20 or 25 cub. ft. of water per foot of grate. Such boilers may and do explode from excess of pressure, or by breaking their backs, but never from mere lowness of water. After this a boiler requiring an ordinary amount of attention is one with a moderate quantity of water in proportion to its grate, as then considerable variations of pressure and water level may occur at not very distant intervals, as in Lancashire or marine boilers, which contain 12 or 15 cub. ft. of water per foot of grate. Again, a boiler requiring more than an ordinary amount of attention is one with a small quantity of water in proportion to its grate, as in most of the water-tube class, which contain only from 3 to 5 cub. ft. of water. With these may also be classed locomotive boilers which, although they have a water capacity of 5 to 7 cub. ft., and a much larger water area than water-tube boilers, have yet an intensity of combustion which more than outweighs these advantages. And lastly, the boiler of all others requiring the most watchful and careful attention is that in which there is very little water and a large grate, as in all fire-engine boilers which contain but little more than 1 cub. ft. of water per foot of grate. So that as regards the least amount of supervision required, we may class boilers thus :—

1. The Egg-end boiler.
2. The Lancashire boiler.
3. The Marine boiler.
4. The Portable boiler.
5. The Water-tube boiler.
6. The Vertical boiler.
7. The Locomotive boiler.
8. The Fire-engine boiler.

And the reason for this classification is more clearly and fully show in Table No. 2, which gives the water capacity, water area, and intensity of fuel combustion for each of the above.

TABLE No. II.

Kind of Boiler.	Water capacity, per foot of grate. Cubic feet.	Water Area, per foot of grate. Square feet.	Coal burned, per foot of grate. Per hour.
Egg-end, ...	15 to 25	6 to 10	6 to 18
Lancashire, ...	13 to 16	5 to 6	15 to 25
Marine, *circular*, ...	10 to 12	2 to 3	18 to 20
Portable, ...	5 to 6	5 to 6	10 to 20
Water Tube, ...	3 to 5	1 to 1·6	15 to 25
Vertical, ...	3 to 4	1·3 to 1·6	10 to 20
Locomotive, ...	5 to 6	3 to 3·5	50 to 70
Fire Engine, ...	1 to 1·3	·67 to ·77	5 to 8

From the point, then, of requiring least attention while working, the "fireless" boiler is of course decidedly pre-eminent, but from the very nature of it, its power must ever be of the most limited and irregular description; in fact, the action of such a boiler is precisely similar to that of a large spring, which although at first powerful, is yet ever decreasing in pressure as it uncoils. But with all ordinary steam boilers worked with fires, or as we may here call them, furnace boilers, the amount of attention they require for each cwt. of coal burned per foot of grate, varies inversely according to the amount of water they contain, and to the area of their water level. And it is the consideration of this fact which seems to point out somewhat of an improvement in the water-tube class of generator, as we see that at present it requires more attention than an ordinary Lancashire boiler, owing to its more rapid fluctuations of pressure and water level. The principle of subdivision carried out in these boilers is however evidently correct for heavy pressures, and what seems to be wanted is merely that this good principle shall not be carried to excess; but that these boilers may be arranged to have a greater water capacity and water area than at present, and thus overcome what for ordinary stationary work is somewhat of a drawback. And so, for such work amongst boilers having equal strength, and being equally economical, that one is most decidedly to be preferred which undergoes the slowest fluctuations of pressure and water level, as with any given class of firemen it will then be safer to work than the others. Some makers claim as an advantage that their boiler raises steam in half an hour, apparently never considering that therefore it will require a much more attentive fireman than one that takes two hours to raise steam, and which may even rival it in economy; for the power of quickly raising steam is no test whatever of small consumption of fuel.

(9.) It may thus be seen that an easy (and as will afterwards be shown in the case of a small generator, the only reliable) way of making a furnace boiler which can take care of itself for a considerable time, is simply to give it a great water capacity and water area. This water, in the most perfect and natural manner possible. acts the part of a heat accumulator, as during a long time it goes on storing up heat within itself, and but very slowly raising the pressure guage; and again during a lengthened period it gives off heat from its store, while yet only slowly reducing the pressure and water levels. Now, this invaluable action of water within a boiler is not carried to any great extent in ordinary locomotives, as there is in them no particular use for it, although on undulating lines it is well known to be of great importance that a boiler should contain a large amount of water. Now, locomotive boilers contain 5 cub. ft. of water, and 3 ft. of water area for each foot of grate, and never require attention oftener, nor indeed so often, as each ten minutes. It is evident, then, that if we give six times as much water capacity and water area, while still keeping the same size of grate, that then as far as safety goes we need only attend to the boiler once in sixty instead of ten minutes. For the given size of grate can only develope a certain amount of heat, and as the water is six times greater in one case than the other, it follows that this grate will take six times as long to raise it to a certain pressure; or again, that for a certain work the water level will take six times as long to fall as before. Now, the above conclusions are simply indisputable, and so we have thus a certain means of constructing a boiler which, as far as its safety is concerned, shall only require attention each forty or sixty minutes; and yet which during this time will give off the most variable amounts of power. Of course this principle, even would it answer any useful purpose, cannot be applied to large locomotive boilers; but for the production of the very few horse power required for a street car, it can be used with the very greatest ease and convenience.

The power required to propel a 44 seat car, including the weight of the propelling mechanism with this large quantity of water, will not on level lines exceed 10 I. HP., although more than this will be required to work heavy roads. Then small boilers and engines will give 10 horse power from each foot of grate, but we had better allow the grate of the car boiler to contain 1·5 ft., and with 30 cub. ft. of water and 18 ft. of water area (both 6 times the ordinary locomotive allowance), we get 45 cub. ft. as the water capacity, and 27 ft. as the area of water level. The furnace should be of considerable depth, not less than 2 ft. below fire-hole, so that before commencing a run it could be filled with fuel, and then left to sink down as it burns away. There must be a water grate to prevent clinkers, as the bars of this narrow deep furnace could not otherwise be cleaned, and as the steam car must work for 15 or 18 hours without ever stopping longer than say 10 minutes at a time. The fuel must be coke or stone coal, to prevent smoke; and as such hard fuel will not burn without a strong blast, a blowing fan must be used, as the ordinary funnel blast cannot be allowed in a street. This combination of a fan and hard fuel is also another reason for using a water grate, as otherwise the fire-bars would run together or burn out in a few hours.

(10.) This accumulator boiler will be worked as follows:—Before commencing a run the driver will pump his boiler full, and raise steam well up say to 130 lbs., fill up the furnace, and then with the greatest confidence allow the boiler to look after itself during the half hour or so required to run his journey, during which it may hold its own, but, from its small grate, will most probably and usually lose a little pressure during the run, so that at the terminus there will generally be only say 110 or 120 lbs. of steam. And it is impossible that the pressure of such a boiler can dangerously rise while running, as however intense the action of the 1 ½ feet of grate may be, yet it cannot supply heat both to drive the car and also to dangerously raise the temperature of the 45 cub. ft. of water surrounding it. So also is the boiler safe from danger arising from lowness of water while running, as suppose that not a single drop of water enters it during the journey, yet still the 27 ft. of water level area is so great, that the total evaporation required for the entire run will only bring it down 2 or 3 inches. For at 40 lbs. of water per I. HP. per hour, 3 inches of evaporation will give more than 20 horse power for half an hour, which is an outside allowance. It might, and of course would, be a matter of convenience to keep the feed pump always partly on while running, yet this is not of the slightest consequence as regards safety, for without any feeding whatever this accumulator boiler will steam a whole run, and even two whole runs, and yet still be as safe from lowness of water as any ordinary boiler. In short, provided that the driver only starts each run with his accumulator boiler full of pure town water, it is almost absolutely impossible that accident can occur from either excess of pressure or lowness of water, and, of course, the inspecting engineer should see that this simple precaution is most rigidly adhered to. And thus we can have the very great convenience of an always powerful furnace boiler, combined with a degree of safety which is practically equal to a fireless receiver. How to work accumulator boiler.

(11.) Now, at first sight it seems well to consider, that as it requires but very little power to propel a street car, and that as fire engines will give out a horse power for each cwt. of their weight, that therefore a small engine and boiler of this class is the very one best adapted for driving a car; yet this consideration is only of weight, *provided that there is a special fireman to attend to this small boiler*, and regulate its ever-changing pressure and water levels. Let any-one watch the boiler of a steam fire-engine at work, and he will allow that of all boilers this is the one requiring the most constant attention. The fire must never be thicker than a few inches, for at a moment's notice the stoker must be ready to bare the bars to check the pointer of the pressure guage, which, on the engine being suddenly stopped, will run round almost as fast as the seconds hand of a watch; or, again, it as rapidly falls back on any extra power being required. And in ordinary work it is usual to have two men for one fire engine, and this notwithstanding that it is for the time being a stationary engine. To put then a boiler of anything approaching to this class into a steam car, where it must of necessity be left almost to itself for, it may be, half an hour at a time, would be a reckless proceeding, and certain to lead to accident, as the pressure might dangerously rise, or the water through priming disappear at such a moment as the driver's whole attention was occupied in driving his car amongst a crowd of other vehicles. And the risk of exploding even a small boiler in a vehicle filled with passengers, and it may be in a crowded street, is certainly not a thing to trifle with; for it is not merely to one steam car, but to the use of hundreds and thousands of them, that we must look and provide for. And for this particular class of work, where only one man can be allowed to both attend to the boiler and also to the driving of the car, and whose whole attention while running must be devoted to the street, it is almost as much out of place to use a vertical boiler of merely ordinary proportions, as in Baxter's steam car, shown in Figure 3; for we see from Table No. 2 that the amount of attention it requires quite unfits it for such work. Such a boiler may, and indeed has, been safely run during a single trial, or even during 1000 trials, conducted under favourable circumstances, but for the ordinary day, and especially night, work of a street car, it is absolutely unfitted. Nor for such work can we seriously consider the application of any device for self-acting fuel and water feeds as in Grantham's steam car shown in Figure 5; such contrivances cannot be altogether depended on, even in the largest stationary boilers, and how much less then in a portable one of the smallest proportions. And if a great number of boiler explosions take place annually from the neglect of the stoker, in situations where he has only to do the one single thing of attending to a boiler which only very slowly fluctuates in pressure and water level, how shall a steam car possibly escape amid the throng of regular work, when these fluctuations take place very rapidly, and when there is no special stoker at all? Accumulator or fireless boilers only to be used.

Considering these things, then, there appears only two classes of steam boilers that should on any consideration whatever be allowed to work in steam cars where there is no special fireman, viz. either a "fireless" or an "accumulator" boiler. And so, almost literally speaking, instead of selecting the lightest, we must rather adopt the heaviest class of boilers for working street cars *having only one attendant*. With these boilers economy is only of secondary importance, as the cost of fuel will only form a small item amongst the various charges of working light street cars by steam power; nor, again, is the extra weight of these boilers of any consequence when compared with their great safety and peculiar fitness for their special work.

(12.) The No. 1 class of country tramways either may or may not be worked with "accumulator" boilers (the "fireless" being here out of place) accordingly as circumstances dictate. In cases where 2 or more cars are run by one locomotive over several miles, it will usually be advantageous, and even necessary, to employ a special fireman, with whom, of course, an ordinary locomotive boiler can be used. Ordinary boilers for certain work.

(13.) We have thus in the accumulator boiler described a convenient, safe, and cheap means of producing power by which street cars can be propelled; yet the mere ability to move How to drive a street locomotive.

along is far from being all that is required of a perfect street locomotive; for on a street railway, of all others, the driver requires perfect break-power, to almost instantaneously control his machine. In a street locomotive, then, of whatever class, the driver should sit right in front of his engine; then his left hand should rest on a conveniently-placed regulator handle, and on his right must be a well-notched reversing handle, as shown in figs. 10 and 11. Then to one side in front—say the left—should be a small frame, lighted at night, in which are the pressure guage and two glass guages, with cocks connected together in pairs, so as to be shut by a touch of the driver's hand, should a glass burst. As we have seen, neither the pressure nor water can dangerously vary while running, yet still the driver should always know how these stand. Then on the left should be the ordinary screw-break, controlling every wheel in the train—this to be used when running down inclines, or pulling up at ordinary stopping-places. And on the right should be a direct acting steam-break, connected with every wheel, with its handle arranged so as to be instantly applied. Yet even still we should be far from having the necessary command over the train; for, as has been mentioned, on the often extremely slippery state of street railroad inclines a car will often run along many yards, even with skidded wheels; and to remedy this, sand must be very liberally used with all locomotive work on such roads. On both the right and left of the driver's seat, then, sand-handles must be placed, both delivering to each side; and the driver will work his engine as follows: He occupies his seat, with his left hand he opens the regulator, and with his right adjusts the reversing handle; then, if the wheels slip, he (with his left hand still on the regulator) works his right sand-handle as long as required. Suppose, now, he must stop very quickly, to avoid a collision, or running over some one who has fallen; his left hand then involuntarily closes the regulator, and his right works the handle of the steam-break. Then, should the road be in bad order, or the danger imminent, he (with his right hand still on the steam-break) works the left sand-handle, and thus brings the train dead up in, it may easily be, only a few seconds, from the very slow speed at which all street railways must ever be worked, especially in crowded thoroughfares. There must also be brushes fixed in front to sweep each line of rails when necessary. For a street railway these brushes had better be arranged so that they will always bear on the rails, and also so that they can be raised out of action by the driver when not required, instead of being simply fixtures, as in ordinary locomotive work. And the working of these brushes and sand-gear will, on most roads, be an important part of the driver's duties, as want of adhesion is one great difficulty to overcome on most street lines. Now all this may seem a great deal for one man to quickly do; yet, judging from considerable experience in driving fast road-engines with somewhat similar arrangements, it will be found extremely easy in practice, and a driver will become quite expert at the work in less than a week's time. In addition to all this, there is, however, yet another thing that is necessary for safely working a street locomotive, and that is a guard-plate, extending right across the front of the engine round the leading wheels, and reaching to within $2\frac{1}{2}$ inches of the rails. For it may happen—and, indeed, in a street must be expected to happen—that persons will at times be found in front of the car; and as the speed of a street locomotive will never be great, and so will almost invariably be nearly stopped before running against a person who may have fallen, we may safely reckon that this guard will prevent bones being broken, or indeed much serious injury. Contrasting in this respect very favourably with the present horse cars, the wheels of which only too frequently either kill persons outright, or maim them for life, even when running at the slowest speeds; for it is not the speed with which a flanged wheel goes over a person that is of consequence, but rather the mere fact that it goes over at all.

Wheel gear for street locomotives.

We have thus considered the means of producing propelling power, and the general arrangement of driving and stopping gear, and now another most important consideration claims attention, viz., the arrangement of wheel gear necessary to enable a locomotive to certainly keep the rails of a street line, when the curves are sometimes less than 30 feet radius, and where the *inner* rail has a super-elevation that the ordinary convex contour of a street may be maintained, and also where the wheel flanges cannot exceed $\frac{1}{2}$ inch in depth. Now, with horse haulage, these points are not of consequence, as the animals always pull to the inner side on a curve, and, if a car does then leave the line, it is easily drawn on again; but when the propelling power is contained within the car itself, the case is then quite different, as the locomotive with, say, four rigid wheels, always tends to move in a straight line, and the very smallest provocation, in the shape of a little speed or dirt in the grooves, will at a curve send such an engine into the middle of the street; and, from its great weight and lack of lateral motion, probably 10 minutes would be the least time in which it could be again railed, as most likely a traversing jack would have to be used. And to be constantly obstructing the ordinary street traffic by the derailment of steam cars, and this especially at the crowded junctions of streets, would be an annoyance not to be tolerated. If, then, our street locomotive consists of a detached engine pulling a car, it may be affirmed that by far the safest and simplest arrangement of wheels will be a single pair of drivers and a leading 4-wheeled bogie, as the engine will then round the sharpest curves without any appreciable friction or grinding, and almost without any tendency to leave the line. Of course it is quite possible, with careful management, to work an engine with 4 rigid wheels round street curves; but such an engine would leave a street rail 10 times for each once of the bogie locomotive; and in winter, when the grooves are full of ice, or when they contain hard mud, the rigid wheeled engine would give endless annoyance from its slight flanges mounting the rails. In a self-contained steam car it is not easy to say what precise arrangement of wheel gear will perfectly meet the requirements of such a machine. For if four rigid wheels are out of place in a detached engine, where the wheel base need not exceed 4 or 5 feet, much more so are they in a combination of engine and carriage, which will be 25 or 30 feet long, and which cannot well be placed on a shorter base than, say, 7 feet. Indeed, such a carriage simply could not work at all on most street lines. Nor is it practicable on the curves of such roads to use 4 coupled wheels and a bogie; and so the only resource seems either to try and balance this long carriage on a pair of single drivers and a bogie, or at once to put it on two bogies. Of course, as in the case of the detached engine, it may be quite possible, with very careful management, to work a steam car on four rigid wheels round a street curve, yet the arrangement is evidently far from meeting the requirements of ordinary street work, especially when considering how small the flanges must be, and that the outer wheel generally runs on the flanges quite unconfined on a flat plate, so that all that keeps the engine on the rails are the ½-inch flanges of the two inner wheels, set at a considerable tangent to the rails.

(14.) It will thus be seen that, without deciding whether a street locomotive shall consist of a self-contained steam car, or of a locomotive pulling a car, or without committing ourselves to any design whatever, we have yet arrived at a considerable number of main features which all street railway engines must possess, and which, for Nos. 2 and 3 classes of traffic, may be recapitulated thus :— *Main features of a perfect street locomotive.*

1. The cars must run at very frequent intervals.
2. They must only have two attendants each.
3. They must be run by steam power.
4. Boiler to be of the " fireless," or " accumulator" class, if the latter, working pressure to be $\frac{1}{10}$ of bursting pressure.
5. Furnace to be deep, with water grate.
6. Fuel to be coke.
7. To have a blowing fan.
8. Exhaust to enter tank and then funnel.
9. Driver's seat to be right in front, with regulator, hand break, sand, glass guages, and pressure guage on the left ; and reversing, steam break, sand, pump, and brush handles on the right hand.
10. Guard round front of engine.
11. All working parts to be protected from sight, mud, and dirt.
12. Outside seats to have an awning, with which funnel head is flush.
13. Cylinder and glass guage cocks to blow off into ash pan, and safety valve into tank.
14. The wheel gear must be so arranged that the locomotive can, with perfect impunity, round 30 ft. flat curves at 5 miles an hour, with only ½ in. wheel flanges.

(15.) Having then obtained these data, let us now examine such mechanical motive-power cars as have yet been made, and test them with these given requirements. *Description of various cars.*

Fig. 1 shows Lamm's ammoniacal gas car, one of which was experimented with in New Orleans in 1871. The arrangement of this is clearly shown, and as we have already condemned ammonia we may let it pass. *Lamm's ammonia car.*

Fig. 2 shows Lamm's fireless locomotive and car, which was experimented with in New Orleans in 1872, and latterly in Chicago and New York, where it has received official permission to run in the outskirts of the city. The boiler contains 60 cub. ft. of water, and is worked thus :—On starting it is nearly filled with cold water, then a connection is made with the steam pipe of a large stationary boiler, working at 200 lbs., when steam rushes into the cold fireless boiler, and in a few minutes raises in it a pressure of about 180 lbs. The connection with the large boiler is then uncoupled, and the fireless locomotive is ready for work ; and it has been found in actual practice that the heat thus stored in this 60 cub. ft. of water, will propel the small engine and car 10 miles along a level, and yet leave 50 lbs. of pressure remaining in the boiler. But, of course, a hilly road vastly lessens the distance the car can run, for an incline of only ·5 per cent. equals the rolling resistance of a street railway, and thus doubles the total resistance ; and a grade of 1 per cent. consumes as much power in 3¼ miles, and a grade of 2 per cent. as much in 2 miles, and one of 4 per cent. as much in 1⅓ miles, as do the 10 miles of level line. Frequent stoppages also tell heavily against the limited power of the fireless locomotive, with which a considerable deduction of pressure per minute must also be made for loss by radiation, etc., from the time that the receiver is charged with heat. For the special purpose in view, however, the principle of the fireless locomotive is a good one, and although not strictly novel, the *modus operandi* having been fully explained in *The Engineer* in 1865, yet still to Dr Lamm belongs the credit of having clearly shown the advantages of a fireless locomotive for propelling street cars. The principle is, however, much better than the somewhat crude arrangement of detached engine and car by which it has as yet been carried into practice, where the driver merely stands on the ordinary car platform, and reaches over to the handles for working the engine. The exhaust is discharged directly into the air, where it forms a considerable cloud of white vapour, as from the boiler being fireless the steam is necessarily damp. An air surface condenser, of limited capacity, has been tried to prevent this, but does not help the matter much, as it is almost impracticable to make a locomotive with an air surface condenser of sufficient capacity to condense all its steam. For the cooling area would require to be so great as five or six times the heating surface, and there must also be powerful fans to drive air through this large condenser, and at the bottom of it a tank into which the condensed water can drain. Seeing, then, that an air surface condenser is, because of weight and bulkiness, inapplicable to an ordinary locomotive, how much less can it be allowed in a "fireless" engine, where the first consideration is that the dead weight shall be reduced to the lowest amount, to compensate for the very limited power of the engine. From this point of view, the fireless engine and car had better be combined in one machine, as then the weight of the engine truck and wheels will be saved, and thus the car will run a greater distance. The entire weight can then also be coupled for adhesion, and to gain sufficient adhesion is a difficult point to overcome in working street railways, as they are much steeper and more slippery than ordinary lines. However, the main idea of using a fireless boiler for street cars is good, and it can undoubtedly be carried into successful practice on level lines, if its constant escape of white vapour does not prove some slight objection to its use. But for most street railways it will, for many reasons, be preferable to use the ever constant and ample power of an accumulator furnace boiler ; as then the car will be more independent, and better able to meet the strain of temporarily increased traffic during certain hours of the day and certain days of the week. And in running a great number of rapidly succeeding cars, if one became *Lamm's fireless locomotive.*

disabled the succeeding car of an accumulator could easily drive this before it, and thus clear the line ; while, with the weak powered fireless engines, the lines would probably be blocked, and the longer the cars waited the less would their propelling power become. It is also possible, and very probable, that the great crowds of public holidays would quite disorganise a traffic carried on by fireless engines, as their power cannot be in any way increased against emergencies ; whereas the accumulator, by running its fan harder or slightly lessening its speed, can vastly increase the total power given out during a run. Then, again, if steam be used at all on tramways, it must be set to collect mud and brush the streets daily, and when required must also quickly clear about 25 ft. of the street centre of snow, all of which would be very imperfectly performed with the limited power of fireless engines. The accumulator car can also run an entire day without coming into the shop, whereas the fireless engine must, at every journey, be run into the shed for that supply of driving heat, which the accumulator boiler is, while at work, constantly receiving from the fuel in its small furnace, and storing for use when required, in precisely the same medium as used in the fireless engine, viz., a great mass of water.

Baxter's steam car.   Fig. 3 shows a steam car, designed by Baxter of Newark, U.S., and experimented with about a year ago in New York. The vertical boiler is 26 inches diameter, and 54 inches high, without any special means of abolishing the ordinary puffing blast or of maintaining the draught. Now, it may be here remarked, that the leading advantage of the ordinary funnel-blast in a locomotive is, that it at all times most perfectly regulates the intensity of the furnace according to the work that the engine is doing ; for whenever the maximum power is required the furnace becomes greatly urged, and thus the pressure does not fall, and when the demand for power is over, so again does the draught almost entirely cease, and thus the pressure will hardly rise at all while standing. And so, in any attempt either in this or other engines to use a locomotive boiler without an artificial blast, one of two results will take place : either the boiler (if of ordinary proportions) must fail to keep steam, or (if made so large as to keep steam with merely a natural draught) it will be impossible to properly regulate the steam pressure, or to keep it from unduly rising when the engine is suddenly stopped. And as this will happen even when a fireman is used, how much worse will the case become when there is no special stoker to incessantly manipulate the damper and fire-doors, as the starting and stopping of the engines may require. The inside cylinder engines are placed below the driving platform, and work on to the leading axle, which is cranked. It has the ordinary 30 inch chilled wheels placed 7 ft. centres, and they are not coupled. Now, on considering the remarks made in paragraphs 8, 11, 13, 14 about boilers, driving and break gear for street railway traffic, it will be seen how very far this design falls short of what is wanted, and how that it cannot be safely run with only a single attendant.

Perkin's road locomotive.   Fig. 4 shows an engine made by Perkins to draw street cars, and tried in London some time since. This engine has a single rubber driving wheel running on the stones between the rails, this being also the steering wheel of the engine. The boiler is of the water-tube class, and carries a very heavy pressure ; the engines have compound cylinders. Now why, after guide rails are already laid in a street, the designer of this engine should deliberately adopt all the risk of steering his engine by hand, is a mystery, the reason for which does not clearly appear. It may also be observed that although it is quite possible and indeed easy to steer an engine at high speed when drawing an ordinary omnibus, yet that to steer this same engine when drawing a car on rails is almost impossible, as but a very slight deviation from truly steering along the centre of the track will draw the car off the rails. Again, no rubber driving wheel will stand the 500 miles a week that any steam car must run. The way to get a high speed rubber driving-wheel to stand long is to make it very large in diameter, and with a great body of rubber, that the amount of kneading per hour suffered by each pound may not be too great ; and thus the driving-wheel of this engine (kept very small to save expense of rubber) would at 500 miles a week be destroyed in a very short time. Indeed, the heat arising from chewing and kneading the rubber below the tread of such a fast revolving wheel would so soften it that it would cease to be able to float up the weight of the engine, and so would squeeze out on all sides.

Grantham's steam car.   Fig. 5 shows a steam car, designed by Grantham, and tried in London a short time since. It has two boilers, 18 inches diameter and 52 inches high, each enclosed in a box in the centre of the car. The cylinders are outside, and work into a pair of the usual 30 inch drivers. The wheel base is 10 ft., and length over all 30 ft. There are self-acting fuel and water feeds for the boilers, which have no special means of avoiding the ordinary puffing blast or of urging the fire. Now, the remarks made in paragraphs 8 and 11 about the danger of such boilers apply strongly to this design, for to suppose that two 18 inch boilers shut up in boxes can safely take care of themselves for half-an-hour at a time (notwithstanding that they have self-acting fuel and water feeds) appears to be simply absurd. To avoid noise the nozzle is made large, and thus the blast is so soft as only to be fit for burning wood ; but the boilers are intended to burn coke to avoid smoke, and coke won't make steam without a heavy blast, but where this heavy blast is to come from with a wide nozzle or without noise in the funnel does not clearly appear. Nor, again, is the tramway yet laid in Britain on which a car can run with a rigid wheel base of 10 ft.

Merits of various cars.   (16.) These various cars all fall far short in either one or other point of being perfect according to the requirements of paragraph 14 ; indeed, to the writer, the only one of all possessing any merit or feature worth preserving is that of Lamn's fireless engine. Reference has not here been made to the elevated street railways at present at work in New York, Chicago, and elsewhere in the States, as they do not actually run amongst the ordinary street traffic. These elevated railways stand about 15 ft. high on a row of posts at the side of the street, quite free from dirt, the ordinary traffic, and even partly from inclines, and it is a very simple matter to work them by steam power. They are an extremely cheap and also a good plan of relieving an evercrowded street, provided their unsightliness be not objected to. Nor, again, has the Lisbon steam tramway been referred to, as although a kind of tramway, yet it certainly is not a *street* tramway, or applicable amongst city traffic ; nor yet still the various so-called steam tramways which have been for years at work in South America, and which are simply ordinary light railways worked with 4 coupled locomotives.

(17.) It is now proposed to give a general outline of the manner in which the main features given in paragraph 14 should be carried into practice in working the three classes of street railway traffic.

TODD'S tramway locomotive on Tramvia de Santander.

Fig. 6 shows a general arrangement for working No. 1 Country traffic, which should generally be done with a detached engine pulling two or more cars or a single, double-bogie car. Figs. 9, 10, 11, 12 13, show the engine enlarged, it being specially designed to comply with the various requirements of paragraph 14. If the route is of sufficient length, a special fireman will be employed, and then the boiler will be of the ordinary type as shown in the engravings, but if the route be short, an "accumulator" boiler will then be used as described in paragraph 9 and shown in figs. 15, 16, 17. The engine is 14 ft. 10 in. long over buffers, 6 ft. 6 in. wide over all, and 14 ft. 5 in. from rail to funnel head, this being equal to a car with outside awning. There are a single pair of 66 in. drivers, 5 ft. 3 in. from which is the bogie with 21 in. wheels placed 3 ft. centres. The driving wheels are without bearing springs, as their large diameter and the very slow speed permits them to roll along with the necessary smoothness, but the small bogie wheels have rubber springs, and thus every wheel takes its proper bearing on the rails. All wheels in the train have solid discs, as these look better in a street and also raise less dust than spoked wheels. The G. S. is 3·5 ft., and H. S. 160 ft. The cylinders are 6½ in. × 9 in., and the crank makes 150 revolutions at 10 miles. The tooth gear consists of a single wheel and pinion, confined in a case, made of steel, and thickly covered with tallow and blacklead. Experience having shown that under such circumstances a single gear will not make any clatter that can be heard above the usual rolling noise of the various carrying wheels of the train. The exhaust drives a 12 in. blowing fan discharging into a close ash-pan, so that the varying intensity of a locomotive draught is thus as perfectly regulated as with the ordinary funnel-blast; for the principle and source of action, viz., the perfect variation of the back-pressure according to the power that the locomotive is at the time exerting, is of course the same in both the exhaust funnel-blast and in the exhaust fan-blast. The exhaust then enters the tank, where part is condensed and all water deposited, the remainder escaping gently through a wide pipe into the funnel where, being small in quantity and free from water, it becomes superheated and passes off noiselessly in an invisible form. The fuel is coke. The two safety valves blow off into the tank, and the cylinder cocks and guages into the ash-pan. The driver's seat and the entire arrangement of gear on the driving platform are placed and worked as described in paragraph 13. The cars are coupled to the locomotive and to each other by rigid draw bars with hardened eyes centered near the axles, which, amongst other advantages, allows the continuous break gear to be of a very simple kind, it being merely a rod passing below the cars, and connected to the steam gear of the engine, which, when it is applied thus, breaks every wheel in the train except those of the engine bogie, and, when out of action, the blocks leave the wheels by means of the usual release springs. Each cross break bar of the cars and each break rod is fitted with rubber springs to equalise the pressure on each block, and to allow the bearing springs some play when the breaks are hard up.

We have thus described an engine designed to fulfil all the various requirements of an efficient street locomotive. It has ample pulling and stopping powers; it can round any street curve; its working parts are unseen, yet quite accessible, and free from mud and dust; it is practically noiseless, smokeless and steamless, and free from glare of fire by night; it can be safely worked by a single attendant; it is not complicated, and is of sightly appearance.

Main features of the "Santander."

(18.)—Fig. 7 shows a design for a self contained steam car with accumulator boiler, shown enlarged in fig. 14, which is in every way proportioned as described in paragraph 9, the water area of 9 ft. being equal to the 27 ft. there mentioned, as an upright has 3 times the vertical rise and fall of a horizontal boiler. It runs on 6 coupled 30 in. chilled wheels with a 7 ft. base, but there are only few street lines that have curves suited for such an engine. Fig. 8 shows a design for an accumulator steam car with double steam bogies for working a street line of 7 per cent grades, but although quite possible to construct such a machine, yet the wear and tear of such a number of small working parts would be very great, as, from their position, they could not be kept free from dirt; and when we carefully consider the various requirements of actually working a street railway by steam power, it seems to be far preferable whenever possible, to use detached engines to pull ordinary cars rather than to attempt the combination of engine, boiler, and passenger carriage into one machine. As in a case where say 50 or 60 cars have to be under steam and on the street daily, it will be at once seen how much easier it will be to repair, clean, and keep in order their boilers and engine motions when these are separate, as the locomotives can then be run into a separate repairing shop, so that the fittings, trimmings, and painting of the passenger carriage are kept clear from the smoke and dirt of the repair shop and also from the lighting up and running shed. With a detached engine also the passenger car is kept perfectly clear from any smell of hot oil or tremour of machinery, and again if any slight escape of steam takes place or accident occurs to the engine the passengers are not needlessly alarmed, as practice has already proved them to be with a self-contained machine. And again there is a strong feeling on this point on the part of the general public, as 99 out of every 100 travellers would prefer to travel in a separate passenger carriage rather than to enter one where part of them would actually sit on top of, and others lean their backs against the boiler. And however successful self-contained steam cars may be from a mechanical point of view, it is doubtful whether such machines will ever become popular favourites. In reference to this some have remarked, that as passengers are not all afraid to go on board a steamer which has a boiler below the deck, that therefore they will not object to the steam cars; but it must be remembered that in the steamer there are a number of skilled men to constantly attend to the boiler and gear; while the leading idea among the present designers of steam cars seems simply to be to stow away one or more boilers out of sight within the car and then leave them and the passengers to take care of themselves.

Remarks about self-contained cars.

It may be mentioned that Figs. Nos. 7, and 8, refer only to schemes, but that all the other engines shown are from actual practice.

(19.) Both the engines just described run always with the same end foremost and must thus be reversed at the end of each journey, if they do not run on a circular rout. This can readily be done by a loop round a block of buildings, monument, or other object; failing which, two quarter circle reverse curves can always be laid into a side street. This necessary turning of the cars is of advantage in causing the chilled wheels to wear equally and thus last longer; as the sharp curves, grooves full of mud, and abrupt crossings of street railways, tell seriously against either one or other of the flanges when not reversed. The line should have shifting points moved by the foot.

**On what lines
to first start
steam power.**

(20.) Three classes of street railway traffic were referred to in paragraph 6, viz., Country, Suburban, and City. On Country lines, it is, or should not be a very difficult matter to work satisfactorily with steam power, as the ordinary traffic is light and the amount of opposition will on such lines be small; with Suburban lines however the case will be more difficult; and with City lines will come the tug of war to overcome prejudice and opposition. Seeing then that this is the case, it may be very enterprising and bold to make a first start with steam power on a purely city line, and to endeavour to cram our untried steam cars down the throats of opposing vestrymen and others, yet certainly it is not a very wise thing to do. Most obviously the best way to commence is on country lines to start some steam trains consisting of separate engines pulling ordinary cars. This is a far easier and safer thing to do than to at once enter into all the difficulties and dangers of combining boiler, engines, and passenger car into one complicated machine, which probably would not suit the public taste when made, for at the present moment almost every railway in existence is worked with locomotives detached and separate from the passenger carriage. Succeeding in this let us then advance to the more difficult suburban traffic, and finally when some lengthened experience of running on street lines is gained let us only then approach the intricate city work, and only then consider whether it appears advisable to attempt the use of self-contained steam cars. For at the present moment there is simply no one at all who has any practical experience of working street railways by steam power, and it is such actual experience of continuous daily work that we now want to assist us in solving the problem, and not merely a great variety of mere scheming.

(21.) The locomotive "Santander," shown in Figs. 7, 9, 10, 11, 12, 13, has been especially designed and constructed to run on the Tramvia de Santander, where the arrangement for the line is such that the locomotive does not require to be uncoupled from the cars at the end of each run, or even during an entire day. While thus carefully fulfilling all the requirements of paragraph 14, it must yet be recollected that it has been specially designed for a certain road, and so may not be a universally or even generally suitable arrangement of engine for other street lines. And as a type of engine more suitable for most ordinary street work than is this "Santander," we will now describe the "New Pony" locomotive shown in Figs. 18, 19, 20, 21, and which equally with the "Santander" thoroughly fulfils all the various requirements of paragraph 14.

(22.) A sectional elevation of the "New Pony" is shown in Fig. 20. It runs on 4 coupled chilled wheels 33 inches diameter, the wheel base shown is 4 feet, but this must be arranged to suit the guage, curves, and speed of any special road. Recollecting the remarks made in paragraph 17, about the difficulty of keeping an engine on the rails of sharp street curves, it will be seen that the base must be as short as possible, in fact, instead of making an engine with a single pair of drivers and a leading logic, we in the "New Pony" virtually use the bogie only, so as to retain full facility of rounding the sharpest curves. But as the centre of gravity in this engine is rather high, the wheel base must not be made too short or the engine will pitch considerably if run fast, or in passing crossings; or again will be inclined to dip heavily in front if suddenly breaked when running fast. There is the usual outside cylinder motion with outside valve gear; all bearings are without exception made with large hardened steel bushes, which can be readily replaced, as they will quickly be worn by the flying dust, from which it will be impossible to perfectly protect them. However, the working motion is as far as possible boxed up from dirt and sight, and there are two doors on each side of the engine, shown in Figs. 18 and 21, through which all the parts are perfectly accessible.

(23.) The boiler is of the accumulator class, 42 ins. dia. × 84 ins. high, proportioned and worked precisely as described in paragraphs 9 and 10. The G. S. shown is 2, and the H.S. 100 square feet, but these must be proportioned to suit circumstances. On referring to these foregoing paragraphs, it will be seen in what way, and for what reason this accumulator boiler can, with perfect safety, be left to itself for, it may be half an hour at a time. The simple fact being that the water capacity is so large in proportion to the grate, that the pressure cannot possibly dangerously rise while the engine is running, nor even rise at all, except very slowly; and again that the water capacity *above* the low water level is equal to the entire evaporation of half an hour, or even an hour's full work. The fire also does not require attention while running, as the deep narrow furnace is merely filled with coke at starting, and is then like a small cupola left to sink down during the half hour's run. And so, provided the driver merely fills his boiler with water and his furnace with coke before starting, he may then with perfect confidence leave it to itself during the run, as the factor of safety is most abundantly great. There are two feed-pumps which the driver will, of course, always keep partly on while running, so as to keep the water level constant, as it would cause a great loss of time to regularly allow the water to run down, and only to pump at the end of each journey, yet, as has been shown, it is in no way essential to safety that even a single drop of water should be pumped into the boiler during the journey. For the production of merely a small power, and where only intermittent attention can be given, this accumulator is essentially and truly a "safety" boiler; indeed it is the only furnace boiler yet designed which can safely be put into a steam car or street locomotive which has *only one attendant*. The accumulator principle is obviously, of course, inapplicable to large boilers, or to the production of great powers, but for the very limited power required for a street car all its parts can readily be kept within ordinary and safe dimensions, and thicknesses of plates.

(24). The "New Pony" is double ended with duplicate driving platforms and gear, the driver's seat, regulator, reversing steam and hand breaks, brush, pump, and sand handles, being arranged precisely as described in paragraph 13. The boiler has double fireholes, and at one side there is a double-ended 4 cwt. coke box, so that it can be stoked from either end of the engine ; while on the other side there is a 100 gallon water tank.

(25). As previously remarked, efficient break gear is of extreme consequence in working all street locomotives ; and in the " New Pony " the *entire* weight of the train is steam breaked. On each driving platform there is the usual screw hand break to control the speed when running down inclines or pulling up at the usual stopping places. Each platform has also a steam break gear, which, as shown, controls the 4 engine wheels, and also by a draw rod directly actuates the ordinary car breaks, which simple arrangement of continuous break gear is rendered possible by the use of the rigid draw rod. Each of the 4 cross break bars is fitted with rubber springs to equalise the strain on all the blocks, and also to allow the bearing springs some play when the breaks are hard up. The car breaks can also be applied by hand from either platform. Thus the entire weight is breaked, and so, by working the engine as described in paragraph 13, it may at any time be brought dead up in merely a few seconds. **Break Gears.**

(26). The engine has a simple wooden buffer beam at each end. Under the ordinary car had better be placed 2 beams about 4 in. square and 30 in. apart, which also carry rigid buffers extending beyond the car platforms or ladders. Spring buffers are here of no use as through the rigid draw bars they never touch while running, and their only use is during shunting, &c. These car beams also carry the draw gear, which consists of strong joints and pins centered near the axles, so as to allow the ends of the car to play up and down as it runs at speed on its narrow wheel base, and also to allow proper swivelling action on curves. There is a rigid drawbar, and also a break rod at each end of the car, the extremities of which extend beyond the buffers, as shown in figs. 18 and 19. These 4 rods always remain coupled to the car, and thus either end of the engine can be coupled to either end of the car in less time than the ordinary horses can be attached. All the eyes and pins of both these break and draw gears are hardened, as they will always be covered with dust. **Buffer and Draw Gears.**

(27). The next point demanding attention in the " New Pony " is the means of keeping steam in almost perfect silence, and yet at all times to have the pressure as perfectly regulated as in a locomotive with the ordinary blast pipe. **How to keep Steam in silence.**

Now the great objection to ordinary locomotives when running in streets is the noise of the puffing blast, which startles horses, and also throws cinders from the funnel-head ; it also requires an open ash-pan, from which a fitful glare of fire is at night projected on the road, a sight which but few horses will approach without dread. The ordinary blast in the funnel has, however, one exceedingly great practical advantage and convenience, in that it at all times most perfectly regulates the intensity of the draught to the ever-varying amount of power that a locomotive gives out. If the engine be going up an incline, the blast becomes very strong, and there is plenty of steam ; again, when descending, the blast is soft, and raises no excess of pressure ; so that, either in running heavily up or lightly down a gradient, the pressure-guage hardly varies. This one advantage is of such very great convenience and utility, that engineers do not like to part with it ; they therefore universally adhere to the contracted exhaust in the funnel ; and in special cases merely try to lessen the noise by making the steam issue through a number of small holes instead of one large one, or through a narrow annular opening ; or they use an adjustable nozzle, or some other device. But with all these schemes, one main fact must not be lost sight of, viz., that the gases *must* issue from the funnel at a certain velocity or the boiler will not keep steam ; and that to maintain this velocity the exhaust *must* be projected into the funnel at a certain great speed. Now, the noise that the exhaust makes depends wholly and entirely upon the speed with which it issues from the blast-nozzle. It is extremely easy to avoid noise, either by making the blast opening sufficiently large, or by making the rate of exit sufficiently slow ; but then of course the velocity of the draught is not maintained, and there is in a locomotive literally no choice between the two evils—either that the exhaust must issue, through whatever kind of opening, at a certain great speed, thereby making noise but keeping steam ; or that, if the noise is reduced, which means that the exhaust has a large opening, then the boiler is spoilt for making steam. **Objections to ordinary locomotives in streets.** **Advantage of ordinary blast.**

Others have entertained the idea, that if the exhaust could be made to issue in a constant stream, instead of separate blasts, that it would then frighten horses less. But this hope has not been realised in practice ; and even were it possible to attain this constant stream, yet still the other objections to a funnel exhaust-blast for a street locomotive remain unremoved. And to show of what small avail this constant stream is in lessening the alarm of horses, it need only be mentioned that an ordinary small jet cock in the funnel frightens horses so much, that it must always be shut off when they are passing, even although the locomotive be standing. The plan has also been tried of fitting road locomotives (having an ordinary proportion of boiler) with an air or other condenser, into which the exhaust can be turned for a short time while passing horses ; but what is wanted in a street is constant, and not intermittent silence. Further, an engine fitted with such a condenser has to depend entirely upon the ordinary blast-pipe for its power of making steam ; and as the exhaust is not constantly in the funnel, it follows that when at work the blast-pipe must do during a certain time work that should have been spread over a longer period. To enable it to do this, the nozzle must be more contracted than usual ; and, so, for the advantage of being silent at certain short times, such an engine pays the penalty of making more noise than ordinary on other longer occasions—a result most out of place in a street. A moment's reflection will also show that a similar and better result than this can be readily attained by merely using an adjustable nozzle, fitted with a hand-lever, so that it can be quickly opened and shut. **Devices to obtain silent blast.**

Again, the plan has been tried of making a vertical locomotive boiler so large in proportion to the amount of power required, that it will fairly be able to make steam without any artificial blast at all, when of course the exhaust can readily be silently disposed of either by partial condensation, and a wide nozzle or otherwise ; indeed, the leading idea of the designer of such an engine seems to be to proportion all the parts of his locomotive after the marine model. But although it is possible thus to run in silence, it will be at once seen how that it is impracticable by this means to even approximately regulate the intensity of combustion, and consequently the steam pressure, according to the ever-varying requirements of a locomotive. A marine engine works against a constant resistance, it may be for weeks together, so that the boiler power required is always constant, and during the very rare occasions when the engine is suddenly stopped, the production of steam can be readily checked by opening the fire and smoke-box doors. But if such a class of boiler is put into a locomotive, how shall the pressure possibly be regulated; for when great power is required on an incline, steam will fall through want of a blast; and again, when running down with breaks on and without steam, this misplaced boiler will go on steaming just as fast as before, which steam can only be disposed of by being blown to waste. Even were there a special fireman to incessantly manipulate the fire and ash-pan doors of such a boiler, still it would be most unsuitable for a locomotive, as the pressure will continuously either be all up or all down, and thus cause no end of annoyance in a street, where of all places annoyance from a locomotive is not wanted. But it has been shown in paragraphs 7 and 8 that only one attendant can be allowed to work a street locomotive, and thus this marine-proportioned boiler must be left to regulate itself for half-an-hour at a time, and how much worse and how much more insufferable than the above will its annoyance then become.

Fans for Locomotives. The only other method of keeping steam in a locomotive, is a blower discharging into a close ash-pan. What, however, has kept fans from coming into use in road locomotives is the old difficulty, viz.:—that with them steam cannot possibly be maintained at anything like a uniform pressure. If driven by a belt from the engine, when going slowly up an incline and steam is wanted, then the fan also goes slowly, and the pressure falls. Or again, when running down at a great speed, and using but little steam, the fan then runs extremely fast, and raises far too much steam, which must be blown off at the safety valve, to startle all horses within hearing. Even should the fan be driven by a donkey engine, as in the dummy engines in the New York main lines, yet still the case is not made much better, as when running the pressure is generally either too high or too low, and the donkey also requires incessantly regulating. In several American road locomotives, and also on the New York Greenwich Street elevated railroad, an induced current steam blower discharging (through 9 holes 1-32 inch in diameter) into the ash-pan is used, but still the intensity of the draught is not self-variable, and the cock for the blower requires constant manipulation by a *special fireman* to maintain a tolerably constant boiler pressure.

Efficiency of exhaust-driven fan. Now, all these contrivances are more or less unsatisfactory. What is wanted, and what any engine intended to work regular passenger traffic in crowded streets *must* have, is some contrivance by means of which it can at all times run in perfect silence, and yet constantly maintain as uniform a pressure as the ordinary puffing blast pipe, so that it may go quietly up an incline, and yet have plenty of steam; or again, run fast down a gradient without accumulating an excess of pressure, and this great desideratum we most perfectly obtain as follows (see figs. 10, 11, 12, 13):—On the axis of a silent fan discharging into a close ash-pan, there is fitted a turbine or bucket wheel; then the usual blast nozzle is taken out of the funnel, and caused to discharge the exhaust steam against this turbine wheel, so as rapidly to rotate the fan. The exhaust is then turned into the water tank, where part is condensed, and all water deposited, the remaining small amount of steam escaping gently through a wide pipe into the funnel, where, being small in quantity, and free from water, it is superheated, and passes off noiselessly in an invisible form. From this arrangement it will be seen that the speed of the fan, and consequently the draught, will be as perfectly regulated as if the blast were in the funnel in the usual manner, for a moment's reflection will show that the two actions depend for their success on precisely the same principle, viz., that in any locomotive, the back pressure of the exhaust varies directly according to the power that the engine is giving out. With the ordinary funnel blast the draught through the boiler is created by *suction*, while with the exhaust-driven fan it is urged by *pressure*. With the latter, whenever the engine starts, the fan starts; if it stops, the fan stops; when going up an incline, the back pressure increases, and the fan runs fast; when going down, it falls away, and the speed of the fan becomes in the most perfect measure reduced. It is thus seen that, as far as relates to their capability of regulating the intensity of a locomotive fire, that the blast pipe and the exhaust-driven fan stand on precisely the same footing; with the blast pipe, however, the exhaust must of necessity be projected rapidly and violently into the atmosphere, while with the steam fan it can, after urging the draught, be still retained in a pipe, and so can be condensed or otherwise noiselessly disposed of.

Economy of exhaust-driven fan. The whole of this apparatus is extremely simple, and is in every way as self-acting as a common blast pipe. The power consumed with it is also not appreciably greater than that lost in the usual back pressure of a locomotive, for a fan is a much more efficient means of forcing air than that of inducing a current by intermittent jets of steam. The fan also saves a considerable amount of fuel which the ordinary suction draught draws through the tubes and sends out of the funnel; it also maintains a constant plenum, instead of the ordinary partial vacuum in a locomotive furnace, which is very favourable to combustion, and which also causes a pressure of heat to impinge against *every part* of the furnace and tubes, whereas the suction draught rapidly draws away the heat which at best it only allows to bear against the upper part of the tubes. However, the ability of by this means making a steam locomotive suitable for street traffic, and not economy of fuel, is the point urged in favour of this contrivance.

Steam raised in silence. A half-inch steam pipe is also fitted to the bucket wheel (as shown in fig. 10), so that the fan can be run when the engine is standing, and steam be raised in perfect silence, and thus the ordinary hissing jet cock in the funnel is not required.

Blast Suppressor. **(28.) This arrangement of exhaust-driven fan we call our "Blast Suppressor," and by it alone, and by no other contrivance, either yet made or proposed, is it possible to continuously work in silence a steam-driven locomotive without greatly impairing its efficiency.**

(29.) It is essential that the exhaust-driven fan be placed in such a position that it can drain into the tank, so that the turbine chamber may not become choked by any priming or condensed water. In the "Santander" it is placed midway between the cylinders and water tank, so that any water naturally drains from the cylinders to the fan, and again from the fan to the tank, while the air pipe is led downwards to the close ash-pan. In the "New Pony" the fan is placed at the side of the boiler, on top of the tank, into which the exhaust enters, and is partly condensed, and then escapes by a wide pipe into the funnel; and the air pipe descends as before into the close ash-pan.

(30.) We have thus described an engine thoroughly well adapted for working ordinary street railways of moderate gradients. It perfectly fulfils all the requirements of paragraph 14, and its leading features may be summed up thus :—

It has ample pulling and stopping powers; it runs in either direction; it can round *Leading features* **any street curve; its working parts are unseen, yet quite accessible, and tolerably free** *of "New Pony."* **from mud and dust; it is practically noiseless, smokeless, and steamless, and free from glare of fire by night; it can be worked with the greatest safety by merely a single attendant; the entire weight of both engine and car is steam breaked; it is not complicated, and is of sightly appearance.**

(31.) LEONARD J. TODD'S PATENTS,
CONNECTED WITH TRAMWAY LOCOMOTIVES.

No. 1.—" Improvements in Steam Carriages, and in Boilers and Elastic wheels for the " same, and applicable otherwise."—*Dated 27th April* 1871."

No. 2.—" Improvements in and connected with Steam Tramway and other Loco- " motives."—*Dated 17th April* 1873.

No. 3.—" Improvements in Tramway Locomotives, and in Boilers for the same."— *Dated 17th January* 1874.

No. 4.—" Improvements in Tramway Locomotives, and in Cars for the same."—*Dated 1st May* 1874.

The Last Word

Phenol

Although this is a volume full of serious, if often exciting, material I really cannot resist the following which is culled from the august pages of nothing less than the *BET Gazette* 15 February 1905 p38. It was particularly apposite during 2009 when the outbreak of 'Spanish', 'Mexican' or 'Swine' 'flu was at its height.

PHENOL MIXTURE

The Potteries Company employees have recently been suffering from and epidemic of sickness, the most prevalent complaint being influenza. Hearing that the North Staffs. Railway and also the North-Western Railway Companies kept supplies of 'Phenol Mixture' at their various depots, and allowed the men to have their doses free, Mr Walklate, the General Manager, laid in a supply of this remedy, which is reputed to be a certain cure for influenza, and is, moreover, extremely cheap. Notices were then issued to the effect that the men could obtain free doses of the mixture by applying to the Chief Inspector. The following is a copy of the notice issued:

The Potteries Electric Traction
Company Ltd.

NOTICE

INFLUENZA-PHENOL MIXTURE

A Sure and Certain Preventative AND CURE FOR
INFLUENZA

DOSE:- For Adults two tablespoons three times
in 24 hours. One dose will be enough to
prevent; three doses enough to cure.

The dose to prevent should not be taken till the
symptoms of Influenza (cold, chill, pains &c.)
show themselves; then one dose will stop it in less than
half-an-hour.

The Company have provided a supply of Phenol
Mixture at each depot so that the men who are
affected with Inflenza Colds can have a few doses
free on applying to the Chief Inspector at his depot.
BY ORDER

General Manager's Office
Stoke-on-Trent February 2nd.,1905

The cost of the mixture is 1s. a gallon, and with bottles and medicine glasses included, the whole expenditure for three gallons does not exceed 5s. or 6s. It is considered that even if the mixture minimises the sickness in the Potteries in only a minor degree, the investment will be justified.

[PHENOL is a combined bacteriacide and germicide only used now as a mouthwash (other than domestically, including the sailor's friend, Jeyes Fluid.) Chemists now would not make the mixture, and as used by the tramway company it must have been heavily diluted as in strength it can kill ALL bacteria – good or bad]

DUDLEY HERALD

22 August 1885

Sedgley, Staffs. To be let.

COTWALL END House and Farm very accessible from Dudley, Wolverhampton, and Tipton, within five minutes of the tram from those towns. 3 rec. 6 bed etc 2 cottages, 70 acres etc.
(Where the jollies were held)

One effect of the war, judging by the condition of the letter-box at TRUTH office, is to increase, to an alarming degree, the weekly output of poetry. If I were a large dealer in this commodity, I could offer the public page after page of it every week; but, unfortunately, I am not. I have picked the following lines, however, out of the last week's arrivals, because they may come home to the hearts of many Londoners, male and female. I hope, too, that they may catch the eye of some sympathetic official at the War Office, and lead to a little more circumspection in the shipping of forage to the Cape. The gallant beasts who have been called from civil life to lay down their lives in the service of their native land ought not to be fed up for slaughter on musty hay :—

THE 'BUS HORSE AT THE FRONT.

Good-by to the pole, and adieu to the trace,
And the man with the painfully rubicund face!
Long enough of the 'bus have I suffered the brunt,
And at last—chuck 'er up—I am off to the front.

In that over-sea land there can never appear
The arm of the " bobby " to check my career,
Nor a hand on a cord to awaken a hell
With the twang of that most diabolical bell.

From the " dozen inside " and the " fourteen without,"
You may guess that my frame is sufficiently stout
To carry a trooper as fat as an ox,
Though he towers a couple of yards in his socks.

They have called me away from the wormwood and gall
Of the hill that is crowned with the shrine of St. Paul,
On account of a gent of that name—but he ain't,
From what I can gather, exactly a saint.

Do you think that I fear to encounter the yell
Of the demon in shrapnel or shriek of the shell ?
Be it mine to collapse, as a quadruped should,
On the field of the fray—not on pavements of wood !

From *"Truth"* magazine, November 1899.

The True Soldier

"We follow only honour's way; be brave, be loyal, be comradely; obey your officers; respect yourselves and your weapons and all other good soldiers; be true to your own company and do not betray your own people by word or deed."

"Meeting and parting are constant in this inconstant world
Where joy and sadness alternate like night and day.
Officials come and go, but justice and righteousness remain
And unchangeable remains forever the Imperial Way."

The top one was from Napoleonic days, the second from the IJAAF soldier's passbook.

Samuel Johnson, 1709-1784, *The Idler*
He that reads and grows no wiser seldom suspects his own deficiency, but complains of hard words and obscure sentences, and asks why books are written which cannot be understood.

Når nøden er størst, er hjelpen næmest
A rough translation is: when the need is greatest, help is at its closest.

SUNDAY CLOSING.

THE Sunday closing of houses for the sale of intoxicating liquors is likely soon to become an accomplished fact, notwithstanding the opposition of the Dudley Town Council, who, in this matter, cannot represent more than a very small minority of their constituents. We believe the majority of publicans themselves would welcome Sunday closing, if made compulsory on all, but for the fear that it may be followed by a demand for the closing of their houses during the remaining six days. It would perhaps have been better if the two questions could have been kept separate; but there is no doubt that a very strong current of public opinion has, during the last few years, set in against the retail sale of intoxicating liquors as at present conducted. The increasing dislike of large numbers of persons to enter, or even to be seen to enter, a public-house has led to the establishment, during the last fifteen years, of an enormous number of dining rooms, coffee shops, and similar places, which now take from the publican the legitimate and unobjectionable part of his business. These, in common with all other traders, close on Sundays. The question is very naturally asked—why should an exception be made in favour of a trade which is generally charged with causing, through the frailty of mankind, a very large proportion of the crime and pauperism which is a reproach to the country? If all others must close their business places on Sunday when no harm results from the sale of their goods, still more requisite is it that those who deal in intoxicating liquors should not carry on their trade on the day of rest.

The reasons given by the Association for Stopping the Sale of Intoxicating Liquors on Sunday are conclusive. The evils of Sunday drinking are well known, and are admittedly such as to call for legislative interference. Public feeling, as shown by a canvass of householders in 400 parishes in England is nearly 9 to 1 in favour of compulsory closing on Sundays. Many of those who frequent public-houses on Sundays, when they have their wages in their pockets and time to spend them unprofitably, would prefer that the temptation should be removed; and it would be a great relief to every publican to have his house for domestic comfort on one day in the week if he were assured that no unfair advantage could be taken by a competitor on that day. Scotland has had this reform for 28 years with decidedly beneficial results, and in nine-tenths of Ireland public-houses have been thus closed since 1878, with a diminution of Sunday drunkenness of sixty-one per cent.

Weekly Mercury, 5 November 1904

"LIKE A RABBIT WARREN

'The Bench thought it was more like a rabbit warren than a civilized home'. This was what the Chairman of the Willenhall Bench told Henry Proffitt, recently of the Turk's Head Yard, who was summoned in connection with the existence of a nuisance caused by overcrowding. There were two small bedrooms in the house, one of which had been occupied by the defendant, a woman, and a little girl, and the other by eight children, ranging from 6 to 15 years of age. Defendant was fined 20s. and costs, and an order made to prevent a continuance of the nuisance."

Situation des chemin der fer 1868

Although slightly before our time this notice shows how far we were in advance of the Continent in railway mileage. Where now are our high speed lines compared with Europe?

ÉTATS.	LONGUEUR EXPLOITÉE.	LONGUEURS	
		Par myriamètres carrés.	Par millions d'habitants.
	kilomètres.	k.	k.
Grande-Bretagne..........	22 228	7,11	747,87
Angleterre proprement dite..	»	10,33	»
Belgique.................	2432	8,23	492,26
Suisse...................	1331	3,27	530,17
Allemagne du centre........	6252	3,60	459,36
France...................	14506	2,71	383,68
Prusse...................	8688	2,47	368,27
Pays-Bas.................	1141	3,23	305,43
Suède et Norvége.........	2036	0,25	350,09
Espagne.................	5111	1,03	324,45
Danemark................	478	1,25	297,25
Italie...................	5030	1,70	201,50
Autriche.................	6147	0,99	188,71
Portugal.................	694	0,73	174,03

St Helens Typhoid

SATURDAY, DECEMBER 8, 1888.

A DEATH PANIC.—The state of the public mind in St. Helens to-day is one which may, without exaggeration, be described as one of panic. The ravages of Typhoid in our midst—striking off victims in the higher grades of society—the death of Mr. Councillor John Lowe, of Elton Head Farm, who was among the healthiest and strongest of leading local men; the equaly-sudden death on Thursday morning, a few hours later, of ex-Councillor Mr. William Longton, of the Grange, and the prostration of Mr. Thomas Walker, chemical manufacturer; Mr. J. O. Swift, solicitor; Mr. Cook, iron founder, and Mr. Ernest Baxter, copper smelter and alkali manufacturer, all of whom were guests at the late Mayoral banquet on the 5th of November, with several others present on that occasion, who have since suffered from indisposition, may well challenge the sympathies and serious thoughts of our prominent men as well as the inhabitants generally. Since this outbreak of typhoid fever, the chairman of the Health Committee, the surveyor, and others of our municipal officials, have been most assiduous in taking preventative measures, as well to avert the spread, as to stamp out the insiduous disease. Disinfectants have been very freely applied to the sewers, and as freely supplied to the public, gratis, and the managers and teachers of our public schools have been urged to a plentiful use of the usual disinfectants. The flushing machine has been set to work; in a word nothing is being spared to cope with the danger, and to protect the health and lives of the people. But whatever the officials of the town may do or wish to do, the people themselves, each in their own house, can best secure their own safety, by a judicious and free use of disinfectants in every part of their habitation, from cellar to attic, and especially by a very bountiful use of water, frequently flushing their slopstones and gullies, and drains, and in larger houses their water closets. Self-help is best help! Cleanliness kills disease !!

John Bull

Since there was some doubt what future existed for "John Bull", the Sydney trial Beyer Peacock engine, throughout the series we have tried to get a definitive answer from the management at Crich, which varied between 'we are an electric tramway museum' to 'it is being mothballed'. This, from the Secretary is both helpful and excellant news.

"I regret that you have been given inaccurate information. The Museum is keen to have an operational steam tram – after all a steam vehicle is always a good draw even if it only runs occasionally, in a similar way to our operation of horse trams. Unfortunately John Bull needs a full overhaul and new bearings to get it operational with a new boiler certificate. Whether this can be achieved without destroying the historical artifact remains unclear at the present."

The Tramway Museum Society, Premises & Registered Office: Crich, Matlock, Derbyshire, DE4 5DP

TOTTENHAM: 8 JULY 1891

"Our Local Police are making a move in the right direction. They are trying to check the rowdyism which disgraces our principal thoroughfares, especially on Saturday and Sunday evenings. It is worse on Sundays than on other days – or else it is more noticeable. Boys and girls now and then fairly take possession of the paths, and decent people are obliged to take to the roads in order to avoid such unpleasant company. But their conduct after all is more tolerable than their language; and it is positively painful to notice how respectable young women are insulted as they are quietly proceeding to or from a place of worship. If Inspector Powell and those under his direction can stamp out this sort of thing they will deserve – and receive – the thanks of the ratepayers of the district."

The Passing of Steam

[This lament, for that is what it is, could well have been written on the passing of the last steam hauled passenger tram, or again towards the very end of scheduled steam operated services on Britain's railways, but instead it was printed on page 522 of the *Railway Magazine* Vol. VIII, no 48, June 1901. And how pleasant it is to see that Mr M. Peters, who wrote these lines, regarded steam as a female – once a girl, now a tired old lady! Ah, so sad]

Steam's getting old. Is she passing away?
Sixty long years, or so, running like mad!
Who could keep up with her – who to this day?
Now she looks drooping, and dying, and sad.

Pain, from her whistle, shrieks out in despair;
All her gay laughter has left her fair face;
All her thin vapours are turned to air;
All her blue cloudlets map out a grimace.

Steam, the old champion, flying apace;
None of her rivals were in it, you know;
Now electricity's entered the race;
What her success will be, Old Time will show.

Greet the New Century – bright morning star!
Welcome new powers – favour for none;
Give all a chance, whatever they are,
Now is there something new under the sun!

Rothbury Mart

Good luck to the hoof and horn
Good luck to the flock and fleece
Good luck to the growers of corn
With blessings of plenty and peace.

Blackpool 1989. A scene we shall not see again as the last true traditional tramway came to its end twenty years later, to be superceded by modern euro-trams. The dark-haired girl watching was my ever-patient wife...

Bradford City Tramways, Thornbury/ Bradford Moor termini. Virtually everything (tramcars, chimneys, wires, rails, man, cow, dog) in this dreich scene has gone even to the very setts. (The late W.A. Camwell)

ACKNOWLEDGEMENTS AND THANKS

Wherever possible routine acknowledgments are in place within each relevant volume of this series. This is therefore by way of being a 'sweeping' exercise. Research into some facets of this series of books (and articles published elsewhere) has been a part of my life for thirty years at least and since many of my colleagues and friends were already elderly all those decades ago commonsense tells us that many have died subsequently, some at a shockingly early age. As an example of this when we were running a museum and I was advisor to another, four full-time staff and ten consultants were involved – I am pretty certain I am the last survivor. Unfortunately, whatever the reason I find myself ill-at-ease with many 'junge' who might have replaced them as fellow scholars and researchers. Perhaps it is true we are all children of our time and cannot break away from the influences that moulded us so many years ago. Interestingly Gerald Hartley who provides our crests and coats-of-arms and with whom I have an easy rapport, follows a modern form of rock 'n' roll – come back Bill Haley, all is forgiven!

So there follows a mélange of names – some no doubt familiar to readers, others lost in the mists of time. If it is true as some philosophers would tell us that man's life is as ephemeral as a sailor's across an ocean then Arthur Hugh Clough clearly understood this:

Where lies the land to which the ship would go?
Far, far ahead, is all her seamen know,
And where is the land she travels from? Away
Far, far behind, is all they can say.

In strictly alphabetical order:
Allan C. Baker for assistance and encouragement, the late Geoff Baddeley, Robin Barnes, Alan Brotchie, Ciaran Cooney, the late Alan Earnshaw, Ric Francis, Foster Frewin, Colin Ganley, the late John Gillham, Adam Gordon for having faith and lots of lovely documents, Ron Grant of New Zealand, Jim Halsall, Ross Hamilton, Peter Hammond of Kirkwall, provider of the photographs of those amazing tram models he builds (skills far beyond mine), Geoff and Shirley Harper for propping me up and for engineering help, David Harvey, George Hearse, Richard Horne for reducing my mistakes in colonial tram matters, the late Fred Jones, Maurice Kelly, Nick Kelly for finding documents I did not know existed, and others I did but needed the day before yesterday... Mrs Jane Kennedy, friend of both my wife and I and very knowledgeable girl, the late Roger Kidner, Colin and Obie Laidler, engineer and wonderful girl respectively, Joe Lloyd, the Beyer Peacock man, Geoff Lumb who found us many items and leads to others, Fred Miller for letting me use his archival studies, David Packer, the late Jim Peden, John Pitt of County Down, Trevor Preece, designer of this and the other six volumes (for only erupting occasionally when yet another document arrived after the closure date), Derek Rayner, Chris Sims, the late Peter L. Smith, once curator of

our museum, Roger Smith for his clear and, more importantly, accurate maps, often prepared at short notice, Iain Stirch, George Toms, the Falcon/Brush historian, Keith Turns, David Voice, and Russell Wear of the ILS., and Graham Whitehead.

As far as Archive offices, Local History Collections and museum collections in their various forms are concerned it would be impossible to list all those consulted during the researching and writing of volumes 1 to 6, but the following gave us assistance in the preparation of this volume.
Staff at:

Accrington, Birmingham, Bury, Colindale (British Library, Newspaper Archive), Cowes (IoW), Dudley (Coseley), Hanley (Stoke-on-Trent), Haslingden, Intellectual Property Office (ex Patent Office Archives), Kew (Public Record Office), Portsmouth, Rochdale (Touchstones), Salford, Smethwick, Southampton, Walsall, Wolverhampton, York Railway Museum (Leeman Road).

The staff at the Institution of Civil Engineers, The staff at the Institution of Mechanical Engineers, The Archivist at the Institute of Mining and Mechanical Engineers, Newcastle, Museumstoomtram Hoorn-Medemblik, The Steam Boat Association of Great Britain, The friendly bunch at the Streetlife Museum, Hull, The Westward Ho! Study Group.

Over time I have been privileged to know a good number of members from the Industrial

Locomotive Society, the Industrial Railway Society, and the Stephenson Locomotive Society who have all added another brick in the edifice.

The editor and staff at the Municipal Journal (a wondrous record of 'behind the scenes' activities.)

Gabriel and Company for permission to reproduce part of their magnificent catalogue. Members of the London & North Western Railway Society.

Then there is an 'inside out' acknowledgement to the handful of people who, for whatever reason, refused, not always too politely, to help us with some detail. But I do thank those who draw our attention to items that I could have read in some relatively obscure publication but missed. It would be impossible for any small number of people to read every tract or pamphlet that has appeared, for example on horse trams or Serpollet cars, even if the budget was elastic enough. Some modifications to previous text appear in this volume, others will be incorporated in any new editions.

Lastly there are personal friends of long ago who taught me the proper meaning of 'honour' and 'belief'; those words so denigrated today. Fanciful though it may sound honour is often the only contract between author and publisher – it is many a long year since I last held a formal legal document – I (or we) contract verbally to write one or more books, and the publisher to do the rest. It is only this honour that binds together two such disparate characters as Adam Gordon and myself who have not met for 30 or more years, and as an extension of this, readers trust us to write honestly and as accurately as we can, without plagiarism or stolen research. This latter is a shocking problem now even in universities (red-brick, blue-brick or chipboard level) where one reads a dissertation and immediately can locate the source, often word-for-word. That in my simple world is an act without honour.

Adolf Bethge taught me how to survive.

Peter Ling, patriot and scholar who said one day that those who we buried in the sand were the lucky ones, for they were fit, strong and did not have to face the possibility of a long drawn out way of dying. Perhaps on reflection he was right.

Pilot-Officers Ryoto and Sato, once of the IJAAF, who held the secret of eternal patience and of chivalry.

And all those others of long ago whose names, but not actions, are lost in the mists of time.

And my three wives and one woman who all affected my life in their own ways; Marika, a beautiful mixture of Arabic and French blood but a Moslem who I last saw surrounded by children outside Marseilles, Anna-Maria dying at 24, Claudie who wandered off to where I know not, and Joyce Marian who wherever she is (be it Valhalla, or Heaven, or Nirvana) no doubt will be laughing at the thought of a 1,008-page book, not on our broad-brush subjects, but a mere 20-year blip in transport history.

Dave Gladwin

Colin Shewring was the photographer who made this delightful study of one of the last of London's tramcars on that last fateful day when their souls joined those of our steam trams in that great shed in the sky. 5 July, 1953.

Index to Volumes 1 to 7

Note: Volume numbers are in **bold**. Names of trams, literature and legislation are in *italics*. Names of tramway systems are indexed if they are specifically mentioned in the main text, or significant information is given in a document, e.g. the extracts from Duncan's Manual from page 334 onwards in volume 7, but generally they are not indexed if details are fairly scant, e.g. the Board of Trade returns on page 271 onwards. The minutes of the Select Committees in section 16 of volume 7 are not indexed in detail because the range of subjects covered is so broad.

The Very Last Words

For perfectly sensible reasons a good number of readers have expressed a liking for the odd aspects of, not of only tramways, but the lives our predecessors led. The main difficulty I have had is that TV gives such a strange 21st century view of the lives of people of the 19th century; all the actors in period costume dramas are so pretty with flawless skins, strong bodies, and are always absolutely clean shaven – both sexes!! But the reality of life then was worse than even that of my wartime childhood, when whooping cough, scarlet fever, chicken-pox, diphtheria, measles (both sorts) polio, smallpox and tuberculosis were some things children had or didn't have. Survival was really a matter of pot-luck. How much more so a century before. But I am also well aware there was an in-built toughness among children that I fear is lost when I see the fat, puffy creatures not only in town, but also more and more in the country. Kids like me swam in the Thames, and for an outing we went on a cycle ride to our friendly marine scrap-yard where providing we saw the night-watchman we could explore what we wanted. So for your delectation here is another batch of what I call 'odds and bobs'.

A Final Couplet

Obviously producing a series of books like this with research spread over two decades, and the writing something over one, office and domestic strains become involved, and mortality within and without the family occurs. My late wife found me this, written by C.S. Calverley (born 1831 and therefore, as she said, even older than me!) which she thought was apposite as a description of how I blew off steam.

Loaf, as I have loafed aforetime,
Through the streets with tranquil mind,
And a long-backed fancy-mongrel
Trailing casually behind.

EDMUND SPENSER. (c.1552 – 1599)   The Faerie Queene
Book I, Can. IX, St.40

'Sleep after toile, port after stormie seas,
Ease after warre, death after life, does greatly please.'

[which takes me back to being a 12 year-old schoolboy...]

Dave Gladwin

Adam Gordon Books

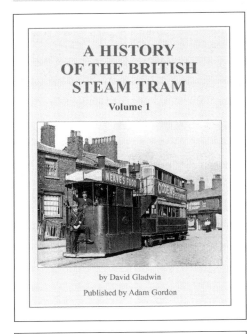

A HISTORY OF THE BRITISH STEAM TRAM

Volume 1

by David Gladwin

Published by Adam Gordon

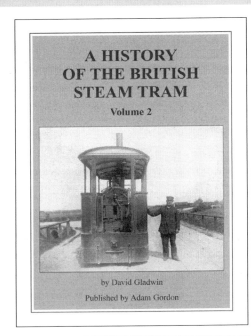

A HISTORY OF THE BRITISH STEAM TRAM

Volume 2

by David Gladwin

Published by Adam Gordon

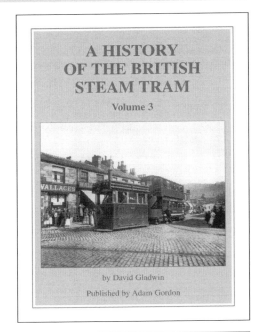

A HISTORY OF THE BRITISH STEAM TRAM

Volume 3

by David Gladwin

Published by Adam Gordon

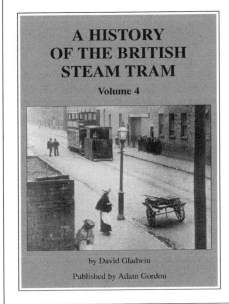

A HISTORY OF THE BRITISH STEAM TRAM

Volume 4

by David Gladwin

Published by Adam Gordon

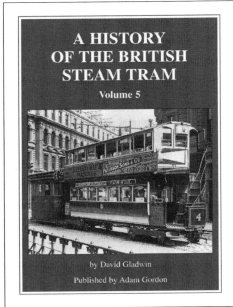

A HISTORY OF THE BRITISH STEAM TRAM

Volume 5

by David Gladwin

Published by Adam Gordon

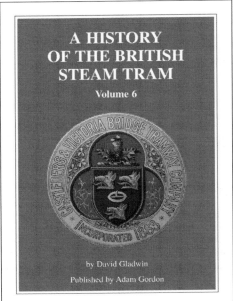

A HISTORY OF THE BRITISH STEAM TRAM

Volume 6

by David Gladwin

Published by Adam Gordon

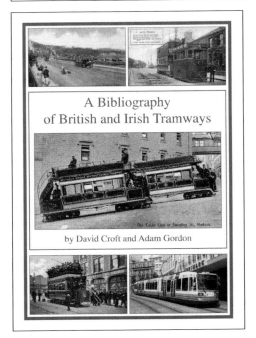

A Bibliography of British and Irish Tramways

by David Croft and Adam Gordon

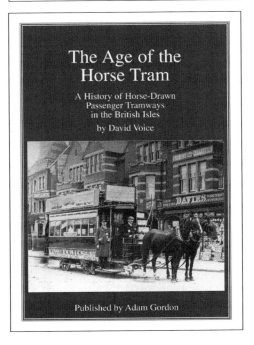

The Age of the Horse Tram

A History of Horse-Drawn Passenger Tramways in the British Isles

by David Voice

Published by Adam Gordon

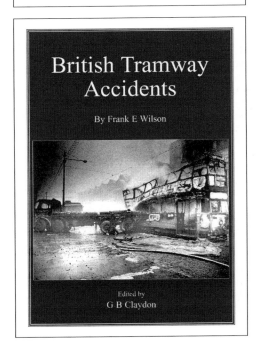

British Tramway Accidents

By Frank E Wilson

Edited by G B Claydon

Adam Gordon Books

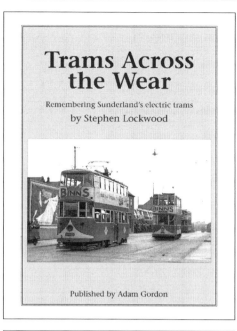

Trams Across the Wear

Remembering Sunderland's electric trams
by Stephen Lockwood

Published by Adam Gordon

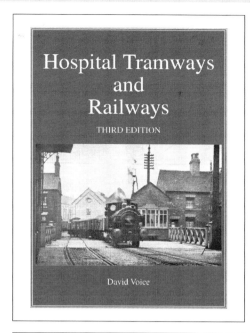

Hospital Tramways and Railways

THIRD EDITION

David Voice

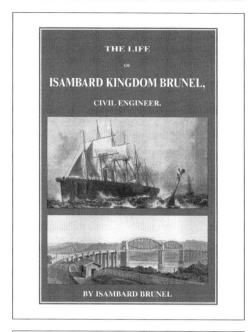

THE LIFE
OF
ISAMBARD KINGDOM BRUNEL,
CIVIL ENGINEER.

BY ISAMBARD BRUNEL

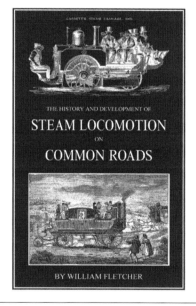

THE HISTORY AND DEVELOPMENT OF
STEAM LOCOMOTION
ON
COMMON ROADS

BY WILLIAM FLETCHER

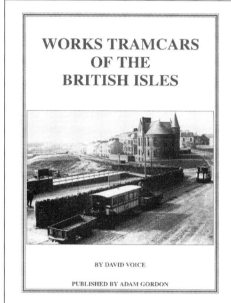

WORKS TRAMCARS OF THE BRITISH ISLES

BY DAVID VOICE

PUBLISHED BY ADAM GORDON

The Wantage Tramway

By S.H. Pearce Higgins
With an Introduction by John Betjeman

The Company Seal

Republished by Adam Gordon

THE DEVELOPMENT OF THE MODERN TRAM

by Brian Patton
Published by Adam Gordon

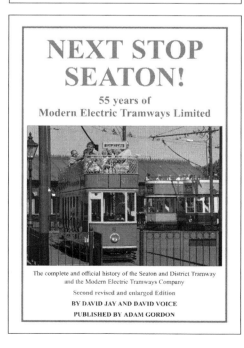

NEXT STOP SEATON!

55 years of
Modern Electric Tramways Limited

The complete and official history of the Seaton and District Tramway
and the Modern Electric Tramways Company
Second revised and enlarged Edition
BY DAVID JAY AND DAVID VOICE
PUBLISHED BY ADAM GORDON

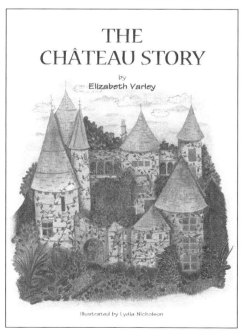

THE CHÂTEAU STORY
by
Elizabeth Varley

Illustrated by Lydia Nicholson

Adam Gordon Books

The Age of the Horse Tram
A history of horse-drawn passenger tramways in the British Isles, D. Voice, hardback, A4, 212pp, £40

Bibliography of British & Irish Tramways
David Croft & Adam Gordon, A4, softback, 486pp, £35

British Tramcar Manufacturers: British Westinghouse and Metropolitan-Vickers
by David Voice, B5, softback, 110pp, £16

British Tramway Accidents
by F. Wilson, edited by G. Claydon, laminated hardback, 228pp, £35

The Life of Isambard Kingdom Brunel
by his son, reprint of the 1870 edition, softback, 604pp, £20

The Definitive Guide to Trams (including Funiculars) in the British Isles,
3rd edition; D. Voice, softback, A5, 248pp, £20

Double-Deck Trams of the World, Beyond the British Isles
B. Patton, A4 softback, 180pp, £18

Double-Deck Trolleybuses of the World, Beyond the British Isles
B. Patton, A4, softback, 96pp, £16

The Douglas Horse Tramway
K. Pearson, softback, 96pp, £14.50

Edinburgh Street Tramways Co. Rules & Regulations
reprint of 1883 publication, softback, 56pp, £8

Edinburgh's Transport, vol. 2, The Corporation Years
1919-1975, D. Hunter, 192pp, softback, £20

Electric Railway Dictionary
R. Hitt, reprint of 1911 publication, 350pp, hardback, £45

The Feltham Car
of the Metropolitan Electric and London United Tramways, reprint of 1931 publication, softback, 18pp, £5

Freight on Street Tramways in the British Isles
by David Voice, B5 softback, 66pp, black and white, £12

Hospital Tramways and Railways
third edition, D. Voice, laminated hardback, 108pp, £25

How to Go Tram and Tramway Modelling
third edition, D. Voice, B4, 152pp, completely rewritten, softback, £20

London County Council Tramways
map and guide to car services, February 1915, reprint, c.12"x17", folding out to 12 sections, £8

Metropolitan Electric, London United and South Metropolitan Electric Tramways
routes map and guide, summer 1925, reprint, c.14"x17", folding out to 15 sections, £8

The Development of the Modern Tram
by B. Patton, all colour, 208pp, world-wide coverage, £40

Modern Tramway, reprint of volumes 1 & 2, 1938-1939
c.A4 cloth hardback, £38

My 50 Years in Transport
A.G. Grundy, 54pp, softback, 1997, £10

Next Stop Seaton!
2nd edition, David Jay and David Voice, B5, softback, 142pp, £20

Omnibuses & Cabs, Their Origin and History
H.C. Moore, hardback reprint with d/w, 282pp, £25

The Overhaul of Tramcars
reprint of LT publication of 1935, 26pp, softback, £6

The History and Development of Steam Locomotion on Common Roads
W. Fletcher, reprint 1891 edition, softback, 332pp, £18

The History of the Steam Tram
H. Whitcombe, hardback, over 60pp, £12

A History of the British Steam Tram, volume 1
D. Gladwin, hardback, coloured covers, 176pp, 312 x 237mm, profusely illustrated, £40

A History of the British Steam Tram, volume 2
D. Gladwin, hardback, size as above, coloured covers, 256pp, £40

A History of the British Steam Tram, volume 3
D. Gladwin, hardback, size as volume 1, coloured covers, 240pp, £45

A History of the British Steam Tram, volume 4
D. Gladwin, hardback, size as volume 1, coloured covers, 256pp, £45

A History of the British Steam Tram, volume 5
D. Gladwin, hardback, size as volume 1, coloured covers, 256pp, £45

A History of the British Steam Tram, volume 6
D. Gladwin, hardback, size as volume 1, coloured covers, 256pp, £45

Street Railways, their construction, operation and maintenance
by C.B. Fairchild, reprint of 1892 publication, 496pp, hardback, profusely illustrated, £40

Toy and Model Trams of the World – Volume 1: Toys, die casts and souvenirs
G. Kuře and D. Voice, A4 softback, all colour, 128pp, £25

Toy and Model Trams of the World – Volume 2: Plastic, white metal and brass models and kits
G. Kuře and D. Voice, A4 softback, all colour, 188pp, £30

George Francis Train's Banquet
report of 1860 on the opening of the Birkenhead tramway, reprint, softback, 118pp, £10

My Life in Many States and in Foreign Lands
G.F. Train, reprint of his autobiography, over 350pp, softback, £12

The Tram Driver (The Art of Tram driving)
by D. Tudor, 72pp, laminated hardback, £20

Trams, Trolleybuses and Buses and the Law before De-regulation
M. Yelton, B4, softback, 108pp, £15

Trams Across the Wear
Remembering Sunderland's Electric Trams, S. Lockwood, hardback, A4, 164pp, £35

Tramway Review, reprint of issues 1-16, 1950-1954
A5 cloth hardback, £23

Tramways and Electric Railways in the Nineteenth Century
reprint of Electric Railway Number of Cassier's Magazine, 1899, cloth hardback, over 250pp, £23

Tramways – Their Construction & Working
D. Kinnear Clark, reprint of the 1894 edition, softback, 812pp. £28

Treatise upon Cable or Rope Traction
J. Bucknall Smith, with other literature on the subject, softback, 434pp, £45

Life of Richard Trevithick
two volumes in one, reprint of 1872 edition, softback, 830pp, £25

The Twilight Years of the Trams in Aberdeen & Dundee
all colour, A4 softback, introduction and captions by A. Brotchie, 120pp, £25

The Twilight Years of the Edinburgh Tram
112pp, A4 softback, includes 152 coloured pics, £25

The Twilight Years of the Glasgow Tram
over 250 coloured views, A4, softback, 144 pp, £25

The Wantage Tramway
S.H. Pearce Higgins, with Introduction by John Betjeman, hardback reprint with d/w, over 158pp, £28

The Wearing of the Green
being reminiscences of the Glasgow trams, W. Tollan, softback, 96pp, £12

Works Tramcars of The British Isles
David Voice, B5, softback, 238pp, £25

TERMS

RETAIL UK – for post and packing please add 10%, but orders £100 and over are post and packing free. I regret that I am not yet equipped to deal with credit/debit cards.

RETAIL OVERSEAS – postage will be charged at printed paper rate via surface mail, unless otherwise requested. Payment please by sterling cash or cheque, UK sterling postage stamps, or direct bank to bank by arrangement.

SOCIETIES, CHARITIES, etc. relating to tramways, buses and railways – a special 50% discount for any quantity of purchases is given **provided my postal charges are paid.**

ADAM GORDON
Kintradwell Farmhouse, Brora, Sutherland KW9 6LU
Tel: 01408 622660   E-mail: adam@ahg-books.com   Website: www.ahg-books.com